The Value of a Dollar

1860—2019

The Value of a Dollar

Prices and Incomes in the United States

1860—2019

By Scott Derks

SIXTH EDITION

Revised by Andrew Schenker

Grey House Publishing

PRESIDENT: Richard Gottlieb
PUBLISHER: Leslie Mackenzie
EDITORIAL DIRECTOR: Laura Mars
EDITORIAL ASSISTANT: Alyssa Hurley
ORIGINAL AUTHOR: Scott Derks
CONTRIBUTOR: Andrew Schenker
PRODUCTION MANAGER: Kristen Hayes
MARKETING DIRECTOR: Jessica Moody

Grey House Publishing, Inc.
4919 Route 22
Amenia, NY 12501
(518) 789-8700
Fax: (845) 373-6390
www.greyhouse.com
books@greyhouse.com

Publisher's Cataloging-In-Publication Data
(Prepared by The Donahue Group, Inc.)

Names: Derks, Scott, author.
Title: The value of a dollar: prices and incomes in the United States, 1860-2019 / by Scott Derks.
Description: Sixth edition. | Amenia, NY: Grey House Publishing, [2019] | Includes bibliographical references and index.
Identifiers: ISBN 9781682179499
Subjects: LCSH: Prices–United States–History. | Wages–United States–History. | Purchasing power–United States–History. | Cost and standard of living–United States–History.
Classification: LCC HB235.U6 D47 2019 | DDC 338.5/2/0973–dc23

Introduction

This sixth edition of *The Value of a Dollar*, like its predecessors, is all about practical economy: what things cost and how much money people have to buy them. The economic conditions of recent years have everyone—from elected officials to electricians—thinking much more carefully about how to spend their money. With this in mind, the comparative nature of *The Value of a Dollar* makes it so much more than a fascinating look into the history of our nation's economy, although it is indeed that. This edition will serve as a valuable study guide to students of American history, economy, and even mathematics. It offers insight into our previous spending habits that could very well guide us into smarter spending in the years to come.

The Value of a Dollar includes the actual pricing of thousands of items that consumers purchased from the Civil War to the present, along with facts about investment options and income opportunities. History shows that consumers do not make personal economic decisions based on models, indexes and trends, but on weighed options: the need to pay a home heating bill versus a desire to buy a new flat screen TV; the short-term pleasure of eating in expensive restaurants measured against the long-term satisfaction of owning an upscale automobile; buying farm fresh produce vs. a fancy cup of coffee.

Pricing is an inexact science. In any given year, the same item—a lawn mower, for example—might be sold at widely varying prices at the same store, based on season, availability, retailer's need for cash, and consumer's demand. Within the same city, the price of a laptop computer for instance, may vary based on the cost of inventory, overhead, competitive pressures, customer demographics, holiday sales promotions, cash flow, or simply the whim of the owner. Although many statistical studies accurately trace wholesale prices, few attempt to define the value of a dollar to the consumer at the point of purchase. The sources of prices reported in *The Value of a Dollar* are the same sources used by consumers at the time: trade cards, newspapers, magazines, catalogues, direct-mail letters, posters, and store websites. In all, more than 500 sources are used.

SECTION ONE: 1860–2019

The first section of this book is divided into nine chapters, all of which follow a standard format. The first chapter covers the era from the Civil War to 1899, when the groundwork was being laid for a national consumer economy. To some degree, less information is available for that period. For most of this first 40-year span, government statistical gathering was in its infancy, few newspapers (and fewer magazines) carried specific product advertising, and ads for jobs were sparse. Trade cards, a handful of publications, and several government reports served as the primary resources for this period.

Subsequent chapters cover 20-year periods: 1900–1919; 1920–1939; 1940–1959; 1960–1979; 1980–1999. The final chapters cover ten-year and five-year periods: 2000-2009; 2010–2014;

2015–2019. Each chapter begins with a background essay describing the major social and economic forces of the period.

Currency Conversion Charts

Currency Conversion Charts appear at the end of each chapter background. To find out what any item in any year would cost in 2019 simply multiply the cost of that item by the dollar amount in the chart. For example, if you know that a man's shirt cost $3.00 in 1950, multiply $3.00 by $10.63 (per chart on page 246) to discover that the same shirt would cost $31.89 in 2019. Each chapter contains price and income reports grouped in five-year subchapters. Each subchapter includes the following elements:

Historical Snapshot

A chronological look at the key economic events and historical happenings. The 1910 creation of the Carnegie Corporation; 1933 default of the city of Chicago; 1955 creation of Chase Manhattan Bank; 1979 prime lending bank rate of 14.5%; 1997 three-year mortgage rate of 7%; 2009 price of crude oil at $46, down from $100 in early 2008; and 2013 lifting of the ban on women serving in combat.

Selected Income

Here you'll find jobs listed in the want ads of major newspapers and reported in the language of the ad. This section represents the types of jobs available and the wages offered across the country, and allows a view of the job market unavailable in average-wage tables. Until fairly recently, for example many ads specified the sex, age, and race acceptable to the employer. When compiling this section, care was taken to include newly created, or trending, jobs, such as advertising copywriters in the 1920s, female factory

workers during World War II, a bilingual administrative assistant in 2009, and a dietician in 2014.

Consumer Expenditures

A report on per-capita consumer prices of the day nationwide serves as a benchmark for specific wage and price information. The information, based on reports compiled by the U.S. Bureau of Economic Analysis, is available annually from 1929 to the present. Before 1929, it was compiled only for certain years (1909, 1914 and, from 1919, in two-year intervals). Prices listed are minus any taxes, and include a wide range of categories, from clothing to health insurance and religious activities.

Investments

A selection of investment returns is compiled from Federal Reserve reports, including a diversified portfolio of common stocks, monitored annually with splits and dividends noted. Dividends were not reported in a standardized fashion until 1927, and thus annual dividends are not included before that date. Use this section to identify the interest rate roller coaster, and volatility of common stock prices.

Standard Jobs

This section provides a selection of national average wages paid for representative jobs traced annually and based primarily on reports compiled by the Bureau of Economic Analysis. Though job opportunities and wages varied from region to region, this section provides a general guide to the wage-earning capacity of the average American. From Construction to Transit Workers, you'll find annual salaries in about 20 industries, with terms based on both SIC and NAICS codes.

SECTION TWO: PRICING TRENDS

The second section of *The Value of a Dollar* compares the cost of everyday products, services and jobs, not only over a specified number of years, but it also shows how those prices compare to today's dollar. Pricing Trends uses both bar charts and numeric tables to illustrate, for example, that a first-class postage stamp was actually more expensive in 1970 (.98 by today's dollar) than in 2019 (.55) and that the salary of the President of the United States is worth considerably less today than in earlier years.

Categorized in seven main headings from Around the House to Travel & Entertainment, Pricing Trends includes about 90 products and services, including a bath towel, major league baseball player's salary, one pound of butter, hiking boots, airline ticket from NYC to Chicago, and a roll of film.

The sixth edition of *The Value of a Dollar 1860–2019*, with a new 2015–2019 chapter, more images, and new Conversion Charts,

is an invaluable research tool for all those researching, or simply curious about, social history: students studying topics that require knowledge about everyday life in the United States; teachers seeking information to enliven classroom discussions while broadening students' understanding of the quality of American life; writers who need access to the basic facts of American commerce; business historians seeking data to establish a framework of wage and price information during a specific period; reporters seeking to enhance a story with economic details. *The Value of a Dollar* is for both the user who simply wants to know what life was like during the time of his or her great-grandparents as well as the serious student engaged in historical research.

In addition to this print book, the sixth edition of *The Value of a Dollar* is available as an eBook. For more information, visit www.greyhouse.com.

—Andrew Schenker

Contents

The Value of a Dollar, 1860–2019

Composite Consumer Price Index; 1860=1

Year	Amount	Year	Amount	Year	Amount	Year	Amount	Year	Amount
1860	$1.00	1895	$1.03	1930	$2.03	1965	$3.81	2000	$20.83
1861	$1.06	1896	$1.03	1931	$1.83	1966	$3.92	2001	$21.42
1862	$1.22	1897	$1.00	1932	$1.67	1967	$4.03	2002	$21.78
1863	$1.53	1898	$1.00	1933	$1.58	1968	$4.22	2003	$22.25
1864	$1.89	1899	$1.00	1934	$1.61	1969	$4.44	2004	$22.86
1865	$1.97	1900	$1.03	1935	$1.67	1970	$4.69	2005	$23.64
1866	$1.92	1901	$1.03	1936	$1.69	1971	$4.89	2006	$24.39
1867	$1.78	1902	$1.03	1937	$1.75	1972	$5.06	2007	$25.08
1868	$1.72	1903	$1.06	1938	$1.69	1973	$5.36	2008	$26.06
1869	$1.64	1904	$1.08	1939	$1.69	1974	$5.97	2009	$25.94
1870	$1.58	1905	$1.06	1940	$1.69	1975	$6.50	2010	$26.39
1871	$1.47	1906	$1.08	1941	$1.78	1976	$6.89	2011	$27.22
1872	$1.47	1907	$1.14	1942	$1.97	1977	$7.33	2012	$27.78
1873	$1.44	1908	$1.11	1943	$2.08	1978	$7.89	2013	$28.07
1874	$1.39	1909	$1.11	1944	$2.14	1979	$8.78	2014	$28.52
1875	$1.33	1910	$1.14	1945	$2.17	1980	$9.97	2015	$28.56
1876	$1.31	1911	$1.14	1946	$2.36	1981	$11.00	2016	$28.92
1877	$1.28	1912	$1.17	1947	$2.69	1982	$11.67	2017	$29.53
1878	$1.22	1913	$1.19	1948	$2.92	1983	$12.06	2018	$30.25
1879	$1.22	1914	$1.22	1949	$2.89	1984	$12.58	2019	$30.63
1880	$1.22	1915	$1.22	1950	$2.92	1985	$13.03		
1881	$1.22	1916	$1.31	1951	$3.14	1986	$13.25		
1882	$1.22	1917	$1.56	1952	$3.19	1987	$13.75		
1883	$1.22	1918	$1.83	1953	$3.22	1988	$14.31		
1884	$1.19	1919	$2.08	1954	$3.25	1989	$15.00		
1885	$1.17	1920	$2.42	1955	$3.25	1990	$15.81		
1886	$1.14	1921	$2.17	1956	$3.28	1991	$16.47		
1887	$1.14	1922	$2.03	1957	$3.39	1992	$16.97		
1888	$1.14	1923	$2.06	1958	$3.50	1993	$17.47		
1889	$1.11	1924	$2.06	1959	$3.53	1994	$17.92		
1890	$1.11	1925	$2.11	1960	$3.58	1995	$18.44		
1891	$1.11	1926	$2.14	1961	$3.61	1996	$18.97		
1892	$1.11	1927	$2.11	1962	$3.67	1997	$19.42		
1893	$1.08	1928	$2.06	1963	$3.69	1998	$19.72		
1894	$1.03	1929	$2.06	1964	$3.75	1999	$20.17		

1860–1899

The Age of Endeavor

PRESIDENTS

Abraham Lincoln*	1861–1865
Andrew Johnson	1865–1869
Ulysses S. Grant	1869–1877
Rutherford B. Hayes	1877–1881
James A. Garfield*	1881–1881
Chester A. Arthur	1881–1885
Grover Cleveland	1885–1889
Benjamin Harrison	1889–1893
Grover Cleveland	1893–1897
William McKinley*	1897–1901

* assassinated

1896 series one-dollar bill.

Historians disagree about whether the Civil War was a revolutionary stimulus to the American economy, a violent interruption of industrial development, or something in between. It is clear that after the war, business and industry came to dominate American life. The combination of advances in technology, increases in manufacturing capacity, the development of a national system of railroads to transport goods, and the accumulation of capital that allowed the industrial barons of the age to build financial empires, established the United States as a world economic power and transformed Americans into the world's most avid consumers.

Railroads were the nation's pioneer big business. They delivered raw materials to manufacturing centers, finished goods to market, food from the farm to the city, and people to centers of commercial opportunity. From 1865 to 1900 track mileage nationwide increased from 35,000 to 192,556. During the same time the total labor force more than doubled, the amount of capital invested in manufacturing increased tenfold, and the gross national product tripled.

The energy required to drive the industrial boom was enormous. Between 1860 and 1900, the total horse-power generated to meet the needs of the economy increased 500 percent, with railroads and factories accounting for 76 percent of the total by 1900.

By 1890, 25 percent of the world output of coal was mined in the United States. Annual production of crude petroleum went from 500,000 barrels in 1860 to 63.6 million in 1900. With the introduction of electricity in the 1870s a powerful energy source was made available that had relatively little effect in the nineteenth century but profoundly affected consumers in the early years of the twentieth century.

Innovation was significant in the Age of Endeavor. Not only were goods manufactured on a scale unimaginable before the Civil War, but entrepreneurs created new products, and ways to produce them. Between 1860 and 1869, 77,355 patents were issued; by 1899 the number rose to 234,749. The Pullman sleeping car and the Westinghouse air brake expanded the uses of trains. Barbed wire, the wind-powered electrical generator, the hay baler, and the twine binder revolutionized farm life; the telephone, typewriter, cash register, and adding machine contributed mightily to the development of commerce.

Despite the financial promise of the Age of Endeavor, the economy was unstable, due partly to irresponsible speculation but more generally to the stubborn adherence of the federal government to a gold standard as the basis of value for currency. Prices went into a steady decline after the Civil War, reaching bottom with the Panic of 1893, and only then beginning a long-term

1

recovery. Congress reacted with increasingly restrictive tariffs to protect American businessmen from foreign competition.

The promise of wealth offered by investment opportunities gave rise to actions that had national repercussions. In September 1873 the failure of the banking house of Jay Cooke & Co., the most prominent in the country, led to a series of failures among banks and brokerage houses, resulting in a five-year decline in the economy despite the continued expansion of industry and increases in equipment purchases. After a brief recovery the depression resumed, reaching its nadir in 1893 with a crisis caused by the failure of Baring Brothers, a British banking house, and the resulting sale of American securities held abroad. The drain of gold caused American reserves to fall to dangerously low levels. Investors panicked; Congress reacted with gold-price supports.

The last half of the nineteenth century saw expansion in the United States. Population went from 31.5 million in 1860 to 76 million in 1900, of whom about 13 million were immigrants. Twelve states were added to the Union, for a total of 45. Alaska, Hawaii, the Philippines, and Puerto Rico were either purchased or annexed. To encourage the economic development of the West, the Homestead Act of 1862 offered any American citizen 160 acres of government land free if the homesteader lived on it for five years; after six months a homesteader could purchase the land for $1.25 per acre. The result was a 700 percent (3.5 million persons) growth in population in the West between 1860 and 1900. The South was now the most populated region of the United States, with over 35 percent of the total population, followed by the North, with 34 percent; at the end of the period the North Central region had grown to nearly 35 percent, followed by the South, with 32 percent.

The social changes imposed by the capitalistic fervor of the Age of Endeavor prompted energetic reform movements. Labor unions protested against the abuse of workers. Wages were low, sixty-hour workweeks were common, and working conditions in factories were often deplorable. Between 1880 and 1900 unions organized twenty-three thousand strikes. By the end of the nineteenth century the newly formed American Federation of Labor had gained supremacy as the chief labor advocate in America. By 1904, eighteen years after it was founded, the AF of L claimed 1.676 million of 2.07 million total union members.

Agricultural reform was advocated by the Granger Movement, which attracted 850,000 farmers seeking cooperative marketing, higher prices for agricultural products, and relief from high railroad freight rates. With support from merchants the Grangers were successful in sponsoring legislation regulating railroad rates and in gaining popular support for their opposition to monopolies.

The most visible social-reform movements were those organized by women suffragists, who fought for women's right to vote, and the temperance crusaders, who sought the prohibition of alcohol. Both issues were hotly debated during the period, and the groundwork was laid for constitutional amendments addressing the reformers' concerns: the 18th Amendment (1919) prohibited the manufacture, sale, or transportation of intoxicating beverages; and the 19th Amendment (1920) extended to women the right to vote.

Year	Dollar Value in 2019	Year	Dollar Value in 2019
1860	$30.63	1880	$24.92
1863	$20.17	1883	$25.17
1865	$15.60	1885	$26.21
1867	$17.18	1887	$26.76
1869	$18.69	1889	$27.63
1870	$19.40	1890	$27.93
1873	$21.18	1893	$28.24
1875	$23.11	1895	$30.26
1877	$24.21	1897	$30.63
1879	$25.42	1899	$30.63

Use this Currency Conversion chart to calculate what any time in the years listed would cost in 2019. Simply multiply the cost of that item by dollar amount in the chart. For example, if you know that a nutmeg grater cost .25 in 1889, multiply by $27.63 to discover that that same nutmeg grater would cost $6.91 in 2019.

HISTORICAL SNAPSHOT 1860–1899

1860

- Abraham Lincoln elected president with 40 percent of the popular vote
- U.S. cotton exports equal $192 million of the nation's export total of $334 million
- John D. Rockefeller enters the oil business
- Elizabeth Cady Stanton urges women's suffrage in an address to a joint session of the New York State Legislature
- Oneida Community grosses $100,000 from the sale of the Newhouse animal trap
- First Pony Express Riders deliver mail from St. Joseph, MO, to Sacramento, CA, in ten days
- Palmolive Soap created using a new soap-milling machine demonstrated at the St. Louis Exposition
- New York's Tiffany & Co. sells a pearl necklace for $1 million
- Checkered Game of Life board game is introduced by Springfield, MA, lithographer Milton Bradley
- U.S. population reaches 31.4 million, double its 1840 level

1861

- Ten Southern states secede from the Union
- Civil War begins when Fort Sumter, in Charleston Harbor, SC, is fired upon
- New York's Bellevue Hospital Medical College is established
- Louis Pasteur refutes the idea of spontaneous generation and advances germ theory
- Congress levies first U.S. income tax; law taxes incomes in excess of $800 at the rate of 3 percent
- U.S. banks suspend payments in gold

- MIT, University of Colorado, University of Washington founded
- I. M. Singer sells more sewing machines abroad than in America, has profits of $200,000
- John Wanamaker opens a Philadelphia menswear shop, becomes pioneer of fixed-price sales
- Elisha G. Otis patents a steam-powered elevator
- The McCormick reaper sells for $150, up from $100 in 1849
- Baltimore canner Isaac Solomon reduces the average processing time for canned goods from 6 hours to 30 minutes using calcium chloride

1862

- Homestead Act provides 160 acres, free to settlers of western land
- Western Union's telegraph forces Pony Express into bankruptcy
- John Hancock Life Insurance Company founded
- Land Grant Act funds land grant college for the education of farmers
- Beer taxed at $1 per barrel to finance war effort

1863

- President Abraham Lincoln's Emancipation Proclamation takes effect, frees nearly 4 million slaves
- Government guarantees Central Pacific and Union Pacific Railroads $16,000 for every mile of track laid, $48,000 per mile through mountains
- Boston College founded
- Travelers Insurance Company created to insure accidents
- Bay Sugar Refining Company starts in San Francisco

1864

- Ulysses S. Grant given command of Union Army

- Inflation devalues Confederate currency to $4.60 per $100
- The University of Kansas and University of Denver formed
- George M. Pullman and Ben Feld patent railway sleeping car
- U.S. wheat prices reach $4 per bushel
- European immigrants pour into United States for Homestead Act free land and factory jobs left vacant due to the war

1865

- Civil War ends and President Lincoln assassinated; War claims a total of 360,222 Union men, 258,000 Confederate
- Union Pacific Railroad construction reaches Kansas City
- Inflation reduces value of Confederate money to $1.76 per $100
- Linus Yale patents Yale Lock
- W.R. Grace & Co. formed to engage in South American trade

1866

- Prices begin rapid rise following war
- Tin can with a key opener is patented
- Breyer's Ice Cream founded
- Jack Daniel's Tennessee Sour Mash Whiskey introduced
- Nebraska admitted to Union

1867

- French engineer George Leclanché invents first practical dry-cell battery
- Pacific Mail Steamship Company begins service from San Francisco to Hong Kong
- University of Illinois and University of West Virginia founded
- More than half of all U.S. working people employed on farms

1868

- House of Representatives votes to impeach President Andrew Johnson
- Navajo chiefs forced to sign treaty establishing 3.5 million-acre reservation
- Metropolitan Life Insurance Company founded under reorganization of National Travelers Insurance Company
- Rand McNally & Co. founded
- U.S. wheat prices fall to 67 cents per bushel
- Tabasco sauce introduced by Edmund McIlhenny

1869

- Union Pacific Railroad and Central Pacific reduce New York to San Francisco travel time from three weeks to eight days
- Wall Street suffers first "Black Friday," ruining many small investors
- Stanley Rule and Level Co. buys patent rights to first metal plane
- Purdue University founded in Lafayette, IN
- First U.S. plow with a moldboard entirely of chilled steel patented

- Armour & Co. adds beef to its line of pork products

1870

- New York's F. A. O. Schwarz toy shop opens on Broadway
- First through railway cars from the Pacific Coast reach New York City
- Steamships account for 16 percent of world shipping
- Smith Brothers Cough Drops are patented by William "Trade" and Andrew "Mark," whose bearded faces serve as trademark

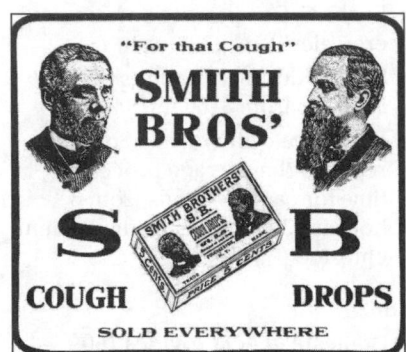

- Women enter University of Michigan for first time since it was founded in 1817
- Texas Christian University founded in Fort Worth
- U.S. corn crop reaches 1 million bushels for the first time

1871

- 1836 Colt redesigned to extend its effective range
- First shipload of bananas lands at Boston, 14 days out of Kingston, Jamaica
- University of Arkansas founded at Fayetteville
- Barnum's Circus opens in Brooklyn, NY; grosses $400,000 in first season
- C. A. Pillsbury & Co. founded by Minneapolis miller Charles Alfred Pillsbury
- U.S. population reaches 39 million, surpassing France, Italy, and Great Britain

1872

- U. S. Grant reelected despite charges of corruption
- Susan B. Anthony arrested for attempting to vote in presidential election
- Commercial production of celluloid begins under a patent obtained by John Wesley Hyatt
- Vanderbilt University founded in Nashville, TN, with a grant from Commodore Vanderbilt
- Congress enacts first consumer protection law, making it illegal to use the mail fraudulently
- Montgomery Ward Co. founded in Chicago, aimed at members of the Grange

1873

- Congress makes gold the sole U.S. monetary standard
- U.S. silver yield reaches $36 million, up from $157,000 in 1860
- Greenback party organized, claiming a shortage of money to be the cause of hard times
- U.S. suffers second "Black Friday"; stocks fall; 5,000 business firms fail
- San Francisco's cable streetcar goes into service
- Henri Nestle's Infant Milk Food introduced in the United States
- Barbed wire exhibited at the DeKalb, IL, county fair

1874

- R. H. Macy & Co. displays doll collection in the world's first Christmas window
- Remington typewriter introduced by E. Remington & Sons; firearms costing $125 each
- Levi Strauss blue jeans add rivets and sell for $13.50 per dozen
- Margarine is introduced in the United States
- Women's Christian Temperance Union founded at Cleveland
- New pressure-cooking technique improves canning process

1875

♦ Prudential Insurance Co. is founded in Newark, NJ

♦ George F. Green patents electric dental drill

♦ Vaseline petroleum jelly introduced by Chesebrough Manufacturing Co.

♦ U.S. cigarette production reaches 50 million

♦ Chinese orchard man in Oregon develops Bing cherry

♦ New York Condensed Milk Co. begins selling canned milk

1876

♦ First Fred Harvey restaurant opens in the Santa Fe Railroad depot at Topeka, KS

♦ Heinz Tomato Ketchup introduced

♦ Bananas introduced as foil-wrapped novelty at the Philadelphia fair costing 10¢ each

♦ W. Atlee Burpee & Co. founded to sell livestock by mail

♦ New York's Central Park completed

♦ BVD underwear introduced by New York's Bradley, Voorhees, and Day

♦ *McCall's* Magazine begins publication under the name *The Queen*

♦ Eli Lilly Company founded

1877

♦ Granola introduced by James Harvey Kellogg

♦ First low-rent housing project opens in Brooklyn, NY. Businessman Alfred Tredway White charges tenants $14 per month

♦ Singer Manufacturing company cuts price of sewing machines in half as depression of 1873 continues

♦ *Washington Post* begins publication, charging 3¢ per copy

♦ Bessemer steelmaking process cuts barbed wire prices from 18¢ per pound to 8¢ per pound

♦ First telephone exchange organized at Lowell, MS

1878

♦ Chase and Sanborn packs first roasted coffee in sealed can

♦ Edison Electric Light Co. founded

♦ 10,500 businesses fail as depression of 1873 continues

♦ Bland-Allison Act makes the silver dollar legal tender

♦ Mennen's Sure Corn Killer introduced by Newark, NJ, pharmacist Gerhard Mennen

♦ 287.42-carat Tiffany diamond discovered in South Africa's Kimberly Mine

♦ Hutchinson Bottle Stopper invented to seal in carbonation of effervescent drinks

1879

♦ Thomas Edison demonstrates first practical incandescent light bulb

♦ Cleveland and San Francisco install arc-lamp streetlights

♦ Standardization of pharmaceutical drugs pioneered by Parke Davis & Company

♦ McCormick's reaper sells for $1,500, up from $150 in 1861

♦ Photography revolutionized by Speed Dry Plate

♦ Scott Paper Company founded in Chester, PA

♦ Lambert Pharmaceutical Company founded in St. Louis

♦ Women given right to practice law before the Supreme Court

1880

♦ 539,000 Singer sewing machines sold, up from 250,000 in 1875

♦ United States has 100 millionaires

♦ New England's ice crop fails because of warm weather; ice prices soar

♦ A&P grocery stores operate 95 stores from Boston to Milwaukee

♦ Plush Del Monte Hotel in Monterey, CA, opens

♦ Halftone photographic illustrations appear in newspapers for the first time

♦ Midwest farmers burn corn for fuel; prices too low to warrant shipping

1881

♦ President James Garfield assassinated

♦ Supreme Court rules 1862 federal income tax law unconstitutional

♦ Diamond Match Co. created

♦ Southern Pacific Railway links New Orleans with San Francisco

♦ Marquette University founded in Milwaukee

♦ Barnum & Bailey's Circus formed through merger of two companies

♦ Marshall, Field & Co. created by reorganization

♦ Chicago meatpacker Gustavus F. Swift perfects refrigerator car to take Chicago-dressed meat to East Coast

1882

♦ An internal combustion engine powered by gasoline is invented by German engineer Gottlieb Daimler

♦ Electric cable cars are installed in Chicago; they travel 20 blocks, averaging less than 2 miles per hour

♦ Only 2 percent of New York homes have water connections

- Andrew Jergens Company founded to produce soaps, cosmetics, and lotions
- Canadian Club whiskey introduced by Hiram Walker distillery
- Van Camp Packing Company Incorporated produces 6 million cans of pork and beans for shipment to Europe and U.S. markets

1883

- Brooklyn Bridge opens

- *Ladies' Home Journal* begins publication; Cyrus H. K. Curtis is publisher
- Thomas Edison invents the radio tube
- First malted milk produced in Racine, WI
- First successful pea-podder machine installed in Owasco, NY, replacing 600 cannery workers

1884

- Linotype typesetting machine patented by Ottmar Mergenthaler, revolutionizing newspaper composing rooms
- More than 80 percent of the petroleum from U.S. oil wells is marketed by John D. Rockefeller's Standard Oil Trust
- National Cash Register Company (NCR) founded
- Waterman pen invented by New York insurance agent Lewis Edson Waterman
- Montgomery Ward catalogue offers 10,000 items

1885

- Westinghouse Electric & Manufacturing Co. founded

- Evaporated milk produced commercially for first time
- Maryland oyster catch reaches 15 million bushels
- Johnson & Johnson Company founded
- Corn crop tops 2 billion bushels per year for first time
- *Good Housekeeping* magazine begins publication
- Parker Brothers founded to market board games

1886

- A record 610,000 workers strike nationwide seeking 8-hour day, better working conditions
- Capture of Geronimo ends last major Indian war
- Commercial aluminum production pioneered
- Johnson's Wax introduced at Racine, WI
- A decade of intermittent drought begins on Great Plains; nearly 60 percent of range livestock dies
- Coca-Cola sold for first time, at Jacob's Pharmacy in Atlanta
- Hires' Root Beer introduced in bottles
- Statue of Liberty dedicated

1887

- Quaker Mill Company registers the first trademark for a breakfast cereal—a man in Quaker garb
- First ready-to-use surgical dressings introduced by Johnson & Johnson
- Railroads ordered by Congress to keep rates fair and reasonable
- Thomas Edison invents first motor-driven phonograph
- Telephone listings surpass 200,000
- Wheat prices fall to 67¢ per bushel
- Log Cabin Syrup introduced by St. Paul, MN, grocer
- White Rock Mineral Springs Company established in Wisconsin
- Ball-Mason jars introduced
- Ice-making machines supercede blocks of ice at Western Cold

Storage Company in Chicago

1888

- Alternating-current electric motor developed
- Anti-Chinese riots erupt in Seattle
- Burroughs adding machine patented
- *National Geographic* begins publication
- First typewriter stencil introduced
- Parker Pen Company started in Janesville, WI
- Immigration from Britain peaks
- Tobacco merchant Washington B. Duke produces 744 million cigarettes
- Ponce de Leon Hotel opened at St. Augustine, FL

1889

- Oklahoma Territory lands formerly reserved for Indians opened to white settlers
- Safety bicycle introduced; more than 1 million will be sold in the following four years
- Electric lights installed in White House
- *Wall Street Journal* begins publication
- I. M. Singer Company introduces first electric sewing machine
- Aunt Jemima pancake flour invented at St. Joseph, MO
- Calumet baking powder created in Chicago

1890

- Congress increases import duty to record highs
- First commercial dry-cell battery introduced
- 3 percent of Americans age 18 to 21 attend college
- *Literary Digest* begins publication
- Population of Los Angeles reaches 50,000, up 40,000 in ten years
- Two-thirds of nation's 62.9 million people live in rural areas
- First aluminum saucepan produced

1891

- Restrictive antiblack "Jim Crow" laws enacted across South
- First full-service advertising agency established in New York City
- First electric oven for commercial sale introduced at St. Paul, MN
- Thousands of Kansas farmers bankrupted by tight money conditions
- $3 million Tampa Bay Hotel completed in Florida
- American Express Traveler's Cheque copyrighted
- Ceresota flour introduced by Northwestern Consolidated Milling Company

1892

- Steelworkers strike Carnegie-Phipps mill at Homestead, PA; violence erupts
- Improved carburetor invented
- General Electric Company created through merger
- $1 Ingersoll pocket watch introduced
- Chicago's first elevated railways go into operation to begin the Loop
- First U.S. motorcar produced at Springfield, MA, by the Duryea brothers
- Hamilton Watch Company founded
- Country has 4,000 millionaires
- First successful gasoline tractor produced by Waterloo, IA, farmer

1893

- Philadelphia and Reading Railroad goes into receivership
- Recession continues; Chicago's Pullman Palace Car Company reduces wages by one-fourth
- First Ford motorcar road tested
- Wrigley's Spearmint and Juicy Fruit chewing gum introduced by William Wrigley Jr.
- Name Sears, Roebuck & Company used for first time
- Cream of Wheat introduced by Diamond Mill of Grand Forks, ND
- New York's 13-story Waldorf Hotel opens

1894

- Income tax imposed on annual incomes of $4,000 or more
- Strikes cripple railroads; federal government intervenes
- 750,000 workers strike during year
- Oil discovered at Corsicana, TX
- Hershey Bar introduced
- Wheat prices down to 49¢ per bushel
- Winchester M1894 lever-action rifle introduced

1895

- Pneumatic tires put on motorcars for first time
- Underwood Typewriter Company founded

- Treasury gold reserves fall to $41 million as depression continues
- *Collier's Weekly* and *Field and Stream* magazines begin publication
- $4.1 million Biltmore House, world's largest private home, completed at Asheville, NC
- Pocket Kodak camera introduced by Eastman Kodak

1896

- Utah admitted to Union
- Bicycle industry reports sales of $60 million; average bike sells for $100
- S&H Green Stamps issued for first time
- Michelob beer introduced
- Cracker Jack and Tootsie Roll candies introduced

- Klondike gold rush begins
- Radioactivity discovered in uranium

1897

- Bituminous coal miners stage 12-week walkout
- Continental Casualty Company founded
- Dow Chemical Company incorporated
- Winton Motor Carriage Company organized
- Mail Pouch tobacco introduced
- Wheat prices rise to $1.09 per bushel
- Jell-O introduced by Pearl B. Wait
- Boston's H. P. Hill uses glass bottles to distribute milk

1898

- First shots of Spanish-American War fired
- Louisiana "grandfather clause" restricts most blacks from voting
- Union Carbide Company is founded
- Motorcar production reaches 1,000 per year
- Goodyear Tire and Rubber Company founded
- *New York Times* drops price from 3¢ to 1¢ daily; circulation triples
- Pepsi-Cola introduced by New Bern, NC, pharmacist Caleb D. "Doc" Bradham
- Uneeda Biscuits created

1899

- J. P. Stevens & Company founded in New York
- Trolley replaces horsecars in Boston
- Automobile production surpasses 2,500
- Wesson Oil developed
- United Mine Workers of America founded
- First concrete grain elevator erected near Minneapolis
- Boll weevil begins spreading across cotton-growing southern states

SELECTED INCOME 1860–1899

Job	Source	Description	Pay
Actor	Philip B. Kunhardt, Philip B. Kunhardt III, and Peter W. Kunhardt, *P.T. Barnum, America's Greatest Showman* (1995)	Three-year contract of Commodore George Washington Morrison Nutt with P. T. Barnum Circus, beginning in 1862	$30,000
Circus Owner	Kunhardt, *P. T. Barnum, America's Greatest Showman* (1995)	Annual income of P. T. Barnum in 1879	$87,850
Composer	Edwin S. Grosvenor and Morgan Wesson, *Alexander Graham Bell* (1997)	Payment to Richard Wagner to compose the patriotic *Centennial March* for the International Centennial Exhibition in 1876, staged in Philadelphia to celebrate the signing of the Declaration of Independence	$5,000
Golfer	Vincent Tompkins, ed., *American Eras: Development of the Industrial United States, 1878-1899* (1997)	Purse to Horace Rawlins in 1895 for winning first U.S. Open	$150 and Gold Medal worth $50
Photographer	James D. Horan, *Mathew Brady: Historian with a Camera* (1965)	Payment to Mathew Brady by Congress in 1875 to purchase his collection of historical and war photographs; the famous photographer was in bankruptcy and forced to sell his life's work (valued at more than $150,000)	$25,000
Photography Retouching	*San Francisco Examiner* (1895)	Ladies, training provided	$10/wk
Political Cartoonist	J. Chal Vinson, *Thomas Nast, Political Cartoonist* (1967)	Annual salary of Thomas Nast at *Harper's Weekly* in 1871; Nast turned down a $50,000 bribe to leave publication from William Magear "Boss" Tweed	$5,000
Teacher	Robert A. Margo, *Race and Schooling in the South* (1990)	Average annual income of black teachers in Alabama in 1890	$255
Teacher	Margo, *Race and Schooling in the South* (1990)	Average annual income of white teachers in Alabama in 1890	$215

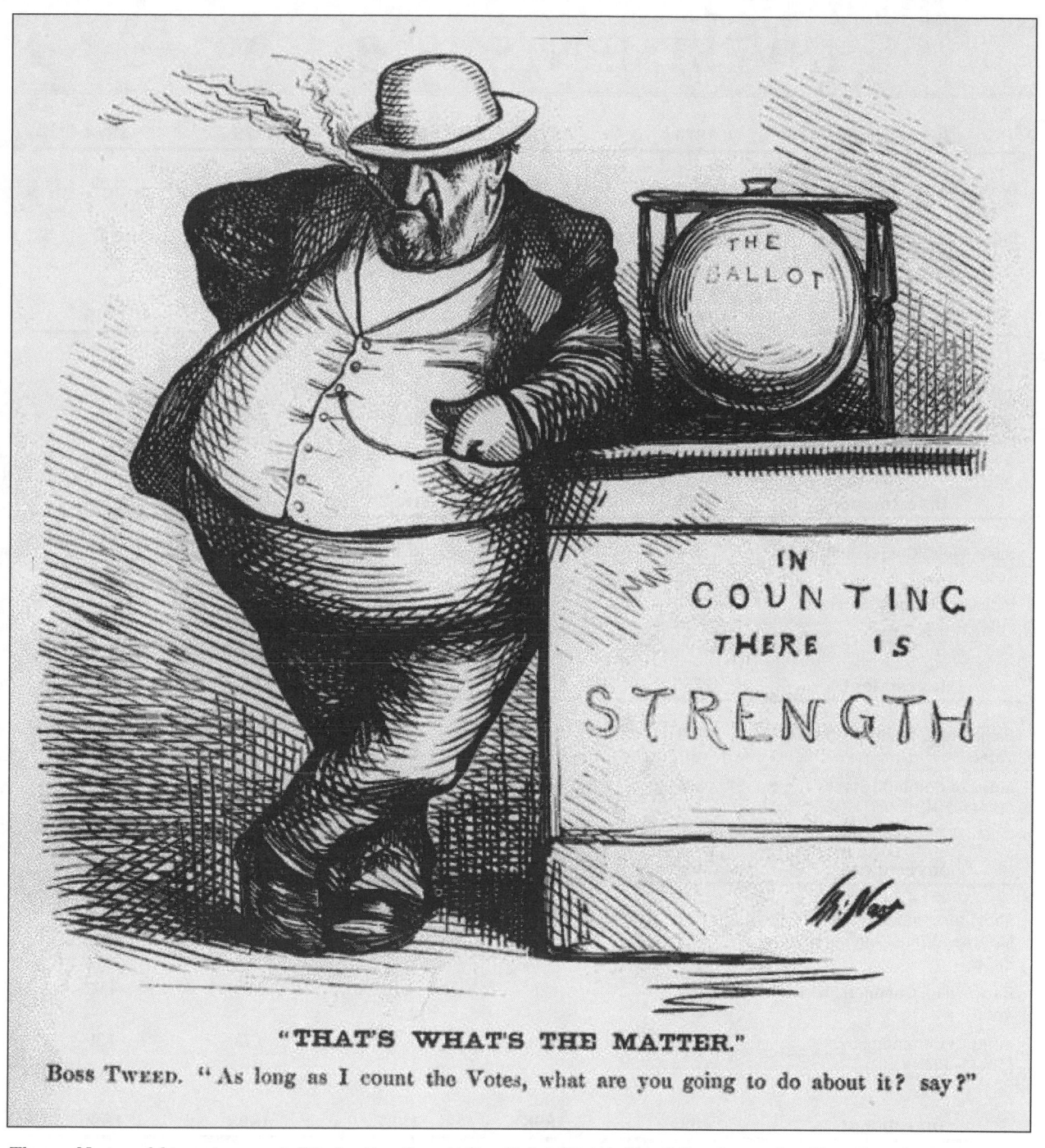

Thomas Nast used his cartoons as political satire. Corrupt New York politician "Boss" Tweed was often his subject. In this Harper's Weekly *cartoon, Nast shows Tweed's source of power: control of the ballot box. "As long as I count the Votes, what are you going to do about it?" (via Wikimedia Commons)*

INVESTMENTS 1870–1899

Investment	1870	1871	1872	1873	1874
Basic Yield, Common Stocks, Total		5.26	5.70	6.54	6.89
Index of Common Stocks (1941 – 1943 = 10)		4.69	5.03	4.80	4.57

Investment	1875	1876	1877	1878	1879
Basic Yield, Common Stocks, Total	6.51	7.02	5.78	5.12	4.70
Index of Common Stocks (1941 – 1943 = 10)	4.45	4.06	3.14	3.38	4.12

Investment	1880	1881	1882	1883	1884
Basic Yield, Common Stocks, Total	4.78	4.84	5.18	5.69	6.31
Index of Common Stocks (1941 – 1943 = 10)	5.21	6.25	5.90	5.63	4.74

Investment	1885	1886	1887	1888	1889
Basic Yield, Common Stocks, Total	5.09	3.85	4.24	4.18	3.88
Index of Common Stocks (1941 – 1943 = 10)	4.60	5.36	5.53	5.20	5.32

Investment	1890	1891	1892	1893	1894
Short-term Interest Rates, 4–6 Months, Prime Commercial Paper	6.91	6.48	5.40	7.64	5.22
Basic Yield, Common Stocks, Total	4.01	4.28	4.16	5.03	4.62
Index of Common Stocks (1941 – 1943 = 10)	5.27	5.03	5.55	4.78	4.39

Investment	1895	1896	1897	1898	1899
Short-term Interest Rates, 4–6 Months, Prime Commercial Paper	5.80	7.02	4.72	5.34	5.50
Basic Yield, Common Stocks, Total	3.97	4.15	3.90	3.72	3.21
Index of Common Stocks (1941 – 1943 = 10)	4.53	4.23	4.45	5.05	6.29

STANDARD JOBS 1860-1864

Job Type	1860	1861	1862	1863	1864
Bricklayers (Massachusetts)	$1.53/day	$1.81/day	$1.79/day	$2.05/day	$2.31/day
Avg hrs/wk	60	61	60	60	60
Carpenters and Joiners (Connecticut)	$1.65/day	$1.50/day	$1.48/day	$1.86/day	$2.05/day
Avg hrs/wk	61	60	60	60	60
Engineers, Stationary (New York)	$1.63/day	$1.82/day	$1.77/day	$1.69/day	$2.04/day
Avg hrs/wk	68	68	70	67	73
Farm Labor (New York)	$0.88/day	$0.88/day	$1/day	$1.13	$1.50/day
Avg hrs/wk	66	66	66	66	66
Firemen (Massachusetts)	$1.33/day	$1.38/day	$1.41/day	$1.48/day	$1.25/day
Avg hrs/wk	70	66	66	66	72
Glassblowers, Bottles (New Jersey)	$2.59/day	$2.44/day	$2.95/day	$2.95/day	$2.95/day
Avg hrs/wk	NR	NR	NR	NR	NR
Hod Carriers (Massachusetts)	$1/day	$1.08/day	$1.18/day	$1.19/day	$1.43/day
Avg hrs/wk	56	61	63	63	63
Marble Cutters (New York)	$2.04/day	$1.62/day	$1.58/day	$1.95/day	$2.52/day
Avg hrs/wk	60	60	60	60	60
Painters (New York)	$1.97/day	$1.93/day	$1.98/day	$2.21/day	$2.93/day
Avg hrs/wk	60	60	60	60	60
Plasterers (Pennsylvania)	$1.69/day	$1.66/day	$1.67/day	$1.92/day	$1.93/day
Avg hrs/wk	60	60	60	60	60
Plumbers (New York)	$1.88/day	$1.88/day	$1.93/day	$2.50/day	$3.50/day
Avg hrs/wk	60	60	60	60	60
Stonemasons (New York)	$2.50/day	$2.50/day	$2.05/day	$1.98/day	$2.35/day
Avg hrs/wk	60	60	60	60	60

STANDARD JOBS 1865-1869

Job Type	1865	1866	1867	1868	1869
Bricklayers (Massachusetts)	$2.59/day	$2.95/day	$3.17/day	$3.76/day	$3.44/day
Avg hrs/wk	60	60	60	60	60
Carpenters and Joiners (Connecticut)	$2.25/day	$2.63/day	$3.03/day	$3.05/day	$2.98/day
Avg hrs/wk	60	61	60	60	60
Engineers, Stationary (New York)	$2.34/day	$2.43/day	$2.63/day	$2.66/day	$2.66/day
Avg hrs/wk	70	70	70	70	69
Farm Labor (New York)	$1.50/day	$1.50/day	$1.50/day	$1.50/day	$1.75/day
Avg hrs/wk	66	66	66	66	66
Firemen (Massachusetts)	$1.51/day	$1.58/day	$1.67/day	$1.64/day	$1.67/day
Avg hrs/wk	66	66	66	66	66
Glassblowers, Bottles (New Jersey)	$3.95/day	$3.95/day	$5.14/day	$5.19/day	$5.19/day
Avg hrs/wk	NR	NR	NR	NR	NR
Hod Carriers (Massachusetts)	$1.55/day	$1.74/day	$1.59/day	$2/day	$1.93/day
Avg hrs/wk	60	60	60	60	60
Marble Cutters (New York)	$2.91/day	$2.94/day	$3.39/day	$3.46/day	$3.69/day
Avg hrs/wk	60	60	60	60	60
Painters (New York)	$2.82/day	$3.35/day	$3.86/day	$3.43/day	$4.29/day
Avg hrs/wk	60	60	60	60	60
Plasterers (Pennsylvania)	$2.29/day	$2.60/day	$3.70/day	$3.67/day	$3.67/day
Avg hrs/wk	60	60	60	60	60
Plumbers (New York)	$3.5/day	$3.50/day	$3.85/day	$3.85/day	$3.85/day
Avg hrs/wk	60	60	60	60	60
Stonemasons (New York)	$2.40/day	$2.73/day	$2.72/day	$2.72/day	$2.72/day
Avg hrs/wk	60	60	60	60	60

STANDARD JOBS 1870–1874

Job Type	1870	1871	1872	1873	1874
Bricklayers (Massachusetts)	$3.97/day	$4.07/day	$3.86/day	$3.88/day	$3.50/day
Avg hrs/wk	60	60	60	60	60
Carpenters and Joiners (Connecticut)	$2.77/day	$2.79/day	$2.73/day	$3.04/day	$2.89/day
Avg hrs/wk	60	60	60	60	60
Engineers, Stationary (New York)	$2.97/day	$2.86/day	$2.62/day	$2.70/day	$2.94/day
Avg hrs/wk	66	70	65	64	67
Farm Labor (New York)	$1.50/day	$1.50/day	$1.50/day	$1.50/day	$1.25/day
Avg hrs/wk	66	66	66	66	66
Firemen (Massachusetts)	$1.73/day	$1.86/day	$1.61/day	$1.67/day	$1.72/day
Avg hrs/wk	66	63	66	66	66
Glassblowers, Bottles (New Jersey)	$5.19/day	$5.17/day	$5.19/day	$5.19/day	$4.96/day
Avg hrs/wk	NR	NR	NR	NR	NR
Hod Carriers (Massachusetts)	$2.12/day	$2.09/day	$1.98/day	$2.03/day	$1.95/day
Avg hrs/wk	60	60	60	60	60
Marble Cutters (New York)	$3.19/day	$3.22/day	$3.27/day	$3.25/day	$3.19/day
Avg hrs/wk	60	60	60	60	60
Painters (New York)	$3.15/day	$3.16/day	$3.12/day	$3.13/day	$3.02/day
Avg hrs/wk	60	60	60	60	60
Plasterers (Pennsylvania)	$2.86/day	$2.88/day	$2.86/day	$2.92/day	$2.86/day
Avg hrs/wk	60	60	60	60	60
Plumbers (New York)	$3.37/day	$3.36/day	$3.22/day	$3.18/day	$3.11/day
Avg hrs/wk	57	57	57	57	57
Stonemasons (New York)	$3.41/day	$3.42/day	$3.38/day	$3.36/day	$2.95/day
Avg hrs/wk	60	60	60	60	60

An 1870 advertisement for the Phoenix Insurance Company, showing horse-drawn fire engines. (via Wikimedia Commons)

STANDARD JOBS 1875–1879

Job Type	1875	1876	1877	1878	1879
Bricklayers (Massachusetts)	$3.48/day	$3.45/day	$2.96/day	$2.90/day	$2.71
Avg hrs/wk	60	60	60	60	60
Engineers, Stationary (New York)	$3.21/day	$3.09/day	$3.10/day	$3.04/day	$2.55/day
Avg hrs/wk	71	70	70	70	72
Farm Labor (New York)	$1.25/day	$1.25/day	$1/day	$0.88/day	$0.88/day
Avg hrs/wk	66	63	63	63	63
Firemen (Massachusetts)	$1.60/day	$1.57/day	$1.51/day	$1.49/day	$1.39/day
Avg hrs/wk	60	60	60	60	60
Glassblowers, Bottles (New Jersey)	$4.64/day	$4.36/day	$3.68/day	$3.68/day	$3.68/day
Avg hrs/wk	NR	NR	NR	NR	NR
Hod Carriers (Massachusetts)	$1.91/day	$1.84/day	$1.79/day	$1.83/day	$1.82/day
Avg hrs/wk	60	60	60	60	60
Marble Cutters (New York)	$3.10/day	$2.93/day	$2.77/day	$2.47/day	$2.38/day
Avg hrs/wk	60	60	60	60	60
Painters (New York)	$3.08/day	$3.02/day	$2.59/day	$2.61/day	$2.84/day
Avg hrs/wk	60	60	60	60	60
Plasterers (Pennsylvania)	$2.88/day	$2.31/day	$1.94/day	$1.94/day	$1.58/day
Avg hrs/wk	60	60	60	60	60
Plumbers (New York)	$3.16/day	$3.13/day	$3.16/day	$3.13/day	$3.12/day
Avg hrs/wk	57	57	57	54	54
Stonemasons (New York)	$3.01/day	$2.52/day	$2.12/day	$2.11/day	$2.47/day
Avg hrs/wk	60	60	60	60	60

STANDARD JOBS 1880-1884

Job Type	1880	1881	1882	1883	1884
Bricklayers (Massachusetts)	$2.68/day	$2.83/day	$3.18/day	$3.23/day	$3.20/day
Avg hrs/wk	60	60	60	60	60
Carpenters and Joiners (Connecticut)	$2.15/day	$2.33/day	2.49/day	$2.57/day	$2.53/day
Avg hrs/wk	61	60	61	60	60
Engineers, Stationary (New York)	$2.48/day	$2.29/day	$2.29/day	$2.24/day	$2.28/day
Avg hrs/wk	65	65	62	64	64
Farm Labor (New York)	$1.25/day	$1.25/day	$1.50/day	$1.25/day	$1.25/day
Avg hrs/wk	63	63	63	63	63
Firemen (Massachusetts)	$1.37/day	$1.42/day	$1.39/day	$1.50/day	$1.48/day
Avg hrs/wk	60	60	60	60	60
Glassblowers, Bottles (New Jersey)	NR	NR	NR	$4.23/day	$4.08/day
Avg hrs/wk	NR	NR	NR	51	51
Hod Carriers (Massachusetts)	$1.82/day	$1.62/day	$1.71/day	$1.94/day	$1.72/day
Avg hrs/wk	60	60	60	60	60
Marble Cutters (New York)	$2.40/day	$2.57/day	$2.05/day	$2.69/day	$2.85/day
Avg hrs/wk	60	60	60	60	60
Painters (New York)	$2.94/day	$2.76/day	$2.86/day	$3.25/day	$3.26/day
Avg hrs/wk	60	58	58	58	58
Plasterers (Pennsylvania)	$1.81/day	$1.97/day	$2.39/day	$2.98/day	$3.25/day
Avg hrs/wk	60	60	60	59	59
Plumbers (New York)	$3.37/day	$3.43/day	$3.50/day	$3.50/day	$3.50/day
Avg hrs/wk	54	54	54	58	60
Stonemasons (New York)	$2.58/day	$2.92/day	$3.22/day	$3.31/day	$3.26/day
Avg hrs/wk	60	60	60	60	60

STANDARD JOBS 1885–1889

Job Type	1885	1886	1887	1888	1889
Bricklayers (Massachusetts)	$3.37/day	$3.50/day	$2.94/day	$3.30/day	$3.46/day
Avg hrs/wk	60	59	58	56	56
Carpenters and Joiners (Connecticut)	$2.32/day	$2.46/day	$2.24/day	$2.56/day	NR
Avg hrs/wk	61	58	55	54	56
Engineers, Stationary (New York)	$2.32/day	$2.34/day	$2.12/day	$2.45/day	$2/day
Avg hrs/wk	64	61	64	63	65
Farm Labor (New York)	$1.38/day	$1.38/day	$1.38/day	$1.40/day	$1.50/day
Avg hrs/wk	63	63	63	63	63
Firemen (Massachusetts)	$1.54/day	$1.63/day	$1.53/day	$1.43/day	NR
Avg hrs/wk	60	57	59	60	NR
Glassblowers, Bottles (New Jersey)	$4.14/day	$4.22/day	NR	$4.95/day	$4.05/day
Avg hrs/wk	52	54	NR	52	54
Hod Carriers (Massachusetts)	$1.66/day	$1.69/day	$1.67/day	$1.73/day	$1.69/day
Avg hrs/wk	60	60	56	58	58
Marble Cutters (New York)	$2.82/day	$2.94/day	$2.98/day	$3.01/day	$2.89/day
Avg hrs/wk	60	60	60	54	54
Painters (New York)	$2.96/day	$3.18/day	$2.93/day	$2.59/day	$3.40/day
Avg hrs/wk	60	54	54	57	55
Plasterers (Pennsylvania)	$3.50/day	$2.85/day	$3/day	$3.50/day	$3.50/day
Avg hrs/wk	54	52	54	54	54
Plumbers (New York)	$3.17/day	$3.28/day	$3.52/day	$3.37/day	$3.59/day
Avg hrs/wk	56	54	52	54	48
Stonemasons (New York)	$3.05/day	$2.75/day	$3.35/day	$3.37/day	$3.32/day
Avg hrs/wk	56	54	56	55	57

STANDARD JOBS 1890–1894

Job Type	1890	1891	1892	1893	1894
Bricklayers (Massachusetts)	$3.55/day	$3.51/day	$3.68/day	$3.75/day	$3.65/day
Avg hrs/wk	55	56	54	54	52
Carpenters and Joiners (Connecticut)	NR	NR	$2.63/day	$2.53/day	$2.26/day
Avg hrs/wk	60	56	56	60	60
Engineers, Stationary (New York)	$2.26/day	$2.26/day	$2.72/day	$2.26/day	$2/day
Avg hrs/wk	63	63	63	63	60
Farm Labor (New York)	$1.49/day	$1.37/day	NR	$1.17/day	$1.25/day
Avg hrs/wk	63	63	66	60	NR
Glassblowers, Bottles (New Jersey)	$3.80	$5.15	$5.15	NR	NR
Avg hrs/wk	51	NR	NR	NR	NR
Hod Carriers (Massachusetts)	$1.80/day	$1.77/day	$2.24/day	$2.22/day	$2.19/day
Avg hrs/wk	57	58	54	54	52
Marble Cutters (New York)	$3.21/day	$3.27/day	$3.38/day	$2.51/day	$2.77/day
Avg hrs/wk	54	50	49	53	54
Painters (New York)	$2.16/day	$2.09/day	$3.43/day	$2.93/day	$2.61/day
Avg hrs/wk	55	51	51	50	54
Plasterers (Pennsylvania)	$3.50/day	$3.20/day	$3.20/day	$2.17/day	NR
Avg hrs/wk	54	48	48	57	NR
Plumbers (New York)	$2.94/day	$2.87/day	$3.58/day	$3.53/day	$3.72/day
Avg hrs/wk	48	48	48	49	48
Stonemasons (New York)	$3.39/day	$3.18/day	$3.90/day	$3/07/day	$3.95/day
Avg hrs/wk	50	49	49	51	48

STANDARD JOBS 1895–1899

Job Type	1895	1896	1897	1898	1899
Bricklayers (Massachusetts)	$3.34/day	$3.87/day	$3.45/day	$3.41/day	$3.60/day
Avg hrs/wk	48	50	48	48	48
Carpenters and Joiners (Connecticut)	$2.27/day	$2.04/day	$2.33/day	NR	NR
Avg hrs/wk	62	60	58	NR	NR
Engineers, Stationary (New York)	$2.52/day	$2.67/day	$3/day	$3.17/day	$3.17/day
Avg hrs/wk	59	63	70	60	56
Glassblowers, Bottles (New Jersey)	NR	NR	NR	$3.97/day	NR
Avg hrs/wk	NR	NR	NR	54	NR
Hod Carriers (Massachusetts)	$2/day	$2.15/day	$2/day	$1.97/day	$2.10/day
Avg hrs/wk	48	49	48	48	48
Marble Cutters (New York)	$2.80/day	$2.83/day	$3.94/day	$4.22/day	NR
Avg hrs/wk	54	54	48	48	NR
Painters (New York)	$2.32/day	$2.96/day	$2.45/day	$2.47/day	$2.57/day
Avg hrs/wk	56	51	49	50	52
Plasterers (Pennsylvania)	NR	$3.19/day	NR	NR	$3.20/day
Avg hrs/wk	NR	NR	49	NR	48
Plumbers (New York)	$3.74/day	$3.49/day	$3.73/day	$3.74/day	$3.92/day
Avg hrs/wk	48	49	48	48	50
Stonemasons (New York)	$3.94/day	$3.92/day	$3.38/day	$3.67/day	$3.06/day
Avg hrs/wk	48	49	48	48	48

A portrait of an African American bricklayers union, circa 1899. (via Library of Congress)

SELECTED PRICES 1860–1899

Item	Source	Description	Price
ADVERTISING			
Advertising Budget	Cecil Munsey, *The Illustrated Guide to the Collectibles of Coca-Cola* (1972)	*Coca-Cola;* amount spent for advertising in 1886	$73.96
Advertising Rate	*The Plantation* (1872)	Full page	$20.00
Advertising Rate	*Demorest's Illustrated Monthly* (1873)	Per line solid agate space	$0.75
APPAREL, CHILDREN'S			
Hat	*Advertising Trade Card* (1892)	Boy's school hat	$0.25
Knee Pants	*The Delineator* (1896)	Boy's; we take remnants of fine woolens, give them to our merchant tailoring department, and make them into boy's knee pants	$0.50-$1.00
Parasol	*New York Times* (1877)	Sun umbrellas	$0.50
School Outfit	*Ladies' Home Journal* (1893)	Our combination suit; extra pair pants and hat to match; for boys 4 to 14 years	$5.00
Shoes	*Advertising Trade Card* (1875)	Button boats; $10,000 worth of boots and shoes better than ever	$0.60
Snap Waist	*Ladies' Home Journal* (1893)	*Cupid;* no more buttons to sew on; no button-holes, no buckles	$1.00
Suit	*Advertising Trade Card* (1885)	Nobby	$2.00
Suit	*Chicago Daily Tribune* (1882)	Jerome suits; 4 to 11 years old	$3.00
Suit	*Ladies' Home Journal* (1893)	Boy's combination; consisting of double-breasted coat, two pairs of knee pants, and a nice hat—all made to match	$5.00
APPAREL, MEN'S			
Clothing	*R. H. Macy & Co. Advertising Flyer* (1881)	Silk walking costumes; in solid colors	$16.84
Collar	*New York Times* (1895)	*Keep's;* best four-ply linen	$0.15
Collar	*Harper's Weekly* (1865)	*American Steel;* snow-white; linen-finished; illusion-stitched	$1.25
Collars and Cuffs	*The Ledger Monthly* (1899)	*Linene;* stylish, convenient, economical, made of fine cloth; the turn-down collars are reversible and give double service; ten collars or five pairs of cuffs	$0.25
Cuff Holder	*Demorest's Family Magazine* (1890)	Invisible; just out; impossible to get out of order	$1.00/2 dozen

Item	Source	Description	Price
Cuffs	*The Youth's Companion* (1898)	*Linene;* reversible; look well, feel well, wear well; made of fine cloth; when soiled, reverse, wear again, then discard	$0.25/5 pairs
Gloves	*Spirit of the Times* (1877)	Kid and dogskin, embroidered backs, all shades	$1.50
Golf Cap	*New York Times* (1895)	*Keep's;* correct styles	$1.00
Half Hose	*Spirit of the Times* (1877)	Elegant; in cotton worsted and merino	$0.40
Hat	*Spirit of the Times* (1877)	*Sola;* made of waterproof duck, dead grass color, and in same style as east India hats; absolute guarantee against sunstroke	$3.00
Hat	*New York Times* (1895)	Fall styles; silk derbies	$6.00
Necktie	*Demorest's Illustrated Monthly* (1873)	Designed to supersede all other methods for fastening the bow to a turn-down collar	$0.10
Necktie	*Demorest's Illustrated Monthly* (1873)	*Demorest's;* black bows in rich red silk	$0.50
Neckwear	*Spirit of the Times* (1877)	Ties, bows, and scarves	$0.25
Pants	*New York Times* (1877)	English trousers; many specialties to order	$9.00
Pants	*Advertising Trade Card* (1885)	Good cassimere pants	$2.00
Shirt	*Spirit of the Times* (1877)	*Wamsutta;* muslin	$1.00
Shirt	*San Francisco Examiner* (1895)	Standard shirts; a shirt that will fit, look, and wear like finest custom-made	$1.50
Shirt Bosoms	*New York Times* (1863)	*Kinzey's gent's;* various styles	$0.28–$0.50
Shirts	*The New Orleans Picayune* (1875)	Stylish shirts	$1.50
Shirts	*New York Times* (1895)	*Keep's;* made to order	$9.00/6
Shoes	*Advertising Trade Card* (1875)	Working; $10,000 worth of boots and shoes better than ever	$0.98
Shoes	*The State* (Columbia, SC) (1891)	*Hanan's;* handmade	$3.00
Shoes	*Advertising Trade Card* (1892)	Man's good working shoes	$1.00
Shooting Coat	*Spirit of the Times* (1877)	*W. H. Holabird;* complete waterproof duck coat	$6.00
Suit	*Advertising Trade Card* (1875)	Fine imported Scotch suits	$10.00
Suit	*Advertising Trade Card* (1875)	Durable working suits	$4.00
Suit	*Advertising Trade Card* (1875)	Fine English cassimere suits	$12.00
Suit	*Chicago Daily Tribune* (1882)	*Putnam Apparel House;* men's single-breast frock suit; made with Scotch cassimere	$12.50
Suit	*New York Times* (1877)	Cheviot; black and blue	$20.00
Suit	*Advertising Trade Card* (1885)	Black cheviot	$7.50
Suspenders	*The Yorkville Enquirer* (Yorkville, SC) (1892)	$0.05 will buy a regular $0.15 suspender	$0.05
Top coat	*New York Times* (1895)	English design	$10.00

Item	Source	Description	Price
APPAREL, WOMEN'S			
Bicycle Skirt	*The Youth's Companion* (1898)	Tailor-made; our new designs in bicycle skirts are recognized everywhere as the most practical skirts for wheeling that have yet been produced	$2.50
Bust Form	*The Delineator* (1896)	*The New Hygeia;* as light as a feather, tastefully covered so that the forms can be removed and the covering washed	$0.50
Cape	*Harper's Weekly* (1875)	Young & Conant; gossamer, waterproof; the best storm garment ever worn; 56" long	$8.25
Corset	*Demorest's Monthly Magazine* (1881)	*Hercules;* supporting; woven, spoon steel, cannot stretch, break or lose its shape, avoids all pressure on the chest	$3.00
Corset	*The Delineator* (1896)	*The Henderson Flexo Girdle;* every inch of it fits	$1.25
Corset	*The Spartan* (Spartanburg, SC) (1898)	*Featherbone;* every one guaranteed	$0.18
Corset	*The Youth's Companion* (1898)	*Warner's* '98 models; the quality is the finest thing to consider in corsets; all figures suited at these prices	$1.00
Dress Shield	*Demorest's Family Magazine* (1890)	*Canfield Seamless;* the only reliable dress shield in the world	$0.25
Dress Shield	*The Delineator* (1896)	OMO: better than rubber, absolutely odorless; impervious to perspiration	$0.25
Glove Hook	*Harper's Weekly* (1887)	*H. H. Tammen;* moss agate	4/$0.05
Gloves	*Advertising Trade Card* (1875)	Perfumed kid gloves; pure elastic; any shade or color Two-button gloves Four-button gloves	 $1.00 $1.50
Gloves	*The Delineator* (1896)	Kayser Patent Finger-Tipped Silk Gloves; the tips wear as long as the gloves	$0.50

From Ladies' Home Journal, *Volume 13 (1895): "Costless comfort and the personification of Elegance—the Cluze Patent Thumb Glove... The peculiar yet simple cut of the thumb piece makes it an ideal glove. There is not a misstich in its entire construction... The cost of the Cluze Patent Thumb Glove isn't any more than for imperfect-fitting and one-day wearing kinds."* (Via Library of Congress)

Item	Source	Description	Price
Hat	*New York Times* (1877)	Trimmed	$2.50
Parasols	*Chicago Daily Tribune* (1882)	*Pardridges'* Semiannual Reduction Sale; satin parasols, regular $5.00	$3.90
Scarf	*New York Times* (1877)	Spanish and Brusells net; 2 1/2 yards long	$0.75
Shoes	*Advertising Trade Card* (1875)	*Lace;* $10,000 worth of boots and shoes better than ever	$0.63
Shoes	*The State* (Columbia, SC) (1891)	*Ziegler's;* button; 100 pairs available	9/$0.05
Shoes	*Advertising Trade Card* (1892)	*Dongola;* button shoes	$1.50
Skirt	*The Delineator* (1896)	Brilliantine	$1.75
Skirt	*The Delineator* (1896)	*Lustre;* wool; the best and lightest all year round skirt, regardless of price; five gored, 3 1/3 yards wide	$2.50
Skirt	*The Delineator* (1896)	Skirt made of heavily figured brilliantine, full flare and ripple back	$2.49
Sleeve Buttons	*Harper's Weekly* (1865)	Ivory and pearl; top quality	$3.00/pair
Suit	*Advertising Trade Card* (1885)	All-wool evening suit	$6.00
Turban	*Ladies' Home Journal* (1893)	Neatly made of cloth and velvet and trimmed in all colors and combinations to match any suit	$0.98
Undergarments	*Ladies' Home Journal* (1893)	Ladies' cotton and wool combination suits, natural color; send bust measurements	$2.00 to $3.00
Waist	*The Delineator* (1896)	*Chicago;* size 6-D; gives such comfort . . . allows perfect freedom of motion and perfect development of the body	$1.00

APPLIANCES

Item	Source	Description	Price
Burner and Chimney	*Harper's Weekly* (1887)	*Royal Argand;* large, white, steady light without a flicker	$1.25

BABY PRODUCTS

Item	Source	Description	Price
Diaper	*Demorest's Family Magazine* (1890)	*The Canfield;* the only article of its kind that affords perfect protection without harmful results	6/$0.05
Shoes	*Advertising Trade Card* (1875)	$10,000 worth of boots and shoes better than ever	$0.15
Soap	*Advertising Trade Card* (1870)	*B. T. Babbitt's;* only the purest vegetable oils used; a certain preventative of chafing, itching, etc.	$2.50

BUSINESS EQUIPMENT & SUPPLIES

Item	Source	Description	Price
Business Cards	*Demorest's Monthly Magazine* (1881)	*Chromo;* in sets of one dozen assorted styles	$0.05
Harness	*Chicago Daily Tribune* (1882)	Double buggy harness	$25.00

Item	Source	Description	Price
Insurance Rates	*The New Orleans Picayune* (1875)	Life insurance, per $1,000, cost per year Age 40 Age 50	 $21.02 $433.17
Printing Press	*Harper's Weekly* (1865)	*Taylor;* double cylinder, five roller, table distribution, bed 38" ×51"	$3,500
Printing Press	*Demorest's Family Magazine* (1890)	Self-inker; printing press with script type outfit	$5.00
Rubber Stamp	*Demorest's Family Magazine* (1890)	With name on, ink pad, pencil & pen; one ring and agent's outfit	$0.10
Typewriter	*Harper's Weekly* (1887)	*Hall;* guaranteed to do better work, and a greater variety, than any other typewriter in the world	$40.00
Typewriter	*The Delineator* (1896)	Anderson's shorthand is taking the place of stenography because it is quickly learned	$25.00

COLLECTIBLES

Item	Source	Description	Price
Engravings	*Harper's Weekly* (1887)	President and Mrs. Cleveland; far superior to lithographs; each portrait 7" × 11"	$0.50
Figures	*The Century Magazine* (1884)	Rogers Group; *The Peddler at the Fair;* these groups are packed without charge to go to any part of the world	$15.00
Photographs	*Ingalls' Home Magazine* (1889)	President and Mrs. Harrison; two cabinet photos	$0.15
Prints	*Spirit of the Times* (1877)	*Currier & Ives;* pictures of the great trotters; all in action, showing just their gait and style; size 13 1/2" × 17 3/4"	$0.20
Stamps	*The Youth's Companion* (1898)	Shanghai, China; 100 rare stamps	$0.10

EDUCATION

Item	Source	Description	Price
Dance Lessons	*San Francisco Examiner* (1895)	Waltz guaranteed in private; 3 months' tuition	$10.00
Fees	*Southern Christian Advocate* (1897)	*Clemson College;* board, washing, fuel, lights for session; 40 weeks	$59.00
Piano Lessons	*New York Times* (1863)	Twenty-four lessons on the piano, at pupils' residences	$8.00
School	*San Francisco Examiner* (1895)	*Miss Bolte's home school;* board; English, French, German, Music, Dancing	$30.00/ month
Tuition	*New York Times* (1868)	*Rockland Female Institute;* for board and English tuition, Nyack on the Hudson	$360/year
Tuition	*New York Times* (1868)	*West Branch Board School;* for boys 10 to 16 years of age, Jersey shore, Lycoming County, Penn.	$225/year
Tuition	*Spirit of the Times* (1877)	Special training for teachers; renowned music school and school of elocution, oratory, modern languages, drawing and painting Classes of three pupils Private	 $10.00/quarter $30.00/quarter

Item	Source	Description	Price
Tuition	*The State* (Columbia, SC) (1896)	*Columbia Female College;* curricula on university plan; students entering every department according to preparation, none held back	$200/year
Tuition	*The Delineator* (1896)	University of the City of New York Law School; Two-year Post-graduate	$200 $125

ENTERTAINMENT

Item	Source	Description	Price
Aquarium Ticket	*New York Times* (1877)	*The Great American Aquarium;* marvelous triple-tailed Japanese fishes, beautiful vari-colored fish, for which $2,000 was offered and refused Children Adult	 $0.25 $0.50
Concert	*The New Orleans Picayune* (1875)	Grand Concert featuring Mlle Corinne Bouligny Per ticket	 $1.00
Concert Ticket	*San Francisco Daily Examiner* (1875)	Grand Concert of Music; Madame Z. Dennis, late of the Italian Opera, Paris and lately from the French Opera, New Orleans, will make her first appearance	$1.00
Concert Ticket	*Spirit of the Times* (1877)	*Gilmore's Concert Garden;* Gilmore's Great Military Band and other eminent artists Per seat Box seating four	 $0.50 $3.00
Exhibition Tickets	*San Francisco Daily Examiner* (1875)	Industrial Exhibition, single season tickets	$3.00
Exhibition Ticket	*New York Times* (1877)	*Academy of Design Painting Exhibition;* the fifty-second Grand Annual Exhibition, 23rd St. and 4th Avenue	$0.25
Exhibition Ticket	*Spirit of the Times* (1877)	*Russian Horse Trotter Exhibition at Fleetwood Park;* a display of all horses as shown at fairs in Russia, with all styles of horse clothing and trappings used there	$1.00
Game Ticket	*Spirit of the Times* (1877)	*Tammy Hall Grand Billiards Match;* for the champion gold medal valued at $600 between Wm. Sexton (champion) and Cyearillic Dion; ladies accompanied by gentlemen free General admission Reserved seats	 $0.50 $1.00
Horse Racing	*Chicago Daily Tribune* (1882)	*Six Great Contests of Speed;* The Cup Day and Chicago Stakes	$0.50
Lecture Ticket	*New York Times* (1863)	*"How To End The War";* lecture by Col. O. T. Beard	$0.25
Museum Ticket	*New York Times* (1863)	*Banvard's Hall of Art;* four Grand Panoramas on the same night Children Adults	 $0.15 $0.25
Museum Ticket	*New York Times* (1863)	*Barnum's American Museum;* featuring the smallest pair of human beings ever seen Children under 10 Adults	 $0.15 $0.25

Item	Source	Description	Price
Museum Ticket	*Harper's Weekly* (1865)	*Barnum's New American Museum;* nothing to offend the most fastidious, but everything to gratify healthy curiosity and refined taste; two performances daily	
		Children	$0.15
		Adults	$0.30
Museum Ticket	*New York Times* (1877)	*P. T. Barnum at Gilmore Gardens;* the very last opportunity to witness the most tremendous amusement combination of modern times	$0.25-$0.75
Opera Ticket	*San Francisco Daily Examiner* (1875)	Grand English Opera, Maguire's New Theatre; *Marriage of Figaro;* reserved seats	$1.00-$2.00
Orchestra Ticket	*New York Times* (1895)	Symphony Orchestra, Walter Damrosch, conductor	$0.25-$1.00
Show Ticket	*Spirit of the Times* (1894)	*Buffalo Bill's Wild West Show;* Ambrose Park, South Brooklyn; twice daily, rain or shine; 20,000 covered seats	
		Children	$0.25
		Adults	$0.50
Skating Ticket	*New York Times* (1863)	*Fifth Avenue Skating Pond;* single ticket	
		Ladies'	$2.50
		Gentlemen's	$5.00
Race Ticket	*Spirit of the Times* (1894)	*Chicago Race-Track at Harlem;* six races each day	$0.75
Theater Ticket	*New York Times* (1868)	*Wood's Museum and Metropolitan Theatre;* Miss Susan Galton will appear in two of Offenbach's comic operettas, introducing the songs of "Home Sweet Home" and "Lo! Hear the Gentle Lark"	
		Children under 10	$0.25
		Adults	$0.50
Theater Ticket	*New York Times* (1877)	*Mark Twain American Drama at Park Theatre;* farewell engagement of John T. Raymond in his creation of Col. Mulberry Sellers	$0.50-$1.50
Theater Ticket	*New York Times* (1895)	*Comic Elephants,* by George Lockhart	$0.40

ENTERTAINMENT, HOME

Item	Source	Description	Price
Card Game	*The Youth's Companion* (1898)	*Dominola;* home card game; fun for young and old	$0.20
Magic Lantern Attachment	*The Ledger Monthly* (1899)	Makes pictures 6' high, plus 36 views	$1.00
Music Box	*Spirit of the Times* (1877)	*Distin;* everything in the musical line	$2.50
Music Box	*The Delineator* (1896)	*The Capital;* self-playing; plays any number of tunes; standard and popular airs	
		44 teeth in comb, 8 tunes	$15.00
		162 teeth in comb, 12 tunes	$75.00
Music Boxes	*Harper's New Monthly Magazine* (1866)	Playing from one to 36 different tunes	$5.50-$6.00
Recording	*Demorest's Illustrated Monthly* (1873)	Elocutionist's Annual	$0.25
Song Sheet	*Spirit of the Times* (1877)	"Life's Wheat Is Full of Tares, My Boy," by H. P. Danks; a motto song of uncommon sense and excellence	$0.30

A stereograph card of two Winnebago women. Images of the American West, and particularly of Native Americans of the West, were popular collectibles in the 19th century. (via New York Public Library)

Item	Source	Description	Price
Stereoscopic Pictures	*New York Times* (1863)	*Leggat Brothers;* magnificent colored pictures	$1.50/dozen

FARM EQUIPMENT & SUPPLIES

Item	Source	Description	Price
Boarding Fee	*Spirit of the Times* (1877)	Horses; for winter at farm in Stamford, Conn.	$8.00/month
Condition Powder for Chickens	*The Youth's Companion* (1898)	*Sheridan's;* to get more eggs there is no better plan than that of daily mixing the food given to poultry	$0.25
Corn Seed	*The Plantation* (1872)	*Dent;* very early and prolific and succeeds well in our (southern) climate	$1.00
Cotton Seeds	*R. H. Macy & Co. Advertising Flyer* (1881)	Duncan's Mammoth Prolific; yields 6590 lbs. seed cotton per acre; for 100 seeds	$0.10
Fertilizer	*The Plantation* (1872)	*Dickson;* ground raw bone	$40/ton
Harness Soap	*Spirit of the Times* (1877)	*Colgate's;* try it and you will use no other	$0.05/cake
Hog	*The Plantation* (1872)	*Berkshire;* one boar, over twelve months old, large and handsome	$40/pair
Hoof Ointment	*Spirit of the Times* (1877)	*Knickerbocker;* for horses; cures quarter cracks, corns, brittle hoofs, and all diseases arising from dryness of the hoof	$1.00/jar
Horse Medicine	*Spirit of the Times* (1877)	*Wilder's Constitution Powders for Horses;* a public blessing to horses and cattle; cures all diseases common to horses, gives vitality, purifies the blood, and gives new lease of life	$0.50/box
Horse Muzzle	*Spirit of the Times* (1877)	*Gedney's;* wire; invaluable for biters and cribbers	$6.00

Item	Source	Description	Price
Horse Muzzle	*Spirit of the Times* (1894)	*Gillespies' Patent;* it prevents bolting and waste of food, it corrects digestion	$2.50
Insecticide	*Spirit of the Times* (1894)	*Tough on Flies;* protect your horses and cattle from any annoyance for flies, gnats, and insects of any kind	$1.00/quart
Oat Seeds	*Spirit of the Times* (1877)	A distinct and hardy winter crop; free from rust; makes good fall pasture	$1.00/bushel
Oats	*The Plantation* (1872)	*Red Rust Proof;* 500 bushels available	$2.00
Raisin Grape Vines	*Demorest's Monthly Magazine* (1881)	Best varieties by mail	3/$0.05
Stud Fee	*Spirit of the Times* (1877)	Trotter *Alamo;* the only son of Almont, the great sire of trotters; mares not proving in foal can return next season free of charge	$50.00

FINANCIAL PRODUCTS & SERVICES

Item	Source	Description	Price
Gold Investments	*The Delineator* (1896)	Ladies and gentlemen investing $100 per month for ten months in our 5 percent bonds receive $1,000 in gold as a premium; no risk, loss impossible	$100
Money Order	*Advertising Trade Card* (1893)	*United States Express;* cheapest, safest, and most convenient $5 to $50 Not over $5 $5–$9.99 $10.00–$19.99 $20–$29.99 $30–$39.99 $40–$50	 $0.05 $0.08 $0.10 $0.12 $0.15 $0.20
Safety Deposit Box Rental	*The State* (1891)	Loan and Exchange Bank (Columbia, SC)	$4 to $12/year

FOOD PRODUCTS

Item	Source	Description	Price
Baking Powder	*Advertising Trade Card* (1870)	*Kenton;* it has few equals and no superior	$0.20
Baking Powder	*Ladies' Home Journal* (1893)	Cleveland's; food raised with Cleveland's baking powder has no bitter taste, but is sweet and keeps sweet and fresh; a quarter-pound can	$0.15
BonBons	*The Delineator* (1896)	*Lowney's Chocolate;* name on every piece	$0.60
Candy	*Demorest's Family Magazine* (1890)	One box candy, 100 colored pictures, 1 pack new cards	$0.06
Candy	*Ladies' Home Journal* (1893)	*Plows';* that's what your Chicago friends bought when you were visiting the World's Fair; tin boxes $0.10 extra	$0.80/pound
Chocolate	*San Francisco Examiner* (1895)	Venard's Eagle chocolate	$0.20/pound
Chocolate Icing	*Ladies' Home Journal* (1893)	*Lang's Readymade;* making chocolate cake easily and successfully; sample can, enough for a three-layer cake	$0.20
Codfish	*The Delineator* (1896)	*Beardsley's;* shredded; clean-wholesome-sweet, requires no boiling or soaking	$0.10/pkg
Coffee	*New York Times* (1863)	Gillies' Old Plantation; to all lovers of fine flavored coffee	$0.25/pound

Advertisement label for Chase & Sanborn's coffee and tea, circa 1892. (left) ; An 1898 advertisement for coffee; J. A. Folger & Co. would become Folgers. (right)

Item	Source	Description	Price
Coffee	*New York Times* (1863)	*Rubia Mills Government;* put up in tin-foil pound papers, 48 in a box	$0.07/pound
Coffee	*The Spartan* (Spartanburg, SC) (1898)	*Chapman's Grocer's;* 11 pounds, parched	$1.00
Corned and Roast Beef	*The State* (Columbia, SC) (1896)	Key cans	$0.10/pound
Crackers	*The Youth's Companion* (1898)	*Baby Educator;* a hard, nutritious cracker, the shape of a ring; six in a box	$0.20
Cream Cheese	*The State* (Columbia, SC) (1896)	Extra fine	$0.15/pound
Extract of Beef	*Ladies' Home Journal* (1893)	*Liebig Company's;* one can will make excellent stock; it is possible to make a quart of good stock at a cost of about $0.10 for the meat flavor	$0.10
Flour	*The State* (Columbia, SC) (1896)	Perfection Half-barrel Barrel	 $2.50 $4.75
Food Supplement	*Demorest's Family Magazine* (1894)	*Ridge's Food for Children;* supplement medicine that brings back strength; the most reliable food on the market for rearing of children	3/$0.05
Gelatin	*Demorest's Family Magazine* (1890)	*Chalmers;* superior to the imported and much cheaper; two-ounce packets	$1.40/dozen
Gelatin	*The Youth's Companion* (1898)	*Knox's;* sparkling; no acids, no odor, no taste; pink gelatin for fancy desserts with every package; two-quart package	$0.15
Instantaneous Chocolate	*Demorest's Family Magazine* (1890)	No trouble, no boiling, the greatest invention of the age; one-pound tin can	$0.75
Lactated Baby Food	*Ladies' Home Journal* (1893)	When four months old we gave him lactated food and since then he has grown strong and healthy	$0.25

Item	Source	Description	Price
Lactated Food	*Advertising Trade Card* (1888)	*Wills Richardson;* 150 meals per can; it makes them healthy, happy, hearty	$1.00
Lactated Food	*Advertising Trade Card* (1890)	It makes them healthy, happy; hearty; that's why they love it; for 150 meals	$1.00
Molasses	*The State* (Columbia, SC) (1896)	Cheap; straight New Orleans molasses, dark colored, but good; by the barrel only	$0.10/gallon
Pineapple Cheese	*The State* (Columbia, SC) (1896)	Picnic; of best quality	$0.40
Pork & Beans	*The Youth's Companion* (1898)	*Van Camp's;* a day's fuel, a day's worry and care, are done away within ten minutes; where economy tastes good	$0.06
Powdered Chocolate	*Demorest's Family Magazine* (1890)	*Wilbur's Cocoa-Theta;* the finest powdered chocolate for family use	$0.10
Rice	*The State* (Columbia, SC) (1896)	Fancy white rice in 240-pound sacks	$0.04/pound
Sarsaparilla	*The Yorkville Enquirer* (Yorkville, SC) (1892)	*Ayer's;* superior to all other preparations claiming to be blood-purifiers; cures catarrh	$1.00
Seeds	*Demorest's Family Magazine* (1890)	Ten varieties best and new and popular annuals	$0.25
Smoked Herring	*The State* (Columbia, SC) (1896)		$0.15/box
Soup	*Ladies' Home Journal* (1893)	*White Label* per case, 2 dozen pint cans 2 dozen quart cans	$2.00 $3.00
Sugar	*The State* (Columbia, SC) (1896)	Best granulated and refined in 100-pound sack	$0.04/pound
Tea	*Demorest's Family Magazine* (1890)	*Sirocco;* direct from our own gardens in India and Ceylon; per tin	$0.60-$1.00
Tea	*The Yorkville Enquirer* (Yorkville, SC) (1892)	Best First-class breakfast tea	6/$0.05
Tea	*The Youth's Companion* (1898)	*Salada Ceylon;* sold only in lead packets	$0.50/pound

FURNITURE

Item	Source	Description	Price
Bed	*San Francisco Daily Examiner* (1875)	Folding bed	$15.00
Bedroom Set	*San Francisco Daily Examiner* (1875)	4 pieces; antique	$11.00
Chair	*San Francisco Daily Examiner* (1875)	New solid oak high-back chairs	$1.00
Safe	*Demorest's Illustrated Monthly* (1873)	*Marvin's;* boudoir; every woman should have one in her dressing room to protect jewelry; highly ornamental	$100

GARDEN EQUIPMENT & SUPPLIES

Item	Source	Description	Price
Chrysanthemums	*The Delineator* (1896)	3 beautiful chrysanthemums	$0.10
Dwarf French Cannas	*The Delineator* (1896)	At prices as low as geraniums; one fine healthy plant	$0.15

Item	Source	Description	Price
Florida Palms	*The Delineator* (1896)	Palms are considered the rich man's plant because so high priced in the north	$0.20
Grapevines	*Demorest's Family Magazine* (1890)	3 sample vines; 100 varieties	$0.15
Pesticide	*The State* (Columbia, SC) (1896)	*Anti-Skeet;* kills mosquitoes; six wafers in a box	$0.10
Plant Sprinkler	*Ladies' Home Journal* (1893)	*Tyrian;* just like rain	$0.75
Roses	*The Delineator* (1896)	Six lovely roses: Snowflake, Maurice Rouvier, Star of Gold, Mde. Sadi Carnot, Mlle F. Kruger, Mde. Schwaller	$0.25
Roses	*The Delineator* (1896)	*Everblooming;* six strong one-year plants	$0.25
Sweet Pea Seeds	*The Delineator* (1896)	Ten full packets	$0.10
Tomato Seeds	*Demorest's Family Magazine* (1890)	*Lorillard;* the most solid and delicious variety grown; a packet	$0.15
Vegetable Seeds	*The Modern Priscilla* (1893)	*Finch's;* packet each of Finch's tree tomato, Mansfield tomato, evergreen cucumber, surehead cabbage, perfection lettuce	$0.30
Vegetable Seeds	*The Youth's Companion* (1898)	Vaughan's; radish 100; beauty lettuce 100; blackest beet 50; early cabbage 100; white onion 100; gem melon 100; cucumber 50; beefsteak tomato 50; giant pumpkin 30; mixed herbs 125	$0.20

HOTEL RATES

Item	Source	Description	Price
Hotel Room	*Spirit of the Times* (1877)	Cincinnati, Ohio; on the European plan	$1.00/day
Hotel Room	*Spirit of the Times* (1877)	New York, New York; European plan, prices reduced	$1.00/day
Hotel Room	*Spirit of the Times* (1877)	Augusta, Georgia; conveniently located, newly fitted up in first-class order; board reduced; special arrangement to theatrical troops	$2.00/day
Hotel Room	*The State* (Columbia, SC) (1891)	Columbia, South Carolina; largest hotel in the city, newly remodeled and refurnished	$2 to $2.50/day
Room	*San Francisco Daily Examiner* (1875)	*Lyon;* for two gentlemen; bedroom and parlor; highly furnished	$20 per month

HOUSEHOLD PRODUCTS

Item	Source	Description	Price
Atomizer and Sprinkler	*Ingalls' Home Magazine* (1889)	Spray appears like fog; best clothes sprinkler in the world	$0.50
Broom Holder	*Demorest's Family Magazine* (1890)	Holds a broom either end up; keeps a wet broom from rotting	$0.15
Cake Tins	*The Delineator* (1896)	*Perfection;* delicate cake removed without breaking; two round layered tins	3/$0.05
Cake Turner	*The Delineator*	Revolving; you press the handle, it turns the cake	$0.20
China	*New York Times* (1868)	*Washington Hadley's White French;* dinner set, 130 pieces	$30.00
Cloth	*Chicago Daily Tribune* (1882)	Silk and wool plaid cloth; worth $0.60 per yard	$0.25

Item	Source	Description	Price
Cloth	*Chicago Daily Tribune* (1882)	44-inch all wool nun's veiling in navy blue, myeartle and bronze green, embroidered with silk flowers; worth $2.25 per yard Special yard price	$0.50
Cloth	*The New Orleans Picayune* (1875)	White linen; per yard	$0.30
Cookie and Biscuit Cutter	*Ladies' Home Journal* (1893)	Dough will not stick to it; saves hours of work; wonderful rotary wire	$0.15
Detergent	*Advertising Trade Card* (1885)	*Boraxine;* saves toil and drudgery; large package	$0.10
Detergent Dye	*The Youth's Companion* (1898)	*Maypole Soap;* home dyeing a pleasure at last; washes and dyes in one operation; all colors	$0.15
Dinner and Tea Set	*The Delineator* (1896)	English decorated dinner and tea set; packed and delivered	$7.00
Dinner Knives	*Demorest's Monthly Magazine* (1881)	Silver plated; orders boxed and placed on car or steamer, free of charge	$3.00/dozen
Dinner Set	*Demorest's Monthly Magazine* (1881)	English porcelain; 100 pieces white china	$14.00
Dishes	*Demorest's Monthly Magazine* (1881)	Dinner set; French china; 149 pieces fine white china	$30.00
Disinfectant	*Demorest's Monthly Magazine* (1881)	*Milson's Patent Ozone;* nature's great disinfectant; includes generator and diffuser, which will purify the atmosphere of dwellings; small size	$8.00
Doilies	*The Ledger Monthly* (1899)	Linen; nine handsome butter doilies stamped on fine white linen	$0.10
Dye	*Demorest's Family Magazine* (1890)	Fancy dyeing at home, fast colors, 50 popular shades for cotton, wool and silk Per package Per dozen	 $0.10 $0.80
Fork	*American Silver Flatware* (1890)	*Graft & Niemann Earl Patent;* for children; the child will naturally place its finger in the shield, which prevents finger slipping and proper control of the fork; sterling; child's size	$2.00
Fruit, Wine, and Jelly Press	*Advertising Trade Card* (1880)	Enterprise; not intended for making cider	$3.00
Glass Cutter and Putty Knife	*Harper's Weekly* (1875)	*Lovejoy's;* will cut glass better than a diamond	$0.50
Linoleum	*The State* (Columbia, SC) (1896)	*A-quality;* laid	$0.80/yard
Nutmeg Grater	*Ingalls' Home Magazine* (1889)	Lady agents wanted in every town to sell this useful article	$0.25
Paint	*Sales Flier* (1892)	Enamel; for decorating tables, chairs, wicker ware, picture frames, baskets, earthenware, metal, glass, etc.	$0.25
Pesticide	*The Ledger Monthly* (1899)	*Stearns Electric Paste;* don't feed roaches and bedbugs on the exterminating powders, which don't even make the bugs sick	$0.25
Polish	*The Delineator* (1896)	*Lemonoide;* the perfect polish, makes your piano or organ conspicuous for its beauty	$0.50

Item	Source	Description	Price
Raisin and Grape Seeder	*Advertising Trade Card* (1880)	*Enterprise;* removes every seed without waste Family size Hotel size	$1.00 $2.50
Rubber Roofing	*Harper's Weekly* (1887)	For house, barn and all out buildings	$2.00/100 sq ft
Shingles	*The Yorkville Enquirer* (Yorkville, SC) (1892)	*North Carolina Heart of Pine;* standard 49 size	$2.50/thousand
Shingles	*The Spartan* (Spartanburg, SC) (1892)	*G. O. Fike Lumber Co.;* we'll sell the best $2 shingles on this market	$2.00
Shower Bath Ring	*The Delineator* (1896)	*Kelly;* prevents wetting the head and floor; nickel-plated rings and 6' of hot waterproof hose	$2.00
Silver Polish	*Demorest's Family Magazine* (1890)	*Electro-Silicon;* silver polish imparts to precious metals the highest degree of brilliancy, without the least detriment; price in stamps for a full-sized bottle	$0.15
Soap	*Advertising Trade Card* (1881)	*Enoch Morgan's Sons Sapolio Cleanser;* no one article known that will do so many kinds of work about the house	$0.10
Soap	*Advertising Trade Card* (1885)	*Boque's;* $100 reward for a bar of Boque's Soap that will not do all that is claimed for it; cakes	$0.25/3
Soap	*Advertising Trade Card* (1885)	*Enoch Morgan's Sons Sapolio;* a cake of Sapolio, a bowl of water and a brush, cloth or sponge, will make housecleaning an easy and quick job	$0.10
Stain	*Sales Flier* (1892)	Ebony black; can be used on woodwork, furniture, etc., to produce an exact imitation of ebony	$0.25
Stove-Polishing Mitten	*The Delineator* (1896)	Polishes the stove better and quicker than a brush	$0.25
Table Covers	*Ingalls' Home Magazine* (1889)	Felt; two yards square, stamped with pansies on the corners	$2.50
Tidies	*Ingalls' Home Magazine* (1889)	Fringed linen; size 15" × 20" including fringe	$0.04
Toilet Set	*Ingalls' Home Magazine* (1889)	Set of 7 pieces stamped on fine Momie cloth, designs of fuchsias, daisies, and roses	$0.60
Vase	*The Century Magazine* (1884)	*West's;* terraline; ready without further preparation to receive Winsor & Newtons, Schoenfelds, or other oil colors without firing or baking	$2.00
Wallpaper	*The Modern Priscilla* (1893)	*Alfred Peats;* handsome gold parlor paper with wide borders and ceilings to match	$0.15/roll
Wallpaper	*The Delineator* (1896)	Over 2 million rolls carried in stock	$0.10/roll
Wallpaper	*The Youth's Companion* (1898)	*Alfred Peats 1898 Prize;* new floral, silk, chintz, delft, denim stripe effects for parlors and bedrooms	$0.03 to $0.10/roll
Window Shades	*The State* (Columbia, SC) (1891)	Per window	3/$0.03

Item	Source	Description	Price
INSURANCE RATES			
Fire Insurance	*Insurance Policy* (1899)	$500 fire coverage two wood frame houses in Columbia, South Carolina	$4.75/year
Insurance Policy	*The Yorkville Enquirer* (Yorkville, SC) (1892)	No salaried officers to support, no capitalist to enrich, no loss—no expense; on $1,000 per annual	$1.50
JEWELRY			
Cuff Buttons	*Ingalls' Home Magazine* (1889)	Oxidized silver jewelry	$0.25/pr
Glove Hook	*Ingalls' Home Magazine* (1889)	Oxidized silver jewelry	$0.10
Pocket Watch	*Harper's Weekly* (1865)	Imperial officer; our whole stock of imported watches being of rich and novel designs, are now offered at reduced prices	$10.00
Pocket Watch	*Spirit of the Times* (1877)	J. Bride & Co.; the greatest imitation gold watch in the market for trading purposes; genuine American movement	$12.00
Scarf Pins	*New York Times* (1863)	For gentlemen	$1/$2/$3
Scarf Pins	*Ingalls' Home Magazine* (1889)	Oxidized silver jewelry	$0.15
Watch	*The Modern Priscilla* (1893)	*Hill;* lady's chatlette; genuine coin; silver case; 14K gold-plated bow and swivel	$5.00

An advertisement for Hampden Watches, an American watch company based in Ohio, circa 1870. (via Wikimedia Commons)

Item	Source	Description	Price
MEALS			
Dinner	*American Silver Flatware* (1868)	Santa Fe route; menu includes: puree of tomato; whitefish stuffed, Spanish sauce; shoulder of mutton, sauce soubise; roast beef; loin of pork, shrimp salad au mayonnaise; ox tongue; rice pudding; apple pie, edam and Roquefort cheese	$0.75
Dinner	*Spirit of the Times* (1894)	*Martin Restaurant;* the best table d'hôtel dinner in New York	$1.25
MEDICAL PRODUCTS & SERVICES			
Artificial Leg	*Harper's Weekly* (1865)	*Weston's;* metallic; lightest, cheapest, most durable, and most natural ever invented	$75.00
Consultation Fee	*New York Times* (1863)	For diseases of the pelvic area; for rupture, piles, varicocele, and fistula, radically cured with the knife or ligature	$5.00
Dental Fees	*Advertising Trade Card* (1880)	Vitalized or gas	$0.25
Dental Fees	*Advertising Trade Card* (1880)	Teeth extracted free when plates are ordered	$5.00
Dental Fees	*Advertising Trade Card* (1880)	Extracting	$0.25
Dental Fees	*Advertising Trade Card* (1880)	Silver Fillings Gold Fillings	$0.50 $1.00
Dental Fees	*Queen City Dentists* (1883)	Teeth extracted free when plates are ordered; gold filling	$1.00
Medical Care	*San Francisco Examiner* (1895)	*The Copeland Institute;* relief from the tortures of chronic diseases; medicines included	$5.00/month
Nonprescription Drug	*New York Times* (1863)	*Dr. Sterling's Ambrosia;* a stimulating oil extract of roots, barks and herbs; it will cure diseases of the scalp and itching of the head; box contains two bottles	$1.00
Nonprescription Drug	*Harper's Weekly* (1865)	*Dr. R. Goodale's Catarrh Remedy;* treatment cures the most hopeless cases	$1.00
Nonprescription Drug	*New York Times* (1868)	*Dr. Hunter's Botanic Cordial;* restores vigor of youth in one week; per bottle	$5.00
Nonprescription Drug	*New York Times* (1868)	*Portuguese Female Monthly Pills;* in all cases of stoppage or irregularity	$5.00/box
Nonprescription Drug	*Harper's Weekly* (1875)	*Dr. Van Holm Perfezione;* strengthens, enlarges, and develops all parts of the body	$1.00
Nonprescription Drug	*Spirit of the Times* (1877)	*Dr. Melvin Capsicum Porous Plaster;* the greatest medical discovery since the creation of man, or since the commencement of the Christian era	$0.25
Nonprescription Drug	*Spirit of the Times* (1877)	*Dr. Van Holm Nervous Debility Pills;* strengthens, enlarges, and develops all parts of the body	$1.00
Nonprescription Drug	*Advertising Trade Card* (1880)	*Horsfords Acid Phosphate;* for mental and physical exhaustion; it makes a delicious drink with water and sugar only	$0.50

Item	Source	Description	Price
Nonprescription Drug	*Advertising Trade Card* (1880)	*Little Hop Pills;* headache is positively cured	$0.25
Nonprescription Drug	*Harper's Weekly* (1887)	*Ayer's Cherry Pectoral;* it saved my life	$1.00
Nonprescription Drug	*Ingalls' Home Magazine* (1889)	Tobacco cure; in one week it will remove all desire for smoking and chewing	$0.50
Nonprescription Drug	Adelaide Hechtlinger, *The Great Patent Medicine Era* (1970)	*Ford's Female Regulator;* effective and reliable medicine in all cases of female complaints, such as amenorrhea, dysmenorrhea, suppressed or irregular menses [cost in 1890]	$0.50
Nonprescription Drug	Hechtlinger, *The Great Patent Medicine Era* (1970)	*Juno Drops;* any woman can bring the blush of health to her cheeks, a perfect plumpness to her figure [cost in 1890]	$1.00
Nonprescription Drug	Hechtlinger, *The Great Patent Medicine Era* (1970)	*Con-Formagen Ointment;* sprinkled on loose or ill-fitting plate makes it conform to mouth and securely fastens it there [cost in 1890]	$0.10
Nonprescription Drug	Hechtlinger, *The Great Patent Medicine Era* (1970)	*Dr. Rose's Obesity Powders;* fat folks, they reduce the weight in a comparatively short time [cost in 1890]	$0.58
Nonprescription Drug	Hechtlinger, *The Great Patent Medicine Era* (1970)	*Dr. Williams Pink Pills for Pale People;* miraculous cure [cost in 1890]	$0.50
Nonprescription Drug	*The Modern Priscilla* (1893)	Root, Bark and Blossom; two months' supply; remedy stomach, liver, kidney, and blood	$1.00
Nonprescription Drug	*New York Times* (1895)	*Rikers Expectorant;* a certain cure for a cough, cold, croup, pneumonia, or any disease of throat or lungs	$0.60
Nonprescription Drug	*The Delineator* (1896)	*Scott's Emulsion of Cod Liver Oil;* it produces force with the whip; to all druggists	$0.50
Nonprescription Drug	*The Delineator* (1896)	*Dr. Edison Obesity Pills;* get thin and well; two months' treatment	$6.00
Nonprescription Drug	*Southern Christian Advocate* (1897)	*Perry Davis Pain Killer;* for cramps, colic, colds	$0.25
Nonprescription Drug	*The Youth's Companion* (1898)	*Hyomei Bronchitis or Incipient Consumption Cure;* it is nature's own remedy, given through the air you breathe Extra inhalant	$1.00 $0.50
Nonprescription Drug	*The Youth's Companion* (1898)	*Arid Air Spiral Spring;* new hospital method, direct cure for coughs, colds, catarrh, asthma; a year without refilling	$0.25
Nonprescription Drug	*The Spartan* (Spartanburg, SC) (1898)	*Bucklen's Arnica Salve;* the best salve in the world for cuts, bruises, sores, ulcers, salt rheum fever sores, tetter, chapped hands, chilblains, corns, and all skin eruptions, and positively cures piles or no pay required	$0.25
Nonprescription Drug	*The Spartan* (Spartanburg, SC) (1898)	*Castoria Medicine;* for infants and children; promotes digestion, cheerfulness and rest; contains neither opium, morphine or mineral; not narcotic; 35 doses per bottle	3 for $0.05
Nonprescription Drug	*The Youth's Companion* (1898)	Morgan's Cod Liver Oil and Horehound Drops; cure your cough; free from taste and odor	$0.05

This advertisement for Hamlin's Wizard Oil claims the medicine remedies 15 different conditions. Circa 1890. (via Wikimedia Commons)

Item	Source	Description	Price
Nonprescription Drug	*The Spartan* (Spartanburg, SC) (1898)	*Mother's Friend Liniment;* good for only one purpose, to relieve motherhood of danger and pain	$1.00
Nonprescription Drug	*The Ledger Monthly* (1899)	*Dr. Campbell's Arsenic Complexion Wafers;* pimples and freckles are things of the past	$0.10
Nonprescription Drug	*The Ledger Monthly* (1899)	*Ayer's Cherry Pectoral;* when a cough medicine is good, it's worth ten times its price	$1.00
Nonprescription Drug	*The Ledger Monthly* (1899)	*Mentholette Cure;* the true Japanese headache cure instantly relieves and cures headache and other pains by simply rubbing	$0.10

MOTORIZED VEHICLE, SUPPLIES, & SERVICES

Item	Source	Description	Price
Automobile	*Sears, Roebuck* (1899)	*The Winton Motor Carriage;* a road locomotive; it does not take an engineer to run it	$1,000
Automobile	*Scientific American* (1899)	*The Winton Motor Carriage;* variable speed up to 8 miles per hour and under perfect control; no agents	$1,000

MUSICAL INSTRUMENTS

Item	Source	Description	Price
Autoharp	*The Delineator* (1896)	Easy to play, easy to buy; the autoharp is a musical instrument in its full range of styles	$7.50
Organ	*Demorest's Illustrated Monthly* (1873)	*Mason and Hamlin;* one to twenty stops	$55 to $500
Organ	*Demorest's Monthly Magazine* (1881)	*Mason & Hamilton Baby;* especially adapted to children	$22.00
Piano	*New York Times* (1863)	Seven-octave; French action, rosewood; cost including stool and cover	$300
Piano	*Demorest's Illustrated Monthly* (1873)	*United States;* first-class 7 octave piano	$290
Piano	*Demorest's Family Magazine* (1890)	*University;* sold direct to families; no middleman	$180
Piano	*San Francisco Examiner* (1895)	Used *Steinway* upright; must have cash	$200
Violin	*Spirit of the Times* (1877)	With bow, case, and instruction book	$5.00
Xylophone	*Spirit of the Times* (1877)	Wood and straw instruments as used in orchestras	$4.50

OTHER

Item	Source	Description	Price
Bow Knot Alphabet	*The Modern Priscilla* (1893)	2 3/4" high, perforated on linen bond paper	$0.10
Buggy Carriage	*Spirit of the Times* (1877)	*Baker & Son;* top side-bar and end-spring road wagon; equal in style, finish, and durability to any made	$135
Carriage	*Demorest's Family Magazine* (1890)	Adjustable top, nickel-plated rod, springs, axles, and braces; wire or wooden wheels same price; delivered free east of the Mississippi	$12.35
Carriage	*The Delineator* (1896)	With iron axles, steel wheels, and parasol top	$3.75 to $31.00

Item	Source	Description	Price
Decalcomania	*Demorest's Illustrated Monthly* (1873)	Chromos, vases, picture frames, passe-partouts, Swiss carved goods, wax flower materials, boxes of assorted wax with tools. For learners.	$5.00
Draft Exemption Fee	*New York Times* (1863)	Civil War; to be arranged by the Secretary of War	$300
Entry Fee	*Spirit of the Times* (1877)	One-mile swimming race; a suitable prize will be given	$1.00
Fire Engine	*New York Times* (1863)	Steam; for Engine Company No. 10, New York City	$4,000
Fountain Pen	*The Yorkville Enquirer* (Yorkville, SC) (1892)	*Rapid Writer;* no. 2 gold mounted	$3.00
Fountain Pen	*Ladies' Home Journal* (1893)	*The Pittsburg;* largest and best pen for the price; solid-gold ink feed, long and short nibs	$3.50
Fountain Pen	*The State* (Columbia, SC) (1896)	*Waterman's;* J. W. Gibbes Stationery Company, Columbia, South Carolina	$4.00
Fountain Pen	*The Ledger Monthly* (1899)	*R. W. Whitney;* 14K pen for bookkeepers, correspondents and stenographers	$1.50
Gas Sunlight Apparatus	*Demorest's Illustrated Monthly* (1873)	A flood of light; consists of a hemispherical cup of flint glass	$2.00
Glass Cards	*Harper's Weekly* (1875)	*F. K. Smith & Co.;* red, blue, white, clear and transparent; beautifully printed in gold	$0.50/dozen
Lottery Ticket	*Spirit of the Times* (1877)	Louisiana State Lottery Co.; capital prize $30,000; 100,000 tickets	$2.00
Magic Inkstand	*Harper's Weekly* (1875)	Ten quarts of fine ink; no refilling fluid	$2.00
Microscope	*New York Times* (1863)	*Craig;* sent with 6 beautiful mounted objects	$3.00
Money Belt	*Harper's Weekly* (1865)	*Howard's;* for soldier; sweat-proof; top quality	$3.00
Pen	*Harper's Weekly* (1865)	*Morton's;* gold; all first quality, in silver-mounted desk-holders; no. 5	$6.25
Photograph Pin	*The Ledger Monthly* (1899)	Your Face On A Button; send photo (cabinet preferred) and receive post-paid, pin-back celluloid medallion with your photo on same	$0.10
Reward	*New York Times* (1863)	Small dog, part terrier breed; hair long and a yellow tan color; nose and eyes brown	$10.00
Silver Engraving	*American Silver Flatware* (1886)	*Benjamin Allen & Co.;* Old English style	$0.10/liter
Silver Engraving	*American Silver Flatware* (1886)	*Benjamin Allen & Co.;* script style on dessert or tablespoons	$0.38/liter
Squirrel Skins	*New York Times* (1868)	500; reported as part of a theft from Solomon Bloomenstock store in New York City	$400
Statuary	*Harper's Weekly* (1875)	*John Rogers';* the tap on the window	$15.00
Ventriloquist Instructions	*Harper's Weekly* (1865)	*M. A. Jagger's;* full instructions by which any person can master the art of ventriloquism in a few hours	$1.00
Weather House	*Harper's Weekly* (1875)	*Lovejoy's;* metallic; indicates the change in the weather, and are pretty mantel ornaments	$2.00
Writing Paper	*Ladies' Home Journal* (1893)	*Metcalf;* linen; the finest made for polite correspondence; for 3 quires (72 sheets) and envelopes to match up	$0.75

Item	Source	Description	Price
PERSONAL CARE PRODUCTS			
Blush	*Demorest's Family Magazine* (1890)	*Extract of Turkish Rose Leaves;* indelible tint for the lips and face, soft as the blush of the rose	$1.00
Cologne	*Spirit of the Times* (1877)	*Mitchell's Memorial;* the most exquisite perfume of the century; small bottle	$0.25
Cologne	*Advertising Trade Card* (1880)	*Austen's Forest Flower;* the most fashionable perfume of the day	$0.25/$0.50/$1.00
Cologne	*Advertising Trade Card* (1883)	*Austen's Forest Flower;* the most fashionable perfume of the day	$0.25/$0.50/$1.00
Cologne	*Advertising Trade Card* (1888)	*Hoyt's German;* fragrant and lasting Trial size Medium size Large size	 $0.25 $0.50 $1.00

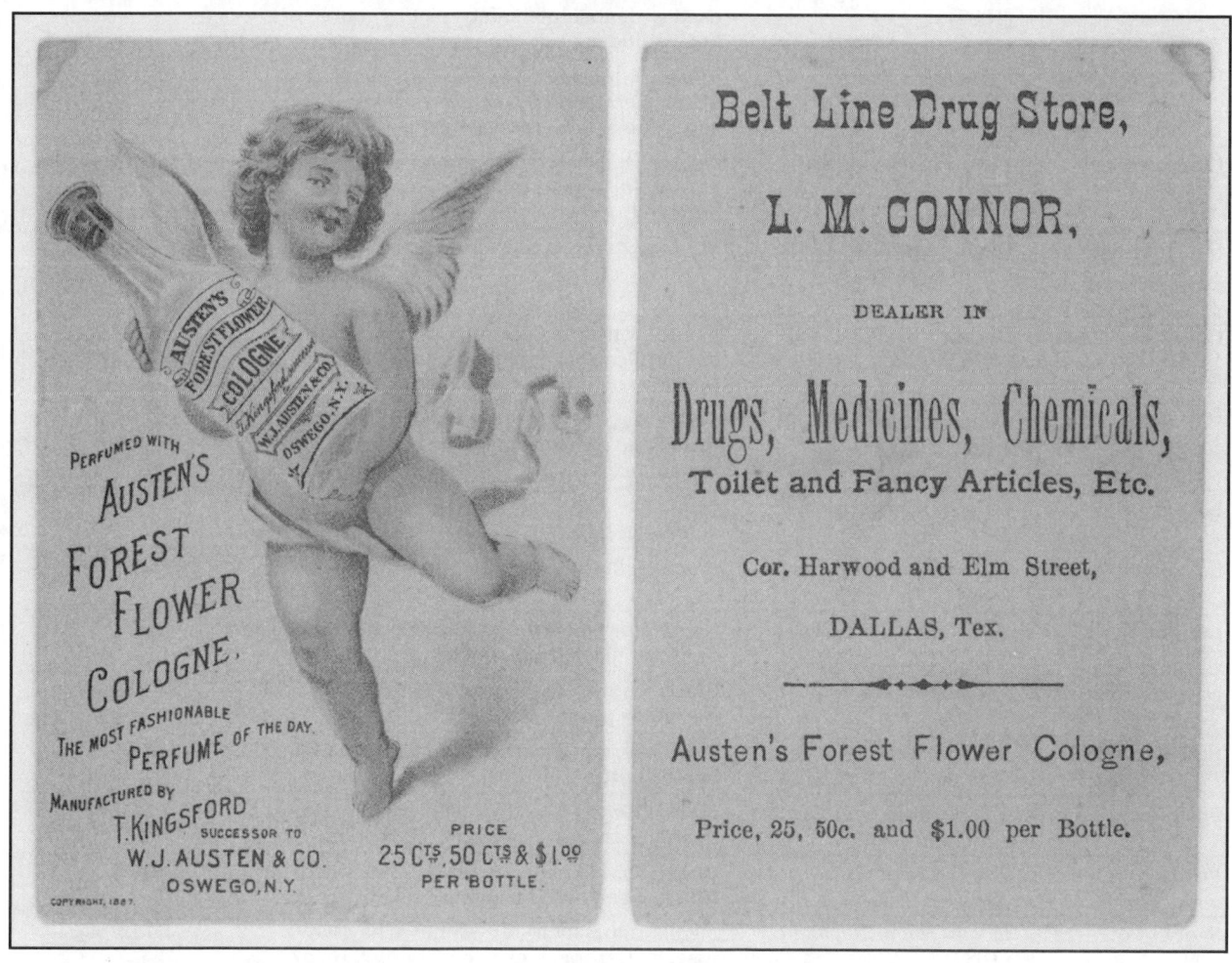

An advertisement for Austen's Forest Flower cologne, circa 1870s. (via SMU Libraries)

Item	Source	Description	Price
Combing Sacque	*The Delineator* (1896)	Of excellent quality of flannelette in pretty pink and blue stripes	$0.98
Dandruff Cure	*The Ledger Monthly* (1899)	*Coke;* if you want to keep your hair, get rid of your dandruff	$1.00
Face Bleach	*The Delineator* (1896)	*Madame Rupert's;* removes tan, pimples, eczema, moth and all diseases the skin is heir to	$2.00
Face Lotion	*The Modern Priscilla* (1893)	*Dr. Hebra's Voila Cream;* removes freckles, pimples, liver-moles, blackheads, sunburn, and tan	$0.50
Face Powder	*The Delineator* (1896)	*Lablanche;* the purest and most perfect face powder that science and skill can produce	$0.50
Facial Cloth	*Ingalls' Home Magazine* (1889)	*Koriza;* removes pimples, blackheads, wrinkles, and crows feet	$0.30
Hair Curler	*Harper's Weekly* (1865)	*Brazilian;* warranted to curl the most straight and stubborn hair into wavy ringlets	$1.00
Hair Curler	*Ingalls' Home Magazine* (1889)	Nickel-plated with enameled handles; can be used with absolute safety, as the source of heat is under perfect control	$0.50
Hair Remover	*Demorest's Family Magazine* (1890)	*(Mme)Thompson's Kosmeo Depilatory;* no blemish so terrible to a pretty woman as superfluous hair upon the face	$1.00
Hair Remover	*The Delineator* (1896)	*Modene;* hair on the face, neck, arms or any part of the person quickly dissolved or removed	$1.00
Hair Restorer	Hechtlinger, *The Great Patent Medicine Era* (1970)	*Princess Tonie* [cost in 1890]	$0.57
Hair Treatment	*Harper's Weekly* (1865)	*Boswell & Warner Colorific;* don't dye the hair; one application, no wash, no trouble; large bottle	$1.00
Hair Wave	*Demorest's Monthly Magazine* (1881)	*Thompson;* natural curly hair; indispensable to all ladies whose front hair is thin or will not remain in crimps	$6 to $12
Lotion	*Demorest's Family Magazine* (1890)	*Planta Beatrice;* a sanitary preparation for the complexion	$1.25
Lotion	*The Modern Priscilla* (1893)	*Hawley's Corn Salve;* cure guaranteed	$0.25
Lotion	*The Delineator* (1896)	*Wrinkleine;* guaranteed to permanently remove wrinkles, flesh worms, etc.	$1.00
Nail Trimmer	*The Ledger Monthly* (1899)	Closes compactly and can be carried in vest pocket or purse	$0.25
Perfume	*Ladies' Home Journal* (1893)	*Seely's Easter Lily;* delicate, fragrant, lasting; one-oz bottle	$0.50
Perfume	*The Delineator* (1896)	*Forest Fringe Violet;* just like a bunch of the freshly gathered flowers of the woods	$1.00
Powder	*The Delineator* (1896)	*Gossamer;* faces fair are made fairer with a touch of Tetlow's Gossamer Powder	$0.25
Sachet Powders	*Ingalls' Home Magazine* (1889)	*Ingalls;* odors include new mown hay, white rose, heliotrope, jockey club, violet, rose, geranium	$0.15/pkg

Item	Source	Description	Price
Shaving Soap	*Advertising Trade Card* (1880)	*Williams;* oldest and most famous shaving soap in the world; for six cakes (one pound)	$0.40
Shaving Soap	*Advertising Trade Card* (1884)	*Williams;* 6 round cakes equal one pound; oldest and most famous shaving soap in the world	$0.40
Shaving-Soap Stick	*Harper's Weekly* (1887)	*Williams;* each stick in a turned-wood case	$0.25
Skin Cleaner	*The Delineator* (1896)	*Campbell's Safe Complexion Wafers;* removes pimples, freckles, moth, blackheads, redness, oiliness and all other beauty marring defects	$1.00
Soap	*New York Times* (1868)	*Phalon's;* for the toilet, bath and nursery	$0.25
Soap	*Demorest's Family Magazine* (1894)	*Wrisley's Cucumber Complexion Toilet Soap;* combines the healthful cleansing of pure sweet soap with the grateful emollient quantities of cucumber juice	1/$0.02
Soap	*The Delineator* (1896)	*Sweet Home;* a chautangua reclining chair or a chautangua desk with a combination box	$0.10
Soap	*The Delineator* (1896)	*Charmant Turkish Wonder Bar;* this is no patent medicine but a soap that has been used in Turkey for hundreds of years; for salve and soap	$1.00
Soap	*The Delineator* (1896)	*Copco Bath Soap;* soap-wise folks say it's a decade in advance of soap making progress	$0.05
Tooth Cleaner	*Demorest's Family Magazine* (1890)	*Rubiform for the Teeth;* deliciously flavored; a perfect liquid dentifrice	$0.25
Tooth Cleaner	*The Youth's Companion* (1898)	*Dr. Sheffield's Creme Dentifrice;* cream in collapsible tubes; it removes from the teeth all stains and whatever would cause decay	$0.25
Tooth Soap	*The Delineator* (1896)	*Arnica;* others imitate; none equals	$0.25
Tooth Soap	*The Delineator* (1896)	*Wright's Myrrh;* without the taste of soap; large china box	$0.25
Whisker and Mustache Grower	*Harper's Weekly* (1865)	*Graham's;* my ointment will force them to grow heavily in six weeks (upon the smoothest face)	$1.00
Wig	*Demorest's Family Magazine* (1890)	Parted bang; made of natural curly hair, guaranteed becoming to ladies who wear their hair parted	$6.00

PUBLICATIONS

Item	Source	Description	Price
Book	*New York Times* (1863)	*Army and Navy Pocket Dictionary;* in flexible leather, marbled edges	$0.75
Book	*Harper's Weekly* (1865)	*Portrait Gallery of the War;* civil, military, and naval; edited by Frank More; full gilt	$7.50
Book	*Harper's Weekly* (1865)	*Speke's Africa;* journal of the discovery of the source of the Nile; by Captain John Hanning Speke; cloth	$4.00
Book	*Harper's New Monthly Magazine* (1866)	*Medical Common Sense;* 400 pages; 100 illustrated	$1.50

Item	Source	Description	Price
Book	*Harper's New Monthly Magazine* (1866)	*New Physiognomy; or Signs of Character;* as manifested through temperament and external forms, and especially in the Human Face Divine	$5.00
Book	*Harper's Weekly* (1875)	*The Ugly Girl Papers: Or Hints for the Toilet*	$1.00
Book	*Spirit of the Times* (1877)	*Scott's Fishing in American Waters;* has an interesting addition to it, such as coast and inland fishing of the South; has numerous new engravings	$3.50
Book	*Demorest's Monthly Magazine* (1881)	*Vick's Floral Guide;* elegant book of 100 pages, one colored flower plate, and 600 illustrations; in English or German	$0.10
Book	*The Century Magazine* (1884)	*Illustrations of Artistic Homes* (Fuller, Wheeler & Prescott); contains 76 full-page illustrations of Queen Anne and Colonial villas and cottages	$3.50
Book	*Harper's Weekly* (1887)	*Harper's Pictorial History of the Rebellion;* containing 1,000 of its famous war pictures; in full Turkey Morocco, gilt edges	$35.00
Book	*Ladies' Home Journal* (1893)	Portrait scrapbooks; scrapbooks made from newspaper pictures are the latest fad For 30 For 70 For 400	 $0.10 $0.20 $1.00
Magazine	*Harper's Weekly* (1865)	*Demorest's Monthly Magazine;* the model parlor magazine of America	$3/year
Magazine	*Harper's Weekly* (1865)	*Harper's Weekly*	$0.10/week
Magazine	*Harper's New Monthly Magazine* (1866)	*American Educational Monthly;* no educator can afford to be without it	$1.50/year
Magazine	*Harper's Weekly* (1887)	*Ridley's Fashion Magazine;* quarterly	$0.15/quarter
Magazine	*Ingalls' Home Magazine* (1889)	*Ingalls' Home Magazine;* monthly	$0.15/month
Magazine	*Demorest's Family Magazine* (1891)	*The Great Divide;* premium: 20 gemstones cut free from the successful monthly of the wild and wooly west	$1.00/year
Magazine	*Demorest's Family Magazine* (1891)	*Demorest's Family Magazine;* monthly	$0.20
Magazine	*Ladies' Home Journal* (1893)	*Ladies' Home Journal* Single issue Per year	 $0.10 $1.00
Magazine	*The Modern Priscilla* (1893)	*The Modern Priscilla;* monthly	$0.50
Magazine	*The Ledger Monthly* (1899)	*The Ledger Monthly;* single copy	$0.05
Newspaper	*New York Times* (1863)	*New York Times;* daily	$0.03/day

Detail of a New York Times *advertisement from 1895.* (via Wikimedia Commons)

Item	Source	Description	Price
Newspaper	*Wall Street Journal* (1890)	Annual subscription	$5.00
Newspaper	*The Weekly Bulletin* (1885)	*The Weekly Bulletin*	$1.00
Pamphlet	*The Delineator* (1896)	Recitations and How to Recite	$0.25
Prohibition Fliers	*Demorest's Family Magazine* (1890)	Logical and convenient tracts for circulation in your neighborhood	$0.05 per 100

REAL ESTATE

Item	Source	Description	Price
Building	*New York Times* (1863)	For sale; four-story; high-stoop basement and under-cellar brownstone house with all modern improvements; near 4th Avenue on 23rd St	$21,000
Business Opportunity	*San Francisco Examiner* (1895)	Saloon; one block off Market Street; daily receipts $20 and over	$650
House	*New York Times* (1863)	For sale; Harlem; two-story and half-frame cottage; 125th Street, near 5th Ave., with gas and water and 2 1/2 lots of ground	$7,800
House	*New York Times* (1863)	For rent; Brooklyn; two-story; Franklin Ave. and Myeartle; with basement and subcellar	$250/year
House	*New York Times* (1863)	For sale; Brooklyn; three-story brick; has marble mantels, gas fixtures, near the Hamilton Ferry	$3,500
House	*New York Times* (1863)	For rent; Brooklyn; three-story; 2nd St. and Williamsburg; with front and back basement near the Ferry	$300/year
House	*New York Times* (1868)	For sale; same block Dr. Cuyler's Church, near Green Ave.; three-story brick and brownstone; basement	$7,000
House	*New York Times* (1868)	For rent; unfurnished, the first-class house; no. 31 Washington Square, four story, low stoop	$2,600/year
House	*New York Times* (1877)	For rent; four-story English; basement; brick; 232 West 43rd St., all improvements	$1,100/year
House	*New York Times* (1877)	For rent; furnished nine rooms, fine view and grounds, well of purest water; 300 fruit trees; one hour from city	$70/month
House	*The Yorkville Enquirer* (York, SC) (1892)	New; six rooms; broad hall, closet, pantry; good well of water on the back porch; one acre, enclosed	$825
Land	*San Francisco Daily Examiner* (1875)	10 acres level land in Alameda County; 1 1/2 acres fruit trees; running water in creek	$1,800
Land Rental	*The New Orleans Picayune* (1875)	618 acres in Red River County, Texas, improved; 200 acres in a good fence and under cultivation Rent per acre	$3.00
Retail Business	*San Francisco Daily Examiner* (1875)	Half interest in oldest and best new books and stationery store in Portland, Oregon; doing $20,000 a year in business	$3,500
Room	*The New Orleans Picayune* (1875)	Furnished room with board; good table, Magazine Street Per month	$25.00

Item	Source	Description	Price
SEWING EQUIPMENT & SUPPLIES			
Cloth	*New York Times* (1863)	*Kinzey's;* sewing cotton; two spools	$0.01
Cloth	*New York Times* (1863)	*Kinzey's;* ladies' fine grass linen; the Eighth Ave. cheap store	$0.25/yard
Cloth	*New York Times* (1877)	Imported black dress silks	$0.80/yard
Cloth	*New York Times* (1877)	Examine our American black silks	$1.30/yard
Cloth	*New York Times* (1877)	Imported stripe silks	$0.60/yard
Cloth	*The State* (Columbia, SC) (1891)	*Sea Island Dress Goods;* yd wide	$0.05
Cloth	*Ladies' Home Journal* (1893)	Evening silks; pongees and silks of a crepe character, two designs in each, all light colorings	$0.50
Cloth	*The Modern Priscilla* (1893)	Waste embroidery silk; 1 oz of silk; assorted colors (equal to 100 skeins) in every box	$0.40
Cloth	*The Delineator* (1896)	Shirting percales	1/$0.03/yard
Cloth	*The Delineator* (1896)	Silk stripe challis; exclusive designs	7/$0.09/yard
Cloth	*The Ledger Monthly* (1899)	Silk remnants for crazy work; from 100 to 120 pieces, carefully trimmed	$0.25
Cross-Stitch Book	*The Modern Priscilla* (1893)	*Priscilla;* contains over 100 patterns	$0.50
Embroidery Frame	*Ingalls' Home Magazine* (1899)	*Priscilla;* 9" without holder, of polished wood	3/$0.05
Embroidery Silk	*Ingalls' Home Magazine* (1889)	For overlaid embroidery; 10 yd skein	$0.03
Oil Colors	*Ingalls' Home Magazine* (1889)	*M. Fuchs & Co.;* German; finest made; tube	$0.05
Pattern	*Demorest's Monthly Magazine* (1881)	Chelsea jacket for child, ornamented with the favorite Capuchin hood, a turned-down collar, and reverse on the double-breasted fronts; sizes for 12 to 16 years	$0.20
Pattern	*The Delineator* (1896)	Combination and decoration for a lady's Louis XIV; 13 sizes, 28" to 48" bust measure	$0.40
Pattern	*The Delineator* (1896)	*Bosquets;* double-breasted ripple basque, with gored sleeves in four sections	$0.30
Pattern	*The Delineator* (1896)	Pattern for lady's basque waist with waist decoration; in thirteen sizes for ladies from 28" to 46" bust measure	$0.30
Quilting Squares	*Demorest's Family Magazine* (1890)	60 beautiful silk and satins, enough to cover 500 square inches	$0.20
Sewing Machine	*Harper's Weekly* (1865)	*Family Gem;* the embodiment of practical utility and extreme simplicity	$5.00
Sewing Machine	*The Delineator* (1896)	*Singer;* buy the improved Singer sewing machine with a complete set of attachments	$9.00
Sewing Machine	*Southern Christian Advocate* (1897)	The best and lightest running machine	$19.50

Item	Source	Description	Price
Sewing-Machine Attachments	*Demorest's Illustrated Monthly* (1873)	*Palmer's;* combination; the perfection of making and arranging every style of dress trimming with as much ease and simplicity as running up an ordinary seam	$3.00
Sewing Needle	*The Delineator* (1896)	Sewing made easy; for each paper	$0.05
Sewing Needles	*The Ledger Monthly* (1899)	Self-threading; can't bend 'em pins; package of four	$0.25
Skirt Binding	*The Delineator* (1896)	*Manhattan Mohair;* yard dyed, seam shrunk and fast color; for five-yd piece	$0.20
Stamping Paint	*Ingalls' Home Magazine* (1889)	*Ingalls;* for stamping felt, velvet, plush, and park goods; large tube	$0.25
Tassels	*Ingalls' Home Magazine* (1889)	*Ingalls;* Chenille; all colors	$0.06
Thread	*Demorest's Family Magazine* (1890)	Twilled lace; for crocheting, makes beautiful lace; per spool, 500 yards	$0.10
Tinsel Cord	*Ingalls' Home Magazine* (1889)	Imported; furnished in light and dark gold, three shades of silver, pink, iridescent, copper	$0.10
Tissue Papers	*Ingalls' Home Magazine* (1889)	*Dennison's;* for flower decoration; beginner's outfit contains 12 half-sheets assorted tissues, wire tubing for stems and leaves, culots, sprays and a book of instructions	3/$0.05
Tracing Wheel	*Demorest's Illustrated Monthly* (1873)	Ladies pentagraph; used for tracing pattern	$0.25
Turkish Rug Patterns	*Ingalls' Home Magazine* (1889)	1/2 yard × 1 yard shows vine of morning glories running around the rug for a border, and a small cluster of flowers in center	$0.40
Work Books	*Ingalls' Home Magazine* (1889)	Fancy; darned lace patterns	$0.15
Yarn	*New York Times* (1863)	*Kinzey's;* French floss; best; spool	$0.02
Yarn	*Ingalls' Home Magazine* (1889)	*Madonna;* crochet cotton; for tidies, lambrequins 25-gram ball	$0.15
Watercolor	*Ingalls' Home* and *Gilding Magazine* (1889)	Perfection; box contains six pans and assorted colors	4/$0.03
Whisk Broom Holder	*Ingalls' Home Magazine* (1889)	Linen; made and bound with designs stamped on them to be worked	$0.20

SPORTS EQUIPMENT

Item	Source	Description	Price
Bait	*Spirit of the Times* (1877)	Artificial; a bait that excels all others for taking black bass	$0.75
Baseball	*Spirit of the Times* (1877)	*Peck & Snyder Treble Match-Ball;* buy our popular brands of baseballs; popular professional ball, red or white; each ball is wrapped in tinfoil and boxed; by mail	$1.50
Baseball Mask	*Spirit of the Times* (1877)	*Peck & Snyder;* catcher's; in case the swift ball misses the catcher's ready grasp and strikes the face, the blow is harmless	$3.00
Bicycle	*New York Times* (1895)	*Waverly Scorcher;* 21 pounds	$85.00
Bicycle	*San Francisco Examiner* (1895)	Waverly	$85.00

Item	Source	Description	Price
Bicycle	*The Delineator* (1896)	*Windsor American Beauties;* for 1896 . . . bicycling should be pure happiness	$85.00
Bicycle	*The Delineator* (1896)	*Columbia;* standard of the world; before buying a bicycle said to be just as good as Columbia, it is well to compare the prices at which the machines sell second hand	$100
Bicycle	*The Delineator* (1896)	*Gladiator Cycles;* perfect machines, strong, light, speedy	$85.00
Bicycle	*The Youth's Companion* (1898)	*Acme*; same grade as agents sell for $75; eight elegant models	$34.50
Bicycle	*Popular Mechanics Picture History of American Transportation* (1952)	*Columbia*; combine the best results of 22 years experience [cost in 1899]	$75.00
Bicycle	*Scientific American* (1899)	*Ideal*; fit every member old and young	$20.00

 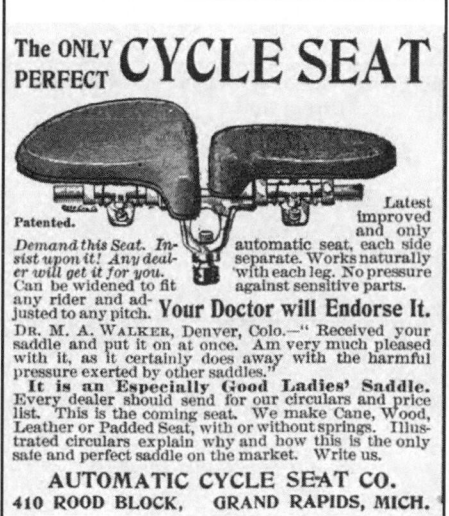 

A bicycle advertisement from Waltham Manufacturing Company, based in Waltham, Massachusetts. (via Library of Congress) (left); An advertisement appearing in Ladies' Home Journal *for a bicycle seat with separate parts for the left and right side. (via Wikimedia Commons) (center); An 1896 Stearns advertisement showcasing a female cyclist. (via Library of Congress) (right)*

Item	Source	Description	Price
Bicycle Lamp	*The Youth's Companion* (1898)	*Klondike*; fine 2 1/2" magnifying lens; colored side lights; perfect ventilation; throws a big light	$2.00
Bicycle Seat	*The Delineator* (1896)	*The Hunt Ladies' Saddle*; especially designed to meet the peculiar requirements of lady cyclists	$5.00
Boxing Gloves	*Spirit of the Times* (1877)	Pecks and Snyders; net price per set, includes two pairs	$2.50 to $6.00
Fishing Rod	*Spirit of the Times* (1877)	*Conroy Bisset & Malleson*; salmon; six-strip, two tips	$50.00
Fly Rod	*Spirit of the Times* (1877)	*Conroy Bissett & Malleson*; split bamboo; six-strip hexagonal rods, two tips	$25.00
Pistol	*Spirit of the Times* (1877)	*W&C Scott & Sons*; .45 caliber; celebrated double-action revolvers; central fire	$20.00
Pocket Gymnasium	*Spirit of the Times* (1877)	*Goodyear No. 6*; for gentlemen of moderate strength, used standing, sitting, or reclining	$1.50
Rifle	*Spirit of the Times* (1877)	*The Remington*; sporting rifle No. 1 model; 30"	$30.00
Skates	*Harper's Weekly* (1875)	*Peck & Snyder's American Club*; the only perfect self-fastening skate that adjusts without heel-plates, shapes or key; fully polished	$7.00

TELEPHONE EQUIPMENT & SERVICES

Item	Source	Description	Price
Telephone Charges	*New York Times* (1895)	600 local messages, two-party line Direct line	$75 $90
		1,000 messages, two-party line Direct line	$105 $120
		1,500 messages, two-party line Direct line	$135 $150

TOBACCO PRODUCTS

Item	Source	Description	Price
Cigar	*The Weekly Bulletin* (1885)	Best nickel cigar in town	$0.05
Cigarette	*Spirit of the Times* (1877)	*L'Amerique*; only best French cigarette paper used; sample pack	$0.15
Pipes	*Hechtlinger, The Great Patent Medicine Era* (1970)	*Cobb*; assorted styles [cost in 1890]	3/$0.03/dozen

TOYS

Item	Source	Description	Price
Game	*Harper's Weekly* (1875)	*Punch and Judy*; jolliest game in the whole world	$1.00
Paper Dolls	*Ingalls' Home Magazine* (1889)	Set contains three paper dolls, 2 girls, 1 boy, and an elegant wardrobe of 30 pieces	$0.15

TRAVEL & TRANSPORTATION

Item	Source	Description	Price
Boat Fare	*Advertising Trade Card* (1885)	Delightful ocean trip to the Point of Pines leaving Foster's Wharf; round trip	$0.40
Boat Fare	*New York Times* (1895)	New York to Boston	$2.00

Item	Source	Description	Price
Boat Fare	*New York Times* (1895)	New York to Southampton	$60.00
Coach Fare	*Spirit of the Times* (1877)	Leaves Brunswick, New York, at 4:30 p.m. and the Getty House, Yonkers, 8 a.m. daily (Box seats $0.50 extra each way)	$1.50
Railroad Fare	Edward L. Throm, ed., *Popular Mechanics Picture History of American Transportation* (1952)	New York Elevated Railway [cost in 1876] Rush hour Regular hours	 $0.05 $0.10
Railroad Fare	*New York Times* (1895)	107 miles from New York on the banks of the Delaware River; round trip	$1.00
Railroad Fare	*The Spartan* (Spartanburg, SC) (1898)	Western Carolina Railroad; Spartanburg, South Carolina, to Augusta, Georgia, round trip for Merry Maker's Week	$4.70
Railroad Freight Charge	Throm, ed., *Popular Mechanics Picture History of American Transportation* (1952)	Charge for barrel of oil from Macksburgh, Ohio, to Marietta, Ohio [cost in 1885] Standard Oil Company All Other Companies	 $0.10 3/$0.05
Steamship	*The New Orleans Picayune* (1875)	New Orleans to Key West Cabin Steerage	 $40.00 $20.00
Steamship Fare	*New York Times* (1863)	New York to Liverpool, payable in gold or its equivalent in U.S. currency Second Cabin Chief Cabin	 $80.00 $132.50
Steamship Fare	*New York Times* (1863)	New York to Nassau	$45.00
Steamship Fare	*New York Times* (1868)	New York to Liverpool, one-way, first-class iron steamship; cabin in gold Steerage First class	 $30.00 $80.00
Steamship Fare	*New York Times* (1868)	*State Line*; New York to Glasgow, Liverpool, Belfast, and Londonderry Second cabin First cabin	 $45.00 $65 to $70
Steamship Fare	*New York Times* (1877)	*Cunard Line*; New York to Liverpool and Queenstown	$80 to $130
Steamship Fare	*Spirit of the Times* (1877)	General TransAtlantic Company; New York to Havre, calling at Plymouth (G.B.); price of passage in gold (including wine) Steerage Third Cabin Second Cabin First Cabin	 $26.00 $35.00 $65.00 $100
Steamship Fare	*New York Times* (1895)	*Cooks Tours Nile Steamers*; New York to Egypt	$675 to $1225
Train	*Chicago Daily Tribune* (1882)	July 4th Excursion to South Park, Chicago; under the auspices of the Women's Christian Temperance Union; good on all suburban trains of the Illinois Central Railroad Roundtrip	$0.25

MISCELLANY 1860–1899

The Barber

A negro came to Green Bay, Wisconsin, to keep a barber's shop. Soon after he opened a Western speculator presented himself to be shaved. His charge was asked: the barber said 25 cents. The customer named several cities he had been shaved at, and all for less money. The negro straightened himself up, and said: "Do you suppose I am going to leave society in the East and come here among you backwoodsmen to shave men for ten cents?"

Harper's New Monthly Magazine, October 1866

Harper's Hand-book for Travellers in Europe and the East

Being a guide through France, Belgium, Holland, Germany, Austria, Italy, Sicily, Egypt, Syria, Turkey, Greece, Switzerland, Russia, Denmark, Sweden, Spain, and Great Britain and Ireland. By W. Pembroke Fetridge. Fifth Year. Large 12mo, Leather, Pocket-Book form. $7.50

Harper's New Monthly Magazine, October 1866

Anesthetics in the Military

The surgeon-general has recommended Congress to pay Dr. G. Morton $200,000 for the use of anesthetics in the army and navy. Dr. Morton personally appeared before the Committee of Ways and Means this morning to urge its adoption.

New York Times, March 3, 1863

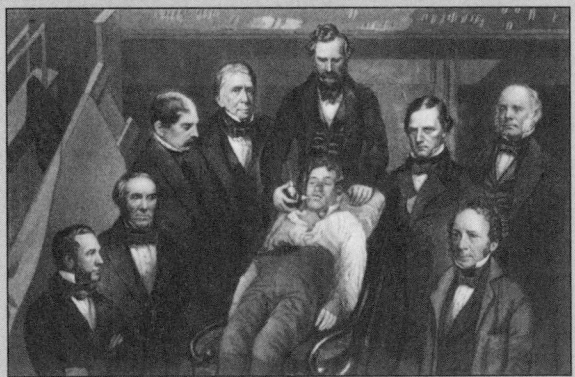

The first public demonstration of anesthetics, performed by Dr. William Morton from Boston. Dr. Morton and the patient are surrounded by medical staff observing the demonstration. (via Wikimedia Commons)

Concerning Dickens's 1869 American Tour

Queuing for tickets to hear Dickens had begun the night before the box office opened; an hour before opening time the queue was already half a mile long; all tickets were sold out in a hectic eleven hours and fourteen thousand dollars were taken in for the first reading in Boston. (Promoter George) Dolby sold tickets at two dollars each. Scalpers were re-selling them at anything up to twenty-six dollars.

Charles Dickens,
An Authentic Account of His Life and Times,
by Martin Fido, 1968

Rental prices in Washington, D. C. in 1865

The Washington city to which (photographer Mathew) Brady returned after the war was a dirty, brawling, lusty city, one step removed from the frontier. In the summer of 1865 living quarters were impossible to find and too expensive. A house which rented for three hundred dollars a season before the war now brought twelve hundred to its owner.

Mathew Brady, Historian with A Camera,
by James D. Horan, 1955

Thomas Nast, Political Cartoonist

Early the next year (1862) he accepted a job at $50 a week from his former employer, Frank Leslie. After a short time, Leslie, perhaps because of financial stress, cut Nast to $30 a week and let him go a month later. After (U. S.) Grant's nomination (1868), however, the journal (Harper's) offered Nast a regular fee of $150 per double page cartoon, five times more than his rate in 1862.

Thomas Nast, Political Cartoonist, by Chal Vinson, 1967

MISCELLANY 1860–1899

Publications and the Civil War

To unite the North, to make the mystical concept of Union a rallying point, Abraham Lincoln encouraged communications in every way. By then, there were 3,000 U.S. publications. Suddenly the Civil War increased circulation substantially. People depended on day-to-day reports from the battlefields. The Union increased mail subsidies and land grants to railroads. It started the Pony Express and then completed the transcontinental telegraph and pushed for a transcontinental railway. The Lincoln Administration established the three-cent postage delivery of a one-ounce letter anywhere in the Union. It initiated free, city-wide postal delivery and collection in 49 cities of 20,000 or more population. It gave newspapers especially low postage rates— half a cent to mail a newspaper, and postage could be billed. Many times papers never paid. Railroad car post offers were now on all important railroads. Registered letters and money orders began.
Sears and Wards: The First Hundred Years Are the Toughest, by Cecil C. Hoge, Sr., 1988

Montgomery Ward Catalog

In the fall (1874), Montgomery Ward issued a 100-page catalog measuring 3 1/2" 3 7". It listed several hundred articles with prices. Sales for Ward passed $100,000 in 1874 . . . In 1878, Montgomery Ward passed $400,000 in sales. For the next few years, the biggest Ward item in dollar sales was the sewing machine. Ward sold sewing machines much cheaper—as low as $26 for a machine which otherwise sold for $50.
Sears and Wards: The First Hundred Years Are the Toughest, by Cecil C. Hoge, Sr., 1988

The One-Price System

In 1878, a successful (Philadelphia) merchant named John Wanamaker had opened what he called a "New Kind of Store," which incorporated something called the one-price system. Instead of negotiating a price with each customer, the merchant marked the price plainly and customers paid the posted price. Wanamaker was not the first merchant to adopt the one-price system— Lord and Taylor in New York used it as early as 1835—but he was the first to adopt it on such a large scale.
Belk, A Century of Retail Leadership, by Howard E. Covington, Jr., 1988

The Centennial Exposition of 1876

The immense buildings that housed the Centennial Exposition of 1876 were mostly taken down when it was over. Highly permanent, however, was another huge structure that also much impressed visitors to Philadelphia that memorable and influential summer—the towered and towering bulk of the new City Hall nearing completion in the square of the middle of town, where seventy years earlier Oliver Evans' wheeled steam monster had been demonstrated. Even in those days of low prices the building cost some $10,000,000. It covers ground enough for almost six football fields and, counting in the 20-foot figure of William Penn on the central tower, rises 450 feet above street level.
The Americans: A Social History of the United States 1587–1914, by J. C. Furnas, 1969

Chinese Labor

In 1870 a New England shoe manufacturer named Calvin T. Sampson fired his unioned workers and imported 75 Chinese laborers from the Pacific coast. The Chinese signed a contract to work for three years at $26 a month, and settled down in North Adams, Massachusetts, where they attended the Methodist Sunday school, saved their money, and reduced Mr. Sampson's costs $840 a week. A writer in *Scribner's* magazine hastened to praise this experiment, saying, "If for no other purpose than the breaking up of . . . labor combinations and 'Trade Unions . . . the advent of Chinese labor should be hailed with warm welcome by all who have the true interests of . . . the laboring classes at heart.'"
The American Past, by Roger Butterfield, 1947

Drug Store for Sale

A Bona-Fide Bargain. A retail drug business in Brooklyn, established 20 years in its present location. Price $4000. F. E. Tower, 482 B. 2nd St., Brooklyn.
Harper's Weekly, January 2, 1875

Method of Cleaning Plaster

The Prussian Government has lately a prize of about $750 for the discovery of a new method of cleaning plaster casts, statues, etc., and one of $2,500 for the invention of a new material possessing the properties of plaster, but which shall not deteriorate by repeated washings.
Harper's Weekly, September 25, 1875

1900–1919

The Progressive Era and World War I

PRESIDENTS

William McKinley*   1897–1901

Theodore Roosevelt   1901–1909

William Howard Taft   1909–1913

Woodrow Wilson   1913–1921

* assassinated

1917 series one-dollar bill.

Social and economic historians divide the first twenty years of the twentieth century into two periods: The Progressive Era (1900–1914), during which Americans confronted the social unrest of early industrialism; and the time of World War I (1914–1918) during which the nation assumed fully the responsibilities of world citizenship and experienced the effects of a centrally managed wartime economy. Despite economic downturns in 1903 and 1907, the beginning of the century was a time of prosperity and stability for the newly emerging middle class; unimaginable profits for the industrial barons; and unrelieved misery for the lower class of workers who toiled, often under unsafe and unhealthy conditions, for a pittance in wages.

"Reform" is the word most often associated with the Progressive Era. The nation had changed too quickly, demographically and economically, to suit the newly prosperous middle class, who sought to maintain their comfortable positions in society while expressing concern about the lack of values in this new age. Big business had been largely responsible for the transformations industrialism brought to American life, and business was an easy target for the misgivings people had about the commercial world. Examples of children, women, and immigrants exploited mercilessly in the cause of commercial enterprise—if not simple greed—were common, and people wanted controls on the excesses of unscrupulous businessmen. The labor movement defended the interests of workers, but its greatest impact came after World War I. Women sought the vote and with it a voice in the business of the nation, but they were not successful until 1920. There was popular sentiment against the monopolistic trusts that threatened to engulf American business, but although antitrust legislation was enacted, most Americans felt the businessmen had their way.

Nationalism had taken on a new meaning in America by 1900. Railway expansion in the middle of the nineteenth century had made it possible to move goods quickly and efficiently throughout the country. As a result, commerce, which had been based largely on local production of goods for local consumption, expanded enormously. Ambitious merchants seized the opportunity to expand their businesses by appealing to broader markets. In 1900 there were 58 chain stores (businesses with more than one retail outlet) in the country; by 1920 the total had risen to 808. The number of clothing chains alone rose from 7 to 125 during the period.

The increase in productivity and consumerism radically changed the character of American life. Manufacturing plants drew people from the country into cities. Between 1900 and 1920 urban population increased by 80 percent compared to just over 12 percent for rural population. During the same time the non-farm work-

57

force went from 783,000 people to 2.2 million. Unlike farmers, these workers drew a regular paycheck and spent it. Government statistics show that disposable income rose from $20 billion to $71.5 billion in the first two decades of this century, during the same time that cars were first available to transport people from home to store. Perhaps the most telling statistic about the change in American lifestyles during this period is that in 1900 only 4,192 automobiles were registered; in 1920 there were 1.9 million.

Moreover, the electrical-energy-generating capacity of the country increased tenfold over the first two decades of the century, with dramatic effects. This new energy supplied the power to operate the plants that provided the expanding workforce with jobs and money. Just as important, it expanded the universe of goods that could be manufactured and sold in the enlarged marketplace. Radios, electric lights, telephones, and powered vacuum cleaners were possible for the first time and quickly established themselves as essential household items. Stimulated by the possibilities of an energized world, inventors were more active than ever before. In 1916, the last year of the period before war-time economic controls went into effect, 43,892 patents were issued, 75 percent more than in 1900.

World War I had a dramatic impact on the American economy. When the war broke out in Europe, American exports were required to support the Allied war effort. America's intervention in 1917 required that two million men be drafted, opening up jobs in home-front industries and requiring production at higher levels than ever before to support the war effort. To finance the war, the federal government issued more money, borrowed from citizens in the form of war bonds, and used the newly enacted income-tax legislation to raise funds (businesses with over $1 million in income were taxed at 77 percent); to control inflation, the government imposed strict price controls, forming the most closely controlled federal economy in American history.

The war forced Americans to confront one more important transformation. The United States had become a full participant in the world economy, and as a result the perimeters of American commerce were extended. The hated tariffs on imported goods were reduced, and exports reached an all-time high in 1919 and 1920, further stimulating American industry. The United States earned the respect of the world during the war; in the postwar years American business capitalized on this attitude.

By 1920 urban Americans had begun to define themselves—for their neighbors and for the world—in terms of what they consumed. It was a turning point in the social and economic history of the nation.

Year	Dollar Value in 2019
1900	$30.49
1903	$29.11
1905	$29.11
1907	$27.25
1909	$28.15

Year	Dollar Value in 2019
1910	$26.96
1913	$25.87
1915	$25.36
1917	$20.01
1919	$14.81

Use this Currency Conversion chart to calculate what any time in the years listed would cost in 2019. Simply multiply the cost of that item by dollar amount in the chart. For example, if you know that a Colt police revolver cost $12.50 in 1900, multiply $12.50 by $30.49 to discover that that same Colt revolver would cost $381.13 in 2019.

HISTORICAL SNAPSHOT 1900–1904

1900

- President William McKinley campaigns for reelection, emphasizing prosperity by using the "Full Dinner Pail" as his symbol
- Average life expectancy at birth is 47 years
- 13,824 motorcars are on the road
- Franklin, Peerless, and Stearns motorcars are introduced
- Hamburger introduced by Louis Lassen in New Haven, Connecticut
- Firestone Tire and Rubber Company founded on patent for attaching tires to rims
- 30,000 trolley cars operate on 15,000 miles of track
- Excavation begins on New York subway system
- U.S. railroads charge an average 75¢ per ton-mile, down from $1.22 in 1883
- First modern submarine, *Holland*, is purchased by navy
- Cripple Creek goldfield in Colorado yields $20 million
- Brownie box camera introduced by Eastman Kodak Company with a sales price of $1.00
- Uneeda Biscuits achieves sales of more than 10 million packages per month

1901

- President William McKinley assassinated; Theodore Roosevelt assumes presidency
- United States Steel Company created by J. P. Morgan
- Monsanto Chemical Company funded with a capitalization of $5,000
- New York City streetcars and elevators convert to electric power

- Andrew Carnegie gives the New York Public Library $5.2 million to open its first branches
- Jergens Lotion for chapped hands introduced King C. Gillette and William Nickerson start American Safety Razor Company with $5,000; becomes the Gillette Safety Razor Company the following year
- Japanese American chemist Satori Kato of Chicago introduces the first soluble "instant" coffee at the
- Pan-American Exhibition

1902

- John Mitchell leads 5-month strike of 147,000 anthracite coal workers
- Price of coal in New York goes from $5 to $30 per ton
- Membership in the AF of L reaches the million mark

- Rayon is patented by U.S. chemist
- A. D. Little
- Carnegie Institute of Washington established with a $10 million gift
- Russian-American Morris Michtom and his wife introduce the teddy bear with movable arms, legs, and head

- Philip Morris Corporation, Ltd., is incorporated in New York
- Charles Lewis Tiffany, founder of Tiffany and Co., dies leaving estate of $35 million
- The first Automat restaurant is opened by Horn & Hardart Baking Company in Philadelphia

1903

- Wright Brothers make first sustained manned flights in a controlled gasoline-powered aircraft
- Twenty-four hp Chadwick motorcar introduced; capable of 60 mph; $4,000
- Massachusetts creates first automobile license plate
- Bottle-blowing machine cuts cost of electric light bulb
- Harley-Davidson motorcycle introduced
- An automatic machine to cut off a salmon's head and tail, and clean it is devised by A. K. Smith
- Sanka Coffee introduced by German coffee-importer Ludwig Roselius

1904

- Marie Curie discovers two new radioactive elements: radium and polonium
- Post Toasties introduced by the Postum Cereal Company
- Joseph Campbell Preserve Company introduces Campbell's Pork and Beans
- St. Louis fair spawns iced tea and the ice-cream cone
- *Ladies' Home Journal* publishes exposé of the U.S. patent-medicine business

59

- Montgomery Ward distributes free catalogues, mailing 3 million books; Sears, Roebuck distributes a million copies of its spring catalogue
- Pope-Toledo motorcar introduced at $650
- E. F. Hutton and Company is founded by Edward Francis Hutton

SELECTED INCOME 1900–1904

Job	Source	Description	Pay
Assistant	*Milwaukee Journal* (1904)	Boy; steady advancement and good chance to learn trade if industrious; no boy who thinks he is 'it' because he swears and smokes cigarettes need apply.	$3.50/wk
Baseball Players	*American Chronicle* (1999)	Each winner's share of the 1903 Baseball World Series	$1,316
Business Representative	*New York Times* (1903)	Wanted—Trustworthy persons in each state to manage business of wealthy corporation; salary in cash each Thursday direct from headquarters; expense money advanced	$18/wk
Businessman	Vincent Tompkins, ed. *American Decades:1900–1909* (1996)	Annual salary of Charles M. Schwab as first president of U.S. Steel in 1903	$2 million
Carpenter	*San Francisco Examiner* (1913)	House carpenter, work on ranch	$3.25/day
Casual Labor	*New York Times* (1903)	Boys, we will give you a perfect timepiece for working for us a few hours. H. W. Wright Co., Baltimore, Md.	Watch
Circular Distributors	*Distributors National Union,* Cincinnati, OH (1902)	Pay advanced; no canvassing	$5/1,000
Clerk	*Chicago Tribune* (1902)	Bookkeeper and Stenographer	$20/wk
Collection Agent	*Chicago Tribune* (1904)	Man—To travel and collect; salary, all expenses, and commission; position will net $4,000 a year; $100 cash security required. Abbott Co.	$100/mo
Collection Agent	*Chicago Tribune* (1902)	German speaking; middle aged or men who cannot work hard	$2/day for 3 days; rest of week commission
Cook	*New York Times* (1900)	Wanted—To remain in the city all summer, a competent, young cook who is also a good laundress and who has first-class city references, wages	$25/mo
Cook	*Chicago Tribune* (1900)	Situation wanted—Competent cook	$50/mo
Cook	*San Francisco Examiner* (1913)	A man cook for hotel, country town	$50/mo
Dressmaker	*New York Times* (1901)	First-class fitter and trimmer; work by day; all latest fancy waists; remodeling	$2.50/day
Editor	Justin Kaplan, *Lincoln Steffens* (1974)	Annual salary of Lincoln Steffens as managing Editor of *McClure's* magazine in 1901	$5,000
Electric Linemen	*New York Tribune* (1902)	Daily pay for nine hours' work as an electric lineman with Pittsburgh and Allegheny Company	$2.50
Letter Carrier	*New York Tribune* (1902)	Yearly pay of America's 75,000 letter carriers is determined by length of service First year 2nd year 3rd year Thereafter	 $600 $800 $1000 $1200

Job	Source	Description	Pay
Light Labor	*Chicago Tribune* (1900)	Situation wanted—Light, by refined young man, 19 years old; some outside work attached	$7/wk
Mine Engineers	*New York Tribune* (1902)	Daily pay of Hoisting Engineers for Amalgamated Copper Company	$4
Nurse	*Chicago Tribune* (1904)	Situated Wanted—by a thoroughly competent nurse to care for an infant and day; wages.	$8/wk
Painter/Wallpaperer	*York (SC) Times* (1901)	Good work done cheap; rooms painted, papered	$1.25/day
Railroad Worker	*Milwaukee Journal* (1904)	Strong Young Men—For firemen and brakemen, Wisconsin and other railroads. Name position preferred. Send stamp for particulars. Railway Association. Firemen, engineers and brakemen conductors	$65/mo $125/mo
Sales	*Chicago Tribune* (1900)	We want a few active hustlers in city to sell our new patent reflectors for Welsbach lights; evening 6 p.m. to 9 p.m.; exclusive territory	$1.50–$3/night
Sales	*Chicago Tribune* (1900)	Agents—introducing our "super-asbestos" wicks; just out; beats electricity; address Fireproof Safety Wick Works.	$3–$5/day
Sales	*Chicago Tribune* (1902)	No experience needed; our circulars teach you the business and our patented goods do the rest; if you are making less than $300 per month write to us	$25/day
Sales	*Milwaukee Journal* (1904)	Wanted—Female Help "Lady"—For census work and distributing sample magazines; steady employment (home work)	$15/wk
Sales	*Milwaukee Journal* (1904)	General Agents—; every businessman buys a new best pocket invention $3. Big holiday business.	$20–$50/wk
Stenographer	*Milwaukee Journal* (1904)	At once—An experienced male stenographer; Smith Premier operator; must also be a bookkeeper. A good position for the right party.	$50/mo
Vaudeville Actor	*American Chronicle* (1999)	Weekly wages of Vaudeville star Lillian Russell in 1902	$3,500
Vaudeville Actor	*American Chronicle* (1999)	Weekly pay of Eva Tanquay at Hammerstein's Victoria Theater	$3,500

INVESTMENTS 1900–1904

Investment	1900	1901	1902	1903	1904
Basic Yield, One-year Corporate	3.97	3.25	3.30	3.45	3.60
Bonds Short-term Interest Rates, 4–6 Months, Prime Commercial Paper	5.71	5.40	5.81	6.16	5.14
Basic Yield, Common Stocks, Total	4.50	3.85	3.71	4.65	4.18
Index of Common Stocks (1941–1943510)	6.15	7.84	8.42	7.21	7.05

COMMON STOCKS, CLOSING PRICE AND YIELD, FIRST BUSINESS DAY OF YEAR

	1900	1901	1902	1903	1904
Allis Chalmers (Inc. 5/7/01)				82 1/8	50
AT & T (5/15/00 first date of issue)		93	96	163	126
Anaconda (Inc. 6/18/1895)	40 1/2	48 5/8	30 5/8	99	76
B & O (Chartered 1827)	58 3/4	85 7/8	108 1/8	101	78 1/2
Corn Products				30 1/2	17 1/2
General Electric (Inc. 4/15/1892)			282	183	170 1/2
(66 2/3% stock dividend, 6/25/02)					
National Biscuit (Inc. 2/3/1898)	90 1/4	41 3/4	43 1/4	45 1/8	36
US Steel (Inc. 2/25/01)			43	36 7/8	11 3/4
Valley Printing Telegraph Co.; name changed to Western Union (1856)	84 3/4	83	92 1/2	88 3/4	86

STANDARD JOBS 1900–1904

Job Type	1860	1861	1862	1863	1864
Average of All Industries, excl. farm labor	$490/yr	$508/yr	$519/yr	$543/yr	$540/yr
Average of All Industries, incl. farm labor	$438/yr	$454/yr	$467/yr	$489/yr	$490/yr
Bituminous Coal Mining	20¢/hr	23¢/hr	24¢/hr	27¢/hr	27¢/hr
Avg hrs/wk	52.60	52.40	52.30	52.20	51.60
Building Trades, Union Workers	37¢/hr	39¢/hr	41¢/hr	44¢/hr	44¢/hr
Avg hrs/wk	48.30	47.50	46.70	46.30	46.10
Clerical Workers in Mfg. & Steam RR	$1011/yr	$1009/yr	$1025/yr	$1037/yr	$1056/yr
Domestics	$240/yr	$243/yr	$264/yr	$270/yr	$277/yr
Farm Labor	$247/yr	$255/yr	$264/yr	$277/yr	$290/yr
Federal Civilian	$940/yr	$974/yr	$967/yr	$1009/yr	$971/yr
Federal Employees, Executive Depts.	$1033/yr	$1047/yr	$1061/yr	$1067/yr	$1066/yr
Finance, Insurance, & Real Estate	$1040/yr	$1037/yr	$1051/yr	$1078/yr	$1099/yr
Gas & Electricity Workers	$620/yr	$615/yr	NA	NA	$556/yr
Lower-Skilled Labor	$459/yr	$471/yr	$481/yr	$501/yr	$512/yr
Manufacturing, Payroll	15¢/hr	15¢/hr	16¢/hr	17¢/hr	16¢/hr
Avg hrs/wk	62.10	61.90	61.50	61.20	61.10
Manufacturing, Union Workers	34¢/hr	35¢/hr	36¢/hr	37¢/hr	37¢/hr
Avg hrs/wk	53.00	52.40	51.80	51.40	51.10
Medical/Health Services Workers	$256/yr	$258/yr	$267/yr	$275/yr	$283/yr
Ministers	$731/yr	$730/yr	$737/yr	$761/yr	$759/yr
Nonprofit Org. Workers	$652/yr	$651/yr	$657/yr	$679/yr	$677/yr

Job Type	1860	1861	1862	1863	1864
Postal Employees	37¢/hr	38¢/hr	37¢/hr	37¢/hr	37¢/hr
Avg hrs/wk	48.00	48.00	48.00	48.00	48.00
Public School Teachers and Local	$328/yr	$337/yr	$346/yr	$358/yr	$377/yr
Govt. Workers	$590/yr	$605/yr	$612/yr	$621/yr	$640/yr
State and Local Govt. Workers	$590/yr	$605/yr	$612/yr	$621/yr	$640/yr
Steam Railroads, Wage Earners	$548/yr	$549/yr	$562/yr	$593/yr	$600/yr
Street Railway Workers	$604/yr	$601/yr	$576/yr	$582/yr	$610/yr
Telegraph Ind. Workers	NA	NA	$544/yr	$573/yr	$601/yr
Telephone Ind. Workers	NA	NA	$408/yr	$397/yr	$392/yr
Wholesale and Retail Trade Workers	$508/yr	$510/yr	$521/yr	$537/yr	$551/yr

FOOD BASKET 1900–1904

Commodity	Year	New York	Atlanta	Chicago	Denver	Los Angeles
Apples, Evaporated, per pound	1900	10¢	10¢	7.67¢	NR	9.67¢
	1901	10¢	10¢	8.67¢	NR	9.33¢
	1902	10¢	10¢	10.71¢	NR	9.83¢
	1903	10¢	10¢	12.50¢	NR	9.67¢
	1904	12¢	10¢	10¢	10¢	10¢
Beans, Dry, per quart	1900	10¢	10¢	8.75¢	NR	5.63¢
	1901	10¢	15¢	8.67¢	NR	5.63¢
	1902	10¢	15¢	8.50¢	NR	7.03¢
	1903	10¢	10¢	10¢	NR	7.50¢
	1904	10¢	10¢	10¢	9.38¢	7.50¢
Beef, Fresh, Roasts, per pound	1900	18¢	18¢	13¢	15.67¢	17¢
	1901	18¢	18¢	13¢	16.67¢	17.67¢
	1902	20.67¢	20¢	14.42¢	21.79¢	18¢
	1903	20¢	17.71¢	14.42¢	21.17¢	18¢
	1904	14.83¢	12.50¢	9.92¢	12.50¢	15¢
Beef, Salt (Corned), per pound	1900	6¢	NR	7.25¢	NR	8.33¢
	1901	6.33¢	NR	7.25¢	NR	8.33¢
	1902	8.83¢	NR	7.75¢	NR	8.33¢
	1903	6.17¢	NR	8¢	NR	8.33¢
	1904	8¢	12.50¢	6.33¢	6.42¢	10¢
Beef, Steaks (Round), per pound	1900	16¢	13.63¢	12¢	12.50¢	10¢
	1901	16.33¢	15¢	12.67¢	14.17¢	10¢
	1902	16.33¢	15¢	13.25¢	14.58¢	11.88¢
	1903	18¢	15¢	12.50¢	11.33¢	12.50¢
	1904	16¢	12.50¢	10.50¢	10¢	12.50¢
Bread, Wheat, per loaf	1900	5¢	5¢	5¢	5¢	5¢
	1901	5¢	5¢	5¢	5¢	5¢
	1902	5¢	5¢	5¢	5¢	5¢
	1903	5¢	5¢	5¢	5¢	5¢
	1904	5¢	5¢	5¢	5¢	5¢
Butter, per pound	1900	26.67¢	28.75¢	22.67¢	27.92¢	25.48¢
	1901	24.67¢	26.25¢	24.58¢	29.17¢	25.24¢
	1902	27.67¢	30.42¢	24¢	31.25¢	28.81¢
	1903	29.33¢	30.83¢	26.58¢	30.83¢	30.48¢
	1904	26.25¢	27.92¢	25.58¢	25.42¢	26.25¢
Cheese, per pound	1900	14.17¢	17.58¢	17.33¢	20¢	18¢
	1901	14¢	17.25¢	17¢	20¢	19.33¢
	1902	17¢	18¢	17.33¢	20¢	20¢
	1903	19.17¢	18.33¢	16.58¢	20¢	20¢
	1904	16.17¢	15.42¢	16.92¢	20¢	20¢
Chickens, per pound	1900	12.50¢	14¢	10.75¢	NR	NR
	1901	12.17¢	15.25¢	10.92¢	NR	NR
	1902	12.75¢	15.33¢	13.25¢	NR	NR
	1903	12.75¢	16.83¢	16.33¢	NR	NR
	1904	18¢	16.04¢	15.42¢	13¢	23.75¢

Commodity	Year	New York	Atlanta	Chicago	Denver	Los Angeles
Coffee, per pound	1900	15.75¢	12.67¢	13.33¢	12.50¢	25¢
	1901	16¢	13¢	13.67¢	12.50¢	25¢
	1902	16¢	11.33¢	13.33¢	12.50¢	25¢
	1903	15¢	11.08¢	15.42¢	12.38¢	25¢
	1904	NR	NR	NR	NR	NR
Cornmeal, per pound	1900	3¢	1.67¢	1.75¢	2¢	2¢
	1901	3¢	2.08¢	2.25¢	2¢	2¢
	1902	3¢	2.08¢	2.50¢	2¢	2.75¢
	1903	3¢	1.77¢	2.50¢	2¢	3¢
	1904	2.95¢	2¢	2.50¢	2.50¢	3¢
Eggs, per dozen	1900	22.83¢	18¢	18.25¢	19.92¢	26.67¢
	1901	22.50¢	19¢	19.17¢	25.21¢	26.25¢
	1902	26.17¢	21¢	22.58¢	25.42¢	29.83¢
	1903	28¢	21.21¢	22.75¢	28¢	29.79¢
	1904	29.17¢	22.13¢	23.92¢	28.33¢	28.33¢
Fish, Fresh, per pound	1900	12¢	12.50¢	11.71¢	NR	10¢
	1901	12¢	12.50¢	11.71¢	NR	10¢
	1902	12¢	12.50¢	11.71¢	NR	10¢
	1903	11.83¢	10¢	11.71¢	NR	9.50¢
	1904	11.50¢	10.83¢	9.25¢	14¢	10¢
Fish, Salt, per pound	1900	9.75¢	14.33¢	6.46¢	NR	NR
	1901	9.33¢	15¢	7.71¢	NR	NR
	1902	9¢	14.92¢	6.17¢	NR	NR
	1903	9¢	15¢	9.17¢	NR	NR
	1904	11¢	12.42¢	10¢	14.81¢	8.33¢
Flour, Wheat, per pound	1900	2.31¢	2.78¢	2.30¢	1.65¢	2.50¢
	1901	2.28¢	3.05¢	2.30¢	1.85¢	2.50¢
	1902	2.61¢	3.05¢	2.30¢	1.90¢	2.50¢
	1903	2.82¢	3.11¢	2.43¢	2.18¢	2.79¢
—per one-eighth barrel bag	1904	81.67¢	84.58¢	74.58¢	61.67¢	73.33¢
Lard, per pound	1900	8.33¢	9.13¢	10¢	10.67¢	NR
	1901	10.21¢	11.08¢	10¢	12.42¢	NR
	1902	12.67¢	12.38¢	11.08¢	14.29¢	NR
	1903	11.33¢	10.46¢	10.67¢	15¢	NR
	1904	11.29¢	9.38¢	10.42¢	10¢	12.50¢
Milk, Fresh, per quart	1900	5¢	8¢	6¢	6.25¢	10¢
	1901	5¢	8¢	6¢	6.25¢	10¢
	1902	4.75¢	8¢	6¢	6.25¢	10¢
	1903	5¢	8¢	6¢	6.62¢	10¢
	1904	6¢	8¢	7¢	6.25¢	9.33¢
Molasses, per gallon	1900	50¢	50¢	60¢	65¢	70¢
	1901	50¢	50¢	60¢	65¢	70¢
	1902	50¢	50¢	60¢	65¢	70¢
	1903	57.50¢	50¢	60¢	65¢	70¢
	1904	53.75¢	50¢	50¢	50¢	50¢
Mutton and Lamb, Leg, per pound	1900	9.75¢	20¢	8¢	15¢	15¢
	1901	10.17¢	20¢	8¢	15¢	15¢
	1902	12.75¢	20¢	8¢	15¢	16.42¢
	1903	12.75¢	17.71¢	10.67¢	11.13¢	18.50¢
	1904	12.42¢	15¢	10.83¢	12.50¢	12.50¢
Pork, Fresh, per pound	1900	14.75¢	NR	9.25¢	12.50¢	15¢
	1901	15¢	NR	9.92¢	14.17¢	15¢
	1902	17.33¢	NR	11.67¢	16.04¢	16.58¢
	1903	18.67¢	NR	10.08¢	13.75¢	17.50¢
	1904	13.38¢	12.50¢	10.25¢	11¢	15¢

Commodity	Year	New York	Atlanta	Chicago	Denver	Los Angeles
Pork, Salt, Bacon, per pound	1900	16.75¢	11¢	12.25¢	13.17¢	13.25¢
	1901	17.58¢	11.17¢	13.75¢	13.71¢	13.75¢
	1902	19¢	12¢	14.58¢	16.42¢	15.50¢
	1903	18¢	17.08¢	15.92¢	17.25¢	17.75¢
	1904	16.33¢	12.96¢	14.50¢	20¢	18¢
Pork, Salt, Dry or Pickled, per pound	1900	13.33¢	NR	8¢	NR	NR
	1901	14¢	NR	10¢	NR	NR
	1902	15¢	NR	12¢	NR	NR
	1903	14¢	NR	12¢	NR	NR
	1904	12.71¢	10¢	11.33¢	11.38¢	12.50¢
Pork, Salt, Ham, per pound	1900	14.08¢	15¢	11¢	13.54¢	14.83¢
	1901	15.08¢	15¢	12.50¢	13.71¢	15.21¢
	1902	14.42¢	15¢	12.50¢	15.96¢	16.08¢
	1903	15.75¢	14.33¢	12.50¢	15.50¢	15.50¢
	1904	20¢	20¢	16.33¢	20¢	20¢
Potatoes, Irish, per bushel	1900	61.33¢	$1.2083	38.64¢	71.25¢	85.75¢
	1901	83.58¢	99.17¢	68.18¢	93¢	94¢
	1902	94.58¢	$1.0250	82.73¢	95.75¢	94.25¢
	1903	99.58¢	90.42¢	71.67¢	93¢	$1.0125
—per peck	1904	30.67¢	19.58¢	18¢	23.81¢	24.69¢
Prunes, per pound	1900	10¢	NR	7.67¢	NR	8.75¢
	1901	10¢	NR	7.33¢	NR	8.33¢
	1902	8¢	NR	7.75¢	NR	8.33¢
	1903	10¢	NR	7.50¢	NR	6¢
	1904	7.83¢	8.33¢	8.50¢	8¢	5¢
Rice, per pound	1900	7¢	7¢	5¢	8.33¢	7¢
	1901	7¢	7¢	5.83¢	8.33¢	7¢
	1902	7¢	7¢	6¢	8.33¢	6.50¢
	1903	7¢	7¢	5¢	8.33¢	6.79¢
	1904	7.58¢	7.50¢	9¢	8.33¢	8¢
Sugar, per pound	1900	5.75¢	5.90¢	5.79¢	5.85¢	NR
	1901	5.92¢	6.04¢	5.71¢	5.74¢	NR
	1902	6¢	5.38¢	5.54¢	5.36¢	NR
	1903	6¢	5.38¢	5¢	5.45¢	NR
	1904	5.58¢	5.67¢	5.33¢	6.25¢	6.35¢
Tea, per pound	1900	50¢	60¢	47.50¢	60¢	50¢
	1901	50¢	61.67¢	50¢	60¢	50¢
	1902	50¢	60¢	50¢	60¢	50¢
	1903	50¢	50¢	50¢	60¢	50¢
	1904	50¢	50¢	50¢	35¢	50¢
Veal, per pound	1900	12.08¢	NR	10.25¢	NR	NR
	1901	12.25¢	NR	12¢	NR	NR
	1902	14¢	NR	12.13¢	NR	NR
	1903	12.75¢	NR	12¢	NR	NR
	1904	20.50¢	15¢	16.33¢	13.96¢	20¢
Vinegar, per gallon	1900	28¢	NR	20¢	NR	40¢
	1901	28¢	NR	20¢	NR	42.50¢
	1902	28¢	NR	20¢	NR	50¢
	1903	32¢	NR	20¢	NR	50¢
	1904	20¢	20¢	20¢	30¢	50¢

SELECTED PRICES 1900–1904

Item	Source	Description	Price
ALCOHOL			
Whiskey	The New Orleans *Picayune* (1903)	White Line Whiskey Gallon Quart	 $3.50 $1.00
Wine	*Atlanta Constitution* (1904)	Zinfandel; 12 quarts	$5.00/case
APPAREL, CHILDREN'S			
Hat	*The New Orleans Picayune* (1903)	Children's lawn or straw hats, trimmed worth $0.98; Special	$0.49
Hosiery	*Ladies' Home Journal* (1904)	Black Cat; serviceable five-thread hose for boys; fine mercerized hose for girls	$0.35/pair
Overcoat	*Yorkville Enquirer* (Yorkville, SC) (1900)	Boy's, 6 to 12 years; best quality	$2.50
Play Suit	*Ladies' Home Journal* (1904)	Little Tudor; a complete top-to-toe garment	$0.50
Silk Bonnet	*Southern Christian Advocate* (1902)	60 Children's silk bonnets; reg $1	$0.50
Suit	*New York Times* (1901)	Three-piece; a camera free with every suit; reg $5	$2.98
Underwear	*The State* (Columbia, SC) (1903)	Jersey ribbed, fleeced, lined vests and pants	$0.15
APPAREL, MEN'S			
Hat	*New York Times* (1901)	Alpines and derbies	$3.49
Heel Cushions	*Ladies' Home Journal* (1904)	*Gilbert's;* make yourself taller; worn inside the shoe; 1/2"	$0.25
Overcoat	*New York Times* (1901)	Spring weight	$6.50
Shirt	*Sears, Roebuck* (1902)	French percale; fast colors, yoke back, pearl buttons	$0.40
Shoes	*New York Times* (1901)	*W. L. Douglas;* My large business permits me to buy the high-grade leathers used in $5 shoes	$3.50
Shoes	*Greenville News* (Greenville, SC) (1902)	Satin calf	$0.93
Suit	*The State* (Columbia, SC) (1903)	*Fitzmaurice;* sack business suit; worn by most businessmen of your acquaintance	$8.50

Item	Source	Description	Price
Suspenders	*Harper's Monthly Magazine* (1903)	President suspenders make walking easy; the "give and take" principle; metal trimmings cannot rust.	$0.50 to $1.00

APPAREL, WOMEN'S

Item	Source	Description	Price
Belt	*The State* (Columbia, SC) (1903)	Silk and elastic; large oxidized buckle, something very swell	$0.50
Corset	*New York Tribune* (1902)	*James McCreery and Company corsets;* straight front, long hip, batiste Value Sale price	 $2.25 $1.45
Crash Skirts	*Atlanta Constitution* (1904)	Linen; black and colors; $1.25 value	$0.69
Dress	*New York Times* (1901)	Spring; percale	$4.88
Handkerchiefs	*New York Times* (1901)	Hemstitched; 1" and 2" hems	$3.00/dozen
Hat	*Sears, Roebuck* (1902)	Jaunty large black turban, with a very richly designed straw braid	$2.25
Hose	*New York Times* (1901)	*Lisle* thread and fine cotton; regularly $0.50	$0.29
Lawn Dress	*New York Times* (1901)	Satin-striped, figured	$10.41
Opera Bag	*The State* (Columbia, SC) (1903)	Positively the newest things	$1.50 to $3.50
Parasol	*Sears, Roebuck* (1900)	Pure white China silk	$1.25
Shoe Inserts	*Harper's Monthly Magazine* (1903)	*Astra* soles keep your feet dry, clean, and healthy—cool in summer and warm in winter. Worn all the year round, they absorb perspiration entirely, prevent catarrh and rheumatism, and save shoes and stockings	$0.25 for 10 pairs
Shoes	*Greenville News* (Greenville, SC) (1902)	*Dongola* shoes	$0.89
Shoes	*Ladies' Home Journal* (1904)	*La France;* the Oxford is the smartest shoe of the season	$3.00
Suit	*New York Times* (1901)	Shirt-waist suit, comfortable successor to the ill-fitting wrapper and house dress	$2.25 to $4.50
Summer Suit	*Ladies' Home Journal* (1904)	Tailored suits Mohair and brilliantine suits Traveling dresses	$8 to $50 $8 to $40 $8 to $30
Undervest	*The State* (Columbia, SC) (1903)	Fleece lined	$0.39

Item	Source	Description	Price
APPLIANCES			
Home Heater	*Sears, Roebuck* (1902)	*Acme Seroco;* hot-blast, air-tight sheet-steel heater for hard or soft coal; 16" diameter	$9.55
Linen Washer and Press	*Harper's Monthly Magazine* (1903)	Washer and heated steel roll mangle; produces crisp, clean linen that can be had in a few minutes; the ideal laundry apparatus for the home	$150 for both
Radiator	*Sears, Roebuck* (1902)	*Acme;* direct steam or water; latest thing in radiator design and construction	$9.45
Range	*Sears, Roebuck* (1902)	*Acme Regal;* 20" × 21" × 4"; steel range is highly nickel plated throughout	$20.55
Range	*Sears, Roebuck* (1902)	Steel; 8" lids; over 17" × 21" × 12"; 475 lbs; terms: $8 cash, $3/mo, no interest	$22.90
Refrigerator	*Sears, Roebuck* (1902)	*Acme Seroco;* ice receptacle holds 125 lbs of ice, and a 100 lb piece will go in easily without any chipping	$27.50
Stove	*The Housewife* (1903)	*Acme Wonder* cook stove; extra fine finish	$4.85

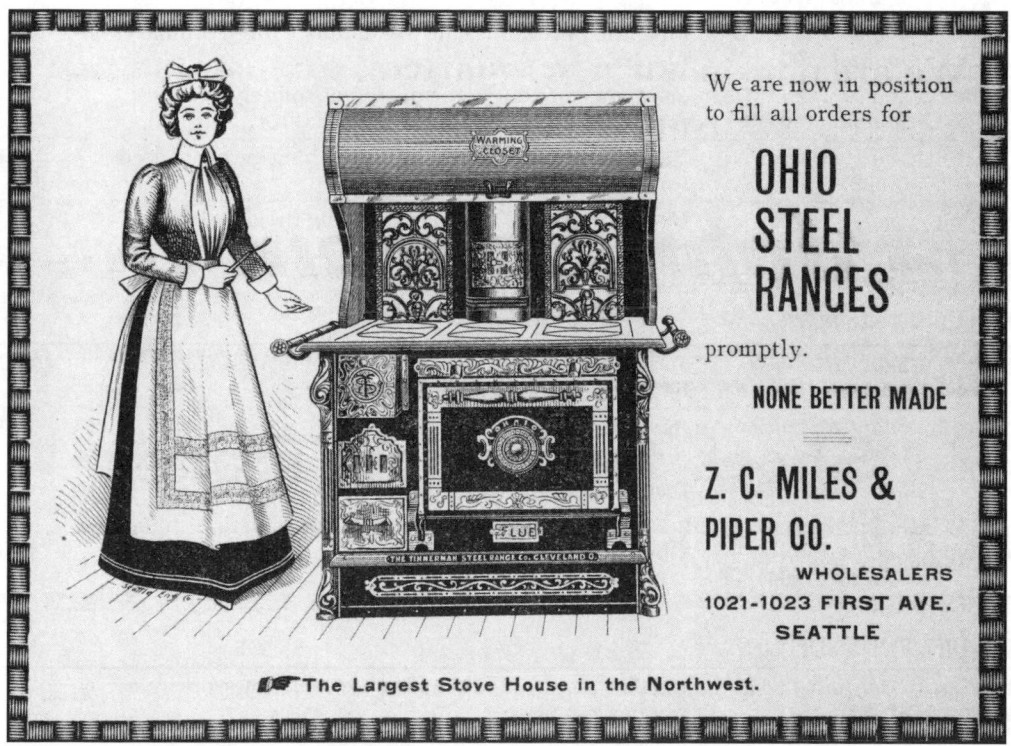

Early kitchen stoves were often ornate, brightly colored, and showcased the artistry of wrought iron. (via Wikimedia Commons)

Item	Source	Description	Price
Washer	*Sears, Roebuck* (1902)	*Fulton American #1;* machine made of white pine, painted and grained as ash color; will wash five shirts clean without the use of a washboard	$4.44
Washing Machine	*The Housewife* (1903)	Wonder washing machine; the equal of washing machines that sell for two or three times the price	$1.95
Water Closet	*Sears, Roebuck* (1902)	Siphon jet water closet; tank copper lined	$19.75

BABY PRODUCTS

Item	Source	Description	Price
Baby Powder	*Sears, Roebuck* (1902)	*Talcum;* nicely perfumed and put up handsomely; decorated metal boxes with sprinkler tops	$0.08/box
Baby Tender	*Ladies' Home Journal* (1904)	*E-Z-Go;* teaches baby to walk	$2.75
Hygienic Absorbent Pads	*Ladies' Home Journal* (1904)	Keep the baby dry and clean; shield wt. 4 oz	$1.50 each
Hygienic Dip Pins	*Ladies' Home Journal* (1904)	*Boston;* if you buy 3, 1 will be sent free	$0.10 each
Infant's Long Dress	*Ladies' Home Journal* (1904)	*Nainsook,* yoke of fine beading and featherstitching	$1.35
Nipple	*Ladies' Home Journal* (1904)	*Clingfast;* pure gum right size; outlasts three ordinary nipples	$0.50/ dozen
Pants for babies	*Ladies' Home Journal* (1904)	*Stork;* made to cover the diaper; absolutely waterproof	$0.05
Rattle Pacifier	*Sears, Roebuck* (1902)	Best rattle, teething ring, and plaything ever invented for the babies	$0.09
Rubber Teething Ring	*Ladies' Home Journal* (1904)	*Bailey's;* expands the gums, keeping them soft; comforts and amuses the child	$0.10

BUGGY CARRIAGES & SUPPLIES

Item	Source	Description	Price
Buggy	*Sears, Roebuck* (1900)	Jump seat; the body is made of good material; 25" × 54"	$59.75
Buggy	*Sears, Roebuck* (1902)	*Acme* Royal Top	$54.90
Buggy Whip	*Sears, Roebuck* (1900)	Black star finish, waterproof cover; 6"	$0.69
Driving Wagon	*Ladies' Home Journal* (1904)	Open trap style; bike gear and 7/8" Kelly rubber tires	$83.00

BUSINESS EQUIPMENT & SUPPLIES

Item	Source	Description	Price
Telephone Rates	*New York Tribune* (1902)	Manhattan rates for business service, New York Telephone Company Per month	$5.00
Wireless Machine	*Ladies' Home Journal* (1904)	*Lambert;* it is a dwarf in size but a giant in its work; complete	$25.00

COLLECTIBLES

Item	Source	Description	Price
Book	*New York Tribune* (1902)	First edition of "The Loving Ballad" by William Makepeace Thackeray	$42.50

Item	Source	Description	Price
Painting	*New York Tribune* (1902)	*The Holy Family* by Peter Paul Rubens sold in auction	$50,000
Painting	*New York Tribune* (1902)	*Harvesting the Poppies* by Jules Breton sold in auction	$35,000
Painting	*New York Tribune* (1902)	*Arabs Crossing a Stream* by A. Schreyer sold in auction	$11,000
Painting	*American Chronicle* (1999)	Anton Mauve's *Sheep Coming Out of the Forest;* sold at auction	$40,200
Proof Sheet	*New York Tribune* (1902)	Original proof sheet of "Charge of the Light Brigade" with margin correction by poet	$440

EDUCATION

Item	Source	Description	Price
Boarding School	*Harper's Monthly Magazine* (1903)	*Dr. Holbrook's School for Boys;* full term begins September 24, 1903; Ossining-on-Hudson, New York	$700
Boarding School	*Harper's Monthly Magazine* (1903)	*Fort Edward Collegiate Institute for Girls;* location unsurpassed; college preparatory; choice of six courses of study; departments also in Music, Art, Elocution, Physical Culture; Fort Edward, New York. Yearly rate	$300 to $400
Boarding School	*Harper's Monthly Magazine* (1903)	*Lawrence Academy;* endowed, limited school for boys over ten; founded 1793. Fits for all colleges, scientific and technical schools; Groton, Massachusetts	$500

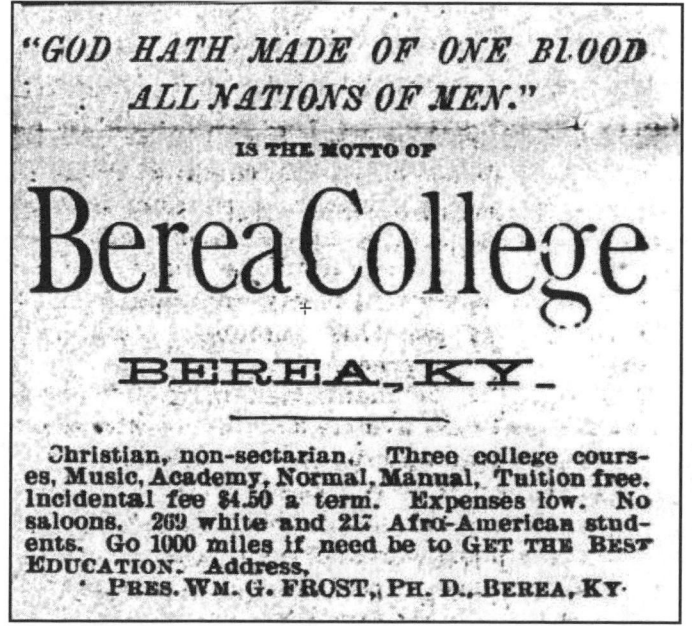

Founded in 1855, Berea College was the first in the Southern United States to offer an education to both men and women of all races. The College is still in operation and charges no tuition. (via Wikimedia Commons)

Item	Source	Description	Price
Boarding School	*Southern Christian Advocate* (1902)	*Wofford College Fitting School;* Spartanburg, South Carolina; board, fuel, lights and all fees	$110
Dance Lessons	*New York Times* (1901)	Waltz, two-step polka, waltz quadrille; five private or four-class lessons	$5.00
Seminary	*Harper's Monthly Magazine* (1903)	*Ashland Seminary;* certificate admits to Wellesley and other colleges. A delightful church school in the heart of the beautiful Blue Grass region. In the Diocese of Lexington, Kentucky; yearly charge	$250

ENTERTAINMENT

Item	Source	Description	Price
Broadway Play	*New York Tribune* (1902)	*Sleeping Beauty and the Beast;* matinee	$50.00 to $1.50
Circus	*New York Tribune* (1902)	Great 4-Paw and Sells Brothers Enormous Shows United; at Madison Square Garden, featuring Diavalo's Loop the Loop	$0.25 to $2.00
Orchestral Concert	*New York Tribune* (1902)	*Wetzler Orchestral Concert;* featuring soloist Paderewski Seats	$1 to $2
Vaudeville	*New York Tribune* (1902)	Big Vaudeville Comedy; 25 star acts Seats Reserved Box	 $0.25-$0.50 $0.75 $1.00
Show Ticket	*Sears, Roebuck* (1901)	Buffalo Bill's Wild West and Rough Riders Show, Madison Square Garden Gallery Second balcony First balcony Arena First-tier boxes Arena boxes	 $0.25 $0.50 $0.75 $1.00 $9.00 $12.00
Theater Ticket	*Atlanta Constitution* (1904)	Eagle Minstrels; Singers, dancers, comedians patriotic first part; funny mock initiation	$0.25-$0.75

ENTERTAINMENT, HOME

Item	Source	Description	Price
Board Game	*Sears, Roebuck* (1902)	*Ouija;* the most interesting and mystifying production of the age	$1.00
Bone Dice	*Sears, Roebuck* (1902)	Square corners, No. 6, 1/2"	$0.09/dozen
Camera	*Sears, Roebuck* (1902)	*Delmar* folding camera	$3.75
Playing Cards	*Sears, Roebuck* (1902)	*Dougherty Climax;* enameled, round-cornered, linen cards	$0.24/pkg
Talking Machine	*Sears, Roebuck* (1900)	*Graphophone;* not a toy but a high-grade and complete graphophone	$5.00
Talking Machine	*Sears, Roebuck* (1902)	Graphophone Grand	$25.00

Item	Source	Description	Price
FARM EQUIPMENT & SUPPLIES			
Dehorning Clippers	*Sears, Roebuck* (1900)	*Keystone;* the latest improved and most powerful instrument for dehorning cattle	$12.00
Pony Plow	*Sears, Roebuck* (1902)	All-steel, wood beam, one-horse plow, 8" cut	$2.39
FINANCIAL PRODUCTS AND SERVICES			
U.S. Money Orders	*Advertising Trade Card* (1900)	$5–$1,000 $2,000–$3,000 $3,000–$4,000 $4,000–$5,000	$0.08 $0.12 $0.15 $0.20
FOOD PRODUCTS			
Breakfast Cereal	*Ladies' Home Journal* (1904)	*Ralston;* over a million people know Ralston is the best	$0.15/pkg
Butter	*Atlanta Constitution* (1904)	*Elgin;* best of this famous brand; delivered on ice	$0.28/pound
Coffee	*Sears, Roebuck* (1902)	Ten-pound tin, special grade	$2.10
Coffee	*Ladies' Home Journal* (1904)	*Pomja;* a selected blend of the highest grades of coffee	$0.30/pound
Coffee	*Ladies' Home Journal* (1904)	*Pomja* coffee; sold in sealed one-pound packages	$0.30
Corn Syrup	*Ladies' Home Journal* (1904)	*Karo;* the great spread for daily bread in air-tight, friction-top tins	$0.10-$0.50
Dessert Jelly	*Ladies' Home Journal* (1904)	*Bro-Man-Gel-On;* the one perfect dessert jelly One package	$0.13
Flour	*Greenville News* (Greenville, SC) (1903)	Virginia flour; ground from selected winter wheat	$4.75/bushel
Gelatin	*Ladies' Home Journal* (1904)	*Bro-Man-Gel-On;* the one perfect dessert jello	13¢/pkg
Jam	*Atlanta Constitution* (1904)	*A&P;* One-pint jar	$0.16/jar
Marshmallows	*Sears, Roebuck* (1902)	Five-pound box	$0.67
Milk Cocoa	*Ladies' Home Journal* (1904)	*Croft's Swiss;* nothing in it but pure pasteurized milk, the finest cocoa beans, and sugar; makes 40 cups	$0.15
Prunes	*Greenville News* (Greenville, SC) (1903)	Large jar	$0.10
Soda Crackers	*Sears, Roebuck* (1902)	Twenty-pound box	$0.99

Item	Source	Description	Price
Sweet Pickled Peaches	*Greenville News* (Greenville, SC) (1903)	Large jars	$0.47
Tea	*Atlanta Constitution* (1904)	*Ceylonia Iced;* highest grade	$0.70/pound
Tea	*Ladies' Home Journal* (1904)	*Ceylon* tea; a delight to all connoisseurs Per package	$0.70
Water	*The New Orleans Picayune* (1903)	*Sparkling Abita;* the perfect table water Per dozen pints	$1.75

FURNITURE

Item	Source	Description	Price
Banquet Lamp	*Sears, Roebuck* (1902)	*Cerise;* globe and bowl are of one dark red shade with the velvet finish, making a very soft light at night; 25" high	$5.90
Bed	*New York Times* (1901)	White enamelled brass, heavy posts	$2.98
Bed	*Sears, Roebuck* (1902)	Brass trimmed iron; baked white-enamel finish, 1/2 brass-top rail on both head and foot	$4.75
Bed	*Atlanta Constitution* (1904)	Sanitary folding; metal, worth $10	$5.00
Bedroom Suite	*Sears, Roebuck* (1900)	With Cheval dresser; made of hardwood	$21.00
Bedroom Suite	*Sears, Roebuck* (1902)	Full-size bed, dresser, 18" × 34" commode, oak	$16.95
Bookcase	*Ladies' Home Journal* (1904)	Sectioned; can be added to as your library grows; 49" high, art glass doors, quarter-sawed oak or mahogany finish	$18.25
Carpet	*Sears, Roebuck* (1902)	Heavy weight; ingrain; all-wool super ingrain carpet in one of the richest dark red backgrounds and newest bright floral designs shown this season	$0.58/yard
Dining Room Suite	*The New Orleans Picayune* (1903)	*The Union Furniture Company;* suite includes one sideboard, one extension table, six cane seat chairs; in solid golden oak	$23.00
Furniture	*New York Times* (1901)	Parlor suits: 3-piece suite, sofa, arm and wall chair; inlaid frames, carved legs, satin damask cover	$90 to $135
Home Desk	*Ladies' Home Journal* (1904)	28" × 40", tambour front; dust proof; quarter-sawed oak; golden finish	$27.00
Lantern	*Sears, Roebuck* (1902)	*Dietz;* a strongly guarded crystal tubular lantern with a glass front instead of tin	$0.68
Mantel	*Harper's Monthly Magazine* (1903)	The newest and most artistic fireplace mantels are made of ornamental brick in Colonial, Elizabethan, Renaissance, Empire, and other styles; any capable brick mason can set them up with our plans	$12.00 and up
Mattress	*Sears, Roebuck* (1902)	You are in luck to sleep on a climax mattress	$10.00
Parlor Suite	*Sears, Roebuck* (1902)	Three-piece; divan, arm chair, and parlor chair; birch construction, mahogany finish; price depending on fabric selection	$9.95–$11.95
Rocking Chair	*Sears, Roebuck* (1900)	High back, richly carved	$2.85

Item	Source	Description	Price
Rolltop Desk	*Sears, Roebuck* (1902)	All oak; 48" long, 30" wide, 46" high; 5 drawers	$11.95

GARDEN EQUIPMENT & SUPPLIES

Item	Source	Description	Price
Fertilizer	*New York Tribune* (1902)	*Bowker's* bone and wood ash fertilizer; 100-pound bag One ton	$2.00 $25.00
Flower Bulb	*Greenville News* (Greenville, SC) (1902)	Calladium	$0.15
Garden Hose	*Greenville News* (Greenville, SC) (1903)	1/2" 3/4"	$0.10/foot $0.125/foot
Lawn Dressing	*New York Tribune* (1902)	*Bowker's* lawn and garden dressing; anyone can apply, sufficient for one-quarter acre 100 pounds	$3.00
Pruning Shears	*Sears, Roebuck and Co. Catalogue* (1902)	*Henry Pattern* pruning shears; high-grade steel blades	$0.27

HOTEL RATES

Item	Source	Description	Price
Hotel Room	*New York Tribune* (1902)	*Hotel Stratford;* ocean front, Atlantic City, New Jersey Per day	$2.50 to $3.00
Hotel Room	*New York Tribune* (1902)	*The Rittenhouse;* Atlantic City, New Jersey, strictly high-class, refined hotel, cuisine and service unsurpassed Spring rates per day Saturday to Monday	$12 to $17 $4.00
Hotel Room	*New York Tribune* (1902)	*Hotel Windsor;* the most reasonably priced first-class hotel in the world, 140 rooms, American plan Per day, per person	$2.50
Hotel Room	*The New Orleans Picayune* (1903)	*Hotel Denechaud;* New Orleans; per day American plan European plan	$2 and up $1 and up

HOUSEHOLD PRODUCTS

Item	Source	Description	Price
Alarm Clock	*Sears, Roebuck* (1902)	Oxidized, no battery necessary; 2 lb	$2.50
Asphalt Coating	*Ladies' Home Journal* (1904)	*Elliott's Durable;* will add at least ten years to the life of a new or old leaky shingle, tin, or felt roof	$0.75/gallon
Blanket	*Yorkville Enquirer* (Yorkville, SC) (1900)	In grey and white	$0.50
Carpet	*Ladies' Home Journal* (1904)	Can be selected at your own fireside from our catalogue; Sultan cottage carpets All-wool extra super ingrains	$0.25/yard $0.59/yard
Carpet Sweeper	*Ladies' Home Journal* (1904)	*Bissell;* it is little short of pathetic to see a woman in this age sweeping with a corn broom	$2.00 to $4.00

Item	Source	Description	Price
Carpet Sweeper	*Sears, Roebuck* (1902)	Acme; does not wear out a carpet like a broom does	$1.65
China	*Sears, Roebuck* (1902)	*Waverly;* 100-piece, semi-porcelain dinner set, service for 12; decorated in green, blue, or brown	$5.98
Cleanser	*Sears, Roebuck* (1902)	*Cleanit Liquid;* the best compound in the world for removing paint or grease stains, 4-oz bottle	$0.15/bottle
Curtains	*The State* (Columbia, SC) (1903)	Very handsome patterns	$3.50/pair
Curtains	*New York Tribune* (1902)	*Lord and Taylor* ruffled muslin curtains; Per pair	$1.00 $2.00
Fleece Blanket	*Ladies' Home Journal* (1904)	*The Suffolk Sanitary;* beautiful to see, healthful to use, light to handle; full-size pair	$1.00
Fountain Brush	*Ladies' Home Journal* (1904)	*The Knickerbocker;* for your bath; 595 little streams and rubber tips bathe and massage at once	$3.50
Glassware	*Sears, Roebuck* (1902)	40-piece outfit; imitation cut glass, includes 6 glass tumblers, 6 goblets, 12 berry saucers"	$1.75
Grille Fencing	*Ladies' Home Journal* (1904)	48" long with pole decorative and inexpensive 60" long	$5.00
Kitchen Cabinet	*Ladies' Home Journal* (1904)	*Hoosier;* storeroom, pantry, kitchen table in one	$14.00
Lead Paint	*The State* (Columbia, SC) (1903)	*Masury's Railroad;* it will stay white	$0.07/pound
Milk Can	*Sears, Roebuck* (1902)	*Wisconsin Pattern;* is in use all over the United States as a wagon can for hauling milk or cream to creameries; 10 gallons	$1.60
Nail Hammer	*Sears, Roebuck* (1902)	*Sears & Roebuck;* 1 1/2", 1 lb claw hammer	$0.53
Paint	*Sears, Roebuck* (1902)	Ready mix	$0.98/gallon
Pesticide	*Sears, Roebuck* (1900)	*Strangle Food;* the surest and quickest death to bugs	$0.25/can
Pillow	*The New Orleans Picayune* (1903)	Large size feather pillows covered with best feather ticking	$0.49
Pineapple Knife and Shredder	*Ladies' Home Journal* (1904)	Seams and eyes quickly and easily removed	$0.25
Porch Shades	*Ladies' Home Journal* (1904)	*Vudor;* shut out the sun and at the same time let in the air, making the porch a cool, cozy, and comfortable room on warm summer days	$2.00
Prepared Wax	*Ladies' Home Journal* (1904)	*Johnson;* the hardwood floor authorities 1 lb can 8 lb can	$0.60 $2.00
Rubber Gloves	*Ladies' Home Journal* (1904)	*Non-Pa-Reil;* preserve the beauty of the hands	$1.00/pair
Saw	*Sears, Roebuck* (1902)	*Henry Disston & Sons;* 22" panel saw, 12 points	$1.13
Sawed Wood	*The State* (Columbia, SC) (1903)	Palmetto Ice Company	$3.25/cord

Item	Source	Description	Price
Sheet	*The State* (Columbia, SC) (1903)	Bleached; 81" × 90"	$0.98
Silver Tea Strainer	*Ladies' Home Journal* (1904)	Made of solid white metal quadruple silver-plated, ebonized handle four inches long	$0.35
Silverware Set	*Sears, Roebuck* (1902)	26 pieces	$4.95
Sponge	*Ladies' Home Journal* (1904)	*Kleanwell;* for perfect hands, the only thoroughly hygienic and sanitary sponge in existence; Toilet size / Bath size	$0.50 / $0.75 to $1.00
Tool Chest	*Sears, Roebuck* (1902)	Made of selected chestnut hardwood moldings; sliding tray; 28" × 15" × 14"	$5.40
Wallpaper	*Sears, Roebuck* (1902)	All-purpose for home; dark gray background with beautiful festoons of daisies; includes 9" border; double roll	$0.09
Washcloth	(1904)	Made by an entirely new process; it cleans itself	$0.05

JEWELRY

Item	Source	Description	Price
Badge or Class Pin	*Ladies' Home Journal* (1904)	Be loyal to your college, school, class, society, or club Silver plate / Sterling silver	$1.00/dozen / $2.50
Pocket Flask	*Sears, Roebuck* (1902)	Pocket drinking flask; glass-covered with leather	$0.80
Pocket Watch	*Sears, Roebuck* (1902)	17-jewel, 20-year guarantee a gold-filled case	$11.00
Watch	*Greenville News* (Greenville, SC) (1903)	Nickel, 21 extra-fine red-ruby jewels	$100

MEALS

Item	Source	Description	Price
Lunch	(1901)	Menu includes: Baked chicken pie; boiled ox tongue with spinach; roast ribs of beef, new golden wax beans, stewed tomatoes, lettuce salad, potato salad, bread and butter, custard pudding	$1.00

MEDICAL PRODUCTS & SERVICES

Item	Source	Description	Price
Alcohol Cure	*Sears, Roebuck* (1902)	It creates an appetite for food instead of liquor	$0.42
Glasses	*New York Times* (1901)	*Keene's Optical*; free exam with purchase of glasses, Regular / Gold-spring eyeglasses	$1.00 / $2.50
Glasses	*Sears, Roebuck* (1902)	Gold-filled spectacles	$1.90
Homeopathic Remedies	*Sears, Roebuck* (1902)	Twelve bottles of homeopathic remedies, medicine case, and instruction sheet free	$1.50
Nonprescription Drug	*Sears, Roebuck* (1900)	*Pasteur's Death of Microbes*; will prevent lagrippe, catarrh, consumption, malaria, blood poison, and rheumatism	$0.80/ half-gallon

Item	Source	Description	Price
Nonprescription Drug	*Sears, Roebuck* (1900)	*Wonderful Little Liver Pills*; constipation, that most hideous and deadly demon of sickness, is an easy enough thing to cure	$0.12/bottle
Nonprescription Drug	Sears, Roebuck (1902)	Dr. Rose's French Arsenic Complexion Wafers; for even the coarsest and most repulsive skin and complexion	$0.35/50 wafers
Nonprescription Drug	*Sears, Roebuck* (1902)	*Electric Liniment*; for rheumatism, sprains, wounds, bruises, lame back, contracted muscles	$0.25
Nonprescription Drug	*Greenville News* (Greenville, SC) (1903)	*Castoria*; remedy for constipation, sour stomach, convulsion, and loss of sleep	$0.35/35 doses
Nonprescription Drug	*Greenville News* (Greenville, SC) (1903)	*Wine of Gardui*; 1,500,000 afflicted women have been cured of female diseases	$1.00/bottle
Nonprescription Drug	*Atlanta Constitution* (1904)	*Botanic Blood Balm*; cures eczema, all skin and blood diseases, cold sores	$1.00/bottle
Painkiller	*Sears, Roebuck* (1902)	At the first sign of a cramp, relief comes at once	$0.25
Teeth	*The New Orleans Picayune* (1903)	*National Dental Parlors*; the Celebrated English Teeth, mounted on Sampson Red Rubber Set of teeth Porcelain crowns Gold fillings	 $3.00 $3.00 $0.75
Tobacco Cure	*Sears, Roebuck* (1902)	Can be chewed the same as tobacco	$0.40
Truss	*Sears, Roebuck* (1900)	*Double scrotal*; we recommend it in very severe cases	$10.00
Truss	*Sears, Roebuck* (1902)	*Lea's*; fitted with improved safety clutch fastenings; elastic; complete with the celebrated water pad; adult size, single adult size, double	 $0.98 $1.75
Witch Hazel Extract	*Sears, Roebuck* (1902)	Useful for sore throat, hemorrhage, wounds, sprains, bruises, sore eyes, stiff joints, burns; ½-pt bottle	$0.12

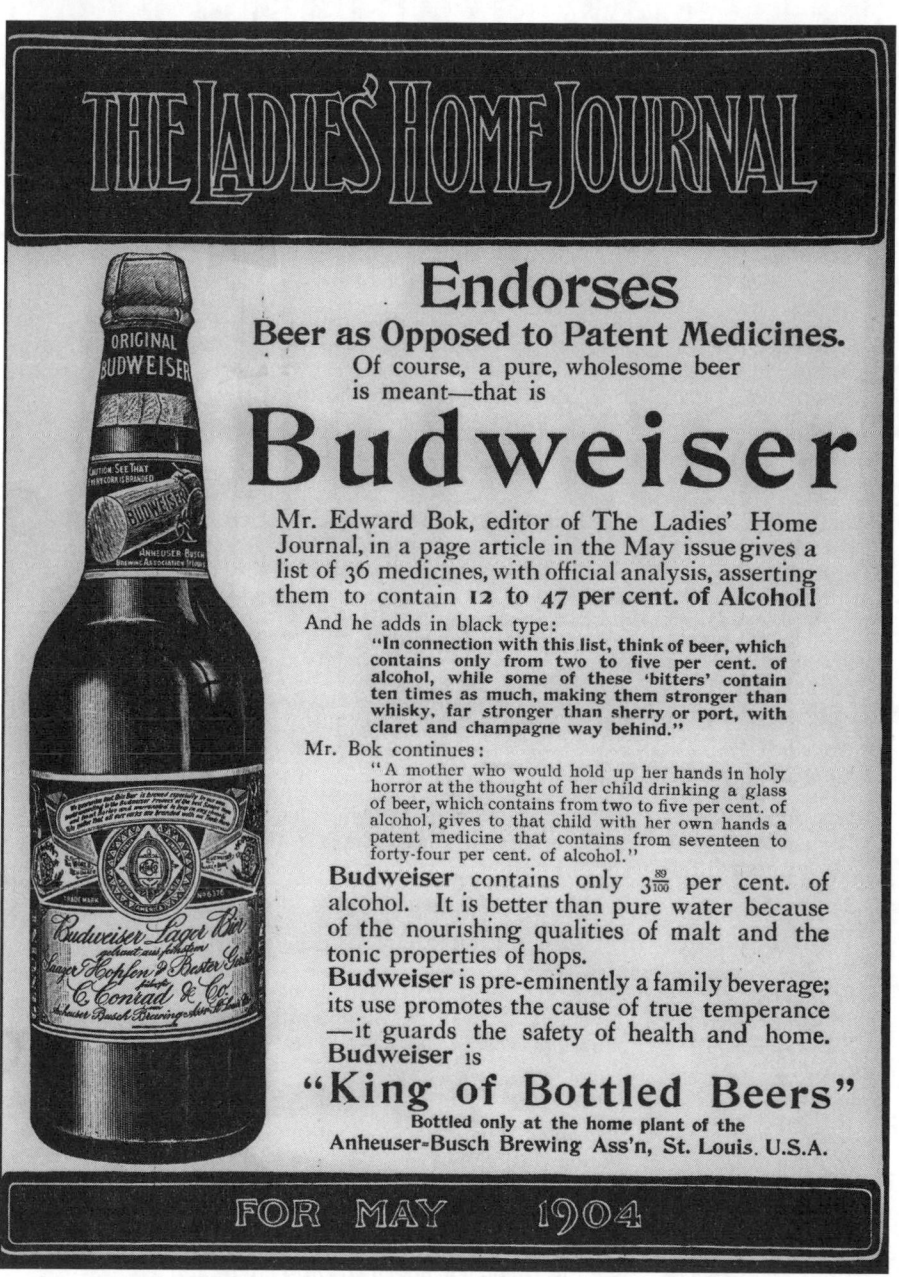

Ladies' Home *Journal endorsed Budweiser in this 1904 advertisement, suggesting that beer was healthier and more effective than other "patent medicines" of the time. Patent medicines were popular in the nineteenth century, often claiming to cure several illnesses at once, and were one of the first major products promoted by the advertising industry. Many of these ads emphasized exotic ingredients and outlandish testimonials. Patent medicines declined in popularity as the Food and Drug Administration and Federal Trade Commission began adding regulations to prevent fraud, unintentional poisoning and deceptive advertising.* (via Missouri History Museum)

Item	Source	Description	Price
MOTORIZED VEHICLES, SUPPLIES, & SERVICES			
Automobile	Schroeder, *The Wonderful World of Automobiles* (1971)	*Hoffman Motor Car*; 8 hp; equal to any $2,500 automobile made [cost in 1902]	$800
Automobile	Schroeder, *The Wonderful World of Automobiles* (1971)	*Rochester Carriage*; new steam model [cost in 1902]	$600
Automobile	*Columbus State Automobile Club* (1902)	*The Santos-Dumont*; in appearance, power, and general results fully the equal of any $6,000 French car on the market	$1,500
Automobile	Schroeder, *The Wonderful World of Automobiles* (1971)	*The Century Tourist*; 7 hp gasoline car; a light touring car at a reasonable price [cost in 1903]	$750
Automobile	Schroeder, *The Wonderful World of Automobiles* (1971)	*The Flint Roadster*; the touring car for two [cost in 1903]	$850
Automobile	Schroeder, *The Wonderful World of Automobiles* (1971)	*The Flint Roadster*; the touring car for two [cost in 1903]	$850
Automobile	Schroeder, *The Wonderful World of Automobiles* (1971)	*Graham Roadster*; complete with lamps and mud guards; wheel steering, if preferred, same price; electric or gasoline [cost in 1903]	$850
Automobile	Schroeder, *The Wonderful World of Automobiles* (1971)	*Jones-Corbin Gasoline Car*; Runabout, 8 hp, 750 lbs Tonneau 9 hp, 1,000 lbs [cost in 1903]	$1,000 $1,500
Automobile	Schroeder, *The Wonderful World of Automobiles* (1971)	*Autocar*; two-passenger; 10 hp; chainless drive; ball-bearing transmission [cost in 1904]	$1,900
Automobile	Schroeder, *The Wonderful World of Automobiles* (1971)	*The Convert*; the ideal light car for town or country [cost in 1904]	$750
Automobile	Schroeder, *The Wonderful World of Automobiles* (1971)	*Crestmobile Model D*; 8 hp to about 1000 lbs weight of vehicle; shaft drive (no chains); slightest possible vibration; [cost in 1904] two-person four-person	$800 $900
Automobile	*Ladies' Home Journal* (1971)	*Oldsmobile*; quality is apparent in every line Standard runabout Touring runabout Light tonneau	$650 $750 $950
Automobile	Schroeder, *The Wonderful World of Automobiles* (1971)	*Packard Voiture Grey World*; broke all American records, running a mile in 46 2/5 seconds and a kilometer in .292/5 seconds [cost in 1904]	$3,000
Automobile	Schroeder, *The Wonderful World of Automobiles* (1971)	*The Santos-Dumont*; high-grade two-cylinder tonneau; fully the equal of any $6,000 French car on the market [cost in 1904]	$1,500
Automobile	*Sears, Roebuck* (1903)	*The Yale Touring Car*; simplicity reduced to a science; starts and stops in a second	$1,750
Motor Bicycle	*Advertising Trade Card* (1902)	*Thomas*; the motor does the work; no hills—no head winds, always coasting—any speed—any distance	$200

Item	Source	Description	Price
MUSICAL INSTRUMENTS			
Autoharp	*Sears, Roebuck* (1902)	23 strings, 5 bars; produces five chords	$2.95
Cornet	*The Housewife* (1903)	*Marceau B Flat cornet;* short model	$6.45
Piano	*New York Times* (1901)	*Waters;* upright; cash price Installments: $10 down and $7/mo	$225
Piano	*Sears, Roebuck* (1902)	Home favorite piano-organ upright; A-grade	$59.45
Violin	*Sears, Roebuck* (1902)	Stradivarius model Genuine Lowendall violin	$2.45 $19.95
OTHER			
Baseball Calendar	*New York Times* (1901)	Part I: July–December 1901	$0.30
Crematory Services	*American Chronicle* (1999)	Adult charges, receptacles free	$30.00
Fine	*New York Tribune* (1902)	Cost of a speeding ticket for automobile dealer Frank Homan of Amsterdam Ave., New York City	$10.00
Fireworks	*Atlanta Constitution* (1904)	Roman candle; 15-ball style	$0.06
Ink	*Sears, Roebuck* (1902)	*Dann's Black;* glass bottle	$0.04/2 ounces
Kid Gloves, Cleaned	*Ladies' Home Journal* (1904)	Scientifically cleaned; ordinary length	$0.10/pair
Palm Reading	*The State* (Columbia, SC) (1903)	Prof. Edwin Chase, psychic; there is no more profit-able and interesting way to spend a half-hour	$2.00
Pencils	*Sears, Roebuck* (1900)	*Dixon's American Graphite;* round, plain, cedar, 7" long, extra quality	$0.05/dozen
Steam-Cleaning	*The State* (Columbia, SC) (1903)	Blankets	$0.50/pair
Steam-Cleaning	*The State* (Columbia, SC) (1903)	Lace Curtains	$0.35 to $1/ pair
Tombstone	*Sears, Roebuck* (1900)	Royal blue Vermont marble; unheard-of value; height 3' 8"	$29.00
Tombstone	*Sears, Roebuck* (1902)	Royal blue marble marker made of unfading Vermont marble; 24" high, 18" wide; 206 lbs	$7.65
Wedding Invitation	*Ladies' Home Journal* (1904)	Worded as you wish, elegant royal vellum stock; 100 cards, double set of envelopes	$2.25
PERSONAL CARE PRODUCTS			
Barber's Razor	*Sears, Roebuck* (1900)	Extra hollow ground, 1/2" blade	$1.50

Item	Source	Description	Price
Bust Developer	*Sears, Roebuck* (1902)	*Princess;* combined with the use of the bust cream or food, forms a full, firm, well-developed bust in a few days' use, per bottle	$1.50/bottle
Comb	*Ladies' Home Journal* (1904)	Utility pompadour; throw away your unhealthy hair rat and use the adjustable comb	$0.25
Cream Paste	Sears, Roebuck (1902)	*Dan's;* embodies the latest results of advanced chemical research in Department of Adhesives	$0.04/1 ounce tube
Electric Belt	*Sears, Roebuck* (1902)	*Heidelberg;* primary; the 20-gauge current is just the right strength for the pains of the back, loins, and groin	$4.00

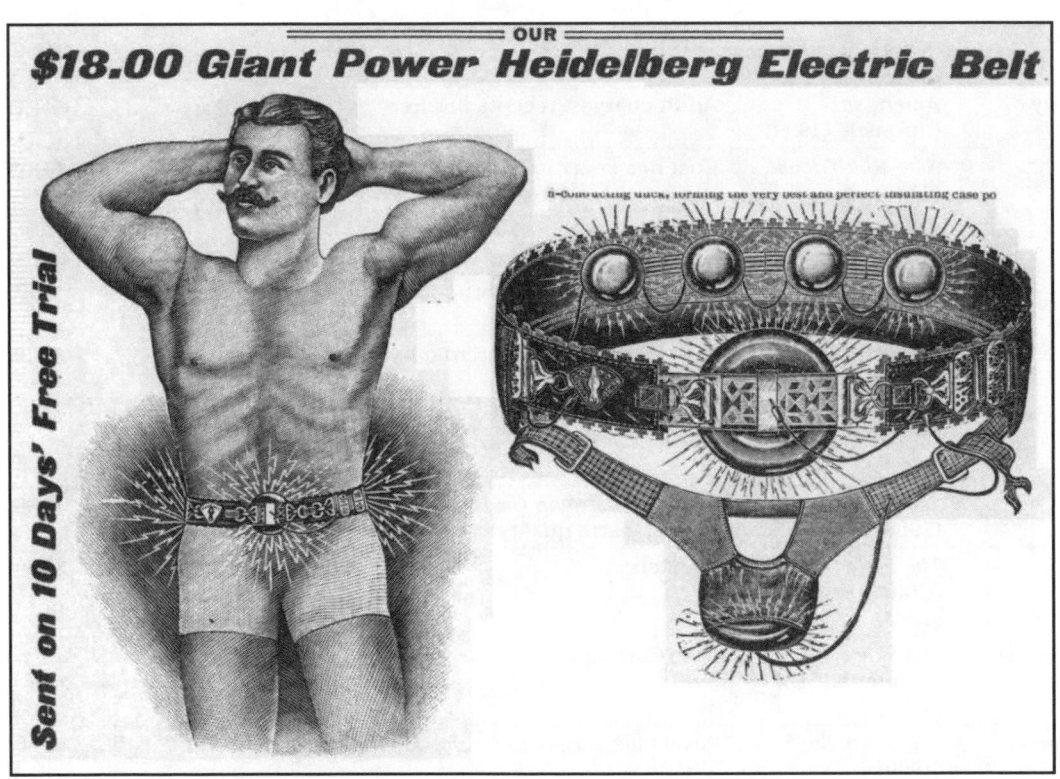

Electric belts, debuting at the 1851 World's Fair, were meant to cure a variety of things, including anxiety, constipation, impotency, and gout. (via James Arboghast/Flickr)

Item	Source	Description	Price
Fountain Comb	*Ladies' Home Journal* (1904)	Scalp-Sprayer; applies any liquid to scalp or hair, no waste, merely press the bulb	$1.00
Hair Bleach	*Sears, Roebuck* (1902)	*Blondine;* the famous hair bleach; small trial-size bottle Large bottle	$0.42 $0.70
Hair Rolls	*Ladies' Home Journal* (1904)	Cool and sanitary, can't injure the hair, braided-wire, 8" 12"	 $0.10 $0.15
Human Hair Wig	*Ladies' Home Journal* (1904)	Natural curly pompadour	$2.50
Skin Cream	*Harper's Monthly Magazine* (1903)	*Hydrozone;* cures eczema, salt rheum, pimples, ring-worm, itch, ivy poison, acne or other skin troubles Trial size	 $0.25
Shoe Dressing	*Ladies' Home Journal* (1904)	*Whittemore's Gilt-Edge Oil;* imparts a beautiful lustre to all black shoes	$0.25/bottle
Soap	*Ladies' Home Journal* (1904)	*Palmolive;* the refinement of soap for gentlefolk	$0.05/bar
Toothbrush	*Sears, Roebuck* (1902)	The highest grade of fine imported French tooth-brushes	$0.25
Trimmer Shears	*Sears, Roebuck* (1902)	8" straight trimmer, Japanned handles, steel-laid blade	3/$0.06

PUBLICATIONS

Item	Source	Description	Price
Book	*New York Tribune* (1902)	My Early Travels and Adventures in America and Asia by Henry M. Stanley, two volumes Regularly Sale	 $3.00 $0.75
Book	*Harper's Monthly Magazine* (1903)	*A History of the American People* by Woodrow Wilson in five volumes; a new, epoch-making, work—the only complete narrative history of the great Republic in existence today	$25.00
Catalogue	*Sears, Roebuck* (1900)	*Sears, Roebuck & Co. Catalogue*	$0.15/year
Catalogue	*Sears, Roebuck* (1902)	*Sears, Roebuck & Co. Catalogue*	$0.50/year
Cook Book	*Ladies' Home Journal* (1904)	From Grandmother's time until now; every improve-ment, as well as famous recipes of Grandma's day. Marion Harland's *New Complete Cook Book*	$2.00
Magazine	*Ladies' Home Journal* (1904)	*Popular Mechanics;* Per copy Per year Per year with easy electrical experiments	 $0.10 $1.00 $1.50
Newspaper	*The Daily Picayune* (New Orleans, LA) (1900)	*The Daily Picayune*	$0.10

Item	Source	Description	Price
Newspaper	*Yorkville Enquirer* (Yorkville, SC) (1900)	*Yorkville Enquirer;* twice weekly	$0.05
Newspaper	*New York Tribune* (1902)	*New York Tribune* Sunday Daily 12 Months	 $0.05 $0.03 $10.00
Periodical	*The Philistine*	*The Philistine;* a periodical of protests Monthly	$1.00

REAL ESTATE

Item	Source	Description	Price
Apartment Building	*New York Times* (1901)	For sale; 20-family, cold-water tenement; five-story; rents over $2,900/year	$3,000
House Plans	*Ladies' Home Journal* (1904)	Large book of 125 plans giving views, plans, description and estimate to build	$0.25
House	*New York Times* (1901)	Country homes in the Palisades	$800
House	*New York Times* (1901)	Prospect Park South; 10–14 room houses, tiled vestibules and two baths	$10,000
House	*New York Times* (1901)	South Midwood, Flatbush Avenue, Brooklyn; 35 minutes from New York City	$7,000 to $12,000
House	*Greenville News* (Greenville, SC) (1903)	Seven-room house, West Washington St., 90'× 200'	$2,800
House	*Ladies' Home Journal* (1904)	California; seashore cottage of Swiss design contains eight rooms and bath	$2,200
House	*Ladies' Home Journal* (1904)	California; shingle bungalow of five rooms; building cost	$1,200
House	*Ladies' Home Journal* (1904)	California; most attractive and spacious cottage of four rooms and bathroom	$1,100
House	*Ladies' Home Journal* (1904)	California; teacher's bungalow and artist's studio	$2,000
Room	*New York Tribune* (1902)	Room with bath; private halls, elegant suite, elevator, hall boy service; Apply at 30 West 128th Street, New York City Per month	 $50.00
Room	*New York Tribune* (1902)	Modern, high-class, absolutely fireproof apartment 1109 Madison Avenue Per year	 $1,600

SEWING EQUIPMENT & SUPPLIES

Item	Source	Description	Price
Broadcloth	*The State* (Columbia, SC) (1903)	52" wide in all colors	$1.00/yard
Cloth	*Sears, Roebuck* (1900)	Fancy percale; both dress and shirting styles in figures, scrolls, and fancy stripes	$0.10/yard
Cloth	*New York Times* (1901)	French batiste all-wool fabrics; reg $0.50	$0.38

Item	Source	Description	Price
Cloth	*Southern Christian Advocate* (1902)	500 yards flannelettes; reg $0.15	$0.10
Cloth	*Sears, Roebuck* (1902)	Broadcloth in all-fashion colors	$1.00/yard
Cloth	*The State* (Columbia, SC) (1903)	Granite stripe madras; new weaves for winter waists	$0.25 to $0.35/yard
Pants Cuffs	*Sears, Roebuck* (1900)	Highwater; enables the wearer to quickly transform regular trousers into bicycle, golf, or riding breeches	$0.25/pair
Pattern	*Ladies' Home Journal* (1904)	Baby wardrobe; 35 patterns for baby's long clothes	$0.25
Sewing Machine	*Sears, Roebuck* (1902)	*Minnesota;* automatic drop desk cabinet	$23.20

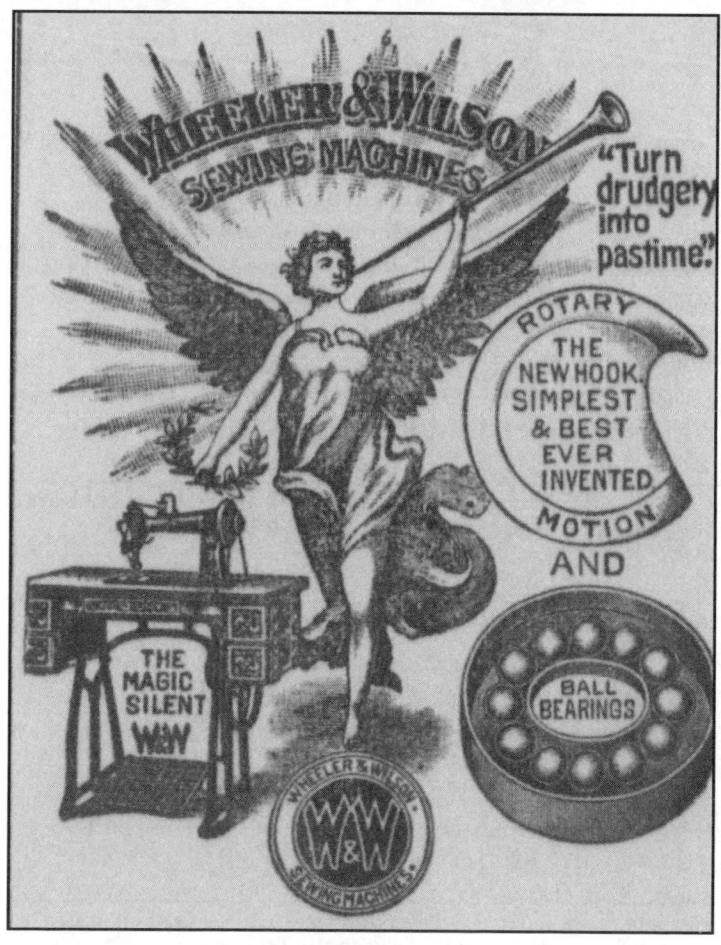

A 1904 ad for various Wheeler & Wilson sewing machines and equipment.
(via Wikimedia Commons)

Item	Source	Description	Price
Sewing Needle Case	*Sears, Roebuck* (1902)	Contains four papers of needles, also other needles and pins	$0.02
Thimble	*Sears, Roebuck* (1902)	Solid silver Solid 14-karat gold	$0.15 $3.75

SPORTS EQUIPMENT

Item	Source	Description	Price
Bicycle	*New York Times* (1901)	*Viking;* special offer	$15.50
Bicycle	*Sears, Roebuck* (1902)	Lady's	$8.95
Bicycle Tire	*New York Times* (1901)	H Rausch	$2.65
Book	*Harper's Monthly Magazine* (1903)	*Practical Golf* by Walter J. Travis, Former Amateur Golf Champion of the United States; profusely illustrated from photographs	$2.00
Carver	*Sears, Roebuck* (1902)	Fancy blade stag-handle carver; 8" knife and fork	$1.62/pair
Field Glasses	*Sears, Roebuck* (1902)	Highest grade genuine Jena	$12.95
Jackknife	*Sears, Roebuck* (1902)	Stag handle, brass lining, finished inside and out	$0.47
League Baseball	*Sears, Roebuck* (1900)	*S. R. & Co.;* made entirely by hand, by old, experienced workmen only	$0.90
Police Revolver	*Sears, Roebuck* (1900)	*Colt;* side-ejecting revolver; 32-caliber, nickel plated	$12.50
Shotgun	*Harper's Monthly Magazine* (1903)	*Iver Johnson* top snap	$7.00

TELEPHONE EQUIPMENT & SERVICES

Item	Source	Description	Price
Telegraph	Susan J. Douglas, *Inventing American Broadcasting* (1987)	Charge to steamship companies to report the arrival of ships at Nantucket [cost in 1901]	$5.00/vessel
Telephone Charges	Douglas, *Telephone: The First Hundred Years* (1987)	Residential rates (Cleveland) for 1901	$48.00/year
Telephone Charges	Douglas, *Telephone: The First Hundred Years* (1987)	Business Rates (Asheville, North Carolina) for 1903	$40.00

TOBACCO PRODUCTS

Item	Source	Description	Price
Cigar	*The New Orleans Picayune* (1903)	*Tulane College* cigar; the leading five-cent cigar; Union Labor; Not in the Trust	$0.05
Pipe	*Sears, Roebuck* (1902)	*Applewood;* wood pipe with silver derrule and rubber stem, 2 1/2" long	$0.04

Item	Source	Description	Price
Pipe	*Sears, Roebuck* (1902)	*Yale Student;* heavy briar pipe with bent Chinese amber bit, heavy Bull-Bitch shape	3/$0.09

TRAVEL & TRANSPORTATION

Item	Source	Description	Price
Cruise	*New York Tribune* (1902)	European Tour, 103-day trip to include Gibraltar, Morocco, Spain, Italy, Austria, Switzerland, Germany, the Rhine, Belgium, France, England	$240 to $975
Ship Fare	*New York Tribune* (1902)	Dominion Line; fast twin screw service Boston to Queenstown to Liverpool Saloon Second saloon	 $50.00 $40.00
Ship Fare	*New York Tribune* (1902)	Mediterranean, service from New York to Gibraltar, Naples, Genoa Saloon Second saloon	 $75.00+ $50.00
Taxi Fare	*New York Tribune* (1902)	Carriage ride from White Star pier in New York City to any point in the city south of 59th Street One person Two or three persons Four persons	 $2.00 $3.00 $4.00

MISCELLANY 1900–1904

Jack Zelig, (1882–1912): Gang Leader and Murderer

A handsome, brutish killer, Big Jack's services were always available for hire to any bidder, high or low. There is no record of the gang leader ever turning down any job of violence. A Zelig henchman once gave the police Big Jack's price list:"

Slash of cheek with knife	$1–10
Shot in leg	1–25
Shot in arm	5–25
Throwing a bomb	5–50
Murder	10–100

The Encyclopedia of American Crime

Liquor Licenses

In 1900, licensed retail liquor saloons annually paid $500 for a license in Chicago, but werecharged $1,100 in Philadelphia. In Boston, innkeepers paid $2000, common victualers, $1,100, while common victualers, second, and third calls, $500.

In Bridgeport, Conn., the amount of the license ran $450—reduced to $250 for the sale of beer only. San Francisco had one of the nation's lowest license fees at $84 a year.

Bulletin of the Department of Labor, September 1901

Nickelodeon

The Sears Roebuck catalog of 1902 offered prospective operators the Edison Projection Kinetoscope (with either an electric arc lamp or a calcium burner) for $105 and a wide selection of titles, some 20 minutes in length. THE FIVE CENT THEATER IS HERE TO STAY—almost any vacant storeroom can be made into a five-cent theater.

Sears and Wards,
The First Hundred Years Are the Toughest

Automobile Production, 1903

Complete statistics from 85 per cent of the automobile manufacturers in the United States to September 3 indicate that the actual sales for the year 1903 will be 11,000 cars, valued at $12,000,000.

This is double the business of 1902, to which must be added to the foreign importation of 200 cars, valued at $800,000. The importation of foreign cars is about the same as last year. Trade in foreign-made cars is probably at its maximum and will slowly decline, as the American manufacturers are rapidly supplying the demand.

Scientific American, January 1904

Twenty-five Flower Beds for Little Money

The prices of the various tender plants, as begonias, geraniums, cannas, and coleus will run at the rate of $5 to $8 a hundred; dahlias, $8 to $10; roses about $10; and hardy plants as day lilies, phloxes and ferns about $10 a hundred. In fewer numbers the prices may be a trifle higher.

Ladies' Home Journal, May 1904

Diamond in the Rough

There has been exhibited in London a diamond which is the second largest gem of its description in the world. It weighs 336 1/2 carats. It is of a yellowish color and worth about $10,000. If the color had been better, the stone would have been worth a fabulous amount. It was recently extracted from the Ottos Kopje diamond mines at Kimberly.

Scientific American, January 1904

Union Dispute

Racine, Wis.—This morning twenty tin shops of Racine went out on strike. The minimum wage scale in the past has been 22 cents an hour, nine hours a day. Their demand is for a minimum scale of 25 cents an hour, nine hours a day. The bosses refused to give the increase in part, claiming that some of the men were worth more than others and refusing to pay it to this class of mechanics. The maximum scale is satisfactory and ranges from25 cents to 35 cents an hour.

Milwaukee Journal (1901)

MISCELLANY 1900–1904

The Chorus Girl of To-Day

There are now employed in New York in musical plays between 1,200 and 1,500 women who appear in the chorus; the salaries range anywhere from $15 to $30 a week. Taking a mean average of $20 a week for the chorus girl, it will be seen that no less than $24,000 is paid out every week in chorus girl salaries alone. In a season of thirty weeks the expenditures in salaries for chorus girls would amount to no less than $720,000.

Sears and Wards: The First Hundred Years Are the Toughest, by Cecil C. Hoge, Sr., 1988

A poster advertising the Gaiety Dancers of Rice & Barton's Big Gaiety Spectacular Extravaganza Co. in 1900, featuring two lines of chorus girls. (via Wikimedia Commons)

Barbers Wanted

Wanted—men to learn barber trade; can nearly earn expenses before finishing; position waiting graduates; $18 weekly; a few weeks completes course.

Atlanta Constitution (1904)

Men's Salaries Compared to Women's

A chart showing the weekly wages in 2,846 Minnesota business establishments in 1890, showed that 13.79 percent of the male workers earned less than $8 per week compared to 81.33 percent of the female workers at that wage. The highest percent-age of male employees received from $9 to $15 per week.

Seventh Biennial Report of the Bureau of Labor of the State of Minnesota, 1899–1900

HISTORICAL SNAPSHOT
1905–1909

1905

- The newly formed Industrial Workers of the World (IWW) attacks AF of L for accepting capitalist system
- A New York law limiting hours of work in the baking industry to 60 per week is ruled unconstitutional by the Supreme Court
- U.S. auto production reaches 15,000 cars/yr, up from 2,500 in 1899
- William Randolph Hearst acquires *Cosmopolitan* magazine for $400,000
- Royal Typewriter Company founded by New York financier Thomas Fortune Ryan

1906

- Excavation of the Panama Canal begins

- Armstrong Linoleum introduced
- Sales of Jell-O reach nearly $1 million
- A-1 Sauce introduced in the United States by Hartford's G. F. Heublein & Bros.
- Planters Nut and Chocolate Company created

- Oklahoma admitted to the Union
- C. W Post creates Post Toasties cornflakes
- Upton Sinclair's The Jungle exposes conditions in U.S. meatpacking industry
- Samuel Hopkins Adams's *The Great American Fraud* exposes the fraudulent claims of many patent medicines

1907

- Economic crises abound with the collapse of the New York Stock Market and runs on banks
- Sears, Roebuck distributes 3 million copies of spring catalogue
- Cadillac is advertised at $800, a Ford Model K at $2,800, horses for $150 to $300
- Wireless telegraphy service links United States to Ireland
- Movie projectionist Donald H. Bell founds Bell and Howell Co., pioneers in motion picture photography and projection
- The first canned tuna fish is packed in California

1908

- U.S. banks close as economic depression deepens
- Model-T Ford introduced; Flivver costs $850.50
- A C Spark Plug Co. founded by Buick Motor Car president W. C. Durant
- Two subway tunnels open to traffic in New York City
- President Theodore Roosevelt calls White House conference on conservation

1909

- 20,000 members of Ladies' Waist Maker's Union stage three-month strike, win most demands
- Westinghouse Electric is placed in receivership
- General Motors acquires Cadillac from Henry H. Leland for $4.5 million
- $17 million Queensboro bridge opens in New York City
- John D. Rockefeller gives
- $350 million for worldwide medical research
- Copyright Act of 1909, significantly extending the rights of authorship, approved by Congress and becomes law

SELECTED INCOME
1905–1909

Job	Source	Description	Pay
Actress	*American Chronicle* (1999)	Salary of Lillian Russell for 33-week engagement at Proctor's 23rd Street Theater in New York	$100,000
Actress	Vincent Tomkins, ed., *American Decades: 1900–1909* (1996)	Earnings of Sarah Bernhardt from "The Divine Sarah" tour in 1906	$1 million

Puzzle in ten postcards showing Sarah Bernhardt in different roles circa 1906.
(via Wikimedia Commons)

Job	Source	Description	Pay
Actuary	*New York Times* (1907)	Western insurance concern	$1,000–$12,000/yr
Bookkeeper and Clerk	*New York Times* (1907)	Manufacturing concern	$780/yr
Boxer	Tomkins, ed., *American Decades: 1900–1909* (1996)	Purse of Jack Johnson for winning Heavyweight Boxing Championship in 1908	$5,000
Boxer	*American Chronicle* (1999)	Purse for heavyweight championship fight between Tommy Burns and Jack Johnson in Sydney, Australia in 1908	$30,000
Cook	*New York Tribune* (1908)	Available through Miss FitzGerald Employment Bureau	$35/month
Cook	*New York Tribune* (1908)	Swedish preferred, capable of soups, entrees, desserts; good managers	$30/month
Department Manager	*Chicago Tribune* (1905)	Familiar with farm implements	$2,000/yr
Domestic	*San Francisco Examiner (1907)*	Chambermaid, Lake Tahoe, fares paid both ways	$25/mo
Draftsman	*Chicago Tribune* (1905)	Electrical experience	$75–$125/mo
Electrical Worker	*Chicago Tribune* (1905)	Machine shop	$4/day
Governess	*New York Tribune* (1908)	Nursery governess	$40/month
Navy Serviceman	*Chicago Tribune* (1905)	Includes board, lodging, medical, $60 uniform free	$16–$70/mo
Nobel Prize	*American Chronicle* (1999)	Theodore Roosevelt's cash award for winning The Nobel Peace Prize recognizing his efforts to mediate the end of the Russo-Japanese War	$40,000
Nurse	*New York Tribune* (1908)	For six-year-old girl	$25/month
Professional Football Player	*American Chronicle* (1999)	Per game pay of Willie Heston to play professional football	$600
Salesman	*Chicago Tribune* (1905)	Man to travel, new line of goods, Chicago	$80/mo
Singer	*New York Times* (1907)	Bass and tenor	$300–$500/yr
Vaudeville Performer	*American Chronicle* (1999)	Weekly pay of Vaudeville headliner Buffalo Bill Cody	$3,000
Waitress	*San Francisco Examiner* (1907)	First class city hotel, room in or out	$30 or $35/mo

CONSUMER EXPENDITURES 1909

Expenditure Type	1909
Clothing	$30.00
Food	$81.43
Auto Purchases	$1.85
Auto Parts	$0.59
Gas & Oil	$1.36
Housing	$61.48
Furniture	$3.25
Utilities	$4.00
Telephone & Telegraph	$0.91
Physicians	$3.24
Dentists	$0.91
Health Insurance	NR
Personal Business	$9.61
Personal Care	$2.88
Tobacco	$6.33
Local Transport	$5.12
Intercity Transport	$2.97
Recreation	$9.49
Religion/Welfare Activities	$9.05
Private Education & Research	$4.59
Per Capita Consumption	$318.42

INVESTMENTS 1905-1909

Investment	1905	1906	1907	1908	1909
Yield, One-year Corporate Bonds	3.50	4.75	4.87	5.10	4.03
Term Interest rates, 4–6 Months, Prime Commercial Paper	5.18	6.25	6.66	5.00	4.67
Basic Yield, Common Stocks, Total	3.53	3.96	5.38	4.93	4.31
Index of Common Stocks (1941 2 1943 5 10)	8.99	9.64	7.84	7.78	9.71

COMMON STOCKS, CLOSING PRICE AND YIELD, FIRST BUSINESS DAY OF YEAR

	1905	1906	1907	1908	1909
Allis Chalmers pfd	21 3/8	22 1/4	16 7/8	5 1/2	15 1/2
AT & T	145	138	135	99 1/2	127 1/2
American Tobacco pfd	145	106	96 1/2	72 3/44	93 1/2
Anaconda	109	289	290	29 1/4	50 1/2
B&O	104 7/8	113 1/8	119 1/2	82 1/2	110
Bethlehem Steel		33 1/2	18 1/8	9 1/2	24
Corn Products	21 1/4	18 5/8	22	10 7/8	17 1/88
General Electric	187	177	160	112 1/2	157
IBM					
International 1 Harvester					65
(Recapitalization: for 2 shares of common stock exchanged for 1 share of common and one share of preferred, 1/8/07)					
National Biscuit	57 1/4	118 1/2	77	67	98 1/2
U.S. Steel	29 7/8	43	48 1/4	26 3/4	53 3/8
Western Union	92 1/2	93 3/8	83 1/2	55	69 1/2
(1 1/4% stock dividend, 1/15/08) (1 1/4% stock dividend, 4/15/08)					

STANDARD JOBS 1905-1909

Job Type	1905	1906	1907	1908	1909
Average of all Industries, excl. farm labor	$559/yr	$571/yr	$593/yr	$564/yr	$594/yr
Average of all Industries, incl. farm labor	$510/yr	$523/yr	$542/yr	$519/yr	$544/yr
Bituminous Coal Mining	30¢/hr	29¢/hr	29¢/hr	29¢/hr	28¢/hr
Avg hrs/wk	51.60	51.60	51.60	51.60	51.60
Building Trades, Union workers	48¢/hr	50¢/hr	51¢/hr	51¢/hr	45¢/hr
Avg hrs/wk	45.90	45.70	45.60	45.60	46.10
Clerical Workers in Mfg. & Steam RR	$1076/yr	$1074/yr	$1091/yr	$1111/yr	$1136/yr
Domestics	$278/yr	$286/yr	$316/yr	$580/yr	$420/yr
Farm Labor	$302/yr	$315/yr	$319/yr	$324/yr	$328/yr
Federal Employees, Executive Depts.	$1072/yr	$1085/yr	$1094/yr	$1102/yr	$1106/yr
Finance, Insurance, & Real Estate	$1115/yr	$1146/yr	$1180/yr	$1218/yr	$1263/yr
Gas & Electricity Workers	$543/yr	$581/yr	$623/yr	$595/yr	$618/yr
Lower-Skilled Labor	$484/yr	$495/yr	$442/yr	$496/yr	$443/yr
Manufacturing, Payroll	18¢/hr	19¢/hr	18¢/hr	18¢/hr	15¢/hr
Avg hrs/wk	60.70	60.60	60.30	60.20	60.10
Manufacturing, Union Workers	38¢/hr	39¢/hr	40¢/hr	39¢/hr	39¢/hr
Avg hrs/wk	51.10	51	50.80	50.40	50.30
Medical/Health Services Workers	$292/yr	$296/yr	$306/yr	$313/yr	$326/yr
Ministers	$773/yr	$759/yr	$831/yr	$833/yr	$831/yr
Nonprofit Org. Workers	$689/yr	$677/yr	$741/yr	$743/yr	$741/yr

97

Job Type	1905	1906	1907	1908	1909
Postal Employees	37¢/hr	38¢/hr	40¢/hr	41¢/hr	38¢/hr
Avg hrs/wk	48.00	48.00	48.00	48.00	48.00
Public School Teachers	$392/yr	$409/yr	$431/yr	$455/yr	$476/yr
State and Local Govt. Workers	$646/yr	$664/yr	$694/yr	$695/yr	$696/yr
Steam Railroads, Wage Earners	$589/yr	$607/yr	$661/yr	$667/yr	$644/yr
Street Railway Workers	$646/yr	$662/yr	$658/yr	$650/yr	$671/yr
Telegraph Ind. Workers	$592/yr	$581/yr	$635/yr	$639/yr	$622/yr
Telephone Ind. Workers	$401/yr	$412/yr	$412/yr	$420/yr	$430/yr
Wholesale and Retail Trade Workers	$393/yr	$580/yr	$593/yr	$609/yr	$561/yr

FOOD BASKET 1905–1909

Commodity	Year	New York	Atlanta	Chicago	Denver	Los Angeles
Apples, Evaporated, per pound	1905	12¢	10¢	12¢	12¢	10¢
	1906	12¢	12¢	13¢	12¢	13¢
	1907	NR	NR	NR	NR	NR
	1908	NR	NR	NR	NR	NR
	1909	NR	NR	NR	NR	NR
Beans, Dry, per quart	1905	10¢	9.44¢	9.33¢	9.38¢	7.50¢
	1906	10.13¢	9.44¢	9.33¢	9.38¢	7.50¢
	1907	NR	NR	NR	NR	NR
	1908	NR	NR	NR	NR	NR
	1909	NR	NR	NR	NR	NR
Beef, Fresh, Roasts, per pound	1905	13.71¢	13.67¢	10.03¢	11¢	12.80¢
	1906	13.02¢	13.98¢	10.29¢	11.14¢	13.35¢
	1907	NR	NR	NR	NR	NR
	1908	NR	NR	NR	NR	NR
	1909	NR	NR	NR	NR	NR
Beef, Steaks (Round), per pound	1905	17.23¢	13.64¢	10.80¢	11.67¢	12.50¢
	1906	17.93¢	13.33¢	10.77¢	11.94¢	12.50¢
	1907	18.13¢	13.75¢	14.25¢	15.20¢	12.50¢
	1908	18.40¢	15¢	14.85¢	15.83¢	12.50¢
	1909	19.20¢	17.50¢	15.93¢	16.55¢	13.19¢
Beef, Salt (Corned), per pound	1905	7.50¢	12.50¢	8.81¢	6.33¢	9¢
	1906	7.72¢	12.50¢	7.31¢	6.33¢	9¢
	1907	NR	NR	NR	NR	NR
	1908	NR	NR	NR	NR	NR
	1909	NR	NR	NR	NR	NR
Bread, Wheat, per loaf	1905	5¢	5¢	5¢	5¢	5¢
	1906	5¢	5¢	5¢	5¢	5¢
	1907	NR	NR	NR	NR	NR
	1908	NR	NR	NR	NR	NR
	1909	NR	NR	NR	NR	NR
Butter, per pound	1905	27.97¢	29.47¢	23.08¢	26.54¢	30.14¢
	1906	29.86¢	29.67¢	23.67¢	26.63¢	33.03¢
	1907	33.14¢	32.75¢	32.04¢	30.28¢	37.64¢
	1908	33.42¢	31.81¢	31.42¢	32.69¢	36.67¢
	1909	35.19¢	37.05¢	32.43¢	34.03¢	37.78¢

Buster Brown was a popular comic strip character created by Richard Felton Outcault in 1902 and used in several advertising campaigns, including this one for Golden West Baking Co. (via Wikimedia Commons)

Commodity	Year	New York	Atlanta	Chicago	Denver	Los Angeles
Cheese, per pound	1905	17.23¢	16.62¢	17.13¢	18.44¢	20¢
	1906	18.50¢	18.54¢	18.37¢	18.44¢	20¢
	1907	NR	NR	NR	NR	NR
	1908	NR	NR	NR	NR	NR
	1909	NR	NR	NR	NR	NR
Chickens, per pound	1905	16.71¢	16.56¢	15.03¢	15.46¢	23.32¢
	1906	17.35¢	16.97¢	14.78¢	15.49¢	24.5¢
	1907	17.83¢	18.67¢	14.39¢	15.31¢	20¢
	1908	18.36¢	22¢	15.29¢	16.22¢	20¢
	1909	19.02¢	20.83¢	16.22¢	18.03¢	22.33¢

Commodity	Year	New York	Atlanta	Chicago	Denver	Los Angeles
Coffee, per pound	1905	18.33¢	25¢	16.80¢	21.67¢	25¢
	1906	19.41¢	25¢	17¢	22.43¢	25¢
	1907	NR	NR	NR	NR	NR
	1908	NR	NR	NR	NR	NR
	1909	NR	NR	NR	NR	NR
Cornmeal, per pound	1905	3.42¢	1.95¢	2.38¢	2.25¢	2.75¢
	1906	3.09¢	2.06¢	2.38¢	2.25¢	2.75¢
	1907	3.17¢	1.96¢	2.57¢	2.56¢	2.97¢
	1908	3.25¢	2.22¢	2.62¢	2.56¢	3.14¢
	1909	3.33¢	2.62¢	2.94¢	2.56¢	3.03¢
Eggs, per dozen	1905	31.93¢	22.69¢	23.32¢	25.69¢	30.69¢
	1906	32.85¢	24.88¢	23.86¢	24.86¢	32.78¢
	1907	32.40¢	23.79¢	26.63¢	27.92¢	32.33¢
	1908	33.38¢	25.65¢	27.62¢	27.64¢	31.95¢
	1909	35.17¢	27.92¢	29.11¢	29.17¢	33.61¢
Fish, Fresh, per pound	1905	12.09¢	11.22¢	10.40¢	14.67¢	10¢
	1906	12.28¢	11.83¢	11.75¢	15¢	10¢
	1907	NR	NR	NR	NR	NR
	1908	NR	NR	NR	NR	NR
	1909	NR	NR	NR	NR	NR
Fish, Salt, per pound	1905	13.24¢	13.96¢	13.13¢	13.87¢	8.33¢
	1906	14.14¢	13.16¢	13.25¢	13.87¢	8.33¢
	1907	NR	NR	NR	NR	NR
	1908	NR	NR	NR	NR	NR
	1909	NR	NR	NR	NR	NR
Flour, Wheat, per one-eighth Barrel Bag	1905	82.84¢	82.22¢	75.93¢	63.47¢	75¢
	1906	78.96¢	81.81¢	63.94¢	49.93¢	75¢
	1907	81.92¢	77.17¢	74¢	$1.18	$1.31
	1908	84.25¢	79.84¢	78.93¢	$1.34	$1.36
	1909	75¢	87.75¢	84.99¢	$1.54	$1.51
Lard, per pound	1905	12¢	10¢	10.88¢	12.50¢	12.50¢
	1906	12.88¢	12.08¢	11.42¢	12.50¢	13.75¢
	1907	14.83¢	12.50¢	12.42¢	15¢	15¢
	1908	14.33¢	12.33¢	12.17¢	15¢	15¢
	1909	15¢	15¢	13.50¢	15¢	15¢
Milk, Fresh, per quart	1905	6¢	8.33¢	7¢	6.25¢	8.25¢
	1906	6¢	8.33¢	7¢	6.40¢	8.50¢
	1907	8.17¢	8.33¢	7¢	7.14¢	9.50¢
	1908	8.17¢	8.33¢	7.17¢	7.14¢	9¢
	1909	8.17¢	8.33¢	7.17¢	7.54¢	9¢
Molasses, per gallon	1905	60¢	50¢	61.67¢	75¢	60¢
	1906	60¢	50¢	65¢	75¢	60¢
	1907	NR	NR	NR	NR	NR
	1908	NR	NR	NR	NR	NR
	1909	NR	NR	NR	NR	NR
Mutton and Lamb, per pound	1905	13.17¢	15.33¢	12¢	15¢	12.50¢
	1906	13.83¢	17.54¢	12.58¢	15¢	13.54¢
	1907	16.67¢	20¢	15¢	15¢	15¢
	1908	16.67¢	20¢	15.33¢	15.17¢	15¢
	1909	16.67¢	17.54¢	16.33¢	15.42¢	15¢

Commodity	Year	New York	Atlanta	Chicago	Denver	Los Angeles
Pork, Fresh, per pound	1905	16.92¢	15¢	11.75¢	12.50¢	15.17¢
	1906	18.17¢	15¢	12.46¢	12.50¢	17¢
	1907	17.33¢	16.67¢	14.67¢	13.75¢	17.50¢
	1908	16.67¢	19.58¢	15¢	13.75¢	17.50¢
	1909	17¢	20.83¢	15.67¢	16.83¢	20.83¢
Pork, Salt, Ham, per pound	1905	15.67¢	19.50¢	13.67¢	25¢	25¢
	1906	16.58¢	20¢	15.17¢	25¢	25¢
	1907	NR	NR	NR	NR	NR
	1908	NR	NR	NR	NR	NR
	1909	NR	NR	NR	NR	NR
Potatoes, Irish, per peck*	1905	32.56¢	22.58¢	16.92¢	15.50¢	22.25¢
	1906	33.33¢	25¢	15.67¢	20.38¢	24.56¢
	1907	NR	29.83¢	21¢	$1.54	$1.95
	1908	NR	25.83¢	25.17¢	$1.58	$1.60
	1909	NR	28.33¢	24¢	$1.58	$1.79
Prunes, per pound	1905	10¢	10¢	8¢	10.63¢	5.25¢
	1906	12¢	10¢	9¢	12.50¢	6.81¢
	1907	NR	NR	NR	NR	NR
	1908	NR	NR	NR	NR	NR
	1909	NR	NR	NR	NR	NR
Rice, per pound	1905	8.67¢	7.33¢	9¢	9.25¢	8.33¢
	1906	10¢	9¢	9.42¢	9.25¢	8.33¢
	1907	NR	NR	NR	NR	NR
	1908	NR	NR	NR	NR	NR
	1909	NR	NR	NR	NR	NR
Sugar, per pound	1905	5.43¢	5.71¢	5.71¢	6.49¢	5.93¢
	1906	5.14¢	5.50¢	5¢	5.85¢	5.49¢
	1907	5.43¢	5.61¢	5.42¢	5.92¢	5.88¢
	1908	5.43¢	5.88¢	5.42¢	6.13¢	6.49¢
	1909	5.43¢	5.72¢	5.50¢	5.83¢	6.25¢
Tea, per pound	1905	50¢	50¢	50¢	60¢	50¢
	1906	50¢	50¢	50¢	60¢	50¢
	1907	NR	NR	NR	NR	NR
	1908	NR	NR	NR	NR	NR
	1909	NR	NR	NR	NR	NR
Veal, per pound	1905	22.75¢	15.42¢	16.83¢	20¢	20¢
	1906	25¢	16.46¢	16.83¢	20¢	22.92¢
	1907	NR	NR	NR	NR	NR
	1908	NR	NR	NR	NR	NR
	1909	NR	NR	NR	NR	NR
Vinegar, per gallon	1905	25¢	30¢	20¢	40¢	50¢
	1906	25¢	30¢	20¢	40¢	50¢
	1907	NR	NR	NR	NR	NR
	1908	NR	NR	NR	NR	NR
	1909	NR	NR	NR	NR	NR

*Prices for 1907 to 1909 for Chicago, Denver, and Los Angeles are listed per 100 pounds.

SELECTED PRICES 1905–1909

Item	Source	Description	Price
ALCOHOL			
Ale	*Chicago Tribune* (1905)	Ye Olde Inn	$1.50/dozen
Beer	*Atlanta Constitution* (1905)	*Bohemian;* the absolute purity and healthful-ness of A. B. C. Beer makes it the safest and best for home use	$1.50/12 pints
Corn Whiskey	*The State* (Columbia, SC) (1905)	*Amulet;* five years old, copper distilled	$2.65/gallon
Whiskey	*The State* (Columbia, SC) (1905)	*Cockade Rye;* 5 years old, smooth and mellow	$3.15/gallon
Whiskey	*The State* (Columbia, SC) (1909)	*Clark's Pure Rye;* 100 Proof	$5.00/gallon
Whiskey	*Atlanta Constitution* (1905)	*H. O. Wise Pure Rye;* Double copper distilled and aged	$3.50/gallon
APPAREL, CHILDREN'S			
Hosiery	*Ladies' Home Journal* (1905)	*Black Cat;* for boys & girls; the highest quality of yarn, the fastest of dyes	$0.25/pair
Knit Waist	*Sears, Roebuck and Co. Catalogue* (1908)	*E. Z. Waist;* thoroughly reinforced over the shoulders and down the back with tubular bands. For boys or girls	$0.19
Shoes	*New York Times* (1905)	Boy's	$1.75
Suit	*San Francisco Examiner* (1908)	*Ruf Wear* for boys; Ruf Wear pertains to the strength of the cloth	$5.00
Underwear	*New York Tribune* (1908)	*Porosknit underwear;* coolest for summer wear Shirts Union suit	 $0.25 $0.50

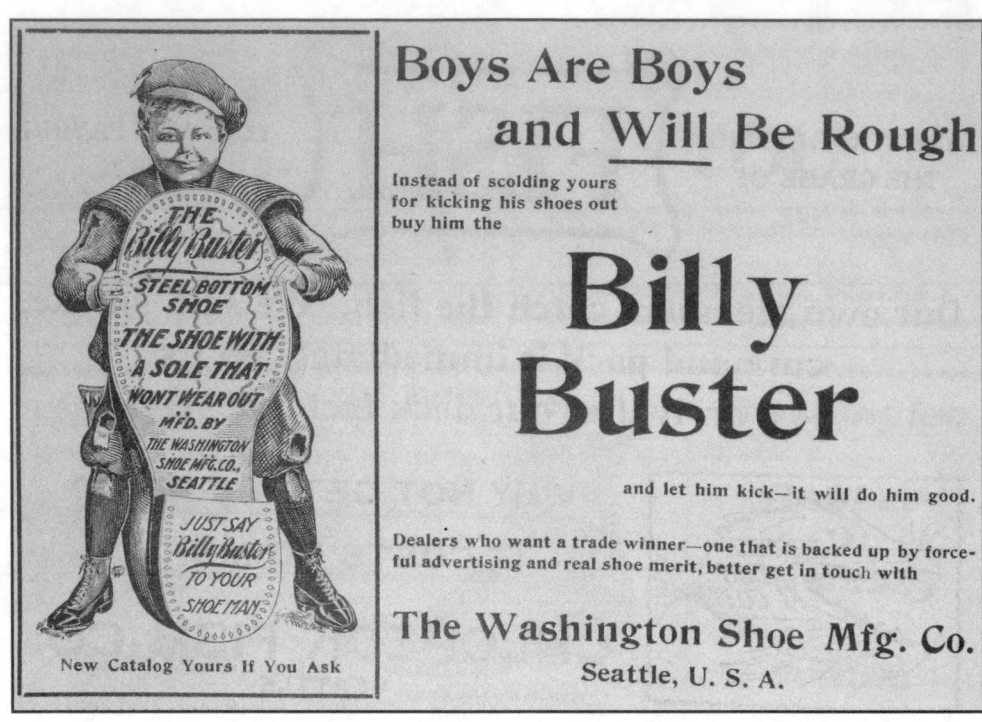

The Washington Shoe company was founded in 1891 and was Seattle's first shoe manufacturer. This ad is for sturdy shoes for boys that won't wear out. (via Wikimedia Commons)

Item	Source	Description	Price
APPAREL, MEN'S			
Collar	*Century Magazine* (1909)	*Arrow* collars; most of the successful styles appear first in *Arrow* collars	$0.15 each
Coat	*New York Times* (1907)	Australian opossum fur automobile coats, long model venetian yoke; regularly $50	$37.50
Coat	*New York Times* (1907)	Raccoon fur automobile coat	$47.50
Cuffs	*Century Magazine* (1909)	*Arrow* cuffs	$0.25/pair
Gloves	*New York Times* (1907)	*Perrin;* regularly $2	$1.30
Handkerchief	*Chicago Tribune* (1905)	White linen hemstitched handkerchiefs; 1/4" to 1/2" hem	$0.50
Hat	*Chicago Tribune* (1905)	Bishop's hat	$3.00
Hat	*New York Times* (1907)	Derby (clear nutria)	$2.75
Hat	*New York Times* (1909)	Deluxe hats	$6.00
Overcoat	*New York Times* (1905)	Spring weight	$15 to $35

Item	Source	Description	Price
Pajamas	*Chicago Tribune* (1907)	Serviceable quality of cheviot, military collars	$1.15
Pajamas	*Sears, Roebuck* (1908)	Military cut; coat and trousers	$0.96
Shirt	*New York Times* (1905)	From the most celebrated looms in Scotland	$4.00
Shirt	*The State* (Columbia, SC) (1905)	*The Emery;* put on a great front	$1.00
Shirt	*New York Times* (1907)	Men's negligee shirt, coat model with cuffs attached	$0.98
Shirt	*New York Times* (1907)	Fine cottons; special designs	$5.50
Shirt	*Century Magazine* (1909)	*Cluett;* dress	$1.50 and up
Shoes	*Atlanta Constitution* (1905)	French tan blucher Oxfords for men; were $5	$3.50
Shoes	*Van Norden Magazine* (1907)	They keep the feet healthy, prevent their getting damp and cold	$4.00
Shoes	*New York Times* (1909)	*Boyden's Famous;* any size, style; per pair regularly $6–$7	$4.75
Socks	*New York Times* (1907)	*Lisle* half-hose for men, lisle thread/instep silk, hand embroidered	$1.00/3 pairs
Suit	*San Francisco Examiner* (1908)	*Cholly Knickerbocker;* 30 styles, 100 colors; the foxiest clothes ever made	$12.50
Suit and Overcoat	*San Francisco Examiner* (1908)	Suits and overcoats	$15 to $45
Suspenders	*Van Norden Magazine* (1907)	Bull Dog	$0.50/pair
Tie	*New York Times* (1907)	Odds and ends sale	$0.27
Trousers	*New York Times* (1907)	Odds and ends sale	$1.35
Work Shirts	*Sears, Roebuck* (1908)	Chambray; lightweight cotton, fine finish	$0.46

APPAREL, WOMEN'S

Item	Source	Description	Price
Clothing	*Chicago Tribune* (1905)	Tailor-made suits for women	$35.00
Coat	*Chicago Tribune* (1907)	Women's fine coats for fall and winter; broadcloth	$40.00
Coat	*New York Tribune* (1908)	Stern Brothers fur-lined coats; long moiré pony coat	$125
Corset	*Ladies' Home Journal* (1905)	W. B.; stitched fan front to restrain and flatten abdomen	$1.50
Corset	*Ladies' Home Journal* (1905)	W. B.; has the new high bust effect	$1.00

Item	Source	Description	Price
Corset	*Sears, Roebuck* (1908)	Are you too stout? Will do what an abdominal corset cannot; size 20–30 size 31–36 size 37–40	 $2.25 $2.50 $2.75
Embroidery Waists	*Chicago Tribune* (1905)	Full blouse front with dainty tucks, form yoke effect	$4.50
Gloves	*Chicago Tribune* (1905)	*Trefousse;* kid gloves; regularly $1.75, sale price	$1.35
Hat	*San Francisco Examiner* (1908)	Pretty hats for Easter with ribbon	$6.50
Hat	*Sears, Roebuck and Co. Catalogue* (1908)	A large flaring mushroom style with long drooping back, rich in trimmings	$2.38
Kimono	*San Francisco Examiner* (1907)	Long lawn kimonos	$0.59
Petticoat	*San Francisco Examiner* (1907)	Heather bloom petticoats	$1.39
Petticoat	*The Taylor-Trotwood Magazine* (1908)	A guaranteed quality Simon's Regatta taffeta silk	$4.95
Shoes	*Ladies' Home Journal* (1905)	*American Lady;* with the character of the woman	$3.00
Shoes	*Van Norden Magazine* (1907)	They keep the feet healthy, prevent their getting damp and cold	$3.00
Shoes	*Sears, Roebuck* (1908)	Made of Conora coltskin, a foot-fitting low shoe	$1.39
Skirt	*San Francisco Examiner* (1907)	Alpaca walking skirt	$2.95
Stockings	*New York Times* (1909)	Pure French silk stockings	$4.50/pair
Suit	*New York Tribune* (1908)	*Saks and Company* tailored suits of fine broadcloths or cheviots; new hipless models, satin lined Regularly $35, special	$19.50
Suits	*San Francisco Examiner* (1907)	Charming new Pony and Eton suits	$14.95

An advertisement for a sale on Spring clothing. (via Wikimedia commons)

Item	Source	Description	Price
APPLIANCES			
Coffee Pot	*Century Magazine* (1909)	The *Marion Harland* coffee pot; full nickel-plated copper cover and silver-plated strainer	
		2-cup size (1 pint)	$1.25
		4-cup size (1 quart)	$1.60
		8-cup size (2 quarts)	$1.90
		12-cup size (3 quarts)	$2.20
Iron Stove	*The State* (Columbia, SC) (1908)	Black	$19.50
Refrigerator	*The State* (Columbia, SC) (1908)	*Big Line Hall;* saves every drop of melted ice as drinking water; you can buy $20 worth of furniture for $2 cash and $0.50 per week	$16.50 and up
Steel Range	*Sears, Roebuck* (1908)	Massive blue steel, six-hole range	$29.27

Item	Source	Description	Price
Washing Machine	*Sears, Roebuck* (1908)	Ball-bearing washing machine	$6.38
Water Heater	*Ladies' Home Journal* (1906)	Heat your home with hot water; average price	$198

BABY PRODUCTS

Item	Source	Description	Price
Baby Carriage	*Sears, Roebuck* (1908)	Finest grade of imported round reeds entirely woven by hand	$16.95
Baby Carriage	*Sears, Roebuck* (1908)	16" steel wheels with 3/8" rubber	$4.25
Baby Walker	*Sears, Roebuck and Co. Catalogue* (1908)	Combination walker, table and swing on a hard-wood frame	$1.80
Cloaks	*Sears, Roebuck and Co. Catalogue* (1908)	Infants' long cloaks in cashmere, Bedford cord and silk Cashmere Cashmere with silk trim	$1.95 $3.29
Gown	*Sears, Roebuck and Co. Catalogue* (1908)	Beautiful Jap silk set; yoke is trimmed with three rows of lace. The underskirt is made of Jap silk Slip and shirt set	$4.25
Ring	*Sears, Roebuck and Co. Catalogue* (1908)	Baby ring, 1 ruby doublet, 2 enamel pearls, size 0 to 4	$0.65

BUSINESS EQUIPMENT & SUPPLIES

Item	Source	Description	Price
Adding Machine	*Forestry and Irrigation* (1905)	*The Locke Adder;* famous calculating machine	$5 to $10
Bowling Alley	*New York Tribune* (1908)	*American Box Ball Company* can put you in the popular bowling game; Alleys pay $25 to $65 each per week Investment	$150 per lane
Carbon Paper	*Van Norden Magazine* (1907)	*Whitfield;* No Smudge, No Blur; 8" × 13"	$0.50/25 sheets
Player Piano	*American Chronicle* (1999)	*Wurlitzer;* 65-note, coin-operated player piano	$700
Pushpins	*Ladies' Home Journal* (1905)	*Moore;* Here's a Pin, Push it in; made of steel and polished glass	$0.10/half-dozen
Typewriter	*New York Tribune* (1908)	Typewriter Exchange, bargains Remingtons Hammonds Franklins	 $15.00 $10.00 $10.00

COLLECTIBLES

Item	Source	Description	Price
Book	*New York Times* (1907)	First edition of *Endymion* (1818) by John Keats	$91.00
Glasses	*American Collector* (1942)	Rare set of eight early green wine glasses, broken pontles, The Loft, West Chester, Pennsylvania [In 1909]	$48.00
Letter	*New York Times* (1907)	By King Ferdinand and Queen Isabella signed 5 May 1495; earliest document mentioning American Indians	$85.00
Painting	*American Chronicle* (1999)	Thomas Gainsborough's *Portrait of John Revett;* sold at auction [In 1907]	$40.00

Item	Source	Description	Price
EDUCATION			
Home Language Lessons	*Century Magazine* (1909)	Learn Spanish, French, Italian, German; taught as if actually in the presence of the teacher	$5/language
Language Classes	*Century Magazine* (1909)	Learn to speak fluently in Spanish, French, Italian or German. Pupils taught as if actually in the presence of the teacher. Ten-week course, per language	$5.00
Preparatory School	*The Taylor-Trotwood Magazine* (1908)	Bethel Military Academy; fifty miles from Washington. Prepares for business, universities and government academies. Warrenton, Virginia	$275
Seminary for Young Women	*Century Magazine* (1909)	Martha Washington Seminary; two-year course for high school graduates Per year	$500
Tuition	*American Chronicle* (1999)	University of Michigan; cost per semester in 1909	$40.00
ENTERTAINMENT			
Concert	*New York Tribune* (1908)	Violin soloist John Spargur; Broadway Theater; all seats reserved	$0.50–$$1.00
Horse Race	*The State* (Columbia, SC) (1909)	Spring; 300 Horses from Big circuit	$0.50

A postcard for a horse race at the Saratoga racetrack in 1909. (via Wikimedia Commons)

Item	Source	Description	Price
Opera Ticket	*New York Times* (1905)	*Die Meistersinger*	$1.00-$3.00
Snake Fight	*New York Times* (1907)	Mr. Rattlesnake v. Mr. Kingsnake	$2.00
Theater	*New York Tribune* (1908)	Klaw and Erlanger's Musical Comedy *Little Nemo*; Wednesday matinee	$1.50
Theater Ticket	*Chicago Tribune* (1905)	Klaw & Erlanger Co. Production	$0.75-$1.50
Theater Ticket	*San Francisco Examiner* (1907)	Novelty Theatre presents Sidewalks of New York	$0.25-$0.50
Theater Ticket	*The State* (Columbia, SC) (1908)	*What Women Will Do*—Friday Night; *Dr. Jekyll and Mr. Hyde*—Saturday Night	$0.15-$0.35
Ticket	*New York Times* (1909)	The greatest girl show ever seen in New York City; table seats	$1.00
Wrestling	*The State* (Columbia, SC) (1908)	Wrestling Dan McLeod v. Charles Conkle; Gallery Balcony Orchestra Stage seats	$0.25 $0.50 $0.75 $1.00

ENTERTAINMENT, HOME

Item	Source	Description	Price
Camera	*Century Magazine* (1909)	*Speed Kodak*; fitted with the Kodak Focal Plane Shutter having a range of automatic exposure from slow instantaneous to 1-1000 of a second	$50
Camera	*Sears, Roebuck* (1908)	*Conley Long Focus*; includes Conley Safety Shutter, 4" × 5"	$13.90
Camera	*Sears, Roebuck* (1908)	*Improved compact*; 4" × 5" size, rack and pinion focus movement	$6.95
Camera	*New York Times* (1909)	*Kodak; N. 4A Speed*; 4 1/4" × 6 1/2" (without lens)	$50.00
Card Game	*Ladies' Home Journal* (1905)	A decided novelty for your friends Gilt edged	$0.50 $0.75
Game	*Sears, Roebuck and Co. Catalogue* (1908)	*Parcheesi*; the popular home game	$0.65
Magic Lantern	*Sears, Roebuck* (1908)	Includes 12 colored slides with four pictures on each slide	$4.98 to $6.98
Playing Cards	*Century Magazine* (1909)	*Bicycle*	$0.25
Playing Cards	*Century Magazine* (1909)	*Congress;* gold edges; 90 picture backs	$0.50
Records	*Sears, Roebuck* (1908)	Wax-cylinder; standard size; your own selection of subjects	$0.18
Records	*Century Magazine* (1909)	Phonograph; in a class by themselves—above price competition; 10" 12"	 $0.60 $1.00
Stereoscopic Views	*Sears, Roebuck* (1908)	St. Louis World's Fair, 100 views	$0.85

Item	Source	Description	Price
Stereoscopic Views	*Sears, Roebuck* (1908)	The siege of Port Arthur; 100 views of the Japanese-Russian War	$0.85
Stereoscopic Views	*Sears, Roebuck* (1908)	50 views of the great plant of Sears, Roebuck & Co.	$0.35
Stereoscopic Viewer	*Sears, Roebuck* (1908)	Standard Special Aluminum	$0.28 $0.49
Talking Machine	*Chicago Tribune* (1907)	Wurlitzer	$29.50
Talking Machine	*Sears, Roebuck* (1908)	*Oxford;* cylinder talking machine	$14.95
Talking Machine	*Century Magazine* (1909)	The actual living, breathing voices of the world's greatest opera singers in all their power, sweetness, and purity	$10.00

FARM EQUIPMENT & SUPPLIES

Item	Source	Description	Price
Bit	*Sears, Roebuck and Co. Catalogue* (1902)	Dexter driving bit; large, heavy cheeks; large, heavy tapered mouthpiece	$0.50
Chicks	*New York Times* (1907)	Barred Rocks, White Leghorns	$0.15/each
Cream Separator	*Sears, Roebuck* and *Co. Catalogue* (1908)	Improved economy cream separator, out skimmed all others. Capacity 250 to 300 pounds per hour, suitable for dairy of two to eight cows	$26.30
Engine	*The Housewife* (1903)	Best gasoline engine made complete with tank, tools and fittings. For pumping water 1-Horsepower 2-Horsepower 3-Horsepower	 $69.00 $95.00 $112.25
Harness	*Sears, Roebuck and Co. Catalogue* (1902)	Iowa single harness; for 900- to 1200-pound horse; weight, boxed, 23 pounds	$8.95
Horse Harness	*Sears, Roebuck and Co. Catalogue* (1908)	*Hercules Farm Harness;* double and stitched trace, 6 feet long, with clip cockeye riveted on. 1 1/2-inch traces	
Incubator	*Wood's Special Poultry Supply Catalog T. W. Wood and Sons Richmond, VA* (1909)	Cyphers' Standard fireproofed incubator, 144-egg size	$20.99 $22.00
Incubator	*Ladies' Home Journal* (1911)	125-egg incubator and brooder	$10.00 for both
Insecticide	*The Ladies' Home Journal* (1910)	*Daisy Fly Killer*—attracts and kills flies. Made of metal; cannot spill or tip over Per box	$0.20
Medicine for Chickens	*Wood's Special Poultry Supply Catalog T. W. Wood and Sons Richmond, VA* (1908)	*Sterling Cholera Cure* is one of the best possible remedies for cholera. Cholera is the most deadly disease affecting poultry	$0.50
Sheep Shears	*Sears, Roebuck and Co. Catalogue* (1908)	Imported English double bow sheep shears, made in Sheffield, England 6 1/2 inch 7 inch	 $1.04 $1.24

Item	Source	Description	Price
Shoe	*Sears, Roebuck and Co. Catalogue* (1908)	Plow shoe; made from Milwaukee oil grain leather	$1.35
Separator	*The Housewife* (1903)	Cream separator; most economical and most thorough hand cream separator	$48.75
Saddle	*Sears, Roebuck and Co. Catalogue* (1902)	Cheyenne Cowboy saddle; made of oiled russet skirting leather on a 15-inch Hidalgo steel fork rawhide covered tree	$19.90
Walking Plow	*Sears, Roebuck* (1908)	They score perfectly	$8.62

FOOD PRODUCTS

Item	Source	Description	Price
Baking Powder	*New York Times* (1905)		$0.38/pound
Baking Powder	*The State* (Columbia, SC) (1905)	Good Luck; positively pure and has unsurpassed leavening qualities	$0.10/pound
Bananas	*Chicago Tribune* (1905)		$0.50 to $1.25/bunch
Beets	*Chicago Tribune* (1905)		$2 to $3.50/ bushel
Beverages	*The Taylor-Trotwood Magazine* (1908)	Teas and coffees, the supplying of Catholic Institutions, clergymen and large consumers a specialty. By the pound Finest teas Finest coffees	 $0.13 $0.18
Catsup	*New York Times* (1905)		$0.20/pint
Cereal	*Ladies' Home Journal* (1905)	*Egg-o-See;* the whole grain of the very best white wheat; a large package	$0.10
Chocolate	*New York Tribune* (1908)	*Taylor-made Sorority Chocolates;* a new sensation One pound box	$0.60
Chocolate Bonbons	*Ladies' Home Journal* (1905)	Caillers	$1.35/pound
Clam Chowder	*Ladies' Home Journal* (1905)	*Scarboro Beach;* appetizing, nutritious, and absolutely pure	$0.10/can
Cracker	*The State* (Columbia, SC) (1908)	*Uneeda Biscuit;* the world's best soda cracker; in dust-tight moisture proof packages	$0.05
Eggs	*The State* (Columbia, SC) (1909)	One-day old; they will cost you more than eggs from two weeks to two months	$0.30/dozen
Flour	*The State* (Columbia, SC) (1908)	*Silver Leaf*	$2.65/98-pound sack
Flour	*The State* (Columbia, SC) (1909)	Piedmont	$0.90/24 pounds
Gelatin	*Ladies' Home Journal* (1905)	*Jell-O;* six flavors	$0.10/pkg
Grape Juice	*Ladies' Home Journal* (1905)	*Welch's;* the food value of a grape	$3.00/dozen

Grape juice was initially used as an alternative to communion wine and was brought to America by British physician and dentist Thomas Welch. Welch's Grape Juice Company was incorporated in 1893. Advertisement circa 1908. (via Wikimedia Commons)

Item	Source	Description	Price
Ham	*The State* (Columbia, SC) (1909)	Swifts Premium	$0.16/pound
Ice Cream	*Ladies' Home Journal* (1905)	*Jell-O;* four kinds	$0.25/2 pkgs
Peanuts	*Sears, Roebuck* (1908)	*Garlandis;* Salted peanuts, 1/2 lb can	$0.21
Potatoes	*The State* (Columbia, SC) (1908)	New York Table	$2.50/sack
Prunes	*The State* (Columbia, SC) (1908)	California; most wholesome food of this season; 25 lb box	$0.10/pound
Sardines	*New York Times* (1905)	Contains 14 fish per can	$0.35/half-can
Soft Drinks	*The State* (Columbia, SC) (1908)	*Bludwine;* King of soft drinks	$0.05/each; $1.90/ 6 dozen
Sugar	*The State* (Columbia, SC) (1909)	Granulated	$1/20 pounds
Sugar Wafers	*Century Magazine* (1909)	*Nabisco;* no other dessert confection has ever so satisfied that wholesome desire for a delicate sweet	$0.10 to $0.25/tin
Tea	*Ladies' Home Journal* (1905)	*Matsuri Tea Co., Importers;* express prepaid	$1.00/pound
Toffee	*Ladies' Home Journal* (1905)	*Mackintosh's;* the great international candy	$1.60/4 pounds
Wafer	*Century Magazine* (1909)	*Nabisco Sugar Wafers;* no other dessert confection has ever so satisfied that wholesome desire for a delicate sweet Small tin Large tin	 $0.10 $0.25

FURNITURE

Item	Source	Description	Price
Bed	*Sears, Roebuck* (1908)	Massive high-grade continuous post brass bed	$28.85
Bed	*Sears, Roebuck* (1908)	Iron bed has corner posts made of drawn steel tubing, finished with white enamel only	$1.89
Chair	*Chicago Tribune* (1905)	Spanish leather-bag cushion rocker	$9.75
Chair	*Sears, Roebuck* (1908)	Golden oak, upholstered seat and back, fabric-covered leather	$4.45
Chair	*The State* (Columbia, SC) (1908)	Back porch rocker; Reed-seat and three-slat back	$2.35
Chair	*Sears, Roebuck and Co. Catalogue* (1908)	Adjustable reclining swing chair, made of oak, figured velour cushion	$6.25
Clock	*Ladies' Home Journal* (1905)	Grandfather; 79" high, regularly $55 Mahogany	$30.00 $34.00
Clock	*Sears, Roebuck*	Mantel; case imitates black Italian marble	$5.05
Clock	*Sears, Roebuck* *(1908)*	Empress design veneered with highly figured quar-tersawed oak; 78" long 3 30" wide	$12.15

Item	Source	Description	Price
Desk	*New York Tribune* (1908)	60-inch Sanitary Rolltop Desk	$37.50
Dining Table	*New York Times* (1907)	Golden oak, round, pedestal base	$11.25
Hall Mirror and Hall Seat	*San Francisco Examiner (1908)*	Hall mirrors Hall seats	$3.00 $10.00
Rug	*Chicago Tribune (1905)*	Oriental; 9.5' 3 13.7', regularly $315	$235

GARDEN EQUIPMENT & SUPPLIES

Item	Source	Description	Price
Flower Bupounds	Childs' Fall Catalogue *of Bupounds and Plants that Bloom* (1908)	*Darwin tulips;* produce only solid self colors and bloom early in May	$0.50 per dozen
Lawn Mower	*The State* (Columbia, SC) (1909)	*Panama;* self-sharpening; 14" cut 16" cut	$6.50 $7.50
Roses	*Ladies' Home Journal* (1905)	Blooming size plants	$1/24 plants
Seeds	*Ladies' Home Journal* (1905)	Giant sweet peas	$0.10/5 pkgs
Tree Protectors	*Forestry and Irrigation* (1905)	Do not wait until rabbits and mice ruin your trees	$0.75/100

HOTEL RATES

Item	Source	Description	Price
Hotel Room	*Century Magazine* (1909)	*The Jefferson Hotel;* the most magnificent hotel in the South. Rooms single and en suite, with and without bath. Richmond, Virginia	$1.50 per day
Hotel Room	*Atlanta Constitution* (1905)	*Hotel Earlington;* rooms with detached bar	$1.00/day
Hotel Room	*Chicago Tribune* (1905)	*Hotel Johnson;* 336 Dearborn, furnished with bath and gas	$2.00/week
Hotel Room	Chicago Tribune (1905)	*The Plaza;* the world's most luxurious hotel With bath With parlor, bedroom, and bath	$2.50/day $4 to $6/day $12 to $20/day
Hotel Room	*Van Norden Magazine* (1907)	*Lenox Hotel;* our rapid electric carriages Exclusively for patrons	$1.50/day

HOUSEHOLD GOODS

Item	Source	Description	Price
Blanket	*Ladies' Home Journal* (1905)	*Suffolk Sanitary Fleece;* superior to woolen blankets	$1.50/pair
Bowl	*Ladies' Home Journal* (1906)	Cut-glass fruit or berry bowl; 7" bowl	$3.00
Bread Maker	*Ladies' Home Journal* (1905)	*Universal;* mixes and kneads bread thoroughly in three minutes; four-loaf capacity, large family size	$3.25

Item	Source	Description	Price
Carriage Bag	*New York Times* (1905)	*Walrus;* vienna covered frame 6", 7", 8", and 9" in tan, brown, and black; value $4	$1.95
Cleaner	*Ladies' Home Journal* (1906)	*Old Dutch;* a natural product, cleanest and cheapest agent that ever blessed the housewife; large cans with sifting top	$0.10
Curtains	*Ladies' Home Journal* (1905)	Lace; Point De Luxe, Motifany, Queen Anne made of real bobbinet	$2.00/pair
Draperies	*Chicago Tribune* (1905)	Cotton; artistically hand-painted cretonnes	$0.13/yd
House Paint	*Sears, Roebuck* (1908)	*Ready* mixed paint ($9.10 for two-story wood frame house)	$0.98/gallon
Liquid Glaze	*Ladies' Home Journal* (1905)	*Varno;* revives all varnished surfaces	$0.30/5-ounce can
Matches	*Sears, Roebuck* (1908)	Red Brand	$0.58/12,000
Mattress	*Ladies' Home Journal* (1905)	*Ostermoor;* 6' 3" long, 3' 6" wide; pure, elastic hand-laid, sheeted mattress not dangerous animal fibre, 4' 6" wide	$11.70 $15.00
Pesticide	*Ladies' Home Journal* (1905)	*Rough on Rats;* Why feed rats? Rough on Rats kills them	$0.15
Plumbing	*Century Magazine* (1909)	*Mott's;* Imperial solid porcelain	$85 to $300
Silver Polish	*Century Magazine* (1909)	*Electro;* silicon; does not scratch or wear	$0.15/jar
Soap	*Ladies' Home Journal* (1905)	*Palmolive;* more than ordinary soap	$0.10
Stove Polish	*Ladies' Home Journal* (1905)	*Black Satin in Can;* the perfect stove polish	$0.25/can
Suitcase	*Atlanta Constitution* (1905)	$4 leather suitcase	$3.00
Tablecloth	*New York Times* (1905)	Irish Satin Damask; 2 yds × 3 yds	$3.00
Tableware	*Sears, Roebuck* (1908)	28 pieces, solid Alaska metal, 6 dinner forks, dinner knives, full-size tablespoons and tea-spoons, 1 butter knife, sugar shell and salt and pepper	$4.66
Tooth Cleanser	*Ladies' Home Journal* (1906)	*Rubifoam;* for a well-kept mouth	$0.25/tube
Towels	*New York Times* (1905)	250 dozen spoke, hemstitched, huckaback	$3.00/dozen
Trunk	*Sears, Roebuck* (1908)	32" × 21" × 23 1/2"	$6.88
Varnish	*Sears, Roebuck* (1908)	Fine carriage varnishes $1.60/ 1/2 gal	4/$0.05/ pint
Water Softener	*The State* (Columbia, SC) (1909)	*Lavadura;* it softens the water and makes easy work of washing the clothes	$0.05 to $0.10/pack

INSURANCE RATES

Item	Source	Description	Price
Fire Insurance	*Insurance Policy* (1908)	$500 fire coverage for two-story wood frame building in Columbia, SC	$4.50

Item	Source	Description	Price
Life Insurance	*Century Magazine* (1909)	Whole life plan (at age 30 equals $50 monthly for 20 years)	$167.35

JEWELRY

Item	Source	Description	Price
Bracelet	*Sears, Roebuck and Co. Catalogue* (1908)	Oval tubing, gold filled, bright polish, patent pull-out spring bracelet	$3.82
Cuff Links	*The State* (Columbia, SC) (1908)	Solid gold cuff; several patterns to select from; regularly $3	$2.00
Watch	*Sears, Roebuck* (1908)	Pocket watch; 7-jewel, nickel plate, size 16	$2.76
Watch	*Sears, Roebuck* (1908)	*Elgin;* pocket watch; 15-jewel; size 16	$8.15
Watch	*Sears, Roebuck* (1908)	Pocket watch; 21-jewel, solid 14K gold, size 16	$32.50
Dinner	*Atlanta Constitution* (1905)	*Hotel Earlington,* New York City; table d'Hôte	$0.75

MEDICAL PRODUCTS & SERVICES

Item	Source	Description	Price
Dentist	*Atlanta Constitution* (1905)	Dr. E. G. Griffin's Gold Crowns and Bridge Work; work at lowest cash prices	$4.00
Dentist	*San Francisco Examiner* (1908)	Fillings Teeth re-enameled Gold plate	$1.00 $2.00 $5 to $8
Glasses	*Sears, Roebuck* (1908)	Man's, cable bow, gold-filled spectacles	$1.98
Nonprescription Drug	*New York Times* (1905)	Castor Oil Tablets	$0.10/box
Nonprescription Drug	*The State* (Columbia, SC) (1905)	*Dr. Bell's Pine-Tar-Honey;* will always prevent a cold if taken on coming in out of the wet	$0.25/bottle
Nonprescription Drug	*Sears, Roebuck* (1906)	*Blackberry Balsam;* a pleasant, safe, speedy, and l effectual remedy for dysentery, diarrhea, looseness, cholera morbus	$0.20/bottle
Nonprescription Drug	*Sears, Roebuck* (1906)	*Carolene;* cures while you sleep; a remedy for whooping cough, asthma, catarrh, diphtheria, croup, colds, cough, etc.	$0.89
Nonprescription Drug	*Sears, Roebuck* (1906)	*Castoria;* the best-known remedy for all stomach and bowel complaints of infants and children; regular price $0.35	$0.26/bottle
Sanitarium	*San Francisco Examiner* (1908)	*Dr. Juilly's;* confinement with ten days' care	$30 to $60

MOTORIZED VEHICLES, SERVICES, & SUPPLIES

Item	Source	Description	Price
Automobile	*Century Magazine* (1909)	The "30" Locomobile shaft drive touring car	$3,500

Item	Source	Description	Price
Automobile	*Sears, Roebuck* (1905)	*Franklin Light Tonneau;* 4-cylinder air-cooled motor	$1,650
Automobile	*Sears, Roebuck* (1905)	*White Steam Car;* the ideal closed automobile	$3,200
Automobile	*Cycle and Automobile Trade Journal* (1905)	*Zent High-grade Car;* the simplest car on earth; has ample power, the 3-cylinder engine developing full 18 hp and over; price for the present	$1,350
Automobile	*New York Times* (1909)	*Rambler Model 44;* 34 hp, seven passengers	$2,250
Automobile Seat	*Sears, Roebuck* (1908)	Two-seat surrey with extension top	$77.45
Boat Steering Gears	*Cycle and Automobile Trade* Journal (1905)	*Edson;* the side steering quadrant will come as a valued aid to the man who wishes to steer his own boat and to run the engine as well	$8.00
Carburetor	*Cycle and Automobile Trade* Journal (1905)	*Schebler;* the heart of the automobile; cost saved through reduced gasoline bills in a few weeks	$18.00
Jack	*Cycle and Automobile Trade* Journal (1905)	*Kenosha;* durable handsomely finished and carefully made in our own factory; everything for the man with the car	$4.00
Marine Motor	*Cycle and Automobile Trade* Journal (1905)	*Clifton;* 1-cylinder; one of the improvements is the use of the jump spark system of ignition	$600
Marine Motor	*Cycle and Automobile Trade* Journal (1905)	*Lawrence;* 2-cycle 12 hp; weighs 600 pounds, runs 450 r.p.m.	$850
Motor Oil	*Cycle and Automobile Trade* Journal (1905)	*Ideal;* for automobile and marine engines; pure hydrocarbon high fire test, low cold test; no gum, no carbon	$0.60/gallon
Motorboat	*Cycle and Automobile Trade* Journal (1905)	18-ft. launch, driven by DuBrie's 2 hp motor, regular speed 8 miles per hour, gasoline consumption about two gallons in 10 hours running; seats 8	$175
Motorcycle	*Popular Mechanics* Picture History of American Travel (1909)	*Curtis;* 7 hp double cylinder	$275
Road Wagon	*Sears, Roebuck* (1908)	Blue Ribbon Runabouts	$32.15 to $34.15

MUSICAL INSTRUMENTS

Item	Source	Description	Price
Piano	*New York Times* (1905)	*Kimball;* New / Used	$450 / $200
Piano	*Sears, Roebuck* (1908)	Special concert grand piano	$195
Piano	*Century Magazine* (1909)	*Steinway;* miniature grand ebonized case	$800
Violin	*Sears, Roebuck* (1908)	*Pisani;* Stradivarius model	$45.00
Violin	*New York Times* (1909)	Student / Regular	$15.00 / $100

Item	Source	Description	Price
OTHER			
College Poster	*Forestry and Irrigation* (1905)	In the colors of the college they represent (14" × 22")	$25.00
Fountain Pen	*Forestry and Irrigation* (1905)	Pocket companion; regularly $3, reduced	$1.00
Photographs	*The State* (Columbia, SC) (1908)	Fine cabinet photos in folders	$3.00/dozen
Photography	*American Chronicle* (1999)	Financier J. P. Morgan's pledge to support a photo collection of North American Indians in 1907	$75,000
Postcards	*New York Times* (1909)	Set of 12, showing 90 hp Locomobile winning 1908 International Race for Vanderbilt Cup	$0.10/set
Stationery	*Ladies' Home Journal* (1905)	*Autocrat;* for social correspondence; special combination cabinet, containing correspondence cards, writing papers and exclusive deep flap envelopes	$0.50
Whiskey Flask	*The State* (Columbia, SC) (1908)	Sterling silver; regularly $12	$9.00
PERSONAL CARE PRODUCTS			
Cold Cream	*Century Magazine* (1909)	*Daggett and Ramsdell's Perfect Cold Cream;* a beauty clean-up in cold weather when pores are contracted and inactive Jar Tube	 $0.35 $0.10
Cold Cream	*Century Magazine* (1909)	The skin needs emollient cleansing	$0.10/tube $0.35/jar
Combination Case	*Ladies' Home Journal* (1905)	Larkin	$10.00
Digestive Aid	*Sears, Roebuck* (1908)	*Essence of Pepsin;* for treatment of indigestion, sour stomach, dyspepsia, bad breath	$0.43/8 ounces
Face Powder	*Ladies' Home Journal* (1905)	*LaBlache;* flesh, white, pink, cream	$0.50/box
Face Whitener	*Sears, Roebuck* (1908)	*White Lily;* great face, neck, and arm whitener; the ladies' favorite toilet preparation	4/$0.05
Razor	*Van Norden Magazine* (1907)	*Razac Ready;* complete outfit, genuine leather case	$3.50
Safety Razor	*Century Magazine* (1909)	*Gillette;* no stropping, no honing; standard set	$5.00

1906 advertisement for the Gillette safety razor. (via Wikimedia Commons)

Item	Source	Description	Price
Skin Cream	*Century Magazine* (1909)	*Strong's Arnica Jelly;* ideal for sunburn, keeps the skin soft and smooth	$0.25
Soap	*Century Magazine* (1909)	*Fairy;* the floating oval cake	$0.50
Sunburn Remedy	*Century Magazine* (1909)	*Arnica Jelly;* ideal for sunburn, keeps the skin soft and smooth	$0.25/tube
Talcum Powder	*Century Magazine* (1909)	*Mennen's Borated;* baby's best brief, relieves and prevents chapped hands and chafing; a non-re-fillable box	$0.25
Toothpaste	*Ladies' Home Journal* (1906)	*Dentacura;* cleans the teeth, destroys bacteria, prevents decay	$0.25
Tooth Soap	*Century Magazine* (1909)	*Arnica;* sweetens the breath, hardens the gums, whitens the teeth; metal package at all druggists	$0.25

Item	Source	Description	Price
PUBLICATIONS			
Book	*Century Magazine* (1909)	*The World I Live In* by Helen Keller, an autobiographical record	$1.20
Book	*Century Magazine* (1909)	*The Trail of the Lonesome Pine;* by John Fox Jr., illustrated	$1.50
Magazine	*Century Magazine* (1909)	*St. Nicholas Magazine;* St. Nicholas is not only a joy to the children for whom it is primarily intended, but has also an unfading attraction for the older folk 12 Issues, One-year subscription	 $3.00
Magazine	*Century Magazine* (1909)	*The American Magazine;* January issue contains a new story by David Grayson One-year subscription	$1.00
Magazine	*Forestry and Irrigation* (1905)	*Scientific American;* anyone sending a sketch and a description may quickly ascertain our opinion on whether an invention is probably patentable	$3.00/year
Magazine	*Van Norden Magazine* (1907)	*The Financial Forum*	$1.00/year
Magazine	*Century Magazine* (1909)	*St. Nicholas Magazine;* monthly for children	$3.00/year
Newspaper	*New York Times* (1905)	*New York Times,* daily issue	$0.01
REAL ESTATE			
Apartment	*New York Tribune* (1908)	*Hoffman Arms Apartments* from 5 to 20 rooms with kitchen or restaurant service; 59th St. and Madison Ave. Rent per year	$1,200 to $4,000
Apartment	*San Francisco Examiner* (1908)	For rent; furnished apartments, gas ranges, sinks, closets	$17.50/ month
Apartment Building	*New York Times* (1907)	For sale; Central Park view apartment house, Central Park West and Eighty-sixth Street, New York City; 100' × 150' plot, 12-story building, 47 apartments	$1,200,000
Farm	*Atlanta Constitution* (1905)	124 acres 16 miles from Atlanta, 1 mile from R. R., heavily timbered, enough timber to pay for place twice	$20.00/acre
House	*New York Tribune* (1908)	Three-story brick dwelling in Flushing, New York; 8 acres, 17 rooms, two bathrooms, large kitchen and laundry in basement	$75,000
House	*Atlanta Constitution* (1905)	10-room home near Peachtree	$4,500
House	*Ladies' Home Journal* (1905)	Three-room house (Carpentry and hardware $675, masonry $125, plumbing $125, painting $75)	$1,000
House	*The State* (Columbia, SC) (1905)	One eight-room dwelling on East Gervais Street, delightful neighborhood	$5,500
House	*Atlanta Constitution* (1905)	For rent; 7-rooms; equipped with furnace heat, gas, and electric lights and all conveniences	$35.00/ month

An advertisement for house units on Clifton Street in Washington D.C. (via Wikimedia Commons)

Item	Source	Description	Price
House	*Atlanta Constitution* (1905)	Lee Street Cottage; $200 cash, balance $15 per month	$1,500
House	*The State* (Columbia, SC) (1908)	For rent; 7 rooms	$19.00/ month
House	*The State* (Columbia, SC) (1908)	For rent; 7-room house, bath both floors, Columbia, SC	$35/month
House	*Sears, Roebuck* (1908)	Plows, all materials for two-story, six-room house	$725
Land	*Chicago Tribune* (1905)	Kansas Wheat	$6 to $12/ acre
Land	*Chicago Tribune* (1905)	Colorado and Nebraska ranch land (payment one-tenth in cash)	$1.75 to $4/ acre
Lot	*Atlanta Constitution* (1905)	50 × 250 lot; This is the place to save your money and we can make you $100 profit on each lot by spring	$250

Item	Source	Description	Price
Lot	*Chicago Tribune* (1905)	24' × 110', old cottage thrown in	$1,800
Lot	*New York Times* (1909)	120 lots in the choicest section of Bogota Estates, Bogota, New Jersey	$250 to $300
Office	*New York Times* (1907)	For rent; Times Square Building; 18 yards × 24 yards, 4th floor, best lighted in New York City, elevators run all night	$1,400/year
Room	*New York Times* (1907)	For rent; eastside New York City, furnished with board, running water, steam heat	$8.00
Room	*New York Times* (1907)	For rent; furnished room, 124th St, 68th East, heated, running water, hall room	$2.00
Warehouse and Factory	*Chicago Tribune* (1905)	244 yds × 130 yds with two-story brick warehouse and factory less than one mile from city hall	$40,000

SEWING EQUIPMENT & SUPPLIES

Item	Source	Description	Price
Cloth	*New York Times* (1907)	Stirling black taffeta silks 26" wide	$1.10/yard
Cloth	*San Francisco Examiner* (1907)	Japanese wash silk in the latest patterns and colorings	$0.39/yard
Sewing Machine	*Sears, Roebuck and Co. Catalogue* (1908)	*Belmont* five-drawer drop head, oak cabinet sewing machine	$9.85
Sewing Machine	*Sears, Roebuck* (1908)	5-drawer, drop head with oak cabinet	$9.85
Sewing Machine	*Sears, Roebuck* (1908)	7-drawer, drop leaf and box cover with oak cabinet	$13.85

SPORTS EQUIPMENT

Item	Source	Description	Price
Baseball Glove	*Sears, Roebuck* (1908)	Made of horsehide, correctly padded	$1.90
Basketball Goal	*Sears, Roebuck* and *Co. Catalogue* (1908)	Regulation style made of iron frame with cotton netting, weight per pair, 12 pounds	$2.74
Bicycle	*Sears, Roebuck* (1908)	Man's Roadster model	$14.95
Bicycle Pump	*Sears, Roebuck* (1908)	Compound action, hose connection will fit all valves	$0.09
Field Glasses	*Sears, Roebuck* (1908)	Highest grade genuine Jena special field glass	$12.95
Fishing Rod	*Sears, Roebuck* (1908)	Two-jointed, 5 1/2" with double cork grip	$1.29
Fishing Tackle	*Sears, Roebuck* and *Co. Catalogue* (1908)	Complete bait casting outfit suitable for bait casting or trolling	$5.98
Pistol	*Sears, Roebuck* (1908)	Automatic self-cocking revolver	$3.75
Shot Gun	*Sears, Roebuck* (1908)	Double-barrel, breech loading	$11.95
Supporter	*Sears, Roebuck and Co. Catalogue* (1908)	Admiral elastic supporters; the most sanitary, most practical jockey strap on the market	$0.44

Item	Source	Description	Price
TELEPHONE EQUIPMENT & SERVICES			
Telephone	*Sears, Roebuck* (1908)	Five-magnet, 1600 ohm, compact, bridging telephone; more power than is required in actual practice	$9.95
Telephone Service	John Brooks, *Telephone The First Hundred Years* (1976)	Annual rates (Pittsburgh) for 1906 Residential Business	$100 $125
Telegraph Charges	Susan J. Douglas, *Inventing American Broadcasting* (1987)	Rates for 1907	$0.05 to $0.25/word
TOBACCO PRODUCTS			
Cigar	*New York Times* (1905)		$0.05
Cigarettes	*Century Magazine* (1909)	*Nestor Cigarettes*; if you must have the very best and ignore the rest, pack of 10, Blue Label Green Label Imported	$0.15/pack $0.25/pack $0.40/pack
Cigarettes	*The State* (Columbia, SC) (1908)	*Piedmont*; famous for the quality of fine old tobacco; packaged in tin foil	$0.05/ten
Cigars	*Sears, Roebuck* (1908)	Perfectos; box of 50	$1.20/box
TOYS			
Doll	*Sears, Roebuck and Co. Catalogue* (1908)	*Full jointed papier maché doll*; natural appearance and beautifully proportioned 19" 24" 30"	$1.19 $2.88 $4.89
Teddy Bears	*Sears, Roebuck and Co. Catalogue* (1908)	*Teddy bears*; the best plaything ever invested, not a fad or campaign article 10" high 12" high 14" high 16" high	$0.75 $1.19 $1.75 $2.38
Wondergraph	*Sears, Roebuck and Co. Catalogue* (1908)	*Wondergraph*; makes, as if by magic, beautiful designs no artist can draw; a child can operate	$0.95
TRAVEL & TRANSPORTATION			
Boat	*New York Tribune* (1908)	*Hudson River Night Lines*; between New York and Albany	$2.65 $1.50
Cruise	*New York Times* (1909)	*To the Orient*; 80 Days	$300
Cruise	*New York Times* (1909)	South America; stopping at all the important cities en route to the Straits of Magellan; duration, 81 days	$350
Cruise	*New York Times* (1909)	*World*; thirty tours to Europe	$250

Promotional literature for the 1905 Scott Special passenger train of the Atchison, Topeka and Santa Fe Railway. (via Wikimedia Commons)

Item	Source	Description	Price
Railroad Ticket	*Atlanta Constitution* (1905)	Weekend railroad tickets, Atlanta to Atlantic Beach (Florida) and return	$8.85
Railroad Ticket	*Chicago Tribune* (1905)	Chicago to San Francisco; The best of everything	$33.00
Railroad Ticket	*New York Times* (1905)	New York to Washington	$12 to $14.50
Railroad Ticket	*New York Times* (1905)	New York to New Orleans for Mardi Gras (Pullman Berth/all meals); round trip	$75.00

Item	Source	Description	Price
Railroad Ticket	*New York Times* (1905)	New York to Pinehurst (Golf Championship) (Pullman Berth/all meals/3 days board at Hotel Carolina)	$35.00
Railroad Ticket	*Forestry and Irrigation* (1905)	St. Paul, Minnesota, to Billings, Montana	$20.00
Railroad Ticket	*Forestry and Irrigation* (1905)	St. Paul, Minnesota, to northern Pacific coastal points	$25.00
Railroad Ticket	*San Francisco Examiner* (1907)	Rock Island Railroad Transportation; *San Francisco* to New Orleans; round trip	$67.50
Railroad Ticket	*San Francisco Examiner* (1907)	Rock Island Railroad Transportation; San Francisco to New York	$108.50
Railroad Ticket	*New York Times* (1907)	New York to Atlantic City, lenten outings; round trip, two days' board	$10 to $12
Railroad Ticket	*The State* (Columbia, SC) (1908)	St. Louis to Portland	$35.50
Steamship	*New York Tribune* (1908)	Steamship *Yale;* fare between New York and Boston	$2.65
Steamship Fare	*New York Times* (1909)	Delightful afternoon excursion from New York to West Point; round trip	$1.00
Train	*Forestry and Irrigation* (1905)	Northern Pacific Railway; train trip to northern Pacific Coast points. From St. Paul, stopovers at will west of Billings, Montana	$25.00
Train	*New York Tribune* (1908)	Special train to Savannah Automobile Races, under direction of Twentieth Century Automobile Club, price includes sleeping accommodations and meals during trip, plus grandstand seats for both racing days	$65.00

MISCELLANY 1905–1909

Auction Results

Several rarities were included in a three day book sale which ended at the Merwin-Clayton rooms, in Eastern Twentieth Street yesterday.

A first edition of "England's Parnassus," by Robert Allot, the earliest poetical anthology of English literature, fetched $120. A first edition of Thomas Bancroft's "Two Books of Epigrammes" sold for $125.

A letter of Ferdinand and Isabella of Spain, Madrid, May 5, 1495, sold for $85. The first edition of John Gay's "Fables" brought $80. The Grolier Club's "Rubaiyat of Omar Khayyam," fetched $148. First editions of "Endymion" and "Lamia" by John Keats, sold respectively for $91 and $101. The letter of Ferdinand and Isabella is said to be the earliest original document extant in America mentioning the American Indians."

New York Times, March 1, 1905

Convenient Schedules via Western and Atlantic Railroad

From Atlanta to the following points and return at the rates named:

Lookout Mountain, Tenn.	$4.10
Dalton, Ga.	$3.00
Monteagle, Tenn.	$6.55

Atlanta Constitution, July 1905

Steam Rate War Ended

The Allen and Donaldson Steamship Lines, after a month of rate cutting, came to terms today with regard to second and third class trans-atlantic passenger tickets. The second-class rate was restored to $35, and the third class to $25.

Atlanta Constitution, August 1, 1905

Wanted to Chop Their Salaries

Somewhat of a stir was created in the House yesterday when the general appropriations bill was under discussion by an amendment offered by Mr. Knight of Berrian, proposing to reduce the salaries of the members of the railroad commission from $2,500 to $1,000 each.

Mr. Knight said $1,000 was all the railroad com missioners were worth, considering the service they rendered the state.

Atlanta Constitution, August 1, 1905

Player Sold to Atlanta

Jackson fans did not relish the parting with their star pitcher, Arthur Raymond, and some harsh things were said of the management for selling him to Atlanta.

The Jackson News said of Raymond: "The regret over Raymond's departure was not one-sided. The big fellow was all broken up over the transaction, notwithstanding the fact that it gives him a salary of $200 per month with a mighty good chance of being in the American or National League next season."

Atlanta Constitution, August 1, 1905

MISCELLANY 1905–1909

Expansion or Inflation

The National Bank Loans for the country increased $395,000,000 during 1906, this increase being almost entirely outside of New York City. A conservative banker from Dakota stated recently that his deposits had decreased because he could not bring himself to compete with his neighbors. Eighteen months ago, farms about his town were selling at $5 to $10 per acre. Now they are held at $125. He loaned only on the old valuation, while others willing to advance more secured the business.

Van Norden Magazine, April 1907

Investor Buys $1,250,000 Apartment House on Central Park West

John H. Berry has sold the Monticello Realty Company to David H. Taylor for investment, the Central Park View apartment house, at the southwest corner at Central Park West and Eighty-sixth Street, a twelve-story structure containing forty-seven apartments, on a plot 100 by 150. The price is reported to have been $1,250,000.

New York Times, March 1, 1907

$439,370 for Paintings

There was a large crowd at Christie's to-day to witness the dispersal of Sir Cuthbert Quilter's famous collection of paintings. Turner's "Venus and Adonis" brought only $20,000. This was far below anticipations, but was considerably above the price paid for the same canvas in 1885, when it sold for $9,250. In 1830 it brought only $215.

Ramney's "Portrait of Mrs. Jordan" for which Quilter had refused $80,000, brought only $24,000.

New York Times, July 25, 1909

HISTORICAL SNAPSHOT 1910–1914

1910

- Western Union abolishes the 40¢ to 50¢ charge for placing telegraph messages by telephone
- *Women's Wear Daily* begins publication in New York
- U. S. cigarette sales reach 8.6 billion cigarettes, with 62 percent controlled by the American Tobacco Trust
- Florida orange shipments rebound to 1894 level
- 70 percent of bread is baked at home, down from 80 percent in 1890
- Flexner Report shows most North American medical schools are inferior to those in Europe

1911

- California women gain suffrage by constitutional amendment
- F. W. Woolworth Co. is incorporated
- Electric self-starter for motorcar perfected and immediately adopted by Cadillac
- Chevrolet Motor Co. founded by race car driver Louis Chevrolet
- First Indianapolis 500-mile race is won by a Marmon Wasp averaging 75 miles per hour

- Carnegie Corporation of New York created through $125 million gift from Andrew Carnegie to encourage education
- Direct telephone link opens between New York and Denver
- New York's Ellis Island has a record one-day influx of 11,745 immigrants

1912

- Congress extends the 8-hour day to all federal employees
- Ford produces more than 22 percent of all U. S. motorcars
- L. L. Bean, Inc., is founded by merchant Leon Leonwood Bean
- SS *Titanic* sinks during maiden voyage
- Oreo biscuits introduced by National Biscuit Company to compete with "biscuit bon bons"
- Merger of U. S. film producers creates Universal Pictures Corp.
- A&P begins rapid expansion based on economy stores that operate on cashandcarry basis
- 1913
- Brillo Manufacturing Corp. founded

- Camel cigarettes introduced by R. J. Reynolds, creating the first modern blended cigarette
- 60-story Woolworth building opens in New York
- Congress strengthens the Pure Food and Drug Law of 1906
- Peppermint Life Savers introduced as a summer seller when chocolate sales are reduced

1914

- World War I begins in Europe
- Henry Ford offers workers a minimum wage of $5 a day
- Panama Canal opens to traffic, linking Atlantic and Pacific across 50 miles of land
- Cleveland installs red and green lights to control traffic
- Gulf Oil distributes the first U. S. automobile maps
- Consumers eat 5 pounds of butter for every pound of margarine
- Mary Phelps Jacob patents elastic brassiere, destined to replace corset

The Titanic sank in April 1912 on its route from Southamptom, England to New York City. It is the fourth deadliest peacetime maritime disaster in history. (via Wikimedia Commons)

SELECTED INCOME 1910-1914

Job	Source	Description	Pay
Accountant	*New York Times* (1911)	Bookkeeper; books opened, audited, system installed; firm not employing bookkeepers	$2.50/wk
Actress	*American Chronicle* (1999)	Mary Pickford's annual salary, following the release of the movie *Tess of the Storm Country* in 1914	$104,000
Address Collection	*Atlanta Constitution* (1914)	Men/Women, to collect all kinds of names and addresses; no canvassing	$25/week
Autoworker	*Atlanta Constitution* (1913)	Colored men taught to build automobiles	$100–$500/mo
Barber	*The New Orleans Picayune* (1912)	Good barber for Saturday and Sunday; wage guaranteed	$4
Ballroom Dancers	Tomkins, ed., *American Decades: 1910–1919* (1996)	Nightly fee for Vernon and Irene Castle in 1913	$1,000
Baseball Player	Tomkins, ed., *American Decades: 1910–1919* (1996)	Annual salary and bonus of Washington Senator pitcher Walter Johnson in 1914	$26,000
Baseball Player	Tomkins, ed., *American Decades: 1910–1919* (1996)	Average salary of a professional baseball player in 1910	$3,000
Baseball Player	Tomkins, ed., *American Decades: 1910–1919* (1996)	Annual salary of Detroit Tigers' Ty Cobb in 1910	$9,000
Bookkeeper	*San Francisco Examiner* (1913)	Complete charge of office and finance	$125/mo
Bookkeeper	New York Times (1914)	Situation Wanted: Practical accountant 14 years' experience modern methods, systematizer, seeks responsible position	$25/wk
Broadway Productions	George Cohan: *Prince of the American Theater* (1943)	Annual income of George Cohan for Broadway productions	$1.5 million
Businessman	American Chronicle (1999)	Annual salary of business executive William Gillette in 1912	$300,000
Carpenter	*San Francisco Examiner* (1913)	House carpenter, work on ranch	$3.25/day
Clerk	New York Times (1912)	Bright office boy about 16; one living within walking distance of Madison Square preferred	$5/wk
Cook	*San Francisco Examiner* (1913)	A man cook for hotel, country town	$50/mo

Job	Source	Description	Pay
Delivery Man	*Atlanta Constitution* (1913)	Colored hustler in each locality; just spare time; experience unnecessary	$100/mo
Detective	*Atlanta Constitution* (1913)	Be a detective; travel over the world	$150–$300/mo
Evangelist	Lyle W. Dorsett, *Bill Sunday and the Redemption of Urban American* (1991)	Annual income of former professional baseball player turned evangelist Billy Sunday in 1914	$200,000
Hotel Manager	*The New Orleans Picayune* (1912)	Total compensation of an assistant manager of The Hotel Plaza in New York, including payment from steamship lines and liquor distributors	$8,400
Hotel Worker	*San Francisco Examiner* (1913)	Janitor, new hotel plus room	$40/mo
Physician	*Atlanta Constitution* (1914)	For lumber company and good outside practice	$125/mo
Railway Mail Clerks	*Chicago Tribune* (1914)	Men 18–35	$75/mo
Raise Mushrooms	*Atlanta Constitution* (1913)	Anybody can earn $20 weekly; raising mushrooms, entire year, in cellars, sheds, boxes, etc.; markets waiting	$20/wk
Sales	*New York Times* (1912)	Young man, let us show you how to make $30 weekly; pleasant outdoor work; no experience necessary	$30/wk
Sales	*Chicago Tribune* (1914)	$18 monthly and expenses to travel, distribute samples and take orders or appoint agents, permanent; Jap-American Co.	$18/mo
Secretary	*Chicago Tribune* (1911)	Situation wanted: stenographer or secretary; well educated and competent; good correspondence; mechanical and sales experience; A-1 references	$90/mo
Situation Wanted	*New York Times* (1911)	Need an assistant? Am nineteen years old and want to connect with firm where attention to business will be rewarded. Want a chance to prove I am worth twelve dollars per week. Shall I call?	$12/wk
Stenographer	*Chicago Tribune* (1910)	At least one year's experience; starting salary according to ability	$10–$12/wk
Stenographer	*New York Times* (1910)	Young man, Christian, neat, careful, accurate, steady, familiar with detail work; not afraid of hard work	$12/wk
Teacher	Margo, *Race and Schooling in the South* (1990)	Average annual income of black teachers in Alabama	$311
Teacher	Margo, *Race and Schooling in the South* (1990)	Average annual income of white teachers in Alabama	$790

Job	Source	Description	Pay
Typist	*New York Times* (1911)	Young woman typist for copy work only; must be expert on Remington machine	$12/wk
World Series Earnings	*The New Orleans Picayune* (1912)	Amount paid in 1911 to each member of the Philadelphia Baseball Team for winning the World Series	$3,654.59

CONSUMER EXPENDITURES 1914

Expenditure Type	1914
Clothing	$29.52
Food	$90.34
Auto Purchases	$4.21
Auto Parts	$1.09
Gas & Oil	$2.35
Housing	$62.78
Furniture	$3.47
Utilities	$4.64
Telephone & Telegraph	$1.13
Physicians	$2.99
Dentists	$0.95
Health Insurance	NR
Personal Business	$9.86
Personal Care	$3.08
Tobacco	$7.39
Local Transport	$6.13
Intercity Transport	$3.32
Recreation	$10.06
Religion/Welfare Activities	$8.44
Private Education & Research	$4.97
Per Capita Consumption	$336.95

INVESTMENTS 1910–1914

Investment	1910	1911	1912	1913	1914
Basic Yield, One-year Corporate Bonds	4.25	4.09	4.04	4.74	4.64
Short-term Interest Rates, 4–6 Months, Prime Commercial Paper	5.72	4.75	5.41	6.20	5.47
Basic Yield, Common Stocks, Total	4.84	4.92	4.85	5.37	5.01
Index of Common Stocks (1941 — 1943=10)	9.35	9.24	9.53	8.51	8.08

COMMON STOCKS, CLOSING PRICE AND YIELD, FIRST BUSINESS DAY OF YEAR

	1910	1911	1912	1913	1914
Allis Chalmers	14 3/4	7 1/2	1 3/8	2	8 3/4
(Foreclosure 4/26/13) (assets acquired by Allis Chalmers Corp.) (1 share common exchanged for .35 share of common and 1 share preferred)					
AT&T	140 5/8	140	137 7/8	139 1/4	117 1/2
American Tobacco pfd	94 1/2	93 1/4	103	103	102
Anaconda	32 3/4	38 1/8	38 1/8	41 1/2	34 1/4
B&O	117 5/8	105 1/8	103 1/4	105 3/4	92 3/4
Bethlehem Steel	33 1/2	29	31 7/8	39 1/4	29 3/4
Corn Products	22 7/8	14 1/4	10 1/2	14 3/4	9 3/8
General Electric (30% stock dividend, 12/31/12)	159	151 1/4	153	185 1/2	139
General Motors					37 3/8
(Inc. 9/16/08; 150% stock dividend, 11/15/09)					37 3/8
Intl Harvester	117	109 1/2	109	112	101
National Biscuit	115	117	140	127	120
US Steel	89 1/8	72 1/8	69	68 7/8	58 3/8
Western Union	76 5/8	72 1/2	78 1/2	74 5/8	59 3/4

STANDARD JOBS 1910–1914

Job Type	1905	1906	1907	1908	1909
Average of All Industries, excl. farm labor	$630/yr	$629/yr	$646/yr	$675/yr	$682/yr
Average of All Industries, incl. farm labor	$574/yr	$575/yr	$592/yr	$621/yr	$627/yr
Bituminous Coal Mining	30¢/hr	31¢/hr	32¢/hr	32¢/hr	32¢/hr
Avg hrs/wk	51.60	51.60	51.60	51.60	51.60
Building Trades, Union Workers	52¢/hr	53¢/hr	54¢/hr	56¢/hr	57¢/hr
Avg hrs/wk	45.20	45	45	44.90	44.70
Clerical Workers in Mfg. & Steam RR	$1156/yr	$1213/yr	$1209/yr	$1236/yr	$1257/yr
Domestics	$337/yr	$343/yr	$350/yr	$357/yr	$355/yr
Farm Labor	$336/yr	$338/yr	$348/yr	$360/yr	$351/yr
Federal Civilian	$1096/yr	$1133/yr	$1140/yr	$1169/yr	$1197/yr
Federal Employees, Executive Depts.	$1108/yr	$1116/yr	$1128/yr	$1136/yr	$1140/yr
Finance, Insurance & Real Estate	$1301/yr	$1355/yr	$1338/yr	$1349/yr	$1368/yr
Gas & Electricity Workers	$622/yr	$648/yr	$641/yr	$661/yr	$651/yr
Lower-Skilled Labor	$506/yr	$496/yr	$521/yr	$536/yr	$492/yr
Manufacturing, Payroll	19¢/hr	19¢/hr	20¢/hr	21¢/hr	21¢/hr
Avg hrs/wk	59.80	59.60	59.30	58.80	58.30
Manufacturing, Union Workers	40¢/hr	41¢/hr	42¢/hr	43¢/hr	44¢/hr
Avg hrs/wk	50.10	49.80	49.50	49.20	48.80
Medical/Health Services Workers	$338/yr	$352/yr	$352/yr	$357/yr	$366/yr
Ministers	$856/yr	$802/yr	$879/yr	$899/yr	$938/yr

Job Type	1905	1906	1907	1908	1909
Nonprofit Org. Workers	$715/yr	$763/yr	$784/yr	$802/yr	$837/yr
Postal Employees	42¢/hr	43¢/hr	44¢/hr	45¢/hr	46¢/hr
Avg hrs/wk	48.00	48.00	48.00	48.00	48.00
Public School Teachers	$492/yr	$509/yr	$529/yr	$547/yr	$564/yr
State and Local Govt. Workers	$699/yr	$712/yr	$724/yr	$779/yr	$788/yr
Steam Railroads, Wage Earners	$677/yr	$705/yr	$721/yr	$760/yr	$795/yr
Street Railway Workers	$681/yr	$685/yr	$674/yr	$704/yr	$737/yr
Telegraph Ind. Workers	$649/yr	$670/yr	$669/yr	$717/yr	$742/yr
Telephone Ind. Workers	$417/yr	$419/yr	$438/yr	$438/yr	$476/yr
Wholesale and Retail Trade Workers	$630/yr	$666/yr	$666/yr	$685/yr	$706/yr

FOOD BASKET 1910-1914

Commodity	Year	New York	Atlanta	Chicago	Denver	Los Angeles
Beef, Rib Roasts, per pound	1910	19.33¢	20¢	17.50¢	18.33¢	20¢
	1911	19.83¢	20¢	19.33¢	18.96¢	20¢
	1912	NR	NR	NR	NR	NR
	1913	NR	NR	NR	NR	NR
	1914	NR	NR	NR	NR	NR
Beef Steaks, (Round), per pound	1910	20¢	20¢	20¢	15.83¢	15¢
	1911	20¢	20¢	16.33¢	20¢	20¢
	1912	25¢	20¢	22¢	25¢	20¢
	1913	25¢	21.10¢	20.20¢	20.90¢	20.80¢
	1914	26.30¢	22.20¢	22.40¢	21.70¢	21.20¢
Bread, Wheat, per loaf	1910	NR	NR	NR	NR	NR
	1911	NR	NR	NR	NR	NR
	1912	5¢	5¢	5¢	5¢	10¢
	1913	6.10¢	5.90¢	6.10¢	5.40¢	6.10¢
	1914	6.20¢	5.90¢	6.10¢	5.50¢	6.20¢
Butter, per pound	1910	39¢	38.33¢	36¢	36.67¢	40¢
	1911	35.17¢	37.50¢	32.17¢	33.75¢	36.25¢
	1912	43¢	37.50¢	40¢	40¢	45¢
	1913	38.20¢	39.90¢	36.20¢	37.30¢	39.60¢
	1914	36.20¢	37.40¢	33.30¢	34¢	35.80¢
Cheese, per pound	1910	NR	NR	NR	NR	NR
	1911	NR	NR	NR	NR	NR
	1912	NR	NR	NR	NR	NR
	1913	19.70¢	25¢	25.20¢	26.10¢	19.50¢
	1914	19.90¢	25¢	25.20¢	26.10¢	20¢
Chickens, per pound	1910	18.67¢	21.67¢	19.83¢	21.33¢	25¢
	1911	19.58¢	22.92¢	17.50¢	17.96¢	25¢
	1912	20¢	20¢	17¢	20¢	20¢
	1913	21.40¢	20.20¢	19.30¢	20.30¢	26.60¢
	1914	21.80¢	21.40¢	19.60¢	20.50¢	27.10¢
Coffee, per pound	1910	NR	NR	NR	NR	NR
	1911	NR	NR	NR	NR	NR
	1912	NR	NR	NR	NR	NR
	1913	27.40¢	32¢	30.50¢	29.40¢	36.30¢
	1914	26.30¢	32.80¢	30¢	29.40¢	36.30¢
Cornmeal, per pound	1910	3¢	2.78¢	3¢	2.75¢	3¢
	1911	3¢	2.68	3¢	2.58¢	2.67¢
	1912	3¢	2.50¢	3¢	2.78¢	3.50¢
	1913	3.40¢	2.50¢	2.90¢	2.50¢	3.33¢
	1914	3.50¢	2.80¢	2.80¢	2.60¢	3.60¢
Eggs, per dozen	1910	36.33¢	31.67¢	30.17¢	28.33¢	30.69¢
	1911	34.92¢	26.88¢	27.25¢	32.08¢	33.75¢
	1912	35¢	40¢	26¢	30¢	45¢
	1913	40.30¢	29.20¢	29.20¢	32¢	38.33¢
	1914	41.30¢	31.10¢	29.80¢	32¢	39.20¢

Commodity	Year	New York	Atlanta	Chicago	Denver	Los Angeles
Flour, Wheat, per one-eighth-barrel bag	1910	90¢	90¢	77.50¢	71.50¢	91.67¢
	1911	90¢	90¢	81.67¢	65.84¢	85¢
	1912	84¢	90¢	70¢	65¢	85¢
	1913	3.20¢	3.60¢	2.80¢	2.60¢	3.50¢ (per lb)
	1914	3.40¢	3.50¢	3.10¢	2.70¢	3.70¢ (per lb)
Ham, Smoked, Sliced, per pound	1910	26¢	27.83¢	24¢	33.33¢	35¢
	1911	25.33¢	28.75¢	24¢	33.75¢	35¢
	1912	28¢	30¢	30¢	25¢	35¢
	1913	29¢	29.80¢	31.80¢	30.20¢	35.30¢
	1914	30.20¢	30.30¢	32.60¢	30.60¢	35.60¢
Lard, per pound	1910	16.67¢	16.25¢	16.17¢	17.50¢	18¢
	1911	14.33¢	13.75¢	12.50¢	13.96¢	18¢
	1912	16¢	15¢	15¢	16¢	18¢
	1913	16.10¢	15.40¢	14.90¢	16.20¢	18¢
	1914	15.70¢	15.60¢	15.10¢	15.90¢	17.50¢
Milk, Fresh, per quart	1910	8.50¢	9.44¢	8¢	8.33¢	9¢
	1911	9¢	10¢	8¢	8.33¢	9.92¢
	1912	9¢	10¢	8¢	8.33¢	10¢
	1913	9¢	10.20¢	8¢	8.40¢	10¢
	1914	9¢	10.30¢	8¢	8.40¢	10¢
Mutton and Lamb, per pound	1910	17.67¢	19.79¢	17.67¢	16.83¢	16¢
	1911	16¢	20¢	17.42¢	16¢	16¢
	1912	16.50¢	20¢	18¢	15¢	17¢
	1913	16.50¢	20.10¢	19.80¢	16.40¢	18.80¢
	1914	16.50¢	20.20¢	19.80¢	17.10¢	19.10¢
Pork, Bacon, Sliced, per pound	1910	25.50¢	27.83¢	28¢	33.33¢	34.17¢
	1911	23.83¢	28.75¢	28¢	33.75¢	34.17¢
	1912	24¢	30¢	28¢	30¢	35¢
	1913	25.10¢	31.70¢	31.60¢	28.30¢	33.70¢
	1914	25.80¢	31¢	31.70¢	28.80¢	34.10¢
Pork Chops, per pound	1910	19.33¢	21.67¢	17.33¢	17.50¢	20¢
	1911	17.83¢	19.79¢	15.25¢	16.88¢	20¢
	1912	20¢	20¢	16¢	17.50¢	25¢
	1913	21.50¢	23.10¢	19¢	19.50¢	25.10¢
	1914	22.90¢	23.50¢	19.80¢	20.80¢	26¢
Potatoes, Irish, per pound	1910	NR	NR	NR	NR	NR
	1911	NR	NR	NR	NR	NR
	1912	40¢ (per peck)	27.50¢ per peck)	20¢ (per 15 lbs)	$1.25 (per100 lbs)	$1.25 (per 100 lbs)
	1913	2.50¢	2.20¢	1.60¢	1.40¢	1.50¢
	1914	2.63¢	2.40¢	1.70¢	1.70¢	1.80¢
Rice, per pound	1910	NR	NR	NR	NR	NR
	1911	NR	NR	NR	NR	NR
	1912	NR	NR	NR	NR	NR
	1913	8¢	8.60¢	8.90¢	8.60¢	7.70¢
	1914	8.30¢	8.60¢	9¢	8.60¢	8¢
Sugar, per pound	1910	5.43¢	5.83¢	5.71¢	6.13¢	6.53¢
	1911	5.91¢	6.44¢	6.50¢	6.54¢	6.28¢
	1912	5.43¢	5.88¢	5.50¢	6¢	5.88¢
	1913	4.90¢	5.70¢	5.10¢	5.50¢	5.40¢
	1914	5.30¢	6.10¢	5.60¢	5.70¢	5.90¢
Tea, per pound	1910	NR	NR	NR	NR	NR
	1911	NR	NR	NR	NR	NR
	1912	NR	NR	NR	NR	NR
	1913	43.30¢	60¢	54¢	52.80¢	54.50¢
	1914	43.33¢	60¢	54.30¢	52.80¢	54.50¢

SELECTED PRICES 1910–1914

Item	Source	Description	Price
ALCOHOL			
Whiskey	*The New Orleans Daily Picayune*	*Hayner Bottled-in-Bond Whiskey;* per quart (1912)	$0.80
Whiskey	*The New Orleans Daily Picayune* (1910)	*Duffy's Pure Malt;* it corrects the defective digestion of the food, increases the appetite, strengthens the heart	$1.00/ bottle
APPAREL, CHILDREN'S			
Army Uniform	*Sears, Roebuck* (1912)	Boy's; the regular army play suit of olive-colored khaki drill	$1.50
Baby Wear	*New York Times* (1910)	*Abraham and Straus;* lawn dress	$0.98
Dress	*Sears, Roebuck* (1913)	Girl's shepherd check; cut in one-piece sailor style with sailor collar	$1.65
Fabric	*Ladies' Home Journal* (1911)	All wool dress serge. Dressmakers' width for family use	$0.75/yard
Hat	*Sears, Roebuck* (1910)	Washable; the entire brim of this hat is of fluted mall, with full double ruffle on edge	$0.44
Hose	*Ladies' Home Journal* (1911)	*Black Cat Hosiery*—a beautiful, fine mercerized hose Girls, per pair	$0.35
Hose Support	*Ladies' Home Journal* (1911)	*Wilson;* children can't stand restraining clothing; that's why their garters are important for comfort	$0.25
Infant's Pants	*Ladies' Home Journal* (1911)	*OMO;* a dainty, comfortable garment that will keep baby's clothes dry and clean	$0.25
Knee Pants	*John M. Smyth Company* (1911)	Boys; these pants are actually worth 75¢—$1.25 per pair	$0.45
Knitted Legging Drawers	*Sears, Roebuck* (1913)	Drawstring at waist	$0.19
Long Cambric Slip	*Sears, Roebuck* (1913)	Infant's; trimmed with lace edge on neck and sleeves	$0.09
Night Gown	*The New Orleans Daily Picayune* (1912)	Soft, fleecy flannelette nightgown	$0.22
Overall Suit	*Sears, Roebuck* (1912)	*Rip-Proof;* neat gray-stripe denim	$1.40
Overcoat	*Sears, Roebuck* (1912)	*Ucanttear;* of strong wool and cotton fabric	$1.75
Stockings	*Sears, Roebuck* (1913)	Girl's tearproof; elastic ribbed black cotton stockings	$0.19

Item	Source	Description	Price
Sweater	*The New Orleans Daily Picayune* (1912)	All-wool sweaters, sizes 20 to 34	$0.50

APPAREL, MEN'S

Item	Source	Description	Price
Automobile Duster	*John M. Smyth Company* (1911)	Man's fancy; made from fancy herring-bone striped natural linen	$1.95
Boots	*The New Orleans Daily Picayune* (1912)	*Dull Calf Blucher boots;* heavy, double sole; splendid shoes for businessmen	$2.45
Coat	*John M. Smyth* Company (1911)	*Alpaca;* the ideal hot weather coat	$1.95
Coat	*John M. Smyth Company* (1911)	English slip-on motor coat; made from fine imported English Roseberry cloth	$10.98
Coat	*John M. Smyth Company* (1911)	*Storm King Mackintosh;* single-breasted with fly front wide black velvet collars, fancy woven plaid lining	$3.98
Coat	*John M. Smyth Company* (1911)	Ministerial coat; made from black Drap D'Ete cloth	$5.00
Coat	*John M. Smyth Company* (1911)	*Presto Model Cravenette Raincoat;* fine black broadcloth	$16.50
Coat	*Sears, Roebuck* (1912)	Sheepskin-lined corduroy; with sheepskin collars	$4.95
Coat	*Sears, Roebuck* (1912)	Waterproof brown duck; made from 8-ounce duck with heavy fancy blanket lining and oiled slicker cloth	$2.10
Coat	*Sears, Roebuck* (1913)	Sweater coat; in popular zig-zag style	$2.48
Collars	*Sears, Roebuck* (1913)	Low style, lots of tie space	$0.59/6
Hat	*Sears, Roebuck* (1913)	*Cornwell;* Lennox Jr. style black or nutria tan	$2.00
Overcoat	*New York Times* (1910)	*Hart, Schaffner and Marx;* large size 40–52	$12.50
Overcoat	*John M. Smyth Company* (1911)	Grey vicuna cloth; full silk lined	$18.00
Pajamas	*Sears, Roebuck* (1913)	Quality madras trimmed with frog fasteners and large pearl buttons	$1.45
Scarf	*Sears, Roebuck* (1913)	Shetland wool motor scarf; veil in medium size mesh with face-knitted border; size about 20" × 54"	$1.05
Suit	*John M. Smyth Company* (1911)	*Glory B;* satin-lined blue serge; the most wonderful suit of the century	$7.98
Suit	*John M. Smyth Company* (1911)	*Smyth Made Model 86;* three-piece, fancy, olive, striped, worsted; a tasteful, elegant, and dressy pattern	$7.98

Item	Source	Description	Price
Suit	*John M. Smyth Company* (1911)	Young man's biplane model; navy blue serge three piece	$7.98
Support Hose	*Sears, Roebuck* (1913)	Elastic; exceptionally good value at $0.25 a pair	$0.12/pair
Trousers	*John M. Smyth Company* (1911)	*Smyth Made Model K;* novelty smoke-gray fancy striped worsted trousers	$3.00
Trousers	*John M. Smyth Company* (1911)	*U.S.A. Khaki;* more popular this season than ever before	$0.98
Trousers	*John M. Smyth Company* (1911)	College style, peg top; made from extra-fine all-wool fancy cassimere	$3.50
Umbrella	*Sears, Roebuck* (1913)	Genuine paragon steel frames with mixed silk taffeta cover and selected boxwood handle	$2.25
Undershirt	*Sears, Roebuck* (1913)	Winter fleeced; extra heavy flat-knit cotton	$0.44
Vest	*John M. Smyth Company* (1911)	Men's fancy vest; every man should have one or two fancy vests in his wardrobe	$1.48
Work Shirt	*Sears, Roebuck* (1913)	Khaki tan; double-yoke shoulders	$0.45

Advertisement for Adler-Rochester Clothes from The Saturday Evening Post, *August 13, 1910.*

Item	Source	Description	Price
APPAREL, WOMEN'S			
Blouse	*Sears, Roebuck* (1913)	Sweater blouse; has high fitting turndown collar	$1.19
Coat	*Sears, Roebuck* (1913)	Furlike; black boucle cloth coat (imitation Persian lamb)	$13.95
Coat	*Sears, Roebuck* (1913)	Misses winter weight; heavy gray cloth coat, double texture plaid trimmed	$8.95
Corset	*Sears, Roebuck* (1910)	Long hip style; our Frances model gives the straight slender effect which is so much desired	$1.38
Corset	*Ladies' Home Journal* (1911)	*W. B. Nuform;* for average or full figures; low bust and low under arms	$2.00
Corset	*Ladies' Home Journal* (1911)	*W. B. Reduso;* for average large figures; medium high bust, long over hips and abdomen	$3.00
Corset	*Ladies' Home Journal* (1911)	Nuform, Style 101—for average figures. Medium high bust, long over hips and back	$1.50
Dress	*The New Orleans Daily Picayune* (1910)	Silk; Pongees, in natural color and light summery shades	$10.95
Dress	*Sears, Roebuck* (1913)	Misses lace-trimmed mohair; looks worth fully twice the price we ask	$5.15
Furs	*The New Orleans Daily Picayune* (1912)	Exclusive Shop; Eastern mink set, regularly $300; on sale	$270
Gloves	*Sears, Roebuck* (1910)	Gauntlet	$0.06
Gloves	*Ladies' Home Journal* (1911)	*Fownes;* silk; it's a Fownes—that's all you need to know about a glove	$0.50
Gloves	*The State* (Columbia, SC) (1911)	Open at wrist 2-clasp, elegant quality pure silk, 16-button length	$0.69
Gloves	*Sears, Roebuck* (1913)	Lined fabric; imported black cashmerette gloves	$0.23
Hair Net	*Ladies' Home Journal* (1911)	*Con-tour;* very convenient and stylish; a favorite with fashionable ladies everywhere	$0.15
Handkerchief	*Sears, Roebuck* (1910)	White Swiss embroidered scalloped handkerchiefs	$0.14
Hat	*New York Times* (1910)	Poke bonnet; made of fancy black braid, trimmed with cluster of royal and pink roses, and silver-lace foliage	$27.89
Hat	*Sears, Roebuck* (1913)	Dressy; a charming poke style turban	$3.15
Hat Pins	*The New Orleans Daily Picayune* (1910)	Rhinestone; a splendid selection of attractive styles	$0.50
Hose	*Ladies' Home Journal* (1911)	*Gordon Dollar Silk;* pure thread silk, heavy lisle soles, heel and toe, extra garter hem protection	$1.00
Muff	*Sears, Roebuck* (1912)	Opossum fur; made in large well-padded semi-barrel style	$8.25
Nightgown	*Sears, Roebuck* (1913)	Misses; very fine quality nainsook Empire style	$0.99

Item	Source	Description	Price
Ostrich Plume	*The New Orleans Daily Picayune* (1912)	Bull Head four-tie willow ostrich plume, black only	$18.00
Petticoat	*New York Times* (1910)	Satin	$7.75
Petticoat	*The New Orleans Daily Picayune* (1910)	White; nainsook tops, lawn flounces	$1.69
Petticoat	*Ladies' Home Journal* (1911)	*Klosfit;* made so that it fits the figure as a silk glove fits the hand	$1.00
Petticoat	*Sears, Roebuck* (1913)	Made of splendid cotton fabric, closely woven	$1.48
Purse	*Sears, Roebuck* (1913)	Silk velvet; ninety-nine steel studs, silver English frame 8"×7"	$1.65
Shoes	*The New Orleans Daily Picayune* (1912)	Maison Blanche Queen Quality shoes; no matter the occasion, whether walking, street or dress wear, you'll find a style suited to your needs	$3.50 to $5.00
Shoes	*The New Orleans Daily Picayune* (1910)	*Queen Quality;* fifty new styles	$3.50
Shoes	*Ladies' Home Journal* (1911)	*Red Cross;* the Red Cross shoe never needs breaking in; You can put it on in the store and wear it home; Oxford style	$3.50
Skirt	*Ladies' Home Journal* (1911)	The *National Maternity Skirt* makes possible outdoor exercise, fresh air, sunshine and health for the prospective mother.	$5.98 to $10.00
Skirt	*Ladies' Home Journal* (1911)	*National Maternity;* it does away with the stay-at-home, the gloom and depression of the maternity period	$5.98
Skirt	*Sears, Roebuck* (1913)	Panama style; made in popular straight hanging style with full length front panel	$2.89
Suit	*New York Times* 1910)	*O'Neill Adams Spring Suit;* an exceedingly smart suit of French serge, with the full-length of coat	$29.75
Supporter	*Ladies' Home Journal* (1911)	Princess Chic supporter produces ideal figure lines State waist measure	$0.50 to $1.00
Union Suit	*Sears, Roebuck* (1913)	Winter weight; elastic-ribbed fleece-lined union suit	$0.48

APPLIANCES

Item	Source	Description	Price
Vacuum Cleaner	*Ladies' Home Journal* (1911)	*Eureka;* no other indoor dry method of cleaning than suction can make your home really clean	$35.00
Vacuum Cleaner	*Sears, Roebuck* (1912)	*Eckhardt;* makes clean houses cleaner	$46.75

BABY PRODUCTS

Item	Source	Description	Price
Baby Walker	*Ladies' Home Journal* (1911)	*E-Z-GO Baby Tender.* Teaches baby to walk in the easy way. Does a large part of a nurse's children's work Express, prepaid	$2.75
Bottle	*Ladies' World* 1910	*Hygeia* nursing bottle, only bottle with a breast; germs of disease have no hiding place 8-ounce bottle and nipple 12-ounce bottle and nipple	$0.38 $0.50

Item	Source	Description	Price
Diaper Cover	*Sears, Roebuck* (1913)	Of white cambric, coated with a specially prepared composition making it waterproof	$0.35
Nipples	*Sears, Roebuck* (1912)	Best black rubber nipples to fit over neck of nursing bottle	$0.10/3
Portable Folding Bathtub	*Sears, Roebuck* (1913)	Tub when open is 36" long, 22" high and 16" wide	$4.98
Wrapper	*The New Orleans Daily Picayune* (1912)	Infant's fleece-lined knit wrapper	$0.17

BUSINESS EQUIPMENT & SUPPLIES

Item	Source	Description	Price
Express Mail Flat Rate	*The New Orleans Daily Picayune* (1912)	Express charge for any package, up to 11 pounds, in United States	$0.27
Typewriter Rentals	*New York Times* (1910)	$100 machines; rental allowed to apply if purchased	$3/mo
Wagon	*The New Orleans Picayune* (1912)	Top delivery wagon	$97.00

COLLECTIBLES

Item	Source	Description	Price
Painting	*American Chronicle* (1999)	Claude Monet's *Fishing Boats*; sold at auction in 1910	$240
Painting	*American Chronicle* (1999)	Rembrandt's *Portrait of Admiral Campbell*; sold at auction in 1910	$4,400
Spade	*The New Orleans Daily Picayune* (1912)	Shovel used by Jane Addams to open The Priscilla Inn, a hotel home for self-supporting women in 1912; spade sold in auction	$900

EDUCATION

Item	Source	Description	Price
Tuition	*American Decades* (1911)	Harvard University	$150/year
Tuition	*American Decades* (1911)	Colgate University	$60.00/year
Tuition	*The Magazine of Wall Street* (1913)	*Raymond Riordon School* (Highland, New York); high school, college preparatory, special courses and department for younger boys	$800

ENTERTAINMENT

Item	Source	Description	Price
Aviation Exhibition	*New York Tribune* (1911)	International Aviation Meet; thirty world-famous men and women aviators demonstrate speed, duration and altitude Admission Seats at starting line Auto space	 $0.50 $1.00 $5.00
Baseball Game	*The New Orleans Picayune* (1912)	Greenwall Theatre; World Series baseball games played on stage by electrical scoreboard; also Monster Burlesque Show Night prices and Ball Game matinees	$0.10 to $0.50
Concert Ticket	*New York Times* (1910)	*Carnegie Hall*; Sembrich Frank LaForge at piano	$2.50
Festival Ticket	*New Orleans Daily Picayune* (1910)	*Grand May Festival and Picnic* at Southern Park; given by the Gardners' Mutual Protective Association; admission to grounds	$0.25 to $1.00

Item	Source	Description	Price
Musical	*The New Orleans Picayune* (1912)	*The Balkan Princess*; includes a special orchestra Nights	$0.25 to $1.50
Musical Comedy	*The New Orleans Daily Picayune* (1912)	*Louisiana Lou* by the La Salle Opera-House Company at Tulane Nights and Saturday matinee, per seat	$0.25 to $1.50
Play	*The New Orleans Daily Picayune* (1912)	*The Confession*; from a successful run at the Broadway Bijou Theatre, New York Nights, seats	$0.15 to $0.75
Theater Ticket	*New Orleans Daily Picayune* (1910)	*American Music Hall*; summer season popular vaudeville; this week Albert Wild, Hilman & Roberts, George Smedley and other features; all seats	$0.10
Theater Ticket	*New York Times* (1910)	*Metropolis;* Harry Bryant's Burlesque Co.	$0.35
Theater Ticket	*New York Times* (1910)	New Amsterdam Theatre; *Madame X;* supreme drama of tears and thrills, best seats	$1.50
Theater Ticket	*New York Times* (1910)	The New Theatre; *The School for Scandal,* Sheridan's delightful comedy	$0.50
Theater Ticket	*San Francisco Examiner* (1913)	Henry W. Savage's play, *The Merry Widow,* all-star revival	$0.50 to $2.00
Theater Ticket	*San Francisco Examiner* (1913)	Thomas A. Edison's Talking Moving Pictures, exclusively at The Orpheum	$0.10 to $1.00

ENTERTAINMENT, HOME

Item	Source	Description	Price
Card Game	*Sears, Roebuck* (1912)	*Old Maid;* too well known to need description	$0.19
Crayons	*Sears, Roebuck* (1913)	*Paragon Drawing;* twenty-eight colors	$0.04
Dominoes	*Sears, Roebuck* (1912)	*Black Cat;* high-grade black composition double six dominoes	$0.33
Game	*Sears, Roebuck* (1912)	*Jolly Coon Race;* a new and very comical game for two or three people; metal figures of darkies with moveable arms, racing along three poles	$0.89
Record	*The Magazine of Wall Street* (1913)	*Columbia Double Disc Phonograph;* fits your machine	$0.65

Columbia Phonograph Company, founded in 1887, began mass-producing their "Double-Faced" discs in 1908, played on the Columbia Granfola "Regent," pictured above. Columbia Phonograph Co. became Columbia Records, which represented such performers as Duke Ellington, ABBA, Alicia Keys, Frank Ocean and others. (via Wikimedia Commons)

Item	Source	Description	Price
Statue	*Sears, Roebuck* (1912)	Musical negroes; darkies playing accordion and flute	$0.98
Talking Machine	*Sears, Roebuck* (1912)	*J. F Oxford;* flower-shaped metal horn, 18" in diameter	$14.95

FARM EQUIPMENT & SUPPLIES

Item	Source	Description	Price
Egg Incubator and Brooder	*Ladies' Home Journal* (1911)	Hot water, copper tanks, double walls, double glass doors, freight paid east of Rockies; 125 egg capacity	$10.00
Milk Bucket	*Sears, Roebuck* (1910)	Tin; flaring open-top pail; 4 1/2 quart capacity	$0.08

FINANCIAL PRODUCTS & SERVICES

Item	Source	Description	Price
Interest Rate	*The New Orleans Picayune* (1912)	Interstate Bank interest payment on savings accounts	4%

FOOD PRODUCTS

Item	Source	Description	Price
Candy	*Sears, Roebuck* (1912)	Peanut Butter Kisses; Preferred by many to the usual taffy; 2 1/2 pound box	$0.46
Cereal	*Ladies' World* 1910	Gigantic kernels of wheat or rice puffed to eight times natural size. Made so porous and crisp that they melt in the mouth Puffed wheat Puffed rice	 $0.10 $0.15
Chocolate	*Ladies' World* 1910	*Baker's Caracas Sweet Chocolate,* a delightful combination of the highest-grade cocoa, pure sugar and vanilla, one package	$0.10
Cracker	*New York Times* (1910)	*Uneeda Biscuit;* made today and packaged snugly in their protecting package	$0.05
Marshmallows	*Sears, Roebuck* (1912)	200 finest soft delicious marshmallows in a box	$0.42
Seasoning	*The New Orleans Daily Picayune* (1910)	*Genuine Creole;* there is no trouble; nothing to learn; regular-size bottle	$0.25
Soup	*Ladies' Home Journal* (1911)	*Campbell's Soup*—a perfect dinner course; 21 kinds	$0.10
Soup	*Ladies' Home Journal* (1911)	Tomato; the way to his heart	$0.10
Wafers	*Overland Monthly* (1910)	*Nabisco Sugar Wafers;* always in good form Two sizes	$0.10 and $0.25

FURNITURE

Item	Source	Description	Price
Bed	*San Francisco Examiner* (1913)	High-class sleigh bed in mahogany or circassian walnut	$39.50
Chair	*The New Orleans Daily Picayune* (1910)	Porch rocker; double cane seat and back, with wide arms and seat	$2.25
Chair	*Ladies' Home Journal* (1911)	*Come-Packt Morris;* in quartered white oak—save half or more buying direct from our factory	$8.75
Chair	*Sears, Roebuck* (1912)	Bowback wooden kitchen chair; made of especially selected northern hardwood	$0.78

Item	Source	Description	Price
Chair	*Sears, Roebuck* (1912)	Morris rocker; solid comfort every minute	$5.35
Furniture Package	*The New Orleans Daily Picayune* (1910)	4-Room outfit consisting of full bedroom suite, Dining suite, parlor suite and kitchen outfit	$147.50
Kitchen Cabinet	*Sears, Roebuck* (1912)	*Wilson Oak;* cupboard and kitchen table in a single piece of furniture	$23.85
Lamp	*Sears, Roebuck* (1912)	*Art Glass;* electric portable; wired complete with chain pull socket	$7.50
Mirror	*The New Orleans Daily Picayune* (1910)	*Chiffonier;* mirror 14" × 22 ", double shaped top 20" ×36 "; full-quartered oak with golden finish, serpentine front	$14.90
Table	*Sears, Roebuck* (1912)	Parlor; made of seasoned quarter sawed oak	$2.85
Tea Wagon	*The Magazine of Wall Street* (1913)	*Willow;* painted to match chintz	$16.50
Turkish Bath Cabinet	*New York Times* (1910)	The best means in the world for breaking up colds or grippe	$4.50 to $18

GARDEN EQUIPMENT & SUPPLIES

Item	Source	Description	Price
Manure Spreader	*Sears, Roebuck* (1912)	*David Bradley;* when not needed to spread, lift off box and you have a splendid farm truck with wheel truck	$69.50
Potato Planter	*Sears, Roebuck* (1912)	*Schofield;* all iron and steel except pole	$19.85

HOTEL RATES

Item	Source	Description	Price
Hotel Room	*The Magazine of Wall Street* (1913)	*Hotel Puritan;* Boston; a public house for those who demand the best single rooms	$2.00/day
Room	*The New Orleans Daily Picayune* (1912)	*Hotel Victoria;* fronting on Fifth Avenue and Broadway, New York City; all rooms have hot and cold running water Rooms Rooms with bath	 $1.50 $2.00
Room	*Overland Monthly* (1910)	*Hotel Normandie,* San Francisco, California; fine air, elevation, location American plan, per day European plan, per day	 $3.00 $1.50
Room	*Overland Monthly* (1910)	*Hotel St. Francis,* San Francisco, California European plan, per day	$2.00
Room	*Overland Monthly* (1910)	*Hotel Windsor,* 308–310 West 58th Street, New York; 100 feet from Broadway; 100 suites, each with bath Per day	 $2.50-$10.00

HOUSEHOLD PRODUCTS

Item	Source	Description	Price
Ammonia	*Sears, Roebuck* (1912)	*Violet;* for the toilet and bath	$0.17
Bedspread	*Sears, Roebuck* (1910)	Pure white, hemmed, crochet, bedspread; 68" × 79"	$0.68

Item	Source	Description	Price
Blanket	*Sears, Roebuck* (1912)	All-wool; splendid wearing qualities and rich appearance	$3.98
Cake Turner	*Sears, Roebuck* (1913)	Steel; length about 12	$0.02
China	*New York Tribune* (1911)	White and gold monogrammed china; 100-piece dinner set with coin gold border	$52.50
Cistern	*The New Orleans Daily Picayune* (1911)	*Cypress cistern,* in good order	$6.50
Cleanser	*Ladies' Home Journal* (1911)	Scour pots and pans with *Old Dutch Cleanser* Large sifter can	$0.10
Couch Covers	*Sears, Roebuck* (1912)	Tapestry; in rich oriental design 2 7/8 yds long by 56" wide	$1.75
Desk	*Sears, Roebuck* (1912)	*Simplex;* single desk; one of our most stable and durable patterns	$1.75
Finish	*Ladies' Home Journal* (1911)	*Johnson's Under-Lac;* a thin, elastic spirit finish far superior to varnish or shellac	$0.70/quart
Flashlight	*Sears, Roebuck* (1912)	*Ever Ready;* the most efficient flashlight of its size ever made with Merchlor battery	$0.98
Floor Wax	*Sears, Roebuck* (1912)	*Seroco;* dirt and dust will not stick to floors waxed with Seroco floor wax	$0.22/ pound can
Hammer	*Sears, Roebuck* (1912)	*Fulton Special;* solid tool steel, full nickel plated; 13 oz.	$0.66
Inlaid Linoleum	*Sears, Roebuck* (1912)	Fine quality domestic inlaid linoleum	$2.35/yard
Lamp Burner	*Sears, Roebuck* (1913)	Brass; by including these items with other goods you usually get them without paying any more freight	$0.04
Lavatory	*Sears, Roebuck* (1912)	Porcelain-enameled one-piece square with nickel-plated model waste and wall hanger	$8.40
Paint	*Sears, Roebuck* (1910)	For entire house; this cottage measures 18' wide × 32' long and 12' high; for body 4 gallons, for trimming 1 gallon	$4.90/ gallon

The text from this 1911 advertisement reads: "The magnificent salons of the monster S. S. Lusitania and of the Great Lakes passenger vessel, Hamonic. the ball-room of the Brooklyn Academy of Music, the New York Public Library, and the New Theatre are notable examples of the extensive use of Vitralite." (via Wikimedia Commons)

Item	Source	Description	Price
Pot Holder	*Sears, Roebuck* (1913)	Iron; asbestos filled	$0.02
Potato Baker	*Ladies' Home Journal* (1911)	*Handi-Kwick;* saves burning your arms and hands, bakes six at a time	$0.10
Rug	*New York Times* (1910)	*Joseph Wild Prairie;* a superior weave of tough grass; carried in plain green or brown; 4' × 7'	$9.50
Shovel	*Sears, Roebuck* (1910)	*Invincible D Handle;* plain back, solid steel	$0.48
Silverware	*The State* (Columbia, SC) (1911)	*1847 Rogers Brothers;* knives and forks warranted 16-dwt pure silver on every dozen (6 knives and 6 forks)	$3.93/ dozen
Soap	*Ladies' Home Journal* (1911)	*Grandma;* borax powdered; Grandma is not a washing powder but a powdered soap	$0.05
Soap	*Sears, Roebuck* (1912)	*Lifebuoy;* removes the dirt you see while destroying the germs which you cannot see	$0.51/12 cakes
Suitcase	*Sears, Roebuck* (1913)	Lightweight cane made over strong wood frame	$4.95

Item	Source	Description	Price
Toilet Paper	*Sears, Roebuck* (1912)	*Jewel;* about 1,000 sheets to roll	$0.27/6 rolls
Trunk	*Sears, Roebuck* (1913)	*Gibraltar;* guaranteed to last a lifetime of ordinary service; 38" × 22" × 24"	$16.95
Umbrella	*New York Times* (1910)	*Abraham and Straus;* woman's style	$2.74
Wallpaper	*Sears, Roebuck* (1912)	*The Eugenia;* red and pink roses in a frame of gilt Border Ceiling	 $0.02 $0.15
Wallpaper	*New York Tribune* (1911)	Fine foreign wallpapers; values $1 to $4; sold in room lot; Now	$0.25 a piece
Wood Stain	*The Magazine of Wall Street* (1913)	*Devoe* wood stain; ready for use after dissolving in water	$0.50/can

INSURANCE RATES

Item	Source	Description	Price
Fire Insurance	*Insurance Policy* (1911)	Rate 2.51; $250 coverage fire damage on brick and frame one-story building in Columbia, SC	$6.27/year

JEWELRY

Item	Source	Description	Price
Diamond Ring	*The New Orleans Daily Picayune* (1910)	Man's solitaire; pure blue-white stone; perfect in cut	$100
Diamonds	*The New Orleans Picayune* (1912)	*Weinfurter's;* blue tinged, finest white diamonds; weight 7/8 and 1/16 carat stone	$185
Watch	*The New Orleans Picayune* (1912)	Waltham gold pocket watch; seventeen jewels	$10.50

MEDICAL PRODUCTS & SERVICES

Item	Source	Description	Price
Dental Crowns	*The New Orleans Daily Picayune* (1912)	*Union Dental Company;* highest quality and workmanship Per tooth	$4.00
False Teeth	*The New Orleans Daily Picayune* (1912)	*Union Dental Company;* a good set of teeth on a rubber base, guaranteed to wear well Per set	$5.00
Laxative	*The New Orleans Daily Picayune* (1912)	*Castoria;* for infants and children; a vegetable preparation for stimulating the food and regulating the stomach and bowels 35 doses per bottle	$0.35

The top of this laxative advertisement can be pulled up to show the laxative in the girl's mouth. (via Wikimedia Commons)

Item	Source	Description	Price
Liquor Cure	*The State* (Columbia, SC) (1911)	From the third day after I started treatment, I can honestly say I have had no desire for a drink of whiskey or beer; includes board, lodging, and necessary attention	$35/mo
Nonprescription Drug	*Sears, Roebuck* (1912)	Elixir pepsin compound; pleasant to take and largely sold for indigestion and stomach complaints	$0.49/16-ounce bottle
Teething Powders	*Ladies' World* (1910)	*Dr. Steedmen's Teething Powders,* absolutely free from morphia or any other alkaloid or constituent of opium; One packet	$0.25

MOTORIZED VEHICLES, SERVICES, & SUPPLIES

Item	Source	Description	Price
Automobile	Throm, ed., *Popular Mechanics Picture History of American Transportation* (1952)	*Black Crow;* biggest, handsomest, greatest value cars ever offered for these prices, 25–30hp	$1,000
Automobile	Joseph J. Schroeder Jr., *The Wonderful World of Automobiles* (1971)	*Franklin 1910;* only one percent of the roads in this country is macadam; the rest are ordinary dirt roads; do you want an automobile that is comfortable only on macadam roads or on all roads?; 4-cylinder, 28 hp, five-passenger touring car	$2,800
Automobile	Schroeder, *The Wonderful World of Automobiles* (1971)	*Glide Special;* 7-passenger, 45 hp touring car [cost in 1910]	$2,500
Automobile	*New York Times* (1910)	*Marmon Thirty-two;* 5-passenger touring car, shaft drive, double system ignition; the positive car	$2,700
Automobile	*New York Times* (1910)	*Mora;* there is no other power plant like it	$1,050
Automobile	*New York Times* (1910)	*Paige-Detroit;* a low-priced, high-powered roadster that at once satisfies the power crank, the speed fiend, and the endurance runner	$800
Automobile	Schroeder, *The Wonderful World of Automobiles* (1971)	*Rambler;* featuring the offset crank-shaft, straight-line drive, spare wheel and new expanding clutch [cost in 1910]	$1,800
Automobile	Schroeder, *The Wonderful World of Automobiles* (1971)	*Sears Motor Car;* so simple that anyone can operate; Model H, 14 hp, air-cooled motor [cost in 1910]	$395
Automobile	Schroeder, *The Wonderful World of Automobiles* (1971)	*American Underslung Traveler Special;* six passengers, the last word in grace and beauty [cost in 1912]	$4,500
Automobile	Schroeder, *The Wonderful World of Automobiles* (1971)	*Elmore Torpedo;* five-passenger light torpedo with top and windshield [cost in 1912]	$1,350
Automobile	Schroeder, *The Wonderful World of Automobiles* (1971)	*Garford Six;* electrically started; all lights are electric; the horn is electric, 60 hp, five-passenger touring car [cost in 1913]	$2,750

Item	Source	Description	Price
Automobile	Schroeder, *The Wonderful World of Automobiles* (1971)	*Jackson*; no hill too steep no sand too deep, 50 hp, 4 cylinder motor, five-passenger [cost in 1913]	$1,800
Automobile	Schroeder, *The Wonderful World of Automobiles* (1971)	*Maxwell Mercury*; an ideal car for touring [cost in 1913]	$1,150
Automobile	Schroeder, *The Wonderful World of Automobiles* (1971)	*Oakland Greyhound*; four-, five-, and seven-passenger touring cars [cost in 1913]	$2,550
Machine Oil	*Sears, Roebuck* (1913)	Best grade of mineral oil for light machinery	$0.06/3 oz.
Transmission Grease	*Sears, Roebuck* (1912)	We cannot use the manufacturer's name for the reason that we are selling it at a greatly reduced price	$0.80/5 lb.
Used Automobile	*The New Orleans Daily Picayune* (1912)	*Stoddard-Dayton* touring car; five-passenger; fully equipped	$600
Windshield	Schroeder, *The Wonderful World of Automobiles* (1971)	*Mezger Automatic*; up or down with one hand without slackening speed [cost in 1910]	$25.00

MUSICAL INSTRUMENTS

Item	Source	Description	Price
Piano	*The New Orleans Daily Picayune* (1912)	Steinway baby grand piano	$2,000
Piano-Organ	*Sears, Roebuck* (1912)	*Beckwith Queen*; leads all others in quality, finish, design and tone	$68.00
Violin	*Sears, Roebuck* (1912)	*Stradivarius Model*; violin outfits of this grade are generally sold for $35	$19.95

OTHER

Item	Source	Description	Price
Film Developer	*The Ladies' World* (1910)	Hayden film tank, the best, simplest and most improved film tank on the market Film printing frame Convertible plate tank 5 3 7	 $0.75 $1.75
Home Plans	*Ladies' Home Journal* (1911)	*MacLagan's*; suburban; 200 building plans of bungalows, suburban and country homes, actually erected costing from $400 up to $10,000; plans and specifications	$5 and up
Mask	*Sears, Roebuck* (1912)	Santa Claus; fancy waxed-cloth mask with heavy eyebrows	$0.09
Plumes	*Ladies' Home Journal* (1911)	French; carefully selected raw material from the male bird; full 15	$1.90
Prize, Billiards Match	*New Orleans Daily Picayune* (1910)	Championship; Harry P. Cline, of Philadelphia, the present title holder at 18.2 balk line billiards, has agreed to meet Willie Hoppe for the world's championship; prize includes championship emblem	$1,000
Wrapping Paper	*Sears, Roebuck* (1912)	Christmas Bells; Red tissue paper; beautiful for Christmas decoration	$0.09/2

Item	Source	Description	Price
PERSONAL CARE PRODUCTS			
Cluster Puffs	*Ladies' Home Journal* (1911)	*Recamier*; just send us a lock of your hair and we will send you this lovely set of Recamier Cluster Puffs	$2.85
Face Powder	*Ladies' Home Journal* (1910)	*Lablache face powder* keeps complexions smooth and velvety Per box	 $0.50
Hair Aid	*Ladies' World* (1910)	Parker's Hair Balsam cleanses and beautifies the hair. Promotes a luxuriant growth; cures scalp diseases and hair falling Small bottle Large bottle	 $0.50 $1.00

Parker's Hair Balsam claimed to promote hair growth as well as recoloring gray hair. (via Digital Commonwealth, Massachusetts Collections Online)

Item	Source	Description	Price
Hair Barrette	*Sears, Roebuck* (1913)	Silvered filigree; 42 rhinestones	$0.49
Soap Dispenser	*New York Times* (1910)	*The Soapator;* supplies soap in the most delightful form, includes soapator and box of assorted soaps	$5.00
Toothpaste	*New York Times* (1910)	*Sanitol;* a perfect dentifrice—you can get it in either powder or paste form	$0.25
Toothpaste	*The New Orleans Daily Picayune* (1910)	*Sanitol;* your general health will be better	$0.25
Tooth Soap	*Sears, Roebuck* (1912)	*Albi-Denta;* for hardening gums and preserving the teeth	$0.10/3 ounce
Toupee	*Sears, Roebuck* (1913)	Man's; made on the finest quality silk gauze foundation	$21.65

PUBLICATIONS

Item	Source	Description	Price
Newspaper	*The New Orleans Daily Picayune* (1912)	Published seven days a week; One-year subscription	$12.00
Magazine	*Overland Monthly* (1910)	*The Jewish Times;* weekly	$3.00
Magazine	*Ladies' Home Journal* (1911)	*Ladies' Home Journal;* biweekly	$0.10
Magazine	*The Magazine of Wall Street* (1913)	*Broadmoor Bungalow;* elevation half-tone reproductions of photographs of California bungalows	$0.50
Magazine	*The Magazine of Wall Street* (1913)	*Collier's;* weekly	$0.05
Magazine	*The Magazine of Wall Street* (1913)	*Illustrated World Magazine;* monthly	$0.05

REAL ESTATE

Item	Source	Description	Price
Apartment	*New York Times* (1910)	West End Ave 712 Apartment A (96th St. subway); Light, heat, hot water; cleanliness	$5.00/week
Apartment	*New York Times* (1910)	2 and 3 rooms, just completed, overlooking Morningside and Central Parks; vacuum cleaning system	$40 to $55/ month
Apartment Building	*New York Times* (1910)	Eight-, nine-, ten-room (3 bath) suites; at 36 Gramercy Park-East	$8,900
House	*Ladies' Home Journal* (1911)	*Aladdin Readi-Cut Houses.* All the materials for a complete house	$557
House	*New York Times* (1910)	Artistic houses	$4,750
House	*The New Orleans Daily Picayune* (1910)	Double, two-story house, New Orleans; 6 rooms each side; driveways, stable, etc.; 938–940 Felicity	$5,100
House	*New York Times* (1910)	New Jersey; 7 rooms, bath, cellar, furnace, gas and electricity, hardwood trim; train and trolly; 15 minutes to city	$5,400
Land	*The New Orleans Daily Picayune* (1910)	Three lots between Freret and Robertson *Streets,* New Orleans	$6,000

Item	Source	Description	Price
Land	*The New Orleans Daily Picayune* (1912)	Texas timberland, walnut, oak, pine, ebony; within 100 miles of gulf port Per acre	$2.00 to $5.00
Land	*The New Orleans Daily Picayune* (1912)	Choice lots in the heart of Mandeville, Louisiana; six blocks from beach and railroad depot Per lot	$30.00
Land	*New York Times (1910)*	Long Island plot; 100 3 145 feet, overlooking Manhasset Bay; water privileges; improvements; eight minutes to either water or station	$3,000
Lots and Commercial Business	*The New Orleans Picayune* (1912)	Sale of The New Orleans Home for Incurables to Transmississippi Terminal Company, two lots	$12,625
Plantation	*The New Orleans Daily Picayune* (1910)	Killoden Plantation Monroe, Louisiana; the plantation contains 3,006 acres of land	$45,675
Room	*New York Times* (1910)	18th St., 26 West; newly furnished, heated	$2.00/week
Room	*New York Times* (1910)	80th St. West, furnished; exceptionally beautiful, exclusive, private residence; three minutes subway L	$10/week
Room	*New York Times* (1910)	28th, 16 East Bachelors; single, double rooms, swimming pool, showers	$6 to $8/week
Room	*The New Orleans Daily Picayune* (1912)	Furnished front room for rent in a private home; includes housekeeping Per month	$7.00
Vineyard	*Overland Monthly* (1910)	28 acres of land, 16 acres in hay, 10 in vines; seven miles from San Jose, California	$5,500

SEWING EQUIPMENT & SUPPLIES

Item	Source	Description	Price
Buttons	*Ladies' Home Journal* (1911)	Buy buttons by the name *Chalmers Pearls* and you buy utmost value Card of 12	$0.05
Buttons	*Ladies' Home Journal* (1911)	*Chalmers;* pearl; you can always match the same style again; 12 buttons per card	5¢/card
Buttons	*Sears, Roebuck* (1913)	Mother of Pearl; choice of three styles	$0.10/dozen
Cloth	*Sears, Roebuck* (1910)	*Zephyr;* dress gingham; new 1910 styling	$0.09/yard
Cloth	*New York Times* (1910)	Crepe Charmeuse; 44" wide; usually $5/yard	$2.25/yard
Cloth	*New York Times* (1910)	Imported dress satin; 35" wide, usually $3.50/yard	$1.78/yard
Cloth	*The State* (Columbia, SC) (1911)	Black taffeta; the wanted quality and weight for summer wear; a regular value, 36" wide	$0.67/yard
Cloth	*The State* (Columbia, SC) (1911)	Marquisette and voile; 40" wide and the cheapest yard in the lot is worth regular price of $0.25/yard	$0.15/yard
Cloth	*Ladies' Home Journal* (1911)	Irish linette; a beautiful sheer fabric will make up into a dress that will attract on account of the simplicity and daintiness of the designs	$0.19/yard
Cloth	*The State* (Columbia, SC) (1911)	Old English poplin; pure snowy white; the finest mercerized in the yarn material for dresses, coat suits, and separate skirts	$0.25/yard

Item	Source	Description	Price
Cloth	*Sears, Roebuck* (1913)	Dress and shirting percale; a very satisfactory cloth at a low price; full yard wide	$0.08/yard
Cloth	*Sears, Roebuck* (1913)	Mohair brilliantine; made in this country; very hard twisted thread	$0.36/yard
Cloth	*Sears, Roebuck* (1913)	Persian silk; neat and attractive in appearance; 19" wide	$1.00/yard
Cloth	*Sears, Roebuck* (1913)	Scotch table damask; every fiber guaranteed pure flax; 66" wide	$0.66/yard
Suiting Cloth	*Sears, Roebuck* (1913)	A heavy all pure-wool serge, soft and smoothly finished 56" wide	$3.00/yard

SPORTS EQUIPMENT

Item	Source	Description	Price
Baseball	*Sears, Roebuck* (1913)	$0.10 value	$0.06
Bicycle	*Sears, Roebuck* (1910)	*Napoleon;* For quality and value our Napoleon is second only to our Peerless.	$15.95
Bicycle	*Ladies' Home Journal* (1911)	*Mead 1911;* with coaster-brakes and puncture-proof tires	$10 to $27

TELEPHONE EQUIPMENT & SERVICES

Item	Source	Description	Price
Telephone	*Sears, Roebuck* (1912)	*Bridging Five Magnet;* Southwestern style price, with two dry batteries	$10.20

TOBACCO PRODUCTS

Item	Source	Description	Price
Cigarettes	*New York Times* (1910)	*Turkey Red;* success has many roads	$0.10/pack

TOYS

Item	Source	Description	Price
Aeroplane	*Sears, Roebuck* (1912)	Splendid copy made of flexible wire and silk	$0.98
Climbing Monkey	*Sears, Roebuck* (1912)	Distinctly a boy's toy; mechanical monkey which moves at will up and down heavy cord	$0.21
Doll	*Sears, Roebuck* (1912)	*Schoenhut;* performing unbreakable art dolls; extra-good quality cloth body with papier maché forearms; height including hat 18	$0.98
Floor Train	*Sears, Roebuck* (1912)	Large 15 1/2" engine and tender, and three 13 1/2" red, white and blue Pullman cars	$1.37
Water Pistol	*Sears, Roebuck* (1912)	Made of metal, nickel finished with hollow rubber handle.	$0.21
Wool Sheep Animal	*Sears, Roebuck* (1912)	Natural bleat, mounted on metal wheels. 13 1/2" × 15"	$1.85

Item	Source	Description	Price
TRAVEL & TRANSPORTATION			
Airplane Fare	*Airports of Columbia Photograph* (1910)	*Stark Airplane Flight;* sightseeing flight over Columbia, South Carolina	$5.00
Bus Fare	Throm, ed., *Popular Mechanics Picture History of American Transportation* (1952)	Hibbing to Alice, Minnesota [cost in 1914]	$0.15
Ocean Liner Fare	*New York Times* (1910)	New York to Rotterdam; Russian American Line on promenade deck	$50.00
Ocean Liner Fare	*New York Times* (1910)	New York to Glasgow; Anchor Line; Glasgow via Londonderry, first cabin	$67.50 to $72.50
Steamship Fare	*The New Orleans Daily Picayune* (1912)	Steamer *New Camelia;* excursions on Tchefuncte River	$0.75
Steamship Ticket	*San Francisco Examiner* (1913)	San Francisco to Los Angeles; round trip	$12.00
Train Fare	*The New Orleans Daily Picayune* (1912)	Roundtrip train ride from New Orleans, Louisiana, to Dallas, Texas; featured attraction, The Dallas Fair	$18.30
Train Fare	*Overland Monthly* (1910)	San Francisco to natural hot sulphur and iron baths in Lake County, California Round trip	$7.00

MISCELLANY 1910–1914

Autograph Auction

An article discussing a recent Rare Autographs Auction at Anderson's in New York City reported, "the autograph receipt for 1,600 ducats of gold by Michelangelo, in part payment for his work on the tomb of Pope Julius II, brought $170. It was dated Rome, June 7, 1513. A Frederick County land survey in George Washington's handwriting, Oct. 22, 1750, went for $74. A civil war letter of W. S. Grant, City Point, Va., March 12, 1865 to Secretary of War Stanton went for $32. Two early Abraham Lincoln legal documents, dated 1844 and 1853, sold respectively, for $37 and $29."

New York Times, March 2, 1910

Public Roads: Mileage and Expenditures

In 1911 the population per mile of road in the United States equalled 41 people, the total estimated expenditures nationwide were $142,144,191 and the expenditure per mile of public road was $64.63.

Statistical Abstract, 1911, U. S. Department of Labor, 1923

The Story of Cotton

Pickers usually carry a sack strapped over their shoulders as they walk or crawl along the rows. The cotton is picked from the stalk by hand and dropped into his sack. Hand labor is expensive and the cost of picking ranges from forty cents to one dollar a hundred pounds.

The New Orleans Daily Picayune, May 15, 1910

Sharecropper Sam Williams (center, holding dog) with his family and cotton field laborers. Williams' wife Diccie is in the center, in white, and their youngest son is seated in front of Sam. (via Library of Congress)

Oyster Legislation

I believe the time has come, said he, when the dredging of our natural oyster reefs must cease, and that the canneries and packers should be given facilities for producing their oysters on state lands. For instance, I believe the State of Louisiana should say to Mr. Packer that after 1913 or 1914, or whatever time may be agreed upon, that they must not dredge on natural reefs of this state.

However, lease to these packers liberal allotments of hard bottoms, on which they can plant oysters and produce them. The state should furnish the seed oysters.

Give the packers a sufficiently long-term lease that it would pay them to enter into the contract: say twenty to twenty-five years: certainly not longer than twenty-five years. The state would furnish police protection and charge them an acreage rental. It should be sufficient to reimburse the state but should not be excessive. Offhand, I should say $1 per acre for the first ten years: $2 per acre for the next ten years, and $5 per acre per year for the last five years.

In that way the state would be recouping its wasted oyster bottoms, and they would be returning a steady income every year during the time.

The New Orleans Daily Picayune, May 15, 1910

Predicts 16-Cent Copper; Adolph Lewisohn Expects an Increased Demand Soon

Adolph Lewisohn, President of the Miami Copper Company and a Director in other mining and smelting companies, predicted yesterday that copper would soon be selling at 10 cents.

"The copper market," he said, "is in excellent condition. Stocks of the metal everywhere have been greatly reduced and are now very moderate. The advance has been gradual on actual demand. At present the price is firm at 15 cents a pound, and only limited quantities are to be had at that figure. I am of the opinion that when the strike situation in England has clarified, demand for the metal in the country will materially increase. I believe copper will further advance and within a reasonable time reach 16 cents a pound. While it is true that most of the large producers are making good profits at present prices, yet it must be taken into consideration

MISCELLANY 1910–1914

that good copper mines are very scarce. The mill of the Miami Copper Company has about been completed, and the company is producing at the rate of approximately 3,000,000 pounds of copper a month. I am extremely optimistic in regard to the future of this property and of the metal market."

New York Times, March 22, 1912

The Minnesota Rate Cases and What They Mean

One of the gravest and most important results of the (rate) reductions under discussion was their effect upon long distance rates. St. Paul lies near the eastern boundary of Minnesota, and practically all freight shipped from States south and east of Minnesota and destined for towns within that State passes through St. Paul. The former through rate from Chicago to Wadena (a small town in the western part of Minnesota) was $1.09 per 100 pounds. But by shipping such freight from Chicago to St. Paul, and then reshipping it from St. Paul to Wadena at the lower interstate rate imposed by Minnesota Commission, the total rate from Chicago to Wadena amounts to less than $1.01 per 100 pounds. *Milwaukee Journal (1901)*

The Magazine of Wall Street, June 1913

HISTORICAL SNAPSHOT 1915–1919

1915

- British steamer *Lusitania* sunk by Germans, killing 1,198, including 128 Americans
- U.S. Pullman-car porters paid $27.50 per month, prompting U.S. Commission on Industrial Relations to ask if wages are too high
- WWI organizer Joe Hill executed by firing squad
- Emory University founded in Atlanta with support of Coca-Cola family money
- Kraft processed cheese introduced by Chicago-based J. L. Kraft and Bros.
- Pyrex glass developed by Corning Glass researchers

1916

- Workman's Compensation Act protects 500,000 federal employees from disability losses
- Kellogg's All-Bran introduced by the Battle Creek Toasted Corn Flakes Co.
- Supreme Court upholds constitutionality of federal income tax
- Hetty Green, the "witch of Wall Street," dies leaving an estate of more than $100 million
- Stanford University psychologist Lewis Madison Terman introduces the term *intelligence quotient* (IQ)

- Lucky Strike cigarettes introduced by American Tobacco, outsells Sweet Corporal and Pall Mall
- Converse basketball shoes and U.S. Keds introduced

1917

- U.S. declares war on Germany
- Charlie Chaplin, Mary Pickford, and Douglas Fairbanks help sell $18.7 billion in Liberty Bonds to support war effort, despite low 3.5% interest rate
- Anchor Oil and Gas Company, founded in 1903, is reincorporated as Phillips Petroleum Company, as oil prices double because of war
- First air-conditioned theater installed in Empire theatre in Montgomery, AL
- Del Monte begins national advertising of canned fruits and vegetables
- Clarence Birdseye pursues commercial exploitation of freezing foods

1918

- Amalgamated Clothing Workers Union stages first of 534 strikes over six years protesting open shops, sweat shops, and piecework pay

- First U.S. airmail stamps issued costing 24 cents as service begins between New York and Washington, DC
- The world's first granulated laundry soap, Rinso, is introduced by Lever Brothers
- Charles Strite patents the first automatic pop-up toaster.
- U.S. corn belt acreage sells for two to three times 1915 price

1919

- Treaty of Versailles assigns Germany sole responsibility for causing the Great War
- Boston police strike against pay scales of 21 to 23 cents per hour for 83- to 98-hour weeks
- Nineteenth Amendment, granting women suffrage, is adopted
- Most of living in New York City up 79 percent from 1914
- Dial telephone introduced in Norfolk, VA
- Grand Canyon National Park established
- Wheat prices soar to $3.50 per bushel as famine sweeps Europe
- U.S. ice cream sales reach 150 million gallons, up from 30 million in 1909

Charlie Chaplin stands on Douglas Fairbanks' shoulders during a Liberty bonds rally. They are at the foot of George Washington's statue in front of the Sub-Treasury (now Federal Hall National Memorial). (via Wikimedia Commons)

SELECTED INCOME 1915–1919

Job	Source	Description	Pay
Actor	Catherine Legrand and Robyn Karney, *Chronicle of the Cinema* (1995)	Payment for three movies to Mary Pickford in 1918	$900,000
Actor	Scott Eyman, *Mary Pickford America's Sweetheart* (1990)	Annual income of Mary Pickford in 1917	$560,000
Actor	Catherine Legrand and Robyn Karney, *Chronicle of the Cinema* (1995)	Weekly income of Douglas Fairbanks in 1917	$10,000
Actor, Director	*American Chronicle* (1999)	Movie star Charles Chaplin's annual salary with Mutual starting in 1916	$675,000
Actor/Producer	*Time* (1916)	Weekly income of Charlie Chaplin in 1916	$10,000
Actress	*American Chronicle* (1999)	Annual pay of movie star Mary Pickford in 1918	$1 million
Barber	*New York Times* (1918)	No Sunday work	$14–20/wk
Baseball Player	Vincent Tomkins, ed., *American Decades: 1910–1919* (1996)	Annual salary of Detroit Tigers' Ty Cobb in 1915	$20,000
Baseball Player	Harvey Frommer, *Shoeless Joe and Ragtime Baseball* (1992)	Annual salary of Chicago White Sox player Joe Jackson in 1919	$6,000

Ty Cobb, Detroit (left), and Joe Jackson, Cleveland (right), standing alongside each other, each holding bats. Cobb was the highest paid baseball player from 1916 to 1921. (via Library of Congress)

Job	Source	Description	Pay
Bookkeeper	*New York Times* (1918)	Assistant, American; in office of large manufacturing concern	$18/wk
Boy Wanted	*New York Times* (1916)	15–16 years old; in advertising business; references required; unusual opportunity for advancement	$5/wk
Boy Wanted	*New York Times* (1918)	Bright boy wanted in large woolen house; splendid chance for advancement	$7/wk
Cabinetmaker	*The Chicago Daily* (1918)	Washington Employment Agency Per week	$18–$20
Driver	*Chicago Tribune* (1915)	Man to drive laundry wagon	$18/wk
Electrical Draftsman	*The Chicago Daily Tribune* (1917)	Must be familiar with isolated plants, installation layouts and interior light and power Per month	$150
Elevator Operator	*New York Times* (1918)	Elderly man desired; steady and easy position	$5/wk
Errand Boy	*New York Times* (1918)	New York office of large textile concern desires boy 16 or 17 to run errands	$5/wk
Football Player	*Tomkins, ed., American Decades: 1910-1919* (1996)	Payment per game to Jim Thorpe, former Olympic Champion and professional football player with Canton, Ohio, Bulldogs in 1915	$250
Foreign Stenographer	*New York Times* (1918)	We are having numerous calls for stenographers in Spanish and English; also French and English; only those experienced in taking dictation in two languages can be used	$20-30/wk
Illustrator	*MastroNet Auction Catalog* (2004)	Fee paid painter Leslie Thrasher to create a "Chew Beech Nut Tobacco" advertisement by P. Lorillard& Co. [In 1918]	$1,500
Movie Actor	*Seventy Years of the Cinema* (1969)	Silent movie actor Charlie Chaplin signed with Mutual for a record salary, annual [1916]	$650,000
Office Worker	*New York Times* (1918)	Boy for office work in wholesale jewelry house	$8/wk
Packers	*Chicago Tribune* (1918)	Boys over 16 years of age to act as packer boys on rotary presses	$12/wk
Racehorse	Vincent Tompkins, ed., *American Decades: 1910-1919* (1996)	One year winnings of Triple Crown winner Sir Barton in 1919	$88,250
Situation Wanted; Accountant	*New York Times* (1916)	Experienced; all lines; books opened, closed, disentangled, audited, systems installed	$2.50/wk
Situation Wanted; Accountant	*Chicago Tribune* (1918)	Just mustered out; accountant or assistant credit manager; experienced; best references; future must be assured	$125–150/mo
Situation Wanted; Bookkeeper	*New York Times* (1916)	Fourteen years' experience	$20/wk
Situation Wanted; Bookkeeper	*Chicago Tribune* (1918)	Married; 33	$20/wk
Situation Wanted; Office Worker	*Chicago Tribune* (1918)	Experienced young man, age 19	$16/wk

Job	Source	Description	Pay
Situation Wanted; Secretary	*Chicago Tribune* (1918)	Young lady, exceptional ability, stenographer, secretary; 6 years' experience	$26/wk
Solicitor	*Chicago Tribune* (1915)	Two magazine men preferred; to call on regular customers; new proposition; permanent employment	$18/wk
Spy	Tomkins, ed., *American Decades: 1910-1919*	Payment to Dr. Heinrich Albert by Germany to sabotage American munitions plants in 1915	$28 million
Stenographer	*Chicago Tribune* (1915)	Excellent appearance, high class, with good personality, Protestant, 16–22; for private office; must be capable; this is a first-class position for a HIGH CLASS GIRL ONLY	$8/wk
Truckers	*The Chicago Daily Tribune* (1917)	Washington Employment Agency Per week	$70 – $80
Wagon Boy	*The Chicago Daily Tribune* (1917)	Must be over 16 years of age Per week	$8

CONSUMER EXPENDITURES 1919

Expenditure Type	1919
Clothing	$55.52
Food	$177.53
Auto Purchases	$12.44
Auto Parts	$5.54
Gas & Oil	$11.73
Housing	$76.98
Furniture	$6.97
Utilities	$6.76
Telephone & Telegraph	$1.93
Physicians	$6.87
Dentists	$2.65
Health Insurance	NR
Personal Business	$19.83
Personal Care	$5.88
Tobacco	$13.67
Local Transport	$7.78
Intercity Transport	$5.43
Recreation	$20.64
Religion/Welfare Activities	$13.92
Private Education & Research	$7.19
Per Capita Consumption	$579.57

INVESTMENTS 1915–1919

Investment	1915	1916	1917	1918	1919
Basic Yield, One-Year Corporate Bonds	4.47	3.48	4.05	5.48	5.58
Short-term Interest Rates, 4–6 Months, Prime Commercial Paper	4.01	3.84	5.07	6.02	5.37
Basic Yield, Common Stocks, Total	4.98	5.62	7.82	7.24	5.75
Index of Common Stocks (1941 – 1943510)	8.31	9.47	8.50	7.54	8.78

COMMON STOCKS, CLOSING PRICE AND YIELD, FIRST BUSINESS DAY OF YEAR

Allis Chalmers	6 1/2	31	27 3/8	19 1/2	32
AT & T	116 1/4	127 1/8	123 3/8	106 3/8	100 1/2
American Tobacco	217 1/2	208 1/2	108 1/2	142 1/8	196
Anaconda	25	90 1/4	83 1/4	62 3/8	60 3/4
B&O	68 1/4	95 3/8	84 1/2	52 3/8	49 5/8
Bethlehem Steel (Dividend 2 shares of Common B @ $120.75, 2/17/17)	46 5/8	458	510	79 1/2	61
Corn Products	8	20 3/8	23 1/4	31 3/4	48 3/8
General Electric (2% stock dividend, 12/7/17) (2% stock dividend, 6/8/17; 2% stock dividend, 12/7/17)	139	174 1/2	168 1/4	134 5/8	151 3/4 37 3/8 37 3/8
General Motors	81	495	138 1/4	115	132 1/2
IBM					
Intl Harvester (Merged with Intl. Harvester of New Jersey 9/19/18; for each share of IH New Jersey, 1 1/2 share of new common; for each share of IH Corp, 2/3 share of new common)	73	75	121	59	113
National Biscuit	118 1/4	124			105
US Steel	49 3/8	88 1/2	109 5/8	95 7/8	95 1/4
Western Union	57 5/8	88 1/2	95 3/4	86 3/4	86 1/2

STANDARD JOBS 1915-1919

Job Type	1915	1916	1917	1918	1919
Average of All Industries, excl. farm labor	$687/yr	$765/yr	$887/yr	$1115/yr	$1272/yr
Average of All Industries, inc. farm labor	$633/yr	$708/yr	$830/yr	$1047/yr	$1201/yr
Bituminous Coal Mining	38¢/hr	48¢/hr	60¢/hr	70¢/hr	34¢/hr
Avg hrs/wk	51.60	49.80	48.70	48.40	51.60
Building Trades, Union Workers	59¢/hr	62¢/hr	68¢/hr	78¢/hr	57¢/hr
Avg hrs/wk	47.50	44.40	44.10	44	44.80
Clerical Workers in Mfg. & Steam RR	$1327/yr	$1427/yr	$1552/yr	$1765/yr	$1999/yr
Domestics	$342/yr	$357/yr	$389/yr	$432/yr	$538/yr
Farm Labor	$355/yr	$388/yr	$481/yr	$604/yr	$706/yr
Federal Civilian	$940/yr	$974/yr	$967/yr	$1009/yr	$971/yr
Federal Employees, Executive Depts.	$1152/yr	$1211/yr	$1295/yr	$1380/yr	$1520/yr
Finance, Insurance, & Real Estate	$1040/yr	$1037/yr	$1051/yr	$1078/yr	$1099/yr
Gas & Electricity Workers	$620/yr	$615/yr	NR	NR	$556/yr
Lower-Skilled Labor	$905/yr	$925/yr	$964/yr	$984/yr	$991/yr
Manufacturing, Union Workers	34¢/hr	35¢/hr	36¢/hr	37¢/hr	37¢/hr
Avg hrs/wk	53.00	52.40	51.80	51.40	51.10
Manufacturing, Payroll	15¢/hr	16¢/hr	17¢/hr	16¢/hr	15¢/hr
Avg hrs/wk	61.90	61.50	61.20	61.10	62.10
Medical/Health Services Workers	$381/yr	$407/yr	$451/yr	$520/yr	$606/yr
Ministers	$730/yr	$731/yr	$737/yr	$761/yr	$759/yr

Job Type	1915	1916	1917	1918	1919
Nonprofit Org. Workers	$652/yr	$651/yr	$657/yr	$679/yr	$677/yr
Postal Employees	38¢/hr	37¢/hr	37¢/hr	37¢/hr	38¢/hr
Avg hrs/wk	48.00	48.00	48.00	48.00	48.00
Public School Teachers	$328/yr	$337/yr	$346/yr	$358/yr	$377/yr
State and Local Govt. Workers	$590/yr	$605/yr	$612/yr	$621/yr	$640/yr
Steam Railroads, Wage Earners	$548/yr	$549/yr	$563/yr	$593/yr	$600/yr
Street Railway Workers	$604/yr	$601/yr	$576/yr	$582/yr	$610/yr
Telegraph Ind. Workers	NR	NR	$544/yr	$573/yr	$601/yr
Telephone Ind. Workers	NR	NR	$408/yr	$397/yr	$392/yr
Wholesale and Retail Trade Workers	$510/yr	$521/yr	$537/yr	$551/yr	$508/yr

FOOD BASKET 1915–1919

Commodity	Year	New York	Atlanta	Chicago	Denver	Los Angeles
Beans, Navy, per pound	1915	8.4¢	9.70¢	7.50¢	7.90¢	7.20¢
	1916	10.90¢	11.20¢	10.90¢	10.10¢	10¢
	1917	17.60¢	17.50¢	18.10¢	17.40¢	14.80¢
	1918	17.60¢	18.60¢	17.20¢	16.60¢	17¢
	1919	12.90¢	14.90¢	12¢	13.20¢	25.30¢
Beef, Rib Roasts, per pound	1915	22.20¢	18.30¢	21.30¢	18.30¢	19¢
	1916	23.20¢	19¢	21.90¢	18.80¢	20¢
	1917	27.40¢	22.90¢	22.30¢	22.30¢	22.10¢
	1918	35.30¢	28.30¢	29.70¢	27.50¢	27.70¢
	1919	39.10¢	30.20¢	31.40¢	29.10¢	28.70¢
Beef, Steaks (Round), per pound	1915	26¢	20.40¢	22.10¢	21.20¢	20.10¢
	1916	27.40¢	20.90¢	22.60¢	21.20¢	21¢
	1917	32.60¢	26.20¢	25.80¢	26.20¢	23.10¢
	1918	42.30¢	34.10¢	32.30¢	38.80¢	29.70¢
	1919	45.70¢	36.50¢	34.30¢	34.50¢	30.50¢
Bread, Wheat, per loaf	1915	6.10¢	6.80¢	5.90¢	5.60¢	6.30¢
	1916	6.20¢	7.20¢	6.10¢	6.20¢	6.30¢
	1917	8.30¢	9.50¢	8.50¢	8.50¢	7.30¢
	1918	NR	10¢	NR	NR	NR
	1919	NR	10¢	NR	NR	NR
Butter, per pound	1915	35.80¢	37.90¢	33.60¢	34.10¢	33.10¢
	1916	39.50¢	40.80¢	37.60¢	37.50¢	37.30¢
	1917	48.80¢	50.60¢	46.40¢	45.80¢	45.90¢
	1918	57.80¢	60.20¢	54.50¢	54.50¢	56.90¢
	1919	68.60¢	70.90¢	63.90¢	65.30¢	67.50¢
Cheese, per pound	1915	23.10¢	23.50¢	23.20¢	24.60¢	24.10¢
	1916	24.60¢	26.20¢	26.10¢	26.20¢	25.10¢
	1917	32.90¢	33.60¢	34.20¢	34.30¢	32¢
	1918	34.90¢	36.80¢	37.30¢	36.70¢	35.90¢
	1919	42.70¢	41.80¢	42.90¢	43.80¢	44.40¢
Chickens, per pound	1915	21.60¢	19.10¢	19¢	19.70¢	25.60¢
	1916	24.50¢	20.50¢	22.30¢	21.50¢	26.70¢
	1917	29.30¢	26.30¢	26.80¢	26.40¢	29.10¢
	1918	39.40¢	35.60¢	33.90¢	34.40¢	39.20¢
	1919	41¢	38¢	36.60¢	37.30¢	46.30¢
Coffee, per pound	1915	28.70¢	29.30¢	30¢	20.60¢	32.70¢
	1916	27.20¢	28.20¢	30¢	29.50¢	32.20¢
	1917	26.40¢	29.20¢	28.90¢	29.90¢	30.70¢
	1918	27.70¢	29.70¢	28.60¢	30.40¢	30.60¢
	1919	39.90¢	43.30¢	39.70¢	44¢	42.10¢
Cornmeal, per pound	1915	3.50¢	2.70¢	3.10¢	2.80¢	3.60¢
	1916	4.10¢	2.70¢	3.30¢	2.70¢	3.90¢
	1917	6.70¢	4.80¢	5.70¢	4.90¢	6.20¢
	1918	7.90¢	5.60¢	6.80¢	6¢	7.60¢
	1919	7¢	5.70¢	6.10¢	5.80¢	7.20¢
Eggs, per dozen	1915	39¢	28.50¢	30.70¢	32.20¢	36.30¢
	1916	42.70¢	33.10¢	33.40¢	36¢	38.90¢
	1917	55.10¢	43.60¢	44.70¢	45.50¢	45.40¢
	1918	64.20¢	52.70¢	52¢	53.70¢	58.30¢
	1919	70.80¢	57.20¢	58.10¢	59.80¢	62.60¢

Commodity	Year	New York	Atlanta	Chicago	Denver	Los Angeles
Flour, Wheat, per pound	1915	4.20¢	4.10¢	3.80¢	3.40¢	4.30¢
	1916	4.50¢	4.40¢	4¢	3.60¢	4.40¢
	1917	7.30¢	6.80¢	6.50¢	5.80¢	6.60¢
	1918	7.20¢	7¢	6.40¢	5.70¢	6.80¢
	1919	7¢	7.30¢	7¢	6.20¢	7.30¢

Newton Colman dressed in a baker's uniform in front of table with sack of flour, cake, pie and loaf of bread. Colman did promotion work with Fisher Flouring Mills ca. 1912-1920. (via Wikimedia Commons)

Commodity	Year	New York	Atlanta	Chicago	Denver	Los Angeles
Ham, Smoked, Sliced, per pound	1915	28.70¢	28.80¢	32.80¢	29.90¢	34.10¢
	1916	31.50¢	31.60¢	34¢	32¢	36¢
	1917	42¢	39.10¢	40¢	42.10¢	46.30¢
	1918	50.20¢	55.40¢	54.70¢	55.40¢	59.90¢
	1919	51.30¢	59.50¢	58.10¢	58.30¢	63.80¢
Lard, per pound	1915	15.20¢	15¢	14.50¢	15.20¢	17¢
	1916	17.40¢	17.90¢	16.80¢	17.70¢	18¢
	1917	27.50¢	27.50¢	26.20¢	28.60¢	27.10¢
	1918	33.20¢	34.20¢	32.20¢	34¢	33.80¢
	1919	36.90¢	37.60¢	35.30¢	38¢	36.10¢
Milk, Fresh, per quart	1915	9¢	10.40¢	8¢	8.40¢	8.50¢
	1916	9.20¢	11.20¢	8.40¢	8.40¢	8.30¢
	1917	11.90¢	14.30¢	10.30¢	10¢	10.40¢
	1918	14.50¢	19.10¢	12.50¢	11.80¢	13.80¢
	1919	16.10¢	21.30¢	14.20¢	12.70¢	14.30¢
Mutton and Lamb, Leg, per pound	1915	18.40¢	17.80¢	21¢	21.10¢	18.40¢
	1916	19.90¢	23.60¢	22.40¢	19.40¢	20.80¢
	1917	26¢	29.50¢	28.20¢	27.40¢	26.70¢
	1918	31.40¢	36.90¢	33.80¢	32.60¢	32.50¢
	1919	31.80¢	38.50¢	35.40¢	31.60¢	32.40¢
Pork, Bacon, Sliced, per pound	1915	25.10¢	29.30¢	30.50¢	26.90¢	33.50¢
	1916	26.40¢	30.70¢	31.80¢	30.30¢	34.60¢
	1917	39.40¢	41.60¢	42.20¢	43.50¢	46.10¢
	1918	50.20¢	55.40¢	54.70¢	55.40¢	59.90¢
	1919	63.80¢	59.50¢	58.10¢	58.30¢	63.80¢
Pork Chops, per pound	1915	21¢	21.50¢	19¢	18.50¢	24.10¢
	1916	23.70¢	23.30¢	21.10¢	20.60¢	25.10¢
	1917	32.70¢	31.90¢	29.40¢	31.30¢	32.90¢
	1918	40.40¢	39.10¢	35.40¢	37.60¢	42¢
	1919	44.40¢	40.30¢	38.30¢	41.10¢	46.20¢
Potatoes, Irish, per peck	1915	1.90¢	1.90¢	1.30¢	1.60¢	1.80¢
	1916	3.30¢	3.20¢	2.50¢	2.50¢	2.60¢
	1917	5.10¢	5¢	4.20¢	4.20¢	3.80¢
	1918	3.80¢	4.10¢	2.70¢	2.70¢	2.60¢
	1919	4.40¢	5¢	3.50¢	3.50¢	3.80¢
Prunes, Dried, per pound	1915	14.50¢	13.60¢	13.80¢	13.70¢	11.30¢
	1916	13.70¢	13.10¢	13.10¢	13.30¢	11.40¢
	1917	15.70¢	16.50¢	15.40¢	16.30¢	14.80¢
	1918	18.30¢	18¢	17.20¢	17.50¢	17¢
	1919	28¢	21.80¢	25.80¢	24.60¢	25.30¢
Rice, per pound	1915	9.20¢	8.50¢	9.50¢	9¢	9.60¢
	1916	9.20¢	7.90¢	9.40¢	9.20¢	9.40¢
	1917	10.30¢	9.60¢	10.10¢	10.60¢	9.80¢
	1918	12.80¢	13.20¢	12.80¢	13.40¢	12.90¢
	1919	14.80¢	14.90¢	14.70¢	15.30¢	14.80¢
Sugar, per pound	1915	5.90¢	6.80¢	6.20¢	7¢	6.50¢
	1916	7.50¢	8.60¢	7.40¢	8¢	7.70¢
	1917	8.80¢	10¢	8.60¢	8.90¢	8.40¢
	1918	9.40¢	9.90¢	9.20¢	9.90¢	9.30¢
	1919	10.40¢	12.50¢	11.40¢	11.60¢	11¢
Tea, per pound	1915	45.20¢	61.50¢	51.20¢	52.10¢	53.10¢
	1916	44.50¢	61.70¢	52.10¢	50¢	55.10¢
	1917	50¢	73.30¢	55.90¢	55¢	55.70¢
	1918	54¢	85.20¢	59.10¢	60.70¢	63.30¢
	1919	55.70¢	88.40¢	63.50¢	69.10¢	69.10¢

SELECTED PRICES 1915–1919

Item	Source	Description	Price
ALCOHOL			
Gin	*New York Times* (1919)	*Imperial Gin*	$2.15/fifth
Rum	*New York Times* (1919)	*Bacardi Rum*	$3.20/fifth
Whiskey	*New York Times* (1919)	*Old Bridgeport Whiskey;* 6 years old	$3.10/fifth
APPAREL, CHILDREN'S			
Baby Shoes	*Powell & Campbell Catalogue* (1915)	*Lyons & Co.;* patent-leather vamp, white-kid top, soft sole	$0.50/each
Dress	*Sears, Roebuck* (1917)	Babies' long white dress; yoke of lace insertions, satin ribbon	$1.33
Gloves	*Chicago Daily Tribune* (1917)	Children's Scotch knit wool gloves, seamless fingers	$0.75
Hood	*Sears, Roebuck* (1917)	Pretty hand-crocheted silk hood	$0.78
Overcoat	*Sears, Roebuck* (1917)	Winter weight; made very large and cut full in every way	$5.48
Shoes	*The Asheville (NC) Times* (1919)	Children's white Oxfords, English toe	$1.45
Skirt	*Sears, Roebuck* (1917)	Girl's; made of all-wool double-twisted wrap serge	$4.38
Suit	*Sears, Roebuck* (1917)	*Knickerbocker;* boys; rich olive-brown cassimere	$6.75
Suit	*Chicago Tribune* (1919)	Boy's suits of excellent quality chambray	$2.95
APPAREL, MEN'S			
Boots	*Powell & Campbell Catalogue* (1915)	Tan elk; oak sole	$21.00
Coat	*Sears, Roebuck* (1917)	80 percent camel hair and 20 percent wool	$4.85
Gloves	*Sears, Roebuck* (1917)	14-ounce canvas gloves, knitted wrists	$1.50/dozen
Hat	*Sears, Roebuck* (1917)	Alpine style; the crown is 5 1/2" high; raw edge brim 2 1/2 " wide	$2.25
Hat	*Chicago Tribune* (1919)	*Newmark;* Easter style; considering style and quality, the lowest prices in town	$5.00

Item	Source	Description	Price
Heel	*Powell & Campbell Catalogue* (1915)	*Foster;* orthopedic; rubber; especially beneficial to people troubled with flat foot; men's whole heel	$0.75/pair
Nightshirt	*Sears, Roebuck* (1917)	Collarless; finished 60 " long with full-size bell-shape body	$1.15
Overcoat	*Sears, Roebuck* (1917)	Chesterfield style; four-button fly front	$9.00
Pants	*Sears, Roebuck* (1917)	*Rip Proof;* inexpensive herringbone-weave brown striped cheviot Rip-Proof work pants	$1.50
Shirt	*Sears, Roebuck* (1917)	Medium weight wool; mixed sacking flannel shirt	$1.49
Shoes	*The Asheville (NC) Times* (1919)	Men's Oxfords in English high toe, button and lace black and tan	$4.95
Suit	*Sears, Roebuck* (1917)	Stylish; good quality pure-wool worsted	$16.50
Suit	*Chicago Tribune* (1919)	*Joseph Sobel;* tailored; made-to-order spring suits, extra pants free	$33.00
Union Suit	*Today's Housewife* (1917)	*Chalmer's Underwear,* as easy to wear as your skin	$1.25
Work Shirt	*Sears, Roebuck* (1917)	Coat style; heavy-weight chambray	$0.75

APPAREL, WOMEN'S

Item	Source	Description	Price
Bloomers	*Altman's Spring Catalogue* (1919)	Of pink or white batiste, elastic band at waist and knee	$0.90
Blouse	*Sears, Roebuck* (1917)	*George;* Crepe daintly adorned with fine white silk embroidery	$5.50
Corset	*Sears, Roebuck* (1917)	Low bust with elastic webbing; designed for exclusive dancing and outdoor wear	$1.59
Corset Cover	*Altman's Spring Catalogue* (1919)	Nainsook; cap sleeves, trimmed with Valenciennes lace; size 36 to 44 in bust	$1.50
Dress	*Sears, Roebuck* (1917)	*Homestead* house dress made of good quality washable gingham	$ 1.59
Dress	*Sears, Roebuck* (1917)	Junior; about one-third wool, shepherd check	$6.25
Dress	*Sears, Roebuck* (1917)	Nobby velveteen corduroy; heart-shaped pockets on the skirt	$5.48
Dress	*Sears, Roebuck* (1917)	For stout woman; half-wool serge; a pretty embroidered dress, especially designed for women of full figure	$8.98
Fur Coat	*Sears, Roebuck* (1917)	Full-length muskrat; natural blue-black Jersey Muskrat coat, with deep square cape effect, collar, cuffs, pocket pieces and button of high-grade	$115
Gloves	*Sears, Roebuck* (1917)	Chamois; wash them like you wash your hands	$1.19
Hose	*Sears, Roebuck* (1917)	Seamless artificial silk; reinforced with cotton at the top	$0.35
Mesh Bag	*Chicago Tribune* (1919)	Silver-plated; in pouch shape, and with plain polished mountings	$7.50

Item	Source	Description	Price
Raincoat	*Sears, Roebuck* (1917)	The outer fabric is a fine twill-wool mixed cashmere	$10.98
Shoes	*Cohan and Harris Theatre Program* (1917)	*Hood Leisure Shoes;* add a touch of distinction to any frock	$3.00 to $4.00
Shoes	*Sears, Roebuck* (1917)	*Sears, Roebuck;* patent-leather button, black brocade cloth top, cuban Louis heel	$3.85
Shoes	*Chicago Tribune* (1919)	*Victory Pumps;* patent leather or dull kid, slender Louis heel.	$5.85
Slippers	*Powell & Campbell Catalogue* (1915)	*P&C;* in patent, mat kid, black satin, black satin	$2.25
Suit	*Sears, Roebuck* (1917)	Fall; made of good wearing quality velveteen; lined throughout	$29.75
Underwear	*Altman's Spring Catalogue* (1919)	Nainsook; Valenciennes lace edge	$1.25
Union Suit	*Sears, Roebuck* (1917)	Nursing; elastic-ribbed wool	$2.68

APPLIANCES

Item	Source	Description	Price
Electric Radiator	*Sears, Roebuck* (1917)	*Majestic;* fine for that cold bathroom, bedroom, small office	$5.75
Indoor Toilet	*Hearth and Home* (1917)	*Kawnear Cabinet;* no more outside back yard inconveniences; no chambers to empty; no sewer or cesspool	$0.01/week/person
Radiator	*The World's Work* (1917)	*American Radiator Company;* ideal boiler and 350 sq. ft. of 38" American radiator will heat a cottage	$1.95
Vacuum Cleaner	*Sears, Roebuck* (1917)	Electric; if your house is lighted by electricity from a central station, you can operate one of the above cleaners	$24.50

BABY PRODUCTS

Item	Source	Description	Price
Blanket	*Sears, Roebuck* (1917)	The most popular baby blankets on the market	$0.75
Safety Pin	*Today's Housewife* (1917)	*Clinton;* send $0.10 for a big $0.10 worth of pins and a dainty pin tray as well	$0.10
Swing	*Today's Housewife* (1917)	*Rock-A-Bye;* baby amuses himself away from dirt, out of drafts; he can't fall out and the swing can't break or wear out	$1.00

BUSINESS EQUIPMENT & SUPPLIES

Item	Source	Description	Price
Telephone Call	*American Chronicle* (1999)	Three-minute long-distance charges between New York and San Francisco in 1915	$20.70
Typewriter	*The World's Work* (1917)	*Corona;* the personal writing machine; makes you independent of your office	$50.00

Item	Source	Description	Price
Typewriter	*Sears, Roebuck* (1917)	*Standard Visible;* writes faster, cleaner, plainer and easier than pen or pencil	$46.50
Typewriter	*The World's Work* (1917)	*Underwood;* guaranteed for five years; includes two color ribbons, back spacer, tabulator, everything complete	$43.85

COLLECTIBLES

Item	Source	Description	Price
Bust	*Sears, Roebuck* (1917)	Bronze-plated metal bust of President Wilson; stands 2 1/2" high	$0.10
Painting	*American Chronicle* (1999)	Sandro Botticelli's *Madonna and Child;* sold at auction in 1915	$20,000

EDUCATION

Item	Source	Description	Price
Tuition	*The Craftsman* (1915)	*The Raymond Riordon School;* Highland, New York; high school, college preparatory, special courses; not merely a recitation hall but a preparation for life's work	$800/year
Tuition	*The World's Work* (1917)	*Cascadilla School for Boys;* a fitting school for Cornell	$675/year
Tuition	*The World's Work* (1917)	*Loomis School for Boys;* Windsor, Connecticut; practical training for boys intending to enter business or farming on graduation	$400/year
Tuition	*American Magazine* (1917)	*Wilbraham Academy;* Wilbraham, Massachusetts; fits for life and college work	$600/year

ENTERTAINMENT

Item	Source	Description	Price
Annual Ball Ticket	*The Playhouse Playbill,* New York City (1916)	The Second Annual Ball of the Allied Arts of the Theatre in behalf of the Actors' Fund of America; Hotel Astor, March 30, 1916, 10 p.m.	$5.00 each
Dance Lessons	*Cohan and Harris Theatre Program* (1917)	Dancing Carnival, 200 instructors, 50,000 square feet of floor space Private lessons, per half hour	 $0.50
Exposition	*Chicago Daily Tribune* (1917)	Home Furnishing Exposition; everything for the home Adults Children	 $0.50 $0.25
Lecture	*Chicago Daily Tribune* (1917)	Captain R. Hugh Knyvett presents "The Real Thing," War lectures Seats	$0.75 $1.00 $1.50
Movie	*The Asheville (NC) Times* (1919)	Mary Pickford in *Rags* Children Adults Including war tax	 $0.10 $0.15

Rags, based on the novel by Edith Barnard Delano, showcased Pickford's fiery persona. She is seen above brandishing a chair at several cowering men. (via IMDB)

Item	Source	Description	Price
Musical	*The Asheville (NC) Times* (1919)	*Flo-Flo;* classy, snappy, catchy, girly musical entertainment	$0.25–$2.00
Opera	*Chicago Daily Tribune* (1917)	*Aida;* by the Boston English Opera Company; Strand Theatre, Chicago Nights	$0.50–$1.00
Theater Tickets	*Cohan and Harris Theatre Program* (1917)	Cohan and Harris Theatre Evening Orchestra, including war tax Saturday Evening Orchestra, including war tax First Balcony, including war tax	$2.20 $2.75 $0.55–$2.20

ENTERTAINMENT, HOME

Item	Source	Description	Price
Camera	*Sears, Roebuck* (1917)	*Kodak Kewpie Kameras;* the Kewpie always gets the picture; for 2 1/2" × 4 1/2" picture	$2.80

Item	Source	Description	Price
Camera	*Sears, Roebuck* (1917)	*Conley Model C;* roll film model; beautifully made in every detail	$16.40
Card Game	*Sears, Roebuck* (1917)	*Rook;* one of the most popular games on the market	$0.42
Game	*Sears, Roebuck* (1917)	*Major League Baseball;* plays all the National League teams with over 240 players	$2.45
Novelty	*Sears, Roebuck* (1917)	Boxing darkies; these little fellows thump each other merrily and heartily as the music plays; rides on needle arm	$1.06
Phonograph	*Sears, Roebuck* (1917)	*Silvertone;* plays every disc record made	$6.95
Phonograph	*The World's Work* (1917)	*Starr;* Jacobean style; for the chosen few of music lovers	$250
Phonograph	*Chicago Tribune* (1919)	*Stark Grafonola;* including Grafonola type D-2 and 14 selections	$65.95
Phonograph Record	*The Craftsman* (1915)	*Columbia;* double disc	$0.65
Phonograph Record	*Chicago Tribune* (1919)	*Columbia;* Ponselle's first *Butterfly* record; a record that justifies the critics' acclaim of Ponselle as the world's greatest dramatic soprano	$1.50

FINANCIAL PRODUCTS & SERVICES

Item	Source	Description	Price
Travelers' Checks	*The World's Work* (1917)	*K. N. & K.;* safer than currency to carry; experienced travelers use them	$0.50

FOOD PRODUCTS

Item	Source	Description	Price
Candy	*Sears, Roebuck* (1917)	*Pep-O-Mint Life Savers;* a dainty confection	$0.05/rl
Cereal	*The Youth's Companion* (1919)	*Quaker Oats;* the best way to cut down your food cost is to breakfast on Quaker Oats Regular size Large size	 $0.12 $0.30
Chewing Gum	*Sears, Roebuck* (1917)	*Wrigley's Doublemint;* 25 packages to each box	$0.73/box
Groceries	Toledo (Ohio) *Weekly Blade* (1917)	Lard, per pound Corn, shelled, per bushel Spring wheat, per bbl Purina whole wheat, per bbl	$0.24 $1.75 $15.50 $15.00
Milk	*Chicago Daily Tribune* (1917)	Bowman Dairy Company perfectly pasteurized milk Quart bottle	$0.12
Macaroni	*Today's Housewife* (1917)	*Skinner's;* made from the highest-grade Durum wheat; cooks in 12 minutes	$0.25
Peanut Sandwich	*The Playhouse Playbill,* New York City (1916)	*National Biscuit Company,* Peanut Sandwich—a generous spread of peanut butter between a slightly salted biscuit Per box	 $0.10
Puffed Rice	*American Magazine* (1917)	No other process makes whole-grain so easy to digest	$0.15/box
Puffed Wheat	*Today's Housewife* (1917)	Puffed grains are all nutrition	$0.15/box

Item	Source	Description	Price
Radium Water	*Cohan and Harris Theatre Program* (1917)	*Muidar Radium Water;* Every glass of water contains radium Case of 50, 24-ounce bottles	$25.00

FURNITURE

Item	Source	Description	Price
Bed and Mattress	*The Gentlewoman* (1919)	*Spiegel, May, Stern Co.;* Sturdy Steel Bed; Colonial design, standard full size, springs and Restwell mattress	$19.95
Bed	*Hearth and Home* (1917)	Feather; full weight 40 lbs	$8.95
Bookcase	*The World's Work* (1917)	*Lundstrom Universal;* solid oak with disappearing glass doors	$8.00
Buffet	*Sears, Roebuck* (1917)	Colonial design; large double-door cupboard, seasoned hardwood, imitation of quarter sawn oak	$14.95
Chair	*The Craftsman* (1915)	Reclining; with adjustable back and spring cushion; with sheepskin cushions	$37.00
Chair	*Sears, Roebuck* (1917)	Morris rocker; artificial black leather upholstery	$7.45
Chair	*Sears, Roebuck* (1917)	Washingtonian-style box-seat dining cushions; the distinctive feature of this fine chair is the extra-high curved back	$4.95
Chair	*Sears, Roebuck* (1917)	Turkish rocker; artificial black leather	$12.55
Chiffonier	*Sears, Roebuck* (1917)	Six drawers with quarter-sawed veneer serpentine front	$11.60
Hall Furniture Rack	*Sears, Roebuck* (1917)	French bevel plate mirror	$9.85
Settee	*The Craftsman* (1915)	7' long, seat 34" deep and 16" high, back 36" high; spring seat cushion of soft leather	$96.50
Table	*The Craftsman* (1915)	*Craftsman;* fumed oak table is suitable for library or living room	$19.00
TeachCart	*Chicago Daily Tribune* (1917)	*John A. Colby and Sons English TeachCart;* finished in old English walnut or brown mahogany	$27.00
Tea Wagon	*The Craftsman* (1915)	*Willow;* new designs in Willow	$16.50

GARDEN EQUIPMENT & SUPPLIES

Item	Source	Description	Price
Seed	*The World's Work* (1917)	*Burpee's Sweet Pea;* 40–50 seeds; packets of Cherub, King White, Margaret Allee, Rosabelle, and Wedgewood	$0.25

HOTEL RATES

Item	Source	Description	Price
Hotel Room	*The World's Work* (1917)	*Hotel Butler;* Seattle, Washington; large airy rooms, care without peer	$1.00/day

HOUSEHOLD PRODUCTS

Item	Source	Description	Price
Canvas Shoe Cleaner	*Powell & Campbell Catalogue* (1915)	*Eagle Brand Nova;* the perfect white cleaner	$0.25/pkg
Clock	*Sears, Roebuck* (1917)	Hanging wall regulator clock; eight-day clock; 35" high, 12" dial	$5.22

Item	Source	Description	Price
Clock	Sears, Roebuck (1917)	National Call 8-day; alarm; an eight-day run on one winding	$2.00
Ice Cream Freezer	Today's Housewife (1917)	Auto vacuum; today's method of making ice cream is automatic, accurate and economical; there's no crank to turn—no labor	$3.00
Kitchen Cabinet	Sears, Roebuck (1917)	Wilson; roll-curtain front cabinet	$19.85
Linoleum and Floor Oil	Sears, Roebuck (1917)	Seroco; cloth finish; puts a coating on linoleum and drys hard	$0.48/quart
Oil	Hearth and Home (1917)	Kibler's All 'Round; the oil with a thousand uses	$0.25/bottle
Oil	Today's Housewife (1917)	3-In-One; a little 3-in-One oil on a damp cloth will restore the lustre and cause surface scratches to vanish	$0.25
Polish	Today's Housewife (1917)	O-Cedar; it cleans as it polishes	$0.25
Polish	Sears, Roebuck (1917)	Whittmore's Albo; cleans and whitens canvas, duck, Nubuck, and suede shoes	$0.08
Rug	Chicago Tribune (1919)	Royal Wilton; 6' × 9'	$43.50
Sheet	Sears, Roebuck (1917)	White cotton; extra-quality regular length; 54" 3 8"	$1.07
Soap	The Asheville (NC) Times (1919)	Grandma's Powdered Soap; just a teaspoon replaces the chipping, slicing, and rubbing Per box	$0.05
Tablespoon	Sears, Roebuck (1917)	Salem; silver plate; Broadfield pattern; set of six	$4.40/set
Tapestry	Sears, Roebuck (1917)	Tallulla; worsted; 9' × 12'	$16.85
Toilet Paper	Sears, Roebuck (1917)	Sterling; large roll	$0.07
Trunk	Sears, Roebuck (1917)	Round cornered Vulcanized fiber; made of three-ply veneer lumber	$18.75
Vacuum Food Jar	Sears, Roebuck (1917)	For salads, stews, hot vegetables; quart size	$3.90
Washing Powder	Today's Housewife (1917)	Fairbank's Gold Dust; to clean pots, pans, refrigerator, and bathroom fixtures; purifies while it cleans	$0.05

INSURANCE RATES

Item	Source	Description	Price
Health Insurance	The World's Work (1917)	Aetna; get $25 a week up to 52 weeks while you are ill	$60.00/year

JEWELRY

Item	Source	Description	Price
Watch	Sears, Roebuck (1917)	Woman's bracelet watch; 10-year gold filled case; fitted with a 7-jewel imported movement	$7.00

MEALS

Item	Source	Description	Price
Dinner	Cohan and Harris Theatre Program (1917)	Murray's, 42nd Street, just west of Broadway Old Dominion Beefsteak Dinner	$1.50

Item	Source	Description	Price
Hot Dog	*American Chronicle* (1999)	Nathan's hotdogs at Coney Island	$0.05 each
Lunch	*Cohan and Harris Theatre Program* (1917)	Murray's Exceptional Luncheon, for tired shoppers and theatergoers	$0.70

MEDICAL PRODUCTS & SERVICES

Item	Source	Description	Price
Cough Drops	*The Playhouse Playbill,* New York City (1916)	*Smith Brothers Cough Drops*—after the show, be sure to bundle up good and take a few S.B. Cough Drops Per box	$0.05
Laxative	*Chicago Daily Tribune* (1917)	*Nujol* for constipation Pint bottle	$0.69
Laxative	*Chicago Daily* Tribune (1917)	Phillips Milk of Magnesia	$0.33
Nonprescription Drug	*The World's Work* (1917)	*Absorbine Jr.;* real help for tired feet	$1.00
Nonprescription Drug	*Today's Housewife* (1917)	*Blue-Jay Corn Medicine;* immediate relief—then the corn comes out in 48 hours	$0.15
Nonprescription Drug	*The World's Work* (1917)	*Brown's Bronchial Troches;* for that hacking cough; speedy, effective, harmless	$0.25
Nonprescription Drug	*The World's Work* (1917)	*Forhan's Pyorrhea Preparation;* at the first sign of inflamed or receding gums	$0.50
Nonprescription Drug	*The World's Work* (1917)	*Luden's Menthol Candy Cough Drops;* throat irritations won't disturb your sleep; in yellow box	$0.05

MOTORIZED VEHICLES, SERVICES, & SUPPLIES

Item	Source	Description	Price
Automobile	*The Playhouse Playbill,* New York City (1916)	Hudson—the super-six motor has made Hudson cars supreme; the motor is 80% more efficient than other like-size motors	$1,675
Automobile	*Cohan and Harris Theatre Program* (1917)	Standard "8", The Magneto Equipped Eight; built by steel masters famous for their railroad rolling stock	$2,450
Automobile	*The Craftsman* (1915)	*King Motor Car;* eight-cylinder, 40–45 hp; too successful to change this year	$1,350
Automobile	Joseph J. Schroeder Jr. *The Wonderful World of Automobiles* (1971)	*Chandler Six;* leads in service, style, and price [cost in 1916]	$1,295
Automobile	Schroeder, *The Wonderful World of Automobiles* (1971)	*Jackson Wolverine Eight;* eight-cylinder car, [cost in 1916]	$1,295
Automobile	Schroeder, *The Wonderful World of Automobiles* (1971)	*Maxwell Touring Car;* completely equipped, includingelectric starter and lights [cost in 1916]	$915
Automobile	Schroeder, *The Wonderful World of Automobiles* (1971)	*Saxon Six;* in the salesrooms of over 2,000 Saxon dealersthroughout the country you will find Saxon Sixes[cost in 1916]	$815

"A Car That Will Out-perform

Any Other in Its Price-class"

Advertisement for the Saxon Six that ran in the November 25, 1916 Country Gentleman. *Manufactured in Detroit from 1914 to 1922, Saxon was one of the top 10 auto manufacturers in sales, selling more than 27,000 units in 1916. Saxons were powered by 4 and 6-cylinder Continental engines.* (via Wikimedia Commons)

Item	Source	Description	Price
Automobile	Schroeder, *The Wonderful World of Automobiles* (1971)	*Allen;* 37 hp, full-floating rear axle, large,easy-acting brakes [cost in 1917]	$795
Automobile	Schroeder, *The Wonderful World of Automobiles* (1971)	*Briscoe 4–24;* the car with the half-million-dollar motor [cost in 1917]	$625
Automobile	*The World's Work* (1917)	*Chandler Six;* seven-passenger touring car	$1,395
Automobile	*The World's Work* (1917)	*Chandler Six;* four-passenger convertible coupe	$1,995
Automobile	*The World's Work* (1917)	*Franklin;* runabout; 2,160 pounds	$1,900

Item	Source	Description	Price
Automobile	*The World's Work* (1917)	*Marion-Handley The Six Pre-Eminent Six-60;* 7-passenger touring, 125" wheelbase	$1,575
Automobile	*The World's Work* (1917)	*Paige Statford Six-51;* 7-passenger car; the most beautiful car in America	$1,495
Automobile	Schroeder, *The Wonderful World of Automobiles* (1971)	*Studebaker Convertible Sedan;* door window lowers into frame, others slide into individual compartments under rear seat [cost in 1917]	$1,700
Automobile	Schroeder, *The Wonderful World of Automobiles* (1971)	*Willys-Knight Touring Sedan;* rear glass lowers, other between rear seat upholstery and tonneau casing [cost in 1917]	$1,950
Carbon Remover	*American Magazine* (1917)	*Johnson;* the engine laxative	$1.00

MUSICAL INSTRUMENTS

Item	Source	Description	Price
Clarinet	*Sears, Roebuck* (1917)	*Lafayette;* 15 keys, 2 rings, in the key of A, B flat, or E flat	$18.45
Player Piano	*Sears, Roebuck* (1917)	*Beckwith;* the versatility of this instrument makes it one of the most desirable of all instruments for home use	$397

OTHER

Item	Source	Description	Price
Cup	*Sears, Roebuck* (1917)	Collapsible; aluminum; just the thing for school children	$0.05
Friction Tape	*Sears, Roebuck* (1917)	Insulating; for electric wires or bicycles	$0.02
Glue	*Hearth and Home* (1917)	*Lepage's;* stronger than nails	$0.10
Home Building Materials	*Today's Housewife* (1917)	*Montgomery Ward Ready Cut;* all lumber, lath, shingles, doors, windows, frames, hardware, pipe, gutter and painting materials for this pretty, roomy bungalow	$548
House Barometer	*The World's Work* (1917)	*Tycos;* make your own weather forecasts	$10
Ink	*Today's Housewife* (1917)	*Payson's Indelible;* ready for use with a common pen	$0.25
Interest Rate	*American Chronicle* (1999)	Interest paid on $2 billion in War Savings Certificates and Liberty Loans to support World War I	3%
Mousetrap	*Sears, Roebuck* (1917)	Easy to set, a sure killer	$0.02
Printing Press	*American Magazine* (1917)	*Multigraph Senior;* produces real printing and form-type-writing rapidly, economically, privately in your own establishment; deluxe model	$765
Telephone Call	*Milwaukee Journal* (1916)	Three-minute call from New York to San Francisco	$20.70
Telephone Call	*Milwaukee Journal* (1916)	Three-minute call from New York to Chicago	$14.45

PERSONAL CARE PRODUCTS

Item	Source	Description	Price
Comb	*Chicago Daily Tribune* (1917)	Ladies' French ivory combs	$0.69

Item	Source	Description	Price
Comb	*Sears, Roebuck* (1917)	4 1/2" ornamental; set with tiny colored beads	$0.43
Comb	*Hearth and Home* (1917)	*Prof. Long's Magnette;* they remove dandruff, stop falling hair; relieve headaches	$0.02
Cream	*Today's Housewife* (1917)	*Ingram's Milkweed;* there is beauty in every jar	$0.50
Deodorant Cream	*Today's Housewife* (1917)	*Mum;* takes all the odor out of perspiration	$0.25
Eye Treatment	*Today's Housewife* (1917)	*Lash-Brow-ine;* nourishes the eyebrows and lashes	$0.25
Face Powder	*Today's Housewife* (1917)	*Nadine;* soft and velvety, adheres until washed off; popular tints: flesh, pink, brunette, white	$0.50
Hair Color	*Hearth and Home* (1917)	*Duby's;* darken your gray hair; package makes one pint	$0.25/pkg
Hair Curlers	*Today's Housewife* (1917)	*West Electric;* wave or curl your hair; every curler electrified—imparting strength to the hair	$0.25
Hair Pins	*Today's Housewife* (1917)	*Hump;* you'll need only one-third as many HUMP Hair pins to get better results; 5 sizes	$0.05
Powder	*Today's Housewife* (1917)	*Air Float Talc;* assorted odors: rose, wisteria, corylopsis, lilac, violet	$0.10
Powder	*Today's Housewife* (1917)	*Delatone;* removes hair or fuzz from face, neck or arm	$1/ounce jar
Powder	*Today's Housewife* (1917)	*Hinds Talcum;* a pure borated talc, powdered to an indescribable fineness	$0.25
Razor Blades	Chicago Daily Tribune (1917)	*Ever-Ready razor* blades Package of 10	$0.33
Shampoo	*Chicago Daily Tribune* (1917)	Hay's Coconut Oil Shampoo	$0.33
Shampoo	*Today's Housewife* (1917)	*Canthrox;* natural beauty and fluffiness of the hair is brought out to its best advantage; 15 exhilarating shampoos	$0.50
Soap	*Chicago Tribune* (1919)	*Kirk's Jap Rose;* opposite Marshall Fields	$0.07

PUBLICATIONS

Item	Source	Description	Price
Book	*The World's Work* (1917)	*Sea Warfare;* Kipling master war correspondent	$1.25
Magazine	*Leslie's* (1919)	*Film Fun;* puts you on speaking terms with your favorite star Per copy Per year	 $0.15 $1.50
Magazine	*The World's Work* (1917)	*The World's Work;* monthly	$0.25
Magazine	*The World's Work* (1917)	*Vanity Fair;* monthly	$0.25
Newspaper	*Wall Street Journal* (1916)	Annual subscription	$12.00
Newspaper	*The Youth's Companion* (1919)	*The Youth's Companion;* The Best of American Life in fiction, fact, and comment; published weekly Per year	$2.00

Item	Source	Description	Price
REAL ESTATE			
Apartment	*Chicago Daily Tribune* (1917)	Seven-room apartment, three baths, overlooking Lake Michigan Per month	$175
Apartment	*Chicago Daily Tribune* (1917)	Near elevated station; four-room flat, stove heat Per month	$12.00
Apartment Building	*Chicago Tribune* (1919)	Highgrade 3-apartment building, Chicago; 1/2 block from lake in Rogers Park	$26,000
Boiler Shop	*Chicago Daily Tribune*	One story brick boiler shop; Halsted Street, Chicago	$20,000
Farm	Toledo (Ohio) *Weekly Blade* (1917)	160-acre farm with 15 acres of corn, 7 of wheat, 3 acres of potatoes, comfortable residence with telephone	$4,500
Farm Land	Toledo (Ohio) *Weekly Blade* (1917)	Low terms for small or large tracts in Michigan's fruit and clover belt Per acre	$15.00 to $25.00
Fruit Farm	*Chicago Daily Tribune* (1917)	Fennville, Michigan 22-acre farm, 500 fruit trees	$6,000
House	*The Asheville (NC) Times* (1919)	Nice house, five rooms with sleeping porch, good neighborhood	$4,200
Land	*The Asheville (NC) Times* (1919)	Six lots in Norwood Park, frontage 250 feet; suitable for handsome residence	$6,500
Land	*Chicago Tribune* (1919)	180 acres, northern Wisconsin; dairy, grain, and stock farm, near town, lake, and river	$9,000
Lot	*Chicago Daily Tribune* (1917)	Vacant corner lot fronting lake and Sheridan Road	$40,000
Room	*Chicago Tribune* (1919)	*The Gibsonia;* Chicago, Illinois; single room; to rent, beautiful large room, separate beds	$4.00/week
SEWING EQUIPMENT & SUPPLIES			
Cloth	*Sears, Roebuck* (1917)	Mixed wool fabric; possess the much desired softness	$0.32/yard
Dress Pattern	*Hearth and Home* (1917)	*Hearth and Home;* this dress has a broad box plait at the center front and the dress fastens under this	$0.10
Sewing Needles	*Sears, Roebuck* (1917)	For sewing machines of any make	$0.15/dozen
SPORTS EQUIPMENT			
Baseball Glove	*Sears, Roebuck* (1917)	*J. C Higgins Professional;* pliable horsehide throughout	$3.00
Golf Bag	*Chicago Tribune* (1919)	5", canvas, leather trim, white or tan; regularly $5	$3.45
Oil	*The Youth's Companion* (1919)	3-in-One Oil; the right oil for guns 3 sizes	$0.15-$0.50
Shotgun	*Sears, Roebuck* (1917)	*Remington Repeating;* six-shot takedown model made in 12-gauge only	$32.70

Item	Source	Description	Price
TELEPHONE EQUIPMENT & SERVICES			
Telephone	*Sears, Roebuck* (1917)	*Bridging;* five-magnet compact bridging telephone with 1,000-ohm ringer; price with two dry batteries	$11.25
TOBACCO PRODUCTS			
Cigarettes	*The Playhouse Playbill,* New York City (1916)	*Murad,* The Turkish Cigarette	$0.15
Cigarettes	*Cohan and Harris Theatre Program* (1917)	*Egyptian Deities;* The utmost in cigarettes Plain end or cork tip, per box	$0.25

Advertisement for "Egyptian Deities" cigarettes, 1919. (via Wikimedia Commons)

Item	Source	Description	Price
Cigars	*Chicago Tribune* (1919)	*Cyro;* the original idea of putting $0.15 worth of smoke in a $0.10 cigar	$0.10
Cigars	*Sears, Roebuck* (1917)	*Berriman's Handmade Havana;* made at Tampa, Florida; can of 25 cigars	$1.27/can
Cigars	*Sears, Roebuck* (1917)	*Sardou;* the sweet domestic cigar; box of 50	$2.47/box
Cigarettes	*Chicago Tribune* (1919)	*Camel;* expertly blended choice Turkish and choice domestic tobaccos	$0.18/pack
Tobacco	*Chicago Tribune* (1919)	*Falk's Serene Mixture;* the great pipe smoke	$0.15/pkg

TOYS

Item	Source	Description	Price
Hobby Horse	*Sears, Roebuck* (1917)	He longs to conquer the fiery steed when placed on a rocking horse like this	$2.98
Wooden Blocks	*Sears, Roebuck* (1917)	Consists of twenty painted square blocks on which are Mother Goose nursery rhymes	$0.79

TRAVEL & TRANSPORTATION

Item	Source	Description	Price
Steamship Fare	*The World's Work* (1917)	From New York to Australia on Sydney Short Line via Honolulu and Samoa aboard splendid 10,000 ton, twin-screw American steamer	$337.50
Streetcar Fare	Edward L. Throm, ed. *Popular Mechanics Picture History of American Transportation* (1952)	Horse and mule; Bleecker Street, New York [cost in 1917]	$0.30
Trolley Fare	*American Chronicle* (1999)	Cost of a cross-town trolley ride in Boston in 1917	$0.05

MISCELLANY 1915–1919

What Price Doctors

Between 1917 and 1923, the eighteen general hospitals reporting to the United Hospital Fund increased their receipts for ward service from $1.46 to $2.67 per day. The average ward rates now charged in the majority of cases are between $3 and $4.

New York Times, May 4, 1919

Liquor and Prohibition

This is the time to acquire your wines and liquors. Prices are advancing daily and will continue to advance whether Prohibition becomes effective July 1, 1919, or January 20, 1920. Henry Hollander 149–151 West 36th Street New York City.

Imperial Gin	$2.15
Doul Gin	$2.30
Gordon Gin	$2.45
Cocktail Rum	$2.75
Bacardi Rum	$3.20
Allash Kummel	$2.60
Old Bridgeport Whiskey	$3.10
Green Creme De Menthe	$3.00

Chicago Tribune, April 19, 1919

MARS adds 17,000 Millionaires to American List

Recent estimates made public at Washington were that not fewer than 17,000 men and women in the United States had graduated into the millionaire class in the last two years. It is estimated that no fewer than 7,000 of their number, and possibly 10,000, are residents of New York.

Chicago Tribune, April 19, 1919

Gas Rates and Politics

As part of his campaign platform for City Council, Charles A. Brady of Columbia, S.C., called for another gas and electric power company, for we need competition, as our rates are too high as compared with other cities.

For 1916, he listed electric current for residence use of 7¢ per KWH in Jacksonville, Fla., 10¢ per KWH for Greenville, S. C., and 7¢ per KWH in New Orleans, La.

Gas prices for residence use were $1.15 per 1000 cu. ft. in Jacksonville, Fla.; $1.35 per 1000 cu. ft. in Greenville, S. C. and $1.10 per 1000 cu. ft. in New Orleans. The rates he was protesting in Columbia, S. C. were 12¢ per KWH and $1.35 per 1000 cu. ft. of gas.

Campaign Flier

Interview with Football Player Red Grange

1.   I started working summers on the ice truck when I was a kid and I kept it up for years, even after I became a professional football player (in 1925). I'd start at six in the morning, and many a day I'd work until seven or eight at night, six days a week. We got five dollars a day until the union came in, and they upped our salary to $37.50 a week.

2.   When I joined the (Chicago) Bears (football team) in 1929, except for my salary the entire payroll—all the coaches and players and even the trainer—was about three thousand dollars a game. I remember some of the early games at Wrigley Field in Chicago; our trainer would wait until they had sold a dozen tickets, then he'd take the ticket money across the street to a drugstore and buy the tape for our ankles. So, help me, that's true.

Robert S. Gallagher, American Heritage Magazine, December 1974

Rapid Dish Washer

At first view, the Rapid Electric Dish Washer appears to be only a beautiful kitchen table with silvery top and spacious lower compartment.

Upon lifting the lid, which extends across a portion of the top, one sees a most interesting interior, consisting of removable racks for dishes, so made that there are spaces for all kinds of china and utensils.

All one has to do in order to operate this machine is scrape the dishes, place them in their proper compartments, pour in eight quarts of boiling water, in which a good washing powder has been mixed, close the lid tight, turn on the current—and go about one's other duties. The price is $40.

Harper's Weekly, January 2, 1875

MISCELLANY 1915–1919

The Price of Fixing

Before 1919 the fixing of baseball games for betting purposes was by no means unheard of. But in that year it went too far: the 'unthinkable' happened; a World Series was fixed by eight star players for the Chicago White Sox. Testimony showed that most of the players had gotten $5,000 for their parts in the fix, while Chicago first baseman Charles Arnold 'Chick' Gandil had kept $35,000 for himself.

The Encyclopedia of American Crime

The eight Chicago White Sox players accused of fixing 1919 World Series. All eight were banned from professional baseball forever. Jackson's involvement has been disputed. (via Wikimedia Commons)

1920–1939

Return to "Normalcy," the Great Depression, and Recovery

PRESIDENTS

Warren G. Harding†   1921–1923

Calvin Coolidge   1923–1929

Herbert Hoover   1929–1933

Franklin D. Roosevelt†   1933–1945

† died in office

1928 series one-dollar bill.

The second twenty years of the twentieth century are divided into two major periods by historians: the Return to Normalcy (1920–1929), following the First World War, a decade of expansion and speculation, and the Great Depression and Recovery (1930–1939), which threw millions out of work and dramatically changed the role of the federal government. The attitude of many Americans during the first half of the era is expressed in President Calvin Coolidge's famous statement, "the chief business of the American people is business"; the role of the federal government remained small and federal expenditures actually declined following the war effort. Harry Donaldson's song "How Ya Gonna Keep 'Em Down on the Farm After They've Seen Paree?" described another basic shift in American society after the war. The 1920 census reported that more than 50 percent of the population—54 million people—lived in urban areas. The move to the cities was the result of changed expectations after the war and the migration of millions of southern Blacks to the industrialized urban North.

The dream of normalcy lasted through most of a fitful decade, during which the United States became more than a land of big cities, big money, and big factories filled with machines. Following the war years, women who had worked men's jobs during the wartime mobilization usually remained in the work force, although at lower wages. Average family earnings increased slightly during the first half of the period while prices and hours worked both declined. The forty-eight-hour work week became standard, providing greater leisure time. At least 40 million per- sons went to the movies every week. Expanding use of electricity, appliances, and automobiles was the consequence of rapidly changing lifestyles. Automobile production rose from 1.5 million in 1921 to 4.8 million in 1929 while the prices declined dramatically. By 1929 one American in five owned an automobile, ushering in weekend trips, tourist cabins, road-sign advertising, and gas stations. Within the home the availability of electricity brought an array of timesaving appliances. Radio brought the world to small-town America; the automobile and expanding railroad service took small-town America to the world.

Despite a growing middle class, the share of disposable income going to the top 5 percent of the population moved from approximately one-quarter to nearly one-third of the total. Fifty percent of the people, by one estimate, lived in poverty. By 1929 the average factory worker made less than $1,500 annually. Coal and textile workers, southern farmers, unorganized labor, the elderly, single women, and most blacks were excluded from the economic giddiness of the period. Union membership declined throughout the 1920s, canceling the gains of the war years, despite a rapidly expanding

193

workforce. Labor strikes also declined during the period from a peak of 4,450 in 1917 to 732 in 1927.

American exports more than doubled during the decade; heavy imports of European goods were virtually halted, a reversal of the progressive movement's flirtation with free trade. Immigration laws were increasingly restrictive during the 1920s. The 1924 National Origins Act limited immigration from each country to a percent of its proportional population of resident aliens based on the census of 1890. It cut immigration to a trickle.

In 1929 America appeared to be in an era of unending prosperity. U.S. goods and services reached an all-time high. Industrial production rose 50 percent during the decade as the concept of mass production was refined and broadly applied. The sale of electrical appliances, radios, refrigerators, and other durable goods skyrocketed. Consumers were able to purchase newly produced goods through the extended use of credit. Debt accumulated faster than wealth. By 1930 personal debt had increased to one-third of personal wealth.

The next decade, following the nightmare on Wall Street in October 1929, was marked by economic paralysis: bank failures, railway insolvency, high unemployment, closed factories, and sharply reduced foreign trade. By 1932 one in four Americans was jobless. One of every four farms was sold for taxes. Five thousand banks closed their doors. Durable goods production did not regain the 1929 peak until 1940. Prosperity had disappeared.

Despite continued assurances to the contrary from government and business leaders, the crash of 1929 was not simply a correction of inflated values. Farm income was cut in half. Members of the middle class lost their savings, their houses, their jobs, and their hope. President Hoover, the great humanitarian of 1928, became regarded as the dupe. The stage was set for change and the New Deal as presented by Franklin D. Roosevelt.

Roosevelt's first series of social experiments was characterized by Relief, Recovery, and Reform. This program carried two key objectives: to raise prices by restricting output while controlling competition, and to inflate the dollar. Believing that the expansion of the United States economy was finished, the Roosevelt administration paid attention to better distribution and planned production. The Civilian Conservation Corps (CCC), for example, put 250,000 jobless young men to work in the forests at $1 a day. By 1935 government deficit spending spurred economic change. By 1937 total manufacturing output exceeded that of 1929; prices and wages rose briskly. Inflation fears forced curtailed spending and restrictions on bank lending, driving the Depression into a serious dip in the late 1930s.

During the second half of the 1930s social security began, and estate and gift taxes were increased, as were the income taxes of large corporations. Organized labor, which hit a low point in 1933, gained expanded rights to organize and rapidly began to use its new-found muscle. Despite progress, 10 million workers were still unemployed in 1938, and farm prices lagged far behind manufacturing progress. Full recovery would not occur until the United States mobilized for World War II.

Year	Dollar Value in 2019	Year	Dollar Value in 2019
1920	$12.81	1930	$15.34
1923	$14.98	1933	$19.70
1925	$14.64	1935	$18.70
1927	$14.72	1937	$17.79
1929	$14.98	1939	$18.43

Use this Currency Conversion chart to calculate what any time in the years listed would cost in 2019. Simply multiply the cost of that item by dollar amount in the chart. For example, if you know that materials for a five-room house cost $1,932 in 1927, multiply $1,932 by $14.72 to discover that those same materials would cost $28,439 in 2019.

HISTORICAL SNAPSHOT 1920–1924

1920

- Chanel No. 5 perfume introduced
- Youngs Rubber Company is founded to make Trojan brand condoms
- Flour consumption falls to 179 pounds per capita from 224 pounds in 1900, as meat, fish, and vegetable consumption rises
- Baby Ruth candy introduced by Curtiss Candy Company, priced at 5 cents
- Coca-Cola sales exceed $4 million
- World sugar price drops from 30 cents per pound to 8 cents
- The Volstead Act, enforcing national prohibition of alcohol, goes into effect
- Soybean harvest reaches 1 million bushels

1921

- Drano drain cleaner introduced
- Wise Potato Chips introduced by Berwick, PA, grocer Earl V. Wise
- Mounds candy bars introduced by the Peter Paul Manufacturing Company
- Molasses prices drop to 2 cents per gallon, down from 20 cents
- Wholesale butter prices fall to
- 29 cents per pound, down from its wartime high of 76 cents
- Salt iodized with potassium iodide
- Cigarette consumption reaches 43 billion cigarettes
- Arrow shirt introduced to meet demand for collar-attached shirts

1922

- New York's Delmonico's Restaurant closes

ARROW SHIRTS

- Thom McAn shoe store introduces mass-produced shoes sold through chain store for $3.99 per pair
- California becomes year-round source of oranges
- Most farmers in deep depression
- First commercially prepared baby food marketed
- Camden, NJ canning company, founded in 1869, changes name to Campbell's Soup Company
- Mah-jongg craze sweeps nation, game sets outsell radio

1923

- Popsicle patented under name Epsicle
- Butterfinger candy bar created and marketed by dropping parachuted bars from airplane
- Commercially canned tomato juice marketed by Libby McNeill & Libby

- First practical electric shaver patented by Schick
- A. C. Nielsen Company founded
- Chicago Radio Laboratory, founded in 1918, is incorporated as Zenith Radio Corporation
- 10 automakers account for
- 90 percent of sales; 108 companies producing cars
- Hertz Drive Ur Self System founded; creates world's first auto rental concern

1924

- Thirty percent of bread baked at home, down from 70 percent in 1910
- First effective chemical pesticides introduced
- *American Mercury* begins publication
- Radio set ownership reaches 3 million
- James Buchanan "Buck" Duke donates $47 million to Trinity College at Durham, NC, which changes its name to Duke
- Ford produces 2 million Model T motorcars; price of touring car falls to $290
- Dean Witter and Company founded
- Maxwell Motor Corporation (run by Walter Chrysler), Ford, and General Motors produce approximately 80 percent of U. S. cars

SELECTED INCOME 1920–1924

Job	Source	Description	Pay
Actor	Legrand and Karney *Chronicle of the Cinema* (1995)	Weekly income of Rudolph Valentino after the release of the silent movie *The Sheik* in 1921	$1,250
Bookkeeper	*San Francisco Examiner* (1921)		$115/wk
Classical Concert Pianist (1922)	*Guinness Book of World Records* (1981)	Single year earnings of classical pianist Ignacy Jan Paderewski	$500,000
Clearing House Clerk	*San Francisco Examiner* (1921)	Bank	$70/wk
Clerk	*Chicago Tribune* (1920)	Young man; bright; willing; experienced at figures	$22/wk to start
Clerk	Chicago Tribune (1920)	Young men 16 and 21; junior clerical position; excellent chance to learn profession while you earn a salary	$14–16/wk
Clerk	*Chicago Tribune* (1922)	Good at figures, reliable, and willing to work some evenings; office experience helpful but not necessary	$35/wk
House Messenger	*Chicago Tribune* (1920)	A boy who wants to start as a house messenger and junior stock clerk, where he can develop and earn a good salary, will find a splendid opportunity now	$17/wk
Industrialist	*American Chronicle* (1999)	Billionaire manufacturer Henry Ford's daily income in 1922	$264,000

The May 1920 issue of The Independent *with Henry Ford on the cover.* (via Wikimedia Commons)

Job	Source	Description	Pay
Mechanical Draftsman	*Chicago Tribune* (1920)	Experienced, preferably with railway experience	$225/mo
Miscellaneous	*Chicago Tribune* (1920)	Boys and young men mechanically inclined; no experience required; steady employment	$15–25/wk
Office Boy	*Chicago Tribune* (1920)	Where is there an office boy with some AMBITION, who wants a good position in an advertising office?	$12/wk
Porcelain	*Chicago Tribune* (1920)	Man—young to learn porcelain work	$15/wk
Sales	*Chicago Tribune* (1920)	No experience necessary; we train you and assist you to make big money	$80–300/wk
Sales	*Chicago Tribune* (1920)	Ambitious and energetic young man 20 years old; married; College education; 5 years successful record in sales promotion	$65/wk
Sales	*Chicago Tribune* (1922)	Men; have openings for some lively young men on special house-to-house work satisfied with $32 to start; selling experience not necessary	$32/wk
Sales	*Chicago Tribune* (1922)	Work with manager on renewals, 20 popular magazine clubs	$40/wk
Sales	*Chicago Tribune* (1922)	Jewish of good personality to represent the largest Jewish publishing house in the world; our work makes an appeal to all classes of Jews, and we can offer you exclusive territory and leads	$100–$125/wk
Secretary	*Chicago Tribune* (1920)	Situation wanted: steno and dictaphone operator; 10 years' experience	$30–35/wk
Sewer	*Picture Play* Magazine (1923)	Decorate pillow tops at home; experience unnecessary; particulars for stamp; tapestry Paint Co., 110 LaGrange, Indiana	$6–18/dozen
Steno-Clerk	*San Francisco Examiner* (1921)	Small Office	$75/wk
Stenographer	*Chicago Tribune* (1920)	The editor and executive of a Catholic publishing house desires to secure the services of a competent stenographer with secretarial experience, preferring one who writes and speaks French	$30/wk to start
Stenographer	*Chicago Tribune* (1920)	Who can do some ledger posting; excellent opportunity for right party	$18/wk
Stenographer	*New York Times* (1923)	Openings for capable refined young women; steno; law	$25–30/wk
Stenographer	*Chicago Tribune* (1924)	Situation Wanted: Steno-Corr; Small office; Loop; efficiency and common sense	$30/wk
Switchboard Operator	*Chicago Tribune* (1920)	Experienced, capable, and competent; small board; some office work. Jewish preferred	$23–25/wk
Telephone Operator	*New York Times* (1923)	Hours 6 a.m. to 2:10 p.m. and from 4-6 p.m. Busy board	$20/wk
Ticket Press	*Chicago Tribune* (1920)	Boys over 16; extra pay for good work	$14/wk
Typist	*Chicago Tribune* (1920)	Good permanent position with chance to advance; dictaphone experience preferred but not necessary	$20/wk to start

CONSUMER EXPENDITURES 1921, 1923

(Per Capita)

Expenditure Type	1921	1923
Clothing	$56.45	$64.52
Food	$128.14	NR
Auto Purchases	$10.66	$20.45
Auto Parts	$3.46	$4.97
Gas & Oil	$11.57	$12.38
Dentists	$1.71	$2.72
Health Insurance	NR	NR
Personal Business	$17.95	$22.17
Personal Care	$5.55	$7.79
Housing	$89.20	$94.80
Furniture	$6.36	$8.78
Utilities	$7.63	$8.97
Telephone & Telegraph	$2.35	$2.71
Physicians	$4.79	$7.15
Intercity Transport	$5.16	$5.22
Recreation	$19.05	$23.44
Religion/Welfare Activities	$12.57	$11.57
Private Education & Research	$6.87	$7.26

Holeproof Hosiery Co. ad with art by Coles Phillips, on the back cover of the June 1922 Photoplay *Magazine.* (via Wikimedia Commons)

INVESTMENTS 1920–1924

Investment	1920	1921	1922	1923	1924
Basic Yield, One-year Corporate Bonds	6.11	6.94	5.31	5.01	5.02
Short-term Interest Rates, 4-6 Months, Prime Commercial Paper	7.50	6.62	4.52	5.07	3.98
Basic Yield, Common Stocks, Total	6.13	6.49	5.80	5.94	5.87
Index of Common Stocks (1941 21943510)	7.98	6.86	8.41	8.57	9.05

COMMON STOCKS, CLOSING PRICE AND YIELD, FIRST BUSINESS DAY OF YEAR

	1920	1921	1922	1923	1924
Allis Chalmers	53 3/8	30 7/8	38	46 7/8	44 1/4
AT&T	97 3/8	96	114 7/8	123 1/2	125 1/4
American Tobacco (75% stock dividend in Common B, 7/15/20)	270	114	129 1/2	155	148 1/2
Anaconda	65	35 1/2	49	49 7/8	38
B&O	33 1/4	36	34	42 3/4	58 3/4
Bethlehem Steel A	93	53	52 5/8	61 3/4	53 5/8
Corn Products	86 3/4	67	93	128 5/8	157
General Electric (2% stock dividend, 6/7/19; 2% stock dividend, 12/6/19) (2% stock dividend, 6/10/20; stock dividend, 12/8/20) (2% stock dividend, 6/8/21; 2% stock dividend, 12/8/21) (5% stock dividend in special stock, 9/7/22) (5% stock dividend in special stock, 9/5/23)	172	122 1/4	137	182	194
General Motors (10 shares for 1 split, 3/1/20; 2 1/2% stock dividend, 7/5/20; 2 1/2% stock dividend, 10/5/20)	338	14 3/8	9 1/2	14 7/8	14 7/8
Intl Harvester (12 1/2% stock dividend, 9/15/20) (2% stock dividend, 1/25/21; 2% stock dividend, 7/25/21) (2% stock dividend, 1/25/22; 2% stock dividend, 7/25/22) (2% stock dividend, 1/25/23)	130	95 3/8	79 1/48	88	79
National Biscuit (4 shares for 1 split, 12/30/22; 75% stock dividend, 12/30/22)	121	NR	123	38 1/2	41 1/4
US Steel	107 7/8	81 1/2	82 1/2	107 1/4	98 7/8
Western Union	88	84	90 5/8	112 1/2	107

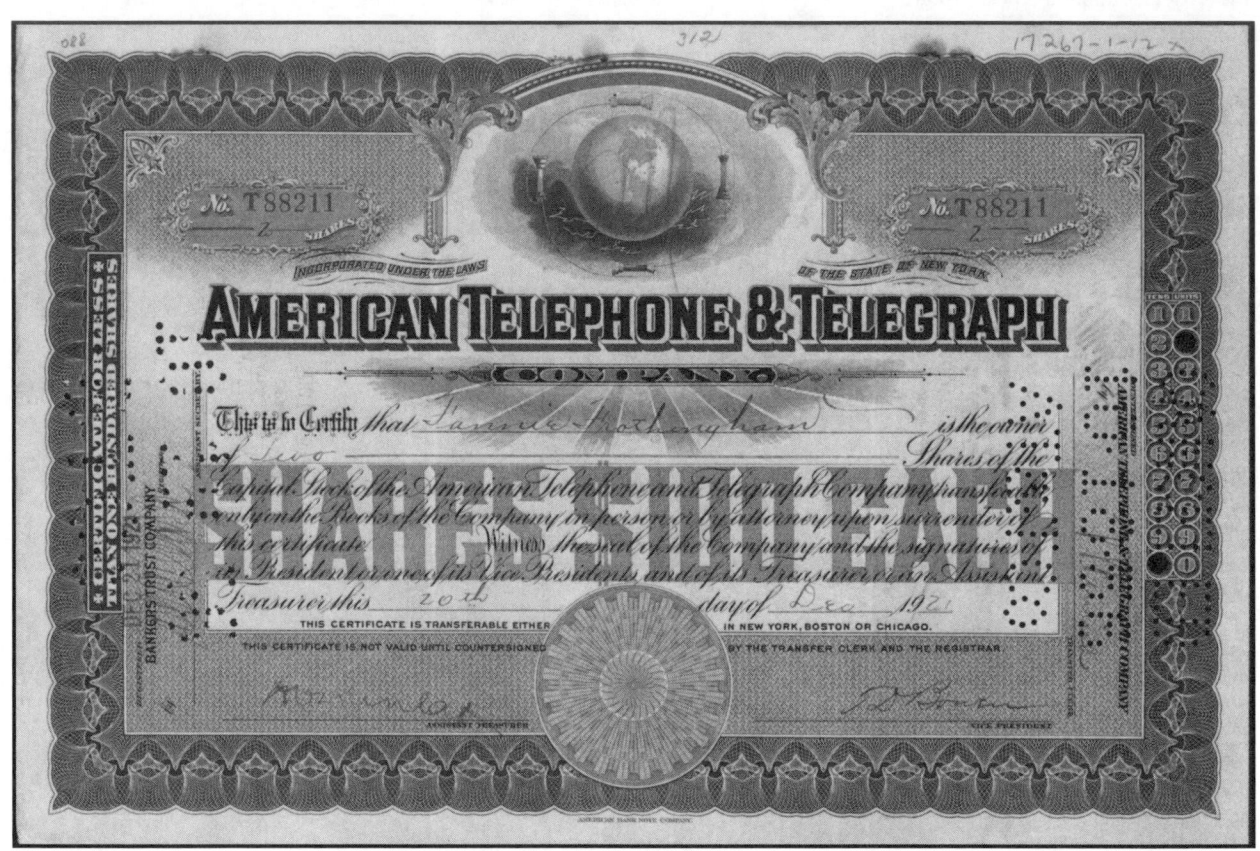

Share of the American Telephone & Telegraph Company, issued December 20, 1921. (via Wikimedia Commons)

STANDARD JOBS 1920–1924

Job Type	1920	1921	1922	1923	1924
Average of All Industries, excl. farm labor	$1489/yr	$1349/yr	$1305/yr	$1393/yr	$1402/yr
Average of All Industries, inc. farm labor	$1407/yr	$1233/yr	$1201/yr	$1299/yr	$1303/yr
Bituminous Coal Mining	85¢/hr	83¢/hr	86¢/hr	81¢/hr	78¢/hr
Avg hrs/wk	48.20	48.40	48.40	48.50	48.20
Building Trades, Union Workers	$1.08/hr	$1.01/hr	$1.11/hr	$1.19/hr	$1.05/hr
Avg hrs/wk	43.80	43.80	43.90	43.80	43.80
Clerical Workers in Mfg. & Steam RR	$2160/yr	$2134/yr	$2067/yr	$2126/yr	$2196/yr
Domestics	$655/yr	$649/yr	$649/yr	$711/yr	$732/yr
Farm Labor	$810/yr	$522/yr	$508/yr	$572/yr	$574/yr
Federal Civilian	$1707/yr	$1683/yr	$1694/yr	$1704/yr	$1747/yr
Federal Employees, Executive Depts.	$1648/yr	$1593/yr	$1625/yr	$1658/yr	$1708/yr
Finance, Insurance, & Real Estate	$1758/yr	$1860/yr	$1932/yr	$1896/yr	$1944/yr
Gas & Electricity Workers	$1432/yr	$1364/yr	$1343/yr	$1339/yr	$1417/yr
Lower-Skilled Labor	$1207/yr	$780/yr	$807/yr	$984/yr	$1128/yr
Manufacturing, Payroll	47¢/hr	44¢/hr	49¢/hr	50¢/hr	56¢/hr
Avg hrs/wk	52.70	53.40	53	52.10	53.50
Manufacturing, Union Workers	88¢/hr	92¢/hr	87¢/hr	91¢/hr	97¢/hr
Avg hrs/wk	45.70	46.10	46.20	46.30	46.10
Medical/Health Services Workers	$752/yr	$983/yr	$912/yr	$845/yr	$845/yr
Ministers	$1556/yr	$1428/yr	$1622/yr	$1620/yr	$1678/yr
Nonprofit Org. Workers	$1286/yr	$1392/yr	$1446/yr	$1454/yr	$1507/yr

Job Type	1920	1921	1922	1923	1924
Postal Employees	76¢/hr	75¢/hr	76¢/hr	78¢/hr	74¢/hr
Avg hrs/wk	47.40	47.40	47.20	47.20	48.00
Public School Teachers	$970/yr	$1109/yr	$1206/yr	$1239/yr	$1269/yr
State and Local Govt. Workers	$1164/yr	$1296/yr	$1316/yr	$1336/yr	$1346/yr
Steam Railroads, Wage Earners	$1817/yr	$1632/yr	$1591/yr	$1585/yr	$1570/yr
Street Railway Workers	$1608/yr	$1539/yr	$1436/yr	$1493/yr	$1544/yr
Telegraph Ind. Workers	$1159/yr	$1145/yr	$1110/yr	$1133/yr	$1150/yr
Telephone Ind. Workers	$980/yr	$1038/yr	$1064/yr	$1069/yr	$1104/yr
Wholesale and Retail Trade Workers	$1270/yr	$1260/yr	$1261/yr	$1272/yr	$1314/yr

FOOD BASKET 1920–1924

Commodity	Year	New York	Atlanta	Chicago	Denver	Los Angeles
Beans, Navy, per pound	1920	12¢	13.50¢	11.60¢	12.70¢	9.90¢
	1921	8.90¢	10¢	7.90¢	9.10¢	8¢
	1922	10¢	11.10¢	9.80¢	10.10¢	9.10¢
	1923	11.60¢	12.80¢	11.10¢	12.10¢	9.80¢
	1924	10.80¢	12.30¢	9.90¢	11¢	9.50¢

Joseph Campbell Company canned beans advertisement in the Saturday Evening Post, *June 18, 1921. Campbell's started using its signature red-and-white can in 1898 and continues to use the design today.* (via Wikimedia Commons)

Commodity	Year	New York	Atlanta	Chicago	Denver	Los Angeles
Beef, Rib Roasts, per pound	1920	40.50¢	30.70¢	33.50¢	28.40¢	30¢
	1921	36.40¢	27.40¢	30.20¢	23.60¢	29.30¢
	1922	35.30¢	26.70¢	28.80¢	22.90¢	28.30¢
	1923	36.30¢	26.90¢	30.20¢	22.40¢	28.10¢
	1924	36.90¢	26.60¢	31.60¢	22.20¢	28.80¢
Beef, Steaks (Round), per pound	1920	47.30¢	36.70¢	34.70¢	34.20¢	32.40¢
	1921	41.30¢	32.80¢	31¢	27.20¢	29.90¢
	1922	39.60¢	31.20¢	29.10¢	25.80¢	28.20¢
	1923	40.80¢	30.90¢	31.50¢	26.40¢	27.60¢
	1924	40.40¢	31.80¢	32.10¢	26.50¢	29.10¢
Bread, per loaf	1920	11.70¢	12.20¢	11.60¢	11.80¢	10.10¢
	1921	10.30¢	11.10¢	10.30¢	10.30¢	9.30¢
	1922	9.50¢	9.90¢	9.70¢	8.30¢	9¢
	1923	9.60¢	9.10¢	9.70¢	8¢	9¢
	1924	9.50¢	9.10¢	9.80¢	7.80¢	8.80¢
Butter, per pound	1920	70.50¢	73.30¢	63.40¢	64.80¢	68.90¢
	1921	52.40¢	54.10¢	48.90¢	47¢	52.40¢
	1922	48.00¢	49.10¢	45.20¢	42.60¢	51.80¢
	1923	55.50¢	56.40¢	53.50¢	51.10¢	57.50¢
	1924	52.20¢	53.80¢	49.80¢	47.30¢	52.50¢
Cheese, per pound	1920	42.10¢	40.20¢	42.20¢	43.90¢	43.90¢
	1921	35.40¢	32.70¢	37¢	36.10¢	38.20¢
	1922	33.30¢	32.40¢	35¢	35.10¢	36.10¢
	1923	37.90¢	35.80¢	40.20¢	38.60¢	37.40¢
	1924	37.10¢	33.30¢	39.20¢	37.40¢	38.20¢
Chickens, per pound	1920	43.50¢	39.50¢	41.60¢	40.80¢	49¢
	1921	42.10¢	33.80¢	36.70¢	35.60¢	44.80¢
	1922	37.40¢	31.30¢	33.70¢	30.70¢	41.30¢
	1923	36.10¢	31.30¢	32.80¢	29.20¢	39.70¢
	1924	37.60¢	31.80¢	34¢	29.40¢	40.20¢
Coffee, per pound	1920	43.10¢	50.30¢	39.70¢	48¢	44.80¢
	1921	32.40¢	34.60¢	33.60¢	36.40¢	37.90¢
	1922	33.50¢	35.90¢	34.50¢	35.50¢	38¢
	1923	34.80¢	37.10¢	38¢	36.60¢	39.50¢
	1924	40.80¢	42.40¢	43.90¢	42¢	47.80¢
Cornmeal, per pound	1920	7.90¢	5.50¢	6.80¢	5.80¢	7.50¢
	1921	6.50¢	3.40¢	6.10¢	3.50¢	5.20¢
	1922	5.40¢	2.90¢	5.20¢	3.10¢	4.30¢
	1923	5.40¢	3.60¢	5.30¢	3.30¢	4.40¢
	1924	5.80¢	4¢	5.60¢	3.60¢	4.70¢
Eggs, per dozen	1920	78¢	69¢	71.20¢	63.40¢	64.50¢
	1921	1.80¢	44.60¢	48.90¢	47.20¢	50.20¢
	1922	53.70¢	38.30¢	42.70¢	40.70¢	44.80¢
	1923	57.10¢	41.40¢	46¢	42.10¢	46.50¢
	1924	57.80¢	43.70¢	47.80¢	43.60¢	46.40¢
Flour, Wheat, per pound	1920	8.70¢	8¢	7.60¢	6.70¢	7.80¢
	1921	5.90¢	6.20¢	5.20¢	4.30¢	5.80¢
	1922	5.20¢	5.50¢	4.60¢	3.90¢	4.90¢
	1923	4.80¢	5.30¢	4.10¢	3.80¢	4.70¢
	1924	5.10¢	5.60¢	4.40¢	3.90¢	4.70¢
Lard, per pound	1920	29.90¢	30.30¢	27.80¢	32.20¢	32¢
	1921	19.10¢	18.90¢	17.30¢	19.80¢	19.20¢
	1922	17.10¢	17.90¢	16.30¢	18.80¢	18.70¢
	1923	18.20¢	18.20¢	17.20¢	19.10¢	19.60¢
	1924	19.60¢	18.90¢	19.10¢	19¢	20.30¢

Commodity	Year	New York	Atlanta	Chicago	Denver	Los Angeles
Milk, Fresh, per quart	1920	16.70¢	25¢	15¢	12.90¢	17¢
	1921	15.1¢	19.10¢	13.40¢	11.40¢	12.10¢
	1922	14.60¢	16.40¢	12¢	10¢	14.20¢
	1923	14.80¢	16.70¢	13.50¢	11.80¢	15¢
	1924	13.80¢	17.60¢	14¢	11.70¢	15.70¢
Mutton and Lamb, Leg, per pound	1920	34.40¢	41.70¢	38.70¢	34.10¢	35.50¢
	1921	32.90¢	34.30¢	33.40¢	31¢	31.40¢
	1922	35.30¢	36.60¢	36¢	34.30¢	32.50¢
	1923	35.80¢	35.50¢	35.60¢	35¢	33.30¢
Pork, Bacon, Sliced, per pound	1920	49.19¢	54.30¢	56.40¢	55.20¢	62.80¢
	1921	40.80¢	43.60¢	50.20¢	46.40¢	54.20¢
	1922	38.20¢	38.60¢	45.90¢	43.40¢	51.50¢
	1923	37.90¢	35.80¢	44.30¢	42.70¢	49.80¢
	1924	36.60¢	34.90¢	42.20¢	41¢	47.70¢
	1924	36.30¢	35.20¢	36.50¢	34.80¢	33.80¢
Pork Chops, per pound	1920	44.10¢	40.50¢	38.10¢	40.40¢	48.90¢
	1921	38.10¢	33.50¢	32.10¢	32.90¢	41.30¢
	1922	35.70¢	31.80¢	30.30¢	30.90¢	38.60¢
	1923	33¢	28.50¢	27.30¢	28.60¢	36.90¢
	1924	33¢	29.10¢	28.40¢	29¢	37.80¢
Pork, Ham, Sliced, per pound	1920	59.90¢	55.80¢	56¢	60.10¢	65.80¢
	1921	53.40¢	48.50¢	50.60¢	53.80¢	60.80¢
	1922	54.60¢	47.60¢	49.40¢	53.60¢	61.20¢
	1923	45.70¢	47.80¢	49.70¢	49.70¢	58¢
	1924	49.90¢	45.20¢	47.30¢	48¢	58.40¢
Potatoes, Irish, per pound	1920	6.60¢	7.70¢	6.60¢	6.40¢	6.35¢
	1921	3.70¢	4¢	2.90¢	2.80¢	3.20¢
	1922	3.40¢	3.90¢	2.70¢	2.50¢	2.90¢
	1923	3.70¢	4¢	2.60¢	2.40¢	3.20¢
	1924	3.40¢	3.60¢	2.60¢	2.70¢	3.50¢
Prunes, Dried, per pound	1920	27¢	27.80¢	28.60¢	30.10¢	27.40¢
	1921	19.30¢	20.70¢	20.60¢	20.30¢	18.10¢
	1922	33.50¢	21.10¢	20.70¢	20.80¢	19.40¢
	1923	17.30¢	19.80¢	19.90¢	20.30¢	18.90¢
	1924	16.10¢	18.10¢	18.80¢	18.40¢	16.90¢
Rice, per pound	1920	16.90¢	16.70¢	16.80¢	17.60¢	16.90¢
	1921	9.20¢	8.40¢	9.40¢	9.40¢	9.90¢
	1922	9.10¢	9.10¢	9.80¢	9.70¢	9.70¢
	1923	9.40¢	8.60¢	10.10¢	9.60¢	9.80¢
	1924	9.80¢	9.50¢	10.60¢	10¢	10.40¢
Sugar, per pound	1920	18.20¢	19.90¢	19.60¢	14.70¢	18¢
	1921	7.20¢	8.30¢	7.50¢	8.60¢	8¢
	1922	6.60¢	7.70¢	6.60¢	8¢	7.40¢
	1923	9.40¢	10.60¢	9.40¢	10.80¢	10.30¢
	1924	8.40¢	9.70¢	8.80¢	9.80¢	9.10¢
Tea, per pound	1920	57.40¢	92.30¢	70.20¢	72.70¢	73.40¢
	1921	52.50¢	90.90¢	65.70¢	71.40¢	69¢
	1922	49.10¢	88.10¢	64¢	69.60¢	70.20¢
	1923	55.40¢	92.90¢	71.30¢	67.70¢	69.80¢
	1924	60.30¢	93.50¢	73¢	68.20¢	70.70¢

SELECTED PRICES 1920–1924

Item	Source	Description	Price
ADVERTISING			
Advertising Budget	Roland Marchand, *Advertising the American Dream* (1985)	Crane Company (plumbing supplies) budget for 1921	$79,000/year
Advertising Budget	Marchand, *Advertising the American Dream* (1985)	*Maxwell House coffee*; for magazine advertisements in 1921	$19,955/year
APPAREL, CHILDREN'S			
Baseball Outfit	*Sears, Roebuck* (1924)	Boy's; quality gray cotton flannel with maroon stripes	$1.79
Bathing Suit	*B. Altman & Co.* (1923)	One-piece; wool jersey in white and navy blue, white-and-rose, or white and copenhagen	$2.95
Camping and Hiking Suit	*B. Altman & Co.* (1923)	Girl's; khaki-colored twill, includes coat, knickers and wrap-around skirt	$14.50
Dress	*B. Altman & Co.* (1923)	Girls; middy; cotton twill, lacing in front, patch pocket	$1.55
Children's Shoes	*The Youth's Companion* (1920)	*Selz Liberty Bell Shoes;* save your children from the foot miseries most adults know	$5.00 and up
Dress	*B. Altman & Co.* (1923)	Baby's; hand-made; long; of nainsook, hand tucks, and hand-hemstitching formed yoke	$2.95
Frock	*B. Altman & Co.* (1923)	Girl's; cotton voile, belted with smocking	$3.85
Night-robe	*B. Altman & Co.* (1923)	Baby's; of cotton stockinette, drawstring at bottom, one year	$0.95
Romper	*B. Altman & Co.* (1923)	Boy's; of chambray in cadet blue on tan	$1.35
Sailor Suit	*B. Altman & Co.* (1923)	Boy's; French blouse; unbleached jean with black trimming	$3.25
Shoes	*B. Altman & Co.* (1923)	Lace; of dark tan calfskin, sizes 7 to 11	$4.50
Shoes	*B. Altman & Co.* (1923)	*Keds;* boy's; of heavy white or brown duck; Goodyear glove band	$0.75
Skirt	*B. Altman & Co.* (1923)	Baby's; long; of nainsook, ruffle of embroidery	$0.85
Suit	*Chicago Tribune* (1920)	*Starr Best;* boy's wash; of plain blue denim trimmed with lighter blue	$2.95
Suit	*B. Altman & Co.* (1923)	Boy's; regulation middy; elaborately trimmed with embroidery and taping; yoke, black silk tie	$2.95
APPAREL, MEN'S			
Bathing Suit	*B. Altman & Co.* (1923)	Of worsted; in black or navy blue	$5.00
Collars	*Sears, Roebuck* (1920)	Vanderbilt style; soft; points 2 1/4"; back 1 1/2"; package of six	$1.25/pkg
Handkerchiefs	*B. Altman & Co.* (1923)	Plain; white lawn, shirred, hemstitched	$1.80/dozen
Hose	*B. Altman & Co.* (1923)	Ribbed wool; half hose; for tennis in white	$1.50/pair

Item	Source	Description	Price
Hose	*B. Altman & Co.* (1923)	*Lisle;* half hose; black, white, cordovan, gray, navy, blue, tan	$0.75/pair
Riding Breeches	*B. Altman & Co.* (1923)	Tan linen crash, with full reinforcement of the material	$12.00
Shirt	*Chicago Tribune* (1922)	*Manhattan;* white Oxford; you're going to like this shirt a lot	$2.75
Shirt	*B. Altman & Co.* (1923)	Polo; white Oxford, with collar attached	$2.50
Shoes	*Chicago Tribune* (1920)	*Henry L. Lytton & Sons Palm Beach Oxford;* made in custom or medium broad toes with solid leather soles	$7.00
Shoes	*B. Altman & Co.* (1923)	Brogue Oxford; of tan or black Norwegian grain leather	$8.50/pair
Slippers	*B. Altman & Co.* (1923)	Of brown or black leather	$3.65
Suit	*Chicago Tribune* (1920)	*Hart Schaffner & Marx;* silk lined; made to sell at $75, $80, $85	$50.00
Suit	*Chicago Tribune* (1922)	*Gold and Sports;* four-piece suits in imported and domestic tweeds	$45.00
Tie	*Sears, Roebuck* (1924)	Fancy knit; of fiber silk	$0.39
Undershirt	*B. Altman & Co.* (1923)	White cotton, gauze-weight, sleeveless	$0.75
Underwear	*Collier's* (1924)	*B.V.D.* knee-length drawers; tailored with balance and grace Each	 $0.85
Union Suit	*B. Altman & Co.* (1923)	White plaid, madras, sleeveless, knee length; webbing at back	$1.15
Union Suit	*National Geographic Magazine* (1924)	*BVD;* there is only one BVD underwear	$1.50
Work Shoe	*Kalamazoo Stove Co.* (1923)	A sturdy genuine brown all-leather, dairy-proof shoe that gives you dependable and long wear	$3.45

APPAREL, WOMEN'S

Item	Source	Description	Price
Apron	*Sears, Roebuck* (1920)	Waterproof; made of cotton material coated with high-grade composition rubber	$0.98
Bathing Suit	*B. Altman & Co.* (1923)	Black sports stain, trimmed with colored stitching	$8.50

The one-piece bathing suit became popular by 1920, though they were still considered risqué. The original text accompanying this image reads: "Bare legs and scanty one piece bathing suits were very much in evidence at the opening of Washingtons municipal bathing beach today. Officials have agreed to disregard as precedents the prohibitory orders issued at Coney Island and Atlantic City." The ban referred to is the ban on wearing bathing suits on city streets. (via Library of Congress)

Item	Source	Description	Price
Bloomers	*B. Altman & Co.* (1923)	Tailored silk model in pink, black or orchid	$3.95
Bloomers	*B. Altman & Co.* (1923)	Mercerized cotton; white or pink	$1.10
Blouse	*Sears, Roebuck* (1920)	Silk crepe de chine; a very special value in a stylish and well-made garment; narrow pin tucks down front panel	$4.95
Blouse	*San Francisco Examiner* (1921)	Forsythe blouse; favorites for tailored and sports wear	$2.95
Boudoir Cap	*B. Altman & Co.* (1923)	Cream net, the crown trimmed with ruffles of Valenciennes lace	$2.95
Boudoir Sacque	*B. Altman & Co.* (1923)	Valenciennes; a slipover model of Georgette crepe	$6.95
Brassiere	*Sears, Roebuck* (1920)	In camisole style	$0.79
Cap	*B. Altman & Co.* (1923)	Maid's cap; fluted white organdie, black ribbon	$0.45
Cape	*Chicago Tribune* (1922)	*The Resale Shop;* made of genuine American mink	$55.00

Item	Source	Description	Price
Coat	*B. Altman & Co.* (1923)	Tailored wool; double breasted, trimmed with leather-covered buttons	$12.75
Corselet and Brassiere	*B. Altman & Co.* (1923)	Pink batiste; very long, with deep elastic gores of hips and back	$3.00
Combination Corset	*B. Altman & Co.* (1923)	*Fasso;* silk; pink figured batiste, daintily trimmed top and bottom with fine net ribbon and silk flowers	$20.50
Dress	*New York Times* (1923)	*Lehman;* cotton; over 300 voiles, crepes, dotted swisses, linens, and chintzes dramatically reduced	$14.00
Dress	*B. Altman & Co.* (1923)	Flowered Georgette crepe; for afternoon wear with wide flowering sleeves that reveal a bit of the arm	$49.50
Fan	*B. Altman & Co.* (1923)	Uncurled ostrich feathers mounted on three amber-colored sticks, in coral, jade, turquoise blue, or American beauty	$7.75
Frock	*B. Altman & Co.* (1923)	Checked gingham smartly trimmed with novelty edging of white organdie	$5.75
Frock	*B. Altman & Co.* (1923)	The chiffon falling in soft panels on each side, and dipping below the skirt give something of an Oriental touch for evening wear	$39.50
Frock	*B. Altman & Co.* (1923)	Cotton voile; the skirt is made with a plaited apron front, irregular in outline, and with panels at the back, which are plaited and these are all trimmed with ribbon	$13.25
Frock	*B. Altman & Co.* (1923)	Black silk braid of interesting design on this frock of navy-blue wool twill	$29.75
Gloves	*B. Altman & Co.* (1923)	*Marvex;* suede and kidskin; eight-button length	$5.50
Gown	*New York Times* (1923)	Lingerie; the workmanship is exquisite with lace	$88.00
Handbag	*B. Altman & Co.* (1923)	Striped moiré silk; silk lined throughout; inside compartment and mirror	$4.90
Hat	*Chicago Tribune* (1920)	*Silk Sport;* fashioned in this season's smartest styles	$13.75
Hat	*B. Altman & Co.* (1923)	Straw and taffeta; with a slightly rolled brim all around	$10.50
Hose	*B. Altman & Co.* (1923)	Cotton; semi-fashioned, black, white, or African brown	$0.35
Hose	*B. Altman & Co.* (1923)	Silk; gossamer weight in black, white, and the fashionable colors	$3.95
Hose	*Chicago Tribune* (1920)	*O'Connor & Goldberg;* pure silk; with semi-fashioned seam	$1.59
Night-robe	*B. Altman & Co.* (1923)	Nainsook trimmed with medallions of embroidery and Valenciennes lace	$1.95
Outercoat	*B. Altman & Co.* (1923)	Coat of bandella cloth, an all-wool material, closing with ornamental clasp at the left side	$75.00
Overblouse	*B. Altman & Co.* (1923)	Crepe de chine of heavy quality with contrasting embroidery of individual design	$18.50
Night-robe	*B. Altman & Co.* (1923)	Nainsook trimmed with medallions of embroidery and Valenciennes lace	$1.95
Pajamas	*B. Altman & Co.* (1923)	Silk; washable; pointed effect at lower edge	$7.95
Panel Collar	*B. Altman & Co.* (1923)	Detachable; cream embroidered net	$3.50

Item	Source	Description	Price
Pantalet	*B. Altman & Co.* (1923)	Cotton gauge; low neck and sleeveless	$0.55
Parasol Umbrella	*Sears, Roebuck* (1920)	Rain or shine; eight-rib paragon steel frame	$5.95
Petticoat	*B. Altman & Co.* (1923)	Radium silk; trimmed with lace insertion and lace edge	$6.85
Robe	*B. Altman & Co.* (1923)	*Eiderdown;* in blue, with collar, cuffs and pockets in blue-and-white checked material	$6.75
Sandals	*New York Times* (1923)	*Novelty;* strap with military, Cuban, and Louis XVI heels	$9.95
Shoes	*B. Altman & Co.* (1923)	Sports Oxford; tie; of white buckskin with patent-leather apron, rubber soles and heels	$11.50
Skirt	*San Francisco Examiner* (1921)	Wool sports skirts; plaids and stripes	$14.95
Slip	*B. Altman & Co.* (1923)	Plaited meteor trimmed with wide Valenciennes lace	$9.75
Slippers	*B. Altman & Co.* (1923)	Of patent leather	$7.50
Suit	*Sears, Roebuck* (1920)	Tailored; all-wool double-twisted warp serge	$27.95
Suit	*B. Altman & Co.* (1923)	Tweed; comprising coat, suit, and knickers—making a serviceable and smart three-piece suit for sports	$36.50
Suit	*B. Altman & Co.* (1923)	Three-piece; both the cape and one-piece dress being of black canton crepe richly embroidered in black	$90.00
Sweater	*New York Times* (1923)	*R. H. Macy & Co.;* sleeveless; coatee model of mohair and fiber, with novel collar	$10.74
Undergarment	*B. Altman & Co.* (1923)	Combination of Nainsook, knickerbocker drawers, drop seat	$1.45
Union Suit	*Sears, Roebuck* (1920)	Elastic-ribbed cotton, double-body, heavyweight	$1.65
Vest	*B. Altman & Co.* (1923)	Silk chemise; machine scalloped and embroidered, in pink, peach color, or orchid, length 21" and 23"	$3.95
Work Boot	*Sears, Roebuck* (1920)	*Cromax;* leather sole; guaranteed to wear six months	$3.98

APPLIANCES

Item	Source	Description	Price
Carpet Sweeper	*The Literary Digest* (1924)	*Bissell Sweeper,* get ten years' of quick, thorough, easy sweeping	$5.00
Electric Cooker	*Kalamazoo Stove Co.* (1923)	*Kalamazoo;* automatic; like an electric range—cooks, bakes, roasts, fries, boils and toasts; just turn the switch and let the electricity heat the food	$28.85
Electric Percolator	*Kalamazoo Stove Co.* (1923)	Coffee tastes better when percolated; 9 cup size	$7.15
Fountain Percolator	*Kalamazoo Stove Co.* (1923)	*Kalamazoo;* six-cup size, aluminum, comes with spreader and valve	$3.87
Gas Grill	*National Geographic Magazine* (1924)	*American Kampkook;* plan to take kitchen convenience with you on your vacation; deluxe model	$15.00

Item	Source	Description	Price
Heating Unit	*Kalamazoo Stove Co.* (1923)	*Vulcan Utility;* with warm and cold air through one big register; it has long been one of our most popular styles	$84.65
Iron	*Kalamazoo Stove Co.* (1923)	*Kalamazoo Comfort;* gasoline; the comfort is ready for use half a minute after lighting	$4.45
Laundry Stove	*Kalamazoo Stove Co.* (1923)	*Kalamazoo;* you can cook and heat irons at the same time—thereby saving fuel	$8.85
Oil Heater	*Kalamazoo Stove Co.* (1923)	*Kalamazoo;* take the chill out of cold rooms; light and convenient	$4.95
Range	*Kalamazoo Stove Co.* (1923)	*Kalamazoo Emperor;* Blue-enamel brass with nickel; improved high closet with smoke pipe behind the clear white-enameled splasher back Cash price Credit price	 $72.25 $79.25
Range	*Kalamazoo Stove Co.* (1923)	*Kalamazoo Prince;* porcelain blue enamel; burns all fuels, regularly furnished with duplex grates for burning soft coal, wood, or coke Cash price Credit price	 $84.95 $93.45
Refrigerator	*Kalamazoo Stove Co.* (1923)	*Kalamazoo North Star;* white, enamel-lined; a dandy little food saver at a little price	$27.95
Refrigerator	*Kalamazoo Stove Co.* (1923)	All steel; for lifetime service, ice capacity 100 pounds	$56.95
Table Stove	*The World's Work* (1923)	*Armstrong;* cooks three things at once, makes waffles too	$12.50
Vacuum Cleaner	*Kalamazoo Stove Co.* (1923)	*Kalamazoo;* put pleasure into your house work; safe for your rugs	$33.95
Waffle Iron	*The World's Work* (1923)	*Armstrong;* electrical dealers in your town will be glad to show you	$4.00
Washer	*Kalamazoo Stove Co.* (1923)	*Kalamazoo;* an electric washer founded upon a washing principle that has been tried and proven in the largest steam laundries—with the revolving wooden cylinder; capacity, six sheets or equal amount of other clothes	$112.50
Wood Heater	*Kalamazoo Stove Co.* (1923)	*Kalamazoo Star;* truly a dandy little air-tight parlor heater; made to burn wood only	$17.80

BABY PRODUCTS

Item	Source	Description	Price
Baby's High Chair	*B. Altman & Co.* (1923)	Of white-enameled reed	$7.00
Crib	*B. Altman & Co.* (1923)	White-enameled metal, drop sides, 28" x 52"	$17.50
Portable Bathtub	*B. Altman & Co.* (1923)	Rubber, with faucet at the bottom made on a wooden folding frame in natural color	$5.75
Wardrobe	*B. Altman & Co.* (1923)	Baby's; white-enameled wicker, with folding drawers	$24.50

BUSINESS EQUIPMENT & SUPPLIES

Item	Source	Description	Price
Steel Pens	*The Youth's Companion* (1920)	*Spencerian Steel Pens;* the standard for over half a century Ten different pens	 $0.10
Typewriter	*The National Geographic Magazine* (1924)	Remington De Luxe Portable typewriter in ivory tone finish with brown leather carrying case	$75.00

Item	Source	Description	Price
Typewriter	*Typewriter Flier* (1921)	*Underwood;* reconstructed; each worn part replaced with a new part	$31.50
Typewriter	*The Mentor* (1923)	*Underwood;* portable; typed words are winged words	$50.00
Typewriter	*National Geographic Magazine* (1924)	*Remington;* portable; an ideal gift for graduates	$60.00
Typewriter Ribbon	*Typewriter Flier Magazine* (1924)	*Condo Typocraft;* medium-black inking; each ribbon foil wrapped in tin box	$3/dozen

EDUCATION

Item	Source	Description	Price
College Tuition	*The Progressive Farmer* (1924)	Clemson College, S. C., for students seeking classes in agriculture Per session	$40.00
Dance Lessons	*San Francisco Examiner* (1921)	Ladies taught by gentlemen; per couple	$1.00

ENTERTAINMENT

Item	Source	Description	Price
Swimming Lessons	*New York Times* (1923)	*Madison Square Garden Gymnasium;* largest swimming pool in United States	$5/6 Lessons
Theater Ticket	*Chicago Tribune* (1920)	*Colonial Theatre Musical Review;* Raymond Hitchcock in his all-new musical revue *Hitchy-Koo 1919;* matinees	$2.00
Theater Ticket	*New York Times* (1923)	*Globe Plays;* fifth annual production of George White's *Scandals;* best seats	$2.50

ENTERTAINMENT, HOME

Item	Source	Description	Price
Camera	*Collier's* (1924)	*Autographic Kodak Camera;* you'll get good pictures from the first	$6.50 and up
Camera	*The Mentor* (1923)	*Kodak No. 1;* autographic; exposures as fast as 1/200 of a second	$50.00
Game	*Sears, Roebuck* (1923)	Mah-jongg; the royal game of China that is sweeping the country like wildfire; ivory pyralin tiles, mahogany box with five compartments	$22.95
Poker Set	*B. Altman & Co.* (1923)	In small leather case, with 100 chips, two packs of playing cards and book of rules	$6.25
Radio	*New York Times* (1923)	*Crosley 50;* Oh, boy! There's London! Last night I had Honolulu and the night before that Puerto Rico	$14.50
Records	*National Geographic Magazine* (1924)	Victor Records featuring The Philadelphia Orchestra; *Carmen*—Prelude to Act I and *March of the Caucasian,* double-faced	$1.50
Talking Machine	*National Geographic Magazine* (1924)	*Victrola No. 405;* walnut case, electric	$290
Table Covers	*The World's Work* (1923)	For Mah-jongg; well made of green, heavy felt, to exactly fit any 30" card table top	$5.00
Talking Machine	*The World's Work* (1923)	*Victrola;* Victor Talking Machine Co., Camden, New Jersey; place your order now while all the 21 instrument styles are available	$25 and up

Item	Source	Description	Price
Talking Machine	*National Geographic Magazine* (1924)	*Victrola;* mahogany, oak or walnut cabinet	$125

FARM EQUIPMENT & SUPPLIES

Item	Source	Description	Price
Hen	*Rhode Island Red Journal* (1923)	S.C. Red; first and color hen at National Red meet at Kansas City, Missouri, 1919	$25.00
Insecticide	*Rhode Island Red Journal* (1923)	*Licecil;* kill the lice the best and sure way	$1.00/bottle
Insect Poison	*The Progressive Farmer* (1924)	*So-Bos-So;* guaranteed to rid your cows of flies and gnats Per 15-gallon drum	$15.00
Medicine for Chickens	*Rhode Island Red Journal* (1923)	*Sunny Life White;* Diarrhea tablets; recommended by thousands of the world's foremost poultry raisers	$0.75/100 tablets
Portable Power Plant	*The Progressive Farmer* (1924)	*Homelite* portable electric light and power plant; power for pumping, grinding, shelling corn, drilling, boring and milking; will run on gasoline, kerosene, fuel oil; Model D-11	$250
Pullet	*Rhode Island Red Journal* (1923)	S.C. Red; sired by a 296-egg cock, out of 247- and 218-egg hens	$5.00
Separator	*Kalamazoo Stove Co.* (1923)	*Kalamazoo;* a cream separator often means as much as $20 extra from every cow; 600 lb capacity	$69.95

FOOD PRODUCTS

Item	Source	Description	Price
Biscuits	*National Geographic Magazine* (1924)	*Huntley & Palmers;* the sweetmeats of kings; special package	$1
Champagne	*New York Times* (1923)	*R. H. Macy's Mount Zircon Ginger Champagne;* bottles by the Moon Tide Spring in Mount Zircon	$0.19
Chocolate	*World's Work* (1923)	*Wilbur Buds;* exquisite morsels of vanilla chocolate, wrapped in pure tin foil	$1.00/1 pound
Chocolate Bars	*Sears, Roebuck* (1922)	*Hershey's;* 24 sweet milk bars	$0.98
Coffee	*New York Times* (1923)	*Macy's Vienna Brand;* a rich and delicious blend of South American Coffees	$0.34/lb
Condensed Soup	*National Geographic Magazine* (1924)	*Campbell's;* look for the red and white label; 21 kinds	$0.12/can
Curry Powder	*New York Times* (1923)	*R. H. Macy Madras;* our own importation from India	$0.29/half-lb
Eggs	*Rhode Island Red Journal* (1923)	S.C. Red; eggs from special color matching for the Southern trade fall hatching	$5.00/15
French Peas	*New York Times* (1923)	*Marceau Brand;* regular size tins; extra fine	$0.37
Gum	*Sears, Roebuck* (1922)	Wrigley Juicy Fruit	$0.39/10 pkgs

July 4th ad for Wrigley's chewing gum that ran in 1920. (via Wikimedia Commons)

Item	Source	Description	Price
Instant Coffee	*National Geographic Magazine* (1924)	*G. Washington's;* even the best roasted coffee can be spoiled in the making; why risk failure?	$0.10
Olives	*New York Times* (1923)	*La Forge Stuffed Spanish Queen;* stuffed with red peppers	$0.29
Salmon	*New York Times* (1923)	*Lily White;* Columbia River fine quality: No. 1 flat can	$0.44
Tenderloin Steak	*San Francisco Examiner* (1921)	From "A" No. 1 prime steer beef	$0.55/pound

Item	Source	Description	Price
FURNITURE			
Bookcase	*Chicago Tribune* (1922)	Sectional; sections are 9" × 11" and 13"	$4.80
Chest	*Kalamazoo Stove Co.* (1923)	Beautiful colonial design; finished in natural cedar and trimmed with satin-polished copper; size: 36"×16"×16"	$12.55
Davenette	*Kalamazoo Stove Co.* (1923)	*Kalamazoo;* two pieces of furniture in one—combining davenette and full sized bed	$46.50
Dresser	*Chicago Tribune* (1920)	Walnut; Louis XVI style; 46" wide, carefully constructed, and has a mirror of generous proportions	$98.00
Furniture Set	*Kalamazoo Stove Co.* (1923)	*Arts and Crafts Oak Mission;* seven-piece set includes arm chair, reception chair, arm rocker, rocker, tabourette, bookends, and table	$28.50
Kitchen Cabinet	*Kalamazoo Stove Co.* (1923)	Oak; modern kitchen efficiency in your home is practically impossible unless you have a convenient place for everything; has a white porcelain top	$32.50
Metal Bed	*Kalamazoo Stove Co.* (1923)	Continuous post; 2" posts, includes bed, mattress and spring	$26.95
GARDEN EQUIPMENT & SUPPLIES			
Birdhouse	*National Geographic Magazine* (1924)	*Dodson's Queen Anne Martin House;* 48 rooms; white with green trim; pine with copper roof; 36" × 26" × 37"	$60.00
Daffodils	*National Geographic*	*Elliott Nursery;* 60-bulb collection	$4.00
Lawn Mower	*The Literary Digest* (1924)	*MontaMower,* no gears, no long blades, trims and cuts at the same time	$18.00
Lawn Mower	*New York Times* (1923)	James McCreery & Co. New England Mower; ball bearing with three 14-inch steel blades	$9.95
Lawn Mower	*National Geographic Magazine* (1924)	Montague MontaMower; the new easy way to cut lawns	$18.00
HOTEL RATES			
Hotel Room	*Chicago Tribune* (1920)	Hotel Wychmere; 150 clean comfortable outside rooms, at exceptionally attractive rates; electric lights, steam heat, running water	$1–$1.50/day
Hotel Room	*New York Times* (1923)	Hotel Monticello New York; 35–37 West 6th Street, between Broadway and Central Park with shower and bath	$3.00/day
Hotel Room	*The Journal of the American Dental Association* (1924)	Waldorf Dallas; with bath, two persons	$4 to $6/day
Room	*National Geographic Magazine* (1924)	Jasper Park Lodge, in Canadian Rockies, American plan	$6.00 per day
HOUSEHOLD GOODS			
Alarm Clock	*Sears, Roebuck* (1921)	National; 8-day alarm	$2.50
Barn Paint	*Kalamazoo Stove Co.* (1923)	Kalamazoo; real insurance against rot and decay	$1.54/gallon
Bath Tub	*Kalamazoo Stove Co.* (1923)	Handee Modern; Handee bath tub includes a stove and water heater combination that gives you real city comfort; Outfit complete	$29.95

Item	Source	Description	Price
Blanket	*B. Altman & Co.* (1923)	All-wool; white, blue, or pink borders; 60" × 84"	$14.50/pair
Bonbon Box	*B. Altman & Co.* (1923)	Engraved glass, sterling silver deposit; with cover	$4.00
Borax	*New York Times* (1923)	Red Star Brand; guaranteed absolutely pure	$0.49/5 pounds
Cookware	*Kalamazoo Stove Co.* (1923)	25-piece aluminum service; includes 5-piece combination cooker and steamer, 2 quart welded spout percolator with spreader, new round toaster, 5 quart tea kettle, 1 quart lipped sauce pan, 2 quart lipped sauce pan, cake turner, soup ladle, 2 bottom cake pans	$10.95
Fence	*Kalamazoo Stove Co.* (1923)	Perfection; open hearth; basic steel, heavily galvanized; a real improvement in farm fencing; 47" high	$0.62/rod
Floor Covering	*Chicago Tribune* (1920)	Texoleum; adapted to use in all parts of the house—on stains, in the halls, upstairs and down	$0.66/sq yd
Floor Paint	*Kalamazoo Stove Co.* (1920)	Kalamazoo; dress up your old floors; colors include yellow, maroon, light gray, buff, oak, and dark gray	$1.95/gallon
Food Jar	*B. Altman & Co.* (1923)	Thermalware; keeps food or liquids hot or cold; capacity one gallon	$10.00
Hat Box	*B. Altman & Co.* (1923)	Circular-shaped of enameled duck; cretonne-lined; leather handle	$5.00
House Paint	*Kalamazoo Stove Co.* (1923)	Kalamazoo; save the surface and you save all	$2.15/gallon
Lamp	*Kalamazoo Stove Co.* (1923)	Nulite Match-Lite; is 20 times as powerful as the old style cool oil lamp, but operates without a wick or grease, lamp black or smell that is so distasteful; burns 14 hours on one filling of three pints of common motor gasoline	$7.35
Meat Platter	*B. Altman & Co. (1923)*	Silver plate; well and tree design; 17"	$10.50
Roaster	*Kalamazoo Stove Co.* (1923)	Aluminum; a roaster that has every modern improvement; with rack	$4.82
Salt and Pepper Set	*B. Altman & Co.* (1923)	Sterling silver; six shakers in case	$4.00/case
Suitcase	*B. Altman & Co.* (1923)	Black enameled duck, cretonne-lined, leather corners and handles; 24" × 15" × 9"	$6.00
Tablecloth	*B. Altman & Co.* (1923)	Fine quality durable satin damask; 72" × 108"	$17.25
Toilet	*Kalamazoo Stove Co.* (1923)	Simply place the sanitary closet in any out of the way place—a closet, under the stairs or wherever a private corner can be found; it is absolutely sanitary and odorless	$6.95
Toilet Cleaner	*National Geographic Magazine* (1924)	*Sani-Flush;* cleans the toilet bowl better than any other means	$0.25
Traveling Bag	*B. Altman & Co.* (1923)	Tan cowhide, leather-lined, size 16"	$10.50
Vacuum Bottle	*B. Altman & Co.* (1923)	Green enamel; aluminum top; capacity one quart	$2.25

Item	Source	Description	Price
INSURANCE RATES			
Fire Insurance	*Insurance Policy* (1920)	*Charleston Insurance And Trust Co.;* $750 fire coverage on one-story frame house	$11.10/year
Fire Insurance	*Insurance Policy* (1921)	*Charleston Insurance & Trust Co.;* (rate $0.68 per $100); $500 fire insurance on brick building in Columbia, South Carolina	$3.40/year
Fire Insurance	*Insurance Policy* (1922)	*New Jersey Insurance Co.;* $2,000 fire insurance; two story, wood frame building	$22.40/year
Life Insurance	*Chicago Tribune* (1920)	*Merchant's Reserve Life Insurance;* pure life insurance; annual premium per $1,000, whole life, age 35	$16.40/year

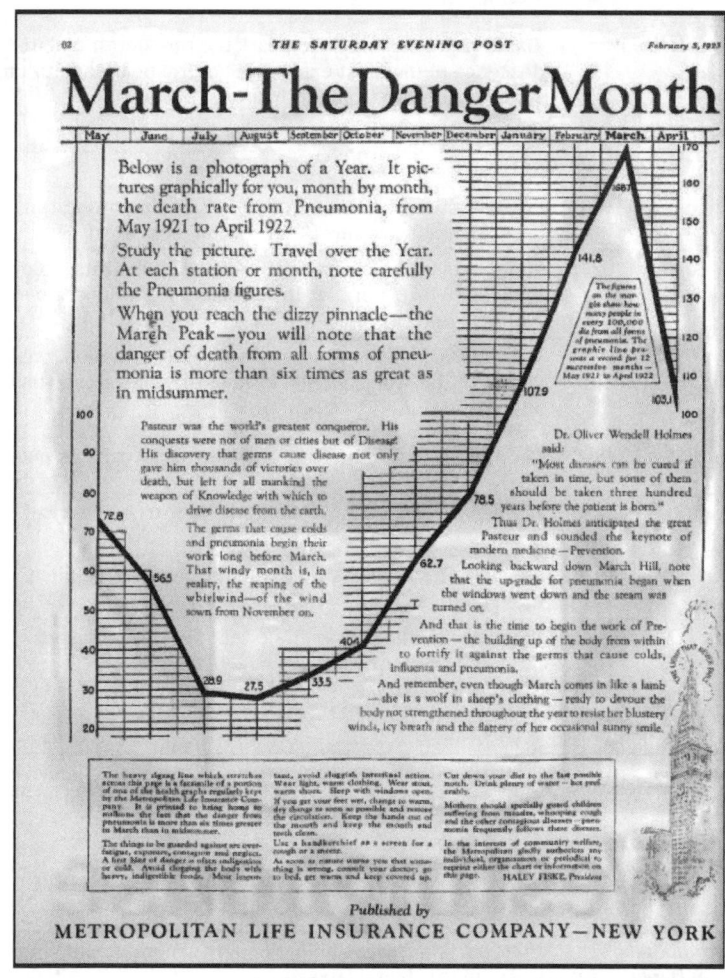

Advertisement from the February 1923 issue of the Saturday Evening Post, *including a graph of pneumonia deaths from May 1921 to April 1922.* (via Wikimedia Commons)

Item	Source	Description	Price
JEWELRY			
Blue Diamond	*National Geographic Magazine* (1924)	*Black Starr & Frost;* the largest blue diamond ever discovered; 1 9/32" by 1 5/32"	$3 million
Cigarette Case	*Sears, Roebuck* (1920)	Sterling silver; engraved ornamentation with shield; gold plated inside	$11.72
Cuff Buttons	*The World's Work* (1923)	*The Baer & Wilde Co. Kum-A-Part Kuff;* the button for soft cuffs that clicks open, snaps shut	$25/pair
Cuff Links	*The World's Work* (1923)	*J.F. Sturdy's Sons & Co. Sta-Lokt;* the perfected separable cuff link	$1.50 to $7.50/pair
Lapel Button	*Reunion Pamphlet, 81st Division Wildcats* (1920)	*Wildcat Insignia Co.;* 81st division Wildcat reunion; screw buttons to be worn on coat lapels; a very neat insignia sterling silver 10-k gold	$1.00 $4.50
Necklace	*The World's Work* (1923)	*The Henshel Co.;* bluebird pearl; the rare depth and iridescence of the most expensive natural pearls; platinum safety clasp with brilliant diamond; 24" long	$85.00
Pendant Earrings	*B. Altman & Co.* (1923)	Imitation pearls in the shower design; French backs	$4/pair
Pin	*B. Altman & Co.* (1923)	Rhinestone bar; set in sterling silver	$2.25
Pocket Watch	*Spiegel Catalog* (1920)	Illinois railroad nickel or gold filled; 18 size; swing-ring case; 21-jewel; genuine Bunn special movement	$43.50
Pocket Watch	*Spiegel Catalog* (1920)	Illinois railroad nickel; twenty-year double strats; gold-filled open face; popular 16 size; fitted with Bunn movement; 23-jewel	$63.50
Ring	*Reunion Pamphlet, 81st Division Wildcats* (1920)	*Wildcat Insignia Co.;* 81st division Wildcat reunion; the center of the seal is a relief form of the wildcat; sterling silver 10-k gold	$3.50 $12.50
Ring	*Chicago Tribune* (1920)	*Lewy Brothers Co.;* sincere, personal service; black pearl	$3,500
Strap Watch	*The World's Work* (1923)	*Hamilton Watch Co.;* all Hamiltons have true beauty of design	$38 to $42
Wristwatch	*Chicago Tribune* (1920)	*Lebolt & Co.;* woman's; 15-jewel movement; gold filled case, hand engraved	$22.00
Wristwatch	*B. Altman & Co.* (1923)	Woman's; sterling silver; 15 jewels; Swiss movement mounted on black ribbon	$20.00
MEALS			
Lunch	*San Francisco Examiner* (1921)	Luncheon: Fruit or combination salad; boiled chicken or boiled steak; mashed potatoes, steamed potatoes, string beans, choice of pudding	$1.00
MEDICAL PRODUCTS & SERVICES			
Electric Heating Oven	*The Journal of the American Dental Association* (1924)	*Buffdentco;* for wax elimination and general heating purposes in the dental laboratory	$55.00
Laboratory Work Bench	*The Journal of the American Dental Association* (1924)	*Alcasco;* designed for the present day restricted working space	$47.50
Medicine	*The Youth's Companion* (1920)	New-Skin—Keeps Little Hurts from Getting Big; it forms a covering that keeps out germs	$0.15 to $0.30

Item	Source	Description	Price
Nonprescription Drug	*Sears, Roebuck* (1921)	Aromatic castor oil; to make it more palatable; 8-oz bottle	$0.69
Nonprescription Drug	*The World's Work* (1923)	*Eno's Fruit Salt Derivative Compound;* just a teaspoonful of ENO's in a glass of water will clear your blood stream and give you a new and happier aspect	$0.75/can
Nonprescription Drug	*Sears, Roebuck* (1924)	*Milk of Magnesia Laxative;* well-known mild laxative and stomach anti-acid corrective; $0.50 size	$0.39
Regulating Dental Appliances	*The Journal of the American Dental Association* (1924)	*Jackson's;* improvement in orthodontic methods enables us to turn out mechanically correctly constructed appliances; gold plated	$7.00
Smock	*The Journal of the American Dental Association* (1924)	*Angelica Jacket Co.;* of finely woven white bleached twill with indestructible knotted tape buttons	$2.00

MOTORIZED VEHICLES, SERVICES, & SUPPLIES

Item	Source	Description	Price
Automobile	*The Literary Digest* (1924)	*Willys-Knight coupe-sedan,* powered by same type engine used in Daimler, Panhard, Mercedes, Minerva	$1,450
Automobile	Joseph J. Schroeder Jr. *The Wonderful World of Automobiles* (1971)	*Hendley Knight;* standard 7-passenger touring car; an ever-increasing appeal to the business man [cost in 1922]	$2,450
Automobile	Schroeder, *The Wonderful World of Automobiles* (1971)	*Kline Car;* Kline lowers manufacturing costs by utilizing its own shops [cost in 1922] Coupe Sedan	 $3,050 $3,090
Automobile	Schroeder, *The Wonderful World of Automobiles* (1971)	*Case;* Sedan; exceptional performance is an outstanding feature of this car [cost in 1922]	$2,790
Automobile	The World's Work (1923)	*1924 Haynes 60 DeLuxe Sedan;* improved six cylinder Haynes-built motor—created from the Haynes motor which had established a wonderful eight-year record for dependability	$1,895
Automobile	Schroeder, *The Wonderful World of Automobiles* (1971)	*Durant Four;* 5-passenger touring car; the new motor is a revelation in power and flexibility [cost in 1924]	$890
Automobile	Schroeder, *The Wonderful World of Automobiles* (1971)	*Buick Standard Six;* open model; 5-passenger touring car [cost in 1924]	$1,175
Automobile	Schroeder, *The Wonderful World of Automobiles* (1971)	*Willys-Overland;* the champion economy car [cost in 1924]	$695
Automobile	*National Geographic Magazine* (1924)	*Chrysler Six Phaeton*	$1,395
Automobile	*National Geographic Magazine* (1924)	*Chandler;* touring car; change speeds without clashing; the traffic transmission is acknowledged to be the most important automotive improvement of the decade	$1,485

Item	Source	Description	Price
Automotive Accessories	*Collier's* (1924)	Oldsmobile Six accessories available at any Oldsmobile dealer:	
		Front bumper	$15.00
		Road spot light	$5.00
		Rear view mirror	$1.75
		Trunk rails, set of four	$6.80
		Windshield wings, pair	$17.00
Heat Indicator	*Collier's* (1924)	*Safe-T-Stat* engine heat indicator; accurate and visible at all times on the dashboard of your car	$10.00
Ignition System	*The Progressive Farmer* (1924)	*Bosch Type 600* ignition system for Fords; insures quick, easy starts	$12.75
Motor Oil	*Collier's* (1924)	*Mobiloil* from Vacuum Oil Company; the new sealed one-quart can is ideal while touring	$0.35

MUSICAL INSTRUMENTS

Item	Source	Description	Price
Piano	*World's Work* (1923)	*Steinway & Sons;* the instrument of the immortals;	
		Upright	$875
		Grand	$1,425
Piano	*New York Times* (1923)	*Mathushek Grand Opera;* size only 36"	$635

OTHER

Item	Source	Description	Price
Adoption	*The American Legion Weekly* (1920)	Cost to adopt a French orphan	$75.00
Dolly Washer	*Kalamazoo Stove Co.* (1923)	Hand powered; it is so constructed that even a child can run it	$15.60
Exercise Program	*Picture Play Magazine* (1923)	*Luthy's Daily Five Minute Basic Physical Exercise;* to keep one agile, healthy and young	$5.00
Exploration	*National Geographic Magazine* (1924)	Cost to National Geographic Society for series of expeditions into Peru to investigate the traces of the Inca race	$50,000
Fountain Pen	*Picture Play Magazine* (1923)	*Waterman Ideal;* self-filling type, mottled with gold-filled level and clip	$7.50
Grid Batteries	*National Geographic Magazine* (1924)	*Philco Diamond;* for low-voltage peanut tubes; east of the Mississippi	$8.00
Incense	*Picture Play Magazine* (1923)	*Temple of Allah;* this rare, choice incense is even used as a cachet by fastidious women; it sweetens the air and keeps away flies and other pests; deluxe set with large metal burner and incense	$1.00
Mail Order House	*National Geographic Magazine* (1924)	*Aladdin;* 7 room; price includes all lumber cut to fit; highest grade interior woodwork, siding, flooring, windows, doors, glass, paints, hardware, nails, lath, roofing, with complete instructions and drawings	$975
Mechanical Pencil	*National Geographic Magazine* (1924)	*Wahl Eversharp;* the superior writing companion; economy model	$3.00

Item	Source	Description	Price
Pen	*National Geographic Magazine* (1924)	*Parker Duofold Duette;* handsomer than gold—mightier than the sword	$7.00
Photographs	*Picture Play Magazine* (1923)	*Homer S. Howry Co.;* movie stars original photos; over 250 stars including Mary Pickford, Doug Fairbanks, Debe Daniels, Betty Compson, Priscilla Dyan; size 8" × 10"	$0.50
Stationery	*The World's Work* (1923)	*Hampshire Paper Co. Old Hampshire;* the stationery of a gentleman; 24 sheets and envelopes of royal club size	$1.50/box

PERSONAL CARE PRODUCTS

Item	Source	Description	Price
Bath Salts	*B. Altman & Co.* (1923)	*Alsam Bouquet*	$1.50/jar
Brush	*B. Altman & Co.* (1923)	*Ideal Hair;* waterproof	$1.65
Dental Cream	*The Mentor* (1923)	*Colgate Ribbon;* cannot roll off the brush	$0.25
Dental Cream	*National Geographic Magazine* (1924)	*Colgate's;* cleans teeth the right way; large tube	$0.25
Dressing Case	*B. Altman & Co.* (1923)	Man's; of black walrus-grain leather; contains comb, ebony-back military brush, ebonized soap box, toothbrush holder, metal shaving-brush holder, metal shaving-soap tube, and space for razor	$5.00
Eyelash Treatment	*Picture Play Magazine* (1923)	*Maybelline;* makes every face more beautiful	$0.75

Advertisement for Lashlux for eye lashes referencing film star "May Allison's Eyes" in the July 1921 issue of Photoplay *magazine.* (via Wikimedia Commons)

Item	Source	Description	Price
Face Cream	*Picture Play Magazine* (1923)	*Hinds Honey and Almond Cream;* an excellent base for face powder, comes in four tints	$0.15
Face Powder	*Picture Play Magazine* (1923)	*Lablache;* protect your complexion; use only a safe powder	$0.50
Hair Comb	*B. Altman & Co.* (1923)	Spanish; crystal-colored celluloid, sapphire studded	$5.25
Hair Remover	*Picture Play Magazine* (1923)	*Neet;* removes hair harmlessly	$0.50
Insect Repellent	*The Progressive Farmer* (1924)	*Black Flag;* kills mosquitoes; just burn a little powder in your bedroom; the smoke is deadly to mosquitoes Powder, per bottle	$0.15
Liniment	*The Literary Digest* (1924)	*Absorbine Jr.,* the antiseptic liniment Per bottle	$1.25

Item	Source	Description	Price
Lipstick	*Picture Play Magazine* (1923)	*Jasmynette;* the latest Parisian novelty; 18kt gold-plated container with mirror	$1.00
Mouthwash	*Sears, Roebuck* (1924)	*Listerine;* $1 size	$0.79
Paste Polish	*Sears, Roebuck* (1924)	*Shinola;* produces a lustrous polish	$0.08
Perfume & Toilet Water	*Picture Play Magazine* (1923)	*Rieger's Flower Drops;* Flower Drops is the most exquisite perfume ever produced; made without alcohol; souvenir box of five 25-cent bottles	$1/5 bottles
Permanent Wave Hairstyle	*New York Times* (1923)	*Permanent Waving Beauty Salon;* Lane Bryant; using the most approved of method—which is absolutely safe and results in a wave that retains its beauty for months; whole head wave (regularly $25)	$15
Shaving Brush	*B. Altman & Co.* (1923)	The brush in this box has been sterilized	$1.25
Shaving Stick	*B. Altman & Co.* (1923)	*Colgate;* handy-grip shaving stick	$0.35
Soap	*Sears, Roebuck* (1921)	*Lifebuoy;* well-known toilet and bath soap	$0.29/3
Soap	*Sears, Roebuck* (1923)	*Pear's Unscented;* three cakes	$0.24
Straight Razor	*Sears, Roebuck* (1922)	*Silverking;* blade of English steel	$2.90
Toothbrush	*The Literary Digest* (1924)	*Dr. West's Toothbrush,* where health hangs in the balance Adult size Youth size Children's size	$0.50 $0.35 $0.25
Toothbrush	*The Journal of the American Dental Association* (1924)	*Pepsodent Co.;* decorator; the new era toothbrush, home style	$0.50
Water Softener	*Picture Play Magazine* (1923)	*Bathasweet;* adorable skin; let softened water help you achieve it and keep it; large size	$1.00

PUBLICATIONS

Item	Source	Description	Price
Book	*Collier's* (1924)	"Love, Marriage and Other Perils" by Uncle Henry; 28 stories from *Collier's*	$1.00
Book	*The Literary Digest* (1924)	*Practical Radio;* know all there is to be known about radio; its amazing development, how radio messages pass through our bodies, how radio outfits are made; 427 pages	$1.75
Book	*Picture Play Magazine* (1923)	*The Long, Long Trail,* by George Owen Baxter; a western story	$1.75
Magazine	*Collier's* (1924)	*Collier's,* The National Weekly Per issue	$0.05

Item	Source	Description	Price
Magazine	*The Progressive Farmer* (1924)	One-year subscription to *The Progressive Farmer*	$1.00
Magazine	*The World's Work* (1923)	*Life;* weekly	$5.00/year

REAL ESTATE

Item	Source	Description	Price
Apartment	*San Francisco Examiner* (1921)	Sacramento at Franklin; 5-room apartment; very attractive new building; rooms finished in ivory; plenty of steam heat	$70/month
Apartment	*San Francisco Examiner* (1921)	A clean, quiet place; 2-room apartment for adults; hot water	$25/month
Grocery Store	*New York Times* (1923)	In best business section of New Rochelle; includes two Dodge delivery cars	$6,000
Hotel	*American Chronicle* (1999)	Cost to construct the 1,200-room Shelton Hotel in New York City in 1923	$8 million
House	*Chicago Tribune* (1920)	For rent; 6-room summer cottage; Fox Lake, Illinois; 100' lake frontage (for season July-Sept.)	$350
House	*New York Times* (1923)	Furnished; New York City; West 50s—23 fine rooms, 6 baths, straight lease	$3,000
Store	*Chicago Tribune* (1920)	For rent; large; with living rooms, steam heat, hot water	$55/month

SEWING EQUIPMENT & SUPPLIES

Item	Source	Description	Price
Bodkin Set	*B. Altman & Co.* (1923)	Sterling silver; 4 pieces, in case	$1.90
Sewing Thread	*Sears, Roebuck* (1924)	*Barbour's;* linen; 100 yds to the spool	$0.09

SPORTS EQUIPMENT

Item	Source	Description	Price
Baseball Glove	*Sears, Roebuck* (1922)	Professional Wagner model; made of high quality, tan color, oil treated horsehide	$4.20
Boat	*New York Times* (1923)	*Cabrilla;* motor yacht; a delightful cruising boat; water-line 110'; beam 12' 6"	$20,000
Canoe	*National Geographic Magazine* (1924)	*Old Town Canoe,* remarkably steady and easy to handle	$64.00
Field Glasses	*The Literary Digest* (1924)	German Army officers' field glasses; finest achromatic day and night lenses; 40mm Slightly used	$9.85
Golf Bag	*B. Altman & Co.* (1923)	Tan or white canvas, with 4 steel stays; hooded top and lock; 5" rawhide bottom	$6.50
Handball Gloves	*Sears, Roebuck* (1924)	*Draper-Maynard Co.;* brown napa leather, stitched front and well padded	$3.50/pair
Tennis Racquet	*B. Altman & Co.* (1923)	Fine quality frame, reinforced at shoulders; strung with best English gut	$10.50

TOBACCO PRODUCTS

Item	Source	Description	Price
Ashtrays	*B. Altman & Co.* (1923)	Nickel-plated, lined with red, blue, green or yellow glass, set of four	$2.75

Item	Source	Description	Price
Cigarettes	*Collier's* (1924)	*Reedsdale Cigarettes;* liked by many smokers of sophisti-cated taste Per package of 20	 $0.20
Cigars	*The World's Work* (1923)	*Robert Burns Panatela*; give a brand that is known for Christmas box of 50	$0.10/each $44.75
Pipe	*B. Altman & Co.* (1923)	Genuine briar; straight stem, mouthpiece of hard rubber	$1.00

TRAVEL & TRANSPORTATION

Item	Source	Description	Price
Airline Ticket	Edward L. Throm, ed. *Popular Mechanics Picture History of American Transportation* (1952)	Los Angeles to San Francisco; one way [cost in 1922]	$50.00
Beach Camping	*The American Legion Weekly* (1920)	*Camp Franklin D'Olier*, the vacation center operated by The Atlantic City Legionnaire Post; spend a week under canvas near the beach; breakfast and light lunch available Per week	 $15.00
Cruise	*The World's Work* (1923)	*Frank C Clark*; around the world in four months on specially chartered Cunarder "Laconia"	$1,000
Cruise	*National Geographic Magazine* (1924)	A joyful week of cruising on four great lakes; meals and berth included	$74.50
Cruise	*National Geographic Magazine* (1924)	*Coates Tours*; world cruises; 30 days of delightful travel	$425
European Tour	*The National Geographic Magazine* (1924)	American Express Travel; Mediterranean tour to Naples with comprehensive European itinerary	$1,370
Hawaii Tour	*The National Geographic Magazine* (1924)	Hawaii in the summer; dark-skinned imps dive for your dimes; travel from Seattle or Los Angeles, includes hotel, sightseeing including visit to Volcano Kilaueachin Hawaii National Park, 3 to 4 weeks	$300 to $400
Motor Tour	*The National Geographic Magazine* (1924)	Yosemite National Park tour covering 240 miles round trip from Merced, California	$35.00
Railroad Ticket	*Chicago Tribune* (1920)	Santa Fe railroad from Chicago direct to San Francisco for National Democratic Convention; round trip from Chicago	$89
Steamship Ticket	*San Francisco Examiner* (1921)	San Francisco to Seattle; round trip; every Tuesday	$75.00
Steamship Ticket	*San Francisco Examiner* (1921)	*Pacific Steamline*; Los Angeles to Alaska; first class; includes berth and meals	$18.00
Steamship Ticket	*New York Times* (1923)	*Colonial Line*; New York to Boston	$5.19
Train Ticket	*The National Geographic Magazine* (1924)	Northern Pacific Railway roundtrip trip from Chicago to Yellowstone Park	$56.50

Item	Source	Description	Price
Train Ticket	*National Geographic Magazine* (1924)	*Pacific Northwest Railroad*; the route will take you to the very gates of five of the nation's greatest scenic attractions: Glacier Park, Yellowstone Park, Crater Lake National Park, Rainier National Park, the Alaskan Tour	$86.00

MISCELLANY 1920-1924

$11,000 Booze Raid in Loop Traps 3 at Bar; Labor Trouble at Still Fills U.S. Cells

Whiskey valued at $11,000 was seized in a saloon at 201 North State Street and the two proprietors and a bartender were arrested yesterday by federal prohibition agents. The men are Edward Stevens and Charles McDermott, owners, and M. J. O'Rourke, the bartender. Bonds were set by Commissioner Lewis F. Mason, at $2,500 for the proprietors and $2,000 for the bartender.

Chicago Tribune, April 17, 1920

Gas Rates Up; It Now Costs $1.15 Per Thousand

Chicago's gas rate was increased from 85¢ to $1.15 a thousand cubic feet by an order of the state public utilities commission yesterday. The commission also fixed a minimum charge of 60¢ a month.

Chicago Tribune, June 16, 1920

L Men Accept Raise; Company to Ask 10¢ Fare

As a result of the 15¢ wage increase awarded the streetcar workers on Monday and the acceptance last night of an equal boost in pay by 2,000 elevated employees, Chicago straphangers are asked to pay an 8¢ street car fare and a 10¢ fare on the overhead lines after July 1.

Chicago Tribune, June 17, 1920

Cement Makers Cut Prices for State Highways

Cement manufacturers today expressed their willingness to do their bit toward maximum highway construction in Illinois in 1922 when they offered to supply 4,000,000 barrels of cement to the state at prices ranging from $1.20 to $1.40 a barrel.

The lowest bid, offering 600,000 barrels at $1.20 a barrel, was made by the Marquette Portland Cement Company, a reduction of 25¢ a barrel from the bids made Jan. 8, which were rejected.

Chicago Tribune, March 6, 1922

Retirement Bonuses

A hundred dollars for each of the fifty years' service was the reward to Rudolph Zimmerman and Louis Moses, who recently completed a half century in the employ of the drug and laboratory firm of Eimer & Amend. At a dinner celebrating the occasion last week each of the veterans, who began as errand boys and are now heads of important departments, received $5,000.

New York Times, June 17, 1923

Americans Pay Lures German Housegirls

Relief appears to be at hand for women who have been wrestling with the servant girl problem. Europe is beginning to send a new and better supply of domestic workers, evidence of this fact having been furnished a few days ago when the Royal Mail liner Orca brought thirty expert servant girls who had embarked at Hamburg and were readily permitted to pass the portals of Ellis Island. They had been earning the equivalent of less than $2 a week in Germany, and when told that many American housewives would gladly pay $10 weekly, their surprise was unbounded.

New York Times, June 17, 1923

Senator David A. Reed of ylvania Urges Cut in Tax on Earned Income

The present system of taxing the earned income is a discrimination in favor of the person whose income is unearned. The man who works for a living can be taxed 58 percent, whereas the man who invests all his capital enjoys exemptions behind which he can take refuge and that man can "get by" with a tax of only 12 1/2 percent.

New York Times, June 17, 1923

Senator David A. Reed in 1922. (via Library of Congress)

MISCELLANY 1920-1924

Letter to the Editor

When these productions are shown for the first time at big theatres, at prices as high as $1.50 or $2.00, the claim is often made in the advertising that they will not be shown in the same city at a lower price within a year. But often within a month, they are shown at the regular movie houses for thirty cents.

Picture Play Magazine, October 1923

Dental Practices for Sale

Indiana Practice for Sale—Light competition. Averaging $6,000 a year cash practice. Many advances to this deal. Salaried Appointment transferable. Practice to go perhaps $10,000 a year with full time. Moderate Investment.

For Sale—Dental practice in Chicago suburb doing $12,000 cash a year.

The Journal of the American Dental Association, September 1924

Valentines

A beautiful assortment from 1/2 ¢ to 25¢ each. Just the kind you may want. Palmetto Drug Co.

Union Progress, Union, SC, February 6, 1924

HISTORICAL SNAPSHOT 1925–1929

1925

- Refrigerator sales reach 75,000, up from 10,000 in 1920
- Florida land prices collapse as investors discover that many lots they bought are underwater; Ponzi scheme gains notoriety
- $10 million Boca Raton Hotel in Florida completed
- Aunt Jemima Mills acquired by Quaker Oats Company for $4 million
- Al Capone takes control of Chicago bootlegging
- Chesterfield cigarettes marketed to women for first time
- Simmons Beautyrest mattress introduced
- President Coolidge opposes cancellation of French and British war debt

1926

- Book-of-the-Month Club founded
- Machine-made ice production exceeds 56 million pounds; up from 1.5 million in 1894
- First ham in a can introduced by Hormel
- Philadelphia's Warwick Hotel opens
- First blue jeans with slide fasteners introduced by H. D. Lee company

- Synthetic rubber pioneered by B. F. Goodrich Rubber Company chemist Waldo Lonsbury Semon

1927

- 20 million cars on roads, up from 13,824 in 1900
- First compulsory automobile insurance law passed in Massachusetts
- Transatlantic telephone service between London and New York begins; call cost $75 for three minutes
- Wonder Bread introduced

1928

- Broccoli marketed in United States
- Rice Krispies introduced by W. K. Kellogg
- Peanut butter cracker sandwich packets sold under the name NAB by National Biscuit Company for 5 cents each
- U.S. per capita consumption of crude oil reaches 7.62 barrels
- Florida's 143-mile Tamiami Trail links Miami to Fort Myers through Everglades at a cost of $48,000 per mile
- Presidential candidate Herbert Hoover calls for "a chicken in every pot and two cars in every garage"

1929

- J. C. Penney goes public
- 513 Americans have incomes of more than $1 million
- Income tax rate is 1.5 percent on first $7,500 of net income
- Auto production exceeds 5 million
- Commercial airlines carry 180,000 passengers, up from 37,000 in 1927
- Delta Air Service, formerly a crop dusting business, inaugurates passenger service and secures airmail contracts
- 20 million telephones in use, double 1918 figures
- Average price of refrigerator falls to $292 from $600 in 1920
- Seven-Up introduced under name Lithiated Lemon
- Coca-Cola has gross sales of $39 million
- Stock market crashes, $30 billion capital disappears.

Men crowd outside of the New York Stock Exchange as the market crashed, October 29, 1929. (via Wikimedia Commons)

SELECTED INCOME 1925-1929

Job	Source	Description	Pay
Actor	Legrand and Karney, *Chronicle of the Cinema* (1995)	Al Jolson's earnings for *The Jazz Singer* (1927), the first motion picture to utilize spoken dialogue	$75,000
Actor	Legrand and Karney, *Chronicle of the Cinema* (1995)	Weekly income of Gloria Swanson when she moved to United Artist to produce her own films in 1926	$20,000
Actor	Legrand and Karney, *Chronicle of the Cinema* (1995)	Weekly income of Greta Garbo after the release of *Flesh and the Devil* in 1927	$5,000
Aviator	Joyce Milton, *Loss of Eden: A Biography of Charles and Anne Morrow Lindbergh* (1993)	Earnings of Charles Lindbergh following his historic transatlantic flight, including $25,000 for the Orteig Prize as the first pilot to fly from New York to Paris, and from the Guggenheim Fund honorarium for his U.S. tour following the flight in 1927	$50,000 $500,000
Barber	*Washington Post* (1928)	Short hours; weekly pay	$30–$35 weekly
Barber	*Washington Post* (1928)	First class; must speak good English; weekly pay	$30 per week 1 commission
Barber	*Washington Post* (1926)	Italian preferred, hours 9:00 a.m. to 7:30 p.m.	$30.00/week
Bookkeeper	*New York Times* (1929)	Experienced; wanted by manufacturing concern to take care of small set of books and do some typing; good appearance required; five-day wk all year	$20.00/week
Carpenter	*Chicago Tribune* (1929)	Situation Wanted: Own tools	$0.60/hr
Chemist	*Popular Science Monthly* (1927)	Annual pay	$4,000
Doorman	*New York Times* (1928)	Prominent automobile company requires services of a courteous, willing, and obliging white man; location Columbus Circle district; steady position with possibilities; uniform furnished	$27.50/week to start
Engineer	*New York Times* (1928)	Junior mechanical engineer at automobile plant close to New York, college-trained preferred	$27/month
Entrepreneur	James Grant, Bernard Baruch, *The Adventures of a Wall Street Legend* (1983)	Investment profits in 1926 of Bernard Baruch from a 1909 investment in Gulf Sulphur Company	$8 million
Gangster (1927)	*Guinness Book of World Records* (1981)	Reported income of Chicago gangster Al Capone, whose enterprises included illegal liquor, gambling, vice and protection racket	$105 million
Inspector	*Popular Science Monthly* (1927)	Weekly pay of Illinois Corn Inspector	$20.00

Job	Source	Description	Pay
Loan Clerk	*New York Times* (1928)	Bank, know securities	$2,400/yr
Miscellaneous	*Chicago Tribune* (1927)	I want 3 men now employed to do some special work for me three evenings a wk.	$30/wk
Pushcart Peddler	*The Youth's Companion* (1925)	Seller of every commodity from fish to umbrellas, occupation of 7,800 people in New York City. Weekly sales	$75 to $126
Plasterer	*Popular Science Monthly* (1927)	Day rate of Union certified plasterer for eight hours	$13.00
Radio Engineer	*New York Times* (1928)	Radio production managers	$10–100/wk
Record Producer	Mary A. Bufwack and Robert K. Oermann, *Finding Her Voice, The Saga of Women in Country Music* (1993)	Income in 1925 of Ralph Peer, country record producer and talent scout	$16,000
Sales	*Washington Post* (1926)	Catholic; if you have sold books, magazines, pictures or insurance and are a hustler, we can offer you a position	$40/wk
Salesman	*Washington Post* (1928)	Salesman with selling experience; exceptional opportunity; small orders bring large commission	$32.50 order brings $6 in advance and bonus
Salesman	*Washington Post* (1928)	Experienced specialty salesman for large manu-facturing firm	$400-$1200 per month
Shipping Room	*Chicago Tribune* (1925)	Young with shipping room experience; ambitious and energetic; must be able to fill orders and pack shipments	$20/wk to start
Stenographer	*Washington Post* (1928)	Office clerk; part-time work, 25 hours Per week Per hour	 $15 $.75
Stenographer	*Chicago Tribune* (1925)	Young man for stenographic position in executive office; large corporation	$125/month
Stenographer	*New York Times* (1926)	Stenographer and typist with knowledge of book-keeping; 18–19 years of age; in customs broker's office; good opportunity for advancement; give previous experience and state religion	$18/wk to begin
Textile Worker	*Time* (1928)	Average wages of workers in New Bedford, Mass. Mills Per week	 $19
Well Digger	*The Farm Journal* (1927)	Average weekly gross income of well digger L. E. Haffner of Donnellson, Iowa using a Lisle Manu-facturing machine	$180.00

CONSUMER EXPENDITURES
1925, 1927, 1929

(Per Capita)

Expenditure Type	1925	1927	1929
Clothing	$62.04	$63.92	$63.24
Food	$160.59	$153.89	$160.14
Auto Purchases	$20.82	$16.76	$21.35
Auto Parts	$6.96	$7.09	$4.92
Gas & Oil	$15.70	$13.39	$14.78
Housing	$98.89	$95.09	$96.08
Furniture	$9.49	$9.43	$9.85
Utilities	$9.82	$10.33	$24.64
Telephone & Telegraph	$5.88	$6.33	$4.93
Physicians	$7.68	$7.79	$8.21
Dentists	$3.26	$3.24	$4.11
Health Insurance	NR	NR	82¢
Personal Business	$27.33	$31.67	$32.85
Personal Care	$7.79	$8.75	$9.03
Tobacco	$13.13	$13.58	$13.96
Local Transport	$9.13	$9.45	$9.03
Intercity Transport	$4.95	$4.77	$4.11
Recreation	$24.52	$26.39	$35.31
Religion/Welfare Activities	$11.31	$12.16	$9.85
Private Education & Research	$7.72	$8.46	$5.75
Per Capita Consumption	$619.45	$626.45	$634.82

INVESTMENTS 1925–1929

Investment	1925	1926	1927	1928	1929
Basic Yield, One-Year Corporate Bonds	3.85	4.40	4.30	4.05	5.27
Short-Term Interest Rates, 4–6 Months, Prime Commercial Paper	4.02	4.34	4.11	4.85	5.85
Basic Yield, Common Stocks, Total	5.19	5.32	4.77	3.98	3.48
Index of Common Stocks (1941 – 1943510)	11.15	12.59	15.34	19.95	26.02

COMMON STOCKS, CLOSING PRICE AND DIVIDEND, FIRST BUSINESS DAY OF YEAR

(PARENTHETICAL NUMBER IS ANNUAL DIVIDEND IN DOLLARS)

	1925	1926	1927	1928	1929
Allis Chalmers	73 1/2	93	39 1/8	117 7/8	190
			(6)	(7)	(3)
AT&T	132 3/8	142 3/4	149 7/8	179 3/8	195
		(9)	(9)	(9)	(9)
American Tobacco	86 3/8	115 3/8	121 3/4	175 3/4	177
(2 for 1 split, 11/28/42)		(8)	(8)	(8)	(8)
Anaconda	47 1/4	49 7/8	47 3/4	58 3/4	118 1/2
		(3)	(3)	(3)	(6)
B&O	30 3/8	94 1/8	107 1/2	117 1/2	123
		(5)	(6)	(4)	(6)
Bethlehem Steel	51	48 1/4	46 1/2	58 1/8	88 (-)
		(-)	(-)	(-)	
Corn Products	41 1/8	42 1/8	47 3/4	64 7/8	91 1/8
		(2)	(2)	(2)	(2)
General Electric	315	326 1/2	83 3/4	137 1/2	125 1/4
(5% stock dividend in special stock, 9/4/24) (share for share distribution of Electric Bond and Share Securities Corp @ 67 1/2, 1/15/25) (5% dividend in special stock, 9/3/25) (4 shares for 1 split, 5/26/26) (10% stock dividend in special, 6/7/26)		(8)	(3)	(4)	(4)
General Motors	65 7/8	118	150 5/8	137 3/4	209
(1 share for 4 reverse split, 9/19/24) (50% stock dividend, 8/21/26) (2 shares for 1 split, 9/16/27)		(6)	(7)	(5)	(5)
International Business Machines	118 3/4	147 1/2	54	119 1/2	154 1/4
(20% stock dividend, 12/1/25) (3 shares for 1 split, 2/16/26) (5% stock dividend, 12/28/28)		(8)	(3)	(5)	(5)
National Biscuit	73 1/4	77 3/4	97	173 1/8	195 1/2
		(3)	(4)	(6)	(6)

Investment	1925	1926	1927	1928	1929
US Steel	120 1/4	136 4/8	155	151 3/4	162 3/4
(40% stock dividend, 6/1/27)		(5)	(7)	(7)	(7)
Western Union	116 1/4	135 5/8	146 1/2	177	182 7/8
		(3)	(8)	(8)	(8)

STANDARD JOBS 1925–1929

Job Type	1925	1926	1927	1928	1929
Average of all Industries, excl. Farm Labor	$1434/yr	$1473/yr	$1487/yr	$1490/yr	$1534/yr
Average of all Industries incl. Farm Labor	$1434/yr	$1473/yr	$1380/yr	$1384/yr	$1425/yr
Bituminous Coal Mining	72¢/hr	$1446/yr	$1342/yr	$1293/yr	72¢/hr
Avg hrs/wk	48.40	NR	NR	NR	48.50
Building Trades, Union Workers	$1.31/hr	$1708/yr	$1719/yr	$1674/yr	$1.23/hr
Avg hrs/wk	43.80	NR	NR	NR	43.90
Clerical Workers in Mfg. & Steam RR	$2239/yr	$2310/yr	NR	NR	NR
Domestics	$741/yr	$748/yr	$756/yr	$725/yr	$731/yr
Farm Labor	$382/yr	$386/yr	$387/yr	$385/yr	$378/yr
Federal Civilian	$1762/yr	$1888/yr	$1907/yr	$1916/yr	$1916/yr
Federal Employees, Executive Depts.	$1776/yr	$1809/yr	NR	NR	NR
Finance, Insurance, & Real Estate	$1997/yr	$2008/yr	$2019/yr	$2043/yr	$2062/y
Gas & Electricity Workers	$1552/yr	$1571/yr	$1558/yr	$1591/yr	$1589/yr
Lower-Skilled Labor	$1095/yr	NR	NR	NR	$1065/yr
Manufacturing, Payroll	49¢/hr	$1502/yr	$1534/yr	$1543/yr	49¢/hr
Avg hrs/wk	52.20	NR	NR	NR	52.20
Manufacturing, Union Workers	99¢/hr	$1.01/hr	NR	NR	NR
Avg hrs/wk	45.90	45.90	NR	NR	NR
Medical/Health Services Workers	$916/yr	$857/yr	$931/yr	$930/yr	$925/yr
Ministers	$1826/yr	$1769/yr	NR	NR	NR
Nonprofit Org. Workers	$1578/yr	$1607/yr	$1647/yr	$1675/yr	$1712/yr

Job Type	1925	1926	1927	1928	1929
Postal Employees	87¢/hr	NR	NR	NR	84¢/hr
Avg hrs/wk	47.20	NR	NR	NR	47.20
Public School Teachers	$1299/yr	$1342/yr	$1393/yr	$1433/yr	$1445/yr
State and Local Govt. Workers	$1377/yr	$1422/yr	$1488/yr	$1500/yr	$1549/yr
Steam Railroads, Wage Earners	$1597/yr	$1613/yr	$1687/yr	$1720/yr	$1749/yr
Street Railway Workers	$1565/yr	$1566/yr	$1549/yr	$1553/yr	$1598/yr
Telegraph Ind. Workers	$1161/yr	$1215/yr	NR	NR	NR
Telephone Ind. Workers	$1108/yr	$1117/yr	NR	NR	NR
Wholesale and Retail Trade Workers	$1416/yr	$1480/yr	$1573/yr	$1594/yr	$1359/yr

FOOD BASKET 1925-1929

Commodity	Year	New York	Atlanta	Chicago	Denver	Los Angeles
Beans, Navy, per pound	1925	11.20¢	12.30¢	9.90¢	10.90¢	10.30¢
	1926	10.40¢	10.60¢	9.40¢	10¢	9.30¢
	1927	10.10¢	10.40¢	9.60¢	9.90¢	9.50¢
	1928	12.37¢	12.78¢	11.91¢	11.50¢	11.60¢
	1929	14.80¢	16¢	13.60¢	12.90¢	13.40¢
Beef, Rib Roasts, per pound	1925	38.80¢	28.50¢	33.60¢	22.60¢	28.60¢
	1926	38.80¢	31.60¢	34.90¢	24.10¢	29.40¢
	1927	40.40¢	32.60¢	35.60¢	25.10¢	30¢
	1928	44¢	35.10¢	39.70¢	30.20¢	33.80¢
	1929	43.60¢	36.60¢	40.40¢	31.10¢	35.40¢
Beef, Steaks (Round), per pound	1925	43.10¢	33.90¢	34.20¢	27.60¢	29.70¢
	1926	43.50¢	36.10¢	35.90¢	30¢	30¢
	1927	45.20¢	38¢	37.20¢	31.30¢	31.10¢
	1928	49.40¢	41.70¢	43¢	36.70¢	35.50¢
	1929	50.90¢	44.60¢	45.70¢	38.10¢	38.40¢
Bread, per loaf	1925	9.60¢	10.30¢	9.90¢	8.30¢	9.30¢
	1926	9.60¢	10.60¢	9.80¢	8.30¢	8.60¢
	1927	9.70¢	10.80¢	9.90¢	8¢	8.50¢
	1928	8.80¢	10.80¢	9.70¢	8¢	8.80¢
	1929	8.60¢	10.50¢	9.80¢	7.60¢	8.60¢
Butter, per pound	1925	55.30¢	57.20¢	52.20¢	50.20¢	57.20¢
	1926	53.90¢	56.30¢	51¢	47.60¢	53¢
	1927	57.20¢	57¢	54.70¢	50.30¢	54.20¢
	1928	57.10¢	57.80¢	54.80¢	51.60¢	55.30¢
	1929	55.60¢	57.50¢	52.90¢	49.90¢	54.70¢
Cheese, per pound	1925	37.40¢	35.20¢	40.80¢	39¢	38.40¢
	1926	38.20¢	35.10¢	41.50¢	37.70¢	39.30¢
	1927	39¢	36.90¢	42.30¢	38¢	38.30¢
	1928	38.50¢	36.50¢	43.40¢	39.80¢	38.50¢
	1929	40.80¢	36.30¢	42¢	38.80¢	38.40¢
Chickens, per pound	1925	38.70¢	32.80¢	36.50¢	29.80¢	42¢
	1926	41.20¢	37.40¢	39.20¢	32.50¢	44.40¢
	1927	39.20¢	35.80¢	37.40¢	30.70¢	42.80¢
	1928	39.50¢	35.50¢	38.90¢	31.10¢	44¢
	1929	41.80¢	37.10¢	41.40¢	32.80¢	38.70¢
Coffee, per pound	1925	47.40¢	50.80¢	52¢	51.90¢	53.20¢
	1926	47.70¢	51.40¢	51.40¢	51.70¢	54.20¢
	1927	45.40¢	49.70¢	48.20¢	49.40¢	51.60¢
	1928	46.10¢	49.70¢	48¢	49.80¢	53.50¢
	1929	44.70¢	51.20¢	47.10¢	49.60¢	53.40¢
Cornmeal, per pound	1925	6.60¢	4.60¢	6.50¢	4.40¢	5.70¢
	1926	6.40¢	4.10¢	6.20¢	4.20¢	5.30¢
	1927	6.50¢	6.70¢	4.40¢	5.40¢	6.50¢
	1928	6.60¢	4.20¢	6.90¢	4.50¢	5.80¢
	1929	6.70¢	4.40¢	6.60¢	4.60¢	5.70¢
Eggs, per dozen	1925	62.90¢	47.20¢	51.50¢	47.50¢	50.50¢
	1926	59.60¢	45.90¢	49.10¢	44.40¢	46.30¢
	1927	57.30¢	43¢	46.20¢	41.10¢	41.60¢
	1928	57.40¢	44¢	48¢	41.40¢	43.70¢
	1929	59.40¢	46.80¢	50.50¢	42.80¢	47.50¢

Commodity	Year	New York	Atlanta	Chicago	Denver	Los Angeles
Flour, Wheat, per pound	1925	6.20¢	6.90¢	5.60¢	5.20¢	5.90¢
	1926	6¢	6.90¢	5.60¢	4.90¢	5.60¢
	1927	5.50¢	6.50¢	5.10¢	4.30¢	5.30¢
	1928	5.20¢	6.60¢	4.80¢	4.30¢	5.20¢
	1929	5¢	6.40¢	4.60¢	3.90¢	4.80¢
Lard, per pound	1925	23.70¢	23.20¢	22.90¢	24.30¢	24.10¢
	1926	22.40¢	21.70¢	21.60¢	22.70¢	23.70¢
	1927	20.20¢	19.10¢	19.30¢	19.60¢	20.20¢
	1928	19.50¢	18.10¢	18.80¢	18.60¢	20¢
	1929	19.30¢	18¢	18.50¢	18.50¢	19.70¢
Milk, Fresh, per quart	1925	14.80¢	17.20¢	14¢	11.40¢	15¢
	1926	15¢	19.40¢	14¢	12¢	15¢
	1927	15.30¢	18.10¢	14¢	12¢	15¢
	1928	15.60¢	17.10¢	14¢	12¢	15¢
	1929	16¢	16.60¢	14¢	12¢	15¢
Mutton and Lamb, Leg, per pound	1925	36.90¢	37¢	38.10¢	35.60¢	37¢
	1926	37.40¢	38.10¢	39.60¢	36.50¢	36.90¢
	1927	37.40¢	40.40¢	39.10¢	36.60¢	36.70¢
	1928	38.40¢	40.40¢	39.40¢	36.70¢	37.70¢
	1929	38.90¢	41.30¢	40.50¢	37¢	38.70¢
Pork Chops, per pound	1925	39.70¢	34.80¢	34.60¢	34.40¢	44.30¢
	1926	42.50¢	37.60¢	38¢	37.30¢	45.70¢
	1927	42.50¢	35.60¢	35.70¢	33.70¢	43.50¢
	1928	38.80¢	34¢	34¢	32.90¢	41.10¢
	1929	39¢	35.20¢	37.20¢	35.30¢	43.50¢
Pork, Bacon, Sliced, per pound	1925	46.69¢	44.50¢	49.80¢	48.40¢	54.90¢
	1926	51.30¢	48.20¢	54.20¢	51.30¢	59.30¢
	1927	48.70¢	45.20¢	51.10¢	47.40¢	55.30¢
	1928	45.90¢	42.40¢	47.90¢	43.20¢	50.90¢
	1929	45.30¢	40.80¢	48.20¢	41.60¢	50.20¢
Pork, Ham, Sliced, per pound	1925	57.70¢	53.40¢	52.70¢	54.90¢	63.90¢
	1926	62.10¢	57.80¢	56.60¢	58¢	69.20¢
	1927	62.10¢	56.60¢	55.70¢	54.60¢	68.40¢
	1928	57.20¢	53.10¢	53.50¢	52.90¢	67.10¢
	1929	58.20¢	56.10¢	54.80¢	54.70¢	68.30¢
Potatoes, Irish, per pound	1925	3.80¢	4.60¢	3.50¢	3.40¢	4.35¢
	1926	5.30¢	6¢	4.80¢	4.20¢	4.70¢
	1927	4¢	5¢	3.70¢	3.60¢	4¢
	1928	3.10¢	3.90¢	2.70¢	2.10¢	2.70¢
	1929	3.60¢	4¢	3.20¢	2.80¢	3.30¢
Prunes, Dried, per pound	1925	16¢	17.50¢	18.40¢	18.80¢	16¢
	1926	15.60¢	18.30¢	18.50¢	18.20¢	16.40¢
	1927	13.50¢	16.70¢	17.40¢	15.60¢	14.10¢
	1928	12.90¢	14.70¢	15.30¢	14.60¢	12.60¢
	1929	14.50¢	16.50¢	17.20¢	16.80¢	15.20¢
Rice, per pound	1925	10.50¢	10.70¢	11.50¢	11.20¢	11.20¢
	1926	10.70¢	11.50¢	11.80¢	11.30¢	11.20¢
	1927	9.90¢	10.10¢	11.20¢	9.90¢	10.20¢
	1928	9.90¢	9.10¢	10.50¢	9.10¢	10.10¢
	1929	9.60¢	9.50¢	10.50¢	8.90¢	9.70¢
Sugar, per pound	1925	6.40¢	7.70¢	6.90¢	7.80¢	6.90¢
	1926	6.10¢	7.30¢	6.60¢	7.40¢	6.70¢
	1927	6.50¢	7.70¢	7.10¢	7.80¢	7¢
	1928	6.30¢	7.60¢	6.90¢	7.50¢	6.80¢
	1929	5.90¢	7.10¢	6.40¢	7.20¢	6.20¢

Commodity	Year	New York	Atlanta	Chicago	Denver	Los Angeles
Tea, per pound	1925	63.80¢	99.10¢	74¢	67.70¢	76¢
	1926	65¢	$1.0480	73.10¢	68.40¢	75.30¢
	1927	66.40¢	$1.0440	72.80¢	68.90¢	74.50¢
	1928	67.80¢	$1.60	69.30¢	69.80¢	74.70¢
	1929	67.60¢	$1.04	70¢	69.40¢	73.80¢

SELECTED PRICES 1925–1929

Item	Source	Description	Price
ADVERTISING			
Advertisement	Roland Marchand, *Advertising the American Dream* (1985)	Full page, four-color in *Saturday Evening Post* [cost in 1926]	$11,000/pg
Advertising Budget	Marchand, *Advertising the American Dream* (1985)	Crane Company (plumbing supplies) [cost in 1925]	$436,000/yr
Advertising Budget	Marchand, *Advertising the American Dream* (1985)	For Maxwell House coffee [cost in 1927]	$509,000/yr
Testimonial Fee	Marchand, *Advertising the American Dream* (1985)	Price paid to a football player for a testimonial for Lucky Strike cigarettes [cost in 1926]	$4,000
APPAREL, CHILDREN'S			
Baby Outfits	*Sears, Roebuck* (1927)	44 pieces including white lawn dress, nainsook dress, white flannelette Gertrude undershirt, booties, bibs, diapers, talcum powder	$9.48
Coat	*Sears, Roebuck* (1927)	Smartly hand-smocked for girls; lovely model adapted in fine quality, silky lustrous all-wool broadcloth; styled on fetching lines	$10.50
Football Pants	*Lorick & Lowrance Hardware* (1928)	Made of good quality 8-oz olive drab duck; Notre Dame-style leg	$7
Hockey Cap	*Sears, Roebuck* (1927)	Knit in double thickness all-wool worsted in fancy pineapple stitch	$0.47
Play Suit	*Sears, Roebuck* (1927)	Boy's; he'll have lots of fun with this khaki drill coat with bright red trimmings; khaki drill pants and headdress	$1.89
Romper	*Sears, Roebuck* (1927)	Boy's; sturdy play suits	$0.59
Shoes	*The Youth's Companion* (1925)	*Keds* athletic shoes. Complete line of canvas rubber-soled shoes	$1.25 to $4.50
Suit	*Store Calendar* (1925)	Two-pants knicker suit and overcoat, sizes 6–18	$10.50
APPAREL, MEN'S			
Chauffeur's Outfit	*Vogue* (1925)	*Brill Brothers;* suit, overcoat, and cap to match	$78
Hat	*Sears, Roebuck* (1927)	A smart and rakish broad-brim fancy-band hat; made of a good-quality fur felt	$3.45

Item	Source	Description	Price
Hose Supporter	*John Martin* (1927)	Velvet grip	$0.12
Hunting Coat	*Lorick & Lowrance Hardware* (1928)	*Red Head;* medium-weight forest-brown regimental duck	$3.50
Overcoat	*Sears, Roebuck* (1927)	Storm proof; heavy all-wool sheep-lined ulster, has a large shawl-style collar of Australian opossum fur	$29.95
Shirt	*Time* (1928)	Custom shirtmaker	$3
Sombrero	*Sears, Roebuck* (1927)	Man's good quality wool felt sombrero work hat; the crown is about 4 3/4" high	$1.98
Suit	*Sears, Roebuck* (1927)	Fancy weaves for fall—pure all-wool worsted	$21.50
Suit and Overcoat	*Store Calendar* (1925)	Two pants, suit and overcoat; the extra pair doubles the wear	$10.50

APPAREL, WOMEN'S

Item	Source	Description	Price
Brassiere Corset	*Vogue* (1925)	*Royal Worcester Bon Ton;* makes you appear slim, supple, and tailored in this smooth-fitting, one-piece garment	$3.50
Coat	*Sears, Roebuck* (1927)	Opossum fur; collegiate style; called the tomboy model, having been especially made for hard strenuous service and cut on loose, comfortable lines	$129
Coat	*Sears, Roebuck* (1927)	All-wool suede velour; true reproduction of French model; satin de chine lining, mandel-fur trimming	$27.50
Corset	*Sears, Roebuck* (1927)	It confines the bust and hip and diaphragm, is light, yet is strong and flexible	$1.69
Frock	*Vogue* (1925)	*Bromely Shepard;* one-piece dress of red jersey with black and red braid	$25
Galoshes	*Sears, Roebuck* (1927)	Silk and wool snap-on	$2.48
Handbag	*Sears, Roebuck* (1927)	Back strap; newest shape and leathers	$2.98
Handbag	*Sears, Roebuck* (1927)	Newest French-tailored; of soft extra-quality smooth calf leather; has three large pockets; coin purse	$4.95
Hose	*Delineator* (1928)	*Allen-A Hosiery;* pure silk the entire length of the hose Per pair	$1.50 to $3.00
Maternity Corset	*Vogue* (1925)	*Lane Bryant;* the best corset in the world	$6.95
Nursing Brassiere	*Sears, Roebuck* (1927)	Fastens with hooks and eyes at each side of panel in front without the least inconvenience	$0.85
Shoes	*Vogue* (1925)	*Shoecraft;* snakeskin and kid model	$22.50
Short Corset	*Sears, Roebuck* (1927)	*Berthe May;* for expectant mothers; very comfortable, no boning over hips	$2.48

Item	Source	Description	Price
APPLIANCES			
Coffee Pot	*Modern Priscilla* (1929)	*Universal;* the percolator that has brought perfect coffee to millions Empire pattern, 4 to 14 cups Continental pattern, electric, 2 to 6 cups	 $4.50 to $6.00 $9.00 to $10.00
Corn Popper	*Sears, Roebuck* (1927)	Enjoy fresh-popped corn, right on your living room table; will make popcorn a daily habit	$1.75
Desk Fan	*Lorick & Lowrance Hardware* (1928)	*Hunter;* electric; alternating current, three speeds, 12" blades	$30
Heating Stove	*Lorick & Lowrance Hardware* (1928)	*Enterprise Burnside;* for coal; 363 pounds	$51
Hot Water Heater	*Delineator* (1928)	American Radiator Company Hotcoil gas water heater; perfect heating at lowest fuel price 20 gallon	 $55.00 plus installation
Iron	*Sears, Roebuck* (1927)	*The Aristocrat;* the ultimate in beautiful design, ease of work, and perfect ironing convenience, full weight, 6 1/2 lbs	$4.95
Iron	*The Farm Journal* (1927)	*Coleman,* self-heating iron; asbestos-lined lid keeps handle cool while iron gets hot	$5.00
Juice Extractor	*Modern Priscilla* (1929)	*Sunkist Junior Orange and Lemon Juice Extractor;* electrically powered; extracts all the juice	$14.95
Omelet Pan	*Modern Priscilla* (1929)	Omelet pan; made from the super-metal Hyb-Lum; is light as aluminum but stronger	$6.75
Range	*The Literary Digest* (1928)	*Campbell Automatic Electric Fireless Cooker;* an electric range with new quick-ring heating elements which actually cook as fast as gas	$25.50
Range	*Lorick & Lowrance Hardware* (1928)	*Supreme Enterprise;* cast with duplex grate for coal or wood	$78
Table Stove	*Sears, Roebuck* (1927)	Heavy cast stoves for kitchenette use; for 110-volt current only	$5.25
Toaster	*Antique Week* (1926)	*Toastermaster Automatic;* pop-up toaster	$12.50
Toaster	*Lorick & Lowrance Hardware* (1928)	*Universal;* electric; has bread-pack drop that never fails to work	$4.95
Vacuum Cleaner	*Delineator* (1928)	*Hoover* vacuum; cleaning that tires you not at all; positive agitation Model 700 Model 543	 $75.00 $59.50
Vacuum Cleaner	*Sears, Roebuck* (1927)	*Greater Energex;* attachments complete and with airizer device for 110-volt city current only	$33.90
Waffle Iron	*Lorick & Lowrance Hardware* (1928)	*Universal;* electric; pure aluminum; 7 1/2" grids that require no greasing	$9.75

Item	Source	Description	Price
BABY PRODUCTS			
Baby Bottle Kit	*Time* (1928)	Sterilizer and carrier; pack it with ice—carry anywhere	$5
BUSINESS EQUIPMENT & SUPPLIES			
Amplifier	*Popular Science Monthly* (1927)	*Thordarson Power Compact* is the only power supply foundation unit available to the home constructor; transform your radio set	$15.00
Bonds	*The Youth's Companion* (1925)	*Smith Bonds;* sold in denominations of $100, $500 and $1,000 with maturities from 2 years to 15 years	7%
Counter	*Popular Science Monthly* (1927)	*Veeder Set-Back Rotary Ratchet Counter;* for presses and metal-stamping machines with reciprocating movement	$11.50
Drill Press	*Popular Science Monthly* (1927)	*Knapp Drill Press,* drills wood, iron, copper, brass, aluminum, lead, slate, bakelite Denver West	$4.50 $4.75
Lathe	*Popular Science Monthly* (1927)	*Junior South Bend Lathe;* practical for handling the finest work in the machine shop, manufacturing plant or tool room	$175
Trucks	*Time* (1928)	White trucks earn the most profit Light delivery, 1 1/2-ton chassis Heavy duty, 3-ton chassis	 $2,125 $4,650
COLLECTIBLES			
Autograph	*The Youth's Companion* (1925)	Signature of Button Gwinnett, one of the 56 signers of The Declaration of Independence, representing Georgia	$14,000
Gun	*Antique Gun and Military Catalog* (1925)	*Kentucky Flintlock Smooth Bore;* with heavy octagonal barrel, 36", 9/16" bore	$50
Gun	*Antique Gun and Military Catalog* (1925)	*Smooth Bore Flint-lock Musket;* 3/4" bore; good, cleaned condition; perhaps made about 1840	$14
Gun	*Antique Gun and Military Catalog* (1925)	Revolving double-barrel flintlock, one hammer with two flash pans, one attached to each barrel	$120
Pistol	*Antique Gun and Military Catalog* (1925)	Pepper-box revolving barrel, 6-shot, top hammer, engraved frame	$12
Rifle	*Antique Gun and Military Catalog* (1925)	*Flintlock 1766;* 21" octagonal barrel, engraved "fowler" on barrel "1766"	$25
EDUCATION			
Camp for Girls	*Delineator* (1928)	*Camp Sequoya* for girls in Allegheny Mountains; water sports, tennis, hockey Bristol, Virginia 8-week term	$225
Cornell University	*Popular Science Monthly* (1927)	Total annual cost of Cornell, including tuition and living expenses	$1,400

Item	Source	Description	Price
Prep School	*Delineator* (1928)	*Dean Academy;* young men and young women find a home-like atmosphere Per year	$500 to $600
School for Boys	*Delineator* (1928)	*Curtis,* a school for 30 young boys, home-life, strong, clean influence, Brookfield, Connecticut	$1,200
School for Boys	*Delineator* (1928)	*Dakotah School for Boys;* a home school in the country for boys under 15; Dakota, Illinois Rates	$600 to $650
School for Boys	*Delineator* (1928)	*Gettysburg Academy;* a school for 100 boys, new gymnasium and swimming pool, Gettysburg, Pennsylvania Per year	$475 to $575

ENTERTAINMENT

Item	Source	Description	Price
Boxing Match	*Guinness Book of World Records* (1981)	Ring-side ticket price for Tunney vs. Dempsey heavy weight title fight in 1926	$27.50
Concert Ticket	*Washington Post* (1926)	London String Quartette; Washington Auditorium	$1–$2

ENTERTAINMENT, HOME

Item	Source	Description	Price
Butterfly Shades	*Modern Priscilla* (1929)	All materials and directions for making exquisite butterfly shade	$5.00
Camera	*Time* (1928)	*Graflex;* Graflex is the only camera which shows the action in the finder exactly as on the negative; Series B, 3 1/4" × 4 1/2"; speed up to 1/1000 second	$80
Camera	*Time* (1928)	*Graflex;* the camera that shows the action in the finder exactly as on the negative Series B, speed up to 1/1000 second	$80.00
Microscope	*Popular Science Monthly* (1927)	*Wollensak Optical* 250 power microscope	$16.50
Radio	*Sears, Roebuck* (1927)	*Model XVIII;* six tube; receiver only	$39.95
Radio	*Sears, Roebuck* (1927)	*Model XX;* six-tube receiver with all accessories; includes two large detector-amplifiers, storage battery, tubes, two large-duty 45-volt "B" batteries; one 100 ampere-hour storage battery, aerial; weight 205 lbs.	$99.95
Radio	*Literary Digest* (1928)	*Atwater Kent Model 30:* powerful one-dial, six-tube receiver	$65
Radio	*Literary Digest* (1928)	*Atwater Kent Model 33;* one dial, six tube receiver with solid mahogany cabinet; effective when distance getting is essential	$75
Radio	*Time* (1928)	*Gembox;* 6-tube electric radio	$65
Radio	*Time* (1928)	*Showbox;* 8-tube AC electric radio	$80

Item	Source	Description	Price
FARM EQUIPMENT & SUPPLIES			
Dog Medicine	*The Farm Journal* (1927)	*Glover's* Mange Medicine	$0.65
		Glover's Imperial Medicated Soap	$0.30
		Glover's Distemper Medicine	$1.25
Fence	*The Farm Journal* (1927)	Kokomo ornamental wire fence, costs less than wood Per foot	$0.06
Horse Treatment	*The Farm Journal* (1927)	*Absorbine* reduces thickened, swollen tissues, curbs filled tendons, soreness from bruises or strains	
		Per box	$2.50
Lamb	*The Farm Journal* (1927)	Average of 29 ewes sold by Caldwell County, Missouri farmer	$16.69
Medicine for Chickens	*Carolina Gazette* (1925)	Absolutely rids chickens of sorehead	$0.35
Plow	*Lorick & Lowrance Hardware* (1928)	*Oliver;* one-horse; right-hand capacity, 4" deep by 7" wide	$8.25
Poultry Medicine	*The Farm Journal* (1927)	*Walko White Diarrhoea Remedy;* reduces chicken loss Per package	$0.50
Spark Plug	*The Farm Journal* (1927)	*Champion X* spark plugs; exclusively for Ford cars, trucks and Fordson tractors	
		Set of four	$2.40
Udder Balm	*The Farm Journal* (1927)	Bag Balm, for dairy cattle udder and teats; will heal between milkings 10-ounce package	$0.60

FOOD PRODUCTS

Item	Source	Description	Price
Milk Chocolate	*Sears, Roebuck* (1926)	*Hershey's;* box of 24 $0.05 bars	$0.97/box

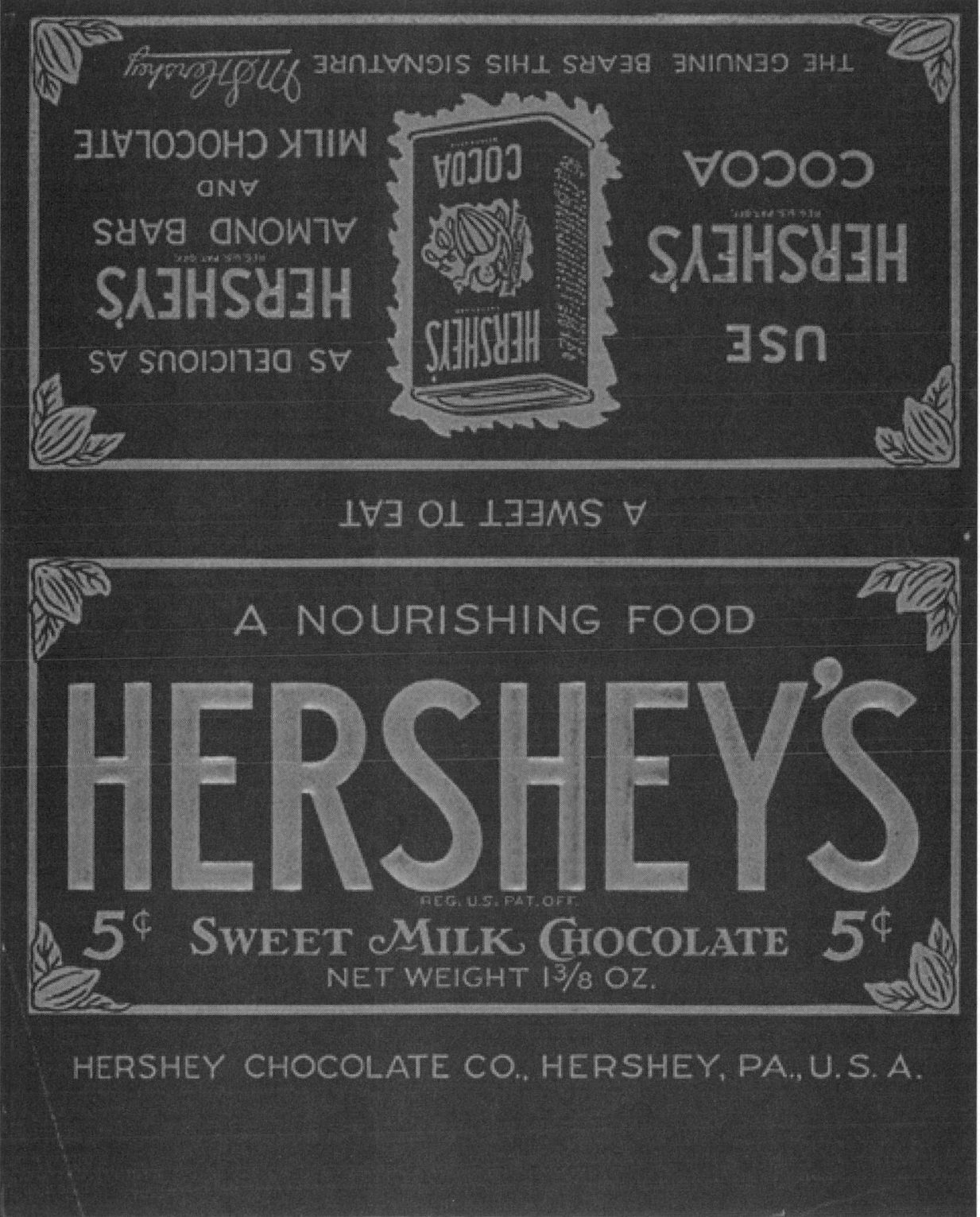

A Hershey's wrapper from 1926. (via Wikimedia Commons)

Item	Source	Description	Price
Strained Vegetables	*Modern Priscilla* (1929)	*Gerber's;* vegetables for baby; fresh to the cooker; per can Strained vegetable soup Strained carrots Strained peas	 $0.25 $0.15 $0.15

HOUSEHOLD PRODUCTS

Item	Source	Description	Price
Blanket	*Modern Priscilla* (1929)	Nashua part wool blanket in color sets Per pair, 72" × 84"	$4.95
Cleaner	*Modern Priscilla* (1929)	*Sani-Flush* cleans closet bowls without scoring Per can	$0.25
Cleaning Fluid	*Modern Priscilla* (1929)	*Energine;* removes spots quickly, dries instantly and leaves no odor Handy sized can	$0.35
Hammer	*Popular Science Monthly* (1927)	*Plumb Ball Pein hammer;* a safe hammer for car or work bench	$1.30
Pots	*Delineator* (1928)	Mirror aluminum pots; cook the new way with vapo-seal lids 10-quart size	 $6.50
Soap	*Modern Priscilla* (1929)	*Super Suds;* beads of soap make clothes whiter, dishes brighter Big box size	$0.10
Tarnish Tissues	*Modern Priscilla* (1929)	*Dexstar Staybrite Tissues;* silverware will not show the slightest tarnish when wrapped in tissues Sample, including 48 sheets (size 20 × 30 inches)	$1.00
Water Softener	*Delineator* (1928)	*Mel'o, a Real Water Softener;* a teaspoon in the dishpan is enough Full-sized can	 $0.10

GARDEN EQUIPMENT & SUPPLIES

Item	Source	Description	Price
Ax	*Lorick & Lowrance Hardware* (1928)	*Kelly Falls City;* single bit; handled, 4 pounds	$1.20
Ax	*Lorick & Lowrance Hardware* (1928)	*Box Scout;* official ax of Boy Scouts of America; 1 1/4 lbs, with Canvas Sheath	$1.65
Plant	*The Literary Digest* (1928)	New water fern; thrives in a vase of water	$0.50
Saw	*Carolina Gazette* (1925)	*Graves;* one-man saw; one man can do the work of two with this saw	$10
Saw	*Lorick & Lowrance Hardware* (1928)	*Handy Hand;* skew-back 24" saw	$2.35
Wheelbarrow	*Lorick & Lowrance Hardware* (1928)	General purpose; weight 43 lbs	$6.25

HOUSEHOLD PRODUCTS

Item	Source	Description	Price
Alarm Clock	*Lorick & Lowrance Hardware* (1928)	*Westclox Big Ben;* mellow toned; rings on back gong	$3.25

Item	Source	Description	Price
Bathroom Fixtures	Marchand, *Advertising the American Dream* (1985)	Meeting the modern demand for color in bathroom fixtures; includes sink, toilet, and tub [cost in 1929]	$157.45
Bathroom Outfit	*Sears, Roebuck* (1927)	*Fairview;* bathtub, lavatory and closet, with lavatory supply and waste pipes to wall	$64.75
Battery	*Lorick & Lowrance Hardware* (1928)	*Ray-O-Vac;* dry-cell A; 1 1/2 volts; diameter 2 1/2"; height 6"	$0.50
Blanket	*Sears, Roebuck* (1927)	Cotton plaid; these best staple cotton blankets are one-fifth lower than they were a year ago; 64" × 76"; weight per pair, 2 1/2 lbs	$1.72
Ceiling Fan	*Lorick & Lowrance Hardware* (1928)	*Hunter;* electric; 52" sweep, four basswood blades, three speeds	$52
Chisels	*Lorick & Lowrance Hardware* (1928)	Cabinet; six different sizes in a box	$10.20/bx
Clothes Pins	*Lorick & Lowrance Hardware* (1928)	One-piece standard pattern; hardwood	$3.50/5 gross case
Comforter	*Vogue* (1925)	*Carlin;* with lamb's wool filling; in Japanese silks	$21
Condiment Set	*Sears, Roebuck* (1927)	Made of Japanese lusterware decorated with cherry blossoms; set consists of one tray, one mustard jar, and one salt and pepper shaker	$0.85
Corn Cake Pans	*Lorick & Lowrance Hardware* (1928)	14 1/4" × 7 5/8" pan; makes 11	$0.85
Egg Beater	*Lorick & Lowrance Hardware* (1928)	*Blue Whirl;* no splash, even when whipping cream or mixing salad dressing	$1
Fireplace Grate	*Lorick & Lowrance Hardware* (1928)	*Cahill;* three-piece frame, 10" opening, 39 lbs., oxidized copper	$10
Fuse Plug	*Lorick & Lowrance Hardware* (1928)	*Universal;* made to fit all Universal electric hollow ware	$1.20
Grist Mill	*Lorick & Lowrance Hardware* (1928)	*Black Hawk;* will grind corn, wheat, rye, rice, or other small grain, beans, peas, spices, etc.	$4
Hacksaw	*Lorick & Lowrance Hardware* (1928)	*Miller Falls;* pistol grip, 10" blade	$2
Ice Cream Disher	*Lorick & Lowrance Hardware* (1928)	*Gilchrist;* automatic; pressing the thumb piece rotates the scraper	$2
Ironing Table	*Lorick & Lowrance Hardware* (1928)	*Daisy;* adjustable to four different heights	$2.35
Knives	*Lorick & Lowrance Hardware* (1928)	*Universal Resistain;* set of six steel paring knives	$0.45
Lantern	*Lorick & Lowrance Hardware* (1928)	*Dietz Monarch;* 13 1/2" height; fount capacity 18 hours	$12.50
Lavatory	*Lorick & Lowrance Hardware* (1928)	*Kohler Columbia;* enameled lavatory 20" × 24"	$50.70
Luggage	*Time* (1928)	Five bags combined in one at practically the price of one	$26.95
Mousetrap	*Lorick & Lowrance Hardware* (1928)	*Victor;* sheet-metal bait trigger	$1.80

251

Item	Source	Description	Price
Nail Hammer	*Lorick & Lowrance Hardware* (1928)	*Plumb;* adze eye, bell face; 1 lb	$1.75
Paint	*Lorick & Lowrance Hardware* (1928)	*Johnston's Dulle Kote;* for interior use; cleans easily with soap and water	$2.75
Pocketknife	*Lorick & Lowrance Hardware* (1928)	*Remington;* pearl handle; three blades	$3.50
Rule	*Lorick & Lowrance Hardware* (1928)	*Lufkin Folding Aluminum Rule;* 69" length, 6" folds	$2.10
Scale	*Vogue* (1925)	*Detecto;* watches your weight	$15
Soap	*Sears, Roebuck* (1927)	Toilet soap	$0.83
Spray Painting Machine	*Time* (1928)	Portable; will cut your maintenance painting costs in half	$115
Toilet	*Lorick & Lowrance Hardware* (1928)	*Kohler;* dorking; vitreous china wash-down closet combination	$35.05
Tool Chest	*Lorick & Lowrance Hardware* (1928)	*Stanley;* includes 12 tools	$15
Turpentine Measure	*Lorick & Lowrance Hardware* (1928)	Capacity 8 qt	$2
Vase	*Sears, Roebuck* (1927)	Imported; made of Japanese tokanabe pottery in antique design; height about 10"	$1.25
Waterproofer	*Sears, Roebuck* (1927)	Will make canvas waterproof and mildew proof; white	$1.25
Wood Varnish	*Lorick & Lowrance Hardware* (1928)	*Luxeberry;* for interior trim	$1.45

INSURANCE RATES

Item	Source	Description	Price
Accident and Sickness	The Literary Digest Insurance (1928)	No medical examination, men and women 16–70 years	accepted $10/yr
Fire Insurance	*Insurance Policy* (1926)	$500 fire coverage on two-story wood-frame building	$9/yr

JEWELRY

Item	Source	Description	Price
Watch	*The Farm Journal* (1927)	*Ingersolls* have earned a reputation for dependability Wrist watch Waterbury pocket watch	 $3.50 $8.00
Wristwatch	*Sears, Roebuck* (1927)	Man's; 14-carat solid white gold; hand engraved bezel and sides; curved back to fit wrist; 15-jewel movement	$38.50

MEALS

Item	Source	Description	Price
Dinner	*Washington Post* (1926)	*The Rendezvous Restaurant;* George Washington Birthday Dinner; home-cooked food at moderate prices	$1

Item	Source	Description	Price
MEDICAL PRODUCTS & SERVICES			
Dust Mask	*The Farm Journal* (1927)	*Dr. Willson's Dust and Spray Mask,* for all dusty farm and factory work	$2.25
Nonprescription Drug	*Time* (1928)	*Gastrogen;* tablets; quick digestive relief and brings no hiccup or gas	$0.20
Sanatorium Care	*Report of the Board of Trustees, Brotherhood of Railroad Trainmen* (1928)	*Thompson Sanatorium;* Kenneiller, Texas	$5/day
MOTORIZED VEHICLES, SERVICES, & SUPPLIES			
Airplane	*Popular Science Monthly* (1927)	Cost of Charles Lindbergh's Ryan Monoplane	$18,000
Auto Camp Fee	*The Farm Journal* (1927)	Connecticut Auto Camp charge per night	$0.50
Automobile	Joseph J. Schroeder Jr., *The Wonderful World of Automobiles* (1971)	*Hudson Coach;* 6-cylinder; world's greatest buy [cost in 1925]	$1,250
Automobile	*Time* (1928)	*Lincoln;* seven-passenger sport touring, restful touring comfort even across a continent	$4,600–$7,300
Automobile	*Time* (1928)	*Plymouth;* 4-cylinder roadster, coupe	$670
Automobile	*Schroeder, The Wonderful World of Automobiles* (1971)	*Chrysler Imperial 80;* town sedan, 112 hp [cost in 1928]	$2,995
Automobile	*The Literary Digest* (1928)	*Packard Custom Eight;* lower prices make it possible for many additional thousands to step up to the possession of America's finest and most modern car	
		2-Passenger Convertible Coupe	$4,150
		4-Passenger Coupe	$4,450
		7-Passenger Limousine	$4,550

Three women and a man are seen sitting in a convertible Packard at Pinehurst, North Carolina. (via Wikimedia Commons)

Item	Source	Description	Price
Automobile	*Washington Post* (1926)	*Peerless Sedan* demonstrator; 5-passenger; 6-cylinder; new car guarantee	$2,100
Automobile, Used	*Washington Post* (1926)	1924 Chevrolet, perfect condition; 4 new tires; wheel lock	$125
Delivery Truck	*Time* (1928)	*White;* delivers the most money-earning miles	$1,545
Motorbike	*Sears, Roebuck* (1927)	High-grade motor bike at fully one-third less than it would cost anywhere else	$25.75
Motorcycle	*Popular Science Monthly* (1927)	*Harley-Davidson Motorcycle;* The single that travels 80 miles per gallon	$235
Radiator Repair	*The Farm Journal* (1927)	*X Liquid* repairs leaky radiators, harmless to metal, rubber and leather For Fords, Stars and Chevrolets	$0.75
Tire Chains	*The Literary Digest* (1928)	*Woodworth Easyon;* don't let your wife drive without them	$0.35
Truck Tire	*Sears, Roebuck* (1927)	*Cushion;* size 30" × 3 1/2"; complete with rim which has four lugs to fit Fords and Chevrolet; ready for mounting	$16.45

Item	Source	Description	Price
MUSICAL INSTRUMENTS			
Harmonica	*John Martin* (1926)	*Hohner;* Anyone can play the Hohner harmonica	$0.50
OTHER			
Christmas Cards	*Modern Priscilla* (1929)	Charming Christmas cards with envelopes for hand coloring	25 per pkg $1.00
Dog Collar Padlock	*Lorick & Lowrance Hardware* (1928)	*Eagle;* assortment	$4.20
Dog Medicine	*The Literary Digest* (1928)	*Glover's Imperial Dog Medicines;* dogs need these aids to health	$0.65
Funeral Expenses	*Report of the Board of Trustees, Brotherhood of Railroad Trainmen* (1928)	D. L. Case	$935
Grave Marker	*Confederate Veteran Magazine* (1928)	"Lest We Forget" markers for Confederate graves; approved by the UDC	$1.50
Lumber	*John Martin* (1926)	*Bildmor Blox;* well-cut building lumber accurately cut on the system of "multiple units" so that interlocking construction is possible	$3.50
Silver Plate Knives	*Delineator* (1928)	Community deluxe stainless knives; blades as sharp as a Turk's scimitar Paul Revere design, per half dozen	$9.00
PERSONAL CARE PRODUCTS			
Cream	*Delineator* (1928)	*Helena Rubinstein's Valaze Pasteurized Face Cream;* cleans the skin immaculately Theatrical size	$1.00 $1.75
Curling Iron Heater	*Sears, Roebuck* (1927)	Heats your iron the safe, clean electric way; strong aluminum tube which keeps the iron warm for some time after the current is turned off	$2.55
Dental Cream	*The Literary Digest* (1928)	*Squibb's*; make your teeth and gums safe at the danger line	$0.40
Eye Care	*Modern Priscilla* (1929)	*Murine* for your eyes; every woman longs for clear, bright eyes Month's supply	$0.60
False Teeth Holder	*The Literary Digest* (1928)	*Klutch*; forms a comfort cushion; holds the plate so snug it can't rock	$0.50
Hair Dryer	*Lorick & Lowrance Hardware* (1928)	*Polar Cub*; electric; for drying hair, shoes, delicate fabrics, motor-driven blower type	$4.95
Hair Treatment	*Sears, Roebuck* (1927)	*Water Waver for Hair;* beautiful deep graceful water waves assured; set of 6	$2.45/set
Hairpins	*Sears, Roebuck* (1927)	*Celluloid;* brown-shell or yellow-amber color; 24 pins per box	$0.23/bx
Lipstick	*Vogue* (1925)	*Tangee;* be beautiful with Tangee	$1

255

Item	Source	Description	Price
Razor	*The Farm Journal* (1927)	*Durham-Duplex Razor*—the blades men swear by, Set includes razor and two $0.50 packages of blades	$1.50
Razor Blade	*Lorick & Lowrance Hardware* (1928)	*Gillette;* double edge; half packet 5 blades	$0.50
Safety Razor	*Lorick & Lowrance Hardware* (1928)	*Enders;* knurled razor handle made of duralumin	$1
Safety Razor	*Lorick & Lowrance Hardware* (1928)	*Gillette New Standard;* genuine-leather-covered case, purple velvet and satin lined	$5
Shaving Lotion	*Sears, Roebuck* (1927)	*Talc for Men*	$0.19
Shaving Soap	*Sears, Roebuck* (1927)	*Colgate's Barber's Bar;* 1 lb equals 8 cakes	$0.49/lb
Suntan Lotion	*Delineator* (1928)	*Helena Rubinstein's Valaze Suntan Lotion*	$2.50
Tissue	*Lorick & Lowrance Hardware* (1928)	*Scott;* the soft, smooth tissue with purity, whiteness and quick absorbency; 50 roll case	$6.50/case
Tissue	Roland Marchand, *Advertising the American Dream* (1985)	*Scott;* now doctors ask you: is your bathroom paper safe? [cost in 1928]	$0.25
Toilet Tissue	*Delineator* (1928)	*A. P. W. Satin Tissue;* soft, absorbent, pure; scientifically safe One year's supply, 10,000 sheets in rolls One year's supply, 9,000 sheets flat	 $2.00 $2.45
Toothpaste	*The Literary Digest* (1928)	*Listerine;* the best paste that scientific knowledge could achieve	$0.25
Toothbrush	*Sears, Roebuck* (1927)	A popular type brush highly recommended by dentists	$0.25
Toothbrush	*The Literary Digest* (1928)	*Prophylactic;* reaches every tooth every time you brush	$0.50

PUBLICATIONS

Item	Source	Description	Price
Article	Marchand, *Advertising the American Dream* (1985)	"Truth is Stranger than Fiction" (1929)	$0.25
Book	*Washington Post* (1926)	*Abraham Lincoln, The Prairie Years* by Carl Sandburg; two-volume set	$10
Book	*Confederate Veteran Magazine* (1928)	*Echoes From Dixie, The Best Collection of the Real Old Songs of the South*	$1
Book	*John Martin* (1927)	*Winnie The Pooh;* amusing as only Christopher Robin's 'Bear of the Little Brain' could make it	$2
Magazine	*The Youth's Companion* (1925)	*The Youth's Companion,* published weekly, one-year subscription	$2.50

Item	Source	Description	Price
Magazine	*The Farm Journal* (1927)	The Farm Journal—inserts no humbug advertising, published monthly One year Four years	$0.25 $1.00
Magazine	*Modern Priscilla* (1929)	*Modern Priscilla Monthly* Per year	$2.00
Newspaper	*Wall Street Journal* (1928)	Annual subscription	$15

REAL ESTATE

House	*The Farm Journal* (1927)	Gordon-Van Tine home; 5 rooms, bath, sun porch; all materials precut and shipped by rail for your construction	$1,932
House	*Carolina Gazette* (1925)	For rent; Bluffton, South Carolina; tent house with four spring cots, mattresses, and pillows	$10/wk
Land	*Popular Science Monthly* (1927)	10 acres near White River in Ozarks	$100 ($5.00 per month)

SEWING EQUIPMENT & SUPPLIES

Cloth	*Sears, Roebuck* (1927)	All-wool flannel shirting; a fine quality twilled flannel in a small check; medium weight; width about 54"	$1.59/yd
Cloth	*Sears, Roebuck* (1927)	Half-wool shirting flannel; makes excellent children's playsuits because it is washable; width about 27"	$0.39/yd
Dye	*Modern Priscilla* (1929)	*Diamond Dyes;* give richer colors to faded or out- of-date dresses	$0.15
Sewing Machine	*Sears, Roebuck* (1927)	Six-drawer, drop-head ball-bearing sewing machine, plain oak woodwork	$33.95
Sewing Machine	*Modern Priscilla* (1929)	*Priscilla Electric Consolette Sewing Machine;* 15 monthly payments of $5	$79.00
Thread	*Modern Priscilla* (1929)	Boil fast mercerized thread; smooth enough to slip without friction through the filmiest chiffons 100-yard spool	$0.05

SPORTS EQUIPMENT

Baseball	*Sears, Roebuck* (1927)	*Wilson Official League;* selected horsehide cover sewed with best linen thread	$1.39
Baseball Bat	*Lorick & Lowrance Hardware* (1928)	*Louisville Slugger;* Ty Cobb style	$2
Baseball Glove	*Sears, Roebuck* (1927)	Youth model first baseman's mitt; good quality, soft and pliable horsehide leather	$1.75
Baseball Glove	*Sears, Roebuck* (1927)	*G. C. Alexander;* professional league model; diverted seams prevent ripping	$3.39

Item	Source	Description	Price
Baseball Glove	*Lorick & Lowrance Hardware* (1928)	*Rawlings Junior;* cross-lace fielder's glove; Willow horsehide, full glovolium oiled	$3
Baseball Mask	*Sears, Roebuck* (1927)	Catcher's; electrically welded dull-black-enameled steel-wire frame	$1.89
Basketball	*Lorick & Lowrance Hardware* (1928)	Made in four sections from tanned pebble grain cowhide	$18
Bicycle	*Lorick & Lowrance Hardware* (1928)	*Williams;* steel; wood-lined rims	$41
Boxing Gloves	*Lorick & Lowrance Hardware* (1928)	*U.S. Army Special;* weight 10 oz	$3.65
Fishing Line	*Lorick & Lowrance Hardware* (1928)	*Mayo;* twisted; made of Irish linen	$5.60
Fishing Plug	*Sears, Roebuck* (1927)	*South Bend Wiz-Oreno;* practically weedless, single hook, swiveling spinner, hackle fly and pork-rind snap	$0.87
Fishing Reel	*Sears, Roebuck* (1927)	*Shakespeare Criterion Level;* winding; 100-yd capacity; full quadruple-multiplying correct-level winding	$4.37
Fishing Reel	*Lorick & Lowrance Hardware* (1928)	*Shakespeare Criterion Level;* winding; capacity 100 yds	$5
Football	*Sears, Roebuck* (1927)	*Glenn F. Thistlewaite;* official; stemless bladder, ready-laced and ready to be inflated	$6.85
Football	*Lorick & Lowrance Hardware* (1928)	*Rawlings Official Intercollegiate;* pebble-grain leather	$12
Football Helmet	*Lorick & Lowrance Hardware* (1928)	Black strap leather; white felt padding	$5.50
Football Pants	*Sears, Roebuck* (1927)	*Red Grange;* boys; made of good quality duck-felt pad at top, reinforced with tape; autographed photograph of Red Grange furnished with each pair of pants	$3.89

A man wearing football equipment in 1929. (via Wikimedia Commons)

Item	Source	Description	Price
Golf Ball	*Time* (1928)	*Dunlop;* Have you ever heard anyone ask for a better ball than a Dunlop? Each	$1.00
Golf Ball	*Time* (1928)	*Practo;* Practo makes perfect; this knitted golf ball will not travel far and it can't break anything	$0.25
Golf Ball	*Lorick & Lowrance Hardware* (1928)	*U. S. Royal;* recessed marking	$1
Golf Club	*Lorick & Lowrance Hardware* (1928)	*Macgregor Master;* driver	$15
Golf Clubs	*Lorick & Lowrance Hardware* (1928)	*Macgregor Duralite Uni-Set;* irons; set of eight	$78
Golf Tee	*Time* (1928)	Be sure you get the original and genuine	$0.25
Golf Tee	*Time* (1928)	*The Reddy Tee* 18 for	$0.25
Gun	*Lorick & Lowrance Hardware* (1928)	*L. C Smith Field Grade;* double-barrel shotgun; made entirely of steel	$40

Item	Source	Description	Price
Gun	*Sears, Roebuck* (1927)	*Winchester Model 94;* solid-frame repeating rifle; the well known lever action style, noted for its simple mechanism, accuracy, and reliability	$31.98
Knife	*Lorick & Lowrance Hardware* (1928)	*Official Boy Scouts of America;* stag handle, four blades	$1.80
Rifle	*The Farm Journal* (1927)	*J. Stevens Arms Company;* manufactured over 10 million arms; single shot, .22 long rifle	$8.00
Rifle	*Antique Gun and Military Catalog* (1925)	*German Breech-loading Target Rifle:* heavy octagonal barrel, fine muzzle front sight, sliding-leaf peep sight	$16
Scooter	*Sears, Roebuck* (1927)	DeLuxe all-steel roller-bearing scooter	$3.98
Shotgun	*Sears, Roebuck* (1927)	Single barrel; matted top rib, trap-style automatic ejector, 12 gauge	$12.35
Shotgun	*Sears, Roebuck* (1927)	Single barrel; barrel is drilled from solid bar of special gun barrel steel, 12 gauge, 20" barrel	$8.95
Shotgun Shells	*Lorick & Lowrance Hardware* (1928)	*Remington New Club;* loaded with blank powder; 12 gauge; case of 100	$37/case
Tennis Racket	*Lorick & Lowrance Hardware* (1928)	*Narragansett;* 3-piece; full-beveled laminated frame, 60 line	$15
Tent	*Sears, Roebuck* (1927)	Army duck waterproofed umbrella style; new popular empire green color, size 9 3/4" × 10 1/2"	$37.85

TELEPHONE EQUIPMENT & SERVICES

Item	Source	Description	Price
Long Distance Charges	*John Brooks, Telephone: The First Hundred Years* (1987)	New York to London [rate for 1927]	$45

TOBACCO PRODUCTS

Item	Source	Description	Price
Pipe Tobacco	*Popular Science Monthly* (1927)	*Old Briar* tobacco is bringing smokers back to the pipe Per box	$0.50 $1.00

TOYS

Item	Source	Description	Price
Board Game	*Sears, Roebuck* (1927)	*Ouija;* apparently answers questions concerning your past, present, and future, equipped with Fauld's new patented transparent indicator	$0.98
Board Game	*Sears, Roebuck* (1927)	*Special Auto Race;* no more exciting game; each kiddie has his own metal racer; two or four can play	$0.39
Cash Register	*John Martin* (1927)	Ask your dealer for Uncle Sam's registering and adding savings banks	$3
Construction Set	*John Martin* (1927)	*Lincoln Logs;* the all-American toy 53 Logs 234 Logs	 $1 $4

Item	Source	Description	Price
Construction Set	*Sears, Roebuck* (1927)	*Tinker Toy Wonder Builder;* will build operating models; an ideal wood construction toy for the younger child	$0.63
Crayons	*John Martin* (1926)	*Rubens Crayola;* 24 bright permanent colors	$0.30
Doll	*John Martin* (1926)	*Amberg Newborn Baskit Babe;* get the guaranteed Amberg Newborn Babe	$1
Doll	*Sears, Roebuck* (1927)	*The New Happy Baby;* smiling-faced, dimpled baby doll, sure to bring Sunshine and Happiness to your little daughter; 23", 4 1/2 lbs	$6.48
Doll	*John Martin* (1927)	*Chase Stockinet;* most prized and loved by the little folks	$3.50
Doll Carriage	*Lorick & Lowrance Hardware* (1928)	Machine-woven flat fibre body, weight 17 lbs	$3.50
Dollhouse Furniture	*John Martin* (1927)	Four-poster bedroom; 14 pieces	$14.25
Doll Embroidery Outfits	*John Martin* (1927)	These attractive outfits for "Dolly" will interest your child in sewing and embroidery	$1
Erector Set	*John Martin* (1926)	Super erector No. 7 builds 533 models	$10
Erector Set With Motor	*Sears, Roebuck* (1927)	235 parts, builds 500 models; a very popular size which will make anybody happy	$4.47
Horseshoes	*Sears, Roebuck* (1927)	*Pitch-Em;* indoor; if in doubt as to how to entertain your friends some evening, just bring out your horseshoe game	$0.89
Juvenile Chevrolet Automobile	*Lorick & Lowrance Hardware* (1928)	Adjustable peddles, 35" long, weight 36 pounds	$11.25
Kitchen Cabinet	*John Martin* (1927)	Just like mother's; 39" high	$11
Motor Driven Toy	*John Martin* (1926)	*Kingsbury;* motor truck 25" long; spring motor, wound crank-fashion from the front	$15
Pedal Car	*Sears, Roebuck* (1927)	Made from heavy-gauge automobile steel; every boy can now haul ice, groceries, wood, anything, and drive it himself	$14.98
Scooter	*Lorick & Lowrance Hardware* (1928)	*American;* steel footboard, 15" long, weight 46 lbs	$2.40
Sewing Machine	*John Martin* (1926)	A real sewing machine for your very own	$5
Stencils	*John Martin* (1927)	*Junior Art-Kraft;* draw and paint artistic pictures, decorate with stencils	$1.50
Toymaker	*John Martin* (1926)	Builds boys as well as toys; boys and girls are now making boats, aeroplanes, radio sets, and many other dandy toys	$2
Train Set	*Popular Science Monthly* (1927)	*Lionel Electric Trains;* real enough for a man to enjoy, simple enough for a boy to operate Sets	$5.75 to $300
Tricycle	*Sears, Roebuck* (1927)	*High Class Fall Tubular Kidobike;* tubular-steel-frame velocipede for youngsters 2 to 4	$3.89

Item	Source	Description	Price
Trucks	*The Youth's Companion* (1925)	*Structo Toys*—for any kid who likes to play with real working toys Giant steam shovel Dump truck Grab bucket Racing auto	 $2.50 $1.20 $1.35 $1.75
Wagon	*Sears, Roebuck* (1927)	*Faultless;* special play wagon for little tots; hardwood bottom, heavy sheet-metal sides	$1

TRAVEL & TRANSPORTATION

Item	Source	Description	Price
Cruise	*The Literary Digest* (1928)	Mediterranean luxury; 71 days of delightful diversion on the *Rotterdam*	$955
Cruise	*The Literary Digest* (1928)	New York to Havana; an entrancing trip of fascinating interest to a gay and scintillating foreign capital; 10 to 17 days	$85
Cruise	*The Literary Digest* (1928)	31 days of tropical contrast; New York to Trinidad	$300
Railroad Ticket	*The Farm Journal* (1927)	Low summer roundtrip fares from Chicago to California	$90.30
Steamship	*Delineator* (1928)	*Floating University;* The World Its Campus, 8 months, 26 countries, all expenses	$2,500 to $4,150
Tour	*The Literary Digest* (1928)	*Collegiate;* Europe; visit five countries, all expenses	$38

MISCELLANY 1925–1929

Random Prices

Cost of the modes nine-room rented house at 21 Massasoit Avenue, Northampton, Mass. rented by President Calvin Coolidge on election day, November, 1928: $32.50 a month.

Wages paid the Marx Brothers for filming a movie version of *The Cocoanuts* for Paramount: $100,000.
*The Year of the Great Crash, 1929, by William K. Klingaman
(New York: Harper and Row)*

What Price Doctors

Excluding the fees of attending physicians and surgeons, actual records selected at random show that a private case of myocardial insufficiency requiring a hospital stay of fifty-five days cost $1,166, approximately half of the expense being for private nursing care and most of the remainder for room and board. A case of appendicitis cost $450; of mastoiditis over $750; of sinus infection $360.
Harpers, 1927

Prices and Wages

In April, 1928, New Bedford, Mass. wages for mill workers manufacturing high quality cloth was cut from $19 to $17 a week.

During an undercover prohibition police raid on Helen Morgan's summer home, outside New York City, a policeman and his wife paid $15 per pint for brandy.
Time, August 13, 1928

Men and Women

In 1928 the Detroit Survey of advertising wages showed that although 50 percent of the men were then receiving salaries of over $5,000 a year, no woman was being paid more than $3,500.
*Advertising the American Dream, by Roland Marchand
(University of California Press)*

Coolidge Raises Pay

President Coolidge approved a schedule of pay increases between $60 and $400 per annum for some 5,400 employees of the Navy Department in offices outside Washington—employees overlooked by the Welch Act.
Time, August 13, 1928

Sears Says We Pay the Postage

Sears, Roebuck and Co. announces with the issuance of this catalog the greatest single step forward in Mail Order merchandising since the establishment of the Parcel Post.

Every article in this catalog which can be conveniently sent by parcel post will be shipped to you postage prepaid.
Sears and Roebuck Catalogue, Spring 1929

Beef Steer Prices

Beef steers attained a strong position at the highest price level of the year during last week. Buyers ran short and scrambled for finished weighty cattle after midweek. New highs were established, prime 1,570 lb beefs for fancy eastern trade at $13.50 being 25¢ above the previous top this year and highest for heavy cattle since the fall of 1925.
Chicago Tribune, March 17, 1927

One Cent A Day Brings $100 A Month

Kansas City, Mo.—Accident insurance at a cost of one cent a day is being featured in a policy issued by the National Protective Insurance Association. The benefits are $1,200 to $1,800 at death. The premium is only $3.65 a year or exactly one cent a day.
Chicago Tribune, March 17, 1927

Borah Turns Back $2,500 Increase in His Pay as Senator

Washington, D.C.—Senator Borah of Idaho has been turning back into the treasury $2,500 of his annual salary since Congress, two years ago, increased the pay of senators and representatives from $7,500 to $10,000. And he says he intends to do so until the completion of his present term in 1931.
Chicago Tribune, March 17, 1927

MISCELLANY 1925-1929

Cost of Medical Service

A study of the cost of medical service was made by the Bureau of Labor Statistics from information secured in the first week of April 1928, from its personnel of 117 persons, other than the commissioner, assistant commissioner, and agents in the field. One hundred and fourteen satisfactory schedules were secured.

The term cost of medical service as used in this study, covers all direct expenditures for health purposes, including the care of the teeth and eyes, medicines, hospital and nursing charges, surgical appliances, etc. as well as the services of physicians and surgeons.

The principal points developed from the study are as follows: the average annual expenditures per employee for medical services were $98.92 for the salary group earning less than $2,000 per year; $146.13 for the salary group $2,000 to

$3,000; and $190.63 for the salary group $3,000 and over. The average medical costs represented 6.2 percent of salary in the lower salary group; 6.3 percent in the middle group; and 5.5 percent in the upper group.

Handbook of Labor Statistics, 1929

HISTORICAL SNAPSHOT 1930–1934

1930

- Unemployment passes 4 million
- University of Pennsylvania professor creates beginnings of Gross National Product Index
- More than 1,352 banks close
- First analog computer is placed in operation by Vannevar Bush
- U.S. has one passenger car per 5.5 persons
- Gasoline consumption rises to nearly 16 billion gallons
- Radio set sales increase to 13.5 million
- Advertisers spend $60 million on radio commercials
- *Fortune Magazine* launched by Henry R. Luce; cost $1 per issue

1931

- Car sales collapse; 1,000,000 auto workers laid off
- Ford halts production of Model A
- 2,294 banks close
- Unemployment reaches 8 million
- Alka-Seltzer introduced by Miles Laboratories
- Chicago gangster Al Capone convicted of evading $231,000 in federal income taxes
- Clairol Hair products introduced by U.S. chemists
- New York's Waldorf-Astoria Hotel opens
- Safeway Stores reach their peak of 3,527 stores

- Birds Eye Frosted Foods sold nationally for first time

1932

- Average weekly wage falls to $17; breadlines form
- Wall Street's Dow Jones Industrials Average drops to 41.22
- AF of L urges that work be spread through a 30-hour week
- Patent application for a parking meter is made by *Oklahoma City News* editor Carl C. Magee
- Beech Aircraft Corporation founded at Wichita, KS
- *Family Circle* magazine begins publication
- Zippo lighter introduced
- Farm prices fall to 40 percent of 1929 levels
- Campbell's tomato juice introduced

1933

- City of Detroit defaults on $400 million debt
- Average earnings for a physician are $3,382; $8,663 for a congressman; $1,227 for a public school teacher
- U.S. abandons the gold standard
- National bank holiday proclaimed March 5
- Gasoline sells for 18¢ a gallon
- General Motors assumes leadership in motorcar sales, followed by Chrysler, then Ford

- IBM enters the typewriter business
- *Esquire* magazine is launched
- Agricultural Adjustment Act approved by Congress
- Ritz Crackers introduced by National Biscuit Company
- A&P stores control 11 percent of grocery stores sales

1934

- United Airlines is created when United Aircraft and Transportation Company, a holding company, is divided into three parts
- Price of gold stabilized by Department of Treasury at $35
- Greyhound cuts business fares in half to $8 between New York and Chicago
- Seagram's 7 Crown blended whiskey introduced
- Soybean acreage increases to 1 million
- Drought reduces corn crop by nearly 1 billion bushels
- Securities and Exchange Commission is created
- 4.7 million families are on relief
- Los Angeles Farmers Market opens; booths cost 50¢ a day
- Royal Crown Cola is introduced

Al Capone's 1931 mug shots. (via Wikimedia Commons)

SELECTED INCOME 1930–1934

Job	Source	Description	Pay
Accountant	*New York Times* (1932)	Certified, diversified experience; public, private position	$45/wk
Actor	*The Scribner Encyclopedia of American Lives*, 1987	Weekly salary of movie star Pat O'Brien, lead in *Flying High* in 1931	$1,750
Actor	Catherine Legrand and Robyn Karney, *Chronicle of the Cinema* (1995)	Weekly income of Johnny Weissmuller to play *Tarzan the Ape Man* in 1932	$250

Johnny Weissmuller in Tarzan the Ape Man, 1932. (via Wikimedia Commons)

Job	Source	Description	Pay
Baseball Player	*Sports Illustrated*	Annual salary of New York Yankees' Babe Ruth in 1930	$80,000
Basketball Player	Victor Bondi, ed., *American Decades: 1930–1939* (1995)	Monthly earnings of Babe Didrikson while touring with a mixed gender professional basketball team in 1934	$1,500
Cook	*Chicago Tribune* (1931)	White, expd. woman. No Sunday work	$15/wk
Cook	*San Francisco Examiner* (1932)	Housework, care for infant; good home	$15/mo
Domestic	*New York Herald Tribune* (1930)	Want white, Protestant girl, with good disposition for cooking and downstairs work in the country. Must be willing to share large corner bedroom and bath with other maid	$75/mo
Domestic	*San Francisco Examiner* (1932)	Spanish-American lady for light housework	$10/mo
Dressmaker	*New Orleans Times-Picayune* (1930)	German; coats, suits, dresses; at home or out	$5/wk
Driver	*New Orleans Times-Picayune* (1931)	Route of 60 families; reliable hustler can start earning and increase rapidly	$35/wk
Government Jobs	*The State* (Columbia, SC) (1930)	Government jobs; men, women; 18 and up; common education usually sufficient; sample coaching; full particulars free	$1,260–$3,400/yr
Miscellaneous	*Chicago Tribune* (1931)	Girls over 21; three permanent positions.	$22.50/wk to start
Miscellaneous	*Chicago Tribune* (1933)	A man, permanent position; old established company only energetic men with best references need apply.	$50/wk
Musicians	Mary A. Bufwack and Robert K. Oerman, *Finding Her Voice, The Saga of Women in Country Music* (1993)	Nightly payment for The Vagabonds' appearance on *The Grand Old Opry* in 1933	$75
Office Assistant	*New York Times* (1934)	Young man, quick and accurate at figures; state age, education, experience if any; references	$15/wk
Painter	*San Francisco Examiner* (1932)	Painting, exterior-interior; ceiling	$2.50/day
Refrigeration Salesman	*New York Times* (1932)	One of the world's largest manufacturers selling nationally known electric refrigerator; leads, promotion; only those willing to work with experienced manager	$30–$50/wk
Routemen	*New York Times* (1933)	With cars, established good routes	$40/wk
Sales	*New York Times* (1933)	Girls (2) inexperienced; attractive personality; cosmetics department, advancement	$15/wk
Sales	*The State* (Columbia, SC) (1930)	Permanent connection with weekly guarantee handling desirable fast-selling specialty; men earning $150 weekly	$40/wk
Sales	*New Orleans Times-Picayune* (1931)	Our business is radio selling and business is good	$30–$50/wk
Sales	*New Orleans Times-Picayune* (1934)	Nationally known concern selling products through wholesale grocery jobbers wants junior salesman. Must own Ford or Chevrolet coach that can be operated cheap.	$100 per month
U.S. President	*Sports Illustrated* (1996)	Annual salary of President Herbert Hoover in 1930	$75,000

CONSUMER EXPENDITURES 1930–1934

(Per Capita)

Expenditure Type	1930	1931	1932	1933	1934
Clothing	$54.39	$45.91	$32.01	$29.44	$36.37
Food	$145.31	$118.41	$91.24	$92.29	$90.13
Auto Usage	$38.15	$30.61	$24.01	$24.66	$29.15
New Auto Purchase	$12.99	$8.86	$4.80	$6.36	$7.91
Auto Parts	$4.06	$3.22	$2.40	$2.39	$2.37
Gas & Oil	$13.80	$12.08	$12.00	$11.93	$12.65
Housing	$90.92	$84.58	$73.63	$64.44	$61.67
Furniture	$7.30	$6.44	$4.00	$3.98	$3.95
Utilities	$25.16	$22.55	$20.81	$20.69	$21.35
Telephone & Telegraph	$4.87	$4.83	$4.00	$3.18	$3.16
Physicians	$7.30	$6.44	$5.60	$4.77	$5.53
Dentists	$4.06	$3.22	$2.40	$2.39	$2.37
Health Insurance	81¢	81¢	80¢	79¢	79¢
Personal Business	$28.41	$25.78	$21.61	$21.48	$21.35
Personal Care	$8.12	$8.05	$6.40	$5.57	$6.32
Tobacco	$12.18	$12.08	$10.40	$9.55	$11.07
Local Transport	$8.93	$7.25	$6.40	$5.57	$6.32
Intercity Transport	$3.25	$2.42	$2.40	$1.59	$2.37
Recreation	$32.41	$26.58	$19.21	$17.50	$18.97
Religion/Welfare Activities	$5.68	$5.64	$4.80	$3.98	$7.12
Private Education & Research	$5.68	$5.64	$4.80	$3.98	$3.95
Per Capita Consumption	$567.74	$487.73	$388.96	$364.39	$406.37

269

INVESTMENTS 1930–1934

Investment	1930	1931	1932	1933	1934
Basic Yield, One-Year Corporate Bonds	4.40	3.05	3.99	2.60	2.62
Short-Term Interest Rates, 4–6 Months, Prime Commercial Paper	3.59	2.64	2.73	1.73	1.02
Basic Yield, Common Stocks, Total	4.26	5.58	6.69	4.05	3.92
Index of Common Stocks (1941— 1943 5 10)	21.03	13.66	6.93	8.96	9.84

COMMON STOCKS, CLOSING PRICE AND YIELD, FIRST BUSINESS DAY OF YEAR

(PARENTHETICAL NUMBER IS ANNUAL DIVIDEND IN DOLLARS)

	1930	1931	1932	1933	1934
Allis Chalmers	49 1/2	34 7/8	11	6 3/8	17 1/4
(4 for 1 split, 9/20/29)	(3)	(3)	(1)	(/)	(/)
AT&T	220	181	112 1/4	103	108 1/2
	(5)	(9)	(9)	(9)	(9)
American Tobacco	201	106	67	55 3/8	67
(2 for 1 split, 9/4/30)	(8)	(5)	(5)	(5)	(5)
Anaconda	72 3/8	32	16 3/8	7 3/8	14 1/8
	(7)	(2 1/2)	(/)	(/)	(/)
B&O	116 3/4	71 7/8	14 7/8	8 7/8	23 3/8
	(7)	(4)	(/)	(/)	(/)
Bethlehem Steel	93 1/4	52 7/8	18 1/2	14 1/2	36 3/8
	(6)	(6)	(4 1/2)	(/)	(/)
Corn Products	89 3/4	80 1/2	38 7/8	53 1/2	75
	(3)	(3)	(3)	(3)	(3)
General Electric	242 1/4	45 3/8	23 1/4	14 7/8	19 1/2
(4 shares for 1 split, 1/24/30)	(1.60)	(1.60)	(1.60)	(.40)	(.40)
General Motors	40 1/2	37 3/8	20 3/4	13 1/8	35
(2 1/2 shares for 1 split, 1/7/29)	(3)	(3)	(3)	(1)	(1)
International Business Machines	164 1/4	152	100	89	142
(5% stock dividend, 1/10/30)	(6)	(6)	(6)	(6)	(6)
Intl Harvester	79	50 3/8	24	20 3/4	39 3/8
	(2)	(2 1/2)	(2 1/2)	(1.20)	(.60)
National Biscuit	177	79	38 3/4	38 3/8	46 1/8
(2 1/2 shares for 1 split, 11/15/22)	(6)	(2.80)	(2.80)	(2.80)	(2.80)
US Steel	167 1/4	142	37 1/8	27 1/8	47 3/4
	(7)	(7)	(4)	(/)	(/)
Western Union	194	134 1/2	33 5/8	26 1/2	53 3/4
	(8)	(8)	(6)	(/)	(/)

STANDARD JOBS 1930–1934

Job Type	1930	1931	1932	1933	1934
Average of all Industries, excl. farm labor	$1494/yr	$1406/yr	$1244/yr	$1136/yr	$1146/yr
Average of all Industries, inc. farm labor	$1388/yr	$1298/yr	$1141/yr	$1045/yr	$1066/yr
Bituminous Coal Mining	$909/yr	$723/yr	$748/yr	$900/yr	$1119/yr
Building Trades	$1233/yr	$907/yr	$869/yr	$942/yr	$1526/yr
Domestics	$676/yr	$584/yr	$497/yr	$460/yr	$473/yr
Farm Labor	$444/yr	$355/yr	$279/yr	$259/yr	$286/yr
Federal Civilian	$1768/yr	$1895/yr	$1824/yr	$1673/yr	$1717/yr
Federal Employees, Executive Depts.	$1492/yr	$1549/yr	$1504/yr	$1213/yr	$1178/yr
Federal Military	$1182/yr	$1164/yr	$1070/yr	$1070/yr	$1191/yr
Finance, Insurance, & Real Estate	$1973/yr	$1858/yr	$1652/yr	$1555/yr	$1601/yr
Gas & Electricity Workers	$1603/yr	$1600/yr	$1542/yr	$1453/yr	$1510/yr
Manufacturing, Durable Goods	$1391/yr	$1127/yr	$1087/yr	$1171/yr	$1556/yr
Manufacturing, Nondurable Goods	$1425/yr	$1352/yr	$1166/yr	$1086/yr	$1139/yr
Medical/Health Services Workers	$933/yr	$919/yr	$865/yr	$810/yr	$801/yr
Miscellaneous Manufacturing	$1466/yr	$1230/yr	$1166/yr	$1195/yr	$1535/yr
Motion Picture Services	$2179/yr	$2175/yr	$1950/yr	$1891/yr	$1844/yr
Nonprofit Org. Workers	$1698/yr	$1653/yr	$1545/yr	$1442/yr	$1440/yr
Passenger Transportation Workers, Local and Highway	$1587/yr	$1500/yr	$1328/yr	$1219/yr	$1310/yr
Personal Services	$1200/yr	$1136/yr	$996/yr	$889/yr	$905/yr
Public School Teachers	$1455/yr	$1463/yr	$1399/yr	$1300/yr	$1265/yr
Radio Broadcasting & Television Workers	$2624/yr	$2732/yr	$2740/yr	$2510/yr	$2198/yr
Railroads	$1717/yr	$1661/yr	$1461/yr	$1439/yr	$1505/yr
State and Local Govt. Workers	$1517/yr	$1497/yr	$1427/yr	$1333/yr	$1289/yr
Telephone & Telegraph Workers	$1410/yr	$1436/yr	$1335/yr	$1245/yr	$1338/yr
Wholesale and Retail Trade Workers	$1569/yr	$1495/yr	$1315/yr	$1183/yr	$1228/yr

FOOD BASKET 1930–1934

(NR=Not Reported)

Commodity	Year	New York	Atlanta	Chicago	Denver	Los Angeles
Beans, Navy, per pound	1930	13.60¢	13.10¢	11.90¢	10.30¢	11.70¢
	1931	10.10¢	8.60¢	7.90¢	7.30¢	7.80¢
	1932	5.70¢	6.10¢	5¢	5.10¢	5.60¢
	1933	5.80¢	6.30¢	4.90¢	5.50¢	5.80¢
	1934	7.50¢	7¢	6¢	6.40¢	6.70¢
Beef, Rib Roasts, per pound	1930	40.50¢	32.40¢	38.20¢	29.10¢	32.90¢
	1931	35.10¢	28.40¢	32.70¢	25.20¢	26.90¢
	1932	30.20¢	24.10¢	26.30¢	20.80¢	22.70¢
	1933	25.20¢	21.30¢	22.30¢	18¢	21.60¢
	1934	27.10¢	21.60¢	23.50¢	18¢	20.90¢
Beef, Steaks, (Round), per pound	1930	47.50¢	42.20¢	43.10¢	34.70¢	35.90¢
	1931	40.10¢	37.30¢	35.10¢	28.50¢	28.30¢
	1932	35.80¢	32.50¢	28.10¢	23.40¢	24.80¢
	1933	29.40¢	27.50¢	23.60¢	21.60¢	24.40¢
	1934	31.90¢	28.40¢	25.40¢	23.90¢	24.70¢
Bread, White, per loaf	1930	8.60¢	9.70¢	9.30¢	7.50¢	8.60¢
	1931	7.70¢	7.90¢	8.70¢	6.50¢	7.50¢
	1932	7.40¢	6.80¢	7.50¢	5.90¢	6.70¢
	1933	7.80¢	7.40¢	6.50¢	6.40¢	7.70¢
	1934	8.90¢	8.90¢	7.40¢	7.60¢	7.80¢
Butter, per pound	1930	46.10¢	50.30¢	44¢	41.50¢	44.90¢
	1931	35.90¢	40¢	34¢	33.20¢	36.10¢
	1932	28.30¢	30¢	26.90¢	25.60¢	28.40¢
	1933	28.90¢	28.70¢	27.50¢	26.20¢	27.30¢
	1934	32.50¢	31.40¢	31¢	30.60¢	31.50¢
Cheese, per pound	1930	38¢	31.50¢	39.60¢	36.70¢	35.30¢
	1931	32.20¢	24.80¢	31¢	28.70¢	28.10¢
	1932	28.60¢	21¢	26.10¢	24.50¢	24.50¢
	1933	26.90¢	20.50¢	25.50¢	24.40¢	23.80¢
	1934	27.40¢	21.10¢	26.50¢	24.20¢	23.60¢
Chickens, per pound	1930	37.30¢	34.20¢	31.50¢	29¢	41.10¢
	1931	32.50¢	28.90¢	32.70¢	26.10¢	35.10¢
	1932	26.50¢	21.80¢	26.10¢	18¢	28.80¢
	1933	22.60¢	18.20¢	21.70¢	18¢	26.30¢
	1934	27.60¢	23.10¢	25.80¢	19.70¢	27.90¢
Coffee, per pound	1930	36.50¢	39.50¢	40.20¢	43.40¢	44.20¢
	1931	31.10¢	34.50¢	33.80¢	40.30¢	37.80¢
	1932	28.70¢	29.10¢	31¢	32.50¢	33.20¢
	1933	25.90¢	25.30¢	27.50¢	32.50¢	30.20¢
	1934	26.90¢	26¢	27¢	31.20¢	30.90¢
Cornmeal, per pound	1930	6.50¢	4¢	6.80¢	4.60¢	5.60¢
	1931	5.90¢	3¢	5.60¢	4.20¢	4.80¢
	1932	5.30¢	2.10¢	5.30¢	4.10¢	4.10¢
	1933	5.10¢	2.30¢	4.90¢	3.80¢	3.50¢
	1934	5.80¢	2.80¢	5.40¢	4.50¢	4.40¢

Commodity	Year	New York	Atlanta	Chicago	Denver	Los Angeles
Eggs, per dozen	1930	51.60¢	39.50¢	41.40¢	35¢	38.80¢
	1931	41.70¢	30¢	33¢	26.60¢	32.80¢
	1932	36.90¢	24.70¢	27.60¢	24.10¢	28.10¢
	1933	35¢	23.60¢	26.40¢	25¢	28¢
	1934	38¢	28.20¢	30.30¢	29¢	30.10¢
Flour, Wheat, per pound	1930	4.40¢	5.50¢	4.10¢	3.60¢	4.40¢
	1931	3.50¢	4.10¢	3.30¢	2.70¢	3.30¢
	1932	3.40¢	3.60¢	2.80¢	2.40¢	2.90¢
	1933	4¢	4.40¢	3.70¢	3.20¢	3.60¢
	1934	5.30¢	4.40¢	4.70¢	4¢	4.50¢
Lard, per pound	1930	17.70¢	16.50¢	17.30¢	16.40¢	17.30¢
	1931	14.10¢	12.70¢	13¢	13.10¢	13.70¢
	1932	9.80¢	8.40¢	8.90¢	8.90¢	9.40¢
	1933	9.90¢	9.10¢	9.10¢	8.60¢	9.50¢
	1934	12.20¢	11.90¢	11.30¢	11.70¢	11.90¢
Milk, Fresh, per quart	1930	15.70¢	16.20¢	14¢	11.40¢	14.50¢
	1931	14.70¢	14.70¢	13¢	10.30¢	12.60¢
	1932	11.90¢	13.30¢	11.20¢	10.10¢	10.60¢
	1933	11.20¢	12.40¢	9.90¢	10¢	10.70¢
	1934	12.40¢	12.20¢	9.50¢	10.10¢	10.80¢
Mutton and Lamb, Leg, per pound	1930	33.90¢	36.50¢	34.90¢	32.10¢	32.30¢
	1931	28.90¢	29.80¢	30.40¢	27¢	25.30¢
	1932	23.20¢	22.70¢	24.20¢	20.80¢	21.30¢
	1933	21.40¢	21.60¢	21.80¢	19.60¢	21.40¢
	1934	25.20¢	23.10¢	24.80¢	22.40¢	24¢
Pork, Bacon, Sliced, per pound	1930	45¢	38.50¢	46.50¢	40.40¢	40.20¢
	1931	39.10¢	31.50¢	40.40¢	35.10¢	38.20¢
	1932	27.40¢	20.50¢	27.20¢	24.10¢	27.90¢
	1933	24.80¢	21.30¢	25¢	21.80¢	21.70¢
	1934	31.40¢	27.20¢	30.40¢	29¢	32.50¢
Pork Chops, per pound	1930	39¢	33.50¢	35.60¢	34.30¢	40.90¢
	1931	32.10¢	27.70¢	29.60¢	28¢	32.70¢
	1932	24.10¢	21.20¢	21.30¢	18.70¢	24.30¢
	1933	21.70¢	19.70¢	19.90¢	17.90¢	25.40¢
	1934	26.60¢	24.60¢	25.40¢	23.80¢	30.20¢
Pork, Ham, Sliced, per pound	1930	55.30¢	51.80¢	55.40¢	52.50¢	65¢
	1931	48.30¢	44.30¢	48.20¢	45¢	53.10¢
	1932	39.10¢	33.20¢	36.10¢	35.10¢	41.40¢
	1933	35.10¢	30.40¢	30.70¢	31.90¢	38.10¢
	1934	39¢	36.20¢	36.60¢	37.40¢	46.40
Potatoes, Irish, per pound	1930	3.80¢	4.40¢	3.70¢	3.40¢	3.65¢
	1931	2.60¢	3.10¢	2.40¢	2.20¢	2.30¢
	1932	2¢	2.30¢	1.80¢	1.80¢	1.90¢
	1933	2.60¢	2.70¢	2.30¢	2.20¢	2.20¢
	1934	2.70¢	2.70¢	2.50¢	2.30¢	2.20¢
Prunes, Dried, per pound	1930	14.90¢	16.90¢	17.10¢	17.30¢	14.80¢
	1931	10.70¢	11.80¢	12.70¢	13.30¢	10.40¢
	1932	8.40¢	9.70¢	10.60¢	10.80¢	8.70¢
	1933	8.80¢	9.40¢	10.90¢	10.90¢	8.60¢
	1934	10.90¢	11.50¢	12.90¢	12.80¢	10.40¢

Commodity	Year	New York	Atlanta	Chicago	Denver	Los Angeles
Rice, per pound	1930	9.10¢	8.50¢	10.10¢	8.90¢	9.20¢
	1931	8¢	7.60¢	8.20¢	7.70¢	7.70¢
	1932	6.50¢	6¢	7.10¢	6.40¢	6.60¢
	1933	6¢	5.70¢	6.50¢	6.20¢	6.10¢
	1934	5.80¢	7.70¢	8.10¢	8.40¢	8.10¢
Sugar, per pound	1930	5.50¢	6.50¢	6.20¢	6.70¢	5.80¢
	1931	5.20¢	6¢	5.70¢	6.20¢	5.40¢
	1932	4.80¢	5.20¢	5.20¢	5.70¢	4.90¢
	1933	5¢	5.60¢	5.40¢	6¢	5¢
	1934	5.30¢	5.80¢	5.70¢	6.10¢	5.10¢
Tea, per pound	1930	66.40¢	96.70¢	72.90¢	71.60¢	73.50¢
	1931	64¢	93.40¢	70.10¢	73.70¢	74.70¢
	1932	57.20¢	80.60¢	66.60¢	71.50¢	73.80¢
	1933	55.80¢	70.10¢	65.90¢	68¢	74¢
	1934	64.20¢	70.90¢	74.30¢	72.60¢	79.50¢

SELECTED PRICES 1930–1934

Item	Source	Description	Price
ADVERTISING			
Advertisement	Roland Marchand, *Advertising The American Dream* (1985)	*Ladies' Home Journal* [cost in 1933]	$12,500/full pg
Advertisement	Marchand, *Advertising The American Dream* (1985)	Weekly advertising cost for *Comic Weekly* and other nationally syndicated Sunday comic supplements [cost in 1933]	$16,000–$17,000/pg
APPAREL, CHILDREN'S			
Baby Skirt	*Montgomery Ward & Co.* (1932)	*Amoskeag Gertrude;* flannelette; skirt long, infant's size only	$0.21
Frock	*Montgomery Ward & Co.* (1932)	*Sunnymorn;* bolero effect youthfully styled	$0.77
Galoshes	*Montgomery Ward & Co.* (1932)	All rubber; three snap fasteners; light-colored lining; reduced from $1.19	$0.98
Gym Suit	*Sears, Roebuck* (1932)	Girl's one-piece; we formerly got $1.89 for this type garment	$1
Knickers	*Montgomery Ward & Co.* (1932)	Boy's; made in golf style, fully lined, and strongly sewn throughout	$0.77
Overalls	*Pee Dee Advocate* Bennettsville, SC (1934)	All sizes at Belk's Department Store	$0.30
Rubber Pants	*Montgomery Ward & Co.* (1932)	Gum; washable; ruffled side ventilation	$0.22/3 pr
Shoes	*Montgomery Ward & Co.* (1932)	Little girl's; patent or calf-grain; extra-good quality; long wearing leather soles	$1.39
Shoes	*Sears, Roebuck* (1932)	*Airway Lightfoot;* fastest shoe on the playground	$0.75
Slip	*Montgomery Ward & Co.* (1932)	*Rayon;* ages 4 to 14 years; ruffled flounce slip with built-up shoulder	$0.39
Sweater	*Sears, Roebuck* (1932)	Girl's; worsted-wool shaker; good quality	$2.19
Vest	*Montgomery Ward & Co.* (1932)	10 percent wool; rayon; striped; pin-back style	$0.35
APPAREL, MEN'S			
Boots	*Montgomery Ward & Co.* (1932)	*Wonderwear* combination rubber soles; double tanned	$1.59
Boots	*Montgomery Ward & Co.* (1932)	All black rubber; absolutely waterproof; great for farm wear	$1.77

Item	Source	Description	Price
Coats	*Curry Brothers Oil Company Catalogue* (1931)	*Fish Brand;* reflex waterproof coats; 44" long	$56/dz
Gloves	*Montgomery Ward & Co.* (1932)	Standard-wear work gloves; the harder the work the better you will like them	$0.79
Handkerchief	*Sears, Roebuck* (1932)	Cotton bandana; neat designs	$0.58/dz
Hat	*Collier's* (1934)	*Dunlap;* America's smartest hats	$5
Hose Supporter	*Sears, Roebuck* (1932)	*Buster Brown;* with non-elastic top	$0.24
Overalls	*Montgomery Ward & Co.* (1932)	Mill shrunk, pure Indigo dyed	$0.85
Shirt	*Montgomery Ward & Co.* (1932)	*Yukon Permana;* Shrunk suede cloth; whatever size you buy stays that size because it's fully guaranteed full shrunk, coat style, with two large button-through pockets	$1
Shirts	*Pee Dee Advocate* Bennettsville, SC (1934)	Heavy covert shirts	$0.65
Shoes	*Montgomery Ward & Co.* (1932)	Plain-toe Oxford tie shoe; black calf-grain leather	$2.48
Shoes	*Sears, Roebuck* (1932)	*Green Grip;* nowhere do we know of stronger, more rugged leather or finer workmanship	$3.98
Suit	*Sears, Roebuck* (1932)	Tailored wool; $1" to $3" lower than for equal quality offered elsewhere	$16.50
Suit	*Montgomery Ward & Co.* (1932)	*Stillson Yale Model;* features all-wool worsted cheviots in a two-button notch lapel coat	$10.88
Sweater	*Montgomery Ward & Co.* (1932)	Men's; all-wool worsted; fits snugly and keeps its shape	$1.88
Trousers	*Montgomery Ward & Co.* (1932)	*Cheviot;* All-wool dress; a new high-rise trouser that will stick with style leaders	$2.89

APPAREL, WOMEN'S

Item	Source	Description	Price
Bag	*Montgomery Ward & Co.* (1932)	Woman's; a new smart steerhide bag of the quality that has been sold everywhere at $2.95	$1.77
Bloomers	*Sears, Roebuck* (1932)	Nainsook; famous for long hard wear	$0.23
Bloomers	*Montgomery Ward & Co.* (1932)	Run-resistant rayon; stout size; flesh, peach; reinforced crotch	$0.55
Coat	*Sears, Roebuck* (1932)	Wool, fur-lined; full length	$13.74
Corselet	*Montgomery Ward & Co.* (1932)	Fine brocade belted; rayon and cotton tricot Jersey top, knitted elastic panels	$1.88
Corset	*San Francisco Examiner* (1932)	Some innerbelt models for heavier women	$1.00
Dress	*Sears, Roebuck* (1932)	Silk; flat crepe; the savings will thrill you	$2.98
Frock	*Montgomery Ward & Co.* (1932)	*Fruit of the Loom;* youthful cotton print; flattering neck line set off with piping and two-tone bow	$1
Girdle	*Montgomery Ward & Co.* (1932)	*Durolastic;* for average height figures; 12" length	$1.74
Gloves	*San Francisco Examiner* (1932)	4-button and fancy kidskins	$1.45
Gloves	*Sears, Roebuck* (1932)	Imported glacé lambskin; usually called kid gloves	$1.95

Item	Source	Description	Price
Handbag	*Sears, Roebuck* (1932)	Back-strap style; calf leather; inverted frame pouch	$1.79
Hat	*Sears, Roebuck* (1932)	Peanut straw body; with the new lifted left-side brim line	$0.95
Hosiery	*Montgomery Ward & Co.* (1932)	*Golden Crest;* pure silk top to toe; medium service weight	$0.89
Mesh Bag	*Sears, Roebuck* (1932)	Lined dresden; predomination colors: green and white; size 4" × 5 3/4"	$2.95
Shoes	*Pee Dee Advocate* Bennettsville, SC (1934)	Suede shoes, regular $2.95—on sale	$1.95
Shoes	*Montgomery Ward & Co.* (1932)	Anita style, smooth calf-grain tip and back	$2.67
Shoes	*Sears, Roebuck* (1932)	*Goodyear Welt;* low heels with rubber top lifts patent leather	$2.48
Slip	*Montgomery Ward & Co.* (1932)	All-silk crepe de chine; nobody ever dreamed of a slip like this; others ask $1.79	$1
Sweater	*Montgomery Ward & Co.* (1932)	All-wool elastic rib knit; a sweater like this is not only practical, but economical	$2.25

APPLIANCES

Item	Source	Description	Price
Batteries	*Pee Dee Advocate* Bennettsville, SC (1934)	Radio batteries recharged Auto batteries recharged	$0.45 $0.75
Cook Stove	*Montgomery Ward & Co.* (1932)	*Juniper Windsor;* heavy all-cast-iron cook stove	$21.50
Electric Heater	*Montgomery Ward & Co.* (1932)	Guaranteed element; in copper bowl, green enamel frame	$1
Electric Washer	*Montgomery Ward & Co.* (1932)	Big value combination! Electric ironer with deluxe porcelain or copper tub	$79.85
Iron	*Montgomery Ward & Co.* (1932)	Electric; don't bother to repair your old iron now—it actually costs less to buy a better one	$1
Iron	*Montgomery Ward & Co.* (1932)	Gasoline; costs 1/2¢ an hour to operate; burns 3 1/2 hours with one filling	$3.98
Mixer	*Dallas Hospitality Magazine* (1932)	*Sunbeam Mix-Master;* mix batters, mash potatoes, beat eggs, extract juice from oranges, etc., make mayonnaise, malted milk	$21
Range	*Montgomery Ward & Co.* (1932)	*Windsor Seminole;* kerosene; 5–burner	$28.95
Toaster	*Montgomery Ward & Co.* (1932)	Electric; it automatically turns the toast when doors are lowered	$1
Vacuum Cleaner	*Montgomery Ward & Co.* (1932)	*Majestic;* beating, sweeping, suction; motor- driven brush	$28.95
Vacuum Cleaner	*Dallas Hospitality Magazine* (1932)	*Premier Duplex;* easy one-hand operation and great ability to pick up threads, etc.	$49.50

Item	Source	Description	Price
Waffle Iron	*Dallas Hospitality Magazine* (1932)	*Westinghouse Crisp-Grid;* it bakes waffles for a houseful of guests at a cost of a couple of cents	$7.95
Washing Machine	*Montgomery Ward & Co.* (1932)	*Wardway DeLuxe Gyrator;* greatest washer value in America; twice winner of the whiteness tests	$57.95

BABY PRODUCTS

Item	Source	Description	Price
Baby Powder	*Montgomery Ward & Co.* (1932)	*Johnson & Johnson;* two $0.25 cans; a real savings	$0.29
Blanket	*Sears, Roebuck* (1932)	*Pepperell;* a woven cotton-twill fabric with a soft downy-fleeced finish	$0.31
Dusting Powder	*Sears, Roebuck* (1932)	*My Baby's;* a cooling, soothing, healing powder	$0.39
Nipple	*Sears, Roebuck* (1932)	*Faultless Wonder;* pure-gum nipple	$0.34
Walker	*Sears, Roebuck* (1932)	Ball bearing walker; non-tipping, with adjustable seat straps	$2.29

BUSINESS EQUIPMENT & SUPPLIES

Item	Source	Description	Price
Typewriter	*Sears, Roebuck* (1932)	*L. C. Smith;* the world's only ball-bearing typewriter	$45
Typewriter	*Montgomery Ward & Co.* (1932)	*Underwood;* portable; four full key rows, 84 characters; paper space up to 9 1/2" wide	$49.50
Typewriter	*Popular Mechanics* (1933)	*International Typewriter Exchange Underwood No. 5;* includes standard 4–row keyboard, backspacer, automatic ribbon reverse, shift-lock key, 2–color ribbon	$39.90
Typewriter	*Popular Mechanics* (1933)	*Underwood;* positively the greatest bargain ever offered; Regular $100 model	$39
Typewriter Ribbons	*Pee Dee Advocate* Bennettsville, SC (1934)	The best silk ribbons	$0.75

ENTERTAINMENT

Item	Source	Description	Price
Concert Ticket	*The Raleigh (NC) Times* (1931)	Ken Hackley's Oklahoma Cowboys Famous Radio Artists, 4 shows daily Matinee Night	 $0.10 to $0.30 $0.10 to $0.40
Movie Ticket	*Pee Dee Advocate* Bennettsville, SC (1934)	*Footlight Parade* starring James Cagney and Ruby Keeler Adults Children Balcony for Colored	 $0.25 $0.10 $0.10

A Kodak Six-20 camera. (via Wikimedia Commons)

Item	Source	Description	Price
ENTERTAINMENT, HOME			
Camera	*Collier's* (1934)	*Kodak Six–20;* with F 6.3 lens, pictures 2 1/2" ×4 1/2"	$20
Cards	*New York Times Magazine* (1931)	*Currier & Ives;* there are 18 subjects, and each subject comes in two sizes 3" × 4" 5" × 6"	 $0.10 $0.15
Microphone	*Popular Mechanics* (1933)	*Master Mike;* with mike ring; reproduces your own voice through your radio; a million dollars worth of fun	$1

Item	Source	Description	Price
Model Airplane	*Popular Mechanics* (1933)	Cleveland Model and Supply Co. Inc. Boeing 247; hailed as a masterpiece in model flying aircraft; nearly 5' span, weight 16 oz	$6.50
Moving Picture Camera and Projector	*Popular Mechanics* (1933)	Get professional moving pictures; uses 50' roll of 16mm film	$13.75
Phonograph Records	*Montgomery Ward & Co.* (1932)	*Paramount Hill Country Melodies;* full 10" size; double-face song *When the Moon Comes Over the Mountain;* lot of five	$0.29
Radio	*Montgomery Ward & Co.* (1932)	*Airline 7–tube Super Heterodyne;* thrilling new power and almost unbelievable realism of tone	$39.85
Radio	*Popular Mechanics* (1933)	*Midwest Radio Corp. Super Deluxe;* 16–tube all wave; world's greatest radio value with new deluxe auditorium-type speaker	$49.50
Radio	*Collier's* (1934)	*Philco 16x All Wave;* no longer is the Atlantic or the Pacific a barrier to your search for radio entertainment	$175
Radio	*Collier's* (1934)	*Philco 8413;* a wonderful little radio in an attractive two-tone cabinet	$20
Radio	*Rock Hill Herald* (Rock Hill, SC) (1933)	*Philco;* make your home the center of the world	$18.75–$295
Shortwave Receiver	*Popular Mechanics* (1933)	*Powertown-Wallace Try-Mo Radio;* price with blue-prints and 1 coil	$14.70
Victrola	*The Raleigh (NC) Times* (1931)	Used portable Victrola with records Contact Raleigh Loan Office	$3.90

FARMING EQUIPMENT & SUPPLIES

Item	Source	Description	Price
Barbed Wire	*Montgomery Ward & Co.* (1932)	Galvanized; 80–rod spool, 53 lbs	$1.43
Barbed Wire	*Sears, Roebuck* (1932)	4–point galvanized cattle wire	$2.28
Cod Liver Oil	*Montgomery Ward & Co.* (1932)	For healthier poultry and livestock	$1.79/gal
Frogs	*Popular Mechanics* (1933)	Breeders lay 10,000 eggs; unlimited market; book, Fortune in Frogs	$1–$3/dz
Hog Troughs	*Montgomery Ward & Co.* (1932)	20–gauge steel, welded and soldered; lots of six	$0.48
Home Hatcher	*Montgomery Ward & Co.* (1932)	*Ward's;* continuous electric entirely eliminates the variation of temperature in the egg chamber	$39.95
Mules and Horses	*Rock Hill Herald* (Rock Hill, SC) (1933)	*W. L. Abernathy* Fort Lawn, South Carolina; the kind to make a cheap crop	$35/$63/$75

FOOD PRODUCTS

Item	Source	Description	Price
Apples	*New York Times Magazine* (1931)	*Jonathan* apples	$3.25/bx
Candy Bar	*Sears, Roebuck* (1932)	*Hershey's Almond;* 25 $0.05 almond bars	$1
Figs	*San Francisco Examiner* (1932)	California Syrup Figs	$0.35

Item	Source	Description	Price
Fruit	*Rock Hill Herald* (Rock Hill, SC) (1933)	*Gator Fruit Store,* Rock Hill, South Carolina; oranges grapefruit bananas	$0.30–$0.40/peck $0.05/2 $0.19/4 lbs
Ice Cream	*The Raleigh (NC) Times* (1931)	Get your favorite flavor at these special prices from White Dairy Products Company One Pint White's Ice Cream Two Pints White's Ice Cream	 $0.25 $0.35
Marshmallows	*Sears, Roebuck* (1932)	*Kraft;* fresh, soft, fluffy vanilla-flavored marshmallows; box of 200	$0.65/bx
Marshmallows	*Montgomery Ward & Co.* (1932)	Creamy; wholesome and nutritious; box of 200	$0.46/bx
Salt Mackerel Fillets	*Collier's* (1934)	18 extra-large mackerel fillets by mail	$3
Vanilla Extract	*Sears, Roebuck* (1932)	*Montclair;* equal of any nationally advertised brand	$0.42

FURNITURE

Item	Source	Description	Price
Bathroom	*Montgomery Ward & Co.* (1932)	*Deerfield;* 3–piece outfit includes bathtub, closet and outfit, Combination and lavatory	$61.45
Bed	*Montgomery Ward & Co.* (1932)	All steel; continuous seamless 2' main posts; includes bed, coil spring, and mattress	$14.35
Bathroom Suite	*Montgomery Ward & Co.* (1932)	3–piece; panel bed, chest, and 36" dresser	$32.75
Cedar Chest	*Montgomery Ward & Co.* (1932)	Solid 3/40, genuine Tennessee red cedar, 40"× 17"× 18 3/4" walnut finish	$12.95
Chair	*Montgomery Ward & Co.* (1932)	Solid oak; positively the first time at this price	$1
Chair	*Montgomery Ward & Co.* (1932)	Nursery; enameled; comfy seat opening, swing over tray	$1
Chair	*Montgomery Ward & Co.* (1932)	Bow-back style; golden oak; made of select hardwood; well-braced, heavy seat	$1
Chifforobe	*Sears, Roebuck* (1932)	Of good-quality seasoned hardwood	$18.95
Clock	*Montgomery Ward & Co.* (1932)	*Gilbert;* mahogany-finished case with burled panels; strikes hours and half hours on cathedral gong	$5.95
Davenport	*Montgomery Ward & Co.* (1932)	*Jacquard;* velour two-tone; serpentine front; never-sag steel under construction	$19.95
Mattress	*Montgomery Ward & Co.* (1932)	Full 50-pound all felted cotton mattress; 54"	$4.65
Radio Bench	*Montgomery Ward & Co.* (1932)	Rich tapestry upholstering	$1
Rug	*Montgomery Ward & Co.* (1932)	Seamless velvet; floral designs on a tan taupe ground; blue border; 9' by 12'	$14.95
Stool	*Sears, Roebuck* (1932)	All metal; eight cross braces; green	$0.97

FUEL

Item	Source	Description	Price
Coal	*Pee Dee Advocate* Bennettsville, SC (1934)	Free burning, grate and stove coal Per ton Per half ton	 $7.50 $4.00

Item	Source	Description	Price
GARDEN EQUIPMENT & SUPPLIES			
Evergreen Shrubbery	*Rock Hill Herald* (Rock Hill, SC) (1933)	*Belk Department Store;* a great variety of large healthy evergreens—broad leaf and conifers	$0.50–$1
Flowers	*New York Times Magazine* (1931)	*Fargo;* 20 double early tulips	$1.10
Lawn Mower	*Montgomery Ward & Co.* (1932)	*Lakeside;* five years ago this same quality mower sold for twice as much; self-adjusting, ball-bearing, quiet and easy running; 9" wheels; 14" blade	$5.49
Plants	*The Raleigh (NC) Times* (1931)	Live ferns from Job P. Wyatt and Sons Company	$0.10 each
Shovels	*Curry Brothers Oil Company Catalogue* (1931)	*Ames 3–Star;* contractor's or digging blade; 9 1/2" × 12 1/4"; handle length 26 1/2"	$25/dz
HOUSEHOLD PRODUCTS			
Blanket	*Montgomery Ward & Co.* (1932)	Fleecy down staple cotton; plain; extra large size; 72"× 84"	$1.25
Blankets	*Sears, Roebuck* (1932)	*Falcon;* all virgin wool	$7.35/pr
Blankets	*Montgomery Ward & Co.* (1932)	All wool; double; extra heavy 6 1/2 lbs; size 70" × 80"	$4.48/pr
Borax	*Sears, Roebuck* (1932)	*Mule Team;* a wonderful and natural water softener for laundry work	$0.27/2 bxs
Bottle Opener and Resealer	*New York Times Magazine* (1931)	*Spear-Cap;* opens and reseals your milk bottle; made of frosted aluminum with nickel-silver spear	$0.10
Brace and Bit Set	*Sears, Roebuck* (1932)	*Fulton;* Brace, 7 auger bits, and screwdriver set	$2.80
Cookery Parchment	*New York Times Magazine* (1931)	*Patapar;* banishes cooking odors, improves flavors, saves food values	$0.10
Dinner Plates	Butler Brothers *Sales Flier* (1934)	*Butler Brother;* imported; plain white semi-porcelain	$0.84/dz
Fire Pails	*Curry Brothers Oil Company Catalogue* (1931)	Round bottom; made of steel, galvanized outside and inside and painted red outside; 10 1/2" × 10 1/2"	$8.55/dz
Flatware	*Sears, Roebuck* (1932)	*Rogers Bros.;* silver plate; 26–piece set	$28.45
Flatware	*Montgomery Ward & Co.* (1932)	*Rogers;* nickel–silver; made to withstand the constant handling of everyday service	$2.79
Grinder	*Popular Mechanics* (1933)	*Chicago Wheel & Mfg. Co. Handee;* just plug in and start grinding—electronically	$10
Hammer	*Curry Brothers Oil Company Catalogue* (1931)	*Stanley Atha Plain Face Adze Eye;* 13 1/2" length overall	$1.50/ea
Hammer	*Montgomery Ward & Co.* (1932)	Ball-peen; size 2/0—12 oz drop forged tempered head	$0.19
Ice Box	*San Francisco Examiner* (1932)	Ideal for the average family	$18.75
Lathe	*Popular Mechanics* (1933)	*South Bend;* back-geared, screw cutting precision lathes, 11" × 4'	$340

Item	Source	Description	Price
Leather Treatment	*Curry Brothers Oil Company Catalogue* (1931)	*Viscol Dressing;* softens and preserves shoes, harnesses, belts, and everything else made of leather; 1/4 pint cans	$2.23/dz
Light Bulbs	*Montgomery Ward & Co.* (1932)	40–watt bulb, package of eight	$1/pkg
Motor Grinder	*Popular Mechanics* (1933)	Powerful; operates on AC or DC, sturdy, durable, and Buffer quality built	$4.95
Oil	*Curry Brothers Oil Company Catalogue* (1931)	*3-In-One;* a blend of animal, mineral and vegetable oils, scientifically compounded 3 oz can 8 oz bottle	 $0.30 $0.60
Oriental Rug	*San Francisco Examiner* (1932)	Approximate size 9' × 12'; the designs are exact copies of priceless Persian pieces	$119.00
Percolator	*Montgomery Ward & Co.* (1932)	9–cup; with guaranteed element and cord set; others ask $1.50	$1
Photography Light Bulb	*Collier's* (1934)	*General Electric Mazda;* photoflood; makes pictures easy to snap indoors	$0.35/ea
Pins	*Sears, Roebuck* (1932)	*Stewart's;* duplex safety pins; box of 6 dozen	$0.39/box
Rule	*Montgomery Ward & Co.* (1932)	*Lakeside;* flexible; length 6', graduated in 16ths; Swedish steel, tempered	$1.59
Salad Bowls	*Butler Brothers Sales Flier* (1934)	*Butler Brothers;* imported; embossed edge; 9 1/2" wide	$1.28/dz
Saw	*Montgomery Ward & Co.* (1932)	*Lakeside Champion Tooth;* one-man and supplementary handles; 3 1/2' length	$1.48
Screwdriver	*Curry Brothers Oil Company Catalogue* (1931)	*Tobrin;* machinists; 9 1/2" overall	$10/dz
Screwdriver	*Montgomery Ward & Co.* (1932)	Spiral Ratchet; works right or left, spiral or ratchet; two size bits	$1
Sheets	*Montgomery Ward & Co.* (1932)	*Longwear;* bleached; size before hemming 81" ×90"	$0.65/ea
Towels	*Montgomery Ward & Co.* (1932)	*Cannon;* fast-color borders	$1/12
Towels	*Montgomery Ward & Co.* (1932)	*Cannon;* only a few weeks ago, the identical quality sold for $0.85/6	$0.65/6
Towels	*Sears, Roebuck* (1932)	Cotton husk; beautiful border on an equally beautiful towel	$0.90/6
Varnish	*Montgomery Ward & Co.* (1932)	*Diamond W; color;* stains and varnishes in one brush stroke	$0.42/qt
Wood Filler	*Popular Mechanics* (1933)	*Plastic Wood;* this canned wood makes home repairs easy	$0.25/tube
Wrenches	*Curry Brothers Oil Company Catalogue* (1931)	*Starrett;* ratchet; for engineers, machinists, and motor mechanics; complete set	$15

Item	Source	Description	Price
JEWELRY			
Pocket Watch	*Illinois Watch Catalogue* (1930)	Man's 23–jewel railroad watch; 60 hour, 6 position, motor barrel 14K filled 14K solid	 $90 $150
Pocket Watch	*Montgomery Ward & Co.* (1934)	*Hamilton Railroad;* the watch of railroad accuracy; 14K white-gold filled	$65
Pocket Watch	*Montgomery Ward & Co.* (1934)	*Ingersoll Buck Rogers;* Buck Rogers and Wilma are shown in action; the hands are shaped like cosmic rays	$0.75
Pocket Watch	*Montgomery Ward & Co.* (1934)	*Ingersoll Mickey Mouse;* "I keep time for 1 1/2 million happy children"; in a gift box	$1.50
Watch	*Delineator* (1928)	*Elgin,* the Madame Jenny; chic and styleful	$35.00
Wristwatch	*Saturday Evening Post* (1930)	*Lady Elgin;* the lowest price ever offered on such an Elgin watch	$25
Wristwatch	*Montgomery Ward & Co.* (1932)	Man's reliable 6–jewel Swiss movement	$5.98
Wristwatch	*Sears, Roebuck* (1932)	*Elgin;* Man's 15–Jewel; 14–karat solid white gold case	$33.25
Wristwatch	*Montgomery Ward & Co.* (1934)	*Ingersoll Mickey Mouse;* the demand is so heavy thatthere is often a scarcity	$2.95
MEALS			
Dinner	*The Raleigh (NC) Times* (1931)	Special Sunday Luncheon and Dinner at California Fruit Store Luncheon Dinner	 $0.50 $0.75
Meal	*Rock Hill Herald* (Rock Hill, SC) (1932)	*Southern Hotel and Dining Room;* the best meal 35 cents can buy	$0.35
Sunday Dinner	*The Raleigh (NC) Times* (1931)	*Wilson's Coffee Shop* open Sundays, specialty juicy western steaks and chops	$0.45
MEDICAL PRODUCTS & SERVICES			
Camphor	*San Francisco Examiner* (1932)	Spirits of Camphor; 2 oz	$0.13
Laxative	*Montgomery Ward & Co.* (1932)	*Milk of Magnesia;* mild laxative, antacid, and mouthwash	$0.46/2 btls
Mineral Oil	*Montgomery Ward & Co.* (1932)	Russian; colorless, odorless, pleasant to take	$0.83/qt
Soda	*San Francisco Examiner* (1932)	Fleet's Phospho-soda	$0.39
Thermometer	*Montgomery Ward & Co.* (1932)	Fever thermometer; tested according to U.S. Bureau of Standards; one-minute style	$0.79
MOTORIZED VEHICLES, SERVICES, & SUPPLIES			
Automobile	*Collier's* (1934)	*Reo Motor Car Co.;* why shackle yourself to a gearshift lever; the Reo self-shifter does it automatically	$795

Item	Source	Description	Price
Automobiles	*The Raleigh (NC) Times* (1931)	Low-priced specials: Used 1929 Olds Sedan Used 1927 Dodge, 4–door	$275 $150
Automobile Cover	*Sears, Roebuck* (1932)	*Society Brand;* slip-on; no fasteners required	$1.45
Car Cleaner	*Sears, Roebuck* (1932)	*Simoniz Kleener;* it makes old cars look new; 12 oz can	$0.44/can
Highway Flare Torches	*Curry Brothers Oil Company Catalogue* (1931)	Made of steel; will burn kerosene or light fuel oil	$24/dz
Jack	*Montgomery Ward & Co.* (1932)	Super-lift hydraulic; capacity 3,080 lbs; lifting range 7 1/2" to 15"	$3.29
Liquid Solder	*Collier's* (1934)	*Warner;* pour a can into the radiator; it finds all leaks and repairs them permanently	$0.50/can
Motor Oil	*Sears, Roebuck* (1932)	*Corona;* for all passenger cars and light trucks	$0.49/gal
Radio	*Collier's* (1934)	*Philco Auto;* featuring a full-size dynamic speaker, four-point tone control, more powerful	$55
Spark Plug	*Sears, Roebuck* (1932)	*Champion;* for Ford Model T	$0.55
Spark Plug	*Popular Mechanics* (1933)	*A. C Spark Plug Co.;* always the quality spark plug offered at the lowest price in Canada	$0.60
Tire	*Sears, Roebuck* (1932)	*AllState;* 6-ply balloon; 31" × 6.50"–19 fits Buick, 1930, 1931; Graham Paige 1928, 1929, 1930	$1.54
Tire and Tube	*Popular Mechanics* (1933)	*Goodyear Firestone Goodrich;* balloon tire; 30" × 5.25"–20 size and rim Tire Tube	 $2.95 $1.15
Tire	*Montgomery Ward & Co.* (1932)	*Chevrolet;* 29 3 4.40-21; 4–ply balloons; order in pairs	$4.65/ea
Tire	*Montgomery Ward & Co.* (1932)	*Studebaker;* 31 3 6.50-19; 6–ply balloons; order in pairs	$11.92/ea
Wax	*Popular Mechanics* (1933)	*Johnson's Wax;* try this amazing new method on your car; enough for 4 or 5 waxings; adds $50–$200 to trade-in values	$0.35/can

MUSICAL INSTRUMENTS

Item	Source	Description	Price
Trombone	*The Raleigh (NC) Times* (1931)	Used sliding trombone, perfect Contact Raleigh Loan Office	$12.50

OTHER

Item	Source	Description	Price
Cooking Fuel	*Montgomery Ward & Co.* (1932)	Sterno Canned Heat; a clean dependable fuel that meets every light cooking need; normally $0.10 per can	$0.29/4 cans
Engine	*Popular Mechanics* (1933)	Briggs-Stratton; 1/2 horsepower, new	$27.50
Memory Course	*Popular Mechanics* (1933)	Bott 15-Minute; how to remember names, faces, numbers, etc.	$1
Microscope Outfit	*Popular Mechanics* (1933)	J. W. Winn Manufacturing Co. Winnerset; complete set contains 100x Wallensak precision-built microscope, dissecting scissors, blade and needle, professional slides, bottle of balsam, specimen jar, tweezers, pipette, book of lens paper, glass rod	$6
Motor	*Popular Mechanics* (1933)	Dumore-Racine Universal; with pulley, cord, and plug; operates on AC or DC, 110 volts	$1.95

Item	Source	Description	Price
Radio Tube	*Montgomery Ward & Co.* (1932)	Trail Blazer; four-prong tube for AC sets; replaces any tube with number ending in 25	$0.42/ea
Signs	*Curry Brothers Oil Company Catalogue* (1931)	Line-O-Graph; highway traffic and safety zone marks; operated by one man; eliminates hand painting	$150
Storage Battery	*Montgomery Ward & Co.* (1932)	Riverside; sturdy, leak-proof composition case with bail handle	$5.19
Valentines	*Montgomery Ward & Co.* (1932)	Cunning and colorful hearts with just the right verse; 16 cards	$0.25

PERSONAL CARE PRODUCTS

Item	Source	Description	Price
Cold Cream	*Montgomery Ward & Co.* (1932)	Tre-Jur; cleans the pores and leaves the skin smooth and glowing; 1 lb jar	$0.49
Comb	*Sears, Roebuck* (1932)	Lightweight dressing; especially suitable for ladies with medium length hair	$0.33
Hair Clipper	*Sears, Roebuck* (1932)	Brown and Sharpe; the choice of professional barbers	$3.87
Hair Color Treatment	*Montgomery Ward & Co.* (1932)	Mary T Goldman; slate color	$1.29/btl
Hair Cut	*Rock Hill Herald* (Rock Hill, SC) (1933)	Sanitary Barber Shop, Rock Hill, South Carolina; why not have the best at this reduced price	$0.20
Hair Lotion	*Montgomery Ward & Co.* (1932)	*Bay Rum;* buy one bottle at Ward's usual low price, $0.36, and get another free	$0.36/2 btls
Hair Tonic	*Montgomery Ward & Co.* (1932)	*Lucky Tiger;* with a free comb	$0.79
Hand Cream	*Montgomery Ward & Co.* (1932)	*Pacquin's;* delightful for chapped hands or face	$0.74
Lotion	*Collier's* (1934)	*Zemo For Skin Irritation;* itching stops the moment Zemo touches the tender and inflamed skin; to clear away rashes, pimples, eczema, ringworm and restore skin	$0.35/$0.60/$1
Powder	*San Francisco Examiner* (1932)	LaBlache face powder	$0.33
Sanitary Napkin	*Sears, Roebuck* (1932)	*Kotex;* the ideal comfort napkin	$0.85/dz
Sanitary Pads	*Montgomery Ward & Co.* (1932)	*Modess;* famous Johnson & Johnson Red Cross quality	$1/5 bxs
Shampoo	*Montgomery Ward & Co.* (1932)	Coconut oil; the favorite of many thousands of our customers; three 50¢ bottles	$0.49
Shave Cream	*Collier's* (1934)	*Colgate Rapid;* de-waterproof your whiskers and make shaving easier; large size tube	$0.25
Soap	*Montgomery Ward & Co.* (1932)	*Woodbury Castile;* made from pure imported Spanish olive oil; bars	$0.57/4

Advertisement for women's shaving razor 1933. (via Wikimedia Commons)

Item	Source	Description	Price
PUBLICATIONS			
Book	*Popular Mechanics* (1933)	*Popular Chemistry Experiment Book;* for junior chemists, adopted by the New York Public Library	$0.50
Magazine	*Popular Mechanics* (1933)	*Popular Mechanics* magazine; monthly	$0.25
Newspaper	*The Raleigh (NC) Times* (1931)	One-year subscription to *The Raleigh Times,* published every evening except Sunday	
		By carrier	$7.50
		By mail	$6.00

Item	Source	Description	Price
REAL ESTATE			
Apartment	*San Francisco Examiner* (1932)	Furnished; 45th Avenue; sunny four rooms; two beds	$25/mo
Room	*The Raleigh (NC) Times* (1931)	Heated room with board, 102 New Bern Avenue Per week	$7.00
SEWING EQUIPMENT & SUPPLIES			
Cloth	*Montgomery Ward & Co.* (1932)	Cotton outing flannel; soft, warmly fleeced on both sides; we've slashed the price and then thrown in 2 extra yards	$1/12 yds
Cloth	*Montgomery Ward & Co.* (1932)	Silk and cotton crepe; here are the prints that will be worn this spring and summer	$0.35/yd
Cloth	*Montgomery Ward & Co.* (1932)	Gold Stripe; stifel rawhide; copper-riveted western style	$0.95/yd
Knitting Yarn	*Sears, Roebuck* (1932)	Golden Crown; a 4-fold yarn mixture of pure wool and rayon	$0.17
Sewing Machine	*Montgomery Ward & Co.* (1932)	*Brunswick;* prices haven't been this low since 1923; golden oak, 5 drawers	$19.95
SPORTS EQUIPMENT			
Baseball	*Sears, Roebuck* (1932)	*J. C. Higgins;* official outseam playground and diamond ball	$0.95
Binoculars	*Sears, Roebuck* (1932)	*Dr. Wobler's;* for sportsmen, marine, or mountain use	$33.48
Boat	*Popular Mechanics* (1933)	*Hammond Lumber Co. Wilson Fold-Flat;* wooden; fold in one minute; carry on running board; 10'; weight 80 lbs; price FOB Los Angeles; slightly higher New York or Chicago	$39
Canoe	*Collier's* (1934)	*Old Town Canoe Co.;* a graceful sweep of cedar, tight planked, strong ribbed, covered with water-tight canvas	$68
Fish Hooks	*Sears, Roebuck* (1932)	Eyed; assorted sizes and patterns	$0.23/100
Fishing Line	*Sears, Roebuck* (1932)	*King Fisher Black Wonder;* silk; extra hard braided	$1.35
Knife	*Sears, Roebuck* (1932)	*Official Boy Scout;* full size 3 5/8", bone stag handle	$1.23
Shotgun	*Sears, Roebuck* (1932)	*Fox Sterlingworth;* double barrel; fitted with Jostam anti-flinch recoil pad	$36.98
Tent	*Sears, Roebuck* (1932)	Boy's camp tent; 5' ×7' with 2' side walls and 4' 8" height at center	$4.95
TELEPHONE EQUIPMENT & SERVICES			
Long Distance Rates	John Brooks, *Telephone: The First Hundred Years* (1987)	*Bell Telephone;* New York to London [cost in 1930]	$30/3 min
TOBACCO PRODUCTS			
Cigarettes	*Collier's* (1934)	*Kool Mild Menthol;* a new champion in throat comfort	$0.15/pk
Pipe	*Popular Mechanics* (1933)	*Drinkless Kaywoodie Presidential Model;* by actual measurement 51% purer smoke, 51% better taste from your tobacco	$3.50
Pony Clamps	*Popular Mechanics* (1933)	*Jorgensen Pony;* fittings go on ordinary 3/4" pipe to make clamps of any length	$3

Item	Source	Description	Price
Smoking Tobacco	*Popular Mechanics* (1933)	Brown & Williamson Tobacco Corp. Sir Walter Raleigh; for pipe and cigarettes	$0.15/tin

TOYS

Item	Source	Description	Price
Bicycle	*Sears, Roebuck* (1932)	*Peerless Junior;* strongly built for safety	$17.50
Croquet Set	*Sears, Roebuck* (1932)	Deluxe; others ask as much as $7.50 for this set	$3.98
Junior Caster Outfit	*Rapaport Catalogue* (1934)	Make your own metal toys; U.S. soldier outfit, baseball player outfit	$2.25
Wagon	*Sears, Roebuck* (1932)	*Chummy Coaster;* child's full-size body, 14 3/4" × 33 3/4" of 20 gauge auto steel	$3.69

TRAVEL & TRANSPORTATION

Item	Source	Description	Price
Bus Excursion	*The Raleigh (NC) Times* (1931)	Weekend bus trips, roundtrip from Raleigh, North Carolina to Wilmington, North Carolina	$3.90
		Charleston, South Carolina	$7.20
		Richmond, Virginia	$4.30
		Washington, D.C.	$7.00

MISCELLANY 1930–1934

Old Money Wanted

Will pay fifty dollars for nickel of 1913 with Liberty head (no buffalo). We pay cash premiums for all rare coins. Send 4¢ for large coin folder.

Popular Mechanics, October 1933

To the Stockholders of Woodside Cotton Mills Company

Your Board of Directors, at a meeting held this day decided that in view of the depressed condition of the cotton textile business throughout the country and its effect on the earnings of this company during the past six months, it is important that all the resources of the company be conserved to the fullest at this time, and that it would be unwise to declare and pay any dividends on the common and preferred stocks this July.

Letter from Woodside Cotton Mills Company, Greenville, S.C., June 26, 1930

Why I Change To Marlboro Contest

I smoked 15-cent cigarettes until I realized that only a few cents are left to buy tobacco—

considering the 6 percent per package U.S. tax and tremendous advertising expenditures.

I smoke Marlboros because they are better—better not because of a more clever catchword or slogan—but better because that extra nickel buys better tobacco. Irwin Shaffer, New York.

New York Times Magazine, October 25, 1931

F. Scott Fitzgerald's Income

F. Scott Fitzgerald's income in 1931 was $37,599. His income statement included nine magazine stories, for which he was paid $4,000 each—minus a 10 percent commission. Royalties from his books that year included $12.90 for *This Side of Paradise* and $17.90 for *The Great Gatsby*. 1931 was Fitzgerald's best year of earnings before he went permanently to Hollywood in 1937.

The Romantic Egoists: Pictorial Autobiography from the Scrapbooks and Albums of Scott and Zelda Fitzgerald

First published by Scribner's in April 1925, The Great Gatsby *received mixed reviews and sold poorly; in its first year, the book sold only 20,000 copies. It has now become an American classic.* (via Wikimedia Commons)

Joseph Aiello

Joseph Aiello and his brothers, Dominick, Antonio, and Andrew, were enemies of Al Capone in the struggle for control of organized crime in Chicago. Aiello tried to have Capone killed in somewhat novel ways, e.g., attempting to bribe a restaurant chef $10,000 to put prussic acid in Capone's soup and, on another occasion, offering a reward of $50,000 for Big Al's head. These efforts called for extraordinary vengeance on Capone's part and he ordered his enemy killed "real good." On October 23, 1930 Aiello was gunned down on North Kolmar Avenue, struck by 59 bullets, weighing altogether well over a pound.

The Encyclopedia of American Crime, June 1934

HISTORICAL SNAPSHOT 1935–1939

1935

- Social Security Act passed by Congress
- Emergency Relief Appropriation Act authorizes $5 billion to create jobs
- Fort Knox becomes repository for U.S. gold bullion
- Kodachrome color film introduced by Eastman Kodak Company
- One-tenth of 1 percent of U.S. corporations earn 50 percent of all corporate income
- Sulfa-drug chemotherapy introduced
- Nylon developed by E. I. Du Pont Corp.
- General Telephone Corporation created
- Beer in cans introduced
- 240 million cases of canned goods shipped
- One-third of farmers receive U.S. Treasury allotment checks for not growing food or crops

1936

- 38 percent of families have incomes of less than $1,000 a year
- Population reaches 127 million
- Ford's V-8 engine unveiled
- *Life* magazine begins publication
- New York's Triborough Bridge opens; charges 25¢ toll
- Mercedes-Benz creates first diesel fuel passenger car

1937

- United Automobile Workers recognized by General Motors as sole bargaining agent for employees
- Principle of minimum wage for women upheld by Supreme Court
- Packard Motor Car Company sells a record 109,000 cars
- General Motors introduces automatic transmission
- Icemen continue to make regular deliveries to more than 50 percent of middle-class households
- Spam introduced by George A. Hormel & Co.
- *Popular Photography* magazine begins publication

1938

- Congress's wage-and-hour law limits work week to 44 hours
- Recovery stumbles, Wall Street's Dow Jones Industrials Average falls to 98.95
- Eastern Airlines created
- Owens-Corning Fiberglass Corporation is incorporated to produce products utilizing newly developed fiberglass
- First high-definition color television demonstrated

- Ballpoint pen patented
- Consumption of beef and dairy produce increases by 3 percent
- First Xerox image produced

- First nylon stockings go on sale

1939

- World War II begins in Europe
- New York's La Guardia Airport opens
- *The Wizard of Oz* is released and one of the first films to use Technicolor
- 42,500 taxpayers declare incomes of more than $25,000
- 5-minute Cream of Wheat introduced
- First food stamp program instituted in Rochester, NY
- 25 percent of American workers are farmers
- Pesticide DDT introduced for crops
- 13,500 motels and tourist courts in business

The original movie poster for The Wizard of Oz, *advertising its use of Technicolor.* (via Wikimedia Commons)

SELECTED INCOME 1935–1939

Job	Source	Description	Pay
Accountant	*Atlanta Constitution* (1937)	For large local concern, age 25 to 30. Must know general accounting, and be familiar with tax work.	$150/wk
Actor	Lee O. Miller, *The Great Cowboy Stars of Movies and Television*	Income in 1938 of William Boyd, better known as Hopalong Cassidy, for eight films	$100,000
Advertising Executive	*Time* (1939)	Annual compensation of Eddie Bernays, promoter of products for Proctor & Gamble	$25,000
Banker	*New York Herald* (1935)	Senior Accountant, factoring or finance experience	$2,600/yr
Bookkeepers	*New York Times* (1936)	Complete charge or assistants	$8–$25/wk
Comic Strip Artist	*Literary Digest* (1936)	Income in 1936 of Bud Fisher for his comic strip *Mutt and Jeff*	$93,600
Cook	*Atlanta Constitution* (1935)	Colored cooks, maids for North Side jobs	$6–$10/wk
Dentist	*New York Times* (1938)	Dentist seeks position, experienced contractor and extractor, careful operator, expert inlays, personality	$40/mo
Draftsman	*Chicago Tribune* (1936)	Sheet metal experience	$125/mo
Driver	*Atlanta Constitution* (1935)	Local tea and coffee route	$60/wk
Engineer	*New York Herald* (1935)	Aircraft designers	$40–$55/wk
Nurse	*New York Times* (1936)	Situation wanted. English; American graduate (24); to care for invalid lady; will travel; New York references	$90/mo
Photographer	*New York Times* (1938)	Commercial still life; bring samples, complete charge	$25/wk
Railway Postal Clerk	*Mechanics Illustrated* (1938)	First year pay; requires travel; clerks on long runs work three days on then three days off	$1,900
Receptionist	*New York Times* (1938)	Attractive college graduate, well poised, good personality	$15/wk
Route Driver	*Atlanta Constitution* (1936)	Automobile offered as bonus for covering local coffee route	$45/wk
Sales	*Atlanta Constitution* (1935)	Ladies wanted immediately to demonstrate actual samples of snag-proofed hosiery to friends	$22/wk206
Sales	*New York Herald* (1935)	Marine Oil Sales Supervisor, under 40, out-of-town	$4,000/yr
Sales	*Chicago Tribune* (1936)	Married man over 35 yrs to call on new and old customers for 75-year-old house furnishings concern. Must have good references. Car furnished and satisfied with commission	$25–$30/wk
Sales	*Chicago Tribune* (1936)	Auto parts	$1,800/yr
Stenographer	*Atlanta Constitution* (1939)	Large North Georgia manufacturer has position available as Assistant Secretary to President	$109/wk

Job	Source	Description	Pay
Stenographer-Bookkeeper	*New York Times* (1936)	Intelligent	$12/wk
Teacher	*Atlanta Constitution* (1939)	Degree men, teach mathematics and coaching	$95/wk
Teacher	*Atlanta Constitution* (1939)	Degree women, grades 2 to 7	$70–$90/wk
Writer	Catherine and Legrand and Robyn Karney, *Chronicle of the Cinema* (1995)	Payment by Metro-Goldwyn-Mayer in 1936 to Margaret Mitchell for movie rights to her book *Gone with the Wind*	$50,000

CONSUMER EXPENDITURES 1935-1939

	(Per Capita)				
Expenditure Type	**1935**	**1936**	**1937**	**1938**	**1939**
Clothing	$39.26	$42.13	$42.65	$42.32	$45.03
Auto Usage	$33.76	$39.01	$41.87	$34.62	$39.69
New Auto Purchase	$11.78	$14.82	$15.51	$9.23	$12.21
Auto Parts	$3.14	$3.12	$3.10	$3.08	$3.82
Gas & Oil	$13.35	$14.82	$16.28	$16.16	$16.79
Housing	$62.03	$63.97	$68.24	$70.79	$71.74
Furniture	$5.49	$6.24	$6.98	$6.16	$6.87
Utilities	$21.98	$23.40	$23.26	$23.08	$23.66
Telephone & Telegraph	$3.93	$3.90	$3.88	$3.85	$4.58
Physicians	$5.49	$5.43	$6.16	$6.92	$6.87
Dentists	$2.36	$2.34	$3.10	$3.08	$3.05
Health Insurance	79¢	78¢	78¢	77¢	$1.53
Personal Business	$22.77	$24.18	$25.59	$23.85	$24.42
Personal Care	$6.28	$7.02	$7.75	$7.69	$7.63
Tobacco	$10.99	$11.70	$13.18	$13.08	$13.74
Local Transport	$6.28	$6.24	$6.98	$6.16	$6.87
Intercity Transport	$2.36	$2.34	$3.10	$2.31	$3.05
Recreation	$20.41	$23.40	$26.36	$24.62	$26.71
Religion/Welfare Activities	$7.07	$7.02	$6.98	$7.69	$7.63
Private Education & Research	$3.93	$3.90	$4.65	$4.62	$4.58
Per Capita Consumption	$438.12	$483.69	$517.21	$493.19	$511.34

INVESTMENTS 1935-1939

Investment	1935	1936	1937	1938	1939
Basic Yield, One-Year Corporate Bonds	1.05	.61	.69	.85	.57
Short-Term Interest Rates, 4–6 Months, Prime Commercial Paper	.75	.75	.94	.81	.59
Basic Yield, Common Stocks, Total (Moody's)	4.01	3.50	4.63	4.30	4.14
Index of Common Stocks (1941 — 1943 = 10)	10.60	15.47	15.41	11.49	12.06

COMMON STOCKS, CLOSING PRICE AND YIELD, FIRST BUSINESS DAY OF YEAR

(PARENTHETICAL NUMBER IS ANNUAL DIVIDEND IN DOLLARS)

	1935	1936	1937	1938	1939
Allis Chalmers	17 1/8	36 1/2	77 3/4	46 1/2	47 3/8
			(1 1/2)	(3.50)	(1.50)
AT&T	105 3/8	158 3/4	185	144 3/4	150
	(9)	(9)	(9)	(9)	(9)
American Tobacco	82 3/4	97 3/8	95	60 3/4	86
	(5)	(5)	(5)	(5)	(5)
Anaconda	11 3/4	29 1/2	53 3/8	29	35 1/4
			(1)	(1.75)	(.50)
B&O	13 7/8	16 1/2	21 1/8	9	8 3/8
Bethlehem Steel	32 1/4	52 1/2	74 7/8	58	79 7/8
			(1 1/2)	(5)	
Corn Products	63 3/4	69 1/2	67	59 1/4	66 1/2
	(3)	(3)	(3)	(3)	(3)
General Electric	22 1/8	38	53 3/4	40 3/4	43 1/2
	(.60)	(.70)	(1)	(2.20)	(.90)
General Motors	34 1/8	55 3/4	62 1/8	29 1/8	50 3/8
	(1)	(2)	(3 1/4)	(3.75)	(1.50)
International Business Machines	152	176 1/2			184 1/4
(2% stock dividend, 1/10/35)	(5)	(6)			(6)
Intl Harvester	43 5/8	61 1/2	105 3/8	61 1/8	59
	(.60)	(1.20)	(2 1/2)	(4)	(1.92 1/2)
National Biscuit	29	33 5/8	31 7/8	18 1/8	25 3/8
	(2)	(1.60)	(1.60)	(1.60)	(1.60)
U.S. Steel	38 1/4	49 3/8	76 1/4	53	
Western Union	33 7/8	74 1/4	77 1/2	24 5/8	
		(2)	(2 3/4)	(2.25)	

STANDARD JOBS 1935–1939

Job Type	1935	1936	1937	1938	1939
Average of all Industries, excl. farm labor	$1195/yr	$1226/yr	$1341/yr	$1303/yr	$1346/yr
Average of all Industries, incl. farm labor	$1115/yr	$1146/yr	$1259/yr	$1221/yr	$1266/yr
Bituminous Coal Mining	$957/yr	$1103/yr	$1170/yr	$1050/yr	$1197/yr
Building Trades	$1027/yr	$1178/yr	$1278/yr	$1193/yr	$1268/yr
Domestics	$485/yr	$506/yr	$558/yr	$527/yr	$544/yr
Farm Labor	$324/yr	$351/yr	$407/yr	$420/yr	$436/yr
Federal Civilian	$1759/yr	$1896/yr	$1797/yr	$1832/yr	$1843/yr
Federal Employees, Executive Depts.	$1183/yr	$1112/yr	$1188/yr	$1149/yr	$1137/yr
Federal Military	$1154/yr	$1152/yr	$1132/yr	$1120/yr	$1134/yr
Finance, Insurance, & Real Estate	$1632/yr	$1713/yr	$1788/yr	$1731/yr	$1729/yr
Gas & Electricity Workers	$1589/yr	$1615/yr	$1705/yr	$1749/yr	$1766/yr
Manufacturing, Durable Goods	$1264/yr	$1376/yr	$1491/yr	$1365/yr	$1479/yr
Manufacturing, Nondurable Goods	$1178/yr	$1210/yr	$1267/yr	$1241/yr	$1263/yr
Medical/Health Services Workers	$829/yr	$851/yr	$876/yr	$899/yr	$908/yr
Miscellaneous Manufacturing	$1244/yr	$1298/yr	$1359/yr	$1274/yr	$1337/yr
Motion Picture Services	$1892/yr	$1896/yr	$1972/yr	$1942/yr	$1971/yr
Nonprofit Org. Workers	$1435/yr	$1465/yr	$1497/yr	$1529/yr	$1546/yr
Passenger Transportation Workers, Local and Highway	$1361/yr	$1433/yr	$1505/yr	$1529/yr	$1569/yr
Personal Services	$915/yr	$940/yr	$978/yr	$992/yr	$1034/yr
Public School Teachers	$1293/yr	$1329/yr	$1367/yr	$1406/yr	$1403/yr
Radio Broadcasting & Television Workers	$2089/yr	$2223/yr	$2361/yr	$2497/yr	$2427/yr
Railroads	$1645/yr	$1724/yr	$1774/yr	$1849/yr	$1877/yr
State and Local Govt. Workers	$1361/yr	$1433/yr	$1505/yr	$1529/yr	$1569/yr
Telephone & Telegraph Workers	$1378/yr	$1420/yr	$1481/yr	$1580/yr	$1600/yr
Wholesale and Retail Trade Workers	$1279/yr	$1295/yr	$1352/yr	$1352/yr	$1360/yr

297

FOOD BASKET 1935–1939

(NR=Not Reported)

Commodity	Year	New York	Atlanta	Chicago	Denver	Los Angeles
Apples, Fresh, per pound	1935	6.50¢	5.50¢	6.50¢	5.90¢	6.20¢
	1936	6.40¢	5.80¢	6.50¢	6.10¢	6.10¢
	1937	NR	NR	NR	NR	NR
	1938	NR	NR	NR	NR	NR
	1939	NR	NR	NR	NR	NR
Beans, Navy, per pound	1935	8.30¢	7.10¢	6¢	6.98¢	7.40¢
	1936	8.90¢	7¢	6.50¢	6.70¢	8¢
	1937	NR	NR	NR	NR	NR
	1938	NR	NR	NR	NR	NR
	1939	NR	NR	NR	NR	NR
Beef, Rib Roasts, per pound	1935	34.10¢	29.20¢	32.20¢	24.20¢	27.60¢
	1936	31.80¢	29.50¢	31.60¢	24.70¢	27.40¢
	1937	NR	NR	NR	NR	NR
	1938	NR	NR	NR	NR	NR
	1939	NR	NR	NR	NR	NR
Beef, Steaks (Round), per pound	1935	39.20¢	36.20¢	34.70¢	31¢	31.30¢
	1936	36.80¢	35.70¢	33.50¢	30.90¢	31.40¢
	1937	NR	NR	NR	NR	NR
	1938	NR	NR	NR	NR	NR
	1939	NR	NR	NR	NR	NR
Bread, White, per loaf	1935	5.60¢	5.60¢	5.20¢	4.10¢	4.50¢
	1936	5.20¢	5.10¢	4.80¢	3.80¢	4.30¢
	1937	NR	NR	NR	NR	NR
	1938	NR	NR	NR	NR	NR
	1939	NR	NR	NR	NR	NR
Butter, per pound	1935	37.10¢	37.50¢	35.60¢	35.40¢	36.50¢
	1936	40.50¢	40¢	39.20¢	38.80¢	39.10¢
	1937	NR	NR	NR	NR	NR
	1938	NR	NR	NR	NR	NR
	1939	NR	NR	NR	NR	NR
Cheese, per pound	1935	28.90¢	24.20¢	28.60¢	27.40¢	27.10¢
	1936	30.50¢	24.50¢	30.40¢	28.50¢	27.70¢
	1937	NR	NR	NR	NR	NR
	1938	NR	NR	NR	NR	NR
	1939	NR	NR	NR	NR	NR
Chickens, per pound	1935	31.80¢	25.10¢	30.30¢	26.50¢	33¢
	1936	33.50¢	26.10¢	32¢	28.90¢	35¢
	1937	NR	NR	NR	NR	NR
	1938	NR	NR	NR	NR	NR
	1939	NR	NR	NR	NR	NR
Coffee, per pound	1935	26¢	24.30¢	26.20¢	30.90¢	28.70¢
	1936	24.50¢	22.90¢	24.70¢	31.80¢	27.30¢
	1937	NR	NR	NR	NR	NR
	1938	NR	NR	NR	NR	NR
	1939	NR	NR	NR	NR	NR

Commodity	Year	New York	Atlanta	Chicago	Denver	Los Angeles
Cornmeal, per pound	1935	6.30¢	3¢	6.10¢	5.40¢	5.10¢
	1936	6.50¢	3¢	6.10¢	5.20¢	4.90¢
	1937	NR	NR	NR	NR	NR
	1938	NR	NR	NR	NR	NR
	1939	NR	NR	NR	NR	NR
Eggs, per dozen	1935	44.20¢	34.60¢	35.60¢	37.10¢	35¢
	1936	43.80¢	34.10¢	36.20¢	35.90¢	32¢
	1937	NR	NR	NR	NR	NR
	1938	NR	NR	NR	NR	NR
	1939	NR	NR	NR	NR	NR
Flour, Wheat, per pound	1935	5.60¢	5.10¢	5.20¢	4.10¢	4¢
	1936	5.20¢	5.10¢	4.80¢	3.80¢	4.30¢
	1937	NR	NR	NR	NR	NR
	1938	NR	NR	NR	NR	NR
	1939	NR	NR	NR	NR	NR
Lard, per pound	1935	19.90¢	19.50¢	19.50¢	20.80¢	22¢
	1936	17.90¢	16¢	17¢	17.40¢	16.30¢
	1937	NR	NR	NR	NR	NR
	1938	NR	NR	NR	NR	NR
	1939	NR	NR	NR	NR	NR
Milk, Fresh, per quart	1935	13¢	14¢	10.70¢	10.80¢	11.20¢
	1936	13.10¢	14.40¢	11.40¢	10.80¢	10.90¢
	1937	NR	NR	NR	NR	NR
	1938	NR	NR	NR	NR	NR
	1939	NR	NR	NR	NR	NR

Milk delivery trucks circa 1939. (via Wikimedia Commons)

Commodity	Year	New York	Atlanta	Chicago	Denver	Los Angeles
Molasses, per gallon	1935	15.70¢	14.70¢	14.40¢	12.60¢	14.10¢
	1936	14.70¢	14.90¢	14.40¢	12.10¢	13.40¢
	1937	NR	NR	NR	NR	NR
	1938	NR	NR	NR	NR	NR
	1939	NR	NR	NR	NR	NR
Mutton and Lamb, Leg, per pound	1935	27.80¢	26¢	28.30¢	24.60¢	26.20¢
	1936	29.10¢	28.20¢	29.70¢	26.20¢	27.60¢
	1937	NR	NR	NR	NR	NR
	1938	NR	NR	NR	NR	NR
	1939	NR	NR	NR	NR	NR
Pork Chops, per pound	1935	36¢	33.20¢	36¢	33.40¢	40.10¢
	1936	34.90¢	32.50¢	34.10¢	32.20¢	39.10¢
	1937	NR	NR	NR	NR	NR
	1938	NR	NR	NR	NR	NR
	1939	NR	NR	NR	NR	NR
Pork, Bacon, Sliced, per pound	1935	42.40¢	38.90¢	43¢	40.40¢	44.60¢
	1936	42.10¢	38.90¢	42.80¢	41.20¢	43.20¢
	1937	NR	NR	NR	NR	NR
	1938	NR	NR	NR	NR	NR
	1939	NR	NR	NR	NR	NR
Pork, Salt, Dry or Pickled, per pound	1935	31.90¢	26.30¢	31¢	26.80¢	29.70¢
	1936	31.20¢	24.20¢	30.10¢	26¢	28.70¢
	1937	NR	NR	NR	NR	NR
	1938	NR	NR	NR	NR	NR
	1939	NR	NR	NR	NR	NR
Pork, Ham, Sliced, per pound	1935	47.30¢	46.80¢	46.40¢	47.80¢	60.40¢
	1936	48.40¢	49.40¢	50.50¢	51.50¢	63.30¢
	1937	NR	NR	NR	NR	NR
	1938	NR	NR	NR	NR	NR
	1939	NR	NR	NR	NR	NR
Pork, Salt, Ham, per pound	1935	31.90¢	26.30¢	31¢	26.80¢	29.70¢
	1936	31.20¢	24.20¢	30.10¢	26¢	28.70¢
	1937	NR	NR	NR	NR	NR
	1938	NR	NR	NR	NR	NR
	1939	NR	NR	NR	NR	NR
Potatoes, Irish, per pound	1935	2.10¢	2.20¢	2.20¢	2.10¢	2.30¢
	1936	3.50¢	3.60¢	3.30¢	3.10¢	3.50¢
	1937	NR	NR	NR	NR	NR
	1938	NR	NR	NR	NR	NR
	1939	NR	NR	NR	NR	NR
Prunes, Dried, per pound	1935	10.80¢	10.80¢	12.30¢	11.90¢	9.80¢
	1936	9.70¢	9.90¢	11.10¢	10.20¢	8.90¢
	1937	NR	NR	NR	NR	NR
	1938	NR	NR	NR	NR	NR
	1939	NR	NR	NR	NR	NR
Rice, per pound	1935	8.80¢	7.90¢	8.50¢	8.40¢	8.80¢
	1936	8.90¢	8.40¢	9.10¢	8.90¢	9.40¢
	1937	NR	NR	NR	NR	NR
	1938	NR	NR	NR	NR	NR
	1939	NR	NR	NR	NR	NR
Sugar, per pound	1935	5.40¢	5.90¢	5.80¢	6¢	5.20¢
	1936	5.40¢	5.70¢	5.80¢	6.10¢	5.10¢
	1937	NR	NR	NR	NR	NR
	1938	NR	NR	NR	NR	NR
	1939	NR	NR	NR	NR	NR

Commodity	Year	New York	Atlanta	Chicago	Denver	Los Angeles
Tea, per pound	1935	64.60¢	76.50¢	81.10¢	78.50¢	74.90¢
	1936	66.10¢	76.90¢	83.20¢	83.10¢	77.40¢
	1937	NR	NR	NR	NR	NR
	1938	NR	NR	NR	NR	NR
	1939	NR	NR	NR	NR	NR
Veal, per pound	1935	44.20¢	36.80¢	36.80¢	34.20¢	41¢
	1936	46.80¢	39.10¢	39¢	35.80¢	42.60¢
	1937	NR	NR	NR	NR	NR
	1938	NR	NR	NR	NR	NR
	1939	NR	NR	NR	NR	NR

SELECTED PRICES 1935–1939

Item	Source	Description	Price
APPLIANCES			
Coffee Mill	*Time* (1939)	*Kitchen Aid Electric Coffee Mill* for the home	$9.75
Fan	*Goodyear Spring and Summer Catalog* (1937)	*Samson Safe-Flex Home Fan;* 30% more breeze and even baby's fingers are safe	$2.90
Fan	*Sears, Roebuck* (1939)	*Cold Wave;* oscillating; guaranteed five years if oiled twice each season	$5.50
Kitchen Range	*Sears, Roebuck* (1939)	Easy cleaning; lustrous surfaces everywhere	$76.95
Refrigerator	*Sears, Roebuck* (1939)	*Cold Spot;* kerosene; costs only $0.04 to $0.07 per day to operate	$169.50
Refrigerator	*Sears, Roebuck* (1939)	*Polar Air;* air-conditioned ice; modern in style and efficiency—a $40 value	$22.98
Stove	*Sears, Roebuck* (1938)	Cast iron; big pull-out hearth for quick firing or easy emptying of ashes	$29.85
Toaster	*Sears, Roebuck* (1938)	*Heatmaster;* record-smashing value	$1.85
Vacuum Cleaner	*Sears, Roebuck* (1938)	*Kenmore DeLuxe;* triple-action cleaning; beating sweeping suction	$31.45
Washing Machine	*Sears, Roebuck* (1939)	*Challenger;* gasoline; does a big day's wash for less than a dime	$39.95
APPAREL, CHILDREN'S			
Slacks	*Sears, Roebuck* (1939)	Boy's; Sanforized-shrunk, heavy weight, washable, deep tone, cotton twill	$0.98
Suit	*Sears, Roebuck* (1939)	Boy's; double-breasted; 1-knicker suit, 40% wool, balance rayon, cotton	$4.98
APPAREL, MEN'S			
Hat	*Collier's* (1938)	*Stetson;* stag brown; he doesn't see how he could afford to wear anything else	$5 to $10
Shoes	*Collier's* (1938)	*Florsheim Brookfield Style;* we lowered the price and raised the value	$8.75
Shoes	*Collier's* (1938)	*Bostonian;* they're walk fitted	$7.50 to $11
Shorts	*Sears, Roebuck* (1938)	Cotton broadcloth; they won't shrink out of fit or rip	$0.22
Sleeping Robe	*Hunting and Life* (1936)	*Woods Arctic Down;* your Woods robe keeps all warmth in, all cold out; large size	$62.50
Socks	*Sears, Roebuck* (1939)	All wool; for work	$0.28
Suit	*Sears, Roebuck* (1939)	Cassimere; herringbone with an overplaid, in a strong all-wool fabric	$13.95

Item	Source	Description	Price
Tie	*Sears, Roebuck* (1939)	Fine rayon	$0.23

APPAREL, WOMEN'S

Item	Source	Description	Price
Charmode	*Sears, Roebuck* (1939)	All-in-one; fits as though it were made for you alone	$2.89
Corset	*Sears, Roebuck* (1939)	Maternity; perfectly designed for correct support before childbirth	$2.98
Dress	*Sears, Roebuck* (1939)	Maternity; spun rayon	$2.98
Frock	*Sears, Roebuck* (1938)	*Eileen Drury;* all-rayon French-type drape	$1.98
Girdle	*Sears, Roebuck* (1939)	Soft-textured 2-way stretch dura-latex	$0.79
Hose	*Time* (1939)	*Davencrepes by Humming Bird;* America's high-style hosiery; every inch is guarded by invisible extra silk Per pair	$1.15
Shoes	*Time* (1939)	*Matrix Originals,* your footprint in leather; oh so comfortable Per pair	$10.00
Slip	*Sears, Roebuck* (1938)	Silk crepe; with shadowproof panels	$1.55
Stockings	*Sears, Roebuck* (1939)	Silk; the same quality that's around $0.29 in most other stores	$0.21

BABY PRODUCTS

Item	Source	Description	Price
Carriage	*Sears, Roebuck* (1936)	Loom-woven baby seat; back and half of sides lined with cotton	$12.98
Crib	*Sears, Roebuck* (1938)	All steel; new Humpty-Dumpty decoration, sides 20" high	$9.15
Hair Treatment	*Sears, Roebuck* (1938)	*Nestle's;* encourages the natural curliness of the hair	$0.83

BUSINESS EQUIPMENT & SUPPLIES

Item	Source	Description	Price
Typewriter	*Sears, Roebuck* (1939)	*Corona Standard;* terms, $5 down, $5/mo	$54.50

COLLECTIBLES

Item	Source	Description	Price
Arrowheads	*Hunting and Fishing* (1936)	100 good ancient arrowheads	$3.00

ENTERTAINMENT

Item	Source	Description	Price
Broadway Play	*Time* (1939)	Actress Tallulah Bankhead in *The Little Foxes* Nightly seating	$0.55 to $3.30

ENTERTAINMENT, HOME

Item	Source	Description	Price
Camera	*Hunting and Fishing* (1936)	*Moviematic;* the camera that has made movie shooting everyone's sport	$5.95
Camera	*Country Life* (1939)	*Kodak Bantam;* with Kodak Anastigmat Special lens, 1/200-second shutter; plunger-type body shutter release	$22.50

Item	Source	Description	Price
Movie Camera	*Time* (1939)	*Bell and Howell,* Filmo 8; makes both color and black-and-white movies; use Filmo indoors or out	$49.50
Radio	*Hunting and Fishing* (1936)	*Tingtone Pocket;* operates without tubes or batteries	$2.90
Radio	*Sears, Roebuck* (1936)	A full-size personal radio in the latest styles; 5-tube	$16.50
Radio	*Goodyear Spring and Summer Catalog* (1937)	*Goodyear Wings Deluxe-8;* home radio	$38.95
Radio	*Sears, Roebuck* (1938)	*A.C. Electric Tuning Radio;* press button, instantly hear the program—no waiting at all	$49.50

FARM EQUIPMENT AND SUPPLIES

Item	Source	Description	Price
Field Tiller	*Sears, Roebuck* (1938)	*David Bradley;* 2-speed transmission	$94.50
Milker	*Sears, Roebuck* (1939)	*Prima;* milking action is similar to the sucking action of a calf	$42.50
Pitchfork	*Sears, Roebuck* (1939)	*Hercules;* heavy, fully polished; 11 tines	$1.35

FINANCIAL PRODUCTS & SERVICES

Item	Source	Description	Price
Traveler's Checks	*Country Life* (1939)	*American Express Travel;* funds that know no frontiers	$0.75/$100

FOOD PRODUCTS

Item	Source	Description	Price
Fish	*Atlanta Constitution* (1935)	Fancy speckled trout	$0.19/ pound
Fish	*Atlanta Constitution* (1935)	Roe Shad	$0.23/ pound
Sausage	*Atlanta Constitution* (1935)	Country sausage	$0.20/ pound
Shrimp	*Atlanta Constitution* (1935)	Cooked, peeled shrimp	$0.23/half pound

FURNITURE

Item	Source	Description	Price
Bathroom Cabinet	*Morgan Millwork Co.* (1936)	*Miami Metal;* 16" × 24"; 3 coats of high-grade baked enamel	$14.00
Bed	*Country Life* (1939)	Louis XIV with Simmons Beautyrest box spring and mattress; custom-made oversize mattress, 6' 4 1/2" long, 6' wide	$345
Bed	*Sears, Roebuck* (1939)	*Lifetime Steel;* complete outfit of bed, mattress, and coil spring	$16.50
Bedroom Set	*Atlanta Constitution* (1935)	12-piece bedroom group; bed, vanity, chest, bench, mattress, 2 pillows, rug, shades, boudoir chair, Simmons coil spring	$89.00
China Cabinet	*Morgan Millwork Co.* (1936)	*Morgan;* designed especially for use in the smaller homes and in apartments; Extra width 2' 9"; height 7'; pine	$32.50
Kitchen Unit	*Morgan Millwork Co.* (1936)	3' 8" wide; 1'10" deep; six wood drawers, two pan and lid racks, one pair of flush doors	$30.38

Item	Source	Description	Price
Mantel	*Morgan Millwork Co.* (1936)	*Morgan Colonial;* with 5' 11" long shelf, 6' 1/2" wide; fancy Greek design	$31.88
Mirror	*Warren's Paint & Varnish Prod.* (1937)	Frameless Venetian; polished v-cut mitered lines are ground on the face side, as well as floral design at the top, peach on blue	$37.72
Sofa and Chair	*Sears, Roebuck* (1939)	Swedish modern; today's most talked of style	$66.85
Table	*Sears, Roebuck* (1936)	Gateleg; with the popular circular leaves opens to 45" × 36"; select hardwoods	$8.69
Table	*Country Life* (1939)	*Hammacher Schlemmer;* rattan serving; easy to carry; firm standing	$10.50
Table	*Country Life* (1939)	*Hammacher Schlemmer;* wrought-iron dining table with glass top	$56.00

GARDEN EQUIPMENT AND SUPPLIES

Item	Source	Description	Price
Ax	*Sears, Roebuck* (1939)	*Merit;* forged-steel head	$0.98
Garden Tractor	*Sears, Roebuck* (1936)	*Handiman;* 4 hp motor	$242
Garden Tractor	*Sears, Roebuck* (1938)	*Handiman;* 2-speed transmission	$299.50

HOTEL RATES

Item	Source	Description	Price
Hotel Room	*Time* (1939)	*Commodore;* New York's best located hotel; 2,000 large outside rooms, all with private baths	From $4.00
Hotel Room	*Time* (1939)	*Hotel Taft* in New York at Radio City; 2,000 rooms with bath and radio	From $2.50 per day
Hotel Room	*Country Life* (1939)	*Copley Plaza Luxury;* Boston, Massachusetts; without pretension and extravagance	$4/night
Room Rates	*Time* (1939)	*Ambassador Hotel;* large, luxurious rooms in New York Single Double Suite	 $6.00 $8.00 $12.00
Room Rates	*Time* (1939)	*Traymore on The Boardwalk,* Atlantic City; cruise ashore European plan With meals	 $5.00 $8.00

Beachgoers in front of the Traymore Hotel in Atlantic City, circa 1935. (via Wikimedia Commons)

Item	Source	Description	Price
Room Rates	*Time* (1939)	*Mayfair of St. Louis;* location, comfort, fine food	
		Single	$3.50 or less
		Double	$5.00 or less

HOUSEHOLD PRODUCTS

Item	Source	Description	Price
Broiler Pan	*Sears, Roebuck* (1936)	Oval aluminum	$0.75
Crock	*Sullivan Hardware Co., Inc.* (1936)	12-gallon stone crock	$1.68
Dinnerware	*Sears, Roebuck* (1939)	Semi-porcelain; service for six, includes 32 pieces	$4.98
Disinfectant	*Sears, Roebuck* (1938)	*Lysol;* Used in the care of the famous Dionne Quintuplets since their birth. Large size	$0.83
Flashlight	*Goodyear Spring and Summer Catalog* (1937)	*Zephyrites Flashlight;* 3-cell, 10 1/16" length, 500' beam; Tiffany of flashlights	$1.39
Flashlight	*Sears, Roebuck* (1939)	*Challenge;* long-range piercing finger of light that reaches 750'	$0.55
Flatware	*Sears, Roebuck* (1939)	*Community Plate;* service for 6	$29.75
Furniture Varnish	*Sears, Roebuck* (1936)	*Seroco;* long-wearing clear, hard gloss	$0.77/quart
Glasses	*Sears, Roebuck* (1939)	Cocktail glasses; 7-piece set, includes 6 glasses and shaker	$0.79
Grill	*Goodyear Spring and Summer Catalog* (1937)	Picnic grill; burns charcoal; folds into small compact carrying carton	$1.95
House Paint	*Warren's Paint & Varnish Prod.* (1937)	*Protex;* a rich linseed oil paint, unexcelled in hiding qualities	$4.08/gal

Item	Source	Description	Price
Kitchen Cabinet	*Sears, Roebuck* (1938)	*Hamper;* heavy spot-welded steel in a smart octagon style	$9.98
Lawn Mower	*Country Life* (1939)	*Stearns;* power; no longer a luxury, 10 models, 6-wheel drive and 4-roll drive	$69.50 to $260
Light Bulbs	*Collier's* (1938)	*Edison Mazda General Electric;* eyestrain season is here; homework and dark winter evenings call for light conditioning 100 watt bulb 150 watt bulb	 $0.15 $0.20
Paint	*Warren's Paint & Varnish Prod.* (1937)	*Southern Colonial Aluminum;* highly recommended for interior work, and for work on radiators, pipes, machinery, etc.	$4.25/gallon
Paintbrush	*Warren's Paint & Varnish Prod.* (1937)	For flat wall paint; 4" width, 2 3/4" length	$0.90
Patching Plaster	*Warren's Paint & Varnish Prod.* (1937)	*Old Newark;* has been on the American market for 118 years; 5 lb package	$0.10
Pressure Cooker	*Sears, Roebuck* (1939)	*Kook-Kwick* 1/3 the time, 1/3 the fuel, 8-quart size	$7.45
Rug	*Sears, Roebuck* (1939)	*Velflor;* the economy rug; 9' × 12'	$8.75
Towels	*Sears, Roebuck* (1936)	*Morninglow;* bath towel; 20" × 40" triple-stripe border	$0.79/4
Wall Clock	*Sears, Roebuck* (1939)	*Ingraham Regulator;* non-striking, for offices, churches, schools, and halls	$6.98
Water hose	*Sullivan Hardware Co., Inc.* (1936)	25' green 5/8' hose	$3.00
Window Cleaner	*Goodyear Spring and Summer Catalog* (1937)	*Windex;* cleans and polishes auto glass without water	$0.39
Wood Filler	*Collier's* (1938)	*Plastic Wood;* this canned wood makes all home repairs easy	$0.35/can
Wood Lathe	*Sears, Roebuck* (1936)	*Companion;* 440 bed, 4-speed	$11.95

JEWELRY

Item	Source	Description	Price
Watch	*Time* (1939)	*Longines President Lincoln* watch for men; 14 carat gold, 17 jewels, pink gold dial	$100
Watch	*Time* (1939)	*Longines Ella Wilcox* watch for women; yellow gold filled, 17 jewels	$47.50

MEDICAL PRODUCTS & SERVICES

Item	Source	Description	Price
Camphor	*Sears, Roebuck* (1938)	U.S.P. quality in cake form; 1 oz cake	$0.29
Laxative	*Sears, Roebuck* (1939)	*Ex-Lax;* chocolated; 18 tablets	$0.19
Nonprescription Drug	*Hunting and Fishing* (1936)	*Dr. Van Vleck's Absorption Treatment;* for the treatment of piles	$1.00

MOTORIZED VEHICLES, SERVICES, AND SUPPLIES

Item	Source	Description	Price
Antifreeze	*Collier's* (1938)	*DuPont Zerone;* get improved engine performance due to better heat dissipation	$1/gallon

Item	Source	Description	Price
Automobile	*Time* (1939)	*Plymouth* stands out; 82-horsepower, L-head engine; price includes front and rear bumpers, bumper guards, spare wheel, tire and tube, foot control for headlight beam, ashtray in front and rear, sun visor, safety glass and big trunk space Coupes start at Sedans start at	 $645 $685
Automobile	*Time* (1939)	*Hudson;* more room for passenger and luggage; safe stopping with Double-Safe Hydraulics; protection when a tire blows	$695
Battery	*Goodyear Spring and Summer Catalog* (1937)	*Goodyear Double Eagle;* a 24-month or 24,000 mile super-feature battery	$16.95
Compass	*Hunting and Fishing* (1936)	*Hull;* this new airplane-type compass constantly tells your direction of travel	$1.95
Fender Guide	*Goodyear Spring and Summer Catalog* (1937)	Illuminated; necessary on the new cars with high hoods and low curved-peak fenders	$1.19
Polish	*Goodyear Spring and Summer Catalog* (1937)	*Duco No. 7 Auto Polish;* just rub it on, let it dry, then wipe it off	$0.59/pint
Radio	*Goodyear Spring and Summer Catalog* (1937)	*Wings Challenger;* auto radio; the gem of the low-price field; 6 tubes	$17.95
Scooter	*Time* (1939)	*Moto-Scoot;* can be ridden standing up; enclosed engine	$109
Seat Covers	*Goodyear Spring and Summer Catalog* (1937)	*Cool Wave;* cool in summer, warm in winter Coupe Sedan	$2.79 $5.85
Spark Plug	*Goodyear Spring and Summer Catalog* (1937)	*Goodyear Spark Plug;* they are built to high standards throughout	$0.60
Tire	*Goodyear Spring and Summer Catalog* (1937)	*Goodyear Double Eagle;* the finest tire the world has ever seen	$18.75
Tire	*Goodyear Spring and Summer Catalog* (1937)	*Goodyear All Weather;* for 1936 Ford	$15.55
Tire Plug	*Goodyear Spring and Summer Catalog* (1937)	*Goodyear Rubber;* can add thousands of miles to tire life	$0.10

MUSICAL INSTRUMENTS

Item	Source	Description	Price
Guitar	*Sears, Roebuck* (1936)	*Lone Ranger;* with he-man figures of radio's most-beloved characters	$4.45
Guitar	*Sears, Roebuck* (1938)	*Supertone Gene Autry;* large concert size	$8.45

A 1939-1940 magazine advertisement for Gibson guitars. (via Wikimedia Commons)

Item	Source	Description	Price
OTHER			
Birdbath	*Country Life* (1939)	*Lombard & Co.;* imported English sandstone	$50.00
Charcoal Briquettes	*Goodyear Spring and Summer Catalog* (1937)	5 lb bag	$0.25
Dog Food	*Hunting and Fishing* (1936)	*Miller's Kibbles;* nearly 1/2 pound beef in every pound	$1/8 pounds
Dogs	*Hunting and Fishing* (1936)	Pair of rabbit hounds; 2 1/2 years old, medium size, long ears, good voices, fast, true, steady drivers; 10 day trial	$20.00
Dogs	*Country Life* (1939)	*Giralda Farms;* English Cocker Spaniel pups sired by Blackmoor Beacon out of imported bitches	$50
Door and Frame	*Morgan Millwork Co.* (1936)	*Morgan Colonial Style Exterior;* door, No. 1 pine, heavy 1 3/4" solid panels, flush on outside with beaded edges	$25.00
Entry Fee	*Hunting and Fishing* (1936)	*National Skeet Championship;* 20-gauge championship at 100 targets (includes targets)	$7.00
Film Enlargement Service	*Hunting and Fishing* (1936)	*Diamond Photo Service;* Kodak film enlarged to 8" × 10", negative returned	$0.29
Fountain Pen	*Collier's* (1938)	*Esterbrook Re-New-Point;* the common sense fountain pen complete fountain pen duracrome renew-point	$1.00 $0.25
House Kit	*Hunting and Fishing* (1936)	*Aladdin's Build It Yourself House;* price includes all lumber, readi-cut, millwork, windows, doors, interior woodwork, hardware, roofing, glass, nails, paints, varnish and stains; we pay freight	$493
Laundry Cleaning	*City Directory* (Greenville, SC) (1937)	*Ideal Laundry;* why wash at home? 15 lbs; ideal damp wash	$0.49
Pedestal Lavatory	*Sears, Roebuck* (1936)	*Mayflower;* it will give your bathroom distinctiveness	$15.00
Shoe Polish	*Sears, Roebuck* (1936)	*Bixby's Jet Oil;* for all-black smooth leather shoes; 13 oz	$0.14
Sunlamp	*Sears, Roebuck* (1939)	*Carbon Arc;* make that flattering tan a year round asset	$6.75
Windows	*Morgan Millwork Co.* (1936)	*Andersen Casement;* twin frame, glazed	$10.03
PERSONAL CARE PRODUCTS			
Bath Salts	*Country Life* (1939)	*Elizabeth Arden Pebble;* make your bath fragrant and restful	$2.50/$6.50
Dental Cream	*Sears, Roebuck* (1939)	*Colgate Ribbon;* an old favorite; 7 oz	$0.33
Dental Cream	*Sears, Roebuck* (1939)	*Milk of Magnesia;* large-size tubes	$0.08
Hair Tonic	*Sears, Roebuck* (1938)	Wildroot	$0.47
Itch Relief	*Hunting and Fishing* (1936)	*Absorbine Jr.;* wonderful relief for just about every kind of trouble that befalls the camper	$1.25/ bottle
Lotion	*Sears, Roebuck* (1936)	*Jergens;* famous for softening dry, harsh, chapped skin; 13 1/2 oz	$0.69
Mouthwash	*Sears, Roebuck* (1939)	*Listerine;* large size, 14 oz	$0.59
Razor Blade	*Hunting and Fishing* (1936)	*Double Keen;* the blades they are talking about at the club	$1.00
Soap	*Sears, Roebuck* (1938)	*Woodbury's;* facial soap; unquestioned purity; 3 cakes	$0.25

Item	Source	Description	Price
Toothbrush	*Collier's* (1938)	*Johnson & Johnson Tek;* using one Tek toothbrush in the morning and one at night, allows the bristles to dry, clean better, and last longer	$0.51/2
Toothpaste	*Collier's* (1938)	*Listerine;* supercharged with luster-foam (C14 H27 O5 Na) regular tube double size tube	 $0.25 $0.40

PUBLICATIONS

Item	Source	Description	Price
Book	*Sears, Roebuck* (1936)	*Ripley's Believe It or Not;* over 350 illustrations	$0.85
Book	*Hunting and Fishing* (1936)	*Sportsman's Encyclopedia,* by William Bruette; 150 illustrations	$1.00
Book	*Sears, Roebuck* (1939)	*Same Sex Life,* by H. W. Long, M.D.; helpful to married couples or those about to marry	$1.85

REAL ESTATE

Item	Source	Description	Price
House	*Country Life* (1939)	Old brick home for sale; 27 miles south of Washington, 9 rooms, 3 baths, basement, steam heat, electricity, hand carved woodwork, 143 acres	$18,000
Land	*Country Life* (1939)	Dairy estate property for sale; 90 miles from New York City; big income, milk retails; illness, sacrifice	$125,000
Land	*Country Life* (1939)	New Hampshire lake shore farm; 400 foot frontage, 150 acres; trout brook; farm house; 2 barns; includes beautiful building site overlooking lake and Mount Monadnock	$15,000

SEWING EQUIPMENT & SUPPLIES

Item	Source	Description	Price
Paper Pattern	*Sears, Roebuck* (1936)	Pattern for Dress. Each pattern may be made up in two or more styles	$0.15
Sewing Machine	*Sears, Roebuck* (1938)	*Franklin Foot Power;* first with all-level sewing surface	$31.95
Yarn	*Sears, Roebuck* (1936)	*Golden Crown Saxony;* threefold territorial wools	$0.23

SPORTS EQUIPMENT

Item	Source	Description	Price
Bait	*Hunting and Fishing* (1936)	Night Crawlers	$1/quart
Basketball	*Sears, Roebuck* (1938)	*J. C. Higgins;* regular pebbled-top-grain cowhide	$3.59
Bicycle	*Goodyear Spring and Summer Catalog* (1937)	*Goodyear;* deluxe boy's bicycle; nothing has been left undone to make it the sort of bike wanted by anyone who appreciates the best there is	$43.95
Bicycle Tires	*Goodyear Spring and Summer Catalog* (1937)	*Goodyear;* balloon bicycle tires; 26" × 2.125"; made of highest quality live rubber	$1.90
Camp Cottage	*Country Life* (1939)	*Hodgson;* simply fit the ready-made sections together and draw them tight with special Hodgson bolts	$200

Item	Source	Description	Price
Camper's Ax	*Sears, Roebuck* (1939)	*Craftsman;* don't miss this $1.70 value	$1.00
Decoys	*Hunting and Fishing* (1936)	*C. A. Frakes;* canvas; light, durable, lasting, lifelike	$2.95/dozen

TELEPHONE EQUIPMENT & SERVICES

Item	Source	Description	Price
Telephone Rates	*Time* (1939)	*Bell System Overseas;* a three-minute, weekday call between New York and Puerto Rico	$11.25

TOBACCO PRODUCTS

Item	Source	Description	Price
Cigar	*Time* (1939)	Webster custom-made cigars; each Golden Wedding Perfecto Chico Queens, 2 for Fancy Tales	$0.10 $0.10 $0.25 $0.15
Pipe	*Sears, Roebuck* (1939)	*Chesterfield;* known for its sweet smoking qualities; 50 size	$0.39
Pipe Filters	*Collier's* (1938)	*Frank Medico Absorbent;* finest briar money can buy	$1.00
Smoking Tobacco	*Hunting and Fishing* (1936)	*Union Leader;* a dime's no longer small change; it's mighty important money when it buys that big red tin of Union Leader tobacco	$0.10
Smoking Tobacco	*Hunting and Fishing* (1936)	*Sir Walter Raleigh;* switch to the brand of grand aroma	$0.15/can

TOYS

Item	Source	Description	Price
Wagon	*Goodyear Spring and Summer Catalog* (1937)	*Playboy DeLuxe Model Wagon;* all-steel safety body; 41" long, 19" wide	$15.45

TRAVEL & TRANSPORTATION

Item	Source	Description	Price
Airline Fare	*Collier's* (1938)	*American Airlines;* let America's flagships-serving 57 major cities give you extra days for living; costs are often less than first-class ground travel; Los Angeles to New York	$149.95
Airline Fare	*Collier's* (1938)	*American Airlines;* New York to Chicago	$44.95
Cruise	*Time* (1939)	*Red Star Line;* one-class travel to Europe; enjoy the run-of-the-ship	$100.50 and up
Cruise	*Time* (1939)	*Norwegian American Line;* from New York to Oslofjord; membership limited to 425	$485 and up

MISCELLANY 1935-1939

Publicity for Salaries

The House Ways and Means Committee has made public every corporate salary of $15,000 or more. In all, 18,000 persons have discovered that their salaries are open to public inspection. Many of them have been printed in the newspapers, and the general feeling of the goldfish is dismay and anger.

Yet it should be recognized that there is a difference between opening up a man's whole income and revealing his salary for the information of the stockholders of his corporation. A corporate officer is only the servant of his stockholder. They are his employers. An employer should know what he is paying his employees. It is not anybody else's business. Neither taxpayers, insurance solicitors, creditors, nor neighbors have any right to the information.

Business Week, January 18, 1936

Down Goes Liquor; 50% Tariff Cut on Imported Liquor and Gin Starts a Wide Series of Price Reductions

Seagram led the parade. Its "V.O." bonded whiskey was cut (in New York) from $2.59 a pt. to $2.09; its Five Crown (blend) went from $1.42 a pt. to $1.19.

Hiram Walker retorted with a cut of its Canadian Club (bonded) from $2.49 a pt. to $2.08; its cheaper blends were reduced to $1.19 a pt.

Business Week, February 1, 1936

Bootleg Wiring; Electrical Industry Makes Drive for More and Better Wiring and Against Unlicensed Work

Ten years ago 2% of the building cost was considered a fair allowance for the wiring of a new home. Recent surveys by *Electrical Contracting* show that 1 1/4% is now a fair average and thousands of six-room houses are being wired today for less than $50.

If 1% of the existing homes were rewired each year to the electrical industry's standard of modern adequacy, it would double the volume of the contracting business.

Business Week, February 1, 1936

Only 9,000,000 Now Idle, Commerce Experts Find

Commerce Department experts reported today that unofficial check-ups indicate there are now fewer than 9,000,000 unemployed.

They said that the number of those out of work has been falling off steadily this year and "was slightly less than 9,000,000 at the end of September."

This compared with their estimates of 11,000,000 for January and 9,550,000 in August.

New York Times, November 11, 1936

Socialists Have Surplus; Report to House Shows Campaign Outlay $2,287 Less Than Gifts

The Socialist Party wound up its Presidential campaign with money in the bank.

A post-election report to the Clerk of the House listed expenditures of $20,937, or $2,287 less than contributions.

Major parties are expected to show deficits of $500,000 or more.

New York Times, November 11, 1936

Are There a Million Aliens on Relief?

There may be as many as one million aliens of illegal entry on our relief rolls, supported by taxpayers, according to Arthur Krock, of *The New York Times.* Mr. Krock offers this as another explanation of the administration's curious hesitation to take a census of the unemployed.

He suggests that Congress may be about to be asked virtually to suspend the naturalization laws, that this army of aliens of illegal entry may quickly be made citizens in as good standing as any other.

Saturday Evening Post, January 23, 1937

MISCELLANY 1935–1939

The Effects of the Gift Tax

Also a Treasury official has testified that a single gift tax of $18,802,978 was paid in 1934, which means that one individual gave another as much as $45,000,000. Just before the tax went into effect, and to avoid its provisions, two taxpayers transferred upward of $150,000,000, according to Treasury information.

Gift-tax rates are three-fourths the estate-tax rates for a given amount and for the same bracket. Thus a rich man saves in two ways by making gifts. He is taxed at a lower rate on the amount given away and he takes the top off his fortune; thereby making another big saving on what is left. If he confines his gifts to $5,000 apiece and to a number of different donees through successive years, he can distribute his whole fortune without incurring any estate-tax obligations.

Saturday Evening Post, February 27, 1937

Clothing Brand Cuts Prices First Time In 15 Years

That department stores are experiencing slowness in the sale of men's clothing was indicated yesterday when one large store cut the price of its leading brand for the first time in fifteen years.

The revision was announced in a mailing to charge account customers only inviting them to a private sale. The amount of the reduction was approximately 15 percent. The sale will be conducted for three days, starting today.

New York Times, October 21, 1937

Radio Would Print News in the Home

F. C. Hamilton, manager of the McClatchy newspapers, announced that an application had been filed with the Federal Communications Commission for a permit to start this form of "radio newspaper" in Sacramento and Fresno. The "radio newspaper" will be two columns wide.

The system is understood to be a modification of stylus radio receiving, which has been in development for many years.

The company intends to broadcast from midnight until 6 a.m., supplementing the regular schedules.

Because the radio facsimile recorder for home use is not yet manufactured in mass quantity, it is planned to acquire 100 of the devices and install them in the homes of fifty Sacramento residents and in the homes of as many Fresno residents to determine the value of the service.

New York Times, October 21, 1937

Farm Group Also Sees President and Proposes 60-Cent Aid for Producers

President Roosevelt, Secretary Wallace, and Secretary Morgenthau prepared today to go ahead with loans to corn producers in advance of the special session of Congress. A loan of about 46 cents a bushel will probably be approved.

New York Times, October 21, 1937

Deepest Hole in the World

And K.C.L. A-2 (in San Joaquin Valley) excels by 1,878 feet the next deepest *producer,* Union Oil Co.'s Rio Bravo discovery well, located about fourteen miles away. Plugged back to 13,180 feet, K.C.L. A-2 is currently producing 450 barrels (or about $520 worth) of crude a day, the allowable permitted under California's proration agreements; and it has produced as much as 3,600 barrels during a twenty-four-hour test, through a one-inch flow bean or choke.

Even beaned down to the present low output,

K.C.L. A-2 is expected to pay out—i.e., return the investment—in about three years. Provided, of course, that K.C.L. A-2's type of crude maintains anything like the current price of $1.15 a barrel.

Fortune, July 1938

MISCELLANY 1935-1939

Akron Disturbed; City Is Startled as Goodrich Plans Big Factory Elsewhere, with Cheaper Labor

A year ago the United Rubber Workers union at the B. F. Goodrich Co.'s Akron plants overwhelmingly voted down a wage cut proposed by the company to its competitive position.

Goodrich, first rubber factory west of the Alleghenies, warned that the city might lose 5,000 jobs if the slash, averaging 12.3% were not accepted. Average hourly earnings for all its Akron workers then were $1.046, while hourly wage rates in all tire and tube plants outside the city averaged but 84¢, Bureau of Labor Statistics showed.

Goodrich, with U.S. Rubber as its main rival, specializes more than other Akron firms in mechanical rubber goods production, where it contended high wages handicapped it more than in the tire and tube end of the business. Outside Akron 59.7¢ was the average hourly wage in 150 mechanical goods plants.

Business Week, May 6, 1939

The Goodrich factory in Akron, Ohio. (via Wikimedia Commons)

Wage-Hour Law on Farm

Not yet satisfied by the House Labor Committee's amendments to the wage-hour law, the farm organizations will try to patch the bill on the floor. The farmer's choler will not block passage, how-ever, for they will take the best they can get rather than let harvest time roll 'round with the law unchanged as it now affects farm hands.

The farm organizations claim that, in liberalizing the hours provisions of the law by allowing a 60-hour week for "first process" workers the House Committee slipped a lot more of the laborers under the wage provisions of the law.

Farmers are afraid, of course, that increased costs will be passed back to them and not ahead to the consumers.

Business Week, May 6, 1939

1940–1959

World War II, Recovery, and the Cold War

1957 series one-dollar bill.

The twenty-year period from 1940 to 1959 includes the turbulent World War II years, when Americans were consumed by the national war effort and recovery, and the contrasting 1950s, when, after resolution of the Korean War, the United States was focused on recovery and increasing the prosperity of the middle class. During the first period the economy was radically disrupted as the workforce, national wealth, and social demographics were realigned. The 1950s brought the flight to the suburbs, the baby boom, and the creation of truly national products and distribution systems. Even inflation and the minor recessions of 1949 and 1957 caused little anxiety.

While the United States struggled with depression in the 1930s, Germany, Italy, and Japan were preparing for war. Slow at first to mobilize, America responded forcefully. Business worked in partnership with government; strikes were reduced. By 1944 the U.S. was producing twice the total war output of the Axis powers combined. Unemployment all but disappeared. By 1943 the wartime demand for production workers pushed average wage-earner income ahead of that of salaried employees. From 1940 to 1945 the gross national product (GNP) more than doubled, from $100 billion to $211 billion, despite rationing and the unavailability of many consumer goods such as cars, gasoline, and washing machines.

By 1945 government expenditures reached $98 billion—$90 billion over the 1936 New Deal peak of $8 billion. Interest rates were low, and the upward pressure on prices remained high, yet from 1943 to the end of the war the cost of living rose less than 1.5 percent. Following the war, as controls were removed, inflation peaked in 1948; union demands for higher wages accelerated. Between 1945 and 1952 confident Americans, and their growing families, increased consumer-credit by 800 percent.

During the war key New Deal labor concessions were retained, including a 40-hour week and time and a half for overtime. Manufacturing demands increased, the labor pool shrank, and wages and union membership rose. As war industry redistributed the population and the demand for labor, the Pacific Coast gained wealth and power, while the South was able to supply its people much-needed war jobs and provide blacks opportunities in fields previously closed to them. Women entered the workforce in unprecedented numbers, reaching 18 million. The net cash income of the American farmer soared 400 percent.

The war years' high employment was followed by the longest sustained period of peacetime prosperity in history. A decade of full employment and pent-up desire produced demands for consumer goods. Businesses of all sizes prospered. Veterans, using the GI Bill of

317

Rights, attended colleges in record numbers. Inflation was the most pressing economic problem, fueled by the Korean War and the Cold War expenditures for defense.

The glamour industries—chemicals, electrical appliances, and electronics—grew at astonishing rates, while the disposable per-capita income more than doubled. The average wage earner benefited more from the industrial system than at any time in national history. The 40-hour workweek became standard in manufacturing. In offices many workers were becoming accustomed to a 35-hour week. During the 1950s an average of seven million new cars and trucks were sold annually. By 1952 two-thirds of all families owned a television set; home freezers and high-fidelity stereo phonographs were considered necessities. Specialized markets developed to meet the consumer needs of such groups as backpackers, amateur photographers, and pet lovers. The adolescent market came of age: shopping malls, supermarkets, and credit cards assumed key roles in the American lifestyle.

By 1960 at least half of all existing dwellings had been built since World War II. Because of Federal Housing Administration and Veterans' Housing Administration programs, a majority of Americans owned their own homes for the first time in the twentieth century. In response to the need for interstate highways, the federal government encouraged the movement from city to suburb. The plan to develop 41,000 miles of highway facilitated the distribution of goods nationally, making national advertising more economical and the concept of a national economy a reality.

Government took on a new role. Following the Korean War, spending remained higher than the 1950 post-World War II low of $45 billion. By 1957 federal spending topped $82 billion—more than half for defense. Big government no longer implied socialism. When Health Education and Welfare secretary Oveta Culp Hobby opposed the free distribution of the polio vaccine as backdoor socialism, the public outcry forced her resignation.

Change was rampant and uneven. By 1950, 25 percent of American wives worked outside the home; by 1960 the number had risen to 40 percent. Scientific innovations and overproduction forced out the small farmer in favor of agribusiness. Up to one-third of the population lived below the government's poverty level, largely overlooked in the midst of prosperity. The Supreme Court's *Brown v. Board of Education* decision to end the "separate but equal" doctrine produced opposition and future opportunities but little immediate equality.

Year	Dollar Value in 2019
1940	$18.30
1943	$14.81
1945	$14.23
1947	$11.49
1949	$10.76

Year	Dollar Value in 2019
1950	$10.63
1953	$9.59
1955	$9.56
1957	$9.12
1959	$8.80

Use this Currency Conversion chart to calculate what any time in the years listed would cost in 2019. Simply multiply the cost of that item by dollar amount in the chart. For example, if you know that a man's shirt cost $3.00 in 1950, multiply $3.00 by $10.63 to discover that that same man's shirt would cost $31.89 in 2019.

HISTORICAL SNAPSHOT 1940–1944

1940

- France, Belgium, the Netherlands, Luxembourg, Denmark, Norway, and Romania fall to Germans
- President Roosevelt's $8.4 billion budget includes $1.8 billion for defense
- 14.6 percent of workforce out of work
- First Social Security checks issued
- Gross National Product is $99 billion
- Arroyo Seco Parkway, first Los Angeles freeway, dedicated
- Chevrolet coupe sells for $659
- Goodyear Dow Corporation formed
- U.S. Blue Cross Insurance programs include 6 million subscribers
- Annual U.S. red-meat consumption reaches 142 pounds per capita
- 33 percent of all farms wired for electric power
- Ford introduces Lincoln Continental

1941

- President's $17.5 billion budget includes nearly $11 billion for defense
- Inflation increases general price level by 10 percent
- U.S. auto production reaches 3.3 million
- Quality Inns founded to franchise motel operations
- Daniel Gerber Fremont Canning Company sells a million cans of baby food weekly

- Cheerios introduced by General Mills
- U.S. food prices up by 61 percent over prewar prices
- Pearl Harbor attacked; U.S. enters war
- Germany declares war on U.S.

1942

- Office of Price Administration formed to control prices
- Tire rationing plan commences; gas rationing begins
- Paine, Webber, Jackson, & Curtis created
- Zinc-coated pennies issued by U.S. Mint
- Florida passes California as leading U.S. producer of oranges
- Kellogg introduces Raisin Bran
- Sunbeam bread introduced
- Maxwell House instant coffee has beginnings in soluble coffee for military's K rations
- Dannon yogurt introduced
- U.S. automobile production halted until 1945

1943

- President Roosevelt's $109 billion budget earmarks $100 billion for war effort
- Congress approves income-tax withholding from paychecks
- Rent controls imposed nationwide
- American Broadcasting Company (ABC) created by Lifesavers millionaire Edward Noble
- Zenith Radio Corporation introduces $40 hearing aid

- Americans rationed three pairs of shoes per year
- Meat rationing set at 28 ounces per week; meat production rises 50 percent
- Sale of sliced bread banned
- Russell Marker pioneers oral contraceptive, Syntex, S.A.

1944

- 176,000 Allied troops land at Normandy beaches; war continues
- President Roosevelt reelected to fourth term
- First automatic, general-purpose digital computer completed at Harvard
- Federal Highway Act establishes interstate highway system
- War costing United States $250 million per day
- GI Bill of Rights enacted to finance college educations for veterans; 4 percent home loans available with no down payment
- U.S. soybean production rises as new uses are found for bean
- Chiquita brand banana introduced
- U.S. grocers test self-service meat markets
- Gasoline averages 21 cents per gallon

A panoramic view of the Omaha beachhead after it was secured, sometime around mid-June 1944, at low tide. Allied forces invaded Normandy on June 6th, popularly known as D-Day. (via Wikimedia Commons)

SELECTED INCOME 1940–1944

Job	Source	Description	Pay
Actress	*Screen Guide* (1941)	Per picture payment to child movie star Carolyn Lee, featured in movie *Virginia*	$10,000
Actor	*Screen Guide* (1941)	Weekly pay of movie actor Henry Fonda	$1,500
Actor	Miller, *The Great Cowboy Stars of Movies and Television* (1979)	Annual income of Gene Autry, King of the Cowboys, in 1941	$600,000
Alderman	*The World Almanac* (1943)	Salary of Chicago Mayor Edward Kelly	$16,200
Army Nurse	*The World Almanac* (1943)	Annual base pay	$1,080
Barber	*Chicago Tribune* (1943)	Steady; good hair cutter; 70% straight; guarantee	$50/wk
Bar Maid	*New Orleans Times-Picayune* (1941)	Colored girl; experienced bar maid and waitress; room and board included	$5 per week
Bartender	*New Orleans Times-Picayune* (1943)	Night work; meals	$25 week
Baseball Player	Victor Bondi, ed., *American Decades: 1940–1949* (1995)	Earnings of New York Yankee Joe DiMaggio in 1941	$35,000
Body Man	*Chicago Tribune* (1941)	Experienced to take over growing body shop	$35/wk
Bookkeeper	*New York Times* (1940)	Full charge; 50–55 year; Scot preferred; good health; non-drinker; able to type; permanent; send details: experience, personal photo (nonreturnable), own handwriting	$20/wk
Bookkeeper	*Greenville Piedmont* (Greenville, SC) (1943)	Male	$2600/yr
Bookkeeper/Office Manager	*New York Times* (1943)	Able to prepare weekly payrolls; 300 men for building subcontractor; keep complete double-entry records	$50/wk
Buffer	*New York Times* (1944)	Plastic	$1 plus/hr
Buyer	*New York Times* (1944)	Assistant trimming buyer, dresses	$50/wk
Cabinet Member	*The World Almanac* (1942)	Annual salary of Department of Justice Solicitor General Charles Fahy	$10,000
Carpenters	*New Orleans Times-Picayune* (1941)	Residential construction; steady work; state experience	$.80 per hour
Clerk (Payroll)	*New York Times* (1943)	40–50 years; experienced	$28/wk
Compositor	*New York Times* (1944)	A-1 man; 48 hrs	$65/wk

Job	Source	Description	Pay
Cook	*New York Times* (1944)	Girls for griddle	$30/wk to start
Cook/Gardener	*New York Times* (1942)	Couple; young cook-houseworker; gardener-houseman; drives	$175/mo
Counter Girl	*New York Times* (1944)	For soda fountain, experienced; 5 1/2 day wk	$35/wk
Dance Instructor	*New York Times* (1944)	Men to teach dancing; no experience	$35–$40/mo
Delivery Man	*The State* (Columbia, SC) (1943)	Colored boy or man	$15/wk
Electrician	*Chicago Tribune* (1943)	Young man 25 to 35 to train for responsible job in electrical industry; must be high-school graduate; night shift; 48-hr wk. Salary during 2-wk training $44.20	$50.83/wk
Elevator Operator	*New York Times* (1944)	Days, Union hrs	$125/mo
Elevator Relief Man	*New York Times* (1944)	18 or over	$122.50/mo
Engineer	*New York Times* (1940)	Wire machinery	$90/mo
Engineer-Draftsman	*Chicago Tribune* (1943)	Long program; 60-hr wk, out of town, all expenses; plant layout; mechanical structural; top men only; confidential	$2.00–$2.50/hr
Factory Girl	*Chicago Tribune* (1941)	Polish or Italian, no experience	$14/wk
Factory War Work	*New York Times* (1943)	Girl, no experience necessary, steady	$25/wk to start
Factory Worker	*Chicago Tribune* (1943)	All trades; men for shops and factories	$40–$50/wk
Factory Workers	*New Orleans Times-Picayune* (1943)	Alert white girls; active elderly women; experience unnecessary; light factory work; 8 hours; half pay for over 40 hours	$2.40 per day
File Clerk	*New York Times* (1943)	Young, personable, thoroughly experienced to organize and maintain files; attractive position, Radio City	$30–35/wk
File Clerk	*New York Times* (1944)	Clerk and typist; 5 days; congenial office	$27/wk to start
Food Handler	*Chicago Tribune* (1943)	You can make more in factory, but this is permanent and living conditions ideal	$50/mo
Hospital Chef	*Chicago Tribune* (1941)	Room and board included	$85/mo
Housekeeper	*New York Times* (1942)	Girl, colored; 5 mornings; references	$6.50/wk
Housekeeper	*New York Times* (1942)	Irish; good cook; excellent references	$80–85/mo
Investigator	*New York Times* (1940)	Beginner with car; 24–28; sales exp; Queens res; H. S. Grad	$140/mo
Judge	*The World Almanac* (1943)	Annual salary of New York City Court Judge Joseph Keller	$17,000
Leather-Goods Workers	*New York Times* (1944)	Experienced; desk pads and sets; 52-hr wk	$65/wk
Leather Sander	*New York Times* (1944)	Man, inexperienced, for leather sanding	$39/wk

Job	Source	Description	Pay
Library Clerk	*Chicago Tribune* (1943)	Young girl for clerical duties in business library; no experience necessary; 5-day wk, 37 1/2 hrs	$25/wk
Machinist	*New York Times* (1944)	First-class; 10 years' experience; 47 1/2 hrs, 5-day wk	$75/wk
Maid	*Chicago Tribune* (1943)	Temporary; colored; 8 hrs	$3/day
Maid-Cleaner	*Chicago Tribune* (1943)	No experience necessary, for north side unfurnished apt. bldg.	$70/mo
Maid-Cook	*Chicago Tribune* (1941)	White; light laundry; gentle family; references; private room	$15/wk
Metallurgist	*New York Times* (1940)	Inorganic analysis	$25–$30/wk
Miscellaneous	*New York Times* (1940)	Boys, 17 yrs old; production department of publishers' reps; experience unnec.	$120/mo
Mother's Helper	*New York Times* (1940)	Schoolgirl mother's helper through vacation	$100/mo
Movie Producer	Catherine Legrand and Robyn Karney, *Chronicle of the Cinema* (1995)	Salary of Orson Welles to produce, direct, write, and appear in the movie Citizen Kane in 1940	$100,000

Citizen Kane was a box office faillure when it was released in 1941. William Randolph Hearst, on whom the title character is based, used his money and influence to limit the release of the film. Hearst's influence in Hollywood resulted in Welles and the film being booed at the 1941 Academy Awars. Citizen Kane is now considered one of, if not the greatest American movie of all time. (via Wikimedia Commons)

Job	Source	Description	Pay
Movie Star	*Screen Guide* (1941)	Weekly pay of actress Judy Garland, star of *The Wizard of Oz*	$2,500
Musicians	Bufwack and Oermann, *Finding Her Voice, The Saga of Women in Country Music* (1993)	Nightly income of *The Texas Playboys* for Saturday night concerts on Pacific Ocean Piers in Los Angeles in 1943	$20,000
Navy Commander	*The World Almanac* (1943)	1942 annual base pay if less than 30 years of service	$3,500
Nurse	*New York Times* (1944)	Reg. charge; small nursing home	$150/mo
Nurse Trainee	*Chicago Tribune* (1943)	Girl who would like to work in doctor's office, room, board	$60/mo
Nursemaid	*New York Times* (1942)	Trained young adult lady; child; days; sleep out	$30/wk
Order Clerk	*New York Times* (1943)	Spanish-English order clerk for long-established firm, representing Latin-American and other foreign publications; pleasant	$120/mo
Order Fillers	*New York Times* (1944)	Girls as order fillers; 5 days 40 hrs	$21/wk
Page Girl	*New York Times* (1944)	Page Girls and messengers	$20–$25/wk
Painter	Steven Naifeh and Gregory White Smith, *Jackson Pollock: An American Saga* (1989)	Monthly income of Jackson Pollock from promoter Pegg Guggenheim's *Art of This Century* gallery in 1943	$150
Pantry Girl	*Chicago Tribune* (1943)	Experienced to work in loop restaurant	$25/wk and meals
Parking	*New Orleans Times-Picayune* (1943)	Young men; 16 or over	$16 wk
Pressman	*New Orleans Times-Picayune* (1943)	Regular jobs; no extra work; 48 hours	$54.60
Pressers	*New Orleans Times-Picayune* (1943)	Women; experienced in wool, linen, silk; steady work assured	$3 per day
Racehorse	Bondi, ed., *American Decades: 1940–1949* (1995)	Earnings for *Pensive* in 1944 *Preakness*	$60,075
Receptionist	*Chicago Tribune* (1943)	Doctor's office	$65/mo
Record Clerk	*Chicago Tribune* (1943)	40-hr wk; no experience necessary if willing to learn; must be neat penman and be able to use typewriter some	$20/wk
Sales	*Chicago Tribune* (1943)	Every home, every store, tavern, business needs 1 or more of this item. You don't have to be a fancy talker	$25/wk
Sales	*Chicago Tribune* (1943)	Follow-up post cards mailed to old accounts; wearing apparel advance comm	$50–$75/wk
Salesman	*New Orleans Times-Picayune* (1943)	Real estate salesman; must own car	$250–$500 per month
Stenographer	*New York Times* (1943)	English-Spanish steno	Up to $45/wk

Job	Source	Description	Pay
Teachers	*The State* (Columbia, SC) (1943)	One teacher for 9th- and 10th-grade industrial arts and aclass in carpentry; college graduate preferred but not necessary	$175/mo
Telephone Solicitor	*New York Times* (1942)	Young man wanted, under 30, with some college education for soliciting of advertising for established publication.	$23.50/wk
Tracers and Letterers	*New York Times* (1940)	Bring samples	$1,200/yr
20-Pin Boys	*Chicago Tribune* (1943)	16 years or over. $0.08 a line.	Up to $10/day
Union President	*The Scribner Encyclopedia of American Lives*, 1987	Annual salary of James Petrillo, president of the American Federation of Musicians in 1941	$46,000
U. S. President	*The World Almanac* (1943)	Annual salary of U. S. President Franklin Delano Roosevelt	$75,000
U. S. Vice President	*The World Almanac* (1943)	Annual salary of U. S. Vice President Henry Wallace	$15,000
Waitress	*New Orleans Times-Picayune*(1943)	Experienced; active; intelligent; first class	$.30/hr. plus tips $35–$50 week
Waitress	*New York Times* (1940)	Neat arm service; small tips	$3.50/day
Writer	Bondi, ed., *American Decades: 1940–1949* (1995)	Payment to writer Edna Ferber for movie rights to her unpublished novel *Saratoga Trunk* in 1941	$175,000

CONSUMER EXPENDITURES 1940–1944

Expenditure Type	(Per Capita)				
	1940	1941	1942	1943	1944
Clothing	$46.93	$53.22	$63.03	$76.79	$83.82
Food	$152.13	$174.66	$210.59	$242.79	$265.18
Auto Usage	$45.41	$53.97	$26.69	$21.21	$21.68
New Auto Purchase	$15.89	$19.49	74¢	73¢	72¢
Auto Parts	$3.78	$5.25	$2.22	$2.93	$2.89
Gas & Oil	$17.41	$19.49	$19.28	$9.51	$10.12
Housing	$73.42	$77.96	$83.05	$86.29	$88.87
Furniture	$8.33	$9.74	$9.64	$8.78	$9.39
Utilities	$25.73	$26.99	$28.92	$29.98	$30.35
Telephone & Telegraph	$4.54	$5.25	$5.93	$7.31	$7.95
Physicians	$6.81	$7.49	$7.42	$8.04	$9.39
Dentists	$3.03	$3.75	$3.71	$3.66	$4.34
Health Insurance	$1.50	$1.49	$1.48	$2.19	$2.17
Personal Business	$24.22	$25.49	$25.21	$27.06	$28.18
Personal Care	$7.57	$8.99	$10.38	$11.70	$13.01
Tobacco	$14.38	$15.74	$17.05	$19.01	$18.71
Local Transport	$6.81	$7.49	$7.42	$8.04	$12.02
Intercity Transport	$3.03	$2.99	$5.19	$7.31	$7.95
Recreation	$28.76	$31.48	$34.85	$39.49	$39.02
Religion/Welfare Activities	$8.33	$8.25	$9.64	$10.97	$12.28
Private Education & Research	$5.29	$5.25	$5.93	$7.31	$7.23
Per-Capita Consumption	$537.38	$605.69	$656.98	$727.66	$781.81

INVESTMENTS 1940-1944

Investment	1940	1941	1942	1943	1944
Basic Yield, One-Year Corporate Bonds	.41	.41	.81	1.17	1.08
Short-Term Interest Rates, 4–6 Months, Prime Commercial Paper	.56	.53	.66	.69	.73
Basic Yield, Common Stocks, Total	5.31	6.25	6.67	4.89	4.81
Index of Common Stocks (1941 2 1943 5 10)	11.02	9.82	8.67	11.50	12.47

COMMON STOCKS, CLOSING PRICE AND YIELD, FIRST BUSINESS DAY OF YEAR

(PARENTHETICAL NUMBER IS ANNUAL DIVIDENDS IN DOLLARS)

	1940	1941	1942	1943	1944
Allis Chalmers	41	36 3/4	30 3/8	26 3/4	38 1/4
	(1.25)	(1.50)	(1.50)	(1)	(1.25)
AT&T	171 7/8	168 3/8	132 1/4	128 1/4	156 1/8
	(9)	(9)	(9)	(9)	(9)
American Tobacco	86 3/4	70 3/4	47 1/2	42 1/8	57 1/2
	(5)w	(5)	(4.50)	(3.25)	(3.25)
Anaconda	30 3/4	27 1/8	28 1/8	24 3/8	25
	(1.25)	(2)	(2.50)	(2.50)	(2.50)
B&O	6 1/4	3 1/2	3 1/2	3 3/8	5 1/2
	(/)	(/)	(/)	(/)	(/)
Bethlehem Steel	82	89	66 1/4	56 3/8	56 1/2
	(1.50)	(5)	(6)	(6)	(6)
Corn Products	64 3/4	44 3/8	55 1/4	55 7/8	55 1/2
	(3)	(3)	(3)	(2.80)	(2.60)
General Electric	40 3/4	34 1/4	28 1/4	30 3/4	37
	(1.40)	(1.85)	(1.75)	(1.40)	(1.40)
General Motors	34 7/8	48 1/4	32	44 1/2	52 1/8
	(1.60)	(3.75)	(3.75)	(2)	(2)
International Business Machines	196	160 1/2			173
(5% stock dividend, 4/1/40)	(6)	(6)			(6)
(5% stock dividend, 1/30/41)					
(5% stock dividend, 1/28/42)					
(5% stock dividend, 1/28/43)					
(5% stock dividend, 1/28/44)					
Intl Harvester	62 1/4	50 1/8	47 3/4	59 1/2	73
	(1.60)	(2.40)	(3.10)	(2.50)	(2.50)
National Biscuit	23 3/4	17 3/4	15 3/4	15 3/4	21 1/4
	(1.40)	(1.60)	(1.60)	(1.30)	(1.20)

Investment	1940	1941	1942	1943	1944
US Steel		70 3/8 (3)		47 7/8 (4)	50 1/4 (4)
Western Union		20 1/8 (1)		27 1/8 (2)	42 1/8 (2)

STANDARD JOBS 1940–1944

Job Type	1940	1941	1942	1943	1944
Average of All Industries, excl. farm labor	$1392/yr	$1561/yr	$1858/yr	$2181/yr	$2360/yr
Average of All Industries, incl. farm labor	$1315/yr	$1492/yr	$1778/yr	$2107/yr	$2292/yr
Bituminous Coal Mining	$1235/yr	$1500/yr	$1715/yr	$2115/yr	$2535/yr
Building Trades	$1330/yr	$1635/yr	$2191/yr	$2503/yr	$2602/yr
Domestics	$554/yr	$601/yr	$706/yr	$919/yr	$1140/yr
Farm Labor	$463/yr	$567/yr	$769/yr	$1002/yr	$1189/yr
Federal Civilian	$1894/yr	$1970/yr	$2265/yr	$2628/yr	$2677/yr
Federal Employees, Executive Depts.	$1125/yr	$1239/yr	$1632/yr	$1792/yr	$1929/yr
Federal Military	$1025/yr	$1113/yr	$1485/yr	$1565/yr	$1763/yr
Finance, Insurance, & Real Estate	$1725/yr	$1777/yr	$1885/yr	$2041/yr	$2191/yr
Gas & Electricity Workers	$1795/yr	$1870/yr	$2040/yr	$2284/yr	$2467/yr
Manufacturing, Durable Goods	$1568/yr	$1840/yr	$2292/yr	$2619/yr	$2774/yr
Manufacturing, Nondurable Goods	$1299/yr	$1440/yr	$1654/yr	$1895/yr	$2081/yr
Medical/Health Services Workers	$927/yr	$955/yr	$1036/yr	$1127/yr	$1262/yr
Miscellaneous Manufacturing	$2320/yr	$1380/yr	$1540/yr	$1882/yr	$2176/yr
Motion Picture Services	$1948/yr	$2016/yr	$2124/yr	$2250/yr	$2379/yr
Nonprofit Org. Workers	$1408/yr	$1379/yr	$1482/yr	$1679/yr	$1795/yr
Passenger Transportation Workers	$1559/yr	$1664/yr	$1990/yr	$2280/yr	$2458/yr
Local and Highway Personal Services	$1062/yr	$1095/yr	$1199/yr	$1386/yr	$1575/yr
Public School Teachers	$1435/yr	$1462/yr	$1512/yr	$1608/yr	$1730/yr
Radio Broadcasting & Television Workers	$2554/yr	$2581/yr	$2667/yr	$2929/yr	$3333/yr
Railroads	$1906/yr	$2030/yr	$2303/yr	$2585/yr	$2714/yr
State and Local Govt. Workers	$1497/yr	$1522/yr	$1574/yr	$1687/yr	$1797/yr
Telephone & Telegraph Workers	$1610/yr	$1633/yr	$1715/yr	$1878/yr	$2035/yr
Wholesale and Retail Trade Workers	$1382/yr	$1478/yr	$1608/yr	$1781/yr	$1946/yr

FOOD BASKET 1940–1944

Commodity	Year	New York	Atlanta	Chicago	Denver	Los Angeles
Apples, Fresh, per pound	1940	NR	NR	NR	NR	NR
	1941	5.90¢	5.40¢	5.80¢	5.90¢	7¢
	1942	7.10¢	6.30¢	7.40¢	8.10¢	7.50¢
	1943	10.10¢	10.50¢	11.90¢	12.60¢	10.70¢
	1944	11.10¢	11¢	11.80¢	12.40¢	11.40¢
Beans, Navy, per pound	1940	NR	NR	NR	NR	NR
	1941	9.90¢	6.90¢	9.90¢	6.40¢	8.60¢
	1942	10.70¢	8.80¢	9¢	7.90¢	10.60¢
	1943	11.30¢	9.60¢	9.90¢	9.50¢	11.10¢
	1944	11.90¢	10.10¢	10.40¢	10.30¢	11.90¢
Beef, Rib Roasts, per pound	1940	NR	NR	NR	NR	NR
	1941	32¢	29.50¢	32¢	27.20¢	34.40¢
	1942	34.20¢	34.10¢	34.50¢	33.60¢	37.60¢
	1943	36¢	33.50¢	34.60¢	34.10¢	36.70¢
	1944	33.60¢	31.70¢	33.30¢	32.40¢	33.90¢
Beef, Steaks (Round), per pound	1940	NR	NR	NR	NR	NR
	1941	41.20¢	35.80¢	38.10¢	34.80¢	38.40¢
	1942	45.40¢	40.70¢	40.90¢	39.80¢	43.30¢
	1943	45.70¢	41.60¢	41.40¢	40.20¢	42.30¢
	1944	42.80¢	40.20¢	39.90¢	39¢	41.60¢
Bread, White, per pound	1940	NR	NR	NR	NR	NR
	1941	9.20¢	9.20¢	7.10¢	7.30¢	7¢
	1942	9.60¢	10¢	7.30¢	7.90¢	7.90¢
	1943	9.60¢	9.80¢	7.60¢	8.60¢	8.10¢
	1944	9.40¢	9.80¢	7.70¢	8.40¢	8.30¢
Butter, per pound	1940	NR	NR	NR	NR	NR
	1941	41.90¢	41.70¢	40.50¢	41¢	42.30¢
	1942	48.10¢	47.90¢	46.20¢	49.10¢	48.70¢
	1943	53.10¢	52.40¢	52.10¢	52.60¢	54.10¢
	1944	50.10¢	49.80¢	49.90¢	50.60¢	51.30¢
Cheese, per pound	1940	NR	NR	NR	NR	NR
	1941	32¢	26.90¢	31.10¢	32.30¢	28.80¢
	1942	36.40¢	31.60¢	34.90¢	37.70¢	35.70¢
	1943	37.70¢	35.60¢	36.50¢	40.70¢	38.30¢
	1944	35.20¢	34.50¢	36.30¢	40.80¢	36.80¢
Chickens, per pound	1940	NR	NR	NR	NR	NR
	1941	34.30¢	27.10¢	32.20¢	29.40¢	34.10¢
	1942	40.10¢	32.40¢	39.90¢	37.40¢	41.30¢
	1943	45.20¢	41¢	44.20¢	40.90¢	47.50¢
	1944	45.40¢	40.70¢	45.30¢	40.60¢	44.30¢
Coffee, per pound	1940	NR	NR	NR	NR	NR
	1941	24.20¢	20.30¢	24.50¢	28.10¢	23¢
	1942	29.20¢	25.40¢	29.20¢	31.60¢	28.10¢
	1943	30.30¢	28.60¢	30.40¢	34.60¢	29.50¢
	1944	30.30¢	31.20¢	30.80¢	34.40¢	29.70¢
Cornmeal, per pound	1940	NR	NR	NR	NR	NR
	1941	6.40¢	2.60¢	5.90¢	4.50¢	4.80¢
	1942	6.70¢	3.40¢	6.50¢	5.90¢	6.40¢
	1943	6.50¢	4.80¢	6.10¢	5.90¢	6.40¢
	1944	6.80¢	5.50¢	6.40¢	6.30¢	8.40¢

Commodity	Year	New York	Atlanta	Chicago	Denver	Los Angeles
Eggs, per dozen	1940	NR	NR	NR	NR	NR
	1941	45.30¢	36¢	38.90¢	33.90¢	39¢
	1942	54.60¢	43.70¢	46.50¢	44.40¢	47.20¢
	1943	60.80¢	53.70¢	57.20¢	54.50¢	57.70¢
	1944	58.50¢	50.80¢	54.60¢	53.10¢	56.10¢
Flour, Wheat, per pound	1940	NR	NR	NR	NR	NR
	1941	5.16¢	5.01¢	4.51¢	4.18¢	4.22¢
	1942	5.74¢	5.90¢	5.28¢	4.72¢	4.96¢
	1943	6.19¢	6.86¢	5.78¢	5.30¢	6.04¢
	1944	6.47¢	7.11¢	6.18¢	5.53¢	6.60¢
Lard, per pound	1940	NR	NR	NR	NR	NR
	1941	13.70¢	12.10¢	12.90¢	12.90¢	13.60¢
	1942	18.10¢	16.20¢	17.30¢	17.70¢	18.40¢
	1943	19.40¢	18.80¢	19.40¢	19¢	20.20¢
	1944	18.50¢	18.70¢	19.30¢	19.20¢	20¢
Milk, Fresh, per quart	1940	NR	NR	NR	NR	NR
	1941	15.70¢	15.20¢	14.50¢	12¢	12.80¢
	1942	16.90¢	16.20¢	16.60¢	13.20¢	14.70¢
	1943	17.40¢	17¢	17.50¢	13.60¢	14.50¢
	1944	17¢	17¢	15.50¢	13.70¢	14.50¢
Molasses, per 18-oz can	1940	NR	NR	NR	NR	NR
	1941	14.40¢	13.80¢	14.20¢	11.60¢	11.20¢
	1942	15.70¢	14.90¢	15.80¢	13.30¢	12.90¢
	1943	16.30¢	14.60¢	16.10¢	15.50¢	15.90¢
	1944	16.20¢	14.90¢	16.40¢	15.50¢	16.50¢
Mutton and Lamb, Leg, per pound	1940	NR	NR	NR	NR	NR
	1941	29.10¢	29.90¢	30.10¢	28.20¢	30.40¢
	1942	34.90¢	34¢	34.50¢	35.10¢	36.20¢
	1943	40.70¢	37.40¢	38.10¢	38¢	39.50¢
	1944	39.90¢	38¢	38.70¢	37¢	39.90¢
Pork, Bacon, Sliced, per pound	1940	NR	NR	NR	NR	NR
	1941	34.40¢	34.40¢	36.90¢	36.20¢	37.80¢
	1942	41.40¢	38.80¢	40.90¢	42.80¢	43.50¢
	1943	43.20¢	38.80¢	40.90¢	42.80¢	43.50¢
	1944	40.20¢	40.80¢	41.30¢	43¢	42.60¢
Pork, Chops, per pound	1940	NR	NR	NR	NR	NR
	1941	34.90¢	32.10¢	35.10¢	31.70¢	39.50¢
	1942	41.50¢	37.50¢	41.60¢	41¢	48.20¢
	1943	49.20¢	39.10¢	39.70¢	40.20¢	48.20¢
	1944	38¢	37.80¢	36.80¢	38¢	38.60¢
Pork, Ham, Sliced, per pound	1940	NR	NR	NR	NR	NR
	1941	50.10¢	47.90¢	50.70¢	51¢	62.10¢
	1942	58.20¢	56.10¢	58.60¢	61.50¢	67.60¢
	1943	54.90¢	54.60¢	55¢	56.20¢	60.50¢
	1944	48.30¢	50¢	50.80¢	51¢	53.40¢
Pork, Salt, per pound	1940	NR	NR	NR	NR	NR
	1941	27.30¢	17.90¢	21.50¢	19.20¢	21.10¢
	1942	30.70¢	22.30¢	25.50¢	24.80¢	24.90¢
	1943	26.20¢	23.20¢	23.80¢	23.70¢	26¢
	1944	24.10¢	22.50¢	22.20¢	22.20¢	23.10¢
Potatoes, Irish, per 15 pounds	1940	NR	NR	NR	NR	NR
	1941	37.30¢	37.90¢	39.90¢	32.20¢	36.70¢
	1942	50.80¢	54.20¢	56.80¢	51.80¢	62.60¢
	1943	68.30¢	69.60¢	70.80¢	59.30¢	68.40¢
	1944	68.10¢	70.90¢	74¢	64.30¢	70.30¢

Commodity	Year	New York	Atlanta	Chicago	Denver	Los Angeles
Prunes, Dried, per pound	1940	NR	NR	NR	NR	NR
	1941	10.20¢	8.30¢	10.80¢	10¢	8.30¢
	1942	13.30¢	11.80¢	14.50¢	14.10¢	13.50¢
	1943	13.30¢	11.80¢	14.50¢	16.10¢	16.70¢
	1944	16.70¢	15.80¢	18.50¢	16.80¢	16¢
Rice, per pound	1940	NR	NR	NR	NR	NR
	1941	8.70¢	9.10¢	8.30¢	8.20¢	9.40¢
	1942	12¢	12.80¢	12.80¢	11.10¢	12.80¢
	1943	12.70¢	12.80¢	12.90¢	12.30¢	13.40¢
	1944	13.40¢	12.40¢	12.90¢	12¢	13.50¢
Sugar, per pound	1940	NR	NR	NR	NR	NR
	1941	5.54¢	5.46¢	5.83¢	6.43¢	5.52¢
	1942	6.60¢	6.40¢	6.90¢	7.90¢	6.70¢
	1943	6.60¢	6.50¢	6.90¢	7.90¢	6.80¢
	1944	6.50¢	6.40¢	7¢	7.40¢	6.80¢
Tea, per pound	1940	NR	NR	NR	NR	NR
	1941	75.60¢	75.60¢	81.60¢	90.80¢	77.60¢
	1942	90¢	91.20¢	95.20¢	$1.0040	89.60¢
	1943	89.20¢	96.40¢	92.40¢	$1.0080	94.40¢
	1944	91.20¢	98.80¢	99.60¢	$1.0720	$1.00
Veal, per pound	1940	NR	NR	NR	NR	NR
	1941	52.80¢	45.90¢	46.40¢	42.30¢	52.30¢
	1942	58.90¢	51.80¢	50.40¢	48.20¢	59.10¢
	1943	52.40¢	46.80¢	47.10¢	44.70¢	53.10¢
	1944	45¢	43.70¢	43.10¢	42.30¢	46.30¢

SELECTED PRICES 1940–1944

Item	Source	Description	Price
ALCOHOL			
Blended Whiskey	*I. Ginsberg Inc. Price List* (1940)	*Seagram's*	$2.70/fifth
Blended Whiskey	*I. Ginsberg Inc. Price List* (1940)	*Seagram's V.O.*	$3.75/fifth
Bourbon	*I. Ginsberg Inc. Price List* (1940)	*Seagram's Five Year*	$3.80/fifth
Cordial	*I. Ginsberg Inc. Price List* (1940)	*Silk Hat*	$1.15/pint
Corn Whiskey	*I. Ginsberg Inc. Price List* (1940)	*Mountain*	$2/quart
Gin	*I. Ginsberg Inc. Price List* (1940)	*Crescent Denby Club*	$1.60/quart
Gin	*I. Ginsberg Inc. Price List* (1940)	*Seagram's King Arthur*	$1.70/fifth
Whiskey	*I. Ginsberg Inc. Price List* (1940)	*Carstairs Blended*	$2.95/fifth
Whiskey	*I. Ginsberg Inc. Price List* (1940)	*Kessler's Private Blend*	$2/fifth
Whiskey	*I. Ginsberg Inc. Price List* (1940)	*Owings Mills Red Moon Corn*	$1.57/quart
Whiskey	*I. Ginsberg Inc. Price List* (1940)	*Seagram's Ancient Bottle Straight Rye*	$3.80/fifth
Whiskey	*I. Ginsberg Inc. Price List* (1940)	*Seagram's Five Crown Blended*	$2.25/fifth
Whiskey	*New York Times* (1940)	*York House Scotch*; outsells the next best-selling famous-label Scotch in Macy's Best Cellar by 8 to 1	$2.79/fifth
APPAREL, CHILDREN'S			
Pants	*Sears, Roebuck* (1941)	Sanforized cool tropicals	$1.19
Pants	*Life Magazine* (1942)	*Kleinert's Softex Pad Pants*; refill pads, completely disposable, are the modern solution to the old-fashioned diaper problem	$0.60
Shoes	*Sears, Roebuck* (1941)	*Classic Saddle*; we don't need to tell you about saddle oxfords	$1.69
Slacks	*Sears, Roebuck* (1941)	Leisure coat and slacks; the style hit of the season	$3.98
APPAREL, MEN'S			
Hats	*Chicago Tribune* (1943)	Dobbs, Stetson and Lee	$5 to $20

Item	Source	Description	Price
Raincoat	*Life Magazine* (1942)	*Rainfair The Grafton;* for businessmen; a fine-quality pied-mont gabardine	$11.50
Shirt	*Chicago Tribune* (1943)	*Arrow White;* magic for any man's appearance—with a variety of collar styles	$2.75
Shoes	*Liberty* (1944)	*Air-o-Magic* shoes for men; hand-moulded innersoles	$6.00 to $7.50
Shoes	*Life Magazine* (1942)	*Winthrop;* action free shoes with a military-type strap oxford, full-leather lined	$9.50
Shoes	*Life Magazine* (1942)	*Roblee;* kodiak brown; harness stitched; overlay blucher; double sole	$6.00
Shoes	*Consumer Reports* (1943)	Thom McAn	$4.20
Shoes	*Consumer Reports* (1943)	Towncraft	$4.79
Sports Jacket	*New York Times* (1940)	*Bloomingdale's;* large selection of wool tweeds and shetlands in shades of blue, grey, brown, and green	$15.00
Suit	*Chicago Tribune* (1941)	*Gulfstream's;* famous gabardine and tropical weaves	$7.95
Tie	*The Saturday Evening Post* (1941)	*Arrow;* as outstanding as Arrow shirts	$1.00
Tie	*Majestic Theatre Program* (1942)	*Arrow;* smart, neat patterns and stripes plus rich fabrics; then, they make the perfect knots	$1/$1.50/$2

APPAREL, WOMEN'S

Item	Source	Description	Price
Brassiere	*Majestic Theatre Program* (1942)	*Model Brassieres;* bias cup; be sure your bra really fits—buy your personal cup depth	$1.00
Brassiere	*Life Magazine* (1942)	*Carole;* wears, gives the beauty and style of a $1 brassiere	$0.59
Brassiere	*Majestic Theatre Program* (1942)	*Bali;* in tea rose, white, black nylon	$1.50 to $5.00
Coats	*Chicago Tribune* (1943)	Tweeds, shetlands, herringbones, fleece, twills, gabardines	$20.00
Dress	*New York Times* (1940)	*Knight in Armor;* our gilt-girdled rayon jersey	$22.75
Dress	*Chicago Tribune* (1941)	Vacation sensation; every one of our entire stock of frocks in that famous carefree fabric	$4.45
Dress	*Chicago Tribune* (1941)	*Russeks Prints;* rayon jerseys, rayon crepes; formerly $29.95–$69.95	$21.00
Dress	*Chicago Tribune* (1943)	*Carson, Pirie Scott & Co.;* a simple tailored dress . . . but not so plain as to be uninteresting and dignified without being mature	$7.95
Fur Coat	*New York Times* (1943)	Muskrat; beautiful in its own right, an impressive imitator . . . hardy, reliable, flattering	$245
Fur Coat	*New York Times* (1943)	*John Wanamaker;* silvery, radiant beaver . . . a subtle flatterer and a congenial companion to casual and formal costumes alike	$595
Fur Coat	*Chicago Tribune* (1943)	Persian lamb; from stock or made to measure	$259

Rita Hayworth poses in a Persian lamb coat by Hollander Furs, 1943. (via Wikimedia Commons)

Item	Source	Description	Price
Gloves	*Life Magazine* (1942)	*Kayser;* double-wearing leatherette glove, double-woven cotton at a single-woven price	$2.50
Handbag	*Chicago Tribune* (1943)	*Edgewood;* bold banner stripe	$5.00
Handkerchief	*Chicago Tribune* (1943)	Lace; delicately feminine are these petite wisps of linen and cotton; finely edged in lace to carry your Easter wishes	$0.25
Hostess Pajamas	*New York Times* (1943)	*Henri Bendel;* cool, flattering, at ease . . . just right for summer teas and supper; gay flower print; of silk and rayon; white background	$45.00
Jerkin	*Sears, Roebuck* (1941)	Gay candy stripes perk up any costume	$0.89
Purse	*Liberty* (1944)	*The Shopper;* the pocket-size purse for the woman with her hands full; includes federal tax	$3.60
Shoes	*Majestic Theatre Program* (1942)	*Anoxnia Deluxe;* women's footwear forerunners for the spring mode; it is never too early to refresh your style	$5.98
Shoes	*Life* (1942)	*Enna Jetticks Shoes, Inc.;* Mae Style	$6.00
Shoes	*Life* (1942)	*Enna Jetticks Shoes, Inc. Phyllis Style;* for mother	$6.00
Shoes	*Chicago Tribune* (1943)	*Red Cross;* the Cupid Bow pump; beauty in gabardine	$6.95
Shoes	*Chicago Tribune* (1943)	Black gabardine tie with embroidered eyelets and a tip of patent; a beautiful shoe	$10.95
Slacks Suit	*Chicago Tribune* (1941)	*Rothley;* with new longer-fitted jackets	$6.95
Slacks	*Sears, Roebuck* (1941)	Wool; styles combine classic perfection with new brands of fashion	$2.98
Slips	*Majestic Theatre Program* (1942)	*Miss Swank Exclusive;* straight-plus-bias ends riding and twisting	$2.25 to $7.00
Sports Coat	*Sears, Roebuck* (1941)	We've put gores or pleats and new trims in every one; cut them beautifully, lined them with rich rayon twill	$7.98
Stockings	*The State* (Columbia, SC) (1940)	*Saxon-Cullum No-Mend Silk;* with silk prices up, this sale is more important to you than ever	$0.98
Suit	*Chicago Tribune* (1941)	Our loveliest of all chambray suits for town and country!	$17.95
Suit	*Chicago Tribune* (1943)	*Rothmoor;* of fine all-wool fabrics	$39.95
Wash frocks	*Sears, Roebuck* (1941)	A famous label with a matchless guarantee; $1 value	$0.79

APPLIANCES

Item	Source	Description	Price
Alarm Clock	*Better Homes and Gardens* (1940)	*Westclox Country Club;* electric; for any room in the house; luminous dial; ivory finish	$3.45
Coffee Percolator	*Liberty* (1944)	Vaculator gives you an insurance policy; make the world's finest cup of coffee	$2.95
Deep Freezer	*Better Homes and Gardens* (1940)	*Motor Products Corporation;* electric; allows right at home the large quantity, frozen-food storage some families enjoy in lock systems	$225
Heater	*Better Homes and Gardens* (1940)	*Arvin Electric;* fan-forced; circulating; standard Model 101; 10" high, green enamel finish	$6.95

Item	Source	Description	Price
Home Incinerator	*Better Homes and Gardens* (1940)	*The Majestic Co.;* just connect to your furnace flue—costs nothing to operate	$29.95
Iron	*Better Homes and Gardens* (1940)	*Knapp-Monarch Co. Steam King;* fully automatic, irons with steam and can be used for dry cleaning	$12.95
Mixer	*Better Homes and Gardens* (1940)	*Kitchen-Aid;* superior food mixing; with juicer	$29.95
Mixer	*Better Homes and Gardens* (1940)	*Sunbeam MixMaster;* lighter, higher cakes due to even mixing and greater aeration; complete with juicer West of Denver	$23.75 $24.50
Oil Burner	*Better Homes and Gardens* (1940)	*General Electric;* can be installed in as short a time as one day; clean, quiet, odorless, fully automatic, easy on oil	$268
Range	*Better Homes and Gardens* (1940)	*Frigidaire;* at last I can afford an electric range; super-sized twin-unit oven, speed-heat cooking units, high-speed broiler	$100
Washing Machine	*Better Homes and Gardens* (1940)	*Maytag;* available in white or gray finish, with or without water discharge pump	$59.95

BABY PRODUCTS

Item	Source	Description	Price
Flannelettes	*Sears, Roebuck* (1941)	Sanforized shrunk; medium-heavyweight embroidered	$0.29
Gown	*Sears, Roebuck* (1941)	*Roly Poly;* combed cotton gown, commended by *Parents Magazine*	$0.47
Training Pants	*Sears, Roebuck* (1941)	The quickest easiest way to teach good habits	$0.13

BUSINESS EQUIPMENT & SUPPLIES

Item	Source	Description	Price
Fountain Pen	*Liberty* (1944)	*Sheaffer's Lifetime Triumph* model pen; 14 karat gold sheath point	$15.00
Typewriter	*Sears, Roebuck* (1941)	Office machine efficiency, portable convenience	$64.50
Typewriter	*Sears, Roebuck* (1941)	*Underwood New Deluxe;* model list price $39.50	$29.75

COLLECTIBLES

Item	Source	Description	Price
Furniture	*American Collector* (1942)	Bow front mahogany Hepplewhite chest of drawers, original with exception of brasses; The Loft, West Chester, Pennsylvania	$125

EDUCATION

Item	Source	Description	Price
Fee	*New York Times* (1940)	Business school; shorthand, beginners, review, typing, stenotypists, reporting	$1/week

ENTERTAINMENT

Item	Source	Description	Price
Concert Ticket	*New York Times* (1943)	Benny Goodman and his orchestra; Hotel Astor; Friday and Saturday	$1.25
Concert Ticket	*New York Times* (1944)	Philadelphia Orchestra; Ormandy conducting	$1.20 to $4.20

Item	Source	Description	Price
Movie Ticket	*New York Times* (1940)	*Gone with the Wind;* air conditioned; Little Carnegie	$1.10
Movie Ticket	*New York Times* (1940)	*The Doctor Takes A Wife;* Loretta Young, Ray Milland; plus big stage show; Roxy	$0.25
Movie Ticket	*Chicago Tribune* (1941)	*Wagons Roll at Night;* Humphrey Bogart; State-Lake Before 6:30 After 6:30	$0.25 $0.40
Movie Ticket	*Chicago Tribune* (1941)	Two features; *That Hamilton Woman* and *The Great American Broadcast;* Oriental; Days Evenings	$0.25 $0.40
Movie Ticket	*New York Times* (1942)	*My Gal Sal;* Rita Hayworth, Victor Mature, Carole Landis; 10:30 a.m. to 5:00 p.m.; Albee	$0.30
Opera Ticket	*New York Times* (1944)	*La Bohéme;* NY City Center Opera Co.	$0.75 to $2.00
Play Ticket	*Majestic Theatre* (1942)	*Lily of the Valley;* Windsor Theatre Matinees Evenings	$0.55 to $1.65 $0.55 to $2.20
Play Ticket	*New York Times* (1942)	*Porgy & Bess;* by DuBose Heyward; one of the finest things in the American theater; Majestic	$2.75
Play Ticket	*New York Times* (1944)	*The Streets Are Guarded;* by Laurence Stallings; Henry Miller's	$1.20–$3.60
Theater Ticket	*New York Times* (1944)	*Carmen Jones;* the lowest-price major musical on Broadway	$3.00

ENTERTAINMENT, HOME

Item	Source	Description	Price
Board Game	*Liberty* (1944)	*Ouija* board; a spine-tingling, electrifying game	$2.00
Camera	*Sears, Roebuck* (1941)	*Eastman Brownie;* compact, easy to operate	$2.56
Home Movie	*Life Magazine* (1942)	*Castle Films; African Pygmy Thrills;* Africa's tiny pygmies, menaced always by vicious man-eating crocodiles; own this astounding movie now 8mm 16mm	 $5.50 $8.75
Record	*Majestic Theatre Program* (1942)	*Decca;* the glorious Gershwin *Porgy and Bess;* four 12" records	 $4.72
Recording Combination	*Better Homes and Gardens* (1940)	*Glamor-tone;* all in one 18" cabinet are radio, phonograph, and home-recording device	$34.50
Recording Disks	*Better Homes and Gardens* (1940)	*Crosley Glameton;* 8" size in cartons of 5	$1.50/carton

FARM EQUIPMENT & SUPPLIES

Item	Source	Description	Price
Chicks	*The State* (Columbia, SC) (1940)	Day old; popular breed, post paid in South Carolina; cash with orders	$7.50/100
Seed	*The State* (Columbia, SC) (1940)	*Coker's Abruzzi;* rye seed, 84 percent germination, 100 percent pure	$1.00/bu
Separator	*Sears, Roebuck* (1941)	America's No. 1 separator; finest precision built into the world's most beautifully designed sanitary cream separator; 400 pounds per hour	$58.50

Item	Source	Description	Price
Tractor Tires	*Sears, Roebuck* (1941)	*Allstate;* makes farming easier; cut costs on every job	$35.15

FOOD PRODUCTS

Item	Source	Description	Price
Artificial Sweetener	*New York Times* (1940)	*Macy's Saccharin Tablets;* 1/4 gr 1000s	$0.54
Candy	*Liberty* (1944)	*Licorice Sweeties;* gay, candy-coated, licorice-flavored for sweet eating Per box	 $0.05
Chocolates	*The Saturday Evening Post* (1941)	*Miss Saylor's;* a tempting lure for lovely ladies; 1 lb tin	$1.00
Chocolates	*The Saturday Evening Post* (1941)	*Whitman's Sampler;* America's outstanding box of fine candy; 5 lb	$5.00
Coffee	*Chicago Tribune* (1943)	*Webb;* ration stamp	$0.33/pound
Drink	*Life* (1942)	*Nesbitt's California Orange Fountain;* favorite for years now in bottles	$0.05
Flour	*Chicago Tribune* (1943)	*Pillsbury;* for pastry, biscuits; not rationed; 24 1/2 lb bag	$1.09
Peanut Butter	*Chicago Tribune* (1943)	*Armours;* 24-oz jar; not rationed	$0.41
Soda Pop	*Better Homes and Gardens* (1940)	*Coca-Cola;* six-pack; delicious and refreshing; plus deposit	$0.25

FURNITURE

Item	Source	Description	Price
Bedroom Suite	*Chicago Tribune* (1943)	4-piece Early American bedroom suite	$49.50
Bunk Bed	*Sears, Roebuck* (1941)	Two beds for the price of one	$10.98
Chair	*Brochure Furniture by Tomlinson* (1940)	*The Riddle Fan Chair;* width 32", depth 28", height 46"	$85.00
Chest	*Brochure Furniture by Tomlinson* (1940)	*Randolph Tall;* 36" wide; will find a multitude of uses in the apartment or average home	$175
Dresser Base	*Sears, Roebuck* (1941)	An $11.50 value; four spacious drawers give plenty of room for clothing	$6.48
Lamp	*Better Homes and Gardens* (1940)	General Electric Mazda 40, 50, 60 Watt 75, 100 Watt	 $0.13 $0.15
Mattress	*Better Homes and Gardens* (1940)	*Simmons Beautyrest;* based on our 10-year guarantee, the price comes down to about a penny a night	$39.50
Radio/ Phonograph Cabinet	*Better Homes and Gardens* (1940)	Stewart Warner Concert Grand Sheraton Model 8D9; for homes where good taste rules	$185
Table	*Brochure Furniture by Tomlinson* (1940)	*Southall;* drop leaf; serves perfectly as a sofa table; top 45" × 26"–68"	$75.00

GARDEN EQUIPMENT & SUPPLIES

Item	Source	Description	Price
Bulbs	*Sears, Roebuck* (1941)	Gladiola; pride of the garden; 10 bulbs	$0.23
Lawn Mower	*Sears, Roebuck* (1941)	We know it sounds unbelievable, but it's TRUE; 18"	$57.50

Item	Source	Description	Price
Pruner	*House and Garden* (1942)	*Seymour Smith & Son, Inc. Snap-cut;* garden scissors, 8"; chrome finish	$2.00
Rose	*Better Homes and Gardens* (1942)	*Jackson & Perkins Dr. Nicolas;* climbing; rose-pink blooms are 5" to 6" across	$1.50
Rose	*House and Garden* (1942)	Wayside Gardens Heart's Desire Red Rose	$1.50
Seeds	*House and Garden* (1942)	*Stumpp & Walter Co.;* multiflora hybrid begonia	$0.35/pkg
Seeds	*House and Garden* (1942)	*W. Atlee Burpee Co.;* marigold garden; twelve distinct kinds	$1/12pkgs

HOTEL RATES

Item	Source	Description	Price
Hotel Room	*New York Times* (1940)	*Berkeley-Carteret;* all inclusive weekend rate; Saturday afternoon and Sunday, room with bath, 3 lavish meals	$5.50
Hotel Room	*New York Times* (1940)	*Kathmere Inn and Beach Club;* private beach, pier; Old Greenwich, Conn.; swimming, tennis, delightful, restricted	$14/week
Hotel Room	*Chicago Tribune* (1941)	*McAlpin;* if business beckons you to New York, stay at the McAlpin; single	$3/day
Hotel Room	*New York Times* (1942)	*Hotel Chesterfield;* room with private bath and radio	$2.50/day
Hotel Room	*Majestic Theatre Program* (1942)	*Chelsea, Atlantic City;* dine royally in our beautiful dining room overlooking the ocean; with meals and bath	$6.50/day
Hotel Room	*New York Times* (1943)	*Hotel Chesterfield;* here's value; room with private bath and radio; at Radio City in Times Square; double	$3.50–$6/day
Hotel Room	*New York Times* (1943)	*The Senator;* Atlantic City; enjoy these famous Senator values; a comfortable room and bath, sun decks, sea water baths, delicious food, just off boardwalk; two to a room	$4/day
Hotel Room	*New York Times* (1943)	*Calderwood;* guest ranch, Ramapo Mountains; northern New Jersey; fine horse, excellent food	$35/week

HOUSEHOLD PRODUCTS

Item	Source	Description	Price
Blanket	*The Saturday Evening Post* (1941)	Lighter, warmer for beauty sleep; 6' × 7 1/2'	$5.95
Casserole	*Better Homes and Gardens* (1940)	*Pyrex;* double duty; cover serves as an extra pie plate; 1 qt size	$0.50
Cheese Slicer	*Better Homes and Gardens* (1940)	*J. C. Brown Hostess;* wire; this sturdy slicer with taut cutting wire is a swifty; at your 5¢ and 10¢	$0.10
Cookware	*Better Homes and Gardens* (1940)	*Wearever Aluminum;* 5-piece matched set is planned to fit the usual oven	$6.40
Cookware	*Sears, Roebuck* (1941)	The kitchen quintuplet 5-purpose cooker	$5.19
Dinnerware	*Sears, Roebuck* (1941)	*Calais;* 32-piece set	$4.98
Draperies	James Bones Wright Jr., *Interiors* (1943)	Glazed chintz	$4/yard
Laundry Tub	*Chicago Tribune* (1943)	2-part concrete construction, less fittings	$9.85
Paint	*Cheatham-Greenville Hardware Co., Inc.* (1943)	*Dulux;* eggshell enamel	$2/quart

Item	Source	Description	Price
Paint	*Cheatham-Greenville Hardware Co., Inc.* (1943)	Light stone porch and floor paint	$4.50/gallon
Paint	*Chicago Tribune* (1943)	*DuPont;* for interiors and exteriors	$2.45/gallon
Paint	*Chicago Tribune* (1943)	*Ultra Luminal;* has the magic-like synthetic resin base	$2.85/gallon
Pressure Cooker	*Better Homes and Gardens* (1940)	*Presto;* just a twist of the lid horizontally seals the cooker; 3-qt size	$10.50
Salad Set	*Chicago Tribune* (1941)	Sterling silver; for summer buffets and little suppers	$4.75
Stoker	*Better Homes and Gardens* (1940)	Iron; fireman; gives abundant automatic low-cost heat; complete with controls	$179.50
Tea Kettle	*Sears, Roebuck* (1941)	Our finest copper teakettle	$3.49
Toast and Jam Set	*Better Homes and Gardens* (1940)	*Toastmaster;* deluxe; includes fully automatic toaster; the handiest of trays, a toast plate and jars for jam or marmalade in colorful Franciscan ware	$17.95
Varnish	*Cheatham-Greenville Hardware Co., Inc.* (1943)	Tufcote	$1.43/quart
Wallpaper	*James Bones Wright Jr., Interiors* (1943)	Dining Room	$1.50/roll
Wax	*Cheatham-Greenville Hardware Co., Inc.* (1943)	*Johnson Paste Wax;* 1/4 pound can	$1.90
Weekend Case	*New York Times* (1940)	Grey or brown-striped canvas	$4.98

JEWELRY

Item	Source	Description	Price
Engagement Ring	*Liberty* (1944)	5-diamond engagement ring, inspired by Lynn Gardner, Columbia Recording star	$265
Cultured Pearls	*New York Times* (1940)	*Gimbel's;* 46 single-strand necklaces, usually $6.95	$1.98
Watch	*Liberty* (1944)	*Gruen Veri-thin Constance* watch for women; 15 jewel movement	$33.75
Watch	*Chicago Tribune* (1943)	*Benrus;* your choice ladies or gents 15 jewel watch	$24.75
Wedding Ring	*Chicago Tribune* (1943)	Five fine-quality diamonds are set in this neatly engraved 18-k solid white or 14-k solid natural gold	$9.75

MEALS

Item	Source	Description	Price
Dinner	*Chicago Tribune* (1941)	*Tracy's Restaurant;* a fresh shrimp cocktail, some relish, then a tender, juicy filet mignon, parsley, new potatoes, and fresh string beans; a farm style salad of fresh cucumbers and sour cream; delicious fresh cherry pie; some hot biscuits and a decanter of coffee	$0.95
Dinner	*New York Times* (1942)	*Taft Grill;* Vincent Lopez and his orchestra; no cover charge	$1.25

Item	Source	Description	Price
MEDICAL PRODUCTS & SERVICES			
Aspirin	*New York Times* (1943)	*St. Joseph*; be sure to insist on genuine St. Joseph aspirin every time; you can't buy aspirin that can do more for you, so why pay more; world's largest seller	$0.35/100
Foot Treatment	*Life* (1942)	*The Mennen Co. Quinsana*; 2-way treatment for athlete's feet	$0.50
Laxative	*Liberty* (1944)	*Inner Clean Herbal Laxative*; helps promote a natural-like movement	$0.30 $0.50 $1.00
Nasal Jelly	*Liberty* (1944)	SNJ for the relief of nose and throat infections Family package, 4 tubes and applicators	$3.00
Nonprescription Drug	*New York Times* (1940)	*Macy's Milk of Magnesia*; 1/2 gallon	$0.61
Nonprescription Drug	*New York Times* (1940)	*Macy's Granular Effervescent Salts*; 1 lb	$0.54
Nonprescription Drug	*Sears, Roebuck* (1941)	*Alka Seltzer*; 8 tablets	$0.24
Nonprescription Drug	*Sears, Roebuck* (1941)	*Listerine*; antiseptic; a favorite in American households for many years	$0.27
Nonprescription Drug	*Sears, Roebuck* (1941)	*Vasoline Camphor Ice*; tube	$0.10
Nonprescription Drug	*Sears, Roebuck* (1941)	Squibb Spirit of Ammonia; 1-oz bottle	$0.23
Vitamins	*Life* (1942	*Vims Vitamin*; contains A, B1, B2, C, D, and P-P; 24 tablets	$1.69
MOTORIZED VEHICLES, SUPPLIES, & SERVICES			
Automobile	Richard M. Langworth and Graham Robson, *Complete Book of Collectible Cars* (1985)	*American Bantam Convertible Coupe* [cost in 1940]	$399–$565
Automobile	Langworth and Robson, *Complete Book of Collectible Cars* (1985)	*Cadillac Series 60 Special*; 4-door sedan [cost in 1940]	$2,090–$3,820
Automobile	Langworth and Robson, *Complete Book of Collectible Cars* (1985)	*Ford V8 De Luxe V8/85 Convertible Coupe* [cost in 1940]	$600–$947
Automobile	Langworth and Robson *Complete Book of Collectible Cars* (1985)	*Lincoln Continental Club Coupe* [cost in 1940]	$2,783–$2,916
Automobile	Langworth and Robson, *Complete Book of Collectible Cars* (1985)	*Buick Series Century Sport Coupe* [cost in 1941]	$1,128–$1,620
Automobile	Langworth and Robson, *Complete Book of Collectible Cars* (1985)	*Chrysler Windsor Town and Country*; 9-passenger wagon [cost in 1941]	$1,412–$1,685
Automobile	Langworth and Robson, *Complete Book of Collectible Cars* (1985)	*Dodge Custom Convertible* [cost in 1941]	$1,162–$1,245
Automobile	Langworth and Robson, *Complete Book of Collectible Cars* (1985)	*Nash Ambassador Six*; 4-door trunkback sedan [cost in 1941]	$925–$1,130

Item	Source	Description	Price
Automobile	Langworth and Robson, *Complete Book of Collectible Cars* (1985)	*Packard One Ten Convertible Coupe* [cost in 1941]	$1,104–$1,375
Automobile	Langworth and Robson, *Complete Book of Collectible Cars* (1985)	*Chevrolet Fleetline Aerosedan* [cost in 1942]	$880
Automobile	Langworth and Robson, *Complete Book of Collectible Cars* (1985)	*DeSoto Deluxe*; featuring air-foil hidden headlamps [cost in 1942]	$1,010–$1,455
Automobile	Langworth and Robson, *Complete Book of Collectible Cars* (1985)	*Oldsmobile Custom 98 Convertible* [cost in 1942]	$1,079–$1,450
Automobile	Langworth and Robson, *Complete Book of Collectible Cars* (1985)	*Packard Clipper 180*; 4-door sedan [cost in 1942]	$2,099–$2,196
Automobile	Langworth and Robson, *Complete Book of Collectible Cars* (1985)	*Pontiac Steamliner Chieftain*; wood-body wagon [cost in 1942]	$1,030–$1,340
Service	*Authorized Buick Service, Eugene B. Smith, Inc.* (1941)	*Eugene B. Smith Buick Service Saver Plan*; 6 chassis lubrications, 1 front wheel lubrication	$4.25

OTHER

Item	Source	Description	Price
Billfold	*Life* (1942)	*Amity Leather Products Co.*; special navy model in dress-block cowhide embossed with official coat of arms	$2.50
Cemetery Plots	*New York Times* (1942)	Four-grave family plot; in beautiful Jewish Memorial Park	$100
Garage Door	*Chicago Tribune* (1943)	Overhead; stock worn 8' × 7'	$7.98
Globe	*Chicago Tribune* (1943)	*Marshall Fields & Co.*; follow this global war on a 10" globe	$2.95
Glue	*Better Homes and Gardens* (1940)	*Casco*; save the cost of a new kitchen table; make it stick with Casco	$0.25/tube
Greeting Card	*The Antique Trader Weekly* (1941)	*Gibson Valentine*; with a cellophane-covered candy heart glued into the printed one	$0.10
Greeting Card	*The Antique Trader Weekly* (1943)	*Norcross Valentine*; with a red diagonal ribbon and bow, alongside one printed rose, set off by a plastic dew drop	$1.00
Haircut	*New York Times* (1940)	For boys; summer holidays just ahead for your son . . . this is the time for him to get a shampoo and haircut in our barber shop; here he'll find barbers, expert at his favorite haircut for camp—side part, crew cut or pompadour	$0.50
Haircut	*New York Times* (1942)	Beautifully yours; 1942 windswept; the hair cut that's sweeping the country; fresh looking and so easy to keep it that way; a flick of the comb after a swim and it's set again	$2.00
Moth Spray	*Chicago Tribune* (1943)	*Enoz*; the ideal product to use on rugs, draperies, things you leave in the open air	$1.29/quart
Mural Kit	*Life* (1942)	150' mural on 3 sides of a barn; by Frank Engebretson in South Wayne, Wisconsin	$165 including paint
Open-Air Sunbathing	*New York Times* (1942)	*Grand Central Palace*; also supervised exercise, iced-alcohol massage, 7 courts for squash and handball, steam-salt baths; luncheon served daily; trial visit	$2.00

Item	Source	Description	Price
Paper Trim	*Better Homes and Gardens* (1940)	*Royledge Shelving Paper;* many a model house owes its kitchen charm to Royledge shelving	$0.05/9 feet
Parking	*Majestic Theatre Program* (1942)	*Corvan Garage Theatre;* parking; 122 and 124 West 54th Street	$0.50/day
Shoe Polish	*Sears, Roebuck* (1941)	Shinola	$0.09
Soles	*Sears, Roebuck* (1941)	Rubber; stick-on; three pairs	$0.42
Stain Remover	*House and Garden* (1942)	*Consolidated Chemical Works Dog-Tex;* removes dog stains, saves rugs, ends odors	$1.25/pt
Tattoo	*Life* (1942)	Snake design on arm	$0.25
Upholstering	*Chicago Tribune* (1941)	Summer bargain sale; sofa or chair	$10.50

PERSONAL CARE PRODUCTS

Item	Source	Description	Price
Bandages	*The Saturday Evening Post* (1941)	*Johnson & Johnson Adhesive;* use a ready-made sterilized Band-Aid instead of fussing around with awkward, home-made bandages; 36 per box	$0.19
Complexion Powder	*Life* (1942)	*Yardley;* mist-blown, graciously scented with Bond Street; ten radiant shades	$1.00
Denture Adhesive	*Better Homes and Gardens* (1940)	*Polident;* she's not ashamed of her false teeth smile	$0.30
Deodorant	*Chicago Tribune* (1941)	*Dresshield;* an easy-to-apply liquid to check and deodorize underarm perspiration; 2 oz bottle	$0.60
Deodorant Powder	*New York Times* (1940)	*Macy's;* 8 oz	$0.39
Hair Oil	*New York Times* (1940)	*Macy's Perfumed Liquid Petroleum for the Hair;* 6 oz	$0.44
Lip Balm	*Life* (1942)	*Fleet's;* guard lips from weather	$0.25
Lipstick	*Majestic Theatre Program* (1942)	*Chanel;* for impeccable grooming—the fashion correct shades of Chanel lipstick	$1.50
Lipstick	*Consumer Reports* (1942)	*Lenthéric Bal Masqué Brune Satine*	$1.50
Lipstick	*Consumer Reports* (1942)	Almay Dark	$1.10
Lipstick	*Consumer Reports* (1942)	L'Adonna Light	$0.50
Lipstick	*Consumer Reports* (1942)	Elizabeth Post Heavenly Pink	$0.10
Lipstick	*Life* (1942)	*Yardley Bond Street;* keeps your lips soft and inviting; in eight shades	$1.00
Makeover	*Majestic Theatre Program* (1942)	*Helena Rubinstein;* complete mid-winter makeover including herbal shampoo, a flattering new coiffure, *posture* exercise, body massage, new make-up	$10.00
Mouthwash	*New York Times* (1940)	*Macy's ZCA's;* 1/2 gallon	$0.71
Perfume Stick	*Life* (1942)	*RIC;* not a liquid; takes perfume off the dressing table and puts it in your purse	$1.00

Item	Source	Description	Price
Razor Blades	*New York Times* (1940)	*Macy's Single Edge;* 50	$0.74
Razor Blades	*Life* (1942)	*Berkeley;* double edge; why pay more, made of fine watch-spring steel; 18 blades to a box	$0.25
Rouge	*Majestic Theatre Program* (1942)	*Coty Air-Spun;* miraculous in the way it clings; buffed by torrents of air	$0.50
Shampoo	*Liberty* (1944)	*Fitch's Saponified Coconut Oil Shampoo;* no dull film remains 6-ounce bottle	$0.50
Shaver	*The Saturday Evening Post* (1941)	*Schick Electric;* new 2-M hollow ground head	$9.95
Skin Lotion	*New York Times* (1940)	Macy's	$0.94/pint
Sun Oil	*New York Times* (1940)	*Macy's;* scented; 8 oz	$0.89
Toothbrush	*Life* (1942)	*Dr. West's Miracle-Tuft;* includes Exton brand bristling, surgically sterile glass packaging, a full year of effective service	$0.50
Tooth Powder	*New York Times* (1940)	*Macy's;* 1 lb	$0.44
Witch Hazel	*New York Times* (1940)	Macy's	$0.82/gallon

PUBLICATIONS

Item	Source	Description	Price
Magazine	*Better Homes and Gardens* (1940)	*Better Homes and Gardens;* monthly	$0.10
Magazine	*Life* (1942)	*Time;* weekly Per issue Per year	 $0.10 $4.50

REAL ESTATE

Item	Source	Description	Price
Apartment	*New York Times* (1940)	For rent; 3 rooms, modern, attractive, refrigeration	$35/month
Apartment	*New York Times* (1940)	For rent; 3 rooms, dinette	$75/month
Apartment	*New York Times* (1940)	For rent; off Central Park; 5 rooms; refrigeration, combination sink, tub, shower; references required	$47/month
Chicken Farm	*Chicago Tribune* (1941)	5 1/2 acres; cash	$200
Farm Suburban Estate	*Chicago Tribune* (1941)	House, 2 acres, beautiful hilltop estate, paved road, interior needs modernization	$2,975
Garden Farm	*Chicago Tribune* (1941)	Black garden soil, on newly paved road; nearly 2 acres, electricity; $100 cash, $8 month	$545
House	*New York Times* (1940)	Garden duplex; 5 rooms 2 baths, fireplace; atmosphere	$1,900
House	*New York Times* (1943)	*Baldwin;* 6-room cottage, extra large, spacious rooms, stall shower and tub; steam-oil; 2-car garage; bus at corner	$6,950
House	*New York Times* (1943)	Owner leaving city offers center hall colonial, short walk to station, bus line or shopping; 3 large bedrooms, tile bath and stall shower, fireplace, modern kitchen. . . complete insulation	$9,000

Item	Source	Description	Price
House	*New York Times* (1943)	Great Neck; price reduced; entirely redecorated; 4 bedrooms, 2 baths; maid's room, bath; sunroom, recreation room with bar; double garage	$16,000
House	*New York Times* (1943)	Exceptionally well-built brick house, painted white, situated on 3 high acres, water view; walking distance of beach and bus; gardens, fruit trees, lovely grounds	$29,500
House	*Chicago Tribune* (1943)	32 minutes to loop; double garage and hen house, good condition	$1,000
House	*Chicago Tribune* (1943)	Frame home, sleeping porch, furnace heat, low taxes	$7,000
House	*Chicago Tribune* (1943)	Cozy 5-room house on large landscaped lot, garage, fruit trees, flowers	$3,800

SEWING EQUIPMENT & SUPPLIES

Item	Source	Description	Price
Cloth	*Sears, Roebuck* (1941)	Monk's cloth; sunfast; plaid; 36" goods	$0.32/yard

SPORTS EQUIPMENT

Item	Source	Description	Price
Golf Clubs	*New York Times* (1942)	*Walter Hagen Power Groove;* set of 5 irons	$12.95
Golf Shoes	*New York Times* (1941)	*Johnny Farrell;* with removable spikes, made on plateau last with selected leather uppers and solid, double-leather outersoles; complete with shoe-horn wrench	$4.99
Head Covers	*New York Times* (1942)	*Poplin Golf Club;* contrasting colors; heavily padded poplin; leather numbers	$1.59/3
Reel	*Sears, Roebuck* (1941)	Top performance; equal quality; the same that costs 1.00/3 more elsewhere; nonbacklash 3-port	$3.79
Shotgun	*Sullivan Hardware Co.* (1940)	*Remington 20/26 Model III;* automatic	$39.30

TOBACCO PRODUCTS

Item	Source	Description	Price
Pipe	*Liberty* (1944)	*Sterling Hall by Briarcraft;* preferred for smoking quality	$3.50

TRAVEL & TRANSPORTATION

Item	Source	Description	Price
Airplane Tickets	*New York Times* (1940)	21 flagships daily; only 75 minutes to Boston; go and return any time One way Round trip	 $11.95 $21.50
Railroad Ticket	*New York Times* (1940)	*New York Central System;* New York-Chicago; the Pacemaker famous deluxe coach train; round trip	$27.25
Railroad Ticket	*New York Times* (1942)	*Montrealer;* round-trip fares to Montreal; summer excursion; upper berth, 60-day return limit	$28.80

347

MISCELLANY 1940–1944

Smith Girls

The job market opens wide for college graduates as war reduces manpower.

The employment boom that is sweeping oldsters, youngsters, and mothers of families into jobs left vacant as men go off to war, last spring invaded the nation's colleges, precipitated many a young girl graduate into a juicy job for which she once would have had to labor long and hard.

At Smith College, whereas $1,200 a year was considered a good starting salary in 1941, this year's candidates averaged $1,600 with the promise of speedy raises after a brief training period.

Anita Livingston Willis of Great Neck, Long Island: She is now employed by Macy's in New York, is going through a nine-month training period. Her starting salary is $30 a week.

Marian Frances Carpenter of Brooklyn, N. Y.: Upon graduation, the Office of Price Administration in Washington put in a bid for her services and she went to work there a fortnight after leaving college. She is in the Research Section of Copper, Aluminum and Ferro-Alloys, starting at a yearly salary of $2,000 with a raise to $2,600 promised soon.

Suzanne Cook Vroom of Worcester, Mass.: The job which she took in July (was) with the Liberty Mutual Insurance Co. in Boston. Having first enrolled in a training class for claims adjusters at a yearly salary of $1,300 plus a bonus of about $150, she is now working in the field, investigating accidents.

Life, September 28, 1942

Cigarette, Liquor Taxes in 2 Days Yield $1,834,386

The state treasury netted $1,834,386 from Illinois's new cigarette and liquor taxes in the first two days the new levies were in effect. Finance Director George B. McKibbin reported today.

McKibbin said the cigarette tax, 2 cents on each package of 20, accounted for $676,790 of revenue and the doubled liquor taxes yielded $1,157,596. The figures covered tax stamps sold by the finance department up to July 3, the taxes having become operative July 1.

Stamps sold during the first two days were largely to cover current stocks of liquors and cigarettes on the shelves of retailers and wholesalers. In the future the stocks will reach retailers prestamped by distributors and manufacturers.

Chicago Tribune, July 8, 1941

Hold Furniture Price Hikes to 5%, U.S. Rules

A ceiling of 5 per cent on price boosts was imposed on the furniture industry yesterday by governmental price fixers. The limit was announced as thousands in the industry gathered in Chicago for the summer home furnishings market, which will be held for two weeks at the American Furniture Mart and the Merchandise Mart.

The price stabilizing order by the Office of Price Administration and Civilian Supply was described as a temporary measure in response to the requests of furniture makers for permission to increase wholesale prices. The markups were made necessary by increasing material and labor costs, manufacturers said.

Chicago Tribune, July 8, 1941

Farm Land Prices Reported Going Up; OWI Warns Against Repetition of Boom in War of 1917–1918 and Subsequent Collapse

The Office of War Information, comparing current price trends of farm lands with those of the last war, warned today against a general rise of values and a subsequent "disastrous" deflation.

Although values were not at the "boom stage which led to the catastrophe of 1921," the OWI said, farm real estate values on March 3, 1943, were noticeably higher than a year earlier.

On that date, the index of the average per acre values (1912–14 being equal to 100) stood at 99 for the country as a whole, as compared with 91 in March 1942, 85 in 1941, and a low of 73 in 1933.

"The low point reached in 1933 was the final aftermath of an inflationary process set in motion during the last war, a process that reached a climax immediately afterward in 1919 and 1920," the OWI stated.

Swollen land values in those two years came about through the demand for farm land that was paying heavy wartime dividends based on excessive prices received for farm products.

MISCELLANY 1940–1944

In 1943, for the first time in twenty years, the annual average of farm prices reached parity with other prices, the OWI said.

Since the outbreak of war, it continued, the average of farm prices had risen more than 90 percent and farm income by about 80 percent, while the average of prices paid by farmers, including interest and taxes, had increased about 25 percent.

The Bureau of Agricultural Economics found that as of March 1, 1943, increases in value over those of the previous year were 20 to 24 percent in thirteen states, 15 to 19 percent in sixteen states, 10 to 14 percent in eleven states and less than 10 percent in six states.

New York Times, July 12, 1943

HISTORICAL SNAPSHOT
1945–1949

1945

- President Franklin Delano Roosevelt dies in office; Harry Truman becomes president
- The United States drops two atomic bombs on Japan; one on Nagasaki and the other at Hiroshima
- Penicillin introduced commercially
- Beechcraft Bonanza two-engine private plane introduced
- U.S. Gross National Product is $211 billion, double the GNP of 1928
- Ballpoint pens, costing $12.50 each, go on sale
- Weed killer 2,4-D patented
- Rationing of all items except sugar ends; shortages continue
- Frozen orange juice pioneered
- Tupperware Corporation formed

1946

- Strikes idle 4.6 million workers with a loss of 116 million man-days, worst stoppage since 1919
- Dow Jones Industrials average peaks at post-1929 high of 212.50
- Wage and price controls end on all areas except rents, sugar, and rice
- U.S. college enrollments reach all-time high of more than 2 million
- Ektachrome color film introduced by Kodak Company
- Tide introduced; by 1949 one in four wash detergent consumers will use it
- Timex watches introduced at $6.95 and up
- Hunt Foods establishes "price at time of shipment" contracts with customers

- U.S. birthrate soars to 3.4 million, up from 2.9 million in previous year

1947

- Taft-Hartley Act restricts organized labor
- New York transit fare doubles to ten cents, the first increase since 1904
- B. F. Goodrich Company introduces first tubeless tire
- Ajax cleanser is introduced by Colgate-Palmolive-Peet Company
- U.S. frozen orange juice concentrate sales reach 7 million cans, up from 4.8 in 1946
- Reddi-Whip whipped cream in a can introduced
- Seagram's 7 Crown becomes the world's largest selling brand of whiskey
- Raytheon Company introduces first commercial microwave oven

1948

- Transistor developed by Bell Telephone Laboratories, permitting miniaturization of electronic devices such as computers, radios, and television
- 360,000 soft-coal workers strike demanding $100 per month in retirement benefits at age 62
- Congress passes Anti-Inflationary Act as cost of living rises
- One million homes have television sets
- Nikon camera introduced to compete with Leica
- Dial Soap introduced as first deodorant soap

- Corn production is now 75 percent hybrid
- Gerber Products Company sells 2 million cans and jars of baby food weekly

1949

- 500,000 steelworkers strike, gain pension demands
- U.S. auto production reaches 5.1 million
- The president's salary is raised to $100,000 per year
- Silly Putty introduced at $1 per ounce
- Sara Lee Cheesecake introduced
- Minimum wage raised from 40 cents to 70 cents per hour
- CBS introduces long-playing vinyl phonograph record

The atomic bombings on Hiroshima and Nagasaki killed between 129,000 and 226,000 people, most of whom were civilians, and remain the only use of nuclear weapons in armed conflict. Japan surrendered 6 days later, effectively ending WWII. (via Wikimedia Commons)

SELECTED INCOME 1945–1949

Job	Source	Description	Pay
Bakery Salesgirls	*Chicago Tribune* (1949)	Experienced; steady; uniforms furnished	$7/day
Baseball Commissioner	Victor Bondi, ed., *American Decades: 1940–1949* (1995)	Annual salary of Albert "Happy" Chandler in 1945	$50,000
Baseball Player	Bondi, ed., *American Decades: 1940–1949* (1995)	Annual salary of New York Yankee outfielder Joe DiMaggio in 1947	$90,000
Baseball Player	Bondi, ed., *American Decades: 1940–1949* (1995)	Salaries for Professional All-American Girls' Baseball League players in 1948	$40–$100/wk

With the entry of the United States into World War II, several major league baseball executives started a new professional league with women players in order to maintain baseball in the public eye while the majority of able men were away. (via Wikimedia Commons)

Job	Source	Description	Pay
Baseball Player	Bondi, ed., *American Decades: 1940–1949* (1995)	Annual salary of Boston Red Sox player Ted Williams in 1949	$125,000
Baseball Player	Arnold Rampersad, Jackie Robinson, *A Biography* (1997)	Earnings of Brooklyn Dodgers Jackie Robinson in 1949	$17,500
Boxer	Bondi, ed., *American Decades: 1940–1949* (1995)	Joe Louis's earnings for heavyweight boxing championship fight with Billy Conn in 1946	$625,916
Cook	Greenville (SC) Piedmont (1945)	Resort; colored woman	$125/mo
Cook	*Atlanta Constitution* (1947)	Good cook and general houseworker; prefer sleeping in; no Thursdays, no Sundays	$20/wk
Counterman	*Chicago Tribune* (1949)		$45/wk
Dictaphone Operator	*Atlanta Constitution* (1947)		$150–175/mo
Director of Home Economics	*Chicago Tribune* (1949)	National food manufacturing company; degree	$7,500/yr
Factory and Warehouse	*Chicago Tribune* (1949)	No experience necessary; choice of shifts	To $1.21/hr
Food Checker	*Chicago Tribune* (1946)	5 days, 9–4; meals included	$25/wk
Football Player	Bondi, ed., *American Decades: 1940–1949* (1995)	Average per player winnings for New York Giants and Chicago Bears Football Championship Game in 1946	$2,000
Golfer	Bondi, ed., *American Decades: 1940–1949* (1995)	Annual winnings of Byron Nelson in 1945	$66,000
Hallicrafters	*Chicago Tribune* (1946)	Builders of high-frequency radios: wirers, solderers, assemblers, stenographers, typists, inspectors, sheet metal workers, layout	$0.80–$1.05/hr
Investigators	*Atlanta Constitution* (1947)	Part-time	$4/day
Machinist	*Chicago Tribune* (1949)	50-hr min; set up and operate; top notch only	$1.25/hr
Maid	*Chicago Tribune* (1946)	White; to do cooking and general housework; must be compatible with family; own room and bath; person with temperament not wanted; must have references	$40/wk
Metal Finisher	*PM* (1977)	Starting hourly wage in General Motors automotive plant in 1947	$1.19
Secretary	*Chicago Tribune* (1949)	For three salesmen	$216/mo
Service Station Attendant	*Atlanta Constitution* (1947)	Experienced; Apply ready to work	$40/wk
Shoemaker	*Greenville* (SC) *Piedmont* (1945)	Good working conditions; West Palm Beach, Florida	$60–70/wk

CONSUMER EXPENDITURES 1945–1949

(Per Capita)

Expenditure Type	1945	1946	1947	1948	1949
Clothing	$93.62	$106.79	$108.24	$114.57	$107.25
Food	$290.15	$334.54	$363.57	$369.64	$351.90
Auto Usage	$29.30	$67.19	$90.19	$105.71	$126.69
New Auto Purchase	NR	$14.15	$27.75	$34.09	$51.61
Auto Parts	$5.00	$9.90	$9.71	$8.87	$8.04
Gas & Oil	$12.86	$24.05	$27.75	$32.74	$35.53
Housing	$91.48	$100.43	$111.01	$122.08	$131.38
Furniture	$10.72	$15.56	$17.35	$19.09	$18.09
Utilities	$32.16	$35.36	$40.24	$45.01	$43.57
Telephone & Telegraph	$8.58	$9.19	$9.71	$10.91	$11.39
Physicians	$10.01	$12.73	$14.57	$16.37	$16.76
Dentists	$4.29	$5.66	$5.55	$5.46	$6.03
Health Insurance	$2.86	$2.83	$5.55	$5.46	$5.36
Personal Business	$29.30	$33.29	$36.08	$38.87	$39.55
Personal Care	$14.29	$14.85	$15.26	$15.69	$15.42
Tobacco	$20.72	$24.05	$25.67	$27.28	$27.48
Local Transport	$12.15	$13.44	$13.18	$13.64	$13.41
Intercity Transport	$7.86	$7.07	$6.94	$6.82	$6.03
Recreation	$43.59	$60.12	$63.83	$66.15	$67.03
Religion/Welfare Activities	$12.86	$14.85	$14.57	$15.69	$15.42
Private Education & Research	$7.15	$7.78	$9.71	$10.23	$11.39
Per Capita Consumption	$854.73	$1017.76	$1123.32	$1192.79	$1119.51

INVESTMENTS 1945–1949

Investment	1945	1946	1947	1948	1949
Basic Yield, One-year Corporate Bonds	1.02	.86	1.05	1.60	1.60
Short-term Interest Rates, 4–6 Months, Prime Commercial Paper	.75	.81	1.03	1.44	1.49
Basic Yield, Common Stocks, Total	1.02	.86	1.05	1.60	1.60
Index of Common Stocks (194121943 5 10)	102	104.8	103.8	100.8	102.7

COMMON STOCKS, CLOSING PRICE AND DIVIDEND, FIRST BUSINESS DAY OF YEAR

(PARENTHETICAL NUMBER IS ANNUAL DIVIDEND IN DOLLARS)

Allis Chalmers	38 1/2	53 3/4	36 7/8	39 1/2	36
	(1.65)	(1.75)	(1.60)	(1.60)	(1.60)
AT&T	163 1/4	190 1/4	171 1/8	152	149 7/8
	(9)	(9)	(9)	(9)	(9)
American Tobacco	65	89 1/4	81	68 1/2	61 1/4
	(3.25)	(3.25)	(3.25)	(3.50)	(3.75)
Anaconda	30	44	39 7/8	34 1/8	33 3/8
	(2.50)	(2.50)	(2.50)	(3)	(3.50)
B&O	12 1/4	25 3/8	21 3/4	13 1/8	10
	(/)	(/)	(/)	(/)	(/)
Bethlehem Steel	65 7/8	95 5/8	91 3/4	103 3/8	31 5/8
	(6)	(6)	(6)	(6)	(2.40)
Corn Products	58 1/2	67 1/4	73 3/4	64	57 3/4
	(2.60)	(2.60)	(2.70)	(3.15)	(3.60)
General Electric	39 3/8	35 1/2	35 7/8	38 7/8	42 3/8
	(1.40)	(1.60)	(1.60)	(1.60)	(1.80)
General Motors	63 7/8	75	54	58	57 3/4
	(3)	(3)	(3.25)	(3)	(4.50)
International Business Machines	185	247 7/8	NR	240	154 1/4
(5% stock dividend, 1/29/45) (5 shares for 4 split, 1/26/46)	(6)	(6)		(6)	(4)
(1 3/4 shares for 1 split, 2/6/48)					
(5% stock dividend, 1/28/49)					
Intl Harvester	80	94 3/4	71 3/4	89 1/4	25 1/2
	(3)	(3)	(3)	(5)	(1.35)
National Biscuit	23 7/8	32 1/2	28	30 1/2	30 1/2
	(1.20)	(1.20)	(1.20)	(2)	(2)

Investment	1945	1946	1947	1948	1949
US Steel	60 1/2	81	71 5/8	77 5/8	69 1/4
	(7)	(4)	(7)	(5.00)	(5.00)
Western Union	45 3/8	51 3/8	19 1/4	20 1/2	15 1/8
	(2)	(2)	(/)	(/)	(1.00)

STANDARD JOBS 1945-1949

Job Type	1945	1946	1947	1948	1949
Average of All Industries, excl. farm labor	$2424/yr	$2529/yr	$2657/yr	$2999/yr	$3075/yr
Average of All Industries, incl. farm labor	$2364/yr	$2473/yr	$2602/yr	$2933/yr	$3000/yr
Bituminous Coal Mining	$2629/yr	$2724/yr	$3212/yr	$3388/yr	$2922/yr
Building Trades	$2600/yr	$2537/yr	$2829/yr	$3125/yr	$3229/yr
Domestics	$1312/yr	$1411/yr	$1463/yr	$1500/yr	$1498/yr
Farm Labor	$1307/yr	$1394/yr	$1479/yr	$1541/yr	$1501/yr
Federal Civilian	$2646/yr	$2904/yr	$3180/yr	$3256/yr	$3481/yr
Federal Employees, Executive Depts.	$2057/yr	$2490/yr	$2843/yr	$2949/yr	$2995/yr
Federal Military	$1931/yr	$2279/yr	$2556/yr	$2676/yr	$2599/yr
Finance, Insurance, & Real Estate	$2347/yr	$2570/yr	$2740/yr	$2954/yr	$3034/yr
Gas & Electricity Workers	$2596/yr	$2697/yr	$2994/yr	$3223/yr	$3383/yr
Manufacturing, Durable Goods	$2732/yr	$2615/yr	$2883/yr	$3163/yr	$3240/yr
Manufacturing, Nondurable Goods	$2211/yr	$2404/yr	$2683/yr	$2892/yr	$2961/yr
Medical/Health Services Workers	$1401/yr	$1605/yr	$1821/yr	$1918/yr	$1995/yr
Miscellaneous Manufacturing	$2401/yr	$2442/yr	$2657/yr	$2808/yr	$2856/yr
Motion Picture Services	$2567/yr	$2978/yr	$3031/yr	$2964/yr	$3028/yr
Nonprofit Org. Workers	$1876/yr	$2070/yr	$2172/yr	$2334/yr	$2465/yr
Passenger Transportation Workers, Local and Highway	$2596/yr	$2886/yr	$3020/yr	$3101/yr	$3164/yr
Personal Services	$1725/yr	$1881/yr	$2011/yr	$2120/yr	$2189/yr
Public School Teachers	$1822/yr	$2025/yr	$2261/yr	$2538/yr	$2671/yr
Radio Broadcasting & Television Workers	$3515/yr	$3972/yr	$4073/yr	$4234/yr	$4380/yr
Railroads	$2711/yr	$3055/yr	$3216/yr	$3611/yr	$3706/yr
State and Local Govt. Workers	$1938/yr	$2093/yr	$2300/yr	$2593/yr	$2670/yr
Telephone & Telegraph Workers	$2246/yr	$2413/yr	$2583/yr	$2776/yr	$2920/yr
Wholesale and Retail Trade Workers	$2114/yr	$2378/yr	$2632/yr	$2832/yr	$2899/yr

FOOD BASKET 1945–1949

(NR 5 Not Reported)

Commodity	Year	New York	Atlanta	Chicago	Denver	Los Angeles
Apples, Fresh, per pound	1945	12.60¢	11.80¢	13.70¢	13.30¢	12.80¢
	1946	13.70¢	13.10¢	13.20¢	14.20¢	14.20¢
	1947	13.10¢	12.90¢	13.20¢	13.50¢	13.50¢
	1948	12.90¢	12.50¢	12¢	12.80¢	13.20¢
	1949	13.60¢	13.20¢	13.20¢	14.20¢	13.80¢
Beans, Navy, per pound	1945	12.90¢	10.40¢	11.60¢	10.50¢	12.50¢
	1946	14.60¢	NR	13.70¢	12.70¢	17.20¢
	1947	22.40¢	20.10¢	20.20¢	18.10¢	25¢
	1948	23.40¢	20.30¢	20¢	19.50¢	24.60¢
	1949	18.50¢	15¢	16.30¢	16¢	18¢
Beef, Rib Roasts, per pound	1945	32.80¢	31.50¢	32.60¢	32.80¢	33.30¢
	1946	NR	41.20¢	44.20¢	41.10¢	45¢
	1947	67.30¢	61.30¢	62.60¢	61.20¢	63.30¢
	1948	76.70¢	73¢	74.30¢	71.40¢	76.20¢
	1949	69.50¢	66.50¢	68.60¢	63.70¢	74.70¢
Beef, Steaks (Round), per pound	1945	41.90¢	39.70¢	39.10¢	39.10¢	41.20¢
	1946	54.70¢	51¢	50.80¢	48.60¢	52.40¢
	1947	80.90¢	76.20¢	73.70¢	71.30¢	70.90¢
	1948	96.20¢	89.20¢	88.70¢	84.80¢	85.40¢
	1949	88.80¢	84.30¢	83.50¢	75.70¢	82¢
Bread, White, per pound	1945	9.40¢	9.70¢	7.70¢	8.60¢	8.50¢
	1946	11.20¢	10.90¢	9.70¢	10.10¢	10.40¢
	1947	13.80¢	13¢	12¢	12.10¢	13¢
	1948	14.90¢	13.90¢	12¢	13.10¢	14.40¢
	1949	14.90¢	13.80¢	13¢	13.30¢	14.40¢
Butter, per pound	1945	50.80¢	50.50¢	50.90¢	51.10¢	52.10¢
	1946	72.60¢	72¢	70¢	71¢	72.80¢
	1947	81.30¢	85.50¢	79.30¢	80.10¢	82.90¢
	1948	88.40¢	92.30¢	84.30¢	85.90¢	89.90¢
	1949	73.40¢	78¢	70.30¢	73.70¢	72.70¢

An advertisement for Swift's Brookfield butter, appearin in a 1948 issue of Ladies' Home Journal. *(via Wikimcdia Commons)*

Commodity	Year	New York	Atlanta	Chicago	Denver	Los Angeles
Cheese, per pound	1945	33.40¢	33.60¢	36.10¢	40.70¢	36.10¢
	1946	NR	48.50¢	47.90¢	NR	70¢
	1947	64¢	55.40¢	57.10¢	57.10¢	65.70¢
	1948	70.80¢	62.30¢	64.40¢	NR	70¢
	1949	NR	NR	NR	NR	NR
Chickens, per pound	1945	46.90¢	40.70¢	47.20¢	41.30¢	47.90¢
	1946	53.20¢	54.10¢	50.60¢	49.60¢	54.10¢
	1947	55¢	58¢	52.50¢	NR	NR
	1948	61¢	62.30¢	58.30¢	51.10¢	63.30¢
	1949	NR	NR	NR	NR	NR
Coffee, per pound	1945	30.80¢	31.10¢	31.20¢	34.80¢	29.70¢
	1946	35.40¢	35.70¢	33.30¢	37.80¢	35.50¢
	1947	47.30¢	47.70¢	44.90¢	49.30¢	47.40¢
	1948	51.50¢	52.70¢	49.70¢	54.90¢	53¢
	1949	55.30¢	53.70¢	52.90¢	58.30¢	58¢
Cornmeal, per pound	1945	7.10¢	5.70¢	6.60¢	6.80¢	8.60¢
	1946	7.70¢	6.60¢	7.40¢	7.80¢	9.40¢
	1947	10.20¢	7.80¢	10.40¢	10.60¢	11.30¢
	1948	12¢	7.60¢	12¢	11.80¢	12.40¢
	1949	11¢	6.70¢	10.70¢	10.20¢	10.80¢
Eggs, per dozen	1945	59.50¢	56.60¢	58.10¢	58.80¢	59.90¢
	1946	62.90¢	56.10¢	57.10¢	57.90¢	62.40¢
	1947	76.20¢	65.70¢	66.30¢	66.60¢	75.50¢
	1948	79.80¢	66¢	67.40¢	68.50¢	75.60¢
	1949	77¢	65.40¢	66.50¢	68¢	71.20¢
Flour, Wheat, per pound	1945	6.61¢	6.86¢	6.18¢	5.55¢	6.69¢
	1946	7.40¢	7.46¢	6.66¢	6.38¢	7.38¢
	1947	9.56¢	10.40¢	9.44¢	8.94¢	9.82¢
	1948	9.70¢	10.60¢	9.42¢	8.50¢	10.30¢
	1949	9.44¢	10.22¢	9.26¢	8.18¢	9.84¢
Lard, per pound	1945	18.30¢	18.70¢	19¢	19.10¢	19.80¢
	1946	NR	26¢	25.20¢	25.90¢	27.90¢
	1947	32.60¢	31.60¢	30.50¢	30.70¢	33.50¢
	1948	30.90¢	28.80¢	28.40¢	29.40¢	31.90¢
	1949	20.40¢	18.40¢	18.30¢	18.80¢	21¢
Milk, Fresh, per quart	1945	17.20¢	17¢	17.50¢	13.60¢	14.50¢
	1946	19.50¢	18.80¢	18.60¢	15.50¢	16.20¢
	1947	21.20¢	22¢	20.10¢	18.20¢	18.30¢
	1948	24.20¢	22.30¢	22.20¢	19.60¢	20¢
	1949	23.30¢	22¢	20.60¢	20.40¢	19.90¢
Molasses, per 18 oz. Can	1945	16.40¢	14.60¢	16.60¢	14¢	15.80¢
	1946	21.20¢	19.50¢	20.80¢	19.30¢	20.30¢
	1947	15.70¢	14.90¢	15.80¢	13.30¢	12.90¢
	1948	NR	NR	NR	NR	NR
	1949	NR	NR	NR	NR	NR
Mutton and Lamb, Leg, per pound	1945	40.30¢	37.60¢	38.20¢	37.80¢	40.50¢
	1946	49.50¢	48.10¢	47.30¢	45.50¢	49.60¢
	1947	62.50¢	72.50¢	63.10¢	62.20¢	65.60¢
	1948	70.50¢	80.20¢	69.20¢	69.30¢	70.70¢
	1949	69.80¢	83¢	72.80¢	71.50¢	71.20¢
Pork, Chops, per pound	1945	37.40¢	37.80¢	36.50¢	38¢	38.60¢
	1946	49.90¢	47.90¢	47.20¢	48.10¢	52.80¢
	1947	72.80¢	69.10¢	71.20¢	70.80¢	81¢
	1948	79¢	70.70¢	77.80¢	72.70¢	87.20¢
	1949	76.60¢	67.50¢	75¢	69.50¢	82.40¢

Commodity	Year	New York	Atlanta	Chicago	Denver	Los Angeles
Pork, Bacon, Sliced, per pound	1945	41¢	40.80¢	40.90¢	43¢	42.60¢
	1946	53.60¢	53.20¢	51.50¢	54.90¢	57.10¢
	1947	80.20¢	76.90¢	76.50¢	81.60¢	82.80¢
	1948	80.10¢	77.70¢	76.60¢	80¢	81.60¢
	1949	69.60¢	66.90¢	66.90¢	68.40¢	70.30¢
Pork, Ham, Sliced, and Whole, per pound	1945	47.30¢	50¢	49.70¢	50.80¢	53.50¢
	1946	NR	NR	NR	64.20¢	NR
	1947	68.80¢	67.10¢	64.70¢	64.70¢	71.90¢
	1948	70.40¢	66.80¢	65¢	63.40¢	70.10¢
	1949	65.10¢	62.30¢	61.10¢	58.40¢	64.60¢
Pork, Salt, per pound	1945	23.70¢	22.40¢	22.40¢	22.50¢	23.40¢
	1946	NR	33.10¢	33.20¢	33¢	NR
	1947	NR	45.50¢	47.50¢	46¢	51¢
	1948	NR	42.40¢	48.20¢	45.20¢	50.20¢
	1949	NR	35.20¢	40.20¢	34.60¢	39.50¢
Potatoes, Irish, per 15 pounds	1945	71.60¢	70.90¢	78.20¢	64.30¢	70.30¢
	1946	72.50¢	70.80¢	75¢	63.30¢	77.10¢
	1947	76.60¢	75.80¢	84.50¢	71.50¢	77.40¢
	1948	80.40¢	84.20¢	$1.00	81.90¢	90.20¢
	1949	82.30¢	86.50¢	93.50¢	77¢	81.20¢
Prunes, Dried, per pound	1945	16.90¢	16.20¢	18.60¢	17.90¢	18.50¢
	1946	19.50¢	18.50¢	19.20¢	NR	19.40¢
	1947	NR	25.10¢	NR	NR	NR
	1948	21.50¢	22.20¢	21.50¢	NR	19.80¢
	1949	23.90¢	24.60¢	23.60¢	NR	20.80¢
Rice, per pound	1945	13.60¢	12¢	13¢	12¢	13.40¢
	1946	14.50¢	12.50¢	13.10¢	NR	14.10¢
	1947	18.90¢	16.40¢	17.60¢	NR	18.90¢
	1948	21.30¢	20.60¢	20.40¢	21.60¢	22.20¢
	1949	18.30¢	17.80¢	18.50¢	18.20¢	20.30¢
Sugar, per pound	1945	6.50¢	6.50¢	7¢	7.30¢	6.70¢
	1946	7.84¢	7.50¢	7.90¢	8¢	7.60¢
	1947	9.60¢	9.60¢	9.90¢	10.10¢	9.50¢
	1948	9.30¢	9¢	9.50¢	9.80¢	9.20¢
	1949	9.30¢	9.10¢	9.70¢	10¢	9.40¢
Tea, per pound	1945	94.40¢	98.80¢	98¢	$1.07	$1.00
	1946	93.60¢	$1.01	93.60¢	$1.08	$1.04
	1947	NR	NR	NR	NR	NR
	1948	NR	NR	NR	NR	NR
	1949	NR	NR	NR	NR	NR
Veal, per pound	1945	44.10¢	42.30¢	42.30¢	44.20¢	46.60¢
	1946	60.10¢	52.30¢	52.20¢	49.60¢	57¢
	1947	90¢	76.10¢	77.40¢	70.60¢	78.40¢
	1948	$1.074	91.40¢	94.10¢	83.50¢	97.70¢
	1949	$1.091	92.30¢	96.70¢	84.90¢	97.80¢

SELECTED PRICES 1945–1949

Item	Source	Description	Price
ALCOHOL			
Gin	*Chicago Tribune* (1946)	Dixie Belle	$3.12/fifth
Liqueur	*Chicago Tribune* (1946)	*Southern Host;* fine 100-proof liqueur	$4.98/fifth
Rye	*Chicago Tribune* (1946)	Mount Vernon	$3.61/fifth
Whiskey	*Chicago Tribune* (1949)	*Old Sunny Brook;* the whiskey that's cheerful as its name	$3.98/fifth
APPAREL, CHILDREN'S			
Cowboy Boots	*Sears, Roebuck* (1946)	Double-tan cowhide	$6.98
Dress	*Sears, Roebuck* (1946)	*Honeysuckle;* for the kindergarten crowd; all have 3" hems, tie sashes	$1.80
Playsuit	*Sears, Roebuck* (1949)	Checked all-in-one in washable cotton percale	$1.49
Shorts	*Sears, Roebuck* (1949)	Clam-digger shorts in Sanforized cotton poplin	$1.39
Socks	*Sears, Roebuck* (1949)	*Boyville;* gaily striped rib-top crew socks	$0.35
Sunsuit	*Sears, Roebuck* (1949)	Cool, summer sun clothes	$0.89
APPAREL, MEN'S			
Boxer Shorts	*Sears, Roebuck* (1946)	Good quality; regular style with grippers or boxer model	$0.65
Hat	*New York Times* (1946)	Pre-shaped Lee	$10.00
Hat	*Chicago Tribune* (1949)	Homburg Distinction by Stetson	$12.50
Neckwear	*New York Times* (1946)	All silk crepe; colorful geometric, floral and all-over patterns	$3.50
Pants	*Sears, Roebuck* (1949)	Stockman-style pants	$4.59
Shirt	*Saturday Evening Post* (1948)	*Lion of Troy;* dress; bold collar; wide and handsome with stitching a full 1/2" from the edge	$5.50
Shirt	*Life* (1949)	*TruVal;* TruVal is able to give you more value per dollar than any other shirt on earth	$2.95
Shirt	*Sears, Roebuck* (1949)	Washable; Sanforized cotton broadcloth; sport-type collar	$2.59
Shoes	*Sears, Roebuck* (1949)	Gold-bond tractor tread	$7.35
Shoes	*New York Times* (1946)	The Freeman shoe; durable soles; strain relieving cradle heels	$10.95
Shorts	*Chicago Tribune* (1949)	*Goldblatts;* 100% nylon; boxer style	$1.94
Socks	*Saturday Evening Post* (1948)	*Sarfert;* now in the new light California weight for spring and summer wear; slack length	$1.50
Suit	*Chicago Tribune* (1946)	*Illinois Clothing Manufacturing;* the largest selection in Chicago	$27.00
Suits	*New York Times* (1948)	Imported and domestic fabrics; many patterns, colours and textures; single and double-breasted	$85.00 to $125
Suspenders	*New York Times* (1946)	Elastic; in stripes or solids	$2.50

Item	Source	Description	Price
Sweaters	*New York Times* (1948)	Washable; virgin wool; pullover	$5.98
Tie	*Fortune* (1949)	*Hickey-Freeman;* silk; knitted; in styles that are not too wide or heavy	$3.50
Topcoat	*New York Times* (1946)	California weight; 2/3 camel hair; 1/3 Australia wool	$110
Underwear	*Life* (1949)	*KOPS Bros. Inc.;* a pantie-girdle with the detachable miracle crotch that custom-fits	$5.95

APPAREL, WOMEN'S

Item	Source	Description	Price
Belt	*Woman's Home Companion* (1949)	*Calderon;* leather	$4.00
Blouse	*Greenville News* (Greenville, SC) (1949)	*Ivey's Jane Holly;* of luscious soft crepe	$4.95
Blousette	*Sears, Roebuck* (1946)	*Kerrybrooke;* Sears brings you that new style sensation; covers you completely, can be worn without a jacket	$2.69
Chemise	*Frederick's of Hollywood* (1947)	*Frederick's Gay Paree;* shorter, barer, sexier than a slip	$5.98
Dress	*Greenville News* (Greenville, SC) (1949)	*Ruth Rowland;* half size; all the bright colors and black; 14 1/2 to 20 1/2	$22.95
Girdle	*Woman's Home Companion* (1948)	*Bestform;* no finer fit at any price	$7.50
Girdle	*Life* (1949)	*Bestform;* to minimize your waist-line, featuring swing-back elastic band for a flat midriff	$6.95
Gloves	*Sears, Roebuck* (1946)	4-button-length slip-ons for all occasion wear; fine imported skins	$4.50
Gloves	*Life* (1949)	*Kayser Afternoon;* dressmaker detailed, suede double-woven cotton	$2.10
Gloves	*Woman's Home Companion* (1949)	*Andre's David;* elbow length doeskin	$18.00
Handkerchiefs	*Greenville Piedmont* (Greenville, SC) (1945)	*Ivey's;* initialed; sheer handkerchiefs of fine batiste in time for Mother's Day	$0.59
Mink Coat	*Chicago Tribune* (1946)	Wild; over 50 masterpieces on display, all made in our factory and priced at savings to 35%	$1,650
Nightgown	*Woman's Home Companion* (1949)	*Jonely;* Sanforized simtex flanlet	$5.00
Panties	*Frederick's of Hollywood* (1947)	*Frederick's Bare Illusion;* to wear under your prettiest things when you want to feel extra alluring and just a little naughty, too	$1.98
Panty Girdle	*Life* (1949)	*Jantzen Foundations;* empire tops to make the ribs flat as a pancake	$8.95
Purse	*Sears, Roebuck* (1946)	*Kerrybrooke;* practical plastics; lightweight, easily kept fresh, every new type: embossed, plastic cord	$4.69
Purse	*Woman's Home Companion* (1949)	*Ronay;* smooth calf satchel with brass handles	$11.00
Rainwear	*Life Magazine* (1949)	*The Alligator Co.;* waterproof fabrics in a variety of styles	$10.75

Item	Source	Description	Price
Scarf	*Woman's Home Companion* (1949)	*Strauss & Mueller;* satin with mink	$3.50
Shoes	*Greenville News* (Greenville, SC) (1949)	*Ivey's Softies by Deb;* in black and brown suede with tooled trim	$8.95
Slip	*Woman's Home Companion* (1948)	*Mary Barron;* nylon satin trimmed at top and hem with Alencon type lace	$6.00
Slip	*Greenville News* (Greenville, SC) (1949)	*Miss Swank;* crepe in white and pink tailored and lace trimmed	$3.95
Stockings	*Chicago Tribune* (1949)	*Boulevard by Belle Sharmeer;* a new deep, deep brown nylon shade	$1.95

APPLIANCES

Item	Source	Description	Price
Carpet Sweeper	*New York Times* (1948)	Electric; can be guided over floors; under furniture; into corners; rubber bumpers	$19.95
Coffee Robot	*New York Times* (1948)	*Farberware;* automatically boils water; stirs brew; keeps coffee for hours without change of flavor	$26.95
Dampness Guard	*EveryWomen's Magazine* (1945)	Dri-Air chemical absorbs dampness in basements, game rooms, store room; kills musty odors	$5.50
Electric Floor	*Woman's Home Polisher* (1948)	*Johnson's;* bring out the beauty of the home *Companion*	$44.50
Electric Knife Sharpener	*New York Times* (1948)	Keeps knives as keen-edged as the day they were bought	$11.95
Hairdryer	*New York Times* (1948)	*Handy-Hanna Electric Hairdryer;* can be held or placed on table stand	$9.95
Humidifier	*Better Homes and Gardens* (1948)	*Fresh'nd-Aire;* guard your family's health; protect your possessions	$59.50
Roaster	*Woman's Home Companion* (1949)	*Westinghouse;* automatic electric roaster; cooks whole meal for eight people	$40.00
Television	*New York Times* (1948)	*Philco* eye-level television consolette; can sit in favorite chair and watch	$349.50
Washer	*Greenville News* (Greenville, SC) (1949)	*Kenmore A;* deluxe model at a standard model price, $5 down, $7 a month	$119.95

BABY PRODUCTS

Item	Source	Description	Price
Baby Swing	*Sears, Roebuck* (1946)	Steel-frame baby swing	$1.85
Car Seat	*Sears, Roebuck* (1946)	Handy baby seat for auto; you can drive undisturbed without worrying about baby	$1.98
Crib Exerciser	*Sears, Roebuck* (1949)	*Novel;* gym crib exerciser amuses baby by the hour, strengthens young muscles	$1.89
Nursers	*Better Homes and Gardens* (1948)	*Evenflo;* breathes as it feeds; includes nipple, bottle, cap	$0.25
Playpen	*Sears, Roebuck* (1946)	Sturdy indoor or outdoor playpen; easy to fold	$11.98
Play Table and High Chair	*Sears, Roebuck* (1946)	Thousands of mothers have found it an indispensable aid in caring for their babies	$7.83

Item	Source	Description	Price
Rattling Toy Set	*Sears, Roebuck* (1949)	Ideal for bath time; for play in crib or pen; 4-piece	$0.98
Shoes	*Sears, Roebuck* (1946)	*Biltwell;* start baby right with supple-leather Biltwell shoes	$1.79

BUSINESS EQUIPMENT & SUPPLIES

Item	Source	Description	Price
Adding Machine	*Fortune* (1949)	*Revolutionary Plus;* economical little key-drive machine to handle the addition	$120
Chrome Furniture	*New York Times* (1946)	Chrome furniture for your showroom and reception room; sales and display room; lobbies, etc.; settee; no sag spring seat; durable leatherette; all colors	$45.00
Display Table	*New York Times* (1946)	All steel; shelf can be raised or lowered; work table, packing table or counter; 6 feet long	$54.50
Steel Trailers	*New York Times* (1946)	Heavy duty; one piece; 4,000-pound capacity	$68.50

COLLECTIBLES

Item	Source	Description	Price
Baskets	*Antiques* (1945)	*Worcester;* circa 1770; a pair of exquisite blue and white china baskets, complete with pierced covers	$225
Book	*Parke-Bernet Galleries* (1946)	1592 printing of *Pierce Penilefse His Supplication to the Diuell,* by Thomas Nash; first edition, one of three known perfect copies	$2,100
Book	*Parke-Bernet Galleries* (1946)	1616 printing of *The Rape of Lucrece,* by William Shakespeare; one of five known copies; sixth edition and the first to bear Shakespeare's name	$3,700
Book	*Parke-Bernet Galleries* (1946)	1653 printing of *The Compleat Angler or the Contemplative Man's Recreation,* by Izaak Walton; being a discourse of fish and fishing, not unworthy of the perusal of most anglers	$400
Book	*Parke-Bernet Galleries* (1946)	1608 printing of the second quarto of *King Lear,* by William Shakespeare	$4,400
Bookcase Desk	*Antiques* (1945)	Chippendale mahogany; kneehole; height 6' 6 1/2" circa 1760 unusual fretwork, top, and mullions	$565
Buttons	*Antiques* (1945)	*Francis Bannerman Son;* British military; Royal Marines light infantry	$0.25
China	*Antiques* (1945)	*Olde Lamps Haviland;* scattered roses, 100 pieces, 12-piece setting	$250
Clock	*Antiques* (1948)	English grandfather clock; Emmanuel Hopperton, Leeds; mahogany case, brass works, inlay carving	$375
Commode	*Antiques* (1945)	Antique; French inlaid; breakfront; 18th century with two drawers, brass ormolu mounts	$325
Coverlet	*Antiques* (1948)	Antique; woven; 82" × 80"; has "North Lima Ohio 1852" in all corners	$60.00
Desk	*Antiques* (1945)	American; small size; walnut; circa 1750 fine serpentine step-up inlaid interior	$975
Figurine	*Antiques* (1948)	*Meissen;* porcelain parrot in brilliant green 11" high plumage perched on rocky base; period 1790	$250
Mirror	*Antiques* (1945)	*The Stuyvesant Shop, Trenton, NJ;* American hand carved; circa 1918; carved from one block of brown mahogany 19 3/4" × 29"	$185
Pin	*Antiques* (1945)	*Old-Mine Diamond;* spray; Louis-Philippe period	$1,850

Item	Source	Description	Price
Sideboard	*Antiques* (1945)	Circa 1810 mahogany sideboard with five inlays 62" wide, 46" high	$595

ENTERTAINMENT

Item	Source	Description	Price
Movie Ticket	*Chicago Tribune* (1946)	*Obsession;* Basil Rathbone, Eugenie Leontovich evenings	$1.20–$3.00
Movie Ticket	*Chicago Tribune* (1949)	*Hamlet;* Academy Award winner; Laurence Olivier; evenings and all day Sunday, all seats	$1.00
Tour	*Fortune* (1949)	*Jungle Garden;* Avery Island, Louisiana; 200-acre jungle garden with its 1,700 varieties of iris, 30,000 azaleas, flame-colored daisies from Africa	$0.25

ENTERTAINMENT, HOME

Item	Source	Description	Price
Board Game	*Sears, Roebuck* (1946)	*Ouija;* mystifying oracle	$1.59
Camera	*Atlanta Constitution* (1947)	Falcon Magni-Vue	$9.95
Changer	*Chicago Tribune* (1949)	*Wurlitzer RCA Victor 45;* this changer brings into your home the amazing 45-rpm system, the new wonder of the world of music	$12.95
Clock Radio	*Life* (1949)	*General Electric Model 65;* wakes you to music-gently without shock; stunning ivory plastic	$36.95
Playing Cards	*Greenville News* (Greenville, SC) (1949)	Canasta; double deck with rules	$1.59
Radio	*Sears, Roebuck* (1946)	*Silvertone Commentator;* self-contained loop aerial, automatic control maintains uniform volume; walnut color plastic case	$11.75
Radio	*Saturday Evening Post* (1948)	*Hallicrafters Model S-28;* four bands bring you thrilling, land, sea, air communications from all parts of the world; perfect for den, library, or office	$47.50
Radio Phonograph	*Saturday Evening Post* (1948)	*Spartan FM;* includes handsome modern design cabinet	$199.95
Radio Phonograph	*Chicago Tribune* (1949)	*Packard-Bell Portable;* home recorder	$99.95
Record	*Music Educators Journal* (1947)	*Carl Fischer;* J. M. Coopersmith's Handel's Messiah; an uncut presentation by the Oratorio Society of New York; vocal score	$1.25
Record Player	*Chicago Tribune* (1949)	*RCA Victor;* this compact attachment plugs into your radio and acts silently with trigger-action speed	$12.95
Television	*Chicago Tribune* (1949)	*General Electric;* see all the action clearly on this 12-channel with big 61-square-inch screen	$189.95
Television	*Chicago Tribune* (1949)	*Emerson AM–FM,* auto-phono; 10"; formerly $495	$295

FARM EQUIPMENT & SUPPLIES

Item	Source	Description	Price
Chicks	*Greenville Piedmont* (Greenville, SC) (1945)	Pay postman on delivery; top quality Pullorum tested, any sex, any breed	$4.95/100
Traps	*New York Times* (1948)	Rats or weasels; 5" × 5" × 18" squirrels or rabbits; 7" × 7" × 24"	$1.75 $3.95

Item	Source	Description	Price
FOOD PRODUCTS			
Baby Food	*Chicago Tribune* (1949)	*Clapp's;* strained	$0.59
Bacon	*Asheville Citizens Times* (Asheville, NC) (1948)	Available at Purity Market, Asheville, North Carolina	$0.59/pound
Boiled Ham	*Asheville Citizens Times* (Asheville, NC) (1948)	Available at Purity Market, Asheville, North Carolina	$0.49/hf pound
Cereal	*Chicago Tribune* (1949)	*American Family Flakes;* large package	$0.27
Cereal	*Chicago Tribune* (1949)	*Nabisco Honey Grahams;* large package	$0.27
Hot Sauce	*Woman's Home Companion* (1948)	*Frank's;* it perks up your taste buds; 3 full oz	$0.10
Ice Cream	*Greenville News* (Greenville, SC) (1949)	*Sealtest Butterscotch Eclairs;* an out-of-this-world dessert treat; box of 4	$0.59
Pears	*Fortune* (1949)	*Royal Riviera;* the business man's favorite gift for customers, associates, employees; gift box of 10 to 14 pears	$2.95
Soda Pop	*Greenville Piedmont* (Greenville, SC) (1945)	*7 Up;* The "fresh up" family drink!	$0.05

A 1948 advertisement for 7 Up. (via Wikimedia Commons)

Item	Source	Description	Price
T-Bone Steak	*Asheville Citizens Times* (Asheville, NC) (1948)	Available at Purity Market, Asheville, North Carolina	$0.59/pound

FURNITURE

Item	Source	Description	Price
Bedroom Suite	*Sears, Roebuck* (1949)	Genuine-walnut veneer, bed, chest, dresser	$89.95
Box Springs	*Sears, Roebuck* (1946)	*Harmony House;* box springs for better sleep, more comfort	$21.98
Cabinet	*Better Homes and Gardens* (1948)	*Fed-Oir;* by day a couch, at night you slide the bed out	$170
Cupboard	*Richmond Times Dispatch* (1949)	*Craftique Hepplewhite;* copied to the last detail out of the same age-old solid mahogany	$179.50
Dinette Set	*Sears, Roebuck* (1949)	5-pc. modern dinette set; 4-legged table, 4 chairs; shining limed oak and chrome	$89.95
Glider	*Richmond Times Dispatch* (1949)	*Troy;* 2-cushion; make your garden your outdoor living room	$59.50
Hassock	*Sears, Roebuck* (1946)	Beauty plus utility best describes this carefully tailored hassock; covered with our finest heavy moleskin-type artificial leather	$7.65
Lamp	*Richmond Times Dispatch* (1949)	Solid brass; 16" opaque drum shade in maroon or green 28" tall	$12.95
Lamp Table	*Better Homes and Gardens* (1948)	*Ruper Lee;* solid cherry; has authentic rose and oak leaf hand-carved pulls; height 25"; top 18" × 14"	$23.45
Mirror	*Better Homes and Gardens* (1948)	Full length; one of the greatest conveniences the well-groomed woman can have	$14.90
Record Cabinet	*Sears, Roebuck* (1946)	Protect your records in these beautiful cabinets	$13.50
Sofa Bed	*Greenville News* (Greenville, SC) (1949)	Duran-plastic; makes into a comfortable bed for two in a jiffy	$79.88
Steel Cabinet Ensembles	*Sears, Roebuck* (1949)	HomArt 3-piece ensemble of matching base units in two sizes	$179.50
Table	*The American Home* (1948)	*Samson;* folding; famous for strength, for comfort, for wear	$12.95

GARDEN EQUIPMENT & SUPPLIES

Item	Source	Description	Price
Bird Food	*Better Homes and Gardens* (1948)	*Banquet;* wild bird; 50 lbs; feed the wild birds this winter	$9.00
Broad Hatchet	*Sears, Roebuck* (1946)	*Craftsman;* for heavy and rough cutting	$1.69
Flowering Pink Dogwood	*Richmond Times Dispatch* (1949)	Virginia's state flower; 18" to 24" size	$2.85
Greenhouse	*The American Home* (1948)	*Orlyt;* comes in sections for easy assembly; size 10' × 11'	$264
Half Hatchet	*Sears, Roebuck* (1946)	*Craftsman;* has the feel and easy swing that only perfect balance can give	$1.45
Hydrangea	*Greenville News* (Greenville, SC) (1949)	*The Flower Shop;* Italy, Texas; get your beautiful hydrangeas, blooming size, 2-foot plants	$1.00

Item	Source	Description	Price
Lawn Mower	*Richmond Times Dispatch* (1949)	*Eclipse Packhound;* power-driven wheels, power driven reel, power-driven sharpener, positive action; 21" cut	$127.50
Lilies	*Better Homes and Gardens* (1948)	*Burpee Orange Trump;* as many as 8 large blooms to a cluster; package of 3 bulbs	$2.75/pkg
Marigolds	*The American Home* (1948)	*Burpee;* glorious large double blooms up to 4" across; normally $0.75	$0.10/pkg
Roses	*Woman's Home Companion* (1948)	*Armstrong Nurseries Nocturne;* all-American award winner, 1948; deep red; package of 3	$5.25
Roses	*Chicago Tribune* (1949)	Two dozen long red roses in vase	$5.00
Rose Bushes	*Sears, Roebuck* (1946)	Sturdy, easy-to-grow everblooming roses	$1.15
Sprinkler	*Saturday Evening Post* (1948)	*Sunbeam Rain King;* automatic; a turn on the red control dial on top sets this sensational Rain King for any desired circle 5 to 50 feet in diameter	$6.95
		West of Denver	$7.25
Tuberous Begonias	*The American Home* (1948)	Your choice of nine lovely colors; package of four	$0.50/pkg

HOTEL RATES

Item	Source	Description	Price
Hotel Room	*New York Times* (1946)	*The Dorset,* Miami Beach; double room	$12.00 and up
Hotel Room	*New York Times* (1946)	*Croydon Arms,* Miami Beach	$16.00
Hotel Room	*Richmond Times Dispatch* (1949)	*Hotel Richmond;* overlooking Capitol Square; 300 rooms	$3.75/day

HOUSEHOLD GOODS

Item	Source	Description	Price
Alarm Clock	*Life* (1949)	Gleaming ivory baked enamel case; one key winds both time and alarm	$4.50
Auto Vents	*Better Homes and Gardens* (1948)	*Maid-O-Mist;* for comfort, humidify; put low cost auto-vents on your steam radiators	$5.00
Bedspread	*Greenville News* (Greenville, SC) (1949)	*Baby Chenille;* full or twin sizes, 8 colors; every spread in this special group is worth five precious dollars	$3.99
China	*Greenville News* (Greenville, SC) (1949)	*Wedgwood Woodstock;* Bone china; 20-piece starter set	$75.60
Clog Remover	*Woman's Home Companion* (1948)	*Drano;* opens clogged drains—keeps them running free	$0.25
Coffee Maker	*Woman's Home Companion* (1949)	Automatic; electric; shifts to low heat when coffee is done	$29.00
Dormitory Trunk	*Sears, Roebuck* (1949)	*J. C. Higgins;* 33" × 18 1/2" × 20 1/2"	$20.34
Electric Broom	*Woman's Home Companion* (1948)	*Regina Electrikbroom;* the new revolutionary vacuum cleaner	$44.95
Electric Liquidizer	*Woman's Home Companion* (1949)	Prepares drinks, salad dressing, soups, children's foods	$35.00
Electric Painter	*Saturday Evening Post* (1948)	*Lowell Thoro-Spray;* the modern answer to home decorating	$34.95
Faucet	*Better Homes and Gardens* (1948)	*Faucet Queen;* a flick of the finger and you have spray or stream	$0.39

Item	Source	Description	Price
Flatware	*Woman's Home Companion* (1948)	*Gorham;* sterling; to love and to cherish; per place setting	$23.00
Flatware	*Greenville News* (Greenville, SC) (1949)	*Gorham Chantilly;* sterling silver; prices are for 6-piece place settings	$25.50
Food Chopper	*Sears, Roebuck* (1946)	New double action, new streamlined design, new chopping efficiency	$2.98
Glasses	*Better Homes and Gardens* (1948)	*Libby;* decorated with a band of white satin-etched leaves; set includes four 12-oz water tumblers; four 6-oz juice glasses; and four 6-oz sherbets	$4.00
Goblets	*Woman's Home Companion* (1949)	*Tudor;* fine handblown lead cut crystal	$30/dozen
Hammer	*Sears, Roebuck* (1946)	*Craftsman;* for the man who wants only the best; 16 oz	$1.39
Humidifier	*Better Homes and Gardens* (1948)	*Magi-tray;* for storing foods which do not require refrigeration; 10" × 6" × 4 1/2"	$2.50
Lamp Bulb	*Life* (1949)	*General Electric;* 60-watt bulbs; there's a right-size lamp to fill the bill	$0.12
Mattress	*Life* (1949)	*Craftmaster's Gold Label;* hundreds of famous inner-springs buried in soft cotton; 15-year guarantee	$54.50
Mattress and Box Springs	*Woman's Home Companion* (1948)	*Serta Perfect Sleeper;* you sleep on it, not in it	$49.50
Mirror	*Sears, Roebuck* (1946)	*Harmony House;* full-length; hang a full-length mirror on your bedroom, hall or closet door; see yourself as others see you—tip to toe	$5.31
Mothproofer	*Woman's Home Companion* (1948)	*Larvex;* penetrates each tiny woolen fibre and makes the cloth itself mothproof for a whole year	$1.19/quart
Open End Wrenches	*Sears, Roebuck* (1946)	*Craftsman;* set of 6	$2.85
Paint	*Greenville Piedmont* (Greenville, SC) (1945)	*Kem-Tone;* the modern miracle wall finish; paste form	$2.98
Paint	*Richmond Times Dispatch* (1949)	*Glidden Spred-Luster Indoor;* for walls that are truly beautiful choose the original resin-emulsion enamel	$4.98/gallon
Plate	*Antiques* (1945)	*Royal Worcester;* 9" plates; light blue and gold in paisley design	$75/dozen
Platter	*Antiques* (1945)	*Staffordshire Amethyst;* 12" × 14 1/2"; Ridgway Oriental pattern	$15.00
Pressing Cloth	*Woman's Home Companion* (1948)	*Weaver Pres-Kloth;* for a perfect steam press; safe for any fabric	$0.89
Rug Cleaner	*Greenville Piedmont* (Greenville, SC) (1945)	*Tavern;* will clean spots or entire rug	$0.59
Shelving Paper	*Woman's Home Companion* (1948)	*Royledge;* put colorful highlights in your kitchen	$0.08/9 feet
Tablecloth	*Sears, Roebuck* (1946)	*TableVogue* by Rosemary; 58" × 54"	$1.69
Travel Clock	*Saturday Evening Post* (1948)	*Sentinel Wayfarer;* a smart chromium-plated watch with black-enamel numeral dial snuggly fitted into a stand-up metal frame that folds flat	$4.95
Vacuum Cleaner	*Chicago Tribune* (1949)	*General Electric Tidy;* maid-of-all-work for floor and above-the-floor cleaning	$39.95
Waffle Iron	*Woman's Home Companion* (1948)	*Handyhot Twin;* electrical products since 1903	$12.95

Item	Source	Description	Price
Wardrobe Trunk	*Sears, Roebuck* (1949)	*J. C. Higgins;* 3-plywood veneer body	$56.70
Water Heater	*The National Police Gazette* (1948)	*Presto;* electric; enjoy the luxury of steaming hot water, anytime, anywhere, simply plug heater's cord in socket and presto you have the hot water you want	$4.98

JEWELRY

Item	Source	Description	Price
Cuff Links	*Fortune* (1949)	*Jaccard;* matching; initialed; 14K natural gold masterfully engraved	$47.50
Pendant	*Woman's Home Companion* (1949)	*Eisenberg;* rhinestone; on velvet band	$7.50
Watch	*Life* (1949)	*Lord Elgin DeLuxe;* men's; the DuraPower mainspring eliminates 99% of watch repairs due to steel mainspring failures	$47.50
Watch	*Greenville News* (Greenville, SC) (1949)	*Elgin DeLuxe;* 17 jewels adjusted; DuraPower mainspring	$55
Wristwatch	*Woman's Home Companion* (1948)	*Harvel;* beautiful 17-jewel, precision-built, gold-filled watches	$47.50
Zircon	*The National Police Gazette* (1948)	1st quality, pure white; 3 zircons; approximate total weight 2 cts	$6.40

MEALS

Item	Source	Description	Price
Dinner	*Chicago Tribune* (1946)	*The Corner House;* open all nite, air conditioned	$0.95
Lunch	*Atlanta Constitution* (1947)	*J. J. Newberry;* smothered pork chop, candied yams, buttered green peas, hot rolls, and muffins and butter	$0.50
Meal	*Chicago Tribune* (1949)	*Hillmans;* broiled jumbo whitefish, with lemon slice; parsley buttered potatoes	$0.50

MEDICAL PRODUCTS & SERVICES

Item	Source	Description	Price
Antacid	*Better Homes and Gardens* (1948)	*Alka-Seltzer;* quick relief for discomfort of colds	$0.30
Antacid	*Chicago Tribune* (1949)	*Tums;* must you avoid favorite foods because of acid stomach?	$0.10
Corn Remover	*Chicago Tribune* (1946)	*Walgreens Freezone;* for corns	$0.16
Skin Whitener Ointment	*Greenville Piedmont* (Greenville, SC) (1945)	*Dr. Fred Palmer's;* loosens blackheads for easy removal	$0.25
Vitamins	*Sears, Roebuck* (1946)	B-Complex capsules; costs only 1 1/3¢ a day; 100-day supply	$1.39
Yeast Tablets	*Sears, Roebuck* (1946)	*Brewer's;* 100 tablets	$0.27

MOTORIZED VEHICLES, SERVICES, & SUPPLIES

Item	Source	Description	Price
Automobile	Richard M. Langworth and Robson, *Complete Book of Collectible Cars* (1985)	*DeSoto Custom Suburban*; 8-passenger sedan [cost in 1946]	$2,093–$2,631
Automobile	Langworth and Robson, *Complete Book of Collectible Cars* (1985)	*Mercury Sportsman Convertible* [cost in 1946]	$2,209

Item	Source	Description	Price
Automobile	Langworth and Robson, *Complete Book of Collectible Cars* (1985)	*Chevrolet Fleetmaster*; 4-door sedan [cost in 1947]	$1,212–$2,013
Automobile	Langworth and Robson, *Complete Book of Collectible Cars* (1985)	*Nash Ambassador Custom Cariolet* [cost in 1948]	$2,345
Automobile	Langworth and Robson, *Complete Book of Collectible Cars* (1985)	*Oldsmobile Futuramic 98 Convertible* [cost in 1948]	$2,078–$2,624
Automobile	Langworth and Robson, *Complete Book of Collectible Cars* (1985)	*Buick Roadmaster Riviera*; two-door hard top [cost in 1949]	$3,203
Automobile	Langworth and Robson, *Complete Book of Collectible Cars* (1985)	*Dodge Wayfarer Roadster* [cost in 1949]	$1,727
Automobile	Langworth and Robson, *Complete Book of Collectible Cars* (1985)	*Packard Super 8 DeLuxe Club Sedan* [cost in 1949]	$2,894–$2,919
Automobile	*Fortune* Magazine (1949)	*Jaguar Sedan;* the finest car of its class in the world	$4,600
Cycle Goggles	*Sears, Roebuck* (1949)	Motorcycle goggles	$3.49
Seat Covers	*Sears, Roebuck* (1946)	*Allstate;* of rich-looking, serviceable fiber, smartly finished with artificial leather	$3.33
Solvent	*Liberty* (1945)	Casite sludge solvent for easy starting Pint can	$0.65

MUSICAL INSTRUMENTS

Item	Source	Description	Price
Bugle	*Sears, Roebuck* (1946)	*Cadet Bugle;* is pitched to the same key as regular army bugle and can be played in any bugle corps	$0.69
Harmonica	*Sears, Roebuck* (1946)	*Silvertone;* American designed and made	$1.79
Organ	*Greenville News* (Greenville, SC) (1949)	*Hammond;* serving over 18,000 churches today	$1,300
Piano Rolls	*Sears, Roebuck* (1946)	*QRS;* favorite selections. choose from 79 popular, patriotic, sacred songs	$0.95/2
Song Flute	*Sears, Roebuck* (1946)	Ideal for children to learn on; grand for servicemen	$0.94
Trumpet	*Chicago Tribune* (1946)	Postwar-model trumpets; complete with case	$135
Valve Oil	*Music Educators Journal* (1947)	*Speedex;* your instrument will play better and last longer	$0.25

OTHER

Item	Source	Description	Price
Audubon Kit	*Woman's Home Companion* (1949)	*Lucey's Workshop;* bird modeling; including roughed-out block for six birds	$2.95
Buttons	*Antiques* (1945)	Civil War; eagle buttons with letters A-D-I-C	$0.10
Dry Cleaning	*Greenville News* (Greenville, SC) (1949)	Men's suits, dresses, men's felt hats; cash and carry	$0.50

Item	Source	Description	Price
Dye	*Woman's Home Companion* (1948)	*Rit;* puts the whole rainbow of colors at your fingertips	$0.25
Flying Lessons	*Airports of Columbia Photograph* (1946)	*Dixie Aviation Aeronca Champion;* America's No. 1 low-cost airplane, easy to fly, easy to buy	$2.00
Hairstyling	*Greenville Piedmont* (Greenville, SC) (1945)	*Ideal Beauty Shop;* creme oil permanents; were $8	$6.50
Heat Sealer	*Better Homes and Gardens* (1948)	*Dobeckmun;* for cellophane bags; seals woolens so moths can't reach them; keeps corsages fresh for days	$7.95
Loom	*Sears, Roebuck* (1949)	*Hearthside;* folding floor-model loom	$99.50
Pen	*Greenville News* (Greenville, SC) (1949)	*Waterman;* ball point; finest quality; regularly $3.50	$0.99
Pen	*Life* (1949)	*Parker 51;* 14 precision advances give true newness; writes dry with wet ink	$13.50
Pen Set	*Fortune* (1949)	*Parker Aero-Metric 51;* set in midnight blue; gold filled caps	$29.75
Pesticide	*The American Home* (1948)	*Mouse Seeds;* kills mice	$0.25
Picture	*The National Police Gazette* (1948)	Full color; heavyweight boxing champions; handsome lithograph suitable for framing for hotels, restaurants club rooms, barber shops, bars, gymnasiums and dens; size 22" × 21"	$1.00
Pictures	*The National Police Gazette* (1948)	Women wrestlers; just what the sport fan wants; 8" × 10"; ready for framing	$4.00/6
Rug Frame	*Sears, Roebuck* (1949)	For waffle-weave rugs, frame and stand	$5.19
Stationery	*Chicago Tribune* (1946)	Letters; random; 40 sheets, envelopes	$0.13
Sunglasses	*Sears, Roebuck* (1949)	Our best men's aviation style	$6.95
Tool Pack	*Woman's Home Companion* (1949)	*Clement Cook Top;* quality light tools for women	$10.00

PERSONAL CARE PRODUCTS

Item	Source	Description	Price
Aftershave	*Woman's Home Companion* (1949)	Mennen Skin Bracer	$0.98
Denture Adhesive	*Sears, Roebuck* (1949)	*Denturfit;* a resilient dental plastic liner for greater comfort and security; 8-oz jar	$0.79
Deodorant	*Woman's Home Companion* (1948)	*Arrid;*don't be half safe	$0.39
Deodorant	*Life* (1949)	*Dryad;* men shy away from a girl who offends with unromantic perspiration odor	$0.10/$0.29/$0.59
Face Cream	*Life* (1949)	*Jergens;* acts as a deep cleaner, a softener, a dry skin cream, and a powder base	$0.20–$1.39/ jar
Hair Rinse	*Woman's Home Companion* (1948)	*Marchand's;* there's a blending shade created especially for you; 6 rinses	$0.25
Hair Styling	*Greenville News* (Greenville, SC) (1949)	*White's Machine;* permanent; machineless or cold wave	$5.00

373

Item	Source	Description	Price
Hand Cream	*Greenville News* (Greenville, SC) (1949)	*Mitchum Esoterica;* new kind of hand cream for fading those brown spots that make your hands look old	$1.50

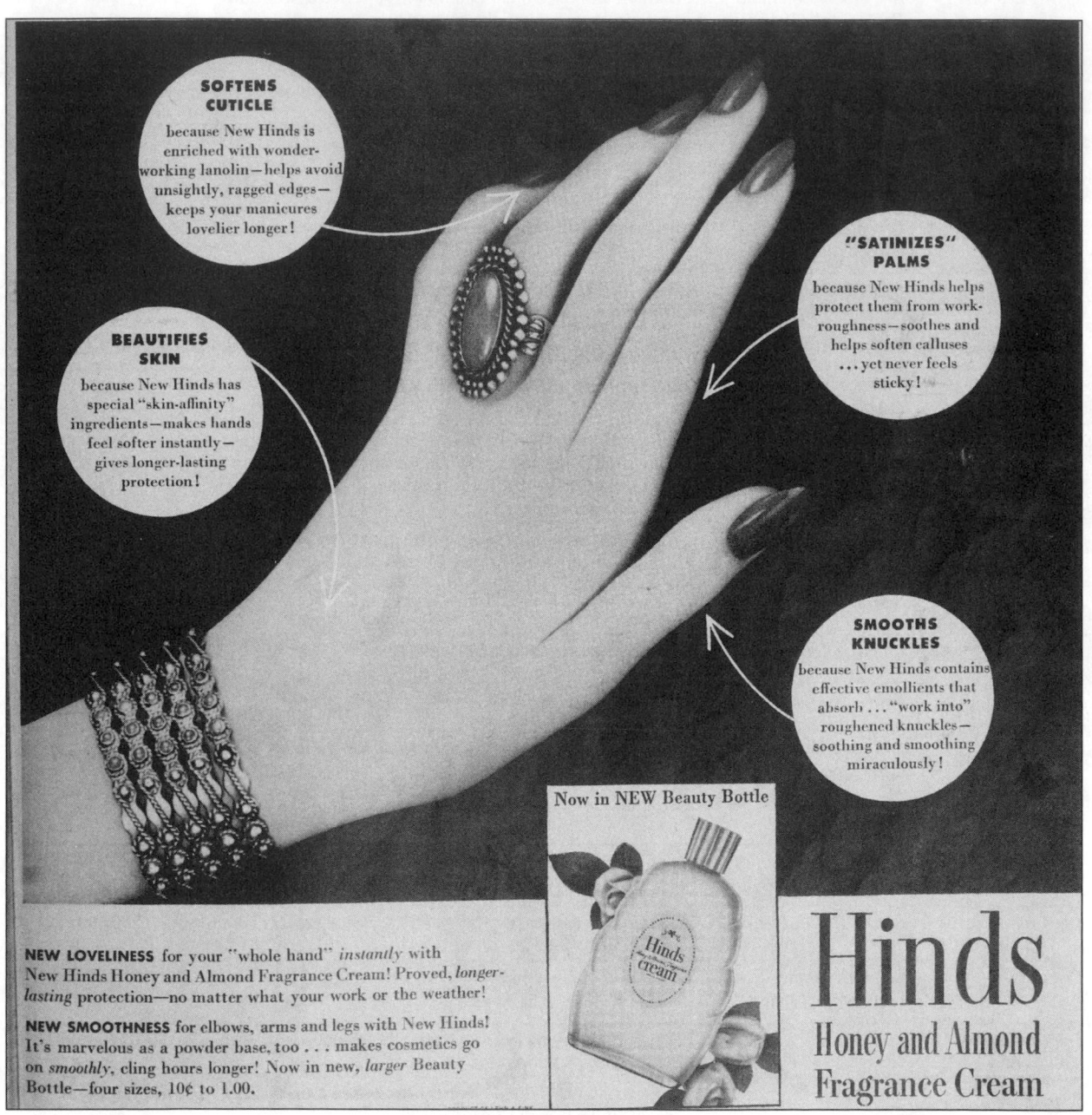

A 1948 advertisement for Hinds hand cream. (via Wikimedia Commons)

Item	Source	Description	Price
Home Permanent Kit	*Sears, Roebuck* (1946)	*Toni;* complete kit; everything you need for a beautiful permanent wave	$1.40
Home Permanent Kit	*Life* (1949)	*Richard Hudnut;* problem hair requires the kindest, safest, gentlest type of home permanent	$2.75
Home Permanent Kit	*Life* (1949)	*Toni;* the secret of lovelier hair is yours with a Toni home permanent; includes plastic curlers	$2.00
Lotion	*Better Homes and Gardens* (1948)	*Jergens Lotion;* finer than ever; more protective, too; large size	$1.00
Manicure Set	*Fortune* (1949)	*Clauss;* handsome, smooth, genuine tan-cowhide case with zipper closing	$15.00
Nail Nippers	*Saturday Evening Post* (1948)	*LaCross;* scientifically curved jaws for close, accurate work	$2.50
Night Cream	*Greenville News* (Greenville, SC) (1949)	*Noxzema;* millions of women use it as a night cream and as a foundation cream; big $0.85 jar	$0.59
Razor	*Life* (1949)	*Gillette Super-Speed;* instant blade changing, real shaving comfort, double-edge economy; 10 blades	$1.00
Razor Blades	*Saturday Evening Post* (1948)	*Marlin;* double-edge; once over and a clean shave; pkg of 12	$0.28
Shampoo	*Chicago Tribune* (1949)	*Walgreens Beauty Brew Beer;* $0.89 regularly	$0.89/2
Shave Cream	*Woman's Home Companion* (1949)	*Woodbury Lather;* shave-cream kit; includes lotion, shampoo, and talc	$1.10
Shaving Lotion	*Saturday Evening Post* (1948)	*Williams Aqua Velva;* after-shave preparation	$0.50
Soap	*Woman's Home Companion* (1948)	*Yardley English Lavender;* you're enchanting when you're wearing the gay-hearted fragrance	$0.40
Soap	*Chicago Tribune* (1949)	*Walgreen Woodbury's;* regular-size cakes; limit four cakes	$0.23
Tissues	*Life* (1949)	*Tender-Touch;* a finer facial tissue that's actually washed in pure, soft water to give it that soft tender touch; box of 300	$0.27
Toothbrush	*Sears, Roebuck* (1949)	Made of heavy-gauge DuPont nylon bristles	$0.59

PUBLICATIONS

Book	*The National Police Gazette* (1948)	*The Babe Ruth Story;* as told to Bob Considine; this important book by two of the greatest names in baseball	$1
Book	*Better Homes and Gardens* (1948)	*Inside USA,* by John Gunther; Book of the Month Club selection	$3.50
Book	*Sears, Roebuck* (1949)	*Bible;* young folks text Bible; leather	$4.71
Magazine	*Sears, Roebuck* (1946)	Popular Mechanics	$3/year
Magazine	*Sears, Roebuck* (1946)	*Jack and Jill;* ten-month subscription	$1.98
Magazine	*Sears, Roebuck* (1946)	Flower Grower	$4/2years
Magazine	*Life* (1949)	*Life;* weekly	$0.20

Item	Source	Description	Price
REAL ESTATE			
Apartment Building	*Chicago Tribune* (1949)	For sale; six flats; two story; four rooms, bath, stove, heat; $5,000 cash	$9,750
Apartments	*Chicago Tribune* (1949)	For sale; two apartments; brick; 5–6 rooms; no leases; separate furnaces	$9,500
Grocery-Deli	*Chicago Tribune* (1946)	Can add liquor and meats; doing $750 week; cash	$6,500
House	*Greenville Piedmont* (Greenville, SC) (1945)	Attractive, practically new 5-room house in Augusta Rd. section; $1,500 down, balance like rent	$5,700
Tavern	*Chicago Tribune* (1949)	For sale; doing good business; 44' bar; ideal for man and wife; includes inventory	$7,000
SEWING EQUIPMENT & SUPPLIES			
Cloth	*Atlanta Constitution* (1947)	*Avondale Cotton Chambrays;* for play clothes, bedroom ensembles	$0.49/yard
Sewing Machine	*Greenville News* (Greenville, SC) (1949)	*Singer Portable;* rebuilt electric machines	$42.50
Toy Sewing Machine	*New York Times* (1948)	Stitches so she can make all her own doll clothes; carrying case	$3.98
SPORTS EQUIPMENT			
Barbell	*The National Police Gazette* (1948)	*Independent Iron Works;* buy direct from factory	$8.95
Belts	*New York Times* (1948)	Ranger belt	$1.95
Boots	*New York Times* (1948)	Cowboy style	$7.95
Reel	*Saturday Evening Post* (1948)	*Ocean City No. 999;* open face; level wind; quadruple; multiplying 100 yds	$9.95
Saddles	*New York Times* (1948)	Especially made for jumping	$160
Saddles	*New York Times* (1948)	Trooper saddle for English-style riders	$25.00
TOBACCO PRODUCTS			
Ashtray	*New York Times* (1948)	Sports ashtray; gamebirds, cowboy or fox-hunt scenes; rimmed with heavy sterling silver	$8.50
Cigarette Holder	*New York Times* (1948)	Sterling silver	$7.50
Cigarette Holder	*Saturday Evening Post* (1948)	*Medico Filtered;* cuts down nicotine; includes box of ten filters	$2.00
Cigarettes	*Chicago Tribune* (1946)	All standard brands; per carton	$1.34

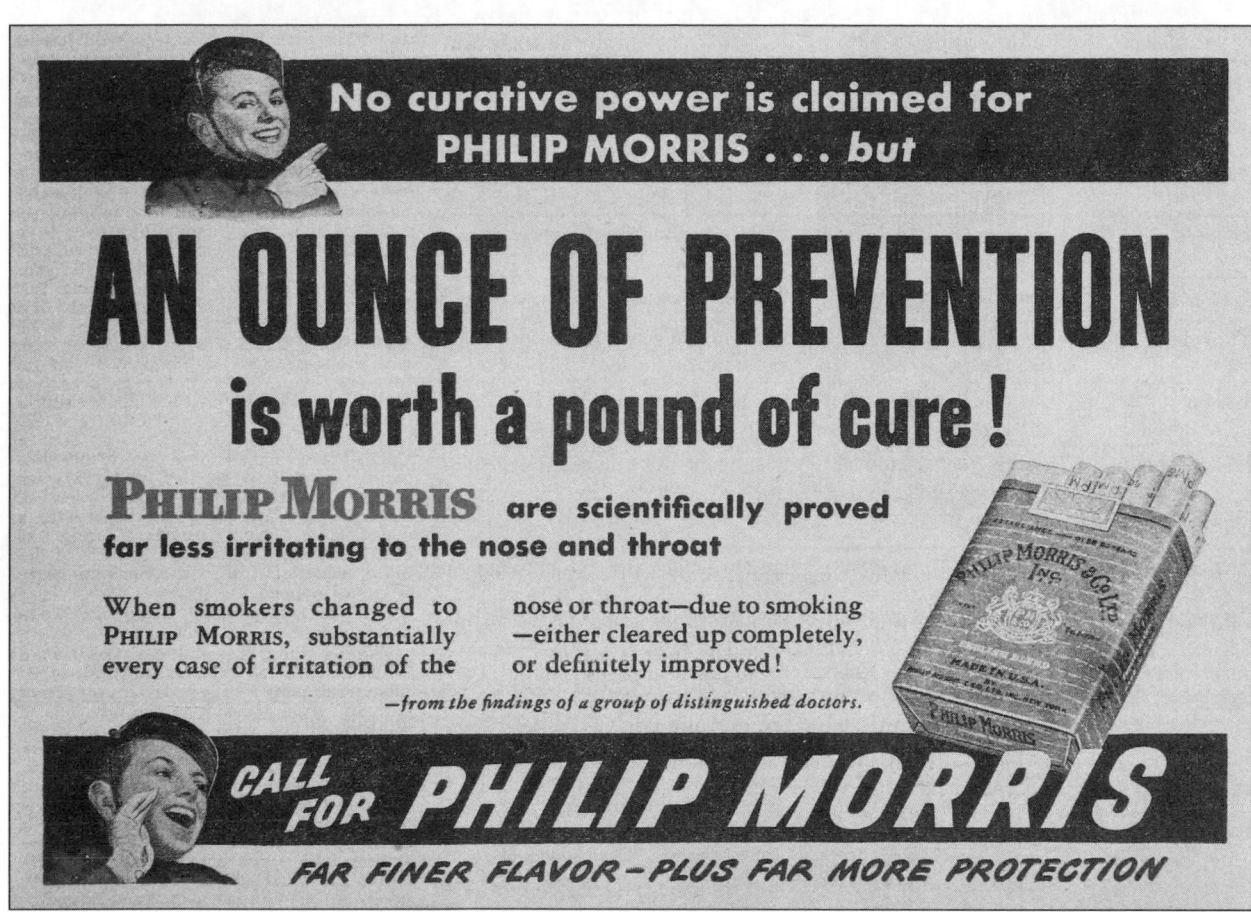

No curative power is claimed for
PHILIP MORRIS . . . *but*

AN OUNCE OF PREVENTION
is worth a pound of cure !

PHILIP MORRIS are scientifically proved
far less irritating to the nose and throat

When smokers changed to
PHILIP MORRIS, substantially
every case of irritation of the
nose or throat—due to smoking
—either cleared up completely,
or definitely improved!

—from the findings of a group of distinguished doctors.

CALL FOR PHILIP MORRIS
FAR FINER FLAVOR—PLUS FAR MORE PROTECTION

A 1945 advertisement for Philip Morris cigarettes. (via Wikimedia Commons)

Item	Source	Description	Price
Cigarette Server	*New York Times* (1948)	It appears to be a lamp; shade pushes down; cigarettes emerge to serve guests	$5.00
Lighter	*Saturday Evening Post* (1948)	*Zippo;* your favorite design engraved on a Zippo lighter; brush finish	$3.25
Pipe Lighter	*New York Times* (1948)	Designed for lighting pipes; when tilted acts like small Bunsen burner; shooting flame into pipe bowl	$5.00
Pocket Lighter	*New York Times* (1948)	Outer jacket of 14 karat gold	$160
Table Lighter	*New York Times* (1948)	Gold plated	$15.00

TOYS

Item	Source	Description	Price
Balls	*Atlanta Constitution* (1947)	Inflated rubber balls; brightly colored	$0.05/3
Doll	*Atlanta Constitution* (1947)	*Sunbabe;* drinking and wetting rubber dolls; complete in box with diaper and bottle	$1.98
Holster Set	*Sears, Roebuck* (1946)	Low-priced Lone Ranger holster set	$1.15

Item	Source	Description	Price
Model Kit	*Sears, Roebuck* (1946)	4 extra-large model kits	$0.89
Model Kit	*Sears, Roebuck* (1946)	6 small hobby model kits	$0.54
Racer	*Atlanta Constitution* (1947)	Hours of fun from this metal racer, in many colors, key attached; 5" long	$0.39
Scooter	*Atlanta Constitution* (1947)	With red and white-rubber tires	$1.59
Telescope	*Sears, Roebuck* (1946)	6-power telescope with precision-ground lenses	$1.00
Tricycle	*Atlanta Constitution* (1947)	Heavy metal with rubber tires; large size painted ivory and blue; originally $15.98	$5.98
Wagon	*Atlanta Constitution* (1947)	Red steel body; medium	$3.29
Walkie-Talkie	*Sears, Roebuck* (1946)	Brand new; adds more excitement to your games	$1.47

TRAVEL & TRANSPORTATION

Item	Source	Description	Price
Airplane Flight	*New York Times* (1948)	LaGuardia one-stop direct to Los Angeles	$99.00
Airplane Flight	*New York Times* (1948)	LaGuardia one-stop direct to Miami	$50.00
Airplane Flight	*New York Times* (1948)	Fly to California overnight	$88.00
Airplane Flight	*New York Times* (1946)	Fly to Miami and back; 21 passengers; complimentary meals aboard	$165
Airline Ticket	*Chicago Tribune* (1949)	*Skycoach;* California from Chicago	$75.00
Railroad Ticket	*Chicago Tribune* (1946)	*Columbian;* Chicago to Washington; round trip	$25.30

MISCELLANY 1945–1949

Bing Signs for New Program $30,000 A Week

Hollywood, Cal. Aug. 15 (AP)—Bing Crosby will return to the radio in October on a weekly program that will be broadcast to 600 stations in the United States, South America, Australia, and Europe.

Everett Crosby, the singer's brother, completed negotiations tonight with James H. Carmine, vice president of Philco Corporation, which will sponsor the programs over the American Broadcasting Company network.

Everett said the salary was the highest ever offered for such a program. Although he declined to specify the amount, other sources indicated Crosby's weekly stipend will be about $30,000, which would be about $2,500 higher than the previous high, paid to Jack Benny.

Chicago Tribune, August 16, 1946

10¢ Buses Open Service to Auto Lots; Fare Hit Some Parkers Balk; Expected 5¢ Trip

Shuttle buses painted in distinctive gray and red to distinguish them from the Chicago Motor Coach company's thru city buses started service yesterday between the automobile parking areas in Grant Park and the Loop.

Patronage was light, as had been expected by traffic experts because the service was new and the weather was favorable to pedestrians. As more motorists become aware of the new, free parking facilities at Soldiers' Field and the shuttle bus service, traffic men said, business will pick up.

Chicago Tribune, August 16, 1946

Estimate Cost to Consumers at $150 Million; Increases Ranging from 3 to 12 Pct.

Washington, D.C. August 25 (AP) Price increases estimated by OPA officials to cost the public "well over 150 million dollars a year" were granted today on such articles as radios, stoves, washing machines, vacuum cleaners, toasters, and irons.

The OPA said the increases were required by the new price controls law which specifies that wholesalers' and retailers' profits must not be cut below their margins on last March 31. Items affected are those on which dealers had been required to absorb part of price increases granted earlier to manufacturers. The OPA said it expects today's increases to be the last on consumers' goods, except for refrigerators, on which the price boost will be announced soon.

The price agency itself announced only that the raises ranged from 3 to 12 per cent. The 150 million dollar estimate was given by an official who would not be quoted by name, in response to a reporter's query on total cost.

Chicago Tribune, August 16, 1946

HISTORICAL SNAPSHOT 1950–1954

1950

- Korean War begins
- Congress increases personal and corporate income taxes and corporation taxes
- Federal Reserve estimates that 4 in 10 families are worth at least $5,000,
- 1 in 10 have assets of at least $25,000
- Gross National Product reaches $284 billion
- Auto registrations show one car for every 3.7 Americans
- Blue Cross programs cover 3.7 million Americans
- Railroads seized by federal troops to avert a strike
- 5 million homes have television sets; 45 million have radios
- Orlon fiber is introduced by E.I. duPont de Nemours
- Otis Elevator installs first passenger elevator with self-opening doors
- More than 75 percent of U.S. farms electrified
- Average farmer produces enough food for 15.5 people
- Coca-Cola's share of U.S. cola market is 69 percent; Pepsi-Cola's share is 15 percent

1951

- President Truman requests a $10 billion war fund
- First power-producing nuclear fission reactor by Atomic Energy Commission
- $71.6 billion budget submitted to Congress

- Wages and salaries frozen
- Margin profit ceilings placed on 200,000 consumer items
- Income-tax receipts reach $56.1 million
- UNIVAC computer introduced
- CBS broadcasts color television programs, although the FCC later approves the RCA color system as the industry standard
- U.S. telephone call rates go from 5¢ to 10¢
- Denver grocery chain begins offering S&H Green Stamps

1952

- General Dwight David Eisenhower elected president
- 600,000 CIO steelworkers stage 53-day strike
- Nation's railroads returned to private control
- 17 million homes have television sets
- Four of five shirts sold in America are white
- Nearly half of U.S. farms have tractors
- First Holiday Inn opens near Memphis

1953

- New York subway fares rise 5¢ to 15¢
- Per capita state taxes average $68.04
- Unemployment hits record lows
- *TV Guide* and *Playboy* begin publication
- New York's Seeman Brothers introduce first instant ice tea

1954

- Sony introduces first pocket-size transistor radio
- Supreme Court declares racial segregation in public schools illegal
- First nuclear-powered submarine, Nautilus, launched
- Gasoline averages 29¢ per gallon
- Texas Instruments introduces first practical silicon transistor
- Taxpayers with incomes of more than $100,000 pay more than $67,000 in taxes
- Sales of Viceroy cigarettes leap as smokers shift to filter-tipped cigarettes
- Open-heart surgery is introduced by Minneapolis physician C. Walton Lillehei
- RCA introduces first color television set
- $13 million, 900-room Fontainebleau Hotel opens at Miami Beach
- Swanson & Sons introduces frozen TV dinners
- Births remain above 4 million per year

The most famous UNIVAC product was the UNIVAC I mainframe computer of 1951, which became known for predicting the outcome of the U.S. presidential election the following year. This incident is noteworthy because the computer predicted an Eisenhower landslide when traditional pollsters all called it for Adlai Stevenson. The numbers were so skewed that CBS's news boss in New York decided the computer was in error and refused to allow the prediction to be read. Instead they showed some staged theatrics that suggested the computer was not responsive, and announced it was predicting 8-7 odds for an Eisenhower win (the actual prediction was 100-1). When the predictions proved true and Eisenhower won a landslide within 1% of the initial prediction, Charles Collingwood, the on-air announcer, embarrassingly announced that they had covered up the earlier prediction. (via Wikimedia Commons)

SELECTED INCOME 1950–1954

Job	Source	Description	Pay
Actor	Legrand and Karney *Chronicle of the Cinema* (1995)	Annual salary of Clark Gable in 1954	$500,000
Actor	Warren G. Harris, *Lucy and Desi: The Legendary Love Story* (1991)	Contract of Lucy and Desi Arnaz for ninety-eight episodes of *"I Love Lucy"* during 1954–1955 season	$4 million
Ad Agency Gal Friday	*New York Times* (1952)	Sten. and ad agency	$85/wk
Attorney	*Chicago Tribune* (1953)	General counsel for independent company; must be well-grounded and experienced corporation lawyer with real-estate experience	$12,000/year
Automechanics	*Chicago Tribune* (1953)	Experienced only	$2/hr
Baseball Player	Rampersad, *Jackie Robinson, A Biography* (1997)	Annual salary of Jackie Robinson in 1951	$39,750
Baseball Radio Announcer	Richard Layman, ed., *American Decades: 1950–1959* (1994)	Annual salary of Red Barber in 1954	$50,000
Biologist	*Chicago Tribune* (1951)	Master's Degree in biology required to be assistant to head of physiology and endocrinology research. Some experience other than academic preferred	$70/wk
Bookkeeper	*New York Times* (1952)	Accounts payable, dress manufacturing experience; 9-5:30, 5 days	$60/wk
Comedian	Layman, ed., *American Decades: 1950–1959* (1994)	Annual contract of Milton Berle with NBC in 1951	$200,000
Comedian	Layman, ed., *American Decades: 1950–1959* (1994)	Two-year contract of Jackie Gleason with CBS for weekly show *The Honeymooners* in 1954	$11 million
Corporate Controller	*New York Times* (1954)	Experience in retail not essential	$25,000
Director of Sales	*New York Times* (1956)	Age 40–55; engineering or physics degree; government contract experience	$25,000
Director of Field Engineering	*New York Times* (1956)	Age 35–55; engineering degree	$19,000
Engineer	*New York Times* (1956)	Senior levels; benefits	$14,000
Executive Accountant	*Chicago Tribune* (1953)	Complete corporation experience for full-charge assignment; manual and machine postings	$10,000/yr
Finance Executive	*New York Times* (1954)	Head of Purchased Paper Department	$10,000
Hairstylist	*San Francisco Examiner* (1950)	Male; with manager's license; refs	$75/wk and commission

Job	Source	Description	Pay
Mechanical Draftsman	*New York Times* (1956)	Senior level	$167 per week
Millwright Foreman	*Chicago Tribune* (1951)	Experienced in maintenance of machine moving and installing all types of equipment, maintenance of brick work, sheet metal; supervise 15–20 workers	$4,500–$5,000
Pianist (1954)	*Guinness Book of World Records* (1981)	Single night earnings of Liberace for concert at Madison Square Garden	$138,000
Product Designer	*New York Times* (1956)	Designing new cameras; camera equipment; must be creative	$8,000
Route Man	*Chicago Tribune* (1954)	Towel supply; perm.; 5 day wk; under 35	$82/wk
Salesman	*Chicago Tribune* (1953)	Hats, shoes, slacks, stead; must be A-1 top man in town; able to start at once	$100–$150/wk
Sales Manager	*New York Times* (1956)	Graduate of accounting; retail experience; must know machine accounting methods	$10,000
Secretary	*Chicago Tribune* (1953)	Situation wanted; top notch; 35; personable appearance	$325/mo
Shipping Clerk Assistant	*Chicago Tribune* (1953)	Good opportunity for reliable man	$1.25/hr
Singer	Bufwack and Oermann, *Finding Her Voice, The Saga of Women in Country Music* (1993)	Dorothy Shay's nightly fee for concerts in 1951	$5,000
Singer	Layman, ed., *American Decades: 1950–1959* (1994)	Annual income of Elvis Presley in 1952	$10 million
Social Worker	*Atlanta Constitution* (1953)	Must have sch. soc. wk. training; exc. conditions; give full Inf., educ. and exp. in first letter	$225/mo
Stenographer	*Atlanta Constitution* (1953)	One-girl office; 5-day week; national concern	$175/mo
Television Host	Layman, ed., *American Decades: 1950–1959* (1994)	Annual contract of Ed Sullivan for TV show *Toast of the Town* in 1951	$125,000

CONSUMER EXPENDITURES 1950–1954

(Per Capita)

Expenditure Type	1950	1951	1952	1953	1954
Clothing	$105.48	$113.42	$116.87	$117.19	$116.39
Food	$354.68	$393.42	$408.39	$409.86	$411.35
Auto Usage	$148.99	$143.24	$142.08	$164.19	$160.72
New Auto Purchase	$67.90	$55.74	$50.97	$69.56	$66.51
Auto Parts	$9.89	$9.72	$10.19	$9.40	$8.01
Gas & Oil	$36.26	$39.54	$43.32	$46.38	$48.03
Housing	$143.06	$157.49	$172.02	$187.38	$198.90
Furniture	$20.44	$20.74	$22.29	$23.19	$23.40
Utilities	$48.13	$51.20	$52.88	$54.52	$57.88
Telephone & Telegraph	$12.53	$14.26	$15.29	$16.92	$17.24
Physicians	$17.14	$17.49	$19.11	$20.68	$22.78
Dentists	$6.59	$6.48	$7.00	$7.52	$8.62
Health Insurance	$5.93	$5.83	$7.00	$8.15	$8.62
Personal Business	$42.85	$46.02	$47.15	$50.76	$54.19
Personal Care	$15.82	$17.49	$18.48	$19.43	$20.94
Tobacco	$28.35	$29.17	$31.22	$31.96	$30.17
Local Transport	$12.53	$12.96	$12.74	$12.53	$11.70
Intercity Transport	$5.93	$6.48	$7	$6.89	$6.16
Recreation	$73.18	$75.83	$78.37	$81.47	$83.13
Religion/Welfare Activities	$15.82	$16.85	$19.11	$19.43	$20.94
Private Education & Research	$11.87	$12.31	$13.38	$13.79	$14.16
Per Capita Consumption	$1266.45	$1348.79	$1395.95	$1457.71	$1476.68

INVESTMENTS 1950–1954

Investment	1950	1951	1952	1953	1954
Basic Yield, One-Year Corporate Bonds	1.42	2.05	2.73	2.62	2.40
Short-term Interest Rates, 4–6 Months, Prime Commercial Paper	1.45	2.16	2.33	2.52	1.58
Basic Yield, Common Stocks, Total	6.27	6.12	5.50	5.49	4.78
Index of Common Stocks (194121943510)	18.40	22.34	24.50	24.73	29.69

COMMON STOCKS, CLOSING PRICE AND YIELD, FIRST BUSINESS DAY OF YEAR

(PARENTHETICAL NUMBER IS ANNUAL DIVIDEND IN DOLLARS)

	1950	1951	1952	1953	1954
Allis Chalmers	32 5/8	45	50 3/4	59	46 3/4
	(2)	(3.25)	(3.50)	(4)	(4)
AT&T	146 1/4	151 1/2	155 3/8	160 1/4	156 1/2
	(9)	(9)	(9)	(9)	(9)
American Tobacco	74 1/2	66 1/4	62 3/8	65 7/8	62 1/2
	(4)	(4)	(4)	(4)	(3)
Anaconda	28 1/2	40 5/8	50 3/8	43 7/8 30	5/8
	(2.50)	(3)	(3.50)	(3.50)	(3)
B&O	10	20 1/2	19 1/8	28	19 1/2
	(/)	(/)	(/)	(.75)	(1)
Bethlehem Steel	31 5/8	50 1/4	51 5/8	56 1/4	51 1/8
	(2.40)	(4.10)	(4)	(4)	(4)
Corn Products	72 7/8	70	70 1/2	70 1/8	73
	(3.60)	(3.60)	(3.60)	(3.60)	(3.60)
General Electric	42 3/8	50 3/8	NR	72 1/2	88 1/4
	(2.50)	(3.40)		(3.00)	(4)
General Motors	70 3/4	7 1/4	31 3/8	68 1/2	60
(2 shares for 1 split, 10/3/50)	(8)	(2.50)	(4)	(4)	(4)
International Business Machines	213	206	207	234	247
(5% stock dividend 1/23/50) (5% stock dividend 1/26/51) (5% stock dividend 1/28/52) (5% stock dividend 1/29/53) (2 1/2% stock dividend 1/28/54) (5 shares for 4 split, 5/10/54)	(4)	(4)	(4)	(4)	(4)
Intl Harvester	27 3/8	32 5/8	28 1/8	32 5/8	28 1/2
	(1.80)	(2)	(2)	(2)	(2)
National Biscuit	39	33	30	35 1/4	36 1/2
	(7)	(2)	(2)	(2)	(2)
US Steel	26 3/8	43	40 1/4	43 1/2	39 7/8
(3 shares for 1 split, 6/2/49)	(1)	(3.45)	(3)	(3)	(3)

Investment	1950	1951	1952	1953	1954
Western Union	41 3/8 (3)	40 5.8 (/)	42 3/4 (2.75)	40 (3.00)	41 5/8 (3)

STANDARD JOBS 1950–1954

Job Type	1950	1951	1952	1953	1954
Average of All Industries, excl. farm labor	$3255/yr	$3526/yr	$3732/yr	$3927/yr	$4033/yr
Average of All Industries, incl. farm labor	$3180/yr	$3452/yr	$3660/yr	$3852/yr	$3953/yr
Bituminous Coal Mining	$3245/yr	$3762/yr	$3718/yr	$4061/yr	$3959/yr
Building Trades	$3377/yr	$3774/yr	$4086/yr	$4354/yr	$4484/yr
Domestics	$1502/yr	$1588/yr	$1707/yr	$1805/yr	$1832/yr
Farm Labor	$1454/yr	$1568/yr	$1594/yr	$1464/yr	$1498/yr
Federal Civilian	$3632/yr	$3924/yr	$4202/yr	$4411/yr	$4507/yr
Federal Employees, Executive Depts.	$3220/yr	$3189/yr	$3326/yr	$3410/yr	$3485/yr
Federal Military	$2897/yr	$2788/yr	$2891/yr	$2927/yr	$2997/yr
Finance, Insurance, & Real Estate	$3217/yr	$3356/yr	$3503/yr	$3663/yr	$3828/yr
Gas & Electricity Workers	$3571/yr	$3851/yr	$4125/yr	$4404/yr	$4579/yr
Manufacturing, Durable Goods	$3483/yr	$3862/yr	$4126/yr	$4383/yr	$4452/yr
Manufacturing, Nondurable Goods	$3154/yr	$3386/yr	$3587/yr	$3784/yr	$3923/yr
Medical/Health Services Workers	$2067/yr	$2143/yr	$2262/yr	$2365/yr	$2417/yr
Miscellaneous Manufacturing	$3020/yr	$3240/yr	$3404/yr	$3560/yr	$3640/yr
Motion Picture Services	$3089/yr	$3269/yr	$3485/yr	$3626/yr	$3929/yr
Nonprofit Org. Workers	$2578/yr	$2720/yr	$2898/yr	$3041/yr	$3179/yr
Passenger Transportation Workers, Local and Highway	$3288/yr	$3489/yr	$3645/yr	$3809/yr	$3914/yr
Personal Services	$2254/yr	$2355/yr	$2462/yr	$2573/yr	$2682/yr
Public School Teachers	$2794/yr	$2998/yr	$3169/yr	$3314/yr	$3510/yr
Radio Broadcasting &Television Workers	$4698/yr	$5017/yr	$5417/yr	$5734/yr	$5957/yr
Railroads	$3778/yr	$4163/yr	$4338/yr	$4418/yr	$4544/yr
State and Local Govt. Workers	$2758/yr	$2758/yr	$2950/yr	$3140/yr	$3281/yr
Telephone & Telegraph Workers	$3059/yr	$3253/yr	$3492/yr	$3720/yr	$3914/yr
Wholesale and Retail Trade Workers	$3034/yr	$3171/yr	$3284/yr	$3446/yr	$3558/yr

FOOD BASKET 1950–1954

(NR = Not Reported)

Commodity	Year	New York	Atlanta	Chicago	Denver	Los Angeles
Apples, Fresh, per pound	1950	12.80¢	12.80¢	13.80¢	12.90¢	11.80¢
	1951	10.90¢	12.50¢	12¢	12.10¢	11.80¢
	1952	NR	NR	16.40¢	16.60¢	15.80¢
	1953	16.30¢	16.10¢	16.50	NR	15.90¢
	1954	14.90¢	16.10¢	16.30¢	NR	16.60¢
Beans, Navy, per pound	1950	17.10¢	14.90¢	14.80¢	16¢	15.40¢
	1951	17¢	15.30¢	15.70¢	19.10¢	17.90¢
	1952	16.90¢	15.60¢	15.70¢	16.70¢	16¢
	1953	17.60¢	16.40¢	16.60¢	17.30¢	24.60¢
	1954	18¢	16.90¢	17.50¢	NR	17.90¢
Beef, Rib Roasts, per pound	1950	75.30¢	75.70¢	74.10¢	72.10¢	80.70¢
	1951	87¢	84.10¢	82.90¢	82¢	88¢
	1952	87¢	NR	83.10¢	81.10¢	89.60¢
	1953	71¢	74¢	66.20¢	NR	79¢
	1954	70.10¢	77.70¢	66.70¢	NR	79.20¢
Beef, Steaks (Round), per pound	1950	98.70¢	95.60¢	88.90¢	86.40¢	88.60¢
	1951	$1.15	$1.11	$1.04	$1.01	$1.06
	1952	$1.17	$1.12	$1.04	$1.00	$1.11
	1953	98.40¢	90.70¢	82.40¢	NR	90.50¢
	1954	97.40¢	92¢	81.80¢	NR	89.40¢
Bread, White, per pound	1950	15.30¢	14.40¢	13.20¢	13.90¢	14.70¢
	1951	16.80¢	15.90¢	14.50¢	15.30¢	15.90¢
	1952	17.30¢	15.90¢	15.20¢	15.30¢	16.40¢
	1953	17.90¢	16.20¢	15.20¢	NR	17.30¢
	1954	18.30¢	17.10¢	16.10¢	NR	18.50¢
Butter, per pound	1950	74.20¢	78¢	70.50¢	72.30¢	72.20¢
	1951	82.60¢	86.40¢	80.20¢	81.30¢	81.30¢
	1952	85.30¢	90.30¢	83¢	86.90¢	86.30¢
	1953	80.20¢	84.30¢	77.20¢	NR	80.70¢
	1954	73.70¢	77.60¢	71.60¢	NR	72¢
Cheese, per pound	1950	55¢	54.10¢	50.90¢	46.70¢	48.60¢
	1951	61.30¢	61.20¢	59.10¢	55.55¢	57.40
	1952	62.20¢	NR	60.50¢	58.90¢	61.10¢
	1953	62.70¢	NR	59.60¢	NR	60.80¢
	1954	59.40¢	NR	58¢	NR	57.80¢
Chickens, per pound	1950	44.30¢	54.20¢	47.50¢	65.80¢	58.40¢
	1951	46.50¢	56.90¢	49.90¢	67.70¢	58.90¢
	1952	47.10¢	56.20¢	48.70¢	68.30¢	60.20¢
	1953	45.50¢	54.30¢	46.60¢	NR	57.70¢
	1954	42¢	47.30¢	NR	NR	NR
Coffee, per pound	1950	79.60¢	77¢	77.40¢	82.90¢	81.10¢
	1951	86.70¢	83.50¢	84¢	92.50¢	90.30¢
	1952	86.90¢	83.10¢	83.70¢	92.20¢	90.30¢
	1953	89.90¢	86.30¢	86.80¢	NR	89.70¢
	1954	$1.13	$1.10	$1.11	NR	$1.07

Commodity	Year	New York	Atlanta	Chicago	Denver	Los Angeles
Cornmeal, per pound	1950	10.60¢	6.40¢	10.40¢	9.90¢	10.60¢
	1951	11.10¢	7.10¢	11.10¢	10.80¢	11.20¢
	1952	11.90¢	7.80¢	12.10¢	17.50¢	18.20¢
	1953	12.10¢	8¢	12.20¢	NR	12.70¢
	1954	12.10¢	7.10¢	12.40¢	NR	12.60¢
Eggs, per dozen	1950	67.10¢	57.20¢	56.70¢	59.50¢	61.90¢
	1951	79.40¢	71.10¢	70.80¢	74.10¢	74.40¢
	1952	71.80¢	63.40¢	64.10¢	68.50¢	67¢
	1953	78.20¢	70¢	69.50¢	NR	69.40¢
	1954	67.20¢	58¢	57.20¢	NR	55.80¢
Flour, Wheat, per pound	1950	9.68¢	10.44¢	9.46¢	9.10¢	9.88¢
	1951	10.28¢	11.06¢	10.04¢	9.86¢	10.38¢
	1952	10.26¢	11¢	10¢	10.06¢	10.74¢
	1953	10.40¢	10.62¢	10¢	NR	10.72¢
	1954	10.64¢	10.76¢	10.40¢	NR	10.88¢
Lard, per pound	1950	20.20¢	19¢	18.30¢	18.70¢	20.60¢
	1951	25¢	24.30¢	23.80¢	24.20¢	25.50¢
	1952	19.20¢	18.20¢	17.60¢	18.10¢	20.70¢
	1953	19.60¢	19.60¢	18.20¢	NR	21.70¢
	1954	25.80¢	25.40¢	24.80¢	NR	27.80¢
Milk, Fresh, per quart	1950	21.90¢	21.90¢	20.90¢	20.60¢	19¢
	1951	25¢	25¢	23.60¢	22.60¢	20.70¢
	1952	25.40¢	25.20¢	25.30¢	23.60¢	22.60¢
	1953	25.90¢	25.80¢	25¢	NR	22.90¢
	1954	26.30¢	25.80¢	24.90¢	NR	21.70¢
Mutton and Lamb, Leg, per pound	1950	72¢	79¢	72.80¢	71.90¢	74¢
	1951	81.40¢	86.80¢	80.90¢	79.80¢	84.10¢
	1952	80¢	84.80¢	79.20¢	81¢	81.80¢
	1953	69.50¢	77.90¢	67.90¢	NR	73.20¢
	1954	68.30¢	76¢	67.80¢	NR	70.30¢
Pork, Bacon, Sliced, per pound	1950	68.20¢	64.70¢	63.20¢	64.10¢	68.30¢
	1951	72.10¢	53.20¢	65.50¢	66.20¢	71.20¢
	1952	68.40¢	64.30¢	63.50¢	65.20¢	67.40¢
	1953	83¢	82.20¢	80.80¢	NR	81¢
	1954	88.50¢	82.20¢	80.80¢	NR	85.40¢
Pork, Chops, per pound	1950	76.20¢	68¢	75.30¢	69.90¢	82.60¢
	1951	81.40¢	86.80¢	80.90¢	79.80¢	84.10¢
	1952	80¢	84.80¢	79.20¢	81¢	81.80¢
	1953	69.50¢	77.90¢	67.90¢	NR	73.20¢
	1954	68.30¢	76¢	67.80¢	NR	70.30¢
Pork, Ham, Whole, per pound	1950	64¢	60.90¢	59.60¢	56.60¢	62.50¢
	1951	67.90¢	64.50¢	64¢	61.60¢	67.10¢
	1952	65.80¢	64.40¢	62.60¢	61¢	65.50¢
	1953	71.60¢	69.20¢	67.70¢	NR	71.10¢
	1954	71.80¢	69¢	68¢	NR	70.80¢
Pork, Salt, per pound	1950	43¢	34.70¢	39.20¢	34.60¢	38.70¢
	1951	44.80¢	38.50¢	43.50¢	37.50¢	44¢
	1952	43.60¢	34.50¢	40.30¢	36.40¢	41.10¢
	1953	NR	NR	NR	NR	NR
	1954	NR	NR	NR	NR	NR
Potatoes, Irish, per 15 pounds	1950	65.70¢	73.60¢	83.70¢	67.60¢	72.70¢
	1951	71.20¢	76.40¢	92¢	73.90¢	83.90¢
	1952	$1.05	$1.20	$1.23	$1.04	$1.15
	1953	71.60¢	83.40¢	97.20¢	NR	93.30¢
	1954	69.70¢	73.10¢	91.70¢	NR	$1.00

Commodity	Year	New York	Atlanta	Chicago	Denver	Los Angeles
Prunes, Dried, per pound	1950	24.80¢	NR	25.20¢	24.80¢	22¢
	1951	27.40¢	NR	28.40¢	28.30¢	24.60¢
	1952	NR	NR	NR	NR	NR
	1953	28¢	29.80¢	29.20¢	NR	26.60¢
	1954	29.70¢	31.30¢	31.20¢	NR	27.80¢
Rice, per pound	1950	17.40¢	16¢	16.20¢	16.10¢	17.20¢
	1951	18.60¢	16.80¢	16.70¢	17.40¢	18¢
	1952	18.70¢	17.40¢	17.10¢	17.50¢	18.20¢
	1953	20.30¢	19¢	18.30¢	NR	19.70¢
	1954	19.90¢	18.60¢	17.70¢	NR	20.50¢
Sugar, per pound	1950	9.36¢	9.40¢	9.82¢	10.30¢	9.66¢
	1951	9.74¢	9.84¢	10.22¢	10.70¢	10.06¢
	1952	9.80¢	9.94¢	10.38¢	10.94¢	10.46¢
	1953	9.94¢	9.98¢	10.64¢	NR	10.54¢
	1954	10¢	9.92¢	NR	10.58¢	10.34¢
Tea, per pound	1950	NR	NR	NR	NR	NR
	1951	NR	NR	NR	NR	NR
	1952	NR	NR	NR	NR	NR
	1953	$1.24	$1.29	$1.30	NR	$1.40
	1954	$1.31	$1.37	$1.37	NR	$1.44
Veal, per pound	1950	$1.20	$1.01	$1.00	97.30¢	$1.08
	1951	$1.39	$1.18	$1.14	$1.12	$1.27
	1952	$1.41	$1.17	$1.15	$1.06	$1.28
	1953	$1.29	$1.01	$1.05	NR	$1.12
	1954	$1.23	98.40¢	$1.05	NR	$1.09

SELECTED PRICES 1950–1954

Item	Source	Description	Price
ALCOHOL			
Blended Whiskey	*New York Times* (1952)	*Old Homestead;* 4/5 quart	$3.19
Bourbon	*New York Times* (1952)	Old Taylor Bonded	$7.35
Bourbon Whiskey	*New York Times* (1952)	*Virginia Lee;* 4/5 quart	$3.69
Canadian Whiskey	*New York Times* (1952)	Seagram's V.O.	$6.10
Cognac	*New York Times* (1952)	Courvoisier V.S.O.P.	$3.68
Grain Gin	*New York Times* (1952)	*Fifth Avenue Gin;* 4/5 quart	$2.88
Rye	*New York Times* (1952)	B.P.R. Bonded	$4.49
Scotch Whiskey	*New York Times* (1952)	*White Abbey;* 4/5 quart	$4.59
APPAREL, CHILDREN'S			
Baseball Suit	*Good Housekeeping* (1950)	*Yankiboy;* Little Leaguers make big hits with these dashingly styled, sturdily made outfits; cotton-flannel shirt and pants, red trim; matching cap	$2.49
Buffalo Bill Costume	*Belk's Christmas Catalog* (1951)	Black-twill pants with chaps, 2-tone flannelette shirt	$2.98
Longies	*Sears, Roebuck* (1952)	Handsome Glen plaid-suspender longies of durable cotton	$1.44
Shirt	*Life* (1950)	*McMullen;* man-tailored shirts get fancy; featuring French cuffs, pique trim, tucked flowed bosom	$10.95–$15.95
Shirt	*Sears, Roebuck* (1952)	Movie star print; has Dale Evans, Roy Rogers, and Trigger on front; old favorites and gay new styles	$0.84
Shoes	*Sears, Roebuck* (1952)	*Jeepers;* Roy Rogers and Trigger imprinted in bright colors to delight every boy, girl	$3.39
Suit	*Good Housekeeping* (1950)	*Botany Eton;* suit for boys; blends the superior quality of Botany Brand 100% virgin worsted with the superb men's wear tailoring of master clothes	$21.00
APPAREL, MEN'S			
Belt	*New York Times* (1952)	Leather	$10.00
Head Warmer	*Woman's Home Companion* (1950)	*Picard;* expert skiers started wearing knitted face-caps last year—now they're your newest perkiest cap for ear-chilling days	$5.00
Jacket	*New York Times* (1952)	Sports jacket, denim striped	$16.50

Item	Source	Description	Price
Jacket	*New York Times* (1952)	Lounging jacket, navy blue silk	$35.00
Pajamas	*New York Times* (1952)	Nylon in gold with navy piping	$14.95
Scarf	*New York Times* (1952)	Silk; in plaids and solids	$10.00
Shirt	*New York Times* (1952)	Clan plaid sports shirt; washable	$16.50
Shirt	*New York Times* (1952)	Oxford cloth button down	$3.95
Shirt	*New York Times* (1952)	Sports shirts; flannels, gabardines or rayon	$3.98
Shirt	*Life* (1950)	*Shirtcraft Airman Model Z;* no buttons on America's newest, smartest business shirt, it zips closed	$3.95
Shirt	*Chicago Tribune* (1951)	Broadcloth; madras	$1.88
Shoes	*Sears, Roebuck* (1952)	Shockless cushion insole; it's smart to be comfortable	$8.98
Shoes	*Sears, Roebuck* (1952)	*Jeepers;* our best quality; pro-type styling	$4.98
Shoes	*New York Times* (1952)	Handsewn moccasins	$13.95
Sweater	*New York Times* (1952)	Sleeveless striped cardigan of imported Alpaca	$23.00
Undershirt	*Life* (1950)	*Arrow;* made by the makers of Arrow shirts	$0.85

APPAREL, WOMEN'S

Item	Source	Description	Price
Brassiere	*Woman's Day* (1950)	*Flexees;* strapless; of satin, elastic and nylon marquisette	$2.00
Brassiere	*Good Housekeeping* (1950)	Embroidered nylon marquisette cups with rayon satin frame and back	$3.00
Brassiere	*Woman's Home Companion* (1950)	*Maidenform Allo-ette;* 2" band in white satin	$2.00
Brassiere	*Chicago Tribune* (1951)	The Magic Insets gently support from below to give lasting uplift, youthful beauty	$3.00
Brassiere	*Today's Health Magazine* (1952)	*Anne Alt;* maternity and nursing; firm, reliable support to enlarging breasts B&C Cups D Cups	 $2.75 $3.00
Brassiere	*Sears, Roebuck* (1952)	Rayon satin or cotton; was $1.19	$0.98
Dress	*McCall's* (1950)	*Clifford;* diagonally tucked bodice; blouse stops at waistline	$23.00
Dress	*McCall's* (1950)	*Margi Spring Lilac;* with yoke and cuffs of ribbed tucks, tucks below the belt are released to make a full skirt	$40.00
Dress	*McCall's* (1950)	*Hi-Dee;* of Irish linen; sleeveless	$30.00
Dress	*Sears, Roebuck* (1952)	Waffle pique; such gay, young new prints	$3.98
Dress	*Ebony* (1954)	One-piece cotton dress has scoop neck and princess-cut wallpaper waist below empire bust	$15.00

Item	Source	Description	Price
Exercise Suit	Chicago Tribune (1951)	Aqua Sheen Slim-Rite; coverall; plastic exercise suit	$3.98
Fur	Chicago Tribune (1951)	Capes, scarfs, stoles, jackets, coats	$175
Girdle	Woman's Day (1950)	Charvin; white nylon girdle, sleek as a slither and twice as cute	$6.95
Girdle	Woman's Day (1950)	Boned front; with side zipper available in tearose, nylon or satin	$12.50
Girdle	Woman's Home Companion (1950)	Bestform; has nylon-taffeta front, sides, and back and boned-nylon diaphragm	$5.95
Girdle	Chicago Tribune (1951)	The Magic Inset eliminates annoying bones, yet it can't roll over, wrinkle, or bind	$5.95
Golf Suit	Good Housekeeping (1950)	Pro-golfer two-piece woman's outfit; smartly fashioned in sanforized fine-combed cotton	$12.00
Gown	Ebony (1954)	Luxite Red Spice; add spicy variety to your lingerie wardrobe; gay, brilliant, beautiful red for a saucy glimpse of color under a dark hem	$5.95
Robe	Woman's Home Companion (1950)	Evelyn Pearson; in pastel or dark rayon crepe, contrast piping	$13.00
Robe	Woman's Home Companion (1950)	In frost white, harvest rose, tawny gold	$9.95
Shoes	Good Housekeeping (1950)	Wohl Natural Poise; beautifully fashioned; blessedly comfortable and they fit precisely—thanks to the exclusive scientific dimensional equalizer	$8.95
Shoes	Good Housekeeping (1950)	Desco Revelations; rest your arches, look divine	$7.95
Shoes	Today's Health Magazine (1952)	Aerotized Walkmaster; the airway design; you'll be delighted with the slipper-like comfort	$8.95
Slip	Woman's Day (1950)	Seamprufe Marybell; daintily adorned with lace and pin tucking; in fine sanforized wamsutta cotton	$4.00
Slippers	Ebony (1954)	Honeybugs; Robert Haynes, co-starring in Return to Paradise, says "My favorite slippers."	$4.99
Suit	Good Housekeeping (1950)	Side-split skirt for walking ease; sheen gabardine	$70.00

APPLIANCES

Item	Source	Description	Price
Electric Range	McCall's (1950)	Deep Freeze; you can buy them with confidence	$159.95
Gas Range	Chicago Tribune (1951)	Imperial; full size; 36"	$99.00
Gas Range	Chicago Tribune (1951)	Marshall DeLuxe; the best cook in the world is helpless with a bulky, inefficient stove	$159
Home Freezer	McCall's (1950)	Deep Freeze DeLuxe Model; 12.3 cubic feet holds more than 430 lbs of assorted frozen foods	$399.95
Refrigerator	McCall's (1950)	Admiral Dual-Temp; no defrosting—no dish covers needed—no bouncing favors	$189.95
Refrigerator	Chicago Tribune (1951)	Frigidaire; has extra-large frozen food super freezer	$199.75
Steam Radiator	The American Home (1954)	Burnham Portable; steam heat	$60-$108

Item	Source	Description	Price
Washing Machine	*Woman's Day* (1950)	*Bendix Home Appliances;* tried and true agitator washing; does 8 pounds of wash at a time	$189.95
Washing Machine	*Woman's Day* (1950)	*Speed Queen;* guarantee yourself the most for your money in home laundry service	$99.95–$139.95
Washing Machine	*McCall's* (1950)	*Thor Automagic Spinner-Washer;* from suds to spin-dry in a single porcelain tub	$199.50
Washing Machine	*Consumer Reports* (1950)	Maytag Nonautomatic	$184.95
Washing Machine	*Chicago Tribune* (1951)	*Speed Queen;* for easier family washings	$99.95

BABY PRODUCTS

Item	Source	Description	Price
Baby Lotion	*McCall's* (1950)	*Johnson's;* hospital-proved the most effective preparation	$0.49/$0.98
Baby Nipple	*Today's Health Magazine* (1952)	*Evenflo;* America's most popular nurser; includes nipple, bottle, cap	$0.25
Baby Oil	*Good Housekeeping* (1950)	*Playtex;* prevent diaper rash with Playtex	$0.79
Crib	*Sears, Roebuck* (1952)	*Honeysuckle;* full-size chest crib; keep baby's pads, shirts, sheets at your fingertips, right where you need them	$49.95
Crib Mattress	*Today's Health Magazine* (1952)	*Bunny Bear;* America's only crib mattress with the unique bonded guarantee	$10.95
Pants	*Woman's Home Companion* (1950)	*Kleinert's;* waterproofed without rubber; three pairs	$3.00
Pants	*McCall's* (1950)	*Playtex;* in pink, white, or blue	$0.69
Pants	*Good Housekeeping* (1950)	*Playtex;* ventilated; it clings gently, gives waterproof fit without cutting off circulation	$0.79
Server	*Good Housekeeping* (1950)	Safety server for babies; prevent tragic highchair accidents; lighten mother's burdens	$15.95
Shoes	*Today's Health Magazine* (1952)	*Moran Wee-Walker;* perfect fit, fine durable leathers	$1.19
Training Pants	*Chicago Tribune* (1951)	White cotton knit; quality	$0.15

BUSINESS EQUIPMENT & SUPPLIES

Item	Source	Description	Price
Adding Machine Tape	*Sears, Roebuck* (1952)	Fits all models	$1.79
Carbon Paper	*Sears, Roebuck* (1952)	*Tower Black;* for typewriter copies	$1.19
Paper Punch	*Sears, Roebuck* (1952)	1/4" diameter holes as close as 1/8" from paper edge	$0.89
Stapler	*Life* (1950)	*Bostitch B8R;* pound it, squeeze it, strike it; fastens it better and faster with wire	$2.60
Stapler	*Sears, Roebuck* (1952)	*Arrow;* use as stapler, plier, or tacker	$2.34
Staples	*Sears, Roebuck* (1952)	*Arrow;* fits all standard staplers; box of 5,000	$0.82

Item	Source	Description	Price

COLLECTIBLES

Item	Source	Description	Price
Book	*Rare Books and Manuscripts; Lathrop C Harper, Inc.* (1953)	*Miguel De Cervantes;* El Ingenioso Hidalgo Don Quijote de la Mancha; Excessively rare second issue of the first edition	$3,500
Book	*Rare Books and Manuscripts; Lathrop C. Harper, Inc.* (1953)	*De Cometis;* First edition of the first printed book on the comets, 1472	$1,250
Coins	*New York Times* (1954)	1953 New Zealand Proof Coin Set; 10 pieces; crown to half-penny in mock leather case; commemorates royal visit of Queen Elizabeth to New Zealand	$14.87
Stamps	*New York Times* (1954)	Triangle stamps from Egypt 100 different 150 different	 $1.50 $3.50

EDUCATION

Item	Source	Description	Price
Course	*McCall's* (1950)	*DuBarry Success Course for Women;* includes twenty beauty, make-up and hair preparations	$28.50
Course	*Good Housekeeping* (1950)	*DuBarry Success Course;* course, with introductory supply of three DuBarry Beauty Preparations	$12.95
Dance Lessons	*New York Times* (1954)	150 dance courses; 2 hr. lessons	$1.00

ENTERTAINMENT

Item	Source	Description	Price
Play Ticket	*Chicago Tribune* (1951)	*Point of No Return;* Henry Fonda; a new comedy by Paul Osborn; evenings	$1.80–$5
Sporting Event Ticket	*Chicago Tribune* (1951)	Polo; fast, dangerous action; double-header games General admission Reserved seats	 $1.00 $2.00
Theater Ticket	*Chicago Tribune* (1951)	*Phil Silvers; Top Banana;* 300 good seats	$2.75
Wrestling Ticket	*Chicago Tribune* (1951)	Wrestling; Vern Gagne, NWA Jr. heavyweight champ	$1.30-$3.90

ENTERTAINMENT, HOME

Item	Source	Description	Price
Board Game	*Woman's Home Companion* (1950)	*Old MacDonald's Farm;* the fun way to be a farmer—corner the market—trade and unload surplus stocks	$2.00
Board Game	*Woman's Home Companion* (1950)	*Parker Brothers Sorry;* an immensely popular board game, unlike any other	$2.50
Board Game	*The American Home* (1954)	*Parker Brothers Monopoly;* the most fascinating game in the world	$3/$4/$10
Camera	*Ebony* (1954)	*Argus;* world's most popular 35 mm camera; perfect for color slides, black and white pictures, action shots	$66.50
Projector	*Ebony* (1954)	*Argus Automatic;* 300-watt projector shows, changes, stores your color slides automatically	$66.50
Record	*Life* (1950)	*Columbia Records; Kiss Me Kate;* up to 50 minutes of music on one record; Alfred Drake, Patricia Morison, and original Broadway cast complete on one record	$4.85

Item	Source	Description	Price
Television	*Chicago Tribune* (1951)	*Scott;* 16"; watch a wonderful world of entertainment—sports, drama, comedy, news and musical events	$299
Television	*The American Home* (1954)	*Crosley;* 17"; fits into a small space	$140

FOOD PRODUCTS

Item	Source	Description	Price
Cake Mix	*Chicago Tribune* (1951)	*Betty Crocker;* white, devil's food, yellow; your choice; 20 oz	$0.35
Candy Bars	*Chicago Tribune* (1951)	*Mounds, Mars, Almond Joy, Jersey;* limit 4	$0.13/2
Chili Con Carne	*Chicago Tribune* (1951)	With beans; with $0.10 newspaper coupon	$0.25
Chili Sauce	*Saturday Evening Post* (1951)	*Bennett's;* last time you tasted chili sauce like this you spooned it out of a Mason jar back home; 8 oz	$0.25
Coffee	*Chicago Tribune* (1951)	*Holleb;* 1 lb	$0.83
Margarine	*Chicago Tribune* (1951)	*Diedrich;* 2 lb	$0.57
Peanut Butter	*Chicago Tribune* (1951)	*Holleb's Supreme;* 12 oz	$0.33
Shortening	*Chicago Tribune* (1951)	*Crisco;* 1 lb	$0.31
Smokie Links	*Chicago Tribune* (1951)	*Oscar Mayer;* deliciously different	$0.59

FURNITURE

Item	Source	Description	Price
Gun Rack	*The American Home* (1954)	*Nimrod;* 6-gun rack with steel guard	$17.95
Hide-A-Bed	*The American Home* (1954)	*T-Cushion;* with Beautyrest seat cushions, in gold Trigger metallic tweed Apartment size Full size	$239.50 $249.50
Hope Chest	*Life* (1950)	*Lane;* a Lane chest is the real love-gift; genuine American walnut with tray	$47.95
Rug	*Woman's Day* (1950)	Glamour-rug; handsome, soft-wood-surface 9' × 12"	$29.95
Table and Chairs	*Good Housekeeping* (1950)	*Daystrom;* the tables with the wonder top; set	$74.50

Though not the first to show a couple sharing a bed on screen, I Love Lucy *detailed the intimacies of marriage more than any other show at the time. The show became so popular that Fashion Trend Furniture sold a replica of the couple's bedroom set. (via Wiki-media Commons)*

Item	Source	Description	Price
GARDEN EQUIPMENT & SUPPLIES			
Garden Hose	*Chicago Tribune* (1951)	*Goodyear Glide;* 50"	$5.95
Lawn Mower	*Chicago Tribune* (1951)	*Davos;* with safety Flex-A-Matic clutch; easy to handle	$88
Trees	*Sears, Roebuck* (1952)	2 Silver Juniper, 4 Pfitzer	$18.95
HOTEL RATES			
Room Rate	*New York Times* (1954)	*The Empress;* European plan available for meals; double occupancy	$14.00
Room Rate	*New York Times* (1954)	*The Broadmoor;* double occupancy	$5.00
HOUSEHOLD PRODUCTS			
Automatic Toaster	*Woman's Home Companion* (1950)	*General Mills;* it's double automatic so toast is always timed to perfection	$22.95
Goblets	*Sears, Roebuck* (1952)	*Harmony House Lace Bouquet;* pattern delicately feminine in design and shape; set of four	$3.35
Gravy Ladle	*Woman's Home Companion* (1950)	*International;* sterling; queen's lace pattern	$10.50
Hair Dryer	*Sears, Roebuck* (1952)	*Ann Barton;* home hair dryer gives you all the convenience of professional shop equipment but right in your own home	$21.50
Ice Cream Freezer	*Woman's Home Companion* (1950)	Homemade ice cream in minutes; 4-qt model	$24.95
Ice Cream Freezer	*The American Home* (1954)	*Silex Freeze-O-Tray;* make delicious ice cream in your own refrigerator	$18.95
Iron	*Woman's Home Companion* (1950)	*General Mills Tru-Heat;* famous for its tapered heel that irons backward as easily as forward	$12.95
Iron	*McCall's* (1950)	*Proctor Champion;* full even heat and over-size soleplate for easier, faster ironing	$9.95
Kitchen Clock	*Woman's Day* (1950)	*General Electric;* things run smoother all day long when you have this accurate, dependable General Electric pantry clock in your kitchen	$3.95

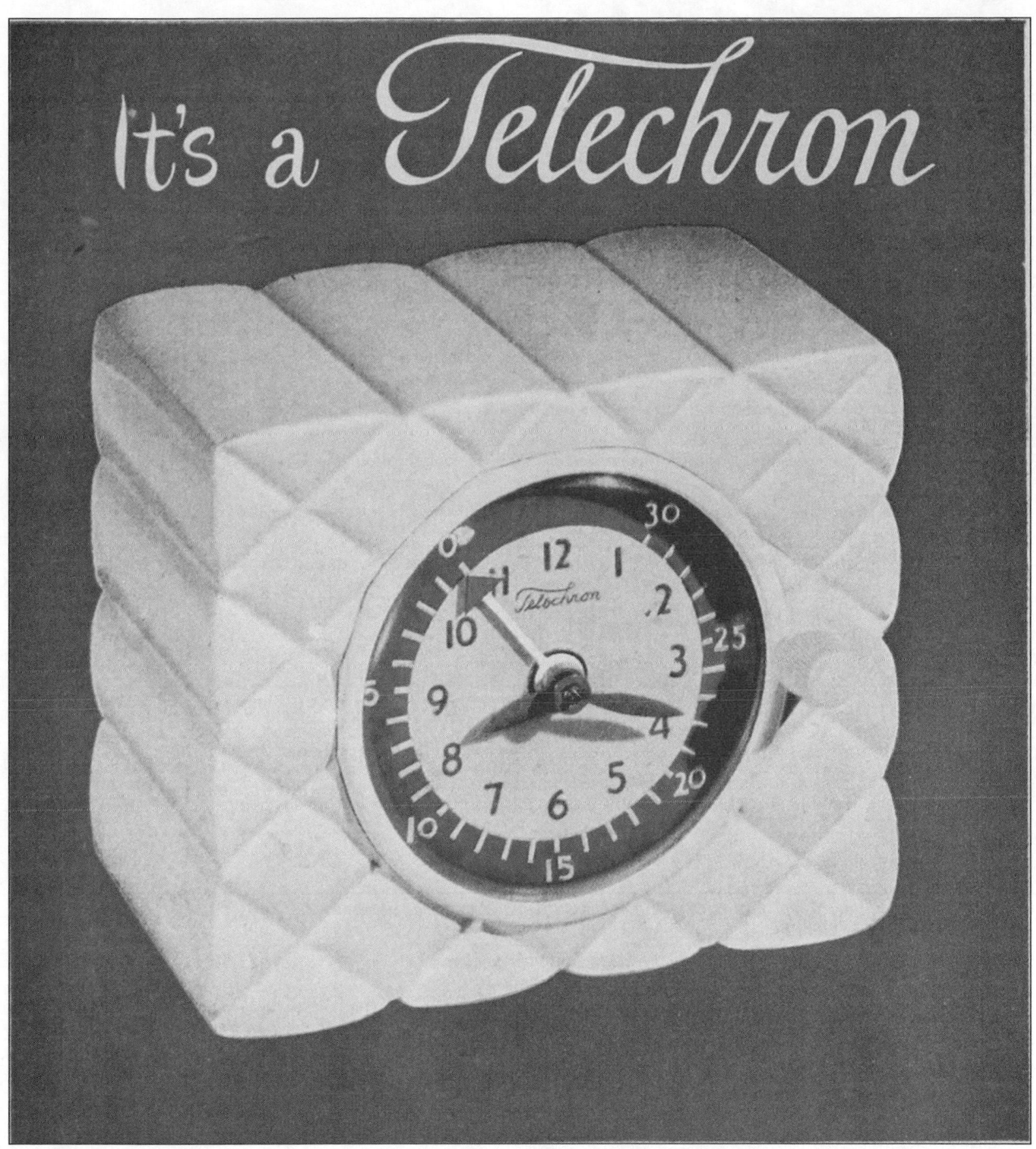

The Telechron company (1912-1992) sought to produce clocks whose designs reflected one of the fundamental principles of the Art Deco movement: to combine modern engineering (including mass-production) with the beauty of simple geometric shapes. (via Wikimedia Commons)

Item	Source	Description	Price
Mattress	*McCall's* (1950)	*Serta Perfect Sleeper;* new improved Serta-foam latex cushioning matching box spring	$49.50
Measure	*Good Housekeeping* (1950)	*Pyrex;* 1-pt size	$0.59
Mixer	*McCall's* (1950)	*General Electric;* to give you faster, more-thorough mixing	$34.95
Mixette	*Woman's Day* (1950)	*Hamilton Beach Portable;* one hand operation, 3-speeds under the thumb	$17.75
		West of Denver	$18.75
Mop	*Good Housekeeping* (1950)	*Dufold Sponge Mop;* does 9 jobs, keeps hands lovely	$5.95
Paint	*Life* (1950)	*Glidden Spread Satin;* new wonder paint makes winter painting practical; no offensive odor; paint with windows closed	$4.49
Pan	*Good Housekeeping* (1950)	*Pyrex;* loaf pan 9 1/8" size	$0.69
Polisher & Scrubber	*The American Home* (1954)	*Regina Twin-Brush;* does your scrubbing, waxing, polishing	$64.50
Portable Mixer	*The American Home* (1954)	*General Electric;* it actually weighs less than three lbs	$19.50
Sander-Polisher	*Saturday Evening Post* (1951)	*Black & Decker;* 1000 ways to speed home and farm jobs	$32.95
Sheet	*The American Home* (1954)	*Dan River;* percale; bordered with tic-tac-toe pattern	$10.50
Towel	*McCall's* (1950)	*Cannon;* buttercup yellow	$1.19
Vaporizer	*Life* (1950)	*Electric Steam Radiator;* the first and only 3 to 24-hour vaporizer that doubles as a room humidifier	$5.95
Weather strip	*The American Home* (1954)	*Mortell;* eliminate unhealthy fuel wasting drafts	$1.25/rl
Wood Cream	*Woman's Day* (1950)	*Gold Sea;* gives you lovelier lustre, leaves no oily film	$0.59/pt

JEWELRY

Item	Source	Description	Price
Brooch	*New York Times* (1952)	*Tiffany's brooch of diamonds and rubies;* divides into two clips	$5200
Diamond	*Saturday Evening Post* (1951)	*De Beers Consolidated Mines;* 1 ct	$550–$1165
Ring	*New York Times* (1952)	Tiffany's twin stone diamond ring	$2750
Watch	*New York Times* (1952)	*Golden mesh band;* costume buckle; 17 jewel surrounded by filigree and pretend pearls	$45.00
Watch	*Ebony* (1954)	*Gruen;* when you give the revolutionary self-winding Gruen autowind, you are giving the finest gift of all time	$125

MEDICAL PRODUCTS & SERVICES

Item	Source	Description	Price
Antacid	*Saturday Evening Post* (1951)	*Tums;* eat like candy, tums for the tummy	$0.10
Aspirin	*Saturday Evening Post* (1951)	100 5-grain tablets; no faster-acting aspirin made	$0.54

Item	Source	Description	Price
Aspirin	*Today's Health* (1952)	*Bayer;* children's size; three ways best for your child; 30 tablets per package	$0.30/pkg
Cough Drops	*Life* (1950)	*Luden's Menthol;* contains more menthol than any other cough drops	$0.05
Glycerine Tablets	*Life* (1950)	*Pine Brothers;* quick throat relief	$0.10
Laxative	*Life* (1950)	*Nature's Remedy NR Tablets;* man's best laxative, 10 herbs in tiny tablet	$0.25
Liniment	*Life* (1950)	*Absorbine Jr.;* the favorite stand-by liniment of many professional athletes for over fifty years	$1.25
Liniment	*Good Housekeeping* (1950)	*Absorbine Jr.;* relieve torturing rheumatic or neuralgic pain; long-lasting bottle	$1.25
Lip Balm	*Life* (1950)	*Chapstick;* keep lips fit	$0.25
Lip Balm	*Saturday Evening Post* (1951)	*Stag;* soothes chapped lips	$0.39
Nail Treatment	*Today's Health* (1952)	*Thumb Nail Biting Medicine;* discourage prolonged and persistent nail biting	$1.20
Nonprescription Drug	*Good Housekeeping* (1950)	*Tabcin;* miserable with cold symptoms?	$0.75
Tincture of Iodine	*Saturday Evening Post* (1951)	First-aid help, with applicator	$0.29

MOTORIZED VEHICLES, SUPPLIES, & SERVICES

Item	Source	Description	Price
Automobile	*New York Times* (1952)	Dodge '52 Coronet	$1895
Automobile	*New York Times* (1952)	Pontiac '52 Club Coupe	$2195
Automobile	*New York Times* (1952)	Buick '51 Riviera	$1995
Automobile	*New York Times* (1952)	*Buick '48;* convertible Roadmaster	$950
Automobile	Richard M. Langworth and Graham Robson, *Complete Book of Collectible Cars* (1985)	*Ford Custom Victoria;* 2-door hardtop	$1925
Automobile	Langworth and Robson, *Complete Book of Collectible Cars* (1985)	*Buick Skylark;* convertible	$5000
Automobile	Langworth and Robson, *Complete Book of Collectible Cars* (1985)	*Cadillac Series 62 Eldorado*	$4,738–$6,286
Automobile	Langworth and Robson, *Complete Book of Collectible Cars* (1985)	*Chevrolet Corvette Roadster*	$2,799–$3,513
Automobile	Langworth and Robson, *Complete Book of Collectible Cars* (1985)	*Nash Rambler;* convertible	$1,550–$2,150

Item	Source	Description	Price
Gasoline Additive	*Saturday Evening Post* (1951)	*Heet*; no more hard starting; prevents frozen gas lines	$0.65

MUSICAL INSTRUMENTS

Item	Source	Description	Price
Chord Organ	*Chicago Tribune* (1951)	*Hammond*; Love music? Then the new Hammond Chord organ is for you, even without musical training	$975
Piano	*McCall's* (1950)	*Lester Spinet*; dollar for dollar your best piano buy	$595

OTHER

Item	Source	Description	Price
Dog Food	*Woman's Day* (1950)	Cooked and ready to use; a nourishing food for dogs	$0.10
Gift Kit	*Woman's Home Companion* (1950)	*Palmolive*; Christmas gift kit; with talc, after-shave lotion and a choice of brushless or latherless shave cream	$1.05
Patent Settlement	*Guinness Book of World Records* (1981)	Settlement paid by Ford Motor Company to the Ferguson Tractor Company in 1952 for a patent-infringement claim filed in 1948.	$9.25 million
Pesticide	*The American Home* (1954)	*Reardon Laboratories Mouse Seed*; kills mice	$0.25
Stationery	*Saturday Evening Post* (1951)	For after-Christmas thank-yous; box of 24 sheets and 24 matching envelopes	$0.49
Wallet	*Sears, Roebuck* (1952)	*Kerrybrooke*; fine-quality leather, smart styling	$3.50

PERSONAL CARE PRODUCTS

Item	Source	Description	Price
Christmas Set	*Woman's Home Companion* (1950)	*Old Spice*; includes aftershave and shaving cream	$1.65
Comb	*Life* (1950)	*Ace*; hard rubber; a type for every purpose	$0.29–$0.39
Cotton Swabs	*Good Housekeeping* (1950)	*Q-Tips*; the largest-selling sterilized swabs; large package	$0.98
Cream	*Good Housekeeping* (1950)	*Sofskin*; new cream softens 3 kinds of dry skin; big jar	$0.25
Cream	*Good Housekeeping* (1950)	*Ponds*; dry skin cream; by day, use lightly under make-up; large jar	$0.89
Cream	*Life* (1950)	*Helena Rubinstein Estrogenic Hormone Cream and Oil Cream;* for hands, face and oil for neck and throat	$3.50
Cream	*McCall's* (1950)	*Jergen's;* doctors' tests show that 8 out of 10 complexions beautifully improved when women used this Vitone-enriched cream	$1.39
Cuticle Scissors	*Sears, Roebuck* (1952)	*Lyric;* fine shaft and rings for holding	$2.00
Deodorant	*McCall's* (1950)	*Stoppette Spray;* 2 1/4 ounces; a quick squeeze checks annoying perspiration, stops odor	$1.25
Deodorant	*McCall's* (1950)	*Odo-Ro-No Cream;* the deodorant without a doubt	$0.25/$0.50
Deodorant	*Today's Health* (1952)	*Heed;* an amazing new underarm deodorant in a lovely cool-green squeezable bottle	$0.59
Electric Shaver	*Life* (1950)	*Schick Colonel;* must outshave blade razors or your money back	$17.50

Item	Source	Description	Price
Hair Color Rinse	*Today's Health* (1952)	*Noreen;* temporary but completely effective	$0.15/$0.30/$0.60
Hair Coloring	*Sears, Roebuck* (1952)	*Ann Barton Glow;* lasting hair color	$1.79
Hair Coloring	*Sears, Roebuck* (1952)	*Clairol;* for easy home use	$0.95
Hair Pomade	*Ebony* (1954)	More hair beauty, more for your money	$0.25
Hair Treatment	*Ebony* (1954)	*Nulox;* 4 oz jar super pre-applied shampoo, 2 oz jar scalp cream; 9 to 12 complete greaseless hair treatment	$2.48
Home Facial	*Woman's Home Companion* (1950)	*Noxzema;* look lovelier in 10 days or your money back; big jar	$0.59
Home Permanent Kit	*Life* (1950)	*Rave;* has the Dial-A-Wave to give you the one right wave for your hair	$2.00
Home Permanent Kit	*Life* (1950)	*Richard Hudnut;* scientific tests show creme waving lotion leaves hair springier and stronger	$2.75
Home Permanent Kit	*Chicago Tribune* (1951)	*Stevens Cold Wave;* you ask for it again and again	$15.00
Lipstick	*McCall's* (1950)	*Barbara Gould;* with exclusive greater stay-on formula	$1.00
Nail Kit	*Woman's Home Companion* (1950)	*LaCross Mariner;* with nail file, nail clip, heavy-duty nail scissors and tweezers; in compact leather case	$5.00
Razor	*Saturday Evening Post* (1951)	*Gillette Super-Speed Razor;* improved 10-blade dispenser in styrene travel case	$1.00
Razor Blades	*Saturday Evening Post* (1951)	*Gillette;* 10 blades; sharpest edges ever honed	$0.49
Shampoo	*Good Housekeeping* (1950)	*Shulton;* perfumed with famous Old Spice; 5 3/4 oz bottle	$0.85
Shaver	*Life* (1950)	*Durham-Enders Razor Cord;* the only genuine one-piece razor; nothing to twist or unscrew; package includes five blades	$0.49
Shaving Cream	*Saturday Evening Post* (1951)	*Stag;* brushless; set up whiskers for quick, close, no-sting, no-nick shaving; jumbo tube	$0.49
Toothbrush	*Saturday Evening Post* (1951)	Five styles, long-wearing nylon bristles	$0.49
Toothbrush	*Today's Health Magazine* (1952)	*Dr. West Miracle-Tuft;* the Exton bristles of this remarkable brush actually repel water	$0.60

Cutex Stay-Fast Lipstick advertisement, 1954. (via Wikimedia Commons)

Item	Source	Description	Price
PUBLICATIONS			
Magazine	*Woman's Day* (1950)	*Woman's Day;* monthly	$0.05
Magazine	*Life* (1950)	*Life;* weekly	$0.20
Magazine	*McCall's* (1950)	McCall's	$0.25
Magazine	*Saturday Evening Post* (1951)	*Saturday Evening Post;* weekly	$0.15
Pamphlets on Communicable Diseases	*Today's Health* (1952)	American Medical Association's topics: common cold, scarlet fever, measles, whooping cough, infantile paralysis	$0.15
REAL ESTATE			
Gas Station and Grocery	*Chicago Tribune* (1951)	Must sell immediately on account of illness	$18,250
House	*Chicago Tribune* (1951)	For sale; ranch bungalow; three bedroom brick	$13,800
House	*Chicago Tribune* (1951)	For sale; nine-room home in excellent condition; 3 1/2 baths, 2 car garage, 2 heated porches; a nice buy	$40,000
House	*Chicago Tribune* (1951)	For sale; 6-bedroom tri-level	$24,750
House	*Chicago Tribune* (1951)	7-room home, 4 bedrooms, 3 baths	$22,500
House Plans	*The American Home* (1954)	*American Home;* traditional stone and wood; one-level plan has three bedrooms, two baths in separate wing	$5.00

Postcard for an open house viewing of a model home. (via Wikimedia Commons)

Item	Source	Description	Price
SEWING EQUIPMENT AND SUPPLIES			
Pinking Shears	*Woman's Day* (1950)	*Griffon;* pinks heavier materials, as it cuts for ravel-proof zig-zag edge	$3.95
SPORTS EQUIPMENT			
Basketball	*Belk's Christmas Catalog* (1951)	*Collette GC;* official size; valve bladder; inflating needle	$2.98
Fishing Rod & Reel	*New York Times* (1952)	*Weak* fish outfit; split bamboo rod; locking reel seat; 150-yd. size; saltwater reel	$6.99
Fishing Rod & Reel	*New York Times* (1952)	Deep sea outfit; solid glass rod; 3 chromium guides; locking reel seat; 250-yd. free spool; star drag reel	$16.99
Reel	*New York Times* (1952)	Pflueger "Templar" Reel	$21.99
Shotgun	*Belk's Christmas Catalog* (1951)	*Louis Max;* double barrel; safety catch; break action loud but safe	$1.98
Sleeping Bag	*Chicago Tribune* (1951)	Vacation special; real U.S. Army	$4.88
TOBACCO PRODUCTS			
Lighter Fluid	*Life* (1950)	*Zippo;* instant lighting, smokeless flame	$0.25
Pipe	*New York Times* (1952)	*Engineer's Desk Pipe;* won't spill ashes	$1.49
Pipe Tobacco	*Saturday Evening Post* (1951)	*Edgeworth;* make your pipe dreams come true; longer lasting; cooler smoking	$0.15
TOYS			
Burp Gun	*Belk's Christmas Catalog* (1951)	*Mattel;* realistically designed even to the trigger; fires 1–50 shots at a touch; plenty of smoke pours from the barrel, lots of noise	$2.98
Cash Register	*Belk's Christmas Catalog* (1951)	*Kampkap;* push the key, correct amount $0.01 to $1 plus No Sale pops up in window; aluminum and red finish	$2.49
Doll	*Belk's Christmas Catalog* (1951)	*Madame Alexander Cissy;* the debutante doll with molded figure, shapely feet that wear high-heeled shoes	$19.95
Doll	*Belk's Christmas Catalog* (1951)	*Betty Bows;* rubber body, vinyl head, locked-in plastic eyes with long lashes	$2.98
Doll	*Belk's Christmas Catalog* (1951)	*Tiny Tears;* American character; with molded hair; wears cotton rompers; layette includes lace-trimmed dress, bonnet, panties, booties; 13 1/2"	$7.95
Doll	*Belk's Christmas Catalog* (1951)	*Goldberger;* in party dress; sleeping eyes; rooted hair that can be fixed; cries when squeezed	$3.98
Double Holster Set	*Belk's Christmas Catalog* (1951)	*Carnell;* 50-shot cap pistol; split-grain cowhide	$2.98
Electric Football	*Belk's Christmas Catalog* (1951)	*Tudor;* real football right at the living room table; size 25" × 15 1/4"	$6.95
Farm Set	*Belk's Christmas Catalog* (1951)	*Auburn Rubber;* jumbo; unbreakable vinyl; silo, barn, team, and wagon, tractor, farmer and wife, plus whole yard full of farm friends	$2.98

Item	Source	Description	Price
Heavy Duty Crane	*Belk's Christmas Catalog* (1951)	Nothing to wind, just push; hand-wind boom, lift, re-movable crane, thick tires	$0.88
Service Station	*Belk's Christmas Catalog* (1951)	*Marx Service Station;* modern as tomorrow; overhead sliding door, cars, garagemen	$3.98
Shooting Gallery	*Belk's Christmas Catalog* (1951)	*Marx;* self-feeding automatic pistol fires steel balls; test of skill	$2.98
Skates	*Sears, Roebuck* (1952)	*J. C. Higgins;* roller skates are fun galore for boys and girls of all ages	$2.45
Steel Refrigerator	*Belk's Christmas Catalog* (1951)	*Wolverine;* revolving shelf, separate freezer, play food, ice cubes; 17" high	$1.98
Tinkertoy	*Belk's Christmas Catalog* (1951)	Now in color; child learns while selecting parts by color; 149 pieces	$1.98
Tool Set	*Belk's Christmas Catalog* (1951)	*Skil-Craft Handy Andy;* steel chest holds saw, pliers, hammer, chisel, coping saw, mallet, screwdriver, try-square, ruler, pencil, sandpaper, manual	$2.98
Vacuum Cleaner	*The American Home* (1954)	*Hoover;* A kid-size Hoover that runs and hums	$14.95
Velocipede	*Belk's Christmas Catalog* (1951)	*Murray Ohio;* strong well-balanced tubular steel frame; 10" ball-bearing front wheel, 1 3/4" tires give speedy ride	$8.95
Washing Machine	*Belk's Christmas Catalog* (1951)	Wind spring, turn switch, it works; rubber drainpipe; just like mother's; fun	$0.88

TRAVEL & TRANSPORTATION

Item	Source	Description	Price
Airplane Flights	*New York Times* (1952)	New York to Cologne; round trip	$474.50
		New York to Munich; round trip	$516.00
		New York to Glasgow; one way	$251.00
		New York to Glasgow; round trip	$382.00
Airplane Flights	*New York Times* (1952)	New York to California; save 10% on return	
		One way	$88.00
		Return	$72.00

MISCELLANY 1950–1954

Shirts for Men

Arrow Shirts for men, sold by Cluett, Peabody and Co., Inc. listed five prices for their line of shirts: $3.65, $3.95, $4.50, $5.50, and $7.50.

Life, January 23, 1950

Family Food Cost Down; Annual Market Basket Drops $100 from Post-War Peak

The Agriculture Department said today the annual cost of the family food market basket had dropped almost $100 from its postwar peak. The retail cost of the market basket in January was put at $615, a drop of $7 from the December cost. The post-war peak cost was $713 in July 1948.

New York Times, March 24, 1950

The Lost Women of Social Security

Social Security is a bargain insurance. If the pension your taxes have earned should be the smallest possible—$10 a month—it is probably worth about $1,500 at current private annuity rates. The average pension is worth $3,900—no trifling gift to the U.S. Treasury on the day you marry.

The instant dream boy slips that gold band on your third finger he becomes your only social security. The personal contributions you have made cease to be worth a nickel. Well, maybe a nickel.

McCall's, April 1950

Aspirin to Stores in War Shut Off; Bayer Head Angered as Price Is Cut to as Low as 4¢ for 100-Tablet Bottle

Hundred-tablet bottles of Bayer aspirin sold for 4¢ yesterday at Abraham & Straus in Brooklyn. Macy's, Gimbels, and other department stores engaged in the price war offered two bottles for 9¢.

The cost to the stores of the aspirin is believed to be in the neighborhood of 43¢. The hundred-tablet bottle carries a fair trade fixed price of 59¢.

A bitter attack on the stores offering its aspirin at rock-bottom prices is made today by the Bayer Company division of Sterling Drug, Inc., the manufacturers. In full-page advertisements in several leading newspapers, the company notifies the shopping public that it has discontinued sales of Bayer aspirin to price-cutting stores.

New York Times, June 15, 1951

New Model Announced by Willys-Overland Motors

The first conventional-type passenger car line to be built by Willys-Overland Motors since 1942 was announced yesterday by the company. Designated the Aero Willys, the new models will go on display tomorrow in dealer showrooms throughout the country.

New York City delivered prices, exclusive of sales tax, were listed as $1,834 for the Aero Lark, DeLuxe two-door sedan; $2,083 for the Aero Wing, super DeLuxe, two-door sedan, and $2,168 for the Aero Ace, custom two-door sedan. Overdrive is optional at extra cost of $86.

New York Times, January 17, 1952

Training Station Salesmen—Key to Shock Absorber Sales

By the end of 1952 there will be 112,000,000 direct action shock absorbers on the road. Since 1907 some 100 types of shock absorbers have been developed, of which only four types have attained general use. Some of these were not only expensive, but were difficult to install. For example, the knee-action type cost from $50 to $75, and installation was a major shop job.

Turning to the question of dealer profit (Houdaille shock absorber representative C. A.) Humphrey pointed out that a Houdaille standard carton, containing a pair of shock absorbers with all needed rubber bushings and fittings, costs the dealer $6.55. The dealer can sell a pair of shocks costing him $6.55 for $12.30, plus an installation charge of $1 per shock, for a total sale of $14.30, leaving a gross profit of $7.75.

National Petroleum News, September 3, 1952

MISCELLANY 1950–1954

Resident Offices Report on Trade: Demand for Ready-to-Wear Found Steady with Lingerie, and Sports Lines Active

A number of buyers were in the wholesale markets here last week but the rush has tapered off, according to McGreevey, Werring & Howell Company, resident buying office. Activity in the ready-to-wear field has been steady, lingerie continued active and sportswear and separates are expected to be very popular for spring.

Reorders were received on all types of suits, with better-priced lines stressing beaded and jewel trims. Reorders began to appear for unlined rayon suits. Full-length spring coats received some attention. January cotton promotions on junior dress lines were successful and stores were filling in on the $8.75 to $14.75 price range on summer merchandise.

New York Times, February 1, 1953

HISTORICAL SNAPSHOT 1955–1959

1955

- Racial segregation on interstate buses and trains ordered to end
- Federal minimum wage rises from 75 cents to $1 per hour
- President Eisenhower submits a 10-year $101 billion highway construction program to Congress
- AF of L and CIO merge
- Merger creates second largest bank, Chase Manhattan Bank
- Whirlpool Corporation merges with Seeger Refrigerator Company and begins producing refrigerators, air-conditioners, and cooking ranges
- *National Review* and *Village Voice* begin publication
- Crest introduced by Procter and Gamble with stannous fluoride
- Special K breakfast food introduced by Kellogg Company
- Suburban shopping centers now number 1,800

1956

- Congress authorizes 42,500 miles of interstate highways costing $33.5 billion
- First Midas Muffler Shop opens in Macon, GA
- Dow Jones Industrials Average peaks at 521.05
- Salem Cigarettes introduced, become leading mentholated brand in 18 months
- Welch's Grape Juice has sales of $40 million

- Merger creates Beech-Nut Life Savers, Inc.
- Jack Daniel's whiskey acquired by Brown-Forman

1957

- Sputnik I launched by Soviet Union is world's first man-made earth satellite
- Painkiller Darvon introduced by Eli Lilly
- University of Wisconsin study shows that 20 percent of Americans live in poverty
- New York's last trolley car retired
- Frisbee introduced by Wham-O Manufacturing
- Per capita margarine consumption exceeds butter for first time
- Record 4.3 million babies born

1958

- Ford Motor Company introduces Edsel
- Cost of 100,000 computerized multiplication computations falls from $1.26 in 1952 to 26 cents
- First U.S. Earth Satellite launched
- Unemployment reaches postwar high
- Upper 1 percent of Americans enjoy 9 percent of nation's total disposable income
- 64 percent of households have incomes above $4,000 per year
- Gasoline costs 30.4 cents per gallon

- Bank Americard credit card introduced
- First-class postal rates climb to 4 cents per ounce
- U.S. television sets reach 41 million
- Sweet'n Low sugarless sweetener introduced
- Pizza Hut chain begins in Kansas City

1959

- Alaska and Hawaii admitted to the Union
- Japanese automakers produce 79,000 cars
- Volkswagen sales in U.S. top 120,000
- Average U.S. automobile wholesales at $1,880
- Supermarkets comprise 11 percent of food stores, but control 69 percent of sales
- 200,000 retailers offer trading stamps
- New York's Four Seasons restaurant opens

Rosa Parks being fingerprinted by Deputy Sheriff D.H. Lackey after her arrest for boycotting public transportation, 1956. (via Wikimedia Commons)

SELECTED INCOME 1955-1959

Job	Source	Description	Pay
Actor	Jeffrey Robinson, Bardot, *An Intimate Portrait* (1994)	Salary of Brigitte Bardot for her role in *Et Dieu A Créa la Femme* (And God Created Woman) in 1957	$11,400
Actor	Legrand and Karney *Chronicle of the Cinema* (1995)	Per-film fee of Marilyn Monroe, not including a percent of profits, in 1955	$100,000
Baseball Player	Bob Rains, St. Louis Cardinals, *The 100th Anniversary History* (1992)	Annual salary of St. Louis Cardinal Stan Musial in 1958	$100,000
Bookkeeping Machine Operator	*Chicago Tribune* (1955)	Typing experience; 5 day wk; insurance	$75/wk starting
Busboys	*Chicago Tribune* (1957)	Meals and uniforms; short hrs; evenings	$1/hr
Cartoonist	Richard Layman, ed., *American Decades: 1950–1959* (1994)	Annual income of Charles Schultz, the creator of *Peanuts*, in 1958	$90,000
Chemical Trainees	*Chicago Tribune* (1957)	Lab technicians will advance as quickly as they can with expanding company; high school chemistry or better starts you; learn and progress	$350–400/mo
Dry Cleaning and Laundry Man	*Chicago Tribune* (1959)	23 to 35, married with sales ability and willingness to work and progress in a very lively organization; salary/commission	$5000-$6000/yr
Engineer	*San Francisco Examiner* (1959)	Jr. Civil, Jr. Elec, Jr. Mech; apply by 11/19/59	$500–600/mo
Golfer	Layman, ed., *American Decades: 1950–1959* (1994)	Average total purse in an official Professional Golf Association event in 1955	$21,722
Housekeeper	*Charlotte Observer* (1956)	Live in; take care three children; white, age 28-45, room and board; maid on duty for housework	$25–35/wk
Insurance Salesman	*San Francisco Examiner* (1959)	National concern has estab. routes avail.; no experience necessary—we train you	$100/wk
Janitor-Assistant	*Chicago Tribune* (1959)	Mechanical electrical experience; state experience in letter	$350/mo
Manager	*Chicago Tribune* (1957)	Bar-restaurant; night work	$7,500/yr
Office Worker	*Chicago Tribune* (1957)	Men age 21–35; h.s. graduate; for responsible positions in truck billing office; salary plus generous shift bonus	$2.15/hr
Private Secretary	*Chicago Tribune* (1959)	Insurance and investment experience; IBM; age 29	$100/wk
Route Salesman	*Chicago Tribune* (1955)	Interesting positions for right men; married preferred	$85/wk and up
Salesman	*New Orleans Times-Picayune* (1956)	Settled married man, 25–35, with high school education, to represent one of the leading companies in its field; most of our salesmen average over $400 per month; this is a wonderful opportunity for man who is willing to apply himself and work hard to get ahead	$60/wk and commission

Job	Source	Description	Pay
Telephone Sales	*Chicago Tribune* (1957)	Men to handle incoming telephone orders 6 evenings a wk, including Friday, Saturday, and Sunday; 37 1/2 hr wk; ideal for intelligent neat appearing man in fifties who has good telephone voice	$1.65/hr

CONSUMER EXPENDITURES 1955-1959

(Per Capita)

Expenditure Type	1955	1956	1957	1958	1959
Clothing	$118.59	$121.86	$120.28	$118.87	$123.71
Food	$414.46	$424.44	$437.89	$447.34	$453.24
Auto Usage	$193.01	$184.88	$196.76	$183.76	$210.88
New Auto Purchase	$83.49	$68.96	$73.57	$55.70	$74.23
Auto Parts	$9.68	$10.11	$11.68	$10.91	$13.49
Gas & Oil	$52.03	$55.88	$59.55	$60.87	$63.54
Housing	$208.14	$218.17	$229.46	$241.18	$253.05
Furniture	$26.62	$27.34	$26.27	$29.29	$26.99
Utilities	$61.72	$64.79	$67.73	$70.63	$72.54
Telephone & Telegraph	$18.76	$19.62	$21.02	$22.39	$23.60
Physicians	$22.99	$24.97	$26.86	$29.29	$30.93
Dentists	$9.08	$10.11	$10.51	$10.91	$11.25
Health Insurance	$8.47	$8.32	$9.34	$8.61	$9.56
Personal Business	$58.69	$63.01	$66.56	$70.06	$74.79
Personal Care	$22.39	$24.37	$26.86	$28.14	$29.24
Tobacco	$30.86	$31.51	$33.28	$34.45	$37.11
Local Transport	$11.49	$11.89	$11.68	$10.91	$11.25
Intercity Transport	$6.66	$6.54	$7.01	$6.32	$6.75
Recreation	$87.73	$91.55	$92.25	$93.03	$98.41
Religion/Welfare Activities	$21.18	$23.18	$23.94	$25.27	$28.12
Private Education & Research	$15.13	$16.64	$18.09	$19.54	$20.24
Per Capita Consumption	$1560.43	$1608.59	$1665.75	$1691.73	$1778.67

INVESTMENTS 1955–1959

Investments	1955	1956	1957	1958	1959
Basic Yield, One-year Corporate Bonds	NR	2.70	3.50	NR	NR
Short-term Interest Rates, 4-6 Months, Prime Commercial Paper	2.18	3.31	3.81	2.46	3.97
Basic Yield, Common Stocks, Total	4.06	4.07	4.33	4.05	3.31
Index of Common Stocks (194121943510)	40.49	42.62	44.38	46.24	57.38

COMMON STOCKS, CLOSING PRICE AND YIELD, FIRST BUSINESS DAY OF YEAR

(PARENTHETICAL NUMBER IS ANNUAL DIVIDEND IN DOLLARS)

	1955	1956	1957	1958	1959
Allis Chalmers	73 3/4	67	34 3/8	24 5/8	29 5/8
	(4)	(4)	(2)	(2)	(1.25)
AT&T	175 1/4	180	171 1/2	170	225 1/2
	(9)	(9)	(9)	(9)	(9)
American Tobacco	66 1/2	82	73 1/2	77 1/2	96 1/8
	(3.40)	(3.40)	(4)	(4)	(4)
Anaconda	52	70 5/8	71 1/8	41 3/8	60 1/2
	(3)	(4.25)	(5)	(3.75)	(/)
B&O	33 7/8	47 5/8	46 3/8	24 3/4	46 3/8
	(1)	(2)	(2)	(1)	(1.50)
Bethlehem Steel	112 1/4	162 3/4	195 3/8	37 1/8	52 5/8
(4 for 1 split, 1/18/57)	(5.75)	(7.25)	(8.50)	(2.40)	(2.40)
Corn Products	84 1/2	27 7/8	29 1/4	34 1/4	54 1/2
	(3.60)	(1.40)	(1.50)	(1.60)	(2)
General Electric	48 1/4	56 3/4	59 5/8	60 7/8	78 3/4
(3 shares for 1 split, 5/5/54)	(.40)	(.50)	(2)	(2)	(2)
General Motors	103 1/8	45 1/4	43 1/8	34 3/8	50 1/8
(3 shares for 1 split, 9/30/55)	(5)	(1)	(2)	(2)	(2)
International Business Machines	360	404	530	302	529
(2 1/2% stock dividend, 1/27/56)	(4)	(4)	(4)	(2.40)	(2.60)
(5 shares for 4 split, 5/14/56)					
(2 shares for 1 split, 5/12/57)					
(2 1/2% stock dividend, 1/28/59)					
(1 1/2 shares for 1 split, 5/18/59)					
Intl Harvester	37 7/8	36 1/4	38	28 1/8	41 3/8
	(2)	(3)	(2)	(2)	(2)
National Biscuit	43 3/8	38 3/4	35	42 1/8	49 7/8
	(2)	(2)	(2)	(2)	(2)

Investments	1955	1956	1957	1958	1959
US Steel	75	56 5/8	71	52 1/2	96 1/4
(2 shares for 1 split, 6/2/55)	(3)	(1.43)	(2.60)	(3)	(3)
Western Union	75	21 1/4	19 1/2	15 1/4	31 7/8
(4 shares for 1 split, 5/23/55)	(3)	(.25)	(1)	(.30)	(1.20)

STANDARD JOBS 1955–1959

Job Type	1955	1956	1957	1958	1959
Average of All Industries, excl. farm labor	$4224/yr	$4445/yr	$4657/yr	$4818/yr	$5069/yr
Average of All Industries, incl. farm labor	$4128/yr	$4342/yr	$4546/yr	$4707/yr	$4965/yr
Bituminous Coal Mining	$4470/yr	$4858/yr	$5086/yr	$4809/yr	$5274/yr
Building Trades	$4607/yr	$4914/yr	$5120/yr	$5305/yr	$5498/yr
Domestics	$1874/yr	$1962/yr	$2050/yr	$2131/yr	$2190/yr
Farm Labor	$1498/yr	$1578/yr	$1657/yr	$1690/yr	$1742/yr
Federal Civilian	$4801/yr	$5025/yr	$5203/yr	$5781/yr	$5852/yr
Federal Employees, Executive Depts.	$3774/yr	$3983/yr	$4073/yr	$4462/yr	$4589/yr
Federal Military	$3237/yr	$3402/yr	$3439/yr	$3697/yr	$3824/yr
Finance, Insurance, & Real Estate	$4005/yr	$4168/yr	$4314/yr	$4523/yr	$4791/yr
Gas & Electricity Workers	$4757/yr	$5000/yr	$5247/yr	$5543/yr	$5815/yr
Manufacturing, Durable Goods	$4737/yr	$4993/yr	$5207/yr	$5478/yr	$5763/yr
Manufacturing, Nondurable Goods	$4134/yr	$4387/yr	$4540/yr	$4725/yr	$4950/yr
Medical/Health Services Workers	$2488/yr	$2532/yr	$2612/yr	$2751/yr	$2881/yr
Miscellaneous Manufacturing	$3789/yr	$4015/yr	$4195/yr	$4408/yr	$4528/yr
Motion Picture Services	$4330/yr	$4587/yr	$4745/yr	$4940/yr	$5315/yr
Nonprofit Org. Workers	$3291/yr	$3395/yr	$3533/yr	$3672/yr	$3815/yr
Passenger Transportation Workers,					
Local and Highway	$4142/yr	$4306/yr	$4449/yr	$4571/yr	$4789/yr
Personal Services	$2766/yr	$2872/yr	$2999/yr	$3140/yr	$3248/yr
Public School Teachers	$3608/yr	$3827/yr	$4085/yr	$4343/yr	$4522/yr
Radio Broadcasting & Television Workers	$6250/yr	$6613/yr	$6756/yr	$7051/yr	$7210/yr
Railroads	$4701/yr	$5085/yr	$5416/yr	$5836/yr	$6099/yr
State and Local Govt. Workers	$3447/yr	$3564/yr	$3747/yr	$3958/yr	$4152/yr
Telephone & Telegraph Workers	$4153/yr	$4298/yr	$4471/yr	$4707/yr	$5091/yr
Wholesale and Retail Trade Workers	$4616/yr	$4883/yr	$5119/yr	$5294/yr	$5558/yr

FOOD BASKET 1955–1959

Commodity	Year	New York	Atlanta	Chicago	Denver	Los Angeles
Apples, Fresh, per pound	1955	14¢	15.90¢	16.40¢	NR	15.80¢
	1956	15.70¢	16.20¢	NR	NR	15.60¢
	1957	16¢	17.80¢	18.70¢	NR	17.80¢
	1958	15.80¢	15.50¢	16.40¢	NR	15.20¢
	1959	14.30¢	15.50¢	15.80¢	NR	16.50¢
Beans, Dried, per pound	1955	18.70¢	16.20¢	18.40¢	NR	19.30¢
	1956	16.90¢	15.20¢	17.40¢	NR	16.30¢
	1957	16.80¢	15.10¢	17.60¢	NR	15.70¢
	1958	18¢	18¢	18.50¢	NR	17.70¢
	1959	17.40¢	16.90¢	17.50¢	NR	17.40¢
Beef, Rib Roasts, per pound	1955	70.20¢	75.60¢	69.10¢	NR	80¢
	1956	68.60¢	76.80¢	68¢	NR	80.30¢
	1957	71.20¢	80.90¢	70.30¢	NR	86.30¢
	1958	78.20¢	87.10¢	78.10¢	NR	94.10¢
	1959	77.40¢	87.80¢	80.10¢	NR	95.90¢
Beef, Steaks (Round), per pound	1955	96.50¢	92.10¢	79.70¢	NR	87.20¢
	1956	94.70¢	89¢	76.50¢	NR	86.90¢
	1957	$1.004	92.4¢	79.50¢	NR	93.40¢
	1958	$1.118	$1.018	89.10¢	NR	98.90¢
	1959	$1.165	$1.085	91.20¢	NR	$1.045
Bread, White, per pound	1955	19.1¢	17.5¢	16.70¢	NR	19.30¢
	1956	18.8¢	17.4¢	17¢	NR	19.70¢
	1957	19.6¢	18.5¢	17.10¢	NR	20.80¢
	1958	20.5¢	19.3¢	17.10¢	NR	22.90¢
	1959	21.5¢	19.3¢	18.40¢	NR	22.90¢
Butter, per pound	1955	72.2¢	75¢	70.30¢	NR	70.30¢
	1956	72.5¢	76.3¢	72¢	NR	71.60¢
	1957	74.1¢	78.8¢	73.70¢	NR	73.70¢
	1958	74.2¢	79.4¢	73.20¢	NR	76¢
	1959	75.3¢	80.7¢	74.50¢	NR	78.40¢
Cheese, per pound	1955	59.4¢	NR	58¢	NR	57.60¢
	1956	58.4¢	NR	58¢	NR	56.90¢
	1957	59¢	NR	58.60¢	NR	57¢
	1958	59.7¢	NR	59.30¢	NR	58¢
	1959	59.8¢	65.4¢	59.90¢	NR	57.80¢
Chickens, per pound	1955	45.4¢	50.1¢	55.40¢	NR	65.80¢
	1956	41.9¢	41.4¢	40.30¢	NR	40.10¢
	1957	NR	42.3¢	43.10¢	NR	57.40¢
	1958	NR	43¢	42.70¢	NR	54.80¢
	1959	41.5¢	39.8¢	38.70¢	NR	48.30¢
Coffee, per pound	1955	94.5¢	90.7¢	93¢	NR	92.50¢
	1956	$1.061	$1.039	$1.043	NR	99.60¢
	1957	$1.038	$1.023	$1.008	NR	99.40¢
	1958	92.3¢	93.2¢	89.30¢	NR	88.70¢
	1959	77.6¢	78.7¢	76.40¢	NR	79.50¢
Cornmeal, per pound	1955	12.5¢	7.2¢	12.40¢	NR	12.30¢
	1956	11.9¢	7.1¢	12.40¢	NR	12.80¢
	1957	12.2¢	7.3¢	12.60¢	NR	12.90¢
	1958	12.3¢	7.6¢	12.90¢	NR	13.40¢
	1959	12.20¢	7.20¢	12.90¢	NR	13.80¢

418

Commodity	Year	New York	Atlanta	Chicago	Denver	Los Angeles
Eggs, per dozen	1955	69.60¢	61¢	59.60¢	NR	57.50¢
	1956	67.60¢	60.70¢	59.90¢	NR	56.50¢
	1957	64.40¢	58.30¢	55.20¢	NR	55¢
	1958	67.60¢	61.80¢	58¢	NR	57.60¢
	1959	60.30¢	52.60¢	49.70¢	NR	NR
Flour, Wheat, per pound	1955	10.60¢	10.04¢	10.28¢	NR	11.14¢
	1956	10.28¢	10.94¢	10.14¢	NR	11.14¢
	1957	10.44¢	11.22¢	10.30¢	NR	12.10¢
	1958	10.70¢	11.48¢	10.32¢	NR	12.66¢
	1959	10.66¢	11.14¢	10.16¢	NR	12.68¢
Lard, per pound	1955	21.90¢	20.10¢	19.80¢	NR	19.80¢
	1956	20.40¢	19.30¢	19¢	NR	21.50¢
	1957	21.90¢	21.80¢	22¢	NR	25¢
	1958	22¢	21.60¢	21.70¢	NR	25¢
	1959	19.40¢	18.40¢	19.30¢	NR	23¢
Milk, Fresh, per quart	1955	26.40¢	25.50¢	26.20¢	NR	21.50¢
	1956	26.50¢	26.50¢	27.80¢	NR	21.70¢
	1957	28.50¢	26.70¢	27.90¢	NR	22.80¢
	1958	30.20¢	27.10¢	25.80¢	NR	23.90¢
	1959	31¢	26.40¢	26.60¢	NR	24.50¢
Mutton and Lamb, Leg, per pound	1955	63.90¢	74.40¢	65.20¢	NR	67.90¢
	1956	64.40¢	76¢	66.60¢	NR	69.50¢
	1957	66.50¢	75.10¢	68.10¢	NR	71.60¢
	1958	73.40¢	82.60¢	73.20¢	NR	77.20¢
	1959	71.10¢	80.70¢	70.90¢	NR	75.20¢
Pork, Bacon, Sliced, per pound	1955	71.10¢	65.90¢	64.40¢	NR	70¢
	1956	61¢	58.70¢	55.50¢	NR	62.40¢
	1957	75.90¢	74¢	71¢	NR	77.90¢
	1958	84.10¢	78.40¢	76.90¢	NR	83.20¢
	1959	72.70¢	66¢	63.90¢	NR	70.10¢
Pork, Chops, per pound	1955	80.80¢	73.10¢	80.90¢	NR	89.90¢
	1956	78.10¢	70.10¢	79.60¢	NR	89.90¢
	1957	87.80¢	76.90¢	85.20¢	NR	98.60¢
	1958	93.80¢	81.50¢	89.80¢	NR	$1.02
	1959	87.80¢	78.50¢	82.50¢	NR	98.40¢
Pork, Ham, Whole, per pound	1955	62.10¢	59.80¢	58.40¢	NR	61.30¢
	1956	60.10¢	58.10¢	58.90¢	NR	60.70¢
	1957	62.80¢	60.80¢	61.40¢	NR	65.60¢
	1958	84.10¢	65.60¢	65.90¢	NR	66.70¢
	1959	64.20¢	60.20¢	60.20¢	NR	61.70¢
Potatoes, Irish, per 10 pounds	1955	51¢	52.10¢	65.80¢	NR	70¢
	1956	59.70¢	65.70¢	78¢	NR	85¢
	1957	50.30¢	55.80¢	63.90¢	NR	70.70¢
	1958	53.80¢	60.60¢	63.90¢	NR	77.80¢
	1959	56.70¢	60.40¢	71.70¢	NR	89.90¢
Prunes, Dried, per pound	1955	32.10¢	34.70¢	34.10¢	NR	31.50¢
	1956	33.50¢	36¢	35.20¢	NR	33.60¢
	1957	32.10¢	33.40¢	33.70¢	NR	30.60¢
	1958	32.50¢	34.70¢	33.40¢	NR	31.80¢
	1959	38¢	40.50¢	39.20¢	NR	38¢
Rice, per pound	1955	19.70¢	19¢	16¢	NR	21.30¢
	1956	19¢	17.60¢	15¢	NR	20.80¢
	1957	19¢	17.90¢	15.50¢	NR	20.80¢
	1958	19.40¢	19.30¢	16.50¢	NR	21.70¢
	1959	19.40¢	19.50¢	NR	NR	22¢

Commodity	Year	New York	Atlanta	Chicago	Denver	Los Angeles
Sugar, per pound	1955	9.94¢	9.80¢	10.50¢	NR	10.32¢
	1956	10.06¢	10.10¢	10.82¢	NR	10.48¢
	1957	10.62¢	10.70¢	11.04¢	NR	10.96¢
	1958	10.92¢	11.16¢	11.02¢	NR	11.30¢
	1959	11.02¢	11.36¢	11.30¢	NR	11.64¢
Tea, Bags, per package of 48 per pound	1955	$1.54	$1.544	$1.592	NR	$1.66
	1956	66.30¢	71.40¢	69¢	NR	74.40¢
	1957	66.30¢	69.30¢	70.80¢	NR	75.30¢
	1958	68.10¢	73.80¢	71.40¢	NR	75.30¢
	1959	69.30¢	73.20¢	71.40¢	NR	75.60¢
Veal, per pound	1955	$1.24	95.60¢	$1.03	NR	$1.07
	1956	$1.26	98.60¢	$1.02	NR	$1.09
	1957	$1.33	$1.04	$1.08	NR	$1.17
	1958	$1.50	$1.20	$1.17	NR	$1.30
	1959	$1.61	$1.31	$1.23	NR	$1.39

SELECTED PRICES 1955–1959

Item	Source	Description	Price
ALCOHOL			
Bourbon	*Ben Arnold Co. Price List* (1955)	*Country Fair;* bottled in bond; straight bourbon	$4.88/fifth
Gin	*Ben Arnold Co. Price List* (1955)	Gordon's	$4.47/fifth
Scotch	*Ben Arnold Co. Price List* (1955)	*Haig & Haig Pinch;* 100% blended scotch	$7.68/fifth
Scotch	*Ben Arnold Co. Price List* (1955)	*Chivas Regal;* 12 years old	$8.06/fifth
Vermouth	*Ben Arnold Co. Price List* (1955)	*Martini & Rossi;* 16-oz bottle	$1.54
Vodka	*Ben Arnold Co. Price List* (1955)	Smirnoff	$5.23/fifth
Whiskey	*Ben Arnold Co. Price List* (1955)	Seagram's	$4.89/fifth
Whiskey	*Ben Arnold Co. Price List* (1955)	Seagram's V.O.	$6.43/fifth
Whiskey	*Chicago Tribune* (1955)	*Sunny Brook;* Kentucky blend; cheerful as its name	$4.30/fifth
APPAREL, CHILDREN'S			
Camp Shorts	*Sears, Roebuck* (1958)	May be worn with or without attachable suspenders	$1.94
Dress Shirt	*Sears, Roebuck* (1958)	Cotton; with cufflinks, bow tie; grown-up styling for little gentlemen	$1.74
Jeans	*Sears, Roebuck* (1958)	Economy price; 10-oz vat dyed; blue denim	$1.64
Necktie	*Sears, Roebuck* (1958)	Redi-tied; junior size with slip knot and gripper fastener	$0.94
Raincoat	*Sears, Roebuck* (1958)	*Ballerina;* collar converts to cozy hood; elastic-hug waist, roomy raglan sleeves	$5.74
Shirt	*Good Housekeeping* (1955)	*Tam o'shanter Beau Brummel;* with matching bow tie, poplin boxer longies, and shirt; 3-piece set	$4.98
Shoes	*Life* (1959)	*Buster Brown;* the shoes you were so proud of when you were little are the same shoes that thrill youngsters most today	$5.99–$7.99
Shoes	*Life* (1959)	*Brown's Pedwin;* young ideas in shoes	$9.95
Sweatshirt	*Boy's Life* (1955)	Official Boy Scout; top-quality cotton yarn, fleece-lined for extra warmth	$1.95
Undershirt	*Sears, Roebuck* (1958)	Lighter weight; sleeveless vest; rib knit of white combed cotton; package of three	$1.11/pkg
Uniform	*Boy's Life* (1955)	Boy Scout; summer; includes field cap, v-neck shirt, shorts, web belt, stockings, handkerchief, and slide	$8.97

Item	Source	Description	Price
APPAREL, MEN'S			
Coat	*Life* (1959)	*The Alligator Company;* America's most wanted gabardine	$42.75
Golf Jacket	*Life* (1959)	*Dow Finsterwald;* swing in comfort and style; lightweight fabric of 65% Dacron, 35% cotton	$11.95
Hosiery	*Life* (1959)	*Kayser-Roth Supp-Hose;* the fashionably sheer way to ease tired legs	$4.95
Shirt	*Sears, Roebuck* (1958)	*Hercules Snap-Front Model;* SNAP—it's open; SNAP—it's closed	$2.34
Shirt	*Life* (1959)	*Jayson;* ready to wear	$5.00
Shirt	*Life* (1959)	*Arrow;* machine-washable, Sanforized fabric	$5.00

In 1946, Monsanto developed and marketed "All" laundry detergent, which they sold to Lever Brothers in 1957. This advertisement is from 1956. (via Wikimedia Commons)

Item	Source	Description	Price
Shoes	*Good Housekeeping* (1955)	*Arch Walker Corrective Step;* the arch oxford that cradles your foot	$5.99–$8.99
Shoes	*Chicago Tribune* (1957)	*Johnston Murphy;* the newest concept in smart styling; low, trim lines with slipper-flex construction	$32.95
Shoes	*Life* (1959)	*Endicott Johnson Johnsonian Guide Step;* fit the feet in action	$10.95–$14.95
Shoes	*Life* (1959)	*Florsheim Perfecto;* a sensationally new shade	$19.95
Shoes	*Life* (1959)	*Rablee;* executive-styled wingtip style; the shoe with the open-collar feeling	$17.95
Slacks	*Life* (1959)	*Lancer;* safeguarded with Scotchgard, repels all stains	$7.88–$12.88
Socks	*Chicago Tribune* (1957)	*Baskin Touch n' Tingle;* unbelievably soft; Dacron and cotton	$1.00
Socks	*Sears, Roebuck* (1958)	Double the wear of ordinary cotton socks; in lots of six pairs	$0.37/pr
Socks	*Life* (1959)	*Esquire;* governor style	$1.00
Stockings	*Life* (1959)	*Burlington Hosiery;* support; the fashionable answer to leg fatigue	$4.95
Suit	*Life* (1959)	*Botany 500;* suits and topcoats made for each other	$59.50
Suit	*Life* (1959)	*Brookfield;* 2 Pants, all wool	$55.00
Suit	*Life* (1959)	*Brookfield;* high-priced luxury; these suits look every bit of $65	$39.95
Sweater	*Life* (1959)	*Robert Bruce Magna Cross;* boatneck pullover for men	$8.98
Topcoat	*Life* (1959)	*Botany 500;* suits and topcoats made for each other	$59.50
T-shirt	*Life* (1959)	*Munsingwear;* America's finest T-shirt; crew neck	$1.50

APPAREL, WOMEN'S

Item	Source	Description	Price
Brassiere	*Good Housekeeping* (1955)	*Warner's Merry Widow;* at the nicest stores here and in Canada	$5.95
Brassiere	*Good Housekeeping* (1955)	*Playtex;* made of elastic and nylon	$3.95
Brassiere	*Life* (1959)	*Maiden Form Star Flower;* white cotton broadcloth, A, B, and C cups	$2.50

An imaginary situation of a partially undressed dream was exploited in Maidenform's advertising in the 1950s and 1960s - "I dreamed I...[doing some ordinary activity]... in my Maidenform bra.", with an illustration of the person wearing only underwear in a public place, appearing proud and cheerful. (via Wikimedia)

Item	Source	Description	Price
Brassiere	*Life* (1959)	*Perma-Lift;* in miracle washeen; the lift that never lets you down	$3.50
Coat	*Life* (1959)	Gold brocade wrap-around coat	$125
Girdle	*Good Housekeeping* (1955)	*Warner's LeGant;* with lend elastic	$13.50
Girdle	*Good Housekeeping* (1955)	*Playtex;* made of wonderful new split-resistant fabricon	$4.95
Gloves	*Life* (1959)	*Pioneer Liquidproof Work Gloves;* nimble fingers; tissue-thin bluettes, knit-cotton lined	$1.49
Hosiery	*Sears, Roebuck* (1958)	*Roy;* purple stretchy garter tops, in white for nurses	$0.97
Nylons	*Good Housekeeping* (1955)	*Kotex Miracle Brand;* stretch; you'll find these full-fashioned nylons a sheer delight	$1.00
Shirt	*Sears, Roebuck* (1958)	Needs little or no ironing	$2.37
Shoes	*Sears, Roebuck* (1958)	*Kerrybrooke;* soft leather drape eased through bold vamp buckle	$3.77
Shoes	*Life* (1959)	*Brown AirStep Americana Tulane;* if activity is your kind of living	$13.95
Shoes	*Life* (1959)	*Brown Paddock;* the shoe with the beautiful fit	$12.95
Stockings	*Good Housekeeping* (1955)	*Cannon;* wear longer, too, just like Cannon towels and sheets	$0.99-$1.65
Suit	*Chicago Tribune* (1957)	*Stevens;* our gay crisp suit gives you a smart casual air	$17.95

BUSINESS EQUIPMENT & SUPPLIES

Item	Source	Description	Price
Boardmaster	*New York Times* (1956)	Graphic pictures of operations at a glance; type or write on cards; snaps in grooves	$49.50 with cards
Lighting	*New York Times* (1956)	Fluorescent and slimline fixtures	$7.60
Photostats	*New York Times* (1956)	Photostats	$0.20 ea.
Shelving	*New York Times* (1956)	Steel Shelving; 24" × 42" × 75"	$12.25
Typewriter	*Sears, Roebuck* (1958)	*Smith-Corona;* here's the first electric typewriter in portable size	$209.35
Typewriter	*Life* (1959)	*Smith Corona;* makes all manual portables old-fashioned	$164.50

COLLECTIBLES

Item	Source	Description	Price
Bowfront Bureau	*Antiques* (1956)	*Israel Sack;* circa 1780–1800, hepplewhite mahogany, small bowfront bureau with retrained inlay, original signature of maker, H. K. Dorsey	$675
Clock	*Antiques* (1956)	Antique grandfather clock; 6'9" mahogany clock with moon phases	$345
Desk	*Antiques* (1956)	Slant top; circa 1775 Chippendale walnut desk, bold ogee bracket feet	$500
Punch Bowl	*Antiques* (1956)	*Plummer Famille Rose;* circa 1790 presented by King George III, diameter 14 1/4"	$950
Rug	*Antiques* (1956)	*Charles W. Jacobsen Oriental;* 14' × 11.4' tabriz from Iran	$690
Settee	*Antiques* (1956)	*Windsor;* circa 1785; 55 1/2" long; very bold cross stretchers	$375
Soup Tureen	*Antiques* (1956)	*Faience;* 18th century tureen in the form of a setting hen on a shaped plateau; size 13" × 15 1/2"	$350

Item	Source	Description	Price
Stand	*Antiques* (1956)	Converts to desk; mahogany and poplar	$265

EDUCATION

Dance Lessons	*New York Times* (1956)	Fred Astaire Dance Club	$25.00

ENTERTAINMENT

Ballet	*New York Times* (1956)	The Royal Danish Ballet	$7.50
Musical	*New York Times* (1956)	Shangri-La	$7.50
Musical	*New York Times* (1956)	Show Boat	$1.10
Play	*New York Times* (1956)	Uncle Vanya	$3.85

ENTERTAINMENT, HOME

Camera	*Life* (1959)	*Kodak Pony II;* 33 mm color; picture as brilliant as autumn	$29.50
Camera	*Life* (1959)	*Graflex Century 35;* combination viewfinder-range finder permits framing	$49.50
Camera	*Life* (1959)	*Argus Match-Matic C-3;* the color-slide camera you can master in less than a minute	$64.95
Loudspeakers	*Consumer Reports* (1958)	*Acoustic Research AR-2;* high-fidelity; 13 1/2" × 24" × 11"; unfinished birch cabinet	$89/pr
Loudspeakers	*Consumer Reports* (1958)	*KLH;* high fidelity	$209
Movie Projector	*Life* (1959)	*Argus M-500;* shows full 400-ft (half-hour-long) reels	$89.95
Organ	*Life* (1959)	*Magnus 500 Electric Cord Organ;* no lessons, beautiful music the same day	$129.95
Pocket Radio	*Consumer Reports* (1957)	*Zenith Royall 500;* seven-transistor	$75.00
Pocket Radio	*Consumer Reports* (1957)	*Emerson 888;* transistor; price varies by color	$44–$48

Happi-Time Pocket Size
Transistor Portable Radio 9.88

Completely portable . . . needs no ground or aerial! All transistor
with Reflex Circuit and volume control. Fits in pocket or purse.
Feather-light. Operates over 500 hours on one battery. Try it!

Newspaper advertisement for the Happi Time transistor radio by Bell Products, 1959. (via Wikimedia Commons)

Item	Source	Description	Price
Record	*Life* (1959)	*RCA Victor;* Puccini, *La Boheme;* two-record set	$9.98
Refrigerator	*Life* (1959)	*Western Auto Wizard;* 80-lb freezer, roll-out shelf	$259
Stereo	*Life* (1959)	*Webcor;* panoramic sound; three stereo speakers; powerful 8-watt amplifier	$37.95–$399.95
Stereo	*Life* (1959)	*Columbia Stereo I;* the new sound of pleasure	$129.95
Television	*Life* (1959)	*Zenith Lafayette Cabinet Model;* includes space command remote control—built right in	$550

FOOD PRODUCTS

Baby Food	*Chicago Tribune* (1955)	*Gerber's;* strained meat for babies; four 3 1/2 oz glasses	$0.87
Candy	*Boy's Life* (1955)	*Tootsie Roll;* the ideal energy candy to take with you on those long hikes	$0.05

427

Item	Source	Description	Price
Chocolate Covered Cherries	*Chicago Tribune* (1955)	*Brach's;* 13-oz box	$0.55
Chop Suey Sauce	*Chicago Tribune* (1955)	*Fuji;* two 3-oz bottles	$0.19
Creamer	*Good Housekeeping* (1955)	*Instant Pream;* 100% dairy product	$0.25
Drink Mix	*Boy's Life* (1955)	*Miracle Aid;* makes cold drinks instantly; 6 tempting fruit flavors; 3/4 oz pkg, makes 1/2 gallon	$0.05
Fruit Cocktail	*Chicago Tribune* (1955)	*None-such;* in heavy syrup; four 16-oz tins	$0.93
Macaroni	*Chicago Tribune* (1955)	*Red Cross;* elbow cut; three 7-oz packages	$0.27
Pork and Beans	*Chicago Tribune* (1955)	*Van Camps;* in tomato sauce; two 15-oz tins	$0.25
Soft Drink	*Boy's Life* (1955)	*Lucky Pop Fizz Tablets;* box of 150 drinks; drop one carbonated flavor pill in an 8-oz glass, in seconds a really refreshing soft drink	$1.00

FURNITURE

Item	Source	Description	Price
Bedroom Set	*New York Times* (1956)	Hand rubbed walnut; brass inlays; 72"; 9-drawer triple dresser; double chest; night tables; headboard	$645
Bed Frame	*Life* (1959)	*Harvard Frames;* with plastic protecto-caps; can't tear bedding	$12.95
Chair	*New York Times* (1956)	*The Oslochair;* 2 reversible innerspring cushions	$39.95
Chandelier	*Antiques* Magazine (1956)	*Paul Crystal Bohemian;* made of the finest crystal in the world; height 23", width 33"; has 12 arms	$425
Lamp	*Good Housekeeping* (1955)	*Johnny One-Light;* with Velon shade; firestone Velon literally lightens your *life*	$11.95
Sofa	*New York Times* (1956)	*Foamland;* caned arm sofa; zippered covers	$99.50
Sofabed	*New York Times* (1956)	Foam rubber sofabed	$69.95
Step Stool	*Good Housekeeping* (1955)	*Cosco Model 4-M;* chromium or black legs with red, yellow, green, charcoal, pink, or chartreuse upholstery	$12.95
Table	*New York Times* (1956)	Rectangular	$39.00
Table	*New York Times* (1956)	Free form	$59.00
Table	*New York Times* (1956)	Butterfly	$59.00

GARDEN EQUIPMENT & SUPPLIES

Item	Source	Description	Price
Lawn Sprinkler	*Good Housekeeping* (1955)	*Tuff-Lite;* underlawn sprinkling system; waters 1000 sq. ft	$16.95
Lawn Sprinkler	*Consumer Reports* (1958)	*Allenco Parkside;* rotating model	$6.50
Lawn Sprinkler	*Consumer Reports* (1958)	*Sunbeam Rain King Automatic K-2A*	$9.95

Item	Source	Description	Price
HOTEL RATES			
Hotel Room	*Asheville Citizen Times* (Asheville, NC) (1957)	*Mount-Vue Motel*	$4/night
Hotel Room	*Complete Guide to New England* (1958)	*Barnum Hotel*; modern city hotel; 200 rooms, coffee shop, dining room	$4.75/night
Hotel Room	*Complete Guide to New England* (1958)	*Hotel Statler*; Hartford, Connecticut; ultra-modern; all air conditioned with radio and TV Single Double	 $7/night $12/night
Hotel Room	*Complete Guide to New England* (1958)	*General Putnam Inn*; Norwalk, Connecticut; small country inn, developed for colonial house; European plan	$4/night
Hotel Room	*Complete Guide to New England* (1958)	*Tremont Motor Court*; New Haven, Connecticut; big, new, modern; 51 air-conditioned units, TV, telephone	$9.50/night
Hotel Room	*Complete Guide to New England* (1958)	*Harbor View Hotel*; Bar Harbour, Maine; near waterfront and next to park; dining room and cocktail lounge; single, in season	$6/night
Hotel Room	*Complete Guide to New England* (1958)	*Bangor House*; Bangor, Maine: commercial-type city hotel, 123 rooms, edge of business district; single	$3.75/night
Hotel Room	*Complete Guide to New England* (1958)	*Green Shutters Inn and Cottages*; Boothbay Harbor, Maine; cottage resort, dining room features New England dishes and seafood; modified American plan; double	$12/night
Hotel Room	*Complete Guide to New England* (1958)	*Hotel Eagle*; Brunswick, Maine; celebrated resort estate, 2 notable dining rooms, Maine specialties, beach and golf course adjacent; per person summer rates	$12/night
Hotel Room	*Complete Guide to New England* (1958)	*Ritz-Carlton Hotel*; Boston, Massachusetts; fashionable, luxurious, and quiet city hotel; main dining room; single	$9/night
Hotel Room	*Complete Guide to New England* (1958)	*Hotel Vendome*; Boston, Massachusetts; transient and residential; 225 rooms; Moulin Rouge supper club and French room restaurant	$5/night
Hotel Room	*Complete Guide to New England* (1958)	*Buzzards Bay Lodge*; Buzzards Bay, Massachusetts; shore setting; 31 modern units, all double or suites, some with TV, many with kitchenette; private beach and dock	$8/night
Hotel Room	*Complete Guide to New England* (1958)	*Commander Hotel;* Cambridge, Massachusetts; across common from Harvard University; all rooms with TV, color TV in apartments; dining room features French cooking Single Double	 $6/night $10/night
HOUSEHOLD PRODUCTS			
Blanket	*Good Housekeeping* (1955)	*Chatham Double;* warmer than blankets that cost almost twice as much; the addition of fabulous Orlon to Purrey's patented weave	$10.95
Can Opener	*Good Housekeeping* (1955)	*Rival Can-O-Mat;* most beautiful can opener made; with magnet	$6.98
Cleaner	*Good Housekeeping* (1955)	*Glamorene Wool Rug Cleaner;* made to dry-clean rugs the easy, quick, modern way; 1/2 gallon; cleans two 9' × 12' rugs	$2.29
Coffee Maker	*Consumer Reports* (1958)	Percolator	$16.88

Item	Source	Description	Price
Coffee Maker	*Consumer Reports* (1958)	*Cory;* vacuum type	$39.95
Cooker	*Good Housekeeping* (1955)	*Presto 700;* cooks three times faster	$12.95
Deodorizer	*Chicago Tribune* (1955)	*Colgate;* aerosol	$0.69
Dishes	*Good Housekeeping* (1955)	International Molded Plastics Brookpark; plastic non-chipping, non-breaking, modern design; 26-piece starter set, service for four	$14.95
Fry Skillet	*Good Housekeeping* (1955)	*Dominion;* electric-automatic; masters every cooking job better and easier	$15.95
Grill	*Good Housekeeping* (1955)	*Capri Roto-Broil 400;* big 8-way rotisserie barbeque	$79.95
Hearth	*Life* (1959)	*Kos-mark;* ready-made; suitable for burning anything from logs to love letters	$250
Heater	*Life* (1959)	*Arvin Model 5912;* portable; electric; economized in every way	$12.95
Iron	*Life* (1959)	*Western Auto Wizard;* steam dry; fully automatic, finger-tip fabric selector	$9.88
Ironing Board Cover	*Life* (1959)	*Magla;* silicone; add zip to your ironing	$1.49
Ironing Table	*Good Housekeeping* (1955)	*Cream City Met-L-Top;* the world's most comfortable ironing table	$13.95
Kitchen Machine	*Good Housekeeping* (1955)	*Rival Kitcheneer;* all-in-one grinder, chopper, slicer, shredder, grater, with interchangeable base	$12.98
Kitchen Towels	*Good Housekeeping* (1955)	*Startex;* so many, many beautiful styles to choose from that you're sure to find just the right patterns for your home	$0.29–$0.49
Mattress	*Life* (1959)	*Serta Perfect Sleeper;* king size at no extra cost	$79.50
Mattress	*Life* (1959)	*Simmons Beautyrest;* the best costs the least	$79.50
Mop	*Good Housekeeping* (1955)	Twice the sponge surface; 5-year written guarantee	$4.98
Paint	*Good Housekeeping* (1955)	*Sherwin-Williams Kem-tone;* paint today, sleep tight tonight; interior paint	$5.59/gallon
Paneling	*Life* (1959)	*Sammara Weldwood;* the only thing expensive is its looks; 12' × 8' wall, 70 panels	$47.00
Photoflash Lamps	*Boy's Life* (1955)	*General Electric M2;* no fuss, no fretting, and they are sure-fire, even on weakened batteries	$0.10
Pillows	*Sears, Roebuck* (1958)	Goose down; extra large, extra soft, and extra comfortable	$14.97
Vacuum Cleaner	*Good Housekeeping* (1955)	*Eureka Super Roto-Matic;* with zip-clip swivel-top and new 4-wheel roto-dolly	$69.95
Vacuum Cleaner	*Good Housekeeping* (1955)	*Electrolux;* world's lightest-weight heavy duty cleaner	$69.75

INSURANCE RATES

Item	Source	Description	Price
Fire Insurance	*St. Paul Fire and Marine Insurance Co.* (1957)	$14,000 coverage on single-family dwelling	$57.40/year

Item	Source	Description	Price
JEWELRY			
Chain	*Life* (1959)	Swank sterling silver; initial on golden tones	$2.50
Watch	*Boy's Life* (1955)	*Timex Boy Scout;* American-made wrist watches with top-quality features	$9.95
Watch	*Life* (1959)	*Bulova Royal Clipper;* slim waterproof watches; 17 jewels, self-winding	$59.50
MEALS			
Hamburger	*Associated Press* (1957)	Burger King Whopper	$0.37
MEDICAL PRODUCTS & SERVICES			
Cough Syrup	*Life* (1959)	*Troutman's;* friend of the family when coughs come	$0.49
Lotion	*Boy's Life* (1955)	*Clearasil;* starves pimples	$0.59–$0.98
Salve	*Life* (1959)	*Blistex;* best for cold sores, chapped lips, fever blisters	$0.39
MOTORIZED VEHICLES, SUPPLIES, & SERVICES			
Automobile	Longworth and Robson, *Complete Book of Collectible Cars* (1985)	*Buick Century;* 2-door hardtop	$2,490–$3,420
Automobile	Longworth and Robson, *Complete Book of Collectible Cars* (1985)	*Chrysler New Yorker DeLuxe Newport;* 2-door hardtop [cost in 1955]	$3,652–$4,243
Automobile	Longworth and Robson, *Complete Book of Collectible Cars* (1985)	*Ford Fairlane;* 4-door town sedan [cost in 1955]	$1,914–$2,272
Automobile	Longworth and Robson, *Complete Book of Collectible Cars* (1985)	*Chrysler Imperial Newport;* 2-door hardtop [cost in 1955]	$3,752–$4,072
Automobile	Longworth and Robson, *Complete Book of Collectible Cars* (1985)	*Lincoln Capri Custom;* 2-door hardtop [cost in 1955]	$3,752–$4,072
Automobile	Longworth and Robson, *Complete Book of Collectible Cars* (1985)	*DeSoto Fireflite;* 2-door hardtop [cost in 1956]	$2,727–$3,615
Automobile	Longworth and Robson, *Complete Book of Collectible Cars* (1985)	*Dodge D-500 Royall;* convertible [cost in 1956]	$2,632
Automobile	Longworth and Robson, *Complete Book of Collectible Cars* (1985)	*Packard Caribbean;* 2-door hardtop [cost in 1956]	$5,495–$5,995
Automobile	Longworth and Robson, *Complete Book of Collectible Cars* (1985)	*Plymouth Fury;* 2-door hardtop [cost in 1956]	$2,866
Automobile	Longworth and Robson, *Complete Book of Collectible Cars* (1985)	*Pontiac Bonneville* [cost in 1957]	$5,782

Item	Source	Description	Price
Automobile	Longworth and Robson, *Complete Book of Collectible Cars* (1985)	*Rambler Rebel*; 4-door hardtop [cost in 1957]	$2,786
Automobile	Longworth and Robson, *Complete Book of Collectible Cars* (1985)	*Ford Thunderbird*; 2-door hardtop [cost in 1958]	$3,631–$4,222
Automobile	*Life* (1959)	*Simca DeLuxe*; imported from Paris by Chrysler	$1,698
Automobile	*Life* (1959)	*Buick Opel Caravan Wagon*; German made American style	$2,292.60
Automobile	Longworth and Robson, *Complete Book of Collectible Cars* (1985)	*Cadillac Eldorado Brougham*; 4-door hardtop [cost in 1959]	$13,075
Automobile	Longworth and Robson, *Complete Book of Collectible Cars* (1985)	*Chevrolet Corvette*; convertible [cost in 1959]	$3,631–$3,934

MUSICAL INSTRUMENTS

Item	Source	Description	Price
Accordion	*Chicago Tribune* (1957)	*Renelli;* 120-bass accordion with 41 treble keys, 2 treble and 4 bass reeds, 2 treble switches; choice of 3 colors, straps and case included; regularly $295	$189
Cornet	*Chicago Tribune* (1957)	*Lyon Healy;* big tone, easy response, gold-lacquered finish; regularly $112.50	$99.50
Guitar	*Chicago Tribune* (1957)	*Washburn;* Spanish flat-top model with clear-grained spruce top; regularly $35	$27.50

OTHER

Item	Source	Description	Price
Air Freshener	*Good Housekeeping* (1955)	*Dazy Spray;* costs less than expensive wicks or throw-away bombs	$0.49
Candygram	*Life* (1959)	*Western Union Candygram;* they'll eat your words	$2.95/pound
Cat Food	*Chicago Tribune* (1955)	*Puss N'Boots;* three 8-oz cans	$0.39
Crystal Prisms	*Antiques* (1956)	Plan colonial; 7" overall	$0.89
Dye	*Good Housekeeping* (1955)	*Rit;* try Rit in your washing machine and amaze yourself	$0.25
Microscope	*Boy's Life* (1955)	*Hy-power;* 100-200–300; 3-turret power	$8.95
Pen	*Life* (1959)	*Listo;* writes on cellophane and everything else	$0.27
Scale	*Good Housekeeping* (1955)	*Health-O-Meter Model 117;* the scale with a lift West of Denver	$8.95 $9.45
Sun and Heat Lamp	*Sears, Roebuck* (1958)	Lets you enjoy the magic of sun-bathing indoors	$72.93

PERSONAL CARE PRODUCTS

Item	Source	Description	Price
Acne Cream	*Good Housekeeping* (1955)	When acne strikes heartache and loneliness often follow	$0.59
Bandage	*Life* (1959)	*Johnson & Johnson Band-Aid;* plastic strips; extra large	$0.69
Dental Cream	*Life* (1959)	*Colgate-Palmolive;* world's largest selling toothpaste	$0.31/$0.53/ $0.69/$0.83

Item	Source	Description	Price
Deodorant	*Life* (1959)	*Tussy;* guard your charms	$1.00
Eyeliner	*Life* (1959)	*Max Factor Hi-Fi;* smearproof, waterproof, long lasting, never flakes	$1.50
Eyelash Curler	*Good Housekeeping* (1955)	*Maybelline;* naturally, it's the best gold tone	$1.00
Face Powder	*Sears, Roebuck* (1958)	Smooth long-lasting veil	$1.38
Facial Treatment	*Sears, Roebuck* (1958)	*Royal Treatment;* look born beautiful; now, famous royal jelly of the Queen Bee can be yours	$5.50
Home Permanent	*Good Housekeeping* (1955)	*Proctor & Gamble Lilt Party Curl;* the only ammonia-free children's home permanent	$1.50
Lipstick	*Good Housekeeping* (1955)	*Cashmere Bouquet Rhythm-In-Red;* stays crimson-bright on your lips	$0.49
Lotion	*Good Housekeeping* (1955)	*Jergens;* positively stops detergent hands	$1.00
Lotion	*Life* (1959)	*Shulton Desert Flower;* contains the very heart of lanolin	$2.00
Makeup	*Good Housekeeping* (1955)	*Tangee;* the miracle makeup; actually lets your skin breathe	$0.39/$0.69
Makeup	*Good Housekeeping* (1955)	*Revlon Love-Pat;* it's pressed powder plus foundation; with Lanolite	$1.35
Makeup	*Life* (1959)	*House of Westmore Tru-glo;* liquid; America's most glamorous women applaud Tru-glo	$0.39
Mouthwash	*Life* (1959)	*Vi-Jon Antiseptic Mouthwash;* for colds, sore throats, bad breath; 16-oz family size bottle	$0.74
Perfume	*Life* (1959)	*Dorothy Gray Volate;* incredibly feminine	$5.00
Razor Blades	*Life* (1959)	*Pal Injector;* 20 blades	$0.79
Shampoo	*Good Housekeeping* (1955)	*Woodbury;* for beautiful hair-dos right after shampooing	$0.59
Shaver	*Life* (1959)	*Lady Norelco;* rotary blades no hand setting	$24.95
Shaving Cream	*Life* (1959)	*Shulton Old Spice;* softens beard better than ordinary push-button lathers; regular or mentholated	$1.00

PUBLICATIONS

Item	Source	Description	Price
Book	*Boy's Life* (1955)	Bruce Catton, *Banners at Shenandoah,* Doubleday; Civil War action novel	$3.00
Magazine	*Boy's Life* (1955)	*Boy's Life;* for all boys; monthly	$0.25
Magazine	*Antiques* (1956)	*Antiques;* monthly	$0.75
Magazine	*Life* (1959)	*Life;* weekly	$0.25

REAL ESTATE

Item	Source	Description	Price
Bungalow	*Chicago Tribune* (1955)	For sale; two-bedroom expandable bungalow, extra kitchen	$14,500
House	*Chicago Tribune* (1955)	For sale, 4 bedrooms, 1/2 acre lot	$34,000

Item	Source	Description	Price
House	*Chicago Tribune* (1955)	For sale; bi-level home; only one left	$17,950
House	*Chicago Tribune* (1955)	For sale; four-bedroom frame, living room, dining room, combination, gas heat, single garage	$19,500
House	*Chicago Tribune* (1955)	For sale; three-bedroom, brick ranch; gas radiant heat, vinyl tile, attic fan, 2-car garage, side drive	$18,300
Studio Home	*Chicago Tribune* (1955)	For sale; terms or contract to qualified couple; garden privileges; large first-floor work or storage area	$5,500

SEWING EQUIPMENT & SUPPLIES

Item	Source	Description	Price
Sewing Machine	*Life* (1959)	*Singer;* young budget portable model built to meet the sewing needs of young families	$119.50

SPORTS EQUIPMENT

Item	Source	Description	Price
Bait Casting Line	*Boy's Life* (1955)	*Cortland Cam-O-Flag;* braided from nylon test 20 lbs; 50 yds	$1.30
Baseball Glove	*Boy's Life* (1955)	Rawlings Little League Stan Musial	$9.95
Baseball Shoes	*Boy's Life* (1955)	*Rawlings;* designed for action, molded rubber soles and cleats	$4.95
Bicycle	*Life* (1959)	*Western Auto Western Flyer;* 26"; features bold Jet-Swept cantilever frame	$64.95
Bicycle Light	*Boy's Life* (1955)	*Delta Electric Rocket Ray;* you'll think you're ready for a flight into space	$2.40
Crow Call	*Boy's Life* (1955)	Philips S. Olt V-16 Junior Model	$1.50
License Plate	*Boy's Life* (1955)	*Better Values;* for bicycles; personalized with name or nickname up to 8 letters	$1.00
Outboard Motor	*Boy's Life* (1955)	*Evinrude;* big twin aquasonic, standard model	$430
Outboard Motor	*Boy's Life* (1955)	*Johnson Motors Sea-horse 25;* 25 HP; for the lift of your life	$430
Race Car Kit	*Boy's Life* (1955)	*Pinewood Derby;* contains 8 pre-sawed blocks of clear pine, plus axle supports, wheels, decals, and instructions	$2.75
Rifle	*Boy's Life* (1955)	*Harrington & Richardson Pioneer;* .22 cal. bolt action single shot rifle model 750	$17.95
Spinning Tackle	*Boy's Life* (1955)	*Airex Larchmont;* a light weight reel with a precision quadrant brake	$25.00
Stationary Bike	*Sears, Roebuck* (1958)	Home riding exercise	$71.50

TOBACCO PRODUCTS

Item	Source	Description	Price
Cigars	*Life* (1959)	*Trend;* mild little cigars blended with fine Havana; you need not inhale to enjoy them; humidor pack of 20 cigars	$0.35
Lighter	*Life* (1959)	*Zippo;* highly polished durable chrome finish	$4.75

A 1957 advertisement for Viceroy cigarettes, featuring famous athletes, including Mickey Mantle. Regulations on tobacco advertising, including a required warning on all advertisements, did not begin until 1971. (via Wikimedia Commons)

Item	Source	Description	Price
TOYS			
Doll	*Good Housekeeping* (1955)	*Gerber Baby Doll;* a-cuddle, sleep sweetly; with 6 Gerber food labels	$2.00
Remote Control Robot	*New York Times* (1956)	Electric motor; eyes flash; arms swing back and forth; walks forward or backwards; all metal	$2.78
Toy	*Life* (1959)	*Revell Dr. Seuss Zoo;* we're nutty and new; set of three	$3.98
Truck	*Life* (1959)	*Buddy-L;* Texaco tank truck; lay away for Christmas	$3.50
TRAVEL & TRANSPORTATION			
Airfare	*Good Housekeeping* (1955)	*TWA;* from New York to London; TWA discount fares; special discounts for couples	
		Round Trip	$482
		Ladies Accompanying Husbands	$282
Airfare	*Chicago Tribune* (1955)	*TWA;* three non-stops to Los Angeles; fly the finest, fly TWA	$76.00
Railroad Fare	*Life* (1959)	Santa Fe Chicago to San Francisco	$63.12
Railroad Fare	*Life* (1959)	*Santa Fe Railroad;* an entire family of four can ride to California and back from Chicago for less than it costs to drive your own car	$212.15

MISCELLANY 1955–1959

Zsa Zsa Gabor

Just discovered why Zsa Zsa Gabor and her daughter, Porfirio Rubirosa, the Herbert Marshalls, Nina Foch, Cy Howard and Gloria Grahame, and Lauritz Melchior are having such a fine time in New York. When one of the richest men in America invited them to his home in Allensville, PA, for his annual New Year's party in honor of his wife, he not only paid all their expenses but gave them an extra check to boot. It was Melchior's third year, but Zsa Zsa claims she got the biggest bonus—$5,000—for being the prettiest guest.

Hollywood entertaining was never like this.

Chicago Tribune, January 8, 1955

Emigrating to the United States in 1941, Zsa Zsa became a sought-after actress with "European flair and style." She was considered to have a personality that "exuded charm and grace," and was very active in the Hollywood social scene. (via Wikimedia Commons)

Installment Credit Up $15 Million in February

Consumer installment credit outstanding rose $15,000,000 in February, the Federal Reserve Board reported yesterday.

February's rise to a total of $27,784,000,000 compared with an increase of $72,000,000 in February, 1955.

The modest size of the latest increase disguised a much larger rise above the 1955 month's level in new installment credit extended. The $2,769,000,000 in new credit was $45,000,000 above the January total and $353,000,000 above that of February, 1955. Repayments rose even more sharply to $2,754,000,000.

New York Times, April 3, 1956

Action Explained in Six Languages; New Gallery Will Be Opened to the Public Tomorrow—Companies to Exhibit

Information about the operations of the American Stock Exchange is now available in English, French, German, Italian, Spanish, and Yiddish. A new gallery, which will be opened to the securities industry today and to the public on Wednesday, is equipped with telephone instructions through which visitors may hear a tape-recorded nine- minute narrative.

New York Times, April 3, 1956

Chain Store Sales Show 15.6% Gain, Best in Six Years

Chain store sales in April registered the sharpest increase over volume of a year earlier since March 1951, according to a survey completed yesterday by the .

The gain for forty-four companies was 15.6 percent, as against 19 percent in March 1951. The strong showing was attributed by company executives to the increase in Easter volume. With the holiday three weeks later this year than in 1956, the bulk of the seasonal trade came in April. Last year it came in March.

New York Times, May 14, 1957

1960–1979

The Vietnam War and the Global Economy

1963 series one-dollar bill.

The 1960s and 1970s were full of hope, revolutionary innovation, and disruptive economic change. The role of government grew and transformed American society. World economics and the Vietnam War altered America's view of its invincibility; inflation played a critical role in prices, wages, and politics; the cold war ended as the Soviet Union and lesser communist regimes behind the iron curtain collapsed.

From 1960 to 1964 the economy expanded. Gross national product and total federal spending increased by nearly 25 percent. Inflation was held in check. The power of the United States internationally was immense. Congress gave the young president John F. Kennedy the defense- and space-related programs he wanted, but few welfare programs. In the years that followed the erection of the Berlin Wall, the Cuban Missile Crisis, and the initial American involvement in the Vietnam War, all of which occurred during the presidency of John F. Kennedy, Americans were forced to think globally—and not always positively. Economic stability during the period was threatened by inflation. From an annual average of less than 2 percent between 1950 and 1965, the inflation rate soared to almost 9.5 percent in the second half of the 1970s. The rate was frighteningly volatile, ranging from 6 percent to almost 14 percent. Banks found it difficult to attract deposits as investors sought better rates of return by shifting their money to other mar-

kets. For savings and loan institutions the funds shift was a disaster leading to thousands of closures.

In 1963 a presidential commission on women responded to the complex of issues related to women's equality. The National Organization for Women and such feminist statements as Betty Friedan's The Feminine Mystique forced women's issues, which are grounded in economics, to the forefront of national attention. By 1980 the two-career family became the norm. Forty-two percent of all American workers were female, and more than half of all married women and 90 percent of female college graduates worked outside the home. Yet, their median wage was 60 percent of that for men.

In 1973 the economic power of foreign oil became alarming. In just two months' time world oil prices shot up from less than $6 to almost $23 a barrel. Shortfalls and long lines at gas stations resulted. The price at the pump doubled. The second oil shock, in 1978, carried oil prices past $34 a barrel and gas at the pump over $1 a gallon. This situation produced an awareness of U.S. vulnerability and widespread inflation. With roughly 6 percent of the world's people, the U.S. consumed one-third of world petroleum.

Attempts to control inflation by tightening the money supply through higher interest rates and frozen prices and wages created a combination of rising living costs and recession known as stagflation. In 1979 the consumer price index rose 13.3 percent. The following year interest rates and inflation each hit 18 percent.

The Cold War became hotter during conflicts over Cuba and Berlin in the early 1960s. Fears over the international spread of Communism led to America's intervention in a foreign conflict that would become a defining event of the decade: Vietnam. Military involvement in this small Asian country grew from advisory status to full-scale war. Vietnam became a national obsession, producing inflation and discontent. In spring 1970 students on 448 college campuses either staged campus strikes or closed down their institutions. The war was the longest in American history; the total cost was $118 billion, 56,000 dead and 300,000 wounded, and the loss of American prestige abroad.

The collapse of communism at the end of the 1980s brought an end to the old world order and set the stage for a realignment of power in which America was still regarded as the strongest nation in the world, but the definition of power was expressed increasingly in economic rather than military terms.

The struggle to bring economic equality to blacks during the period produced massive government spending for school integration, especially in the 1960s. By 1963 the peaceful phase of the civil rights movement ended; street violence, assassinations, and bombings marked the period. In 1967, forty-one cities experienced major disturbances, but by 1972 nearly half of Southern black children sat in integrated classrooms, and about a third of black families had risen economically into the ranks of the middle class.

Year	Dollar Value in 2019
1960	$8.65
1963	$8.37
1965	$8.13
1967	$7.67
1969	$6.98

Year	Dollar Value in 2019
1970	$6.60
1973	$5.77
1975	$4.76
1977	$4.23
1979	$3.53

Use this Currency Conversion chart to calculate what any time in the years listed would cost in 2019. Simply multiply the cost of that item by dollar amount in the chart. For example, if you know that a zigzag sewing machine cost $119.95 in 1965, multiply $119.95 by $8.13 to discover that that same sewing machine would cost $975.19 in 2019.

HISTORICAL SNAPSHOT 1960–1964

1960
- Organization of Petroleum Exporting Companies (OPEC) meets for first time
- Coal supplies 45 percent of power needs
- Sprite introduced by Coca-Cola Company
- Laser perfected
- Gross national product is $503 billion
- More than 25 million taxpayers declare incomes of $5,000 or more; 5.23 million claim $10,000 or more
- Corporate mergers total 844
- Auto registrations show one passenger car for every three Americans
- Television plays a key role in the Nixon-Kennedy presidential election
- Paperback book sales reach 300 million annually
- 10 percent of workforce is on the farm
- Beef consumption reaches 99 pounds a year per capita
- Enovid 10 contraceptive, known widely as the Pill, sells for 55 cents each, costing $11 per month

1961
- DNA genetic code broken
- New York's First National Bank offers fixed-term certificate of deposit
- IBM Selectric typewriter introduced
- Merger creates Harper & Row
- Cigarette makers spend $115 million on television advertising

- R. J. Reynolds acquires Pacific Hawaiian Products Company to diversify
- Canned pet foods are among the three top-selling categories in grocery stores

1962
- Cuban missile crisis pits United States against Soviet Union
- President Kennedy reduces tariff duties to stimulate foreign trade
- Electronic Data Systems founded by H. Ross Perot
- 90 percent of households have at least one television set
- American Broadcasting Company (ABC) begins color telecast for 3.5 hours per week
- *Silent Spring* by U. S. biologist Rachel Carson published
- Diet-Rite Cola introduced as first sugar-free soft drink
- Tab-opening aluminum drink cans introduced

1963
- President Kennedy assassinated; Lyndon Johnson becomes President
- Congress enacts equal-pay-for-equal- work legislation for women
- Jersey Central Power and Light installs first commercial nuclear reactor
- Two-thirds of the world's automobiles are in United States
- Valium introduced by Roche Laboratories
- U.S. factory workers average more than $100 weekly for first time

- Federal budget reaches nearly $100 billion
- First-class postal rates increase to 5cents per ounce
- Weight Watchers founded in Queens, NY
- Average per capita meat consumption reaches 170.6 pounds; chicken consumption is 37.8 pounds

1964
- Congress approves Tonkin Gulf resolution in North Vietnam
- Civil Rights bill approved
- Soviet coup strips Nikita Khrushchev of power
- 24th Amendment, making poll taxes unconstitutional, goes into effect
- Studebaker-Packard Corporation makes seat belts standard equipment
- Ford introduces Mustang
- Gasoline prices are 30.3 cents per gallon
- Zip codes adopted by U.S. Post Office
- Sales through vending machines total $3.5 billion

President Kennedy in the limousine in Dallas, Texas, on Main Street, minutes before his assassination. Also in the presidential limousine are Jackie Kennedy, Texas Governor John Connally, and his wife, Nellie. (via Wikimedia Commons)

SELECTED INCOME 1960–1964

Job	Source	Description	Pay
Account Executive	Chicago Tribune (1964)	High-caliber man; successful organization servicing established accounts assures you of excellent commission; direct sales experience required	$15,000–$18,000/yr
Accountant	New York Times (1961)	Prefer sr.'s or semi's with CPA experience or experience as auditor, controller or F/C bookkeeper; 35–65 years old	$116–$160/wk
Actor	Legrand and Karney Chronicle of the Cinema (1995)	Warren Beatty's salary for his role in Splendor in the Grass in 1961	$200,000
Actor	Miller, The Great Cowboy Stars of Movies and Television (1979)	Clint Eastwood's salary for his role in the movie A Fistful of Dollars in 1964	$15,000
Actor	Robinson, Bardot, An Intimate Portrait (1994)	Brigitte Bardot's salary for Contempt in 1963	$530,300
Administrative Assistant	New York Times (1961)	Male; administrative office of industry-wide pension, welfare & vacation plans; college graduate preferred; must be able to coordinate, handle detail & possess writing ability; liberal FREE benefits	$125/wk to start
Advertising Trainees	Chicago Tribune (1962)	You will get your feet wet as the department contact man	$500/mo
Agency Director	Chicago Tribune (1964)	Life insurance	$17,000/yr
Airlines Trainees	Chicago Tribune (1964)	No experience needed; free travel privileges	$385/mo
Assistant Civil Engineer	San Bernardino Evening Telegram (1963)	Person desired is college graduate with two years responsible experience in municipal engineering Per month	$708 to $848
Boiler Engineer	New York Times (1961)	New York, New Jersey, Florida	$7,000/yr
Broker	Chicago Tribune (1962)	Famous brokerage firm needs 3 young men over 20 to learn stock trading; some college helpful; your ability to learn will assure you this spot	$400/mo
Businessman	Harry Hunt III, Texas Rich: The Hunt Dynasty from the Early Oil Days Through the Silver Crash (1981)	Gross income of Nelson Bunker Hunt from Sarir oil field, Libya, in 1961	$6 billion
Cartoonist	National Public Radio Interview (2004)	Sid Couchy's pay per cartoon page to pencil Richey Rich comic books in 1961	$15

An advertisement in Scientific American *calling for qualified candidates to work at NASA's Jet Propulsion Lab.* (via Wikimedia Commons)

Job	Source	Description	Pay
Computer Sales Trainee	*Chicago Tribune* (1964)	Opportunity of a lifetime; fastest growing industry in America; this company will train college men for permanent positions that will earn $25,000–$30,000 annually within four years	$9,000–$11,000/yr
Cook	*Chicago Tribune* (1962)	Chef-sous; chef-sauciers; bakers; institutional cooks	$100–$250/wk
Customer-Service Technicians	*Chicago Tribune* (1964)	General chemical know-how, plus careful training by the employer will make you a top-notch customer-relations representative	$8,000–$9,500/yr
Delivery Man	*San Bernardino Evening Telegram* (1963)	Family man, neat appearing and friendly, to take over local and delivery route Per week to start	$120
Director Public Relations	*Chicago Tribune* (1962)	Industrial background; work with president in all financial areas	$18,000/yr
Editor	*Minneapolis Morning Tribune* (1964)	Editor Trainee to edit monthly house organ and weekly sales magazine Per month	$475
Electrician	*Minneapolis Morning Tribune* (1964)	Alaska Lumber & Pulp Co.; job requires 5 years industrial equipment experience; pulp and mill experience preferred. Rate per hour	$4.10
Executive Assistant	*Chicago Tribune* (1964)	Busy executive will train right young man to assist him; degree not essential	$115/wk
Export Sales	*Chicago Tribune* (1962)	You will get in on this corporation's plans to expand its foreign sales staff! They will hire you and train you in the home office until you are familiar with the operation	$90–$100/wk
Factory Girls	*New York Times* (1961)	No experience; day/night	$65/wk
Factory Men	*New York Times* (1961)	Foundry type operation; 2 yrs recent metal-working experience	$1.56/hr to start
Guard	*New York Times* (1961)	Train as guard; 20 years and over; no experience	$75–$85/wk, plus lunch
Housekeeper	*San Bernardino Evening Telegram* (1963)	Must have driver's license; work from 12:30 to 5:30 pm Per month	$100
Industrial Sales Manager	*New York Times* (1964)	Shipyard or heavy industrial experience leading company, Philadelphia area	$12,000 to $16,000
Machinist	*New York Times* (1961)	Helpers Machinists	$1.75 $3.25
Model Trainees	*New York Times* (1961)	Size 12; coats	$55/wk
Musicians	*Life* (1964)	Payment to the Beatles for their landmark appearance on *The Ed Sullivan Show* in 1964	$4,000
Organic Research Chemist	*Minneapolis Morning Tribune* (1964)	For Minneapolis area, per year	$12,000
Pages (Girl-Woman)	*New York Times* (1961)	Company pays fee; 16 years; housewives ok	$55–$70/wk
Patrolman	*San Bernardino Evening Telegram* (1963)	San Bernardino policeman; high school degree, minimum height 5 9"; minimum weight 155 lbs. Per month	$529-$639

Job	Source	Description	Pay
Programmer Trainees	*New York Times* (1961)	College graduate; math-statistics, research work; top publisher; no skills	$80–$100/ wk
Public Information	*Chicago Tribune* (1964)	Stable work background; no experience; under 50; 37 1/2 -hour week	$400/mo
Public Opinion Interviewing	*New York Times* (1961)	Part-time; reliable men living in Manhattan needed for evening interviewing in Manhattan	$1.75/hr
Recording Studio	*New York Times* (1961)	College graduate; work in classical music area	$70/wk
Route Runner	*Chicago Tribune* (1962)	Capable of handling part of our north-side vacation routes with help of supervisor. Permanent position with commission good chance for advancement.	$140/wk plus
Sales	*Minneapolis Morning Tribune* (1964)	Pharmaceutical sales in St. Cloud, Fargo and St. Paul; pay includes car Yearly salary	 $6,000
Sales Assistant	*Chicago Tribune* (1964)	To vice president; electrical or mechanical education; will train to apply company products to OEM equipment	$11,000– $13,500
Social Security	*San Bernardino Evening Telegram* (1963)	Average Social Security payment at age 65; per month	$127
Tool and Die Maker	*Chicago Tribune* (1964)	Job shop experience necessary; top pay; best working conditions	$110/wk
Trainee	*Chicago Tribune* (1962)	General factory; experienced; semiskilled	$60–$120/ wk
Typist	*New York Times* (1964)	For publishing company Per week	$80
U.S. President	*Look Magazine* (1961)	Annual salary of President John F. Kennedy in 1961	$100,000
Veterinarian	*Chicago Tribune* (1964)	Many Loop positions now open; any armed forces clerical, medical, or technical background qualifies; excellent futures	$375–$450/ mo

CONSUMER EXPENDITURES
1960–1964

Expenditure Type	1961	1962	1963	1964	1965
Clothing	$123.98	$125.21	$129.73	$131.58	$141.23
Food	$457.74	$462.19	$466.93	$472.94	$492.99
Auto Usage	$218.63	$207.41	$229.44	$245.72	$256.39
New Auto Purchase	$77.49	$65.87	$79.26	$90.89	$93.57
Auto Parts	$13.84	$14.15	$15.01	$15.85	$16.68
Gas & Oil	$66.42	$65.33	$67.55	$68.69	$70.87
Housing	$266.78	$278.73	$293.24	$306.49	$319.98
Furniture	$26.01	$26.13	$27.34	$29.06	$31.79
Utilities	$74.72	$76.21	$79.34	$82.96	$85.47
Telephone & Telegraph	$24.91	$26.13	$27.34	$29.06	$31.27
Physicians	$32.10	$32.12	$34.85	$36.46	$42.73
Dentists	$11.07	$11.43	$12.33	$12.15	$14.07
Health Insurance	$9.96	$10.89	$11.79	$11.63	$12.51
Personal Business	$79.70	$65.87	$79.26	$90.36	$95.89
Personal Care	$30.99	$33.21	$38.59	$39.63	$39.09
Tobacco	$38.19	$38.65	$38.59	$39.63	$39.61
Local Transport	$11.07	$10.89	$10.72	$10.57	$10.42
Intercity Transport	$7.19	$7.62	$8.04	$7.93	$8.86
Recreation	$101.84	$103.98	$110.43	$117.84	$127.16
Religion/Welfare Activities	$29.34	$29.94	$31.09	$32.33	$37.00
Private Education & Research	$21.59	$22.32	$24.12	$25.36	$27.09
Per Capita Consumption	$1830.39	$1856.92	$1943.21	$2016.99	$2133.00

445

INVESTMENTS 1960–1964

Investment	1960	1961	1962	1963	1964
Basic Yield, One-year Corporate Bonds	NR	NR	NR		
Short-term Interest Rates, 4–6 Months, Prime Commercial Paper	3.85	4.50	4.50		
Basic Yield, Common Stocks, Total	3.60	3.07	3.37		
Index of Common Stocks (1941 2 1943 5 10)	55.85	66.27	62.38		

COMMON STOCKS, CLOSING PRICE AND YIELD, FIRST BUSINESS DAY OF YEAR

Investment	1960	1961	1962	1963	1964
Allis Chalmers	35 3/4	25	21 7/8	15 3/8	16 5/8
(2 for 1 split, 6/15/56)	(1)	(1.50)	(1.25)	(.75)	(.50)
AT&T	80 3/8	103 1/2	133 5/8	115	139 1/2
(3 for 1 split, 4/24/59)	(3.30)	(3.30)	(3.60)	(3.60)	(3.60)
American Tobacco	107	65 1/4	100 1/4	29 1/4	28 1/
(2 for 1 split, 4/7/60)	(4)		(2.30)	(1.50)	(1.50)
(2 for 1 split, 4/5/62)					
Anaconda	64 7/8	44 1/8	49 1/21/2	41	48
	(2.50)	(2.50)	(2.50)	(2.50)	(2.50)
Bethlehem Steel	56 3/8	41	43	29	32 1/2
	(2.40)	(2.40)	(2.40)	(1.50)	(1.50)
B&O	41 1/4	28 5/8	22 3/8	29 1/8	
(Merged with Chesapeake & Ohio)	(1.50)	(.60)	(/)	(/)	
(B&O shares voluntarily exchanged for 1 share					
Chessie Systems plus $1.69/ share. Shares not exchanged by 5/7/74 were canceled and exchanged for 1 share Chessie Systems)					
Corn Products	56 1/2	78 3/4	56 3/4	49 3/4	60 1/2
	(2)	(2.40)	(1.30)	(1.40)	(1.50)
General Electric	96 5/8	72 1/4	74 3/4	76 3/8	86 3/4
	(2)	(2)	(2)	(2)	(2.20)
General Motors	54 1/2	41 1/2	56 3/8	58 1/4	80 1/4
	(2)	(2)	(2)	(2)	(4)

Investment	1960	1961	1962	1963	1964
International Business Machines	437	582 1/2	572	384 3/4	517
(1 1/2 shares for 1 split, 5/16/61)	(2.40)	(3)	(2.40)	(3)	(5)
(5 shares for 4 split, 5/15/64)					
Intl Harvester	49	43 1/4	52 1/8	49 7/8	58 5/8
	(2.40)	(2.40)	(2.40)	(2.40)	(2.40)
National Biscuit	55 1/2	72 1/2	85	43 1/2	57
(2 shares for 1 split, 5/11/62)	(2.40)	(2.80)	(2.80)	(1.50)	(1.60)
US Steel	101 3/8	76 1/8	77 1/8	43 3/4	54 7/8
	(3)	(3)	(3)	(2.75)	(2)
Western Union	50 1/8	40	39 3/4	27	32 3/8
	(1.40)	(1.40)	(1.40)	(1.40)	(1.40)

STANDARD JOBS 1960–1964

Job Type	1960	1961	1962	1963	1964
Average of All Industries, excl. farm labor	$5260/yr	NR	NR	NR	NR
Average of All Industries, incl. farm labor	$4816/yr	$4961/yr	$5155/yr	$5343/yr	$5609/yr
Bituminous Coal Mining	$5367/yr	$5357/yr	$5507/yr	$5786/yr	$6162/yr
Building Trades	$5750/yr	$5938/yr	$6174/yr	$6364/yr	$6709/yr
Domestics	$2336/yr	$2356/yr	$2364/yr	$2418/yr	$2471/yr
Farm Labor	$1848/yr	$1929/yr	$2044/yr	$2166/yr	$2413/yr
Federal Civilian	$6073/yr	$6451/yr	$6643/yr	$6995/yr	$7518/yr
Federal Employees, Executive Depts.	$4721/yr	$4812/yr	$4861/yr	$5137/yr	$5503/yr
Federal Military	$3872/yr	$3813/yr	$3807/yr	$3997/yr	$4284/yr
Finance, Insurance, & Real Estate	$4910/yr	$5203/yr	$5353/yr	$5522/yr	$5797/yr
Gas, Electricity, Sanitation Workers	$6150/yr	$6390/yr	$6655/yr	$6941/yr	$7303/yr
Manufacturing, Durable Goods	$5894/yr	$6048/yr	$6291/yr	$6512/yr	$6842/yr
Manufacturing, Nondurable Goods	$5081/yr	$5250/yr	$5416/yr	$5570/yr	$5836/yr
Medical/Health Services Workers	$3414/yr	$3636/yr	$3831/yr	$4051/yr	$4277/yr
Miscellaneous Manufacturing	$4648/yr	$4753/yr	$4883/yr	$5039/yr	$5301/yr
Motion Picture Services	$5444/yr	$5871/yr	$6008/yr	$6168/yr	$6603/yr
Nonprofit Org. Workers	$3584/yr	$3684/yr	$3787/yr	$3896/yr	$4000/yr
Passenger Transportation Workers, Local and Highway	$4877/yr	$4966/yr	$5081/yr	$5202/yr	$5409/yr
Personal Services	$3665/yr	$3810/yr	$3968/yr	$4063/yr	$4267/yr
Public School Teachers	$4762/yr	$4991/yr	$5291/yr	$5446/yr	$5653/yr
Radio Broadcasting & Television Workers	$7429/yr	$7384/yr	$7713/yr	$8011/yr	$8435/yr
Railroads	$6241/yr	$6440/yr	$6651/yr	$6823/yr	$7105/yr
State and Local Govt. Workers	$4527/yr	$4721/yr	$4987/yr	$5159/yr	$5342/yr
Telephone & Telegraph Workers	$5532/yr	$5793/yr	$6078/yr	$6335/yr	$6687/yr
Wholesale and Retail Trade Workers	$5756/yr	$5932/yr	$6172/yr	$6419/yr	$6703/yr

FOOD BASKET 1960–1964

Commodity	Year	New York	Atlanta	Chicago	Denver	Los Angeles
Apples, Fresh, per pound	1960	16.30¢	17.50¢	18.40¢	NR	18.50¢
	1961	17.70¢	18.10¢	19.10¢	NR	19.80¢
	1962	16.80¢	18.60¢	18.10¢	NR	20.40¢
	1963	18.20¢	17.90¢	19.20¢	NR	19.90¢
	1964	19¢	NR	17.60¢	NR	18.60¢
Beans, Dried, per pound	1960	16.20¢	16.60¢	17.50¢	NR	17.40¢
	1961	15.90¢	17.10¢	16.80¢	NR	17.90¢
	1962	16.60¢	16.30¢	17.10¢	NR	19.80¢
	1963	17.20¢	16.90¢	18.30¢	NR	18.90¢
	1964	16.60¢	NR	17¢	NR	18.70¢
Beef, Rib Roasts, per pound	1960	75.50¢	87.80¢	81¢	NR	95.90¢
	1961	73.50¢	86.20¢	81.50¢	NR	94.60¢
	1962	78¢	89.20¢	86.20¢	NR	97¢
	1963	77¢	89¢	88¢	NR	$1.00
	1964	78.20¢	NR	85.60¢	NR	96.70¢
Beef, Steaks (Round), per pound	1960	$1.16	$1.09	89.60¢	NR	$1.00
	1961	$1.14	$1.08	89.20¢	NR	$1.00
	1962	$1.19	$1.10	94.80¢	NR	$1.00
	1963	$1.18	$1.08	91.20¢	NR	98.40¢
	1964	$1.18	NR	88.50¢	NR	94.40¢
Bread, White, per pound	1960	22.80¢	19.40¢	18.90¢	NR	23.40¢
	1961	23.80¢	19.40¢	19¢	NR	24.80¢
	1962	23.90¢	19.30¢	19.80¢	NR	28¢
	1963	25¢	19.40¢	19.50¢	NR	28.60¢
	1964	24.10¢	NR	18.90¢	NR	28.70¢
Butter, per pound	1960	73.80¢	80.50¢	74.60¢	NR	79.40¢
	1961	75.30¢	82.20¢	76.40¢	NR	79.60¢
	1962	74.10¢	81.50¢	74.90¢	NR	76.80¢
	1963	73.90¢	80.40¢	75.80¢	NR	75.50¢
	1964	73.50¢	NR	76.50¢	NR	75.90¢
Cheese, per pound	1960	67¢	67.60¢	66.80¢	NR	72.20¢
	1961	70.20¢	71¢	71.20¢	NR	77¢
	1962	70¢	69.40¢	71¢	NR	77.60¢
	1963	70.40¢	70.60¢	71.60¢	NR	77.60¢
	1964	71¢	NR	72.80¢	NR	78.20¢
Chickens, per pound	1960	43¢	40.90¢	39.20¢	NR	48.60¢
	1961	38.60¢	35.60¢	35.30¢	NR	43.50¢
	1962	41.70¢	37.30¢	38.20¢	NR	43.60¢
	1963	41.50¢	NR	38.10¢	NR	43.50¢
	1964	40.10¢	NR	36.80¢	NR	41.10¢
Coffee, per pound	1960	75¢	78.60¢	74.60¢	NR	77.20¢
	1961	74.60¢	77.30¢	73.90¢	NR	70.60¢
	1962	72.20¢	75.10¢	73.70¢	NR	63.60¢
	1963	69.50¢	72.80¢	72.10¢	NR	64.70¢
	1964	81.10¢	NR	82.30¢	NR	79.50¢

449

Commodity	Year	New York	Atlanta	Chicago	Denver	Los Angeles
Cornmeal, per pound	1960	12.20¢	7.20¢	12.90¢	NR	14¢
	1961	12.80¢	7.50¢	13¢	NR	14.60¢
	1962	13.30¢	7.70¢	13.60¢	NR	16.20¢
	1963	14.10¢	7.80¢	13.80¢	NR	16.90¢
	1964	NR	NR	NR	NR	NR
Eggs, per dozen	1960	63.40¢	56.80¢	55.10¢	NR	55.90¢
	1961	63.30¢	56¢	56¢	NR	55.10¢
	1962	60.80¢	52.30¢	52.60¢	NR	51¢
	1963	60.90¢	53.60¢	53.20¢	NR	50.70¢
	1964	58.30¢	NR	51.80¢	NR	50.90¢
Flour, Wheat, per pound	1960	10.58¢	11.13¢	10.40¢	NR	13.04¢
	1961	10.62¢	11.36¢	10.68¢	NR	13.04¢
	1962	10.88¢	11.74¢	10.50¢	NR	12.22¢
	1963	11.14¢	11.92¢	10.52¢	NR	11.90¢
	1964	11.26¢	NR	10.84¢	NR	11.70¢
Lard, per pound	1960	19.10¢	17.70¢	18¢	NR	21.50¢
	1961	20.70¢	19.40¢	19.50¢	NR	23.40¢
	1962	20.10¢	18.50¢	19.10¢	NR	23.60¢
	1963	19.70¢	17.80¢	19.30¢	NR	23¢
	1964	NR	NR	NR	NR	NR
Milk, Fresh, per quart	1960	31.80¢	27¢	28.10¢	NR	NR
	1961	31.50¢	27.20¢	28.70¢	NR	25.80¢
	1962	31.20¢	27.20¢	29.30¢	NR	22.80¢
	1963	27¢	26.90¢	29.50¢	NR	23.40¢
	1964	30.50¢	NR	28.95¢	NR	26.95¢
Mutton and Lamb, Leg, per pound	1960	70¢	76.50¢	70.10¢	NR	74.80¢
	1961	65.10¢	73.40¢	66.40¢	NR	72.20¢
	1962	66.70¢	76.60¢	70.20¢	NR	72.50¢
	1963	67.20¢	77.10¢	69.80¢	NR	73.40¢
	1964	$1.33	NR	$1.36	NR	$1.44
Pork, Bacon, Sliced, per pound	1960	68.50¢	65.60¢	64.20¢	NR	67.90¢
	1961	73.20¢	70.80¢	68.80¢	NR	72.70¢
	1962	74.40¢	69.60¢	67.70¢	NR	71.10¢
	1963	73.40¢	68.60¢	65.90¢	NR	67.40¢
	1964	70.30¢	NR	66¢	NR	66.30¢
Pork, Chops, per pound	1960	89.60¢	78.60¢	86¢	NR	98.10¢
	1961	90.20¢	81.40¢	87.30¢	NR	$1.00
	1962	92.80¢	84.10¢	87.80¢	NR	$1.01
	1963	92.20¢	79.70¢	85.10¢	NR	$1.00
	1964	$1.33	NR	$1.36	NR	$1.44
Pork, Ham, Whole, per pound	1960	62.70¢	59.10¢	58.40¢	NR	59.20¢
	1961	63.60¢	60.50¢	59.30¢	NR	59.70¢
	1962	66.20¢	61.20¢	60.60¢	NR	59.20¢
	1963	65¢	59.50¢	58.50¢	NR	58¢
	1964	63¢	NR	58.40¢	NR	57.30¢
Potatoes, Irish, per 10 pounds	1960	67.30¢	65.30¢	78.30¢	NR	$1.04
	1961	54.90¢	57.70¢	71.50¢	NR	81¢
	1962	57¢	60.70¢	75¢	NR	83¢
	1963	60.30¢	64.30¢	77.60¢	NR	86.90¢
	1964	75.30¢	NR	86.70¢	NR	99.80¢

Commodity	Year	New York	Atlanta	Chicago	Denver	Los Angeles
Prunes, Dried, per pound	1960	37.90¢	39.80¢	39.40¢	NR	37.80¢
	1961	39.20¢	42.50¢	41¢	NR	41.10¢
	1962	38.20¢	40.90¢	40.10¢	NR	39.70¢
	1963	32.70¢	39.20¢	39.60¢	NR	38.70¢
	1964	NR	NR	NR	NR	NR
Rice, per pound	1960	18.70¢	20.70¢	18.70¢	NR	22.10¢
	1961	19.10¢	21.30¢	19¢	NR	22.30¢
	1962	19.90¢	22.70¢	19.30¢	NR	22.50¢
	1963	20.20¢	23.10¢	19.20¢	NR	22.70¢
	1964	19.80¢	NR	19¢	NR	22.30¢

A 1964 advertisement for Riceland rice. (via Flickr)

Commodity	Year	New York	Atlanta	Chicago	Denver	Los Angeles
Sugar, per pound	1960	11.06¢	11.40¢	11.30¢	NR	12.18¢
	1961	11.40¢	11.52¢	11.50¢	NR	11.62¢
	1962	11.38¢	11.52¢	11.58¢	NR	10.88¢
	1963	13.76¢	13.88¢	12.86¢	NR	12.50¢
	1964	13.14¢	NR	12.58¢	NR	12¢
Tea bags, per pound or package of 48	1960	69.60¢	74.40¢	69.60¢	NR	75.90¢
	1961	70.20¢	75¢	72.30¢	NR	75.60¢
	1962	70.50¢	74.40¢	72.90¢	NR	75¢
	1963	91.60¢	95.10¢	90.40¢	NR	95¢
	1964	59.60¢	NR	66¢	NR	67¢
Veal, per pound	1960	$1.59	$1.31	$1.22	NR	$1.42
	1961	$1.60	$1.31	$1.24	NR	$1.42
	1962	$1.67	$1.35	$1.28	NR	$1.47
	1963	$1.72	$1.34	$1.30	NR	$1.52
	1964	$1.71	NR	$1.30	NR	$1.47

SELECTED PRICES 1960–1964

Item	Source	Description	Price
ALCOHOL			
Scotch	*New York Times* (1964)	*Clan MacGregor Rare Scotch;* 4/5 quart	$4.79
Whiskey	*New York Times* (1964)	*Canadian Club Whiskey;* full quart	$7.85
APPAREL, CHILDREN'S			
Blouse	*Ivey's of Charlotte, NC* (1963)	*Liberty;* print cotton; Bermuda collar, roll sleeves; cranberry or loden	$4.00
Blouse	*Ivey's of Charlotte, NC* (1963)	*Smarteens;* print cotton blouse; red and blue on beige	$3.00
Boy Scout Uniform	*Boy's Life* (1962)	Complete uniform including field cap, shirt trousers, web belt, cotton socks, one-color neckerchief, braided slide, metal slide	$10.75
Brassiere	*Ivey's of Charlotte, NC* (1963)	*Teenform Pretty Please Gro-Cup;* helanca nylon stretch lace cups	$1.75
Briefs	*Ivey's of Charlotte, NC* (1963)	*Atkinson;* cotton knit for boys; fit smoothly with just the right amount of snugness	$2/3pr
Coat	*Ivey's of Charlotte, NC* (1963)	*N. Y. Mackintosh;* winter coat for girls; with DuPont Orlon acrylic pile liner with full sleeves	$18.00
Coat	*Ivey's of Charlotte, NC* (1963)	*Atkinson;* muted plaid; all-weather coat with an iridescent gleam	$23.00
Cullotte	*Ivey's of Charlotte, NC* (1963)	*College Teens;* wool flannel, in grey or camel	$8.00
Dress	*Ivey's of Charlotte, NC* (1963)	*Little Star;* plaid cotton dress; deep tones keep fresh through hardest play; black watch or red plaids	$5.00
Duster	*Ivey's of Charlotte, NC* (1963)	*Pettirobe;* printed quilted cotton; a self-ruffle circles the collar cuffs	$8.00
Hat and Bag	*Sears, Roebuck* (1964)	Cotton velveteen	$4.57
Jumper	*Ivey's of Charlotte, NC* (1963)	*Maybro;* madras-inspired wool jumper; fashion-noted with a bateau neckline, self-belt	$11.00
Overalls	*Ivey's of Charlotte, NC* (1963)	*Kid-Bits;* completely washable, long-wearing corduroy	$3.00
Pajamas	*Sears, Roebuck* (1964)	Boys; here's the whole TV gang: Deputy Dog, Terry Bears, Pepino Mouse	$1.99
Parka	*Ivey's of Charlotte, NC* (1963)	*Walter Jerome of Tidykins;* for girls; reversible quilted nylon, filled with ultra-warm Kodel polyester	$23.00
Shirt	*Ivey's of Charlotte, NC* (1963)	*Atkinson;* combed cotton; for teens; tasteful good looks, just wash-n-wear	$3.00
Shirt	*Ivey's of Charlotte, NC* (1963)	*Atkinson;* short sleeves; cotton knit; wonderfully washable, always handsome with its trimmed fashion collar	$3.00

453

Item	Source	Description	Price
Shirt	*Sears, Roebuck* (1964)	*Ban-Lon;* knit	$2.97
Shoes	*Boy's Life* (1962)	*Buster Brown Cub Scout Shoe;* sizes 1 to 6; can take it over the roughest trails	$9.99
Shoes	*Ivey's of Charlotte, NC* (1963)	*Jumping Jack The Sabot;* black patent or velvet 8 1/2 to 12 12 1/2 to 14 Big teens	 $6.98 $7.98 $8.98
Shoes	*Ivey's of Charlotte, NC* (1963)	*Jumping Jack Loafers;* for girls; in new cordo brown	$7.98
Shoes	*Sears, Roebuck* (1964)	Classic saddle	$3.97
Shoes	*Life* (1964)	*Calumet;* V-toe shoe for teens	$9.99
Ski Hood	*Ivey's of Charlotte, NC* (1963)	*Maybro;* for teens; nylon shell, zipper front, drawstring hood and waist; elastic cuffs	$6.00
Slacks	*Ivey's of Charlotte, NC* (1963)	*Danskin;* stretch nylon; will stay in place, won't ride up; wash easy	$5.00
Slacks	*Ivey's of Charlotte, NC* (1963)	*Atkinson;* combed cotton for teens; Ivy model; wash-n-wear Slims Huskies	 $4.00 $5.00
Slicker	*Ivey's of Charlotte, NC* (1963)	*Spatz;* waterproof; fashioned just like a sou'wester with metal-snap fasteners and a protective matching helmet	$4.00
Slip	*Ivey's of Charlotte, NC* (1963)	*Alice Aiken;* blouse slip; DuPont Dacron polyester- cotton; delicate lace trim	$4.00
Snowsuit	*Sears, Roebuck* (1964)	*Convert-A-Babe;* a bunting at 6 months; a bootee suit at 12 months; an outdoor suit to 24 months	$9.80
Sweater	*Ivey's of Charlotte, NC* (1963)	*Jacquard;* v-neck cardigan for boys; of DuPont orlon acrylic; charcoal, red	$5.00
Sweater	*Ivey's of Charlotte, NC* (1963)	Scandinavian-type ski sweater for teens; features a colorful snowflake pattern	$7.00

APPAREL, MEN'S

Item	Source	Description	Price
Coat	*Time* (1962)	Forget wrinkles this fall; Dacron is here	$90.00
Coat	*Sears, Roebuck* (1964)	Pile lining adds even more warmth	$19.70
Garters	*Sears, Roebuck* (1964)	Double grip	$1.44
Shirt	*Time* (1960)	*Manhattan Mansmooth* shirt; the no-iron 100 percent cotton shirt that stays neat and wrinkle-free all day, Each	$5.00
Shirt	*Time* (1960)	*Sir Pendleton;* when leisure and dignity mix; 100 percent virgin wool shirt with impeccable tailoring	$17.50
Shirt	*New York Times* (1964)	Silk and knit sport shirt; tailored for comfort	$7.95
Shirt	*Chicago Tribune* (1962)	*Hathaway;* the world's coolest sport shirt	$8.95
Shirt	*Life* (1963)	*Manhattan Golf;* because it's 65% Dacron, 35% combed cotton, it's light; solids, iridescents, white	$5.00
Shoes	*Chicago Tribune* (1962)	*Johnston & Murphy;* regularly $29.95 and $34.95	$21.90

Item	Source	Description	Price
Shoes	*Chicago Tribune* (1962)	*Johnston & Murphy;* hand-sewn moccasins; regularly $16.95 and $17.95	$10.90
Shoes	*Saturday Evening Post* (1964)	*Nunn-Bush;* ankle-fashioning provides superior, tensile, coddling fit	$19.95–$39.95
Shoes	*Sears, Roebuck* (1964)	The priceless-looking wing-tip	$21.70
Slacks	*Sears, Roebuck* (1964)	Finely tailored all-wool worsted slacks	$11.90
Socks	*Life* (1960)	*Supp-hose;* how to be supported in style	$4.95
Suit	*Time* (1960)	*Michaels, Stern & Company;* gray worsted plaid suit	$80.00
Suit	*Time* (1961)	*Worsted-Tex;* the 10-monther suit; all-climate suit	$69.50
Suit	*Time* (1962)	Wrinkles are now obsolete for fall; and Dacron did it	$90.00

APPAREL, WOMEN'S

Item	Source	Description	Price
Blazer	*Life* (1961)	*McGregor Meteor;* lined with batik-printed cotton	$25.95
Brassiere	*Life* (1961)	*Formfit;* lifts me lovely, and ends under-cup curl-up forever	$3.00
Dress	*Seventeen* (1960)	*DuPont 100% Dacron polyester fiber dress;* upkeep is almost non-existent	$20.00
Dress	*Seventeen* (1960)	*Lord & Taylor* dress; the dating costume in pure silk print; junior sizes 5 to 15	$24.95
Dress	*Chicago Tribune* (1962)	*Miller's Fashion Plate;* a divine shirtdress of exquisite Dacron and cotton; newest Italian collar; price includes 3-letter monogram	$14.95
Dress	*Chicago Tribune* (1962)	*Norman;* cool-as-a-garden patio casual	$6.00
Dress	*Sears, Roebuck* (1964)	The positive flair for after five	$22.00
Dress	*Life* (1964)	*Macy's;* navy; flare-skirted, trimmed with gold braid	$120
Hair Bow	*Sears, Roebuck* (1964)	Double-fabric cotton and rayon grosgrain	$1.00
Hat	*Sears, Roebuck* (1964)	Pleated pillbox; veil	$3.97
Purse	*Seventeen* (1960)	*Princess Gardner French Purse;* made of lustrous leather	$5.00
Shoes	*Minneapolis Morning Tribune* (1964)	*QualiCraft Dress Shoes;* lots of styles	$2.99
Socks	*Seventeen* (1960)	Adler worsted wool knee-high socks	$2.00
Shoe Cover	*Life* (1960)	*Rain Dears;* for all but spike heels	$2.00
Slacks	*Life* (1961)	*McGregor Meteor;* a terrific blend of 50% Dacron polyester and 50% cotton	$10.00
Stockings	*Chicago Tribune* (1964)	Ultra-sheer seamless; box of 6 prs	$5.28
Stole	*Sears, Roebuck* (1964)	Natural brown mink; 5 skins	$149
Sweater	*Greenville News* (1963)	*Belk's;* ribbon-front cardigan; in six fashion colors	$7.99
Swimsuit	*Life* (1963)	Rose Marie Reid Vanessa; based on bold nylon print	$24.00
Veil	*New York Times* (1964)	Imported French silk lace veiling; for keeping coiffures from the wind	$5.00

Item	Source	Description	Price
APPLIANCES			
Air Conditioner	*Chicago Tribune* (1962)	*Admiral*; 5800 btu	$158
Air Conditioner	*Chicago Tribune* (1962)	*Kelvinator 6700 btu*; 7∧/2 amp	$169
Air Conditioner	*New York Times*(1964)	*RCA Whirlpool Air Conditioners*; 1 HP, 7 1/2 AMP	$179
Dryer	*Minneapolis Morning Tribune* (1964)	*Hamilton Gas Dryer*; ideal for all fabrics	$188
Hot Water Heater	*Sears, Roebuck* (1964)	*Gas-type burner, oil fired*; 30-gal glass lined tank	$229.95
Humidifier	*Minneapolis Morning Tribune* (1964)	*Air King humidifier*; sends out fresh air to many rooms;	$49.00
Mixer	*The Saturday Evening Post* (1961)	*Sunbeam's Deluxe Mixmaster Mixer*; the quality mixer that does everything	$49.95
Portable Radio	Seventeen (1960)	Zenith's Royal 50; the smallest pocket radio plays up to 75 hours on 40 cents worth of batteries	$29.95
Refrigerator	*Chicago Tribune* (1964)	Admiral; 11.1 cu ft; no money down—only $1.50 a week	$158.88
Refrigerator	*San Bernardino* Evening *Telegram* (1963)	Frigidaire Frostproof Refrigerator; absolutely no frost, no defrosting, 162 lb. Freezer Easy Terms	$478.88
Stove	*San Bernardino* Evening *Telegram* (1963)	Modern Maid Gas Cook-Top; drop-in type with thermal eye top 28" × 21"	$72.20
Stove	*Sears, Roebuck* (1964)	Automatic from top to bottom	$249.95
BABY PRODUCTS			
Bath Set	*Sears, Roebuck* (1964)	Attaches firmly to tub with 4 suction cups for bath-time safety	$2.57
Car Seat	*Sears, Roebuck* (1964)	Extra-safe style made of strong flexible, high impact styrene	$6.95
Doll	*San Bernardino* Evening *Telegram* (1963)	*Baby Doll in Cradle*; 15" fully jointed doll with rooted hair and moving eyes; regular $5.98	$3.99
Feeding Set	*Sears, Roebuck* (1964)	*3-piece; features the Flintstones*; will delight any child	$1.99
BUSINESS EQUIPMENT AND SERVICES			
Briefcase	*Ivey's of Charlotte, NC* (1963)	*Digby*; sturdy vinyl and split-cowhide brief bag is roomy 16"	$8.00
Dictating System	*Time* (1960)	*Sound Scriber*; dictating system for the office of the space age; complete satellite system	$161.00
Fountain Pen	*Time* (1960)	*Sheaffer's PFM*; pen for men; with unique inlaid point and snorkel pen cleaning action	$14.95
Microfilm	*Time* (1961)	*Recordak*; 100-foot roll of 16mm microfilm, including processing cost	$4.90
Name Purchase	*The Scribner Encyclopedia of American Lives* (1987)	Price paid by Ray Kroc to obtain unrestricted use of the name McDonalds in 1961	$2.7 million
Store Rental	*San Bernardino* Evening *Telegram* (1963)	*Northland Center*; attractive 16' × 50' store building at Highland's newest commercial center on Base Line just west of Palm Per month	$125

456

Item	Source	Description	Price
Typewriter	*Ivey's of Charlotte, NC* (1963)	*Royalite*; with latest feature, carry case, standard space age keyboard, pica or elite complete satellite system	$49.95

EDUCATION

Item	Source	Description	Price
Dance Lessons	*Chicago Tribune* (1962)	*Fred Astaire*; introductory offer, reg $56;	$19.50
Driving Lessons	*Chicago Tribune, Illinois* (1962)	*Goldblatt's Learn to Drive*; Easy Method; beginner's course	$46.88
Public School Education	*Time* (1961)	Per pupil expenditure in Delaware Mississippi	 $460 $225
Tuition	*Boy's Life* (1962)	*Augusta Military Academy*; distinguished ROTC school in *Shenandoah Valley*; boys 8–20introductory offer, reg $56	$1,300/yr

ENTERTAINMENT

Item	Source	Description	Price
Broadway	*New York Times* (1964)	*Luv*; a new comedy; Booth Theatre Monday to Thursday evenings, Orchestra Friday and Saturday evenings, Orchestra	 $6.90 $7.50
Dance Concert	*San Bernardino Evening Telegram* (1963)	Beach Boys, The Astronauts, and The Torquays; you might even be on TV. Channel 18 will telecast the dance from 9:30 p.m. to 10:30 p.m., so no jeans, capris or toreadors; couples only In advance At the door	 $4.00 $4.50
Drive-In Movie	*San Bernardino Evening Telegram* (1963)	Mt. Vernon Motor-In Theatre; Rock Hudson in A Gathering of Eagles Per Car	$1.50
Hockey Game	*Minneapolis Morning Tribune* (1964)	*Professional Hockey*; Minneapolis vs. Cincinnati; per seat	$1.50-$2.50
Ice Skate Show	*Minneapolis Morning Tribune* (1964)	*Ice Capades*; six nights	$2.00-$3.50
Movie	*Minneapolis Morning Tribune* (1964)	Walt Disney's The Sword and the Stone, children	$0.50
Movie	*Minneapolis Morning Tribune* (1964)	Metro-Goldwyn-Mayer's *How the West Was Won*	$2.25
Movie Ticket	*Greenville Times* (Greenville, SC) (1963)	*Promises, Promises!*; Jayne Mansfield; uncut and uncensored European version	$0.75
Symphony	*Minneapolis Morning Tribune* (1964)	*Minneapolis Symphony Orchestra;* Andre Watts, pianist	$2.75 to $5.00
Theater Ticket	*Chicago Tribune* (1962)	*The Sound of Music;* Schubert Theater; evenings Friday and Saturday	$2.50–$6.60

ENTERTAINMENT, HOME

Item	Source	Description	Price
Board Game	*San Bernardino Evening Telegram* (1963)	*Parker Brothers Monopoly;* fun for all	$3.33
Camera	*Boy's Life* (1963)	*Kodak Brownie Super 27;* includes camera, neck strap, flash bulbs, batteries, film, instruction book	$22.00
Camera	*Chicago Tribune* (1964)	*Bell and Howell Canon 7;* F/1.8 lens	$149.50

Item	Source	Description	Price
Camera	*Chicago Tribune* (1964)	Polaroid 100	$99.95
Camera	*The Saturday Evening Post* (1961)	*Kodak;* The Brownie Starmite Camera; most compact camera with built-in flash ever offered	$12.00
Hi-Fi	*Seventeen* (1960)	*Webcor Hi-Fi Fonografs;* with the record changer that keeps things going	$29.95
High-Fi	*Time* (1961)	*Stereophonic Console Phonograph;* The Voice of Music; preserve the natural musical beauty of the live performance	$350
Movie Camera	*Popular Mechanics* (1962)	*Kodak Electric 8;* automatic; no lens setting, an electric eye automatically adjusts the super-fast F/1.6 lens to the light	$1,000
Projector	*Time* (1960)	*Keystone;* 8mm movie projector with motorized action-editor; with case	$220
Radio	*New York Times* (1964)	*Emerson Clock Radio;* wakes you to music; 5 tube chassis for crisp, clear highs, resonant lows	$19.88
Record	*Chicago Tribune* (1964)	Peter, Paul & Mary	$1.77
Record	*Chicago Tribune* (1964)	Ella Fitzgerald	$2.77
Record	*Chicago Tribune* (1964)	Leontyne Price	$2.77
Record Club	*Life* (1960)	*Columbia Record Club;* any 5 records, regular or stereo	$1.97
Stereo	*Saturday Evening Post* (1964)	*Admiral Playmate;* full-automatic phonograph with a long-distance radio	$59.95
Stereo	*Sears, Roebuck* (1964)	Four great speakers create a living wall of sound	$124.95
Stereo Phonograph	*Time* (1960)	*Magnavox Imperial Classic;* stereophonic high-fidelity phonograph with superb FM/AM radio	$650
Stereo Theater	*Life* (1961)	*Magnavox Broadway;* superb stereophonic high fidelity; big optically filtered 23" television, FM/AM radio; automatic record player	$495
Tape Recorder	*Time* (1962)	*RCA Victor;* tape cartridge recorder; ends forever the loose tape worries of conventional reel to reel recorders	$99.95
Tape Recorder	*Time* (1960)	*Webcor Regent Cornet;* professionally engineered for three-speed, 4-track stereo (and monaural) record and playback	$139.95
Television	*Sears, Roebuck* (1964)	All channel; 19" with VHF remote control	$179.95
Television	*Life* (1964)	*General Electric;* portable; black and white; 12-lb personal portable with 11" screen	$99.95
Television	*Chicago Tribune* (1964)	*General Electric;* 23" console; with lifetime circuit board guarantee	$179.88
Television	*Chicago Tribune* (1964)	*General Electric;* 19" portable	$139.95

FOOD PRODUCTS

Apples	*Greenville News* (Greenville, SC) (1963)	Red Delicious	$0.10/lb

458

Item	Source	Description	Price
Baby Food	*Chicago Tribune* (1962)	*Clapp's;* what a variety to choose from; you can keep baby healthy 'n happy with all kinds of meal variety; 4-oz jar	$0.25/3
Baby Food	*San Bernardino Evening Telegram* (1963)	Beech-Nut Strained Baby Food	$0.29/ 3 jars
Bacon	*Chicago Tribune* (1962)	*Corn King;* fresh corn-country flavor	$0.49/lb
Baked Beans	*Chicago Tribune* (1962)	*Heinz Pork and Beans;* for outdoor suppers	$0.12
Bananas	*Minneapolis Morning Tribune* (1964)	Golden Ripe Bananas, per pound	$0.10
Bologna	*Minneapolis Morning Tribune* (1964)	*Swift's Premium Large Bologna* by the piece; per pound	$0.39
Bread	*Greenville News* (Greenville, SC) (1963)	*Big Star;* 14 oz; sandwich bread; per loaf	$0.19
Butter	*Minneapolis Morning Tribune* (1964)	*Land O' Lakes Sweet Cream Butter;* 1 pound carton	$0.69
Cake Mix	*Minneapolis Morning Tribune* (1964)	*Pillsbury Cake Mixes;* 4 packages	$1.00
Catsup	*Chicago Tribune* (1962)	*Hunt's;* a tangy sauce for picnic foods; 14-oz bottle	$0.39/2
Cheese	*Minneapolis Morning Tribune* (1964)	*Bongards Natural Cheddar Cheese;* 2 pound package	$0.89
Coffee	*Greenville News* (Greenville, SC) (1963)	Maxwell House	$0.38/lb
Crackers	*Chicago Tribune* (1964)	*Nabisco;* 16-oz package	$0.25
Dates	*San Bernardino Evening Telegram* (1963)	*Mac's Date Shop;* new crop 3 pounds	$0.98
Diet Drink	*Time* (1960)	Metrecal by Mead Johnson and Company reducing liquid drink, 8 oz. Can	$1.29
Drink Powder	*San Bernardino Evening Telegram* (California) (1963)	*Nestle's Quik;* nutritious chocolate drink; two pound tin	$0.66
Fish	*Minneapolis Morning Tribune* (1964)	*Booth's Frozen Walleye Fillets;* 12 ounce package	$0.59
Fish	*Minneapolis Morning Tribune* (1964)	*Del Monte Chunk Style Tuna Fish;* 6 1/2 ounce can	$0.22
Flour	*Greenville News* (1963)	*Golden Rose;* 5-lb bag	$0.28
Green Beans	*Chicago Tribune* (1962)	*Fresh;* just can't find fresher finer produce; 2 lbs	$0.29
Ham	*Greenville News* (1963)	*K-Mart;* cooked	$0.46/lb
Margarine	*Chicago Tribune* (1962)	Bluebrook margarine melts quickly and deliciously on steaming fresh buns, adding just the right moistness and flavor	$0.15/lb
Meat	*Minneapolis Morning Tribune* (1964)	*Braunschweiger;* 1 1/2 pound chub	$0.59
Meat	*Chicago Tribune* (1962)	*National Food Stores;* Boston Butt steak or roast	$0.35/lb
Milk	*Greenville News* (1963)	*Big Star;* tall can	$0.10
Peanut Butter	*Chicago Tribune* (1964)	*Jif;* plain or crunchy; 18-oz jar	$0.51
Peas	*Greenville News* (1963)	*Argo;* June peas	$0.05

Item	Source	Description	Price
Pie	*Greenville News* (1963)	*Morton's*; pumpkin pie; 20-oz package	$0.25
Potato Chips	*Chicago Tribune* (1962)	*So Fresh*; crisp .fresh; twin pack; 1-lb box	$0.49
Potatoes	*Minneapolis Moring Tribune* (1964)	*Burbank Russet Potatoes*; U.S. No. 1, B size, 20 pound	$0.49
Salad Dressing	*Chicago Tribune* (1964)	*Kraft Miracle Whip*; quart jar	$0.43
Shortening	*Greenville News* (1963)	*Snowdrift*; 3-lb can	$0.48
Shrimp	*San Bernardino Evening Telegram* (1963)	*Crystal Seafood*; shrimp, per pound	$1.00
Soup	*Chicago Tribune* (1962)	*Campbell Chicken Noodle*; quick to fix—nourishing too	$0.16
Sweet Peas	*Chicago Tribune* (1964)	*Del Monte;* 16-oz cans	$0.33/2
Veal	*Minneapolis Morning Tribune* (1964)	*Swift's Premium Boneless Rolled Veal Roast;* per pound	$0.59

FURNITURE

Item	Source	Description	Price
Bed	*Greenville News* (Greenville, SC) (1963)	Cherry poster; spool bed; double size	$89.99
Bed	*Sears, Roebuck* (1964)	Triple decker bunk	$149.95
Bed	*Sears, Roebuck* (1964)	Colonial divan; cloud soft comfort; becomes 72" × 53" bed	$194.95
Cigarette Table	*Sears, Roebuck* (1964)	Cut from the central core of the walnut tree	$28.95
Desk	*Greenville News* (Greenville, SC) (1963)	*Ethan Allen;* dresser desk; 4' 8"; 4 drawer	$85.60
Lounge	*Chicago Tribune* (1964)	*Estee Sleep Shops;* our popular Empress foam lounge; not the skinny lounges you've seen at this price but afull 30" × 74" foam cushion; 4" thick	$49.88
Patio Umbrella	*New York Times* (1964)	Giant 8-foot lawn umbrella with automatic lift	$29.95
Sofa	*Greenville News* (Greenville, SC) (1963)	*Custom Built Furniture;* demand to be shown the U.S. Naugahyde trademark seal on the back of the fabric you are buying	$19.97
Sofa	*Greenville News* (Greenville, SC) (1963)	*Kirby Quinn;* walnut; modern; purple; list $182	$139.99

GARDEN EQUIPMENT AND SUPPLIES

Item	Source	Description	Price
Chain Saw	*San Bernardino Evening Telegram* (1963)	Homelite chainsaw	$149.95
Fence	*San Bernardino Evening Telegram* (1963)	Chain Link fence installed, per foot	$0.85
Ladder	*New York Times* (1964)	Heavy Duty Aluminum Extension Ladder; automatic steel locks	$19.99

Item	Source	Description	Price
HOTEL RATES			
Room Rate	*San Bernardino Evening Telegram* (1963)	*Clark Hotel,* Los Angeles; central location Per day	$5.00
Room Rate	*Time* (1960)	*Essex House on the Park;* make this executive suite your office in New York; per night Single from Double from Executive Suites from	 $16.00 $20.00 $30.00
HOUSEHOLD PRODUCTS			
Baby Walker	*New York Times* (1964)	*Dennis Mitchell Baby Walker;* extra-wide wheel base	$5.99
Can Opener	*Chicago Tribune* (1964)	*Westinghouse;* automatic electric; truly automatic—just slide the switch on and can opens; no fuss, no holding, just a clean rolled edge	$8.44
Carpet	*Greenville News (Greenville, SC)* (1963)	*Wunda Weve;* surplus stock	$9.88/sq yd
Cleaner	*San Bernardino Evening Telegram* (1963)	*Mr. Clean* household cleaner; giant 20 oz. size	$0.59
Cooker	*Chicago Tribune* (1962)	*Sunburst Broil-Mate;* play it cool this summer—don't cope with stifling oven temperatures in the kitchen	$5.99
Cookware	*San Bernardino* Evening Telegram (1963)	*Ekco Stainless Steel flint cookware;* sauce pan with cover; magic radiant heat; 4 quart size	$5.98
Detergent	*San Bernardino Evening Telegram* (1963)	*Tide Detergent powder,* giant size	$0.69
Doorknob	*Sears, Roebuck* (1964)	Provincial knob; antique English finish	$0.46
Drill	*Life* (1964)	*Black & Decker U-100;* 1/4" power drill	$9.88
Humidifier	*Sears, Roebuck* (1964)	Put a fresh breath of spring into dry parched air	$64.95
Kitchen Gloves	*Life* (1961)	*Pioneer Ebonettes;* neoprene to outlast rubber in fast acting cleaning aids	$0.98
Level	*Sears, Roebuck* (1964)	68" magnesium level	$18.50
Light	*Popular Mechanics* (1962)	*Magna-Lite* shop light; put the light where it's needed; with magnet base	$6.95
Light Bulbs	*Boy's Life* (1962)	*El-Tronics, Inc. Solar;* handy six-pack	$1.50
Mailbox	*Sears, Roebuck* (1964)	What an elegant way to get mail	$8.25
Midget Pliers	*Sears, Roebuck* (1964)	Cutting pliers for fast accurate bench work	$2.64
Percolator	*Chicago Tribune* (1964)	Universal Coffiesta	$9.88
Sander	*Popular Mechanics* (1962)	*Millers Falls;* 12 times faster than hand sanding	$34.95
Sander-Polisher	*Sears, Roebuck* (1964)	It's almost like having three sanders and polishers in one	$48.99
Saw	*Popular Mechanics* (1962)	*Dremel Model 572;* in one compact, portable unit you have a jig saw, disc sander, buffing wheel, bench grinder and a flexible shaft machine	$49.95

461

Item	Source	Description	Price
Silverware	*Seventeen* (1960)	*Reed & Barton* solid silver patterns; six-piece place setting	$35 to $45
Soap	*San Bernardino Evening Telegram* (1963)	*Cascade* for automatic dishwashers; 20 oz. size	$0.33
Soldering Gun	*The Saturday Evening Post* (1961)	*Weller Soldering Gun Kit;* a tool for repairs, electrical work and hobbies	$7.95
Switch Plate	*Sears, Roebuck* (1964)	Gleaming white ceramic accented with gold trim; double	$1.99
Tools and Tool Chest	*Popular Mechanics* (1962)	*Craftsman;* 59-piece set; regular separate prices total $69.95; all tools fit in 18" × 8" × 9" steel toolbox	$39.99

JEWELRY

Item	Source	Description	Price
Bracelet	*Sears, Roebuck* (1964)	*From West Germany*	$3.30
Jewelry Box	*Seventeen* (1960)	*Mele Jewel Case;* the Pandora, the ultimate in luxury	$19.98
Necklace	*Chicago Tribune* (1962)	*Pakula;* new year-round tones; browns, blues, greens, orange; in a three-strand Cleopatra choker	$3.00
Necklace	*Sears, Roebuck* (1964)	*Gold-color metal,* intriguing textured balls strung on supple chain	$5.50
Ring	*New York Times* (1964)	*Lambert Brothers* oval diamond engagement ring	$350
Watch	*San Bernardino Evening Telegram* (1963)	*Timex Wrist Watch;* ladies' and men's	$6.95 to $39.95
Watch	*Time* (1960)	*Omega Ladymatic* watch with stainless steel case, water and shock resistant	$115
Watch	*Seventeen* (1960)	*Bulova Senator Watch;* 17 jewels; shock-resistant	$35.75
Watch	*Boy's Life* (1962)	*Timex;* Boy Scout wristwatch; takes a licking and keeps on ticking	$9.95
Watch	*Saturday Evening Post* (1964)	*Longines Admiral Jubilee;* 5-star Admiral automatic watch	$125
Watch	*Saturday Evening Post* (1964)	*Longines-Wittnauer;* with the world's most advanced, self-powered wristwatch movement	$125
Watch	*Sears, Roebuck* (1964)	*Barbie's picture is on the dial,* a reminder of her favorite doll	$8.95

MEALS

Item	Source	Description	Price
Breakfast	*Chicago Tribune* (1962)	*Walgreens Cafeterias;* this week's breakfast buy; 2 hot cakes, 2 strips bacon, and maple syrup	$0.33
Dinner	*San Bernardino Evening Telegram* (1963)	*San Franciscan Steak House;* family buffet Thanksgiving dinner; roast young Tom turkey and ham Adults Children	 $2.50 $1.50
Dinner	*San Bernardino Evening Telegram* (1963)	*B&B Rancho;* broiled steak and lobster combination	$3.25

Item	Source	Description	Price
Dinner Theatre	*New York Times* (1964)	*Restaurant Voisin;* dinner menu and courtesy limousine service to theatre Prix-Fixe Price	$9.50
Lunch	*Chicago Tribune* (1962)	*Walgreens Cafeterias;* delicious home-cooked flavor; chicken pot pie with garden vegetables under a flaky crust	$0.49
Lunch	*San Bernardino Evening Telegram* (1963)	*Taco Aqui;* taco, tostada and beans Tacos, 5 for	$0.50 $0.95

MEDICAL PRODUCTS AND SERVICES

Item	Source	Description	Price
Acne Medicine	*Boy's Life* (1962)	*Clearasil;* the man's way to clear pimples fast	$0.98
Analgesic Powder	*Life* (1961)	*Stanback;* quick relief of pain due to headache, neuralgia, cold	$0.98
Antacid	*San Bernardino Evening Telegram* (1963)	*Maalox Antacid;* non-constipating, 12 oz. Size	$0.96
Antacid	*Life* (1961)	*Tums;* for acid indigestion; per roll	$0.12
Cold Medicine	*Saturday Evening Post* (1964)	*Contac;* over 600 tiny time pills in each Contac capsule keeps working all day or night; 10 continuous-action capsules	$1.49
Lip Balm	*Life* (1961)	*Chap-et;* relieves chapped dry lips	$0.35
Make-Up Cream	*Seventeen* (1960)	*Dermacare,* a new plan for blemish control; per tube	$1.25

MOTORIZED VEHICLES, SUPPLIES, AND SERVICES

Item	Source	Description	Price
Air Conditioner	*Chicago Tribune* (1962)	*Mark IV;* air condition your present car with Mark IV	$279
Air Conditioner	*American Motorist* (1963)	Be cool this summer, completely installed	$299.95
Air Conditioner	*American Motorist* (1963)	*Mark IV;* commuter, air conditioner; fits many American cars; starts cooling in seconds; completely installed	$289.50
Airplane	*Time* (1961)	*Cessna 310F;* leave your competitors behind	$62,500
Alignment	*American Motorist* (1963)	All American cars; foreign cars and parts additional	$3.95
Auto Leasing	*San Bernardino Evening Telegram* (1963)	*Travel Leasing Company* Per Day Per Mile	$7.00 $0.07
Automobile	*Minneapolis Morning Tribune* (1964)	*Plymouth 2-Door Hardtop;* V-8 engine; 5-year, 50,000 mile warranty	$2,706
Automobile	*Life* (1961)	*Renault Dauphine;* have you ever jealously watched a Dauphine scoot in and out of heavy city traffic? You also get just a little bit more mileage than most other imports give, a lot more mileage than any bigger car	$1,385
Automobile	*Life* (1961)	*Chrysler Newport;* 60's price surprise; this is no junior edition; this is the full-size Chrysler Newport with a small-size price tag	2,964
Automobile	*Life* (1961)	*Rambler America;* look into Rambler excellence, classic 6	$1,845

Item	Source	Description	Price
Automobile	*Esquire* (1961)	*Chevrolet Corvair Monza;* suggested price $200 more than the '61 Corvair Monza with all sports options	$2,850
Automobile	*Esquire* (1961)	Maserati	$3,200
Automobile	*Popular Mechanics* (1962)	*Saab '96;* this car was built to be better and safer, not different	$1,895
Automobile	*Time* (1962)	*Peugeot;* the steel in a Peugeot is .9mm thick; you could overturn the car and remain unscathed; not that we recommend it, but Peugeots at the factory are tested this way	$2,250
Automobile	*Greenville News* (Greenville, SC) (1963)	*Ford Fastback Coupe;* radio, heater, whitewall tires	$3,095
Automobile	*Chicago Tribune* (1964)	Pontiac Grand Prix	$2,895
Automobile Painting Service	*American Motorist* (1963)	*Rainbow Auto Painters;* Washington's largest and busiest auto paint shop	$49.95
Automobile, Used	*Greenville News* (Greenville, SC) (1963)	*1957 Plymouth Belvedere;* hardtop coupe; v-8 powerflyte, radio, heater, whitewall tires, clean	$595
Automobile, Used	*Chicago Tribune* (1964)	*1963 Tempest;* here's a fine sedan 4 dr with low mileage	$1,593

A Cadillac advertisement for the Dietrich Motor Car Company, the first franchised auto dealership in Allentown, PA. (via Wikimedia Commons)

Item	Source	Description	Price
Automobile, Used	*San Bernardino Evening Telegram* (1963)	*1959 Cadillac Fleetwood Sedan;* 4-door hardtop	$2,895
Automobile, Used	*San Bernardino Evening Telegram* (1963)	*1957 Dodge V-8 Lancer;* radio, heater, overhauled transmission, power steering and brakes	$595
Battery	*Chicago Tribune* (1964)	Installed free; guaranteed 24 months	$7.88
Brake Service	*Chicago Tribune* (1964)	*Korvette Tire Center;* all four wheels relined; free installation	$12.88
Car Bed	*New York Times* (1964)	*Teddy Tot's "Zip apart";* goes from car bed to car seat in a zip	$12.95
Convertible Tops	*Sears, Roebuck* (1964)	Appearance and pinpoint grain same as original equipment on most 1964 cars	$31.70
Floor Mats	*New York Times* (1964)	*Rubbermaid Heavy Duty Floor Mat* to protect your car Rear Front	$6.99 $9.50
Garage Door Opener	*Minneapolis Morning Tribune* (1964)	*Auto-Mate Overhead Garage Door Operator;* completely installed	$159.95
Radio	*American Motorist* (1963)	*Motorola;* all transistor; installed free; with free antenna	$29.95
Repair	*San Bernardino Evening Telegram* (1963)	Ring and valve grind special; includes labor and parts, new rings, wrist pins, grind valves and seats 6 cylinder 8 cylinder	 $48.50 $58.50
Seat Belts	*New York Times* (1964)	*Hickok Seat Belt;* Royal Traveler; Insist on Hickok, the largest manufacturer of seat belts	$12.95
Seat Covers	*Sears, Roebuck* (1964)	Channel quilted, all-vinyl seat covers	$23.49
Tires	*San Bernardino Evening Telegram* (1963)	*Dary's Deluxe Retreads;* black wall Plus tax and tire exchange	$7.88
Tires	*American Motorist* (1963)	*Fisk's;* 4-ply; custom tubeless nylon tires; rugged nylon carcass for added strength	$12.77
Tires	*Minneapolis Morning Tribune* (1964)	*B. F. Goodrich Black Tubeless Tires;* 6.50–13; per tire	$14.95
Washcloth	*American Motorist* (1963)	*Kozaks;* made by people you can depend on to do the right thing	$3.00

MUSICAL INSTRUMENTS

Item	Source	Description	Price
Clarinet	*Sears, Roebuck* (1964)	With standard B-flat Boehm style	$79.95
Keyboard Harmonica	*Sears, Roebuck* (1964)	25 keys, 2 octaves	$11.95
Organ	*San Bernardino Evening Telegram* (1963)	Estey Electric Organ, used	$149.50

OTHER

Item	Source	Description	Price
Autograph Hound	*Ivey's of Charlotte NC* (1963)	*Sutton;* the whole crowd will sign on Snippy, the long, autograph hound	$2.00

Item	Source	Description	Price
Bird Food	*San Bernardino Evening Telegram* (1963)	*HAP Parakeet Seed*; contains millet, canary seed	$0.29
Charcoal	*Chicago Tribune* (1962)	*Easy Life*; 20-lb bag	$0.85
Dog	*San Bernardino Evening Telegram* (1963)	*Registered Dachshund puppies*; small deposit holds until Christmas Each	$35.00
Dog	*New York Times* (1964)	*Poodle*; all mamas had pups at once; special this week;	$85.00 each
Flag	*Boy's Life* (1962)	*American flag set*; includes 3' × 5' printed cotton flat, 1-piece 6' pole of sturdy aluminum, metal wall bracket, halyard, flag courtesy holder	$3.95
Flower Delivery	*Life* (1963)	*FTD*: Mother's Day flower arrangement; glads, carnations, pompons and greens, delivered any place in the United States and Canada	$7.50
Glasses	*Chicago Tribune* (1964)	*Wieboldt's*; single vision; white lenses and frame	$9.95
Marker	*Life* (1960)	*Carter (1960) Marks-a-Lot*; with felt tip	$0.59
Model Paint	*Boy's Life* (1963)	*Testors*; look at the models that win competitions and you'll see the difference PLA enamels make, matching colors	$0.15
Paneling	*San Bernardino Evening Telegram* (1963)	*Wickes*; plywood paneling, ½" width; 4' × 8' prefinished V groove sheets; per sheet Rustic Birch Philippine Mahogany Knotty Cedar Walnut	 $5.60 $4.00 $6.40 $10.08
Pen	*Ivey's of Charlotte , NC* (1963)	*Parker-T-Ball Jotter*; in black, light grey, green, bright red, dark blue	$1.98
Pen	*Saturday Evening Post* (1964)	*Scripto Tilt-Tip*; with skip-proof tungsten ball for smooth writing	$1.98
Pen/Pencil	*Boy's Life* (1962)	*Scripto*; official, dependable, rugged, slim, lightweight, vest-locking, smooth-writing	$1.95
Portrait	*New York Times* (1964)	*Stern's Father Day Special*; three photographs of you or your child; 5"x7" portrait	$4.95
Schoolbag	*Ivey's of Charlotte, NC* (1963)	*Digby's*; in ginger, tan, olive; serv-a-lon	$3.00
Sea Horses	*Boy's Life* (1962)	*Florida Sea Horse Co.*; live; pair of dwarf species of living sea horses from Florida	$3.50
Slide Rule	*Popular Mechanics* (1962)	4"; non-warp with 2-color scales on white nitrate face	$2.95
Umbrella	*Ivey's of Charlotte, NC* (1963)	Your little girl's name personalized on the handle	$3.00
Wood	*Minneapolis Morning Tribune* (1964)	*Dry firewood*; per stove cord	$11.00

PERSONAL CARE PRODUCTS

Item	Source	Description	Price
Bathroom Tissue	*San Bernardino Evening Telegram* (1963)	*Chiffon Tissue;* assorted colors, first quality Per roll	$0.10
Cologne	*San Bernardino Evening Telegram* (1963)	*Shulton Old Spice for Men* Set	 $1.25 and up

Item	Source	Description	Price
Face Lotion	*Esquire* (1961)	*English Leather After Shave;* after shower, after hours	$2–$10
Hair Cream	*San Bernardino Evening Telegram* (1963)	*Brylcreem Hair Dressing;* king size tube	$0.59
Haircut	*Life* (1964)	Rothschild Barber Shop in Beverly Hills, California	$2.50
Lip Cream	*The Saturday Evening Post* (1961)	*Blistex;* cure; sore lips, cold sores, chapped lips, fever blisters	$0.39
Make-Up	*Seventeen* (1960)	*Pond's Angel Touch Liquid Make-Up;* nine soft-and- subtle shades; per bottle	$1.00
Makeup Kit	*Life* (1961)	*Merle Norman 3 Steps to Beauty;* includes all-purpose cold cream, miracle powder base	$6.50
Mouthwash	*Life* (1960)	*Vi-Jon;* for bad breath, colds, sore throat; 6-oz size bottle free with purchase of family size	$0.49
Perfume	*Seventeen* (1960)	*Lentheric Miracle* perfume; 1/2 ounce	$10.00
Perfume	*Seventeen* (1960)	*Chanel No. 5* spray perfume; good things come in small packages	$5.00
Perfume	*New York Times* (1964)	*Elizabeth Arden Blue Grass Flower Mist,* 4 ounces	$2.00
Permanent	*San Bernardino Evening Telegram* (1963)	*Bella Dona Beauty Salon;* Brush Back Permanent special	$4.50
Permanent Wave	*Chicago Tribune* (1962)	*Helene Curtis Baroness Rhapsody;* permanent wave	$7.50
Shaver	*Seventeen* (1960)	*Lady Ronson Superbe Electric Shaver;* two different cutting actions	$16.50
Soap	*Minneapolis Morning Tribune* (1964)	*Dial Soap;* 4 regular bars	$0.49
Tissues	*Chicago Tribune* (1964)	*Scott;* 2 packages of 400	$0.39
Toothbrush	*Chicago Tribune* (1964)	*Sunbeam;* electric; cordless	$11.44
Washcloth	*New York Times* (1964)	*Wash-Away,* disposable washcloth with instant suds	$1.00

PUBLICATIONS

Item	Source	Description	Price
Book	*Hobbies* (1963)	*New Manual of Model Ship-Building* by P. M. Wright	$6.95
Book	*Time* (1960)	*Victory in the Pacific* by Samuel Eliot Morison; Atlan-tic- Little-Brown, publisher	$6.50
Dictionary	*Time* (1961)	*Webster's New World Dictionary*; 142,000 entries, 1,760 pages	$5.57
Magazine	*Life* (1961)	*Life* Magazine; weekly	$0.20
Magazine	*Boy's Life* (1962)	*Boy's Life*; monthly	$0.25
Time Magazine	*Time* (1960)	*The Weekly News* Magazine Per issue Per Year	$0.25 $7.00

REAL ESTATE

Item	Source	Description	Price
Apartment	*San Bernardino Evening Telegram* (1963)	Clean bachelor apartment completely furnished; Civic Center location	$57.50/mo

Item	Source	Description	Price
Apartment	*San Bernardino Evening Telegram*(1963)	Starlite Apartments; new two-bedroom units; colored fixtures in kitchen, snack bar, carpet and drapes	$127.50
Apartment	*Chicago Tribune* (1964)	For rent; 3 1/2 rooms; gas included; newly decorated; near Lincoln Park golf course	$110/mo
Apartment	*Chicago Tribune* (1964)	For rent; 5 rooms, 2 bedrooms	$135/mo
Apartment Building	*New York Times* (1964)	East Bronx five-story walk-up; 16 apartments, 83 rooms; rent $12,725	$49,000
Apartment Building	*Chicago Tribune* (1964)	For sale; deluxe 3 flats; excellent income property at this preopening price for a limited time only	$47,500
Cooperative Apartment	*New York Times* (1964)	Apartments of 3 1/2, 4, 5, 6 rooms; some terraces; centrally air conditioned; gas and electric Priced from	$16,250
Cottage	*Chicago Tribune* (1962)	For sale; Valparaiso, Indiana; on choice, spectacular lakefront; nice summer cottage; 72' × 30'; full basement, private parking lot and boat; completely furnished; cash or contract	$7,850
Home	*New York Times* (1964)	Bucks County, Pennsylvania summer home; knotty pine; 3 bedrooms; modern conveniences; good fishing	$3,600
House	*Chicago Tribune* (1962)	For rent; 3 bedrooms, 1 bath, attached garage	$125/mo
House	*San Bernardino Evening Telegram* (1963)	Raintree Valley View Homes; 4 bedrooms, near College site	$17,100
Land	*Greenville News* (1963)	For sale; 55 acres, highway 296, near Five Forks, ,700 ft river frontage; lovely open land, passenger and wooded area; Greenville, South Carolina area	$9,950
Lot	*Chicago Tribune* (1962)	For sale; 1/2 acre corner; paved streets; close in; 700 ft river frontage; lovely open land, passenger and wooded area; nice homes in area	$1,900
Mobile Home	*San Bernardino Evening Telegram* (1963)	Great Lakes home; Belmont; two-bedroom, 10' × 50'	$3,895
Townhome	*Chicago Tribune* (1962)	For rent; 2 bedrooms	$106/mo

SEWING EQUIPMENT AND SUPPLIES

Item	Source	Description	Price
Cloth	*San Bernardino Evening Telegram* (1963)	*Heavy sport cottons*; plain or print; per yard	$0.79

SPORTS EQUIPMENT

Item	Source	Description	Price
BB Gas Rifle	*Boy's Life* (1962)	*Benjamin Super 100*; no pumping, uniform high power	$19.95
BB Gun	*Dell Comic Book 6 Black Horses* (1962)	*Daisy 1894*; a spitting image of the model 94 Winchester; easy 2-way cocking action	$12.98
BBs	*Dell Comic Book 6 Black Horses* (1962)	*Daisy*; copper coated from the world's largest manufacturer of B-Bs; per tube	$0.05-$0.25
Fishing Lure	*Boy's Life* (1962)	*Fred Arbogast Hawaiian Wiggler*; for heavy brush and cover	$1.25
Fishing Reel	*Boy's Life* (1963)	*Zebco 20Z*; the lowest-priced foolproof spinning reel made in America	$5.95

Item	Source	Description	Price
Knife	*Boy's Life* (1962)	*Boy Scout*; brass-lined knife has four tempered carbon-steel blades	$1.75
Sailboat	*New York Times* (1964)	*The Sea Shark*; lightweight, unsinkable; 11 feet long; sail area 45 square feet	$99.75
Shotgun	*Boy's Life* (1962)	*O. F. Mossberg & Son*; boy's; single-shot .410 gauge; with youth-size stock and short barrel so you can shoulder accurately	$27.95
Sunraft	*Chicago Tribune* (1962)	*Abercrombie & Fitch*; inflatable; almost 20 sq ft of sunning surface	$29.95
Waders	*Sears, Roebuck* (1964)	Chest high	$16.50
Weights	*Sears, Roebuck* (1964)	*Vinyl jacketed*; 110-lb set with 2 dumbbells	$20.00

TELEPHONE EQUIPMENT AND SERVICES

Telephone	*Popular Mechanics* (1962)	*Western Electric*; late-model dial phone same as used by all the telephone companies; cost $40 new	$6.95

TOBACCO PRODUCTS

Lighter	*Saturday Evening Post* (1964)	*Scripto Goldenglo*; compact Vu-Lighter	$5
Pipe	*Time* (1960)	*Kaywoodie*; for flavor, mildness, relaxation without inhaling Standard Relief Grain Connoisseur	$5.95 $7.95 $15.00
Pipe	*Popular Mechanics* (1962)	*Kirsten*; patented radiator stem means cool smoking	$3.95

TOYS

Art Board	*San Bernardino Evening Telegram* (1963)	*Enlarg-A-Graph*; complete with many figures and scenes to enlarge; operates on D cell batteries, not included	$5.98
Board Game	*Boy's Life* (1963)	*Cadaco All-Star Baseball*; select your lineup from 40 present-day stars and 20 all-time greats	$3.00
Boat	*San Bernardino Evening Telegram* (1963)	*Mighty Matilda Nuclear Aircraft Carrier*; with 100 man crew; 3 feet long	$8.88
Cannon	*San Bernardino Evening Telegram* (1963)	*Remco Mighty Mo Cannon;* breech loading, remote control firing	$9.88
Cars	*Boy's Life* (1962)	*Matchbox;* made in England of die-cast metal	$0.50
Chemistry Set	*San Bernardino Evening Telegram* (1963)	*Gilbert Chemistry Set* of plastic and glass; make dozens of exciting glass objects	$7.98
Doll	*San Bernardino Evening Telegram* (1963)	*Ideal Doll; Bitsy;* she eats then bubbles like a real baby	$12.88
Doll Clothes	*Barbie and Ken Catalogue* (1963)	*Barbie Nighty-Negligee;* luxurious full-length gown; Grecian bodice with embroidered flowers	$3.00
Doll Clothes	*Barbie and Ken Catalogue* (1963)	*Barbie Icebreaker;* red velveteen skating skirt top with furry white jacket; red knit leotard with turtleneck and long sleeves, long stockings and skates complete the set	$3.00
Doll Clothes	*Barbie and Ken Catalogue* (1963)	*Barbie American Airline Stewardess;* Barbie takes off for sky adventures in her flight blue uniform with flight insignia on cap and jacket	$3.50

Item	Source	Description	Price
Model Kit	*Boy's Life* (1962)	*Hubley;* scale model metal kit; 1930 Packard Sport Phaeton, die cast in durable metal	$2.98
Model Kit	*Boy's Life* (1962)	*Hawk;* starfighter airplane; each model is actually metal plated with a coat of real aluminum and then covered with a high glass lacquer	$2.00
Model Kit	*Popular Mechanics* (1962)	*Aurora;* who would prefer a pokey loco going around in circles to the pulse-pounding action of a road race; includes land-changing crisscross layout	$21.98

TRAVEL AND TRANSPORTATION

Item	Source	Description	Price
Airline Fare	*Time* (1964)	*American Airlines;* starting January 15; we reduced our first-class fares and our coach fare for families; New York to Los Angeles; first class	$160.90
Cruise	*American Motorist* (1963)	*Canada Steamship Lines;* through French Canada; Richelieu cruises, six days; steamer your hotel throughout	$149.50
Cruise	*American Motorist* (1963)	*Canada Steamship Lines Aristo;* 8 days includes Ritz-Carlton, Manoir Richelieu; Chateau Frontenac hotels	$204.50
Cruise	*New York Times* (1964)	Cruise on Queen Elizabeth; the World's largest liner; New York to Europe, roundtrip Tourist Cabin First Class	 $316 $406 $660
Land Sales Trip	*Chicago Tribune* (1964)	*Mackie Brothers;* special; all expense trip to Deltona, Florida; including meals, lodging and transportation for only	$50.00
Subway Token	*Life* (1963)	New York City	$0.15
Tour	*Time* (1962)	*Lufthansa;* visit Europe on a Budget tour	$485
Travel Kit	*New York Times* (1964)	Celebrity's travel kit with two zipper compartments, removable vinyl case with plastic fitting	$5.00
Trip	*American Motorist* (1963)	*AAA Travel Service;* Washington to Waikiki by jet; 14-day tour including hotel accommodations	$640

American Airlines used their stewardesses as an advertising strategy in the 1960s. (via Wikimedia Commons)

MISCELLANY 1960-1964

People

To help raise money for taxes, friends of the London Library put several prized manuscripts on the block of a local auctioneer. The final hand-written draft of A Passage to India, the great West confronts East novel by E. M. Forster, was knocked down for $18,200—said to be the highest price ever paid for a living author's manuscript. The buyer, a Manhattan rare books dealer, also picked up (for another client) a hand copy of T. S. Eliot's The Wasteland, faithfully duplicated by the poet in his own script because the original—last seen many years ago in Manhattan—is missing and presumed lost. Price: $7,840.

The Encyclopedia of American Crime

Plenty of Sugar

When President Eisenhower last week decided to give Fidel Castro his lumps, he set off a flurry of excitement on the New York Coffee and Sugar Exchange, clearinghouse for much of the world's sugar. Just before Ike announced a slash of 700,000 tons in the amount of sugar that the United States would buy from Cuba during the rest of 1960, world sugar prices dropped 3 to 8 points, i.e., hundredths of a cent a pound, in expectation of the cut—and in fear that Cuba would dump its surplus sugar on the world market. Instead, Cuba raised its minimum export price from $3 to $3.25 a hundred pounds in an effort to recover part of its losses on sugar sales. Thereupon, in heavy trading world sugar futures shot up again, only to level off at week's end.

Time, July 18, 1960

The Yankee Tinkerers

The most fascinating phenomenon on Wall Street these days is the spectacular rise of the growth and glamour stocks. For investors who know how to choose well, they have made some tidy profits. They have also created a new class of management millionaires who rank with the Rockefellers and the big rich of Texas, and who prove that—despite high taxes—it is still quite possible in the United States to get impressively rich in a short time.

Among listed growth stocks, none has risen faster than one that appears on the ticker tape as FAV—the Fairchild Camera & Instrument Corp. An investor who bought $1,000 worth of Fairchild stock when it was selling at its 1958 low of 19 1/2, and held onto it, last week would have had nearly $18,000 worth of stock. Fairchild makes a long list of imaginative products, ranging from a new silicon superconductor to the first 8-mm. home sound motion-picture camera. It is one of the street's most cherished buys, ranking with such rapid risers as Texas Instruments (72 1/8 to 214 1/4 in 18 months), Polaroid (97 1/4 to 245 1/2) and Universal Match (46 1/4 to 271 1/8 on a presplit basis).

Time, July 25, 1960

N.Y.U. Operating Giant Computer; $3,000,000 Device Digests 750,000 Facts a Second

The Courant Institute of Mathematical Sciences at New York University has begun operating an IBM 7090—the most powerful computer in use at any Eastern university.

The computer, which cost $3,000,000, will be used by the Atomic Energy Commission's Computing and Applied Mathematics Center at N.Y.U., as well as by scientists and institutions engaged in basic and applied mathematical research.

New York Times, November 2, 1961

Liquor Revenues Rose 4.6% In Year

Governmental revenues from alcoholic beverages in 1961 came to $4,687,872,807, or 4.6 per cent above the level of 1960, and brought the total collected since Repeal twenty-eight years before, to 76,747,276,116. The report noted that the Federal excise tax on distilled spirits is $10.50 a gallon and on beer, $9 a barrel of thirty-one gallons. The tax on a still wine gallon is as follows: Wine not over 14 per cent alcohol by volume, 17 cents; more than 14 and not exceeding 21 per cent, 67 cents; over 21 and not exceeding 24 per cent, $2.25.

New York Times, September 2, 1962

MISCELLANY 1960–1964

Greenwich Homes' Cost Highest in Connecticut

The median value of one-family homes in this town was the highest in the state in 1960, according to a survey by the Connecticut Department of Public Works.

The survey was based on owner estimates in the 1960 census. It showed that the median value—midpoint between the upper and lower halves—of Greenwich homes was $32,800. The town of Woodridge in New Haven County was second with a median value of $30,600.

Other Fairfield County figures were:

New Canaan	$26,862;
Darien	$26,298;
Westport	$26,082;
Weston and Wilton	$25,000;
Stamford	$23,800;
Norwalk	$20,600;
Bridgeport	$16,000;
Bethel	$15,376.

New York Times, September 2, 1962

HISTORICAL SNAPSHOT
1965-1969

1965

- Vietnam War intensifies
- President Lyndon Johnson's "Great Society" plan unveiled
- Americans buy $60 million worth of prescription weight-loss drugs
- Production of soft-top convertibles peaks at 507,000
- Avis Rent-A-Car acquired by International Telephone and Telegraph
- Saint Louis's Gateway Arch completed
- 1,250-room Washington Hilton opens in Washington, D.C.
- U.S. immigration bill abolishes national origin quotas

1966

- Student Protest against Vietnam War begins
- National Organization for Women (NOW) is founded
- Largest year-to-year rise in cost of living since 1958 announced—2.8 percent
- 2,377 corporate mergers take place
- New York subway fares rise to 20 cents
- Per capita consumption of processed potatoes reaches 44.2 pounds per year

- Taster's Choice freeze-dried instant coffee introduced

1967

- 2,975 corporate mergers occur
- 41 percent of nonwhite families make less than $3,000 annually
- *New York World Journal & Tribune* closes; *Rolling Stone* magazine founded
- 2.7 million Americans receive food stamp assistance
- Nearly 10,000 farmers receive more than $20,000 each in subsidies
- Annual beef consumption reaches 105.6 pounds
- Burger King Corporation acquired by Pillsbury Corporation
- U.S. population passes 200 million

1968

- Vietnam War and protests intensify
- Richard Nixon elected president
- 4,462 corporate mergers take place
- Bank Americard holders number 14 million, up 12 million in two years
- Automobile production reaches 8.8 million
- Volkswagen captures 57 percent of U.S. import market

- Oil discovered on Alaska's North Slope
- Television advertising revenues hit $2 billion, twice that of radio
- First-class postage rates climb to 6 cents
- Uniform Monday Holiday Law enacted by Congress, creating 3-day holiday weekend
- Average farm subsidy is nearly $1,000

1969

- Neil Armstrong walks on moon
- Average U.S. automobile wholesales at $2,280
- Panty hose production reaches 624 million pairs, up from 200 million in 1968
- Average U.S. farm produces enough food for 47 people
- Blue Cross health insurance covers 68 million Americans
- *Penthouse* magazine begins publication; *Saturday Evening Post* folds
- National Association of Broadcasters begins cigarette advertising phaseout

Members of the military police keep back anti-Vietnam War protesters during their sit-in at the Mall Entrance to the Pentagon, 1967. (via
Wikimedia Commons)

SELECTED INCOME 1965–1969

Job	Source	Description	Pay
Assistant	*Milwaukee Journal* (1904)	Boy; steady advancement and good chance to learn trade if industrious; no boy who thinks he is 'it' because he swears and smokes cigarettes need apply.	$3.50/wk
Accounting	*Chicago Tribune* (1966)	Accounting Clerks	$500/mo
Actress	Legrand and Karney, *Chronicle of the Cinema* (1995)	Elizabeth Taylor's salary for her role in *Cleopatra* in 1963	$1 million
Actress	Legrand and Karney *Chronicle of the Cinema* (1995)	Audrey Hepburn's salary for *My Fair Lady* in 1964	$1 million
Advertising Copywriter	*New York Times* (1965)	Fine NYC agency wants package-goods TV writer; 2–5 years 4A experience; no job hoppers	$15,000–$40,000/yr
Airline Trainees	*New York Times* (1965)	No experience; train as reservationist	$75–$100/wk
Baseball Player	Jim Hunter, *Catfish: My Life in Baseball* (1988)	Salary of Oakland Athletics pitcher Jim "Catfish" Hunter in 1967	$13,000
Basketball Star	*Time* (1968)	Annual salary of professional basketball center Wilt Chamberlain	$250,000
Chauffeur	*New York Times* (1967)	With or without experience	$65–$160/wk
Clerk	*New York Times* (1967)	Shipping Stock	$70–$100/wk
Comparative Analyst	*New York Times* (1965)	Know major medical coverage; college degree	$8500/yr
Comptroller	*Chicago Tribune* (1966)	Any age to 42. Degree not required, varied duties, good future	$12,000/yr
Counterman	*Chicago Tribune* (1966)	For retail building supply; capable of selling plywood, paneling, tile, etc.; 5 days	$2.75/hr to start
Dishwasher	*Chicago Tribune* (1968)	Nights or days; experienced; car needed for transportation	$100/wk
Doctors	*Time* (1968)	Average annual pay of U. S. doctors	$31,160
Editor/Assistant	*New York Times* (1967)	BA Engineering, rewriting, editing	$100/wk
Executive Director	*New York Times* (1965)	Washington, D.C., youth agency	$11,000/yr
Football Player	*Time* (1968)	Minimum annual salary for a second-year professional football player in the National Football League	$12,000

Job	Source	Description	Pay
Girl Friday	*Chicago Tribune* (1966)	To baby doctor; no medical experience needed to welcome tiny patients and their parents, announce their arrival, escort them to examination rooms where you help by weighing babies	$90/wk
Girl/Man Friday	*New York Times* (1967)	Park Avenue management consultant needs takeover right hand for top-level work	$150/wk
Greeter	*Chicago Tribune* (1968)	100% public contact; chance of lifetime for girl with light office skills, a nice smile and friendly personality	$125/wk
Highway Designers	*Chicago Tribune* (1966)	From trainees to actual experience	$150–$175/wk
Hospital Receptionist	*Chicago Tribune* (1966)	Age to 40; will be front-desk receptionist for famous Chicago hospital; will answer phones, screen calls, do customer service, greet new patients, process new patients through hospital	$382/mo
Industrial Relations	*Chicago Tribune* (1966)	College graduate; train under the industrial relations manager of a world-famous Chicago-based company	$600/mo
Inventor's Apprentice	*Chicago Tribune* (1966)	He'll train jack-of-all-trades	$475–$600/mo
Judges	*Time* (1968)	Average annual pay of General Court judges across America	$20,620
Keypunch Operator	*New York Times* (1965)	A/N; good at punctuation; paid overtime	$85/wk
Manager	*New York Times* (1965)	College degree; 1 year supervisory experience; manager of a world-famous Chicago-based company	$6,500/yr
Model	*Playboy* (1996)	Modeling fee of Victoria Valentino, the Playboy Playmate for September, 1963	$1,000
Painter	James E. B. Breslin, *Mark Rothko:A Biography*(1993)	Annual earnings of Mark Rothko in 1967	$129,451
Porter	*Chicago Tribune* (1968)	For AM shift in north suburban nursing home; must have transportation	$2.50/hr
Programmer Trainee	*New York Times* (1967)	College graduates, any degree; immediate hire	$7,000 1/yr
Programmer Trainee	*Chicago Tribune* (1968)	HS Graduate with good figure aptitude; top firm offers	$725/mo
Purchaser	*New York Times* (1967)	Relocation paid to Manila, including housing and car	$12,000/yr
Sales Promotion	*Chicago Tribune* (1968)	National firm with home office in Chicago needs men who can meet and talk with management-level executives of their clients	$8,400/yr
Sales Trainee	*New York Times* (1965)	MBA preferable for wholesaling	$9,000/yr
Sales Trainee	*Chicago Tribune* (1966)	Pharmaceuticals	$550/mo
Security Management	*Chicago Tribune* (1968)	Ex-GIs: this is a terrific opportunity for you to put your service experience to work; very little training is necessary; this multi-million-dollar firm has had great success in the past with young vets	$150/wk

Elvis became a pop culture phenomenon in the late 1950s and remains an icon today, often referred to as the "King of Rock and Roll." (via Wikimedia Commons)

Job	Source	Description	Pay
Singer	*Guinness Book of World Records* (1981)	Single year earnings of singer/actor Elvis Pressley in 1965	$4.7 million
Technical Writers	*New York Times* (1967)	Top metro electronic career	$8,000–$10,000/yr
Teletype	*New York Times* (1965)	Days or nights; light experience and ability to read tape	$450/mo
Trainee	*Chicago Tribune* (1966)	Learn new products tests; high school enough	$435/wk
Troubleshooter	*Chicago Tribune* (1968)	All around the plant into everybody's hair, training everywhere!	$110–$160/wk
TV Station Receptionist	*Chicago Tribune* (1966)	HURRY this choice position will not last long; meet and greet TV stars, help answer fan mail and be on the inside of the television world	$400/mo

Job	Source	Description	Pay
TV Trainee	*New York Times* (1965)	Job future; join #1 TV company; reach management fast	$5,200/yr
Typist	*Chicago Tribune* (1966)	Any typing; hunt and peck, slow or fast; if you type at all we have the jobs right now	$90/wk
Typist	*Chicago Tribune* (1968)	TV-Radio Studio; long-term assignment to start immediately	$3/hour
Wall Street Sales Trainee	*New York Times* (1965)	MBA preferable for wholesaling	$9,000/yr
Writers	*Time* (1968)	Daily rate of Presidential historians assigned the task of recording President Lyndon Johnson's accomplishments	$50

CONSUMER EXPENDITURES 1965–1969

Expenditure Type	1965	1966	1967	1968	1969
Clothing	$147.19	$158.73	$164.06	$178.87	$189.96
Food	$519.81	$555.05	$565.14	$605.86	$643.88
Auto Usage	$283.58	$294.06	$299.43	$338.80	$361.66
New Auto Purchase	$110.14	$106.84	$100.65	$122.07	$123.84
Auto Parts	$18.01	$19.33	$20.13	$22.92	$26.64
Gas & Oil	$76.17	$81.40	$86.05	$92.67	$101.15
Housing	$336.59	$353.58	$372.90	$397.09	$428.27
Furniture	$33.45	$35.61	$38.71	$39.36	$41.45
Utilities	$89.55	$93.10	$97.13	$100.15	$105.09
Telephone & Telegraph	$33.45	$35.61	$38.75	$41.35	$45.89
Physicians	$43.75	$46.29	$50.23	$54.31	$61.18
Dentists	$14.41	$15.26	$15.60	$19.93	$21.22
Health Insurance	$13.89	$15.26	$15.60	$19.93	$20.72
Personal Business	$107.56	$117.52	$128.83	$141.00	$144.07
Personal Care	$41.69	$45.79	$49.32	$52.81	$54.77
Tobacco	$41.69	$43.24	$44.79	$46.83	$48.35
Local Transport	$10.81	$10.68	$11.70	$11.96	$13.32
Intercity Transport	$10.29	$11.70	$13.59	$15.45	$18.26
Recreation	$137.93	$156.69	$166.57	$182.85	$196.86
Religion/Welfare Activities	$39.63	$43.24	$47.30	$51.32	$54.27
Private Education & Research	$41.99	$39.68	$43.78	$49.33	$54.77
Per Capita Consumption	$2288.18	$2450.14	$2563.01	$2785.67	$2978.63

INVESTMENTS 1965–1969

Investment	1960	1961	1962	1963	1964
Basic Yield, One-year Corporate Bonds	4.14	5.00	5.29	6.29	7.05
Short-term Interest Rates, 4–6 Months, Prime Commercial Paper	4.38	5.55	5.10	5.90	7.83
Basic Yield, Common Stocks, Total	3.06	3.57	3.35	3.22	3.42
Index of Common Stocks (Moody's)	21.03	13.66	6.93	8.96	9.84

COMMON STOCKS, CLOSING PRICE AND YIELD, FIRST BUSINESS DAY OF YEAR

(Parenthetical number is annual dividend in dollars)

	1960	1961	1962	1963	1964
Allis Chalmers	19 5/8	33 1/8	21 7/8	35 3/4	30 1/2
	(.50)	(.75)	(1)	(1)	(1)
AT&T	69 1/2	61 1/2	54 3/8	51 5/8	53 1/2
(2 for 1 split 5/28/64)	(2)	(2.20)	(2.20)	(2.40)	(2.40)
American Tobacco	33 7/8	36 1/2	31 3/4	32 1/4	39
	(1.60)	(1.70)	(1.80)	(1.80)	(1.90)
Anaconda	52 3/4	84 1/8	81 1/2	47 3/8	64
(split 2 shares for 1, 6/9/67)	(2.50)	(3.75)	(5)	(1.25)	(2.50)
Bethlehem Steel	35	39 7/8	30 3/8	33 1/2	31 1/4
	(1.50)	(1.50)	(1.50)	(1.50)	(1.60)
Corn Products	54 3/4	53	46 3/8	40 1/2	42 5/8
	(1.50)	(1.60)	(1.70)	(1.70)	(1.70)
Delta Air Lines	61 1/4	70 1/2	116 1/8	33 7/8	36 1/2
(2 for 1 split 12/13/65)	(1.60)	(1)	(1)	(.40)	(.40)
(3 for 1 split 11/16/67)					
General Electric	91 1/8	116 7/8	89	95 5/8	94 7/8
	(2.20)	(2.60)	(2.60)	(2.60)	(2.60)
General Motors	95 3/8	102 5/8	68 7/8	82 3/4	80 1/8
	(4.45)	(5.20)	(4.55)	(3.80)	(4.30)
International Business Machines	405 1/8	493 1/2	369	613 1/2	313 3/4
(3 shares for 2 split, 5/17/66)	(5)	(6)	(4.40)	(4.40)	(2.60)
(2 1/2% stock dividend, 6/10/67) (2 shares for 1 split, 5/23)					

Investment	1960	1961	1962	1963	1964
Intl Harvester	74 1/8	45 3/4	34 7/8	35 5/8	37 1/8
(2 shares for 1 split, 4/9/65)	(2.80)	(1.50)	(1.80)	(1.80)	(1.80)
National Biscuit	58 3/8	54 3/8	47	43 1/2	50 1/8
	(1.70)	(1.80)	(1.90)	(2)	(2.10)
U.S. Steel	50 3/4	51 7/8	38 1/2	42 1/8	43 1/2
	(2)	(2)	(2.40)	(2.40)	(2.40)
Western Union	30 3/8	49 1/2	37	36 3/4	42 7/8
	(1.40)	(1.40)	(1.40)	(1.40)	(1.40)

STANDARD JOBS 1965–1969

Job Type	1965	1966	1967	1968	1969
Bituminous Coal Mining	$6543/yr	$7398/yr	$7663/yr	$8169/yr	$8582/yr
Building Trades	$6921/yr	$7363/yr	$7738/yr	$8332/yr	$9049/yr
Domestic Industries	$5812/yr	$6062/yr	$6312/yr	$6759/yr	$7230/yr
Domestics	$2657/yr	$2780/yr	$2961/yr	$3254/yr	$3543/yr
Farm Labor	$2661/yr	$2923/yr	$3136/yr	$3327/yr	$3646/yr
Federal Civilian	$7859/yr	$8170/yr	$8257/yr	$9002/yr	$9690/yr
Federal Employees, Executive Depts.	$5763/yr	$5921/yr	$5993/yr	$6520/yr	$7010/yr
Federal Military	$4477/yr	$4650/yr	$4732/yr	$5148/yr	$5526/yr
Finance, Insurance, & Real Estate	$5962/yr	$6239/yr	$6516/yr	$6994/yr	$7400/yr
Gas, Electricity, & Sanitation Workers	$7480/yr	$7801/yr	$8191/yr	$8666/yr	$9316/yr
Manufacturing, Durable Goods	$7001/yr	$7228/yr	$7475/yr	$8002/yr	$8454/yr
Manufacturing, Nondurable Goods	$5950/yr	$6172/yr	$6413/yr	$6849/yr	$7257/yr
Medical/Health Services Workers	$4410/yr	$4565/yr	$4861/yr	$5292/yr	$5845/yr
Miscellaneous Manufacturing	$5365/yr	$5548/yr	$5849/yr	$6252/yr	$6620/yr
Motion Picture Services	$7125/yr	$7397/yr	$7503/yr	$7946/yr	$8318/yr
Nonprofit Org. Workers	$4138/yr	$4280/yr	$4402/yr	$4655/yr	$5138/yr
Passenger Transportation Workers, Local and Highway	$5553/yr	$5737/yr	$5926/yr	$6279/yr	$6623/yr
Personal Services	$4375/yr	$4551/yr	$4705/yr	$4960/yr	$5254/yr
Private Industries, incl farm labor	$5810/yr	$6098/yr	$6342/yr	$6772/yr	$7237/yr
Public School Teachers	$5848/yr	$6142/yr	$6605/yr	$7129/yr	$7623/yr
Radio Broadcasting & Television Workers	$8515/yr	$8833/yr	$9000/yr	$9563/yr	$10,085/yr
Railroads	$7460/yr	$7708/yr	$8116/yr	$8663/yr	$9317/yr
State and Local Govt. Workers	$5558/yr	$5834/yr	$6284/yr	$7255/yr	$7894/yr
Telephone & Telegraph Workers	$6604/yr	$6858/yr	$7063/yr	$7506/yr	$8044/yr
Wholesale and Retail Trade Workers	$6981/yr	$7345/yr	$7690/yr	$8142/yr	$8685/yr

FOOD BASKET 1965–1969

(NR=NOT REPORTED)

Commodity	Year	New York	Atlanta	Chicago	Denver	Los Angeles
Apples, Fresh, per pound	1965	20.10¢	NR	16.30¢	NR	20.50¢
	1966	21.20¢	NR	19¢	NR	21.20¢
	1967	23.30¢	NR	20.50¢	NR	23¢
	1968	26¢	23.90¢	24¢	NR	27.60¢
	1969	26¢	23.50¢	24.20¢	NR	26.90¢
Beans, Dried, per pound	1965	16.80¢	NR	17.70¢	NR	21¢
	1966	19.80¢	NR	20¢	NR	22.30¢
	1967	18.60¢	NR	18.50¢	NR	20¢
	1968	20.30¢	16.30¢	19.70¢	NR	23.20¢
	1969	17.40¢	17.40¢	18.80¢	NR	23.10¢
Beef, Rib Roasts, per pound	1965	84.70¢	NR	91¢	NR	$1.01
	1966	88.30¢	NR	95.70¢	NR	$1.01
	1967	88.70¢	NR	97.60¢	NR	99.30¢
	1968	91.50¢	99.40¢	99.60¢	NR	$1.08
	1969	$1.00	$1.19	$1.11	NR	$1.20
Beef, Steaks (Round), per pound	1965	$1.23	NR	91.90¢	NR	96.70¢
	1966	$1.27	NR	93.70¢	NR	99.80¢
	1967	$1.26	NR	93.10¢	NR	$1.01
	1968	$1.31	$1.09	96.30	NR	$1.05
	1969	$1.45	$1.26	$1.09	NR	$1.15
Bread, White, per pound	1965	24.20¢	NR	19.20¢	NR	29.40¢
	1966	25.20¢	NR	21.30¢	NR	27.80¢
	1967	25.40¢	NR	21¢	NR	26.50¢
	1968	26.30¢	22¢	21.50¢	NR	26.20¢
	1969	27¢	22.10¢	22.80¢	NR	26.10¢
Butter, per pound	1965	75¢	NR	77.70¢	NR	76.80¢
	1966	81.90¢	NR	86.30¢	NR	84.70¢
	1967	82.90¢	NR	87.10¢	NR	85.60¢
	1968	84¢	90.50¢	87.70¢	NR	84.70¢
	1969	85.10¢	91.80¢	87.50¢	NR	85.50¢
Cheese, per 8 ounces	1965	36.20¢	NR	36.90¢	NR	39.30¢
	1966	40.30¢	NR	41.50¢	NR	44.70¢
	1967	41.10¢	NR	42.40¢	NR	47¢
	1968	42.70¢	42.70¢	44.10¢	NR	46.80¢
	1969	45.30¢	45.70¢	48.40¢	NR	49.90¢
Chickens, per pound	1965	41.60¢	NR	37.10¢	NR	40.10¢
	1966	44.20¢	NR	39.60¢	NR	40¢
	1967	41.40¢	NR	36.10¢	NR	37.20¢
	1968	44.30¢	39.30¢	37.80¢	NR	38¢
	1969	47.20¢	40.20¢	41.10¢	NR	42.10¢
Coffee, per pound	1965	83.70¢	NR	85.30¢	NR	79.40¢
	1966	83.50¢	NR	84.60¢	NR	74.10¢
	1967	77.30¢	NR	77.80¢	NR	69.80¢
	1968	75.80¢	79.50¢	78¢	NR	70.50¢
	1969	74.50¢	76.50¢	79.10¢	NR	94.20¢

Commodity	Year	New York	Atlanta	Chicago	Denver	Los Angeles
Cornmeal, per pound	1965	19.08¢	NR	21.80¢	NR	21.20¢
	1966	21¢	NR	23¢	NR	22¢
	1967	25.10¢	NR	27.90¢	NR	26.90¢
	1968	25.20¢	25.20¢	28.40¢	NR	26.80¢
	1969	NR	NR	NR	NR	NR
Eggs, per dozen	1965	56.70¢	NR	51.40¢	NR	48.90¢
	1966	64.70¢	NR	58.60¢	NR	55.60¢
	1967	51.30¢	NR	48.60¢	NR	47.90¢
	1968	56.20¢	51.70¢	54.40¢	NR	48¢
	1969	66.90¢	61.50¢	62.30¢	NR	56.20¢
Flour, White, per pound	1965	11.44¢	NR	11.26¢	NR	12.02¢
	1966	11.64¢	NR	11.76¢	NR	11.62¢
	1967	12.06¢	NR	11.58¢	NR	11.80¢
	1968	11.70¢	12.84¢	11.56¢	NR	11.90¢
	1969	11.58¢	12.52¢	11.46¢	NR	12.14¢
Lamb Chops, Loin, per pound	1965	$1.45	NR	$1.46	NR	$1.59
	1966	$1.52	NR	$1.54	NR	$1.70
	1967	$1.57	NR	$1.57	81¢	$1.66
	1968	$1.66	$1.38	$1.71	NR	$1.73
	1969	$1.77	$1.48	$1.83	NR	$1.86
Margarine, per pound	1965	29.70¢	NR	30.20¢	NR	28¢
	1966	30.70¢	NR	31.40¢	NR	27.70¢
	1967	29.90¢	NR	30.50¢	NR	27.60¢
	1968	29.70¢	29.10¢	30.10¢	NR	27.20¢
	1969	30.10¢	29.50¢	29.80¢	NR	27.60¢
Milk, Fresh, per quart	1965	29.75¢	NR	27.10¢	NR	27.55¢
	1966	31.40¢	NR	28.45¢	NR	28.25¢
	1967	31¢	NR	30.30¢	NR	29¢
	1968	32.30¢	30.55¢	33.35¢	NR	30.75¢
	1969	33.10¢	31.60¢	33.80¢	NR	31.45¢
Pork, Bacon, Sliced, per pound	1965	85.50¢	NR	81.10¢	NR	78.40¢
	1966	$1.02	NR	94.90¢	NR	91.30¢
	1967	90.40¢	NR	84.10¢	NR	76.10¢
	1968	87.30¢	83.50¢	82¢	NR	75¢
	1969	91.60¢	90.10¢	90.10¢	NR	82¢
Pork, Chops, per pound	1965	$1.03	NR	91.50¢	NR	$1.06
	1966	$1.14	NR	$1.02	NR	$1.14
	1967	$1.08	NR	92.60¢	NR	$1.09
	1968	$1.11	$1.01	90.20¢	NR	$1.08
	1969	$1.22	$1.09	98.10¢	NR	$1.19
Pork, Ham, Whole, per pound	1965	68¢	NR	64.10¢	NR	62.50¢
	1966	76.20¢	NR	69.90¢	NR	69.40¢
	1967	71.10¢	NR	62.70¢	NR	65.70¢
	1968	70.40¢	64.60¢	62.50¢	NR	65.20¢
	1969	75.60¢	65.40¢	69.70¢	NR	70¢
Potatoes, Irish, per 10 pounds	1965	90.70¢	NR	$1.10	NR	$1.18
	1966	79.20¢	NR	79.50¢	NR	85.20¢
	1967	75.30¢	NR	90¢	NR	88.90¢
	1968	76.80¢	75.10¢	93.60¢	NR	95.10¢
	1969	82.80¢	81.80¢	$1.07	NR	$1.00

Commodity	Year	New York	Atlanta	Chicago	Denver	Los Angeles
Rice, per pound	1965	20.10¢	NR	19¢	NR	22.60¢
	1966	20.30¢	NR	19.60¢	NR	23.30¢
	1967	20.70¢	NR	19.30¢	NR	23.30¢
	1968	20.70¢	21.50¢	19.40¢	NR	23.20¢
	1969	20.90¢	19.30¢	19.90¢	NR	23.50¢
Sugar, per pound	1965	11.90¢	NR	12¢	NR	10.78¢
	1966	12.40¢	NR	12.22¢	NR	11.18¢
	1967	12.40¢	NR	11.70¢	NR	11.80¢
	1968	12.48¢	12.20¢	11.90¢	NR	11.76¢
	1969	12.76¢	12.30¢	12.16¢	NR	11.74¢
Tea, Bags, package of 48	1965	58.10¢	NR	66.40¢	NR	65.60¢
	1966	55.90¢	NR	66.40¢	NR	66.70¢
	1967	56.70¢	NR	60.70¢	NR	66¢
	1968	57.70¢	61.90¢	61.20¢	NR	64.40¢
	1969	57.90¢	64.20¢	61.80¢	NR	64.80¢
Veal, per pound	1965	$1.74	NR	$1.35	NR	$1.58
	1966	$1.85	NR	$1.46	NR	$1.68
	1967	$1.95	NR	$1.52	NR	$1.76
	1968	$2.09	$1.56	$1.68	NR	$1.78
	1969	$2.32	$1.89	$1.85	NR	$2.04

SELECTED PRICES 1965–1969

Item	Source	Description	Price
ALCOHOL			
Beer	*Chicago Tribune* (1968)	*Schlitz;* 12-oz quick chill cans; 6 pack	$0.99
Rum	*Chicago Tribune* (1968)	*Virgin Island Brugal;* choice of dark or light	$2.98/fth
Scotch	*New York Times* (1965)	*Clan MacGregor Rare Scotch;* light and smooth Full quart	$6.19
Whiskey	*New York Times* (1965)	*Four Roses Blended Whiskey;* per fifth sized bottle	$4.99

A woman unpacks a box of Schlitz beer. Schlitz was known as "the beer that made Milwaukee famous" and was advertised with the slogan "When you're out of Schlitz, you're out of beer". (via Wikimedia Commons)

Item	Source	Description	Price
APPAREL, CHILDREN'S			
Briefs	*Life* (1969)	*Fruit of the Loom;* Dacron and cotton is what makes our golden line of underwear the buy it is; package of 3	$2.65
Clothing	*Sears, Roebuck* (1967)	Sports set; yellow broadcloth blouse with shoulder epaulette; navy-and-white-striped denim culottes	$5.97
Dancing Shoes	*Sears, Roebuck* (1967)	*Sparking;* tap shoe	$5.77
Dress	*New York Times* (1965)	High-waisted sundress with bright carrot appliqués across the front	$12
Shorts	*Sears, Roebuck* (1967)	One low price for three pairs of smart snappy play shorts	$2.97
Slip	*Sears, Roebuck* (1967)	*Magic Grow;* packages of three; white cotton percale; one with nylon lace and schiffli embroidery; two with schiffli embroidery	$2.97
APPAREL, MEN'S			
Boots	*Sears, Roebuck* (1967)	Cowboy; olive-brown 12" boot has fine water-buffalo calf uppers	$26.80
Hat	*Chicago Tribune* (1968)	*Bonds;* famous Executive Group hats with the hand-detailed extras that add to your wearing pleasure	$7.99
Jacket	*The Sporting News* (1966)	Major league warm-up jacket; satin jacket with team name in script	$12.95
Jacket	Sears, Roebuck (1967)	Authentic western wear	$5.27
Shirt	*Life* (1968)	*Arrow;* available in 19 solid colors; sanforized-plus-2 in a blend of Dacron polyester and cotton	$7.50
Shoes	*Chicago Tribune* (1968)	Scotch-grain supple; long-wearing leathers with the added comfort of heel-to-toe-full leather lining	$13.80
Slacks	*Sears, Roebuck* (1967)	Fashion-right plaid slacks in smooth-weave fabric of Fortrel and combed cotton	$6.97
APPAREL, WOMEN'S			
Brassier	*New York Times* (1965)	Longline with flatter band, B cup, 32 to 40	$11.00
Clothing	*Sears, Roebuck* (1967)	The weekend set; jacket, skirt and pants; crisp white with floral print	$9.90
Coat	*Sears, Roebuck* (1967)	Imported leather suede or cabretta; snappily seamed and shaped	$38.90
Dress	*New York Times* (1965)	Chiffon for Evening at *Bonwit Teller;* in blue and white or pink and white	$90.00
Dress	*New York Times* (1965)	*B. Altman & Company;* cotton and acetate dress and matching jacket	$70.00
Girdle	*New York Times* (1965)	Youthcraft's Long Leg "Shift" Girdle	$11.00
Hat	*Sears, Roebuck* (1967)	Garden party pillbox; high rounded dome covered with flowers	$4.97
Pullover	*Life* (1968)	*James Douglas Goodson;* challis; makes a splashy beach cover-up	$28.00

Item	Source	Description	Price
Shirt	*Life* (1968)	*Gregory Sheer;* printed with challis-like flowers	$20.00
Shoes	*Sears, Roebuck* (1967)	It's time for flats; young and impish	$6.97

APPLIANCES

Item	Source	Description	Price
Air Conditioner	*Western Auto Catalog* (1965)	*Wizard Ex-pand-O;* 8,000 btu, featuring the panelmatic cover that snaps off for instant cooling	$189.95
Air Conditioner	*Chicago Tribune* (1966)	*Goldblatt's;* whole house; completely installed at a new low price; includes unit and installation	$498.88
Air Conditioner	*Sears, Roebuck* (1967)	The only window air conditioners with separate controls for humidity and temperature; 11,000 btu	$254.95
Dishwasher	*Western Auto Catalog* (1965)	Fully automatic built-in dishwasher; two separate spray arms to clean every dish without pre-rinsing; special loading	$207.95
Dishwasher	*Life* (1968)	*General Electric;* now you can take your dishes from the table to the dishwasher to the cupboard	$119.25
Dryer	*Western Auto Catalog* (1965)	*Wizard;* electric; 8-cycle sunshine ozone lamp in drum freshens, sanitizes, and prevents mildew	$169.95
Freezer	*Western Auto Catalog* (1965)	*Wizard;* 21" chest; economical to operate, saves on electricity bills; coiling system is welded to sides of heavy-duty steel liner	$232.95
Oven	*Western Auto Catalog* (1965)	*Wizard;* built-in; new eye-level check-it oven pre-heats, thaws frozen food fast, warms finest china safely	$154.95
Oven	*Western Auto Catalog* (1965)	Automatic electric; lets you cook meals while away from home; includes roll-out broiler with 2-pc porcelain pilots	$164.95
Range	*Western Auto Catalog* (1965)	*Wizard Citation;* the convenience of a full-size 30" range, plus, a separate eye-level rotary broiler	$299.95
Refrigerator	*Chicago Tribune* (1968)	*Frigidaire;* 12.3 cu ft; keeps food really cool	$208
Refrigerator-Freezer	*Western Auto Catalog* (1965)	*Wondermart 15;* no-frost; 4.8-cu-ft-bottom freezer holds 171 lbs; never any frost in 9.69-cu-ft refrigerator	$299.95
Vacuum	*Sears, Roebuck* (1967)	Built-in; you can install system in existing or new home for floor-to-ceiling vacuuming and cleaning	$195
Washer	*Western Auto Wizard Catalog* (1965)	Citation; 7-cycle; does everything but put the laundry in and take it out	$247.95
Washer	*Western Auto Wizard Catalog* (1965)	Economical 10-lb capacity washer, wringer adjusts for all fabrics	$99.88

BABY PRODUCTS

Item	Source	Description	Price
Auto Harness	*Sears, Roebuck* (1967)	Helps guard baby while you drive	$2.99
Bottles	*Sears, Roebuck* (1967)	34-piece feeding kit	$7.99
Crib	*Western Auto Catalog* (1965)	Portable crib and play yard; fits easily into car seats; masonite floor raises to make dressing table	$22.95
Gate	*Western Auto Catalog* (1965)	Portable; easiest way of letting baby have lots of room to play; yet keeps him out of places he shouldn't be	$3.95

Item	Source	Description	Price
Play Yard	*Western Auto Catalog* (1965)	Nylon mesh; A-frame construction is far more rigid, durable, and easier to fold than models with corner legs	$19.25
Sterilizer	*Western Auto Catalog* (1965)	Baby bottle; aluminum; has a lift-out storage rack; quick heating allows you to prepare day's formula in one sterilization	$3.99
Stroller	*Sears, Roebuck* (1967)	Two-seater stroller sleeper	$29.95
Walker-Stroller	*Western Auto Catalog* (1965)	Deluxe 3-in-1; easy-to-clean plastic coated snap-on fabric in ice-sparkler pattern	$18.95

BUSINESS EQUIPMENT AND SERVICES

Item	Source	Description	Price
Calculator	*Time* (1968)	Friden Electric Printing Calculator	$1,495
Calculator	*New York Times* (1965)	Remington Electric Calculator	$189.50
Calculator	*Time* (1966)	Friden Model 132; a division of Singer; how much faster is an electronic calculator? On accounts payable, Gimbels' found it 43% faster; with automatic square root	$1,950
Stapler	*Sears, Roebuck* (1967)	Variable-compression stapler	$10.79
Tape Recorder	*New York Times* (1965)	Roberts 1640 4-track stereo tape recorder with two speakers	$198.95
Typewriter	*Western Auto Wizard Catalog* (1965)	Imperial; manual; finger-tip control panel, push-button tabulator; stamped-steel frame	$89.95

COLLECTIBLES

Item	Source	Description	Price
Candelabra	*Antiques* (1969)	Sheffield; circa 1820, 22" high	$425
Clock	*Antiques* (1969)	Seth Thomas; pillar and scroll; running order circa 1809–1813	$600
Creamer	*Antiques* (1969)	Silver; creamer 7 1/2"; John Curry; Philadelphia circa 1830	$250
Desk	*Antiques* (1969)	Lloyds of New York; reproduction directoire; length 48", depth 24", height 30"	$545
Figurines	*Antiques* (1966)	Chelsea boy and girl; 10" high, 9" wide	$450
Harp	*Antiques* (1966)	Gilt; early-nineteenth-century harp by Sébastien Érard	$790
Print	*Antiques* (1969)	Rare folio; Mark Catesby, 1754; birds, animals, fish, snakes	$35.00
Printed Broadsheet	*Guinness Book of World Records* (1981)	Price paid in 1969 for one of the 16 known copies of The Declaration of Independence, printed in 1776 by Samuel T. Freeman & Co.	$404,000
Rug	*Antiques* (1966)	Keshan; 12' × 9'	$1,250
Rug	*Antiques* (1966)	Herez; 15.4' × 11.2'	$925
Sideboard	*Antiques* (1966)	Hepplewhite; circa 1790–1800; shaped front; hepplewhite legs ending in spade feet	$2,200
Statue	*Antiques* (1966)	Bronze; Ming horse and noble rider, height 20", width 17 1/2"; weight 13 lbs	$750
Sugar and Creamer	*Antiques* (1969)	Silver; 6" to 7"; circa 1830–1840	$450

Item	Source	Description	Price

EDUCATION

| Dance Lessons | *Chicago Tribune* (1966) | Fred Astaire; take a tranquilizer; learn to dance; 8 private 1/2-hour lessons | $13.95 |

ENTERTAINMENT

Ballet	*New York Times* (1965)	New York City Ballet; Apollo Orchestra	$4.95
Concert Ticket	*Life* (1969)	Newport Jazz Festival; featuring Buddy Rich, B.B. King, and Johnny Winter	$3.50–$6.50/day
Movie	*New York Times* (1965)	*The Yellow Rolls-Royce* at Radio City Music Hall Noon Afternoon Evenings	 $0.99 $1.35 $1.85
Opera Ticket	*Chicago Tribune* (1968)	D'Oyly Carte Opera Company; Gilbert & Sullivan's *HMS Pinafore*	$3.50–$6.50
Play	*New York Times* (1965)	*Kiss Me, Kate* at New York City Center; Special Cole Porter Memorial Production Orchestra 2nd Balcony	 $4.95 $1.95
Play Ticket	*Chicago Tribune* (1968)	Neil Simon's *Plaza Suite*; Forrest Tucker and Betty Garrett; evening, Monday through Thursday, orchestra	$5.95

ENTERTAINMENT, HOME

Camera	*Time* (1968)	Kodak Instamatic 814 Camera; drop-in film cartridge	$240
Camera	*Western Auto Catalog* (1965)	Argus; 35mm cartridge; instant loading; with flash and slide reviewer	$69.95
Camera	*Life* (1968)	Polaroid Color Pack; the 60-second excitement	$50.00
Camera	*Life* (1969)	Kodak Instamatic S-10; it fits your pocket; palm or purse	$35.00
Camera and Projector	*Western Auto Catalog* (1965)	Mansfield; 8mm holiday electromatic; retain those once-in-a-lifetime occasions on film; includes a projector, camera combination and shadow box and wall screen; camera carrying case and accessories	$99.99
8 mm Camera	*New York Times* (1965)	Fujica 8mm Electric Power Zoom Reflex Camera; normal, slow motion and sound speeds	$129.95
Film	*Western Auto Catalog* (1965)	*Technicolor;* 35mm indoor/outdoor color slide film; high-quality color film with the Hollywood difference	$2.49
Film Editor	*Western Auto Catalog* (1965)	*Mansfield Action Editor;* see your processed movie film in clear, sharp detail; in forward and reverse action or single-frame stills	$19.95
Slide Viewer	*Time* (1968)	6AF Ansochrome Color Slide Film Viewer	$2.45
Movie Outfit	*Chicago Tribune* (1968)	*Kodak Super 8;* movie outfit; it's the instant-loading camera that uses drop-in 50 ft film	$24.66
Radio	*Western Auto Catalog* (1965)	*Custom 7;* transistor; PM speaker for clear reception; includes handsome carrying case	$12.95

Item	Source	Description	Price
Radio	*National Geographic* (1966)	*Admiral All World Transistor;* portable radio; tune in the world; 10 bands for world-wide reception	$200
Slide Projector	*National Geographic* (1966)	*Kodak Carousel 600;* dependable as gravity because it works by gravity	$80.00
Slide Projector	*Time* (1966)	*Honeywell;* there are a lot of other built-in conveniences, too, including the handiest edit/preview gate on the market	$149.50
Slide Projector	*Life* (1968)	*Sawyer;* automatic focusing; you focus the first slide, the machine does the rest	$60.00
Stereo	*Western Auto Catalog* (1965)	*Truetone Skylark 200;* portable stereo; with console-like features	$64.95
Stereo	*Western Auto Catalog* (1965)	*Provincial 3000;* cabinet; enjoy the exciting depth of living stereophonic sound	$499.95
Tape Player	*Sears, Roebuck* (1967)	*Stereo;* play the new 8-track stereo tape cartridges on your present music system	$67.95
Television	*Western Auto Catalog* (1965)	*Truetone;* color; cabinet model; 21" long-*life* laminated etched picture tube	$629.95
Television	*Western Auto Catalog* (1965)	*Truetone Riviera;* 16" black & white portable; 16,000 volts of power for a bright, clear picture; weighs less than 24 pounds	$149.95
Television	*National Geographic* (1966)	*Magnavox;* contemporary S24 color; walnut with remote control	$650

FARM EQUIPMENT AND SUPPLIES

Item	Source	Description	Price
Arc Welder	*The Progressive Farmer* (1968)	*Wel-Dex Arc Welder;* does the work of an $85 welder; fits ordinary 110 outlet	$18.95
Bearing Lubricator	*The Progressive Farmer* (1968)	*T&M Sealed Bearing Lubricator;* made for farmers by farmers	$2.95
Cattle	*The Progressive Farmer* (1968)	Holstein heifers, two to four weeks old, each	$45.00
Chickens	*The Progressive Farmer* (1968)	Red Cross chicks, per 100	$6.75
Ducks	*The Progressive Farmer* (1968)	Muscovy Ducks, pair	$5.00

FOOD PRODUCTS

Item	Source	Description	Price
Bread	*New York Times* (1965)	*la Vie's* sourdough bread; available at Bloomingdale's; per pound	$0.49
Catsup	*Chicago Tribune* (1968)	*Hunts;* 14-oz bottle	$0.22
Chocolate Covered Cherries	*Chicago Tribune* (1968)	*Brach's;* 12 oz; light or dark chocolate	$0.47
Coffee	*Chicago Tribune* (1968)	*Folgers;* 2-lb can	$1.27
Cola	*Chicago Tribune* (1968)	*Pepsi;* no deposit, 10-oz bottles; 6 pack	$0.59
Juice Drink	*Chicago Tribune* (1968)	*Del Monte;* pineapple-grapefruit; 46-oz can	$0.25

Item	Source	Description	Price
Liquid Diet	*Chicago Tribune* (1968)	*Sego;* 4 cans	$0.99

FURNITURE

Item	Source	Description	Price
Bunk Bed	*Western Auto Catalog* (1965)	Wagon-wheel; early American bunk bed; solid oak; bunkie mattress	$69.95
Cabinet	*Western Auto Catalog* (1965)	Multi-purpose; rich walnut finish, adds style; storage is an excellent room divider	$22.95
Chair	*American Home* (1966)	*Viking;* made of solid, clear birch	$11.95
Desk	*Western Auto Catalog* (1965)	Three-drawer; spacious dovetailed drawers with authentic antique-brass-finished hardware	$47.88
Dinette Set	*Western Auto Catalog* (1965)	High-pressure laminated plastic top; tapered legs; tubular branching; seats 8	$99.95
Dinette Set	*Western Auto Catalog* (1965)	Early American; 5 piece; 42 in table with leaf; laminated plastic table top, plus four chairs	$119.88
Living Room Suite	*Western Auto Catalog* (1965)	7-piece living room group; nylon frieze sofa and chair; 3 marproof occasional tables; 2 table lamps	$169.77
Mattress	*Western Auto Catalog* (1965)	*Englander;* innerspring or foam; quilted damask covers; twin or full	$59.95
Nightstand	*Western Auto Catalog* (1965)	Solid-oak construction with full-depth drawer and magazine shelf	$25.95
Recliner	*Western Auto Catalog* (1965)	King-size; pillow back; reinforced super glove-soft plastic; wears like iron; is easy to care for	$59.95

GARDEN EQUIPMENT AND SUPPLIES

Item	Source	Description	Price
Arbor	*Sears, Roebuck* (1967)	Aluminum; has baked-on white enamel finish so it never needs painting	$19.50
Bird Bath	*Sears, Roebuck* (1967)	Plastic bird bath; designed with the look of alabaster; fill the base with sand for stability	$2.89
Chaise	*Western Auto Catalog* (1965)	Redwood; three position; ideal for relaxing on lawn or patio	$25.95
Duster	*The Progressive Farmer* (1968)	*Whatley's Roller Duster;* dust 100 ft. per minute; use on Mason jar	$1.00
Edge-Trimmer	*Western Auto Catalog* (1965)	*Wizard;* 3 wheel, 2 hp, gas power; gives your lawn a manicured look	$9.96
Fertilizer	*Western Auto Catalog* (1965)	Weed and Feed; 20-10-5 fertilizer and 2-40 kills weeds;	$3.89
Hose	*Western Auto Catalog* (1965)	Red rubber; 50'; inner tubes reinforced with strong rayon-cord body and vulcanized	$7.95
Lawn Chair	*Western Auto Catalog* (1965)	Aluminum-web folding; 6 vertical, 5 horizontal webs in seat and back	$5.99
Lawn Flamingo	*Sears, Roebuck* (1967)	Our loveliest flamingos in natural pink	$3.69
Lawn Mower	*Western Auto Catalog* (1965)	Wizard Holiday Alum-Lite; 21"; has 3 hp Briggs and Stratton engine; 5 select-a-height trim size adjustments	$79.95

Item	Source	Description	Price
Outdoor Vacuum	*Sears, Roebuck* (1967)	Vacuum clean your lawn, hedges, patios, walks, and driveway	$194
Rider-Tractor	*Western Auto Wizard Holiday Catalog* (1965)	has everything for easiest mowing; Stratton engine; select-a-height trim size adjustments	$352.95
Seeds	*The Progressive Farmer* (1968)	Morris Heading collard seeds, per pound	$2.00
Sprinkler	*Western Auto Wizard Catalog* (1965)	Set 'N Spray; oscillating; covers up to 2600 sq ft with just a twist of a dial Stratton engine; 5 select-a-height trim size adjustments	$9.19
Tiller	*Western Auto Wizard Catalog* (1965)	Imperial; deep-digging; 4 hp, with power reverse	$140.95
Wagon	*Western Auto Catalog* (1965)	Town & Country; rugged wagons feature 10 in double-disc fit grip handles and self-lubricating bearings	$18.50

HOUSEHOLD PRODUCTS

Item	Source	Description	Price
Blender	*Chicago Tribune* (1968)	Proctor; 4 speeds, 6 pushbuttons, a perfect gift for the home	$13.49
Carpet	*The Progressive Farmer* (1968)	DuPont 501 Nylon Carpet; resists crushing and withstands the stiffest wear	$5.95/sq. yd.
Carpet	*Western Auto Catalog* (1965)	9' × 12' carpet; get extra service; extra-heavy-duty loop pile of 100% nylon at low cost	$38.95
Carpet	*American Home* (1966)	Cabin Crafts Briarwood; makes a great show of elegance, but it's really a toughie at heart	$10.95/yard
China	*Western Auto Catalog* (1965)	Estate; the classic swirl design of estate dinnerware, accented by a fine platinum band;57-piece service	$49.95
Clock	*Western Auto Catalog* (1965)	Sunburst; wall clock; brilliant 23" brass spokes radiate from 7" diameter; battery operated	$16.25
Clock	*Western Auto Catalog* (1965)	General Electric; sparkle alarm clock; a shadow-box crystal enhances the white dial and black numerals and hands	$5.98
Clock Radio	*Western Auto Catalog* (1965)	Truetone Imperial; AM/FM; all the beauty and style of a console; 4" × 6" heavy magnet speaker	$62.95
Coffee Maker	*Chicago Tribune* (1966)	*West Bend;* perks and serves 12 to 230 cups of full flavored coffee automatically	$9.95
Coffee Maker	*Western Auto Catalog* (1965)	*General Electric Peek-a-Brew;* with a transparent indicator that actually lets you see the coffee level	$19.95
Disinfectant Spray	*American Home* (1966)	*Florient;* why pay $0.98 for the high-priced spray	$0.59
Drill	*Western Auto Catalog* (1965)	*Wizard;* 2-speed electric drill; 1/4" drill develops 1/4 hp, drills through 1/4" steel, 1/2" hardwood	$19.95
Drill	*Chicago Tribune* (1968)	*Black & Decker;* 1/4" electric; your very best value in a general-purpose powerful drill	$10.99
Electric Blanket	*Western Auto Catalog* (1965)	*Wizard;* electric; non-allergenic, machine wash, dry; snap fit corners; double size	$19.35
Fan	*Western Auto Catalog* (1965)	*Imperial;* 3-speed; reversible window fan; 20"; has a push-button switch control panel and automatic thermostat that shuts fan off at pre-set temperature	$44.95
Fan	*Western Auto Catalog* (1965)	*Wizard;* box fan; 20", 2-speed suitable-type handle on top for easy portability	$21.45

Item	Source	Description	Price
Fan	*Western Auto Catalog* (1965)	*Wizard Imperial;* oscillating fan; 12", 3-speed; highly polished; deep-pitched aluminum blades	$19.95
Fireplace Tools	*Western Auto Catalog* (1965)	Hanging; wrought iron; solid-polish brass pull chains; black fire-screen mesh	$.95
Food Processor	*Western Auto Catalog* (1965)	*Wizard Meal Maker;* use as a juicer, mixer or grinder; seven speeds—from slow for easy blending to fast for grinding meats, vegetables	$39.95
Glasses	*Western Auto Catalog* (1965)	*Western Auto;* cut-glass water set; clear crystal; beauty and economy; includes six 9-oz tumblers and one 72-oz pitcher	$2.49
Ice Cream Maker	*Chicago Tribune* (1966)	*Proctor;* makes delicious homemade ice cream	$16.95
Ice Cream Maker	*Western Auto Catalog* (1965)	Electric; turns smoothly easily; 4-qt capacity	$27.95
Iron	*Western Auto Catalog* (1965)	*Wizard Imperial;* economically priced iron with unusually fine performance	$6.95
Ironing Table	*Western Auto Catalog* (1965)	12-way all-metal queen-of-the-ironing table; weighs only 15 lbs	$7.99
Lamp	*American Home* (1966)	*Stiffel;* with base; early Renaissance in character with Mediterranean overtones; height 22"	$72.50
Light Bulbs	*Western Auto Catalog* (1965)	*Wizard Long Life;* each bulb in handy 4-pack lasts 3 *times* longer; pack contains two 100 watt; one 75 watt	$1.29
Mirror	*American Home* (1966)	*Pittsburgh Plate Glass Mirror;* Spanish provincial style 32" × 46"	$7.00
Ovenware	*Western Auto Catalog* (1965)	*Western Auto;* 12-pc, withstands oven temperature includes 6 5-oz custard cups, gelatin molds, round 1-qt pudding pan; 1 deep loaf pan for bread, meat loaf, 9" pie plate; baking utility dish; 1 1/2-qt casserole dish and cover	$3.95
Paint	*Western Auto Catalog* (1965)	latex; interior flat; one application is all you need; balanced formula for high hiding power	$5.55/ gallon
Pillow	*Western Auto Catalog* (1965)	Machine washable; foam; made from 100% virgin urethane flaked foam; non-allergic	$4.98/pair
Plate	*American Home* (1966)	Pottery; creamy white, 10" pottery plate has bamboo pattern and border	$6.00
Pliers	*Western Auto Catalog* (1965)	Needle nose; slender jaws give long reach; hardened wire-cutter edges	$2.95
Polish	*Antiques* (1966)	Old Patina; furniture polish and feeder with beeswax; wire-cutter edges	$2.25/pt
Rods	*Sears, Roebuck* (1967)	Gleaming rods for café curtains; solid brass 30" to 52"	$4.89
Roller Pan Set	*Chicago Tribune* (1968)	Lightweight and easy to use. . .makes your painting job a breeze	$0.49
Router	*American Home* (1966)	Stanley Works Rout-About; compact 1/4 hp unit that spins at 25,000 rpm	$34.95
Rug	*Antiques* (1966)	Semi-antique Persian Sehna-Kurd Oriental rug; 7 '× 4' gold medallion on blue field, orange-red design	$345
Saw	*Chicago Tribune* (1968)	Black & Decker; 7 1/4" circular saw; cuts 2" × 4"'s at 45 degree angle	$27.77
Scale	*Sears, Roebuck* (1967)	Get the type of scale the professionals use	$42.37

Item	Source	Description	Price
Slip Covers	*Sears, Roebuck* (1967)	Crystal clear; show off the beauty of your furniture; chair cover	$3.99
Socket Set	*Western Auto Catalog* (1965)	57-piece; includes 1/2", 3/8", and 1/4" drive parts	$56.95
Tableware	*Western Auto Catalog* (1965)	Paris Night; stainless steel; is exactly as its name; 69-piece service for 8	$19.95
Tile	*Western Auto Catalog* (1965)	Vinyl asbestos tile for kitchen floors; 9" square; made for long lasting life even in areas of critical wear	$12.50
Toaster	*Western Auto Catalog* (1965)	Imperial; this toaster gives you fingertip control	$11.39
Toaster-Broiler-	*Western Auto Catalog* (1965)	Use as a baker one way, flip over for a broiler-toaster	$15.25
Tool Set	*Sears, Roebuck* (1967)	Craftsman; 155-piece set	$128.60
Vacuum Cleaner	*Western Auto Catalog* (1965)	Canister; power to spare, return original carpet beauty, get floors, walls really clean; includes 13-piece set	$69.95
Varnish	*Western Auto Catalog* (1965)	Spar Varnish; with china-wood oil; can be used inside on trim, woodwork, or outside to protect wood surfaces	$5.79

HOTEL RATES

Item	Source	Description	Price
Room Rate	*Time* (1968)	Hotel Thomas Jefferson in Birmingham, Alabama; completely new throughout Commercial Single Rate	$8.50
Room Rate	*New York Times* (1965)	Hotel Shelburne; Boardwalk, Atlantic City; 100% central system air conditioned; per room; two in a room	$7.00
Room Rate	*New York Times* (1965)	*Griswold Hotel and Country Club;* 4 days and 3 nights Per person	$59

JEWELRY

Item	Source	Description	Price
Necklace	*Western Auto Catalog* (1965)	*Hallmark;* cultured pearl; perfectly matched set of cultured pearls; hand knotted graduated pearl necklace	$29.95
Pin	*Sears, Roebuck* (1967)	Abstract-shaped dramatic accent to current fashion	$5.00
Pocket Watch	*Sears, Roebuck* (1967)	Fob watch; railroad type; minute-marked dial	$5.49
Ring	*Western Auto Catalog* (1965)	Diamond; 4-prong Tiffany or Illusion setting; 1 ct; 14k yellow or white gold	$795
Watch	*New York Times* (1965)	*Longines Watch;* self-winding automatic; two years to pay with small down payment	$135
Watch	*New York Times* (1965)	*Belforte Electronic* watch for men	$49.95
Watch	*Western Auto Catalog* (1965)	*Timex Marlin;* radiolite dial for telling time in the darkest room; chrome-plated bezel	$11.95
Watch	*Western Auto Catalog* (1965)	*Waltham Ultra-thin Guardsman;* man's; white gold finished case; 17 jewel	$28.95

Item	Source	Description	Price
Watch	*Western Auto Catalog* (1965)	*Timex Cavatina;* lady's; beautifully styled, keeps perfect time; lasting chrome-plated bezel, comfortable nylon-cord band	$9.95

MEALS

Item	Source	Description	Price
Dinner	*New York Times* (1965)	*Astrojet Room;* interesting people are just part of the fascination of airport dining; complete Dinners Supreme from	$2.95
Lunch	*New York Times* (1965)	*Paddy's Clam House;* Maine Lobsters a Specialty; lunch, 4-course fish meal	$1.48

MEDICAL PRODUCTS AND SERVICES

Item	Source	Description	Price
Acne Solution	*Hit Parade* (1968)	Wipe away pimples, blackheads, and other embarrassing surface symptoms; an 8-wk solution	$2.98

MOTORIZED VEHICLES, SUPPLIES, AND SERVICES

Item	Source	Description	Price
Air Conditioner	*Western Auto Catalog* (1965)	1800 btu model; 2 big rotary blowers cool you with 315 cu ft minimum of refrigerated air	$269.95
Automobile	*Time* (1968)	*Datsun;* value wagon of the year; all synchromesh 4-speed	$2,196
Automobile	*Life* (1968)	*Volkswagen;* station wagon; half a Volkswagen station wagon holds as much as most whole wagons hold	$2,602

Advertisement for a 1969 Volkswagen 1600. (via Wikimedia Commons)

Item	Source	Description	Price
Battery	*Western Auto Catalog* (1965)	*Wizard Deluxe;* for cars; new inter-cell construction to give your car 25% more starting power	$12.88
Car Wax	*Western Auto Catalog* (1965)	*Simonize;* durable paste wax puts a gleaming shine on your car's finish that lasts for months	$0.99
Dimmer	*Western Auto Catalog* (1965)	Automatic headlight dimmer; less than half the cost of previous models, automatic or manual	$26.95
Exhaust Kit	*Sears, Roebuck* (1967)	Dual-exhaust kit for Corvair	$18.45
Header Set	*Sears, Roebuck* (1967)	Dual-header set for Falcon and Comet	$64.95
Radio	*Western Auto Catalog* (1965)	Truetone; 11-transistor AM/FM auto radio; have the pleasure and relaxation of FM listening while you drive; plus the added enjoyment of an AM radio—both in one radio	$84.95
Resonator Pipes	*Sears, Roebuck* (1967)	Heavy 18-gauge steel tubing; Ford 1957–1960	$1.29
Seat Belt	*Western Auto Catalog* (1965)	Borg-Warner Maji-Buckle; automatically adjusts to fit everyone in your family	$12.45
Seat Covers	*Western Auto Catalog* (1965)	Suburban Jetspun; polypropylene-coated Jetspun fibers are durable, resist stains, fading, burns, scuffs; jewel tone pattern	$24.45
Spray Paint	*Western Auto Catalog* (1965)	Dupli-Color; quick, easy way to touch up your car; 6-oz can	$1.49
Tire	*Western Auto Catalog* (1965)	Davis Safety Sentry; new wrap-around tread design adds style, handling ease; black-tube type	$16.48
Tire	*Western Auto Catalog* (1965)	Davis Super Highway; 7.50 × 16; 6-ply rating, tube type	$26.95
Tires	*The Progressive Farmer* (1968)	Premium Each, with trade	$19.98

MUSICAL INSTRUMENTS

Item	Source	Description	Price
Guitar	*Western Auto Catalog* (1965)	Truetone Jazz King; masterful guitar construction; 4-way selector switch	$97.95
Guitar	*Sears, Roebuck* (1967)	Electric; hollow body; triple pickup, each with tone and volume controls	$199.95
Organ	*Western Auto Catalog* (1965)	Truetone Regency; electric cord; voice selector switch, 8 pedal buttons for bass tones	$379.95
Trumpet	*Western Auto Catalog* (1965)	Barclay; student; perfect for the beginner; durable nickel-plated valves and mouthpiece	$79.50

OTHER

Item	Source	Description	Price
Baseball Cards	*The Sporting News* (1966)	Topps; 1966 complete set	$11.95
Bookkeeping Record	*Life* (1968)	Dome; simplified weekly bookkeeping record; America's most widely used single entry system	$3.75
Cosmetic Case	*Sears, Roebuck* (1967)	14" × 9" × 8"	$15.67
Film Developing	*Life* (1968)	United Film Club; CX 35 mm-20, Kodapak cartridge; with new film	$5.99

Item	Source	Description	Price
Flag Set	*Western Auto Catalog* (1965)	United States; includes 3' × 5' printed flag; 6' jointed metal pole, plus rope halyard	$44.88
Flight Bag	*Sears, Roebuck* (1967)	Unzips to hang for easy packing	$39.47
Gasoline Container	*Western Auto Catalog* (1965)	5 gal; made of rugged dependable 28-gauge steel	$3.05
Knife	*Western Auto Catalog* (1965)	Kutmaster; two-bladed pocketknife; stag-type handle	$1.00
Parking Fee	*Life* (1969)	Watergate, Washington, D.C.	$3,500/yr
Photograph	*Hit Parade* (1968)	Friendship Photos; plastic laminate of favorite photo with deep-sunk embossing; 30 pictures	$1.00
Portable Kitchen	*Western Auto Catalog* (1965)	Deluxe oblong; all-aluminum; chrome-plated hinged grid 30" high for no-stoop cooking;	$37.95
Reupholstery	*Chicago Tribune* (1966)	Goldblatt's; new fabrics, new colors; flawless workmanship; sofa	$94.00
Service Weapons	*Time* (1968)	Booty money paid in Vietnam for captured Communist Weapons AK-47 Assault Rifle 120-mm Mortar	$25 $200

PERSONAL CARE PRODUCTS

Item	Source	Description	Price
Artificial Fingernails	*Hit Parade* (1968)	Nu-Nails; artificial fingernails, pink, rose, platinum	$0.49/10
Barber Set	*Sears, Roebuck* (1967)	17 piece	$10.88
Electric Shaver	*Sears, Roebuck* (1967)	Lady Kenmore; distinctive cameo styling plus convenient built-in light	$13.97
Electric Toothbrush	*Western Auto Catalog* (1965)	Trident; re-chargeable battery-powered motor in handle; four individual snap-in brushes	$12.50
Hair Dryer	*Western Auto Wizard Holiday Catalog* (1965)	Dries like a console, yet it carries like a portable	$29.95
Hair Spray	*Chicago Tribune* (1968)	Just Wonderful; 12-oz can	$0.47
Razor Blades	*Chicago Tribune* (1968)	Gillette; $1.59 size, cartridges of 10	$0.99
Shaver	*Western Auto Catalog* (1965)	Remington 25; for men; contour head has six rows of diamond-honed cutters	$25.95
Shaving Cream	*Chicago Tribune* (1968)	Gillette Foamy; regular, menthol, or lemon-lime; 11-oz can	$0.59
Strop	*Sears, Roebuck* (1967)	Craftsman; leather strop	$5.77
Toothpaste	*Chicago Tribune* (1968)	Colgate; 6.75-oz tube	$0.55
Vitamins	*Western Auto Catalog* (1965)	contains more than the known minimum daily requirement; 100 tablets	$1.49

PUBLICATIONS

Item	Source	Description	Price
Book	*Time* (1868)	*This Timeless Moment: A Personal View of Aldous Huxley* by Laura Archera Huxley	$6.95
Book	*New York Times* (1968)	*Always Ask a Man*, Arlene Dahl's Key to Femininity	$5.95
Book	*New York Times* (1965)	*Portrait of A People* by Charles Raddock; *The Story of the Jews from Ancient to Modern Times*; three-volume set	$18.75
Book	*New York Times* (1965)	*Note 3 For Treason* by Brian Cleeve; a Random House Mystery	$3.95

Item	Source	Description	Price
Encyclopedia	*Western Auto Catalog* (1965)	World University; 12-volume set, a treasury of information	$59.00
Magazine	*Antiques* (1966)	*Antiques* Magazine; monthly	$12/yr
Magazine	*Life* (1968)	*Life*; weekly	$0.40

REAL ESTATE

Item	Source	Description	Price
Apartment	*Life* (1969)	Watergate, Washington, D.C.; cost of Attorney General John Mitchell's apartment	$140,000
Farm Land	*The Progressive Farmer* (1968)	740 acre farm bordering river in Culpepper, Virginia; 3 houses, 5 barns, 4 silos	$395/acre
House	*New York Times* (1965)	Bayside Hills Home in Queens; 3 bedrooms, 1 1/2 baths	$35,000
House	*New York Times* (1965)	Sea Cliff home in Nassau—Suffolk area; 3 bedrooms	$34,000
House	*Chicago Tribune* (1968)	3 bedroom, 1 1/2 bath, large closets, family room, many extras; fenced yard	$25,500
House	*Chicago Tribune* (1968)	Outstanding 3-bedroom ranch; garage, screened-in porch; drive out today	$23,500
Loft	*New York Times* (1965)	Manhattan lofts; 2nd Ave.; 16,000 to 27,000 square feet	$1.50/sq. ft.
Lot	*New York Times* (1965)	Brooklyn lot; 16 St. W; 40 × 120 lot in unrestricted area	$10,500

SEWING EQUIPMENT AND SUPPLIES

Item	Source	Description	Price
Cloth	*American Home* (1966)	Bloomcraft Art Nouveau; printed cotton; has a protective finish, is about 54" wide, and has sufficient body to be used for draperies, slip covers or upholstery	$3.50/yard
Cloth	*Sears, Roebuck* (1967)	Man-made fabrics and blends, three 4' pieces; enough for three smart dresses	$5.97
Electric Scissors	*Western Auto Catalog* (1965)	Dritz; electric; cut pattern in a fraction of time	$7.45
Electric Scissors	*Sears, Roebuck* (1967)	Reduces cutting time and makes cutting so much easier	$7.65
Sewing Machine	*Western Auto Catalog* (1965)	Wizard Imperial Zig-zag; sews 101 fancy stitches, monograms, embroiders, buttonholes with ease	$119.95
Sewing Machine	*Sears, Roebuck* (1967)	Kenmore 95; with new stretch stitch for elasticized fabrics	$149.95
Sewing Machine	*Life* (1968)	Singer Touch & Sew; solid-state speed control, exclusive push-button bobbin	$149.95
Yarn	*Sears, Roebuck* (1967)	3-ply cotton	$2.37

SPORTS EQUIPMENT

Item	Source	Description	Price
Baseball Bat	*Western Auto Catalog* (1965)	Revelation Little League; 32 in; sturdy white ash, natural color	$2.25
Baseball Catcher's Mask	*Western Auto Catalog* (1965)	Wilson; full-size professional quality mask; made of lightweight magnesium	$11.50
Baseball Glove	*Western Auto Catalog* (1965)	Revelation; fielders; has wide, deep, and rugged professional styling	$8.95
Baseball Glove	*Western Auto Catalog* (1965)	Wilson. . .Harvey Kuenn; fielders; a glove good enough for the majors	$15.95

Item	Source	Description	Price
Bicycle	*Chicago Tribune* (1968)	Power King; adjustable polo saddle and hi-rise handlebar	$29.99
Bow	*Western Auto Catalog* (1965)	Ben Pearson Cougar; durable, laminated construction; the ideal bow for adult beginners or the accomplished archer	$22.95
Fishing Bait	*Western Auto Catalog* (1965)	Doc's Prepared Catfish Bait; choice of 4 scents; 12-oz jar	$.69
Fishing Lure	*Western Auto Catalog* (1965)	DeLong Red Worm; best for bluegill, perch; package of 3	$0.49
Fishing Lure	*Western Auto Catalog* (1965)	Heddon Toni; yellow body; jewelry blade finish; 1/4 oz	$0.89
Fishing Lure	*Sears, Roebuck* (1967)	Lucky Dozen; actual replicas of 12 of the fish-takingest lures ever designed	$5.22
Fishing Reel	*Western Auto Catalog* (1965)	Shakespeare Wonder-Cast; push button; aluminum frame; full-circle micro-drag	$12.95
Golf Shoes	*New York Times* (1965)	Woman's spiked oxford golf shoes; exceptionally lightweight	$22.00
Gun Scope	*The Sporting News* (1966)	Weaver K4 Scope; see the magnified target in clear, sharp detail	$34.50
Pool Table	*Western Auto Catalog* (1965)	Imperial; 8'; our very best table; laminated slatite precision playing bed; 100% virgin-wool billiard cloth assures you a hard, smooth surface	$334.50
Rod and Reel	*Western Auto Catalog* (1965)	Zebco 606; spin-cast rod-reel fishing combination; 2-piece, solid glass rod, 4 guides; tip top; cork handle	$9.99
Rod and Reel	*Western Auto Catalog* (1965)	Zebco 777; fishing-spinning combination; Zebflex 6 1/2', 2-piece tubular glass rod and 777 open-face spinning reel	$15.49
Sailboat	*Sears, Roebuck* (1967)	Puffer; 10' sailing dinghy can be used with motor or oars	$385
Sleeping Bag	*Western Auto Catalog* (1965)	Duraloft; 3 lb washable; 100% polyester insulation; 36" × 80" cut size	$17.95
Softball	*Western Auto Catalog* (1965)	Voit Collegiate; official size and weight	$1.65
Table Tennis Set	*Western Auto Catalog* (1965)	Revelation; deluxe; complete set for 4 players includes 3-ply rubber-faced paddles with tapered walnut handles; extra-heavy posts; green cord netting; adjustable metal ends, 4 official table-tennis balls	$6.95
Table Tennis Set	*Sears, Roebuck* (1967)	Complete set	$10.00
Table Tennis Table	*Western Auto Catalog* (1965)	our very best table; 5' × 9' tournament size; formed by two 4 1/2' × 5' sections	$43.95
Tennis Ball	*Western Auto Catalog* (1965)	Wilson Championship; Dacron-nylon-wool cover for best wear, approved U.S. International and Professional Lawn Tennis Association	$2.65/can
Tennis Racket	*Western Auto Catalog* (1965)	Autograph; a perfect racket for the economy-minded beginner; laminated frame	$1.95
Tennis Racket	*Western Auto Catalog* (1965)	*Spalding Pancho Gonzales;* our very best racket; laminated ash and beech shoulder overlays for extra strength	$10.85
Tent	*Western Auto Catalog* (1965)	*Eagle;* wall tent; excellent for rough Boy Scout use; cut size; 5' × 7'	$17.75

Item	Source	Description	Price
Water Skis	*Western Auto Catalog* (1965)	*Wizard;* combine regular and slalom skiing, graceful, fast, banana-shape style	$19.95

TOBACCO PRODUCTS

Item	Source	Description	Price
Cigarettes	*New York Times* (1965)	Pink cigarettes for weddings and other occasions; carton of 200	$9.50

TOYS

Item	Source	Description	Price
Backyard Amusement Set	*Western Auto Catalog* (1965)	Includes lawn glider; 2 swings; 2 gym rings; trapeze, sky-shooter; pumper swing, 7 1/2' platform slide	$34.95
Bicycle	*Western Auto Catalog* (1965)	*Western Flyer Cosmic Flyer;* for boys; features a new double-strength frame with twin center bars	$49.95
Bicycle	*Western Auto Catalog* (1965)	*Western Flyer Standard Flyer;* for girls or boys; rugged and built to last; 26"	$31.95
Croquet Set	*Western Auto Catalog* (1965)	Regulation size; 4-player; knurled 3 3/8" rock maple balls	$6.95
Doll	*Western Auto Catalog* (1965)	*Mattel Teenage Barbie;* easy to dress; arms, legs and head move; 11 1/2" with stand	$2.29
Doll	*Western Auto Catalog* (1965)	*Mattel Midge Bride;* Barbie's best friend; wears Barbie's clothes	$3.49
Doll	*Western Auto Catalog* (1965)	*Mattel Ken;* Barbie's boyfriend; a living doll; neatest crew cut; big blue eyes; 12 1/2" with stand	$2.69
Doll	*Sears, Roebuck* (1967)	*Eeyore;* 10" high; 14" long; removable tail	$4.99
Lead Pellets	*Western Auto Catalog* (1965)	*Crossman;* .177 cal, 250 per can	$0.95
Locomotive	*Railroad Model Craftsman* (1966)	*Tyco Prairie Santa Fe;* locomotive and tender; 2-6-2 with operating headlight	$16.77
Motorcycle	*Western Auto Catalog* (1965)	*Western Flyer Thunder Rod;* roaring engine; hi-rise handlebar, pneumatic tires; banana seat	$34.95
Pistol	*Western Auto Catalog* (1965)	*Daisy;* CO2 pistol; shoot regular .177 caliber bb's; semi-automatic	$16.95
Racing Set	*Western Auto Catalog* (1965)	*Aurora HO;* two speed controls allow you and your opponent to brake the cars and control them on curves; set comes with track, powerpack, and two lightning fast cars—Corvette Sting Ray and Jaguar XKE	$19.77
Rifle	*Western Auto Catalog* (1965)	*Daisy 51 Scope Smoker Rifle;* shoots a captive cork with a pop and a shower of sparks and a puff of smoke; 21" long	$0.97
Rifle	*Western Auto Catalog* (1965)	*Daisy golden 750;* lever action air rifle; our most popular model Daisy; carbine styled, 750-shot lever-action repeater	$7.50
Rifle	*Western Auto Catalog* (1965)	*Hy-Score;* single-shot pellet; shoots .177 caliber pellets; single-breaking action cocks rifle	$19.95
Robots	*Chicago Tribune* (1968)	*Ideal Zeroids;* the workers of the future—robots that obey your every command; they grab, throw, push, haul, and much more	$3.97
Space Man	*Chicago Tribune* (1968)	*Eldon's Billy Blast-Off;* 9" high miniature space man in space suit; comes with his own 7-piece set of space equipment	$3.99

Item	Source	Description	Price
Sports Car	*Western Auto Catalog* (1965)	*Western Flyer;* pedals easy; steers easy; 33 1/2" long	$11.95
Station Wagon and Camper	*Western Auto Catalog* (1965)	*Buddy L;* an authentic replica of the Tee Pee Trailer; hi-impact plastic tent, tufted bed; tent flaps	$5.66
Tricycle	*Western Auto Catalog* (1965)	*Western Flyer;* 10"; sturdier, huskier frame for young Rough Riders	$7.95
Truck	*Western Auto Catalog* (1965)	*Tonka;* pick-up truck; features snap-open tailgate, glassed-in cab and rubber tires; 9 1/8" long	$1.69
Wading Pool	*Western Auto Catalog* (1965)	*Western Auto Playmate;* custom-styled steel wading pool; 147-gallon capacity	$8.45

TRAVEL AND TRANSPORTATION

Item	Source	Description	Price
Air Fare	*New York Times* (1965)	New York to San Francisco by Jet	$217.65
Airline Fare	*Chicago Tribune* (1966)	*Delta;* Miami; Delta's got up to 11 jets daily; up to 4 non-stops on weekend; it's just 24 hours to Florida's most famous resort city; Day Jetourist	$74.70
Hawaii Tour	*Time* (1968)	Trans International Airlines offers two weeks in Hawaii; complete tour	$599 and up

MISCELLANY 1965–1969

Giving Is Growing

The annual survey of 50 U.S. colleges and universities by New York's John Price Jones Co., professional fund raisers, shows that gifts spurted 1 1/3% last year over 1963—from $335,456,000 to

$373,446,000. Contributions from individuals still provide the biggest single source of such funds (39.3%), but foundation grants are growing (now 33.1%), while bequests (16.9%) and corporations (10.7%) provide the rest. The gifts of the past four years alone total more than a fourth of the $4.8 billion that the Jones surveys have tabulated in their 44 years of existence.

The top ten beneficiaries in 1964:

Harvard	$38,812,000
Stanford	$36,078,000
Cornell	$27,695,000
Yale	$22,538,000
M.I.T.	$21,233,000
Chicago	$20,555,000
California	$16,602,000
Princeton	$16,416,000
Columbia	$16,001,000
N.Y.U.	$15,741,000

Time, February 26, 1965

$8,000 a Year

By far the most controversial part of the President's program was a plan to provide direct subsidies, for rent or mortgage payments, for some 500,000 city families with incomes as high as $8,000 a year. Initially, the aid would be limited to families displaced by Government projects such as urban renewal and highway construction, to those presently in substandard housing, to the impoverished elderly, and to displaced or ill-housed families capable of increasing their income in the future. In general, the formula would call for such families to pay 20% of their income for housing—and the Government would make up any necessary difference. Critics might wonder if an $8,000-a-year family really ought to be on a dole, but the President insisted that this section might "prove the most effective instrument of our new housing policy."

Time, March 12, 1965

Divorced

By Mary Costa, 36, blonde and beautiful lyric soprano, who left a $150,000-a-year job as TV's Chrysler girl for an opera career, making her widely acclaimed 1964 Metropolitan debut as Violetta in La Traviata; Frank Tashlin, 53, Hollywood writer director of slapstick comedies (The Man from the Diners' Club); on grounds of cruelty; after twelve years of marriage, no children; in Santa Monica, Calif.

Time, April 22, 1966

Shape of Events from One Year to Next

And capital is in shorter supply. The American economy, the powerhouse of world progress these last few years, went under severe monetary restraint in 1966. The transition was not too skillfully handled—1966 should have seen, but did not see, a tax increase—and the economy entered 1967 with every prospect of a lower growth rate, if not an end to its unprecedented six-year boom. Yet the demands on that economy will not grow less. The rising costs of Vietnam were matched by a growing list of domestic problems ranging from smog to transportation, from ghettos to inadequate schools.

Life, January 1967

Killebrew to Get $65,000 for 1967; Slugger and Twins Agree to Terms for This Season

Harmon Killebrew, one of the leading sluggers in baseball, has agreed to a 1967 contract for a salary estimated at $65,000, the Minnesota Twins said today.

Killebrew hit 281 last season, smashing 39 home runs and driving in 110 while playing first base, third base and the outfield for the American League club. He was second to Frank Robinson

of the Baltimore Orioles in both homers and runs batted in.

New York Times, February 23, 1967

MISCELLANY 1965–1969

Watergate West

The interior of Watergate West's free-form superstructure includes a number of "luxury features." The lobby is resplendent with fake Chou Dynasty lamps and curtains handwoven in Swaziland. The elevators are flooded with Muzak, and the bathrooms are paved with marble and equipped with bidets and golden faucets. The 143 apartments vary as much in design as they do in price (from $28,000 for a one-bedroom to $186,000 for a penthouse). Many living and dining rooms are trapezoids or obtuse-angled triangles, while a few entranceways are circles.

Life, August 1969

Advertisement: Getting Rid of $176,000,999 Isn't as Easy as You Think

The next time you sit down to balance your checkbook, think about what it would be like if you had the job of balancing a bank's bank account.

Especially when the bank is the biggest in Michigan. And when the job has to be done not just once a month, but every day, all day long.

Time, August 8, 1969

HISTORICAL SNAPSHOT 1970–1974

1970

- Man-made fibers control 56 percent of U.S. textile market
- Gross National Product reaches
- $977 billion
- New York subway rates reach 30¢
- Daily volume on New York Stock Exchange nearly three times that of 1960 at 11.6 million shares
- 25.5 million Americans live below the $3,908 per year poverty level
- President Nixon calls for voluntary wage and price controls

1971

- President Nixon orders 90-day freeze on wages and prices
- The average taxpayer gives the government $400 for defense, $125 to fight the war in Indochina, $40 to build roads, $30 to explore space, and $315 for health activities
- First-class postal rates rise to 8 cents per ounce
- Chicago's 1,107-foot Standard Oil of Indiana building opens
- Annual per capita beef consumption reaches 11 pounds
- *Look* magazine ceases publication

1972

- Richard Nixon reelected; Watergate burglary occurs

- Nearly 30 percent of U.S. petroleum is imported
- Wages, prices, and profits remain controlled by Phase II economic measures
- Dow Jones closes at 1003.15 on November 14, above 1,000 for first time
- San Francisco Bay Area Rapid Transit System opens
- *Ms.* magazine begins publication; *Life* magazine suspends publication
- Polaroid SX-70 system produces colored print
- New York's 110-story World Trade Center opens
- Birth rate falls to 15.8 per 1,000, lowest since 1917

1973

- McDonald's introduces Egg McMuffin, pioneering fast-food breakfast
- U.S. troops leave South Vietnam
- Median sales price of an existing single-family house reaches $28,900
- Average farmer produces enough food for 50 people
- Farm labor represents 5 percent of workforce
- President Nixon orders freeze on all retail food prices

- Vodka outsells whiskey for first time
- Energy crisis and soaring grain prices produce economic recession

1974

- Pocket calculator marketed
- President Nixon lowers highway speed limit to 55 mph to save gasoline
- 110,000 clothing workers stage nationwide strike
- Unemployment reaches 6.5 percent, highest since 1961
- Universal product code designed for supermarket industry
- Year-long daylight savings time adopted to save fuel
- 3M develops Post-it to stick paper to paper
- ITT's Harold Geneen is highest paid executive at $791,000 per year
- Time, Inc., issues *People* magazine, devoted to celebrity journalism
- Walgreen's drug chain exceeds $1 billion in sales for first time
- President Nixon resigns

507

Richard Nixon boarding Army One upon his departure from the White House after resigning the office of President of the United States following the Watergate Scandal in 1974. (via Wikimedia Commons)

SELECTED INCOME 1970-1974

Job	Source	Description	Pay
Accountant	*New York Times* (1971)	Park Avenue Public Co.	$15,000/ yr
Accounting Clerks	*New York Times* (1971)	Night Students	$160/wk
Actor	Legrand and Karney, *Chronicle of the Cinema* (1995)	Mae West's fee for 10 days' work in the movie *Myra Breckinridge,* her first screen appearance since 1943	$335,000
Art Designer	*New York Times* (1973)	Children's book designer	$11,000/ yr
Art Gallery Clerk	*New York Times* (1973)	Good appearance; sales personality	$150– $125/wk
Baseball Umpire	John Feinstein, *Play Ball: The Life and Troubled Times of Major League Baseball* (1993)	Annual salary of Bruce Froemming in 1972	$10,000
Bookkeeper	*New York Times* (1973)	Midtown music company seeks several assistant bookkeepers	$125– $170/wk
Branch Manager	*New York Times* (1970)	Bank seeks branch manager for operations, credit and new business; per year	To $16,000
Caretaker	*Chicago Tribune* (1970)	Free apartment, plus food; retired or nonretired couple; care for home on lake	$150/mo
Chess Player	*Life* (1972)	Prize money offered to Boris Spassky and Bobby Fisher to play chess in Iceland	$125,000
Clerk	*Chicago Tribune* (1970)	Maintain technical society membership records	$100/wk
Cocktail Waitress	*Chicago Tribune* (1970)	Nights	$120/wk
Dancer	*Chicago Tribune* (1972)	No experience necessary; daily pay	$350/wk
File Clerk	*New York Times* (1970)	Law firm seeks persons with light experience; legal experience helpful; per week	$100 to $110
Girl/Man Friday	*New York Times* (1971)	No stenography necessary; lovely office; 9–5	$110– $135/wk
Hostess	*Chicago Tribune* (1972)	Days-nights; full charge of 25 girls; seating capacity 150	$125/wk to start
Hotel Desk Clerk	*New York Times* (1971)	5 days, relief shift; must know NCR 4200	$125/wk
Hotel Room Clerk	*New York Times* (1973)	4–12 or nights	$541/mo
Housekeeper	*Chicago Tribune* (1970)	Experienced pleasant woman to live in	$80/wk
IBM Typist	*Chicago Tribune* (1970)	Must type 65 words per minute accurate and neat for small print shop	$2.90 1/ hr

Job	Source	Description	Pay
Ice Skater	*Guinness Book of World Records* (1981)	Annual earnings of professional ice skater Janet Lynn [1974]	$750,000
Inventory Clerk	*Chicago Tribune* (1972)	Mail-order book concern in Niles needs intelligent young adult for inventory records	$520/mo
Keypuncher	*Chicago Tribune* (1970)	For a world-famous airline; junior	$450/mo
Keypuncher	*New York Times* (1971)	3 mos 1 experience	$130/wk
Manager	*New York Times* (1971)	IBM System 3	$15,000/yr
Metallurgist	*Chicago Tribune* (1974)	Heat treat supervisor	$14,000/yr
Navy Recruit	*Life* (1972)	Monthly pay of Navy recruit, plus free food, free clothing	$288
Nurse	*Chicago Tribune* (1970)	Situation wanted: practical nurse; will care for elderly or invalid person; will live-in and give 24 hr care 6 days	$150/wk
Part-Time Typist	*Chicago Tribune* (1974)	Large publishing firm located in Loop area needs permanent part-time typist	$3.63–$4/hour
Psychiatric Social	*Chicago Tribune* (1974)	Immediate opening; ACSW with three years or worker with more experience	$11,138/yr
Sales-Buyer	*Chicago Tribune* (1974)	Must love to sell and work; must be talented in sales, office skills and want to grow with a large wholesale firm	$200/wk
Secretary	*New York Times* (1970)	Will work as right-hand to dynamic executives in high profit brokerage firm; per week	$135 to $175
Truck Driver	*Chicago Tribune* (1974)	Must have good work and driving record	$14,000/yr
Wall Street Analysts	*New York Times* (1970)	Institution seeks topnotch senior analyst in oil	$40,000/year
Writer	Patrick H. Samway, *Walker Percy: A Life* (1997)	Payment to Walker Percy for paperback rights to his novel *Love in the Ruins* (1971)	$75,000

CONSUMER EXPENDITURES 1970–1974

Expenditure Type	1970	1971	1972	1973	1974
Clothing	$194.26	$208.99	$225.83	$248.22	$261.86
Food	$693.58	$710.26	$755.114	$831.02	$926.33
Auto Usage	$362.16	$419.43	$460.70	$500.69	$506.89
New Auto Purchase	$106.89	$135.79	$150.55	$159.97	$126.25
Auto Parts	$29.77	$34.19	$38.11	$41.99	$44.42
Gas & Oil	$106.89	$111.72	$116.25	$132.60	$168.81
Housing	$458.81	$494.56	$534.07	$579.02	$627.06
Furniture	$41.98	$44.30	$45.55	$55.68	$58.45
Utilities	$110.79	$119.43	$131.02	$144.87	$169.74
Telephone & Telegraph	$49.29	$52.97	$59.08	$66.54	$72.48
Physicians	$68.33	$73.68	$79.09	$86.83	$94.92
Dentist	$23.92	$24.56	$26.68	$31.15	$34.14
Health Insurance	$21.48	$23.59	$28.59	$30.20	$29.93
Personal Business	$156.19	$169.51	$183.42	$196.31	$216.04
Personal Care	$57.59	$58.27	$61.46	$66.54	$72.01
Tobacco	$52.71	$54.42	$58.75	$62.29	$65.93
Local Transport	$14.64	$15.89	$16.19	$16.52	$17.30
Intercity Transport	$19.52	$21.19	$24.77	$27.84	$32.27
Recreation	$210.37	$221.51	$244.88	$272.29	$297.39
Religion/Welfare Activities	$59.06	$65.01	$72.42	$76.92	$84.17
Private Education & Research	$61.01	$65.97	$71.94	$78.34	$85.57
Per Capita Consumption	$3155.52	$3372.32	$3658	$4002.19	$4338.01

INVESTMENTS 1970–1974

Investment	1960	1961	1962	1963	1964
Basic Yield, One-year Corporate Bonds	8.51	7.94	7.63	7.80	8.98
Short-term Interest Rates, 4–6 Months, Prime Commercial Paper	7.72	5.11	4.69	8.15	4.87
Basic Yield, Common Stocks, Total	3.83	3.14	2.84	3.06	4.47
Index of Common Stocks (194121943510)	83.22	98.29	109.20	107.43	82.85

COMMON STOCKS, CLOSING PRICE AND YIELD, FIRST BUSINESS DAY OF YEAR

(Parenthetical number is annual dividend in dollars)

Allis Chalmers	21 7/8	15 3/4	13	12 1/2	8 7/8
	(/)	(.05)	(.05)	(.20)	(.26)
American Brands	35 5/8	45 1/8	42 1/8	43	33 1/2
	(2)	(2.10)	(2.20)	(2.29)	(2.38)
AT&T	49 3/8	48 3/4	44 3/4	53 1/4	50
	(2.60)	(2.60)	(2.60)	(2.80)	(3.08)
Anaconda	30 3/4	21 1/8	16	19 3/4	27 3/4
	(1.90)	(1.90)	(/)	(.12)	(.50)
Bethlehem Steel	27 1/8	22 1/2	29 1/4	29 3/8	32 1/2
	(1.80)	(1.80)	(1.20)	(1.20)	(1.60)
CPC Intl (Name changed from Corn Products, 4/22/69)	32 3/8	33 5/8	32 5/8	32 1/2	26 3/4
	(1.70)	(1.70)	(1.70)	(1.77)	(1.86)
Delta Air Lines	30 3/4	33 1/2	48	66	39 7/8
	(.40)	(.50)	(.50)	(.50)	(.60)
General Electric (2 shares for 1, 4/29/71)	76 5/8	93 7/8	63	73 7/8	62 5/8
	(2.60)	(2.60)	(1.40)	(1.40)	(1.60)
General Motors	71 1/4	78 7/8	79 3/4	82 1/8	46
	(4.30)	(3.40)	(3.40)	(4.45)	(5.25)
International Business Machines	364 3/4	313	333	409	242 3/4
	(4)	(4.80)	(5.20)	(5.40)	(4.48)
Intl Harvester	26 1/8	27 1/2	29 3/4	38 3/4	26 3/4
	(1.80)	(1.80)	(1.40)	(1.40)	(1.50)
National Biscuit (Name changed to Nabisco 4/27/71)	49 3/4	52 1/4	57 7/8	60 7/8	37 1/2
	(2.20)	(2.20)	(2.20)	(2.30)	(2.30)
US Steel	34 3/4	32 1/4	30 1/2	31 1/8	37 1/4
	(2.40)	(2.40)	(1.60)	(1.60)	(1.60)
Western Union	44 1/4	40 1/2	44 5/8	48 5/8	14 3/8
	(1.40)	(1.40)	(1.40)	(1.40)	(1.40)

STANDARD JOBS 1970–1974

Job Type	1970	1971	1972	1973	1974
Domestic Industries	$7747/yr	$8255/yr	$8794/yr	$9326/yr	$10,017/yr
Private Industries, incl. farm labor	$7679/yr	$8144/yr	$8634/yr	$9154/yr	$9867/yr
Bituminous Coal Mining	$9790/yr	$10,331/yr	$11,323/yr	$12,335/yr	$13,580/yr
Building Trades	$9810/yr	$10,473/yr	$10,747/yr	$11,251/yr	$12,192/yr
Domestics	$3847/yr	$4159/yr	$4478/yr	$4833/yr	$5260/yr
Farm Labor	$3787/yr	$3783/yr	$3900/yr	$4391/yr	$4776/yr
Federal Civilian	$10,921/yr	$11,767/yr	$12,596/yr	$13,464/yr	$14,080/yr
Federal Employees, Executive Depts.	$8040/yr	$8995/yr	$10,331/yr	$11,003/yr	$12,446/yr
Federal Military	$6319/yr	$7139/yr	$8603/yr	$9070/yr	$9594/yr
Finance, Insurance, & Real Estate	$7823/yr	$8347/yr	$8861/yr	$9270/yr	$9853/yr
Gas, Electricity, & Sanitary Workers	$10,028/yr	$10,696/yr	$11,420/yr	$12,156/yr	$13,031/yr
Manufacturing, Durable Goods	$9810/yr	$10,473/yr	$10,747/yr	$11,251/yr	$12,192/yr
Manufacturing Nondurable Goods	$7691/yr	$8167/yr	$8636/yr	$9099/yr	$9925/yr
Medical/Health Services Workers	$6593/yr	$7043/yr	$7499/yr	$7980/yr	$8727/yr
Miscellaneous Manufacturing	$7097/yr	$7355/yr	$7800/yr	$8080/yr	$8679/yr
Motion Picture Services	$8359/yr	$8441/yr	$8882/yr	$9172/yr	$10,108/yr
Nonprofit Org. Workers	$5449/yr	$5924/yr	$6088/yr	$6645/yr	$7130/yr
Passenger Transportation Workers, Local and Highway	$6996/yr	$7309/yr	$7496/yr	$7973/yr	$8645/yr
Personal Services	$5636/yr	$5892/yr	$6268/yr	$7079/yr	$7459/yr
Public School Teachers	$8299/yr	$8813/yr	$9284/yr	$9774/yr	$10,249/yr
Radio Broadcasting & Television Workers	$10,712/yr	$10,885/yr	$11,575/yr	$12,168/yr	$12,779/yr
Railroads	$10,110/yr	$11,360/yr	$11,991/yr	$13,775/yr	$14,240/yr
State and Local Govt. Workers	$7894/yr	$8443/yr	$8898/yr	$9466/yr	$10,020/yr
Telephone & Telegraph Workers	$8512/yr	$9350/yr	$10,518/yr	$11,397/yr	$12,503/yr

FOOD BASKET 1970–1974

(NR=NOT REPORTED)

Commodity	Year	New York	Atlanta	Chicago	Denver	Los Angeles
Apples, Fresh, per pound	1970	25¢	22.40¢	20.20¢	NR	24.20¢
	1971	26.60¢	25.10¢	19.90¢	NR	NR
	1972	26.50¢	25¢	25.30¢	NR	28.40¢
	1973	32.10¢	31.30¢	31.70¢	NR	32.10¢
	1974	37.70¢	51.70¢	36.70¢	NR	39.60¢
Beans, Dried, per pound	1970	20.10¢	17.50¢	18.30¢	NR	21.70¢
	1971	22.60¢	18.30¢	19.40¢	NR	24.70¢
	1972	25.30¢	20.30¢	20.80¢	NR	29.20¢
	1973	32¢	30.30¢	29.70¢	NR	34¢
	1974	94¢	$1.02	50.30¢	NR	73.30¢
Beef, Rib Roasts, per pound	1970	$1.02	$1.19	$1.09	NR	$1.25
	1971	$1.70	$1.27	$1.11	NR	$1.27
	1972	$1.17	$1.39	$1.25	NR	$1.40
	1973	$1.41	$1.65	$1.42	NR	$1.65
	1974	$1.51	$1.85	$1.41	NR	$1.63
Beef, Steaks (Round), per pound	1970	$1.54	$1.32	$1.09	NR	$1.16
	1971	$1.64	$1.37	$1.14	NR	$1.21
	1972	$1.77	$1.49	$1.22	NR	$1.30
	1973	$2.02	$1.83	$1.49	NR	$1.58
	1974	$2.12	$1.89	$1.90	NR	$1.64
Bread, White, per pound	1970	28.50¢	22.90¢	24¢	NR	26.40¢
	1971	30.10¢	24.30¢	24.30¢	NR	26.80¢
	1972	30.30¢	24.10¢	24.60¢	NR	41.20¢
	1973	33.20¢	26.70¢	28.20¢	NR	28¢
	1974	40.90¢	32.70¢	35¢	NR	33.70¢

A 1972 advertisement for Wonder Bread appearing in Ebony Magazine. (via Flickr)

Commodity	Year	New York	Atlanta	Chicago	Denver	Los Angeles
Butter, per pound	1970	88.10¢	93¢	86.70¢	NR	87.20¢
	1971	90.10¢	93¢	87.30¢	NR	88¢
	1972	89.50¢	91.10¢	87.40¢	NR	87.90¢
	1973	93.30¢	98.20¢	93.90¢	NR	91.30¢
	1974	97¢	$1.02	93.50¢	NR	92.90¢
Cheese, per 8 ounces	1970	49.10¢	50.20¢	51.10¢	NR	53.20¢
	1971	58.40¢	52.50¢	55.10¢	NR	55.30¢
	1972	52.10¢	53.60¢	57.80¢	NR	57.90¢
	1973	58¢	61.30¢	63.70¢	NR	64.70¢
	1974	72.40¢	73.50¢	74.30¢	NR	77.10¢
Chickens, per pound	1970	46.40¢	38.90¢	39.90¢	NR	39.70¢
	1971	46.90¢	39.20¢	40.40¢	NR	39.20¢
	1972	46.40¢	41.10¢	40.60¢	68.30¢	40.50¢
	1973	63.40¢	58.70¢	59.50¢	NR	57.40¢
	1974	60.60¢	55.30¢	55.80¢	NR	52.70¢
Coffee, per pound	1970	91¢	93.80¢	94.10¢	NR	85.30¢
	1971	93¢	95.80¢	97.60¢	92.50¢	86.20¢
	1972	91.80¢	93.90¢	96.60¢	NR	86.10¢
	1973	$1.03	$1.01	$1.08	NR	98.3¢
	1974	$1.24	$1.22	$1.29	NR	$1.11
Eggs, per dozen	1970	66.80¢	61.40¢	60.70¢	NR	56.20¢
	1971	57.90¢	53.20¢	52.50¢	NR	46.80¢
	1972	57.10¢	52.80¢	51.50¢	NR	9.20¢
	1973	83.50¢	77¢	77.10¢	NR	77¢
	1974	85.60¢	78.30¢	81¢	NR	72.30¢
Flour, White, per pound	1970	11.78¢	12.76¢	11.10¢	NR	12.12¢
	1971	11.72¢	13.40¢	10.90¢	NR	12.46¢
	1972	11.26¢	13.42¢	10.94¢	NR	12.62¢
	1973	14.62¢	16.04¢	14.72¢	NR	15.24¢
	1974	20.06¢	21.64¢	20.74¢	NR	19.90¢
Lamb Chops, per pound	1970	$1.84	$1.46	$1.89	NR	$1.90
	1971	$1.92	$1.51	$1.93	NR	$1.94
	1972	$2.03	$1.69	$2.09	NR	$2.08
	1973	$2.29	$2.34	$2.30	NR	$2.25
	1974	$2.49	$2.56	$2.36	NR	$2.75
Margarine, per pound	1970	32.70¢	31.80¢	31.40¢	NR	29.50¢
	1971	37.40¢	35.50¢	34.60¢	NR	32.30¢
	1972	37¢	37.50¢	35.10¢	NR	33.10¢
	1973	41.50¢	39.30¢	37.70¢	NR	36.50¢
	1974	63.50¢	58.70¢	58.20¢	NR	55.10¢
Milk, Fresh, per quart	1970	35.60¢	32.85¢	34.95¢	NR	33.85¢
	1971	36.85¢	33.65¢	36.25¢	NR	35.05¢
	1972	37.05¢	34.40¢	37.10¢	NR	35.25¢
	1973	40.55¢	38.70¢	41.70¢	NR	36.95¢
	1974	41.80¢	44.95¢	39.20¢	NR	34.75¢
Pork, Bacon, Sliced, per pound	1970	$1.02	92.70¢	98.90¢	NR	88.70¢
	1971	92.40¢	78.60¢	83.10¢	NR	72.70¢
	1972	$1.02	97.70¢	$1.03	NR	88.20¢
	1973	$1.38	$1.34	$1.39	NR	$1.21
	1974	$1.41	$1.365	$1.37	NR	$1.21

Commodity	Year	New York	Atlanta	Chicago	Denver	Los Angeles
Pork, Chops, per pound	1970	$1.30	$1.17	$1.01	NR	$1.21
	1971	$1.25	$1.09	93.70¢	NR	$1.12
	1972	$1.40	$1.22	$1.11	NR	$1.32
	1973	$1.66	$1.56	$1.44	NR	$1.67
	1974	$1.67	$1.65	$1.59	NR	$1.69
Pork, Ham, Whole, per pound	1970	82.40¢	71.30¢	73¢	NR	78.20¢
	1971	79¢	67.40¢	65.10¢	NR	72.20¢
	1972	84.80¢	78.50¢	71.60¢	NR	78.40¢
	1973	$1.10	$1.02	94.20¢	NR	$1.08
	1974	$1.12	98.50¢	$1.16	NR	$1.08
Potatoes, Irish, per 10 pounds	1970	94.40¢	$1.09	$1.15	NR	$1.00
	1971	94.20¢	$1.14	$1.10	NR	91.60¢
	1972	99.90¢	$1.27	$1.20	NR	$1.04
	1973	$1.47	$1.65	$1.57	NR	$1.47
	1974	$1.76	$1.89	$2.05	NR	$1.72
Rice, per pound	1970	22.10¢	19.40¢	19.90¢	NR	24.40¢
	1971	23.70¢	20.40¢	19.80¢	NR	25.20¢
	1972	23.70¢	20.80¢	20.60¢	NR	24.70¢
	1973	30.40¢	27¢	29¢	NR	32.10¢
	1974	51.20¢	44.80¢	46.60¢	NR	55.90¢
Sugar, per pound	1970	13.48¢	12.84¢	13.02¢	NR	12.34¢
	1971	13.90¢	13.42¢	14.10¢	NR	13.10¢
	1972	14.08¢	13.92¢	14.40¢	NR	13.84¢
	1973	15.50¢	15.12¢	15.32¢	NR	14.74¢
	1974	33.60¢	33.18¢	32¢	NR	30.80¢
Tea, Bags, per package of 48	1970	60.80¢	66.50¢	62.30¢	NR	65.20¢
	1971	62¢	66.10¢	64.10¢	NR	64.60¢
	1972	60.80¢	66.70¢	64¢	NR	65.20¢
	1973	62.10¢	65.40¢	65.80¢	NR	64.80¢
	1974	66.80¢	71.40¢	73¢	NR	69.50¢
Veal, per pound	1970	$2.65	$2.00	$1.98	NR	$2.11
	1971	$2.88	$2.10	$2.19	NR	$2.26
	1972	$3.29	$2.28	$2.77	NR	$2.77
	1973	$3.90	NR	$2.94	NR	$3.1
	1974	$3.92	NR	$3.18	NR	$4.06

SELECTED PRICES 1970–1974

Item	Source	Description	Price
ALCOHOL			
Whiskey	*New York Times* (1970)	*Canadian Club whiskey;* C.C., Canada's best tasting initials; per fifth	$7.10

A 1974 advertisement for Jim Beam bourbon, featuring Bette Davis. (via Wikimedia Commons)

Item	Source	Description	Price
APPAREL, CHILDREN'S			
Dress	*New York Times* (1970)	*Pandora;* ruffly-edged coat dress with white collar	$13
Jacket and Knit Cap	*Sears, Roebuck* (1974)	NFL; authentic team emblem on the left front	$17.99
Pajamas	*Sears, Roebuck* (1974)	Perma-press knit; features irresistible characters screen printed on chest Tigger, Snoopy, and Woodstock Scooby-Doo	 $5.49 $5.99
Robe	*Sears, Roebuck* (1974)	Plaid-flannel robe	$8.99
Shoes	*New York Times* (1970)	*Penaljo* footwear for girls; ultra-comfortable walker	$19.95
Sweater	*New York Times* (1970)	*Justin Charles;* easy care Orlon acrylic sweater; monogram with three initials or first name	$7
APPAREL, MEN'S			
Belt	*Smithsonian* (1973)	*Austral Enterprisers;* braided calfskin; 1 1/2" wide, pliant, comfortable, hand-braided from sixteen strands of specially tanned calfskin	$12.50
Belt	*Sears, Roebuck* (1973)	*Buck suede;* lucite-plastic insert buckle mixes textures with buck suede	$7
Jacket	*Ebony* (1972)	*Smith House of Leather, leather;* colors include black, brown, red, and blue	$80
Jacket	*Sears, Roebuck* (1973)	Lightweight; stitch-trimmed western style in smooth-grain leather	$65
Pants	*Ebony* (1972)	*Jaymar,* hemmed slack is fashioned of 100% Trevira polyester in a rare range of colors	$22.50
Shirt	*Sears, Roebuck* (1973)	*Kings Road;* lightweight double-knit polyester stretch sports shirt with collar and placket	$7
Shoes	*Ebony* (1972)	*Flagg Brothers Outta Sight;* tan and brown leather wingtip lace-up; flared maxi heel	$16.99
Shoes	*Ebony* (1972)	*Navarro Brothers;* baby sharkskin slip-ons; benchmade by Mexico's finest shoemaker	$39.50
Shoes	*Smithsonian* (1973)	*Norm Thompson;* handcrafted moccasins from golden-tan deerskin for unbelievable comfort indoors or out	$15
Underwear	*Ebony* (1972)	*Kayser-Roth;* Paris zig-zag-colored boxer shorts; lily-white underwear was your Mother's idea	$4
Underwear	*Penthouse* (1973)	Imported Norwegian see-thru fish-net weave bikini briefs keep you cool in the summer, warm in the winter; 3 to a pack	$8.95
APPAREL, WOMEN'S			
Blouse	*Ebony* (1972)	*Frederick's of Hollywood;* a shirtmaker that goes from prim to pow; buttons to the chin; blue or pink nylon	$9
Body Suit	*Sears, Roebuck* (1973)	High band-neck with 6-button placket adds a great look to this figure-hugging rib-knit stretch nylon body suit; was $7.97	$4.77

Item	Source	Description	Price
Coat	*New York Times* (1970)	*Bergdorf Goodman;* fierce tiger fake with natural brown Australian opossum borders; a sash of real leather holds everything in place	$260
Coat	*The New York Times Magazine* (1971)	*John Meyer* velvet midi coat	$80
Dress	*New York Times* (1970)	*The Young Individualist;* black velvet overalls with satin work-shirt top; rhinestone buckles	$60
Dress	*The New York Times Magazine* (1971)	*Kay Windsor* dress; spirited knit, squared off with eye-catching accents; Dacron polyester double knit	$32
Jeans	*Sears, Roebuck* (1973)	Our lowest price in five years; corduroy	$4.88
Overcoat	*Ebony* (1972)	*Swank Shirt Shop;* jazz-age wrap, featuring 47" wool velour, cashmere hand wrap	$74.50
Pants	*Ms.* (1972)	*Lady Wrangler;* corduroy flares	$15
Pantsuit	*The New York Times Magazine* (1971)	*ENKA Pantsuit* made of Encron polyester by Adamo Knits; will never wrinkle or crush	$26
Shirt	*Sears, Roebuck* (1973)	For today's individualist; great ways to express yourself; be creative in versatile coordinates	$11
Shoes	*Sears, Roebuck* (1973)	Sandals; cross straps for comfort	$12.99
Shoes	*The New York Times Magazine* (1971)	*B. Altman & Company* offers suede shoes with an Oxford accent; made by Sandler of Boston	$17
Skirt	*The New York Times Magazine* (1971)	*Alberoy Tie-Back Boot-Topper;* birch, beet, and brick	$28
Skirt	*Ebony* (1972)	*Smith House of Leather,* leather; colors include blue, black, red, and burgundy	$19.00
Underwear	*Sears, Roebuck* (1973)	Brassiere and panties; suit-your-size; Antron nylon knit in yellow, green, and pink print on orange	$7

APPLIANCES

Item	Source	Description	Price
Air Cleaner	*The New York Times Magazine* (1971)	*General Electric Air Cleaner;* keeps dirt off your furniture and out of the air you breathe	$319.95
Chain Saw	*Southern Living* (1973)	*Remington Mighty Mite Bantam Chain Saw;* weighs just 6 1/2 pounds	$89.95
Microwave Oven	*New York Times* (1970)	*Radarange Microwave Oven;* cook cool with electronics; so quick that usual cooking time is reduced up to 75%	$450
Reading Light	*The New York Times Magazine* (1971)	*Love Lights* for your bed; each reader has his or her own light source	$45

BABY PRODUCTS

Item	Source	Description	Price
Bed-wetting Alarm	*Sears, Roebuck* (1973)	*Wee-alert Buzzer,* buzzer alarm helps keep sleeper dry and more comfortable by conditioning him to stop bedwetting	$19.95
Quilt	*The New York Times Magazine* (1971)	*Triboro Quilt* cuddles babies with a pram suit and comforter; with Disney characters	$5

Item	Source	Description	Price

BUSINESS EQUIPMENT AND SERVICES

Item	Source	Description	Price
Welding Torch	*Southern Living* (1973)	*Pyro Welding Torch kit;* produces 5000 degrees heat for welding, soldering and brazing	$24.88

COLLECTIBLES

Item	Source	Description	Price
Bowl	*Gourmet* (1973)	*Haviland & Co.;* Louis XV carette porcelain bowl	$33.50
Calendar	*Ms.* (1972)	*Reid & Reid Books;* Marilyn Monroe photo calendar, 1954; extremely rare	$10
Egg Box	*Gourmet* (1973)	*Georg Jensen;* sterling	$145
Painting	*Guinness Book of World Records* (1981)	Price paid in 1971 for painter Mary Cassatt's Summertime	$150,000
Paintings	*New York Times* (1970)	*Gimbels* magnificent collection of framed reproductions; Sunflower by Borg; walnut frame	$29.99
Plate	*New York Times* (1970)	*Franklin Mint;* annual Christmas collector's plate by Norman Rockwell; a sound investment	$100
Print	*Gourmet* (1973)	Nineteenth-century Chinese, on rice paper	$50
Sculpture	*Gourmet* (1973)	Cybis porcelain birds, limited edition, sold as a pair	$1,800
Sculpture	*Smithsonian* (1973)	Porcelain original; by conservationist Lowell Davis, 17 1/2" long, limited edition of 950 pieces	$1,000
Shop Box	*Gourmet* (1973)	Decoupage and lacquer	$75

ENTERTAINMENT

Item	Source	Description	Price
Antique Show	*Southern Living* (1973)	High Museum Antiques Show and Sale in Atlanta, Georgia; featuring furniture influenced by 17th and 18th century China	$2.50
Concert Ticket	*New York Times* (1973)	*Mostly Mozart;* Philharmonic Hall, Lincoln Center; all seats reserved	$4.50
Theater Ticket	*New York Times* (1971)	*Hair,* Monday—Thursday evenings Rear Mezzanine Front Mezzanine Orchestra	$5–$9 $11 $12
Theater Ticket	*New York Times* (1971)	*Oh! Calcutta!;* evenings	$5–$15
Theater Ticket	*New York Times* (1973)	American Shakespeare Theatre; Measure for Measure; The Country Wife; Macbeth Saturday Matinee; Saturday Evening; Sunday Matinee All Other Shows	$5.50 $8
Theater Ticket	*New York Times* (1973)	*Sportsmen's Show;* 2 Hollywood stars Children Adult General Admission	$0.75 $1.50

An advertising poster for the Spectrum Arena in Philadelphia, PA. The arena also housed a number of sporting events. The building was demolished in 2010. (via Wikimedia Commons)

Item	Source	Description	Price
ENTERTAINMENT, HOME			
Camera	*Life* (1972)	*Kodak* introduces the pocket camera; Just drop in the new little film cartridge and shoot.	$28
Camera	*Life* (1972)	*Polaroid's Focused Flash 400;* You can forget burnouts, you can forget blackouts	$70
Camera	*Life* (1971)	*Cannon Canonet QL 17;* this carry-it-anyplace camera gives you quick and precise rangefinder focus	$165
Camera	*Life* (1971)	*Polaroid's Square Shooter,* brings 60-second color pictures down to about the cost of shots you have developed at the factory	$35
Camera	*Popular Mechanics* (1972)	*Kodak Electric 8 Automatic Movie Camera;* no lens setting, an electric eye automatically adjusts the super-fast f/1.6 lens to the light.	$1,000
Camera	*Smithsonian* (1973)	*Kodak Pocket Instamatic 40;* an electronic shutter and CIS electric eye give you automatic exposure control	$68
Camera Outfit	*Ebony* (1972)	*Kodak Hawkeye Instamatic X;* includes camera, film, magicube, wrist strap, and instruction book	$22.95
Camera Outfit	*Smithsonian* (1973)	*Polaroid Minute Maker Kit;* contains everything you need to take instant pictures, including Square Shooter 2 camera, 2 Sylvania Blue Dot flashcubes, a pack of square color film, and a coupon for 3 free copies of a favorite instant picture	$36
Cassette Tapes	*Sears, Roebuck* (1974)	60-minute; 3 in package	$1.99
Projector	*Southern Living* (1973)	*Kodak Carousel Custom H Projector;* The slide projector that lives in the living room	$180
Radio	*New York Times* (1970)	*Hitachi Solid State AM/FM Radio;* works with batteries or AC; reduced from $79.99, now	$49.99
Record Album	*New York Times* (1970)	Simon & Garfunkel's *Bridge Over Troubled Water*	$5.98
Record Album	*New York Times* (1970)	Neil Young's *After the Gold Rush*	$4.98
Stereo	*Life* (1972)	*The Voice of Music;* This graduation gift is brought to you in glorious color by the class of '72; includes four speed, automatic changer; orange peel color, Model 346	$79.95
Television	*Ebony* (1972)	*Sears, Roebuck;* portable 19" screen; color with one-button tuning	$220
FOOD PRODUCTS			
Eggs	*Chicago Tribune* (1972)	*Sunnybrook;* fresh grade A	$0.39/dz
Pecans	*New York Times* (1970)	*Sunnyland Farms;* paper-shell pecans 5 lb. Box	$6.45
Shrimp	*Chicago Tribune* (1972)	Peeled and de-veined; 1 1/2 lb bag	$3.69
FURNITURE			
Buffet	*The New York Times Magazine* (1971)	*Bennington* solid pine antiqued Welch buffet	$429

Item	Source	Description	Price
Chair	*New York Times* (1970)	*Beach Hill Furniture;* Wendell open-arm chair, tufted seat in muslin	$425
Chair	*New York Times* (1970)	Bean bag chair; sold everywhere for $50 or more; full adult size	$29.99
Chest	*New York Times* (1970)	*Beacon Hill Furniture;* Harcourt chest; oriental design, lacquer finish	$525
Mattress	*The New York Times Magazine* (1971)	*Sealy Posturepedic Mattress;* your back has to last a long time Queen size, 2 piece set King size, 3 piece set	$399.95 $499.95
Table	*New York Times* (1970)	*Maurice Villency;* stainless steel tables; made any size with glass top; dining table 36" × 60" × 28" with 1/2" glass top	$418

GARDEN EQUIPMENT AND SUPPLIES

Item	Source	Description	Price
Flower	*Smithsonian* (1973)	African Amaryllis; pre-planted, exotic Amaryllis grows nearly an inch a day	$5.95
Hedge Trimmer	*Life* (1972)	*Disston* cordless electric lawn products; the lightweight way to save trimming time Heavy duty model	$59.99
Wheelbarrow	*The Updated Last Whole Earth Catalog* (1974)	For brick and tile; carries up to 120 bricks; made of rugged, seasoned hardwood	$34.95

HOTELS

Item	Source	Description	Price
Room Rate	*New York Times* (1970)	*Barbizon-Plaza Hotel,* 106 Central Park South, New York City; 24 hour operator attended elevators; choice doubles	$26 to $34
Room Rate	*New York Times* (1970)	*Sheraton Inn at LaGuardia;* free bus to/from LaGuardia Airport, free parking; singles, per night from	$22
Room Rate	*The New York Times Magazine* (1971)	*Downingtown Inn,* Downingtown, Pennsylvania; tour Penna Dutch Amish land; 3 days and 2 nights with gourmet meals; each	$60
Room Rate	*Southern Living* (1973)	*Del Webb's Hotel Sahara;* three days, two nights, two dinner shows; per person, double occupancy required	$43

HOUSEHOLD PRODUCTS

Item	Source	Description	Price
Blanket	*New York Times* (1970)	Thickly woven 100% virgin wool reversible animal design blanket from Peru	$22.50
Bundt Pan	*Sears, Roebuck* (1973)	Perfect for use with the Bundt-pan cake mixes; 12-cup colored aluminum Bundt pan with Teflon lining	$2.99
Capita Set	*Penthouse* (1973)	*Jose Cuervo;* hand-made, hand-painted potter tray	$2.50
China	*Gourmet* (1973)	*Royal Worchester;* teacup and saucer; Royal Garden porcelain set	$15
Cleanser	*Chicago Tribune* (1972)	*Janitor in a Drum;* industrial strength; 64 oz.	$0.99
Cocktail Shaker	*Gourmet* (1973)	*Reed & Barton;* sterling; milk-can design	$47
Coffee Set	*Gourmet* (1973)	*Gorham;* pewter; 3-piece set includes 40 oz coffee pot, creamer, and sugar bowl	$125
Cookware Set	*Sears, Roebuck* (1973)	*Corning Ware;* 9-piece; the newest pattern and shape in freezer-to-oven; save $9.31	$34.99

Item	Source	Description	Price
Detergent	*Chicago Tribune* (1972)	*Dove;* liquid; 22-oz bottle	$0.57

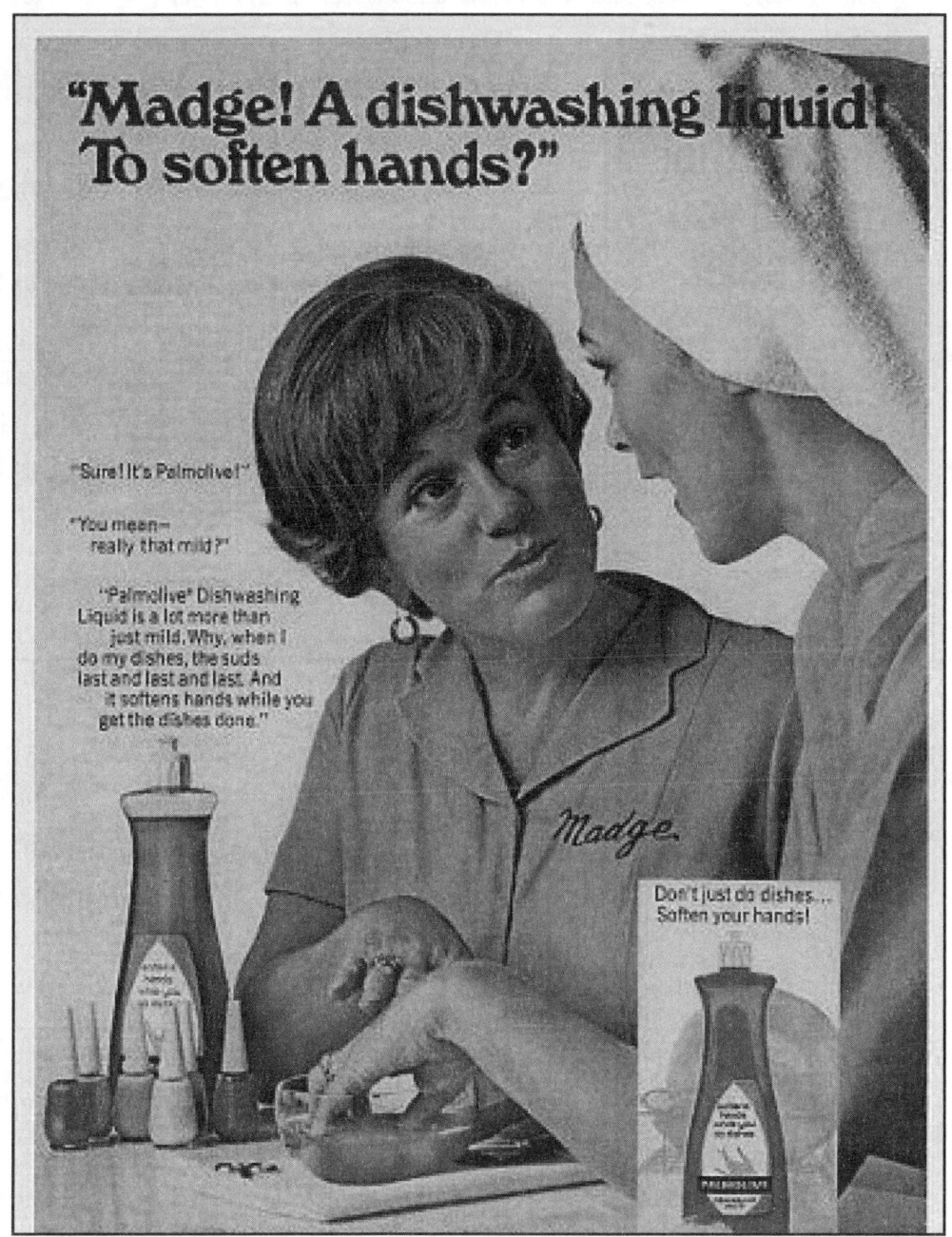

A Palmolive advertisement claiming that their dish detergent was safe and beneficial for hands. (via Wikimedia Commons)

Item	Source	Description	Price
Dish	*Gourmet* (1973)	*Bonniers Dansk;* porcelain; statement style, ovenproof	$18.50
Fabric Softener	*Chicago Tribune* (1972)	*Downy;* 64-oz bottle; with coupon in this ad	$0.99
Flatware	*Gourmet* (1973)	*Bergdorf Goodman;* stainless-steel Spectro style; 5-piece place setting	$10
Grill	*Gourmet* (1973)	Wrought iron; fish shaped	$12
Mattress and Box Spring	*Life* (1971)	*Sealy Posturepedic Sleep System;* queen-size mattress and posturepedic foundation	$249.95
Pasta Machine	*Gourmet* (1973)	*Bazaar De La Cuisine;* Italian chrome-plated machine	$30
Pepper Grinder	*Gourmet* (1973)	*Cartier;* 11" tall and handsome is our silver and mahogany pepper grinder	$35
Preserve Dish	*Gourmet* (1973)	*Wedgwood Queensware;* melon design	$20
Pressure Cooker	*Sears, Roebuck* (1973)	Non-electric; lets you cook complete meals in minutes and still keep food moist and flavorful	$18.99
Shoe Bag	*Gourmet* (1973)	*Louis Vuitton;* cotton bag	$8.50
Staple Gun	*Southern Living* (1973)	*Tru-Test Staple Gun* set; heavy-duty	$4.95
Valise	*Gourmet* (1973)	*Mark Cross;* canvas and leather	$175
Water Softener	*Sears, Roebuck* (1973)	Even at this low price, a manual water softener with up to 36,000 hardness-grain capacity	$99.95
Wok	*The Updated Last Whole Earth Catalog* (1974)	16" spun steel; one with a handy steel-ring base to sit on gas burners	$17.50

JEWELRY

Item	Source	Description	Price
Bracelet	*New York Times* (1970)	*Tiffany & Company;* wide link bracelet of 18 karat gold	$1400
Brooch	*Gourmet* (1973)	Yellow sapphire and diamond; one of a kind	$6,500
Jewel Case	*Gourmet* (1973)	*Gucci;* leather with yellow and red accents	$99
Pendant	*Life* (1971)	*Alva Museum;* dragon; gold electroplated facsimile	$6.50
Ring	*New York Times* (1970)	Beautifully styled dome ring; approximately 3 karats of matched diamonds; 18 karat gold setting	$975
Watch	*Life* (1972)	*Haverhill's;* Get a fine Swiss diver's watch	$9.95
Watch	*Penthouse* (1973)	*Rolling Stones;* wristwatch; Swiss made	$15.95

MEALS

Item	Source	Description	Price
Breakfast	*Chicago Tribune* (1972)	*Elliott's,* served all day	$0.95
Dinner	*Chicago Tribune* (1972)	*Magical Lamp of Aladdin;* imported turbot, sautéed with dainty mushrooms	$5.95
Dinner	*Chicago Tribune* (1972)	All you can eat; dessert included	$2.45
Dinner	*Gourmet* (1972)	*Coventry Forge Inn;* Coventryville, Pennsylvania; prix fixe	$12.50
Dinner	*Gourmet* (1973)	*Antolotti's,* New York, New York; table d'hôte	$8.25
Dinner	*Gourmet* (1973)	*Constantine's,* Mobile, Alabama; table d'hôte	$2.85
Dinner	*Gourmet* (1973)	*L'Etoile;* San Francisco; table d'hôte	$12
Dinner	*Gourmet* (1973)	*Alfio's La Trattoria;* Washington, D.C.; table d'hôte	$3.75

Item	Source	Description	Price
Meal	*Chicago Tribune* (1972)	*Sir Whoopee;* where a sandwich is a meal; chicken at 1/2 price with this coupon; 8 piece; regular price $2.40	$1.20

MEDICAL PRODUCTS AND SERVICES

Item	Source	Description	Price
Bed Pan	*Sears, Roebuck* (1973)	Hospital quality; contoured design for more comfortable and easier use	$4.98
Biofeedback Monitor Kit	*Smithsonian* (1973)	*Edmund Scientific Co.;* for greater relaxation, concentration, listen to your Alpha and Theta brain waves	$125.50
Cold Remedy	*Chicago Tribune* (1972)	*Neo-synephrine;* 1 oz drops; $1.06 value	$0.66
Eye Drops	*Chicago Tribune* (1972)	*Visine;* regular $1.33; for irritated eyes	$0.99
Nonprescription Drug	*Chicago Tribune* (1972)	*Bayer;* aspirin; manufacturer's list price $1.17; everyday low price; 100 tablets	$0.79
Nonprescription Drug	*Chicago Tribune* (1972)	*Excedrin;* 100 count; 1.69 value	$0.89
Weight Loss Tablets	*Sears, Roebuck* (1973)	*Naturama;* protein; to help you lose weight	$2.19
Wheelchair	*Sears, Roebuck* (1973)	Even at this low price a wheelchair with chrome-plated rims and handrims	$70

MOTORIZED VEHICLES, SUPPLIES AND SERVICES

Item	Source	Description	Price
Automobile	*Life* (1972)	*Renault 12 Sedan;* front wheel drive, front disc brakes, independent front suspension	$2,295
Automobile	*Life* (1971)	*Volkswagen;* 4-door sedan; a big car as good as a Volkswagen	$2,999
Automobile, Used	*Chicago Tribune* (1972)	*Cougar;* 1969 model	$2,998
Automobile, Used	*Chicago Tribune* (1972)	*Oldsmobile Sport Coupe;* 1970 model; Oldsmobile V-8; never buy before you try	$2,899
Automobile, Used	*New York Times* (1971)	*Oldsmobile Cutlass;* 1968 model; 4 dr; A/C, power steering, power brakes, alarm, excellent condition	$1,850
Automobile, Used	*New York Times* (1971)	*BMW 2002;* early 1970 production; white; 5,000 miles, showroom condition	$2,900
Automobile, Used	*New York Times* (1971)	Datsun; 1966 model; sedan; good condition	$475
Automobile, Used	*Chicago Tribune* (1972)	Ford Wagon; 1968 model; full-size ranch wagon with 6-cylinder automatic and power	$545
Tires	*The New York Times Magazine* (1971)	General Safety-Jet Tires for Volkswagen owners; radial; Each plus $1.74 Federal Excise Tax	$16.95

OTHER

Item	Source	Description	Price
Beekeeping Set	*The Last Walter T. Kelly's Complete Updated Whole Earth Catalog* (1974)	The necessary items that you need in starting with one hive of bees, including bees, necessary tools, and a book of instructions	$30
Bowhunter's License	*Southern Living* (1973)	Arkansas license fee for non-resident for bow hunting deer	$10
Cane	*Sears, Roebuck* (1973)	Pistol-grip; 1" thick maple shaft; walnut finish; 35"	$4.98

Item	Source	Description	Price
Center Punch	*Sears, Roebuck* (1973)	Craftsman; automatic; adjusts for light, heavy impression; steel; 5" long	$5.04
Christmas Tree	*Sears, Roebuck* (1974)	This Canadian pine is our best-selling 6' Christmas tree of all time; now reduced $6 to our lowest price ever	$29.95
Combination Square	*Sears, Roebuck* (1973)	Craftsman; hardened, ground-steel blade	$25.99
Dog Tag	*New York Times* (1970)	Silver plated dog bone shaped tag with animal's name, area code, phone number, city and state engraved	$7.50
Folding Chair	*Sears, Roebuck* (1973)	Aluminum-frame yacht chair	$11.65
Light	*Popular Mechanics* (1972)	Magna-Lite; shop light; put the light where it's needed; with magnet base	$6.95
Metal Detector	*Ebony* (1972)	Relco; finds buried gold, silver, and coins	$19.95
Potter's Wheel	*Smithsonian* (1973)	Gilbert's Potterycraft; create your own ceramics; seat and flywheel adjust for adults or teenagers	$55
Puppy	*New York Times* (1970)	American Kennels; The Dog Department Store; Yorkshire Terrier Lhasa Apso Pekingese Husky	$199 $249 $99 $150
Rule	*Sears, Roebuck* (1973)	Craftsman; stainless steel; chrome plated	$1.99
Rule	*Sears, Roebuck* (1973)	Stainless steel; not Craftsman; flexible, 6" long	$0.89
Sander	*Popular Mechanics* (1972)	Millers Falls; 12 times faster than hand sanding	$34.95
Saw	*Sears, Roebuck* (1973)	9" saw; manual brake for stopping blade quickly; performs the same operations as our 12" saw on a smaller scale	$164
Saw	*Popular Mechanics* (1972)	Dremel Model 572; in one compact, portable unit you have a jig saw, disc sander, buffing wheel, bench grinder, and a flexible shaft machine	$49.95
Slide Rule	*Popular Mechanics* (1972)	4"; non-warp with 2-color scales on white nitrate face	$2.95
Tool Set	*Popular Mechanics* (1972)	Craftsman; 59-piece set; regular separate prices total $69.95; all tools fit in 18" × 8" × 9" steel toolbox	$39.99
Tropical Fish Motor	*Life* (1971)	Dynaflo; never change aquarium water filter	$13.50
Weight Loss Pants	*Life* (1971)	Sauna Belt; the amazing space-age slenderizer that is so sensationally effective	$13.50

PERSONAL CARE PRODUCTS

Item	Source	Description	Price
Bath Oil	*Chicago Tribune* (1972)	Calgon Bath Oil Beads; 16-oz package	$0.98
Condoms	*Penthouse* (1973)	*Trojan;* made so thin, they're ultra-sensitive; special sampler includes 9 condoms	$3
Deodorant	*Chicago Tribune* (1972)	*Ban Roll-On;* 1 1/2-oz size; save $0.50; limit 1	$0.49
Hair Spray	*Chicago Tribune* (1972)	*Adorn Hard to Hold;* regular or unscented; 13 oz; $2.35 value	$1.09

Item	Source	Description	Price
Hair Treatment	*Ebony* (1972)	*LaCade Hormone Hair Growth Treatment;* with vitamins A and D	$3
Hair Treatment	*Ebony* (1972)	Murray's Natural Sheen	$1
Hair Treatment	*Ebony* (1972)	*Drake Persulan Blow-Out Creme;* make Afro twice as big	$2.25
Skin Cream	*Ebony* (1972)	*Bleach and Glow;* does beautiful things for your skin	$1.50
Soap	*Penthouse* (1973)	*English Leather Shower Soap;* our soap on a rope is tied to a great tradition	$2
Soap	*Chicago Tribune* (1972)	*Lifebuoy;* $0.07 off label; bath size	$0.40/2
Wig	*Ebony* (1972)	*Valmor High Fashion;* soul wig, hand styled; 100% human hair	$29.99
Wig	*Ebony* (1972)	*Valmor High Fashion;* Afro-American natural wig	$9.99

PUBLICATIONS

Item	Source	Description	Price
Book	*New York Times* (1970)	*A White House Diary* by Lady Bird Johnson; published by Holt, Rinehart and Winston, 806 pages	$10.95
Book	*New York Times* (1970)	*The Supreme Commander: The War Years of General Dwight D. Eisenhower* by Stephen E. Ambrose; published by Doubleday; 732 pages	$10.00
Book	*New York Times* (1970)	*Lawn Beauty the Organic Way* by Glenn Johns; Rodale Press books	$6.95
Book	*New York Times* (1973)	*Breakfast of Champions,* by Kurt Vonnegut, Jr.	$7.95

The first edition, 1973 cover of Kurt Vonnegut's Breakfast of Champions. The book spent 56 total weeks on the New York Times Bestseller List, though Vonnegut himself was disappointed with the novel, grading it a "c." (via Wikipedia)

Item	Source	Description	Price
Book	*New York Times* (1973)	*Once Is Not Enough*, Jacqueline Susann	$7.95
Book	*New York Times* (1973)	*The Joy of Sex*	$12.95
Book with Cassette	*Sears, Roebuck* (1974)	You'll be enchanted when you pop in a cassette and hear a fairy tale dramatized complete with music and voices; fourteen-page story book follows the action; has full-color illustrations	$1.79
Magazine	*Ebony* (1972)	*Ebony* magazine; Johnson Publishing Co.; monthly	$0.75
Magazine	*Gourmet* (1973)	*Gourmet;* monthly	$0.50
Magazine	*Penthouse* (1973)	*Penthouse;* monthly	$1
Magazine	*Smithsonian* (1973)	*Smithsonian;* monthly	$1

REAL ESTATE

Item	Source	Description	Price
Apartment	*New York Times* (1971)	For rent; 80s and Madison; a skyline view East and South; 2 bedrooms, 2 baths; year-round pool, doorman, security system; 16 months sublet or possible new lease	$680/mo
Apartment	*New York Times* (1971)	For rent; renovated brownstone; 2 bedrooms; large living room; working fireplace; A/C; all electric heat	$475/mo
House	*New York Times* (1971)	For sale; 2-bedroom ranch; double garage; 1 1/2 baths screened patio with triple-Hollywood pool; 1/2 acre beautifully landscaped; immaculate	$38,000
House	*New York Times* (1971)	For sale; must sell magnificent 7-room, 2 1/2-bath colonial; professionally landscaped and decorated;heated concrete pool, cabana and many extras; sacrifice	$55,500
House	*Chicago Tribune* (1972)	For sale; ranch style triplex in Florida; good income from three 2-bedroom apartments	$25,500
Hunting and	*New York Times* (1973)	For sale; 440 acres with 50 acre private lake near Fishing Lodge, Minocqua, Wisconsin; year-round lodge with two guest houses plus garage and out-camp hunting table	$75,000

SPORTS EQUIPMENT

Item	Source	Description	Price
Archery Set	*Sears, Roebuck* (1974)	Bear Target; includes bow, arrows, quiver, and target	$28.95
Basketball	*Sears, Roebuck* (1974)	Our lowest price this season for any basketball	$4.98
Basketball Goal	*Sears, Roebuck* (1974)	Portable; so stable, rebound action matches most permanent goals	$99.90
Binoculars	*New York Times* (1970)	Quazar 2000 Binocular; made in West Germany; weighs a mere 18 1/2 ounces	$149.95
Life Vest	*Sears, Roebuck* (1973)	Meets USCG specifications; adult ski vests	$20.59
Striking Bag Set	*Sears, Roebuck* (1974)	Wall mount; help develop your body while you sharpen timing, reflexes and coordination	$34.95
Tent	*Sears, Roebuck* (1973)	Pitches anywhere; even on solid rock or sand because it needs no stakes, and its frame anchors to tent, not in ground; plus tent fly adds additional protection from rain	$89

Item	Source	Description	Price
Tent	*Sears, Roebuck* (1973)	Two-man nylon pack; 5' × 7' sleeping area; tent with nylon case	$29.99
Weight Bench	*Sears, Roebuck* (1973)	500-lb capacity; adjustable back and adjustable barbell arms	$3,5.87

TELEPHONE EQUIPMENT AND SERVICES

Item	Source	Description	Price
Telephone	*Popular Mechanics* (1972)	Western Electric; late-model dial phone same as used by all the telephone companies; cost $40 new	$6.95

TOBACCO PRODUCTS

Item	Source	Description	Price
Cigarette Box	*Gourmet* (1973)	Bergdorf Goodman; ceramic	$12
Cigarette Lighter	*New York Times* (1970)	A great little lighter with a big difference; works on butane fuel, ignites electronically, never needs flints; gold tone metal case	$30
Pipe	*Popular Mechanics* (1972)	Kirsten; patented radiator stem means cool smoking	$3.95
Pipe	*Penthouse* (1973)	Kaywoodie; custom-crafted smoking pipe; new relief grain; custom cut	$3.95
Tobacco	*Life* (1971)	Laredo; menthol filter blend cigarette tobacco; smoke the freshest menthol filter cigarettes ever for less than $0.20 a pack	$1

TOYS

Item	Source	Description	Price
Baby Doll	*Sears, Roebuck* (1974)	Tenerella; cut $2; this lovely 19" doll has long, dark, rooted hair, sparkling go-to-sleep-eyes and smooth vinyl skin	$12.99
Buggy Kit	*Sears, Roebuck* (1974)	Assemble your own collection of NFL buggies; an officially licensed NFL product	$5
Coloring Book	*Chicago Tribune* (1972)	Regularly $0.29	$0.10
Doll	*Sears, Roebuck* (1974)	Rub-A-Dub Dolly; 17"; wash her, dry her, then bundle her up after the bath	$8.94
Doll	*Sears, Roebuck* (1974)	Smokey the Bear; acrylic pile and blue denim	$4.94
Doll Clothes	*Sears, Roebuck* (1974)	2-piece hand-knit outfits for 12"–18" baby dolls	$3.49
Race Track	*Popular Mechanics* (1962)	*Aurora;* who would prefer a pokey loco going around in circles to the pulse-pounding action of a road race; includes land-changing crisscross layout	$21.98
Stuffed Animal	*Sears, Roebuck* (1974)	*Fashionable Friends;* cotton felt animal with pert cotton-print dresses and bonnets	$3.47
Toy Set	*Sears, Roebuck* (1974)	Get an entire wagonload of 5 of our all-time favorite toys, and we'll include the red wagon for just $1 more; here's what you get: Bugs Bunny toothbrush; 40-piece medical kit; all-steel cash register; 10-piece nesting blocks; talking telephone	$21.78
Walkie-Talkie	*Sears, Roebuck* (1974)	Pocket-size; keeps you in voice contact with your fellow secret agents	$19.99

Item	Source	Description	Price
TRAVEL AND TRANSPORTATION			
Air Fare	*The New York Times Magazine* (1971)	New York to Aruba on KLM or American Airlines; one way	$89.50
Airfare	*New York Times* (1973)	*American Airlines;* California and the West round-trip; purchase only 7 days in advance; regular coach fare $336; you save $156.05	$179.95
Airfare	*Smithsonian* (1973)	*American Airlines;* roundtrip group airfare from California to Sydney, Australia; includes 10-day lodging and Hertz Ford Falcon rental car with 500 free miles	$683
Bus Ticket	*Ebony* (1972)	*Greyhound Ameripass;* good for 60 days of almost limitless travel; a new way to see more of America on $2.50 a day	$149.50
Cruise	*Smithsonian* (1973)	*Orient Overseas Services;* 4-month cruise to Acapulco, Panama Canal, Rio de Janeiro, Santos, Buenos Aires, Cape Town, Durban, Lourenco Marques, Singapore, Hong Kong, Kaohsiung, Kobe, Vancouver, San Francisco; up to 40 days in port	$3,105
European Tour	*Southern Living* (1973)	Icelandic; one-week car tour, per person, from New York, features roundtrip jet to Luxembourg and self-drive car with unlimited mileage	$250
Hawaiian Tour	*Southern Living* (1973)	Braniff International makes it easy for you to spend seven days and six nights discovering Hawaii; includes accommodations at The Outrigger Surf or Outrigger West hotel in Waikiki; all transfers between airport and hotel; a city tour of Honolulu; from Kansas City, per person	$356.31
Sponge Diving Tour	*Southern Living* (1973)	25-minute trip on Anclote River, Tarpon Springs, Florida, where a diver will demonstrate the technique of sponge diving and bring up live sponges Adults Children	 $1.50 $.75
Safari	*Smithsonian* (1973)	East Africa; in-depth viewing of abundant, various wildlife concentrations in famous national parks and reserves of Kenya and Tanzania	$1,519
Trip	*Chicago Tribune* (1972)	*Cartan Travel;* Hawaii; lovely enchanting islands; enjoy 4 islands, top hotels, great sightseeing entertainment, 9 days in outer islands; 5 days in Honolulu, Waikiki Beach	$575
Trip	*Chicago Tribune* (1972)	*VIP Travel Service;* Las Vegas; 3 nights, 4 days; strip hotel	$149
Trip	*Chicago Tribune* (1972)	*Mr. Travel;* San Francisco, Los Angeles, Las Vegas; two weeks; jet to all three	$289

MISCELLANY 1970–1974

The Mafia Sells

Mafia business is not precisely booming these days, but business about the Mafia has never been better. There are nearly 1,000,000 Godfather hard covers in print, and over 10 million paperbacks. Jimmy Breslin's best-selling comic novel That Gang Couldn't Shoot Straight—said to be a take-off of the chaotic exploits of Brooklyn's Gallo gang—was recently reincarnated as a movie. Gay Talese's Honor Thy Father, a detailed and understanding portrait of the son of Mafia Boss Joseph Bonanno, has been on the bestseller lists for four months, and recently brought a beefy $451,000 for paperback rights.

Time, February 26, 1965

U.S. Compensating Kin of Raid Dead; Cambodians in Town Hit by Error Will Get $400 Each

The United States made formal restitution to Cambodia today for an accidental American air raid Aug. 6 against the Mekong River town of Neak Luong in which 137 civilians and Cambodian Government soldiers were killed and 282 wounded.

Under an agreement signed today by the Cambodian and American Governments, the United States will pay surviving relatives of each of the dead the equivalent of about $400.

Time, March 12, 1965

Divorced

By Mary Costa, 36, blonde and beautiful lyric soprano, who left a $150,000-a-year job as TV's Chrysler girl for an opera career, making her widely acclaimed 1964 Metropolitan debut as Violetta in La Traviata; Frank Tashlin, 53, Hollywood writer director of slapstick comedies (The Man from the Diners' Club); on grounds of cruelty; after twelve years of marriage, no children; in Santa Monica, Calif.

New York Times, August 23, 1973

The Aging American Indian

The indicators of Indian suffering are appalling. Their life expectancy is 44 years, compared with 71 for white Americans. The average income for each Indian family living on a reservation—and more than half do—is only $1,500. The average years of schooling is 5.5, well behind that of both the black and Mexican American. Some officials rate 90% of reservation housing as substandard. Unemployment ranges from a low of 20% on the more affluent reservations to 80% on the poorest. The birthrate of Indians is 2 1/2 times that of whites—a majority of Indians are under 20 years old. The average family has to carry water for its daily needs at least a mile. It is usually done afoot.

Time, February 9, 1970

Price Panel Okays Bra Price Stretch

The Price Commission granted Warmaco Inc. permission Monday to lift prices on brassieres and girdles.

As the Price Commission put it, the company will be permitted to raise prices on the following items by the stated maximum amount: Bras-fiber, filler, 12 percent; bras, soft cup, 10 percent; bras, Love Touch, 7.5 percent; bras, Love Lace, 7.5 percent; coresellettes, 4.8 percent; and girdles, controlled 9 percent.

In another case, the commission approved requested price increases by Diamond International on toothpicks, clothes pins, and wooden ice cream sticks. The request ranged from 2.95 percent to 5.02 percent.

Atlanta Constitution, February 15, 1972

$5.50 Kit Tells If You're Pregnant

Mrs. Earl Callan's menstrual period was eight days overdue. The Toronto, Ontario, housewife decided to wait no longer to determine if she was pregnant. As she completed the family shopping for the day, she stopped in the neighborhood drugstore and picked up a three-inch square paper box bearing the brand name of Confidelle. She paid $5.50 for it and hurried home.

Atlanta Constitution, February 17, 1972

MISCELLANY 1970–1974

PBA Plans a Job Action to Gain Pay Raise

In his brief news conference yesterday, Mr. Kiernan said that patrolmen were not satisfied with the money among other things in the rejected contract. The proposed increases would have raised the salaries of patrolmen $2,150 between Jan. 1, 1971, and Jan. 1, 1973, when the final $750 increase would have gone into effect. Thus, their pay would have gone from the present $12,150 to $14,308.

Various other benefits, such as night differential, paid holidays, uniform allowance, annuity fund payments, medical plan costs and city contributions to the PBA health and welfare fund, according to the PBA's computations, would have raised the annual wage and benefits of a patrolman to $16,894 as of Jan. 1, 1973.

Mr. Kiernan said that the delegates, representing the city's 27,000 patrolmen, had decided also to start a public relations program to tell people of the city why policemen should be paid more than firefighters and sanitation men.

New York Times, June 7, 1972

Gold Price Rises to a Record of $62.37; A Commercial Shortage Brings Heavy Buying in Long Market

A new gold rush prompted by a commercial shortage of the metal shot its price to new peaks today in Europe's free markets.

The flow of buying orders swept the price to a record closing level of $62.37 an ounce in London. This was more than $24 above the official United States price for monetary gold. The previous closing high was yesterday at $59.55.

The picture was much the same in Zurich, Switzerland, the other major trading center. Gold rose to $62.25 an ounce in Zurich, before it closed at $62. The previous recording in Switzerland just topped the $60 mark on May 31.

In Frankfurt active buying pushed the price to a record of $59.22, compared with the previous high of $58.49 last Friday, dealers said. In France, where the market is controlled the price was a more modest $58.16, up from $57.19 yesterday.

New York Times, June 7, 1972

HISTORICAL SNAPSHOT
1975–1979

1975

- First desktop microcomputer available
- Pet rocks go on sale, featuring obedience, loyalty, and low maintenance costs
- Unemployment hits 9.2%
- Minnesota first state to require businesses, restaurants, and institutions to establish no-smoking areas
- New York City averts bankruptcy with $2.3 billion federal loan
- Beef consumption falls 9%; chicken consumption rises nearly 35%
- McDonald's opens its first drive-thru restaurants
- Time-sharing of vacation real estate introduced in the United States
- Record 120,000 Americans declare personal bankruptcy

1976

- Jimmy Carter elected president
- Cuisinart home food processor introduced
- $68 million football stadium opens in East Rutherford, NJ
- Colossus Cave, first computer game, designed at Princeton
- 3,420 lobbyists registered in Washington, DC
- Congress passes law to admit women in military academies
- ABC offers industry's first $1 million per-year contract, to Barbara Walters of NBC
- Clothier Abercrombie & Fitch declares bankruptcy
- 100 companies sponsor 76% of network TV ads

- Mobil Petroleum buys Montgomery Ward for $1 billion

1977

- Balloon angioplasty developed for reopening diseased arteries of the heart
- United States and Canada sign pact to build gas pipeline from Alaska to Midwest
- 1.9 million women operate businesses
- 20,000 shopping malls generate 50% of total retail sales
- Pepsi tops Coca-Cola in sales for first time
- Three major networks control 91% of prime-time audience
- American Express becomes first service company to top $1 billion in sales

1978

- Airline Deregulation Act eliminates federal controls on fares and routes
- California voters adopt Proposition 13 to control property taxes
- Gold sells for $245 per ounce
- Tax code permits 401(k) savings plans for first time
- 8 airlines control 81% of domestic market
- 26 major-league baseball teams show average profit of $4,526
- PepsiCo acquires Mexican fast-food chain Taco Bell
- President Carter signs legislation raising the mandatory retirement age to 70
- Unemployment rises to 6 percent
- First class postal rate goes to 15 cents per ounce

1979

- New York City's Citicorp Building completed
- Multiple-mirror telescope installed at Mount Hopkins in Arizona
- Sony Walkman, a portable tape player with headphones, is introduced
- Gold sells for more than $400 per ounce
- First Jiffy Lube fast oil-change automotive service center opens
- Avon products acquires Tiffany & Co.
- Ford Motor Co. acquires 25% of Japan's Mazda Motor Co.
- The second oil crisis occurs due to the Iranian Revolution
- Three-Mile Island near meltdown arouses antinuclear forces
- Inflation worst in 33 years; prices increase over 13.3%
- Prime lending rate at banks hits 14.5%

535

A line of automobiles at a gas station in Maryland, June 1979. The 1979 oil crisis occurred due to decreased oil output in the wake of the Iranian Revolution. This was the second oil crisis the United States experienced, the first in 1973. Though the second crisis was not as severe as the first, it led to widespread panic and long lines at the gas station for the American people. Gas prices did not return to pre-crisis amounts until the mid-1980s. (via Library of Congress)

SELECTED INCOME 1975–1979

Job	Source	Description	Pay
Account Executive	*Chicago Tribune* (1978)	Prefer college degree and background in teaching, sales or management	$15,000/yr to start
Accountant	*Los Angeles Times* (1978)	Min 2 yrs experience in general accounting; diversified corporation in sales and distribution	$18,000/yr
Accountant	*Los Angeles Times* (1978)	Semi-sr to strong srs, audit and heavy tax positions; permanent with small to "BIG 8" firms	$30,000/yr
Accounting Clerk	*Los Angeles Times* (1978)	Accounting personnel service	$900/mo
Actor	*Guinness Book of World Records* (1981)	Per single episode fee paid to Peter Falk for his role in the television show *Columbo* [1976]	$350,000
Administrator	*New York Times* (1977)	Children's theater association	$13,000/yr
Author	*Guinness Book of World Records* (1981)	Advance paid by Bantam Books to Judith Krantz for Princess Daisy	$3.2 million
Baseball Player	*USA Today Sports Weekly* (2004)	Salary of Minnesota Twins baseball player Rod Carew in 1978	$150,000

Carew with the Minnesota Twins warming up before a game in Cleveland in 1975. Carew was an 18 times All-Star and his number (29) is retired for both the Minnesota Twins and the Los Angeles Angels. (via Wikimedia Commons)

Job	Source	Description	Pay
Baseball Player	*New York Times* (2004)	1975 annual salary of relief pitcher Tug McGraw, Philadelphia Phillies	$75,000
Bookkeeper	*Los Angeles Times* (1978)	Full charge; CPA office	$18,000/yr
Bowler	*Guinness Book of World Records* (1981)	Earnings of professional bowler Mark Roth [1978]	$134,500
Bowling-alley Trainees	*Los Angeles Times* (1978)	Desk sales	$184/wk
Business Executive	*Guinness Book of World Records* (1981)	Salary, bonus, stock and other benefits paid to David Tendler of Engelhard Minerals and Chemical Corp. and President of Philipps Brothers trading division [In 1979]	$2,202,938
Business Manager	*Los Angeles Times* (1978)	Multimember university medical practice; billing and organization experience necessary	$18,000/yr
Cashier (Restaurant)	*New York Times* (1977)	Nights, 5–6 days	$3.50/hr
Chef	*Los Angeles Times* (1978)	Seafood	$1,500/mo
Executive Secretary	*Los Angeles Times* (1978)	Fast notes or light shorthand; one person only in busy sales firm	$1,200/mo
Football Player	*The State Newspaper* Columbia, SC (2004)	Payment in 1978 to each member of the Dallas Football team for winning the Super Bowl	$18,000
Golfer	*Guinness Book of World Records* (1981)	Earnings of professional golfer Nancy Lopez [In 1979]	$197,488
Industrial Engineer	*Chicago Tribune* (1978)	National consulting firm, enjoying 20 years of continuing growth, has opening for qualified engineer for consulting assignments involving full range of industrial-engineering disciplines	$22,000–$25,000/yr to start
Keypunch Operator	*New York Times* (1978)	3742 or Key Disc; minimum one year's experience; 35 hours, 5 days a week; per week	$130 to $180
Nobel Prize Award (1979)	*Guinness Book of World Records* (1981)	Amount paid to each of the 1979 Nobel Prize winners in Physics, Chemistry, Medicine and Physiology, Literature, Peace and Economics	$192,775
Programmer/Analyst	*Chicago Tribune* (1978)	Do you know or want to learn any of the following applications: IMS, MRP, CICS, MVS, IOMS, VSAM, DB/DC, A/R, or A/P?	$1,450–$2,100/mo
Race Car Driver	*Guinness Book of World Records* (1981)	Earnings of NASCAR driver Richard Petty [In 1979]	$531,292
Receptionist	*New York Times* (1977)	Exciting Sportswear designer anxious to hire outward individual	$170–$190/wk
Receptionist	*Los Angeles Times* (1978)	Greet clients, handle phones; a variety of public contact and general office duties for top law firm	$850/mo
Research Coordinator	*New York Times* (1977)	Well-known Fifth Avenue firm seeks sharp, personal individual to act as coordinator in research effort	$12,800/yr
Respiratory Therapist	*Los Angeles Times* (1978)	2-year graduate or CRTT	$944/mo

Job	Source	Description	Pay
Rodeo Cowboy	*Kristine Fredriksson, American Rodeo* (1985)	Annual winnings of Tom Ferguson in 1976	$114,000
Sales	*Chicago Tribune* (1978)	Art sales; long term security; fast advancement; no experience necessary	$800/wk, plus commission
Sales	*Chicago Tribune* (1978)	Dialysis equipment	$22,000–$24,000/yr
Secretary	*New York Times* (1978)	Gal/Guy Friday; Executive Secretary for health management company; per year	$10,000 to $12,000
Secretary	*Chicago Tribune* (1978)	Fantastic world-famous ad agent will train you to work with him on million-dollar account	$13,000/yr
Secretary/Clerk	*New York Times* (1977)	2 days wkly, Tuesday & Thursday	$5/hr
Social Secretary	*Chicago Tribune* (1978)	Secretary will receive telephone messages and correspondence for employer	$175/wk
Stunt Man	*Guinness Book of World Records* (1981)	Fee paid to Dar Robinson for a 1,100-foot-high leap off the CN Tower in Toronto for the movie *High Point* [In 1979]	$100,000
Tennis Player	*Guinness Book of World Records* (1981)	Earnings of professional tennis player Martina Navratilova [In 1979]	$747,548
Wine Consultant	*Chicago Tribune* (1978)	Immediate openings with PIEROTH, a 371-year old internationally known German winery. Ours is an exclusive guaranteed-high-quality product.	$25,000/yr

CONSUMER EXPENDITURES 1975–1979

Expenditure Type	1975	1976	1977	1978	1979
Clothing	$279.66	$300.41	$326.01	$359.86	$377.68
Food	$1011.70	$1082.39	$1161.92	$1259.09	$1390.33
Auto Usage	$550.53	$654.02	$748.73	$808.68	$885.12
New Auto Purchase	$135.67	$175.20	$201.59	$217.89	$219.06
Auto Parts	$47.69	$52.29	$58.57	$60.65	$63.98
Gas & Oil	$183.82	$197.22	$212.95	$225.08	$294.15
Housing	$680.64	$740.71	$815.02	$906.17	$1006.86
Furniture	$59.27	$64.67	$74.76	$80.87	$90.20
Utilities	$196.32	$222.89	$251.54	$274.95	$309.26
Telephone & Telegraph	$81.95	$90.81	$97.62	$107.37	$114.19
Physicians	$108.81	$118.33	$134.39	$146.01	$163.52
Dentists	$37.97	$42.65	$46.77	$50.77	$54.65
Health Insurance	$30.56	$32.10	$42.68	$53.46	$55.09
Personal Business	$245.40	$273.81	$300.13	$359.41	$397.68
Personal Care	$77.32	$83.47	$93.99	$103.33	$111.53
Tobacco	$69.92	$77.05	$77.19	$82.22	$85.31
Local Transport	$18.52	$20.18	$21.79	$21.56	$21.33
Intercity Transport	$33.80	$39.44	$44.95	$49.87	$58.21
Recreation	$331.53	$328.28	$392.30	$435.79	$487.44
Religion/Welfare Activities	$91.22	$102.28	$112.60	$132.53	$148.85
Private Education & Research	$94.92	$102.74	$108.97	$119.95	$132.41
Per-Capita Consumption	$4745.50	$5242.74	$5773.33	$6384.98	$7036.95

540

INVESTMENTS 1975–1979

Investment	1960	1961	1962	1963	1964
Basic Yield, One-Year Corporate Bonds	9.57	9.01	8.43	9.07	10.12
Short-Term Interest Rates, 4–6 Months, Prime Commercial Paper	6.33	5.35	5.60	7.99	10.91
Basic Yield, Common Stocks, Total	4.31	3.77	4.56	5.28	5.46
Index of Common Stocks (194121943 5 10)	85.17	102.01	98.18	96.11	107.94

COMMON STOCKS, CLOSING PRICE AND YIELD, FIRST BUSINESS DAY OF YEAR

(Parenthetical number is annual dividend in dollars)

Investment	1960	1961	1962	1963	1964
Allis Chalmers	6 3/4	12 1/8	26 1/2	24 3/4	29 5/8
	(.26)	(.40)	(.90)	(.60)	(1.70)
American Brands	31 1/2	38 3/4	45 1/4	42 1/2	50 3/8
	(2.56)	(2.68)	(2.80)	(3.04)	(4)
Anaconda	14 1/2	(1)	17 1/8	30	
(Merged as wholly owned subsidiary of Atlantic Richfield, 1/12/77)		(.60)	(.60)		
Bethlehem Steel	24 7/8	33 1/2	39 7/8	20 3/8	19 7/8
	(4)	(2)	(2)	(1)	(1)
CPC Intl	33	43	46 7/8	45 3/4	49 1/2
	(2)	(2.14)	(2.30)	(2.50)	(2.70)
Delta Airlines	29 1/8	37 5/8	39 1/4	39 1/8	42
	(.60)	(.60)	(.70)	(.70)	(1)
General Electric	33 3/4	46 5/8	55 3/8	48 3/4	47
	(1.60)	(1.60)	(1.80)	(2.20)	(2.60)
General Motors	31 7/8	58 3/8	78	61 1/2	55
	(3.40)	(2.40)	(5.55)	(6.80)	(6)
IBM	168 7/8	226 1/2	276 1/2	268 3/4	303 1/2
(5 shares for 4 split, 5/10/73)	(6)	(7)	(9)	(11.52)	(13.76)
(4 shares for 1 split, 5/31/79)	364 3/4	313	333	409	242 3/4
Intl Harvester	20 1/4	23 1/8	32 7/8	29 5/8	36 7/8
	(1.70)	(1.70)	(1.85)	(2.10)	(2.30)
Nabisco	22 3/4	38 5/8	50 1/2	46 1/2	25 3/8
	(2.30)	(2.30)	(2.40)	(2.52)	(1.50)

Investment	1960	1961	1962	1963	1964
US Steel	38 1/2	65 3/8	49 3/8	31 3/8	22 1/8
	(4)	(2.80)	(2.20)	(2.20)	(1.60)
Western Union	9 1/4	16 1/4	20 1/4	16 7/8	15 1/2
	(1.40)	(1.40)	(1.40)	(1.40)	(1.40)

STANDARD JOBS 1975-1979

Job Type	1975	1976	1977	1978	1979
Wages per Full-Time Employee	$10,817/yr	$11,585/yr	$12,370/yr	$13,263/yr	$14,373/yr
Private Industries, incl. farm labor	$10,655/yr	$11,430/yr	$12,222/yr	$13,143/yr	$14,310/yr
Bituminous Coal Mining	$15,924/yr	$17,018/yr	$18,292/yr	$20,160/yr	$22,363/yr
Building Trades	$13,447/yr	$14,242/yr	$14,639/yr	$15,394/yr	$16,785/yr
Domestics	$5774/yr	$6479/yr	$6844/yr	$7206/yr	$7912/yr
Farm Labor	$5073/yr	$5416/yr	$6021/yr	$6438/yr	$7154/yr
Federal Civilian	$15,024/yr	$16,238/yr	$17,488/yr	$18,905/yr	$19,907/yr
Federal Employees, Executive Depts.	$12,446/yr	$13,153/yr	$13,980/yr	$15,068/yr	$15,961/yr
Federal Military	$10,064/yr	$10,420/yr	$10,854/yr	$11,570/yr	$12,316/yr
Finance, Insurance, & Real Estate	$10,609/yr	$11,386/yr	$12,184/yr	$13,207/yr	$14,326/yr
Gas, Electricity, & Sanitation Workers	$14,231/yr	$15,653/yr	$16,916/yr	$18,277/yr	$19,697/yr
Manufacturing, Durable Goods	$12,594/yr	$13,622/yr	$14,730/yr	$15,841/yr	$17,212/yr
Manufacturing, Nondurable Goods	$10,901/yr	$11,710/yr	$12,578/yr	$13,564/yr	$14,738/yr
Medical/Health Services Workers	$9624/yr	$10,465/yr	$11,248/yr	$12,179/yr	$13,276/yr
Miscellaneous Manufacturing	$9407/yr	$10,148/yr	$10,678/yr	$11,494/yr	$12,563/yr
Motion-Picture Services	$10,614/yr	$11,987/yr	$13,209/yr	$14,910/yr	$16,821/yr
Nonprofit Org. Workers	$7407/yr	$7701/yr	$8297/yr	$8933/yr	$9564/yr
Passenger-Transportation Workers, Local and Highway	$9462/yr	$10,121/yr	$10,780/yr	$11,590/yr	$12,266/yr
Personal Services	$7459/yr	$7943/yr	$8322/yr	$9048/yr	$9723/yr
Public-School Teachers	$11,182/yr	$12,038/yr	$12,738/yr	$13,391/yr	$14,306/yr
Radio Broadcasting & Television Workers	$13,475/yr	$14,705/yr	$15,708/yr	$16,879/yr	$18,329/yr
Railroads	$14,987/yr	$17,292/yr	$18,784/yr	$20,605/yr	$23,021/yr
State and Local Govt. Workers	$10,831/yr	$11,594/yr	$12,359/yr	$13,022/yr	$13,879/yr
Telephone & Telegraph Workers	$13,948/yr	$15,756/yr	$17,279/yr	$19,032/yr	$20,646/yr
Wholesale and Retail Trade Workers	$12,930/yr	$13,684/yr	$14,584/yr	$15,711/yr	$17,113/yr

FOOD BASKET 1975–1979

(NR=NOT REPORTED)

Commodity	Year	New York	Atlanta	Chicago	Denver	Los Angeles
Apples, Fresh, per pound	1975	35.60¢	40.30¢	34.30¢	NR	40¢
	1976	35.90¢	39.30¢	32.40¢	NR	36¢
	1977	41.50¢	45.10¢	38.50¢	NR	43.80¢
	1978	NR	NR	NR	NR	NR
	1979	NR	NR	NR	NR	NR
Beans, Dried, per pound	1975	52¢	43.90¢	39.90¢	NR	42.50¢
	1976	57.90¢	43.70¢	41.20¢	NR	53¢
	1977	50.20¢	38.80¢	43.20¢	NR	44.10¢
	1978	NR	NR	NR	NR	NR
	1979	NR	NR	NR	NR	NR
Beef, Rib Roasts, per pound	1975	$1.77	$1.99	$1.64	NR	$1.86
	1976	$1.75	$1.96	$1.58	NR	$1.75
	1977	$1.80	$1.97	$1.40	NR	$1.88
	1978	NR	NR	NR	NR	NR
	1979	NR	NR	NR	NR	NR
Beef, Steaks (Round), per pound	1975	$2.25	$1.99	$1.64	NR	$1.71
	1976	$2.12	$1.91	$1.49	NR	$1.59
	1977	$2.09	$1.78	$1.37	NR	$1.59
	1978	NR	NR	NR	NR	NR
	1979	NR	NR	NR	NR	NR
Bread, White, per pound	1975	42.30¢	33.50¢	35.30¢	NR	36.30¢
	1976	42.40¢	34¢	35.70¢	NR	35¢
	1977	41.20¢	34.10¢	35.80¢	NR	34.90¢
	1978	35.5¢ (U. S. Average)				
	1979	NR	NR	NR	NR	NR
Butter, per pound	1975	$1.05	$1.06	98.80¢	NR	$1.03
	1976	$1.32	$1.26	$1.21	NR	$1.24
	1977	$1.41	$1.37	$1.34	NR	$1.31
	1978	$1.33 (U. S. Average)				
	1979	NR	NR	NR	NR	NR
Cheese, per pound	1975	77.90¢	79.10¢	75.10¢	NR	80.80¢
	1976	86.70¢	89.60¢	80.40¢	NR	89.30¢
	1977	89.80¢	91.60¢	85.50¢	NR	89.70¢
	1978	NR	NR	NR	NR	NR
	1979	NR	NR	NR	NR	NR
Chickens, per pound	1975	68.20¢	61.20¢	63.80¢	NR	61.90¢
	1976	66¢	58.60¢	59.40¢	NR	61.10¢
	1977	65.40¢	56.40¢	59.60¢	NR	63.30¢
	1978	NR	NR	NR	NR	NR
	1979	NR	NR	NR	NR	NR
Coffee, per pound	1975	$1.40	$1.33	$1.35	NR	$1.22
	1976	$1.99	$1.80	$1.91	NR	$1.74
	1977	$3.58	$3.46	$3.39	NR	$3.37
	1978	$3.42 (U. S. Average)				
	1979	NR	NR	NR	NR	NR

Commodity	Year	New York	Atlanta	Chicago	Denver	Los Angeles
Eggs, per dozen	1975	84.60¢	77¢	73.90¢	NR	72¢
	1976	91.40¢	82.40¢	83.80¢	NR	78.70¢
	1977	88.50¢	79.70¢	81¢	NR	79¢
	1978	82.30¢ (U. S. Average)				
	1979	NR	NR	NR	NR	NR
Flour, Wheat, per pound	1975	19.78¢	21.50¢	20.06¢	NR	19.28¢
	1976	19.04¢	19.34¢	19.02¢	NR	16.28¢
	1977	17.86¢	17.80¢	17.48¢	NR	14.54¢
	1978	NR	NR	NR	NR	NR
	1979	NR	NR	NR	NR	NR
Lamb, Chops, per pound	1975	$2.80	$2.65	$2.75	NR	$2.74
	1976	$3.10	$3.09	$2.93	NR	$3.00
	1977	$3.21	$3.58	$2.94	NR	$3.14
	1978	NR	NR	NR	NR	NR
	1979	NR	NR	NR	NR	NR
Margarine, per pound	1975	68.70¢	68.50¢	63.10¢	NR	61.80¢
	1976	59¢	56.90¢	53.60¢	NR	53¢
	1977	63.20¢	62.60¢	60.90¢	NR	58.60¢
	1978	57.20¢ (U. S. Average)				
	1979	NR	NR	NR	NR	NR
Milk, Fresh, per quart	1975	41.40¢	45.40¢	38.75¢	NR	34.80¢
	1976	42.80¢	49.30¢	41.20¢	NR	34.40¢
	1977	43.05¢	51.15¢	42.35¢	NR	34.10¢
	1978	83.90¢ (U. S. Average)				
	1979	NR	NR	NR	NR	NR
Pork, Bacon, Sliced, per pound	1975	$1.85	$1.81	$1.80	NR	$1.60
	1976	$1.85	$1.70	$1.69	NR	$1.54
	1977	$1.69	$1.50	$1.62	NR	$1.45
	1978	$1.56 (U. S. Average)				
	1979	NR	NR	NR	NR	NR
Pork, Chops, per pound	1975	$1.92	$1.92	$1.79	NR	$1.95
	1976	$1.92	$1.85	$1.72	NR	$1.91
	1977	$1.85	$1.83	$1.62	NR	$1.90
	1978	$1.81 (U. S. Average)				
	1979	NR	NR	NR	NR	NR
Pork, Ham, Whole, per pound	1975	$1.26	$1.03	$1.05	NR	$1.28
	1976	$1.47	$1.17	$1.22	NR	$1.35
	1977	$1.40	$1.11	$1.14	NR	$1.33
	1978	NR	NR	NR	NR	NR
	1979	NR	NR	NR	NR	NR
Potatoes, Irish, per 10 pounds	1975	$1.41	$1.75	$1.75	NR	$1.24
	1976	$1.61	$1.87	$1.90	NR	$1.17
	1977	$1.67	$2.16	$2.08	NR	$1.16
	1978	$1.49 (U.S. Average)				
	1979	NR	NR	NR	NR	NR
Rice, per pound	1975	49.80¢	33.50¢	40.50¢	NR	51.50¢
	1976	47.70¢	39.40¢	34.70¢	NR	45.20¢
	1977	44.80¢	35.70¢	34.60¢	NR	40.40¢
	1978	40¢ (U. S. Average)				
	1979	NR	NR	NR	NR	NR

Commodity	Year	New York	Atlanta	Chicago	Denver	Los Angeles
Sugar, per pound	1975	39.72¢	40.94¢	35.82¢	NR	35.24¢
	1976	25.24¢	25.58¢	24.52¢	NR	22.46¢
	1977	22.36¢	20.54¢	22.94¢	NR	20.22¢
	1978	$1.08 (U. S. Average)				
	1979	NR	NR	NR	NR	NR
Tea, Bags, per package of 48	1975	86.80¢	87.60¢	82.90¢	NR	84¢
	1976	89.10¢	82.60¢	87.90¢	NR	86.40¢
	1977	$1.04	$1.03	$1.19	NR	$1.03
	1978	NR	NR	NR	NR	NR
	1979	NR	NR	NR	NR	NR
Veal, per pound	1975	$3.68	NR	$3.16	NR	$2.75
	1976	$3.54	$3.05	$2.97	NR	$2.51
	1977	$3.45	$3.71	$2.84	NR	$2.88
	1978	NR	NR	NR	NR	NR
	1979	NR	NR	NR	NR	NR

SELECTED PRICES 1975–1979

Item	Source	Description	Price
ALCOHOL			
Beer	*Chicago Tribune* (1978)	*Stroh's;* 6-pack	$1.49
Vodka	*Chicago Tribune* (1978)	*Smirnoff;* 80-proof; 1.75 liter	$8.59
Wine Butler	*New York Times* (1978)	Never spill another drop of wine when you pour with Wine Butler; made from space-age material that cuts off the last drop cleanly, returning it to the bottle; with sterling silver crown	$24.50
APPAREL, CHILDREN'S			
Belt	*Sears, Roebuck* (1976)	Leather strap with all around three-hole perforations and three-prong metal buckle	$3.99
Boots	*Sears, Roebuck* (1976)	*Winnie-the-Pooh;* over the foot pull-on boot	$10.99
Briefs	*Sears, Roebuck* (1976)	Rib knit with two-way stretch	$2.99
Coat	*Sears, Roebuck* (1976)	*Winnie-the-Pooh;* all-weather trench coat	$19
Coat	*Sears, Roebuck* (1976)	*Balmecaan;* single-breasted styling	$8.99
Coverall	*Sears, Roebuck* (1976)	Corduroy	$3.99
Dress	*Sears, Roebuck* (1976)	No-iron dresses at low prices; save $1 when you buy any 2 dresses in any style, in any size	$5.49
Dress	*Sears, Roebuck* (1976)	Picture-perfect no-iron dresses	$3.49
Dress	*Sears, Roebuck* (1976)	*Winnie-the-Pooh;* dresses never need ironing	$10
Gown	*Sears, Roebuck* (1978)	Screen-printed across yoke, "My Heart Belongs to Daddy"	$4.99
Jacket	*Sears, Roebuck* (1976)	Denim jackets with screen-print back; motorcycle, *Budweiser,* American eagle	$9.99
Jeans	*Sears, Roebuck* (1976)	Perma-prest; denim jeans; wise buys for thrifty shoppers	$3.88
Jeans	*Sears, Roebuck* (1976)	*Toughskins;* the toughest of Sears, Roebuck tough casual jeans; lab tests prove it	$5.99
Pajamas	*Sears, Roebuck* (1978)	*Winnie-the-Pooh;* has pants that are hem-stitched at ankle	$5.99
Play Suit	*Sears, Roebuck* (1976)	*Winnie-the-Pooh;* our finest sleep 'n' play suit; heavyweight stretch-knit terry	$4.99
Raincoat	*Sears, Roebuck* (1976)	Water-repellent vinyl raincoat; boys' sizes 6 to 16	$3.79
Shirt	*Sears, Roebuck* (1976)	Cat appliqué	$6.99

Item	Source	Description	Price
Shirt	*Sears, Roebuck* (1976)	Perma-prest knit shirt	$2.99
Shirt	*Sears, Roebuck* (1976)	Tie-dyed shirt	$5.99
Shirt	*Sears, Roebuck* (1976)	Wet-look shirt	$5
Shoes	*Sears, Roebuck* (1976)	T-strap	$10.99
Slippers	*Sears, Roebuck* (1976)	Mom will love these slippers as much as the kids because they're so easy to keep clean; just machine wash, warm	$4.99
Socks	*Sears, Roebuck* (1976)	Novelty knee-high socks; multicolor florals	$1.59
Socks	*Sears, Roebuck* (1976)	Tube socks; three pairs	$2.97
Sweatshirt	*Sears, Roebuck* (1976)	Hooded sweatshirt	$5.99
Tank Top	*Sears, Roebuck* (1976)	Pullover contrast rib-knit trim at U-neck and sleeve openings	$4.99
Tights	*Sears, Roebuck* (1976)	Stretch nylon in opaque knit	$1.67
Underwear	*Sears, Roebuck* (1976)	Perma-prest underwear for girls and boys; three in package	$2.99
Vest	*Sears, Roebuck* (1976)	Girl's rosebud print vest	$2.99

APPAREL, MEN'S

Item	Source	Description	Price
Briefs	*New York Times Magazine* (1975)	*Bravos;* bikinis and fly front briefs	$1.99
Coat	*New York Times Magazine* (1975)	*Antartex Main Shop;* from Scotland; 9 skin colours, 8 sheep-skin types	$175
Jeans	*Sears, Roebuck* (1977)	100% cotton denim jeans; 3 proportioned cuts mean your jeans will fit and feel better; prewashed blue	$13
Jeans	*Sears, Roebuck* (1977)	*Toughskin;* casual jeans	$6.39
Moccasin	*Smithsonian* (1976)	*J&M After Hours Swanee I;* moccasin toe, clip-on styling for good looks and comfort	$37.50
Pants	*New York Magazine* (1975)	*Cable Car;* cotton corduroy hobby pants; fuller cut, pleated for leisure, travel, golf, or puttering	$19
Robe	*Smithsonian* (1976)	*L. L. Bean;* chamois cloth; a high grade 100% cotton flannel, thickly napped on both sides	$33
Shirt	*Popular Mechanics* (1977)	*Canadian Mist Chamois* cloth shirt; long sleeves and long tuck-in tails	$12.50
Shirt	*New York Times Magazine* (1975)	*Bravos;* tank shirt; bold, individually expressed in DuPont's 100% 2-ply stretch nylon	$2.99
Shirt	*Sears, Roebuck* (1977)	*Perma-Prest;* long-point banded collar; permanent stays; 65% polyester, 35% chambray	$7.99
Shirt	*Sears, Roebuck* (1977)	Rugby-style long-sleeve knit shirts	$4.49

Storm Striders—Here's a ruggedly handsome way to cut through the chills. Just suit up in this blanket-lined Lee Rider storm jacket accented by a corduroy collar (about $26.) and step out in matching pre-washed denim jeans featuring a lean boot-cut flare leg (about $15.). Top it all off with a Lee plaid flannel shirt (about $16.) and you've got another great Lee outfit going for you. The Lee Company, 640 Fifth Avenue, New York 10019. (212) 765-4215.

A Lee clothing advertisement appearing in a 1976 issue of Playboy magazine. (Flickr)

Item	Source	Description	Price
Socks	*New York Times Magazine* (1975)	Interwoven satin stripe; the handsome alternating stripes of Antron nylon add just right lustre	$2
Socks	*Smithsonian* (1976)	*Eddie Bauer;* goose down; fully insulated and quilted in tough nylon taffeta	$9.95
Ties	*Smithsonian* (1976)	*Wm. Chelsea, Ltd.;* Tin Lizzie design, select blue or brown	$10
Touring Cap	*New York Times Magazine* (1975)	*L. L. Bean;* attractive and sturdy sports cap of brushed-pig-skin leather	$7.50
Vest	*Smithsonian* (1976)	*Austral Enterprises;* Welsh sheepworker's; a casual top for work or leisure; made of the best 12-oz Welsh flannel; 100% wool	$27.50

APPAREL, WOMEN'S

Item	Source	Description	Price
Blazer	*New York Times Magazine* (1975)	*Lord & Taylor;* smoothly knit; personal and Dacron, America's finest polyester	$50
Blouse	*New York Times Magazine* (1975)	*Lydia;* Edwardian; of white lawn with embroidery Anglaise and Irish-lace trimming	$200
Body Briefer	*Sears, Roebuck* (1977)	Featherweight all-in-one of sheer, glistening Antron nylon and spandex lets your clothes fall in sensuous unbroken lines; especially desirable under close-fitting outerwear	$16
Coatdress	*Sears, Roebuck* (1977)	Double-knit polyester; multicolor pali-print bodice with pique texture	$21
Coverup	*Sears, Roebuck* (1977)	Front-tie closing at rounded neckline, shirring at front and back yoke	$13
Gown	*New York Times* (1977)	*Elizabeth Arden Salon;* innocence is Blass; and very in	$125
Jacket Dress	*Atlanta Journal and Constitution* (1978)	*Lady Carol;* sleeveless striped dress and matching short-sleeve jacket, 100% encron polyester	$32
Jumpsuit	*Sears, Roebuck* (1977)	Easy-fitting step-in-style with a front-button opening	$21
Jumpsuit	*Sears, Roebuck* (1977)	Pre-washed denim; sized to be worn over underwear	$31.99
Kimono	*New York Times Magazine* (1975)	*Saks Happy Coat;* in woven textured polyester; traditional length 36"	$35
Maternity Top	*Sears, Roebuck* (1977)	Pull-over style with sweetheart neckline; front yoke of broadcloth with an inset of denim	$9
Maternity Top	*Sears, Roebuck* (1977)	With Mom motif	$8
Pants	*New York Times Magazine* (1975)	*Koret of California;* seersucker; creating resort wardrobes that set the pace for summer fashion; 65% Dacron polyester, 35% cotton	$20
Pants	*Sears, Roebuck* (1977)	Tailored; extra-smooth heavyweight single-knit polyester that looks woven	$12
Panty	*Sears, Roebuck* (1977)	Knee length; smoothes from waist through thighs	$10.38
Shirt	*New York Times Magazine* (1975)	*Koret of California;* printed polo; creating resort wardrobes that set the pace for summer fashion; 65% Dacron polyester, 35% cotton	$15

Item	Source	Description	Price
Shoes	*Atlanta Journal and Constitution* (1978)	*Bakers;* glazed cork; sure allure on 4" heels; from our collection of urethane beauties, timed for day or disco	$19.99
Shoes	*Atlanta Journal and Constitution* (1978)	*K-Mart Lighthearted Sandals;* cut out for fun, 3-tier upper bands in white vinyl, bone, or teak urethane	$4.91
Shoes	*Rolling Stone* (1975)	*Kalso Earth Shoe;* the theory of pure walking	$23.50
Shoes	*Sears, Roebuck* (1977)	Oxford with two-eyelet tie	$7.99
Shoes	*Sears, Roebuck* (1977)	Wedge pump; pillow-soft shoe insole of cushioned vinyl	$12.99
Slack-Companion	*Sears, Roebuck* (1977)	Calf-length panty gives a smooth line; stretch lace leg bands	$12.38
Suit	*Atlanta Journal and Constitution* (1978)	*Walden Classics;* 3-piece set; includes sleeveless dress, tailored blazer, and bias skirt; spring weight polyester in pink or blue plaid	$40
Sweater	*New York Times Magazine* (1975)	*Beldoch Popper;* a carefree rib-turtle by Sandy Starkman of luxurious Qiana nylon	$20
Sweater	*Sears, Roebuck* (1977)	Pullover; has a pointed collar, open-front placket, short sleeves and turn-back cuffs, a square bottom	$11
Sweatercoat	*New York Times* (1977)	*Rodier's Ravissant;* boot-brushing belted, beautifully ribbed	$140
Swimsuit	*Sears, Roebuck* (1977)	Bikini; bra-halter style with V-neckline, tie-bow trim, and princess seams; pants; pull-on style elasticized waist and leg opening	$13
Swimsuit	*Sears, Roebuck* (1977)	One-piece stretch; smooth knit of Antron nylon and Lycra	$20

APPLIANCES

Item	Source	Description	Price
Circular Saw	*Popular Mechanics* (1977)	*Rockwell* 7 1/4" circular saw, cuts at 5800 RPMs	$22.88
Coffee Maker	*Chicago Tribune* (1978)	*Norelco;* 12-cup automatic drip filter coffeemaker; coffee never boils so it's never bitter	$23.88
Computer	*Cox News Service* (2004)	*Apple I;* [In 1976]	$666.66
Computer	*Cox News Service* (2004)	*Apple II;* [In 1977]	$1300

An Apple II advertisement from the December 1977 issue of Byte *magazine. Between September 1977 and September 1980, annual sales grew from $775,000 to $118 million.* (via Wikimedia Commons)

Item	Source	Description	Price
Dryer	Sears, Roebuck (1977)	Kenmore; this model has cycles for cotton, sturdy, and permanent press as well as an air-only cycle too	$149
Espresso Maker	New York Times Magazine (1975)	Brews four to six demitasses the Italian way by steam pressure	$40
Food Processor	Sears, Roebuck (1977)	Helps you prepare meals from everyday to gourmet, slices thick or thin, shreds most fruits and vegetables, nuts, cheese	$39.99
Food Sealer	Sears, Roebuck (1977)	Seal-N-Save; seals 8" individual pouches or holds 8" or 10" wide continuous rolls of pouch material for sealing long items	$16.49
Freezer	Chicago Tribune (1978)	8.3 cu. ft. compact freezer	$199.88
Freezer	Sears, Roebuck (1977)	Upright 16 cu. ft. conventional defrost model with painted steel interior	$219
Kitchen Machine	Sears, Roebuck (1977)	Basic outfit includes power unit plus attachments for grinding, blending, mixing, juicing	$99.99
Microwave Oven	Chicago Tribune (1978)	Big microwave oven cooks fast and cool	$168
Slow Cooker	Sears, Roebuck (1977)	Yellow metal exterior; glass lid; recipes and instructions	$13.79

BABY PRODUCTS

Item	Source	Description	Price
Baby-Basket Set	Sears, Roebuck (1976)	3-piece set; save $1; includes print liner, hoodless basket, basket pad	$24.97
Baby Carrier	Sears, Roebuck (1976)	Pak-A-Poose; patented frame distributes baby's weight evenly; for babies from 4 months old to 35 pounds	$14
Baby Holder	Sears, Roebuck (1976)	Johnny Jump-Up; for babies 4 months old to 24 pounds	$6.99
Child Carrier	Sears, Roebuck (1976)	Sports denim-look rear-mount carrier	$11.88
Cradle	Sears, Roebuck (1976)	Automatic; converts cradle	$34.99
Food Grinder	Sears, Roebuck (1976)	Handy-size food grinder; convenient size for travel; only 5" high; serve fresh natural foods right at the table	$4.50
Mattress Pad	Sears, Roebuck (1976)	Our finest crib-size mattress pad; it's quilted, waterproof	$5.99
Nurser	Sears, Roebuck (1976)	26-piece disposable nurser kit; presterilized bag collapses as baby drinks, so baby takes in less air	$5.99
Pajamas	Sears, Roebuck (1976)	One-piece style; gripper snaps down front, crotch, both legs; short sleeves	$2.79
Pants	Sears, Roebuck (1976)	Corduroy boxer pants; 2 in package	$3.99
Seat Carrier	Sears, Roebuck (1976)	Lightweight, portable; cradles baby for feeding, rocking, toting from place to place	$9.99
Sleeper	Sears, Roebuck (1976)	Winnie-the-Pooh; our finest stretch terry sleep 'n' play suit	$4.99
Slippers	Sears, Roebuck (1976)	Infant's slippers and bag set; a cuddly combination that's sure to please; set includes Pooh slippers plus matching and handy hanging hook	$5.99

Item	Source	Description	Price
Stroller	*Sears, Roebuck* (1976)	Swivel-wheel stroll 'n' fold; handy ideas for outgoing swivel front wheels take corners easily, umbrella-type mother; handle totes easily on mother's arm, leaves both handles free	$24.99
Walker	*Sears, Roebuck* (1976)	Circular; easy to disassemble for compact storage	$10.88
Waterproof Sheets	*Sears, Roebuck* (1976)	Reversible waterproof sheets; two layers of warm fleeced cotton flannelette laminated to a pure gum rubber core; package of 2; 27" × 26"	$3.99

BUSINESS EQUIPMENT AND SUPPLIES

Item	Source	Description	Price
Briefcase	*Smithsonian* (1976)	*Paul McAfee & Friends;* natural leather; legal size, 11" by 16 3/4" case	$35.95
Calculator	*Chicago Tribune* (1978)	*Texas Instruments;* pocket calculator	$74.95
Calculator	*Chicago Tribune* (1978)	*Texas Instruments Exactra;* electronic calculators; adds, subtracts, multiplies, and divides; battery operated and easy to use	$29
Copier	*New York Times* (1977)	*Saxon;* plain paper; we'd like to demonstrate the reasons for our success	$2,995
Drill Press	*New York Times* (1978)	*Chicago Power Tools;* cast iron head, 1/2 horsepower 1725 motor; 5 speed	$199
Phone Rates	*New York Times* (1978)	*Bell System;* three-minute call from United States to Paris, Berlin or Amsterdam; station-to-station	$6.75

COLLECTIBLES

Item	Source	Description	Price
Automobile	*Guinness Book of World Records* (1981)	Price paid in 1979 for a 1936 Mercedes-Benz Roadster	$421,040
Bedside Cupboard	*Antiques* (1977)	With tambour door; circa 1790	$690
Book	*Art & Antiques* (1993)	William Falkner's one-act play entitled *"Marionettes,"* hand-lettered by author, sold at auction in 1975	$34,000
Bookcase	*Antiques* (1977)	Antique Chippendale cherry; especially noteworthy for its ventilated cornice, double-raised panel doors; circa 1790	$6,600
Camera	*Guinness Book of World Records* (1981)	1856 J. B. Dancer stereo camera sold in 1977	$42,000
Card Table	*Antiques* (1977)	Chippendale fold-over table; circa 1760; mahogany with cabriole legs and claw-and-ball feet	$1,950
Clock	*Antiques* (1977)	Nineteenth-century country French Horloge cherry clock; height 7' 9 1/2", width 19 1/2", depth 11 1/2"	$2,800
Dough Table	*Antiques* (1977)	Rare Watervliet, New York Community dough table, signed "E. L."; height 30 1/2", depth 21", length 47"; circa1830	$1,650
Drum Table	*Antiques* (1977)	Georgia Coromandel wood; a charming, small antique table; circa 1780	$2,390
Figurine	*New York Times Magazine* (1975)	Steuben; glass penguin; height 6 1/2";send $3 for 1975 catalogue of Christmas gifts	$130
Figurine	*Smithsonian* (1976)	Burgues; nature in porcelain; young walrus; 9" wide by 5 1/2" high; issue of 950	$225

554

Item	Source	Description	Price
Figurine	*Smithsonian* (1976)	Steuben; glass Stars and Stripes; crystal prism, cut and engraved	$160
Print	*Antiques* (1977)	Antique Audubon quadrupeds; 21" × 27"	$150
Print	*Antiques* (1977)	Antique Wilson birds; 1810; 13" × 6"	$17.50
Print	*Antiques* (1977)	Catesbury; bird; 1771 edition; 14" × 20"	$150
Print	*Antiques* (1977)	Gould's Birds of Great Britain; hand colored, 1862; 15" × 20"	$50
Rug	*Antiques* (1977)	Oriental; Tabriz; 9' 10" × 11' 2", from Iran	$1,950
Rug	*Antiques* (1977)	Persian Bakhtiari rug; 6' 4" × 4"; a fascinating combination of large-scale stylized floral design in a scatter rug size	$1,850
Sculpture	*Guinness Book of World Records* (1981)	Price paid in 1977 of a 4th-century BC bronze statue of a youth attributed to the school of Lysippus	$3.9 million
Seats	*New York Times* (1978)	Original reserved seats from Yankee Stadium; removed for the recent renovation Pair, connected	$45
Teddy Bear	*New York Times Magazine* (1975)	Antique; American Hurrah; circa 1910	$100
Tilt-Top Table	*Antiques* (1977)	Mahogany table; circa 1780; 31" diameter	$750

EDUCATION

Item	Source	Description	Price
Golf School	*New York Times* (1978)	Concord Golf School; six days and five nights based on double occupancy, per person; intense instruction	$650
TV/Audio	*Popular Mechanics* (1977)	NRI School; A complete course in black and white and color TV servicing, including 48 lessons, 10 special reference texts and 11 training kits	$550

ENTERTAINMENT

Item	Source	Description	Price
Hockey Ticket	*Chicago Tribune* (1978)	Stanley Cup playoffs; Black Hawks vs. Boston	$6.50–$18.75
Movie Ticket	*Chicago Tribune* (1978)	Dirty Mary Crazy Larry; carload	$4
Movie Ticket	*Chicago Tribune* (1978)	Golden Voyage of Sinbad	$1
Movie Ticket	*Chicago Tribune* (1978)	Serpico; Al Pacino	$0.75
Resort Package	*New York Times* (1978)	Granit Hotel and Country Club; the only resort catering exclusively to adults; weekly package, 8 days, 7 nights, per person, double occupancy	$196–$229
Theater Ticket	*New York Times* (1977)	Beatlemania; phenomenal; a case example of the theater's miracle; Saturday evening	$11/$13/$15
Theater Ticket	*New York Times* (1977)	*A Chorus Line;* Pulitzer prize for drama, winner of 9 Tony awards; orchestra and boxes	$17.50
Theater Ticket	*Chicago Tribune* (1978)	*Rustic Barn Confidence Game;* 3-act comedy; dinner theater; play; gratuity; choice of 5 dinner entrees	$8.95

Item	Source	Description	Price
ENTERTAINMENT, HOME			
Camera	*Smithsonian* (1976)	*Kodak EK$ Instant;* pictures that develop in minutes, the image protected by an elegant, textured, satinlux finish; automatic exposure control and electronic shutter	$54
Camera	*Smithsonian* (1976)	*Kodak Trimlite Instamatic 48;* has a superb f/2.7 Ektar lens and a coupled range finder	$129
CB Base Station and Walkie Talkie	*Atlanta Journal and Constitution* (1978)	*K-Mart;* AM/CB receiver with morse code function; transmits on channel 14	$16.97
CB Radio	*Chicago Tribune* (1978)	Basic 40-channel mobile CB radio	$39.88
Game	*New York Times* (1978)	*Pachinko Pinball Game;* A fast, challenging game of action	$22.50
Projector	*Smithsonian* (1976)	*Kodak Carousel Custom 850H;* auto-focus; quiet dependability	$275
Radio	*Sears, Roebuck* (1978)	Stereo headphone radio; plays anytime and anyplace	$39.50
Stereo Cassette System	*Smithsonian* (1976)	*Sony CF-580;* the first complete stereo cassette system that's portable	$400
Stereo Receiver	*Rolling Stone* (1975)	*Pioneer SX-737;* offers a level of performance that can only be described as awesome	$400
Turntable	*Rolling Stone* (1975)	*Dual 1225;* fully automatic, single-play/multi-play; viscous damped cue-control; pitch control	$199.95
FARM EQUIPMENT			
Tractor	*Guinness Book of World Records* (1981)	65-ton *Northern Manufacturing Company* 8-wheeled, 16V-747 tractor	$325,000
FOOD PRODUCTS			
Alaskan King Crab	*Chicago Tribune* (1978)	Al's Fishery; split; precooked; 3 lb bag; reg. $3.99; while supply lasts	$2.50/lb
Crackers	*New York Times* (1978)	Carr's Table Wafers; 12 ounce can	$3.99
Fruit Cake	*New York Times Magazine* (1975)	Marty's Ol Fashion; fresh to you in time for the holidays; three one-pound loaf cakes	$6
Groceries	*New York Times* (1978)	The Country Grocer; the first all natural supermarket in New Jersey Organic Roast Beef, per 1/2 pound Turkey Breast, cooked on premises, per 1/2 pound Alta Dena flavored Yoghurt, sweetened with honey, 8 oz	 $1.99 $1.89 $.49
Soup	*New York Times* (1978)	Pepperidge Farm cold fruit soups; fresh off-the-vine taste; strawberry, prune, peach, cherry, apricot and orange, Per 10 3/4 ounce can	$1.19
FURNITURE			
Bean Bag	*Sears, Roebuck* (1977)	Wet-look vinyl; graphic prints	$37.95
Bunk Beds	*Sears, Roebuck* (1977)	Bunk outfit with 6 storage drawers and two bookcases	$439.95
Chair	*Atlanta Journal and Constitution* (1978)	James David; contemporary; designs in thick gleaming chrome with deep foam cushions covered in beautiful, durable rust corduroy	$109

Item	Source	Description	Price
Chair	*New York Times* (1978)	Breuer Chairs; black with hand-caned seat and back; the authentic Italian import	$32.50
Chaise Group	*Atlanta Journal and Constitution* (1978)	3-piece; includes chaise, armless love seat, cocktail table	$699
Cocktail Table	*Atlanta Journal and Constitution* (1978)	Woodmere; 32" square table, wormy chestnut finish	$139
Mate's Bed	*Sears, Roebuck* (1977)	With two storage drawers, mattress, and foundation	$169.95
Stereo Wall System	*Atlanta Journal and Constitution* (1978)	Brazil Contempo; units finished in exotic mercuro laminate; feature tempered-glass door, lighted cabinets and chrome trim; all units are a full 15" deep × 72" high 30" wide	$199
Trestle Table	*New York Times Magazine* (1975)	Great North Woods; butcher block; made from natural 2"-thick hard-rock maple and finished by hand; 24" × 60"	$62.40
Trestle Table and Benches	*Sears, Roebuck* (1977)	3-piece set includes table and 2 side benches	$289.95

GARDEN EQUIPMENT AND SUPPLIES

Item	Source	Description	Price
Fence	*New York Times* (1975)	Chain link and stockade fences; standard 2 inch mesh natural 2"-thick hard-rock maple and finished by hand; 24" × 60"	$.80 Per running foot
Flower	*Smithsonian* (1976)	Christmas crocus; twelve Holland bulbs, preplanted and ready to grow	$11.95
Hummingbird Feeder	*Smithsonian* (1976)	Droll Yankee; has three feeding stations, a three-year guarantee	$13.50
Lawn Sweeper	*Sears, Roebuck* (1977)	Self-propelled; brush adjusts to 9 different heights to whisk up grass, leaves; 3 1/2 hp	$229.99
Lawn Sweeper and Bagger	*Sears, Roebuck* (1977)	Lawn Valet; vacuum, compactor, and bagger; clears a 25" path; converts to blower to clear an 8' path; reduces 4 bushels of leaves to 1; no lower price since 1975	$186
Seeds	*Chicago Tribune* (1978)	Excel; flower and vegetable seeds; limit 6 packs	$0.59

HOTEL RATES

Item	Source	Description	Price
Hotel Room	*New York Times Magazine* (1975)	St. Moritz on the Park; handsome views of New York's Central Park	$31/day
Hotel Room	*Chicago Tribune* (1978)	Schwartz Resort Hotel; 6 days, 5 nights	$110
Room Rate	*Guinness Book of World Records* (1981)	Cost of staying at the Celestial Suite on the 9th floor of the Astro Village Hotel, Houston, Texas Per day	$2,500
Room Rate	*New York Times* (1978)	Stouffer's Inn of Westchester; Get out of the jungle this weekend; swim, jog and exercise; enjoy in-room movies; per person based on double occupancy	$72
Room Rate	*New York Times* (1978)	Barbizon Plaza Hotel; Enjoy Central Park in bloom across the street; single anytime, per night	$35.90
Room Rate	*New York Times* (1978)	Jeronimo's Place in the Country; No big name stars; no planned activities; no yoga, reducing or any other courses; no rap sessions; no hassles; per person, per day	$30

Item	Source	Description	Price
HOUSEHOLD PRODUCTS			
Apron	*Gourmet* (1976)	Cotton and polyester; adjustable	$12
Bath Scale	*Sears, Roebuck* (1977)	Extra-large bath scale has handle for easy portability	$17.99
Bedspread	*Sears, Roebuck* (1977)	Woven; an early American touch; no-iron coordinates	$34.96
Bedspread	*Atlanta Journal and Constitution* (1978)	Singapore by Croscill; twin; fully quilted spread is covered in polyester/cotton with Kodel polyester fiberfill	$39
Blanket	*Popular Mechanics* (1977)	Canadian Mist American Trapper blanket; 85% wool, 15% nylon; 71" × 90"	$26.75
Brief Bag	*New York Times Magazine* (1975)	Chisholm Classics; leather; hand-rubbed chestnut brown leather, brass hardware, legal size	$52
Casserole	*Gourmet* (1976)	Metal; two-quart flameproof casserole	$58
Cookware	*Sears, Roebuck* (1977)	Stainless-steel cookware, aluminum-clad bottom; save $10	$69.96
Drapes	*Sears, Roebuck* (1977)	Rod pocket draperies; tufted medallion design; 63" × 72"	$9.96
Drill Stand	*Sears, Roebuck* (1977)	Portalign; holds drill for perpendicular exact-angle holes	$19.99
Extension Cord	*Popular Mechanics* (1977)	Carol heavy-duty 25-foot extension cord; all purpose for indoor and outdoor use	$3.89
Fabric	*New York Times* (1978)	Upholstery Fabric; save on the best in designer seconds for your home Per yard	$4.95
Faucet	*Sears, Roebuck* (1977)	Our best single-control washerless faucet; chrome-plated, brass handle	$36.99
Floor Lamp	*Smithsonian* (1976)	Light Crafters Wonderful Sight Light; up to 5 times the light of conventional lamps; traditional style	$78.50
Garbage Can	*New York Times* (1978)	Dapol Blow Mold 30 gallon garbage can	$5.99
Ice Bucket	*New York Times Magazine* (1975)	Modern classic in stainless steel from Finland	$80
Ice Cream Machine	*Smithsonian* (1976)	Salton's; nothing tastes better than homemade ice cream	$24.95
Lamp	*Gourmet* (1976)	Jean-Paul Beaujard; French brass with glass shade	$95
Luggage	*Chicago Tribune* (1978)	Amelia Earhart	$12.90
Massage Shower Head	*Sears, Roebuck* (1977)	This massage shower is two showers in one; just turn for massage action or regular spray	$26.95
Nail Spinner	*Sears, Roebuck* (1977)	Sets in finishing nails without predrilling	$4.99
Platter	*Gourmet* (1976)	Diane Love; handmade; earthenware	$25
Plywood Sheet	*New York Times* (1978)	Interior plywood sheet; 4' × 8' × 1/4"	$6.99
Pressure Cooker	*Chicago Tribune* (1978)	Presto; 6-qt pressure cooker; speed, convenience and economy; cooks food 3 to 10 times faster	$10.88
Punch Bowl	*New York Times Magazine* (1975)	Le Grenier; hand-blown glass, a French import that holds over a gallon	$35
Quilt	*New York Times Magzine* (1975)	Continental Quilt Shoppe; dreamy white European Goose down, light as a cloud; you'll never make your bed again because the continental quilt eliminates a top sheet	$109.95
Restroom Radio	*Sears, Roebuck* (1978)	AM radio was $6.99 in our 1974 Christmas book	$5.95
Sheets	*New York Times Magazine* (1975)	Satin twin; flat and fitted; slip into the luxury of these acetate satin sheets	$12

Item	Source	Description	Price
Sheets	*Sears, Roebuck* (1977)	Perma-prest muslin sheets in fun prints; Peanuts, Dumbo, Tiger-Tiger, Budweiser; twin	$4.99
Sheets	*Atlanta Journal and Constitution* (1978)	*Country Lace by Suzanne Pleshette;* twin; a stylized gingham check, made of no-iron cotton/polyester percale from Utica	$7
Storm Windows	*Sears, Roebuck* (1977)	Triple-track insulating aluminum frame storm-screen windows; requires minimal maintenance	$32.95
Towel	*Atlanta Journal and Constitution* (1978)	In thick all-cotton terry, and measuring a generous 32" × 65"; imported from Brazil	$9.99
Trash Bags	*New York Times* (1978)	*Plastic City* trash bags; Our bags are double strength because they're virgin poly not repro; box of 500, 10-gallon size	$19.95
Vacuum Cleaner	*Chicago Tribune* (1978)	*Eureka;* bigger bag capacity to work harder, longer; fewer changes	$49.88

JEWELRY

Item	Source	Description	Price
Cigarette Case	*New York Times Magazine* (1975)	*Colibri;* French enamel; precision-crafted with old world pride of craftsmanship, in Colibris hand-surfaced Cloisenamel finish	$34.95
Earrings	*New York Times Magazine* (1975)	*S. Marsh & Sons;* exquisite pave diamond earrings, with 96 full-cut diamonds weighing 4.53 karats, 18K gold and platinum	$2,290
Necklace	*New York Times Magazine* (1975)	*International Museum Talisman of Love;* the apple of Solomon—a love charm and talisman; 2" in diameter, struck in solid bronze	$22
Necklace	*Sears, Roebuck* (1977)	His or hers; elegant fine-link construction	$9
Watch	*New York Times Magazine* (1975)	*Baume & Mercier;* woman's; excitement in 14 karat gold	$650
Watch	*New York Times Magazine* (1975)	*Concord;* man's wristwatch; 18K gold electroplated; the second generation in digital watches by Concord	$395
Watch	*New York Times Magazine* (1975)	*Gruen Telestar;* clip bracelet for women; at the press of a button, brings you the hours, minutes, seconds, month and day; bracelet is in sterling silver with gold-filled highlighting	$300
Watch	*New York Times Magazine* (1975)	*Movado;* ladies wristwatch; sophisticated interwoven bracelet of 14K yellow gold	$925

MEALS

Item	Source	Description	Price
Meal	*Chicago Tribune* (1978)	*Lobster Tail;* home of famous San Francisco sourdough bread	$7.95
Meal	*Chicago Tribune* (1978)	*Medium Rare;* featuring complete all inclusive dinners of prime rib of beef, fresh filet of red snapper, flaming shish kebob; or fixed price includes 2 cocktails before dinner, glass of wine with dinner, and one after dinner drink	$6.95
Meal	*Chicago Tribune* (1978)	*Nordic Steak 'n Pub;* broiled African lobster tail; huge salad bar	$6.95

Item	Source	Description	Price
Meal	*Chicago Tribune* (1978)	*Port of Entry;* featuring complete all inclusive dinners of prime filet mignon; African lobster tails; prime rib or beef succulent barbeque ribs; with your choice of 2 cocktails before dinner, a glass of vintage wine with dinner, and 1 after dinner drink; Sunday—Tuesday	$6.95

MOTORIZED VEHICLES, SUPPLIES AND SERVICES

Item	Source	Description	Price
Automobile	*Popular Mechanics* (1977)	*1977 Toyota Corolla;* two door sedan; EPA 49 miles highway, 36 in the city	$2,788
Automobile	*Popular Mechanics* (1977)	*Oldsmobile Cutlass;* Cutlass style and Cutlass comfort	$4,811
Automobile	*Time* (1976)	Volkswagen Rabbit	$3,500
Battery	*Los Angeles Times* (1978)	*Firestone Forever;* maintenance-free battery; any size; 12-volt exchange	$59
Car Stereo	*Sears, Roebuck* (1977)	*Citizens Band Transceiver;* 40-channel with built in AM/FM stereo radio	$269.99
Electronic Engine Tune-Up	*Los Angeles Times* (1978)	Most 4-cylinder cars; foreign or American	$29
Motorcycle	*Popular Mechanics* (1977)	*Kawasaki 250cc F-11, Enduro;* two-stroke engine mated to five-speed transmission	$699
Motor Oil	*Chicago Tribune* (1978)	10W30 all-weather oil; one-quart can	$0.39
Tire	*Sears, Roebuck* (1977)	Steel-belted radials; warrantied 40,000 miles	$42
Tires	*Popular Mechanics* (1977)	*Sears Guardsman* 4-ply tires for mid-sized cars, 6-78-14 black wall prices, plus $2.23 for Federal excise tax	$21

OTHER

Item	Source	Description	Price
Batteries	*New York Times* (1977)	For all electronic watches, installed by experts	$2.95
Charcoal Starter	*Chicago Tribune* (1978)	*Gulf Lite;* for quick starts; one-quart can	$0.57
Charitable Donation	*New York Times Magazine* (1975)	*Save the Children Federation;* for sponsorship of a child in one of 27 countries	$16/mo
Stationery	*Atlanta Journal and Constitution* (1978)	*Sheridan;* 100 sheets and envelopes, antique vellum	$6.95
Sunglasses	*Sears, Roebuck* (1977)	Large sunglasses have radiant, smoke-color scratch-resistant plastic lenses	$7.99
Trophies (1978)	*The State Newspaper* Columbia, SC (2004)	Value of Vince Lombardi Trophy, given to the winner of the football Super Bowl game	$2000

PERSONAL CARE PRODUCTS

Item	Source	Description	Price
Bandages	*Chicago Tribune* (1978)	*Curad;* box of 30 assorted sizes	$0.69
Bath Powder	*New York Times Magazine* (1975)	Chanel No. 19	$7

Item	Source	Description	Price
Compact	*New York Times Magazine* (1975)	*Miss Dior;* solid perfume designer miniature; brushed-silver toned oval has the famous Dior signature in gold-plated letters with long-lasting Miss Dior solid perfume inside	$4.50
Hair Dryer	*Chicago Tribune* (1978)	*Presto;* here's the quickest, easiest, most convenient hair dryer	$3.88
Makeup	*New York Times Magazine* (1975)	*Revlon Ultima II;* creme; 1.5 oz in Aurora, Beige, Bronze, Umber, Honey Tan, Tuscan Beige	$8.50
Mouthwash	*Chicago Tribune* (1978)	*Listerine;* 48-oz. mouthwash; price includes $0.50 off label	$1.99
Perfume	*New York Times Magazine* (1975)	*Chanel No. 19;* spray; it's another feeling; it's Chanel	$9.50
Razor Blades	*Chicago Tribune* (1978)	*Comfort II;* reg $1.79 packs	$1.29
Toothpaste	*Chicago Tribune* (1978)	*Ipana;* 7-oz tube of toothpaste	$0.59
Wrinkle Cream	*New York Times Magazine* (1975)	*Revlon Ultima II;* translucent	$15

PUBLICATIONS

Book	*New York Times* (1978)	Isaac Bashevis Singer's *Shosha,* a love story set between the two World Wars	$8.95

REAL ESTATE

Apartment	*New York Times* (1977)	For rent; Ocean Avenue and Avenue Y; modern-elevator building; 3 1/2 rooms	$240/mo
Condominium	*New York Times* (1977)	For rent; 8 rooms, 4 baths	$1,025/mo
Country House	*Antiques* (1977)	For sale; 12 rooms built in 1929 in the English tradition; more than 207 acres	$300,000
Home	*New York Times* (1978)	Flushing, New York; six rooms, solid brick, 3 bedrooms, garage, gas heat	$48,500
Home	*New York Times* (1978)	Woodside/Queens Boulevard, New York; ranch type family home, garage, mint condition, modern kitchen, basement	$44,990
Rental	*New York Times* (1978)	Boca Raton, Florida; magnificent view of the ocean; furnished, 2 bedrooms, 2 baths, pool and recreation room; season rental (four month minimum)	$6,400
Summer Home	*New York Times* (1978)	Stratford, Connecticut; six room summer home; just completely remodeled and carpeted; on Long Island Sound	$49,900

SEWING EQUIPMENT AND SUPPLIES

Cloth	*Atlanta Journal and Constitution* (1978)	*K-Mart;* double knits; polyester yarn-dyed prints and double-blister crepes, 58–60 wide	$1.33/yd
Sewing Machine	*Chicago Tribune* (1978)	Heavy-duty zigzag sewing head	$69.88

Item	Source	Description	Price
SPORTS EQUIPMENT			
Basketball	*Sears, Roebuck* (1976)	Even at this low price, a basketball with long-wearing pebble-grain vinyl/rubber cover	$4.89
Basketball Goal	*Sears, Roebuck* (1976)	Adjustable-height goal for players 6–12 years old; you can set height from 7' to regulation 10'	$49.99
Bicycle	*Sears, Roebuck* (1976)	24" youth lightweights; for the shorter youth or the petite miss	$99
Bicycle	*Sears, Roebuck* (1976)	26" midweight bike is built for comfort	$64.99
Boat Motor	*Sears, Roebuck* (1977)	*Gamefisher;* 30-speed twin prop motor; whisper quiet electric fishing motors	$119
Motorcycle Helmet	*Sears, Roebuck* (1977)	Meets DOT safety specs where applicable	$30.99
Pump	*Sears, Roebuck* (1976)	Inflating pump; steel with 8" barrel	$2.80
Telescope	*Smithsonian* (1976)	*Edmund Newtonian Field Reflector;* clearest, brightest, most spectacular wide-angle view of moon, stars, comets, galaxies ever	$129.95
Tennis Balls	*Chicago Tribune* (1978)	*Wilson Pro;* yellow; package of 3	$2.29
Tricycle	*Sears, Roebuck* (1976)	With flowered basket	$16.99
Unicycle	*Sears, Roebuck* (1976)	Beginners	$21.88

TELEPHONE EQUIPMENT AND SERVICES

Item	Source	Description	Price
Telephone Charges	*New York Times* (1977)	*Bell System;* wherever in the world you do business, a station-to-station call is the cheapest way to get there; France, Italy, Germany	$6.75

TOYS

Item	Source	Description	Price
Baby Doll	*Sears, Roebuck* (1978)	*Tenerella;* cut $2; this lovely 19" doll has long, dark, rooted hair, sparkling go-to-sleep eyes, and smooth vinyl skin	$12.99
Big Slider Gym	*Sears, Roebuck* (1977)	Has three activities including 9 1/2' long slide that goes over the top	$64.99
Bird Model Kits	*Smithsonian* (1976)	*Ariel;* little owl card sculptures of wild birds in flight; easy to make in a few hours	$5.95
Car Set	*Sears, Roebuck* (1978)	Matchbox	$4.47
Collector's Case	*Sears, Roebuck* (1978)	*Matchbox;* store and carry up to 72 mini-cars in this collector's case	$6.97
Crazy Buggy	*Sears, Roebuck* (1978)	The do-anything stunt car set	$9.95
Dome Climber	*Sears, Roebuck* (1977)	When your muscles tire, take climber into a clubhouse, just cover with old sheets or blankets	$44.99
Fun Tunnel	*Sears, Roebuck* (1978)	*Winnie-the-Pooh;* a crawl-through tunnel of fun that's 22" in diameter; 9' long; plenty of room for roaming	$10.95

Item	Source	Description	Price
Horse and Wagon	*Sears, Roebuck* (1978)	*Weebles West;* mosey on down to the corral and hitch the Weebles' roly-poly cowpony to the 8" covered wagon	$2.97
Merry-Go-Round	*Sears, Roebuck* (1977)	2-seat; 6' diameter, seat height 24"	$43.99
Remote-Control Racer	*Smithsonian* (1976)	*JS&A;* computer logic has added a new fun way to control remote control products	$49.95
Rocks and Minerals Set	*Sears, Roebuck* (1978)	*Learning by Doing;* start a lifetime hobby	$3.66
Sno-Cone Maker	*Sears, Roebuck* (1978)	Crank out sno-cones from ice cubes; add flavors	$5.66
Top	*Sears, Roebuck* (1978)	*Winnie-the-Pooh* spinning top	$4.49
Viewer	*Sears, Roebuck* (1978)	*View Master 3D;* touch and see your world; one reel of 7 scenes	$17.44

An advertisement for the ViewMaster toy, which showed a different scene with every click. (via Flickr)

Item	Source	Description	Price
Wagon	*Sears, Roebuck* (1976)	Remove green hardwood side panels to convert to coaster wagon	$28.87

TOBACCO PRODUCTS

Pipe	*New York Times* (1978)	*Connoisseur Pipes;* Bent Dublin	$18.75

TRAVEL AND TRANSPORTATION

Item	Source	Description	Price
Airfare	*New York Times* (1978)	*Aerolineas Argentinas;* APEX fares from New York to Rio; requires minimum 29-day stay in Argentina; round trip	$775
Airfare	*New York Times* (1978)	TWA round trip fares from New York to San Francisco Monday-Thursday: Night Coach Day Coach Friday-Sunday: Night Coach Day Coach	 $229 $252 $275 $298
Airplane Fare	*New York Times* (1977)	*United;* save to Los Angeles/San Francisco; freedom fare round trip; your savings $86	$342
Airplane Fare	*Los Angeles Times* (1978)	*TWA;* new economy coach for our lowest price; you'll save up to 56%; Los Angeles to Boston	$230
Cruise	*Chicago Tribune* (1978)	*Chandris Lines;* 7 nights, 8 days	$6.99
Ferry	*Chicago Tribune* (1978)	*Chessie;* the good ferry rides again between Michigan and Wisconsin; one-way adult	$8
Trip	*Chicago Tribune* (1978)	TWA from Chicago to Las Vegas; round trip; open bar & meals; 4 days at the hotel Frontier	$179.95

MISCELLANY 1975–1979

Now, The No-Frills House

Thanks to inflation and the continuing energy shortage, the compact car seems here to stay. Now, with driveway ready, comes the compact house. In suburban areas around the country, builders are turning out no-frills houses that sell for prices ranging in most areas from about $20,000 to $36,000. Aimed at buyers who would not otherwise be able to afford a home of their own in today's market, the small houses in some areas are breaking sales records in a recession-dogged industry.

Time, February 23, 1976

Hemingway Should Have Had It So Good

Former Domestic Affairs Chief John Ehrlichman, who received a $50,000 advance from Simon & Schuster for his first novel, has now peddled film rights to the book to Paramount Pictures. His price: an estimated $75,000. Titled The Company and due in the stores by May, it is about a U.S. President who dabbles in domestic spying, then faces blackmail by the CIA. "If I stick to a routine and don't get too loose, I can write 15 to 25 pages a day," says Ehrlichman. Now appealing his 1975 conviction for Watergate-related crimes, he has already started work on a second book, which he describes as another "purely fictional novel about Washington, D.C." So far, no nibbles from Hollywood.

Time, March 1, 1976

College Graduates Found to Earn More

Finance Facts, a monthly statistical bulletin issued by the National Consumer Finance Association says that a college education continues to play "a major determining role" in household income.

Its most recent survey based on 1975 figures, indicates that households headed by a college graduate averaged $21,734 in annual income, compared with $13,779 for all households.

Where the head of the household had completed only one to three years of college, income averaged $15,500. It slipped to $13,905 where the household head was only a high school graduate. At lower levels of education, average income ran still less, the survey found.

A wide discrepancy persists between households headed by men and women, the organization says. In fact, households headed by males average $15,873—or a little more than double the $7,201 average where a female headed the family.

Time, March 1, 1976

Rubber

The breakthrough in the 16-week strike by 60,000 members of the United Rubber Workers came after a 70-hour bargaining marathon, when union negotiators and Firestone agreed to a new pay package giving workers a 36% increase in wages and benefits over three years. The Firestone agreement, which will set the pattern for the other struck members of rubber's Big Four (Goodyear, Goodrich, and Uniroyal), will boost the industry's average hourly wage in the first year by 88¢ to $6.38. In addition, the rubber workers got an escalator that provides an extra 1¢ an hour for each .4% increase in the cost of living index.

Time, August 23, 1976

1980–1999

From Recession to the Era of Possibilities

1993 series one-dollar bill.

The decade of the 1980s began with serious economic problems. Both interest rates and inflation rates reached a staggering 18 percent. The economy was at a standstill and unemployment was rising. By 1982, America was in its deepest depression since the Great Depression that spanned most of the 1930s. One in 10 Americans was out of work. Convinced that inflation was the primary enemy of long-term economic growth, the Federal Reserve Board brought the economy to a halt in the early days of the decade. It was a shock treatment that worked. By 1984 the tight money policies of the government, stabilization of world oil prices and labor's declining bargaining power brought inflation to four percent, the lowest level since 1967. Despite the pain, the plan to strangle inflation succeeded; Americans not only prospered, but many began to believe it was their right to be successful. The decade came to be symbolized by self-indulgence and a soaring stock market. The Dow Jones Industrial Average tripled from 1,000 in 1980 to nearly 3,000 a decade later. In the center of the recovery was Mr. Optimism, President Ronald Reagan. During his presidential campaign he promised a "Morning in America" and during his eight years, his good nature helped transform the national mood. The collapse of communism at the end of the 1980s brought an end to the old-world order of Cold War and set the stage for a realignment in which America was still regarded as the strongest nation in the world. However, in the postcommunist world, it was a strength defined by both military might and economic reach. As democracy swept across Eastern Europe in the 1990s, the U.S. economy began to feel the impact of a peace dividend generated by many corporations' willingness to invest in the newly created economies of countries such as Russia, its former satellites and the awakening giant of Asia, China.

Even though the 1990s opened heavily burdened by a ballooning national debt, the chaotic collapse of the savings and loan industry and a war in Iraq, economists marvel at the prosperity achieved during this decade, driven by dramatic improvements in technology, a willingness by consumers to assume more personal debt, and the race toward globalization. Innovative advances in technology produced more personal efficiency, but contributed to job losses, most of which were blamed on globalization, especially the off-shoring of American manufacturing jobs. At the end of World War II, the U.S. economy accounted for almost 50 percent of the global economic product; by 1993 the U.S. share was less than 23 percent and declining. This need for a global reach inspired corporate mergers as companies searched for efficiency, market share, new products, or advanced technology.

The increase in consumer credit fueled the boom years and led to an increase in personal bankruptcy. At the same time, the two-career family became the norm. Forty-two percent of American workers were female; the rise of women in the workforce, brought great social change, affecting married life, child rearing, family income, office culture, and the growth of the national economy.

The 1990s was labeled the "Era of Possibilities" by Fortune magazine and had produced the longest economic expansion in the nation's history. The stock market set a succession of records throughout the period, attracting thousands of middle-class investors. This market boom eventually spawned new wealth and brought early retirement to legions of aging baby boomers. At the turn of the twentieth

century, 63 percent of all men over the age of 65 were in the workforce; by 1948 it was 47 percent, and by the mid-1990s, less than 16 percent. The economic boom did not benefit everyone, however, as many new jobs were within the low wage sector. At the same time, the workplace was changing. As companies expanded and contracted adjusting to the new global economy, American job security was threatened, and the cost of health insurance was rising. Workers became more willing to learn new job skills, establish their own companies, and use dramatic improvements in technology to lessen the impact of distance and geography. Profit sharing became more common. Retirement programs and pension plans became more flexible, serving the needs of a highly mobile workforce.

Year	Dollar Value in 2019
1980	$3.11
1983	$2.57
1985	$2.38
1987	$2.25
1989	$2.07

Year	Dollar Value in 2019
1990	$1.96
1993	$1.77
1995	$1.68
1997	$1.60
1999	$1.54

Use this Currency Conversion chart to calculate what any time in the years listed would cost in 2019. Simply multiply the cost of that item by dollar amount in the chart. For example, if you know that a general admission ticket to the Indiana University Baroque Orchestra cost $10.00 in 1987, multiply $10.00 by $2.02 to discover that that same ticket would cost $20.20 in 2019.

HISTORICAL SNAPSHOT 1980–1984

1980

- Sixty-five million Americans read daily newspapers
- 4,225 cable-television channels, 750 commercial television stations, and over 7,500 radio stations now in operation
- Mount St. Helen's erupts in Washington, killing 57 people
- EPA superfund created to clean up toxic waste sites
- Japan surpasses the United States as world's largest auto producer
- The Rubik's Cube is introduced at the International Toy Fair
- Double-digit inflation continues; prices rise 12.4 percent
- Ted Turner establishes CNN
- John Lennon is murdered

1981

- IBM Personal Computer marketed
- 12,000 striking air-traffic controllers fired by President Ronald Reagan
- Public debt hits $1 trillion
- U.S. prime interest rate reaches 21.5 percent, highest since Civil War
- The Space Shuttle *Columbia* is launched
- U.S. first-class postal rates go to 18¢, then 20¢

- AIDS is recognized by the Centers for Disease Control and Prevention
- U.S. population hits 228 million
- MTV is launched, airing "Video Killed the Radio Star" by The Buggles

1982

- Court order breaks up AT&T, U.S. telephone monopoly, into AT&T long lines and regional telephone companies
- The movie *E.T.* is released
- *USA Today,* first national general-interest daily newspaper, introduced
- 2.9 million women operate businesses
- United Auto Workers (UAW) agree to wage concessions with Ford Motor Co.
- U.S. Steel acquires Marathon Oil
- Unemployment reaches 10.8 percent
- First successful embryo transfer is performed
- Michael Jackson releases *Thriller*, which becomes the world's best-selling album within a year

1983

- Martin Luther King Day becomes a national holiday

- One-of-a-kind Cabbage Patch dolls become overnight sensation
- 26 major league baseball teams show total loss of $45 million
- Wall Street's Dow Jones Industrials Average closes at new high 1258.64
- 35.3 million live below poverty line
- Motorola introduces the first mobile phones in the U.S.
- The U.S. Embassy in Beirut, Lebanon is bombed

1984

- President Reagan reelected
- Laser disc computer data storage system becomes available
- Book publishers sell 2.164 billion books; total receipts reach $9.12 billion
- Three major networks control 73% of prime-time viewership
- New York State imposes first mandatory automobile seat belt law
- Inflation drops to 1972 levels
- Trivial Pursuit board game has sales of $777 million
- Average price of single-family house tops $101,000

The United States embassy in Beirut, Lebanon was bombed in April 1983, killing 32 Lebanese, 17 Americans and 14 visitors and passers-by. It was the deadliest attack on a U.S. diplomatic mission up to that time, and was considered the beginning of Islamist attacks on U.S. targets. (via Wikimedia Commons)

SELECTED INCOME 1980–1984

Job	Source	Description	Pay
Adjuster	*New Orleans Times-Picayune* (1983)	1 to 2 yrs. multi-line exp.; 20% comp, 50% gen. liability, 30% comm lines; this position offers good advancement potential	$20,000/yr
Administrative Assistant	*New Orleans Times-Picayune* (1983)	For fund-raising director of non-profit organization; responsibilities include special events, proposal and grant writing, record-keeping and some typing; experience required	$12,000–$15,000/yr
Baseball Player	Bob Rains, *St. Louis Cardinals: The 100th Anniversary History* (1992)	Annual income of Milwaukee Brewers pitcher Don Sutton in 1982	$700,000
Boxer	*Guinness Book of World Records* (1981)	Purse paid to boxer Sugar Ray Leonard for a welter weight title fight against Roberto Duran in 1980	$8.5 million
Dancers-Hostesses	*Chicago Tribune* (1981)	No experience necessary; full or part-time	$500–$700/wk
Housekeeper-Cook	*Chicago Tribune* (1983)	Live-in; private room and bath; 3 adults; must speak English; RECENT reference; 5-day week	$200/wk to start
Keypunch Operator	*San Francisco Examiner* (1982)	Min. 2 yrs. exper. nec.; 15,000 strokes/hr; IBM 129 exper. helpful	$6.45/hr
Mechanic	*San Francisco Examiner* (1982)	Will train; exc. co. benefits; flexible hours	$8–$10/hr
Medical Secretary	*Chicago Tribune* (1981)	No medical experience necessary; you'll deal with patients, get information for charts, histories; talk with hospital personnel to set up surgeries, therapy; good typing skills desired; no Saturdays; exceptional benefits; employer pays fee	$1,250/mo
Nurse	New York Times (1981)	LPN; Candidates must have a license to practice as a Practical Nurse in New York State	$10,755/yr
Performer	*Guinness Book of World Records* (1981)	Annual payment to television's *Tonight Show* host Johnny Carson for 125 days a year	$2.5 million
Playwright	*Life Magazine* (1983)	Payment in 1983 to Tennessee Williams for rights to a television remake of his 1947 play *A Streetcar Named Desire*	$750,000
Produce Stand Vendor	*San Francisco Examiner* (1982)	Pleasant Hill area; must have truck	$2,000/mo
Rehabilitation Assistant	New York Times (1981)	Bachelor's degree and 1 year experience in the care or rehabilitation of mental patients or a Masters degree in an appropriate field of study essential	$14,245/yr
Salesman	*Chicago Tribune* (1983)	Outside sales person for health organization; possible inside management position available	$300–$600/mo, plus weekly commission

Job	Source	Description	Pay
Teacher	*New York Times* (1981)	Special Ed; work on transdisciplinary team serving multi-handicapped	$14,500–$17,000/yr
Tennis Instructor	*Chicago Tribune* (1981)	600 hrs of group lessons per year plus private lessons; U.S.P.T.A. sanction preferred	$13/hr

CONSUMER EXPENDITURES
1980–1984

(Per Capita)

Expenditure Type	1980	1981	1982	1983	1984
Clothing	$394.35	$424.88	$435.45	$470.77	$511.35
Food	$1592.31	$1597.77	$1662.57	$1733.28	$1820.24
Auto Usage	$943.71	$1028.07	$1034.58	$1144.28	$1270.61
New Auto Purchase	$203.76	$220.49	$229.57	$282.55	$328.34
Auto Parts	$65.43	$66.97	$64.88	$70.85	$73.19
Gas & Oil	$380.73	$425.75	$405.30	$398.21	$399.84
Housing	$1120.68	$1248.56	$1339.96	$1428.11	$1532.94
Furniture	$90.90	$94.37	$90.45	$100.72	$112.97
Utilities	$356.14	$390.09	$425.55	$458.82	$480.23
Telephone & Telegraph	$121.20	$134.38	$151.18	$155.79	$163.39
Physicians	$187.95	$219.18	$237.76	$263.77	$291.10
Dentists	$60.16	$70.02	$74.94	$79.81	$85.89
Health Insurance	$56.21	$63.49	$77.09	$79.39	$82.51
Personal Business	$446.16	$471.85	$525.91	$626.98	$670.64
Personal Care	$118.13	$124.81	$127.92	$144.69	$156.13
Tobacco	$91.78	$99.15	$104.66	$121.21	$127.36
Local Transport	$21.08	$21.74	$23.26	$25.61	$28.35
Intercity Transport	$70.70	$76.11	$77.09	$79.81	$89.28
Recreation	$516.43	$567.53	$603	$662.41	$731.14
Religion/Welfare Activities	$169.51	$189.61	$206.31	$224.08	$248.79
Private Education & Research	$147.55	$164.82	$179.61	$195.48	$210.71
Per Capita Consumption	$7676.57	$8376.79	$8869.32	$8788.88	$10409.87

INVESTMENTS 1980–1984

Investment	1980	1981	1982	1983	1984
Basic Yield, One-year Corporate Bonds	12.75	15.06	14.84	12.78	13.49
Short-term Interest Rates, 4–6 Months,					
Prime Commercial Paper	12.29	14.76	11.89	8.89	10.16
Basic Yield, Common Stocks, Total	5.25	5.41	5.81	4.40	4.64
Index of Common Stocks (1941–1943 5 10)	118.71	128.05	119.71	160.41	160.50

COMMON STOCKS, CLOSING PRICE AND YIELD, FIRST BUSINESS DAY OF YEAR

(PARENTHETICAL NUMBER IS ANNUAL DIVIDENDS IN DOLLARS)

	1980	1981	1982	1983	1984
Allis Chalmers	33 1/2	36	15 7/8	9 5/8	16 1/8
	(2)	(2)	(/)	(/)	(/)
American Brands	66 7/8	77 1/8	36 3/4	45 1/2	59 3/8
(2 for 1 split, 5/8/81)	(5.50)	(6.20)	(3.25)	(3.50)	(3.60)
AT&T	51 3/4	48 7/8	58 1/2	59 7/8	62 1/2
	(5)	(5)	(5.40)	(5.40)	(5.40)
Bethlehem Steel	20 7/8	26 1/4	23 1/2	19 3/4	27 7/8
	(1.60)	(1.60)	(1.60)	(1)	(.60)
CPC Intl	58 1/2	62 1/2	35	40 1/4	38 7/8
	(3)	(3.40)	(1.92)	(2.10)	(2.20)
Delta Airlines	37 1/4	59	24 5/8	41 1/2	40 3/8
(2 for 1 split, 12/1/81)	(1.20)	(1.20)	(1)	(1)	(.60)
General Electric	49 3/8	61 7/8	58 3/8	91 3/4	57 5/8
(2 for 1 split, 4/23/83)	(2.80)	(3)	(3.20)	(3.40)	(2)
General Motors	49 3/8	45 3/8	39 3/4	61	74 1/8
	(5.30)	(2.95)	(2.40)	(2.40)	(2.80)
Intl Harvester	37	25 3/8	7 1/4	4 3/8	11 5/8
	(2.50)	(1.20)	(/)	(/)	(/)
Nabisco	21 5/8	26 3/4	30 5/8	36	40 7/8
(merged as wholly owned subsidiary of R. J. Reynolds Industries, Inc.)	(1.62)	(1.80)	(1.85)	(2.05)	(2.28)
U.S. Steel	18	25 5/8	30	20 3/4	31
	(1.60)	(1.60)	(2)	(1)	(1)
Western Union	20 3/8	25 3/8	35 7/8	43 3/4	36 7/8
	(1.40)	(1.40)	(1.40)	(1.40)	(1.40)

STANDARD JOBS 1980–1984

Job Type	1980	1981	1982	1983	1984
Wages Per Full-Time Employees	$15,757/yr	$17,197/yr	$18,430/yr	$17,524/yr	$18,356/yr
Private Industries, incl. Farm Labor	$15,721/yr	$17,144/yr	$18,331/yr	$17,420/yr	$18,200/yr
Bituminous Coal Mining	$24,555/yr	$27,283/yr	$29,110/yr	$29,796/yr	$32,292/yr
Building Trades	$18,571/yr	$20,355/yr	$21,868/yr	$20,488/yr	$20,748/yr
Domestics	$8576/yr	$9327/yr	$10,260/yr	$6,665/yr	$6,760/yr
Farm Labor	$7434/yr	$7989/yr	$8781/yr	$6552/yr	$6864/yr
Federal Civilian	$21,206/yr	$23,029/yr	$24,452/yr	$23,972/yr	$25,083/yr
Federal Employees, Executive Depts.	$17,217/yr	$19,079/yr	$20,689/yr	$21,666/yr	$25,655/yr
Federal Military	$13,498/yr	$15,537/yr	$17,384/yr	NR	NR
Finance, Insurance, & Real Estate	$15,871/yr	$17,343/yr	$18,966/yr	$19,552/yr	$20,695/yr
Gas, Electricity, & Sanitation Workers	$21,701/yr	$23,959/yr	$26,185/yr	$27,508/yr	$29,276/yr
Manufacturing, Durable Goods	$19,014/yr	$20,810/yr	$22,256/yr	$21,476/yr	$22,568/yr
Manufacturing, Nondurable Goods	$16,323/yr	$17,739/yr	$19,272/yr	$19,188/yr	$19,916/yr
Medical/Health Services Workers	$14,728/yr	$16,288/yr	$17,861/yr	$17,108/yr	$17,888/yr
Miscellaneous Manufacturing	$13,990/yr	$15,169/yr	$16,680/yr	$17,680/yr	$18,512/yr
Motion Picture Services	$17,868/yr	$19,856/yr	$21,452/yr	$23,712/yr	$25,428/yr
Nonprofit Org. Workers	$10,400/yr	$11,153/yr	$11,971/yr	$10,504/yr	$10,972/yr
Passenger Transportation Workers, Local and Highway	$13,447/yr	$14,446/yr	$15,224/yr	$13,780/yr	$14,508/yr
Personal Services	$10,615/yr	$11,195/yr	$11,752/yr	$9308/yr	$9776/yr
Postal Employees	$20,280/yr	$23,384/yr	NR	$25,262/yr	$26,417/yr
Public School Teachers	$15,438/yr	$16,606/yr	$18,061/yr	$19,040/yr	$20,031/yr
Radio Broadcasting & Television Workers	$19,538/yr	$20,813/yr	$22,550/yr	$21,944/yr	$23,504/yr
Railroads	$25,372/yr	$27,452/yr	$29,692/yr	$21,840/yr	$22,724/yr
State and Local Govt. Workers	$15,078/yr	$16,362/yr	$17,762/yr	$17,160/yr	$18,252/yr
Telephone & Telegraph Workers	$22,515/yr	$25,090/yr	$27,313/yr	$27,716/yr	$28,574/yr
Wholesale and Retail Trade Workers	$18,822/yr	$20,324/yr	$21,694/yr	$21,476/yr	$22,724/yr

575

FOOD BASKET 1980–1984

Commodity	Year	U.S. Average	North East	North Central	South	West
Bananas, per pound	1980	33.39¢	34.80¢	34.30¢	33.30¢	33.10¢
	1981	37.70¢	37.10¢	37.80¢	39.60¢	36.10¢
	1982	37.20¢	36.60¢	36.60¢	38.80¢	36.70¢
	1983	43.80¢	45.30¢	41.70¢	46.60¢	41.80¢
	1984	38.60¢	38.40¢	37.60¢	38.90¢	39.10¢
Beef, Ground, Hamburger, per pound	1980	$1.85	$1.87	$1.78	$1.88	$1.87
	1981	$1.78	$1.80	$1.69	$1.83	$1.83
	1982	$1.78	$1.79	$1.73	$1.85	$1.74
	1983	$1.77	$1.79	$1.69	$1.83	$1.79
	1984	$1.69	$1.71	$1.58	$1.73	$1.74
Beef, Steak, T-bone, per pound	1980	$3.64	NR	$3.66	$3.80	$3.32
	1981	$3.57	NR	$3.55	$3.68	$3.24
	1982	$3.89	NR	$3.90	$3.99	$3.73
	1983	$3.88	NR	$3.86	$3.73	$3.82
	1984	$4.06	NR	$4.01	$4.16	$3.82
Bread, White, per pound	1980	51.90¢	60¢	48.40¢	47¢	48.70¢
	1981	51.90¢	58.30¢	50.70¢	47.60¢	51.50¢
	1982	52.90¢	61.40¢	52.50¢	49.20¢	49.10¢
	1983	54.20¢	62.70¢	51.80¢	51.70¢	52.80¢
	1984	54.10¢	67¢	50¢	50.90¢	53.30¢
Butter, per pound	1980	$1.99	$1.98	$1.95	$2.08	$1.93
	1981	$1.99	$1.94	$2.02	$2.06	$1.93
	1982	$2.05	$1.98	$2.10	$2.12	$2.00
	1983	$2.07	$2.01	$2.06	$2.17	$2.06
	1984	$2.11	$2.06	$2.07	$2.20	$2.14
Chickens, per pound	1980	76.60¢	79.70¢	74.20¢	74.30¢	79.70¢
	1981	73.40¢	76.90¢	71.70¢	70.60¢	75.40¢
	1982	72¢	75¢	71.50¢	68.70¢	73.50¢
	1983	68.70¢	72.20¢	70.20¢	65.60¢	72.10¢
	1984	82.90¢	91.40¢	77.70¢	79.30¢	85.50¢
Coffee, per pound	1980	$2.19	$2.96	$2.90	$2.90	$2.80
	1981	$2.56	$2.48	$2.65	$2.53	$2.45
	1982	$2.56	$2.54	$2.56	$2.60	$2.57
	1983	$2.45	$2.51	$2.40	$2.49	$2.43
	1984	$2.60	$2.59	$2.60	$2.63	$2.59
Corn on the Cob, per pound	1980	40.90¢	NR	39.30¢	43.80¢	45.80¢
	1981	45.50¢	NR	42.90¢	64.70¢	53.90¢
	1982	46.80¢	43.10¢	50.10¢	42.90¢	56.90¢
	1983	56.70¢	NR	60.70¢	56.70¢	NR
	1984	45.80¢	60¢	46.70¢	41.30¢	34.90¢
Eggs, per dozen	1980	91.17¢	99.40¢	88.10¢	88.50¢	90.50¢
	1981	90.04¢	99.80¢	83.70¢	87.50¢	92.60¢
	1982	84.20¢	93.70¢	80¢	80.40¢	87.30¢
	1983	86.50¢	94¢	81.90¢	83.50¢	93.80¢
	1984	87.60¢	96.80¢	78¢	87.20¢	96.10¢

Commodity	Year	U.S. Average	North East	North Central	South	West
Crackers, Salted, per pound	1980	82¢	86.50¢	79.60¢	81.20¢	76.40¢
	1981	87.20¢	89.50¢	86.40¢	85.10¢	89.30¢
	1982	88.20¢	NR	87.30¢	85.10¢	NR
	1983	94.70¢	NR	94.70¢	89.60¢	NR
	1984	$1.00	NR	95.70¢	97.30¢	NR
Lettuce, Iceberg, per pound	1980	52.20¢	59.60¢	51.90¢	55.40¢	42.60¢
	1981	44.10¢	47¢	46.30¢	46.90¢	37.30¢
	1982	51.80¢	57.80¢	51.50¢	53.50¢	44.70¢
	1983	58¢	58.40¢	58.60¢	57.10¢	58.30¢
	1984	43.60¢	48.20¢	43.50¢	49¢	31.40¢
Margarine, per pound	1980	73.10¢	NR	70¢	NR	69.40¢
	1981	73¢	NR	68.80¢	NR	75.80¢
	1982	NR	NR	NR	NR	NR
	1983	NR	NR	NR	NR	NR
	1984	80¢	81¢	78.20¢	76.20¢	91.30¢
Milk, Fresh, per half-gallon	1980	$1.08	$1.03	$1.08	$1.22	$1.03
	1981	$1.11	$1.06	$1.10	$1.24	$1.06
	1982	$1.12	$1.10	$1.11	$1.24	$1.05
	1983	$1.12	$1.11	$1.11	$1.23	$1.05
	1984	$1.12	$1.09	$1.09	$1.27	$1.06
Orange Juice, Frozen, per 16 ounces	1980	$1.14	$1.31	$1.08	$1.04	$1.20
	1981	$1.41	$1.55	$1.37	$1.35	$1.42
	1982	NR	NR	NR	NR	NR
	1983	$1.36	$1.45	$1.27	$1.36	$1.44
	1984	$1.66	$1.66	$1.63	$1.68	$1.69
Pork, Chops, per pound	1980	$2.05	$2.07	$1.91	$2.13	$2.20
	1981	$2.05	$2.07	$1.94	$2.10	$2.20
	1982	$2.32	$2.33	$2.16	$2.37	$2.52
	1983	$2.41	$2.39	$2.22	$2.51	$2.62
	1984	$2.43	$2.42	$2.26	$2.48	$2.63
Pork, Bacon, Sliced, per pound	1980	$1.68	$1.80	$1.64	$1.64	$1.65
	1981	$1.53	$1.61	$1.49	$1.49	$1.52
	1982	$1.98	$1.97	$2.00	$1.94	$2.00
	1983	$1.95	$1.98	$1.93	$1.92	$1.97
	1984	$1.90	$2.02	$1.80	$1.91	$1.87
Pork, Ham, Rump or Shank Half, per pound	1980	$1.39	$1.57	$1.32	$1.33	$1.53
	1981	$1.19	$1.31	$1.11	$1.13	$1.45
	1982	$1.38	$1.44	NR	$1.35	NR
	1983	$1.3230	$1.2810	NR	$1.30	NR
	1984	$1.2710	$1.2870	NR	$1.19	NR
Potato Chips, 16 ounces	1980	$2.13	$2.10	$2.03	$2.32	$2.13
	1981	$2.27	$2.30	$2.14	$2.35	$2.32
	1982	$2.40	$2.46	$2.25	$2.41	$2.51
	1983	$2.53	$2.53	$2.41	$2.52	$2.76
	1984	$2.57	$2.62	$2.50	$2.56	$2.67
Potatoes, per 10 pounds	1980	$2.20	$2.11	$2.32	$2.23	$2.15
	1981	$2.75	$2.59	$2.85	$2.93	$2.59
	1982	$2.29	$2.05	$2.29	$2.21	$2.67
	1983	$2.09	$2.12	$2.03	$2.34	$1.89
	1984	$2.99	$3.15	$3.12	$3.04	$3.17

Commodity	Year	U.S. Average	North East	North Central	South	West
Rice, per pound	1980	52¢	60.30¢	NR	43.20¢	55.50¢
	1981	57.20¢	64.40¢	NR	47.30¢	59.50¢
	1982	50.80¢	66.60¢	NR	42.60¢	49.20¢
	1983	46.80¢	NR	NR	38.50¢	49.10¢
	1984	48.40¢	59.40¢	NR	39.80¢	51.50¢
Sugar, per pound	1980	55¢	61.20¢	53.40¢	55.10¢	48.90¢
	1981	44.60¢	49.70¢	42.90¢	42.70¢	43.60¢
	1982	33.50¢	37.70¢	30.90¢	32.50¢	35.35¢
	1983	35.50¢	40.30¢	33.40¢	34.50¢	35.90¢
	1984	35.80¢	38.60¢	35.60¢	33¢	39.70¢
Soft Drink, Cola, per 16 ounces	1980	44.60¢	42.80¢	45.70¢	NR	45.50¢
	1981	46.40¢	45.50¢	47.60¢	45.50¢	46.60¢
	1982	47.30¢	47.50¢	48.40¢	46.30¢	47.40¢
	1983	46.90¢	45.40¢	48.70¢	46¢	47.50¢
	1984	47.50¢	49.80¢	49.20¢	46.50¢	46¢
Tuna, Light, Chunk, per pound	1980	$2.55	$2.46	$2.54	$2.64	$2.54
	1981	$2.58	$2.48	$2.59	$2.63	$2.62
	1982	$2.58	$2.54	$2.51	NR	$2.42
	1983	$2.38	$2.47	$2.34	$2.34	$2.46
	1984	$2.16	$2.05	$2.12	$2.16	$2.18

SELECTED PRICES 1980–1984

Item	Source	Description	Price
ADVERTISING			
Advertising Rate	*Guinness Book of World Records* (1981)	Price of a single minute of television advertising on Super Bowl XIV in 1980	$468,000
Business Advertising Rate	*Guinness Book of World Records* (1981)	Price of a four-color back cover of Parade Magazine; circulation 21 million in1980	$152,475
ALCOHOL			
Beer	*Los Angeles Times* (1981)	Pabst; 12 pack, 12-oz cans	$3.19
Bourbon	*Los Angeles Times* (1981)	Old Crow; 1.75 liter	$9.49
Vodka	*Los Angeles Times* (1981)	Count Vasya; 80 proof; 1.75 liter	$6.99
Wine	*Los Angeles Times* (1981)	Bolla Soave; dry white; 750 ml; save $1.40	$2.99
Wine	*Guinness Book of World Records* (1981)	1822 bottle of rare Château Lafite wine bought in 1980	$31,000
APPAREL, CHILDREN'S			
Shoes	*Yankee* (1981)	Kangaroos; Sebago's most noted quality casual shoes	$38.95
APPAREL, MEN'S			
Boots	*Field & Stream* (1982)	Browning Featherweight; soft leather boot	$102.95
Cap	*Sears, Roebuck* (1983)	Genuine leather with acetate lining	$22
Gloves	*Sears, Roebuck* (1983)	Leather driving-style; soft, rich cowhide shell	$17
Gloves	*Sears, Roebuck* (1983)	Canvas-cloth work gloves	$6.49
Hat	*Field & Stream* (1982)	Gunslinger western style; flat crown, 4 1/4" high with oval indentations; made of 100% wool felt	$15.50
Hunting Suit	*Field & Stream* (1982)	Cabela; camouflage; reversible orange and camouflage; 2-piece suit	$74.95
Jacket	*The Scottish Lion Catalog* (1984)	Irish tweed; a washing in the River Eske in Ireland to soften the yarn is part of the special handling these jackets have been receiving since 1866	$185
Pants	*New York Times* (1981)	Genuine U.S. Marine; camouflage	$39
Pants	*Bon Appétit* (1984)	REI Woolrich; comfort in action; have fun and good fit in these Rugby-style pants	$18.95

Item	Source	Description	Price
Shirt	*Field & Stream* (1982)	L. L. Bean; chamois cloth shirt; in green, red, navy, ivory, tan, and slate blue	$18.25
Shoes	Yankee (1981)	Deerskin Trading Post; pile-lined suede mocs; sturdy cowhide suede lined with fleecy acrylic	$12.99
Shoes	Sears, Roebuck (1983)	Wing-tip oxford	$39.99
Socks	Sears, Roebuck (1983)	Even our very low-priced work socks are cotton-terry lined; 6 pairs in package	$5.99/pkg
Socks	*Sears, Roebuck* (1983)	Wool blend for boots	$5.99
Sport coat	*Sears, Roebuck* (1983)	In a rich array of colors, patterns, and sizes	$59.99
Work Gloves	*Sears, Roebuck* (1983)	Long-wearing; split-cowhide leather palm	$4.99

APPAREL, WOMEN'S

Item	Source	Description	Price
Bag	*The Scottish Lion* Catalog (1984)	Two thistle; 100% cotton canvas tote bag; zippered top opens to a roomy 12" × 10" × 4 1/2" interior	$25
Blouse	*Sears, Roebuck* (1983)	Coordinating Dacron polyester blouses with ties; solid colors; misses sizes	$12
Blouse	*The Scottish Lion* Catalog (1984)	In 100% Irish silk, tie front, dry clean	$85
Caftan	*Yankee* (1981)	Chain stitched embroidered caftan; 100% cambric cotton	$22
Dress	*The Scottish Lion* Catalog (1984)	*Liberty of London;* 100% cotton; top stitching around the collar, waist band, and placket front	$125
Jacket	*The Scottish Lion* Catalog (1984)	Belted; made in Scotland of 70% mohair, 23% wool, 7% nylon	$110
Kimono	*Bon Appétit* (1984)	*Horchow Collection;* Japanese cotton kimono robe	$29.50
Nightshirt	*The Scottish Lion* Catalog (1984)	Seersucker shortie; 100% cotton, button on the front placket and cuffs; made in Scotland	$19
Pocketbook	*The Scottish Lion* Catalog (1984)	Lovely leather bag from Wales; can be carried on the shoulder or the arm; wine, black, or navy	$49
Shoes	*Los Angeles Times* (1981)	*Lady Wellco The Mesh;* walking shoe; plenty of soft comfort in this mesh shoe	$19.99
Skirt	*The Scottish Lion* Catalog (1984)	Striped skirt; from Scotland; 100% linen in bold natural, black and red design	$59
Sweater	*The Scottish Lion* Catalog (1984)	Cardigan; 100% pure new wool with high crewneck for warmth	$95

APPLIANCES

Item	Source	Description	Price
Air Conditioner	*Chicago Tribune* (1983)	*Hotpoint;* 5,950 btu	$299
Computer	*Cox News Service* (2004)	*Apple Macintosh;* easy graphic user interface, includes mouse	$2500
Fan	*Sears, Roebuck* (1983)	Manually reversible 2-speed window fan	$34.99

Item	Source	Description	Price
Fan	*Sears, Roebuck* (1983)	Whole-house window fans can pull at least twice as much air through your home as any other fan sold on this page; 24"; 3-speed; with temperature control	$179.99
Gas Grill	*Los Angeles Times* (1981)	*Turco Saratoga;* deluxe twin-burner gas grill	$179.99
Microwave Oven	*Sears, Roebuck* (1981)	*GE Spacemaster;* 1.3 cu ft; mounts like range hoods to cook, vent, illuminate; all without using an inch of valuable counterspace	$689.99
Vacuum Cleaner	*Los Angeles Times* (1981)	*Eureka;* high-performance upright; originally $150	$119.95
Vacuum Cleaner	*Food & Wine* (1984)	*Eureka Mini Mite;* the cordless rechargeable hand vacuum, the eighties answer to a dustpan and broom	$39.95
Washer	*Sears, Roebuck* (1983)	*Kenmore;* 2 speed; 5 fabric care cycles	$529.95
Washer	*Chicago Tribune* (1983)	*Westinghouse;* single speed	$318
Washer and Dryer	*Sears, Roebuck* (1983)	*Kenmore;* all-in-one; installs permanently	$719.95

BABY PRODUCTS

Item	Source	Description	Price
Baby Bag	*Yankee* (1981)	*The Baby Bag;* warmer and easier to use than a snowsuit; fits children 3 months to two years	$32.50
Cradle	*Sears, Roebuck* (1983)	Suspends from hooks mounted on stand posts, swings or can be locked in stationary position	$79.99
Crib	*Sears, Roebuck* (1983)	*Homestead;* features a pine-frame crib with carved detail on the footboard	$129.99
Crib	*Sears, Roebuck* (1983)	*Laura Lynn;* has a pine frame and turned spindles; choose pine or maple finish	$119.99
Crib Set	*Sears, Roebuck* (1983)	Mattress and bumper pad; save $6; separate prices total$165.97; includes crib, 80-coil mattress, and polyurethane foam bumper pad	$159.97
Dressing Table	*Sears, Roebuck* (1983)	1" thick polyurethane foam pad covered in vinyl Sunny Days print that reverses to white	$79.99

BUSINESS EQUIPMENT AND SUPPLIES

Item	Source	Description	Price
Attaché Case	*Sears, Roebuck* (1983)	Our finest cowhide attaché won't open when upside down	$44.99
Attaché Case	*Sears, Roebuck* (1983)	Dark brown pigskin leather; molded handle; leather- look vinyl interior wipes clean; brass-plated double combination lock	$89.99
Chair	*Los Angeles Times* (1981)	*Ford Office Furniture;* secretary posture chair; list $70	$39.95
Computer	*New York Times* (1984)	*Panasonic Sr. Partner;* more powerful than IBM or Compaq portables plus a built-in printer	$2,195
Computer	*New York Times* (1984)	*IBM;* 256K RAM that's expandable to 512K	$1,795
Computer	*New York Times* (1984)	*Macintosh; 128K;* includes MacWrite and MacPaint	$1,788
Copier	*Los Angeles Times* (1981)	Xerox 2300	$2,995

Item	Source	Description	Price
Desk	*Los Angeles Times* (1981)	*Ford Office Furniture;* full executive desk, 36" × 72"	$139.95
Paper Shredder	*New York Times* (1984)	*Destroyit;* styled to fit into executive office	$474.95
Portfolio	*Sears, Roebuck* (1983)	Our business case collection; genuine pigskin leather	$49.99
Printer	*New York Times* (1984)	*Epson RX-80;* frills on a no-frills budget	$239

COLLECTIBLES

Item	Source	Description	Price
Furniture	*Atlanta Constitution* (1983)	Antique pub table	$150
Painting	*Guinness Book of World Records* (1981)	Price paid in 1980 for J. M. W. Turner's *Juliet and Her Nurse,* 1836	$6.4 million
Painting	*Guinness Book of World Records* (1981)	Auction price in 1980 of Picasso's 1923 portrait of an acrobat Saltimbanque	$3 million
Poster	*Bon Appétit* (1984)	By Robert Rauschenberg; 1984 Olympic; fine-art poster; 24" × 36"	$30

ENTERTAINMENT, HOME

Item	Source	Description	Price
Camera	*New York Times* (1984)	*Canon Super Sure-Shot;* autofocus	$128.50
Movie Camera	*Sears, Roebuck* (1983)	Low-light silent movie camera; 2-to-1 manual zoom	$109.99
Movie Projector	*Sears, Roebuck* (1983)	*Dual 8;* silent movie projector	$99.99
Turntable	*Los Angeles Times* (1981)	*Sony;* direct-drive turntable; fully automatic straight-line tonearm tracks any record more accurately	$200
Video Camera	*Village Voice* (1981)	Panasonic PK 750	$645
Video Camera	*New York Times* (1984)	*Sharp;* save on world's smallest portable video cameras	$359.50
Video Disc Player	*Village Voice* (1981)	Pioneer VP 1000	$539
Video Games	*New York Times* (1981)	*Bally Professional Arcade Plus;* includes three built-in games, two hand controls; color calculator; Bally Basic cartridge worth $54.95	$299.95
Video Tapes	*Village Voice* (1981)	Maxwell T-120	$13.49

An advertisement for the video game Tron, based on the film released in 1982. (via Flickr)

Item	Source	Description	Price
ENTERTAINMENT			
Circus Ticket	*Los Angeles Times* (1981)	*Ringling Bros. and Barnum & Bailey Circus;* all seats reserved	$5–$8.50
Concert	*Village Voice* (1981)	*Musical Medicine Show;* General Mineral's musical comedy, Floating Hospital Children's Theater Adults Children	 $2 Free
Concert Ticket	*New York Times* (1984)	Pete Seeger at Carnegie Hall	$8.50–$10.50
Movie	*Village Voice* (1981)	*Mickey Mouse and Silly Symphonies;* Whitney Museum	$2
Music Concert	*Village Voice* (1981)	*Jazz in the Park;* Danny Holgate Ensemble and tap dancer Sandman Sims Each	 $2.50
Museum Ticket	*Mini-Vacation in the Mid-Atlantic* (1980)	*The Hagley Museum;* a complex of 19th-century industrial buildings on the site of the original DuPont black powder works	$2.50
Museum Ticket	*Mini-Vacation in the Mid-Atlantic* (1980)	*Old Dutch House Museum;* reputedly the oldest brick dwelling in the state	$0.50
Theater Ticket	*New York Times* (1984)	Dance; Ailey at City Center; evenings and Sunday matinee; orchestra and mezzanine	$30
FOOD PRODUCTS			
Beef Jerky	*Los Angeles Times* (1981)	*Lowry's;* in plastic jar with screw top lid; 4 oz size	$1.99
Beef Roast	*New York Times* (1981)	USDA Choice grade; top round, sirloin, tip round, bottom round	$1.89/lb
Candy	The Scottish Lion Catalog (1984)	Scottish Butterscotch; 1 lb; individually gold-foil wrapped, packed in assorted reusable tin of English shops; 4 1/2" × 3" × 3"	$7
Carrots	*New York Times* (1981)	3 1-lb bags	$1
Crabmeat	*Food & Wine* (1984)	*Stone Harbor;* whole; backfin lump crabmeat; now you can enjoy delicious Crab Louis or Crab Imperial; 12 6 1/2 oz tins; regular $70.95; introductory price	$62.95
Cran-apple Juice	*Los Angeles Times* (1981)	*Ocean's Spray;* 32-oz jar	$0.93
Elephant Garlic	*Food & Wine* (1984)	*Willacrick Farm;* great gift item, contains over 2 pounds	$15
Lobster	*Bon Appétit* (1983)	*Barker's;* four 1 1/4-pound Maine lobsters with four pounds of live, clean Ipswich steamers	$79.50
Marmalade	The Scottish Lion Catalog (1984)	*Dundee;* four 1-lb jars of orange, lemon, grapefruit and 3-in-1 blend	$16
Milk	*Los Angeles Times* (1981)	*Sunnydell;* 1/2 gallon homogenized	$1.01
Pork Loin	*New York Times* (1981)	*Wilson;* rib end	$0.99/lb
Tomatoes	*New York Times* (1981)	Hard, ripe; selected for slicing; 18 oz package	$0.79

Item	Source	Description	Price
Yogurt	*New York Times* (1981)	*Breyers;* assorted flavors; 8-oz containers; 2 containers	$0.89

FURNITURE

Item	Source	Description	Price
Chair	*New York Times* (1981)	*Wild Boar;* taupe; regularly $1,795; sale	$895
Dresser	*New York Times* (1981)	*Welch;* dresser; regularly $2,405	$1,599
Sofa	*New York Times* (1981)	Green and pink floral contemporary; 80"; parsons style; upholstered; regularly $1,995	$1,495

GARDEN EQUIPMENT AND SUPPLIES

Item	Source	Description	Price
Lawn Mower	*Sears, Roebuck* (1983)	*Craftsman;* standard Eager-1 engine; 3.5 reserve power	$299.99
Plants	*Atlanta Constitution* (1983)	Ground covers; English Ivy, Pachysandra, or Vinca Minor; bundle of 25, per bundle	$7.25
Plants	*Atlanta Constitution* (1983)	Azaleas, full 6" pots; dwarf and tall, each	$.99
Shears	*The Scottish Lion Catalog* (1984)	Japanese gardeners' hedge shears; the stainless-steel model has a 6 1/2" blade, is 25" overall and weighs 30 oz	$19.95
Soil	*Atlanta Constitution* (1983)	*Hyponex Professional Mix Potting Soil;* sphagnum peat moss, vermiculite, perlite, humus, charcoal, 16 quart	$3.88

HOTEL RATES

Item	Source	Description	Price
Hotel	*Great Outdoors Vacation & Lodging Guide* (1980)	*Baranof Hotel;* Juneau, Alaska; 218 rooms and suites, the Latch-string restaurant, sauna and exercise room; double	$48.50/ngt
Hotel	*Great Outdoors Vacation & Lodging Guide* (1980)	*Holiday Inn;* Flagstaff, Arizona; 157 excellent rooms, restaurant, coffee shop, cocktail lounge, heated pool; double	$35/ngt
Hotel	*Great Outdoors Vacation & Lodging Guide* (1980)	*Ramada Inn;* Lake Havasu City, Arizona; 100 excellent rooms, restaurant, cocktail lounge, heated pool; double	$27/ngt
Lodge	*Great Outdoors Vacation & Lodging Guide* (1980)	*Afognak Wilderness Lodge;* Kodiak Island, Alaska; accommodations for 10 guests at a time; rates cover lodging, all meals, and boat travel	$100
Lodge	*Great Outdoors Vacation & Lodging Guide* (1980)	*Alexander Lake Lodge;* rustic fly-in resort in lowland lake country 50 miles northeast of Anchorage, offers unspoiled fishing; rates include all meals, lodging and boat service; per person	$75
Lodge	*Great Outdoors Vacation & Lodging Guide* (1980)	*Garland's Oak Creek Lodge;* Arizona; located in the heart of Oak Creek Canyon, surrounded by stunning red-rock mountains; rates include breakfast, dinner, and lodging; per couple, per night	$58
Resort	*Great Outdoors Vacation & Lodging Guide* (1980)	*Indian Rock Resort;* Fairfield Bay, Arkansas; guest-house for 4, located on 40,000 acre Greers Ferry Lake	$60

Item	Source	Description	Price
HOUSEHOLD PRODUCTS			
China	*The Scottish Lion Catalog* (1984)	English, fine bone; 10-piece tea-for-two set includes 2-cup teapot with cover, sugar and creamer, 2 teacups and saucers, 2 6 1/2" plates	$69
Chisel Set	*The Scottish Lion Catalog* (1984)	*Marples;* beveled-edge chisel set; made of Sheffield steel; set of six: 1/4", 3/8", 1/2", 5/8", 3/4", 1"	$51.95
Clock	*The Scottish Lion Catalog* (1984)	Chiming, carriage; beautiful brass clock with silver face is made in Norfolk County in England; quartz movement	$115
Curtains	*Yankee* (1981)	*Country Curtains;* classic tightly woven pinwale corduroy curtains in colonial blue, bright red, natural or deep brown; 63" or 72" long; per pair	$37
Flatware	*Bon Appétit* (1984)	*International Lyon;* 60-piece service for 12, queen's fancy style	$219.95
Folding Rule	*The Scottish Lion Catalog* (1984)	Hardwood; 3', 4-fold rule, subdivided in 8ths, 16ths	$6.95
Footlocker	*Sears, Roebuck* (1983)	Antique-look burled-design vinyl exterior with nickel- plated steel hardware	$49.99
Furniture Finish	*Yankee* (1981)	Lemon oil with beeswax furniture polish; leaves no film; two 8 oz Bottles	$4.98
Gadget Bag	*Sears, Roebuck* (1983)	Rugged, yet lightweight; great for carrying all your photographic equipment	$19.99
Hammer	*The Scottish Lion Catalog* (1984)	*Stanley;* 13 oz; hickory; rim-tempered face, curved claw, hickory handle; Stanley list price $12.25	$8.95
Handsaw	*The Scottish Lion Catalog* (1984)	*Model D-95;* precision set and beveled to provide smooth, accurate cuts, 26" × 8 points	$19.95
Knife	*Bon Appétit* (1984)	*Sabatier Gingko International;* 6" chef's knife, crafted of high-carbon stainless steel in La Monnerie, France	$10
Mattress Set	*Atlanta Constitution* (1983)	Queen size, regular $399.95 to $649.95 Sale on sets	$165 to $292
Screwdriver	*The Scottish Lion Catalog* (1984)	*Stanley Blackhawk;* professional quality, forged-steel blades; set of 4; Stanley's list price $26.95	$14.95
Tray	*Bon Appétit* (1983)	*Bombay Raffles;* serving tray; adapted from our popular Raffles table; mahogany finished	$9
Workbench	*The Scottish Lion Catalog* (1984)	Swedish; woodworking; top is arctic birch; the body is three-layer laminated hardwood; 50 1/2" long, includes five drawers	$259.95

An advertisement for a Morton Hearth Furnace, published in Country Living magazine, November 1984. (via Flickr)

Item	Source	Description	Price
JEWELRY			
Brooch	*The Scottish Lion Catalog* (1984)	Irish harp; a lyrical, lovely and treasured gift; British gold	$115
Pendant	*The Scottish Lion Catalog* (1984)	Thistle amethyst; a symbol of unity and pride in Scottish history; gold	250
Pendant	*Food & Wine* (1984)	*Diamond Desires;* heart; it's scandalous what diamonds do to me	$1,650
Wristwatch	*New York Times* (1984)	*Rolex Oysterquartz Date;* just peerless performance, timeless style	$2,725
Wristwatch	*New York Times* (1984)	*Seiko 12-L;* ladies ultra thin	$84.95
MOTORIZED VEHICLES, SUPPLIES AND SERVICES			
Automobile	*Atlanta Constitution* (1983)	*1983 Honda Civic* wagon; five speed transmission, air conditioning, stereo cassette, pin stripes; list price $8,317.85, now	$7,517.85
Automobile	*Sports Illustrated* (1980)	*Pontiac Firebird;* Pontiac takes on the imports	$6,132
Automobile	*Los Angeles Times* (1981)	*Cadillac Eldorado;* 1981	$19,700

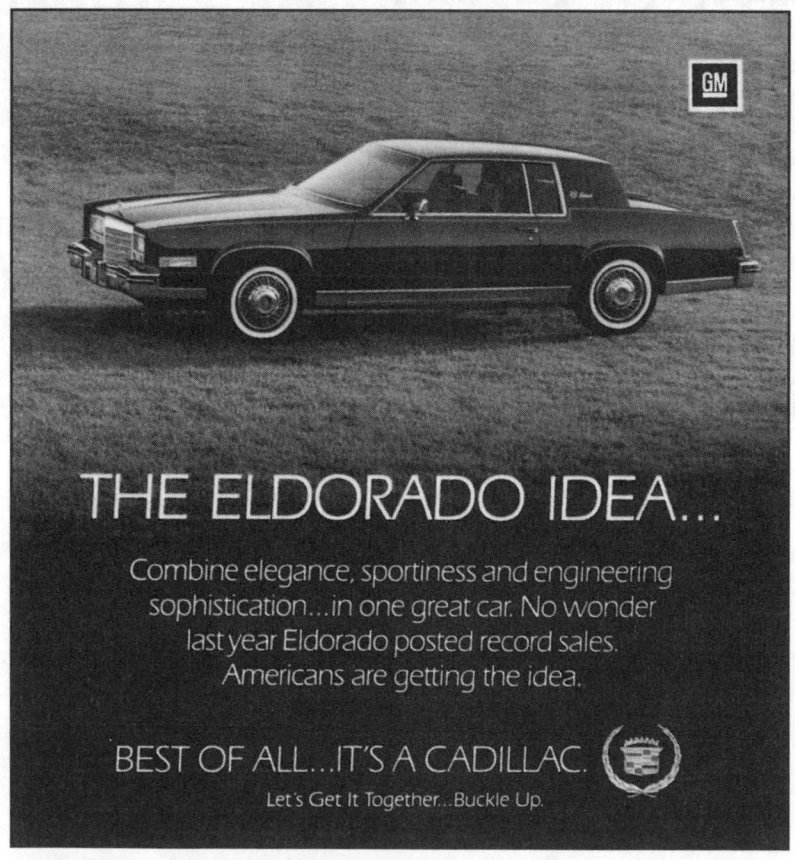

An advertisement for a 1984 Cadillac Eldorado. (via Flickr)

Item	Source	Description	Price
Car Stereo	*Sears, Roebuck* (1983)	*Sanyo Automatic;* music-select system; auto reverse with locking fast forward and reverse	$179.99
Rental	*Food & Wine* (1984)	*Budget;* Budget has more Lincolns than Hertz, Avis, and National combined; so when you want a Lincoln call Budget	$44.95/day
Truck	*Field & Stream* (1982)	*Dodge Ram 50;* pick-up; now the world has turbo-diesel pick-ups	$5,999

OTHER

Item	Source	Description	Price
Carving Kit	*Yankee* (1981)	Learn to carve a Cardinal; a complete kit, including ready to carve pine bird, material for eyes, legs and feet	$11.95
Figurine	*The Scottish Lion Catalog* (1984)	Blue Tit bird; a very lifelike pose; ceramic is signed by the sculptor; 3 1/2" height	$65
Photo Album	*Sears, Roebuck* (1983)	100-page loose-leaf album	$12.99
Photo Finishing	*New York Times* (1981)	*First Class Photo;* any size film, 110–126 and 35mm too; per picture from roll	$0.14
Tree Lease	*Food & Wine* (1984)	*North County Corp.;* rent Mother Nature; lease a sugar- maple tree or a sap bucket for one year	$25

PERSONAL CARE PRODUCTS

Item	Source	Description	Price
Cuticle Nipper	*Yankee* (1981)	*German Cutlery;* cuticle nipper, precision ground	$10.95

PUBLICATIONS

Item	Source	Description	Price
Book	*Food & Wine* (1984)	*The Gold and Fizdale Cookbook,* by Arthur Gold and Robert Fizdale; asparagus, ampergios, and anecdotes	$19.95
Magazine	*Village Voice* (1981)	52 weeks	$26
Newspaper	*Atlanta Constitution* (1983)	*The Atlanta Constitution* (mornings) and *Atlanta Journal* (afternoons); 13 weeks	$25
Videotape	*Food & Wine* (1984)	*Video Manufacturing Concepts; The Videotape Italian Cookbook;* the perfect holiday gift for those with VHS/Beta recorders	$42.50

REAL ESTATE

Item	Source	Description	Price
Apartment	*Chicago Tribune* (1983)	For rent; top of the line; deluxe 2 bedroom	$489/mo
Apartment	*Chicago Tribune* (1983)	For rent; 1 bedroom with underground parking	$400/mo
Apartment	*Chicago Tribune* (1983)	Furnished; elegant 3 1/2 rooms, 2 bedroom; carpeted, with appliances and furniture; all utilities paid	$350/mo
House	*Chicago Tribune* (1983)	The 5-bedroom fully furnished main residence, 4-room coach house, and enclosed horse arena/barn are situated on 7 wooded acres; originally priced at $475,000	$185,000
House	*New York Times* (1984)	Doctor's home; custom details throughout; huge living room, fireplace, formal dining room, 4 bedrooms, 3 baths	$156,000

Item	Source	Description	Price
House	*New York Times* (1984)	Very special; stunning colonial inside and out; living room with fireplace, dining room, new kitchen, screened terrace, playroom, and office	$225,000
House	*New York Times* (1984)	Exciting; sprawling California contemporary ranch	$659,000

SPORTS EQUIPMENT

Item	Source	Description	Price
Bicycle	*Sears, Roebuck* (1983)	*FS300;* 20" has mag-style wheels, gumwall knobby tires, and × BMX pads	$139.99
Bicycle	*Sears, Roebuck* (1983)	*FS500;* 24" track-certified bike for competitive use	$179.99
Boat	*Field & Stream* (1982)	*Bass Tracker 1;* boats that can do the same job as the expensive $12,000–$15,000 fiberglass boats but not carry the additional weight, cost, and inefficiency	$3,795
Boat	*Field & Stream* (1982)	*Harrison-Hodge Sea Eagle;* inflatable; lightweight, 81-pound boat has 1200 pound capacity	$540
Fishing Spool	*Field & Stream* (1982)	*Lew Childre & Sons;* fresh water light bait casting reel; 9.7 ounces	$95
Fly Reel	*Field & Stream* (1982)	*Shakespeare;* 6 oz; takes up to no. 8 fly line	$29.95
Golf Balls	*New York Times* (1981)	*Spalding Top-Flite;* 15-ball bonus packs	$13.99
Golf Clubs	*New York Times* (1981)	*Wilson;* 11-piece pro-style	$219.99
Heater	*Field & Stream* (1982)	*Kero-Sun Omni;* portable; ideal to heat extra-large areas; operates up to 18 hours on a 2-gallon tankful of kerosene	$289.95
Knee Pads	*Sears, Roebuck* (1983)	Red and white elastic	$5.99/pr
Rifle	*Field & Stream* (1982)	*Beeman Feinwerkbau 124 Air Rifle;* .177 caliber, 18.3", 12-groove rifled barrel, single shot	$299.50
Rod and Reel	*Field & Stream* (1982)	*Daiwa 4-Minimite;* ultra/light skirted spool spinning system	$59.95
Shotgun	*Field & Stream* (1982)	*Olin/Winchester;* pigeon grade lightweight, 12-gauge; 25 1/2" barrel	$1,200
Skateboard	*Sears, Roebuck* (1983)	Our longest, widest board for stability; kicktail on board aids in trick riding; king bolts adjust for ease of turning	$59.99
Skates	*Sears, Roebuck* (1983)	*Young Star;* with sealed-greased bearings and durable nickel-plated steel chassis that resists corrosion	$24.99
Sleeping Bag	*Field & Stream* (1982)	*Coleman;* 31 lbs, spring to late fall comfort range	$32
Tackle Box	*Field & Stream* (1982)	*Plano Molding;* measures 19" × 19 1/2" × 13 5/8"; front panel opens and slides under bottom drawer	$89.95

TELEPHONE EQUIPMENT AND SERVICES

Item	Source	Description	Price
Long Distance Rates	*Chicago Tribune* (1983)	Chicago to Detroit; 10 minutes	$3.08
Long Distance Rates	*Chicago Tribune* (1983)	Indianapolis to New York; 5 minutes	$1.78

Item	Source	Description	Price
Telephone	*New York Times* (1984)	*Cobra;* national best-seller; cordless	$139.95

TOBACCO PRODUCTS

Cigars	*Food & Wine* (1984)	*Thompson Cigar;* you don't need Castro's permission to smoke Cuban-seed handmade cigars; sampler	$10.90

TOYS

Blocks	*Yankee* (1981)	We call this one Triple Up because the object of the game is to be the first to get three blocks of your color in a row; per set	$4.95
Doll	*Yankee* (1981)	*Yankee Doodle Dancer,* Dancer Folk Toy; an educational rhythm toy	$8.50

TRAVEL AND TRANSPORTATION

Airfare	*Village Voice* (1981)	Ventura seaplane to Fire Island from 23rd Street, New York City	$40
Airfare	*Great Outdoors Vacation & Lodging Guide* (1980)	*Air Alaska;* from Anchorage to Brooks Lodge on Brooks River, Alaska; round trip	$135
Boat Tour	*Mini-Vacation in the Mid-Atlantic* (1980)	*Potomac Boat Tours;* cruises daily 10–9	$3
Cruise	*Yankee* (1981)	*Emerald Seas;* sailing from Miami to the Bahamas; three night cruise to Nassau, per person On season Off season	 $230–$475 $215–$460
Expedition	*Great Outdoors Vacation & Lodging Guide* (1980)	*Alaska Discovery;* Yukon River 10-day canoeing and camping excursion; per person	$600
Festival	*Village Voice* (1981)	*Reggae Sunsplash, Jamaica's Music Festival;* one week includes roundtrip airfare from New York to Chicago Montego Bay; double occupancy hotel, admission to music events	$499
Houseboat Trip	*Great Outdoors Vacation & Lodging Guide* (1980)	*Colorado River Houseboat;* a unique means of vacation transport on 500 miles of the Colorado River and the entire expanse of Lake Havasu; rate includes 6 days on a 43-ft craft	$755
River Trip	*Great Outdoors Vacation & Lodging Guide* (1980)	*Miller's Float Services;* Cotter, Arkansas; one-day float trip for two on White River	$90

MISCELLANY 1980–1984

Sony Unit Links Camera to Recorder

In twin presentations in Tokyo and New York yesterday, the Sony Corporation introduced a single-unit combination video camera and video cassette recorder weighing 4.4 pounds, substantially more compact than existing equipment with the same functions.

The new Video Movie, as the product is called, is a prototype, however, and will not be commercially available until 1985.

The new single-unit prototype, which will sell for under $1,000, apparently offers an entirely new product to further stir the percolating video- recording field.

New York Times, July 2, 1980

Prices Farmers Get Fell 0.7% from May

Prices that farmers get for their raw products fell seventh-tenths of one percent in June from the May level but still averaged 11 percent more than in June of last year, the Agriculture Department said today.

The department's Crop Reporting Board, in releasing its preliminary estimates for June, said lower prices for wheat, soybeans, corn, hay, and lettuce led the month's drop. These declines were partly offset, however, by higher prices for hogs, tomatoes, potatoes, broilers, and turkeys.

New York Times, July 1, 1981

Video Games Go to Hollywood

Hollywood is cashing in on the video game craze. In 1981, game cartridges that can be plugged into home television sets and coin-operated arcades were an $8 billion business, while audiences paid less than $3 billion at U. S. movie theater box offices. In the past few weeks, nearly every movie studio has announced a joint venture or new division meant to siphon off some of those impressive video game revenues.

Each studio is aiming its laser guns and spaceships down a different path, but all share at least one goal—replacing games titled "Pac-Man," "Berzerk," and "Frogger" with games called, "Jaws," "9 to 5," "Star Wars," and "Star Trek."

New York Times, July 1, 1982

Tobacco Market Opens Sluggishly

"We had anticipated a strong market opening. The quality was good, but the overall interest of the (buying) companies was something less than we expected," said [U.S. Senator Sam] Irvin. Georgia tobacco farmers are expected to produce a 117-million-pound crop this year.

The average opening day buying price ranged from $145 to $170 per hundred pounds, depending on the quality and grade, the commission said. Last year's average price was $162.50.

Atlanta Constitution, July 22, 1982

HISTORICAL SNAPSHOT 1985–1989

1985

- Single optical fiber carries 300,000 simultaneous phone calls in Bell Laboratory tests
- Coca-Cola introduces new-formula Coke; public outcry brings back old formula as Classic Coke one year later
- Capital Cities Communications buys television network ABC for $3.5 billion
- First genetically engineered microorganisms are licensed for commercial purposes
- The U.S. and the Soviet Union meet for the first time in six years
- Supreme Court upholds affirmative-action hiring quotas
- World oil prices collapse, bottoming out at $7.20 per barrel
- First Windows operating system for computers is introduced
- U.S. national debt tops $2 billion
- Pete Rose breaks the record for most career hits in MLB history

1986

- Sears celebrates its 100th anniversary
- Office Depot, one of the first office supply warehouse-type stores, opens in Lauderdale Lakes, FL
- The Challenger Space Shuttle explodes on launch, killing seven people, including school teacher Christa McAuliffe
- Seven million people link hands across the United States as part of the Hands Across America campaign
- Reports start coming out on the Iran-Contra affair
- *The Oprah Winfrey Show* begins airing

- A nuclear accident happens at the Chernobyl Nuclear Power Plant in the Ukraine
- Halley's Comet passes overhead for the first time since 1910
- The antidepressant Prozac becomes available as a prescription drug

1987

- Supercomputer capable of 1,720 billion computations per second goes on-line
- President Reagan visits Berlin and urges Gorbachev to "Tear down this wall!"
- The stock market experiences a record 22.6% drop on what became known as 'Black Monday'
- Clean water bill passed to address pollution of estuaries and rainwater
- Stock market plunges 508 points in one day (October 19), largest drop in history
- New York Stock Exchange seat sells for $1.5 million
- Trade deficit hits record $16.5 billion
- The first major condom commercial is aired in San Francisco by the brand Trojan

1988

- Robots are used for fruit picking
- Unemployment falls to 5.4 percent
- Philip Morris buys Kraft for $12.9 billion
- U.S. savings and loans lose $13.44 billion
- Iran accepts a UN-sponsored peace treaty, ending the 8-year Iran-Iraq war
- Nike begins using their famous "Just Do It" slogan

- Compact discs (CDs) outsell vinyl records for the first time
- A draught in the United States causes intense heat waves and wildfires
- The first World AIDS Day is observed
- The Morris Worm was one of the first computer worms distributed via the Internet

1989

- The Berlin Wall falls, essentially ending the Cold War
- Media conglomerates Warner Communications and Time, Inc. merge
- Exxon oil tanker runs aground off Alaska coastline, causing worst U.S. oil spill; costs Exxon $1.7 billion in lawsuits
- Stock market plunges 190.58 points in single day (October 17), 2nd largest drop in history
- Federal government spends $159 billion to bail out savings and loan industry
- President George H. W. Bush declares a "War on Drugs"
- Hundreds of people die in the Tiananmen Square massacre in Beijing
- General Motors acquires half of Sweden's Saab
- The Human Genome Project is initiated
- The first episode of *The Simpsons* airs

Photograph of President Reagan and his staff watching a televised replay of the Space Shuttle Challenger *explosion, which occurred on January 28th, 1986. Millions of Americans watched the explosion live on television. All seven people on board died in the accident, including school teacher Christa McAuliffe, who was selected in the NASA Teacher in Space project.* (via Wikimedia Commons)

SELECTED INCOME 1985–1989

Job	Source	Description	Pay
Accountants	*New York Times* (1988)	Temporary	$12/hr
Administrative Assistant	*New York Times* (1988)	French/English; Gourmet Foods; work for top exec	$22,000/yr
Advertising	*New York Times* (1988)	Direct response account executives	$30,000–$40,000/yr
Assistant Service Manager	*New York Times* (1988)	Ford experience preferred; modern shop; excellent benefits	$30,000/yr
Attorney	*New York Times* (1988)	Major law firm seeks corporate SEC attorney; early responsibility and extensive client contact; 2–4 years experience	$50,000–$60,000/yr
Bookkeeper A/R	*New York Times* (1988)	You will know this leading sportswear importer; phenomenal growth has created this position for an experienced A/R adjuster	$15,000–$17,000/yr
Bookkeeper Billing Coordinator	*New York Times* (1988)	Brooklyn-based manufacturer; prerequisites include capacity to supervise small staff in all phases of computerized billing	$16,000–$21,000/yr
Carpenter	*New York Times* (1988)	Experienced kitchen/bathroom installer; fine carpentry; driver's license necessary	$11/hr
Chauffeur	*New York Times* (1988)	Early retiree ok; no violations; heavy OT; mature	$19,000/yr
Chef	*New York Times* (1988)	Candidate must have at least 5 years experience in the industry and have formal culinary training in United States or abroad	$37,000/yr
Conference Planner	*Chicago Tribune* (1986)	Nat'l Association located near O'Hare offers excellent career opportunity for experienced conference planner who is skilled in working with volunteer program committees and hotel facilities	$20,000 (mid)/yr
Customer Service	*Chicago Tribune* (1986)	Entry level; will train; front-office appearance base salary	$14,400/yr
Delivery Driver	*Chicago Tribune* (1986)	Use your own vehicle; excellent part-time earnings; weekdays and weekends	$20/delivery
Drafters	*New York Times* (1988)	Experienced inter or exter/detailing	$20,000/yr
Driver	*Chicago Tribune* (1986)	Pizza; Top pay! Part & full time plus tips	$1.75/delivery,
Driver	*Chicago Tribune* (1986)	Pizza; work for Chicago's top pizzeria; full or part time	$6/hr
EDP Auditor	*New York Times* (1988)	Prominent financial service organization is expanding its EDP audit division; candidate should possess 1 year experience in audit reviews and programming	$28,000/yr
Golfer	Victor Bondi, ed., *American Decades: 1980–1989* (1996)	Average total purse in an official Professional Golf Association Event in 1985	$538,000

Job	Source	Description	Pay
Industrial Engineer	*New York Times* (1988)	Major international bank seeks IE for operations analyst position; individual will perform work measurement studies; analyze manual and auto systems and review clerical procedures	$26,000–$30,000/yr
Insurance Claims	*Chicago Tribune* (1986)	Accident, health; two raises 1st year; looking for experienced major medical claims adjuster with willingness to grow with us	$19,000/yr
Mechanical Artist	*New York Times* (1988)	Excellent entry-level career opportunity for art school graduate with at least one year experience to work in lively magazine art department of major publishing house	$230–$250/wk
Media Manager	*New York Times* (1988)	Media planning pro with strength in broadcasting to oversee agencies, assist managers; develop manufacturing and media strategies	$42,000/yr
Model	*Playboy* (1986)	Modeling fee of Christine Richters, the Playboy Playmate for May, 1986	$15,000
Print Estimator	*New York Times* (1988)	21 years agency media department	$16,000/yr
Production Manager	*New York Times* (1988)	Experienced residential interior retails	$45,000/yr
Salesman	*Chicago Tribune* (1986)	Manager trainees, students welcome	$7/hr part time; $360/wk full time
Secretary	*New York Times* (1988)	German/English; diverse position for secretary to assist in lively office of European co.; skills in English a plus	$18,000–$20,000/yr
Transfer Supervisor	*New York Times* (1988)	Supervise 10 clerks; legal, transfer area	$20,000–$24,000/yr

CONSUMER EXPENDITURES 1985–1989

Expenditure Type	1985	1986	1987	1988	1989
Clothing	$542.22	$576.75	$611.98	$648.44	$706.29
Food	$1891.67	$1981.67	$2062.43	$2177.51	$2406.31
Auto Usage	$1398.52	$1411.96	$1447.16	$1538.05	$1567.01
New Auto Purchase	$366.51	$416.77	$385.06	$412.16	$403.07
Auto Parts	$75.90	$76.46	$77.42	$84.47	$131.39
Gas & Oil	$406.35	$331.18	$348.82	$354.62	$338.79
Housing	$1645.94	$1752.69	$1863.52	$1975.92	$2158.48
Furniture	$119.93	$130.06	$135.90	$138.75	$135.84
Utilities	$500.28	$487.41	$495.43	$519.48	$563.17
Telephone & Telegraph	$179.48	$187.40	$195.21	$204.86	$196.89
Physicians	$319.96	$349.46	$401.53	$451.33	$456.84
Dentists	$92.68	$97.65	$106.25	$113.85	$117.24
Health Insurance	$95.19	$91.83	$98.84	$107.73	$119.67
Personal Business	$775.37	$891.31	$963.68	$1040.59	$982.82
Personal Care	$167.32	$180.22	$195.21	$209.75	$211.44
Tobacco	$132.93	$137.54	$144.14	$147.72	$168.59
Local Transport	$31.03	$32.83	$32.95	$33.87	$35.98
Intercity Transport	$93.93	$94.32	$104.19	$114.26	$118.05
Recreation	$787.95	$846.84	$921.26	$1007.14	$1068.93
Religion/Welfare Activities	$265.45	$292.12	$312.99	$350.95	$335.15
Private Education & Research	$228.54	$245.16	$263.98	$292.18	$259.96
Per Capita Consumption	$11,185	$11,845	$12,569	$13,450	$13,948

INVESTMENTS 1985-1989

Investment	1985	1986	1987	1988	1989
Basic Yield, One-year Corporate Bonds	12.05	9.71	9.91	10.18	9.66
Short-term Interest Rates, 4–6 Months,					
Prime Commercial Paper	8.01	6.39	6.85	7.68	8.80
Basic Yield, Common Stocks, Total	4.25	3.48	3.08	3.64	3.45
Index of Common Stocks (1941–1943 5 10)	186.84	236.34	287.00	265.88	323.05

COMMON STOCKS, CLOSING PRICE AND YIELD, FIRST BUSINESS DAY OF YEAR

(PARENTHETICAL NUMBER IS ANNUAL DIVIDENDS IN DOLLARS)

Allis Chalmers	6 1/8	4 1/4	2 3/4	1 3/8	
(Ch 11 Bankruptcy 12/2/88; 1 share common exchanged for .122039 new common)	(2)	(2)	(2)	(2)	
American Brands	63 3/4	65 1/2	43 3/8	48 1/2	62 1/4
(2 for 1 split, 9/10/86)	(3.75)	(3.90)	(2.08)	(2.20)	(2.44)
AT&T	19 1/4	24 5/8	25 1/4	28 1/4	28 5/8
	(1.20)	(1.20)	(1.20)	(1.20)	(1.20)
Bethlehem Steel	17 1/4	15 3/8	7	17 3/4	22 5/8
	(.60)	(2)	(2)		
CPC Intl	40	51	81 1/4	41 3/4	51
	(2.20)	(2.20)	(2.48)	(1.44)	(1.60)
Delta Airlines	43 7/8	39 1/4	48	37 3/4	49 3/8
	(.60)	(1)	(1.00)	(1.20)	(1.20)
General Electric	56	71 7/8	87 3/8	46 1/2	44
(2 shares for 1 split, 4/23/87)	(2.20)	(2.32)	(2.52)	(1.40)	(1.64)
General Motors	77 5/8	70 7/8	66 7/8	63 1/4	82 1/4
(distribution of 1 share of class E common stock @39 for each 20 shares of common held, 12/10/84) (distribution of 1 share of class H common stock 2 shares for 1 split, 2/17/89)	(4.75)	(5)	(5)	(5)	(5)
Intl Harvester	8 1/8	8 3/8			
	(2)	(2)			

Investment	1985	1986	1987	1988	1989
Nabisco	51				
(Merged as wholly owned subsidiary of R. J. Reynolds Industries, 9/10/85)	(2.48)				
U.S. Steel	25 3/4	26 1/2	21 7/8	31 1/2	29 1/4
(Name changed to U.S.X. 7/9/86)	(1)	(1.20)	(1.20)	(1.20)	(1.40)
Western Union	8 1/2	12 3/8	4 1/4	2 3/4	1 3/8
	(/)	(/)	(/)	(/)	(/)

STANDARD JOBS 1985–1989

Job Type	1985	1986	1987	1988	1989
Wages Per Full-Time Employee	$19,188/yr	$21,915/yr	$22,872/yr	$24,032/yr	$22,568/yr
Private Industries, incl. farm labor	$18,980/yr	$21,699/yr	$22,629/yr	$23,794/yr	$22,256/yr
Bituminous Coal Mining	$32,968/yr	$34,837/yr	$35,924/yr	$36,660/yr	$37,908/yr
Building Trades	$21,372/yr	$23,590/yr	$24,537/yr	$25,872/yr	$25,220/yr
Domestics	$7072/yr	$10,061/yr	$10,289/yr	$11,353/yr	$8736/yr
Farm Labor	$7228/yr	$10,216/yr	$10,156/yr	$10,472/yr	$7904/yr
Federal Civilian	$25,591/yr	$27,833/yr	$28,828/yr	$29,957/yr	$28,775/yr
Federal Employees, Executive Depts.	$26,598/yr	$24,273/yr	$25,239/yr	$28,725/yr	$29,951/yr
Finance, Insurance, & Real Estate	$22,308/yr	$25,778/yr	$27,750/yr	$27,716/yr	$28,288/yr
Gas, Electricity, & Sanitary Workers	$31,096/yr	$33,222/yr	$34,730/yr	$35,308/yr	$36,972/yr
Manufacturing, Durable Goods	$23,868/yr	$27,147/yr	$27,899/yr	$129,170/yr	$27,768/yr
Manufacturing, Nondurable Goods	$20,800/yr	$23,313/yr	$24,141/yr	$25,407/yr	$23,764/yr
Medical/Health Services Workers	$18,668/yr	$21,652/yr	$23,724/yr	$25,665/yr	$23,608/yr
Miscellaneous Manufacturing	$18,200/yr	$20,145/yr	$20,918/yr	$20,904/yr	$21,528/yr
Motion Picture Services	$27,040/yr	$28,363/yr	$32,308/yr	$27,716/yr	$34,060/yr
Nonprofit Org. Workers	$11,440/yr	$14,350/yr	$15,017/yr	$15,635/yr	$13,832/yr
Passenger Transportation Workers, Local and Highway	$12,589/yr	$16,239/yr	$16,710/yr	$17,356/yr	$14,092/yr
Personal Services	$10,088/yr	$13,403/yr	$13,889/yr	$14,758/yr	$12,012/yr
Postal Employees	$26,995/yr	$26,362/yr	$27,262/yr	$28,364/yr	$28,479/yr
Public School Teachers	$20,973/yr	$21,920/yr	$22,940/yr	$23,992/yr	$22,413/yr
Radio Broadcasting & Television Workers	$25,064/yr	$28,721/yr	$31,125/yr	$30,857/yr	$28,860/yr
Railroads	$23,036/yr	$37,673/yr	$39,456/yr	$40,862/yr	$36,039/yr
State and Local Govt. Workers	$18,363/yr	$21,949/yr	$23,075/yr	$24,284/yr	$22,440/yr
Telephone & Telegraph Workers	$29,276/yr	$33,705/yr	$35,623/yr	$37,210/yr	$35,906/yr
Wholesale and Retail Trade Workers	$23,764/yr	$26,119/yr	$27,269/yr	$27,820/yr	$28,652/yr

FOOD BASKET 1985–1989

(NR = Not Reported)

Commodity	Year	New York	Atlanta	Chicago	Denver	Los Angeles
Bananas, per pound	1985	35.60¢	40.30¢	34.30¢	NR	40¢
	1986	41¢	35¢	NR	41¢	49¢
	1987	35¢	33¢	38.50¢	43¢	30¢
	1988	41¢	34¢	NR	31¢	32¢
	1989	NR	39¢	NR	48¢	48¢
Beef, Ground, Hamburger, per pound	1985	NR	NR	NR	NR	NR
	1986	$1.37	$1.13	NR	$1.26	$1.29
	1987	$1.59	$1.22	NR	91¢	$1.28
	1988	$1.59	$1.56	NR	$1.15	$1.09
	1989	NR	$1.71	NR	$1.13	$1.49
Beef, Steak, T-bone, per pound	1985	NR	NR	NR	NR	NR
	1986	$4.17	$4.49	NR	$3.54	$2.52
	1987	$4.25	$3.99	NR	$3.85	$3.22
	1988	$4.07	$3.98	NR	$3.95	$2.89
	1989	NR	$5.99	NR	$4.18	$4.02
Bread, White, per 24 ounces	1985	NR	NR	NR	NR	NR
	1986	71¢	50¢	NR	54¢	75¢
	1987	72¢	54¢	NR	45¢	59¢
	1988	69¢	57¢	NR	48¢	52¢
	1989	NR	65¢	NR	66¢	92¢
Chickens, per pound	1985	NR	NR	NR	NR	NR
	1986	88¢	79¢	NR	78¢	$1.25
	1987	77¢	84¢	NR	57¢	80¢
	1988	75¢	60¢	NR	50¢	51¢
	1989	NR	63¢	NR	67¢	99¢
Cheese, Parmesan, Grated, per 8 ounces	1985	NR	NR	NR	NR	NR
	1986	$2.75	$2.35	NR	$2.77	$2.09
	1987	$2.99	$2.29	NR	$2.76	$2.68
	1988	$2.93	$2.38	NR	$2.37	$2.74
	1989	NR	$2.52	NR	$2.39	$2.82
Coffee, per pound	1985	NR	NR	NR	NR	NR
	1986	$3.41	$3.97	NR	$2.96	$3.53
	1987	$2.97	$3.55	NR	$3.20	$2.86
	1988	$2.71	$2.34	NR	$2.52	$2.23
	1989	NR	$2.92	NR	$2.82	$3.05
Corn, Whole Kernel, Frozen, per 10 ounces	1985	NR	NR	NR	NR	NR
	1986	53¢	70¢	NR	53¢	46¢
	1987	55¢	65¢	NR	55¢	46¢
	1988	57¢	62¢	NR	55¢	50¢
	1989	NR	78¢	NR	52¢	64¢
Eggs, per dozen	1985	NR	NR	NR	NR	NR
	1986	92¢	68¢	NR	88¢	94¢
	1987	99¢	84¢	NR	83¢	$1.25
	1988	89¢	65¢	NR	72¢	$1.25
	1989	NR	78¢	NR	93¢	$1.56

Commodity	Year	New York	Atlanta	Chicago	Denver	Los Angeles
Cereal, per 18 ounces	1985	NR	NR	NR	NR	NR
	1986	$1.54	$1.30	NR	$1.57	$1.44
	1987	$1.57	$1.40	NR	$1.73	$1.46
	1988	$1.73	$1.42	NR	$1.74	$1.41
	1989	NR	$1.55	NR	$1.66	$1.71
Margarine, per pound	1985	NR	NR	NR	NR	NR
	1986	85¢	59¢	NR	62¢	68¢
	1987	91¢	58¢	NR	61¢	68¢
	1988	65¢	52¢	NR	45¢	64¢
	1989	NR	61¢	NR	64¢	78¢
Lettuce, per 1 1/4 pound	1985	NR	NR	NR	NR	NR
	1986	71¢	56¢	NR	80¢	43¢
	1987	75¢	62¢	NR	71¢	34¢
	1988	$1.23	92¢	NR	82¢	$1.16
	1989	NR	83¢	NR	99¢	64¢
Milk, Fresh, per half gallon	1985	NR	NR	NR	NR	NR
	1986	$1.27	$1.46	NR	$1.22	$1.02
	1987	$1.29	$1.40	NR	$1.22	$1.02
	1988	$1.15	$1.22	NR	$1.16	$1.02
	1989	NR	$1.33	NR	$1.12	$1.13
Pork, Bacon, Sliced, per pound	1985	NR	NR	NR	NR	NR
	1986	$2.61	$2.72	NR	$2.30	$2.14
	1987	$2.99	$2.82	NR	$3.10	$2.22
	1988	$2.59	$2.39	NR	$2.72	$2.22
	1989	NR	$1.42	NR	$1.95	$1.42
Potatoes, per 10 pounds	1985	NR	NR	NR	NR	NR
	1986	$2.28	$1.86	NR	$1.65	$1.46
	1987	$2.27	$1.74	NR	$1.25	$1.36
	1988	$1.97	$2.39	NR	$1.76	$1.34
	1989	NR	$2.90	NR	$3.14	$2.15
Sugar, per 5 pounds	1985	NR	NR	NR	NR	NR
	1986	$1.83	$1.44	NR	$1.36	$1.55
	1987	$1.69	$1.33	NR	$1.19	$1.62
	1988	$1.73	$1.32	NR	96¢	$1.46
	1989	NR	$1.55	NR	$1.17	$1.80
Soft Drink, Cola, per 2 liters	1985	NR	NR	NR	NR	NR
	1986	$1.23	$1.11	NR	$1.12	$1.44
	1987	$1.09	$1.19	NR	$1.26	$1.69
	1988	$1.03	$1.49	NR	$1.04	$1.24
	1989	NR	$1.03	NR	$1.51	97¢
Tuna, Canned, per 6 1/2 ounces	1985	NR	NR	NR	NR	NR
	1986	76¢	74¢	NR	59¢	95¢
	1987	85¢	74¢	NR	59¢	64¢
	1988	99¢	66¢	NR	64¢	72¢
	1989	NR	64¢	NR	65¢	68¢

SELECTED PRICES 1985–1989

Item	Source	Description	Price
ALCOHOL			
Beer	*New York Times* (1988)	*Michelob;* 12-oz n/r bottles	$9.95/case

Item	Source	Description	Price
Cocktails	*New York Times* (1988)	Martini for two	$1.08
Liqueur	*New York Times* (1987)	*Kahlua;* coffee liqueur	$9.97/btl
Wine	*New York Times* (1987)	Liebfraumilch	$3.99/btl

APPAREL, CHILDREN'S

Item	Source	Description	Price
Disposable Diaper	*Consumer Reports* (1987)	"In light of the unmitigated rave reviews for Pampers Super, it might be difficult to choose another model of disposable diaper." Medium / Large	$.21 ea / $.31 ea
Jackets	*Los Angeles Times* (1988)	Boys; express twill classics in fall colors	$12.70–$21.20
Socks	*Sears, Roebuck* (1988)	More of our crew-length tube socks; package of six pairs	$4.99
Underwear	*Sears, Roebuck* (1988)	A fun new underwear idea for the little guy; no problem; just choose GI Joe or our Fruit of the Loom Funpals Alf	$5.49

APPAREL, MEN'S

Item	Source	Description	Price
Shirt	*Sears, Roebuck* (1988)	100% cotton-knit shirts never had it so good and neither will you	$15.88
Shirt	*New York Times* (1988)	Velour	$14.92
Shoes	*New York Times* (1987)	*Asics Tiger GT IIGEL;* this is the most advanced running shoe for serious runners	$89.95
Suit	*New York Times* (1988)	*Dunhill Tailors;* ready-to-wear suit for fall; the dollar remains strong	$525–$650
Sweater	*New York Times* (1988)	Long sleeve, bulk knit	$29.25
Sweatshirt	*European Travel & Life* (1987)	European trade sweatshirts	$17.95–$19.95

APPAREL, WOMEN'S

Item	Source	Description	Price
Blouse	*Sears, Roebuck* (1988)	Take a closer look at this soft laundered fabric that's so versatile it goes from beach to business with a quick change of accessories	$26
Clogs	*Better Homes and Gardens* (1986)	Genuine leather clog; lightweight, perforated to let your feet breathe	$19.95
Dress	*Charlotte Observer* (1986)	Strapless dress with sequin bodice and white ruffled organza skirt	$215
Fur	*Chicago Tribune* (1986)	Tibetan lamb jackets in white or pink; regularly $750	$399
Hose	*Sears, Roebuck* (1988)	Our sheerest nylon hosiery for your fanciest occasions; three pairs per package	$8.07
Jumpsuit	*Los Angeles Times* (1988)	Cotton sheeting with front snaps	$34.99

Item	Source	Description	Price
Shoes	*New York Times* (1987)	*Naturalizer;* cool comfort for spring; genuine leather uppers with cutout detail on a medium heel	$45
Skirt	*Sears, Roebuck* (1988)	Swirl potential; soft, full skirt with an easy wearing elastic waist	$26

APPLIANCES

Item	Source	Description	Price
Camcorder	*Charlotte Observer* (1986)	*RCA Small Wonder Camcorder;* 3-way AC/DC versatility	$994
Can Opener	*Los Angeles Times* (1988)	*Sunbeam;* electric; originally $25; sharpens knives; opens cans and plastic bags	$19.99
Coffee Maker	*Consumer Reports* (1987)	*Mr. Coffee,* the brand that fomented the drip-coffee revolution, still rules the market in terms of numbers	$36.00
Heater	*Popular Mechanics* (1985)	*Arvin;* radiant; instant fan-forced heat	$23.88
Microwave	*Sears, Roebuck* (1988)	*Kenmore;* solid-state electronics; digital readout that doubles as time-of-day clock and 100-minute countdown timer; variable power settings from 100 to 700 watts	$199.99
Range	*Sears, Roebuck* (1988)	*Lady Kenmore;* 30" range; gives you cooking and cleaning convenience	$559.99
Refrigerator	*Sears, Roebuck* (1988)	America's smartest refrigerator; no one has an electronic system this innovative	$1,769.99
Vacuum Cleaner	*Popular Mechanics* (1985)	*Shop-Vac Mighty Mini-Vac;* hardware can be the perfect gift	$44.88
Water Heater	*Sears, Roebuck* (1988)	*Kenmore;* compact style; tank has limited 5-year warranty against leaks; polyurethane or fiberglass insulation; adjustable thermostat with energy-saving setting	$89.99

BABY PRODUCTS

Item	Source	Description	Price
Bicycle Child Carrier	*Sears, Roebuck* (1988)	Hi-impact molded plastic carrier has contoured seat	$14.99
Bronze Shoes	*Better Homes and Gardens* (1986)	Baby's first shoes bronze-plated in solid metal	$5.99
Canisters	*Sears, Roebuck* (1988)	Clear-acrylic nursery canisters with My Bears decoration; come with vinyl-covered wire tray; safer than glass	$12.99
Car Seat	*Charlotte Observer* (1986)	*Century Car Seat;* meets Federal safety standards	$54.99
Diapers	*Charlotte Observer* (1986)	*Pampers Ultra Plus 64 Larger Diapers;* after $3 refund offer	$13.99
Dressing Table	*Sears, Roebuck* (1988)	*Cosco Quick Change;* dressing table has four interlocking plastic cubes that are used in a variety of ways; includes dressing table pad with wipe clean bin cover and safety strap	$77.99
Stroller	*Charlotte Observer* (1986)	*Graco Stroll-a-Bed;* features one hand opening and closing	$56.97

BUSINESS EQUIPMENT AND SUPPLIES

Item	Source	Description	Price
Briefcase	*Gourmet* (1988)	*Lladro;* Spanish leather	$565
Calculator	*New York Times* (1987)	*Casio;* printing; 12 digit, 2 color	$54.95

Item	Source	Description	Price
Computer	*New York Times* (1987)	*Leading Edge Model D;* one-drive system	$895
Computer	*New York Times* (1987)	Apple IIGS	$795
Desk Set	*European Travel & Life* (1987)	Italian pearl wood desk set lined with calfskin	$250
Floppy Disks	*New York Times* (1987)	*Fuji;* 5 1/4" DS/DD; per box	$9.95
Modem	*New York Times* (1987)	*Maxum;* internal, 1,200 baud; 1/2 card	$119.95
Overhead Projector	*New York Times* (1987)	*Bell & Howell;* 14" triple lens	$262.99
Printer	*New York Times* (1987)	*Epson;* 48 cps nlq mode	$429
Software	*New York Times* (1987)	*Lotus;* spreadsheet	$339
Tape Backup	*New York Times* (1987)	*Mountain Filesafe 7000;* external 60 mb	$1,295

COLLECTIBLES

Item	Source	Description	Price
Antique Automobile	*Guinness Book of World Records* (1986)	*1931 Berline de Voyage Royale;* greatest price paid for used car; one of six Bugatti Royales	$8,100,000
Cel Animation	*Art & Antiques* (1993)	Cel and background for movie *Who Framed Roger Rabbit* sold at auction in 1989	$7,150
Coin	*Guinness Book of World Records* (1989)	The highest price paid at auction for a single coin; for a U.S. 1804 silver dollar in proof condition at Rarcoa's, Chicago, Illinois	$990,000
Quilt	*Village Voice* (1989)	*Kentucky Quilt Company;* individually hand-made at home in the foothills of the Appalachian Mountains	$299 to $499
Table	*Art & Antiques* (1993)	Console table once owned by Marie Antoinette; sold at auction in 1988	$2.97 million

ENTERTAINMENT

Item	Source	Description	Price
Ballet Ticket	*Chicago Tribune* (1986)	*The Nutcracker;* Arie Crown Theatre, McCormick Place; main floor; Saturday and Sunday	$18
Concert Ticket	*New York Times* (1987)	*Indiana University Baroque Orchestra* Student General Admission	 $5 $10
Concert Ticket	*New York Times* (1988)	*Victor Borge;* Carnegie Hall	$10–$30
Membership	*Village Voice* (1989)	YMCA summer membership; There's swimming, jogging, weights, fitness classes; the whole summer, one price	$125
Movie Ticket	*Chicago Tribune* (1986)	*Lady and the Tramp;* General Cinema; all showings before 6 pm	$2
Play Ticket	*Chicago Tribune* (1986)	*Pump Boys and Dinettes;* Tuesday-Thursday; 8 pm	$19.50

Item	Source	Description	Price
ENTERTAINMENT, HOME			
Audio Tape	*New York Times* (1987)	*Sony;* high power; uniaxial; blank; three pack	$7.99
Camcorder	*Chicago Tribune* (1986)	*Kodak 3440;* modular; weighs slightly over 4 lbs; save $102	$893
Camcorder	*Audubon* (1989)	*Sharp 8x;* VHS; record your memories for years to come	$1,799.99
Camera	*New York Times* (1987)	Nikon FP-Program	$189.99
Cassette Player	*Chicago Tribune* (1986)	*Sony Walkman;* make great gifts	$19.95
Cassette Player and Recorder	*Chicago Tribune* (1986)	*Panasonic;* two 5" dynamic speakers, continuous-tone control, one-touch recording; regular $59.95	$37
Compact Disc	*Los Angeles Times* (1988)	Top hits	$11.99
Compact Disc Player	*New York Times* (1987)	*Technics;* programmable; fine-focus single-beam system	$229.95
Computer Game	*Sears, Roebuck* (1987)	*New York Times Fidelity;* par excellence; 5.0 computer chess	$149
Scanner	*Sears, Roebuck* (1988)	*Regency Informant;* instantly monitors 9 bands with the push of a button	$299.99
Telescope	*Popular Mechanics* (1985)	*Bausch & Lomb Criterion 400;* high-quality amateur telescope	$695
Television	*Chicago Tribune* (1986)	*Sony Watchman;* pocket-size black-and-white television; 2" screen with crisp, bright high-contrast picture; reference price $129.95	$95
Television	*New York Times* (1987)	*Sharp;* 19" color	$209.99
Television Satellite Dish	*Popular Mechanics* (1985)	*Radio Shack;* brings you over 100 channels of quality entertainment	$1,995

Item	Source	Description	Price

FOOD PRODUCTS

Item	Source	Description	Price
Cereal	*Los Angeles Times* (1988)	*Kellogg's Corn Flakes;* 18-oz package	$1.59
Cheese	*Los Angeles Times* (1988)	*Kraft American;* cheese food; 1-lb singles	$2.79
Corn	*Los Angeles Times* (1988)	Fresh barbecue sweet corn; 5 ears	$1
Fruit	*Charlotte Observer* (1986)	Washington Fancy Red Apples; per pound	$.29
Fruit	*Charlotte Observer* (1986)	California Sweet Cantaloupe; large size; each	$.79
Fruit	*Charlotte Observer* (1986)	Oranges; Florida new crop; 5 pound bag	$1.59
Ice Cream	*Time* (1985)	*Dove Bar;* they're expensive, but they're worth it	$1.45
Meat	*Charlotte Observer* (1986)	Ground Beef, fresh family pack; per pound	$.99
Milk	*Chicago Tribune* (1986)	2 percent; plastic carton	$1.59
Olive Oil	*European Travel & Life* (1987)	*Green Gold;* the Christmas gift for the host who has everything	$8.28
Potato Chips	*Chicago Tribune* (1986)	*Ruffles;* 6 1/2-oz bag	$1.19
Potatoes	*Charlotte Observer* (1986)	U.S. No. 1 spuds; 10 pound bag	$.99
Pot Pie	*Charlotte Observer* (1986)	*Morton Chicken Pot Pies;* three for	$.99
Soft Drink	*New York Times* (1988)	*Coke;* 2 liter	$1

FURNITURE

Item	Source	Description	Price
Chair	*Better Homes and Gardens* (1986)	*Adirondack;* remember lawn chairs; they're back	$129
Chair	*New York Times* (1987)	*Bon Marche;* all steel; black or white	$57.50
Chair	*New York Times* (1987)	*Scandinavian Gallery;* leather tub chair	$399.95
Chair	*Audubon* (1989)	*Adirondack;* outdoor chair and ottoman; made of kiln-dried western pine	$119.95
Coffee Table	*Better Homes and Gardens* (1986)	Quaint Victorian with imported marble top	$89.95
Couch	*New York Times* (1988)	*Eclectic Furniture of Manhasset;* sectional; two pieces with queen sleeper	$799
Entertainment Center	*Village Voice* (1989)	Complete wall unit and entertainment center	$699
Grandfather Clock	*Better Homes and Gardens* (1986)	*European Clock Company;* do-it-yourself kits; build your own grandfather clock	$280

Item	Source	Description	Price
Modular System	*New York Times* (1987)	*Bon Marche;* black or white hard melamine laminate; per unit	$85
Sofa	*Los Angeles Times* (1988)	*Eastman West;* full size 82"; imported leather; smooth, supple, sumptuous	$599
Table	*New York Times* (1988)	Handcrafted Italian marble table; 71" × 37"	$998
Table Pad	*Better Homes and Gardens* (1986)	Save 50% by buying direct	$49.95

GARDEN EQUIPMENT AND SUPPLIES

Item	Source	Description	Price
Azalea	*New York Times* (1987)	6" pot	$3.99
Easter Lily	*New York Times* (1987)	*Plant Shed;* special	$4.99
Lawn Mower	*Consumer Reports* (1987)	The *Homelite-Jacobsen HSD20* was judged a Best Buy	$300

HOUSEHOLD PRODUCTS

Item	Source	Description	Price
Bedspread	*Sears, Roebuck* (1988)	The look your star athlete will love; let the game begin; whether it's a kick-off or the first ball thrown your special athlete can be part of the action with these coordinates; bunk size	$16.99
Carving Set	*Gourmet* (1988)	*James Robinson;* ebony-handled, stainless steel, set of four	$675
Compote	*Gourmet* (1988)	*By Design;* frosted glass, large size, designed by Sugahara	$21.95
Dinner Plate	*Gourmet* (1988)	*Majolica;* Italian hand-painted plates, designed by Jackie Rice	$80
Flatware	*House & Garden Gardens* (1986)	*Oneida Heirloom;* 48-piece stainless set	$229.95
Glass	*House & Garden* (1987)	*Block;* full-lead crystal; Atlantis Chartres pattern designed by Gerald Gulotta	$37.50
Glue Gun	*Sears, Roebuck* (1988)	*Craftsman;* the best of both worlds is yours with this	$24.99
Light Bulb	*Popular Mechanics* (1985)	*DieHard;* has an average life of 6,000 hours—about six times longer than conventional bulbs; 2 bulb pack	$4
Pillow	*House & Garden* (1987)	*Hermes;* lotus design; 13" × 17"	$75
Pillow	*European Travel & Life* (1987)	*HedBed;* end stiff necks	$11
Plate	*Gourmet* (1988)	*Umbra;* on rubber feet; large frost-glass plate	$24
Plate and Knife	*Gourmet* (1988)	Cheese; earthenware	$45
Rug	*Chicago Tribune* (1986)	Handmade wool rugs from India; oriental King and Spring Garden pattern in blue; pure wool; 6' × 9'; regularly $1,199	$499
Shade	*Better Homes and Gardens* (1986)	*Burlington Voile Pouf Shade;* when delicate almost lacy romance is your style	$50
Sham	*Gourmet* (1988)	Cotton with lace trim; European-square, circa 1920	$95
Silk Azalea	*Sears, Roebuck* (1988)	Lovely azalea bush has 132 leaves, 48 rosy blooms in an 8" diameter whitewash rattan basket	$24.99

Item	Source	Description	Price
Silk Geranium	*Sears, Roebuck* (1988)	Double jumbo geranium has 294 leaves, 54 buds and an incredible 234 gorgeous blooms	$54.99
Silk Spider Plant	*Sears, Roebuck* (1988)	Double jumbo spider plant has 240 leaves and an unbelievable 80 bouncing babies	$54.99
Soufflé Dish	*Gourmet* (1988)	Frosted glass	$22
Tape/Rule	*Popular Mechanics* (1985)	*Master Mechanic;* 69 pocket tape rule free when you buy the 25" power tape in rugged cycolac case	$8.99

JEWELRY

Item	Source	Description	Price
Bracelet	*New York Times* (1987)	Sapphire and diamond	$129
Earrings	*New York Times* (1987)	Sapphire earrings surrounded by diamonds; regularly $690	$190
Necklace	*New York Times* (1987)	Italian 14 kt gold herringbone chains; 16"; regularly $225	$79

MEALS

Item	Source	Description	Price
Dinner	*Village Voice* (1989)	*Meson Toledo;* complete daily dinner with wine or Sangria; 318 W. 23rd Street, New York	$16.95
Dinner	*Village Voice* (1989)	*Kinoko;* Sushi, all you can eat	$15
Meal	*Gourmet* (1988)	*Shun Lee Restaurant;* New York City; Szechuan seafood salad	$13.50

MOTORIZED VEHICLES, SUPPLIES AND SERVICES

Item	Source	Description	Price
Alignment	*Charlotte Observer* (1986)	Front Wheel Alignment; set front wheel castor, camber and toe on cars with adjustable suspension	$29
Automobile	*House & Garden* (1987)	*Mazda RX-7 Roadster;* the sensible sports car to buy	$22,000
Automobile	*New York Times* (1987)	*1988 Dodge Medallion;* 4-door sedan	$8,995
Automobile	*New York Times* (1987)	*1987 Wrangler;* 4-wheel drive; soft-top	$8,395
Car Phone	*Chicago Tribune* (1986)	*Metrocom;* the superior car phone; plus free hands-free speaker phone	$995
Luggage Carrier	*Sears, Roebuck* (1988)	X-cargo roof-top carrier provides 21 cu ft of storage; for mobile homes, RVs, and vans	$169.99
Radio	*New York Times* (1987)	*Alpine;* removable car radio	$199
Stereo	*New York Times* (1987)	*Audiovox;* car stereo; cassette player and quartz clock	$89
Tires	*Charlotte Observer* (1986)	*Eagle GT Radial Tire;* no trade needed; outline white letters	$78.70

Item	Source	Description	Price
MUSICAL INSTRUMENTS			
Guitar	*Sears, Roebuck* (1988)	Beginner's guitar; comes with everything needed to get on the road to stardom	$89.99
Synthesizer	*Sears, Roebuck* (1988)	*Yamaha PSS-470;* our lowest price ever; custom drummer	$188.88
OTHER			
Book Club Membership	*New York Times* (1987)	*Literary Guild;* you can't beat our benefits; unlimited time to buy; easy at-home shopping; 5 books	$1
Currency Calculator	*European Travel & Life* (1987)	Currency; calculator; clock; one-touch currency conversion to and from dollars	$32
Decals	*European Travel & Life* (1987)	Authentic international auto decals from Europe	$5
Pen Set	*House & Garden* (1987)	*Cross* for women; gray; pen and pencil set	$30
Radar Detector	*Chicago Tribune* (1986)	*Fuzzbuster;* detects all types of police radar at 10 times their effective range; advanced filter system; reference price $89.95	$69
Sneaker Nameplates	*Better Homes and Gardens* (1986)	Stylish way to tag and identify your sports and jogging shoes	$2.50
Yacht	*Popular Mechanic* (1985)s	*Hatteras 77;* lets you cruise the world	$1,700,000
PERSONAL CARE PRODUCTS			
Hand Lotion	*Los Angeles Times* (1988)	*Corn Huskers;* heavy-duty hand lotion	$1.59
Insect Repellent	*Consumer Reports* (1987)	*Off!* 6 oz aerosol style; 15% active ingredient of DEET	$2.99
Perfume	*Guinness Book of World Records* (1984)	Most expensive perfume; the Chicago-based firm Jovan marketed from March 1984 a cologne called Andron that contains a trace of the attractant pheromone androstenol	$2,750/oz

A 1986 Christmas advertisement for Evyan's Most Precious fragrance. (via Flickr)

Item	Source	Description	Price
Skin Moisturizer	*Consumer Reports* (1986)	*Sea Breeze Moisture Lotion* "felt less greasy than most" and "has a more pleasant consistency than most."	$3.31

PUBLICATIONS

Catalogue	*House & Garden* (1987)	*P. E. Guerin;* everything from bathroom faucet sets to door knobs to decorative hardware	$7.50

REAL ESTATE

Apartment	*Chicago Tribune* (1986)	For rent; Willow West; 2 bedroom, all carpeted; heat; air conditioning; all appliances; pool	$520/mo
Apartment	*Chicago Tribune* (1986)	For rent; furnished; newly decorated 3 rooms in quiet neighborhood; includes heat	$275/mo
Co-Op Condo	*Village Voice* (1989)	Sunny one bedroom in luxurious building; 1000 square feet; 4th Street, East, New York	$225,000
House	*Chicago Tribune* (1986)	Quick sale price; interesting price-wise buy for alert buyer; cute and cozy secluded cottage nestled in convenient Rogers Park	$50,000
Hotel	*Guinness Book of World Records* (1989)	Sale of hotel Bel-Air in Los Angeles; sold to Sekitei Kaihatsu Company of Tokyo, Japan; per room	$1,200,000
House	*Village Voice* (1989)	Crown Heights; one family, four story, 15 rooms, four baths	$240,000
House	*Charlotte Observer* (1987)	Ashebrook Villas Townhouses, York, South Carolina; 3 bedrooms, 2 baths; lots of room for living	$67,900

SEWING EQUIPMENT AND SUPPLIES

Labels	*Better Homes and Gardens* (1986)	Personalized sewing labels; your originals deserve these washable woven rayon taffeta labels	$4.95/20

SPORTS EQUIPMENT

Bicycle	*European Travel & Life* (1987)	*Aero Urban Cowboy;* perfect for city biking; it takes potholes like a Cadillac	$600
Gun Kit	*Popular Mechanics* (1985)	*Weller Soldering;* give a gift that will come in handy	$19.99
Helmet	*Sears, Roebuck* (1988)	Use of a helmet while biking is an investment in protection for you and for your child	$19.99

TELEPHONE EQUIPMENT AND SERVICES

Long Distance Rates	*Newsweek* (1985)	*AT&T ReachOut America;* you get an hour of AT & T long distance calls	$9.45
Long Distance Rates	*House & Garden* (1987)	*AT&T;* United States to Holland, standard rate from 7 am to 1 pm	$1.18/min
Long Distance Rates	*Gourmet* (1988)	*AT&T;* 6 pm to midnight, 10-minute call, United States to Brazil	$0.96/min

An advertisement for a Radio Shack push-button phone from 1985. (via Flickr)

Item	Source	Description	Price
TOBACCO PRODUCTS			
Cigars	*Los Angeles Times* (1988)	*Wm. Penn Invincible;* corona cigars; $5 value	$1.99
TOYS			
Doll	*Charlotte Observer* (1986)	*Playskool Doll;* My Buddy Wink or Kid Sister Wink; each	$24.97
Toy	*Charlotte Observer* (1986)	*Playskool;* Sesame Street Poppin Pals; 5 different activities	$11.97
Game	*Charlotte Observer* (1986)	*Fisher Price Bowling* game; easy set-up pins	$9.97
TRAVEL AND TRANSPORTATION			
Airfare	*Village Voice* (1989)	*New York to Osaka;* Seil Travel America	$715
New Orleans Weekend	*Village Voice* (1989)	New Orleans Labor Day Weekend Getaway; includes airfare, 3 nights with breakfast, transfers, each	$520
Tour	*Audubon* (1989)	*Wood Star;* birding tour of Argentina; 21 day trip	$3,595
Trip	*New York Times* (1988)	St. Kitts; the Royal St. Kitts Hotel & casino; includes round-trip air via BWIA; manager cocktail party; $25 casino chips, tennis, and admission to disco; 7 nights	$403
Trip	*New York Times* (1988)	Cupecoy Beach Resort; roundtrip American; Tuesday, Wednesday, Thursday departures; 8 days/7 nights; 1-bedroom suite	$545
Trip	*New York Times* (1988)	Deer Valley this year, don't just ski Deer Valley; live it; 7 nights/6 days; December 8–16; January 3– February 9	$499
Trip	*New York Times* (1988)	Paradise Island; 8 days/7 nights; including airfare	$249

MISCELLANY 1985–1989

Metromedia to Sell Mobile Phone Operations

The Southwestern Bell Corporation has agreed to buy the paging and mobile telephone businesses of Metromedia, Inc. for $1.65 billion in cash.

The sale will vastly enrich John W. Kluge, already one of the nation's wealthiest men, who owns 93 percent of the voting stock of Metromedia.

Southwestern Bell, for its part, will become the largest investor in cellular telephones in the country. Its existing cellular operations, joined with Metromedia's interests in such major cities as New York, Chicago, and Washington, would service markets with a total population of 45 million.

New York Times, July 1, 1985

Texas Instruments vs. Japan

To survive in a world market increasingly dominated by the Japanese, such American semiconductor manufacturers as the Intel Corporation and Advanced Micro Devices, Inc. have withdrawn to segments they think they can still defend.

Others, including Motorola, Inc. and Fairchild Semiconductor Corporation, are teaming up with their Japanese rivals.

But even though its semiconductor operations lost $89 million in 1985 and barely broke even in 1986, the battle cry at Texas Instruments, Inc. is never give an inch to the Japanese.

New York Times, July 1, 1987

Mutual Fund Sales Decline

Monthly mutual fund sales fell to $7.1 billion in May, compared with $9 billion in April and $13.5 billion in May 1987, the Investment Company Institute said today.

Year-to-date mutual fund sales through May were $42.1 billion, compared with $111.2 billion for the comparable 1987 period, the institute said.

New York Times, July 1, 1988

Investor Group Buying South Carolina Resort Island

Charles S. Way Jr. and his associates have bought themselves some choice real estate: a sparkling South Carolina sea island that had been in the hands of Kuwaiti investors.

Mr. Way said yesterday that his group had paid $105 million for the 10,000 acre Kiawah Island near Charleston, making it one of the biggest real estate transactions in South Carolina history.

The Kuwaitis bought the island in 1974 for $17.4 million, and Mr. Way said they had sunk $200 million into its development as a resort.

New York Times, July 1, 1988

HISTORICAL SNAPSHOT 1990–1994

1990

- U.S. deploys combat aircraft to Persian Gulf to defend Saudi Arabia
- Banks are allowed to trade stocks
- Atlanta awarded 1996 Olympic Summer Games
- General Electric Foundation allots $2.1 million to 30 universities to attract women, African Americans, American Indians, and Hispanics to careers in science and business
- East and West Germany united after 45 years of separation
- The Hubble Space Telescope is launched during a Space Shuttle *Discovery* mission
- The first contraceptive implant in approved by the FDA
- Smoking in domestic airplane flights is banned

1991

- United States and allies wage war with Iraq
- U.S. Postal Service increases first-class postage stamp rate from 25 to 29 cents
- U.S. Supreme Court ends forced busing, originally designed to end racial segregation
- Federal Reserve slashes interest rates by 1/2 percent to spur economy
- National Commission on AIDS approves needle exchange program to reduce spread of the disease
- Congress approves family leave allowing up to 12 weeks for family emergencies
- General Motors announces plans to close more than 20 plants over several years, eliminating more than 70,000 jobs

1992

- TWA Airlines files bankruptcy
- President of United Way of America forced out by excessive spending allegations
- United Auto Workers end five-month-old strike against Caterpillar, maker of heavy equipment
- *Endeavor* astronauts repair $150 million communications satellite in space
- Third party presidential candidate Ross Perot withdraws from race, then reenters
- British Airways invests $750 million in US Air
- U.S. launches spacecraft to study Mars
- Bill Clinton elected president of the United States

1993

- Blast injures hundreds in World Trade Center bombing in New York City
- Major League baseball owners announce new initiatives on minority hiring
- Law agents raid religious cult in Waco, Texas
- Women receive combat roles in aerial and naval warfare
- Civil rights advocate Ruth Bader Ginsburg named to U.S. Supreme Court
- IBM announces $8.9 billion restructuring of world's largest computer maker; eliminates 60,000 jobs
- President Bill Clinton supports easing ban on homosexuals in military
- Chicago Bulls basketball star Michael Jordan retires to play professional baseball

- American novelist Toni Morrison wins Nobel Prize for literature
- Inflation rate remains at 2.7%, lowest in seven years

1994

- Supreme Court rules abortion clinics may sue violent antiabortion protesting groups for damages
- Viacom buys Paramount for $10 billion in cash and securities
- Astronauts grow crystals, melt metals, and test magnets and new drugs in low-gravity conditions aboard shuttle *Columbia*
- U.S. renews China's trade status despite human rights policy
- Tobacco companies accused of nicotine manipulation
- Major League baseball players go on strike, World Series canceled
- United States ends policy of accepting Cubans fleeing by sea
- United States, French, and British troops leave Berlin without foreign presence for first time since World War II
- Hartford, CT, public schools hire private firm, Education Alternatives, to manage city schools
- Steven Spielberg, David Geffen, and Jeffrey Katzenberg form DreamWorks, a new Hollywood studio

President George H.W. Bush riding in a Humvee with General Schwarzkopf in Saudi Arabia during the Gulf War. The war was waged
by coalition forces from 35 nations led by the United States against Iraq in response to Iraq's invasion and annexation of Kuwait arising
from oil pricing and production disputes.
(via Wikimedia Commons)

SELECTED INCOME 1990-1994

Job	Source	Description	Pay
Administrative Assistant	*Atlanta Journal Constitution* (1994)	Must know Microsoft Word and Harvard Graphics	$20,000–$23,000/yr
Banker	*New Orleans Times-Picayune* (1993)	Demand Deposit Manager	$70,000/yr
Bookkeeper	*Atlanta Journal Constitution* (1994)	Office administrator and bookkeeper to calculate payroll of 120 employees and handle receivables	$25,000/yr
Budget Analyst	*Atlanta Journal Constitution* (1994)	City of Marietta; must have knowledge of state and city budgeting regulations	$22,693/yr
Business Executive	*Fortune* (1994)	Salary of CEO Billy Payne, Atlanta Committee for Olympic games in 1994	$600,000/yr
Business Executive	*San Francisco Examiner* (1994)	Eight months' salary and bonus for Apple Computer Chairman Gilbert Amelio in 1994	$3 million
Chemist	*New Orleans Times-Picayune* (1993)	Research and development; PhD; 10 years specialty in chemistry	$70,000/yr
Chief Financial Officer	*Wall Street Journal* (1993)	Major U.S. university	$175,000/yr
Chief Information Officer	*Wall Street Journal* (1993)	Medical college seeking candidates for planning, managing and orchestrating the use of Information Systems	$75,000–$80,000/yr
Collections	*Atlanta Journal Constitution* (1994)	Commercial collections representative; for calling on past-due accounts	$7.25/hr
Computer Support	*Chicago Tribune* (1990)	Wang Programmer	$35,000/yr
Computer Support	*Chicago Tribune* (1990)	Tape Librarian	$18,000/yr
Crafts	*Chicago Tribune* (1990)	Assemble craft items at home	To $525/wk
Dancer	*New Orleans Times-Picayune* (1993)	Go-Go dancer, guaranteed pay, good tips	$300/wk
Driver	*Chicago Tribune* (1990)	Pizza delivery	$6.50/hr
Finance and Administrative Director	*Wall Street Journal* (1993)	Global Environmental Fund; Responsible for all internal functions relating to accounting, financial management, information systems	$50,000–$65,000/yr
Football Player	*New Orleans Times-Picayune* (1993)	Three-year contract signed by Pittsburgh Steeler Kevin Greene in 1993	$5.3 million
Golfer	*Milwaukee Journal* (1991)	Earnings of John Daly for winning the Professional Golfers' Association Championship in 1991	$230,000
Investment Analyst	*Wall Street Journal* (1993)	Entails developing sophisticated strategies for the financing of goods sold by U.S. exporters premised on innovative structuring of credit facilities and discounting trade debt	$87,000/yr
Investment Director	*Wall Street Journal* (1993)	Emerging Market Investments Director	$80,000–$100,000/yr

Job	Source	Description	Pay
Legal Secretary	*San Francisco Chronicle* (1996)	Don't be on the wrong side of the door when opportunity knocks	up to $42,000/yr
Marketing Trainee	*Chicago Tribune* (1990)	National Wholesale Management Trainee; no experience	$25,000–$35,000/yr
Mason	*Milwaukee Journal* (1991)	Employment for brick layers; quality a must	$23/hr
Model	*Playboy* (1993)	Modeling fee of 1993 Playmate of the Year, Anna Nicole Smith	$100,000 plus automobile
NFL Coach	*USA Today* (2004)	Annual salary, Washington Redskin Football Coach Joe Gibbs	$1.6 million
Phone Operator	*Chicago Tribune* (1990)	Switchboard operator	$7/hr
Postal Clerk	*Chicago Tribune* (1990)	No experience	$11.57/hr
Sales	*Chicago Tribune* (1990)	Engineering sales, two years experience in machine tools or robotics	$40,000/yr
Sales Manager	*Wall Street Journal* (1993)	U.S. West Communications needs manager to direct all sales activities targeting home-based business customers within a 14-state region	$75,000/yr
Sales Manager	*Wall Street Journal* (1993)	Sell franchises, distributorships, joint ventures	$100,000/yr
Stockers	*Chicago Tribune* (1990)	Major department store now hiring	$4.00–$4.75/hr

CONSUMER EXPENDITURES 1990–1994

Expenditure Type	1900	1901	1902	1903	1904
Clothing	$622	$667	$694	$670	$657
Food	$2,485	$2,651	$2,643	$2,735	$2,712
Auto Usage	$1,642	$1,741	$1,776	$1,843	$1,953
New Auto Purchase	$445	$414	$452	$486	$556
Auto Maintenance	$235	$245	$244	$248	$272
Gas & Oil	$402	$382	$389	$390	$394
Housing	$1,860	$1,996	$2,164	$2,166	$2,274
Furniture	$119	$113	$126	$126	$127
Utilities	$499	$527	$544	$581	$599
Telephone	$227	$237	$249	$263	$276
Health Care	$569	$597	$653	$710	$702
Health Insurance	$223	$252	$290	$320	$326
Personal Business	$996	$1,071	$1,100	$1,163	$1,175
Personal Care	$140	$153	$154	$154	$158
Tobacco	$105	$105	$110	$107	$103
Public Transportation	$116	$116	$116	$125	$152
Entertainment	$546	$566	$600	$650	$626
Per Capita Consumption	$10,915	$11,390	$11,938	$12,276	$12,692

INVESTMENTS 1990–1994

Investment	1990	1991	1992	1993	1994
Basic Yield, One-Year Corporate Bonds	9.69	9.46	8.56	7.55	8.41
Short-Term Interest Rates, 4–6 Months, Prime Commercial Paper	8.06	6.21	3.95	3.40	5.02
Basic Yield, Common Stocks, Total	3.39	3.28	3.05	2.80	2.90
Index of Common Stocks S&P 500	358.02	371.16	408.14	450.53	444.27

COMMON STOCKS, CLOSING PRICE AND YIELD, FIRST BUSINESS DAY OF YEAR

(PARENTHETICAL NUMBER IS ANNUAL DIVIDENDS IN DOLLARS)

	1990	1991	1992	1993	1994
AT&T	30 61/64	20 1/2	26 5/8	34 45/64	35 23/32
(Name changed from American	(1.29)	(1.32)	(1.32)	(1.32)	(1.32)
Telephone & Telegraph Company,					
4/21/94) (1 per 16 spin-off, 12/13/96)					
NationsBank N/C Bank of America			40 3/8	51 1/8	48 3/8
(NCNB & C&S Sovran combine			(0.76)	(0.82)	(0.94)
to form NationsBank, 1/2/92)					
(2 for 1 split, 2/7/97)					
(NationsBank combines					
with Bank of America, 10/1/98)					
CPC Ind. N/C Best Foods	17 5/32	19 3/8	21 3/64	23 9/16	22 5/32
(Pfd rights redepmt., 4/1/91)	(0.50)	(0.54)	(0.59)	(0.63)	(0.67)
(2 for 1 split, 4/2/92)					
(1 per 4 spin-off, 12/15/97)					
(Name changed to Best Foods, 1/2/98)					
(2 for 1 stock split, 3/31/98)					
Bethlehem Steel	18 1/2	14 7/8	14	16	20 3/8
(1 per 1 poison pill rights, 10/18/98)	(0.40)	(0.40)	(0.00)	(0.00)	(0.00)
Delta Airlines	34 1/8	27 7/8	33 1/16	25 7/16	27 5/16
(2 for 1 split, 11/2/98)	(0.60)	(0.60)	(0.60)	(0.10)	(0.10)
American Brands N/C Fortune Brands	29 3/8	26 15/32	28 45/64	25 53/64	21 13/64
(2 for 1 split, 10/9/90)	(1.41)	(1.59)	(1.81)	(1.97)	(1.99)
(1 per 1 spin-off, 5/29/97)					
(Name changed to					
Fortune Brands, Inc., 5/30/97)					
General Electric	16 1/8	14 11/32	19 1/8	21 3/8	26 7/32
(2 for 1 split, 4/28/94)	(0.47)	(0.51)	(0.56)	(0.63)	(0.72)
(2 for 1 split, 4/28/97)					

Investment	1990	1991	1992	1993	1994
GM/E Electronic Data Sys.	13 21/32	19 5/16	31 1/2	32 7/8	29
(2 for 1 split, 2/16/90)	(0.28)	(0.32)	(0.36)	(0.40)	(0.48)
(2 for 1 split, 2/14/92)					
(Each share of CL "E"					
converted into 1 share of					
Electronic Data Systems, 6/10/96)					
General Motors	39 59/64	32 31/64	27 9/32	30 15/32	51 55/64
(1 spin-off, 12/17/97)	(3.00)	(1.60)	(1.40)	(0.80)	(0.80)
Microsoft	2 27/64	4 3/16	9 17/64	10 43/64	10 5/64
(2 for 1 split, 3/26/90)	(0.00)	(0.00)	(0.00)	(0.00)	(0.00)
(3 for 2 split, 6/18/91)					
(3 for 2 split, 6/3/92)					
(2 for 1 split, 5/6/94)					
(2 for 1 split, 11/22/96)					
(2 for 1 split, 2/6/98)					
Ind Harvester N/C Navistar Int'l	38 3/4	22 1/2	26 1/4	22 1/2	23 5/8
(Name change to Navista	(0.00)	(0.00)	(0.00)	(0.00)	(0.00)
International Corp., 2/20/86)					
(1 for 10 split, 6/30/93)					
Nabisco/RJ Reynolds Inc.	-	-	53 3/4	43 1/8	31 7/8
(1 for 5 split, 4/12/95)	(0.00)	(0.00)	(0.00)	(0.00)	(0.00)
USX-U.S. Steel Group	36	29 3/4	27 5/8	33 1/8	42 1/8
(Formerly USX Corp.; each share of USX Corp. was divided into 1 share of USX-Marathon Group and 2 shares of USX-U.S. Steel Group eff. 5/6/91)	(1.00)	(1.00)	(1.00)	(1.00)	(1.00)
Wal-Mart	47 1/8	30 (0.08)	59 1/8	62 7/8	25 1/2
(2 for 1 split, 6/15/90) (2 for 1 split, 2/2/93)	(0.07)		(0.10)	(0.12)	(0.16)
Warner Lambert	118 1/2	67 1/4	77 3/4	68 1/2	66 7/8
(2 for 1 split,5/2/90) (2 for 1 split,5/3/96) (3 for 1 split,5/8/98)	(0.25)	(0.29)	(0.34)	(0.38)	(0.41)

STANDARD JOBS 1990–1994

Job Type	1990	1991	1992	1993	1994
Wages Per Full-Time Employee	$23,602	$24,578	$25,897	$26,361	$26,939
Private Industries, incl. Farm Labor	$23,258	$24,178	$25,547	$25,934	$26,494
Bituminous Coal Mining	$38,552	$39,988	$39,649	$40,493	$42,236
Building Trades	$25,504	$25,945	$26,227	$26,739	$27,677
Domestics	$9,284	$9,527	$9,926	$10,275	$10,466
Farm Labor	$14,203	$14,493	$14,735	$15,019	$15,294
Finance, Insurance & Real Estate	$29,683	$31,008	$34,824	$36,013	$36,061
Gas, Electricity, & Sanitary Workers	$32,945	$33,940	$35,035	$36,755	$38,010
Manufacturing Durable Goods	$24,375	$25,112	$25,939	$26,992	$28,286
Manufacturing Non-Durable Goods	$21,049	$21,823	$22,541	$23,181	$23,905
Medical/Health Services Workers	$17,593	$18,522	$19,367	$20,091	$20,637
Miscellaneous Manufacturing	$18,678	$19,107	$20,042	$20,508	$21,154
Motion Picture Services	$31,833	$35,152	$35,417	$37,541	$40,811
Non Profit Org. Workers	$12,999	$13,368	$13,853	$14,094	$14,513
Passenger Transportation Workers, Local & Highway	$16,126	$16,770	$17,379	$17,802	$18,424
Postal Employees	$31,877	$33,210	$36,877	$37,609	$37,050
Public School Teachers	$23,653	$24,561	$25,270	$25,816	$26,372
Radio Broadcast and Television Workers	$27,679	$28,455	$29,543	$30,702	$31,382
Railroads	$37,794	$36,772	$38,291	$40,672	$40,874
State & Local Government Workers	$24,818	$25,863	$26,611	$27,369	$28,121
Telephone & Telegraph Workers	$30,253	$31,034	$32,454	$33,871	$34,941
Total Federal Government	$30,286	$32,609	$35,066	$36,940	$38,038
Wholesale & Retail Trade Workers	$12,588	$12,930	$13,277	$13,597	$14,056

FOOD BASKET 1990–1994

Commodity	Year	U.S. Average	North East	North Central	South	West
Bacon, sliced, per pound	1990	$1.971	$2.094	$1.952	$1.942	$1.895
	1991	$2.261	$2.409	$2.266	$2.265	$2.102
	1992	$1.948	$2.232	$1.979	$1.757	$1.822
	1993	$1.861	$2.115	$1.793	$1.707	$1.830
	1994	$2.028	$2.209	$2.077	$1.894	$1.930
Bananas, per pound	1990	43.2¢	47.4¢	42.2¢	41.3¢	41.8¢
	1991	44.1¢	48.9¢	42.5¢	40.9¢	44.1¢
	1992	42.9¢	45.1¢	42.9¢	38.9¢	44.6¢
	1993	43.0¢	46.1¢	40.4¢	37.8¢	47.8¢
	1994	44.3¢	48.0¢	42.2¢	41.3¢	45.5¢
Beef, Ground 100% beef, per pound	1990	$1.545	NR	$1.566	$1.569	$1.501
	1991	$1.632	NR	$1.623	$1.657	$1.615
	1992	$1.597	NR	$1.615	$1.576	$1.600
	1993	$1.054	NR	$1.601	$1.561	NR
	1994	$1.533	NR	$1.588	$1.531	$1.480
Bread, white pan, per pound	1990	72.0¢	87.1¢	66.3¢	59.7¢	74.8¢
	1991	72.9¢	87.6¢	69.6¢	59.6¢	74.6¢
	1992	74.2¢	90.5¢	72.6¢	60.0¢	73.8¢
	1993	76.5¢	86.7¢	76.6¢	64.6¢	78.2¢
	1994	79.2¢	87.6¢	80.6¢	63.9¢	84.8¢
Butter, salted, grade AA, stick, per pound	1990	$2.103	$2.195	$2.036	$2.074	$2.108
	1991	$1.941	$2.070	NR	$1.812	NR
	1992	$2.010	$2.010	NR	NR	NR
	1993	$1.927	$1.927	NR	NR	NR
	1994	$1.696	$1.835	$1.557	NR	NR
Chicken, fresh, whole, per pound	1990	89.9¢	$1.087	85.0¢	77.6¢	88.3¢
	1991	90.7¢	$1.050	84.3¢	80.7¢	92.8¢
	1992	89.3¢	$1.057	83.9¢	78.7¢	89.0¢
	1993	89.8¢	$1.059	83.3¢	78.4¢	91.4¢
	1994	91.8¢	$1.027	88.3¢	79.1¢	97.1¢
Coffee, 100%, ground roast, all sizes, per pound	1990	$2.912	$3.041	$2.765	$3.077	$2.764
	1991	$2.932	$3.028	$2.744	$3.060	$2.897
	1992	$2.656	$2.870	$2.562	$2.602	$2.589
	1993	$2.348	$2.615	$2.241	$2.413	$2.122
	1994	$2.533	$2.777	$2.478	$2.470	$2.408
Cola, nondiet, cans, 6 pack, 12-oz cans per 16 ounces	1990	41.7¢	NR	NR	NR	41.7¢
	1991	NR	NR	NR	NR	NR
	1992	NR	NR	NR	NR	NR
	1993	NR	NR	NR	NR	NR
	1994	NR	NR	NR	NR	NR
Corn on the cob, per pound	1990	NR	NR	NR	NR	NR
	1991	NR	NR	NR	NR	NR
	1992	NR	NR	NR	NR	NR
	1993	NR	NR	NR	NR	NR
	1994	NR	NR	NR	NR	NR

Commodity	Year	U.S. Average	North East	North Central	South	West
Crackers, soda, salted, per pound	1990	$1.249	NR	NR	$1.249	NR
	1991	$1.334	NR	NR	$1.334	NR
	1992	NR	NR	NR	NR	NR
	1993	$1.138	NR	NR	$1.138	NR
	1994	$1.023	NR	NR	$1.023	NR
Eggs, Grade A, large, per dozen	1990	$1.232	$1.356	$1.148	$1.193	NR
	1991	$1.135	$1.300	$1.093	$1.013	NR
	1992	94.5¢	$1.138	81.0¢	88.6¢	NR
	1993	92.3¢	$1.083	82.2¢	86.3¢	NR
	1994	94.6¢	$1.128	83.3¢	87.8¢	NR
Lettuce, iceberg, per pound	1990	61¢	68.6¢	54.9¢	61.4¢	59.0¢
	1991	69.2¢	77.8¢	67.3¢	69.6¢	62.0¢
	1992	58.2¢	63.5¢	59.2¢	58.8¢	51.4¢
	1993	62.8¢	70.0¢	62.9¢	63.8¢	54.5¢
	1994	50.7¢	57.1¢	49.1¢	52.0¢	44.6¢
Margarine, soft, tubs, per pound	1990	$1.138	NR	$1.090	NR	$1.186
	1991	NR	NR	NR	NR	NR
	1992	$1.097	NR	$1.097	NR	NR
	1993	NR	NR	NR	NR	NR
	1994	$1.076	NR	$1.076	NR	NR
Margarine, stick, per pound	1990	86.8¢	90.8¢	84.3¢	76.1¢	95.9¢
	1991	87.1¢	NR	86.0¢	80.3¢	94.9¢
	1992	87.2¢	80.2¢	78.5¢	98.1¢	91.9¢
	1993	86.5¢	NR	75.5¢	88.6¢	95.3¢
	1994	81.6¢	NR	82.8¢	80.3¢	NR
Milk, fresh, whole, fortified, per 1/2 gallon	1990	$1.444	$1.400	$1.457	$1.664	$1.255
	1991	$1.390	$1.379	$1.274	$1.593	$1.313
	1992	$1.364	$1.365	$1.393	NR	$1.335
	1993	$1.348	$1.325	NR	NR	$1.370
	1994	$1.461	$1.364	NR	NR	$1.558
Potatoes, frozen, French fried, per pound	1990	85¢	94.2¢	82.8¢	78.1¢	NR
	1991	85.7¢	98.5¢	87.6¢	71.1¢	NR
	1992	96.3¢	$1.019	95.3¢	91.6¢	NR
	1993	90.9¢	$1.014	89.6¢	81.8¢	NR
	1994	59.7¢	NR	88.0¢	91.2¢	NR
Steak, T-Bone, U.S. Choice, bone-in, per pound	1990	$5.199	NR	$5.134	$5.263	NR
	1991	$5.232	NR	$4.974	$5.489	NR
	1992	$5.159	NR	$5.145	$5.173	NR
	1993	$5.334	NR	$5.473	$5.194	NR
	1994	$5.716	NR	$5.731	$5.701	NR
Sugar, white, all sizes, per pound	1990	42.3¢	45.6¢	40.9¢	40.9¢	41.7¢
	1991	44¢	49.0¢	43.3¢	40.8¢	42.8¢
	1992	43¢	49.2¢	38.9¢	40.7¢	43.3¢
	1993	42¢	51.0¢	36.3¢	38.8¢	41.8¢
	1994	41.2¢	48.5¢	36.3¢	39.5¢	40.4¢
Tuna, light, chunk, per pound	1990	$1.986	NR	$2.057	$1.915	NR
	1991	$2.042	NR	$1.995	$2.088	NR
	1992	$2.064	$2.228	$1.979	$1.986	NR
	1993	$1.973	$2.240	$1.912	$1.768	NR
	1994	$2.074	$2.261	$2.016	$1.901	$2.116

627

SELECTED PRICES 1990–1994

Item	Source	Description	Price
ALCOHOL			
Gin	*New Orleans Times-Picayune* (1992)	*Seagram's Extra Dry Gin;* 1.75 liter	$14.39
Liquor	*Chicago Tribune* (1990)	*Grand Marnier Creme;* 750 ml	$6.99
Rum	*New Orleans Times-Picayune* (1992)	*Bacardi Rum;* 1.75 liter	$15.99
Vodka	*New Orleans Times-Picayune* (1992)	*Absolut Vodka;* 750 ml	$12.29
Whiskey	*New Orleans Times-Picayune* (1992)	*Seagram's 7 Crown;* blended whiskey; 750 ml	$6.79
Whiskey	*New Orleans Times-Picayune* (1992)	*Jack Daniel's Black Label;* 750 ml	$11.39
Whiskey	*New Orleans Times-Picayune* (1992)	*Canadian Mist;* 1.75 liter	$14.49
Wine	*New Orleans Times-Picayune* (1992)	*Glen Ellen White Zinfandel;* 750 ml	$3.99
APPAREL, CHILDREN'S			
Coat	*Chicago Tribune* (1990)	*Pacific Trail;* boy's ski jacket; waterproof nylon	$49.96
Jacket	*Sears Flyer* (1993)	Crinkle nylon jacket	$18
Leggings	*Sears Flyer* (1993)	Bends more the way you do	$15
Overalls	*Sears Flyer* (1993)	OshKosh B'gosh overalls	$22
Pants	*Milwaukee Journal* (1991)	*Wild Thunder;* cotton canvas and twill with drawstrings	$19.99
Shirt	*New Orleans Times-Picayune* (1992)	*Blitz;* knit shirt; 100% cotton; crew-neck styling	$5.50
Shoes	*New Orleans Times-Picayune* (1992)	McGregor Boot Oxfords	$9.96
Socks	*New Orleans Times-Picayune* (1992)	*Keds;* 4-pack cuff anklets, cotton-nylon blend	$4
Sweater	*Natural History Magazine* (1993)	Charming, handmade sweater with dinosaur design	$68
Tee Shirt	*Sears Flyer* (1993)	Skateboard tee shirt, rainbow hued, hand sprayed and sponged front and back	$9
APPAREL, MEN'S			
Baseball Cap	*New Orleans Times-Picayune* (1992)	Choice of color	$2.99
Blazer	*Sears Flyer* (1993)	Wool blend	$95
Coat	*Chicago Tribune* (1990)	*Edelweiss Glenn;* nylon-fiber shell	$99.96

Absolut began an advertising campaign in the early 1980s that emphazied simplicity. The company created hundreds of advertisements in this style, tweaking the design slightly to market their product to different locations and events. This advertisement is specifically for the black currant flavor of the vodka. (via Flickr)

Item	Source	Description	Price
Jacket	*Sears Flyer* (1993)	Cotton polyester with poplin shell	$45
Jacket	*Natural History* (1993)	Genuine leather U. S. Army field jacket; available	$199
Pants	*Milwaukee Journal* (1990)	*Maxx;* cargo pockets, tapered legs, matching belt	$14.99
Shirt	*Atlanta Journal Constitution* (1993)	*Spalding;* golf shirt; cotton blend	$14.98
Shirt	*Atlanta Journal Constitution* (1993)	*Kensington;* cotton pinpoint dress shirt	$29.99
Shoes	*New Orleans Times-Picayune* (1992)	*Brittania;* leather boat oxfords	$16
Shoes	*Milwaukee Journal* (1990)	*Nike Air;* cross-trainer	$58.99
Shoes	*Milwaukee Journal* (1990)	*Reebok Sir Jam;* basketball high top	$58.99
Shoes	*Atlanta Journal Constitution* (1993)	*Etonic Stableair Base 11;* running shoe	$49.96
Tennis Shoes	*Sears Flyer* (1993)	Converse All Stars	$24
Tie	*Natural History* (1993)	Dashing Dinosaur tie made exclusively for the American Museum of Natural History	$35
Underwear	*Milwaukee Journal* (1990)	*Hanes;* red-label briefs; 3 per pack	$4.49

APPAREL, WOMEN'S

Item	Source	Description	Price
Blazer	*Sears Flyer* (1993)	Lined rollback cuffs, notched lapels, patch pockets	$38
Bodysuit	*Sears Flyer* (1993)	Figure hugging stretch cotton, lace trims neck and sleeves	$26
Cardigan	*Sears Flyer* (1993)	Bold graphics with shoulder pads	$40
Coat	*Chicago Tribune* (1990)	*Columbia Bugaloo;* parka; zip-out fleece liners	$119
Formal Wear	*Milwaukee Journal* (1990)	Mother-of-the-bride polyester georgette dress, in mauve or silver blue	$44.99
Girdle	*Sears Flyer* (1993)	Hi waist style	$25
Handbag	*New Orleans Times-Picayune* (1992)	Ladies' vinyl handbags, assortment of dressy or casual styles	$9.44
Jumpsuit	*Milwaukee Journal* (1990)	*Bonjour;* chambray jumpsuit	$29.99
Polo Shirt	*Sears Flyer* (1993)	Oversized	$18
Shirt	*Milwaukee Journal* (1990)	*Willow Bay;* ladies' rugby-stripe mock neck blouse	$7.99
Shoes	*New Orleans Times-Picayune* (1992)	*Gitano;* comfort walkers	$10.87

Item	Source	Description	Price
APPLIANCES			
Air Conditioner	*Sears Flyer* (1993)	Window air conditioning unit	$474.99
Air Purifier	*Sears Flyer* (1993)	Cleans up to 2250 sq. ft. per hour; 4 speed fan control	$234.50
Dishwasher	*Sears Flyer* (1993)	5 cycle, 5 option with Quiet Pack; plus installation	$629.99
Dishwasher	*New Orleans Times-Picayune* (1992)	*Whirlpool;* 5-cycle built-in dishwasher	$299
Microwave Oven	*Milwaukee Journal* (1990)	Ten-power microwave; touch control	$99
Refrigerator	*Milwaukee Journal* (1990)	*Frigidaire;* 18 cubic feet	$396
Refrigerator	*Sears Catalog* (1990)	*Kenmore Space Saver;* two-door, frostless model	$425.97
Vacuum Cleaner	*New Orleans Times-Picayune* (1992)	*Hoover Elite II;* vacuum with 5 amp motor	$89.96
Vacuum Cleaner	*New Orleans Times-Picayune* (1992)	*Dustbuster;* cordless vacuum; lightweight and compact	$17.99
Water Heater	*Sears Flyer* (1993)	40 gallon unit	$549.99
BABY PRODUCTS			
Car Seat	*Sears Flyer* (1993)	Converts to carrier or rocker	$65
Car Seat	*Sears Catalog* (1992)	*Travel 700 Car Seat;* padded shield and push-button release	$80
Chest	*Sears Flyer* (1993)	4 drawer chest, some assembly required	$200
Crib	*Sears Flyer* (1993)	Honey oak finish, double drop sides with stabilizer bar	$190
Crib Sheets	*Sears Flyer* (1993)	3 piece, Mickey Mouse design	$40
Diapers	*New Orleans Times-Picayune* (1992)	*Walgreen;* disposable diapers for boys or girls	$6.99
Dressing Table	*Sears Flyer* (1993)	Honey oak finish	$100
BUSINESS EQUIPMENT AND SUPPLIES			
Calculator	*New Orleans Times-Picayune* (1992)	*Tozal;* compact desktop dual power with 8-digit display	$3.99
Computer	*Atlanta Journal Constitution* (1993)	*Apple MacIntosh PowerBook;* 180 4/80	$3,799
Office Machine	*Atlanta Journal Constitution* (1993)	*Brother Intellifax-600;* Home Office Fax Machine with cutter	$353.43
Pager	*New Orleans Times-Picayune* (1992)	*Motorola Lifestyle;* digital pager	$7.95/mo
Photocopier	*Sears Catalog* (1990)	*Xerox;* personal copier	$899.99
Telephone	*Atlanta Journal Constitution* (1993)	Oki-810; car phone, includes installation and antenna	$149

Item	Source	Description	Price
COLLECTIBLES			
Bottle	*Glass-Works Auctions East Greenville, PA* (1992)	*Wahoo & Calisaya Bitters Bottle—Jacob Pinkerton;* medium amber semi-cabin 9 7/8" high, smooth base, applied mouth	$400
Boxing Trunks	*Art & Antiques* (1993)	Boxer *Muhammad Ali's* satin boxing trunks, sold at auction in 1992	$13,200
Calendar	*Natural History Magazine* (1993)	*Insects of the New World;* wall calendar	$12.85
Coin	*Boy's Life* (1992)	1652 Colonial Massachusetts silver sixpence	$35,200
Comic Book	*Art & Antiques* (1993)	*Superman* Comic Book, No. 1, from June 1938; good condition, sold at auction in 1992	$82,500

Item	Source	Description	Price
Furniture	*Art & Antiques* (1993)	Porcelain and tulipwood jewel casket and stand, once owned by Marie Antoinette; sold at auction in 1991	$4.93 million
Photograph	*Art & Antiques* (1993)	Photographer Nic Nicosia's scenes from daily life, each	$3,500
Photograph	*Boy's Life* (1992)	Simulated Special Edition of *Boy's Life* cover with your favorite picture plus $3.50 for postage and handling	$19.95
Political Button	*David J. Frent Political Auction* (1994)	George Washington, 1789 Inaugural Shank Button; GW raised in center with "Long Live the President" above in semicircular channel	$1,408
Snuff Box	*Art & Antiques* (1993)	18th century snuff box reading "On Thy Sweet Lips, To Print A Kiss, Is My Dear Girl The Price Of This"	$700
Sports Card	*Art & Antiques* (1993)	Baseball card for Honus Wagner, from 1910; sold at auction in 1991	$451,000
Stamp Collection	*Natural History Magazine* (1993)	Endangered species stamp collection; U.N. postal administration	$8.50
Stamps	*Boy's Life* (1992)	109 stamps from around the world	$0.50

EDUCATION

Item	Source	Description	Price
Annual Tuition	*Boy's Life* (1994)	Military academy, Gainesville, Georgia, grades 8–12	$9,400
Camp	*Boy's Life* (1994)	Lake Toxaway, NC	$3,100
Tuition	*Boy's Life* (1992)	Carson Long Military Institute; New Bloomfield, Pennsylvania	$7,500/yr

ENTERTAINMENT

Item	Source	Description	Price
Antique Show	*Art & Antiques* (1993)	*The Original Miami Beach Antiques Show;* 33 years in the same location; Miami Beach Convention Center Admission	$7
Camp	*Boy's Life* (1992)	*Northern Michigan Wilderness Camp;* backpacking, canoeing, and bicycling, two weeks	$515
Festival Ticket	*New Orleans Times-Picayune* (1993)	*New Orleans Jazz and Heritage Festival;* Friday night	$25 reserved seat
Lecture	*Natural History* (1993)	Natural History Museum presents the latest scientific findings from the Hubble Space Telescope; slide-show illustrated lecture, each	$8
Tour	*Natural History Magazine* (1993)	American Museum of Natural History; Predators, Prey, and their Habitats	$10

ENTERTAINMENT, HOME

Item	Source	Description	Price
Camcorder	*New Orleans Times-Picayune* (1992)	*RCA* compact 8mm 8:1 zoom camcorder with remote control	$699
Camera	*New Orleans Times-Picayune* (1992)	*Kodak Star 435;* 35mm camera, focus-free, built-in flash	$29.96
CD/Cassette Player	*New Orleans Times-Picayune* (1992)	*Sony;* three-piece portable CD and cassette player; 34-track programming	$166
Television	*Chicago Tribune* (1990)	*Mitsubishi;* Big-screen TV; 35"; stereo digital monitor	$2,599

Item	Source	Description	Price
Television	*New Orleans Times-Picayune* (1992)	*Zenith;* 25"; remote monitor receiver	$388
VCR	*Chicago Tribune* (1990)	*JVC;* VHS Hi-Fi stereo sound	$399
VCR	*Milwaukee Journal* (1990)	*Toshiba;* programmable VHS with remote	$227
VCR	*Sears Catalog* (1990)	*RCA;* 2 heads and up to 110 cable-compatible channels	$294.97
Videotape, Blank	*Milwaukee Journal* (1990)	3 T120 JVC videotapes	$8.49
Videotape, Prerecorded	*New Orleans Times-Picayune* (1992)	Walt Disney's *Jungle Book*	$19.76
Videotape, Prerecorded	*Fine Woodworking Magazine* (1994)	*School of Classical Woodcarving; Acanthus Leaf Training;* 72 minutes	$52.50

FOOD PRODUCTS

Item	Source	Description	Price
Apples	*New Orleans Times-Picayune* (1993)	Washington State Delicious apples	$0.59/lb
Chocolate	*New Orleans Times-Picayune* (1992)	*Hershey's Chocolate Kisses;* 14 oz	$1.97
Crackers	*Milwaukee Journal* (1990)	*Nabisco Ritz Bits;* box	$1.69
Eggs	*New Orleans Times-Picayune* (1993)	Large	$0.89/dz
Fish	*Chicago Tribune* (1990)	Farm-raised catfish	$2.29/lb
Flour	*New Orleans Times-Picayune* (1993)	*Gold Medal Flour;* 5-lb bag	$0.79
Shrimp	*Chicago Tribune* (1990)	Cooked tail-on shrimp; 12 oz	$8.99
Squid	*Chicago Tribune* (1990)	Federally inspected whole squid	$0.79/lb
Turkey	*New Orleans Times-Picayune* (1993)	10–22 lb average	$0.59/lb

FURNITURE

Item	Source	Description	Price
Bed	*New Orleans Times-Picayune* (1992)	Cherrywood full-size bed	$399.88
Bed	*Atlanta Journal Constitution* (1993)	Solid pine bunk bed	$69
Dining Set	*Milwaukee Journal* (1990)	5-piece oak dining set, 42" round table, 4 high back	$499
Easy Chair	*Milwaukee Journal* (1990)	*La-Z-Boy;* wall recliner; matching pair	$599
Lamp	*Atlanta Journal Constitution* (1993)	Brass lamps, 26" high	$36
Sofa	*Sears Catalog* (1990)	Sofa sleeper; has recessed handle sleeper mechanism with one-piece design	$499

Item	Source	Description	Price
Table	*Atlanta Journal Constitution* (1993)	Pine dinette with 2 benches	$99
Wall Shelves	*New Orleans Times-Picayune* (1992)	*Thomasville;* hand-crafted wall system; 3-piece wall system of cherry solids and veneers	$1,599
Wicker Furniture	*Sears Catalog* (1990)	Chaise lounge; frame and cushion	$493.99

GARDEN EQUIPMENT AND SUPPLIES

Item	Source	Description	Price
Ant Poison	*New Orleans Times-Picayune* (1992)	*Hyponex;* fire ant killer; 4 lb	$2.94
Fertilizer	*New Orleans Times-Picayune* (1992)	*Scott's Turf Builder;* lawn fertilizer; 5,000 square ft coverage	$7.88
Flowers	*New Orleans Times-Picayune* (1992)	4" flowering annuals, begonias, coleus, or salvia	$0.72
Hose	*Milwaukee Journal* (1991)	3 gauge sprinkler hose; 50'	$7.99
Lawn Mower	*New Orleans Times-Picayune* (1992)	*Lawn-Boy;* 4 HP 21" power mulch push mower; two cycle commercial grade engine	$289
Seed	*Chicago Tribune* (1990)	Wild bird food; 20 lbs	$2.99
Shrubbery	*New Orleans Times-Picayune* (1992)	1 gallon azalea, brilliant colors	$0.99
Spreader	*New Orleans Times-Picayune* (1992)	*Precision Green Drop;* 12" rubber tires	$54.75
Weed Killer	*Milwaukee Journal* (1991)	*Monsanto Round-Up;* 24-ounce; gallon	$16.99

HOTEL RATES

Item	Source	Description	Price
Hotel Room	*Atlanta Journal Constitution* (1993)	*Sheraton New York;* New York City; Sure Saver Rate	$169/night
Hotel Room	*Atlanta Journal Constitution* (1993)	*Sheraton Boston;* Boston, Massachusetts; Sure Saver Week-end Rates	$104/night

HOUSEHOLD PRODUCTS

Item	Source	Description	Price
Alarm Clock	*Milwaukee Journal* (1990)	*Ingraham;* wood clock; round, square or octagonal shape	$9.99
Alarm Clock	*New Orleans Times-Picayune* (1992)	*Spartus;* electronic eurostyle	$9.99
All Purpose Cleaner	*New Orleans Times-Picayune* (1992)	*Formula 409;* 32-oz	$1.79
Bath Set	*Milwaukee Journal* (1990)	5-piece bath rug set and 2-piece tank cover	$12.99
Blinds	*Sears Catalog* (1990)	Kenney contoured mini blinds; ready-made; 35" × 42"	$15.99
Caulk	*New Orleans Times-Picayune* (1992)	*Red Devil Speed Demon;* latex caulk; 10.3 oz tube	$0.89
Cleanser	*New Orleans Times-Picayune* (1992)	*Comet;* 14 oz	$0.49
Coffee Filters	*New Orleans Times-Picayune* (1992)	*Mr. Coffee;* basket type	$0.29/50

Item	Source	Description	Price
Coffee Maker	*Milwaukee Journal* (1990)	*Regal Drip Coffeemaker;* 1–10 cup capacity	$7.99
Comforter	*Sears Catalog* (1990)	Quilted comforter has polyester fill; twin 68"× 86"	$26.88
Cookware	*New Orleans Times-Picayune* (1992)	*Anchor Hocking;* Microwave 20-piece pop top set; 9 containers and 4 cup pitcher with lids	$7.96
Cookware	*New Orleans Times-Picayune* (1992)	7-piece cookware set, non-stick interior	$10
Dishes	*New Orleans Times-Picayune* (1992)	*Corelle Livingware;* 16-piece dinnerware	$17.97
Flashlight	*New Orleans Times-Picayune* (1992)	*First Alert;* rechargeable	$7.99
Grill	*New Orleans Times-Picayune* (1992)	*Hibachi;* 2 adjustable grids	$6.99
Knife	*New Orleans Times-Picayune* (1992)	*Washington Forge;* 4-piece steak knife set	$3.50
Laundry Basket	*Milwaukee Journal* (1990)	Rubbermaid	$2.99
Laundry Cleaner	*New Orleans Times-Picayune* (1992)	*Ultra Tide;* 128 oz	$5.94
Light Bulb	*Atlanta Journal Constitution* (1993)	Halogen Accent Bulb	$8.96
Light Bulb	*Atlanta Journal Constitution* (1993)	*Philips Bag-A-Way;* 2 bulbs	$1.61
Light Bulb	*Atlanta Journal Constitution* (1993)	*Philips Director;* 150 watt	$2.09
Luggage	*New Orleans Times-Picayune* (1992)	*American Tourister;* garment bag	$39.96
Mattress	*Atlanta Journal Constitution* (1993)	*Loving Care Supreme Mattress;* queen size	$189.95
Mattress	*Milwaukee Journal* (1990)	*Sealy;* queen size; extra firm; 10 year warranty	$324
Paint	*New Orleans Times-Picayune* (1992)	*Woolsey;* gloss-white paint	$14.95/gal
Paint Additive	*Country Living Magazine* (1996)	Zinsser's Blend and Glaze Decorative Painting Liquid	$25/gal
Paint Roller	*New Orleans Times-Picayune* (1992)	*EZ Painter;* free frame with three covers	$6.88
Paper Towels	*New Orleans Times-Picayune* (1993)	Mardi Gras	$0.50
Plastic Wrap	*New Orleans Times-Picayune* (1992)	*Reynolds Wrap;* 100 sq ft	$1.99
Resin	*New Orleans Times-Picayune* (1992)	Fiberglass resin with hardener	$16.95/gal
Saw	*Chicago Tribune* (1990)	7 1/4" circular saw; 2 1/3 H.P. motor	$59.99
Sheets	*New Orleans Times-Picayune* (1992)	Smooth-touch twin sheet, fitted	$8.99
Sheets	*New Orleans Times-Picayune* (1992)	Percale sheet set; permanent press; cotton and polyester; 4-piece set	$17.96

Item	Source	Description	Price
Sheets	*New Orleans Times-Picayune* (1992)	Waterbed sheet set; cotton; queen size	$19.96
Shower Curtain	*Sears Catalog* (1990)	Priscilla-style shower curtain has mock valance	$19.77
Smoke Detector	*New Orleans Times-Picayune* (1992)	Family guard detector with test button and battery	$5.99
Tape	*New Orleans Times-Picayune* (1992)	Duct tape; 45 yds, 2" wide	$2.99
Teapot	*New Orleans Times-Picayune* (1992)	6-cup porcelain teapot, designs licensed by Corning	$5.50
Towel	*New Orleans Times-Picayune* (1992)	*JC Penney;* bath towel	$4.90
Trash Bag	*New Orleans Times-Picayune* (1992)	*Hefty;* 33 bonus size bags	$2.88
Trash Bag	*Milwaukee Journal* (1990)	*Hefty;* 20-count; 30-gallon size	$2.22
VCR	*Sears Catalog* (1990)	*RCA;* 2 heads and up to 110 cable-compatible channels	$294.97

JEWELRY

Item	Source	Description	Price
Gold Chain	*New Orleans Times-Picayune* (1992)	Ladies 18" 14k gold diamond cut rope	$79.99
Ring	*Sears Catalog* (1992)	Round pearl ring	$79.99
Ring	*Sears Catalog* (1992)	Emerald cluster ring	$99.99
Ring	*Atlanta Journal Constitution* (1993)	*ArtCarved* high-school class ring	$69.95
Watch	*New Orleans Times-Picayune* (1992)	*Citizen;* men's	$149.90
Watch	*Chicago Tribune* (1990)	*Raymond Weil;* white dial with 18k gold bezel and black sharkskin strap; men's	$750
Watch	*New Orleans Times-Picayune* (1992)	Timex Analog Quartz	$14.99
Watch	*Natural History* (1993)	Your dog on a wristwatch; see your favorite dog walk around the dial	$29.95

MEALS

Item	Source	Description	Price
Dinner	*Milwaukee Journal*(1990)	*Hales Corner Restaurant;* 8 oz filet mignon, relish tray, salad, soup and potato, cherries jubilee	$7.95
Easter Sunday	*New Orleans Times-Picayune* (1993)	*Salvatore Ristorante;* Easter Sunday menu	$15.95

MEDICAL PRODUCTS AND SERVICES

Item	Source	Description	Price
Hydrogen Peroxide	*New Orleans Times-Picayune* (1992)	16-oz bottle	$0.39
Nonprescription Medicine	*Atlanta Journal Constitution* (1993)	*Nyquil;* 10-oz bottle	$4.93

Item	Source	Description	Price
Nonprescription Medicine	*Milwaukee Journal* (1990)	*Advil;* caplets, 100-count package	$6.68
Nonprescription Medicine	*New Orleans Times-Picayune* (1992)	*Dramamine;* for nausea, dizziness, and vomiting; 12 tablets	$2.39
Ointment	*Milwaukee Journal* (1990)	*Preparation H;* 1-oz tube	$2.88

MOTORIZED VEHICLES, SUPPLIES, AND SERVICES

Item	Source	Description	Price
Anti-Freeze	*Milwaukee Journal* (1990)	*Prestone;* antifreeze/coolant	$5.45
Automobile	*Milwaukee Journal* (1990)	1990 *Ford Escort*	$5,999
Automobile	*Milwaukee Journal* (1990)	1990 *Ford Taurus;* 4 doors; fully equipped	$9,999
Automobile	*Chicago Tribune* (1990)	1991 *Oldsmobile Ninety-Eight Regency Elite*	$20,999
Automobile	*Atlanta Journal Constitution* (1993)	1992 *Miata*	$14,978
Automobile	*Atlanta Journal Constitution* (1993)	1993 *Nissan Altima GXE*	$14,484
Automobile	*Atlanta Journal Constitution* (1993)	1993 *Toyota Previa*	$20,893
Automobile, Used	*Atlanta Journal Constitution* (1993)	1990 *Cadillac Seville*	$11,900
Automobile, Used	*Atlanta Journal Constitution* (1993)	1990 *Eldorado*	$15,900
Automobile, Used	*Chicago Tribune* (1990)	1987 *Toyota Supra*	$11,995
Automobile, Used	*Chicago Tribune* (1990)	1988 *Chrysler LeBaron*	$8,495
Battery	*Atlanta Journal Constitution* (1993)	*Marine Deep Cycle;* 500 CCA	$39.99
Motor Oil	*New Orleans Times-Picayune* (1992)	*Quaker State;* 10W-30	$0.99/qt
Oil Filter	*Atlanta Journal Constitution* (1993)	FRAM	$2.99
Tire	*Milwaukee Journal* (1990)	*Goodyear 54S;* radial, two steel belts	$41.95
Tire	*Atlanta Journal Constitution* (1993)	*Dunlop;* steel radial P195/70SR14	$65.77
Tire Cleaner	*Atlanta Journal Constitution* (1993)	No Touch Tire Care	$2.79

OTHER

Item	Source	Description	Price
Christmas Tree	*Chicago Tribune* (1990)	Artificial 7' Blue Alpine Fir	$124.99

Item	Source	Description	Price
PERSONAL CARE PRODUCTS			
Contact Lens Solution	*New Orleans Times-Picayune* (1992)	*Boston Advance conditioner;* 4-oz bottle for gas permeable lenses	$4.99
Mouthwash	*New Orleans Times-Picayune* (1992)	*Listerine;* 6-oz bottle	$1.79
Razor	*New Orleans Times-Picayune* (1992)	*Gillette;* disposable razors, with $2 rebate	$2.99
Scale	*Sears Flyer*(1993)	Bathroom scales, weighs up to 300 pounds	$27.99
REAL ESTATE			
Home	*Art & Antiques* (1993)	10,000 square foot house in Dallas, Texas suburb designed by architect Frank Lloyd Wright in 1958	$5.5 million
SEWING EQUIPMENT AND SUPPLIES			
Sewing Machine	*New Orleans Times-Picayune* (1992)	*Brother;* lightweight free arm; sews 16 different stitches	$150
SPORTS EQUIPMENT			
Backpack	*Natural History* (1993)	Leather backpack; plus $3.95 shipping	$29.95
Baseball Bat	*Atlanta Journal Constitution* (1993)	Louisville Slugger TPXBBL	$79.96
Baseball Glove	*Atlanta Journal Constitution* (1993)	*Wilson Roger Clemens;* all leather	$34.98
Basketball Backboard	*Chicago Tribune* (1990)	Fiberglass backboard with rim and pole	$99.98
Binoculars	*Sears Catalog* (1992)	*Tasco;* 8–20 power × 50 mm	$139.99
Exercise Bicycle	*Chicago Tribune* (1990)	*Airgometer;* exercise cycle	$249.99
Exercise Equipment	*Natural History Magazine* (1993)	*Lifestep;* Model 550; proven effective in the nation's finest health clubs	$1,589
Exercise Equipment	*Natural History Magazine* (1993)	*Nordic Track;* takes weight off and keeps it off	$399.95
Exercise Machine	*Natural History* (1993)	*Lifestep 5500 Aerobic Trainer;* 20 minutes to a healthier body	$1,598
Golf Clubs	*Atlanta Journal Constitution* (1993)	*Dunlop Solution Golf Set;* stainless-steel woods and irons	$249
Knife	*Milwaukee Journal* (1990)	Wormark Fish 'n Fillet	$9.99
Pistol	*New Orleans Times-Picayune* (1993)	*Smith & Wesson;* 38 caliber; SST, S-shot	$309
Pool Table	*Chicago Tribune* (1990)	*Canterbury;* 69	$699
Rod and Reel	*Milwaukee Journal* (1990)	Garcia Lite Plus Casting Combo	$59.99
Scuba Equipment	*New Orleans Times-Picayune* (1993)	Pro scuba mask; list $79.95	$24.95

Item	Source	Description	Price
Scuba Equipment	*New Orleans Times-Picayune* (1993)	Scuba tank; 80 cu ft; 3000 PSI	$119.95
Tennis Racket	*Atlanta Journal Constitution* (1993)	*Wilson;* 3.0 tennis frame; wide-body graphite/kevlar construction	$129.97
Tent	*Atlanta Journal Constitution* (1993)	*Camel Genesis Sixty Second Tent*; 7' × 8' dome	$89.98

TOYS

Item	Source	Description	Price
Tilt Walker	*Boy's Life* (1994)	Develops coordination	$21.95
Water Balloon Launcher	*Boy's Life* (1994)	200 yard model	$13.50

Popular children's toys in an advertisement for KayBee toys. (via Flickr)

Item	Source	Description	Price
TRAVEL AND TRANSPORTATION			
Airline Ticket	*New Orleans Times-Picayune* (1993)	*American Airlines;* New Orleans to Miami	$290
Airline Ticket	*Chicago Tribune* (1990)	*Midway Airlines;* Chicago to Boston one way	$99
Airline Ticket	*Chicago Tribune* (1990)	*Midway Airlines;* Chicago to Saint Thomas; one way	$179
Airline Ticket	*New Orleans Times-Picayune* (1993)	*Trans World Airlines;* New Orleans to Honolulu	$612
Cruise Ticket	*Natural History Magazine* (1993)	Alaska cruise; If you want authentic Alaska, don't gamble on another cruise	$2,395/person

MISCELLANY 1990–1994

Bordeaux Wines

At $40 or more for a bottle from a well-known chateau, a good Bordeaux wine comes at a price that can cramp the style of all but the most well-heeled wine lovers. Some Bordeaux producers have done something about this. Look for the 1990 Maitre d'Estournel ($8), 1989 Michel Lynch ($8.50), 1989 Christian Moueix Merlot ($10) and 1989 Mouton-Cadet ($8). They're ally very good wines and real values.

Bon Appétit, February 1993

Cheap Gas—For Now

Happy anniversary, drivers! Just a year after Iraqi troops conquered Kuwait and gasoline prices began spiking, a new study by oil historian Daniel Yergin says pretax, inflation adjusted gasoline prices are at their lowest point since 1947.

Even with recent increases in federal and state fuel taxes, gasoline costs Americans 44% less in real terms than it did in 1980, and surprisingly, 24% less than it did in the halcyon days of 1960, before anyone had heard of Saddam Hussein or OPEC.

Time, August 5, 1991

Remember Cost Control

Eighteen months ago, everyone agreed that the bottom line to healthcare reform had to be controlling the skyrocketing costs that are busting the federal budget—and devastating families, businesses, and the economy as a whole. Today you'd have to scour the Congressional Record for a mention of that goal. Instead, national leaders compete over who can give the most generous benefits to the most constituents . . . Consider the stark numbers. In 1993 the United States spent an estimated 14.3 percent of its gross domestic product on health care. That translates into $3,400 per person, more than three and a half times as much as the amount 30 years ago, even taking inflation into account.

Newsweek, July 25, 1994

PGA Championship Prize

Golfer John Daly has plans for at least part of the $230,000 first-place check (he earned as winner of the Professional Golfers' Association Championship).

"Pay off my house, van and BMW," said Daly, who bought the car for his fiancée. "I'm going to donate $30,000 to charity, whatever the PGA wants to donate it to."

Milwaukee Journal, August 21, 1991

HISTORICAL SNAPSHOT 1995–1999

1995

- Michael Jordan leaves baseball, returns to professional basketball's Chicago Bulls
- United States opposes Microsoft's planned $2 billion merger with Intuit
- Longest Major League Baseball strike in history, 234 days, ends
- Courts force the Citadel Military College to admit first female cadet
- Oklahoma City Federal Courthouse bombed, the worst act of terrorism in U.S. history at that time
- Twenty-fifth anniversary of Earth Day celebrated
- United States renews trade privileges with China despite human rights record
- United States space shuttle docks with Russian Space Station
- Federal Drug Administration rules nicotine an addictive drug, moves to regulate
- The trial against O. J. Simpson, a former football player accused of murdering his ex-wife, begins
- Chemical Bank and Chase Manhattan merge to create nation's biggest bank
- Forty thousand African American men meet in Washington, DC, pledge to take responsibility for their lives and communities
- Twenty-five percent of Americans continue to smoke cigarettes despite health warnings

1996

- U.S. approves fat substitute olestra for snacks
- Budget crisis shuts down Federal Government temporarily
- Networks introduce Television Rating System
- General Motors strike settled after 16 days
- Federal Drug Administration approves U.S. marketing of abortion pill RU-486
- Centennial Summer Olympics in Atlanta, GA, disrupted by bombing
- Jobless rate lowest in six years
- Incumbent U.S. president Bill Clinton defeats Bob Dole
- Minimum wage increased 90 cents to $5.15 per hour
- Wall Street's Dow Jones Industrial average surpasses 6,000 barrier
- Department of Agriculture says the cost of raising a child to age 17 is $149,820
- Dow ends year at 6,448

1997

- Thirty-year mortgage falls to 7 percent
- Leading tobacco companies make $368 billion settlement with states to settle smoking death claims
- Scottish researchers announce the first cloning of an adult mammal, a sheep named Dolly
- Despite a one-day plunge of 554 points, stock market soars; Dow up 20 percent for third straight year
- President Clinton gains line-item veto power for first time
- Affirmative Action programs, designed to aid minorities, come under attack

1998

- Tobacco companies make a $260 billion settlement with states for smoke-related illnesses
- Dow Jones industrial average closes year at 9,181, up 16%
- Inflation rate falls to 1.6%
- The Unabomber pleads guilty to all charges and accepts a sentence of life without parole
- Impeachment is initiated against President Bill Clinton who admits to an affair with White House intern Monica Lewinsky
- In professional baseball Mark McGuire and Sammy Sosa compete to break Roger Maris's 1961 home run record; both succeed; Sosa hits 66 and McGuire hits 70
- Melissa Ward becomes the first black female captain in commercial aviation
- The television game show *The Price is Right* airs its 5,000th episode
- India resumes nuclear testing after Pakistan successfully tests its first nuclear weapon
- The search engine Google is created

1999

- Over 10,000 people protest the World Trade Summit in Seattle, Washington
- The United States officially hands over control of the Panama Canal to Panama
- Pokémon, a card game, is the largest toy craze of the year
- The cartoon movie *South Park* is released and found to have the most curse words per minute, of any movie ever distributed
- NATO bombs Serbia to stop Serbian aggression against the Croats
- The USA Women's soccer team wins the World Cup
- George W. Bush, son of former president George Bush, announces that he will run for president of the United States

Pepper spray is applied to the protestors of the World Trade Organization Summit in Seattle, 1999. (via Wikimedia Commons)

SELECTED INCOME 1995-1999

Job	Source	Description	Pay
Administrative Assistant	*San Francisco Chronicle* (1996)	Collections, pull credit reports, create spreadsheets	$20,000–$26,000/yr
Administrative Assistant	*San Francisco Chronicle* (1996)	International bank seeks French speaking candidate	$30,000/yr
Administrative Assistant	*New York Times* (1998)	Chairman looking for an articulate assistant to coordinate all meetings and presentations	$52,000/yr plus bonus
Animal Control Officer	*San Francisco Chronicle* (1996)	Good people and animal handling skills required; law enforcement background preferred	$10.75/hr
Attorney	*San Francisco Chronicle* (1996)	City of Oakland, California; Deputy City Attorney	$7,094–$8,709/mo
Baseball Player	*People Weekly* (1998)	Annual salary of St. Louis Cardinal baseball player Mark McGwire	$9 million
Book Advance	*People Weekly* (1998)	Amount paid to Monica Lewinsky to write a tell-all book about her affair with President Bill Clinton	$600,000
Bus Driver	*Washington Post* (1999)	Require clean driving and criminal record. Must pass physical with drug test	$9/hr
Comedian	*San Francisco Examiner* (1997)	Per episode salary of television comic star Jerry Seinfeld in 1997	$1 million
Computer Engineer	*New York Times* (1998)	LAN/WAN engineer, routers, frame, SNA, ATM, NT	to $100,000
Dentist	*New York Times* (1998)	Endo, ortho, implants	$2,000/day
Football Player	*San Francisco Examiner* (1997)	Salary and bonus of San Diego Chargers player Junior Seau in 1997	$6.88 million
Hockey Player	*San Francisco Examiner* (1997)	Annual salary of Philadelphia hockey player Eric Lindros in 1997	$8 million
Housekeeper	*San Francisco Chronicle* (1996)	9 A.M. to 4 P.M. M-F	$15/hr
Housekeeper	*San Francisco Chronicle* (1996)	Must have car; English speaking	$1,000/mo
Housekeeper	*Washington Post* (1999)	Live-in, Monday through Friday, experience and references required	$225/wk
Informant	*People Weekly* (1998)	Reward paid to David Kaczynski for identifying his brother, Ted, as the Unabomber	$1 million
Legal Secretary	*San Francisco Chronicle* (1996)	Don't be on the wrong side of the door when opportunity knocks	up to $42,000/yr
Medical Faculty	*Look Smart Website* (2000)	Annual salary of Dermatology faculty in 1999	$153,498
Medical Faculty	*Look Smart Website* (2000)	Annual salary of Internal Medicine faculty in 1999	$120,000
Packers	*Atlanta Constitution* (1999)	Warehouse has openings from 7:00 A.M. to 4:00 P.M.	$8/hr
Secretary	*San Francisco Chronicle* (1996)	Human Resources Department; part-time; MS Word/Excel required	$12–$13/hr

Job	Source	Description	Pay
Store Manager	*Atlanta Constitution* (1999)	If you have clean motor vehicle record, with 2 years college or management experience, are able to lift 75 lbs., we want you	$33,000/yr
Systems Administrator	*Washington Post* (1999)	Must have ability to maintain small Windows NT 4.0 network	$45,000/yr
Television Anchor	*People Weekly* (1998)	Annual salary of television's *Today* host Katie Couric	$7 million
U.S. President	*The Christian Science Monitor* (1996)	Annual salary of President Bill Clinton in 1996	$200,000
Wrestler	*People Weekly* (1998)	Estimated annual income of wrestler Stone Cold Steve Austin, not including merchandising royalties	$2 million

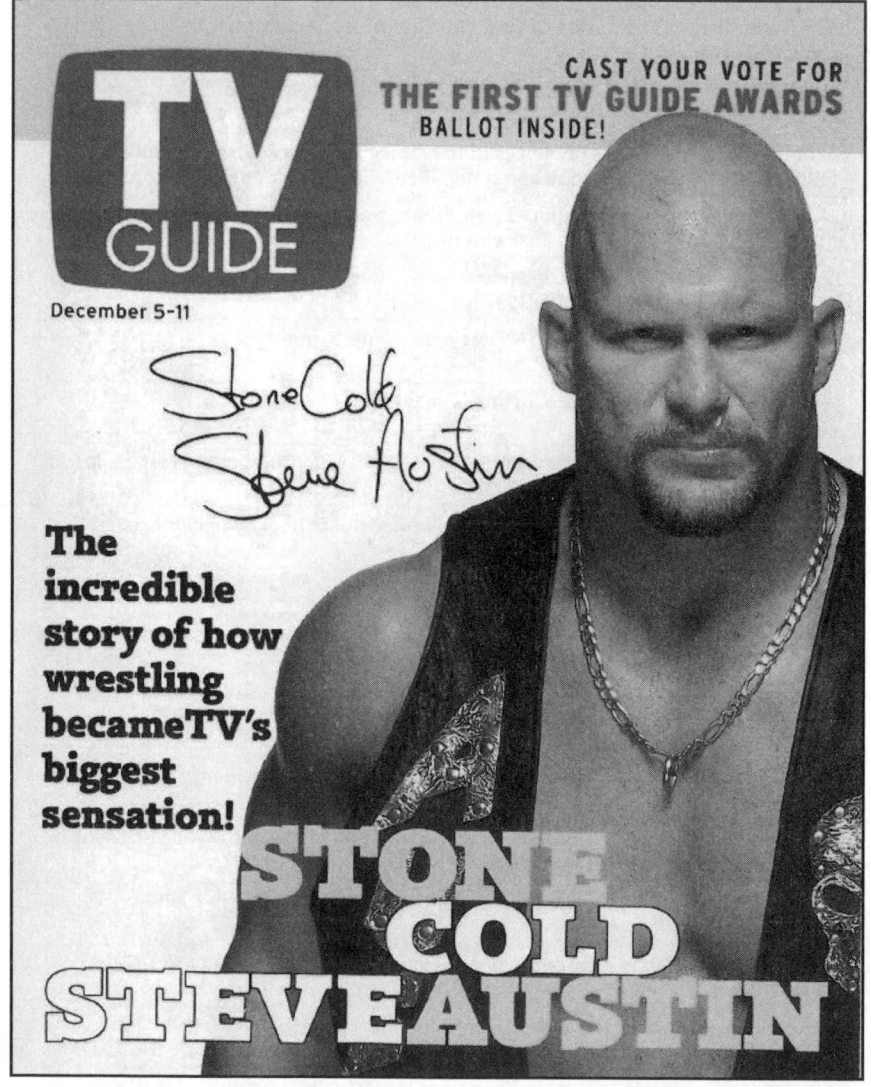

A 1998 TV Guide featuring Steve Austin on the cover. Austin's wrestling career spanned from 1989 to 2003. (via Flickr)

CONSUMER EXPENDITURES 1995–1999

Expenditure Type	1995	1996	1997	1998	1999
Clothing	$991	$886	$866	$961	$933
Food at Home	$1,401	$1,461	$1,354	$1,408	$1,449
Food Away from Home	$1,098	$1,138	$1,225	$1,232	$1,236
Auto Usage	$2,921	$3,197	$3,239	$3,331	$3,536
Auto Purchase (new)	$1,042	$1,189	$1,244	$1,362	$1,507
Auto Maintenance	$393	$381	$391	$392	$382
Gas and Oil	$530	$582	$567	$529	$565
Housing	$7,030	$7,095	$7,586	$7,843	$8,206
Utilities	$1,421	$1,488	$1,563	$1,536	$1,551
Telephone	$506	$544	$583	$581	$592
Health Care	$1,110	$1,155	$1,249	$1,220	$1,336
Personal Taxes	$2,013	$1,828	$2,011	$2,040	$2,218
Tobacco	$172	$166	$169	$175	$189
Public Transportation	$239	$305	$280	$297	$250
Entertainment	$992	$1,002	$1,011	$999	$1,040
Total Average Expenditures	$21,859	$22,417	$23,338	$23,906	$24,990

INVESTMENTS 1995–1999

Investment	1995	1996	1997	1998	1999
Basic Yield, One-Year Corporate Bonds	7.54	7.96	7.63	6.23	7.64
Short-Term Interest Rates, 4–6 Months, Prime Commercial Paper	5.79	5.61	5.65	4.80	5.71
Basic Yield, Common Stocks, Total	2.53	2.21	1.77	NR	NR
Index of Common Stocks (S&P-500)	544.75	670.63	885.14	1229.23	1469.25

COMMON STOCKS, CLOSING PRICE AND YIELD, FIRST BUSINESS DAY OF YEAR

(PARENTHETICAL NUMBER IS ANNUAL DIVIDENDS IN DOLLARS)

	1995	1996	1997	1998	1999
Allis Chalmers	1	3/8	1	3 5/8	3.50
AT&T	34 3/16	44 3/64	41 1/4	58.82	77.88
(Name changed from American Telephone & Telegraph Company, 4/21/94) (1 per 16 spin-off, 12/13/96) (3 for 1 split, 4/99; 1 for 5 split, 11/02)	(4.40)	(4.40)	(4.40)	(4.40)	(4.40)
NationsBank N/C Bank of America	45 3/4	69 3/8	97 3/8	60 3/4	60.50
(NCNB&C&SSovrancombine to form Nations-Bank, 1/2/92) (2 for 1 split, 2/7/97) (NationsBank combines with Bank of America, 10/1/98)	(1.04)	(1.20)	(1.37)	(1.80)	(1.85)
Delta Airlines	25 1/4	36 13/16	35 7/16	59 1/2	51.94
(2 for 1 split, 11/98)	(.10)	(.10)	(.10)	(.10)	(0.10)
American Brands N/C Fortune Brands	23 59/64	28 3/8	31 21/32	37.06	31.25
(2 for 1 split, 10/9/90) (1 per 1 spinoff, 5/29/97) (Name changed to Fortune Brands, Inc., 5/30/97)	(2.00)	(2.00)	(1.41)	(1.67)	(1.99)
General Electric	25 1/2	36	49 7/16	73.31	100.56
(2 for 1 split,4/28/94) (2 for 1 split,4/28/97) (3 for 1 split, 5/00)	(.82)	(.92)	(1.04)	(1.20)	(1.29)
GM/E Electronic Data Sys.	38 3/8	52	43 1/4	43 15/16	
(2 for 1 split, 2/16/90) (2 for 1 split, 2/14/92) (Each share of CL "E" converted into 1 share of Electronic Data Systems, 6/10/96)	(.52)	(.60)	(.60)	(.60)	
General Motors	39 13/16	49 31/32	52 11/16	60 3/4	70.87
(1 spinoff, 12/17/97)	(1.10)	(1.60)	(2.00)	(2.00)	(2.00)

Investment	1995	1996	1997	1998	1999
Microsoft	5 9/32	21 15/16	41 5/16	64 5/8	141.00
(2 for 1 split,3/26/90)					
(3 for 2 split,6/18/91)					
(3 for 2 split,6/3/92)					
(2 for 1 split,5/6/94)					
(2 for 1 split, 11/22/96)					
(2 for 1 split, 2/6/98)					
(2 for 1 split, 3/99; 2 for 1 split, 2/03)					
Ind Harvester N/C Navistar Int'l	15 1/8	10 5/8	9 1/8	24 13/16	27.75
(Name changed to Navistar)					
(no dividends)					
International Corp.,					
(1 for 10 split, 6/30/93)					
Nabisco/RJ Reynolds Inc.	27 1/2	30 3/4	34	37 1/2	n/a
(1 for 5 split, 4/12/95)	(1.50)	(1.76)	(2.00)	(2.05)	(1.55)
USX-U.S. Steel Group	35 5/8	31 7/8	32 1/8	34 7/8	n/a
(Formerly USX Corp; each share of USX Corp was divided into 1 share of USX-Marathon Group and .2 shares of USX-US Steel Group eff. 5/6/91)	(1.00)	(1.00)	(1.00)	(1.00)	
Wal-Mart	20 7/8	23 1/4	23	39 3/8	80.63
(2 for 1 split, 6/15/90)	(.10)	(.11)	(.14)	(.16)	(.19)
(2 for 1 split, 2/2/93)					
(2 for 1 split, 4/99)					
Warner Lambert	76 1/2	98 1/2	74	125 7/8	n/a
(2 for 1 split,5/2/90)	(.43)	(.46)	(.51)	(.64)	
(2 for 1 split,5/3/96)					
(3 for 1 split,5/8/98)					

STANDARD JOBS 1995–1999

Job Type	1995	1996	1997	1998	1999
Wages Per Full-Time Employee	$27,845/yr	$28,946/yr	$25,272	$26,260	$27,092
Private Industries, incl. Farm Labor	$27,440/yr	$28,581/yr	$28,170	$28,990	$28,640
Bituminous Coal Mining	$42,711/yr	$44,769/yr	$44,535	$44,811	$44,582
Building Trades	$28,465/yr	$28,846/yr	$33,649	$35,068	$36,379
Domestics	$10,854/yr	$11,173/yr	$11,180	$11,596	$12,636
Farm Labor	$15,863/yr	$15,316/yr	$14,196	$14,612	$15,808
Finance, Insurance, & Real Estate	$38,577/yr	$41,728/yr	$41,808	$42,380	$42,990
Gas, Electricity, & Sanitation Workers	$38,936/yr	$39,398/yr	$42,549	$44,592	$45,274
Manufacturing, Durable Goods	$28,507/yr	$28,366/yr	$30,122	$31,006	$32,051
Manufacturing, Nondurable Goods	$24,387/yr	$24,203/yr	$29,403	$29,767	$31,190
Medical/Health Services Workers	$21,234/yr	$21,555/yr	$21,667	$22,431	$23,290
Miscellaneous Manufacturing	$21,798/yr	$21,688/yr			
Motion Picture Services	$39,585/yr	$39,842/yr	$39,906	$40,606	$40,777
Nonprofit Org. Workers	$15,016/yr	$15,538/yr	$15,540	$16,030	$16,106
Passenger Transportation Workers, Local & Highway	$18,525/yr	$18,167/yr	$19,662	$21,149	$20,320
Postal Employees	$35,797/yr	$37,776/yr	$35,204	$35,412	$36,244
Public School Teachers	$27,130/yr	$27,875/yr	$34,060	$34,892	$35,776
Radio Broadcast and Television Workers	$32,223/yr	$32,822/yr	$32,811	$33,117	$33,222
Railroads	$42,175/yr	$42,983/yr	$42,328	$44,148	$42,432
State & Local Government Workers	$29,023/yr	$30,160/yr	$30,784	$31,824	$31,824
Telephone & Telegraph Workers	$35,844/yr	$36,571/yr	$33,696	$35,412	$36,140
Total Federal Government	$38,520/yr	$34,944/yr	$35,568	$36,088	$37,908
Wholesale & Retail Trade Workers	$14,412/yr	$14,415/yr	$20,332	$21,320	$21,892

FOOD BASKET 1995–1999

Commodity	Year	U.S. Average	North East	North Central	South	West
Bacon, Sliced, per pound	1995	$1.921	$2.252	$1.969	$1.661	$1.801
	1996	$2.177	$2.353	$2.093	$2.207	$2.054
	1997	$2.658	$2.854	$2.595	$2.599	$2.585
	1998	$2.64	$2.78	$2.67	$2.51	$2.73
	1999	$2.52	$2.77	$2.61	$2.27	$2.64
Bananas, per pound	1995	50.6¢	56.2¢	47.3¢	47.5¢	51.3¢
	1996	46.7¢	50.0¢	43.2¢	43.1¢	50.3¢
	1997	50.3¢	54.3¢	46.9¢	46.6¢	53.2¢
	1998	$0.47	$0.52	$0.44	$0.43	$0.51
	1999	$0.48	$0.49	$0.48	$0.44	$0.55
Beef, Ground 100% beef, per pound	1995	$1.364	NR	$1.384	$1.343	$1.365
	1996	$1.305	NR	$1.297	$1.402	$1.215
	1997	$1.404	NR	$1.315	$1.492	NR
	1998	$1.45	NR	$1.42	$1.49	NR
	1999	$1.38	NR	$1.32	$1.42	NR
Bread, White Pan, per pound	1995	78.2¢	85.2¢	76.1¢	69.2¢	82.2¢
	1996	86.8¢	90.3¢	84.6¢	81.7¢	90.5¢
	1997	87.1¢	89.0¢	87.4¢	81.4¢	90.6¢
	1998	$0.85	$0.96	$0.84	$0.75	$0.94
	1999	$0.87	$1.01	$0.87	$0.77	$0.89
Butter, Salted, Grade AA, Stick, per pound	1995	$1.610	$1.610	NR	NR	NR
	1996	$1.784	$1.771	$1.908	$1.673	NR
	1997	$1.959	NR	NR	$1.959	NR
	1998	$2.35	NR	NR	NR	NR
	1999	$3.00	NR	NR	$2.79	NR
Chicken, Fresh, Whole, per pound	1995	91.7¢	$1.058	86.4¢	79.5¢	95.0¢
	1996	96.2¢	$1.100	93.8¢	82.9¢	98.2¢
	1997	$1.029	$1.074	$1.000	93.6¢	$1.104
	1998	$1.02	$1.10	$0.97	$0.91	$1.15
	1999	$1.07	$1.21	$1.13	$0.98	$1.11
Coffee, 100%, Ground Roast, all sizes, per pound	1995	$4.478	$4.739	$4.236	NR	$4.459
	1996	$3.336	$3.097	$3.451	$3.254	$3.543
	1997	$3.333	$3.661	$3.135	NR	$3.204
	1998	$4.02	$4.40	$3.77	$3.89	$4.01
	1999	$3.43	$3.69	$3.17	$3.37	$3.48
Crackers, Soda, Salted, per pound	1995	NR	NR	NR	NR	NR
	1996	$1.306	NR	NR	$1.306	NR
	1997	$1.441	NR	NR	$1.441	NR
	1998	$1.66	NR	NR	$1.49	NR
	1999	$1.59	NR	NR	$1.41	NR
Eggs, Grade A, Large, per dozen	1995	92.4¢	$1.115	78.6¢	87.0¢	NR
	1996	$1.193	$1.330	$1.046	$1.202	NR
	1997	$1.167	$1.312	$1.052	$1.138	NR
	1998	$1.12	$1.20	$1.04	$1.11	NR
	1999	$1.05	$1.17	$1.00	$1.00	NR

Commodity	Year	U.S. Average	North East	North Central	South	West
Lettuce, Iceberg, per pound	1995	82.1¢	98.6¢	75.3¢	82.0¢	72.5¢
	1996	76.3¢	83.1¢	73.2¢	81.0¢	67.7¢
	1997	64.7¢	67.2¢	57.4¢	70.6¢	63.7¢
	1998	$1.07	$1.16	$0.82	$1.15	$1.13
	1999	$0.64	$0.70	$0.59	$0.66	$0.62
Margarine, Soft, Tubs, per pound	1995	NR	NR	NR	NR	NR
	1996	NR	NR	NR	NR	NR
	1997	NR	NR	NR	NR	NR
	1998	NR	NR	NR	NR	NR
	1999	NR	NR	NR	NR	NR
Margarine, Stick, per pound	1995	80.9¢	NR	81.8¢	80.0¢	NR
	1996	NR	NR	NR	NR	NR
	1997	NR	NR	NR	NR	NR
	1998	NR	NR	NR	NR	NR
	1999	NR	NR	NR	NR	NR
Milk, Fresh, Whole, Fortified, per 1/2 gallon	1995	$1.446	$1.319	NR	NR	$1.572
	1996	$1.481	$1.327	NR	NR	$1.635
	1997	$1.616	$1.441	NR	NR	$1.790
	1998	NR	NR	NR	NR	NR
	1999	NR	NR	NR	NR	NR
Potatoes, Frozen, French Fried, per pound	1995	81¢	NR	78.0¢	83.2¢	81.9¢
	1996	83.5¢	NR	80.3¢	86.7¢	NR
	1997	90.8¢	NR	88.3¢	93.3¢	NR
	1998	$0.98	$1.13	NR	$0.87	NR
	1999	$1.00	$1.19	NR	$0.95	NR
Steak, T-Bone, U.S. Choice, Bone-in, per pound	1995	$5.660	NR	$5.577	$5.743	NR
	1996	$5.667	NR	$5.691	$5.643	NR
	1997	$5.799	NR	$5.776	$5.822	NR
	1998	$5.82	NR	NR	NR	NR
	1999	$6.36	NR	$6.04	NR	NR
Sugar, White, All Sizes, per pound	1995	40.1¢	45.3¢	36.1¢	39.4¢	39.6¢
	1996	40.9¢	43.4¢	37.7¢	41.0¢	41.5¢
	1997	43.5¢	45.2¢	43.7¢	42.9¢	42.2¢
	1998	$0.43	$0.45	$0.42	$0.41	$0.43
	1999	$0.43	$0.46	$0.42	$0.42	$0.44
Tuna, Light, Chunk, per pound	1995	$2.022	$2.122	$1.950	$1.922	$2.093
	1996	$2.016	$2.067	$2.007	$1.858	$2.132
	1997	$2.063	$2.087	$2.090	$1.911	$2.165
	1998	$2.10	NR	$2.15	$2.03	NR
	1999	$2.09	NR	$2.30	$1.93	NR

SELECTED PRICES 1995–1999

Item	Source	Description	Price
ALCOHOL			
Wine Bottle Holder	Playboy (1997)	Hand-crafted by artist Eric Kaposta; limited edition; bust of Bacchus	$150
Wine	*Playboy* (1997)	1994 Cakebread Cellars Chardonnay Reserve	$36
Wine	*Viansa Catalog* (1998)	*Viansa;* 1997 Sauvignon Blanc, made from Napa Valley grapes	$12
APPAREL, MEN'S			
Belt	*Coldwater Creek Catalog* (1998)	Fine-grained Italian leather, 1" wide	$42
Field Jacket	*Lands' End Catalog* (1998)	Gently stonewashed 7-oz cotton canvas, with corduroy collar	$69.50
Jacket	*Soccer Madness Catalog* (1997)	*Adidas Santiago Polar Fleece;* two-tone sleeves and body	$69.95
Jeans	*Los Angeles Times* (1997)	Todd Oldham style	$50
Shoes	*Los Angeles Times* (1997)	Bass Brompton style	$59.99
Shoes	*Coldwater Creek Catalog* (1998)	Loafers of flexible nappa leather	$68
Soccer Cleats	*Soccer Madness Catalog* (1997)	*Predator Touch liga;* features jets, fins, and ridges which offer better ball control and spin	$129.95
Suit	*Los Angeles Times* (1997)	*Savane;* double-gabardine suit	$149.99
Suit	*Boston Globe* (1997)	Hickey-Freeman	$760
Suit	*Boston Globe* (1997)	Oxford suit	$1,320
APPAREL, WOMEN'S			
Brassiere	*Boston Globe* (1997)	Maidenform	$12.99
Brassiere	*Boston Globe* (1997)	Best Form	$5.99
Brassiere	*Los Angeles Times* (1997)	*Olga;* push-up sensuous solution style	$20.63
Brassiere	*Los Angeles Times* (1997)	*Vanity Fair;* underwire skin-to-skin style	$18
Dress	*Los Angeles Times* (1997)	*Versace;* stretch scuba dress	$295
Fur Coat	*Boston Globe* (1997)	Beaver jacket	$495

653

Item	Source	Description	Price
Fur Coat	*Boston Globe* (1997)	Blush fox coat	$2,595
Fur Coat	*Boston Globe* (1997)	Russian sable coat	$7,995
Handbag	*Los Angeles Times* (1997)	*Tignanello;* one-touch leather bag	$69.99
Hat	*Smith & Hawken* (1998)	Double-chenille stuffs into backpack or purse	$39
Jacket	*Boston Globe* (1997)	Cashmere-blend jacket	$69.99
Pants	*The State* (Columbia, SC) (1998)	*Diane Richard* washable flannel pants, styled in poly/rayon	$28
Purse	*Los Angeles Times* (1997)	*Kenneth Cole;* leather reaction bag	$148.50
Shoes	*Boston Globe* (1997)	*Salmon Evolution* 7.1 boots	$189.95
Shoes	*Los Angeles Times* (1997)	Hush Puppies	$29.99
Shoes	*Atlanta Constitution* (1999)	*Brooks Paragon;* cross-training tennis shoe	$55
Turtleneck Underwear	*Lands' End Catalog* (1998)	Pure silk; just as lightweight yet warm as our long, full bodied underwear	$32.50

APPLIANCES

Item	Source	Description	Price
Bread maker	*Consumer Reports* (1997)	*The Breadman TR800* made the best bread	$100
Vacuum Cleaner	*Consumer Reports* (1998)	*Hoover WindTunnel Deluxe* weighs 18 lb.; better than most on carpeting and at edge-cleaning	$280
VCR	*Consumer Reports* (1998)	*The Panasonic PV-8662* is a fine all-around performer that offers features for a range of family uses	$240
Whirlpool Tubs	*Consumer Reports* (1998)	*American Standard Luxury System II* is spacious and comfortable; holds 25 to 63 gallons	$1,660

BUSINESS EQUIPMENT AND SUPPLIES

Item	Source	Description	Price
Computer	*Boston Globe* (1997)	*Apple MacIntosh Performa;* 6115CD	$2,699
Computer	*Boston Globe* (1997)	*Apple MacIntosh Performa;* 475	$1,099
Computer	*New York Times* (1999)	*Compaq Presario 1235;* all-in-one color notebook	$1,199
Electronic Organizer	*Newsweek* (1998)	*The Palm III;* connected organizer keeps names, phone numbers, schedules, memos, and e-mail at your fingertips	$369
Envelope	*Los Angeles Times* (1997)	9" × 12" Brown Kraft Clasp Envelope	$4.65/100
Fax Machine	*Boston Globe* (1997)	*Brother Plain Paper Fax Machine;* features quickscan, 30-page document feeder	$799.99
Printer	*Newsweek* (1998)	*Epson Stylus;* color printers have the exclusive perfect- picture imaging system; Model 740	$279
Software	*Boston Globe* (1997)	Microsoft Office 4.2	$248.99
Software	*Boston Globe* (1997)	Meca Managing Your Money 2.0	$39.99
Telephone	*Boston Globe* (1997)	Handheld cellular with alpha memory	$49.99

Item	Source	Description	Price

ENTERTAINMENT

Item	Source	Description	Price
Art Exhibit	*New York Times* (1999)	*Baule: African Art/Western Eyes;* Museum for African Art	$8
Museum	*Southern Living* (1999)	*Reedville Fisherman's Museum,* Reedville, Va.	$2

ENTERTAINMENT, HOME

Item	Source	Description	Price
Audio Tape	*Boston Globe* (1997)	*TDK audio tape;* 7-pack D90	$5
Camcorder	*Consumer Reports* (1999)	"The digital *Sony DCR-PC10* delivered the best image, but it's still extremely expensive."	$2,700
Camera	*Consumer Reports* (1999)	The *Nikon Coolpix 900* has 1.280 ×960-pixel resolution, compact flash memory card and Adobe Photo Deluxe 2.0 for Windows 95, Mac 05 7.2	$800
Camera	*American Photo* (1998)	*Canon;* EOS-3 35mm with eye control	$1,900.00
Film	*Boston Globe* (1997)	*Kodak Gold;* 110 film; 24 exposures; 3-pack; 200 speed	$6
Piano	*Atlanta Constitution* (1999)	*Yamaha;* digital piano	$997
Television	*Boston Globe* (1997)	*Zenith;* 19"; Digital; Color	$139
Television	*Playboy* (1997)	*Projectavision;* Digital Home Theater TV; combines 60" rear-projection TV with computer display	$10,000
Videotape, Prerecorded	*Playboy* (1997)	Farrah Fawcett, *All of Me*	$19.98
Videotape, Prerecorded	*Boston Globe* (1997)	Disney's *Lion King*	$29.97
Videotape, Prerecorded	*Atlanta Constitution* (1999)	Lethal Weapon	$15.99

FOOD PRODUCTS

Item	Source	Description	Price
Cookies	*Viansa Catalog* (1998)	*Amaretti;* soft almond cookies in assorted fruit and nut flavors in spaghetti tin	$18
Jam	*Williams-Sonoma Catalog* (1997)	*La Trinquelinette;* organically grown fruits; 13-oz jar	$9
Olive Oil	*Viansa Catalog* (1998)	Extra-virgin oil from three olive varieties; comes in a hand etched glass decanter, 23 oz	$32
Salt	*Williams-Sonoma Catalog* (1997)	*Brittany Grey Sea Salt;* 2 lb 2 oz box	$10.50
Tea	*Los Angeles Times* (1997)	*Tetley Iced Tea Mix;* 42 Servings	$0.99
Water	*Los Angeles Times* (1997)	*Niagara Pure Drinking Water;* 1.5 liter	$0.49

FURNITURE

Item	Source	Description	Price
Armoire	*Atlanta Constitution* (1999)	Port Royal entertainment armoire, holds 32" TV	$899
Bed	*Atlanta Constitution* (1999)	Campaign bed, made from steel with a protective coating; queen size	$699

Item	Source	Description	Price
Cabinet	*Boston Globe* (1997)	54" Utility cabinet, ready to finish	$44
Chair	*Boston Globe* (1997)	*La-Z-Boy;* 18 different elevations; 3-position foot rest	$332.99
Chair	*Los Angeles Times* (1997)	Global Leather Task Tilter	$99.99
Desk	*Los Angeles Times* (1997)	Recycled office furniture; 60" × 18"	$128
Ladderback Chair	*New York Times* (1998)	Walnut construction with rush seat	$195

GARDEN EQUIPMENT AND SUPPLIES

Item	Source	Description	Price
Arbor	*Southern Living* (1999)	Vinyl arbor	$495
Bulbs	*Fine Gardening Magazine* (1996)	100 pink/white lily-flowering tulips; delivered	$43
Garden Label	*Fine Gardening Magazine* (1996)	Flag-style markers	$20.95/100

HOTEL RATES

Item	Source	Description	Price
Hotel Room	*Chicago Tribune* (1996)	*The Talbott Hotel;* includes deluxe accommodations, $20 Marshall Field's gift certificate, and holiday keepsake; available weekends	$160
Room Rate	*Southern Living* (1999)	Kiawah Island, SC	$260

HOUSEHOLD PRODUCTS

Item	Source	Description	Price
Answering Machine	*Playboy* (1998)	*Bang & Olufsen Beotalk 1100;* uses digital chip recorder to forward messages to three mailboxes	$250
Bath Towel	*The Company Store Catalog* (1998)	*Silhouette;* 100% cotton long terry loop, 27" × 54"	$24
Bath Tub Reglaze	*The State* (Columbia, SC) (1998)	Don't replace your old tub, reglaze it	$170
Battery	*Boston Globe* (1997)	*Eveready;* D-size; 2-pack	$6
Blender	*Los Angeles Times* (1997)	*Krups Power X;* 330-watt; 14 speeds	$49.99
Bowl Set	*Williams-Sonoma Catalog* (1997)	11-piece glass bowl set; tempered glass from France	$32
Bread maker	*Los Angeles Times* (1997)	*Welbilt;* 2-lb convection bread machine	$129.99
Ceiling Fans	*Consumer Reports* (1998)	*Hunter Sojourn* is a very efficient fan with	$190
Cell Phone	*Consumer Reports* (1998)	*Motorola StarTAC* has excellent overall reception purity With contract Without contract	$199–$550 $349–$799
China	*Los Angeles Times* (1997)	5-piece place setting; festive pattern	$28.75
Cleanser	*Los Angeles Times* (1997)	*Purex All Purpose Cleaner;* 32 oz	$0.99
Cleanser	*Boston Globe* (1997)	*Ultra Downy;* 20 oz	$2
Cleanser	*Boston Globe* (1997)	*Ultra Mr. Clean;* 14 oz; Lemon Fresh	$2

Item	Source	Description	Price
Comforter	*Los Angeles Times* (1997)	*Quallowarm II;* hypoallergenic polyester fiberfill; king size	$160
Cookware	*Williams-Sonoma Catalog* (1997)	All-clad master soup pot; stainless steel; 12 qt	$230
Cookware	*Williams-Sonoma Catalog* (1997)	International clay pot; ideal for the health conscious	$14.95
Deodorizer	*Los Angeles Times* (1997)	Arm & Hammer Pet Fresh Carpet and Room Refresher	$0.99
Faucet	*Boston Globe* (1997)	Acrylic-handle lavatory faucet	$43
Flatware	*Williams-Sonoma Catalog* (1997)	Sierra four-piece setting; bakelite handles	$40
Food Processor	*Williams-Sonoma Catalog* (1997)	*Cuisinart;* perfect size to meet most families' day-to-day needs	$139
Glasses	*Williams-Sonoma Catalog* (1997)	Monogrammed beer mugs; 20-oz; 4 3/4" high	$40
Glue	*Boston Globe* (1997)	*Krazy Glue;* .07-oz tube	$1
Knife	*Los Angeles Times* (1997)	*J. A. Henckels;* 4-piece steak knife set	$39.99
Knife	*Williams-Sonoma Catalog* (1997)	*Schaaf;* forged 5" tomato knife	$44.95
Lamp	*Atlanta Constitution* (1999)	*Cresswell;* iron floor lamp; 60"	$69.99
Low Flush Toilets	*Consumer Reports* (1998)	*Gerber Ultra Flush* did an outstanding job of clearing waste and cleaning the bowl with each flush	$270
Luggage	*Playboy* (1998)	*Willis & Geiger;* leather chart case with multiple compartments and pockets	$470
Luggage	*Los Angeles Times* (1997)	*Samsonite 750;* jumbo hardside cart	$399.99
Mold	*Williams-Sonoma Catalog* (1997)	Butter molds; create rose- and leaf-shape pats with ease; one of each	$10
Mortar and Pestle	*Williams-Sonoma Catalog* (1997)	Process a small amount of peppercorns or spices with this porcelain tool	$9
Oriental-Style Rugs	*New York Times* (1998)	Geometrics from Pakistan, 9' 1" × 12' 1"	$2,458
Paint Additive	*Country Living Magazine* (1996)	Zinsser's Blend and Glaze Decorative Painting Liquid	$25/gal
Pillow	*Los Angeles Times* (1997)	European square 26" pillow with cotton cover	$15
Plates	*Williams-Sonoma Catalog* (1997)	Grape-leaf salad plates, green-grape-leaf design; 8" diameter, set of 4	$49
Roaster	*Los Angeles Times* (1997)	*Calphalon;* double roaster	$99.99
Silverware	*Southern Living* (1999)	Sterling, 46 piece setting	$2,999
Slumber Bag	*The Company Store Catalog* (1998)	Soft, bright and totally fun; 30 × 66	$89.99
Stairs	*Southern Living* (1999)	Victorian spiral stairs	$3,300

Item	Source	Description	Price
Tissue	*Los Angeles Times* (1997)	*Kleenex;* 150 count	$0.99
Toilet	*Boston Globe* (1997)	White, water-saver 1.6 gallon flush	$49
Towel	*Los Angeles Times* (1997)	*Fieldcrest Softique;* bath towel; 8 colors	$12
Trash Bag	*Boston Globe* (1997)	*Sure-Tuff Trash Bag;* 26-gallon size	$0.50/10
Vegetable Slicer	*Williams-Sonoma Catalog* (1997)	*Benriner;* shreds and juliennes fruits and vegetables	$45

JEWELRY

Item	Source	Description	Price
Bracelet	*Atlanta Constitution* (1999)	Garnet and diamond hugs and kisses bracelet in 18k gold over sterling	$160
Necklace	*Atlanta Constitution* (1999)	Cultured pearl necklace, 18" strand	$425
Ring	*New York Times* (1998)	*Givenchy;* sterling silver cross band ring with cubic zirconia; woman's	$40
Watch	*Newsweek* (1998)	*Pulsar Solar;* charges with any light source, man's	$215
Watch	*Los Angeles Times* (1997)	*Kirium Chronometer;* men's	$1,695
Watch	*Playboy* (1997)	*Picasso Watch Collection;* featuring Pablo Picasso's "The Face"	$165

MEALS

Item	Source	Description	Price
Buffet	*The State* (Columbia, SC) (1998)	Daily seafood buffet, 60 items include crab legs, mussels, scallops, shrimp, fish, beef, and chicken dinner	$6.50
Dinner	*San Francisco Examiner* (1996)	*North India Restaurant;* featuring Baingan Bharta, mesquite-smoked eggplant	$7.95

MEDICAL PRODUCTS AND SERVICES

Item	Source	Description	Price
Dental Services	*The State* (Columbia, SC) (1998)	Extractions, per tooth	$25
Nonprescription Drug	*Boston Globe* (1997)	*Pepto Bismol;* 8 oz	$4
Nonprescription Drug	*Boston Globe* (1997)	*Robitussin DM;* cough suppressant; 4 oz	$3

MOTORIZED VEHICLES, SUPPLIES, AND SERVICES

Item	Source	Description	Price
Automobile	*Southern Living* (1999)	1999 *Chevy Malibu*	$16,535
Automobile, New	*The State* (Columbia, SC) (1998)	1998 *Volvo S70* sedan	$26,895
Automobile, Used	*The State* (Columbia, SC) (1998)	1996 *Lincoln Mark VIII*	$20,292

Item	Source	Description	Price
Garage Door Opener	*Los Angeles Times* (1997)	*Lift Master 2000;* installed	$275
Radar Detector	*Playboy* (1997)	*SOLO Radar and Laser Detector;* cordless	$199
Tire	*Boston Globe* (1997)	Bridgestone High Performance 65 HR 15	$85

OTHER

Item	Source	Description	Price
Bird Bath	*Smith & Hawken* (1998)	Cast-stone sundial design, 15" square with pedestal and base, including shipping	$236
Cat Food	*Boston Globe* (1997)	*Purina Cat Chow;* 20-lb bag	$7.99
Telescope	*Coldwater Creek Catalog* (1998)	*Bushnell;* compact spotting scope that weighs just over a pound; magnifies 20 to 50 times.	$225
Wreath	*Smith & Hawken* (1998)	Victorian Rose wreath combines rose buds, cedar tips, winter wheat and pink larkspur on a 12" grapevine base	$59

PERSONAL CARE PRODUCTS

Item	Source	Description	Price
Denture Adhesive	*Boston Globe* (1997)	*Fixodent;* 1.4-oz cream	$2.50
Deodorant	*Boston Globe* (1997)	*Secret;* 1.7 oz	$1.50
Deodorant	*Boston Globe* (1997)	*Old Spice;* 2 oz	$1.79
Hand Lotion	*Boston Globe* (1997)	*Lubriderm Lotion;* relieves dry, chapped skin; 16-oz	$7
Shampoo	*Boston Globe* (1997)	*Vidal Sassoon Hair Care;* 13 oz	$2.50
Shaving Cream	*Los Angeles Times* (1997)	*Wilkinson Cream;* 11 oz	$0.99
Toothpaste	*Boston Globe* (1997)	*Crest;* gel, 6.4-oz Tartar Control	$2

PUBLICATIONS

Item	Source	Description	Price
Book	*Williams-Sonoma Catalog* (1997)	*Mediterranean Cooking Kitchen Library;* 108 pages; hardback	$14.95
Book	*Fortune Magazine* (1996)	*Success and the Fear of Success in Women,* by David Krueger, M.D.; paperback	$25
Book	*Times Past Catalog* (1998)	VW Beetle: A Comprehensive Illustrated History of the World's Most Popular Car	$24.98
Book	*Times Past Catalog* (1998)	Roadside Memories: A Collection of Vintage Gas Station Photographs	$29.95
Catalog	*Country Living Magazine* (1996)	*Waterworks Sink and Plumbing Fixtures Catalogue*	$8
Catalog	*Fine Gardening Magazine* (1996)	*Heirloom Old Garden Roses Catalog and Reference Guide*	$5
Magazine	*People Weekly* (1998)	Annual subscription to *People Weekly* magazine; published weekly	$103.98

Item	Source	Description	Price
SPORTS EQUIPMENT			
Bicycle	*Playboy* (1997)	*Hotta TT;* racing bike; carbon-fiber monocoque frame	$4,000
Bicycle	*Boston Globe* (1997)	*Rand Barbie;* 12" girl's bike	$49.97
Exercise Equipment	*Boston Globe* (1997)	*Weider Jane Fonda Manual Treadmill*	$299.96
Exercise Equipment	*New York Times* (1999)	*Pro-Form* cage machine; multi work-out positions, weights not included	$299.99
Rollerblade Skates	*Boston Globe* (1997)	*Variflex*	$34.97
Soccer Ball	*Soccer Madness Catalog* (1997)	*Diadora;* signature ball; hand sewn	$69.95
TOYS			
Bank	*Times Past Catalog* (1998)	*Mr. Potato Head* coin bank	$19.95
TRAVEL AND TRANSPORTATION			
Airline Ticket	*Los Angeles Times* (1997)	*Southwest Airlines;* Los Angeles to Chicago	$198
Airline Ticket	*Los Angeles Times* (1997)	*Southwest Airlines;* Ontario to Salt Lake City	$69
Trip	*Boston Globe* (1997)	*Cancun Clipper Club;* includes round-trip airfare; seven nights in January	$399
Trip	*Boston Globe* (1997)	Lake Tahoe; includes round-trip airlines; 3 nights' hotel accommodations; ski lift discounts	$594
Trip	*Boston Globe* (1997)	*Radisson Inn;* Sanibel Island, Florida; package includes round-trip from Boston; 3 hotel nights; 3-day economy Alamo Rent-A-Car	$389
Trip	*Boston Globe* (1997)	Rex Saint Lucian; includes round-trip airfare, seven nights	$749

MISCELLANY 1995-1999

Expect to Spend $60,000 or More for Net Commerce

Online commerce "used to be an 'If you build it, they wouldn't have come,' situation because the audience was fearful of it," said Anita Bloch, president of Red Dot Interactive, San Francisco. "I don't think the technology has changed much, but the perception has changed that [the Web] is no less secure than any other credit card transactions." Medium-size sites wishing to include more secure transactions will face higher start-up costs, partially due to the need for "secure" servers such as those distributed by Netscape.

Transactions like this could cost a company a median price of $21,250, according to our developers. Many sites have incorporated "shopping carts" on their transaction-based sites. This technology allows users to browse through a site and add items to their "cart" as they go. A site with a huge catalog of varied products would find this ideal, but could expect to pay a median price of $62,500 to set it up.

Advertising Age, January/February 1997

The Cost of Bringing Up Baby

Rene Bellerive knew that bringing up a baby would cost a bundle. But $149,820? That's how much the Department of Agriculture says Bellerive and average new parents like her will spend to raise their newborns to age 17. The 1996 survey of 12,850 two-parent households and 3,395 single-parent households found that housing took the biggest chunk—33 percent, or $49,710. Food was No. 2, at $26,130; followed closely by transportation, clothing and child care. It costs about $8,300 a year, or $694 a month, to raise one child in a two-child, two-parent, middle-class family, the survey found. A generation earlier, raising a child cost one-sixth as much. Several expenses, such as child care, weren't a factor in earlier times. In 1960, the first year the department conducted the survey, raising a child cost $25,229.

San Francisco Examiner, November 25, 1997

Same Price, More PC

Here's what you get in a $4,000 Gateway 2000 PC today compared with one in 1988:

$4,000 in 1988
—Intel 386 running at 20 megahertz
—DOS 3.3
—80-megabyte hard drive
—1 meg of RAM, expandable to 8
—3.5-inch disc drive
—5.25-inch disc drive

$4,000 in 1995
—Intel Pentium running at 133 megahertz
—Windows 95
—1.62-gigabyte hard drive
—16 megs of RAM
—3.5-inch disc drive
—6X CD-ROM drive
—28.8-kilobaud fax modem
—Surround Sound speakers with subwoofer
—Microsoft Office software

Newsweek: Computers and The Family, Fall/Winter 1995

Football Business

If the NFL ever changes some of the fundamental ways it does business, especially revenue sharing, it will impact old football stadiums. No less than 86% of the Green Bay Packers' revenue comes from shared sources—63% from the league's television contract and another 23% from ticket receipts, licensing agreements and other income that the NFL divides among its teams. Right now, business is booming. The Packers have a rainy-day fund of $21 million.

Beginning last year they picked up an additional $2.5 million in annual skybox revenue by dropping an arrangement under which they placed three games a season at Milwaukee County Stadium.

Sports Illustrated, January 13, 1997

2000–2009
9/11, the War on Terror, and the Aftermath

PRESIDENTS

William J. Clinton   1993–2001

George W. Bush   2001–2009

Barack H. Obama   2009–2017

2009 series one-dollar bill.

History will record that the twenty-first century began in the United States on September 11, 2001, when four American commercial airliners were hijacked and used as weapons of terror. The tragedies of the World Trade Center in New York; Shanksville, Pennsylvania; and the Pentagon, in Washington DC, made Americans feel vulnerable to a foreign invasion for the first time in decades. Citizens in every part of the nation, even those thousands of miles away from the targets, immediately began to question their safety and personal priorities. As a result, the United States economy—already reeling from the stock market crash in overpriced technology stocks—slowed to a crawl. This recession would stretch for 36 months as cautious companies reduced planned expansions, slowed product development, and looked for technology-driven productivity gains capable of driving down costs. The slowdown allowed a rapidly expanding global economy to catch its breath, while creating a rise in unemployment across most U.S. sectors.

America's military response to the 9/11 attacks was to dispatch U.S. forces around the world in a War on Terror. United in grief and outrage, America mobilized its intelligence, law enforcement, diplomatic and financial resources in a counterattack. The first stop was the mountains of Afghanistan, where a new breed of suicidal terrorist known as Al Qaeda, were collected into an army of self-styled Islamic warriors determined to destroy America. Under the protection of the country's ruling Taliban, al Qaeda had trained thousands of terrorists. America's military response was swift and uncompromising. The stated goal was to hunt down and kill the al Qaeda leadership and free Afghanistan from Taliban rule. The initial fighting force used billion-dollar U.S. technology to attack distant primitive cave targets from the air using space-age laser-guided missiles. The Taliban was quickly routed, but insurgent activity continued requiring a constant military presence in the country. The prime target of the assault, al Qaeda leader Osama bin Laden, escaped capture and was still at large when President George W. Bush left office in 2009.

Shortly after the invasion of Afghanistan the United States shifted its focus to Iraq, home of leader Saddam Hussein. Despite stout opposition from Germany, France, Spain, and the United Nations, President Bush launched Operation Iraqi Freedom to eliminate Hussein and the possibility of his employing weapons of mass destruction. As in the invasion of Afghanistan, the United States achieved a rapid military victory but struggled to bring peace and stability to the nation and failed to find the fearsome weapons of mass destruction. Sectarian violence soon evolved into civil war in Iraq, and little economic or political progress

663

was made despite the presence of 144,000 troops. As casualties rose above 3,000 and the monthly cost of the war topped $10 billion, the American people lost patience and turned against the Republican administration punishing the 2006 Republican Congressional candidates at the polls.

But the twin wars in Afghanistan and Iraq were pushed off the front pages in 2007 and 2008 by a collapse of the U.S. economy that was first compared to the recession of 1981–1982 and then to the Great Depression that started with the stock market crash in 1929. For years the economy had been fueled by a laissez-faire capitalism that embraced inexpensive borrowing, extensive deregulation, and a tax policy that tended to concentrate America's wealth among the most affluent three percent. Real income gains for the working and middle-class stagnated, even as their personal debt structure grew. Beginning in August 2007 the Federal Reserve and the Treasury Department attempted to address weakness following the bursting of the housing bubble. Fueled by low-cost borrowing, exotic new financial instruments, and lax oversight by a wide range of well-established financial institutions, banks worldwide suffered substantial losses on mortgage-related securities. Home foreclosures soared into the hundreds of thousands throughout the United States. The problems, which continued into 2009, required the federal government to allocate $700 billion to stem the credit crisis. In the process the financial industry was largely reorganized, and federal deficits soared. Substantial, well-respected investment houses disappeared overnight; the American automobile industry appeared to be on the point of collapse, and consumers found that credit was both more difficult to obtain and less affordable.

The crisis was the first severe economic slump since the overhaul of the welfare system or governmental cutbacks in job training and housing assistance—traditional safety net tools for managing the recession. At the same time America's industry was undergoing a transformation, outsourcing many of its manufacturing jobs to China, South America, or India. The result for President Bush was a dramatic decline in popularity in public opinion polls, hovering in the 20s—comparable only to President Herbert Hoover, whose administration was in power at the time of the Great Depression.

The unpopularity of the wars, rising energy costs, and the crippling state of the economy, propelled America to embrace the fresh promise of Democrat Barack Obama, who won the presidential election on November 4, 2008 on the twin themes of change and hope. When he was sworn in January 2009, his priorities included the revitalization of the American economy, diversification of America's energy policy, the proper conduct of two wars, and fixing an over-burdened medical health system. The nation was also divided by decades of cultural wars concerning issues such as abortion, gay rights, and the definition of marriage.

Year	Dollar Value in 2019
2000	$1.49
2003	$1.39
2005	$1.31
2007	$1.24
2009	$1.19

Use this Currency Conversion chart to calculate what any time in the years listed would cost in 2019. Simply multiply the cost of that item by dollar amount in the chart. For example, if you know that a freshwater cultured pearl necklace cost $105.00 in 2000, multiply $105.00 by $1.49 to discover that that same necklace would cost $156.45 in 2019.

HISTORICAL SNAPSHOT 2000-2004

2000

- The human genome is decoded after furious work including competition between private and government scientists
- George W. Bush wins the presidency in a disputed election after the U.S. Supreme Court rules that the Florida presidential vote will stand without a recount
- Los Alamos Scientist Dr. Wen Ho Lee is accused of spying and later found to be innocent
- The Whitewater investigation finally ends after six years; neither Bill nor Hillary Clinton is indicted
- Google, a popular search portal, indexes one billion websites
- *How the Grinch Stole Christmas* becomes the highest grossing film of the year, taking in over $260 million
- The intifada starts in Israel over the breakdown of the peace talks
- Vermont approves same sex marriages
- Britain ends self-rule in Northern Ireland after the IRA misses a deadline to disarm

2001

- American businessman Dennis Tito becomes the first space tourist after paying the Russian space program millions of dollars for the experience of space travel
- Oklahoma City bomber Timothy McVeigh is executed
- Terrorists hijack four airliners on September 11th; two are flown into the Twin Towers in New York City, a third into the Pentagon, while the fourth goes down 80 miles outside of Pittsburgh

- The United States invades Afghanistan in retaliation for its unwillingness to hand over Osama bin Laden, the head of al Qaeda, the group responsible for the September 11 attacks. The Taliban is deposed
- Enron, one of the world's largest energy trading firms, collapses because of massive fraud and accounting problems
- A U.S. spy plane collides with a Chinese fighter jet, igniting an international incident
- Harry Potter and the Sorcerer's Stone is the highest grossing movie of 2001

2002

- The euro debuts in 12 European countries, officially beginning the process of creating a common economy
- Arthur Andersen, one of the four largest accounting firms in the United States, collapses for its part in the Enron scandal
- Roadside snipers terrorize the Washington, DC area, killing
- 10 people before being apprehended
- The United Nations passes a unanimous motion calling on Iraq to disarm or face serious consequences
- *Spiderman* is the highest grossing movie of 2002, with over $400 million in ticket sales
- Reacting to the spate of high-profile fraud and bankruptcies at U.S. companies, Congress passes sweeping new anti-corruption laws
- Record companies continue to blame internet music downloading

for flat music sales; the industry responds by suing consumers
- North Korea admits to making nuclear bombs in defiance of signed treaties

2003

- Space shuttle Columbia explodes on reentry; seven astronauts are killed
- After Britain and the United States lose their attempt for UN resolution authorizing war against Iraq, they attack on March 19; coalition forces capture the Iraqi capital of Baghdad on April 9
- The Supreme Court upholds Affirmative Action
- Apple Music begins to sell songs for $0.99 over the Internet
- The Massachusetts Supreme Court rules that the legislature must craft a bill that gives gay couples the right to marry
- President George Bush signs a 10-year, $350 billion tax cut, the
- third-largest tax cut in U.S. history
- The Congressional Budget Office reveals that the deficit will be $480 billion in 2004 and projects a deficit of up to $5.8 trillion by 2013
- The European Union expands by 10 members

2004

- The Detroit Pistons beat the heavily favored Los Angeles Lakers in five games to win the National Basketball Association Championship
- American armed forces hand over partial sovereignty to Iraq; widespread violence persists throughout the country

- Kenneth Lay, the CEO of Enron, is indicted in connection with the giant energy company's collapse in 2001
- Massachusetts Senator John Kerry wins the democratic nomination and picks North Carolina Senator John Edwards as his runningmate
- Abu Ghraib prison in Iraq becomes an international anti-American symbol after prisoner abuse by United States soldiers is uncovered
- Former President Ronald Reagan dies at age 93 after years of suffering from Alzheimer's disease
- Michael Moore releases the movie *Fahrenheit 9/11*, an attack on President George W. Bush, causing a political firestorm; the film becomes the highest grossing documentary of all time
- The U.S. Supreme Court rules that all prisoners of war and enemy combatants held at Guantanamo Bay, Cuba are to be allowed access to a lawyer and the courts
- Jeopardy contestant Ken Jennings wins over a million dollars competing on the popular television game show

Plumes of smoke billow from the World Trade Center towers in Lower Manhattan after a Boeing 767 hit each tower during the September 11 attacks. (via Wikimedia Commons)

SELECTED INCOME 2000-2004

Job	Source	Description	Pay
Advertising Director	New York Times (2000)	Per day fee of Charles Stone III, Ad Director, Budweiser's "Whassup" campaign	$18,000/day
Attorney	The State Newspaper Columbia, SC (2004)	Average annual income of lawyers in Myrtle Beach, South Carolina in 2002	$95,610
Bartender	New York Times (2000)	Bartender in fashionable restaurant in New York City	$600/night
Baseball Player	USA Today Sports Weekly (2004)	Salary of Minnesota Twins pitcher J. C. Romero	$820,000
Book Advance	New York Times (2004)	Fee paid in advance to John Welch, Jr., former Chairman of General Electric, to write a book on winning in the business world	$4 million
Carpet Cleaner	San Francisco Chronicle (2004)	Stanley Steemer; will train; weekly pay	$300 to $500
Chemist	American Chemical Society Annual Survey (2002)	Starting salary of a chemistry graduate with a master's degree	$45,000
Clerical	San Francisco Chronicle (2004)	General office work with benefits	$20.70/hr
Disc Jockey	New York Times (2000)	Nightly pay for DJ Mark Ronson	$7,500
Dog Walker	New York Times (2000)	Half hour walk for one dog	$20/half hr.
Endorsement Fee	Charlotte (NC) Observer (2004)	Amount paid to horse Smarty Jones' jockey Stewart Elliott to wear the logo for Infone, a telephone concierge service, during Belmont Stakes horse race	$200,000
Engineer	Society of Fire Protection Engineers Website (2001)	Fire protection engineers annual salary	$78,000
Focus Panelist Fee	New York Times Magazine (2003)	Amount paid for two hours of participation in a focus panel concerning the Iowa Democratic presidential caucus	$60
Football Player	USA Today Sports Weekly (2004)	Annual salary of back-up quarterback Kurt Warner, St. Louis Rams	$9.5 million
Football Player	The State Newspaper Columbia, SC (2004)	Payment in 2004 to each member of the winning team in the Super Bowl	$68,000
Foundation Director	New York Times (2000)	Annual average salary for director of a nonprofit foundation in New York City	$224,000
Garbageman	New York Times (2000)	Starting annual salary for sanitation worker in city of New York; high school diploma or GED required	$27,842
Information Manager	Tech Target Survey (2003)	Annual salary of storage architect	$80,836
Massage Therapist	New York Times (2000)	Average hourly wage of a massage therapist in a New York health club	$35
Massage Therapist	New York Times (2000)	Average hourly wage of a massage therapist working privately	$55
Medicine	Ivy Tech State College Survey (2000)	Annual salary of medical laboratory technician	$25,771

Job	Source	Description	Pay
Medicine	*Ivy Tech State College Survey* (2000)	Top salary paid to radiology technician	$33,384
Model	*New York Times* (2000)	Hourly fee of super model Gisele Bundchen	$8,000/hr.
Movie Star	*Wall Street Journal* (2004)	Nicole Kidman's salary as lead in Sydney Pollack movie *The Interpreter*	$15 million
Movie Star	*Wall Street Journal* (2004)	Ben Affleck's salary as star of movie *Gigli*	$12.5 million
Musicians	*New York Times* (2000)	New York Philharmonic cellist	$91,260
Nurse	*New York Times* (2001)	Dialysis RN	$45/hr.
Physical Therapist	*New York Times* (2004)	Home health care in all boroughs of New York City	$80,000
Physician	*New York Times* (2000)	Starting OB/GYN salary	$160,000
Physician	*American College of Physicians* (2002)	Median annual salary of doctor of internal medicine with ten years' experience	$162,872
Plumber	*Ivy Tech State College Survey* (2000)	Average hourly wage of plumber/pipefitter	$25
Policeman	*New York Times* (2000)	Average salary of first year police officer in New York City	$31,305
Police Sergeant	*New York Times* (2000)	Average salary of a New York City police sergeant	$59,299
Professor	*Association of Collegiate Schools of Planning* (2004)	Average salary of full professor at *Oklahoma State University* in 2001	$86,591
School Principal	*New York Times* (2004)	Rye City School District in Westchester County, New York	$117,000–$141,000
Software Developer	*SearchNetworking. com* (2004)	Annual salary of software developer in northwest United States	$87,000
Teacher	*U. S. Department of Labor* (2004)	Median annual earnings of preschool teachers in 2002	$19,270
Teacher	*U. S. Department of Labor* (2004)	Annual salary of beginning teachers with a bachelor's degree in 2000	$30,719
Teacher	*New York Times* (2000)	Average wage of a New York City teacher with a master's degree	$42,625
Triathlete	*San Francisco Chronicle* (2004)	Winning prize for *The Escape from Alcatraz Triathlon;* includes 1.5 mile swim; 18 mile bike ride and 8 mile run	$5000
Writer	Salary.com (2004)	Median salary of a copywriter with an advertising agency	$34,603

CONSUMER EXPENDITURES 2000-2004

(One Person)

Expenditure Type	2000	2001	2002	2003	2004
Food	$2,825	$2,835	$2,913	$2,831	$3,095
Food at home	$1,477	$1,533	$1,558	$1,525	$1,681
Food away from home	$1,348	$1,302	$1,356	$1,306	$1,414
Alcoholic beverages	$325	$314	$285	$280	$359
Housing	$8,189	$8,371	$8,619	$8,768	$9,244
Shelter	$5,054	$5,253	$5,465	$5,614	$5,841
Owned dwellings	$2,332	$2,491	$2,605	$2,692	$2,916
Rented dwellings	$2,435	$2,505	$2,538	$2,679	$2,659
Utilities, fuels, and public service	$1,628	$1,799	$1,712	$1,758	$1,830
Natural gas	$208	$276	$225	$254	$274
Electricity	$569	$642	$600	$621	$649
Telephone services	$607	$620	$624	$623	$634
Water and other public services	$175	$189	$201	$190	$188
Apparel and services	$1,028	$862	$921	$837	$949
Transportation	$3,732	$4,012	$3,890	$3,839	$3,941
Vehicle purchases (net outlay)	$1,456	$1,805	$1,662	$1,692	$1,600
Cars and trucks, new	$797	$832	$791	$1,027	$796
Cars and trucks, used	$628	$934	$846	$620	$776
Gasoline and motor oil	$682	$659	$646	$674	$806
Other vehicle expenses	$1,272	$1,275	$1,306	$1,217	$1,281
Vehicle maintenance and repairs	$396	$419	$437	$362	$404
Public transportation	$322	$273	$276	$256	$254
Health care	$1,488	$1,441	$1,522	$1,558	$1,697
Entertainment	$1,026	$1,097	$1,193	$1,041	$1,162
Personal care products and services	$338	$297	$310	$316	$355
Reading	$113	$111	$108	$93	$97
Education	$407	$423	$562	$498	$629
Tobacco products and smoking supplies	$203	$203	$210	$193	$167
Cash contributions	$1,047	$1,063	$998	$1,032	$1,027
Personal insurance and pensions	$1,778	$1,960	$2,055	$1,948	$2,184
Miscellaneous expenditures	$561	$518	$602	$423	$517
Total average annual expenditures	$23,059	$23,507	$24,190	$23,657	$25,423

Expenditure Type	2000	2001	2002	2003	2004
Personal Taxes (1)					
Money income before taxes	$24,977	$26,650	$27,042	$27,131	$28,143
Personal taxes	$2,090	$1,829	$1,815	$1,592	$1,383
Federal income taxes	$1,621	$1,403	$1,396	$1,180	$990
State and local income taxes	$360	$334	$327	$304	$280
Other taxes	$109	$91	$93	$107	$113
Income after taxes	$22,886	$24,822	$25,226	$25,539	$26,761

Notes: Totals may not add up to component items due to rounding errors; (1) Components of income and taxes are derived from complete income reporters only through 2003. Beginning in 2004 income imputation was implemented. As a result: Source: U.S. Department of Labor, Bureau of Labor Statistics, Consumer Expenditure Surveys, 2000–2006 (Table 4. Size of Consumer Unit: Average Annual Expenditures and Characteristics)

INVESTMENTS 2000–2004

Investment	2000	2001	2002	2003	2004
Moody's Yield on Seasoned Corporate Bonds—All Industries, AAA (1)	7.62	7.08	6.49	5.66	5.63
90-Day AA Nonfinancial Commercial Paper Interest Rate (2)	6.31	3.65	1.69	1.11	1.41
Federal Funds Effective Rate (3)	6.24	3.88	1.67	1.13	1.35
Bank Prime Loan Rate (4)	9.23	6.91	4.67	4.12	4.34
Certificate of Deposit (CD), 6-month Rate (5)	6.59	3.66	1.81	1.17	1.74
U.S. Treasury Note, 10-year (6)	6.03	5.02	4.61	4.01	4.27
Mortgage Rate, 30-year Fixed (7)	8.06	6.97	6.54	5.82	5.84
Index of Common Stocks (S&P 500)	1,320.28	1,148.08	879.82	1,111.92	1,211.92
Dividend Yield in Percent, S&P 500 (8)	1.23	1.37	1.83	1.61	1.60

(1) Moody's AAA rates through December 6, 2001, are averages of AAA utility and AAA industrial bond rates. As of December 7, 2001, these rates are averages of AAA industrial bonds only.

(2) Interest rates interpolated from data on certain commercial paper trades settled by The Depository Trust Company. The trades represent sales of commercial paper by dealers or direct issuers to investors (that is, the offer side).

(3) The daily effective federal funds rate is a weighted average of rates on brokered trades. Annualized using a 360-day year or bank interest.

(4) Average majority prime rate charged by banks on short-term loans to business, quoted on an investment basis. Rate posted by a majority of top 25 (by assets in domestic offices) insured U.S.–chartered commercial banks. Prime is one of several base rates used by banks to price short-term business loans.

(5) Average rate on 6-month negotiable certificates of deposit (secondary market), quoted on an investment basis.

(6) Market yield on U.S. Treasury securities at 10-year constant maturity, quoted on investment basis.

(7) Contract interest rates on commitments for 30-year fixed-rate first mortgages.

(8) Based on research by Aswath Damodaran from the Stern School of Business.

Source: The Federal Reserve (H.15 Selected Interest Rates—http://www.federalreserve.gov/releases/h15/data.htm) except where otherwise noted.

COMMON STOCKS	2000	2001	2002	2003	2004
AT&T (T)	47.00	50.38	39.90	28.91	26.14
Dividend	1.00	1.02	1.07	1.37	1.25
Bank of America (BAC)	48.44	46.75	62.96	70.68	79.09
Dividend	2.06	2.28	2.44	2.88	2.50
2:1 Stock Split, Aug. 30, 2004					
Boeing (BA)	40.19	62.00	38.10	33.88	41.99
Dividend	0.56	0.68	0.68	0.68	0.77

COMMON STOCKS	2000	2001	2002	2003	2004
General Electric (GE)	150.00	43.75	40.95	25.48	31.12
Dividend	0.84	0.66	0.73	0.77	0.82
3:1 Stock Split, May 8, 2000					
General Motors (GM)	74.62	52.19	48.64	38.95	53.64
Dividend	2.00	2.00	2.00	2.00	2.00
Kellogg Co. (K)	29.87	26.31	29.97	34.87	37.80
Dividend	1.00	1.01	1.01	1.01	1.01
Microsoft (MSFT)	116.56	43.38	67.04	53.72	27.45
Dividend	0.00	0.00	0.00	0.24	3.16
2:1 Stock Split, March 29, 1999; 2:1					
Stock Split Feb. 18, 2003					
Navistar International Corp. (NAV)	46.12	26.31	39.12	25.22	47.33
No Dividend					
Pfizer (acquired Warner-Lambert Feb. 2000)	31.87	46.13	39.90	31.53	35.55
Dividend	0.36	0.44	0.52	0.60	0.68
2:1 Stock Split, July 1, 1999					
Procter & Gamble Co. (PG)	107.19	78.50	80.00	87.81	98.99
Dividend	1.34	1.46	1.86	1.73	1.46
2:1 Stock Split, June 21, 2004					
Reynolds American Inc. (RAI)	17.04	51.00	57.64	42.37	57.61
(previously R.J. Reynolds Tobacco)					
Dividend	3.10	3.30	3.73	3.80	3.80
2:1 Stock Split, Aug. 15, 2006					
United States Steel Corp. (X)	31.81	17.19	17.50	13.65	35.52
Dividend	1.00	0.55	0.20	0.20	0.20
Wal-Mart (WMT)	66.81	53.88	58.05	51.60	52.30
Dividend	0.24	0.28	0.30	0.36	0.52
2:1 Stock Split, Apr. 20, 1999					
Yahoo (YHOO)	475.00	28.19	18.63	17.60	45.40
No Dividend					
2:1 Stock Split, Feb. 8, 1999; 2:1 Stock Split, Feb. 14, 2000;					
2:1 Stock Split, May 12, 2004					

Source: Yahoo! Finance

STANDARD JOBS 2000–2004

Based on SIC codes	2000	Based on NAICS codes	2001	2002	2003	2004
Total, all industries	$35,323	Total, all industries	$36,219	$36,764	$37,765	$39,354
Total, all industries, private	$35,337	Total, all industries, private	$36,157	$36,539	$37,508	$39,134
Federal government	$46,228	Federal government	$48,940	$52,050	$54,239	$57,782
State government	$36,296	State government	$37,814	$39,212	$40,057	$41,118
Local government	$32,387	Local government	$33,521	$34,605	$35,669	$36,805
Bituminous coal underground mining	$53,224	Bituminous coal underground mining	$54,335	$54,052	$55,780	$58,428
Construction	$36,622	Construction	$38,412	$39,027	$39,509	$40,521
Private households (domestics)	$13,236	Private households (domestics)	$13,904	$14,466	$15,108	$15,377
Crop production	$18,779	Crop production	$19,241	$19,844	$20,138	$20,973
Finance, insurance and real estate	$56,029	Finance and insurance	$63,687	$62,762	$64,956	$70,129
Wholesale trade	$46,740	Wholesale trade	$48,791	$49,241	$50,835	$53,310
Retail trade	$18,430	Retail trade	$22,667	$23,232	$23,804	$24,415
Electric, gas, and sanitary services	$61,478	Utilities	$65,561	$67,374	$68,651	$72,403
Elementary and secondary schools	$31,594	Elementary and secondary schools	$32,794	$33,559	$34,475	$35,372
Manufacturing	$44,776	Manufacturing	$42,969	$44,097	$45,916	$47,861
Postal service	$41,933	Postal service	$42,240	$44,424	$45,511	$49,713
Communication	$57,929	Telecommunications	$56,492	$57,149	$59,192	$63,635
Radio and television broadcasting	$51,324	Radio and television broadcasting	$51,704	$51,576	$53,450	$55,737
Motion pictures	$34,549	Motion picture and video industries	$45,875	$45,572	$47,122	$49,598
Health services	$34,945	Ambulatory health care services	$42,963	$44,062	$44,719	$46,455
Membership associations and organizations	$23,007	Membership associations and organizations	$25,050	$26,034	$27,047	$28,199
Rail transportation	$38,682	Rail transportation	$37,839	$31,255	$31,397	$33,411
Local and interurban passenger transit	$42,601	Transit and ground passenger	$42,031	$43,222	$44,555	$45,099

Note: The QCEW survey switched from SIC to NAICS codes in 2001. Data may not be directly comparable. Items in bold changed dramatically between 2000 and 2001.

Source: Bureau of Labor Statistics, Quarterly Census of Employment and Wages (QCEW), 2000–2007

FOOD BASKET 2000-2004

(NR = Not Reported)

Commodity	Year	U.S. Average	Atlanta	Chicago	Denver	Los Angeles	New York
Bananas, per pound	2000	51¢	53¢	NR	62¢	56¢	73¢
	2001	51¢	54¢	NR	57¢	58¢	76¢
	2002	51¢	52¢	61¢	63¢	60¢	79¢
	2003	51¢	49¢	63¢	57¢	61¢	66¢
	2004	50¢	49¢	66¢	51¢	60¢	57¢
Beef, Ground 100% beef, per pound	2000	$1.54	$1.72	NR	$1.53	$1.52	$2.55
	2001	$1.63	$1.82	NR	$1.90	$1.76	$2.59
	2002	$1.71	$1.95	$2.39	$1.83	$1.94	$2.79
	2003	$1.80	$1.81	$2.28	$1.85	$1.94	$2.74
	2004	$2.08	$1.92	$2.89	$2.11	$1.90	$2.90
Bread, white, per loaf	2000	92¢	$1.04	NR	98¢	$1.10	$1.16
	2001	95¢	$1.06	NR	$1.01	$1.05	$1.10
	2002	99¢	$1.16	$1.17	$1.11	$1.11	$1.10
	2003	$1.00	$1.16	$1.15	$1.11	$1.22	$1.18
	2004	$1.04	$1.16	$1.34	$1.13	$1.20	$1.41
Cereal, Corn Flakes, 18 oz	2000	$2.56	$2.72	NR	$2.32	$2.87	$3.87
	2001	$2.63	$2.80	NR	$2.53	$3.09	$3.83
	2002	$2.70	$2.84	$3.33	$2.92	$3.13	$3.83
	2003	$2.72	$2.80	$3.37	$2.67	$3.75	$4.07
	2004	$2.74	$2.73	$3.39	$2.78	$3.69	$4.20
Cheese, grated Parmesan, 8 oz	2000	$3.69	$3.39	NR	$4.03	$4.01	$5.12
	2001	$3.67	$3.26	NR	$4.08	$4.03	$5.19
	2002	$3.73	$3.60	$4.24	$4.28	$4.09	$5.01
	2003	$3.61	$3.24	$4.01	$4.23	$4.06	$5.22
	2004	$3.49	$3.04	$4.01	$4.07	$4.05	$5.13
Chicken, whole uncut, price per pound	2000	96¢	89¢	NR	95¢	$1.11	$1.41
	2001	98¢	$1.01	NR	99¢	$1.06	$1.37
	2002	97¢	92¢	$1.28	$1.02	$1.03	$1.39
	2003	99¢	85¢	$1.29	$1.00	$1.35	$1.39
	2004	$1.04	91¢	$1.22	$1.10	$1.35	$1.43
Coca-Cola, 2 liter	2000	$1.14	99¢	NR	94¢	$1.01	$1.52
	2001	$1.17	$1.03	NR	$1.08	$1.01	$1.54
	2002	$1.18	$1.22	$1.42	$1.08	$1.21	$1.42
	2003	$1.18	$1.18	$1.26	$1.04	$1.15	$1.49
	2004	$1.20	$1.13	$1.19	$1.09	$1.23	$1.42
Coffee, vacuum-packed, 11.5 oz	2000	$2.80	$2.87	NR	$3.76	$3.79	$4.03
	2001	$2.64	$2.48	NR	$3.69	$3.27	$3.87
	2002	$2.45	$2.31	$2.68	$2.95	$3.21	$3.86
	2003	$2.61	$2.63	$3.07	$3.22	$3.22	$4.00
	2004	$2.62	$2.64	$3.06	$3.35	$3.48	$3.64
Corn, whole kernel frozen, 16 oz	2000	$1.10	$1.09	NR	$1.40	$1.40	$1.74
	2001	$1.14	$1.07	NR	$1.44	$1.34	$1.70
	2002	$1.20	$1.13	$1.35	$1.48	$1.25	$1.64
	2003	$1.21	$1.07	$1.34	$1.57	$1.26	$1.78
	2004	$1.19	96¢	$1.30	$1.50	$1.28	$1.79

Commodity	Year	U.S. Average	Atlanta	Chicago	Denver	Los Angeles	New York
Eggs, 1 dozen, grade A or AA, large	2000	98¢	99¢	NR	$1.06	$2.14	$1.59
	2001	$1.05	$1.07	NR	$1.12	$2.01	$1.56
	2002	$1.03	$1.01	$1.57	$1.08	$1.81	$1.70
	2003	$1.15	$1.10	$1.70	$1.24	$2.12	$1.65
	2004	$1.32	$1.28	$1.88	$1.45	$2.18	$1.79
Lettuce, Iceberg, head (approx. 1-1/4 lb)	2000	$1.15	$1.19	NR	$1.55	99¢	$1.79
	2001	$1.07	$1.20	NR	$1.34	98¢	$1.66
	2002	$1.31	$1.36	$1.42	$1.61	99¢	$2.10
	2003	$1.14	$1.17	$1.70	$1.21	$1.12	$1.62
	2004	$1.18	$1.26	$1.52	$1.06	$1.22	$1.55
Margarine, 1 lb, stick form	2000	73¢	64¢	NR	72¢	58¢	$1.71
	2001	80¢	69¢	NR	78¢	70¢	$1.82
	2002	86¢	.82¢	$1.03	83¢	74¢	$1.91
	2003	.89¢	91¢	97¢	$1.06	$1.02	$1.95
	2004	90¢	83¢	99¢	$1.11	$1.06	$1.87
Milk, whole, 1/2 gallon	2000	$1.68	$1.99	NR	$1.92	$2.06	$1.70
	2001	$1.74	$1.99	NR	$1.98	$2.16	$1.78
	2002	$1.76	$1.76	$2.13	$2.09	$2.40	$2.01
	2003	$1.74	$1.71	$1.69	$2.10	$2.47	$1.87
	2004	$1.84	$1.75	$1.97	$2.26	$2.57	$1.97
Orange Juice, fresh, 64 oz	2000	NR	NR	NR	NR	NR	NR
	2001	$1.57	$1.70	NR	$1.78	$1.77	$2.19
	2002	$1.56	$1.73	$1.68	$1.51	$1.77	$2.19
	2003	$1.59	$1.54	$1.47	$1.65	$1.69	$2.26
	2004	$2.70	$2.55	$3.01	$2.67	$3.56	$2.77
Peaches, halves or slices, 29 oz can	2000	$1.64	$1.59	NR	$2.17	$1.53	$2.01
	2001	$1.65	$1.55	NR	$2.24	$1.63	$2.02
	2002	$1.67	$1.55	$1.82	$1.97	$1.72	$2.19
	2003	$1.67	$1.59	$1.91	$2.11	$1.92	$2.15
	2004	$1.69	$1.62	$2.03	$2.18	$2.09	$2.07
Peas, sweet, 15 oz can	2000	68¢	65¢	NR	87¢	84¢	99¢
	2001	73¢	67¢	NR	90¢	83¢	$1.01
	2002	78¢	78¢	94¢	85¢	85¢	$1.03
	2003	.78¢	82¢	97¢	90¢	90¢	$1.15
	2004	78¢	81¢	95¢	93¢	95¢	$1.13
Potatoes, 10 lb sack, white or red	2000	$2.58	$3.59	NR	$2.78	$2.24	$3.61
	2001	$2.76	$3.18	NR	$2.53	$2.51	$4.85
	2002	$3.67	$4.63	$4.71	$3.68	$2.33	$3.53
	2003	$3.45	$4.20	$5.30	$3.03	$3.18	$3.95
	2004	$3.28	$3.87	$4.58	$3.33	$2.83	$4.36
Sausage, pork, 1 lb	2000	$3.20	$3.06	NR	$3.70	$4.53	$4.30
	2001	$3.21	$3.11	NR	$3.86	$3.96	$4.50
	2002	$3.33	$3.26	$3.94	$4.39	$4.28	$5.38
	2003	$3.33	$3.14	$3.67	$4.51	$4.30	$5.49
	2004	$3.36	$2.94	$3.84	$4.70	$4.80	$4.91
Shortening, all-vegetable, 3 lb can	2000	$3.06	$3.17	NR	$3.16	$3.56	$4.70
	2001	$3.07	$3.21	NR	$3.14	$3.51	$4.72
	2002	$3.15	$3.32	$3.69	$3.17	$3.51	$4.55
	2003	$3.24	$3.45	$3.85	$3.19	$3.92	$4.53
	2004	$3.36	$3.62	$4.07	$3.32	$4.03	$4.93

Commodity	Year	U.S. Average	Atlanta	Chicago	Denver	Los Angeles	New York
Steak, T-bone, per pound	2000	$6.43	$7.22	NR	$6.32	$7.21	$9.99
	2001	$6.75	$7.31	NR	$7.03	$7.56	$10.31
	2002	$6.69	$7.65	$7.31	$7.31	$8.02	$11.17
	2003	$7.22	$7.04	$7.34	$7.59	$8.49	$11.89
	2004	$8.04	$7.68	$8.27	$8.85	$8.55	$11.48
Sugar, white, 4–5 lb	2000	$1.58	$1.45	NR	$1.54	$1.65	$1.99
	2001	$1.57	$1.61	NR	$1.56	$1.86	$2.12
	2002	$1.60	$1.72	$1.67	$1.72	$1.90	$1.95
	2003	$1.59	$1.64	$1.40	$1.52	$1.97	$1.86
	2004	$1.59	$1.55	$1.65	$1.62	$1.83	$1.93
Tuna, chunk light, 6.0 oz can	2000	66¢	58¢	NR	89¢	74¢	$1.34
	2001	68¢	61¢	NR	86¢	68¢	$1.34
	2002	70¢	64¢	93¢	75¢	61¢	$1.33
	2003	68¢	60¢	$1.01	80¢	75¢	$1.32
	2004	68¢	60¢	82¢	75¢	81¢	$1.19

Notes: data for New York covers Manhattan only; data for 2000 covers Q4 only; data for 2001–2007 are 4-quarter averages; NR not reported

Source: Council for Community and Economic Research (formerly ACCRA), Cost of Living Index, 2000–2007

SELECTED PRICES 2000-2004

Item	Source	Description	Price
ALCOHOL			
Beer	*Charlotte Observer* (NC) (2003)	*Budweiser,* 12-pack, bottles	$8.99
Beer	*The State Newspaper* Columbia, SC (2002)	*Coors Light;* 18-pack, 12 oz cans	$8.99
Champagne	*San Francisco Chronicle* (2004)	*Roederer Estate Brut;* per bottle	$15.99
Wine	*Charlotte Observer* (NC) (2003)	*Gallo of Sonoma Chardonnay;* 750 ml. bottle	$9.99
Wine	*San Francisco Chronicle* (2004)	*La Crema Chardonnay;* per bottle	$11.99
Wine	*The State Newspaper* Columbia, SC (2002)	*Robert Mondavi;* 1.5 liter bottle	$11.49
APPAREL, CHILDREN'S			
Pants	*Campmor Catalog* (2004)	*Campmor* girls capri pants; 100% quick dry nylon; back zippered security pocket; value $32	$14.99
Shoes	*Orlando* (Fl.) *Sentinel* (2004)	Boy's *Michael James* shoes	$17.99
Shorts	*Orlando* (Fl.) *Sentinel* (2004)	*Russell Athletic* reversible shorts Regular On sale	$16.00 $10.99
Shorts	*Goody's Flyer* (2004)	*Levi's* side-vent denim shorts for juniors 1–13, regular $30	$14.99
Shorts	*J C Penney Catalog* (2004)	*Big Flirt* active skorts; junior sizes; original $19.99	$9.99
Shorts	*J C Penney Catalog* (2004)	*Arizona* camper shorts; girls sizes 7–17; original $16.99	$8.49
Shorts	*J C Penney Catalog* (2004)	*Arizona* beach shorts; boys sizes 8–20; original $21.99	$9.99
Tank Tops	*J C Penney Catalog* (2004)	*Energie and One Step Up* tanks and halters; junior sizes; original $14.99	$7.49
Tee shirts	*Goody's Flyer* (2004)	*Choppers* screen tees for young men, regular $19.99	$12.99
APPAREL, MEN'S			
Boots	*Campmor Catalog* (2004)	*Dunham* men's waffle stomper mid-leather boots; list $110	$49.97
Boxers	*Kohl's Flyer* (2004)	Patriotic boxers and lounge pants for men; original $12–$20; sale	$6–$10
Fleece Top	*Campmor Catalog* (2004)	*Campmor* microfleece zip-T neck; 100 weight micro-denier fleece with anti-piling technology; 12.5" zipper front opening; value $45	$19.99

Item	Source	Description	Price
Hat	*Seventeen* (2000)	*Stetson* style hat; black	$600
Pants	*Goody's Flyer* (2004)	*Duck Head* classic twill pants; in pleated and flat-front styles, regular $40	$20
Sandals	*J C Penney Catalog* (2004)	*St. John's Bay* men's Cayman leather sandals; regular $49.95	$24.96
Shirts	*Goody's Flyer* (2004)	*Ivy Crew* short sleeve rayon shirts, regular $29.99	$14.99
Shirts	*J C Penney Catalog* (2004)	*Pierre Cardin* boxed dress shirt and tie sets, regular $55	$27.50
Shoes	*San Francisco Chronicle* (2004)	*Adidas* men's trail running shoes; originally $74.99	$39.99
Shorts	*Campmor Catalog* (2004)	*Columbia Shoshoni Falls* water trunks; list $30	$19.95
Shorts	*Kohl's Flyer* (2004)	*Dockers* shorts for men; original $38	$18.99
Shorts	*Kohl's Flyer* (2004)	*Lee Dungaree* shorts; twill or denim style; original $34	$16.99
Tee Shirts	*Kohl's Flyer* (2004)	Novelty screen printed muscle and short-sleeved tees for young men; original $18	$9

APPAREL, WOMEN'S

Item	Source	Description	Price
Bra	*Seventeen* (2000)	*Playtex* bras; regularly $22.00 to $29.50	$10.97 to $13.97
Dress	*Coldwater Creek Catalog* (2004)	A darted, side-wrapped dress; USA made of imported polyester; back zip closure	$69
Dress	*Seventeen* (2000)	*Ann Linn* slip dress; bright designs	$86
Dress	*Seventeen* (2000)	*All That Jazz* floral pink dress	$54
Dress	*Charlotte Observer* (NC) (2004)	*Donna Morgan* silk leopard print halter dress	$79
Formal Dress	*Seventeen* (2000)	*Zum;* sequin-embroidered organza ballgown with three frog enclosures in back; polyester	$185
Handbag	*Seventeen* (2000)	*Jill Stuart* sequined handbag	$175
Handbag	*Seventeen* (2000)	Rampage Blue Bag	$28
Handbag	*Orlando* (Fl.) *Sentinel* (2004)	*St. John's Bay* EZ organizers	$19.99
Hat	*Coldwater Creek Catalog* (2004)	Handwoven hat of red-hot rice paper that springs back fresh; one size fits most	$25
Linen Shirt	*jjill Catalog* (2004)	Light weight, softly shaped, scoop neckline; pure linen. Machine wash. Petite Size Women's Size	$69 $79
Pants	*Goody's Flyer* (2004)	*Dockers* twill capris for misses 4–18, regular $38	$21.99
Poncho	*Seventeen* (2000)	*Tibi* crocheted poncho	$165
Purse	*Coldwater Creek Catalog* (2004)	Straw, twisted and woven with long leather-like straps; full-fabric lining and zip top	$25
Sandals	*Coldwater Creek Catalog* (2004)	Soft, glossy leather slingbacks with stretchy sides and flexible soles; 7/8" heel; red, blue, or black	$49
Shirt	*J C Penney Catalog* (2004)	*DCC* shirts; misses sizes; original $30	$14.99

Item	Source	Description	Price
Shoes	*San Francisco Chronicle* (2004)	*New Balance* women's running shoes; originally $49.99	$39.99
Sleepwear	*Kohl's Flyer* (2004)	*Nine and Company* sleepwear separates for women; original $18	$8.99
Socks	*Kohl's Flyer* (2004)	Novelty socks for women; original $5	$2.50
Tank Tops	*J C Penney Catalog* (2004)	*Worthington* tank tops; misses sizes; original $20	$9.99
Tote Bag	*Seventeen* (2000)	*Old Navy* totes featuring the skyline of Seattle, San Francisco, New York, and Chicago; each	$12.50
Underwear	*Orlando* (Fl.) *Sentinel* (2004)	Delicate lace boy shorts Regular Two	$12 $18

APPLIANCES

Item	Source	Description	Price
Air Conditioner	*Chicago Tribune* (2004)	*Sears* window air conditioner	$99.99
Blender	*New York Times Sunday Magazine* (2003)	*Oster's* beehive blender	$80.00
Cordless Drill	*Washington Post* (2004)	*DeWalt* 12-volt cordless drill and driver kit	$129
Dishwasher	*Asheville* (NC) *Times Citizen* (2003)	Maytag Jetclean II	$429.00
Electrical Cord	*Washington Post* (2004)	*Doitbest* Heavy-Duty Outdoor Extension Cord, 100'	$19.99
Fireplace Gas Logs	*The Roanoke Times* (Va.) (2004)	*Appalachian Stove;* 30" log set, manual control, 16,000 to 31,500 btu	$399
Gas Grill	*The State Newspaper* Columbia, SC (2004)	*The Big Easy,* 36,000 btu gas grill and smoker with side burner	$259
Gas Grill	*Sears Flyer* (2004)	*Kenmore Gas Grill;* wide body cooking system; 580 sq. inches total cooking area	$134.99
Grill	*Chicago Tribune* (2003)	*George Foreman* 14" round grill; nonstick grilling surface, adjustable temperature	$29.99
Heater	*New York Times* (2004)	*Toastmaster;* fully automatic compact heater; thermo-statically controlled	$19.95
Iron	*Kohl's Flyer* (2004)	*Black & Decker* steam 3 iron; regular $34.99	$17.49
Lantern	*Asheville* (NC) *Times Citizen* (2003)	Multi-function lantern; includes 5.5" black and white TV, AM/FM and weather band radio, fluorescent lantern, thermometer, flashlight, audible siren, compass and auto AC/DC adapter. Regularly $60	$39.99
Microwave	*Chicago Tribune* (2003)	*Kenmore* microwave; 1.4 cu. ft., 1100-watt. 6 quick touch sensor cooking keys	$64.99
Refrigerator	*Charlotte Observer* (NC) (2004)	*Whirlpool* no frost refrigerator; 17.6 cubic feet; upfront temperature control knobs	$397
Stereo System	*Belk Flyer* (2004)	*Dolby* executive stereo system; top loading CD player; black lit LCD readout; built-in AM/FM tuner; full function remote; desk or wall mount; regular $70	$49.99
Television	*Sears Flyer* (2004)	*Samsung* 42" wide-screen tabletop projection HDTV monitor; 30 watt audio system	$999.99
Walkman	*Men's Fitness* (2004)	*Sony* walkman; downloads tunes 10 times faster than previous model	$200
Wine Cooler	*San Francisco Chronicle* (2004)	*Urbina* design wine storage cooler; electronic cooling technology; 18 bottle size	$269.95

Item	Source	Description	Price

BABY PRODUCTS

Item	Source	Description	Price
Diapers	*Charlotte Observer* (NC) (2004)	*Pampers Easy Ups* training pants; 40 per package	$14.99
Play Suits	*J C Penney Catalog* (2004)	*Baby Okie-Dokie* summer sets; original $12.99	$6.99
Sleep Outfit	*The Roanoke* (Va.) *Times* (2004)	*Little Me Stretchies;* each	$7.97

BUSINESS EQUIPMENT AND SERVICES

Item	Source	Description	Price
Computer	*Office Depot Flyer* (2004)	*Presario* desktop computer bundle with Intel celeron processor; 2.7GHz	$417.49
Computer Line	*Chicago Tribune* (2004)	*SBC Yahoo!* DSL line; up to two computers; price reduced when ordered online; per month	$26.95
Handheld Computer	*New York Times* (2003)	*Palm One* handheld; 8M8 memory	$99.99
Phone	*Martinsville* (Va.) *Bulletin* (2004)	*Telos* camera flip phone; *Audiovox* 8900	$99
Printer	*Office Depot Flyer* (2004)	*HP* flatbed all-in-one printer	$178.22
Rotary Tool Kit	*Home Depot Flyer* (2004)	*Dremel* MultiPro rotary toolkit	$59.97
Scanner	*Office Depot Flyer* (2004)	*Canon CanoScan* flatbed scanner	$49.00
Software	*New York Times* (2003)	*Microsoft Office* standard edition 2003; full version	$349.99
Telephone	*Martinsville* (Va.) *Bulletin* (2004)	*Motorola T731* color screen phone	$79.95
Tool Set	*Sears Flyer* (2004)	*Craftsman* 137-piece mechanic's tool set; 82 sockets, 8 wrenches; includes case	$99.99
Want Ad	*San Francisco Chronicle* (2004)	Chronicle of available jobs; five days	$12
Wireless Telephone	*The Roanoke Times* (Va.) (2004)	*Verizon Wireless* color flip-phone *Audiovox CDM-8600;* retail $109.99, less $30 mail-in rebate and $40 instant savings	$39.99

COLLECTIBLES

Item	Source	Description	Price
Movie Memorabilia	*Associated Press* (2004)	Ray gun from *Super Mario Brothers* film	$75
Painting	*Art & Antiques Magazine* (2002)	Karl Schmidt-Rottluff 1912 painting *Die Lesende* of a woman reading a book	$3.9 million
Painting	*Art & Antiques Magazine* (2002)	Norman Rockwell painting of *Rosie the Riveter,* which appeared on the May 29, 1943 cover of *The Saturday Evening Post*	$4.9 million
Sculpture	*Art & Antiques Magazine* (2002)	Carved Mezcala stone figure from Mexico dating from pre-classic period (circa 300–100 B.C.)	$71,700
Television Memorabilia	*Associated Press* (2004)	Set of yellow school lockers from the television series "Dawson's Creek"	$100
Used Automobile	*USA Today* (2004)	1970 *Pontiac GTO Convertible,* sold at auction	$27,000

Item	Source	Description	Price
Wine	*San Francisco Chronicle* (2004)	Case of 1999 *Pillar Rock;* sold at auction in 2001	$11,500

EDUCATION

Item	Source	Description	Price
College Tuition	*Website* (2004)	*St. John's College* annual tuition	$30,570
Private High School	*Wall Street Journal* (2004)	*Hotchkiss School,* Lakeville, Connecticut annual tuition	$24,500
Summer Camp	*New York Times* (2004)	*Camp Caribou,* Winslow, Maine; seven-week program; per child	$7,150

ENTERTAINMENT

Item	Source	Description	Price
Boxing	*San Francisco Chronicle* (2004)	Professional live boxing event, Marco Angel Perez vs. Sergio Macias; Longshoreman's Hall, San Francisco Ringside Main Floor Balcony	$75 $50 $25
Concert Ticket	*Chicago Tribune* (2004)	An evening with *Lyle Lovett;* Chicago Pavilion	$60
Concert Ticket	*Chicago Tribune* (2004)	*Dave Brubeck Quartet; Marian McPartland Trio; Ramsey Lewis Trio;* Chicago Pavilion	$40
Concert Ticket	*Direct Mail Solicitation* (2003)	*Handel's Messiah,* David Tang, conducting Oratorio Singers of Charlotte, First United Methodist Church	$20.00
Concert Ticket	*Rolling Stone* (2004)	*Madonna* at the Forum, Los Angeles, California	$58.50 to $354.50

A ticket for Madonna's 2004 Re-Invention tour in Portugal. (via Flickr)

Item	Source	Description	Price
Concert Ticket	*Times-News* (Hendersonville, NC) (2004)	*Flat Rock Music Festival* with Ralph Stanley and the Clinch Mountain Boys, Snake Oil Medicine Show and Ras Alan and The Lions; weekend pass	$60
Dance Lessons	*Times-News* (Hendersonville, NC) (2004)	*Dance Lovers USA;* Foxtrot, Swing, Waltz, Rumba, and Cha-Cha; 12-week course	$91.25
Movie Ticket	*Chicago Tribune* (2004)	*Harry Potter and the Prisoner of Azkaban;* Davis Theatre	$7.50
Pool	*Charlotte Observer* (NC) (2004)	*Intex* easy set pool; 10' by 30'; includes pool, filter pump, and set-up video	$49.99
Theater Ticket	*San Francisco Chronicle* (2004)	*The Buddy Holly Story,* the hit rock 'n roll musical	$35

ENTERTAINMENT, HOME

Item	Source	Description	Price
Cable Television	*Martinsville* (Va.) *Bulletin* (2004)	*Adelphia* cable service; up to 140 channels; per month	$24.95
Camcorder	*Chicago Tribune* (2003)	*Samsung* mini-DV digital camcorder, *Sears* low price 2.5". color LCD, built-in digital still camera	$399.99
Camera	*Sears Flyer* (2003)	*Canon Rebel SLR* digital camera; 6.3 mega-pixels	$999.99
Camera	*Men's Fitness* (2004)	*Olympus Stylus 410;* 4 mega-pixel digital camera can shoot short videos with sound	$800
Disposable Camera	*Publix Flyer* (2004)	*Kodak Max HQ Camera;* 27 exposure film	$7.99
DVD	*New York Times* (2004)	*The Lord of the Rings;* DVD	$21.85
DVD Deck	*Sears Flyer* (2003)	*Sony* DVD/VCR dual desk	$179.99
Electronic Game System	*Charlotte Observer* (NC) (2004)	*Game Boy* advance SP system; features backlit screen	$99.99
Electronic Game Software	*Charlotte Observer* (NC) (2004)	*Harry Potter and the Prisoner of Azkaban* on *Gameboy Advance*	$29.99
Exercise Equipment	*Chicago Tribune* (2003)	*ProForm* 545S treadmill	$599.99
Exercise Equipment	*Wall Street Journal* (2004)	*Precor EFX 5.23* elliptical trainer; keeps track of customized exercise routines for two different users	$3,999
iTunes Album	*USA Today* (2004)	*Dark Side of the Moon* by Pink Floyd	$16.99
Music	*Charlotte Observer* (NC) (2004)	*Bob Dylan* MTV Unplugged; DVD	$10.99
Radio/CD Player	*Direct Mail* Letter (2003)	*Bose* Wave Radio/CD	$499
Television Combination Set	*Sears Flyer* (2003)	*Toshiba* 24" TV/DVD/VCR combination	$499.99
Television	*Sears Flyer* (2003)	*Pioneer* 50" PureVision plasma HDTV monitor	$7,999
Video Camera	*Sears Flyer* (2003)	*Fisher Digital CameraCorder;* combines 3.0 mega-pixel digital camera with digital camcorder	$899.99
Water Filtration System	*Kohl's Flyer* (2004)	*PUR Ultimate,* faucet mount; regular $39.99	$19.99

FOOD PRODUCTS

Item	Source	Description	Price
Apples	*Charlotte Observer* (NC) (2003)	*Granny Smith* apples per pound	$.99

Item	Source	Description	Price
Bananas	*Charlotte Observer* (NC) (2003)	*Chiquita* bananas per pound	$.39
Beer	*Publix Flyer* (2004)	*Heineken* beer, 12-pack	$11.49
Bottled Water	*Publix Flyer* (2004)	*Deer Park Spring Water;* 25-pack, 26.9 oz bottles	$4.99
Bread	*Publix Flyer* (2004)	*Publix Bakery* sourdough French bread; 16 oz Loaf	$1.99
Bread	*The State Newspaper* Columbia, SC (2002)	French bread; each	$.99
Broth	*Charlotte Observer* (NC) (2003)	*Swanson* beef broth 14.5 oz can	$.59
Carrots	*The State Newspaper* Columbia, SC (2004)	Organic carrots; 5 lb bag	$2.99
Cereal	*The State Newspaper* Columbia, SC (2004)	*Nature's Patch* organic cereal	2 for $5
Chicken	*The State Newspaper* Columbia, SC (2002)	Split chicken breasts; bonus pack, per lb	$1.29
Coffee	*Bi-Lo Flyer* (2003)	*Maxwell House* coffee; 39 oz can	$2.99
Coffee Cake	*Publix Flyer* (2004)	*Publix Bakery* cinnamon nut coffee cake, 11 oz size	$3.39
Cooking Oil	*Publix Flyer* (2004)	*Mazola Oil;* assorted varieties; 48 oz bottle	$2.49
Deli Meat	*The State Newspaper* Columbia, SC (2002)	*Sahlen's* deli ham; per lb	$4.99
Fish	*The State Newspaper* Columbia, SC (2004)	Wild Alaskan sockeye salmon fillets; per lb	$7.99
Frozen Food	*San Francisco Chronicle* (2004)	*Banquet Crock-Pot Classics;* 41.5 oz package	$4.99
Fruit	*The State Newspaper* Columbia, SC (2002)	*Athena* cantaloupes, each	$1.79
Ham	*Charlotte Observer* (NC) (2003)	*Armour Hostess* canned ham; 4 lbs	$7.99
Juice	*Charlotte Observer* (NC) (2003)	*Ocean Spray* cranberry juice 64 oz bottle	$2.69

OceanSpray's regular and diet Cran-Lemonade. (via Flickr)

Item	Source	Description	Price
Sour Cream	*San Francisco Chronicle* (2004)	*Daisy* sour cream; 16 oz cup	$1.39
Sour Cream	*Publix Flyer* (2004)	*Publix* sour cream; 16 oz cup; comes in regular, fat free and light	$1.09
Steak	*Publix Flyer* (2004)	Beef ribeye steak; bone in, per lb	$7.99
Steak	*Bi-Lo Flyer* (2003)	T-bone bonus pack, per lb	$4.99
Vegetables	*The State Newspaper* Columbia, SC (2002)	Zucchini squash; per lb	$.69
Yogurt	*The State Newspaper* Columbia, SC (2004)	*Stonyfield Farm* organic yogurt; low fat blueberry	4 for $3

FURNITURE

Item	Source	Description	Price
Bed	*New York Times* (2004)	*Campaign* bed; queen-sized hand forged iron	$999
Bookcase	*San Francisco Chronicle* (2004)	*Akio* two-shelf bookcase	$119
Chair	*San Francisco Chronicle* (2004)	*La-Z-Boy Pinnacle* recliner; leather finesse; two chairs	$999
Chair	*Charlotte Observer* (NC) (2004)	*Revista* magazine chair; retail price $1,067	$640
Chandelier	*Home Depot Flyer* (2004)	*Easy Street* 6-light chandelier; champagne marbled glass shades	$199
Computer Desk	*Havertys Flyer* (2004)	*Oak Canyon* computer desk with return; oak solids and veneers	$999
Queen Bed	*Havertys Flyer* (2004)	*Broyhill's Generation X;* built of hardwood solids and walnut veneers; was $499	$399
Recliner	*Havertys Flyer* (2004)	*Lane Home Furnishings* Montana mission-style high-leg recliner	$799
Reclining Sofa	*Havertys Flyer* (2004)	*Lane Home Furnishings* Markham collection; sofa with burgundy leather; pillow top arms and seating; was $1199	$1099
Rug	*J C Penney Catalog* (2004)	Accent rug; 22" × 36"; regular $25	$12.50
Sofa	*San Francisco Chronicle* (2004)	*Gatsby* Italian leather sofa	$899
Table & 2 Side chairs	*Havertys Flyer* (2004)	*Havertys' British Inn* collection; 42" round drop-leaf table with two side chairs; was $349	$299

GARDEN EQUIPMENT AND SUPPLIES

Item	Source	Description	Price
Birdhouses	*Michaels Arts & Crafts Store Flyer* (2003)	Ready to finish wood birdhouses; each	$3.99
Fencing	*The State Newspaper* Columbia, SC (2002)	Chain-link fencing; 48" × 50' roll	$39.90
Flowers	Jackson & Perkins 2004 Catalog	10 giant begonias, produce huge 6"–9" blooms on 24' stalks	$29.95
Lawnmower	*Home Depot Flyer* (2004)	*Murray* 6.5 hp, 22" high wheel mower; *Briggs & Stratton* engine	$219
Mulch	*Martinsville* (Va.) *Bulletin* (2004)	*Rubberific* mulch; 10 bags and one free; covers 250 square feet	$273
Patio Furniture	*San Francisco Chronicle* (2004)	Teak grade A bow bench	$375

Item	Source	Description	Price
Plants	*Martinsville* (Va.) *Bulletin* (2004)	Geraniums; 6 1/2" pot	$5.99
Plants	*Martinsville* (Va.) *Bulletin* (2004)	Hosta; each	$3.59
Roses	Jackson & Perkins 2004 Catalog	Hybrid tea rose plant, each	$17.95
Storage Building	*The State Newspaper* Columbia, SC (2002)	Gable style lap building; 10' × 16' × 10'	$1,249
Torch	*Charlotte Observer* (NC) (2004)	Copper torch for outdoor living; regular $59	$19.99
Weedwacker	*Sears Flyer* (2004)	*Craftsman* 13" electric weedwacker line trimmer with extra line	$29.99

HOTEL RATES

Item	Source	Description	Price
Room Rate	*New York Times* (2004)	*Henryetta Inn and Dome* near Okemah, Oklahoma, birthplace of *Woody Guthrie*, per night	$81
Room Rate	*Chicago Tribune* (2004)	*Cincinnati Hotel;* weekend getaway package at four-star luxury hotel in Ohio; one night, luxury queen	$175
Room Rate	*New York Times* (2004)	*Delta Bow Valley Hotel*, Calgary, Alberta, Canada; per night	$137

HOUSEHOLD PRODUCTS

Item	Source	Description	Price
Bathroom Tissue	*The State Newspaper* Columbia, SC (2002)	*Charmin* bath tissue, 24 double rolls	$9.99
Batteries	*Charlotte Observer* (NC) (2003)	*Duracell* 8-pack "AA" batteries	$3.99
Beach Towel	*Belk Flyer* (2004)	*Home Accents* beach towels; 34" × 64", regular $20	$10
Brushes	*A. C. Moore Flyer* (2002)	*Surprize Ink* game books; regular $4.99	$3.99
Charcoal	*Publix Flyer* (2004)	*Kingsford Original* charcoal briquets; 20 lb bag	$5.99
Charcoal	*Bi-Lo Flyer* (2003)	*Southern Home* instant light charcoal; 8 lb bag	$3.29
Crystal Figurines	*Belk Flyer* (2004)	*Godinger* crystal animal figurines; regular $40	$19.99
Cutlery Set	*Kohl's Flyer* (2004)	*Basic Essentials* 22-piece cutlery and tool set; regular $19.99, sale	$9.99
Dish Detergent	*Publix Flyer* (2004)	*Dawn Dish Liquid;* assorted varieties; 20.2 oz to 25-oz	$2.19
Drill	*New York Times* (2004)	*Stanley* model H131 drill	$19.95
Glasses	*New York Times Sunday Magazine* (2003)	*Deborah Ehrlich's* stemware	$200.00/ pair
Glue	*A. C. Moore Flyer* (2002)	Super tacky glue; four oz size	$.79
Glue Sticks	*A. C. Moore Flyer* (2002)	Hot metal glue sticks; -4", each	$.04
Luggage	*Belk Flyer* (2004)	*Ciao Roll-A-Ton* rolling duffel; black/blue or black/red; regular $50	$19.99
Pepper Grinder	*Chicago Tribune* (2004)	*Michael Graves* design pepper mill	$12.99
Pillow	*Belk Flyer* (2004)	*Carpenter* comfort pillows; sensafoam pillow with100% Visco-elastic "memory" foam; regular $80	$39.99
Punch	*A. C. Moore Flyer* (2002)	*Fiskars* border punch	$10

Item	Source	Description	Price
Sheets	*Seventeen* (2000)	*Springs Registry* cotton sheet set	$29.99
Tape Measure	*Home Depot Flyer* (2004)	*MaxSteel* 25' and 12' tape measure combination	$19.99
Trees	*Michaels Arts & Crafts Store Flyer* (2003)	6' ft silk Ficus trees; each	$19.99

JEWELRY

Item	Source	Description	Price
Bracelet	*Seventeen* (2000)	*Tarina Tarantino* coil bracelet	$80
Cross	*Parisian Gift Guide* (2003)	*Faith* bronze cross	$28
Earrings	*Coldwater Creek Catalog* (2004)	Sterling silver and stabilized turquoise; 1 1/8" long; in posts or clips	$34
Necklace	*Seventeen* (2000)	Freshwater cultured pearl necklace	$105
Necklace	*J C Penney Catalog* (2004)	*Omega and Slide;* reversible necklace; 10k gold; regular $249.99	$99.99
Necklace	*Kohl's Flyer* (2004)	10k gold diamond accent initial pendant; regular $100	$34.99
Necklace	*Chicago Tribune* (2004)	*Ono* pendant in 18k gold with diamonds	$2,495
Pin	*Coldwater Creek Catalog* (2004)	Matte gold tone pin 2 3/8"; USA-made	$24
Sports Watch	*Campmor Catalog* (2004)	*Timex Kids Tattoo You* analog watch; water resistant; rotating disc design; elastic fabric straps; list $19.95	$5.97
Watch	*Parisian Gift Guide* (2003)	*Fossil* watch; ladies' stainless steel with adjustable bangle band; silver dial	$55

A ladies Fossil watch with diamonds. (via Flickr)

Item	Source	Description	Price
Watch	*Men's Fitness* (2004)	*Tommy Hilfiger;* multi-dial	$125

MEALS

Item	Source	Description	Price
Buffet	*Martinsville* (Va.) *Bulletin* (2004)	*Aloha Wok;* Mother's Day buffet, Collinsville, Virginia Adult Child	 $6.95 $3.95
Oyster Roast	*The State Newspaper* Columbia, SC (2004)	*Ducks Unlimited Annual Oyster Roast* per person	$25
Pizza	*Atlanta Constitution* (2002)	*Little Caesars;* one large pizza with topping	$12.95
Steak	*Menu* (2003)	*Morton's Steak House,* San Francisco, prime rib	$48

MEDICAL PRODUCTS AND SERVICES

Item	Source	Description	Price
Eye Surgery	*Charlotte Observer* (NC) (2004)	*Lasik* New Wave Front Zyoptix Technology; per eye, starting at	$299.00
Eye Examination	*Martinsville* (Va.) *Bulletin* (2004)	Professional eye exam	$43
Fertilization	*New York Times* (2003)	*In vitro* fertilization with donor eggs	$35,000
Pain Reliever	*CVS Pharmacy Flyer* (2004)	*Aleve;* 100 count	$5.99
Pain Reliever	*Bi-Lo Flyer* (2003)	*Advil;* 50 count	$3.99
Pain Reliever	*CVS Pharmacy Flyer* (2004)	*Afrin No Drip Nasal Spray;* per bottle	$4.99
Plastic Surgery	*New York Times* (2004)	Female breast reduction, 2003 average	$5,351
Plastic Surgery	*New York Times* (2004)	Liposuction, 2003 average	$2,578
Skin Care	*CVS Pharmacy Flyer* (2004)	*Scarguard;* Improves the appearance of old and new scars	$29.99
Vitamins	*CVS Pharmacy Flyer* (2004)	*One A Day Vitamins;* 100 count	$5.99

MOTORIZED VEHICLES, SUPPLIES, AND SERVICES

Item	Source	Description	Price
Airplane	*Wall Street Journal* (2003)	2004 *Hawker 400XP,* cruising speed 529 mph, passenger capacity 7	$387,500
Automobile	*Wall Street Journal* (2003)	2003 *Jaguar X-Type 2.5;* manual with single-disc CD player; permanent all-wheel drive	$279/mo
Automobile	*Orlando* (Fl.) *Sentinel* (2004)	2004 *Honda Element EX,* 4 × 4 Total cost 48-month lease	$19,990 $249 per month
Automobile	*Orlando* (Fl.) *Sentinel* (2004)	2005 *Chevy Equinox;* automatic transition, towing package, power driver's seat Regular Sale price	 $24,175 $18,995
Automobile	*Orlando* (Fl.) *Sentinel* (2004)	2004 *Ford F-250* super duty *Harley-Davidson* edition; V-10 engine Base price Fully equipped	 $35,930 $48,805
Automobile	*San Francisco Chronicle* (2004)	2004 *Jaguar XK;* 294-horsepower engine	$899 per month

Item	Source	Description	Price
Automobile	*Asheville* (NC) *Citizen-Times* (2004)	*Isuzu 2004 Ascender;* 4-wheel drive; seven passenger	$26,990
Automobile	*The State Newspaper* Columbia, SC (2004)	*Isuzu Rodeo* 2004 Model	$16,995
Automobile	*Men's Fitness* (2004)	*Nissan 350Z* Roadster	$33,850
Automobile	*The State Newspaper* Columbia, SC (2004)	*Toyota Prius* hybrid automobile; designed to get50 to 66 miles per gallon	$20,810
Gasoline	*Times-News* (Hendersonville, NC) (2004)	Price of one gallon of regular gasoline	$1.78

Walt Wyvill celebrates 35 years of ownership of his gas station in Amherst, Ohio. Walt put his gasoline on sale for 99 cents per gallon on August 31, 2001, selling 1,500 gallons during the one-hour sale. (via Flickr)

Item	Source	Description	Price
Navigation	*USA Today* (2003)	*Delphi;* portable in-car GPS navigation system	$999.99
Parking Cost	*Times-News* (Hendersonville, NC) (2004)	Cost to park in a metered space in downtown Hendersonville, N.C.	$.25/hr.
Radio	*The Roanoke Times* (Va) (2004)	Sirius Satellite Radio equipment and service Parts Labor Radio subscription per month	 $30 $30 $12.95
Tires	*Charlotte Observer* (NC) (2004)	Tires and wheels; four 225/60R 16; 16×7 MBM 747	$449
Used Automobile	*San Francisco Chronicle* (2004)	1997 *Chevrolet Suburban;* fully loaded 4×4	$15,500
Used Automobile	*San Francisco Chronicle* (2004)	2000 *Jeep Wrangler,* 70,000 miles; air conditioning; tow package	$12,500
Used Motorcycle	*San Francisco Chronicle* (2004)	1997 *Harley Davidson Custom Softtail;* 12,000 miles	$17,500

OTHER

Item	Source	Description	Price
Carpet Cleaning	*Direct Mail* (2003)	*Stanley Steemer Carpet Cleaner;* 6 areas cleaned and protected	$224
Dog Food	*The State Newspaper* Columbia, SC (2004)	*One Earth* natural adult dry dog food; 17.6 lbs.	$18.99
Figurines	*Parisian Gift Guide* (2003)	*A Breed Apart;* dog and cat figurines, each	$34
Kitchen Counters	*San Francisco Chronicle* (2004)	Granite kitchen counters; custom made in choice of 100 colors; as low as	$1,849
Puppies	*San Francisco Chronicle* (2004)	Chihuahua pups; 11 weeks; first shots Each	 $350
Puppies	*San Francisco Chronicle* (2004)	English Bulldog puppies; male or female Each	 $1,200
Trophies	*The State Newspaper* Columbia, SC (2004)	Value of *Vince Lombardi Trophy,* given to the winner of the football *Super Bowl* game	$2000
Water and Sewer Rates	*Times-News* (Hendersonville, NC) (2004)	Monthly cost of water and sewer service in Hendersonville County, N.C.; based on a 5,000 gallon a month Inside city of Hendersonville Outside city	 $29.80 $47.10

PERSONAL CARE PRODUCTS

Item	Source	Description	Price
Bathroom Tissue	*CVS Pharmacy Flyer* (2004)	*Scott Tissue;* 12 pack	$5.49
Body Gems	*Seventeen* (2000)	*Natural Desire's Girlstuff Birthstone Body Gems in Topaz;* star and moon-shaped glitter bits for shoulders, cheeks or hair	$9.99
Deodorant	*San Francisco Chronicle* (2004)	*Right Guard Extreme Deodorant;* 2 oz package	$3.49
Feminine Pads	*San Francisco Chronicle* (2004)	*Kotex Maxi Pads;* 14 count	$2.50
Lipstick	*Seventeen* (2000)	*Maybelline's East Mystique* brush blush in Pink Tangerine; cach	$4.70
Shampoo	*CVS Pharmacy Flyer* (2004)	*Pantene* hair care; 5.1 oz size	$2.99

Item	Source	Description	Price
Shampoo	*Bi-Lo Flyer* (2003)	*Pantene* shampoo; 13.5 oz size, two	$7
Sunglasses	*Campmor Catalog* (2004)	*Julbo Sherpa;* blocks 100% UVA, Band C light; leather side shields; black nylon frame with amber polycarbonate lens; includes hard case	$29.99
Toothpaste	*Charlotte Observer* (NC) (2003)	*Colgate Simply White Toothpaste,* mint, 4 oz tube	$3.49
Whitestrips	*CVS Pharmacy Flyer* (2004)	*Crest Whitestrips;* dental whitening system, 56 count	$24.99

PUBLICATIONS

Item	Source	Description	Price
Book	*Rock & Ice* (2001)	Fearless on Everest, the Quest of Sandy Irvine	$18.95
Book	*Charlotte Observer* (NC) (2004)	*Killer Smile* by Lisa Scottoline	$18.00
Book	*Seventeen* (2000)	*Playing Botticelli* by Liza Nelson; G. P. Putnam & Sons	$23.95
DVD	*San Francisco Chronicle* (2004)	*Speaking to the Big Dogs: A Boardroom Survival Kit;* features comments of 17 top corporate executives	$239
Magazine	*USA Today* (2003)	*USA Today Sports Weekly.* Baseball and pro football coverage for 52 weeks	$39.95
Magazine	*Men's Fitness* (2004)	*Men's Fitness* magazine, 12 issues	$12

REAL ESTATE

Item	Source	Description	Price
Co-Op	*New York Times* (2004)	Washington Heights, New York City, 2-bedroom, 1-bath 1,050 square foot co-op in a pre-war tutor-style building	$435,000
House	*Asheville* (NC) *Citizen-Times* (2004)	Weaverville, N.C.; three bedrooms, two baths, open floor plan, new construction	$179,900
House	*Chicago Tribune* (2004)	1844 North Burling, Chicago, five bedroom, 5.5 bath custom home in all brick and limestone; 6,200 square feet	$3.7 million
House	*Chicago Tribune* (2004)	West Grale, Chicago, four bedroom, 3 bath home with open floor plan	$799,000
House	*New York Times* (2004)	Stonington, Connecticut, Mason's Island; Georgian style	$1.8 million
Loft	*Chicago Tribune* (2004)	South Loop location, granite in bathrooms, open layout	$294,999
Lot	*Wall Street Journal* (2004)	Sun West Ranch on The Madison River, Ennis, Montana; private community of 55 homesites on 2000 acres	$335,000
Residential Water Use Rates	*The Roanoke Times* (Va.) (2004)	Henry County, Virginia, based on a monthly minimum of 6,000 gallons; per month	$24
Studio Apartment	*New York Times* (2001)	46th St. & 9th Ave., NYC, studio, furnished, with separate kitchen, 3rd floor walk-up	$1300/ month
Townhouse	*Chicago Tribune* (2004)	North Damen Ave., Chicago; 3 bedroom, 2 bath, chef's kitchen, granite countertops; designer appliances	$419,000

SEWING EQUIPMENT AND SUPPLIES

Item	Source	Description	Price
Beads	*Michaels Arts & Crafts Store Flyer* (2003)	*Halcraft Bead Boxes;* each	$4.88
Ribbon	*Michaels Arts & Crafts Store Flyer* (2003)	*Tulle Circles Ribbon;* 100 yd roll	$6.88

Item	Source	Description	Price
Scissors	*Michaels Arts & Crafts Store Flyer* (2003)	*Provo Craft Decorative Edge Scissors;* three pair	$2

SPORTS EQUIPMENT

Item	Source	Description	Price
Basketball Goal	*San Francisco Chronicle* (2004)	Lifetime World Class Acrylic Portable Basketball System	$124.50
Binocular Set	*Belk Flyer* (2004)	*Meade;* binocular gift set; regular $50	$29.99
Boot	*Rock & Ice* (2001)	*Salomon Super Mountain 9* with memofit lacing system and contragrip soles; regularly $375	$219
Compass	*Campmor Catalog* (2004)	*Lensatic Compass* with sighting mechanics and cover; weighs 2 1/2 oz	$7.99
Daypack	*Campmor Catalog* (2004)	*Eddie Bauer Ocean Daypack* with zippered bottom hideaway pocket and organizer compartment with key clip; detachable cell phone pocket; weighs 2 pounds; list /$34.99	$14.97
Fishing Reel	*San Francisco Chronicle* (2004)	*Shimano Spheros* spinning reel	$99.99
Glove	*Men's Fitness* (2004)	*Wilson A900 3X* glove; triple welted constructed	$99
Shotgun	*San Francisco Chronicle* (2004)	*Legacy Escort;* 12-gauge fast pump action	$189.50
Sleeping Bag	*Campmor Catalog* (2004)	*Cocoon Ripstop Nylon/Fleece KidBag;* 71" × 30"; temperature rating 58 degrees F; navy blue; stuff sack included; list $65	$29.96
Tent	*San Francisco Chronicle* (2004)	*Coleman* 13' × 11' Hex Dome Tent	$74.99
Tent	*Rock & Ice* (2001)	*TNF Perigrine* two-person tent; two door; ample ventilation; seven lbs.	$239
Tennis Racquet	*San Francisco Chronicle* (2004)	*Prince* tennis racquets; on sale	$79.99
Travel Chair	*Campmor Catalog* (2004)	*Travel Chair Company* deluxe hi-back chair; armrests with drink holder; matching storage/carrying bag with shoulder strap and drawstring closure; regular $39.99	$29.97
Treadmill	*Sears Flyer* (2004)	*Proform 350S* treadmill with hand weights; 2 hp; 16" × 45" treadbelt; was $499.99	$399.88

TOBACCO PRODUCTS

Item	Source	Description	Price
Cigarettes	*Charlotte Observer* (NC) (2003)	*Marlboro Cigarettes;* flip top box Carton	$21.99

TOYS

Item	Source	Description	Price
Car	*Parisian Gift Guide* (2003)	*Tyco's* canned heat cars; runs on batteries	$24.95
Chalk	*A. C. Moore Flyer* (2002)	*Crayola* 20-piece box of sidewalk chalk	$.99
Game	*New York Times* (2004)	*Radica 20Q* names the object you are thinking about	$9.99
Kit	*Parisian Gift Guide* (2003)	*Supermag Genius* 50-piece construction kit	$21.95
Scooter	*Seventeen* (2000)	*Razor Scooter;* runs up to 40 minutes at speeds up to 10 mph	$79.97

A girl rides a Razor scooter. (via Flickr)

Item	Source	Description	Price
Slide	*Charlotte Observer* (NC) (2004)	*Wham-O Heat Wave Slip 'N Slide;* 22' long with *Drench-O-Mat-ic* overhead hydrant system; as seen on TV	$19.99
Wiffle Ball	*Men's Fitness* (2004)	Wiffle ball and bat	$3.69

TRAVEL AND TRANSPORTATION

Item	Source	Description	Price
Airline Fare	*Wall Street Journal* (2004)	New York to Miami; *U. S. Airways* Business Class Leisure Class	 $667 $257
Airline Fare	*The State Newspaper* Columbia, SC (2004)	Roundtrip ticket on *Independence Air* from Columbia, SC to Newark, NJ	$178.30
Airline Fare	*New York Times* (2004)	*Continental;* New York City to Tulsa, Oklahoma	$450
Cruise	*San Francisco Chronicle* (2004)	*Norwegian Spirit Cruise* to Alaska; six nights	$658
Getaway	*San Francisco Chronicle* (2004)	Costa Rica Eight-Day Package; *Villa Sol Hotel;* includes air-fare, hotel, and transfers from San Francisco	$749
Mountain Climb	*San Francisco Chronicle* (2004)	Mount Kilimanjaro in Tanzania; 15-day tour of Mount Kilimanjaro, visits to wildlife sanctuaries and game drive Per person, land-only	$2,799
Tour	*San Francisco Chronicle* (2004)	Four-day trip to Santa Fe, New Mexico, sponsored by *Oakland Museum* of California; includes private tours; per person, double occupancy and meals	$1,725

MISCELLANY 2000–2004

Permissions on Digital Media Drive Scholars to Lawbooks

When some 20,000 first-year American medical students reported to their schools last summer, they received a free 20-minute multimedia collage of music, text, and short video clips from television doctor dramas, past and present, burned onto a CD-ROM.

"The patients you meet in the coming years may have doubts about you because of the doctors they see on prime-time television," the introduction reads. "The aim of this presentation is to explore why that is, and suggest what you can do about it."

But the CD was perhaps more of an education for its developer, Joseph Turow, a professor at the University of Pennsylvania's Annenberg School for Communication.

"It's crazy," Professor Turow said of the labyrinth of permissions, waivers, and fees he navigated to get the roughly three minutes of video clips included on the CD, which was paid for by a grant from the Robert Wood Foundation. The process took months, Professor Turow said, and cost about $17,000 in fees and royalties paid to the various studios and guilds for the use of the clips. The film used ranged from, for example, a 1961 episode of "Ben Casey" to a more recent scene from "ER."

This Friday, Professor Turow and other experts will meet at a conference sponsored by the Annenberg School to debate how digital media fits into the concept of "fair use"—a murky safe harbor in copyright law that allows scholars and researchers limited use of protected materials for educational or commentary purposes.

The New York Times, June 14, 2004

Fed Expected to Raise Rate

The price of borrowing money is going up. The Federal Reserve Board today begins a two-day meeting that will lead to the first increase in its key interest rate since May 2000.

The Fed has cut its key interest rate 13 times since then, propping up an economy choked by recession, terrorism, corporate scandals, and war.

On Wednesday, it is expected to raise the target for its federal funds rate to 1.25 percent, up a quarter of a percentage point.

The move is a shot across the bow at inflation. The nation's inflation rate jumped 3.2 percent in the first

three months of this year, significantly more than the 1 percent increase in the first quarter of 2003.

The federal funds interest rate is what banks pay when they make short-term loans to each other. It is a benchmark used directly or indirectly to set other interest rates.

The State, (Columbia, SC) June 29, 2004

The Ultimate Luxury Item Is Now Made in China

Zhongshan, China—Among the carp ponds, duck farms and moldering plywood huts that have long lined the bank of a Pearl River estuary here, a most incongruous newcomer has appeared: a long, towering shed for building very large luxury yachts, a product that has no market in mainland China.

Lion dancers bobbed and weaved as strings of firecrackers sizzled and boomed on July 3 at the official opening of the yacht factory—an emblem of how China is shifting its sights upmarket. Having mastered the manufacture of many inexpensive goods for mass consumption here and abroad, the country is getting into luxury goods, the kinds coveted by the world's most demanding buyers. China's competitive advantage is that it is doing this at lower cost.

Increasingly expensive brands of shoes, clothing, and furniture are being made in this country, mostly for domestic consumption but sometimes for export. BMW has begun assembling some of its latest models in China for sale here, and Mercedes and Cadillac are preparing to do the same.

With yachts, though, China is braving a market where it has little recent experience or demand at home.

The New York Times, July 13, 2004

Meet Me Online

When running a small business, you don't always have the space to hold meetings with staff and clients. And renting a hotel conference room or meeting site for a day or two can cost a small fortune. So, how do you get your team together to work on projects? Consider Web collaboration.

What is Web collaboration? It's a way for teams to work on a project together—online and off—while eliminating travel costs and paper. Online collaboration works pretty much like this:

MISCELLANY 2000-2004

One person signs up and sets up a virtual meeting room. That person then informs the rest of the group where to meet online. It's a bit like a personal chat room, where members can communicate and work securely.

In addition to Microsoft's NetMeeting (www.microsoft.com), which is free, there are several services that let you collaborate with far-flung clients and employees. Punch Networks' WebGroups (www.punchnetworks.com), for example, lets you automatically and securely work on important projects. WebGroups also features document management tools such as version tracking, audit trails, and automatic change notification.

Black Enterprise, July 2001

The Pajama Game: Not Just for Bedtime

What do you do when pulling on a sweat suit for a trip to the corner Starbucks is too much effort? How about just keeping on your pj's? Everyone from carpooling moms to yoga-bodied Hollywood celebs is taking the concept of dressing down a few notches lower by turning their pajamas into outerwear. Classic men's cuts in fun colors and prints, often more than $100 a pair, are being worn in pieces: bottoms only with a T-shirt, a camisole or a swimsuit; or just the long-sleeved top over a sexy T-shirt as a jacket for the evening. "My daughter at college in Santa Barbara wants to sell pj bottoms out of her dorm," says Dory Forge, designer of the spirited pj line Lounge Act. "Kids there are living in them."

Time, March 3, 2003

Closing the Pay Gap

In 1999, the weekly pay of American women with full-time jobs was 76.5% of what men got, up from 61% in 1974. That's a big gain. But progress has stalled since the mid-1990s. A study by Cornell University economists Francine D. Blau and Lawrence M. Kahn, to be published in the fall 2000 issue of the *Journal of Economic Perspectives*, argues that the stall is only temporary, and that the gap should narrow in the years ahead.

The primary reason for the shrinking pay gap in the 1980s and early 1990s was a rise in the full-time work experience of women, Blau and Kahn say. At the outset of the 1980s, men had an average of 7.5 more years of work experience than women. That's important, because work experience increases both productivity and pay. By the end of the 1980s, the experience disparity had fallen to 4.6 years.

Women also caught up because more of them went into professional and managerial jobs, and because of a decline in union membership, which hurt the wages of men more than those of women. Although the government scaled back anti-discrimination enforcement in this period, Blau and Kahn believe it's likely that discrimination still decreased in those years. Employers, they argue, began to realize that women were more committed to staying on the job than they had been in the past. Also, they say, changes in social attitudes made gender bias "increasingly unpalatable."

BusinessWeek, August 21–28, 2000

For Many Low-Income Workers, High Gasoline Prices Take a Toll

Tampa, Fla.—Denise Quenneville drives 30 miles each way to her $7-an-hour job as a cashier at a Krispy Kreme doughnut shop here. With this year's surge in gas prices, she's paying $23 every couple of days to fill up her car, up from about $19 a year ago.

"A $4 difference is a lot," says Ms. Quenneville, who now is pouring about a quarter of her take-home pay into the tank of her blue 2000 Oldsmobile Alero. To keep her car on the road, the 19-year-old has run up a balance of about $500 on her gas-company credit card.

The cost of gas, currently averaging $1.89 a gallon nationwide, is creating a new burden for everyone who drives a car. But the toll is particularly heavy among low-income workers, for whom higher gas prices amount to a palpable pay cut.

The average U.S. price of a gallon of regular unleaded gasoline topped $2 this spring for the first time. That's cheaper in inflation-adjusted terms than during the price peaks of the early 1980s, and prices have begun to fall over the past month. But at $1.89, the average price still is up 40 cents, or 27%, from a year ago.

At that level, assuming a car travels 15,000 miles a year, which is typical, and gets 21 miles per gallon, approximately the national average, its driver will spend $1,350 annually on gas, or

$286 more than last year. Families that need two or three cars to get around, as many do, could be spending $3,000 or $4,000 a year on gas.

The Wall Street Journal, July 12, 2004

HISTORICAL SNAPSHOT 2005-2009

2005

♦ The search for weapons of mass destruction in Iraq was officially ended

♦ The Kyoto Protocol went into effect, without the support of the United States and Australia

♦ Pope John Paul II died; Cardinal Joseph Ratzinger was elected pope and took the name Benedict XVI

♦ Tens of thousands of demonstrators, many of them supporters of Shi'a cleric Moqtada al-Sadr, marched through Baghdad to denounce the U.S. occupation of Iraq

♦ Hurricanes Katrina and Rita struck the Louisiana, Mississippi, and Alabama coasts causing widespread destruction and political turmoil

♦ North Korea agreed to stop building nuclear weapons in exchange for aid

♦ U.S. Secretary of State Condoleezza Rice promoted a strategy for victory in Iraq that she described as "clear, hold and build"

♦ Iran's president, Mahmoud Ahmadinejad, called for Israel to be "wiped off the map" and condemned the peace process

♦ Sizzling housing sales lured speculators to buy houses with the idea of selling them fast for the sake of profit

♦ The average retail gas price was $1.78 a gallon nationwide

♦ Cancer passed heart disease as the top killer of Americans

♦ The New England Patriots won their third Super Bowl in four years

♦ The New York medical examiner stopped trying to identify victims of the 2001 terror attack on the World Trade Center, leaving more than 1,000 victims unidentified.

♦ Former FBI official Mark Felt acknowledged he was "Deep Throat," the secret source who helped *Washington Post* reporters uncover Watergate

2006

♦ The world's population was calculated at 6.5 billion; the population of the United States topped 300 million

♦ The U.S. Supreme Court ruled that President George W. Bush had overstepped his authority by

♦ ordering military war-crime trials for Guantánamo Bay detainees

♦ After 34 days of fighting, a truce between Israel and Hezbollah was declared

♦ President George W. Bush signed the Secure Fence Act, which called for the building of 700 miles of fence along the U.S. Mexican border

♦ The United Nations reported that Norway, Iceland, Australia, Ireland, and Sweden were the best five countries to live in; the United States was ranked eighth place, after Canada and Japan

♦ Scientists at Rice University discovered a way to reduce arsenic contamination of groundwater

♦ During the 78th Academy Awards ceremony, *Crash* won Best Picture, Ang Lee (*Brokeback Mountain*) captured Best Director, while Reese Witherspoon (*Walk the Line*) was named Best Actress, and Philip Seymour Hoffman (*Capote*) the Best Actor

♦ The *New York Times* reported that in Baghdad, Iraq "at least 10 neighborhoods that a year ago were mixed Sunni and Shiite are now almost entirely Shiite"

♦ A revolutionary scramjet engine designed to fly at 7 times sonic speed was successfully tested in Australia

♦ Deposed Iraqi leader Saddam Hussein was hanged

♦ Protests of the U.S. immigration reform bill attracted 500,000 people in Los Angeles, California, 50,000

♦ in Denver, Colorado, and 20,000 in Phoenix, Arizona

2007

♦ Nancy Pelosi became the first female speaker of the United States House of Representatives

♦ Apple Inc. introduced the highly anticipated iPhone at the 2007 Macworld Conference & Expo

♦ President George W. Bush unveiled a war plan known as "the surge" to station 21,500 additional troops in Iraq

♦ China successfully tested a ground-based ballistic missile capable of destroying satellites in orbit, drawing criticisms from other countries

♦ The International Red Cross and Red Crescent Movement adopted the Red Crystal as a non-religious emblem for use in its overseas operations

♦ A 2100-year-old melon was discovered by archaeologists in western Japan

♦ NASA's *Messenger* spacecraft made its second fly-by of Venus en route to Mercury

- The final book of the Harry Potter series, *Harry Potter and the Deathly Hallows,* sold over 11 million copies in the first 24 hours, becoming the fastest selling book in history
- Track and field star Marion Jones surrendered the five Olympic medals she had won in the 2000 Sydney Games after admitting to using banned performance enhancing drugs
- Reformation Sunday was observed by Lutherans and other Protestants around the world, to commemorate the 490th anniversary of the Ninety-Five Theses, which began the Protestant Reformation
- Vladimir Putin, President of Russia, was named *Time* magazine's 2007 Person of the Year
- A group of activist Lakota Indians attempted to secede from the Union as the Republic of Lakotah

2008

- USDA approved production and sale of foods from cloned animals
- The Earth Liberation Front set fires to five model luxury homes in Woodinville, Washington in an act of eco-terrorism
- Discovery of Rings of Saturnian moon Rhea, the first known rings around a moon, was announced
- The U.S. Senate passed legislation providing for more rigorous inspection of toys and other playthings imported into the United States
- The U.S. House of Representatives failed to override President Bush's veto of a bill outlawing waterboarding and other aggressive interrogation techniques

- The price of gold reached $1000 per troy ounce for the first time
- NASA said it would concentrate more on the outer Solar System and less on Mars exploration in the future, due to budget cuts
- Ford Motor Company sold its British luxury-car brands Jaguar and Land Rover to India's Tata Motors for $2.3 billion
- The oldest known recording of a human voice, created with a phonautograph by Édouard-Léon Scott de Martinville on April 9, 1860, was replayed by American researchers
- Cities around the world participated in Earth Hour, in which households and businesses turned off lights and non-essential electrical appliances between 8–9pm
- The U.S. Department of State renewed the contract of Blackwater Worldwide to provide security in Iraq despite ongoing investigation
- The United States Supreme Court upheld the constitutionality of lethal injection as a form of capital punishment over Eighth Amendment "cruel and unusual punishment" challenges
- Mars, Inc. bought the Wm. Wrigley Jr. Co., the world's largest chewing gum manufacturer, in a deal worth $23 billion
- After five years of searching, the Caribbean Monk Seal is declared officially extinct
- The first global study of coral reefs found that one-third of coral-building species face extinction
- Democrat Barack Obama was elected President of the United States, the first African American to hold that position

2009

- Fierce fighting erupted in the Gaza Strip between Israeli military forces on Hamas militants
- *Slumdog Millionaire* captured four awards at the Golden Globes ceremony including best drama
- Manufacturing activity sank to its lowest point in 28 years
- The price of crude oil began the year at $46 per barrel, down dramatically from $100 per barrel a year earlier
- Base stealer Ricky Henderson and hitter Jim Rice were named to the Baseball Hall of Fame
- The congressionally chartered National Safety Council advocated a ban on cell phone use while driving
- Electric cars, designed to run on batteries, dominated 2009 auto show in Detroit
- Barack Obama was inaugurated as the 44th President of the United States

Barack Obama takes the Oath of Office, becoming the 44th President of the United States and the first African American to hold the office. (via Wikimedia Commons)

SELECTED INCOME 2005–2009

Job	Source	Description	Pay
Activist	*Village Voice* (2005)	PAC environmental activist, fighting to open more national forests to logging and mining	$300–$500/wk
Actor/Model	*Village Voice* (2005)	All ages & sizes for fashion shows, magazines, catalogs, music videos, reality shows, commercials, film & TV. No experience necessary	$1,500 per day
Actress	*Atlanta Constitution* (2005)	Amount paid to actress Angelina Jolie in 2005	$27,000,000
Administrative Assistant	*Village Voice* (2005)	Working in Fashion Showroom, answering phones and typing	$35,000
Art Director	www.salary. com (2008)	Median salary for art director in advertising agency in 2008	$131,776
Artist	*Atlanta Constitution* (2005)	Amount artist Todd Persche made in 2005	$25,000
Athlete	www.parade.com (2008)	Annual salary of professional baseball player Barry Bonds	$15 million
Attorney	www.indeed.com (2008)	Legal services for area adoption office, intensive foster care & clinical services, relating to child protection, foster care, adult protection and economic services	$44,825.00–$82,930.00
Author	www.parade.com (2008)	Annual salary of author Stephen King	$52.1 million
Automotive Technician	*Atlanta Constitution* (2006)	Experienced ASE/Master Tech	$700 to $1,500 per week
Business Development Manager	Craigslist (2009)	Management and co-ordination of translators, software engineers and DTP specialists Planning, scheduling and monitoring the progress of multiple projects. Basic awareness of HTML/XML.	$60K
Bi-lingual Administrative Assistant	Monster.com (2009)	Bilingual (English/Spanish) Administrative Assistant needed for the Austin, (TX) office of a flooring manufacturer/supplier. Day-to-Day duties include reception, filing, faxing, copying and drafting correspondence. Knowledge of MS Word Outlook Explorer	$11–$14/hr
Bureau of Protective Services Officer	www.indeed.com (2008)	Maintains security at Chambers of the Legislature, Governor's mansion, State Capitol Complex and other state buildings; provides protection for Governor, Lieutenant Governor, and their families.	$29,910.00–$31,154.00
Cardiovascular Technologist (Senior)	www.healthcare source.com	Prospecting new staff, is a resource for equipment and procedures and in charge as needed. 2 years college education; 5 years Cath Lab experience; Registry or Certification Required; Special Training in cardiac monitoring, imaging and recording equipment.	$18.54/hr
Carpet & Vinyl Tile Installer	*Washington Post* (2005)	Protective covering mechanic for maintenance, installation and repair of various floor coverings	Starts $27,479
Chef	www.parade.com (2008)	Annual salary of chef & TV host Emeril Lagasse	$7.2 million
Cleaning Service	*Atlanta Constitution* (2006)	Restaurant kitchen exhaust cleaning company; mostly nights; some travel	$8.00/hr and up

Job	Source	Description	Pay
Cyclist	*Atlanta Constitution* (2005)	Amount paid to professional cyclist, Lance Armstrong in 2005	$19,000,000
Custodian	www.indeed.com (2008)	Routine, manual custodial duties such as window cleaning, dusting, vacuuming, cleaning and polishing	$13,624.00– $15,000.00
ESL Instructor	*Boston Globe* (2007)	ESL instructors for area schools BA/BS in Education; MA; certified teacher preferred; sensitivity to adult learners	$20.00/hr
Executive Recruiter	*Atlanta Constitution* (2006)	Banking industry recruiter	$100,000
Human Resources Director	*Boston Globe* (2007)	Manage Human Resources Department and employee relations; develop personnel policies; manage position classifications; oversee training	$68,503–$89,232
Highway Patrol Officer	www.indeed.com (2008)	Enforce laws; patrols state highways; investigates collisions; serves as a witness in criminal and civil courts; provides information to public regarding vehicle laws; responsible for public funds	$29,881–$46,033
"Inauguration" Event Chauffeur	*Washington Post* (2009)	Special event chauffeurs for Presidential Inauguration	$1,000
Jr. Software Engineer	*Atlanta Constitution* (2006)	E-Comm/ Web Development Skills using MySQL; Program Analyst in PHP	$39,000 to $41,000
Laborer/Machine Operator	*Boston Globe* (2007)	2nd Shift; F/T; Lift up to 60 lbs	$11.00/hr +Daily and Weekly bonuses
Legal Assistant	*Washington Post* (2005)	Works in all aspects of real estate transactions; including UCC searches; analysis of property titles, surveys, closing and reviewing leases	$80,000+ based on experience
Marketing Manager	Monster.com (2009)	Brand representative on a global cross functional team, working with Marketing Director, Artwork &Packaging, Regulatory, Legal, Customer Care and Sales and Finance providing business analysis and development of marketing plan.	$100–$130K
Mascot	*Village Voice* (2005)	Interacts with tourists and promotes attraction; must be 6' to 6'3" to operate costume	$17.00/hr
Mechanical Engineer	*Boston Globe* (2007)	Plan, design mechanical systems, repair products and systems, design and review specifications and manuals to determine feasibility of design	$30,000
Nurse (Occupational)	*Washington Post* (2005)	Conduct health screenings and pre-employment physicals; counsel associates with health problems; provide nursing treatments; dispense medication; maintain medical records; order medical supplies	$45,000–$50,000
Payroll (Accountant)	*Atlanta Constitution* (2006)	Part Time (20 hrs), ADP experience	$12.00-$13.00/hr
Plumber	www.salary.com (2008)	Median salary for plumber in South Carolina	$55,022.00
Physician – Anesthesiology	www.salary.com (2008)	Median salary of anesthesiologist	$253,133.00– $364,764.00
Probation Officer	www.indeed.com (2008)	Needs BA with 15 semester hours in social or behavioral science; must have passed Department's reading comprehension exam.	$26,522.00– $34,084.00
Promotions Representative	*Boston Globe* (2007)	Manage promotions at various retailers, public events, and sporting events	$600.00–$1,200 weekly

Job	Source	Description	Pay
Public Relations Specialist	www.careerbuilder.com (2008)	For library: assists in conducting media relations; identifies newsworthy stories; writes and distributes news releases; maintains media relationships	$33,754
Retail Automotive Store Manager	*Career Builder* (2009)	Knowledge of the automotive industry, including experience with diagnostics, general repairs and maintenance. ASE certifications helpful.	$60,000–$80,000
Singer/Personality	*Atlanta Constitution* (2005)	Amount paid to singer/personality Jessica Simpson in 2005	$4,000,000
Social Worker	*Washington Post* (2005)	BSW or MSW and licensed in DC; Assesses elderly for needed service; performs group and individual counseling; case management & outreach	$35,000
Software Developer	Monster.com (2009)	Develop and support multiple software applications. Provide guidance and recommendations on direction of software development. Develop integration and usage strategies into MM system. Follow systems requirements guidelines. Report and consolidate documentation to Project/Reporting Manager.	$50–$70/hr
Software Engineer	*Boston Globe* (2007)	Design, develop, code, maintain and test complex realtime multitasking embedded software systems for building automation systems	$105,000
Speech Teacher	*Career Builder* (2009)	Evaluation and treatment of children with speech and language difficulties in both one-on-one and group settings. The position also requires periodic training of staff on speech and language disorders in children, and creating behavior management systems.	$26.24–$29.74/hr
Store Detective	*Village Voice* (2005)	Males/Females; no experience necessary	$15.00/hour
Swimmer	*Atlanta Constitution* (2005)	Amount paid to Olympic Medalist Michael Phelps in 2005	$1,000,000
Talkshow Host	www.parade.com (2008)	Annual salary of David Letterman, host of the *Late Show*	$33.6 million
Teacher	*Boston Globe* (2007)	After/Pre-School; teacher PT or FT	$12.00–$14.00/hr
Teacher (Nurse)	*Washington Post* (2005)	Nursing instructor; teach 10 months with summers off	up to $80,000
Traffic Planner	*Atlanta Constitution* (2006)	Works on transportation planning processes along with travel demand theory/practice.	$37,869.00–$77,720.00
Truck Driver	*Atlanta Constitution* (2006)	Free Training for CDL	$35,000 to $75,000
Writer (Technical)	www.monster.com (2008)	Writes policy, process/procedure documentation using the Infrastructure Library framework; have experience with documentation, procedures, tasks and instruction and working with end users.	$25.00/hr

The Late Show began airing in 1993, with David Letterman as the original host. Letterman retired in 2015, at which point Stephen Colbert took over as host. (via Wikiedia Commons)

CONSUMER EXPENDITURES 2005-2009

Expenditure Type	2005	2006	2007	2008	2009
Food	$3,073	$3,249	$3,328	$3,620	$3,460
Food at home	$1,638	$1,728	$1,814	$1,975	$1,953
Food away from home	$1,435	$1,521	$1,514	$1,645	$1,507
Alcoholic beverages	$327	$428	$428	$374	$355
Housing	$9,835	$11,067	$11,269	$11,507	$11,388
Shelter	$6,179	$7,187	$7,212	$7,511	$7,376
Owned dwellings	$3,055	$3,651	$3,628	$3,686	$3,495
Rented dwellings	$2,889	$3,235	$3,228	$3,480	$3,513
Utilities, fuels, and public service	$2,024	$2,153	$2,206	$2,265	$2,298
Natural gas	$312	$361	$325	$340	$314
Electricity	$719	$771	$804	$832	$868
Telephone services	$664	$684	$706	$702	$722
Water and other public services	$230	$244	$264	$260	$309
Apparel and services	$980	$950	$971	$922	$975
Transportation	$4,030	$4,433	$4,539	$4,439	$4,182
Vehicle purchases (net outlay)	$1,395	$1,558	$1,478	$1,217	$1,441
Cars and trucks, new	$673	$826	$743	$553	$791
Cars and trucks, used	$669	$726	$683	$605	$606
Gasoline and motor oil	$1,032	$1,188	$1,276	$1,384	$1,022
Other vehicle expenses	$1,336	$1,324	$1,461	$1,523	$1,417
Vehicle maintenance and repairs	$437	$419	$471	$443	$470
Public transportation	$267	$363	$324	$314	$303
Health care	$1,750	$1,827	$1,790	$1,821	$2,007
Entertainment	$1,335	$1,464	$1,413	$1,655	$1,510
Personal care products and services	$328	$361	$364	$388	$345
Reading	$103	$91	$97	$88	$87
Education	$500	$477	$621	$602	$492
Tobacco products and smoking supplies	$227	$227	$223	$214	$253
Cash contributions	$1,313	$1,611	$1,219	$1,314	$1,268
Personal insurance and pensions	$2,409	$2,528	$2,491	$2,620	$2,518
Miscellaneous expenditures	$563	$662	$533	$558	$565
Total average annual expenditures	$26,773	$29,374	$29,285	**$30,120**	**$29,405**
Personal Taxes (1)					
Money income before taxes	$30,290	$31,557	$31,962		

Expenditure Type	2005	2006	2007	2008	2009
Personal taxes	$1,425	$1,602	$1,423	$32,994	$32,780
Federal income taxes	$1,016	$1,170	$1,033	$1,205	$1,395
State and local income taxes	$286	$314	$269	$1,147	$967
Other taxes	$124	$118	$121	$287	$312
Income after taxes	$28,864	$29,955	$30,539	$135	$118

Notes: Totals may not add up to component items due to rounding errors; (1) Components of income and taxes are derived from complete income reporters only through 2003. Beginning in 2004 income imputation was implemented. As a result: Source: U.S. Department of Labor, Bureau of Labor Statistics, Consumer Expenditure Surveys, 2000–2009 (Table 4. Size of Consumer Unit: Average Annual Expenditures and Characteristics)

INVESTMENTS 2005–2009

Investment	2005	2006	2007	2008	2009
Moody's Yield on Seasoned Corporate Bonds— All Industries, AAA (1)	5.23	5.59	5.56	5.63	5.26
90-Day AA Nonfinancial Commercial Paper Interest Rate (2)	3.42	5.10	4.92	2.13	0.26
Federal Funds Effective Rate (3)	3.22	4.97	5.02	1.92	0.16
Bank Prime Loan Rate (4)	6.19	7.96	8.05	5.09	3.25
Certificate of Deposit (CD), 6-month Rate (5)	3.73	5.24	5.23	3.14	0.87
U.S. Treasury Note, 10-year (6)	4.29	4.80	4.63	3.66	3.26
Mortgage Rate, 30-year Fixed (7)	5.86	6.41	6.34	6.04	5.04
Index of Common Stocks (S&P 500)	1,248.29	1,418.30	1,468.36	903.25	1115.1
Dividend Yield in Percent, S&P 500 (8)	1.79	1.77	1.89	3.12	2.05

(1) Moody's AAA rates through December 6, 2001, are averages of AAA utility and AAA industrial bond rates. As of December 7, 2001, these rates are averages of AAA industrial bonds only.

(2) Interest rates interpolated from data on certain commercial paper trades settled by The Depository Trust Company. The trades represent sales of commercial paper by dealers or direct issuers to investors (that is, the offer side).

(3) The daily effective federal funds rate is a weighted average of rates on brokered trades. Annualized using a 360-day year or bank interest.

(4) Average majority prime rate charged by banks on short-term loans to business, quoted on an investment basis. Rate posted by a majority of top 25 (by assets in domestic offices) insured U.S. –chartered commercial banks. Prime is one of several base rates used by banks to price short-term business loans.

(5) Average rate on 6-month negotiable certificates of deposit (secondary market), quoted on an investment basis.

(6) Market yield on U.S. Treasury securities at 10-year constant maturity, quoted on investment basis.

(7) Contract interest rates on commitments for 30-year fixed-rate first mortgages.

(8) Based on research by Aswath Damodaran from the Stern School of Business.

Source: The Federal Reserve (H.15 Selected Interest Rates—http://www.federalreserve.gov/releases/h15/data.htm) except where otherwise noted.

COMMON STOCKS	2005	2006	2007	2008	2009
AT&T (T)	25.59	24.71	34.95	41.00	29.42
Dividend	1.29	1.33	1.42	1.60	n/a
Bank of America (BAC)	46.46	47.08	53.33	40.56	14.33
Dividend 2:1 Stock Split, Aug. 30, 2004	1.90	2.12	2.40	n/a	n/a
Boeing (BA)	50.97	70.44	89.17	86.62	45.25
Dividend	1.00	1.20	1.40	1.60	n/a
General Electric (GE)	36.59	35.37	37.97	36.76	17.07
Dividend 3:1 Stock Split, May 8, 2000	0.91	1.03	1.15	n/a	n/a

COMMON STOCKS	2005	2006	2007	2008	2009
General Motors (GM)	40.30	18.90	29.45	24.41	3.65
Dividend	2.00	1.00	1.00	n/a	n/a
Kellogg Co. (K)	44.36	43.72	50.45	51.74	45.05
Dividend	1.06	1.14	1.20	n/a	n/a
Microsoft (MSFT)	26.74	26.84	29.86	35.22	20.33
Dividend 2:1 Stock Split, March 29, 1999; 2:1 Stock Split Feb. 18, 2003	0.32	0.37	0.41	n/a	n/a
Navistar International Corp. (NAV)	43.89	28.78	34.01	54.70	24.43
No Dividend					
Pfizer (acquired Warner-Lambert Feb. 2000)	26.45	23.78	26.29	22.91	18.27
Dividend	0.76	0.96	1.16	1.28	n/a
2:1 Stock Split, Jul. 1, 1999					
Procter & Gamble Co. (PG)	55.19	58.78	64.54	72.31	62.80
Dividend	1.09	1.21	1.36	1.55	n/a
2:1 Stock Split, June 21, 2004					
Reynolds American Inc. (RAI) (previously R.J. Reynolds Tobacco)	78.50	96.50	65.35	65.60	40.39
Dividend	4.20	4.00	3.20	n/a	n/a
2:1 Stock Split, Aug. 15, 2006					
United States Steel Corp. (X)	49.29	49.44	71.31	113.64	39.51
Dividend	0.38	0.60	0.80	n/a	n/a
Wal-Mart (WMT)	53.35	46.23	47.55	46.90	57.18
Dividend	0.60	0.67	0.88	n/a	n/a
2:1 Stock Split, Apr. 20, 1999					
Yahoo (YHOO)	38.18	40.91	25.61	23.72	12.85
No Dividend					
2:1 Stock Split, Feb. 8, 1999; 2:1 Stock Split, Feb. 14, 2000;					
2:1 Stock Split, May 12, 2004					

Source: Yahoo! Finance

STANDARD JOBS 2005–2009

Based on NAICS codes	NAICS	2005	2006	2007	2008	2009
Total, all industries	10	$40,677	$42,535	$44,458	$45,563	$45,559
Total, all industries, private		$40,505	$42,414	$44,362	$45,371	$45,155
Federal government		$59,864	$62,274	$64,871	$66,293	$67,756
State government		$42,249	$43,875	$45,903	$47,980	$48,742
Local government		$37,718	$39,179	$40,790	$42,274	$43,140
Bituminous coal underground mining	2121112	$62,699	$65,205	$68,155	$70,959	$76,666
Construction	1012/23	$42,100	$44,496	$46,784	$49,013	$49,322
Private households (domestics)	814	$15,715	$16,320	$16,999	$17,519	$16,880
Crop production	111	$21,761	$22,796	$23,830	$24,570	$24,581
Finance and insurance	52	$73,385	$78,566	$84,952	$85,268	$79,793
Wholesale trade	42	$55,262	$58,046	$60,719	$61,483	$61,595
Retail trade	44–45	$24,930	$25,567	$26,124	$26,179	$26,162
Utilities	221	$75,208	$78,341	$82,275	$84,153	$84,877
Elementary and secondary schools	6111	$36,166	$37,664	$39,173	$33,762	$34,790
Manufacturing	31–33	$49,287	$51,427	$53,489	$54,400	$54,873
Postal service	491	$48,640	$52,208	$52,609	$25,640	$27,537
Telecommunications	517	$64,866	$67,385	$70,490	$71,639	$70,683
Radio and television broadcasting	5151	$57,794	$60,553	$62,791	$64,206	$63,918
Motion picture and video industries	5121	$51,403	$52,912	$54,267	$56,101	$56,716
Ambulatory health care services	621	$47,700	$49,160	$50,675	$52,234	$53,369
Membership associations and organizations	813	$29,246	$30,544	$32,086	$33,476	$34,449
Rail transportation	4821	$35,777	$43,788	$42,692	$45,106	$42,698
Transit and ground passenger	485	$46,139	$47,403	$49,279	$25,244	$25,217

Note: The QCEW survey switched from SIC to NAICS codes in 2001. Data may not be directly comparable. Items in bold changed dramatically between 2000 and 2001.

Source: Bureau of Labor Statistics, Quarterly Census of Employment and Wages (QCEW)

FOOD BASKET 2005–2007

(NR = Not Reported)

Commodity	Year	U.S. Average	Atlanta	Chicago	Denver	Los Angeles	New York
Bananas, per lb	2005	51¢	49¢	69¢	49¢	62¢	69¢
	2006	51¢	48¢	66¢	49¢	67¢	74¢
	2007	51¢	47¢	54¢	51¢	59¢	.77¢
Beef, Ground, price per lb	2005	$2.44	$2.08	$3.23	$2.32	$2.75	$3.10
	2006	$2.52	$2.39	$2.91	$2.56	$2.95	$3.66
	2007	$2.58	$2.82	$3.05	$2.44	$2.41	$4.29
Bread, white, per loaf	2005	$1.10	$1.17	$1.39	$1.20	$1.56	$1.53
	2006	$1.15	$1.16	$1.46	$1.20	$1.80	$1.84
	2007	$1.24	$1.24	$1.34	$1.28	$1.71	$2.64
Cereal, Corn Flakes, 18 oz	2005	$2.89	$2.84	$3.36	$2.94	$3.51	$4.25
	2006	$2.94	$2.95	$3.15	$2.87	$3.98	$4.46
	2007	$3.17	$3.32	$3.39	$3.37	$3.44	$5.33
Cheese, grated Parmesan, 8 oz	2005	$3.44	$3.22	$4.17	$4.12	$4.35	$4.88
	2006	$3.38	$3.03	$4.13	$4.03	$4.21	$4.99
	2007	$3.44	$2.94	$3.77	$4.19	$4.04	$5.62
Chicken, whole uncut, price per lb	2005	$1.09	81¢	$1.30	$1.25	$1.54	$1.39
	2006	$1.06	88¢	$1.42	$1.14	$1.43	$1.63
	2007	$1.12	$1.17	$1.23	$1.06	$1.32	$2.07
Coca-Cola, 2 liter	2005	$1.25	$1.14	$1.14	$1.12	$1.41	$1.56
	2006	$1.29	$1.31	$1.17	$1.18	$1.66	$1.59
	2007	$1.36	$1.36	$1.17	$1.18	$1.42	$1.91
Coffee, vacuum-packed, 11.5 oz	2005	$2.99	$2.95	$3.40	$4.00	$3.88	$3.87
	2006	$3.15	$3.26	$3.57	$4.09	$4.05	$4.33
	2007	$3.31	$3.44	$4.14	$4.08	$3.92	$5.46
Corn, whole kernel frozen, 16 oz	2005	$1.20	89¢	$1.43	$1.38	$1.63	$2.10
	2006	$1.23	92¢	$1.46	$1.47	$1.91	$2.21
	2007	$1.27	92¢	$1.26	$1.91	$1.80	$2.46
Eggs, 1 dozen, grade A or AA, large	2005	$1.08	$1.04	$1.81	88¢	$2.09	$1.89
	2006	$1.09	97¢	$1.64	96¢	$2.13	$1.86
	2007	$1.52	$1.30	$1.56	$1.31	$2.10	$2.62
Lettuce, Iceberg, head (approx. 1-1/4 lb)	2005	$1.22	$1.25	$1.37	$1.05	$1.20	$1.82
	2006	$1.20	$1.23	$1.35	$1.08	$1.30	$2.03
	2007	$1.29	$1.36	$1.46	$1.06	$1.58	$2.36
Margarine, 1 lb, stick form	2005	88¢	.62¢	99¢	$1.14	$1.09	$1.86
	2006	86¢	61¢	99¢	$1.00	$1.09	$1.81
	2007	85¢	79¢	$1.12	88¢	$1.05	$2.10
Milk, whole, 1/2 gallon	2005	$1.99	$1.83	$2.34	$2.41	$2.48	$2.17
	2006	$1.97	$1.98	$2.34	$2.19	$2.35	$2.16
	2007	$2.13	$2.14	$2.05	$2.20	$2.40	$2.47
Orange Juice, fresh, 64 oz	2005	$2.73	$2.67	$2.62	$2.71	$3.92	$3.44
	2006	$2.79	$2.85	$2.78	$2.71	$3.73	$3.40
	2007	$3.26	$3.43	$3.46	$3.14	$3.32	$4.08
Peaches, halves or slices, 29 oz can	2005	$1.74	$1.65	$2.00	$2.46	$2.25	$2.03
	2006	$1.78	$1.71	$2.05	$2.38	$2.36	$2.13
	2007	$1.92	$1.87	$1.92	$2.62	$2.40	$2.49

Commodity	Year	U.S. Average	Atlanta	Chicago	Denver	Los Angeles	New York
Peas, sweet, 15 oz can	2005	84¢	83¢	$1.07	$1.16	$1.09	$1.14
	2006	85¢	.93¢	88¢	$1.05	$1.05	$1.22
	2007	87¢	94¢	95¢	92¢	$1.00	$1.45
Potatoes, 10 lb sack, white or red	2005	$3.18	$3.94	$4.16	$3.01	$2.82	$4.66
	2006	$3.65	$4.44	$4.37	$3.32	$3.33	$4.63
	2007	$3.89	$4.96	$4.12	$3.90	$4.49	$6.10
Sausage, pork, 1 lb	2005	$3.55	$3.23	$4.00	$5.09	$5.14	$4.04
	2006	$3.29	$3.02	$3.22	$3.74	$4.57	$4.40
	2007	$3.16	$3.27	$3.45	$3.76	$3.01	$4.88
Shortening, all-vegetable, 3 lb can	2005	$3.48	$3.51	$4.34	$3.43	$4.04	$4.41
	2006	$3.52	$3.77	$4.45	$3.62	$4.31	$4.14
	2007	$3.83	$4.07	$4.54	$4.47	$4.76	$4.43
Steak, T-bone, per lb	2005	$8.60	$8.16	$8.02	$9.71	$8.82	$11.52
	2006	$8.49	$8.51	$8.07	$9.40	$8.22	$12.60
	2007	$8.93	$9.37	$10.37	$9.05	$7.98	$11.97
Sugar, white, 4–5 lb	2005	$1.60	$1.44	$1.93	$1.97	$2.13	$2.25
	2006	$1.72	$1.70	$1.71	$2.23	$2.38	$2.39
	2007	$1.92	$2.01	$2.02	$2.22	$2.12	$2.87
Tuna, chunk light, 6.0 oz can	2005	$72¢	56¢	$1.00	76¢	87¢	$1.09
	2006	74¢	.66¢	97¢	82¢	92¢	$1.06
	2007	76¢	70¢	80¢	71¢	$1.07	$1.57

Notes: Data for New York covers Manhattan only; data for 2000 covers Q4 only; data for 2001–2007 are 4-quarter averages; Data could not be found for 2008-2009 Source: Council for Community and Economic Research (formerly ACCRA), Cost of Living Index, 2000–2007

SELECTED PRICES 2005-2009

Item	Source	Description	Price
ALCOHOL			
Beer	*Boston Globe* (2005)	*Bud & Bud Light;* 30 pk	$19.99
Beer	*Boston Globe* (2005)	*Corona;* 12 oz Bottles; Loose Case	$20.99
Beer	*Boston Globe* (2005)	*Bass Ale;* 12 pk Bottles	$11.99
Champagne	Wine.com (2005)	*Dom Perignon* 2000	$159.99
Liquor	*Boston Globe* (2009)	*Jim Beam;* 80; 1.75 ltr.	$19.99
Liquor	*Boston Globe* (2005)	Tequila; *Jose Cuervo Gold;* 80; 1.75 ltr.	$31.99
Liquor	*Boston Globe* (2005)	*Bushmills;* 80; 1.75 ltr.	$34.99
Liquor	*Boston Globe* (2005)	*Grand Marnier;* 80; 750 ltr.	$26.99
Wine	*Boston Globe* (2005)	*Blackstone;* Merlot, Pino Noir or Chardonnay	$7.99
Wine	*Boston Globe* (2005)	*Clois du Bois;* Merlot	$11.99
Wine	*Boston Globe* (2005)	*Duboeuf Beaujolais-Villages;* Nouveau 2005	$6.99
Wine	*Boston Globe* (2005)	*Taylor Fladgate;* Port; 2003	$83.99
APPAREL CHILDREN'S			
Jeans	*Target Flyer* (2007)	Boys *Cherokee* Jeans; in several washes and fits; regular, slim, and husky sizes	$9.99
Pants	*Target Flyer* (2007)	Boys; *Cargo* pants	$9.99
Pants	*Target Flyer* (2007)	Girls; 4–16 Straight legged pants; 100% Cotton	$9.99
Sleepwear	gap.com (2009)	Girls 100% cotton pajama set	$19.99
T-shirt	*Target* Flyer (2007)	Boys or girls attitude or licensed-character styles	2 for $12.00
APPAREL, MEN'S			
Coat	*Charlotte Observer* (NC) (2005)	Leather coat	Sale $69.99 and up
Coat	*Charlotte Observer* (NC) (2005)	Sport coat	Sale $29.99 and up
Jeans	*Sears Flyer* (2007)	*Lee;* regular or relaxed fit	$19.99
Jeans	*Sears Flyer* (2007)	*Lee;* boot cut jeans	$24.99
Shirt	*Sears Flyer* (2007)	*Canyon River Blues;* Young Men's	$9.99
Shirt	*Sears Flyer* (2007)	Young men's novelty and screen-printed tees	$9.99

709

Item	Source	Description	Price
Shirt	*L.L. Bean Catalog* (2008)	Chamois cloth shirt	$34.50
Shirt	*L.L. Bean Catalog* (2008)	Scotch plaid flannel shirt	$29.50
Shirt	*L.L. Bean Catalog* (2008)	Wrinkle resistant chino shirts	$29.50
Shoes	*Charlotte Observer* (NC) (2005)	*Cotulla* boots	Sale $89.99
Shoes	*Charlotte Observer* (NC) (2005)	*Cole Haan* loafers	Sale $89.99 and up
Sweatshirt	*L.L. Bean Catalog* (2008)	Rugged, Heavyweight, Zip Front Sweatshirt	$49.50
Tuxedos	*Atlanta Journal Constitution* (2006)	Groom's free rental & preview	Starts at $49.00

APPAREL, WOMEN'S

Item	Source	Description	Price
Coat	*Talbots Catalog* (2008)	Timeless trench coat in Polished cotton/ polyester/ spandex sateen; fully Lined	$188.00
Dress	*American Baby Magazine* 2008	*Maternal America* tie dress	$128.00
Dress	*Talbots Catalog* (2008)	Red dress and jacket; double weave wool/ spandex	$198.00
Handbag	*Atlanta Journal Constitution* (2006)	*Satchels,* hobos, top-zips, totes and more, in leather, PVC or fabric; Originally $50.00–$220.00	$12.50–$110.00
Shirt	*Sears Flyer* (2007)	Misses *Apostrophe* lace layered top	$19.99
Shirt	*Sears Flyer* (2007)	Misses novelty knit top	$19.99
Shoes	*Atlanta Journal Constitution* (2005)	Ladies' *Cole Haan* shoes; *Air Vail* mule in bamboo, red or black leather; Originally $165.00	$99.99
Shoes	*Atlanta Journal Constitution* (2005)	Ladies' *Cole Haan* shoes; *Air Marquesa* clog in salt or black Nubuck; Originally $135.00	$99.99
Skirt	*American Baby Magazine* (2008)	*Maternal America* Flutter skirt	$88.00
Sweater	*Sears Flyer* (2007)	Misses *Apostrophe* layered sweater	$24.99
Top	*American Baby Magazine* (2008)	*Bump Couture* Marilyn top	$66.00

APPLIANCES

Item	Source	Description	Price
Beer Dispenser	*Macy's Flyer* (2008)	For perfectly chilled draft beer at home; keeps beer fresh for up to 30 days after tapping	$279.99
Dishwasher	*Sears Flyer* (2007)	*Whirlpool* 5 level wash; quiet with tail tub design	$399.99
Dryer	*Sears Flyer* (2007)	Large, 6 temperatures; 5 cycles	$699.99
Microwave	bestbuy.com (2009)	1200W, 11power levels, 7-digit 2-color lighted display, 9 sensor cook options, Keep Warm feature, 16"glass turntable, child lock function	$349.99
Mixer	*Macy's Flyer* (2008)	*KitchenAid Artisan* 5 qt stand mixer; tilt head design	$299.99

The KitchenAid standard design has remained relatively unchanged since the 1930s. The silhouette has since been made a registered trademark with the U.S. Patent and Trademark Office. In 1997 the San Francisco Museum of Modern Art selected the KitchenAid stand mixer as an icon of American design. (via Flickr)

Item	Source	Description	Price
Refrigerator	*Sears Flyer* (2007)	*Kenmore* 24.8 cubic foot with gallon door storage, advanced temperature control system and pull out freezer drawer	$1,488
Stereo	*Sears Flyer* (2007)	*Emerson* portable sound system with IPod docking station; AM/FM stereo radio; backlit digital frequency display; digital clock with timer	$39.99
Stove	*Sears Flyer* (2007)	*Kenmore* gas range; 4.1 cubic foot capacity; 4 9,000 btu burners	$329.99
Television	*Sears Flyer* (2007)	*Samsung* 26"; LCD; HDTV	$949.99
Television	*Sears Flyer* (2007)	*Sylvania* 26"; LCD TV; 2 HDMI inputs; 1 PC input	$479.99
Television	Sears Flyer (2007)	Samsung 52"; 1080p LCD HDTV; PC Input; 3 HDMI; 2 Components; 2 S-Video	$3,999.99
Washing Machine	*Sears Flyer* (2007)	Large, quiet; 5 temperatures; 5 cycles	$799.99
Washing Machine	bestbuy.com (2009)	4.7 cu. ft. 14-cycle, large capacity washer, front-loading	$1,699.99

Item	Source	Description	Price
BABY PRODUCTS			
Announcement Cards	*Vista Print Flyer* (2008)	Birth announcements, folded, 10	$4.99
Baby Carrier	*American Baby Magazine* (2008)	Organic cotton carrier	$100.00
Baby Portraits	*Target Flyer* (2008)	Portrait package: 1 8"×10"; 2 5"×7"s; 4 3.5"×5"s; 16 Wallets	$8.99
Body Suit	*American Baby Magazine* (2008)	Organic cotton; bright colored suits	$24.00
Books	*Scholastic Flyer* (2008)	8 *Disney* storybooks and free backseat organizer	$1.99 plus shipping and handling
Crib	potterybarn.com (2009)	Wooden sleigh crib, adjustable mattress platform, available in different finishes	$999
Cups	*Target Flyer* (2007)	2-pk; 9 oz spill proof cups	2 for $8
Diaper Bag	*American Baby Magazine* (2008)	From recycled plastic bottles stuffed with *Seventh Generation* products	$200.00
Diapers	*Walmart Flyer* (2007)	*Pampers* jumbo pack	$7.87
Movies	*Disney Movie Club Flyer* 2008	4 *Disney* movies	$1.99
Sleep Sacks	*American Baby Magazine* (2008)	Organic cotton sleep sacks	$45.00
Stroller	*American Baby Magazine* (2008)	*Vista* stroller	$650.00
Toy	*American Baby Magazine* (2008)	*Zoobie Pet; 3* in one plush animal head stuffed with blanket; works as pillow	$34.00
Toy	*American Baby Magazine* (2008)	*Grip & Grasp* with two silly toys and holds a drink	$20.00
Toy	*American Baby Magazine* (2008)	*Big Baby Keys* that squeak and rattle	$9.00
Toy	*American Baby Magazine* (2008)	Classic wooden toy blocks made from sustainable hardwood	$56.00
BUSINESS EQUIPMENT AND SUPPLIES			
1GB USB 2.0 Flash Drive	*Atlanta Journal Constitution* (2006)	With $15 mail-in rebate; limit one per customer	$39.99
ATI Radeon 9200 AGP Video Card	*Atlanta Journal Constitution* (2006)	128Mb DDR Memory; VGA & TV output; OpenGL Compliant	$69.99
Laptop	*Atlanta Journal Constitution* (2006)	*Fujitsu Intel Centrino* mobile technology notebook; 15.4" Wide XGA display; 740 Processor	$1,149.99
Paper	*Staples Flyer* (2007)	*Hammermill* copy and multipurpose paper with case	$29.99
Pressure Washer	*Home Depot Flyer* (2006)	*Husky* 1750 PSI electric pressure washer	$99.00
Printer	*Boston Globe* (2007)	Print/fax/scan; 50 sheet document feeder with built in wireless networking and scan resolution up to 4800dpi	$299.00
Shredder	*Staples Flyer* (2007)	24-sheet strip cut shredder with reverses function and easy glide pull-out basket; 8 gallon bin	$129.99

Item	Source	Description	Price
Software	*Best Buy Flyer* (2008)	Office home and student 2007 with *Word, Excel, Power-Point* and *One-Note*	$99.99
Software	*Atlanta Journal Constitution* (2006)	Learn a second language; CD-ROM Curriculum with 20 activities in each of 92 lessons Level 1 Level 2 Level 1 & 2	 $175.50 $202.50 $269.10
Water Cooler	*Atlanta Journal Constitution* (2007)	Bottled water cooler for cold & room temperature water $88.88	
Wireless Router	*Best Buy Flyer* (2008)	Stream HD and more at speeds faster than standard wireless with better range	$99.99

COLLECTIBLES

Item	Source	Description	Price
Autographed Guitar	hardrockstageproductions.com (2009)	Signed by Billy Ray & Miley Cyrus	$649.00
Baseball	*Boston Globe* (2007)	Jonathan Papelbon autographed baseball	$99.95
Baseball Bat	*Boston Globe* (2007)	2004 World Series Champions bat with box scores of each game engraved on back	$99.95
Braves Winter Fan Fest	*Atlanta Journal Constitution* (2006)	Autograph sessions with players and coaches; $20 donation gives unlimited access to autograph stations with Chipper Jones, Andrew Jones Jeff Francoeur, Tim Hudson, Édgar Rentería and others	Free
Photograph	*Boston Globe* (2007)	Johnny Pesky/Ted Williams photo autographed and framed 8 × 10	$89.99

ENTERTAINMENT

Item	Source	Description	Price
Concert Ticket	*Boston Globe* (2005)	*Boston Baroque* on New Year's Eve and Day	$28.00 & $64.00
Concert Ticket	*City Magazine*, Lynchburg VA (2008)	Diamond Rio in concert from Nashville In advance At gate	 $25.00 $30.00
Concert Ticket	*Charlotte Observer* (NC) (2005)	A Scots-Irish Twelfth Night at the Hezekiah Alexander House and Open House Tour and Colonial Crafts	$6.00 per person
Football Game Package	*Charlotte Observer* (NC) (2005)	Steelers playoff game with bus from Charlotte, hotel and tickets	$475 per person
Theater Ticket	*Boston Globe* (2005)	*Disney's Beauty & The Beast* musical in Boston's children's theatre tradition of live theatre	$20.00 & $22.00
Theatre Ticket	*Charlotte Observer* (NC) (2005)	*Outback Steakhouse* Family Dinner Theatre Night with dinner and *Beauty and the Beast* Adults Students	$20.00 $15.00
Theatre Ticket	*Atlanta Journal Constitution* (2006)	*Atlanta Passion,* play	$10.00–$25.00
Theater Ticket	broadway.com (2009)	*Jersey Boys* at August Wilson Theater in NYC, Sat, mezzanine	$97.00
Wine Expo Ticket	*Boston Globe* (2005)	The largest consumer wine event in the country; 2-day pass Sunday Only	$95.00 $60.00
Concert Ticket	*City Magazine*, Lynchburg VA (2008)	Toby Mac in concert, with special guest The Beautiful Republic In advance At gate	 $25.00 $30.00

Item	Source	Description	Price

ENTERTAINMENT, HOME

Item	Source	Description	Price
Camera	*Atlanta Journal Constitution* (2005)	*Cannon Rebel* XT; 8 million pixels; 2000 zoom lens	$999.99
Camera	*Boston Globe* (2007)	*Olympus* 8MP; EVOLT E-500; two lens outfit; 2.5 LCD	$589.99
DIRECTV	*Charlotte Observer* (NC) (2005)	125 Channels with local channels; 3 rooms free; includes satellite dish; 3 standard receivers and remotes; and standard installation	$39.99 per month
DVD Player	*Boston Globe* (2005)	*Mintek* 7 Portable DVD Player plays DVD's, CDs CDRWs and *Kodak* picture CDs	$129.99
DVD/CD Player	*Atlanta Journal Constitution* (2006)	*jWIN* DVD/CD player	$28.88
Game	*Best Buy Flyer* (2008)	PSP game; Tiger Woods PGA Tour '09	$39.99
Game	*Best Buy Flyer* (2008)	PC Game; SIMS 2—Apartment Life	$29.99
Ink Jet Printer	*Atlanta Journal Constitution* (2005)	*Epson* R200 ink jet printer; 6-color inks; border free; 8.5"×11" photos; easy USB connection	$99.99
Internet	*Charlotte Observer* (NC) (2005)	*Altell* DSL high-speed internet	$26.95 Month
Photo Viewer	*Atlanta Journal Constitution* (2005)	*Epson* P2000 photo viewer; 40 GB hard drive; 3.8 LCD Screen	$499.99

FOOD PRODUCTS

Item	Source	Description	Price
Bananas	*Ingles Flyer* (2005)	*Delmonte* bananas	3 lbs for $1.00
Beef	*Ingles Flyer* (2005)	USDA choice beef; London broil	$1.98 lb
Bread	*Kroger Flyer* (2005)	*Kroger* buttercrust bread	$0.88 ea.
Chicken	*Ingles Flyer* (2005)	*Perdue* bone-in split chicken breast	$1.38 lb
Chicken	*Kroger Flyer* (2005)	Fresh whole fryers	$0.69 lb
Cookie	*Kroger Flyer* (2005)	12" message cookie	$6.99
Eggs	*Kroger Flyer* (2005)	Dozen large eggs	$0.77 ea.
Green Beans	*Kroger Flyer* (2005)	*Georgia Crown*	$0.99 lb
Jumbo Raw Shrimp	*Boston Globe* (2005)	Frozen 2 lb. bag; 26/30 ct.	$4.99 lb
Jumbo Sea Scallops	*Stop & Shop* (2009)	Wild caught, under 20 per lb.	$13.99 lb
Milk	*Kroger Flyer* (2005)	*Springdale* 2%, 1% or skim gallon jug	2 for $5.00
Ribeye Roast	*Boston Globe* (2005)	Whole semi-boneless	$4.59 lb
Soft Drink	*Ingles Flyer* (2005)	*Coke* 12-pack; 12oz cans	3 for $9.99 limit 6
Yams	*Boston Globe* (2005)	Louisiana yams	$.079 lb

Item	Source	Description	Price
Mushrooms	*Boston Globe* (2005)	10 oz pack	$1.79 ea.
Artichokes	*Boston Globe* (2005)	Fancy	$0.99 ea.
Coffee	*Boston Globe* (2005)	*Hilltop* 1 lb bag	2 for $5.00
Lettuce	*Boston Globe* (2005)	California red leaf; green leaf; Boston lettuce	$0.98 ea.
Eggplant	*Boston Globe* (2005)	Fancy Florida eggplant	$0.78 lb
Apples	*Boston Globe* (2005)	Premium quality sweet crisp, Red Delicious, and Golden	$0.98 lb
Oranges	*Boston Globe* (2005)	Extra large, sweet California Navel oranges	$0.98 lb
Tangerines	*Boston Globe* (2005)	Orchard Fresh, large; sweet Florida tangerines	$0.98 lb
Pizza	*Atlanta Journal Constitution* (2006)	*Tombstone* frozen pizza, assorted varieties; 16–32 oz package	2 for $5.00
Chicken	*Atlanta Journal Constitution* (2006)	BBQ rotisserie chicken	$5.99
Top Round London Broil	*Atlanta Journal Constitution* (2006)	Premium certified beef	$3.49 lb
Shrimp	*Atlanta Journal Constitution* (2006)	Medium Florida pink shrimp; 41–50 per lb	$5.99 lb
Sirloin Strip Steak	*Boston Globe* (2007)	Family pack sirloin strip steak	$5.44 lb
Baby Back Ribs	*Boston Globe* (2007)	Baby back ribs	$2.99 lb
Water	*Kroger Flyer* (2008)	*Glaceau Vitamin water* assorted varieties	10 for $10.00
Spice	*Kroger Flyer* (2008)	*McCormick Spice* grinders; .85–2.12 oz	10 for $10.00
Eggs	*Kroger Flyer* (2008)	Large 18 ct eggs	$1.88 each

FURNITURE

Item	Source	Description	Price
Bar	*Atlanta Journal Constitution* (2005)	*Carter* bar; 9" tall × 8' × 8' pine also available	$3,995; Pine $2,995
Bedroom Set	*Atlanta Journal Constitution* (2005)	*Cottage Grove'* bedroom set; crafted in solids and veneers; headboard panels on queen bed; dresser, armoire, mirror, wood rails	$999.99
Chair	*Macy's Flyer* (2008)	Reclining chair & ottoman with leather seating and vinyl sides and back	$649.00
Chaise Lounge	raymourflanigan.com (2009)	Microfiber, with rich wood trim, matching pillow	$769.95
Mattress & Box Spring	*Charlotte Observer* (NC) (2005)	2 PC queen set; euro pillowtop premium	$677.00
Settee	*Charlotte Observer* (NC) (2005)	Settee in woven fabric; regular $1,249.00	$679
Sofa	*Charlotte Observer* (NC) (2005)	Sofa with accent pillows and two chairs; regular $3,918.00	$1699.00
Sofa and Chair	*Boston Globe* (2007)	All leather sofa and chair	$599.00

Item	Source	Description	Price
GARDEN EQUIPMENT AND SUPPLIES			
Composter	homedepot.com (2009)	124 gallon continuous composter	$249 incl. shipping
Flowers	*Home Depot Flyer* (2005)	Pansies 6pk	$0.99 ea.
Hose	homedepot.com (2009)	75 ft. industrial garden hose	$44.97
Landscape Designs	*Atlanta Journal Constitution* (2005)	1.5 hr consultation	$149.00
Lawnmower	*Home Depot Flyer* (2006)	2005 *John Deere* model; LT30 rigid lawn mower; 23 Horsepower; Originally $2,499.00	$1,999.00
Plant	*FreeTimes*— Abode Special section (2008)	*Woodley's Garden Centers,* Sagos	$29.00/gal
Shed	*Boston Globe* (2007)	*American Classic* 10×12	$2,499.00
Shovel	*Home Depot Flyer* (2005)	Garden tools with fiberglass handle	$9.97
HOTEL RATES			
Room Rate	*Boston Globe* (2005)	Riverside Tower Hotel; Hudson River Views Singles Suites	$84.00; $199.00
Room Rate	www.hilton.com (2008)	Hilton San Francisco	$259.00 per night
Room Rate	www.hilton.com (2008)	Hilton Columbia Center	$159.00 per night
Room Rate	www.hilton.com (2008)	Hilton Charlotte Center City	$229.00
Room Rate	www.motel6.com (2008)	Motel 6 Chicago O'Hare—Schiller Park	$53.19
Room Rate	www.motel6.com	Motel 6 Las Vegas Downtown	$39.99
HOUSEHOLD PRODUCTS			
China	*Atlanta Journal Constitution* (2005)	*Mikasa* parchment or *Platinum Crown* china service for 8	$199.99
Crockpot	*Atlanta Journal Constitution* (2005)	*Rival* crock pot; 2 heat settings; rinse clean	Sale $19.99
Curtains	*Boston Globe* (2005)	72" thermal backed drapery pairs in burgundy, blue, gold & beige	$19.99
Iron	*Atlanta Journal Constitution* (2005)	*Rowenta Power Glide* with stainless steel soleplate; vertical/variable/burst of steam; center pivoting cord	$39.99
Knives	*Atlanta Journal Constitution* (2005)	15 pc stainless steel cutlery set; kitchen knives; steak knives; shears, and more in block	$37.99
Mattress	*Atlanta Journal Constitution* (2005)	*Sealy Posturepedic Beasley Plus* Queen King	$599.00 $899.00
Microwave Oven	*Atlanta Journal Constitution* (2005)	*Sharp* 0.8 cu. ft. microwave oven; 800 watts of power with digital display, auto touch control	$49.99

Item	Source	Description	Price
Pots and Pans	*Atlanta Journal Constitution* (2005)	*Simply Calphalon* 10-pc cookware set, nonstick; 1 and 2qt covered saucepans; 6qt covered stockpot; 3qt covered sauté pan with helper handle; 8" and 10" omelet pans	$199.99
Sheets	*Atlanta Journal Constitution* (2005)	*Cambridge* 6pc sheet set, queen or king; 250 thread count; cotton	$27.99
Sheets	*Boston Globe* (2005)	220 ct. percale sheet sets, king	$19.99
Carpet	*Boston Globe* (2007)	13.6" × 24" Golden Floral	$1,000
Charcoal BBQ Grill	*Atlanta Journal Constitution* (2006)	*Char-Broil* BBQ grill	$38.88
Hand Vacuum	*Atlanta Journal Constitution* (2006)	*SHARK* hand vacuum	$28.88
Laundry Detergent	*Walmart Flyer*(2007)	*Tide* liquid laundry detergent 100 fluid oz	$10.00

Introduced in 1946, Tide is the highest selling detergent brand in the world, with an estimated 14.3 percent of the global market. (via Flickr)

Item	Source	Description	Price
Panini Press	williams-sonoma. com (2009)	*Breville Ikon,* fits wide range of breads, fillings, non-stick plates wipe clean	$99.95
Silicone Tongs	williams-sonoma.com (2009)	Heat-resistant up to 575°F, protects cookware from scratches	$15.00
Stove	*Atlanta Journal Constitution* (2006)	300 electric range with storage drawer	$218.88
Table Pads	*Boston Globe* (2007)	Custom table pads	$49.99
Towels	*Sears Flyer* (2008)	*Colormate* bath towels 30" × 54"	$9.99
Wine Cooler	*Atlanta Journal Constitution* (2006)	Wine cooler with glass door	$98.99

JEWELRY

Item	Source	Description	Price
Bracelet	*Macy's Flyer* (2008)	Diamond cut bangles	$80.00
Earrings	*Sears Flyer* (2008)	Diamond earrings	$259.90
Earrings	*Macy's Flyer* (2008)	Sterling silver with semi-precious stone	$50.00
Engagement Ring	*Boston Globe* (2007)	*Tiffany* diamond engagement rings in platinum	$4,230–
Fashion Jewelry	*Atlanta Journal Constitution* (2006)	Earrings, necklaces and bracelets in gold tone and silver	$15.00–$150.00
Necklace	*Macy's Flyer* (2008)	Semi-precious stone and natural shell pendant	$60.00

MEALS

Item	Source	Description	Price
Dinner	www.hennessyssc. com (2008)	Maryland Crab Cakes with Hennessy's secret mixture of jumbo lump crabmeat and herbs	$19.95
Dinner	www. ristorantedivino.com (2008)	Roasted stuffed double rack of Berkshire pork, roasted garlic mashed potatoes, and southern greens	$25.95
Lunch	www.villatronco.com (2008)	Baked Escolar and Eggplant Napoleon	$10.00
Lunch	www.villatronco.com (2008)	Lemon Pepper Chicken	$9.00
Red Snapper Meal	*Charlotte Observer* (NC) (2005)	Horseradish Encrusted Red Snapper at Renaissance Charlotte Suites Hotel	$17.95
Restaurant	*Boston Globe* (2005)	New Year's Eve Meal at Dolphin Seafood	$32.95/person
Restaurant	*Charlotte Observer* (NC) (2005)	Friday Night Special, Seafood Festival Buffet	$9.99

MEDICAL PRODUCTS AND SERVICES

Item	Source	Description	Price
Dentures	*Boston Globe* (2007)	Same day dentures with extractions; all insurance plans accepted	$199.00
Eye Surgery	*Atlanta Journal Constitution* (2006)	Lasik Surgery	$299.00
Laser Hair Removal	*Charlotte Observer* (NC) (2005)	Underarms	$300.00

Item	Source	Description	Price
Laser Hair Removal	*Charlotte Observer* (NC) (2005)	Bikini Line	$487.00
Laser Hair Removal	*Charlotte Observer* (NC) (2005)	Entire Body	$2,850.00

MOTORIZED VEHICLES, SUPPLIES AND SERVICES

Item	Source	Description	Price
Automobile	*Atlanta Journal Constitution* (2005)	2006 *Saturn* *0/t2; 140 IPSTFQPXFS; 2.2- MJUFS; DOHC engine; OnStar*dent resistant polymer panels; theft deterrent system	$13,530
Automobile	*Atlanta Journal Constitution* (2005)	2005 *Mitsubishi Galant;* power windows & locks; cruise; AM/FM/CD	$15,995
Automobile	*Atlanta Journal Constitution* (2005)	2005 *Honda Element;* 4WD; graphite interior	$20,990
Automobile	*Charlotte Observer* (NC) (2005)	2005 *Dodge Neon*	$19,949
Automobile	*Charlotte Observer* (NC) (2005)	2008 *GMC Yukon*	$28,800
Automobile	*Atlanta Journal Constitution* (2006)	2006 *Tacoma* with access cab	$17,920
Automobile	*Atlanta Journal Constitution* (2006)	2006 *VW Passat*	$24,655
Automobile	*Atlanta Journal Constitution* (2006)	2006 *VW Jetta*	$16,995
Tires	*Atlanta Journal Constitution* (2005)	*Harmony;* long mileage; excellent traction	$89.90
Tires	*Atlanta Journal Constitution* (2005)	All-Terrain T/A KO; light truck or SUV	$102.83
Tires	*Atlanta Journal Constitution* (2006)	*Goodyear* triple tread with 80,000 mile warranty	$89.00

MUSICAL INSTRUMENTS

Item	Source	Description	Price
Piano	*Atlanta Journal Constitution* (2005)	New grand piano	$5,990.00
Piano	*Atlanta Journal Constitution* (2005)	Digital piano	$1,799.00
Trumpet	www.kkmusicstore.com (2008)	*Cecilio* 2 Series gold lacquer finish Bb trumpet w/ Monel Valves	$189.99
Violin	www.audubon strings.com (2008)	*SNOW* professional violin *SIMONA* finished by William Hu of selected aged European tonewoods with spirit and oil varnish mix	$3,150.00

OTHER

Item	Source	Description	Price
Cemetery Lot	*Atlanta Journal Constitution* (2006)	2 tandem crypts in Sunrise Chapel on outside wall	$24,500
Cremation	*Atlanta Journal Constitution* (2005)	Direct cremations	$695.00
Hardwood Flooring	*Atlanta Journal Constitution* (2005)	Hardwood flooring	$0.99 sq. ft.

Item	Source	Description	Price
Portraits	*Charlotte Observer* (NC) (2005)	8" × 10"; 2- 5" × 7"; 4- 3" × 5"; 12 wallets	$19.95
Windows	*Atlanta Journal Constitution* (2005)	Any size installed	$189.00

PERSONAL CARE PRODUCTS

Item	Source	Description	Price
Back Massager	*Boston Globe* (2005)	Shiatsu back massager with 3 settings	$149.99
Day Spa	*Boston Globe* (2005)	Dayle's European Skin Care & Day Spa; ultrasound facial treatment; manicure; pedicure	$99.00
Electric Shaver	*Boston Globe* (2005)	Norelco speed XL shaver with 3 tracks and car charger	$129.99
Electric Toothbrush	*Boston Globe* (2005)	Sonicare electric toothbrush	$79.99
Moisturizer	*Boston Globe* (2007)	Pore minimizing skin refinisher, 1.0 oz.	$46.50
Perfume	*Atlanta Journal Constitution* (2005)	4.2 oz spray; Pure Turquoise by Ralph Lauren	$72.50
Toothpaste	*Rite Aid Flyer* (2008)	Crest toothpaste	$73.00
Vitamins	*Rite Aid Flyer* (2008)	Centrum Cardio vitamins	$2.49

PUBLICATIONS

Item	Source	Description	Price
Book	*Boston Globe* (2005)	Meet Mr. Cool with over 75 photos of Tom Brady; Game Summaries of 2001, 2003 & 2004 Super Bowl Seasons	$22.95
Book	*Atlanta Journal Constitution* (2006)	Strapped: Why America's 20 and 30 Somethings Can't Get Ahead by Tamara Draut; Doubleday; 288p	$22.95
Book	*Atlanta Journal Constitution* (2006)	Happiness: A History by Darrin M. McMahon; 560 p	$27.50
Book	*Atlanta Journal Constitution* (2006)	Cosmopolitanism: Ethics in a World of Strangers Kwame Anthony Appiah; W.W. Norton, 256p	$23.95
Book	*Boston Globe* (2007)	Armed Americans: Portraits of Gun Owners in Their Homes; photographs by Kyle Cassidy; 208p	$30.00
Book	*American Baby Magazine* (2008)	Autism Heroes	$35.00
Newspaper Subscription	*Boston Globe* (2007)	7-day subscriptions; 26 weeks; receive a $40.00 Dunkin Donuts card	$104.00

REAL ESTATE

Item	Source	Description	Price
Condominium	*Atlanta Journal Constitution* (2006)	2 swimming pools; granite countertops in kitchens and baths; covered parking; 24-hr fitness center; concierge 1 Bdrm 2 Bdrms 3 Bdrms	$140,000; $190,000; $220,000
Home	*Boston Globe* (2007)	Includes membership at country club with two 18 hole championship golf courses; private cabana club with oceanfront pool and white sand beach	$765,000

Item	Source	Description	Price
House	http://realestate.nytimes.com (2008)	Upper Eastside NYC in limestone mansion; five floors with an additional garden level and a full sub-basement comprising a total of approximately 21,000 1/2 sq ft.	$75,000,000
Loft	*Atlanta Journal Constitution* (2006)	20' ceilings; granite countertops; hardwood floors; stainless steel appliances; swimming pool with cabana; lighted tennis court; fitness center; on-site dry cleaning; wine tasting room	$209,000

SPORTS EQUIPMENT

Item	Source	Description	Price
Basketball Goal	www.sportsauthority.com (2008)	*Mammoth* 54" clear glass in ground basketball system	$1,199.99
Golf Club	*Boston Globe* (2007)	*TaylorMade;* Rac OS2 irons	$700.00
Paintball Gun	www.sportsauthority.com (2008)	*US Army Paintball Alpha Black Tactical Edition* paintball marker power pack	$169.99
Soccer Ball	www.sportsauthority.com (2008)	*Reusch* viper soccer ball	$19.99
Treadmill	*Atlanta Journal Constitution* (2005)	*Life Fitness* treadmill	$2,799.00
Wakeboard	www.sportsauthority.com (2008)	*World Industries* battle youth wakeboard (124cm)	$144.99

TELEPHONE EQUIPMENT AND SERVICES

Item	Source	Description	Price
Cell Phone	*Charlotte Observer* (NC) (2005)	Camera phone	$29.99
Cell Phone	*Charlotte Observer* (NC) (2005)	Camera phone with flash	$29.99
Cell Phone	*Charlotte Observer* (NC) (2005)	Office quality speaker phone	$49.99
Cell Phone	*Atlanta Journal Constitution* (2006)	*Samsung* X49; w/ music ringtones	$19.99
Cell Phone	*Atlanta Journal Constitution* (2006)	*Nokia* 6102 video camera phone	$29.99
Cell Phone	*Atlanta Journal Constitution* (2006)	A560 *Samsung;* full color display; SMS text messaging enabled; built in speaker phone	Free with contract
Cell Phone Plan	*Atlanta Journal Constitution* (2005)	*T-mobile,* 1,000 minutes	$39.99
Phone Plan	*Boston Globe* (2007)	*Verizon* FiOS TV, Internet and phone	$99.99/ month

TOBACCO PRODUCTS

Item	Source	Description	Price
Cigarettes	*Ingles Flyer* (2005)	*Marlboro* carton	$27.48
Cigarettes	*Ingles Flyer* (2005)	*Winston* carton	$23.98
Cigarettes	*Ingles Flyer* (2005)	*Camel* carton	$24.48

Item	Source	Description	Price
TOYS			
Pool Table	*Atlanta Journal Constitution* (2005)	Regulation slate pool table	$790.00
4 Wheeler	www.happyscooters.com (2008)	50CC ATV 4 Wheeler- QUAD with alarm system, remote start/stop; rear engine cut out valve	$579.95
Fire Truck	www.fatbraintoys.com (2008)	American retro classic pedal deluxe fire truck, true to the original 1940s classic fire engine ride-on toy	$318.00
Lightsaber	www.thinkgeek.com (2008)	Glowing blades with realistic power-up/down effects, authentic sound effects, durable metal hilt, sturdy blade that's permanently attached to the hilt, and custom-designed display stand	$119.99
TRAVEL AND TRANSPORTATIONS			
Airfare	*Atlanta Journal Constitution* (2006)	One way based on round-trip purchase from Atlanta to Maui, Hawaii	$259.00
Cruise	*Atlanta Journal Constitution* (2006)	Tahiti by *Gauguin*	$1,995

Paul Gauguin Cruises operates the luxury cruise ship, the Paul Gauguin, to Tahiti, French Polynesia and the South Pacific. (via Wikimedia Commons)

Item	Source	Description	Price
Getaway	*Atlanta Journal Constitution* (2005)	Garden Hotel, Historic Savanah; dinner and show package for two	$199.00
Getaway	*Atlanta Journal Constitution* (2005)	Crowne Plaza; Hilton Head Island Resort; three nights for the price of two Nightly rates: October November December	 $139.00 $119.00 $99.00
Getaway	*Atlanta Journal Constitution* (2005)	Cancun Mexico, Aquamarina Beach Hotel; five nights	$549.00
Getaway	*Atlanta Journal Constitution* (2005)	Atlantis, the Caribbean's largest casino with the world's largest open-air marine habitat; rates from Atlanta, 4 day/3 night resort package	$499
Resort	*Atlanta Journal Constitution* (2006)	Winter Escapes include air from Atlanta, oceanfront hotel 7 nights	$1,599.00
Spa Trip	*Atlanta Journal Constitution* (2005)	Tennessee Fitness Spa; one week, per person	$650.00

MISCELLANY 2005–2009

The Next Big Thing Is Us, by Lev Grossman

It goes against everybody's inner cynic to read (or for that matter to write) a sentence like the following: We are on the verge of the greatest age of creativity and innovation the world has ever known. It smacks of treacly dotcomism. It smacks of I Love the '90s. My inner cynic is a tiny bit queasy right now. But lately it's a conclusion I've had a hard time avoiding. Consider the following idea. Things, broadly speaking, used to be invented by a small, shadowy élite. This mysterious group might be called the People Who Happened to Be in the Room at the Time. These people might have been engineers, or sitcom writers, or chefs. They were probably very nice and might have even been very, very smart. But however smart they were, they're almost certainly no match for a less élite but much, much larger group: All the People Outside the Room.

Historically, that latter group hasn't had much to do with innovation. These people buy and consume whatever gets invented inside the room, but that's it. The arrow points just the one way. Until now it's been kind of awkward getting them involved in the innovation process at all, because they're not getting paid; plus it's a pain to set up the conference call.

But that's changing. The authorship of innovation is shifting from the Few to the Many. Take as an example something called the open-source movement. The basic idea is that while most soft-ware is produced by the aforementioned People in the Room, open-source software is offered to the entire world as a collaborative project. Somebody posts a piece of software on the Internet and then throws the joint wide open. It's like American Idol for software. In the open-source model, innovation comes from hundreds of thousands of people, not just a handful of engineers and a six-pack of Code Red. One open-source program, the truly excellent Web browser *Firefox*, has been downloaded 150 million times. *SourceForge.net* a website that coordinates open-source work, is currently host to almost 15,000 projects. Internet behemoth *AOL*, which shares a corporate parent with this magazine, open-sourced its instant-messaging service just last week.

The idea that lots of people, potentially everybody, can be involved in the process of innovation is both obvious and utterly transformative, and once you look for examples you start seeing them everywhere. When Apple launched iTunes and the iPod it had no idea that podcasting would be a big deal. It took the rest of us to tell Apple what its product was for. Companies as diverse as Lego, Ikea, and BMW are getting in on this action. And it exists in the cultural realm too. Look at websites like *YouTube*, or *Google Video*. Anybody anywhere can upload his or her little three-minute movies, and the best ones bubble to the top. Who knows what unheralded, unagented Soderbergh will come crawling out of that primordial tide pool? Granted, some of the movies are of people falling off jungle gyms. But some of them are brilliant. Some of them are both.

Two things make this kind of innovation possible, one obvious and one not. The obvious one is—say it with me—the Internet. The other one, the surprising one, is a curious phenomenon you could call intellectual altruism. It turns out that given the opportunity, people will donate their time and brainpower to make the world better. There's an online encyclopedia called *Wikipedia* written entirely by anonymous experts donating their expertise. It has the unevenness you'd expect from anything that's user-created and user-edited, but it's still the most useful reference resource anywhere on- or off-line; earlier this month *Wikipedia* posted its 1 millionth article.

You would think corporations would be falling all over themselves to make money off this new resource: a cheap R&D lab the approximate size of the earth's online population. In fact, they have been slow to embrace it. Admittedly, it's counterintuitive: until now the value of a piece of intellectual property has been defined by how few people possess it. In the future the value will be defined by how many people possess it. You could even imagine a future in which companies scrapped their R&D departments entirely and simply proposed questions for the global collective intelligence to mull. All that creative types like myself would have to do is sit back and harvest free, brilliant ideas from the brains of billions. Now that's an idea my inner cynic can get behind.

Time, March 20, 2006

MISCELLANY 2005-2009

With Ambitious Campaign, Obama Is Both Big Spender and Penny Pincher, by Michael Luo and Mike McIntire

Sen. Barack Obama's presidential campaign has collected a record shattering $640 million, but only two of his staff members are among the 15 highest paid workers in the general election, according to campaign finance records. The rest, including the three highest paid, are employed by Sen. John McCain.

The Obama campaign, despite having more than 700 field offices across the country, compared with 400 for Mr. McCain, has paid slightly less on rent than its counterpart.

And even though Mr. Obama has raised $400 million more than Mr. McCain, he has spent less on fund-raising consultants.

Mr. Obama has devoted enormous sums in this election to nearly everything, including more than $240 million for advertising and $31 million for the payroll. His half-hour primetime commercial on Wednesday (October 29), which cost more than $3 million, was perhaps the most visible flexing of his financial muscle.

The New York Times, October 31, 2008

Digital Mystery Tour: The Beatles First Video Game

If you've always bragged that you could play the drum part in "Helter-Skelter" better than Ringo Starr, you may soon get your chance to prove it in a video game based on the music of the Beatles.

The game developer Harmonix and the publisher MTV Games, creators of the music game Rock Band, announced in a conference

call on Thursday that they had entered into a partnership with the Beatles' Apple Corp. Ltd. to produce an interactive game that would offer players "an experimental journey" through the Fab four's music and history, according to Alex Rigopulos, chief executive of Harmonix. Paul McCartney and Mr. Starr, as well as Olivia Harrison and Yoko Ono, have approved the as-yet-untitled game. Giles Martin, son of the Beatles' producer, George Martin, will serve as the project's music producer.

The New York Times, October 31, 2008

Watch and Listen

Multitasking is increasingly second nature for young Americans, who consume a growing share of their media out of the corner of their eyes, or ears. A new study from the Kaiser Family Foundation surveyed students in grades seven through twelve on their media consumption habits, and found that 58 percent usually consumes some form of media while they read, another 63 percent typically multitask while listening to music, 62 percent usually do so while using the computer. The students surveyed were slightly less likely to multitask while watching television, which probably reflects the sheer amount of time the teenagers spend watching TV and DVDs. Overall, the teenagers surveyed spend more time watching (or half watching) television than they spent reading, writing e-mail, surfing the Internet, and playing video games combined.

The Atlantic, April 2007

Snail Mail 2.0 by Duncan Graham-Rowe

My eighth grader who has finished introductory geometry can tell you the shortest distance between two points is a line, but any postal worker who is hauled a mailbag along a 10 kilometer route can tell you that figuring out the shortest distance between 400 or more addresses is nearly impossible. Software aimed at doing just that recently made its commercial debut, in Denmark, with the hope of shortening mail delivery times and slashing postal service costs.

The software, developed by Paris-based company Eurobio, takes a novel approach to what is known as the "traveling salesman problem," which has stymied mathematicians for decades. The central challenge: adding a single new address multiplies the number of possible paths by the total number of addresses, so calculating an ideal route quickly becomes untenably time consuming. (At present, using a standard PC to compare every possible route spanning just 100 addresses would take years.) Computer scientists have developed various programs that solve the traveling salesman problem for limited research purposes. But according to Dave Cliff, a complexity expert at the Hewlett-Packard's Bristol laboratories in England, the vast scale of postal systems meant

MISCELLANY 2005-2009

that "until recently it wasn't worth looking at computer modeling methods, because the processing power wasn't there."

Technology Review, April 2005

Purple Heart Is Ruled Out for Traumatic Stress

The Pentagon has decided that it will not award the Purple Heart, the hallowed medal given to those wounded or killed by enemy action, to war veterans who suffer from posttraumatic stress disorder because it is not a physical wound.

The decision, made public on Tuesday, for now ends the hope of Iraq and Afghanistan veterans who have the condition and believed that the Purple Hearts could honor their sacrifice and help remove some of the stigma associated with the condition.

New York Times, January 7, 2009

United Airlines to Offer Wi-Fi on Its Premium Flights

Some friendly skies are about to become a Wi-Fi hot spot.

Passengers on selected transcontinental *United Airlines* flights soon will be able to check e-mail and surf the Web via their Wi-Fi-enabled laptops, BlackBerries and iPhones.

On Wednesday, United is expected to unveil plans to roll out its first broadband offering during the second half of this year. The project will involve 13 *Boeing* 757 jets used for p.s., the Chicago-based carrier's premium service for business travelers who trek from New York City to Los Angeles and San Francisco.

Chicago Tribune, January 14, 2009

2010–2014
New Beginnings

PRESIDENT

Barack H. Obama   2009–2016

2013 series one-dollar bill.

The second decade of the twenty-first century suffered from a massive hangover brought on by the Great Recession of 2008, when job losses went into freefall, the housing boom went bust, and credit virtually disappeared. Officially, the deepest economic crisis since the Great Depression ended in June 2009, yet its shadow lingered. Unemployment remained high, and underemployment for millions diminished the expectations of American families. To stimulate growth, Federal Reserve Chairman Ben Bernanke embarked on a round of asset purchases that kept borrowing rates low. Critics complained that he risked inducing high inflation and a rapid acceleration in prices. Although that didn't happen, the stimulus failed to quickly bring down unemployment. It was a jobless recovery. Surveys showed that half of those aged 45–75—the Baby Boomers—were being forced to delay retirement, thus decreasing the number of jobs available for the younger generation, who relied on technological innovation to create new jobs. By 2014 the recovery—though languid—was underway. The stock market established new, record highs, and the housing market was showing signs of improvement as new building permits and average home prices began to rise again. Consumer confidence, which propels spending, surged to the highest level in nearly six years. New car sales increased. The jobless rate, which had hit a high of 10 percent in Oc-

tober 2009, fell to below 8 percent amidst predictions of better times.

Despite the poor economy in 2012, incumbent President Barack Obama won reelection, proudly promoting the first-term passage of the Affordable Care Act, designed to make healthcare insurance available and affordable for all Americans. The new law drew the ire of the right wing of the Republican Party and was forced to survive three dozen repeal votes in the House of Representatives.

Politically, the decade will be recognized for the rapid rise and resilience of the Republican-based Tea Party movement, known for a no-compromise approach to a reduction in the national debt and federal budget deficit through dramatic cuts in government spending and taxes. Determined not to compromise to either the Republicans or the Democrats, Tea Party members held the government budget and debt ceiling hostage on several occasions, shutting down the federal government and placing the American debt rating in jeopardy. Frustrated by a divided government, Americans' approval rating of Congress plunged into the single digits.

The Occupy Movement spontaneously held national demonstrations to protest the shrinking middle class and the concentration of wealth in the top one percent of the nation's population. The first

Occupy protest to receive widespread attention was Occupy Wall Street in New York City's Zuccotti Park, which began on September 17, 2011. By October 9, Occupy protests had taken place or were ongoing in 600 communities in the United States. At the same time, extreme poverty in the nation, meaning households living on less than $2 per day before government benefits, doubled from 1996 levels to 1.5 million households in 2011, including 2.8 million children. The wealthiest 10 percent of the population possessed 80 percent of all financial assets.

Significant also were several self-appointed cyber watchdogs who exposed U.S. government secrets through massive data dumps via the Internet. Julian Assange of WikiLeaks was hailed as both a traitor and a hero when he released secret documents concerning the Iraq War and private diplomatic State Department cables. The releases ignited strong disapproval and condemnation from most world governments, which criticized WikiLeaks for potentially jeopardizing international relations and global security. A similar firestorm erupted in 2013 when Edward Snowden exposed the ongoing operational details about the U.S. National Security Agency's (NSA) global surveillance of foreign nationals and U.S. citizens. A significant portion of the full cache of 1.5 million documents was later published by media outlets worldwide. The disclosure provided impetus for the creation of social movements against mass surveillance, such as Restore the Fourth. The Electronic Frontier Foundation joined a coalition of diverse groups filing suit against the NSA. Several human rights organizations urged the Obama administration not to prosecute, but rather to protect, "whistleblower Snowden."

On the energy front, the United States became a leader in the production of natural gas by using a controversial water injection technique known as fracking. This brought the country greater energy independence, as did an expanded search for offshore oil. On April 20, 2010, a British Petroleum oilrig exploded in the Gulf of Mexico, giving the company the dubious distinction of causing the worst oil spill in U.S. history, surpassing the damage done by the Exxon Valdez tanker, which had spilled 11 million gallons of oil into the ecologically sensitive Prince William Sound in 1989. It is estimated that over 205 million gallons of oil were released into the Gulf.

Meanwhile, social media officially surpassed newspapers as a primary way for Americans to obtain news. By 2014, YouTube boasted one billion monthly users with four billion views per day; the number of Facebook users climbed to 1.11 billion; Twitter had 500 million registered users with more than 200 million active; and Apple's customers had downloaded over 50 billion apps as iPads were revolutionizing social games. Clearly, there was no turning back.

Year	Dollar Value in 2019
2010	$1.17
2011	$1.14
2012	$1.12
2013	$1.10
2014	$1.08

Use this Currency Conversion chart to calculate what any time in the years listed would cost in 2019. Simply multiply the cost of that item by dollar amount in the chart. For example, if you know that a Rolex watch cost $8,550.00 in 2010, multiply $8,550.00 by $1.17 to discover that that same watch would cost $10,003.50 in 2019.

HISTORICAL SNAPSHOT 2010-2014

2010

- Google was the target of a cyber attack from China
- The Supreme Court ruled that the First Amendment prohibits
- restrictions on independent political expenditures by corporations, associations, and unions
- In his first State of the Union Address, President Barack Obama emphasized the nation's economy, job creation, putting an end to the "Don't ask, don't tell" policy in the military, and restated his commitment for healthcare reform
- The Tea Party movement that had gained momentum in 2009 during the national healthcare debate hosted its first convention in Nashville, Tennessee
- In Super Bowl XLIV, the New Orleans Saints defeated the Indianapolis Colts 31–17 and won their first world championship
- In one of the largest environmental disasters in U.S. history, an explosion on the *Deepwater Horizon* oil rig killed 11 workers and caused a massive oil spill in the Gulf of Mexico
- China allowed the yuan to rise against the U.S. dollar after Congress threatened to penalize China unless it did so, causing widely imported Chinese goods to the United States to become more expensive and to raise demand for American goods
- Bans on texting while driving went into effect in half a dozen states
- Forty U.S. billionaires announced plans to give half of their wealth to charitable organizations

- Former Solicitor General Elena Kagan was sworn in as an Associate Justice of the Supreme Court
- The Medal of Honor was awarded for the first time since the Vietnam War to Army Staff Sergeant Salvatore Giunta for his actions during the War in Afghanistan
- Citing obesity concerns, the San Francisco Board of Supervisors banned Happy Meal toys served by McDonald's
- General Motors returned to trading on the New York Stock Exchange after declaring bankruptcy 16 months earlier
- The last U.S. combat troops left Iraq

2011

- Super Bowl XLV, won by the Green Bay Packers over the Pittsburgh Steelers 31–25, was the most watched television program in U.S. history, with 111 million viewers
- AOL purchased online publisher *The Huffington Post* in a $315 million deal
- At the 83rd Academy Awards, *The King's Speech* won four Oscars including the Academy Award for Best Picture
- Frank Buckles, America's last surviving World War I veteran and one of only three verified surviving veterans of the war worldwide, died at the age of 110
- When the Space Shuttle *Discovery* landed at the Shuttle Landing Facility in Florida on its final mission, the vehicle had clocked 365 days in orbit during its 27-year career

- Archaeologists found new artifacts in an archaeological site in Texas indicating human existence in America 15,500 years ago—about 2,000 years earlier than the benchmark Clovis culture
- In response to the Barack Obama citizenship conspiracy theories circulating that the president was not born in the United States, Obama released his original birth certificate
- Osama bin Laden, founder and leader of the militant Islamist group Al-Qaeda and America's most-wanted fugitive, was killed during an American military operation in Pakistan

- The Supreme Court ruled that warrantless searches do not violate the Fourth Amendment when it is believed that there is an "imminent destruction of evidence"
- Oprah Winfrey hosted the finale of her syndicated talk show, which was on the air for 25 years
- The Supreme Court ruled in a case involving Roche's HIV PCR test that inventors do not give up their patent rights to their employers if that employer received federal funding

729

♦ The Food and Drug Administration required new warning labels on cigarette packs featuring graphic images depicting the dangers of smoking

♦ The Bureau of Alcohol, Tobacco, Firearms, and Explosives (ATF) lost track of 1,400 guns involved in Operation Fast and Furious, aimed at tracing the flow of weapons to Mexican drug cartels

♦ The NFL Players Association unanimously accepted a 10-year pay deal with team owners in the National Football League (NFL)

♦ President Obama signed legislation to raise the debt ceiling to avert the 2011 debt ceiling crisis

♦ Google acquired Motorola Mobility

♦ In a court case concerning the theft of Kevlar-related trade secrets, DuPont was awarded $920 million in damages

♦ In the 63rd Primetime Emmy Awards, *Mad Men* won for Outstanding Drama and *Modern Family* for Outstanding Comedy

♦ The U.S. military officially ended its policy of "Don't ask, don't tell," allowing gay and lesbian personnel to publicly declare their sexual orientation

♦ The St. Louis Cardinals defeated the Texas Rangers in seven games to win their 11th World Series

2012

♦ Utah banned discounts or specials on alcoholic drinks, essentially eliminating the Happy Hour

♦ Arizona, Oregon, Washington, Montana, Colorado, Ohio, Vermont, and Florida raised their minimum wage; San Francisco raised its minimum wage to over $10 per hour, making it the highest in the country

♦ Classified documents were leaked detailing a range of advanced non-lethal weapons proposed or in development by the U.S. Armed Forces, including a laser-based weapon designed to divert hostile aircraft, an underwater sonic weapon for incapacitating SCUBA divers, and a heat-based weapon designed to compel crowds to disperse

♦ Two American scientists, Robert Lefkowitz and Brian Kobilka, won the 2012 Nobel Prize in Chemistry for their research on discovering the inner workings of G protein-coupled receptors

♦ Trayvon Martin, an unarmed black 17-year-old, was fatally shot by George Zimmerman in Sanford, Florida, igniting a nationwide debate over racism in the United States

♦ Kodak filed for bankruptcy protection

♦ The Kellogg Company purchased snack maker Pringles from Procter &Gamble for $2.7 billion

♦ The Supreme Court decided that law enforcement officials did not need to issue Miranda warnings to prison inmates under questioning if these inmates were warned that they may end the interrogation at any time

♦ *The Artist* won five Academy Awards, including Best Picture, the first silent film to win the award since *Wings* in 1927

♦ The *Encyclopædia Britannica*, the oldest encyclopedia still in print in the English language, announced that it would no longer be producing printed versions but continuing online editions

♦ The University of Kentucky defeated the University of Kansas to win the 2012 NCAA Men's Division I Basketball Tournament

♦ The Supreme Court ruled 5–4 that law enforcement officials can strip-search newly admitted jail inmates even if the holding charge is minor

♦ Shakeel Afridi, a Pakistani physician who helped the CIA track down Osama bin Laden by collecting DNA samples from residents of bin Laden's compound, was sentenced to 33 years' imprisonment for treason

♦ Arizona defeated South Carolina to win its first College World Series title since 1986 and fourth overall

♦ In a 5–4 decision, the Supreme Court upheld the Patient Protection and Affordable Care Act as constitutional under the taxing and spending clause

♦ A California jury ruled that Samsung Electronics owed Apple Inc. over $1 billion for patent infringement

♦ Felix Baumgartner broke the world human ascent by balloon record before space diving out of the *Red Bull Stratos* helium-filled balloon over Roswell, New Mexico

♦ *Newsweek* announced it would cease print publication and move to an online-only format

♦ Hostess Brands, maker of Twinkies, filed for bankruptcy, stating that a bakery union's worker strike stemming from contract disputes "crippled" its operations

♦ Texas A&M University quarterback Johnny Manziel became the first freshman ever to win the Heisman Trophy as the most outstanding player in U.S. college football

2013

- Cyclist Lance Armstrong admitted to doping during his interview with Oprah Winfrey
- Secretary of Defense Leon Panetta lifted the ban on women serving in combat
- Dell went private after a $24 billion leveraged buyout deal with a consortium led by founder Michael Dell
- The U.S. Post Office announced plans to end first-class mail delivery on Saturdays
- US Airways and the bankrupt American Airlines announced a merger to form the world's largest air carrier, trading as American Airlines
- Berkshire Hathaway and 3G Capital bought H.J. Heinz for $28 billion
- With his portrayal of the title character in *Lincoln*, Daniel Day-Lewis became the only actor to have won the Academy Award for Best Actor three times
- Private First Class (PFC) Bradley Manning pled guilty to 10 counts out of 22 against him for leaking classified material to WikiLeaks
- Google agreed to pay a $7 million penalty to settle an investigation into the collection of emails, passwords, and other sensitive information sent over wireless networks from 2007–2010 in the United States
- Qari Abdul Saeed was arrested in Pakistan for the 2002 beheading of *Wall Street Journal* reporter Daniel Pearl
- A study published in the *Journal of Pediatrics* asserted that there is no scientific evidence of a link between vaccines and autism
- Thirty-five teachers and administrators from Atlanta, Georgia, were indicted on fraud charges for facilitating cheating on standardized tests dating back to 2001

- Two explosions near the finish line of the Boston Marathon left three people dead and 260 injured

- The Boy Scouts of America lifted its longstanding ban on gay youth members
- The Supreme Court ruled that naturally occurring human genes may not be patented, with significant implications for future medical research
- In a 5–4 decision, the Supreme Court struck down Section 4 of the Voting Rights Act of 1965, which had required states with a history of discrimination to get permission from the federal government to change their election procedures in any way
- At the 65th Primetime Emmy Awards, *Breaking Bad* won for Outstanding Drama and *Modern Family* for Outstanding Comedy
- The shutdown of the federal government by opponents of the Affordable Care Act resulted in the furloughing of hundreds of thousands of federal government workers and represented a major threat to the U.S. economy
- In Major League baseball, the Boston Red Sox won the World Series, defeating the St. Louis Cardinals in the first series to be won in Boston by the Red Sox since 1918

2014

- Numerous provisions of the Patient Protection and Affordable Care Act, popularly referred to as Obamacare, go into effect
- Colorado and Washington states allow the sale of recreational cannabis from legally licensed businesses
- The 2014 North American polar vortex breaks coldest temperature records throughout the country
- The cost of first-class mail stamps increases to $0.49
- The Seattle Seahawks win their first Superbowl
- President Obama raises minimum wage for federal contract workers to $10.10
- *12 Years a Slave* wins Best Picture at the 86th Academy Awards
- Flint, Michigan, switches its water source to the Flint River, beginning the ongoing Flint water crisis, which has caused lead poisoning in up to 12,000 people
- The West Africa Ebola outbreak kills American health worker Patrick Sawyer, causing panic in the country
- A policeman kills unarmed 18-year-old African American Michael Brown in Ferguson, Missouri, leading to both peaceful protests and riots
- Academy Award-winning actor Robin Williams commits suicide at his home at the age of 63
- The largest earthquake to hit San Francisco since 1989 registers a 6.0 magnitude and injures 120 people

- ISIS militants in Iraq behead several American journalists in response to airstrike campaigns
- The US Department of Labor announces that the unemployment rate is the lowest since 2008 at 5.6%
- The Supreme Court decides not to hear cases on same-sex marriage appeals, thus immediately legalizing same-sex marriage in 5 states
- The new One World Trade Center opens in New York City

- Actor and comedian Bill Cosby accused of sexual assault by at least 26 women
- Protests erupt in New York City after the officers who killed Eric Garner, and unarmed African American, is not indicted
- Senate Democrat release a highly redacted report showing CIA interrogation methods to be inhumane and largely ineffective
- President Obama announces the end of the US's embargo against Cuba, the first time since 1961

- The United States and United Kingdom officially withdraw their troops from Afghanistan
- American poet Maya Angelou dies at the age of 86

In 2013, the Black Lives Matter movement began on social media after the acquittal of George Zimmerman in the shooting death of African-American teen Trayvon Martin in February 2012. Black Lives Matter became nationally recognized for its street demonstrations following the 2014 deaths of two African Americans: Michael Brown—resulting in protests and unrest in Ferguson, Missouri—and Eric Garner in New York City. A protester is holding a sign with the names of other African American men killed by police. (via Wikimedia commons)

SELECTED INCOME 2010-2014

Job	Source	Description	Pay
Accounting Manager	jobs.aol.com/listings	Landform of Central Florida, Inc,	$40,000
Activity Aide, Nursing Home	houston.salary.com (2014)	Rochester, NY	$24,209
Actuary	payscale.com (2013)	South Atlantic U.S. Region	$58,800–$99,283
Administrative Assistant	aol.careerbuilder.com (2013)	Fresno, CA	$12,000–$20,000
Air Traffic Controller	bls.gov (2012)		$117,200
Airline Pilot	careerprofiles.info (2012)		$141,100
Alumni Relations Officer	chron.com (2014)	Hartford, CT	$47,931
Ambulance Driver	bls.gov (2012)		$40,380
Anesthesiologist	cnn.com (2010)		$292,000
Animal Control Worker	bls.gov (2012)		$31,680
Animal Obedience Trainer	www.bls.gov/oes/current (2012)	Philadelphia, PA	$27,990
Appraiser, Residential	houston.salary.com (2014)	Little Rock, AR	$40,492
Architect	careerprofiles.info (2012)		$64,200
Art Director	designsalaries.aiga.org (2011)	Salt Lake City, UT: Advertising, marketing, PR	$72,500
Art Director	www.bls.gov/oes/current (2013)		$94,260
Assistant Buyer, Retail	jobstat.net (2011)		$41,255
Assistant Director of Accounting	jobs.aol.com/listings (2013)	Florida A&M University	$60,000
Assistant Manager	www.glassdoor.com (2013)	Walgreens	$39,000
Automotive Mechanic	usnews.com (2011)		$36,180
Bailiff	careerprofiles.info (2010)		$32,690
Bank Teller	glassdoor.com (2012)		$11.43 per hr
Bilingual Caseworker	aol.careerbuilder.com (2013)	Dover, DE	$30,000
Bill and Account Collector	bls.gov (2012)		$35,420
Bingo Caller	chron.com (2014)	Los Angeles, CA	$23,697
Budget Analyst	bls.gov (2012)		$78,170
Bursar	chron.com (2014)	Columbia, SC	$62,712
Bus Driver	usnews.com (2011)		$35,720
Business Analyst	www.glassdoor.com (2013)	Electronic Data Systems	$54,000
Cannery Worker	houston.salary.com (2014)	New Orleans, LA	$25,314
Carpenter	jobsradar.com (2012)	Carpenter in Queens, NY	$13–$20 per hr
Case Worker, Home Care	houston.salary.com (2014)	Detroit, MI	$41,309
Cashier	careerprofiles.info (2012)		$16,800
Children's Caseworker	aol.careerbuilder.com (2013)	Philadelphia, PA	$25,000–$29,000
Chiropractor	houston.salary.com (2014)	Cambridge, MA	$145,550
City Legislator	www.bls.gov/oes/current (2012)	St. Louis, MO	$24,390
Claims Adjuster	www.glassdoor.com (2013)	Progressive Insurance	$44,000
Coatroom Attendant	www.bls.gov/oes/current (2012)	Chicago, IL	$20,570

Job	Source	Description	Pay
Computer and Information Systems Manager	careerprofiles.info (2012)		$94,000
Computer Programmer	careerprofiles.info (2012)		$65,500
Construction Worker	bls.gov (2010)		$26,300
Crane and Tower Operator	bls.gov (2012)		$65,760
Crossing Guard	careerprofiles.info (2012)		$21,100
Customer Service Worker	jobs.aol.com/listings (2013)	Walmart	$8.00 per hr
Day Care Center Teacher	chron.com (2014)	Detroit, MI	$27,462
Dietician	chron.com (2014)	Providence, RI	$57,781
Driver	www.glassdoor.com (2013)	UPS	$74,000
Electrician	usnews.com (2011)		$84,240
Embalmer	www.bls.gov/oes/current (2012)	Fort Lauderdale, FL	$44,010
Engineer	www.glassdoor.com	Exxon Mobil	$97,000
Executive Chef	salary.com (2013)	New York City	$80,663
Fast Food Worker	jobs.aol.com/salaries (2013)	McDonald's	$8.25 per hr
Federal Air Marshal	careerprofiles.info (2010)		$84,739
Firefighter	bls.gov (2012)		$55,200
Fish and Game Warden	careerprofiles.info (2011)		$42,000
Flight Attendant	houston.salary.com (2014)	Juneau, AK	$75,487
Forest and Conservation Worker	careerprofiles.info (2011)		$20,800
Forklift Operator	jobs.aol.com/listings (2013)	Dayton, NJ	$11.50 per hr
Foundry Worker	houston.salary.com (2014)	New Orleans, LA	$31,066
Funeral Director	bls.gov (2011)		$61,460
Ghostwriter	careerprofiles.info (2011)		$61,000
Graphic Designer	careerprofiles.info (2010)		$39,900
Hairstylist	salary.com (2012)		$24,255
Hazardous Materials Removal Worker, Mfg.	recruiter.com (2010)		$44,880
Heart transplant surgeon	salary.com	San Francisco, CA	$627,299
High School Coach	www.bls.gov/oes/current (2012)	Chicago-Joliet-Naperville, IL	$32,290
High School Teacher	payscale.com (2013)	Columbus, Ohio	$35,000–$51,500
Highway Maintenance Worker	recruiter.com (2012)		$30,000
Hotel, Motel, and Resort Desk Clerk	bls.gov (2012)		$25,520
Housekeeper, Hotel	houston.salary.com (2014)	Atlanta, GA	$22,552
Insurance Agent	careerprofiles.info (2012)		$43,900
Interior Design Sales Consultant	aol.careerbuilder.com (2013)	Ethan Allen, Hartsdale, NY	$45,000–$100,000
Janitor	usnews.com (2011)		$22,370
Labor Relations Director	houston.salary.com (2014)	Hartford, CT	$141,304
Lawyer	cnn.com (2010)		$115,000
Legal Secretary	indeed.com (2012)	Commercial corporate legal secretary in Boston, MA	$66,000
Librarian	careerprofiles.info (2012)		$51,400

Job	Source	Description	Pay
Lifeguard	careerprofiles.info (2012)		$17,200
Locksmith	bls.gov (2012)		$32,000
Logging Worker	vocationary.com (2012)		$30,720
Mail Carrier	www.glassdoor.com (2013)	US Postal Service	$51,000
Maintenance Housekeeping	usnews.com (2011)		$19,390
Major League Umpire	chron.com (2012)		$120,000–$350,000
Market Researcher	houston.salary.com (2014)	Richmond, VA	$49,317
Mathematician	careerprofiles.info (2011)		$86,900
Medical Social Worker	houston.salary.com (2014)	Tampa, FL	$48,642
Meeting and Event Planner	houston.salary.com (2014)	Richmond, VA	$56,005
Middle School Teacher	careerprofiles.info (2012)		$46,300
Mortgage Document Imaging Specialist	aol.careerbuilder.com (2013)	Eagan, MN	$12.00 per hr
Mover	www.bls.gov/oes/current (2012)	Nashville, TN	$28,340
Multimedia Artist	www.bls.gov/oes/current (2012)	Seattle-Bellevue-Everett, WA	$68,980
Museum Research Worker	houston.salary.com (2014)	Boston, MA	$53,737
Nanny	aol.careerbuilder.com (2013)	Full-time, live-out, NJ	$500–$900 per wk
Paralegal	cnn.com (2010)		$65,600
Paramedic	chron.com (2014)	Oklahoma City, OK	$36,731
Pharmacist	www.glassdoor.com (2013)	Walgreens	$116,000
Pharmacy Technician	www.glassdoor.com (2013)	CVS Caremark	$10.00 per hr
Plumber	usnews.com (2011)		$47,750
Postdoctoral Fellow	jobs.aol.com/articles (2013)	National Institutes of Health (NIH)	$45,000
Probation Officer	www.bls.gov/oes/current (2012)	Houston, TX	$40,480
Program Manager	www.glassdoor.com (2013)	Expedia	$91,000
Project Manager	www.glassdoor.com	Hewlett-Packard	$95,000
Psychiatrist	cnn.com (2010)		$177,000
Radio Announcer	www.bls.gov/oes/current (2012)	Atlanta-Sandy Springs-Marietta, GA	$59,290
Ranch Manager	houston.salary.com (2014)	Helena, MT	$31,564
Refuse and Recyclable Materials Collector	chron.com (2012)		$34,420
Registered Nurse	careerprofiles.info (2011)		$60,400
Reporter	www.bls.gov/oes/current (2012)	Philadelphia, PA	$37,050
Research Fellow	Queensland Brain Institute (2012)	Applicants must hold a PhD in a relevant field and have extensive post-doctoral experience with demonstrated evidence of research productivity	$81,857
Restaurant Cook	usnews.com (2011)		$22,080
Sailor	recruiter.com (2010)		$38,370
Security Guard	usnews.com (2011)		$23,900
Security Officer	jobs.aol.com/listings (2013)	Securities US, Boulder, CO	$10.00–$12.00 per hr

Job	Source	Description	Pay
Service Station Attendant	chron.com (2014)	Phoenix, AZ	$20,222
Social Worker	careerprofiles.info (2012)		$37,500
Speech and Language Pathologist	chron.com (2014)	Providence, RI	$74,765
Speech Writer, Government	chron.com (2014)	Washington, DC	$122,437
Stagehand	jobs.aol.com/listings (2013)	Carnegie Hall, NY	$420,000
Stock Clerk	bls.gov (2012)		$26,310
Stonemason	usnews.com (2011)		$50,760
Store General Manager	aol.careerbuilder.com (2013)	McAlister's Deli, Dayton, OH	$45,000
Tailor	salary.com (2012)		$27,118
Tax Preparer	bls.gov (2012)		$33,730
Taxi Driver	careerprofiles.info (2012)		$20,400
Technical Writer	cnn.com (2010)		$67,400
Telemarketer	recruiter.com (2012)	Boston, MA	$34,140
Teller	www.glassdoor.com (2013)	Wells Fargo	$11.00 per hr
Town Manager	wickedlocal.com (2010)	Concord, MA	$158,000
Translator	usnews.com (2011)		$44,160
Translator	www.bls.gov/oes/current (2012)	Boston-Cambridge-Quincy, MA	$63,510
TSA Screener	careerprofiles.info (2010)		$28,000
Upholsterer	indeed.com (2012)		$28,000
Urban and Regional Planner	cnn.com (2010)		$66,200
Usher/Ticket Taker	houston.salary.com (2014)	Denver, CO	$18,492
Veterinarian	cnn.com (2010)		$83,900
Vice President	www.glassdoor.com (2013)	Merrill Lynch	$120,000
Video Editor	www.bls.gov/oes/current (2012)	Washington-Arlington-Alexandria, DC-VA-MD-WV	$76,870
Warehouse Associate	aol.careerbuilder.com (2013)	Aerotek Louisville, KY	$11.40 per hr

CONSUMER EXPENDITURES 2010-2014

(Per Person)

Expenditure Type	2010	2011	2012	2013	2014
Food	$3,450	$3,638	$3,497	$3,654	$3,637
Food at home	$1,877	$2,072	$1,964	$2,126	$2,101
Food away from home	$1,573	$1,567	$1,533	$1,528	$1,536
Alcoholic beverages	$322	$370	$344	$339	$322
Housing	$11,223	$11,456	$11,532	$11,751	$12,348
Shelter	$7,246	$7,176	$7,437	$7,530	$8,057
Owned dwellings	$3,477	$3,438	$3,412	$3,384	$3,600
Rented dwellings	$3,404	$3,443	$3,715	$3,837	$4,098
Utilities, fuels, and public services	$2,331	$2,380	$2,291	$2,341	$2,448
Natural gas	$292	$284	$229	$260	$280
Electricity	$906	$927	$903	$939	$974
Telephone services	$720	$745	$736	$735	$746
Water and other public services	$307	$311	$326	$310	$336
Apparel and services	$804	$1,021	$865	$861	$802
Transportation	$4,011	$4,367	$4,599	$4,952	$4,617
Vehicle purchases (net outlay)	$1,036	$1,235	$1,377	$1,592	$1,470
Cars and trucks, new	$481	$582	$653	$705	$612
Cars and trucks, used	$516	$629	$713	$847	$825
Gasoline and motor oil	$1,164	$1,399	$1,420	$1,373	$1,300
Other vehicle expenses	$1,495	$1,418	$1,472	$1,676	$1,510
Maintenance and repairs	$483	$500	$525	$529	$515
Public and other transportation	$316	$316	$330	$311	$337
Healthcare	$2,027	$2,112	$2,339	$2,375	$2,517
Entertainment	$1,441	$1,522	$1,485	$1,547	$1,622
Personal care products and services	$360	$388	$380	$360	$400
Reading	$81	$90	$83	$74	$71
Education	$600	$782	$675	$643	$849
Tobacco products and smoking supplies	$268	$255	$251	$244	$232
Cash contributions	$1,242	$1,446	$1,484	$1,382	$1,428
Personal insurance and pensions	$2,570	$2,588	$2,535	$2,558	$2,540
Miscellaneous	$752	$577	$647	$509	$602
Total average annual expenditures	**$29,149**	**$30,613**	**$30,716**	**$31,248**	**$31,987**

Expenditure Type	2010	2011	2012	2013	2014
Personal taxes					
Money income before taxes	$32,979	$34,540	$34,102	$32,292	$33,487
Personal taxes	$1,117	$1,378	$1,546	$3,838	$4,397
Federal income taxes	$730	$998	$1,114	$3,085	$3,512
State and local income taxes	$291	$293	$346	$715	$821
Other taxes	$97	$87	$86	$38	$65
Income after taxes	**$31,862**	**$33,162**	**$32,556**	**$28,455**	**$29,090**

Source: U.S. Department of Labor, Bureau of Labor Statistics, Consumer Expenditure Surveys 2008–2014 (Table 4. Size of consumer unit: Average annual expenditures and characteristics)

INVESTMENTS 2010–2014

Investment	2010	2011	2012	2013	2014
Moody's Yield Seasoned Corp Bonds AllIndustries AAA	5.01	3.93	3.65	4.99	4.75
90-Day AA Nonfinancial Commercial Paper Int Rate	0.24	0.17	0.19	0.10	0.09
Federal Funds Effective Rate	0.18	0.1	0.14	0.10	0.09
Bank Prime Loan Rate	3.25	3.25	3.25	3.25	3.25
Certificate of Deposit—6-Month Rate	0.44	0.42	0.44	0.25	
US Treasury Note—10-Year	3.22	2.78	1.8	2.13	2.53
Mortgage Rate—30-Year Fixed	4.69	4.46	3.66	3.91	4.13
S&P 500 Index—Price	1257.64	1257.6	1426.19	1,611	1,934
S&P 500 Index—Dividend Yield	1.84	2.12	2.18	1.94	1.92

STOCK PRICES AND DIVIDENDS

	2010	2011	2012	2013	2014
AT&T (T)	25.02	27.27	32.04	35.40	35.23
Dividends	0.42	0.43	0.44	0.45	0.46
Bank of America (BAC)	13.18	5.52	11.58	12.95	15.31
Dividends	0.01	0.01	0.01	0.01	0.01
Boeing (BA)	61.21	70.48	74.16	103.22	127.66
Dividends	0.42	0.42	0.44	0.485	0.73
General Electric (GE)	16.68	16.9	20.5	22.32	25.26
Dividends	0.12	0.15	0.17	0.19	0.22
General Motors (GM)	36.86	20.27	28.83	33.52	36.25
Dividends	0	0	0	0	0.3
Kellogg Co. (K)	46.84	47.86	54.65	440.36	575.16
Dividends	0.4	0.43	0.44	0	0
Microsoft (MSFT)	25.86	24.69	26.12	64.03	65.48
Dividends	0.16	0.2	0.23	0.44	0.46
Pfizer	15.77	20.31	24.46	34.41	41.86
Dividends	0.18	0.2	0.22	0.23	0.28
Navistar International Corp. (NAV)	57.91	37.88	21.77	28.00	37.65
Dividends	0	0	0	0	0
Procter & Gamble Co. (PG)	58.46	62.58	65.84	27.97	29.61
Dividends	0.48	0.53	0.56	0.24	0.26
Reynolds American Inc. RAI	28.05	37.7	39.81	77.02	78.87
Dividends	0.45	0.53	0.59	0.6015	0.6436
United States Steel Co. (X)	57.22	26.05	23.67	24.44	30.31
Dividends	0.05	0.05	0.05	0	0
Wal-Mart (WMT)	50.29	57.25	66.98	74.99	75.27
Dividends	0.3	0.36	0.39	0.47	0.48

Investment	2010	2011	2012	2013	2014
Yahoo (YHOO)	16.63	16.13	19.9	17.67	26.32
Dividends	0	0	0	0.05	0.05

STANDARD JOBS 2010–2014

Based on NAICS Codes	NAICS	2010	2011	2012	2014
Total, all industries	10	$46,751	$48,043	$49,289	$51,364
Total, all private industries		$46,455	$47,815	$49,200	$51,296
Federal government		$69,198	$73,001	$73,340	$75,797
State government		$48,960	$50,252	$51,366	$54,179
Local government		$43,493	$43,926	$44,373	$46,155
Bituminous coal underground mining	2121112	$80,990	$84,698	$83,625	$87,643
Construction	1012/23	$49,597	$50,693	$52,298	$55,037
Private households (domestics)	814	$17,462	$16,917	$15,264	$23,117
Crop production	111	$25,109	$25,988	$27,160	$29,191
Finance and insurance	52	$84,518	$88,292	$91,218	$97,380
Wholesale Trade	42	$63,629	$66,142	$68,226	$71,043
Retail trade	44–45	$26,652	$27,118	$27,731	$28,742
Electric, gas, and sanitary services	221	$86,791	$90,609	$93,722	$98,123
Elementary and secondary schools	6111	$35,196	$35,927	$36,680	$38,409
Manufacturing	31–33	$57,526	$59,210	$60,496	$63,976
Postal Service	491	$28,095	$28,875	$28,619	$28,900
Telecommunications	517	$72,207	$75,024	$77,391	$80,632
Radio and television broadcasting	5151	$65,878	$67,792	$70,926	$75,882
Motion picture and video	5121	$59,175	$61,319	$63,435	$66,603
Health care and social assistance	621	$54,143	$54,832	$55,995	$45,857
Membership associations and organizations	813	$35,410	$36,061	$37,221	$39,531
Rail transportation	4821	$40,700	$47,186	$44,537	$48,915
Transit and ground passenger transportation	485	$25,596	$26,133	$26,653	$27,418

Source: Bureau of Labor Statistics

741

FOOD BASKET 2010–2014

Commodity	Year	U.S. Average	Atlanta	Chicago	Denver	Los Angeles	New York
Bananas, per lb.	2010	56¢	59¢	71¢	49¢	67¢	85¢
	2011	59¢	62¢	70¢	55¢	71¢	86¢
	2012	59¢	63¢	61¢	51¢	70¢	86¢
	2013	58¢	60¢	52¢	54¢	69¢	87¢
	2014	58¢	61¢	48¢	56¢	69¢	60
Beef, Ground, per lb.	2010	$2.70	$2.44	$2.73	$2.50	$2.75	$3.59
	2011	$3.03	$3.63	$2.63	$2.81	$3.10	$3.97
	2012	$3.38	$3.81	$3.68	$3.07	$3.71	$4.65
	2013	$3.52	$3.89	$3.28	$3.52	$3.61	$4.39
	2014	$3.77	$3.84	$4.22	$4.99	$3.91	$4.18
Bread, white, per loaf	2010	$1.39	$1.29	$1.54	$1.47	$1.41	$2.28
	2011	$1.41	$1.63	$1.50	$1.66	$1.54	$2.26
	2012	$1.48	$1.76	$1.63	$1.44	$1.50	$2.40
	2013	$1.49	$1.68	$1.46	$1.50	$1.47	$2.49
	2014	$1.50	$1.64	$1.49	$1.49	$1.42	$2.38
Cereal, Corn Flakes, 18 oz.	2010	$3.41	$3.37	$4.27	$3.40	$3.44	$5.38
	2011	$3.51	$3.83	$4.15	$3.63	$3.81	$5.01
	2012	$3.57	$3.80	$3.39	$3.21	$4.02	$5.08
	2013	$3.49	$3.25	$3.63	$3.60	$3.91	$5.48
	2014	$3.42	$3.49	$3.19	$3.47	$4.09	$5.32
Cheese, grated Parmesan, 8 oz.	2010	$3.84	$3.22	$4.97	$4.37	$4.98	$5.82
	2011	$3.75	$3.32	$4.87	$4.41	$4.89	$6.84
	2012	$3.89	$3.87	$4.77	$4.04	$4.49	$6.82
	2013	$3.80	$3.89	$4.06	$3.86	$4.44	$6.47
	2014	$3.82	$3.88	$4.07	$4.19	$4.71	$7.32
Chicken, whole uncut, per lb.	2010	$1.16	$1.17	$1.16	$1.08	$1.17	$1.77
	2011	$1.18	$1.16	$1.33	$1.16	$1.16	$1.78
	2012	$1.22	$1.37	$1.30	$1.20	$1.06	$1.88
	2013	$1.26	$1.09	$1.48	$1.32	$1.48	$1.83
	2014	$1.35	$1.26	$1.54	$1.35	$1.53	$1.47
Coca-Cola, 2 liter	2010	$1.48	$1.01	$1.52	$1.41	$1.49	$2.00
	2011	$1.53	$1.81	$1.67	$1.48	$1.63	$2.10
	2012	$1.56	$1.73	$1.68	$1.36	$1.68	$2.00
	2013	$1.56	$1.55	$1.90	$1.58	$1.71	$2.07
	2014	$1.56	$1.61	$1.89	$1.51	$1.76	$2.00
Coffee, vacuum-packed, 11.5 oz.	2010	$3.66	$3.49	$4.81	$4.94	$4.84	$5.82
	2011	$4.41	$4.30	$5.57	$5.18	$5.55	$5.85
	2012	$4.76	$5.11	$6.32	$5.71	$6.09	$5.65
	2013	$4.26	$4.93	$5.86	$5.11	$5.56	$6.14
	2014	$4.15	$4.85	$5.43	$5.13	$5.09	$6.06
Corn, whole kernel frozen, 16 oz.	2010	$1.40	$1.20	$1.40	$1.85	$1.57	$2.51
	2011	$1.38	$1.38	$1.56	$1.72	$1.62	$1.96
	2012	$1.44	$1.57	$1.77	$1.45	$1.53	$2.34
	2013	$1.36	$1.70	$2.07	$1.61	$1.65	$2.20
	2014	$1.34	$1.17	$1.86	$1.89	$1.67	$1.78
Eggs, 1 dozen grade A or AA, large	2010	$1.47	$1.16	$1.35	$1.25	$1.97	$2.67
	2011	$1.66	$1.65	$1.72	$1.71	$2.28	$2.55
	2012	$1.74	$1.81	$2.16	$1.63	$2.09	$2.71
	2013	$1.74	$1.66	$1.84	$1.89	$2.21	$2.89
	2014	$1.93	$1.80	$1.87	$2.10	$2.46	$2.83

Commodity	Year	U.S. Average	Atlanta	Chicago	Denver	Los Angeles	New York
Lettuce, iceberg head (approx. 1 1/4 lb.)	2010	$1.37	$1.45	$1.14	$1.17	$1.14	$2.16
	2011	$1.38	$1.51	$1.57	$1.44	$1.34	$2.42
	2012	$1.33	$1.36	$1.30	$1.28	$1.28	$2.28
	2013	$1.37	$1.59	$1.67	$1.47	$1.31	$2.10
	2014	$1.38	$1.43	$1.26	$1.42	$1.21	$1.83
Margarine, 1 lb., stick form	2010	93¢	78¢	$1.38	98¢	$1.02	$1.95
	2011	97¢	73¢	$1.20	$1.03	$1.06	$1.87
	2012	$1.06	$1.05	$1.12	96¢	$1.29	$2.01
	2013	$1.01	83¢	$1.10	$1.06	$1.11	$1.91
	2014	$1.01	$1.17	$1.03	98¢	$1.01	$1.93
Milk, whole, 1/2 gallon	2010	$2.02	$1.75	$2.25	$1.74	$2.01	$2.47
	2011	$2.22	$2.12	$2.67	$1.87	$2.18	$2.26
	2012	$2.27	$2.09	$2.51	$2.09	$2.20	$2.34
	2013	$2.31	$2.22	$2.11	$1.98	$2.22	$2.23
	2014	$2.40	$2.45	$1.93	$2.05	$2.51	$2.13
Orange juice, fresh, 64 oz.	2010	$3.08	$3.18	$3.13	$2.85	$3.16	$4.94
	2011	$3.20	$3.35	$3.46	$3.08	$3.26	$4.60
	2012	$3.36	$3.94	$3.65	$3.23	$3.25	$4.38
	2013	$3.42	$3.41	$3.72	$3.84	$3.50	$4.11
	2014	$3.39	$3.48	$3.88	$3.66	$3.20	$4.19
Peas, sweet, 15 oz. can	2010	$1.07	$1.08	$1.17	95¢	$1.07	$1.58
	2011	$1.06	$1.05	$1.30	$1.05	$1.15	$1.65
	2012	$1.15	$1.19	$1.49	90¢	$1.61	$1.70
	2013	$1.15	$1.10	$1.26	95¢	$1.58	$1.82
	2014	$1.12	$1.38	$1.20	$1.11	$1.20	$1.71
Potatoes, 10 lb. sack, white or red	2010	$2.80	$4.45	$3.36	$2.39	$2.59	$4.67
	2011	$3.04	$3.79	$3.08	$3.05	$3.36	$3.72
	2012	$3.07	$3.79	$3.31	$2.42	$3.32	$3.79
	2013	$3.00	$3.74	$2.56	$2.24	$2.30	$4.88
	2014	$3.09	$3.78	$2.55	$2.51	$2.82	$4.65
Sausage, pork, 1 lb.	2010	$3.38	$3.19	$3.42	$3.71	$4.12	$4.35
	2011	NR	NR	NR	NR	NR	NR
	2012	$3.83	$4.35	$4.76	$3.45	$4.60	$5.22
	2013	$3.73	$3.50	$4.66	$3.63	$5.03	$4.65
	2014	$4.18	$4.05	$4.49	$4.25	$4.62	$4.64

Commodity	Year	U.S. Average	Atlanta	Chicago	Denver	Los Angeles	New York
Steak, T-bone, per lb.	2010	$9.03	$9.76	$8.69	$9.79	$10.36	$13.93
	2011	$9.28	$9.79	$9.04	$9.80	$9.99	$14.00
	2012	$9.80	$10.90	$9.60	$10.17	$9.53	$15.52
	2013	$10.12	$11.52	$10.63	$11.46	$10.46	$12.78
	2014	$10.37	$11.61	$10.81	$10.29	$9.88	$13.33
Sugar, white, 4–5 lb.	2010	$2.25	$2.12	$2.29	$2.51	$2.36	$3.38
	2011	$2.38	$2.37	$2.38	$2.55	$2.55	$3.60
	2012	$2.65	$2.63	$2.97	$2.39	$2.64	$3.75
	2013	$2.58	$2.62	$2.75	$2.55	$2.80	$3.63
	2014	$2.26	$2.25	$2.65	$2.74	$2.57	$3.57
Tuna, chunk light, 6 oz. can	2010	92¢	85¢	$1.15	90¢	95¢	$1.74
	2011	89¢	87¢	99¢	83¢	79¢	$1.57
	2012	99¢	$1.00	$1.02	95¢	96¢	$1.53
	2013	$1.05	$1.18	$1.14	$1.16	$1.09	$1.72
	2014	$1.03	$1.26	$1.18	$1.53	$1.07	$1.48

Notes: Data are annual averages, derived from averaging data for the first 3 quarters.Source: Council for Community and Economic Research (formerly ACCRA), Cost of Living Index

SELECTED PRICES 2010–2014

Item	Source	Description	Price
ALCOHOL			
Absinthe	Liqueurs de France (2013)	Authentique, 750 ml	$110.00
Beer	Food Lion newspaper insert, Virginia (2013)	24 pack of Natural Light, 12 oz cans	$12.99
Gin	abcliquorsandlounge.com (2013)	Tanqueray, 750 ml	$32.99
Scotch Whiskey	westconcordliquors.com (2010)	Macallan, 12-year-old, 750 ml	$65.99
Vodka	liquormart.com (2013)	Absolut, 1.75 liters	$36.99
Vodka	liquormart.com (2013)	Grey Goose, 1.75 liters	$64.99
Wine	westconcordliquors.com (2010)	Gnarly Head Cabernet Sauvignon	$13.99
Wine	westconcordliquors.com (2010)	Besieged Merlot/Cabernet blend	$26.99
APPAREL, CHILDREN'S			
Dress	Sunny Fashion (2012)	Girl's tank embroidered dress with flower trim	$15.90
Hat And Mitten Set	Urban Boundaries (2011)	Boy's Acrylic Knit Hat and Mitten Set (Ages 2–4)	$17.99
Hoody	sales-fashion.com (2014)	Ecko Unlimited Boys 8–20 Lined Hoody	$34.99
APPAREL, MEN'S			
Bandanna	Horizon Industries (2011)	Paisley (Black)	$2.35
Bandanna	sunshine_joy.com (2012)	X-Spiral tie-dyed bandanna	$12.48
Jeans	*Belk Catalog* (2013)	Levis 501 button fly jeans	$47.99
Kimono	The House of Rice Store (2011)	Traditional kimono with crane design	$90.90
Shirt	J.C.'s 5 Star Outlet Flier (2013)	Select men's fashion dress shirts	$7.62
Slippers	Isotoner.com (2013)	ACORN Men's polar moccasin, black	$36.00
Swim Trunks	Nordstrom's (2013)	Speedo	$42.00
T-Shirt	Computer Gear & More Catalog (2013)	Shirt reads: The Past, Present and Future walked into a bar—It was Tense	$19.99
T-Shirt	Truth Soul Armor (2011)	Short-sleeve T-shirt	$15.00
T-Shirt	Computer Gear & More Catalog (2013)	Shirt reads: Anyone who thinks "the customer is always right" never worked in tech support	$19.99

Item	Source	Description	Price
Wallet	Value on Style (2011)	Leather trifold wallet, soft lamb skin leather, black	$11.98

APPAREL, WOMEN'S

Item	Source	Description	Price
Burqa	Zarinas.Com (2013)	Afghan burqa, blue	$24.99
Choker	The Wizard's Chest (2011)	Women's leather studded choker	$14.63
Coin Purse	BeltOutlet.com (2010)	Mundi leather	$11.90
Corset	Bslingerie.com (2012)	Women's Faux Leather Zipper Front Boned Corset	$19.99
Dress	*Belk Catalog* (2012)	Junior, Chevron print dress, 50% off	$21.99
Handbag	Gucci (2013)	Gucci Soho shoulder bag	$2,240.00
Handbag	*Belk Catalog* (2012)	New Directions totes, originally $78.00	$39.99
Hat	*Redbook* (2012)	Fedora, Protect your face (and hide a weird hair day)	$42.00
Jeans	Lee.com (2010)	Lee, Classic Fit	$24.99
Nightshirt	*National Catalog* (2012)	Carole nightshirt, medium	$22.42
Shoes	*Belk Catalog* (2013)	Flats and mocs: LifeStride Equilla	$37.50
Shoes (Basketball)	lastpairs.com (2011)	Converse Chuck Taylor All-Star Hi-Top Pink women's	$52.98

A variety of Converse Hi-Tops. (via Flickr)

Item	Source	Description	Price
Sundress	Windorshore.Com (2012)	Embrace to sundress. Few things feel as liberating on a sweltering day	$44.90
Wristband	Grim Reapers (2011)	Studded leather wristband	$5.39

APPLIANCES

Item	Source	Description	Price
Deep Fryer	Macy's (2010)	Waring DF280 Pro Deep Fryer	$139.99
Dishwasher	Sears (2013)	Kenmore 24" Built-In Dishwasher—White	$299.99
Espresso Machine	bedbathandbeyond.com (2010)	De'Longhi Lattissima Plus EN520R Pump Automatic Espresso/Latte/Cappuccino Machine	$399.99
Food Processor	cuisinart.com (2013)	Cuisinart Elite Collection 12-Cup Food Processor	$249.00
Slow Cooker	jcpenney.com (2013)	Hamilton Beach® 6-qt. Programmable Oval Slow Cooker	$55.00
Toaster Oven	bestbuy.com (2010)	Frigidaire—Professional Infrared Convection Toaster Oven—Stainless Steel	$149.99

ART SUPPLIES

Item	Source	Description	Price
Canvas	Utrecht Art Supplies (2010)	Utrecht traditional primed cotton canvas roll, 72" × 6 yds.	$174.99
Oil Paint	Utrecht Art Supplies (2010)	Windsor Newton cobalt blue deep, 37 ml. tube	$30.09
Palette Knife	Utrecht Art Supplies (2013)	Trowel, made in Italy	$5.19

BABY PRODUCTS & SUPPLIES

Item	Source	Description	Price
Bathrobe	Baby Aspen (2013)	Let the Fin Begin Terry Shark Robe, Blue, 0–9 Months	$38.00
Carrier	Infantino (2013)	Union Ergonomic Carrier, Gray	$29.99
Crib	wayfair.com (2013)	Babyletto Hudson Convertible Crib	$379.00
Crib	toysrus.com (2013)	Babi Italia Pinehurst 3-in-1 Classic Convertible Crib	$299.99
Gate	Regalo (2013)	Easy Step Walk Thru Gate, White	$32.00
Monitor	Infant Optics (2012)	Infant Optics DXR-5 2.4 GHz Digital Video Baby Monitor with Night Vision	$169.99
Pant And Shirt Set	Hudson Baby (2012)	Long Sleeve Bodysuit and Pant Set	$12.99
Swing	Fisher-Price (2012)	Cradle 'N Swing	$139.00

BUSINESS EQUIPMENT & SUPPLIES

Item	Source	Description	Price
Bubble Wrap	ValueMailers.com (2011)	½". × 125' × 24".	$34.76
Desk Lamp	IKEA (2013)	Grey. You can easily direct the light where you want it because the lamp arm and head are adjustable	$39.99
Packing Tape	Sealer Supply (2012)	12 rolls commercial grade packing tape 2"× 55 yds.	$26.44
Planner	At-A-Glance (2010)	Yearly/Weekly Planner Book	$24.99
Push Pins	Staples (2010)	500/tub, assorted colors	$7.49

Item	Source	Description	Price
COLLECTIBLES			
Blanket	Penny Lane Gifts (2010)	Jimi Hendrix Blanket—Playing Guitar & Logo with Ornate Artwork & Tie Dye Background, 50"	$33.99
Collectible	Fastcoin (2012)	1946 S Gem BU Silver Dime	$9.95
Poster	fineartamerica.com (2013)	Joan Jett poster	$15.00
COMPUTERS, PHONES & ACCESSORIES			
Bluetooth Speaker	www.usa.philips.com (2014)	Philips SBT30/27 SoundShooter Wireless Portable Bluetooth Speaker	$44.69
Buddy Box	Dynamic Product Distribution (2012)	Rugged Rubber Combo Hybrid Hard Back Cover Case for iPhone 4/4s + Screen Protector	$12.50
Cable Clips	Amamax (2013)	Cable clips, white (100 pieces per bag)	$4.49
Computer Headset	logitech.com (2011)	Logitech ClearChat headset	$15.99
Computer Wallet	Computer Gear & More Catalog (2013)	Tear resistant, water resistant, recycled Tyvek	$14.99
Dvd-R	Verbatim (2012)	Verbatim 95079 4.7 GB up to 16x DataLifePlus White Inkjet Printable, Hub Printable Recordable Disc DVD-R 50-Disc Spindle	$12.95
Ipad	Apple Store (2012)	iPad Air, 16GB	$499.00
Ipad App	iTunes.com (2013)	The cosmos story app such children explore the universe is iPad is the visual. The perspective is based on your child's exact geographic location	$3.00
Iphone	Apple Store (2013)	iPhone 5, 32 GB	$299.00
Iphone Case	Digital Gadget Store (2013)	My Sweet Barbie iPhone 5 Case (Black Long-Dress)	$52.99
Iphone Case	Etsy (2013)	iPhone 4 case	$12.99
Ipod Touch MP3 Player	Target (2013)	Apple 5th generation MP3 player	$214.99
Keyboard And Mouse Bundle	E-3lue E-Blue (2013)	E-3LUE Cobra Wired Gaming Keyboard& Mouse Bundles/Combos 1 USB Cable interface	$59.99
Laptop Bag/Briefcase	Vicenzo Leather Bag Company (2011)	Full Grain Leather Laptop/Briefcase Bag	$125.00
Laptop Computer	Office Depot (2013)	HP Pavilion, 17.3 "	$429.99
MP3 Player	Best Buy (2013)	Sony Walkman video MP3 player	$64.99
Mobile Reader	Rolling Stone (2012)	Kindle fire, All the content, half the price; movies and TV shows, music, apps and games, millions of books and Amazon Silk, the cloud-accelerated web browser	$199.00
Mouse Pad	Best Buy (2013)	HandStands—Memory Foam Mouse Mat with Wrist Rest—Black/Gray	$14.99
Notebook PC	Tigerdirect.Com (2013)	Asus K55 Notebook PC	$359.99
Paper	Staples (2012)	Staples copy paper, 8 1/2" 3 11", ream	$5.79
Power Adapter	Brightgate Inc (2011)	Bluecell Black USB Power Adapter for iPhone	$2.00
Printer/Fax/Scanner	BestBuy.com (2010)	HP OfficeJet All-in-One	$590.02
Printer Ink	Toner Planet (2010)	HP combo pack 3-pack inkjet, 2 HP 96 (black) 1 HP 97 (color)	$71.00
Remote Pointer	Brainydeal (2013)	AGPtek® USB Wireless Remote Pointer Control PowerPoint Presentation presenter with Laser Pointer	$13.99

Item	Source	Description	Price
Smartwatch	Http://Toq.Qualcomm. Com (2014)	Qualcomm® Toq™ smartwatch for Android, the revolutionary smartwatch with a Qualcomm® Mirasol™ color touchscreen display	$299.99
Software	Adobe.Com (2013)	Adobe Photoshop v. 6	$99.00
Software	Software Office.Com (2013)	Microsoft Office Home & Business 2013	$219.99
Speaker	Elektronic Evolution (2011)	Sonpre Mini Micro Speaker System for PC, Phone, Tablet, Apple iPod Touch, iPhone 4, iPad, MP3 Player	$8.99
Speaker Stands	World Wide Stereo (2014)	Sunfire HRS-SATSTAND Stand for High Resolution Series Satellite Speaker—Pair (Black)	$326.00
Tablet	Hewlett-Packard (2013)	HP Slate 7 8G	$139.99
Tablet PC	J.C.'S 5 Star Outlet Flier (2013)	ZEKI 7 in. dual-core android tablet PC; capacitive multi-touch hi screen; built in Wi-Fi	$74.62
Travel App	Google Store (2012)	FlightTrack for Android	$4.99
Usb Connector	Nextronics (2012)	SuperSpeed USB 3.0 Type A Male to Type A Female Cable	$6.99
Wireless Reading Device	Amazon Digital Services, Inc. (2010)	Kindle 3G 1 Wi-Fi, 6" display, graphite	$195.98
Wrist Strap	Forrest Shopping (2011)	Bluecell 10 pcs Black Nylon Round Hand Wrist Strap Lanyard for Camera Cell Phone iPod MP3 MP4 PSP Wii and Other Electronic Devices	$1.99

EDUCATION

Item	Source	Description	Price
Art Classes	*Washington Post* (2013)	Uncork'd Art, 2-hour painting class with wine	$25.00
Language Course	Fluenz (2012)	Spanish (Latin America) 112131415 with supplemental Audio CDs and Podcasts	$398.00
University Tuition (Public)	Pennsylvania State (2011)	Pennsylvania State per year	$15,250

ENTERTAINMENT

Item	Source	Description	Price
Apple Picking	*Washington Post* (2013)	Ridgefield Farm and Orchard, 2 bags of pick-your-own apples	$10.00
Oktoberfest	*Washington Post* (2013)	V.I.P. ticket with up to 8 beers plus lunch	$32.00
Paintball Rental	*Washington Post* (2013)	PEV's Paintball, full-day gameplay and equipment rental for 3 people	$59.00
Restaurant Meal	*The New Yorker* (2013)	ABC Cocina is a "modern global exchange" restaurant, entrees	$7–$24.00

ENTERTAINMENT, HOME

Item	Source	Description	Price
Billiard Table	sears.com (2013)	MD Sports 7-1/2 ft. Courtland Billiard Table with Bonus Cue Rack	$251.99
Board Game	kmart.com (2012)	SCRABBLE	$17.99
Board Game	kmart.com (2012)	Monopoly	$12.99

A shelf full of Monopoly variations. (via Flickr)

Item	Source	Description	Price
Boombox	VCT Electronics (2012)	Sony ZS-S2iP CD boombox with iPod dock	$199.32
CD Set	secamvhs.com (2011)	Bessie Smith: The Complete Recordings, Vol. 4, 2 CDs	$50.09
Computer Game	Oh the Very Best Deals (2011)	Twisted Metal for Sony PlayStation 3	$14.98
Gas Grill	sears.com (2010)	Kenmore 4-Burner Stainless Steel Gas Grill	$349.99
Grill Briquettes	homedepot.com (2010)	Bradley Smoker Hickory Briquettes (48-Pack)	$16.48
Home Video	PBS Home Video Catalog (2013)	Voyage to the Galapagos; Alan Alda follows in Charles Darwin's footsteps, meeting the animals and birds that inspired Darwin's theory of those evolution	$17.99
Home Video	PBS Home Video Catalog (2013)	Inspector Robert Lewis steps out of the shadow of his mentor, the inimitable Inspector Morse, in this highly acclaimed series, from pilot to series 6	$99.99
Home Video	PBS Home Video Catalog (2013)	The sweeping *Downton Abbey* saga continues with the fourth season of drama, romance, and family intrigue. Season four DVD Blue ray	 $49.99 $54.99

Item	Source	Description	Price
Lounge Cover	World Class Inc. (2011)	GSI super quality outdoor chaise lounge chair cover, waterproof and weather resistant	$18.83
Patio Fire Pit	avantgardendecor.com (2013)	CobraCo™ Diamond Mesh Fire Pit	$179.64
Smoker Grill	homedepot.com (2012)'	Masterbuilt 30 in. Vertical Digital Electric Smoker with Remote Control	$289.00
Speaker	The GroupDeal (2012)	StrongVolt POP360 Hands Free Bluetooth Speaker With 360 Degree Sound	$34.99
Swing Set	Global Supplies (2010)	Flexible Flyer "Triple Fun" Swing Set, a four-leg ivory color frame gym set with 6' midnight blue wave slide three midnight blue kid comfort seat swings with vinyl covered adjustable height chains a two child See-Saw with midnight blue deluxe seats with handles	$220.00
Television	Samsung.com (2012)	32" LED TV	$379.99
Trampoline	walmart.com (2013)	Airzone 12' Trampoline with Safety Enclosure	$199.00

FARM EQUIPMENT & SUPPLIES

Item	Source	Description	Price
Chicken Coop	TRIXIE Pet Products (2013)	Chicken Coop with a View, suitable for 2 standard size chickens or 4 bantams, nesting house with hinged roof and removable divider, sleeping house with hinged roof and removable roosting pole	$419.99
Chicken Wire	B&G (2013)	48" × 50' 2" Galvanized Mesh Hexagonal Poultry Netting	$29.99
Generator	Northern Tool + Equipment (2013)	Powerhorse Portable Generator with Electric Start—9000 Surge Watts, 7250 Rated Watts	$849.99
Herb Seeds	zziggysgal.com (2013)	Culinary herb set, 12 packets of high-quality seeds	$14.95

FOOD PRODUCTS

Item	Source	Description	Price
Canned Pasta	Food Lion newspaper insert, Virginia (2013)	Chef Boyardee canned pasta, 15 oz	$0.88
Cocoa	Trader Joe's (2010)	Droste, 8.8 oz	$8.99
Florida Oranges	Save a Lot food stores advertising circular (2012)	3 pound bag	$2.49
Green Peppers	ALDI newspaper insert (2013)	Per three pack	$1.29
Mushrooms	ALDI newspaper insert (2013)	White mushrooms, 8 oz package	$0.79
Peter Pan Peanut Butter	Save a Lot Food Stores advertising circular (2012	Creamy or crunchy, 16.3 oz	$1.99
Russet Potatoes	Save a Lot food stores advertising circular (2012)	5 pound bag	$1.49
Steak	Food Lion newspaper insert, Virginia (2013)	New York strip steak, per pound	$6.99
Sugar	ALDI newspaper insert (2013)	Baker's Corner powdered sugar, 32 oz	$1.19
Tea	Vita Cafe (2013)	Black Tea Organic Golden Peach, 25 bags	$5.16
Toffee	Trader Joe's (2014)	Trader Joe's English Toffee with Nuts, 1 lb.	$8.99

Item	Source	Description	Price

FURNITURE

Item	Source	Description	Price
Bathroom Mirror	Lowe's (2013)	Gatco 31-1/2" H × 23-1/2" W Tiara Rectangular Tilting Frameless Bathroom Mirror with Chrome Hardware and Beveled Edges	$93.75
Bookcase	Kohl's (2010)	Sauder 5-Shelf Split Bookcase, engineered wood, assembly required	$214.99
Child's Pillow	Blablakids.com (2013)	Hold me tight mustache pillow	$52.00
Cotton Bedding	Gaiam Living (2013)	Organic cotton premium sateen bedding Quilt Pillow Shams	$229 $129 $59
Dining Table	Sears.com (2013)	Keter Symphony expandable dining table	$299.24
Loveseat	Jordan's Furniture (2010)	Reclining Loveseat	$600.00
Mirror	Gaiam Living (2013)	Sunburst Driftwood mirror. Wood "rays" are distressed to give the look of driftwood, then layered around a mirror for a sunburst effect	$350.00
Painted Bench	*Redbook* (2012)	Sigurd bench; less than 17" wide, so it's great for a tight hallway	$79.99
Urban Lounge Gear	*Rolling Stone* (2012)	Sumo Lounge offers the best selection of huge bean bags	$149.00
Vanity Bench	bedbathandbeyond.com (2013)	The Victoria Vanity Bench takes its cues from the past-with sweeping romantic lines and French-inspired scrollwork; gracefully crafted with swirled iron legs, this vanity bench features a comfortable plush grey cushion	$150.99

GARDEN EQUIPMENT & SUPPLIES

Item	Source	Description	Price
Garden Hose	Metal Fittings (2013)	50' expandable garden hose	$24.00
Garden Stakes	botanicalinterests.com (2013)	10-pack	$2.98
Herb Seeds	botanicalinterests.com (2013)	Chives	$1.99
Indoor Gardening System	*Rolling Stone* (2012)	My Grow Buddy, comes with everything you need except plant	$499.00

HOLIDAY & RELIGIOUS SUPPLIES

Item	Source	Description	Price
Buddha Statue	Cultural Elements (2013)	Hand Carved Wood Sitting Buddha Statue, measures 6" s high, made in India	$32.00
Christmas Ornament	Toys on Earth (2013)	Lenox Annual Spire Snowflake Ornament	$80.00
Hindu Statue	Shambala Shop (2013)	Dancing Ganesh Statue: Beautifully crafted statue of Lord Ganesh in the dancing pose made in India. Heavyweight brass; measures approximately 4.5" H × 1.25" W × 1.4" L	$18.99
Hoodoo Herb Spell Kit	Witch SuperCenter (2014)	19 herbs and book	$20.99
Kwanzaa Decoration	African Heritage Collection (2013)	Kwanzaa Arc Candleholder & Celebration Set—Made in Ghana. Set includes Kinara, cup, set of 7 candles, mat and information sheet	$79.95

Item	Source	Description	Price
Kwanzaa Mat	African Heritage Collection (2013)	Colorful Bamboo Kwanzaa Mat	$4.99
Menorah	World of Judaica (2013)	Menorah Candles from Paraffin with Bold Color Design from Safed Candles	$95.00
Ramadan Cookie Cutters	Eidway (2013)	Islamic Eid & Ramadan Cookie Cutter Set—5 Stainless Steel Cutters	$16.95
Ramadan Decoration	Enchanted Gift Gallery (2013)	Green Glass Moroccan Lantern, 4-1/2" × 3-3/4" × 10-1/4" high	$19.50
Shinto Ornamental Shrine/Shelf	Sanai Trading Works Japan (2013)	Miniature Kamidana Golden Ornament Japanese Shinto Shrine God Shelf	$36.00
Wicca Spellbook	amazon.com (2014)	The Wicca Spellbook: A Witch's Collection of Wiccan Spells, Potions, and Recipes by Gerina Dunwich	$47.00
Classic Hotel Room	lenoxhotel.com (2013)	The Lennox Hotel, Boston, Massachusetts	$215.00
Standard Hotel Room	windsurfercrs.com (2013)	Essex Inn, Chicago, Illinois, per night	$139.00
Standard Hotel Room	theroosevelthotel.com (2013)	Roosevelt Hotel, New York City	$289.00

HOUSEHOLD ITEMS

Item	Source	Description	Price
Absinthe Glass	Kegworks (2013)	Authentic Absinthe Glass—2 Pack	$26.00
Alarm Clock	Eek Technology (2011)	Elgin battery-operated analog alarm clock	$14.00
Aroma Diffuser	Gaiam Living (2013)	Balance mind, body and spirit by engaging the senses. The handcrafted Maplewood and hand-blown glass piece itemizes pure essential oils are playing traditional Japanese music	$369.00
Base Plate	De-Sta-Co (2012)	Machined Base Plate	$11.75
Blanket	Great Gift Ideas, Etc. (2011)	Super Soft 100% Alpaca Wool Reversible Throw Blanket	$185.95
Bread Box	J.C.'S 5 Star Outlet Flier (2013)	Anchor stainless steel bread box	$9.62
Bucket	toolboxsupply.com (2010)	Rubbermaid Neat 'N Tidy kitchen bucket	$10.09
Candle	Belk Catalog (2013)	Yankee Candle home fragrance warmers and refills, flour	$20.00

A Yankee Candles storefront. (via Flickr)

Item	Source	Description	Price
Candles	Quick Candles (2011)	10-hour white unscented votive candles set of 72	$21.98
Candleholder	Furniture Creations (2010)	Spanish mission metal cathedral stand	$11.75
Charging Cradle	Toner Warehouse Direct (2011)	Motorola MC9000 4 Slot Charging Cradle	$489.00
Chef's Knife	Chef's Resource (2010)	Victorinox, 8" chef's knife	$29.99
Coffee Grinder	Abt Electronics (2010)	KitchenAid small coffee grinder	$27.99
Comforter	Belk Catalog (2013)	Biltmore Festival comforter set, queen size, includes shams	$199.99
Cookie Jar	Target (2013)	Threshold™ Stoneware Figural Owl Cookie Jar—white	$19.99
Cookware	Kohl's (2013)	Calphalon 12" nonstick covered jumbo skillet	$89.99
Cookware Set	Belk Catalog (2013)	Cook's Tools, 19-pc. nonstick cookware set in Red or black. With Belk card	$42.49
Dinnerware	Belk Catalog (2013)	Pfaltzgraff everyday 16-pc. dinnerware set	$59.99
Dinnerware	Pfaltzgraff (2013)	Rustic Leaves 16 pc Dinnerware Set	$170.00
Dish Towels	Keeble Outlets (2013)	Kitchen towels, white with blue stripe, highly absorbent, low lint, 100% cotton	$27.99

Item	Source	Description	Price
Door Knocker	Pottery Barn (2010)	Ella Door Knocker, made of substantial hand-hammered brass with a ring and simple, stepped striking plate. 4.5" wide × 1.75" deep × 7" high; mounting hardware included	$59.00
Drinking Glasses	J.C.'S 5 Star Outlet Flier (2013)	Anchor 20-pc. glassware set	$24.99
Duraflame Logs	Life And Home (2013)	Six-pack	$23.49
Fireplace Screen	Plowhearth.Com (2010)	Two-Door Floral Fireplace Screen with Beveled Glass Panels	$69.95
Fly Swatter	Geroy's (2010)	Willert Home Products fly swatter	$6.24
Furnace Filter	The Home Depot (2011)	Filtrete 16" × 20" × 1" Micro Allergen FPR 7 Air Filter (4-Packs, Case of 3)	$47.86
Glassware	etailz.Com (2013)	HOME ESSENTIALS Grand Diamond 18-pc.drinkware set	$28.00
Juicer, Electric	Bed Bath & Beyond (2013)	Breville Ikon multi-speed juice fountain	$199.99
Hangers	Unbeatablesale, Inc. (2012)	super heavyweight hangers, 18-pack	$22.99
Household Cleaner	Americarx (2010)	Tilex Mold & Mildew Remover, 16 fl. oz.	$9.05
Kitchen Bags	Supreme Hardware (2011)	Glad Quick-Tie tall kitchen bags, 13 gallon, 80 bags	$15.86
Light Bulbs	Light Bulbs Etc., Inc. (2012)	4 of 25-watt incandescent light bulbs, frosted	$6.39
Light Bulbs	E Plus (2011)	Ecosmart 14-watt daylight bulb, compact fluorescent, set of 4	$32.23
Mattress Topper	Belk Catalog (2013)	Isotonic Ultimate foam mattress topper with cover; the 2" memory foam construction molds to the shape of your body	$109.99
Mortar and Pestle	toysngamesetc.com (2013)	5" stone granite mortar and pestle	$27.95
Picture Frame	Adorama Camera (2010)	MCS fashion wood bullnose frame for 8" × 10" photograph, black	$5.49
Picture Hangers	Perfect Utopia (2013)	Picture hangers, support up to 100 pounds,	$4.79
Pineapple Slicer	Dinami Product (2011)	Pineapple Cutter Makes Perfect Pineapple Rings in Seconds, Slices, Cores, Peels	$17.95
Placemat Set	Lone Buck Enterprises (2012)	EKCO 12-pc. bamboo placemat coaster chopstick set	$28.19
Rug Protector	officesupplies.Com (2012)	Chair mat rug protector, 36" × 48"	$54.93
Salad Tosser	inmod.com (2013)	Water drop Teakwood salad tosser	$47.00
Sauna	costco.com (2013)	Dynamic Venice 2-person FAR Infrared Sauna	$1,399.99
Shower Curtain Ring Set	Big Ten (2010)	Clear shower curtain rings, 12-pack	$11.99
Silverware Tray	Madesmart (2012)	Six-compartment cutlery tray	$11.99
Solar Panel	homedepot.com (2013)	Grape Solar 250-Watt Monocrystalline Solar Panel	$374.99
Soup Pot and Bowls	Chefs (2013)	Five-pc. Tuscan soup pot and bowls	$99.99
Summer Plates	*Redbook* (2012)	Sea Life collection plate, set of four	$40.00
Switch Plate	switchhits.com (2013)	Hand-painted ceramic light switch plate, 1 toggle	$21.50
Telephone	Eek Technology (2010)	AT&T Trimline, corded	$17.99
Telephone	DFW Computer Supply (2010)	Motorola digital expandable cordless phone with corded base and answering system	$315.19

Item	Source	Description	Price
Toilet	The Renovators Supply (2013)	White w/gold, blue Vitreous China, Sheffield Deluxe Bowl Only	$399.00
Towels	Belk Catalog (2013)	Egyptian Luxe towels by Home Accents	$5.99
Wall Sconce	houzz.com (2013)	Morgan 1-light sconce; elegant off-white linen shades trimmed in bronze silk combine with crystal ball accents and petite square arms	$99.00
Wine Bucket	Red Envelope (2013)	Nickel-plated stainless steel	$89.95

JEWELRY

Item	Source	Description	Price
Engagement Ring	zales.com (2014)	3/4 CT. T.W. Diamond Double Frame Bridal Set in 14K White Gold	$2,139.00
Pendants	Cool Rings (2010)	Stainless Steel Couples Eternal Love Pendants Necklace Set	$45.99
Men's Watch	Macy's (2011)	Fossil Townsman mechanical twist stainless steel bracelet	$225.00
Women's Watch	overstock.com (2012)	Gino Franco's silver and tan watch	$90.00

MEDICAL PRODUCTS & SERVICES

Item	Source	Description	Price
Acupuncture	massagetherapyworks.com (2013)	One hour	$110.00
Eye Exam	*Washington Post* (2013)	Eye exam plus $200 towards glasses at Khalil Eye Care	$49.00
First Aid Kit	My First Aid Company (2013)	Ever Ready First Aid Fully Stocked First Responder Kit, Orange	$98.99
Glucose Meter	Buy Wholesale Prices (2010)	ACCU-CHEK Compact Plus Meter Kit, lancet technology makes testing less painful, attachable lancet device allows you to easily carry the system, pre-loaded 17-test drum helps remove struggling with test strips	$19.95
Heating Pad	Shefi (2011)	Knee and Elbow Reusable Pain Relief Instant130F Heat Therapy Gel pad and a Pouch kit (pouch and two medium size purpose designed Heat pads)	$79.95
Home Hospital Bed	spinlife.com (2013)	Medline Basic Full-Electric Bed, battery backup, remote with large buttons	$799.00
Lab Flask	Lake Charles Manufacturing (2013)	Karter Scientific Glass Erlenmeyer Flask 5 Piece Set 50, 150, 250, 500, & 1000 ml	$23.00
Lab Pipette	Electronix Express (2013)	Plastic Transfer Pipettes 3ml, Graduated, Pack of 100	$4.95
Lab Petri Dish	Scientific Equipment of Houston (2013)	100 × 15 mm 20/Pk	$9.95
Latex Gloves	ShopDirectSource.com (2010)	Latex gloves, 1,000	$46.75
Pill Reminder	GroupMedShop.com (2012)	Apex 7-day medical planner	$7.80
Prescription	azmarijuana.com (2013)	Medical marijuana: Green Kryptonite, per gram	$18.00
Prescription	azmarijuana.com (2013)	Medical marijuana: Blue Dream pre-roll, one	$12.00
Reading Glasses	LianSan (2012)	Super Light 100% Titanium Fashion Rimless Reading Eyeglasses	$25.00

Item	Source	Description	Price
Stethoscope	globalindustrial.com (2013)	Cardiology III Stethoscope, 28"	$225.95
Surgery	Blue Mountain Clinic, Montana (2013)	Vasectomy	$700.00
Surgical Mask	globalindustrial.com (2013)	1500 Series N95 Respirator and Surgical Mask, MOLDEX 1517, Box of 20	$26.95
Therapeutic Massage	massagetherapyworks.com (2013)	Half-hour	$55.00
Wheelchair	spinlife.com (2013)	Heavy Duty with 12" Rear Wheels, removable desk length armrests, 22" wide seat	$235.00

MOTORIZED VEHICLES, SERVICES, & SUPPLIES

Item	Source	Description	Price
Automobile	*Washington Post* (2013)	New 2013 Toyota Highlander plus V6	$28,789
Automobile	*Washington Post* (2013)	2013 Cadillac ATS 2.0 sedan, North American car of the year, exclusive luxury upgrade event, lease per month	$299.00
Car Trunk Organizer	CoolKarStuff (2011)	Trunk Organizer. Foldable. Tough and Heavy Duty Material. Buckles Nicely to Stay Together for Easy Carry Around	$29.95
Gasoline	eia.gov/dnav/pet (2011)	New York City, Gallon	$3.69
Gasoline	eia.gov/dnav/pet (2012)	Los Angles, California, Gallon	$4.13
Gasoline	eia.gov/dnav/pet (2010)	Boston, Massachusetts, Gallon	$2.80
Jump Starter	qualitytoolsforless.com (2014)	Clore JNC300XL 'Jump-N-Carry' 900 Peak Amp Ultraportable 12V Jump Starter with Light, CEC Compliant	$73.99
Recreational Vehicle	fleetwoodrv.com (2014)	Southwind 32VS Length: 33.5 ft. Pewter Mist interior décor with Cinnabar wood cabinetry	$133,889
Tire, Regular	ntb.com (2013)	Goodyear Eagle RS-A	$139.99
Tire, Winter	tirebuyer.com (2013)	Firestone Winterforce, high-sipe density for powerful traction in wet, snowy, and icy weather, 3D directional tread design, accepts #12 metal studs for extra traction in wintry conditions	$67.96

MUSICAL INSTRUMENTS

Item	Source	Description	Price
Amplifier	Fender.com (2012)	Excelsior Guitar Amp	$399.99
Drum Microphone	Sam Ash Music Direct (2012)	AKG D40 Professional Dynamic Instrument Microphone	$99.00
Electric Guitar	The Guitar Center (2011)	Fender Nitro Satin Series Stratocaster Electric Guitar	$799.99
Flute	lotmusic (2012)	Traditional Handmade Chinese Musical Instrument Bamboo Flute, Key of G	$21.99
Harmonica	Guitar Center (2013)	Hohner 1896 Marine Band Harmonica	$37.35
Trumpet	Brook Mays(2011)	Bach Prelude trumpet	$266.98
Trumpet Mute	Brook Mays (2011)	Bach straight trumpet mute	$18.47

Item	Source	Description	Price
OTHER			
Absinthe Dripper	Absinthes.com (2014)	Absinthe Dripper: glass, high quality	$16.00
Business Cards	Vistaprint (2010)	250 cards	$29.99
Can Holder	The Paper Store (2013)	Boston Red Sox	$9.99
Cocktail Shaker	Deluxe Buys (2012)	Barware Styles Best Premium Large 24 oz Classic & Elegant Style Stainless Steel Martini & Cocktail Shaker, Deluxe, 3-Piece, Silver Mixer Bottle Won't Rust or Leak	$34.95
Desktop Ornament	Computer Gear & More Catalog (2013)	Powered by the heating and cooling of steam, this precision handcrafted desktop engine is an engineer's dream	$224.99
Diary	The BD Store (2013)	Handmade Art Writing Diary Journal with Natural Material in Diamond Stripe and Heart Design with Natural Wooden Bead Elasticized Bracelet	$32.95
Dinosaur Poop	Computer Gear & More Catalog (2013)	By studying coprolite, fossilized dinosaur dung, scientists learn about the met metabolism, physiology, behavior and environment of the dinosaur that produced it. Each boxed.	$14.99
Floor Mat	The Andersen Company (2014)	Andersen 2295 WaterHog Eco Premier PET Polyester Fiber Entrance Indoor/ Outdoor Floor Mat, SBR Rubber Backing, 8.4' Length × 3' Width, 3/8" Thick, Red	$49.95
Gift Wrap	Buttons Bags and Bows (2011)	New premium bright red gift wrap wrapping paper 16' roll	$14.95
Grumpy Cat Doll	Computer Gear & More Catalog (2013)	Will satisfy curmudgeons, cat lovers, and fans of the frown all year long	$24.99
Hookah	Fire Sale Merchant (2011)	Never Exhale 11" Premium 1 Hose Hookah Shisha Complete Set	$11.95
Incense	Penny Lane Gifts (2011)	Morning Star Sandalwood Incense (200 Sticks and Holder)	$7.69
Incense	Penny Lane Gifts (2011)	Nippon Kodo, Morning Star, patchouli, 200 sticks and holder	$13.34
Lock	Walmart.com (2010)	Master Lock X-treme combination lock	$11.67
Map	Rand McNally (2013)	Deluxe Laminated Wall Map (United States)	$19.39
Maple Leaf Sticky Notes	Computer Gear & More catalog (2013)	Leave nature inspired notes in the home or office	$9.99
Moving Boxes	The Home Depot (2010)	Pratt Retail Specialties Wardrobe Box with Metal Hanging Bar (3-Pack)	$28.84
Mug	Zazzle.com (2013)	"Happy Hanukkah" coffee mug	$19.99
Pen	Nilmee (2011)	BIC Atlantis stic ball pen, medium point (1.2 mm), black, 12 pens	$15.16
Photo Scans	*Washington Post* (2013)	PhotoBin: scan any combination of 350 photos, slides and/or negatives	$39.00
Postage	U.S. Post Office (2013)	Letter, Ounce	$0.46
Postage	U.S. Post Office (2012)	Letter, Ounce	$0.44
Postage	U.S. Post Office (2012)	Letter, Ounce	$0.45
Roses	1800Flowers.com (2012)	Two dozen with vase	$49.99

Item	Source	Description	Price
Spiral Notebook	Office Max (2013)	Schoolio One Subject Notebooks, 70 sheets, 10.5" × 8"	$1.49
Sunglasses	Red's Gear (2011)	Tifosi Roubaix iron frame/smoke, one size	$49.09
Watch Battery	JustCalculators.com (2013)	Panasonic watch battery button cell (pack of 5)	$5.35
Zombie Heart and Brain Gelatin Mold	Computer Gear & More catalog (2013)	Eat your heart out! Literally with this fun gelatin mold set; anatomically correct heart and zombie brain	$17.99

PERSONAL CARE PRODUCTS & SERVICES

Item	Source	Description	Price
Bath Brush	Pendergrass Inc. (2010)	Long handle wooden bath brush	$18.68
Bath Gift Set	Caswell-Massey (2011)	Lilac gift set	$36.95
Bath Sponge	Detroit Sponge & Chamois Co. (2010)	Large, natural sea sponge	$10.80
Blush	giorgioarmanibeauty-usa.com (2013)	Giorgio Armani powder blush	$49.00
Chapstick	Walgreens (2010)	ChapStick Moisturizer Skin Protectant/ Sunscreen SPF 15 Raspberry Cream	$1.69

Packaging for the Spearmint flavor of ChapStick. (via Flickr)

Item	Source	Description	Price
Dental Floss	AmericaRx (2012)	Reach Gentle Gum Care woven dental floss, fluoride, 50-yard dispensers (pack of 6)	$19.81
Eye Drops	Sam's Online (2013)	Bausch & Lomb lubricant eye drops, hydration, dry eye therapy 0.5 fl oz	$11.75
Eye Makeup Removal	*Redbook* (2012)	Almay's Soothing and Depuffing gentle eye makeup remover pads; 80 pads	$5.99
Eye Shadow	giorgioarmanibeauty-usa.com (2013)	Eyes to Kill Acqua Collection	$33.00
Eyeliner	soap.com (2013)	CoverGirl LineBlast 24HR Eyeliner	$7.99
Facial	Bella Santé (2013)	Decléor Harmonie Extreme Facial, soothes, calms, also softens with liquorice derivatives, blueberry extracts, and active essential oils. (For the most sensitive of skin types.) All facials include a hand, foot, or scalp massage. 50 minutes	$115.00
Facial Tissues	CVS.com (2013)	65 Kleenex Facial Tissues Lotion Aloe & E	$2.39
Fingernail Gloss	*Redbook* (2012)	CoverGirl Outlasts Stay Brilliant Nail gloss in peaches and cream	$5.49
Gel Blush Cosmetics	*Redbook* (2012)	We like Estée Lauder Pure Color Chic Rush in Techno Jam	$28.00
Haircut	Haircuts, LTD (2013)	Men's/Women's	$15.95
Hairbrush	bigflysports.com (2012)	Phillips light-touch cushion hairbrush	$13.99
Hand Lotion	Walmart (2010)	Aroma Naturals Body Butter Pure Shea 3.3 oz	$9.97
Lint Brush	Grady's Online (2013)	Evercare Magik brush	$6.77
Makeup	lancome-usa.com (2013)	Lancôme Teint Visionnaire, per ounce	$60.00
Makeup	Target (2012)	Maybelline	$5.99
Manicure	Bella Santé (2013)	OPI Gel Manicure is a breakthrough in the nail industry. OPI's Gel manicures last up to two weeks without chipping, smudging or cracking. With over fifty different shades to choose from you will not be disappointed. 45 minutes	$52.00
Mascara	Walgreens (2012)	CoverGirl Queen Collection Lash Fanatic Mascara	$7.99
Men's Shower Gel	Natural Bath & Body Shop (2010)	Apollon men's bath and shower gel	$11.19
Nail Dryer	sunvalleytek (2011)	USpicy® MACARON USND-3603 Professional UV Acrylic Gel & Shellac Curing Nail Dryer/ Lamp/Light (White, 36W)	$32.99
Natural Soap	VitaminLife.com (2014)	Sappo Hill Natural Oatmeal Glycerine Cream Soap Fragrance Free, 1 bar	$1.61
Organic Tampons	soap.com (2014)	Seventh Generation Tampons, Super Plus, 20 ct., 2 pk	$10.25
Pedicure	1 on 1 Self-Indulgence Spa (2013)	Cuticle removal, exfoliating the skin, callus removal, moisturizing foot mask and massage and finished with a beautiful polish application	$55.00
Perfume	Aromachology (2012)	Eau de Parfum Spray, 1.7 fl oz	$100.00
Razor Blades	Derby (2011)	100 Double-Edge Blades	$8.00
Scale, Digital	Season International Corporation (2013)	Bluetooth Digital Bathroom Scale Body Fat w/ Large Backlit Display and Step-On Technology for iPhone5S, iPhone5C, iPad mini	$79.99

Item	Source	Description	Price
Shower Caddy	toolboxsupply.com (2012)	Grayline large-size shower caddy, white	$16.27
Shower Cap	sallybeauty.com (2010)	Betty Dain stylish design, mold resistant	$7.99
Soap	Caswell Massey (2012)	One almond and aloe soap bar	$10.00
Spa Package	1 on 1 Self-Indulgence Spa (2013)	Exfoliate using Dead Sea Salt, rinse off in a calming Remineralizing Sea Bath in our jetted Hydro Tub, Moor Mud treatment that contains minerals and sea extracts, invigorating scalp massage using warm essential oils, refreshing, rinsing shower and soothing moisturizing application.	$160.00
Sunspot Remover	*Redbook* (2012)	Philosophy Help Me Retinol Tonight Treatment	$47.00
Terry Cloth Back Scrubber	drugstore.com (2014)	Extra Long Exfoliating Back Scrubber—Terry Cloth & Nylon with Plastic Handles	$6.99

PERSONAL SAFETY PRODUCTS

Item	Source	Description	Price
Beverage Testing Kit	exit15.com (2013)	Bodyguard Beverage Testing Kit, pack of 3, don't fall prey to date rape, test your drinks for GHB, Rohypnol, and ketamine	$15.00
Pepper Spray	sabrered.com (2013)	SABRE Red Pepper Spray: Making Grown Men Cry Since 1975. The Magnum 120 Flip-Top contains 4.4 oz of SABRE RED protection and delivers up to 40 shots at a range of 12 feet	$19.99
Safety Chick Kit	sabrered.com (2013)	Kit Includes: Date Rape Drug Test Coasters—Quickly tests drinks for the two most common date rape drugs. Door Wedge Alarm—120dB alarm will alert you to a potential intruder BEFORE they get inside. Personal Safety Alarm—120 dB alarm and flashing strobe light draws attention and can signal for help! SABRE RED Pepper Spray	$39.99
Stun Gun	sabrered.com (2013)	SABRE 500,000v Stun gun is 6" tall with a belt clip and wrist strap, uses two 9 volt alkaline batteries.	$65.00

PET SUPPLIES

Item	Source	Description	Price
Litter Box	MMP Living (2011)	Enclosed cat pan, large, assorted colors	$24.07
Litter Box Liners	Litterboy Products (2011)	Neat 'N Tidy litter sifting liners	$11.99
Aquarium Tank	Maija Pet Supply (2013)	Glass Standard Extra High Aquarium Tank, 30-Gallon, measures 24" length by 12" width by 24" height	$107.60

PUBLICATIONS

Item	Source	Description	Price
Book	Barnes & Noble (2013)	*The Midwife of Hope River*, Paperback	$11.99
Harlequin Kiss Novel	Parenting (2013)	Free e-book on *Waking Up Married* from the new Harlequin Kiss book collection approximate retail value of $4.99	Free
Book	American Civil Liberties Union (2014)	The Constitution of the United States of America	Free

Item	Source	Description	Price
REAL ESTATE			
Commercial Space	The New York Times (2013)	Upper East side New York city property, suitable for commercial operation; 630 sq. ft.; Annual lease	$52,800
House	MountainX.com (2013)	Tiny treetop home on large lot with mountain view; Hardwood floors, sunroom, garage, two bedrooms, one bath, shopping, entertainment nearby	$124,000
Apartment	MountainX.com (2013)	Two bedroom, one bath rental apartment with heat pump; Black Mountain, N.C. location, no pets, per month	$585.00
Commercial Building	The New York Times (2014)	Five-story commercial bldg. in NYC; This mixed-use, 1950s building includes 5422 ft. located at 352 E. 55th St.	$4.35 million
SEWING EQUIPMENT & SUPPLIES			
Crochet Hooks	joann.com (2012)	Wrights Gift Box With 8 Aluminum Hooks	$12.99
Knitting Needles	yarn.com (2012)	Knitter's Pride Nova 14" Single Pointed Needle Set includes 9 pairs of needles in US sizes 4, 5, 6, 7, 8, 9, 10, 10.5, and 11. These needles have an exceptionally smooth surface and sharp, gradually tapered points that make them ideal for a variety of knitting projects	$51.99
Yarn	yarn.com (2013)	Merino wool, 400 yds	$30.00
Sewing Machine	sears.com (2014)	SINGER Heavy Duty Sewing Machine with Metal Frame and Stainless Steel Bedplate	$199.99
SPORTS & OUTDOOR EQUIPMENT			
Backpack	Endless_Possibilities (2012)	JanSport Classic SuperBreak Backpack	$31.99
Beach Bag	Traders and Company (2011)	Moroccan straw summer beach/shopper/tote bag 16" × 6" × 12.5"	$45.49
Beach Towels	Redbook (2012)	Sun Valley 33" × 66" towel	$35.00
Blanket	The Source Group (2012)	NFL Premium Oversized Fleece Blanket 62" × 90"	$16.95
Camera	bestbuy.com (2013)	Nikon–D3200 Digital SLR Camera with 18–55mm VR Lens—Black	$499.99
Camera Bag	bestbuy.com (2010)	Trax–170 Camera Bag compatible with most DSLR cameras with an attached lens, 1 or 2 additional lenses and accessories; polyester material; lightweight design	$24.99
Canoe	walmart.com (2013)	Sun Dolphin Mackinaw 15.6' Canoe	$439.00
Cycling Helmet	REI (2010)	Bell Volt Bike Helmet, Fusion In-mold technology bonds both the top microshell and bottom wrap to an expanded polystyrene (EPS) foam layer to make a sturdy, solid and protective helmet	$155.00
Compass	Prime Scuba (2012)	Wrist Compass with hose mount Waterproof Underwater for Scuba Diving, Camping, Hiking, Climbing other outdoor recreation sports	$39.95

Item	Source	Description	Price
Inflatable Raft	rei.com (2013)	Friday Harbor Commander 9 Inflatable Raft suitable for paddling on lakes, mild rivers, bays and estuaries, durable, heavy-gauge PVC provides superb puncture resistance, tough padding resists abrasion in wear-prone spots and a landing plate enhances durability when coming ashore	$229.95
Kayak	rei.com (2013)	Perception Tribe 13.5 Tandem Sit-On-Top Kayak	$649.00
Picnic Basket Set For Two	potterybarn.com (2010)	Woven of textural natural rattan, this classic basket includes everything you need for a picnic–plus plenty of room for food and wine. Lined with cotton canvas and filled with two wine glasses, two plates, flatware and a wine opener, it makes a perfect gift for a summer wedding	$89.00
Ski Gloves	The Source Group (2011)	Women's Thinsulate-lined waterproof ski gloves	$15.99
Skis, Downhill	Alpine Sporting Goods (2013)	K2 Hellbent Schizo 12	$479.00
Sleeping Bag	REI (2012)	REI Radiant Down Sleeping Bag, high-quality duck down is warm, lightweight and compressible; bag has a temperature rating of 20°F	$199.00
Snorkeling Mask	Get Wet Store (2013)	Promate Junior Snorkeling Scuba Diving Mask DRY Snorkel Set for Kids	$39.95
Snowboard	Alpine Sporting Goods (2013)	Jones Carbon Flagship Snowboard 2014	$849.00
Tent	REI (2010)	Marmot Limelight 3-Person Tent, large side doors provide convenient access; 2 vestibules offer storage space for personal gear	$279.00
Travel Cooler and Warmer	invertersrus.com (2010)	Rubbermaid Travel Cooler/Warmer VEC223RB, 14 Can Capacity	$74.99
Tripod	Davis & Sanford (2012)	Vista Explorer 60-Inch Lightweight Tripod with Tripod Bag	$26.50

TELEPHONE EQUIPMENT & SERVICES

Item	Source	Description	Price
Cell Phone Service	ATT.com (2013)	Unlimited talk and data with 16 GB of storage	$85.00
Cell Phone Service	Washington Post (2013)	Sprint gives you unlimited talk, text, and data while on the Sprint network on the My Way plan, per month	$80.00

TOBACCO PRODUCTS

Item	Source	Description	Price
Cigarettes	theawl.com (2012)	Per pack in New York	$12.50
Cigarettes	theawl.com (2012)	Per pack in West Virginia	$4.84
E-Z Wider Rolling Papers	rollingpaperdepot.com (2013)	Per pack	$2.45

Item	Source	Description	Price
TOOLS			
Brackets	Country Art House (2012)	5 complete sets security hanger hardware	$12.96
Chain Saw	Washington Post (2013)	MS 251 chain saw, features great power to weight ratio for quick work of firewood cutting, 18-in. bar	$349.95
Hardware	Grizzly (2011)	wood screw assortment 100 pcs.	$9.65
Ladder	Home Depot (2010)	Werner 20' ft. Aluminum Extension Ladder with 225 lb Load Capacity Type II Duty Rating	$125.00
Scroll Saw	Woodcraft Flier (2013)	Excalibur 21" scroll saw package	$849.99
Snow Thrower	Northern Tool 1 Equipment (2010)	Husqvarna Single Stage Snow Thrower—21" Clearing Width, 208 cc Snow King Engine	$649.99
Tape Measure	homedepot.com (2014)	Stanley PowerLock 25' Tape Measure	$9.97
Tension Wrench	Empekay LLC (2011)	Lock Technology tension wrench	$19.98
Tile Grout	Farm & Home Supply Center (2014)	Elmer's E873 Tile Grout 6 oz	$3.58
Toolbox	Sears (2013)	Stack-On 16" multi-purpose steel toolbox	$27.13
Wood Glue	Woodcraft flier (2013)	Titebond glue, designed for professionals,	$19.79 per gallon
Wood Lathe	Woodcraft Flier (2013)	NOVA DVR XP lathe with electronic variable speed	$1,849.99
Wrench	Tools Plus (2013)	10-in. MaxGrip locking adjustable wrench	$14.91
TOYS			
Crayons	quill.com (2014)	Crayola® Crayons; 24-count Box	$2.29
Electric Scooter	toysrus.com (2013)	Razor Daisy E100 Electric Scooter	$99.99
Maze Game	Toys"R"Us (2013)	PlaSmart Perplexus 3D	$19.99
TRAVEL & TRANSPORTATION			
Flight	Travelocity (2012)	Round-trip ticket: Boston to Seoul, South Korea	$1,160.00
Luggage	Samsonite Company Stores (2012)	Samsonite 30" spinner	$185.59
Luggage	J.C.'s 5 Star Outlet Flier	3-pc. expandable luggage set, includes 20"×, 24" and 28" uprights; Regularly $357.00	$79.62
Train Ticket	Amtrak (2013)	Round-trip ticket: Boston to New York City	$144.00
Travel Alarm Clock	DBROTH (2010)	FLY on Time lightweight, 4 alarm settings	$11.98
Travel Handbag	Kloud City(2011)	Nylon Travel Handbag	$8.49
Travel Organizer	eBags (2012)	Belle Hop ID document organizer	$21.29

MISCELLANY 2010-2014

$1 Million to Inventor of Tracker for A.L.S.

BOSTON—Tracking the inexorable advance of amyotrophic lateral sclerosis, the deadly neuromuscular ailment better known as Lou Gehrig's disease or A.L.S., has long been an inexact science—a matter of monitoring weakness and fatigue, and making crude measurements of the strength of various muscles.

This imprecision has hindered the search for drugs that could slow or block the disease's progress. But now, a neurologist at Beth Israel Deaconess Medical Center here has won a $1 million prize—reportedly the largest ever for meeting a specific challenge in medical research—for developing a reliable way to quantify the small muscular changes that signal progressive deterioration.

The winner, Dr. Seward Rutkove, showed that his method could halve the cost of clinical trials to screen potential drugs for the disease, said Melanie Leitner, chief scientific officer of Prize4Life, the nonprofit group that created the competition.

The method does not provide a target in the body at which to aim drugs, nor will it help doctors better diagnose the disease. But Dr. Merit Cudkowicz, a professor of neurology at Massachusetts General Hospital and a chairwoman of the Northeast A.L.S. Consortium, compared Dr. Rutkove's discovery to the way magnetic resonance imaging expedited the development of drugs for multiple sclerosis.

The New York Times, February 3, 2011

"E-Readers Catch Younger Eyes and Go in Backpacks,"

Something extraordinary happened after Eliana Litos received an e-reader for a Hanukkah gift in December.

"Some weeks I completely forgot about TV," said Eliana, 11. "I went two weeks with only watching one show, or no shows at all. I was just reading every day."

Ever since the holidays, publishers have noticed that some unusual titles have spiked in e-book sales. The "Chronicles of Narnia" series. "Hush, Hush." The "Dork Diaries" series.

At HarperCollins, for example, e-books made up 25 percent of all young-adult sales in January, up from about 6 percent a year before—a boom in sales that quickly got the attention of publishers there.

"Adult fiction is hot, hot, hot in e-books," said Susan Katz, the president and publisher of Harper-Collins Children's Books. "And now it seems that teen fiction is getting to be hot, hot, hot."

In their infancy, e-readers were adopted by an older generation that valued the devices for their convenience, portability and, in many cases, simply for their ability to enlarge text to a more legible size. Appetite for e-book editions of best-sellers and adult genre fiction—romance, mysteries, thrillers—has seemed almost bottomless.

But now that e-readers are cheaper and more plentiful, they have gone mass market, reaching consumers across age and demographic groups, and enticing some members of the younger generation to pick them up for the first time.

"The kids have taken over the e-readers," said Rita Threadgill of Harrison, N.Y., whose 11-year-old daughter requested a Kindle for Christmas.

In 2010, young-adult e-books made up about 6 percent of the total digital sales for titles published by St. Martin's Press, but so far in 2011, the number is up to 20 percent, a spokeswoman for the publisher said.

The New York Times, February 4, 2011

Safety on the Home Front, the Latest News from the American Academy of Pediatrics

Just eight weeks before the tragedy in Newtown, Connecticut, the American Academy of Pediatrics (AAP) called for new community safety efforts and gun control legislation. But the buck does not stop on Capitol Hill or the offices of your local school district. It's important for parents to make similar steps in their own homes. Did you know that a three-year-old has the finger power to pull the trigger of a gun? That's scary, especially since more than a third of American families own guns, and many of them are stored loaded and unlocked. Firearms-related injuries are one of the top three causes of death in children.

"Young children are curious and are often unable to remember to follow safety rules," said Marion Burton, M.D., a past president of the AAP. "Older

MISCELLANY 2010-2014

children and teens naturally tend to be moody and impulsive. When you combine these traits with access to guns, the consequences can be tragic and permanent."

Parenting, March 2013

Open the Door and Let 'em In, The Opponents of Immigration Reform Are Hampering the Economy—and Hurting All of Us

From an economic standpoint, the battle over immigration reform has always been utterly baffling to me. Immigrants, or the children of immigrants, founded 40 percent of the country's Fortune 500 firms and untold millions of smaller businesses. They are the key reason the U.S.'s population growth, and thus its economic growth, is predicted to be higher than that of most of the rest of the rich world over the next couple of decades. Immigrants are the difference between an economy growing at a healthy 3 percent rate and a sluggish 2 percent. Why wouldn't we want to get as many of them as we can get?

Sadly, many House Republicans, who have been debating the issue in recent days, don't agree. That means the Immigration Reform bill that passed the Senate with bipartisan support a few weeks ago is likely to be scuppered. Conservatives continue to insist that creating a job path to citizenship for undocumented immigrants would unleash a torrent of new low-skilled workers from Mexico that would drive down U.S. wages.

The truth is that the net flow of immigrants from Mexico into the United States has been slowing for a decade. It has now essentially stopped and is likely to reverse later this year, with the number of Mexicans returning home from the United States exceeding the number crossing over to America. Increased border patrols and tougher U.S. laws have clearly played a part, but a more important reason is that the economic calculus of immigration has changed. The recession hurt prospects in the United States. Meanwhile, a booming Mexican economy and better educational and job opportunities in Mexico have led many Mexican immigrants—who make up 28 percent of the native-born population of the United States—to go home.

Time, July 22, 2013

After SAC Plea, Fellow Funds May Pay

In striking its $1.2 billion settlement with SAC Capital Advisors, the government set a record for insider trading penalties. For the hedge fund industry, the hidden costs of the deal are even bigger.

Tougher regulatory scrutiny since the financial crisis and changes in the law have forced hedge funds to spend millions of dollars a year on new compliance measures to make sure that they are not ensnared in the same net as SAC. This has added to the cost of doing business, which can cut into returns.

"It is getting much more expensive for hedge funds," said Thomas A. Sporkin, a partner at Buckley Sandler and a former enforcement lawyer at the Securities and Exchange Commission. "What kind of returns are you going to need to make in this business given the compliance and regulatory burdens?"

The New York Times, November 6, 2013

2015–2019
A Fractured Country

2017 series one-dollar bill.

The years from 2015 and 2019 have seen the American economy largely recover from the Great Recession of the late 2000s and early 2010s. By September 2015, the unemployment rate had fallen back to its pre-crisis levels, and it has continued to fall in the years since. As the recovery continued, it became the second largest on record by April 2018. The United States remains the world's largest national economy as well as the world's largest producer of oil and gas. Despite the decline of the manufacturing sector, the United States is still the second largest manufacturing nation in the world. In 2016, the country's industrial output totaled $3.6 trillion and the total value of exported goods was a robust $1.62 trillion.

Nonetheless, despite these positive markers, the American economy is not as dominant or as equitable as it once was. The country that ranks number one in manufacturing output, China, has proved a challenging negotiating partner for the United States. Although China stopped manipulating its currency in 2014, it has entered a new trade war with the United States centering on the issue of tariffs. Because so many Chinese goods reach the American market and China is the second largest holder of U.S. debt, a trade balance has ensued that the U.S. government has sought to correct, largely through the imposition of tariffs on Chinese goods.

Inequality has long been a problem in the United States, but after the Great Recession and the recovery, the difference in wealth between the top earners and the bottom earners has increased dramatically. In 2016, the economists Peter H. Lindert and Jeremy G. Williamson noted that income inequality was at the highest level it had ever been. This lack of opportunity for so many Americans was on the minds of voters during the 2016 election in which the Democratic nominee Hilary Clinton was upset by the Republican candidate Donald Trump. Despite having no political experience, Trump's campaign with its promise to "Make American Great Again," and its not-so-veiled racism and xenophobia, appealed to many white Americans who felt that they were disenfranchised and who feared the nation's changing demographics. The election was plagued with controversy, as evidence of possible interference on multiple fronts by Russia was detected and is the subject of an ongoing investigation by Special Counsel and former FBI Director Robert Mueller.

Trump's victory in the Electoral College, coupled with his losing the popular vote by several million, pointed up the increasingly divided nature of the country, in which every facet of life suddenly took on the feel of being politicized. Venues such as football, in which Colin Kaepernick's using of the National Anthem to protest racist police violence, brought forth extreme responses from both liberals and conservatives who seemed unable to agree on anything, showed the widening scope of the schism. This disagreement continued to be reflected in the actions of Congress, in which Democrats and Republicans voted almost exclusively along party lines. The result was that little legislative activity was achieved during this time and on December 22, 2018, the government shut down for what would be a record 34 days.

The years 2015–2019 also saw a rise in the awareness and visibility of racial issues. In response to the acquittal of George Zimmerman in the killing of the unarmed African American teenager Trayvon Martin in 2013 and the later police killing of another unarmed African American teenager, Michael Brown, in Ferguson, Missouri, in 2014, the Black Lives Matter movement was founded. An international activist movement, BLM campaigns against violence and systemic racism directed against African Americans. Meanwhile, police killings of unarmed black men and boys continued to make headlines, drawing divisive reactions from both anti-racist advocates and pro-police supporters. The rise of the alt-right, a white nationalist movement whose prominence coincided with the campaign of Donald J. Trump further reflected the tense and fractured racial tensions in the country. This trend had its most visible flowering in the Unite the Right Rally, a gathering of white supremacists in Charlottesville, Virginia, on August 11 and 12, 2017 that resulted in the murder of a counter-protestor and outrage on the part of many observers.

Meanwhile, social media continued to play a central role in people's lives and a chief means of receiving information, although not without controversy. Facebook, in particular, came under fire for its role in the 2016 election, both from the ways it was used to spread fraudulent news stories and for its partnership with Cambridge Analytica, a British consulting firm that was given access to user's data that they then manipulated for political purposes. More generally, a growing awareness of the ways in which people's personal information was being harvested by social media companies led to a backlash and to many tech conglomerates revising their policies. Nonetheless, social media remains as big a part of Americans' lives as it ever has been.

Year	Dollar Value in 2019
2015	$1.06
2016	$1.05
2017	$1.02
2018	$1.00
2019	$1.00

Use this Currency Conversion chart to calculate what any time in the years listed would cost in 2019. Simply multiply the cost of that item by dollar amount in the chart. For example, if you know that a Rolex watch cost $9,220.00 in 2015, multiply $9,220.00 by $1.06 to discover that that same watch would cost $9,773.20 in 2019.

HISTORICAL SNAPSHOT 2015-2018

2015

- The New England Patriots defeat the Seattle Seahawks 2—24 in Super Bowl XLIX amidst allegations of cheating in a scandal that came to be known as Deflategate
- RadioShack files for bankruptcy after experiencing 11 straight quarterly losses
- *NBC Nightly News* suspends anchor Brian Williams for six months after it was revealed he fabricated his experiences in Iraq
- The 87th Academy Awards are held, with *Birdman* winning four awards, including Best Picture and Best Director for Alejandro González Iñárritu
- The U.S. Federal Communications Committee (FCC) votes to uphold net neutrality, applying the Communications Act of 1934 and the Telecommunications Act of 1996 to the Internet
- Former CIA director David Petraeus pleads guilty in federal court of mishandling classified information, having leaked secrets to his biographer and lover Paula Broadwell
- Indiana Governor Mike Pence signs Indiana Senate Bill (SB) 101 into law, allowing discrimination against LGBT people on religious grounds and sparking much controversy
- Barack Obama and Cuban President Raul Castro meet to discuss normalizing relations between the United States and Cuba. Soon after, Obama removes Cuba from the list of State Sponsors of Terrorism. Later in the year, the two countries establish full diplomatic ties
- Protests in Baltimore break out over the death of Freddie Gray, a young African American man who died in police custody. Looting and property damage ensues, leading Maryland Governor Larry Hogan to declare a state of emergency and send in the National Guard.
- Dzhokhar Tsarnaev is sentenced to death for his role in carrying out the Boston Marathon bombings
- Caitlyn Jenner, formerly known as Bruce, comes out as a trans woman and becomes the first transgender person to appear on the cover of *Vanity Fair*
- Nine people are shot and killed during a service at the historically black Emanuel African Methodist Episcopal Church in Charleston, South Carolina, by white supremacist Dylann Roof
- In *King vs. Burwell*, the Supreme Court upholds the constitutionality of tax credits under the Patient Protection and Affordable Care Act by a 6–3 decision
- In *Obergefell vs. Hodges*, the Supreme Court rules that the Constitution ensures a right to same sex marriage by a 5–4 decision
- The unemployment rate drops to 5%, finally returning to pre-Great Recession levels
- Fourteen people are killed in a mass shooting in San Bernardino, California, at a facility for the mentally disabled

2016

- Several armed militias take over the Malheur National Wildlife Range in Harney County, Oregon. The FBI is called in, staging a shootout in which one militiaman is killed and five are arrested, including ringleader Ammon Bundy
- The Denver Broncos defeat the Carolina Panthers 24–10 in Super Bowl 50
- *Spotlight* takes the top prize at the 88th Academy Awards. Alejandro González Iñárritu wins Best Director for the second straight year for his film *The Revenant.*
- In Super Tuesday primary voting, Hilary Clinton and Donald Trump both win seven states, emerging as front-runners for the Democratic and Republican presidential nominations respectively
- Barack Obama nominates Merrick Garland to fill the Supreme Court seat vacated by Antonin Scalia's death. The Republican majority in the Senate refuses to hold a hearing or vote on this nomination
- Pharmaceutical companies Pfizer and Allergan call off an intended merger because of new laws on tax inversion
- Omar Mateen opens fire at the gay nightclub Pulse in Orlando, killing 49 and wounding 53, making it the largest mass shooting in U.S. history.
- FBI director James Comey recommends against bringing charges against Hilary Clinton for using a private e-mail server while Secretary of State and Attorney General Loretta Lynch ends the investigation. Nonetheless, both the State Department and the FBI later reopens the investigation
- Despite losing the popular vote by nearly 3 million, Donald Trump is elected president, defeating Hilary Clinton in the Electoral College 304–227.
- Four states vote to legalize the sale and use of recreational marijuana. The states are California, Nevada, Maine, and Massachusetts

- The CIA informs lawmakers that it is confident that Russia engaged in cyberattacks to help influence the U.S. election in favor of Donald Trump. Congress vows to hold an investigation
- The withdrawal of U.S. troops from Afghanistan is completed, although 8,400 troops were left behind

2017

- Donald Trump is inaugurated as the 45th President of the United States
- 2.9 million people attend the Women's March, protesting Trump's election. It becomes the largest protest in U.S. history
- President Trump signs an executive order banning the entry of all citizens of 7 predominantly Muslim countries for 90 days. This leads to widespread protest and a lawsuit from the American Civil Liberties Union (ACLU)
- The New England Patriots stage a stunning comeback to defeat the Atlanta Falcons 34–28 in Super Bowl LI
- In a surprise, *Moonlight* upsets heavy favorite *La Land* to win Best Picture at the 89th Academy Awards
- Trump fires FBI head James Comey, citing his manhandling of the Hilary Clinton e-mail case. Many feel the real reason is that he doesn't want Comey to investigate ties between Russia and his campaign. Soon after, the Justice Department names Robert Mueller special counsel to launch a full-scale investigation into these alleged ties.
- The Unite the Right Rally, a gathering of various white nationalist groups in Charlottesville, Virginia, turns fatal when a car ploughs into a group of counter-protestors, killing 32-year-old Heather Heyer

- North Korea continues to escalate its nuclear program, launching a ballistic missile over northern Japan. Trump says that "all options are on the table" in terms of a U.S. response.
- Hurricane Maria decimates the U.S. territory of Puerto Rico, leaving millions of people without power or homes. Trump's tepid response is widely criticized.
- Steven Paddock opens fire at the Route 91 Harvest Festival in Las Vegas. Fifty-nine people are killed and 851 are injured, surpassing the Pulse shooting, and making it the deadliest mass shooting in modern U.S. history
- The #Me Too movement begins as numerous accusations of sexual misconduct are brought against famous men such as Matt Lauer, Louis C.K. and Kevin Spacey, changing the conversation about sexual abuse and male power
- The Senate approves the Tax Cuts and Job Acts of 2017 by a 51–49 vote. The Act is the first major overhaul of the tax code since the 1980s.

2018

- Amazon opens an Amazon Go store in Seattle. It is the first completely cashier-less grocery store in existence.
- The Eagles win their first-ever Super Bowl, defeating the New England Patriots 41–33
- A mass shooting breaks out at Marjorie Stoneman Douglas High School in Parkland, Florida, killing 17. It is the deadliest school shooting in U.S. history.
- The 90th Academy Awards are held. *The Shape of Water* takes home four awards, including Best Picture.
- Secretary of State Rex Tillerson is fired and replaced with former CIA Director Mike Pompeo

- Facebook suspends Cambridge Analytica, a data analysis company that manipulated user data to help elect Donald Trump
- Trump announces tariffs on up to $60 billion of Chinese goods, hoping to correct the trade imbalance. The Dow Jones drops sharply. Soon after, China announces its own tariffs on U.S. goods.
- The unemployment rate falls to 3.9, its lowest rate in nearly two decades
- Trump meets with North Korean leader Kim Jong-un in Singapore
- Supreme Court Justice Anthony Kennedy announces his retirement. He is eventually replaced by controversial nominee Brett Kavanagh.
- Donald Trump's former lawyer, Michael Cohen, pleads guilty to five criminal charges on the same day that his former campaign chairman, Paul Manafort, is found guilty on eight charges of bank and tax fraud
- *Washington Post* columnist Jamal Khashoggi is killed inside the Saudi consulate in Istanbul, leading to a diplomatic crisis between the United States and the Saudi government, who initially denied the event altogether
- In the mid-term elections, the Democrats retake the House of Representatives,
- while losing two seats in the Republican-controlled Senate. The Democrats also gain seven new governorships
- The government shuts down after the two parties fail to agree on a budget. At stake is the border wall that Trump insists be funded as part of the agreement.

The "Cuban thaw" was a warming of Cuba–United States relations that began in December 2014, ending a 54-year stretch of hostility between the nations. In March 2016, Barack Obama became the first U.S. President to visit Cuba since 1928. (via Wikimedia Commons)

SELECTED INCOME 2015-2019

Job	Source	Description	Pay
Accounting Manager	payscale.com (2019)		$69,271
Activity Aide, Nursing Home	indeed.com (2019)	Sullivan County, NH	$26,936–$36,358
Actuary	bls.gov (2016)	Austin, TX	$97,070
Administrative Assistant	careerbuilder.com (2019)	St. Louis, MO	$31,000-$38,000
Air Traffic Controller	bls.gov (2015)		$122,950
Airline Pilot	bls.gov (2017)		$111,930
Alumni Relations Officer	salary.com (2019)		$53,009
Ambulance Driver	bls.gov (2017)		$33,380
Anesthesiologist	glassdoor.com (2019)		$371,527
Animal Control Worker	bls.gov (2017)		$22,950
Animal Obedience Trainer	indeed.com (2019)	Methuen, MA	$31,200–$41,600
Appraiser, Residential	salary.com (2019)	Houston, TX	$54,568
Architect	usnews.com (2017)		$78,470
Art Director	indeed.com (2019)	New York, NY	$70,000–$80,000
Assistant Buyer, Retail	salary.com (2019)		$47,921
Assistant Director of Accounting	glassdoor.com (2019)		$77,384
Assistant Manager	glassdoor.com (2019)	Walgreens	$38,040
Automotive Mechanic	usnews.com (2017)		$39,550
Bailiff	payscale.com (2018)		$40,101
Bank Teller	glassdoor.com (2019)		$23,200
Bilingual Caseworker	indeed.com (2019)	San Francisco, CA	$37,440–$41,600
Bill and Account Collector	glassdoor.com (2019)		$33,446
Bingo Caller	salary.com (2019)		$25,170
Budget Analyst	bls.gov (2017)		$75,240
Bursar	salary.com (2019)	New York, NY	$78,223
Bus Driver	usnews.com (2017)		$40,780
Business Analyst	indeed.com (2019)	New York, NY	$40,000–$45,000
Cannery Worker	salary.com (2019)	New Orleans, LA	$27,366
Carpenter	indeed.com (2019)	Albertson, NY	$30,000–$40,000
Case Worker, Home Care	salary.com (2019)		$63,743
Cashier	payscale.com (2019)		$19,240
Children's Caseworker	careerbuilder.com (2019)	Phoenix, AZ	$27,500
Chiropractor	salary.com (2019)		$147,316
Claims Adjustor	indeed.com (2019)	Grand Junction, CO	$40,000–$50,000
Coatroom Attendant	ziprecruiter.com (2019)		$26,162
Computer and Information Systems Manager	glassdoor.com (2017)		$91,587
Computer Programmer	payscale.com (2019)		$61,240

Job	Source	Description	Pay
Construction Worker	bls.gov (2017)		$33,450
Crane and Tower Operator	recruiter.com (2019)	Nevada	$74,180
Crossing Guard	recruiter.com (2019)		$26,600
Customer Service Worker	indeed.com (2019)	Wal-Mart	$19,510–22,880
Day Care Center Teacher	salary.com (2019)		$31,939
Dietician	glassdoor.com (2019)		$59,660
Driver	truckdriversalary.com (2019)	UPS	$57,866
Electrician	ziprecruiter.com (2019)	California	$47,475
Embalmer	bls.gov (2017)		$42,780
Engineer	glassdoor.com (2018)	Exxon Mobil	$106,031
Executive Chef	glassdoor.com (2019)	New York, NY	$72,381
Fast Food Worker	indeed.com (2019)	McDonald's	$17,019

Protesters gather outside the McDonald's restaurant at University Avenue and Marion Street in St. Paul and call for a $15 per hour minimum wage, paid sick days, and union rights. (via Wikimedia Commons)

Job	Source	Description	Pay
Federal Air Marshal	glassdoor.com (2016)	Dept. of Homeland Security	$95,000
Firefighter	bls.gov (2017)		$49,080
Fish and Game Warden	bls.gov (2015)		$54,970
Flight Attendant	indeed.com (2019)	Denver, CO	$38,480
Forest and Conservation Worker	salary.com (2019)		$53,349
Forklift Operator	indeed.com (2019)	Mamaroneck, NY	$37,440
Foundry Worker	salary.com (2019)		$33,472
Funeral Director	ziprecruiter.com (2019)	Maryland	$47,965
Ghostwriter	ziprecruiter.com (2019)		$65,756
Graphic Designer	payscale.com (2019)		$43,270
Hairstylist	glassdoor.com (2019)		$21,650
Hazardous Materials Removal Worker	payscale.com (2019)		$41,442
Heart Transplant Surgeon	salary.com (2019)		$618,203
High School Coach	ziprecruiter.com (2019)		$45,024
High School Teacher	usnews.com (2017)		$59,170
Highway Maintenance Worker	recruiter.com (2019)	California	$49,600
Hotel Clerk	recuiter.com (2019)	Massachusetts	$26,340
Housekeeper, Hotel	usnews.com (2017)		$24,630
Insurance Agent	salary.com (2019)		$49,846
Interior Design Sales Consultant	indeed.com (2019)	Landover, MD	$50,000–$60,000
Janitor	salary.com (2019)		$29,510
Labor Relations Director	salary.com (2019)		$156,435
Lawyer	usnews.com (2017)		$119,250
Legal Secretary	indeed.com (2019)	New York, NY	$40,000–$45,000
Librarian	ziprecruiter.com (2019)	Montana	$47,500
Lifeguard	glassdoor.com (2019)		$22,852
Locksmith	bls.gov (2017)		$40,680
Logging Worker	bls.gov (2017)		$38,840
Mail Carrier	glassdoor.com (2019)	US Postal Service	$36,000
Major League Umpire	chron.com (2019)		$120,000–$350,000
Market Researcher	usnews.com (2017)		$63,230
Mathematician	bls.gov (2017)		$103,310
Medical Social Worker	salary.com (2019)		$62,136
Meeting and Event Planner	usnews.com (2017)		$52,630
Middle School Teacher	payscale.com (2019)		$46,870
Mover	bls.gov (2017)		$25,870
Multimedia Artist	ziprecruiter.com (2019)		$43,973
Museum Researcher	salary.com (2019)		$53,349
Nanny	indeed.com (2019)	Cohasset, MA	$36,400–$40,040

Job	Source	Description	Pay
Paralegal	payscale.com (2019)		$46,619
Paramedic	glassdoor.com (2019)	New York, NY	$54,584
Pharmacist	salary.com (2019)		$132,263
Pharmacy Technician	glassdoor.com (2019)		$29,276
Plumber	ziprecruiter.com (2019)	Wisconsin	$52,000
Probation Officer	indeed.com (2019)		$44,733
Program Manager	glassdoor.com (2019)	Expedia	$99,827
Project Manager	glassdoor.com (2019)	Hewlett-Packard	$87,255
Psychiatrist	ziprecruiter.com (2019)	Virginia	$244,966
Radio Announcer	bls.gov (2017)		$32,450
Ranch Manager	salary.com (2019)		$43,774
Registered Nurse	nurse.org (2017)	South Carolina	$63,630
Reporter	glassdoor.com (2019)	New York Times	$105,963
Research Fellow	indeed.com (2019)		$51,463
Restaurant Cook	usnews.gov (2017)		$25,180
Sailor	recruiter.com (2017)		$37,500
Security Guard	glassdoor.com (2019)		$28,963
Service Station Attendant	indeed.com (2019)		$22,401.60
Social Worker	glassdoor.com (2019)		$53,950
Speech Pathologist	ziprecruiter.com (2017)	Florida	$87,303
Speech Writer	glassdoor.com (2019)	U.S. Senate	$86,360
Stagehand	glassdoor.com (2019)		$34,540
Stock Clerk	salary.com (2019)		$35,532
Stonemason	recruiter.com (2019)		$39,900
Store General Manager	payscale.com (2019)		$53,998
Tailor	indeed.com (2019)	Men's Warehouse	$30,971.20
Tax Preparer	ziprecruiter.com (2019)		$43,763
Taxi Driver	salary.com (2019)		$35,098
Technical Writer	payscale.com (2019)		$58,581
Telemarketer	usnews.com (2017)		$27,670
Translator	salary.com (2019)		$47,044
TSA Screener	federallawenforcement.org (2019)		$25,518–$44,007
Upholsterer	bls.gov (2017)		$35,060
Urban and Regional Planner	bls.gov (2017)		$71,490
Usher/Ticket Taker	salary.com (2019)		$20,048
Veterinarian	usnews.com (2017)		$94,420
Vice President	glassdoor.com (2019)	Merrill Lynch	$142,668
Video Editor	glassdoor.com (2019)		$50,584
Warehouse Associate	payscale.com (2019)		$27,248

CONSUMER EXPENDITURES 2015-2017*

| | (Per Person) | | |
Expenditure Type	2015	2016	2017
Food	$3,989	$3,829	$4,425
Food at home	$2,185	$2,049	$2,323
Food away from home	$1,805	$1,780	$2,101
Alcoholic beverages	$393	$358	$390
Housing	$12,393	$13,125	$13,529
Shelter	$8,069	$8,478	$8,735
Owned dwellings	$3,321	$3,305	$3,574
Rented dwellings	$4,382	$4,772	$4,710
Utilities, fuels, public services	$2,348	$2,407	$2,353
Natural gas	$286	$242	$249
Electricity	$926	$945	$938
Telephone services	$752	$818	$747
Water and other public services	$308	$340	$352
Apparel and services	$957	$1,019	$1,007
Transportation	$4,960	$4,746	$5,155
Vehicle purchases (net outlay)	$1,851	$1,625	$1,761
Cars and trucks, new	$998	$795	$832
Cars and trucks, used	$816	$767	$896
Gasoline and motor oil	$1,085	$1,007	$999
Other vehicle expenses	$1,632	$1,728	$1,961
Maintenance and repairs	$512	$544	$794
Public and other transportation	$393	$386	$435
Healthcare	$2,638	$2,852	$2,967
Entertainment	$1,711	$1,696	$1,660
Personal care products and services	$417	$434	$496
Reading	$80	$105	$80
Education	$735	$758	$743
Tobacco products and smoking supplies	$253	$243	$240
Cash contributions	$1,400	$2,260	$1,403
Personal insurance and pensions	$2,897	$3,065	$3,093
Miscellaneous	$685	$709	$773
Total average annual expenditures	**$33,508**	**$35,199**	**$35,960**

Expenditure Type	2015	2016	2017
Personal Taxes			
Money income before taxes	$35,522	$36,171	$35,889
Personal taxes	$5,129	$5,013	$4,793
Federal income taxes	$4,076	$4,042	$3,884
State/local income taxes	$968	$929	$886
Other taxes	$85	$43	$23
Income after taxes	**$30,393**	**$31,158**	**$31,095**

2017 is the most recent year with reliable data

Source: U.S. Department of Labor, Bureau of Labor Statistics, Consumer Expenditure Surveys 2012–2017 (Size of consumer unit: Average annual expenditures and characteristics)

INVESTMENTS 2015-2018

Investment	2015	2016	2017	2018
Moody's Yield Seasoned Corp Bonds—All Industries AAA	5.10	4.68	4.64	4.83
90-Day AA Nonfinancial Commercial Paper Int Rate	0.17	0.46	1.16	2.06
Federal Funds Effective Rate	0.13	0.40	0.91	1.90
Bank Prime Loan Rate	3.25	3.50	4.25	5.00
Certificate of Deposit-6-Month Rate				
US Treasury Note-10 Year	2.33	1.53	2.21	2.88
Mortgage Rate-30 Year Fixed	3.87	3.56	3.90	4.54
S&P 500 Index-Price	2,107	2,031	2,437	2,727
S&P 500 Index-Dividend Yield	2.11	2.03	1.84	2.09

STOCK PRICES AND DIVIDENDS

	2015	2016	2017	2018
AT&T (T)	35.59	43.42	37.84	32.16
Dividends	0.47	0.48	0.49	0.50
Bank of America (BAC)	17.25	13.37	24.46	28.08
Dividends	0.05	0.05	0.075	0.12
Boeing (BA)	141.29	129.54	187.41	330.69
Dividends	0.91	1.09	1.42	1.71
General Electric (GE)	25.67	30.27	26.12	12.96
Dividends	0.23	0.23	0.24	0.12
General Motors (GM)	33.61	28.69	34.52	39.08
Dividends	0.36	0.38	0.38	0.38
Google (GOOG)	524.73	692.20	912.18	1,099.00
Dividends	0	0	0	0
Kellogg Co. (K)	62.70	81.44	69.58	69.59
Dividends	0.49	0.5	0.52	0.54
Microsoft (MSFT)	44.46	51.13	69.33	98.10
Dividends	0.31	0.36	0.39	0.42
Navistar International Corp. (NAV)	22.75	11.76	26.50	40.32
Dividends	0	0	0	0
Pfizer	33.56	35.15	33.48	36.00
Dividends	0.28	0.3	0.32	0.34
Procter & Gamble Co. (PG)	78.39	84.52	87.40	77.50
Dividends	0.6629	0.6695	0.6896	0.7172
Reynolds American Inc. (RAI)	37.42	54.00	64.46	
Dividends	0	0	0	
Wal-Mart (WMT)	71.60	73.13	75.84	85.65
Dividends	0.49	0.5	0.51	0.52

Investment	2015	2016	2017	2018
United States Steel Co. (X)	20.77	16.70	22.17	34.50
Dividends	0.05	0.05	0.05	0.05

STANDARD JOBS 2015–2018

Based on NAICS Codes	NAICS*	2015	2016	2017	2018
Total, all industries	10	$52,942	$53,621	$55,390	$57,265
Total, all private industries		$52,876	$53,515	$55,338	$57,198
Federal government		$77,900	$78,379	$80,432	$83,666
State government		$55,878	$57,168	$58,802	$60,731
Local government		$47,573	$48,440	$49,720	$51,507
Bituminous coal underground mining	2121112	$86,682	$83,842	$88,817	$92,153
Construction	1012	$57,009	$58,647	$60,735	$62, 732
Private households (domestics)	814	$23,870	$24,501	$25,288	$26,378
Crop production	111	$30,317	$31,587	$32,794	$34,052
Finance and insurance	52	$100,286	$101,210	$106,185	$109,247
Wholesale Trade	42	$73,363	$73,710	$75,904	$77,879
Retail trade	44-45	$29,742	$30,299	$31,217	$32,357
Electric, gas, and sanitary services	221	$101,445	$102,868	$107,194	$109,947
Elementary and secondary schools	6111	$39,288	$40,166	$41,234	$42,233
Manufacturing	31-33	$64,305	$64,870	$66,840	$68,528
Postal Service	491	$30,061	$29,882	$29,841	$31,290
Telecommunications	517	$82,996	$85,976	$87,515	$89,221
Radio and television broadcasting	5151	$76,858	$78,411	$81,997	$85,356
Motion picture and video	5121	$66,504	$64,737	$67,484	$70,835
Health care and social assistance	62	$47,296	$47,956	$49,076	$50,328
Membership associations and organizations	813	$41,142	$42,348	$43,941	$45,445
Rail transportation	4821	$45,299	$48,345	$47,398	$50,152
Transit and ground passenger transportation	485	$28,345	$30,152	$31,602	$34,427

Source: Quarterly Census of Employment and Wages from the Bureau of Labor Statistics

*The North American Industry Classification System (NAICS) is a classification of business establishments by type of economic activity (process of production). It is used by government and business in Canada, Mexico, and the United States of America. The first two digits designate the largest business sector, the third digit designates the subsector, the fourth digit designates the industry group, the fifth digit designates the NAICS industries, and the sixth digit designates the national industries.

FOOD BASKET 2015–2017*

Commodity	Year	U.S. Average	Atlanta	Chicago	Denver	Los Angeles	New York
Bananas, per lb.	2015	57¢	64¢	55¢	58¢	69¢	60¢
	2016	57¢	60¢	40¢	60¢	69¢	51¢
	2017	57¢	60¢	49¢	59¢	69¢	75¢
Beef, Ground, per lb.	2015	$4.47	$4.69	$5.71	$5.09	$4.27	$6.09
	2016	$3.91	$4.30	$4.57	$4.77	$4.60	$6.10
	2017	$3.79	$3.88	$4.33	$3.88	$4.77	$5.38
Bread, white, per loaf	2015	$1.48	$1.46	$2.05	$1.54	$1.48	$2.28
	2016	$3.15	$4.14	$3.05	$2.85	$3.19	$3.73
	2017	$3.22	$4.13	$2.94	$3.25	$3.11	$3.86
Cereal, Corn Flakes 18 oz.	2015	$3.43	$3.30	$3.50	$3.43	$3.93	$3.96
	2016	$3.44	$3.61	$3.71	$3.54	$4.43	$3.88
	2017	$3.47	$3.69	$3.79	$3.57	$4.81	$4.78
Cheese, grated Parmesan, 8 oz.	2015	$3.91	$4.07	$4.46	$3.97	$4.41	$6.21
	2016	$3.92	$3.97	$4.37	$3.97	$4.99	$5.59
	2017	$3.91	$3.85	$4.14	$3.99	$4.78	$5.40
Chicken, whole uncut, per lb.	2015	$1.40	$1.42	$1.43	$1.50	$1.56	$1.49
	2016	$1.34	$1.35	$1.67	$1.40	$1.24	$2.04
	2017	$1.33	$1.27	$1.28	$1.35	$1.00	$2.08
Coca-Cola, 2 liter	2015	$1.62	$1.73	$2.09	$1.63	$1.86	$2.14
	2016	$1.61	$1.60	$1.79	$1.54	$1.99	$2.04
	2017	$1.65	$1.72	$1.99	$1.43	$2.10	$2.23
Coffee, vacuum-packed, 11.5 oz.	2015	$4.34	$4.58	$4.92	$5.49	$5.27	$6.09
	2016	$4.20	$4.55	$4.45	$5.67	$6.04	$5.72
	2017	$4.24	$4.66	$4.53	$4.59	$6.42	$5.70
Corn, whole kernel frozen, 16 oz.	2015	$1.28	$1.32	$1.84	$1.34	$1.39	$1.69
	2016	$1.26	$1.29	$1.36	$1.24	$1.10	$2.18
	2017	$1.30	$1.34	$1.47	$1.23	$1.10	$2.27
Eggs, 1 dz. grade A or AA, large	2015	$2.18	$2.07	$2.39	$1.99	$2.35	$1.89
	2016	$1.95	$1.73	$1.69	$2.88	$2.49	$2.72
	2017	$1.39	$1.58	$1.65	$1.83	$2.11	$2.48
Lettuce, iceberg head	2015	$1.42	$1.34	$1.41	$1.10	$1.43	$1.70
	2016	$1.43	$1.46	$1.88	$1.14	$1.53	$2.15
	2017	$1.34	$1.41	$2.10	$1.05	$1.58	$2.54
Milk, whole ½ gallon	2015	$2.23	$2.30	$2.39	$1.99	$2.35	$1.89
	2016	$1.98	$1.99	$1.94	$1.78	$2.03	$2.45
	2017	$1.95	$1.98	$1.95	$1.72	$2.24	$3.24

Commodity	Year	U.S. Average	Atlanta	Chicago	Denver	Los Angeles	New York
Orange juice, fresh, 64 oz.	2015	$3.52	$3.75	$4.05	$4.05	$3.54	$4.14
	2016	$3.43	$3.45	$4.44	$3.91	$3.87	$4.15
	2017	$3.50	$3.56	$4.55	$3.52	$3.65	$4.74
Peas, sweet, 15 oz. can	2015	$1.10	$1.36	$1.41	$1.03	$1.42	$1.26
	2016	$1.07	$1.28	$1.36	$1.01	$1.55	$1.36
	2017	$1.06	$1.37	$1.37	$1.03	$1.60	$1.72
Potatoes, 10 lb. sack, white or red	2015	$2.98	$3.59	$3.17	$2.29	$2.93	$4.07
	2016	$2.93	$2.86	$3.51	$2.81	$2.66	$3.78
	2017	$2.99	$3.75	$3.79	$2.33	$2.63	$4.12
Sausage, pork 1 lb	2015	$4.36	$4.36	$4.48	$4.42	$4.88	$5.24
	2016	$3.90	$3.83	$4.35	$4.24	$4.16	$5.41
	2017	$3.83	$3.87	$4.38	$3.83	$4.60	$5.36
Steak, T-bone, per lb	2015	$10.97	$12.83	$11.95	$10.92	$11.05	$13.31
	2016	$11.31	$13.69	$11.76	$12.85	$10.63	$14.30
	2017	$11.17	$12.05	$12.22	$12.90	$12.10	$12.88
Sugar, white, 4-5 lb	2015	$2.27	$2.52	$3.06	$2.76	$2.59	$3.32
	2016	$2.22	$2.42	$3.10	$2.90	$2.85	$3.06
	2017	$2.15	$2.29	$2.33	$2.33	$3.00	$3.47
Tuna, chunk light, 6 oz. can	2015	.99¢	98¢	$1.45	$1.17	$1.10	$1.51
	2016	97¢	97¢	$1.18	$1.76	$1.11	$1.55
	2017	98¢	$1.04	$1.13	$1.09	$1.13	$1.48

*2017 is the most recent year with reliable pricing information.

Notes: Data are annual averages, derived from averaging data for the first 3 quarters.

Source: Council for Community and Economic Research (formerly ACCRA), Cost of Living Index

SELECTED PRICES 2015–2019

Item	Source	Description	Price
ALCOHOL			
Absinthe	absinthes.com	Absinthe Exitus, 500 ml	$37.00
Beer	liquormart.com	Bud Light, 24 pack of 12 ounce cans	$21.99
Gin	boxed.com	Tanqueray, London Dry Gin, 750 ml	$31.99
Scotch Whiskey	mashandgrape.com	Highland Journey, Blended Malt Scotch Whiskey 750 ml	$49.99
Vodka	boxed.com	Absolute Vodka, 750 ml	$37.99
Vodka	boxed.com	Smirnoff No. 21 Vodka, 750 ml	$16.99
Wine	wine.com	The Prisoner Wine Company, 2017 California Red, 750 ml	$49.99
Wine	wine-searcher.com	Domaine de la Chevalerie Diptyque Borgueil, Cabernet Franc, 750 ml	$14.99
APPAREL, CHILDREN'S			
Bowtie	J Crew	Boy's patterned silk bowtie	$19.50
Dress	Macys.com	Bonnie Jean Little Girls Floral Shantung Dress	$68.00
Hat and Mitten Set	Amazon.com	Simple Joy by Carter's, Baby and Toddler's Boy's Hat and Mitten Set	$15.99
Hoodie	Hanna Anderson	Jersey lined boy's hoodie in French terry	$48.00
APPAREL, MEN'S			
Bandana	The Gap	Elephant bandana, Adirondack green or Chambray blue	$15.00
Jeans	J.C. Penney	Levi's 505 regular fit jeans	$39.99
Kimono	Zaful.com	Dragon-printed kimono-front open jacket, black	$20.74
Shirt	L.L. Bean	Wrinkle-free twill sport shirt	$44.95
Slippers	Vineyard Vines	Men's suede slippers with 100% shearing lining and rubber sole	$98.50
Swim Trunks	L.L. Bean	Vacationland stretch swim trunks, 8"	$44.99
T-Shirt	Banana Republic	Soft wash crew-neck t-shirt	$29.50
Wallet	Shinola	Five-pocket card case	$125.00
APPAREL, WOMEN'S			
Basketball Shoes	Zappos.com	Nike Air Precision II FlyEase	$69.95
Choker	Sundance Catalog	Good faith choker, leather with sterling silver cross and delicate labradorite stones at the clasp	$120.00
Coin Purse	Aspinal of London	Small zipped coin purse	$75.00
Corset	Frederick's of Hollywood	Ramona corset, black vegan leather	$47.00

Item	Source	Description	Price
Fedora Hat	*Sundance Catalog*	Wool Corbin fedora with leather band	$98.00
Handbag	Newchic.com	Oil leather tote handbag	$31.31
High Heels	J.C. Penney	Worthington Beckwith pumps	$18.99
Hijab	The Hijab Store	Linen hijab with fringes	$4.99
Nightshirt	J.C. Penney	Liz Claiborne essential knit nightshirt	$17.40
Skirt	UNIQLO	Front-button circular skirt	$29.90
Sundress	Lulus	Emina navy blue-striped button-front mini-dress	$45.00
Women's Jeans	J.C. Penney	Lee relaxed fit jeans	$29.99
Wristband	Amazon.com	Studded leather wristband	$12.99

APPLIANCES

Item	Source	Description	Price
Deep Fryer	Walmart	Hamilton Beach 2 Liter professional deep fryer	$22.88
Dishwasher	Sears	Kenmore 24" built-in dishwasher	$429.99
Espresso Machine	Home Depot	DeLonghi 15 bar espresso and cappuccino machine	$166.22
Food Processor	Williams-Sonoma	Magimix food processor, 12 cup, white	$299.95
Slow Cooker	Home Depot	7 quart manual slow cooker	$29.99
Toaster Oven	Kohl's	Hamilton Beach 4 slice toaster oven	$24.99

ART SUPPLIES

Item	Source	Description	Price
Canvas	Utrecht Art Supplies	Utrecht masters acrylic primed cotton canvas roll, medium texture	$202.07
Oil Paint	Utrecht Art Supplies	Atelier Interactive artist's acrylic paint, cerulean blue, 250 ml jar	$62.57
Palette Knife	Utrecht Art Supplies	Blick palette knife by RGM	$16.39

BABY PRODUCTS & SUPPLIES

Item	Source	Description	Price
Car Seat, Toddler	Target	Graco TurboBooster Highback LX car seat	$69.99
Carrier	Ergobaby	Ergobaby Original ergonomic baby carrier	$96.00
Crib	buybuyBaby	DaVinci Jade 4-in-1 convertible crib	$239.99
Gate	Target	Regalo wooden expandable safety gate	$14.99
Monitor	Nanit	Nanit Plus smart baby monitor	$299.00
Pant And Shirt Set	Kohl's	Baby Boy Carter's 3-piece nautical bodysuit, suspenders, and white pants set	$32.20
Swing	Walmart	Graco Simple Sway Baby Swing	$75.99

BUSINESS EQUIPMENT & SUPPLIES

Item	Source	Description	Price
Bubble Wrap	ULINE	Bubble roll, 12" × 300 '	$27.00
Desk Lamp	J.C. Penney	Simple Designs desk lamp	$40.00
Packing Tape	The Packaging Group	Clear packing tape, 2" × 110 yds.	$2.06
Planner	Daytimer.com	Mini weekly-monthly planner	$14.99

Item	Source	Description	Price
Push Pins	Staples	Plastic push pins, 200 pack	$2.19

COLLECTIBLES

Item	Source	Description	Price
Blanket	Etsy	Fleece blanket, rock and roll theme, 64" × 60"	$29.00
Collectible Poster	Framedart.com	Champagne Vicomte de Mouillac 24" × 30" framed poster	$108.99
Collectible Poster	Art.com	Framed photograph of The Rolling Stones, 1967, 18" × 14"	$149.99

COMPUTERS, PHONES, & ACCESSORIES

Item	Source	Description	Price
Copy Paper	Staples	Ream of 500 sheets, 8.5" × 11" copy paper	$7.49
iPad	Walmart	Apple iPad, 32 GB, Wi-fi	$259.00
iPhone	Apple.com	iPhone XR	$449.00

The iPhone X, released in 2017, with packaging and accessories. (via Wikimedia Commons)

Item	Source	Description	Price
iPhone Case	Velvet Caviar	iPhone 8 case, floral design	$30.00
Laptop Bag	Best Buy	Sling sleeve carrying case for 13" Apple computers	$60.99
Laptop Computer	Dell.com	Dell Inspiron 15 3000 (4M cache)	$299.99
Mouse Pad	Amazon.com	Steel Series QcK gaming surface, 12.6" × 10.8"	$9.99
Power Adapter	Dell.com	45-watt AC adapter	$49.99
Printer Ink	HP.com	HP 60 2 pack black/tri-color ink cartridges	$47.99
Printer/Scanner	Staples	HP Office Jet Pro All-in-One Inkjet Printer	$89.99
Smartwatch	Att.com	Apple Watch, Series 4, 44mm	$849.99
Software	Adobe.com	Adobe Photoshop, per year	$239.88
Software	Microsoft.com	Microsoft Office 365, Home Edition, per year	$69.99
Speaker	Dell.com	Stereo speaker system	$19.99
USB Connector	Dell.com	10' USB cable	$14.99
Wireless Reading Device	Amazon.com	Kindle Paperwhite, waterproof, 8 GB storage	$129.99

EDUCATION

Item	Source	Description	Price
Art Classes	Time Out New York	Paint and Sip Class Party at the Art Studio, New York	$34.43
Language Course	Fluenz	Spanish (Latin America), download all 5 levels of study	$378.00
University Tuition	Harvard University	one-year tuition	$46,340
University Tuition	Pennsylvania State University	one-year in-state tuition	$18,436

ENTERTAINMENT

Item	Source	Description	Price
Apple Picking	The Billfold	8 lbs of apples	$11.20
Movie Ticket	IFC Center	IFC Center, New York, evening movie	$16.00
Oktoberfest	Mountsnow.com	Mount Snow Oktoberfest, Vermont, one-day adult pass	$35.00
Paintball Rental	Skirmish.com	Skirmish Paintball, Pennsylvania, open play, per person	$29.99
Restaurant Meal	Gramercytavern.com	Gramercy Tavern, New York, 3-course prix fixe dinner	$134.00

ENTERTAINMENT, HOME

Item	Source	Description	Price
Billiard Table	Walmart	EastPoint Sports 87" billiard table	$399.99
Blu Ray Player	Best Buy	Sony UBP-X800 Blu Ray player	$199.99
Board Game	Amazon	Monopoly	$33.59
Computer Games	Best Buy	Anthem, EA games, for Windows	$59.99
Gas Grill	Target	Char-Broil classic 2-burner gas grill	$109.99
Grill Briquettes	Amazon	21st Century, 60 piece gas grill ceramic briquettes	$12.36
Television	Best Buy	Samsung 50" television	$349.99

Item	Source	Description	Price
Trampoline	Jumpflex.com	Jumpflex Flex 120 12' trampoline	$549.99
Video Game System	Best Buy	Playstation 4 Pro Console	$399.99

FARM EQUIPMENT & SUPPLIES

Item	Source	Description	Price
Chicken Coop	Wayfair	Freddy chicken coop with outdoor run	$236.98
Chicken Wire	Lowe's	Gray steel poultry netting, 24" roll	$21.48
Generator	Walmart	Sportsman 3000 watt invertor/generator	$469.99
Herb Seeds	Amazon	Assortment of 12 culinary herb seeds	$11.94

FURNITURE

Item	Source	Description	Price
Bathroom Mirror	Serena and Lily	Circular, unadorned rattan mirror	$248.99
Bookcase	Hayneedle	Remington heavy duty bookcase, 48"	$141.98
Child's Pillow	Kohl's	Sonoma cloud-shaped children's throw pillow	$24.99
Dining Table	Wayfair	Artefama Flora dining table	$519.99
Loveseat	Walmart	Noble House reclining loveseat	$294.98
Sofa	Joss & Main	Garren sofa	$315.99
Vanity Bench	Wayfair	Brewen Estate vanity bench	$83.99

GARDEN EQUIPMENT & SUPPLIES

Item	Source	Description	Price
Garden Hose	Williams Sonoma	Professional series garden hose, orange, 50 ft	$69.95
Garden Stakes	Greenhouse Mega Store	25 pack of bamboo stakes, 6' × 1/2"	$13.00
Indoor Gardening System	Amazon	Vertical NFT hydroponics system, 6 LED grow light, timer, pump, and reservoir with 24 pods	$359.99

HOTEL RATES

Item	Source	Description	Price
Hotel Room	Booking.com	W Hotel, New York, room with 1 king bed, per night	$349.00
Hotel Room	Booking.com	The Fontaine, Kansas City, standard king room, per night	$169.00

A standard 2 Queen room at the Renaissance Marriott in Columbus Ohio costs $179 a night in 2019. (via Wikimedia Commons)

Item	Source	Description	Price
Motel Room	Priceline.com	Sleep Inn, Albuquerque Airport, per night	$48.00

HOUSEHOLD ITEMS

Item	Source	Description	Price
Alarm Clock	K-Mart	Sharp SPC137 digital alarm clock	$23.99
Aroma Diffuser	Aroma 360	Mini i360 SL, silver	$199.99
Base Plate	Scaffold Express	7" × 9" shoring base plate	$7.40
Bread Box	Amazon	Bamboo bread box	$27.99
Bucket	Berlin Packaging	3.5 gallon black steel open head bucket	$14.27
Candleholder	Oriental Trading Company	White candle holder set, 3 piece set	$15.98
Candles	Quickcandles.com	Richland pillar candle, 3" × 3", dark green	$3.49
Chef's Knife	Wayfair	Nero hammered 12 piece block set	$91.99
Coffee Grinder	The Home Depot	8 oz Burr Mill stainless steel coffee grinder	$39.59
Cookie Jar	Overstock.com	Home Basics cookie jar with metal top	$28.99
Cookware Set	Kohl's	Food Network, 10 piece ceramic cookware set, brown	$84.99
Dinnerware Set	Bed, Bath and Beyond	Salt soft square 16-piece dinner set, white	$19.99

Item	Source	Description	Price
Dish Towels	Crate and Barrel	Indigo textured terry dish towels, set of 2	$12.95
Door Knocker	Build.com	Delaney 4" door knocker with 160 degree viewer	$6.24
Drinking Glasses	Williams Sonoma	Open kitchen tumblers, set of 6	$24.00
Fireplace Screen	Pottery Barn	Lattice single screen, small	$199.99
Fly Swatter	Duluth Trading Company	Cork/bamboo fly swatter	$11.95
Furnace Filter	Gamut.com	Pleated air filters, pack of 12	$68.28
Hangers	Boxed.com	Ivory non-slip hangers, 35 count	$9.99
Household Cleaner	Staples	Sustainable Earth all-purpose cleaner, 1 gallon	$10.79
Juicer, Electric	Best Buy	Breville Juice Fountain, compact electric juicer, silver	$99.99
Kitchen Bags	Boxed.com	Hefty ultra-strong, tall kitchen bags, 110 count	$14.99
Light Bulbs	1000bulbs.com	60-watt frosted bulbs	$1.38
Mortar And Pestle	West Elm	White marble mortar and pestle	$15.00
Picture Frame	West Elm	Gallery frame, 4" × 6"	$19.00
Placemat Set	Amazon	Set of 6 woven vinyl washable table placemats	$12.99
Rug Protector	ULINE	Carpet chair mat 36" × 36"	$41.00
Salad Tosser	Everythingkitchens.com	Oxo steel salad spinner	$54.99
Shower Curtain Ring Set	West Elm	Shower curtain rings, polished nickel	$15.00
Silverware Tray	Amazon	Large 6-compartment silverware tray, granite	$8.99
Solar Panel	Theinverterstore.com	120 watt solar panel	$209.00
Soup Pot And Bowls	Amazon	BW Brands colorful mini casserole pots with lids, 4 piece	$22.42
Switch Plate	Wallplatesonline.com	Century brushed nickel	$2.37
Telephone	Dell.com	Ooma DP1-T wireless home phone	$89.99
Toilet	Home Depot	Colony 2 piece, single flush toilet, white	$91.40
Towels	J.C. Penney	Home Expressions solid bath towels	$3.74
Wall Sconce	West Elm	Sculptural glass sconce	$32.00
Wine Bucket	Crate and Barrel	Callaway wine/champagne bucket	$39.95

JEWELRY

Item	Source	Description	Price
Bracelet	Pandora	Silver charm bracelet with heart clasp	$65.00
Engagement Ring	Angara	Princess Diana-inspired garnet ring with diamond halo	$779.00
Men's Watch	Watches.com	Skagen multi-function analog watch	$155.00
Pendants	Sundance Catalogue	Mountain spirits cross pendant necklace	$138.00
Women's Watch	Swarovski	Graceful lady watch with leather strap	$149.50

Item	Source	Description	Price
MEDICAL PRODUCTS			
First Aid Kit	ULINE	10 person first aid kit	$24.00
Glucose Meter	Walmart	ReliOn Prime blood glucose monitoring system	$9.00
Heating Pad	Amazon	Sunbeam heating pad, 6 heat settings with auto-shutoff, 12" × 15"	$25.00
Home Hospital Bed	Progress Mobility	Fully electric hospital bed set	$845.00
Lab Flask	The Lab Depot	Erlenmeyer flask	$21.00
Lab Petri Dish	Growing labs	Sterilin petri dishes, 20 pack	$16.00
Latex Gloves	ULINE	Industrial latex gloves, 100 count	$8.00
Pill Reminder	Amazon	7-day pill box, set of 3	$9.98
Reading Glasses	Readers.com	The Dean black reading glasses	$15.95
Stethoscope	SupremeMed	Electronic stethoscope, 27" tube	$363.95
Surgical Mask	ULINE	Surgical mask, carton of 50	$7.00
Wheelchair	Walmart	Drive medical blue streak wheelchair, 16" seat	$118.77
MOTORIZED VEHICLES & SERVICES			
Automobile	Kelley Blue Book	2019 Ford Escape SE sport utility vehicle	$27,595
Automobile	Kelley Blue Book	2018 Honda Civic Sedan	$19,835
Car Trunk Organizer	Mark and Graham	Calistoga 2-in-1 car organizer, olive waxed canvas	$66.99
Gasoline	Speedway	Hudson, NY, per gallon, regular unleaded	$2.60
Jump Starter	Tire Rack	Weego Jump Starter 22	$90.00
Recreational Vehicle	RV Trader	2019 Forest River Pursuit 27DS	$86,990
Tire, Regular	Tire Rack	Continental Extreme Contact tire	$108.99
Tire, Winter	Tire Rack	Pirelli Winter Cinturato tires	$62.75
MUSICAL INSTRUMENTS			
Amplifier	Guitar Center	Rogue G10 10 watt guitar amp	$34.99
Drum Set	Sweetwater	Ludwig Questlove pocket kit drum set	$249.00
Electric Guitar	Guitar Center	Squier Special Edition Bullet Stratocaster SSS electric guitar, sea foam green	$129.99

All six factory colors for the Squier Bullet Special guitar. (via Wikimedia Commons)

Item	Source	Description	Price
Flute	Woodwind & Brasswind	Allora student series flute	$179.99
Harmonica	Sweetwater	Hohner Blues Band harmonica in C	$7.49
Trumpet	Amazon	Yamaha YTR-2330 standard B-flat trumpet	$775.98
Trumpet Mute	Woodwind & Brasswind	Harmon B Model aluminum trumpet wow-wow mute	$32.99

OTHER

Item	Source	Description	Price
Business Cards	Vistaprint	Personalized business cards, set of 500	$9.99
Cocktail Shaker	Williams Sonoma	Large stainless steel cocktail shaker, 60 ounces	$34.95
Desktop Ornament	Hayneedle	Woodstock 12" desk gong	$60.00
Diary	Montblanc	Notebook #147, open diary, black	$42.00
Fidget Spinner	Amazon	Magtimes rainbow fidget spinner	$11.99
Floor Mat	ULINE	Waterhog carpet mat, 18" × 27"	$25.00
Gift Wrap	Amazon	Brown craft wrapping paper, 30' × 15'	$8.85
Grumpy Cat Doll	Google Express	11" plush doll	$31.99
Hookah	Hookah-shisha.com	33' Shika Egyptian flag hookah	$119.99
Incense	ssense.com	Wacko Maria grey kuumba edition, pack 15 bamboo incense sticks	$30.00
Lock	ULINE	Master Lock combination lock	$9.00
Map	Zoro.com	Rand McNally laminated world wall map, 50" × 32"	$19.52
Moving Boxes	ULINE	12" × 12" × 12", set of 25	$18.25
Mug	Discountmugs.com	16 oz Miami two-tone bistro mugs	$1.95
Pen	Amsterdam Printing	Delane Softex Pen, set of 50	$34.50

Item	Source	Description	Price
Postage	USPS	First class letter, up to 1 ounce	$0.47
Roses	1800Flowers.com	Two dozen red roses with ginger vase	$24.99
Spiral Notebook	Schoolspecialty.com	1 subject spiral college-ruled notebook, 8" × 10.5"	$1.33
Sunglasses	Sunglass Hut	Oakley full rim sunglasses	$103.00
Watch Battery	Zoro.com	Energizer 2032bp-4 lithium coin cell battery	$3.34

PERSONAL CARE PRODUCTS

Item	Source	Description	Price
Bath Brush	Bloomingdale's	The Organic Pharmacy skin brush	$19.00
Bath Gift Set	Knack	Just Breathe tropical spa and bath gift set	$76.00
Bath Sponge	Murchison-Hume	Natural sea sponge	$21.00
Blush	Macy's	Estee Lauder pure color envy sculpting blush, peach passion	$35.00
ChapStick	Amazon	ChapStick Classic, 12 stick pack	$18.99
Dental Floss	Boxed.com	Oral-B Glide Pro-Health Advanced, 6 pack	$17.99
Eye Drops	MSC Industrial Supply	Eye saline 32 oz single disposable eyewash bottle	$14.55
Eye Shadow	Macy's	Bobbi Brown eye shadow, 0.08 oz	$27.00
Eyeliner	Barney's New York	Givenchy Beauty liner couture, No. 1 black	$33.00
Facial Tissues	Target	Kleenex Cool Touch facial tissue, 50 count	$1.59
Fingernail Gloss	J.C. Penney	O.P.I. Infinite Shine 2 nail lacquer	$9.75
Hairbrush	Nordstrom	Aveda wooden paddle brush	$27.00
Hand Lotion	Dead Sea Premier	Classic luxury hand cream	$16.99
Lint Brush	J.C. Penney	Honey-Can-Do 60-sheet adhesive roller, 4 pack	$18.75
Lipstick	Target	Maybelline Compulsion lipstick, 0.1 oz	$6.99
Makeup Remover	Ogee	Organic makeup-removing face wipes, 3 packs of 10	$26.00
Mascara	FragranceNet.com	Estee Lauder sumptuous extreme waterproof mascara, black	$23.30
Men's Shower Gel	FragranceNet.com	Coach for Men shower gel, 5 oz	$22.67
Nail Dryer	Vanity Planet	Glow dry portable LED nail dryer	$39.99
Organic Tampons	The Honest Company	Organic cotton tampons, hypoallergenic, 20 count	$5.95
Perfume	The Body Shop	White musk Eau de Parfum, 1.69 fl. oz	$24.50
Razor Blades	Boxed.com	Shick Intuition razor cartridges, 12 count	$33.99
Scale, Digital	Wayfair	Digital body fat scale with tempered glass platform	$31.99
Shower Caddy	Wayfair	Basket shower caddy, frosted white	$25.99
Shower Cap	Tanga.com	Mademoiselle designer shower cap with pouch	$8.99
Soap	Boxed.com	Dove sensitive skin, 16 count	$15.39
Terry Cloth Back Scrubber	Amazon	Terry cloth back strap sponge/scrubber, beige	$4.39

Item	Source	Description	Price
PERSONAL SAFETY PRODUCTS			
Beverage Testing Kit	Sabre	Drink test kit, helps determine if your drink has been tampered with	$9.99
Pepper Spray	Amazon	Mace triple action self defense pepper spray	$9.99
Safety Chick Kit	Amazon	Sabre Red Safety Chick Kit, includes date rape drug test coasters, door wedge alarm, personal safety alarm, and pepper spray	$32.99
Stun Gun	Amazon	Avenger defense portable stun gun	$22.97
PET SUPPLIES			
Aquarium Tank	PetSmart	Great Choice aquarium starter kit, 10 gallons	$29.99
Dog Food	Chewy.com	Blue Buffalo Life Protection Formula, chicken and brown rice recipe, 6 lbs	$15.74
Dog Leash	Chewy.com	Frisco nylon dog leash, blue, 6' 3/4"	$4.29
Litter Box	Chewy.com	IRIS open top liter box	$8.69
Litter Box Liner	Chewy.com	Petmate litter box liners, 15 count	$2.84
REAL ESTATE			
Commercial Building	Century 21	Warehouse style commercial building, Greenpoint, Brooklyn, 45,000 square feet	$40,000,000
House	Homes.com	Johnstown, PA; 3 bedroom/3 bath house, 2,012 square feet	$159,000
Apartment	Streeteasy.com	3 bedroom/1 bath luxury rental in Chelsea, Manhattan, monthly rent	$5,740
Tiny House	Tinyhouselistings.com	The "Maverick" Tiny House, 210 square feet, Tipp City, Ohio	$69,900
SEWING EQUIPMENT & SUPPLIES			
Crochet Hooks	Joann	Clover soft-touch crochet hooks, set of 7 assorted hooks	$6.99
Knitting Needles	Walmart	Quicksilver single point knitting needles, 10"	$7.28
Sewing Machine	Home Depot	Singer 23-stitch sewing machine	$168.99
Yarn	The Knitted Purl	Malabrigo silky merino	$9.60
SPORTS & OUTDOOR EQUIPMENT			
Backpack	Everlane	Modern snap backpack	$68.00
Beach Bag	Land's End	Extra-large natural open top canvas tote bag, ivory	$25.20
Beach Towel	Target	Sun Squad shark-themed beach towel	$10.00
Camera	Walmart	Canon PowerShot digital camera, black	$229.00
Camera Bag	Best Buy	Lowepro format 160 camera bag, black	$15.99
Canoe	Dick's Sporting Goods	Field and Stream scout canoe, small	$479.99
Compass	Amazon	Classic pocket style camping compass	$5.89
Cycling Helmet	Walmart	Free Agent steel helmet	$30.00

Item	Source	Description	Price
Inflatable Raft	Walmart	Intex Mariner 3-person inflatable river/lake dinghy	$163.96
Kayak	Dick's Sporting Goods	Pelican Trailblazer 100 NXT kayak, green	$199.99
Ski Gloves	L.L. Bean	Women's Ultralight 850 down gloves, medium	$44.99
Skis, Downhill	REI	Rossignol Smash 7 skis with bindings, men's	$299.93
Sleeping Bag	L.L. Bean	Camp sleeping bag, flannel-lined	$79.99
Snorkeling Mask	Snorkel-Mart	Vista Vue full face snorkel	$49.95
Snowboard	Backcountry.com	Burton Instigator wide snowboard, 155 cm	$279.97
Tent	Dick's Sporting Goods	Coleman Highline 4-person dome tent, small	$39.98
Travel Cooler	Frontgate	Barebones Trekker cooler, holds up to 6 12 oz cans	$25.00
Tripod	Amazon	Amazon Basics 60" lightweight tripod with bag	$23.49

TELEPHONE SERVICES

Item	Source	Description	Price
Cell Phone Service	AT & T	AT&T Unlimited & More Premium plan, single line, per month	$48.00
Cell Phone Service	Verizon	Unlimited plan, single line, per month	$40.00

TOBACCO PRODUCTS

Item	Source	Description	Price
Cigarettes	Expatistan.com	Pack of Marlboro cigarettes in New York	$14.00
Cigarettes	Expatistan.com	Pack of Marlboro cigarettes in Richmond, VA	$4.85
Rolling Papers	Rolling Paper Depot	Pack of E-Z Wider rolling papers	$2.50

TOOLS

Item	Source	Description	Price
Brackets	Global Industrial	Wall mounting bracket	$1.94
Chain Saw	Lowe's	Husqvarna 120 38 cc 2-cycle 14" gas chainsaw	$179.00
Ladder	Lowe's	Werner 6' aluminum 250 lb-capacity step ladder	$49.96
Tape Measure	ULINE	Accu-Lock tape measure, 1" × 25'	$10.00
Tile Grout	Aquaquality Pools and Spas	Perma-Tile grout, 5 lb	$29.99
Toolbox	Global Industrial	19" toolbox with tote tray and lid	$14.50
Wood Glue	Target	Gorilla Wood Glue, 4 oz	$2.99
Wood Lathe	Baileigh Industrial	Woodworking lathe	$3,995.00
Wood Saw	Home Depot	Husky 15" wood handle tooth saw	$9.97
Wrench	Amazon	Crescent combination wrench set, 10 pieces	$13.85

TOYS

Item	Source	Description	Price
Crayons	Staples	Crayola 64 crayon box	$3.99
Frisbee	Catchsurf.com	Beach Day flying disc	$15.00
Hoverboard	Walmart	Razor Hovertrax 2.0 self-balancing hoverboard	$178.00
Maze Game	Oriental Trading Company	STEM maze activity	$51.49
Scooter	Walmart	Razor Carbon Lux kick scooter, black	$49.97

Item	Source	Description	Price
TRAVEL & TRANSPORTATION			
Flight	Justfly.com	Round-trip ticket: Boston to Seoul, South Korea	$1,014.76
Luggage	Ebags.com	Travelpro Maxlite 4, 25"	$99.99
Train Ticket	Amtrak	Round-trip ticket: New York to Boston	$191.00
Travel Alarm Clock	Amazon	Digital travel alarm clock, "no bells, no whistles"	$9.97
Travel Handbag	Tumi.com	Ruma crossbody, women's travel bag	$175.00
Travel Organizer	L.L. Bean	Personal organizer/toiletry bag, medium	$29.95

MISCELLANY 2015–2019

U.S. Economy Grew 3% in 2nd Quarter, Fastest Pace in 2 Years

The current recovery has entered its ninth year—long by economic standards—but it is showing some unexpected vigor.

The Commerce Department said on Wednesday that the economy had expanded at an annual rate of 3 percent in the second quarter of the year, better than initially estimated, and a substantial acceleration over the first quarter's lackluster 1.2 percent pace.

The revised figure is still well below President Trump's goal of 4 percent growth, but it is the economy's best quarterly showing in two years.

Mr. Trump talked up the latest figures in a speech on Wednesday in Springfield, Mo., laying out his plans for tax overhaul. Despite nearly uniform skepticism from mainstream economists, he insisted that much faster economic growth was within reach.

"I happen to be one who thinks we can go much higher than 3 percent," the president said. "There is no reason why we should not."

There are several reasons that his goal is probably far-fetched, namely the country's aging workforce and slower population growth than in the past. Combine that with low productivity growth, and hitting Mr. Trump's target begins to look like a Sisyphean challenge.

The president also suggested that other economies overseas were growing at two or three times the American rate. "You look at other countries and what their G.D.P. is, they are unhappy when it is 7, 8, and 9," he said.

No major Western economy is growing close to that rate—and none has in years. The fastest-growing large economy, China's, grew 6.7 percent last year.

Still, with personal consumption accounting for nearly 70 percent of economic output, the new willingness of shoppers to open their wallets is a good sign.

The New York Times, August 30, 2017

Unrest in Virginia

Violence erupted in the college town of Charlottesville on Aug. 12 after hundreds of white nationalists and their supporters who gathered for a rally over plans to remove a Confederate statue were met by counter-protesters, leading Virginia's governor to declare a state of emergency.

Clashes broke out between the white nationalists and counter-protesters; the "Unite the Right" rally at a park once named for Confederate Gen. Robert E. Lee was deemed unlawful. At one point in the afternoon, a vehicle drove into a crowd of counter-protesters marching through the downtown area before speeding away, resulting in one death and leaving more than a dozen others injured. State police later reported the crash of a helicopter that was monitoring the events in Charlottesville, killing two troopers.

President Trump addressed the violence in televised remarks from New Jersey, condemning an "egregious display of hatred, bigotry and violence on many sides" and calling for the "swift restoration of law and order." Among his critics was Sen. Ron Wyden of Oregon. "What happened in Charlottesville is domestic terrorism," Wyden tweeted. "The President's words only serve to offer cover for heinous acts."

The night before Saturday's violence, hundreds of white nationalists marched through the University of Virginia campus while carrying burning torches.

Time Magazine, August 2017

Coal-mining Jobs are Holding Steady Under Trump's Watch

President Donald Trump's campaign trail vow to revive the coal industry may not have come to pass, but two years into his presidency, the miners have at least halted the plunge in employment over the last 30 years.

Since Trump took office, coal miners have kept employment steady at about 51,000 to 53,000 positions. Over the next two years, it could become harder for the industry to hold the line, as a surge in U.S. coal exports is expected to lose steam.

In February, the industry employed about 52,800 workers, figures from the Bureau of Labor Statistics showed on Friday. That's up from a reading of 50,900 in February 2017.

However, because of the way BLS measures employment, the bureau's economists have not been able to say whether employment actually rose or fell significantly throughout much of the last two years. Instead, they usually say employment held steady.

MISCELLANY 2015-2019

Still, that is a welcome reprieve for the coal-mining industry, which has shed more than 100,000 jobs over the last three decades.

CNBC, March 8, 2019

Federal Judge Lets Amazon Off the Hook for Hoverboard Fire that Killed Two Dogs

A federal judge has ruled that Amazon.com Inc cannot be held liable for selling a hoverboard that allegedly set a California family's home on fire.

U.S. District Judge Jon Tigar in San Francisco in a decision on Wednesday said the online reseller owed no duty of care to the family, since the hoverboard was sold on Amazon by a Chinese manufacturer who is not a party to the litigation.

Reuters, March 21, 2019

A.I. Is Flying Drones (Very, Very Slowly)

A drone from the University of Zürich is an engineering and technical marvel. It also moves slower than someone taking a Sunday morning jog.

At the International Conference on Intelligent Robots and Systems in Madrid last October, the autonomous drone, which navigates using artificial intelligence, raced through a complicated series of turns and gates, buzzing and moving like a determined and oversized bumblebee. It bobbed to duck under a bar that swooshed like a clock hand, yawed left, pitched forward and raced toward the finish line. The drone, small and covered in sensors, demolished the competition, blazing through the course twice as fast as its nearest competitor. Its top speed: 5.6 miles per hour.

A few weeks earlier, in Jeddah, Saudi Arabia, a different drone, flown remotely by its pilot, Paul Nurkkala, shot through a gate at the top of a 131-foot-high tower, inverted into a roll and then dove toward the earth. Competitors trailed behind or crashed into pieces along the course, but this one swerved and corkscrewed through two twin arches, hit a straightaway, and then blasted into the netting that served as the finish line for the Drone Racing League's world championship. The winning drone, a league-standard Racer3, reached speeds over 90 miles per hour, but it needed a human to guide it. Mr. Nurkkala, known to fans as Nurk, wore a pair of goggles that beamed him a first-person view of his drone as he flew it.

Artificial intelligence, or A.I., has been on a hot streak, besting humans in competitions over the past five years. AlphaGo, a program built by Deep-Mind, the artificial intelligence arm of Google parent Alphabet, went from learning the basics of the game Go to beating the world's best human player in a little over three years. More recently, the A.I. AlphaStar, also by DeepMind, was able to beat a top player in the complex strategy video game "StarCraft II," shutting out its human competitor five games to zero.

But the real world can be an immensely noisy place, and many A.I.-powered, and autonomous, vehicles still struggle to excel in it.

The New York Times, March 26, 2019

Pricing Trends
1910–2019*

This *Pricing Trends* section is the result of suggestions from the readership of the previous editions. To fully understand the practical economy in which we live, it is often necessary to study the cost of buying common objects, such as an automobile or a vacuum cleaner, over long periods of time. Although it is helpful to know the cost of a man's dress shirt in any given year, which is the essence of *The Value of a Dollar,* it is truly insightful to view that same knowledge over a 100-year panorama. New products, innovations, competition, new materials and fads can all impact what we are willing to pay for something we desire. *Pricing Trends* helps unravel the mystery of price over time.

With this knowledge we can understand the relative value—and financial strain—placed on owning a tennis racquet in 1910 versus 1990. *Trends* provides insight into what percentage of the family's income is required to buy a candy bar, or a dozen eggs, or a lovely skirt throughout the last 100-plus years. During the last several years, students, librarians, social studies teachers, historians, journalists and friends have asked for the relative meaning of an individual price as it changes over time. In hundreds of conversations, the suggestion has been made that this edition of *The Value of a Dollar* include a way to look at pricing from a historical perspective. Thus, *Trends* was created, thanks to you.

Each section has been arranged within topics such as *Travel & Entertainment,* where theater tickets can be found; *Outdoors,* which includes the cost of a Harley-Davidson motorcycle or a hammock; and even *Help Wanted,* which features a variety of jobs from coal miner to professional baseball player. Hopefully, each of these miniature pricing profiles can breathe new fascination into ordinary data.

At the same time, each pricing chart includes an index to current pricing. The indexing of these long pricing trends provides us another way of seeing how much each item would cost in today's terms. While it is essential to know what people were willing to pay for a certain item in a given year, it is also important to understand how those prices change over a long period of time. In this way, we are provided a window into the minds of consumers we have never met. Is it more or less expensive to attend professional football's premier event, the Super Bowl, today versus 10 years ago? How does the actual cost and relative cost of a Broadway play in 1920 compare to 1980? When were price changes over time the most dramatic and what influenced those costs? Historians and economists use this type of information to study the value of money and how it relates to human events. Their purpose often is to comprehend how values influence economic and cultural events—not just on the national level, but also the individual level. For all of us, this data allows us to anticipate events that may occur in the future, especially as it relates to how we spend our money.

By employing indexes based upon consumer expenditures, economists and historians can look back and compare monetary trends over periods of time. If we know that a comic book was worth $0.10 in 1939, we can compare the price to the Consumer Price Index and determine what it was worth in the dollar value of the year being compared. If one compares the value of the comic book in 2019 dollars, the 1939 comic book would cost approximately $1.84. The United States government did not focus on actual inflation rates and indexing consumer pricing until the twentieth century. During World War I, prices were rising rapidly, especially in shipbuilding centers in the United States. It was during this period that the federal government started compiling an index essential for calculating cost-of-living adjustments in wages. Most of this work began around 1917, but the government developed indexes with estimates back to 1913. This information is compiled today by the U.S. Department of Labor under the Bureau of Labor Statistics.

When developing the charts for *The Value of a Dollar,* information was often not available prior to 1913. To include the material prior to 1913, an alternative index was utilized based upon John J. McCusker's principle of determining the value of money prior to 1913. Charts in this book expressing values prior to 1913 should be viewed as approximations when compared to 2019 dollars. Charts that begin at or after 1913 used the Consumer Price Index and provide a closer comparison of actual dollars in 2019.

The use of indexing in this way gives each of us a deeper knowledge of economics. For example, the often discussed inflation index is a product of thousands of issues and items. Using individual trend data, we no longer look only at an average cost of change over time, but a specific change. This additional information then tells us that while most items experience price increases decade to decade, the relative price of many is less than it was 100 years ago. Thanks to improved agricultural tech-

niques, many products—such as a dozen eggs—have a lower relative cost today and thus have a lower impact on the family budget.

As noted before, pricing is an inexact science. In any given year the same item—a woman's dress, for example—might be sold at widely varying prices in the same store, based on the season, the availability, the retailer's need for cash, or the consumer's demand. View this same item over 100 years and the variables—from workmanship to material quality, innovations in manufacture, changing fashion or the type of store selling the item—all have an impact. For that reason every effort has been made to appropriately price items. For example, the Broadway ticket price shows the best seat available, and indicates such in the description. The automobile pricing is the lowest list price over time, before dozens of extras are added in. Most of the prices came from catalogs and advertisements, meticulously traced back for 100 years. Some were provided by the companies themselves, recognizing that products, like a lawn mower, bear little resemblance to the whirling push device first employed decades ago. No mention is made of whether yesterday's sun was really hotter or the weeds more stubborn.

*The range of years will vary slightly from item to item, based on available data.

AROUND THE HOUSE

BATH TOWEL

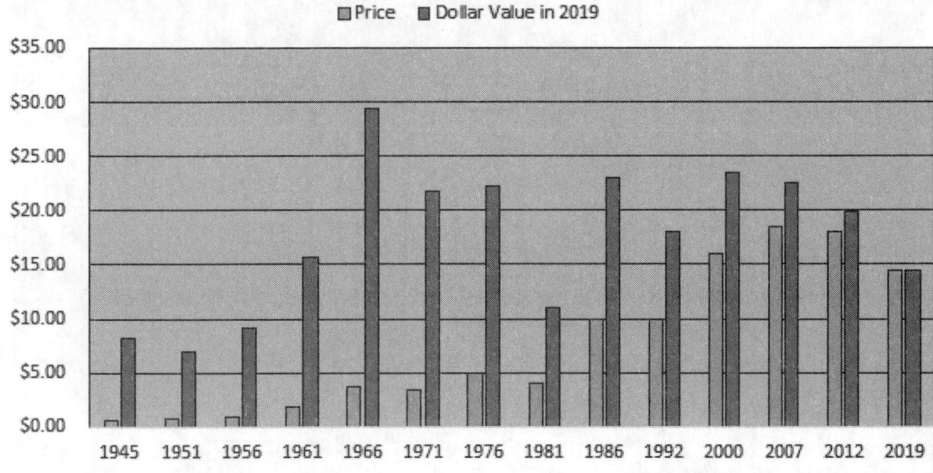

	1945	1951	1956	1961	1966	1971	1976
Price	$0.59	$0.72	$0.98	$1.86	$3.77	$3.48	$4.99
Dollar Value in 2019	$8.29	$7.00	$9.11	$15.72	$29.41	$21.72	$22.17

	1981	1986	1992	2000	2007	2012	2019
Price	$3.99	$9.99	$10.00	$15.99	$18.50	$18.00	$14.39
Dollar Value in 2019	$11.10	$23.04	$18.02	$23.47	$22.55	$19.82	$14.39

Listerine ad with "What? Tooth Powder in a Tube?" (1937). Clockwise from Cupid in the top right: Rubifoam at 25 cents (1899); Listerine toothpaste at 25 cents (1933); mom showing daughter the benefits of brushing with Colgate in ad that offers "proof" but no price (1950); wife doting on lounging husband for Ipana toothpaste (1933); Listerine toothpaste at 40 cents a quarter pound (4 ounces) for the "double size" or 25 cents regular size (1937); 99 cents for Colgate (2013); Dr. Graves tooth powder in 25 cent and 50 cent sizes; Pebeco toothpaste (1928); Colgate with "if it's kissin' that you're missin'" (1942) and Colgate cartoon ad with a sailor and gal (1944).

AROUND THE HOUSE

CAMERA

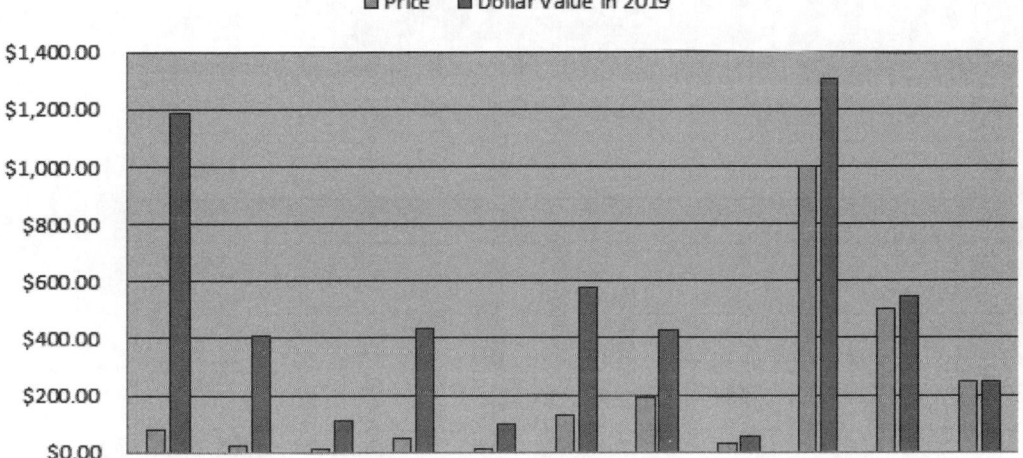

	1928	1939	1947	1959	1964	1976
Price	$80.00	$22.50	$9.95	$49.50	$12.00	$129.00
Dollar Value in 2019	$1,189	$411.48	$113.42	$432.41	$98.40	$576.31

	1987	1992	2005	2013	2019
Price	$189.99	$29.96	$999.99	$499.99	$249.99
Dollar Value in 2019	$425.14	$54.28	$1,302	$545.59	$249.99

AROUND THE HOUSE

CELL PHONE

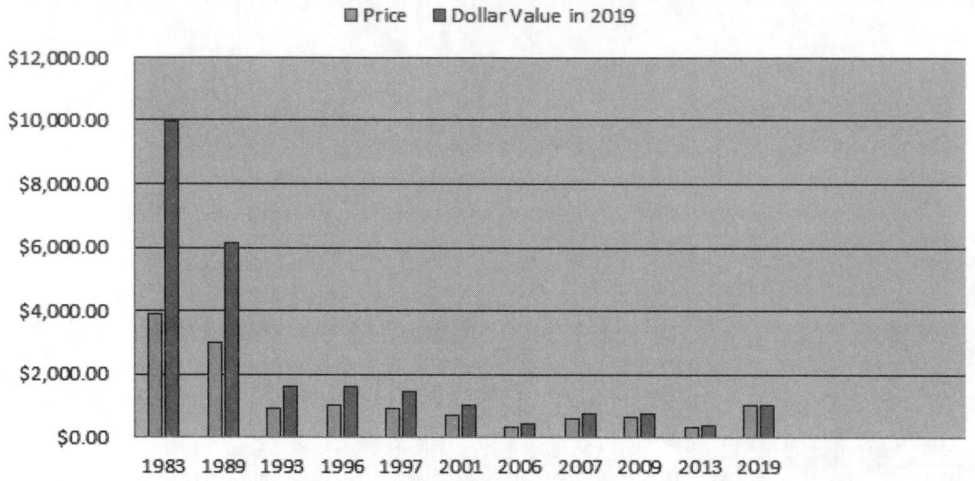

	1983	1989	1993	1996	1997	2001
Type of Phone	Motorola DynaTAC	Motorola MicroTAC	Simon Personal Communicator	Motorola StarTAC	Nokia 6110	Handspring Treo
Price	$0.05	$0.05	$0.05	$0.10	$0.10	$0.15
Dollar Value in 2019	$0.73	$0.93	$0.71	$0.95	$0.81	$0.71

	2006	2007	2009	2013	2019
Type of Phone	BlackBerry Pearl	iPhone	Samsung Galaxy	Google Nexus 5	iPhone XS
Price	$0.50	$0.70	$0.75	$1.19	$1.12
Dollar Value in 2019	$1.18	$1.17	$1.08	$1.46	$1.24

Excerpts from Ad Descriptions

1980: *Telecom Mobile Phone*—A Telecom Mobile Phone aboard your cruiser or yacht, let's you command local, STD or ISD calls direct—perfect for captains of industry.

1988: *Radio Shack CT-300*—Price and Technology Breakthrough! Lightweight Handheld Cellular Phone. Carry it along with you to make or take calls wherever you go!

1996: *Mitsubishi MT-20*—It has a clock, calendar, calculator; it records voice memos; and you can store appointments on it with a reminder alarm, just in case you're prone to amnesia.

2003: *Samsung V200*—Capture the truth with rotating lens (marketing campaign in conjunction with the film *The Matrix Reloaded*)

2007: *Apple iPhone*—Your life in your pocket. The ultimate digital device.

2016: *Google Pixel*—It has the highest rated smartphone camera. Ever. A battery that lasts all day. Unlimited storage for all your photos and videos.

AROUND THE HOUSE

CHICAGO DAILY TRIBUNE: DAILY PAPER

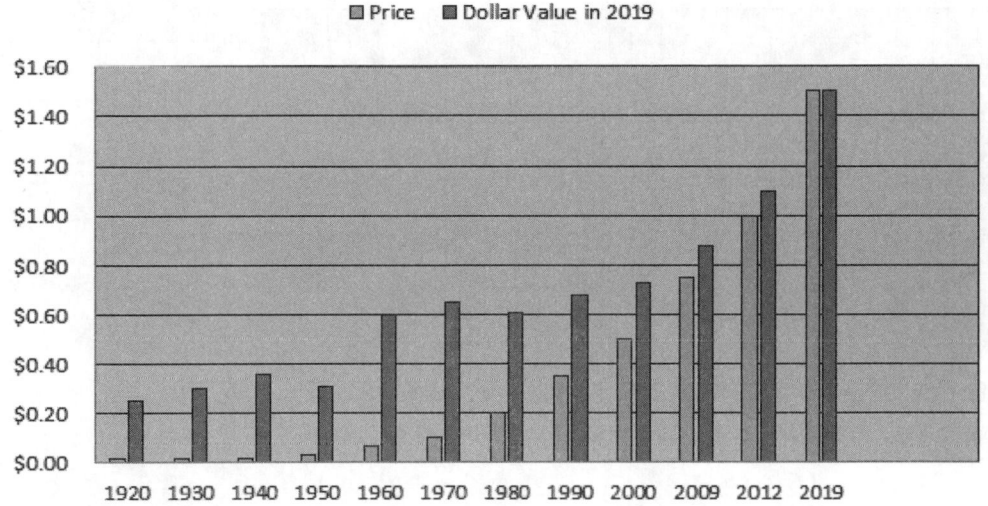

	1920	1930	1940	1950	1960	1970
Daily Price	$0.02	$0.02	$0.02	$0.03	$0.07	$0.10
Dollar Value in 2019	$0.25	$0.30	$0.36	$0.31	$0.60	$0.65
	1980	**1990**	**2000**	**2009**	**2012**	**2019**
Daily Price	$0.20	$0.35	$0.50	$0.75	$1.00	$1.50
Dollar Value in 2019	$0.61	$0.68	$0.73	$0.88	$1.10	$1.50

AROUND THE HOUSE

ELECTRIC IRON

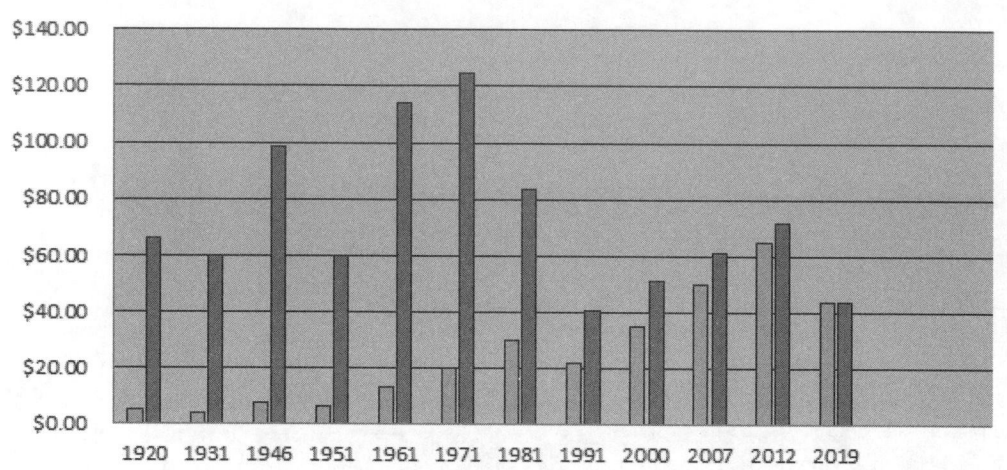

	1920	**1931**	**1946**	**1951**	**1961**	**1971**
Price	$5.25	$3.95	$7.60	$6.19	$13.50	$19.95
Dollar Value in 2019	$66.35	$59.79	$98.52	$60.18	$114.13	$124.52

	1981	**1991**	**2000**	**2007**	**2012**	**2019**
Price	$29.99	$21.95	$35.00	$50.00	$64.99	$43.99
Dollar Value in 2019	$83.40	$40.74	$51.38	$60.96	$71.55	$43.99

AROUND THE HOUSE

ELECTRIC WASHING MACHINE

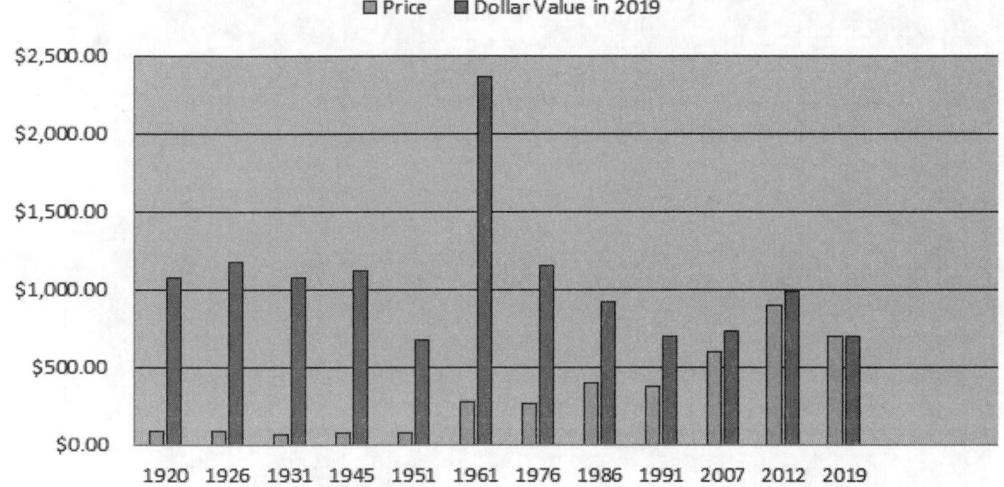

□ Price   ■ Dollar Value in 2019

	1920	**1926**	**1931**	**1945**	**1951**	**1961**
Price	$84.75	$82.50	$64.50	$79.95	$69.95	$279.95
Dollar Value in 2019	$1,071.14	$1,178.19	$1,072.64	$1,122.75	$680.06	$2,355.71

	1976	**1986**	**1991**	**2007**	**2012**	**2019**
Price	$259.35	$399.99	$374.99	$600.00	$899.00	$698.40
Dollar Value in 2019	$1,154.82	$922.52	$695.95	$731.48	$989.77	$698.40

Powel Crosley, Jr. (1886-1961), the inventor of refrigerator door shelves, became rich making affordable radios in the 1920s. He started making refrigerators in 1930, but sold the appliance business in 1945 to make a short-lived line of small cars. Clockwise from top left: The Leonard ice box (1889); Bohn ice box (1905); Frigidaire, a brand created by General Motors in 1918 that became synonomous with the electric refrigerator, at $850+ (1922); Kelvinator at $98+ (1933); Crosley Shelvador refrigerator (1944); Crosley Hotshot roadster (1949); Whirlpool (1980) and Kenmore Elite for $1,999.99 (2013).

AROUND THE HOUSE

EUREKA VACUUM CLEANER

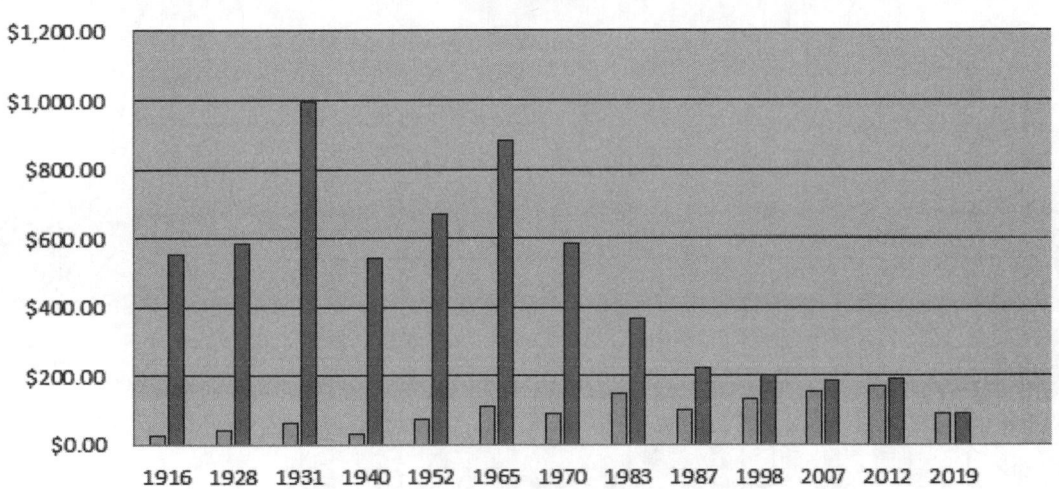

	1916	1928	1931	1940	1952	1965	1970
Price	$23.75	$39.50	$59.95	$29.95	$69.95	$109.95	$89.95
Dollar Value in 2019	$550.77	$583.93	$996.97	$540.76	$667.23	$882.31	$586.01

	1983	1987	1998	2007	2012	2019
Price	$145.00	$99.97	$129.99	$150.00	$169.99	$88.11
Dollar Value in 2019	$368.00	$222.45	$201.58	$182.81	$187.15	$88.11

AROUND THE HOUSE

FLASHLIGHT BATTERY

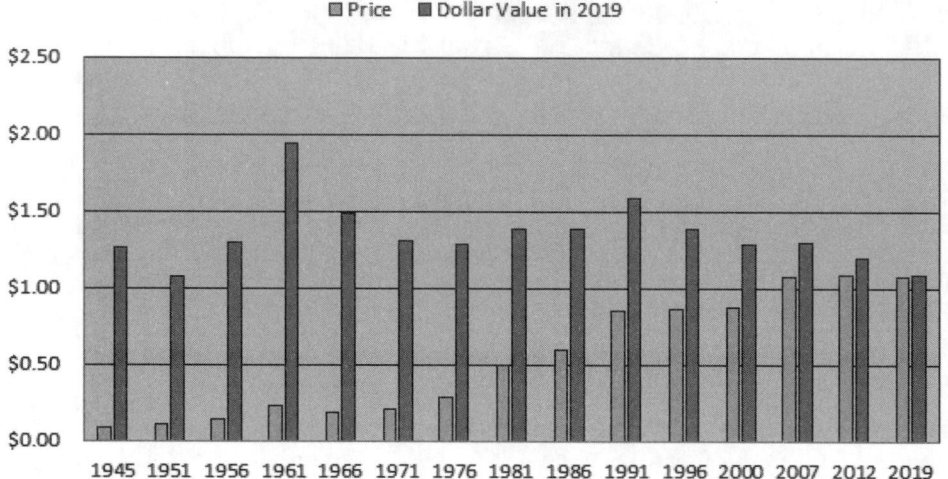

	1945	1951	1956	1961	1966	1971	1976	1981
Price	$0.09	$0.11	$0.14	$0.23	$0.19	$0.21	$0.29	$0.50
Dollar Value in 2019	$1.26	$1.07	$1.30	$1.94	$1.48	$1.31	$1.29	$1.39

	1986	1991	1996	2000	2007	2012	2019
Price	$0.60	$0.85	$0.86	$0.88	$1.07	$1.09	$1.20
Dollar Value in 2019	$1.38	$1.58	$1.39	$1.29	$1.30	$1.20	$1.09

AROUND THE HOUSE

NEW HOME*

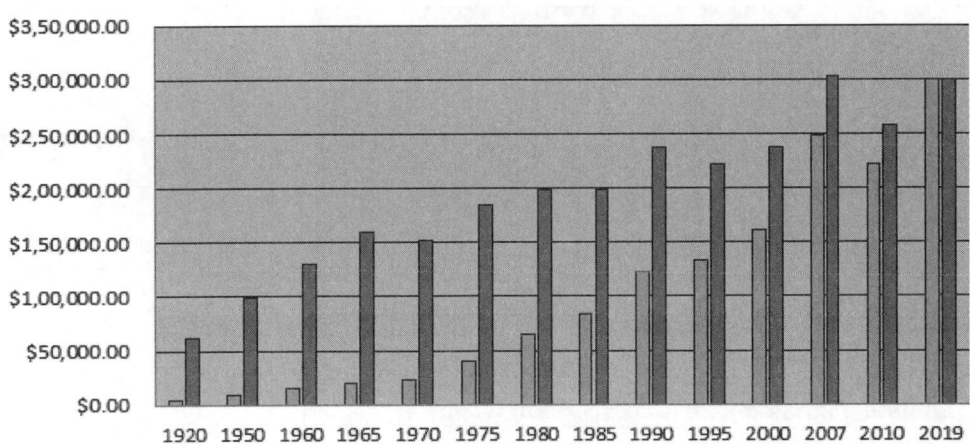

	1920	**1950**	**1960**	**1965**	**1970**	**1975**	**1980**
Home Price	$4,938	$9,422	$15,200	$20,000	$23,400	$39,300	$64,600
Dollar Value in 2019	$62,410	$98,824	$129,804	$160,493	$152,447	$184,649	$198,171

	1985	**1990**	**1995**	**2000**	**2007**	**2010**	**2019**
Home Price	$84,300	$122,900	$133,900	$161,400	$247,900	$221,800	$300,000
Dollar Value in 2019	$198,039	$237,691	$222,091	$236,922	$302,221	$257,116	$300,000

*Median Sales Price

AROUND THE HOUSE

NEW YORK TIMES: DAILY PAPER*

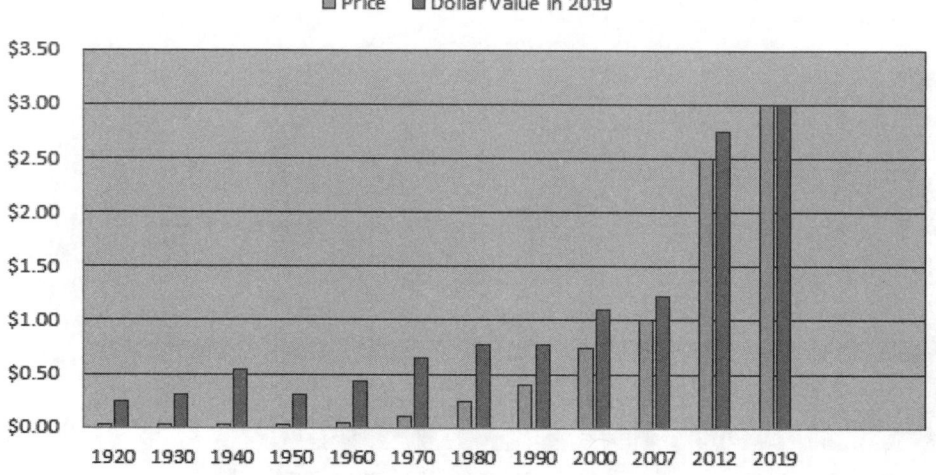

	1920	1930	1940	1950	1960	1970
Daily Price	$0.02	$0.02	$0.03	$0.03	$0.05	$0.10
Dollar Value in 2019	$0.25	$0.30	$0.54	$0.31	$0.43	$0.65

	1980	1990	2000	2007	2012	2019
Daily Price	$0.25	$0.40	$0.75	$1.00	$2.50	$3.00
Dollar Value in 2019	$0.77	$0.77	$1.10	$1.22	$2.75	$3.00

*Cost is for papers purchased in the New York City area (within 200 mile radius of New York City).

AROUND THE HOUSE

NEW YORK TIMES: SUNDAY PAPER*

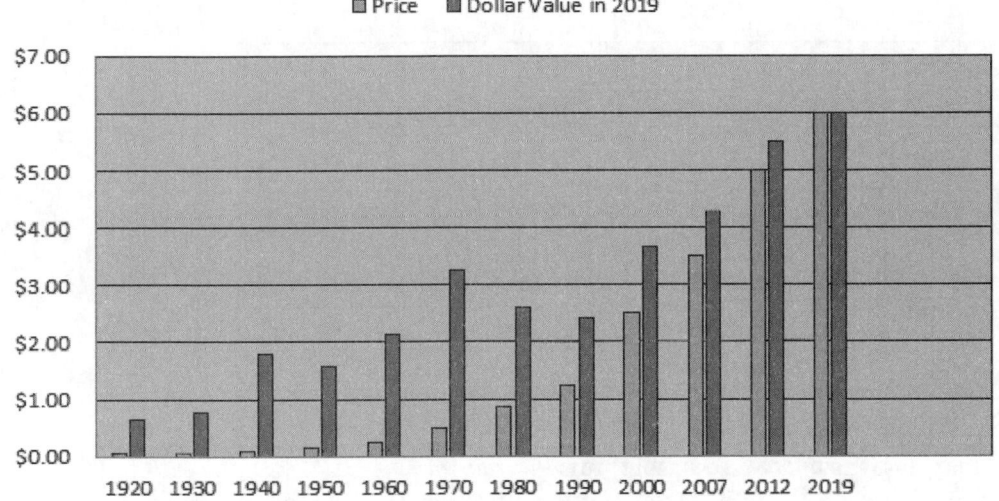

	1920	**1930**	**1940**	**1950**	**1960**	**1970**	**1980**	**1990**
Price	$0.05	$0.05	$0.10	$0.15	$0.25	$0.50	$0.85	$1.25
Dollar Value in 2019	$0.63	$0.76	$1.81	$1.57	$2.13	$3.26	$2.61	$2.42

	2000	**2007**	**2012**	**2019**
Price	$2.50	$3.50	$5.00	$6.00
Dollar Value in 2019	$3.67	$4.27	$5.50	$6.00

* Cost is for papers purchased in the New York City area (within 200-mile radius of New York City)

AROUND THE HOUSE

PERSONAL COMPUTER

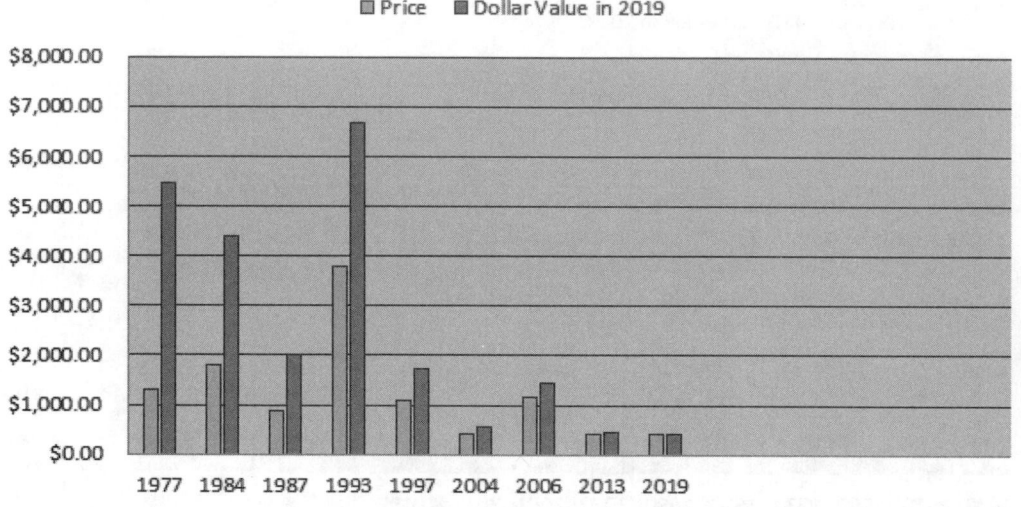

	1977	1984	1987	1993	1997
Price per serving	$1,300	$1,795	$895	$3,799	$1,099
Dollar Value in 2019	$5,453	$4,392	$2,0003	$6,683	$1,741

	2004	2006	2013	2019
Price per serving	$417	$1,149	$430	$420
Dollar Value in 2019	$561	$1,449	$469	$420

AROUND THE HOUSE

POSTAGE STAMP FOR 1 OZ FIRST CLASS MAIL

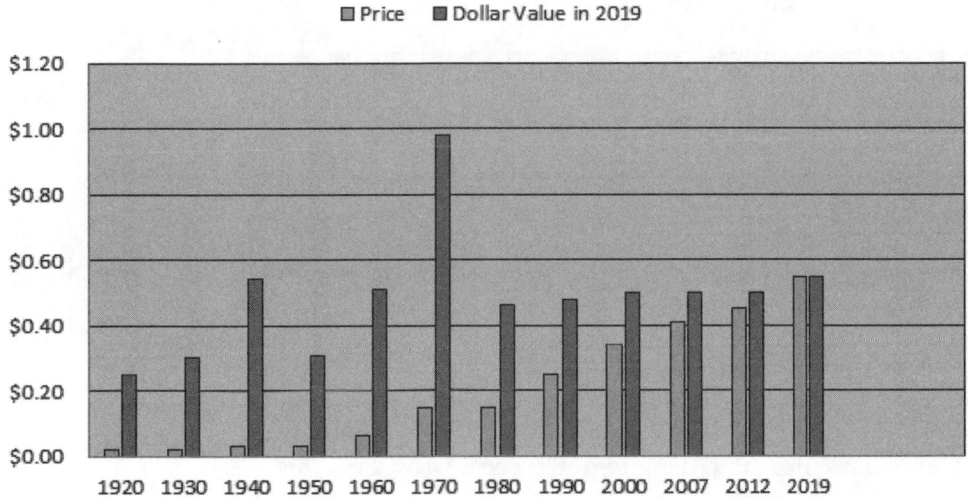

	1920	**1930**	**1940**	**1950**	**1960**	**1970**
Price	$0.02	$0.02	$0.03	$0.03	$0.06	$0.15
Dollar Value in 2019	$0.25	$0.30	$0.54	$0.31	$0.51	$0.98

	1980	**1990**	**2000**	**2007**	**2012**	**2019**
Price	$0.15	$0.25	$0.34	$0.41	$0.45	$0.55
Dollar Value in 2019	$0.46	$0.48	$0.50	$0.50	$0.50	$0.55

AROUND THE HOUSE

SUNBEAM TOASTER

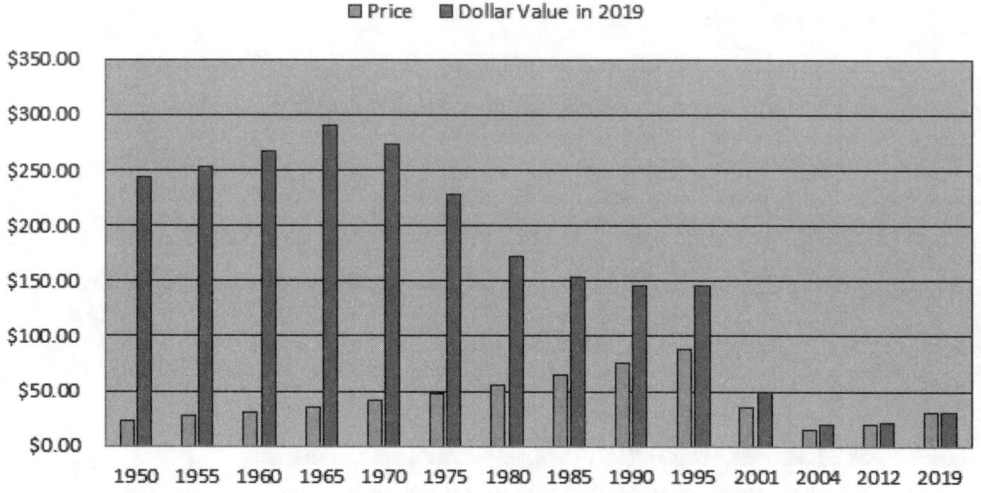

	1950	1955	1960	1965	1970	1975	1980
Price	$23.17	$26.90	$31.20	$36.10	$41.85	$48.50	$56.25
Dollar Value in 2019	$243.02	$253.72	$266.44	$289.69	$272.65	$227.87	$172.56

	1985	1990	1995	2001	2004	2012	2019
Price	$65.25	$75.50	$87.65	$34.99	$15.00	$19.99	$29.99
Dollar Value in 2019	$153.29	$146.02	$145.38	$49.97	$20.07	$22.01	$29.99

The ad for the Sunbeam Coffeemaster appeared in Life magazine in June 1944 a year before World War II ended. Production was halted on this and many other consumer products during the war. The Sunbeam Coffeenmaster had sold for $16 in 1940, and would sell for $32 in 1949. Clockwise from top right: Sunbeam Coffeemaster assembled for brewing (1944); Maxwell House Coffee ad (1928); "An Electric Percolator" ad (1919); 1-quart "Granite Dripper Coffee Pot" for 45 cents (1895); 1-quart Granite Coffee Pot for 15 cents (1899); ad for $90 Cuisinart (2013); and Proctor Silex for $16 (1979).

AROUND THE HOUSE

SUPERMAN COMIC BOOK

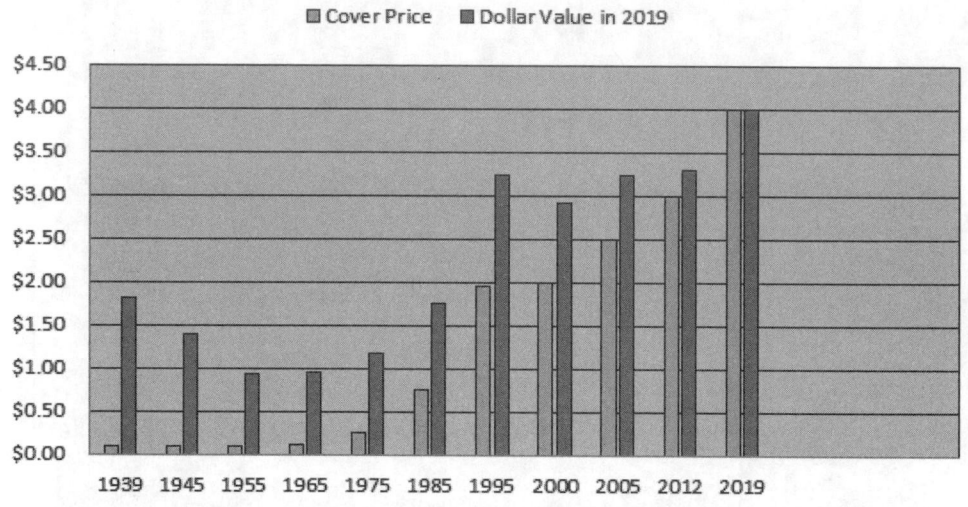

	1939	1945	1955	1965	1975	1985
Cover Price	$0.10	$0.10	$0.10	$0.12	$0.25	$0.75
Dollar Value in 2019	$1.82	$1.40	$0.94	$0.96	$1.17	$1.76

	1995	**2000**	**2005**	**2012**	**2019**
Cover Price	$1.95	$1.99	$2.50	$2.99	$3.99
Dollar Value in 2019	$3.23	$2.92	$3.24	$3.29	$3.99

AROUND THE HOUSE

THE ATLANTIC MONTHLY: YEARLY SUBSCRIPTION

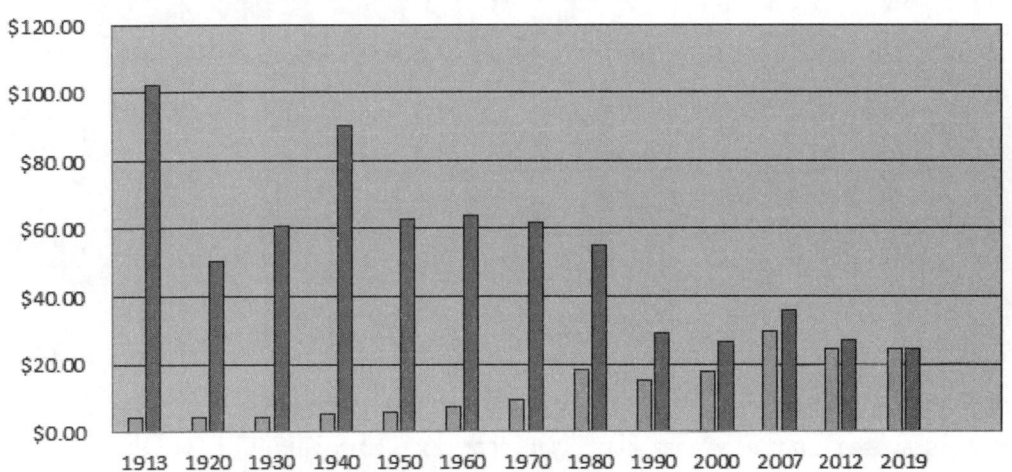

	1913	1920	1930	1940	1950	1960	1970
Price	$4.00	$4.00	$4.00	$5.00	$6.00	$7.50	$9.50
Dollar Value in 2019	$102.13	$50.56	$60.55	$90.28	$62.93	$64.05	$61.89

	1980	1990	2000	2007	2012	2019
Price	$18.00	$14.95	$17.94	$29.50	$24.50	$24.50
Dollar Value in 2019	$55.22	$28.91	$26.33	$35.96	$26.97	$24.50

AROUND THE HOUSE

TIME MAGAZINE: YEARLY SUBSCRIPTION

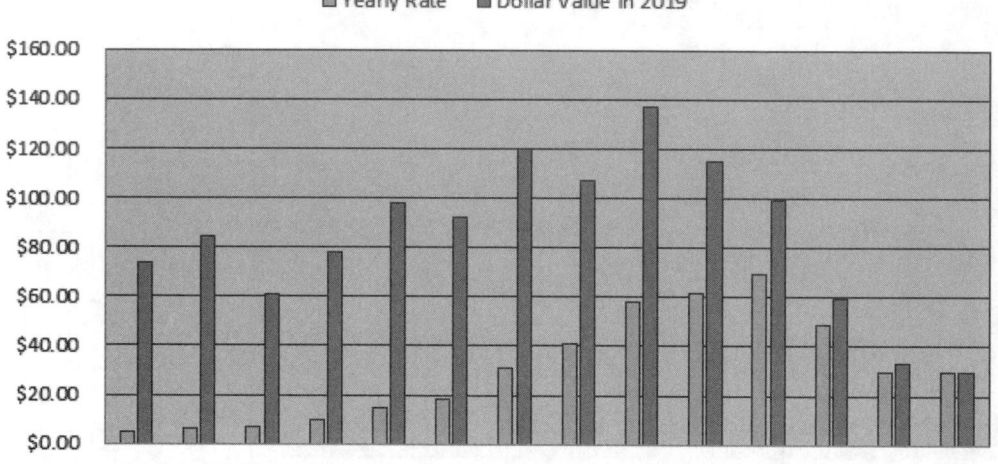

	1924	1946	1958	1966	1970	1974	1978	1982
Yearly Rate	$5.00	$6.50	$7.00	$10.00	$15.00	$18.00	$31.00	$41.00
Dollar Value in 2019	$73.91	$84.26	$61.23	$78.02	$97.72	$92.29	$120.18	$107.40

	1985	1991	2001	2007	2012	2019
Yearly Rate	$58.24	$61.88	$69.66	$49.00	$30.00	$30.00
Dollar Value in 2019	$136.82	$114.84	$99.48	$59.74	$33.03	$30.00

AROUND THE HOUSE

VOGUE MAGAZINE: SINGLE ISSUE

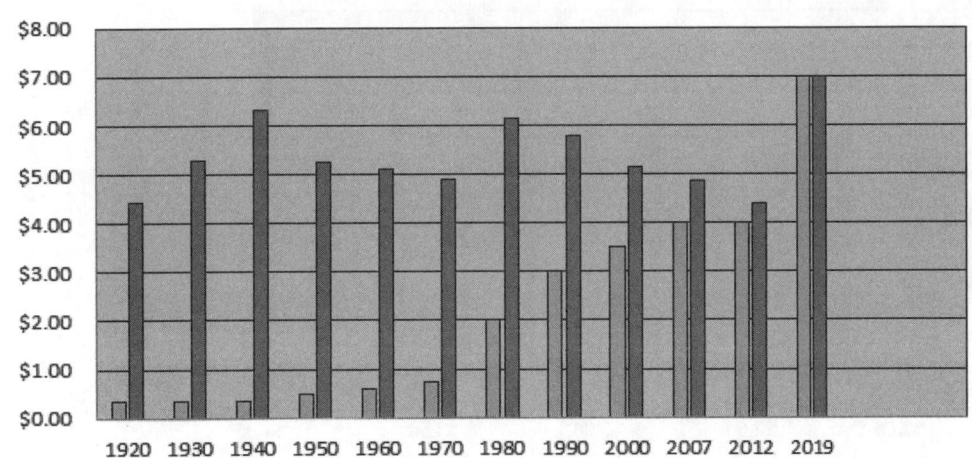

	1920	1930	1940	1950	1960	1970
Price	$0.35	$0.35	$0.35	$0.50	$0.60	$0.75
Dollar Value in 2019	$4.42	$5.30	$6.32	$5.24	$5.12	$4.89

	1980	**1990**	**2000**	**2007**	**2012**	**2019**
Price	$2.00	$3.00	$3.50	$3.99	$3.99	$6.99
Dollar Value in 2019	$6.14	$5.80	$5.14	$4.86	$4.39	$6.99

AROUND THE HOUSE

ZIPPO STANDARD BRUSH CHROME LIGHTER

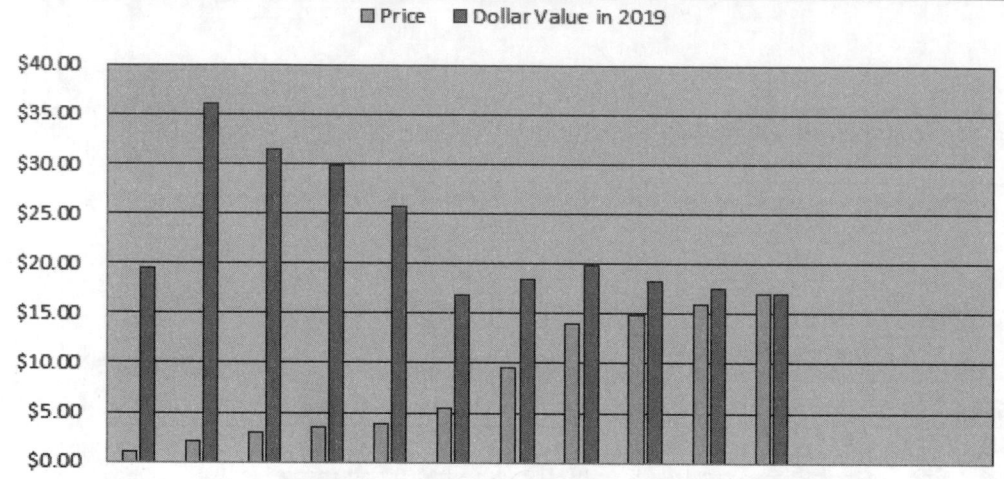

◼ Price ◼ Dollar Value in 2019

	1933	1940	1950	1960	1970	1980
Price	$1.00	$2.00	$3.00	$3.50	$3.95	$5.50
Dollar Value in 2019	$19.44	$36.11	$31.47	$29.89	$25.73	$16.87

	1990	2001	2007	2012	2019
Price	$9.50	$13.95	$14.95	$15.95	$16.95
Dollar Value in 2019	$18.37	$19.92	$18.23	$17.56	$16.95

Excerpts from Ad Descriptions:

1945: Zippo is in the War! Sorry, you can't buy your favorite wind proof, trouble proof lighter until the needs of war have all been filled—so keep yours in good repair.

1955: The Lossproof Zippo. A "built-in" elastic lanyard holds the LOSSPROOF ZIPPO securely to belt, jacket or shirt.

1962: This is the original Zippo lighter—made in 1932. It still works today. If any Zippo ever fails to work, we'll fix it free.

1978: (Christmas ad)—For each name on your list / There's a Zippo just right / So it's Zippos to all / And to all a good light

1987: The name Zippo has become a tradition in quality gifts. Why not stay with a tradition?

1997: Music by The Screaming Lizards. T-shirt by your cousin Danny. Encore by Zippo.

2009: We are thrilled to unveil Zippo BLU in Zippo's most enduringly popular finish.

2018: Riveted and riveting, the crown jewel of the Choice collection is an Armor High Polish Chrome with 360° MultiCut engraving and a clean industrial design.

DANFORTH, Druggist Shaving sets with a good Torrey razor, lather and per... design traveling cases 75c. Our prices low.

It cuts the beard clean — shaves close and smooth — yet leaves the skin without smart or roughness. It is the famous Torrey edge that does this — the edge that it has taken thirty years to bring to its present state of perfection.

Why not use this real man's razor?

Torrey Razors

What, $5 for a Razor?

Gillette Razor, $5.00.

What, $5 for a Razor? To be sure, but it will be the finest razor he ever used. Besides it is not one razor, but 24 razors. Follow us and we'll try to make you understand:

The Gillette Razor is a safety razor. It is unlike any other razor on the market. It is double-edged and your gentleman shaves with either side. The wafer blade fits into a concave base of triple silver plate, the handle is hollow to admit a tube which screws down, thus holding the razor securely in place.

No part of the razor can be affected by rust, for all best triple-plated silver, except the wafer blade and Damascus steel. The razor does not require honed—you do not even have to use pa... It is the most wonderful contrivance... was ever invented for man's tons... sonably soft beard, we calculate, c... us and never have to raise the que...

British invader.

WILKINSON SWORD STAINLESS 15 cents a blade.

$29⁹⁹ SALE Norelco 6945 razor

PHILIPS NORELCO

I HAD SAD EXPERIENCES WITH MISFIT BLADES—THEY LEFT MY FACE UNCOMFORTABLE AND RAW. YOU CAN'T GET A BETTER

Gillette BLADES

"Best investment I ever made"...

says S...

SCHICK

Schick Super $22.50

udio FOR MEN

Clockwise from top: Torrey Razor travel case for 75 cents (1896); Torrey, a "real man's razor," (1910); "What, $5 for a (Gillette) Razor?" (1904); Wilkinson Sword blades at 15 cents each (1964); Walgreens disposable razors at 12 for $3.29, or 27 cents each (2014); Schick Super electric shaver at $22.50 (1950); Norelco electric at $29.99 (2013); Remington electric shaver at about $25 (1972); 10 Gillette replacement blades at 25 cents (1937).

FASHION

BROOKS BROTHERS WHITE BUTTONDOWN SHIRT

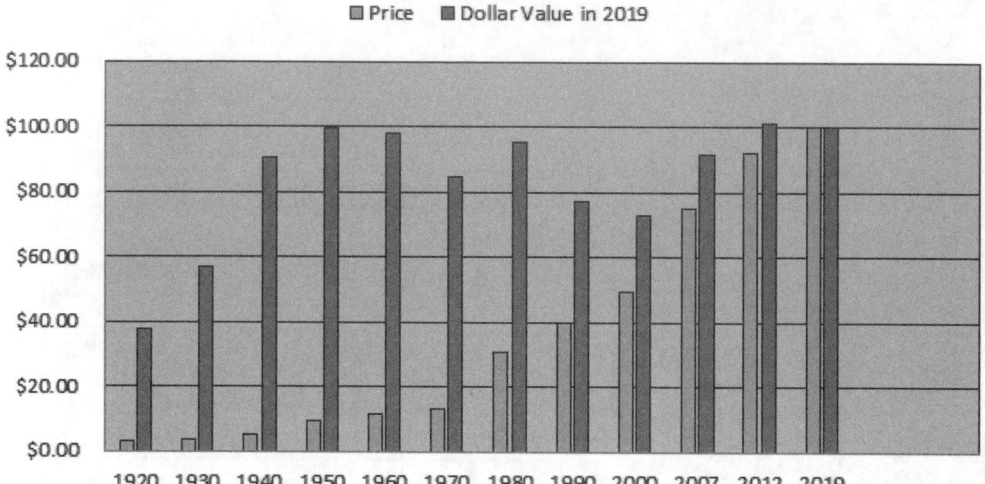

	1920	1930	1940	1950	1960	1970
Price	$3.00	$3.75	$5.00	$9.50	$11.50	$13.00
Dollar Value in 2019	$37.92	$56.76	$90.28	$99.64	$98.21	$84.69

	1980	1990	2000	2007	2012	2019
Price	$31.00	$40.00	$49.50	$75.00	$92.00	$100.00
Dollar Value in 2019	$95.10	$77.36	$72.66	$91.43	$101.29	$100.00

FASHION

MEN'S BLACK LEATHER DRESS SHOES

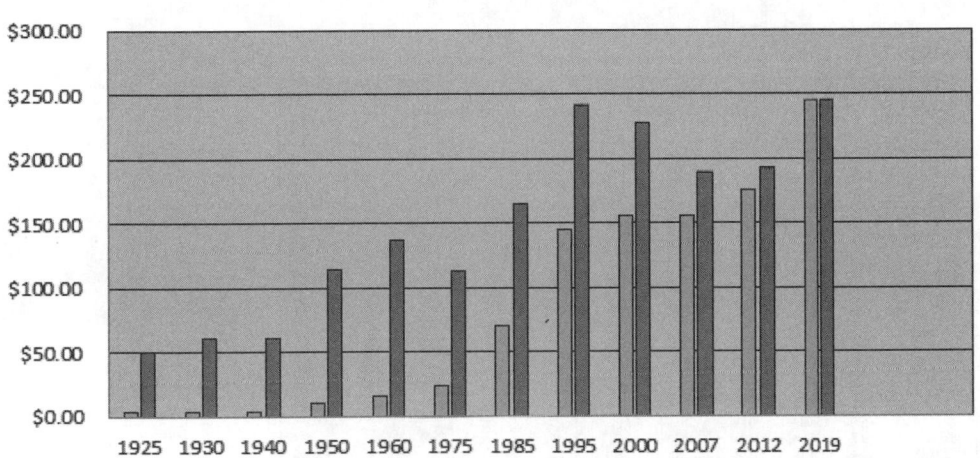

Price   ■ Dollar Value in 2019

	1925	1930	1940	1950	1960	1975
Price	$3.48	$4.00	$3.39	$10.95	$15.97	$23.99
Dollar Value in 2019	$50.27	$60.55	$61.21	$114.85	$136.38	$112.72

	1985	1995	2000	2007	2012	2019
Price	$70.00	$145.00	$155.00	$155.00	$175.00	$245.00
Dollar Value in 2019	$164.45	$240.50	$227.53	$188.96	$192.67	$245.00

Excerpts from Ad Descriptions

1925: *The Brogue:* We think these splendid looking black or brown GENUINE GOODYEAR WELT oxfords are the best bargains we know of. Rubber heels for comfort.

1940: *Peg Shanks:* French toes –"must haves" for every shoe wardrobe. Pegged shanks, steel arch supports … rubber heels.

1960: *Cushion Insole GOLD BONDS.* Wing tip with bold, distinctive rugged looks. Supple, premium leather uppers. Pacifate twill vamp lining. Pliant leather sole and rubber heel. Goodyear welt construction.

1985: Luxurious, lightweight ghillie tie dress shoe. Designed of incredibly soft and supple leather uppers, unlined for comfort and flexibility. Stacked leather heel has leather and rubber toplift. Imported from Italy.

2012: *Florsheim Shoe* commands attention with your polished style wearing these wing-tip oxfords.

2019: *Aldo Shoes Walker-R:* A luxurious leather derby shoe, featuring a wood-stacked heel, gets tough with a fractioned sole.

FASHION

MEN'S DRESS (OVER/TRENCH) COAT

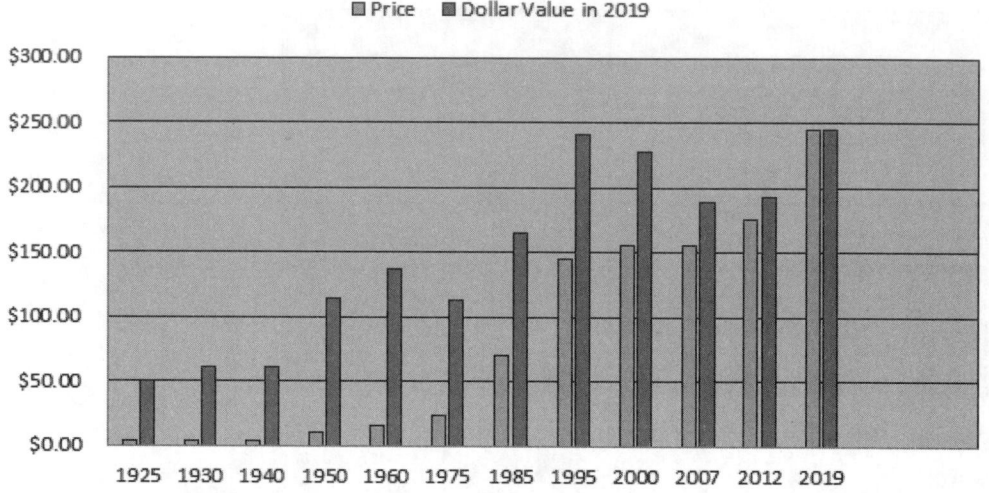

	1920	1930	1945	1950	1960	1975
Price	$28.50	$19.35	$17.95	$32.95	$29.90	$59.80
Dollar Value in 2019	$360.21	$292.89	$252.07	$345.60	$255.34	$280.97

	1980	1990	2000	2007	2012	2019
Price	$70.00	$74.75	$89.99	$89.99	$125.00	$134.99
Dollar Value in 2019	$214.74	$144.57	$132.10	$109.71	$137.62	$134.99

FASHION

MEN'S DRESS SHIRT

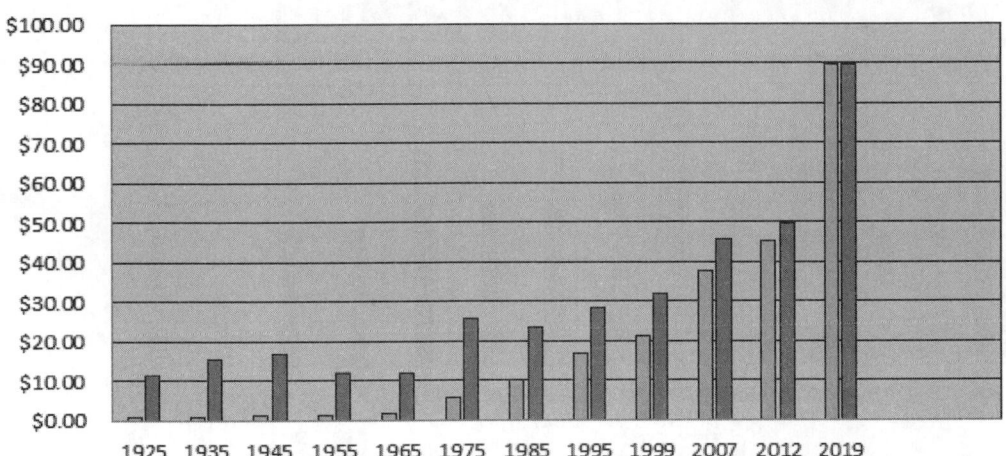

	1925	1935	1945	1955	1965	1975
Price	$0.79	$0.84	$1.18	$1.25	$1.46	$5.47
Dollar Value in 2019	$11.41	$15.50	$16.57	$11.79	$11.72	$25.70

	1985	1995	1999	2007	2012	2019
Price	$9.99	$16.99	$21.00	$37.50	$45.00	$89.50
Dollar Value in 2019	$23.47	$28.18	$31.86	$45.72	$48.54	$89.50

FASHION

MEN'S DRESS SLACKS

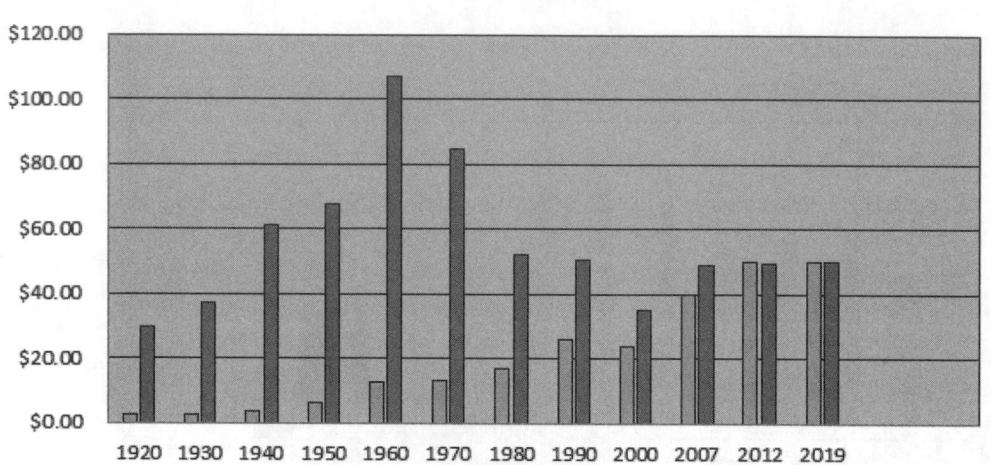

	1920	1930	1940	1950	1960	1970
Price	$2.35	$2.45	$3.39	$6.45	$12.50	$12.95
Dollar Value in 2019	$29.70	$37.08	$61.21	$67.65	$106.75	$84.37

	1980	1990	2000	2007	2012	2019
Price	$16.99	$26.00	$23.99	$40.00	$49.99	$49.97
Dollar Value in 2019	$52.12	$50.28	$35.22	$48.77	$49.54	$49.97

Excerpts from Ad Descriptions

1920: Striped trousers always popular, neat self -stripe worsted trousers furnished in dark blue, brown or green colors

1940: 12 1/2 oz. All wool navy blue "Famo" serge, durable serge–color-fast, smoothly finished.

1960: Men's slacks go casually continental…, scotchgard treated sheen gabardine of 100% virgin wool worsted.

1980: The coordinated slacks, Dacron polyester double knit. Slanted front pockets' set in black.

2000: Barrington dress slacks, comfortable polyester/rayon blend

2012: Calvin Klein Flat Front; make a solid investment in these dress pants from Calvin Klein that have a slim fit for a truly modern look.

2019: Tailored fit flat front micro tweed dress pants; A stylish classic. These micro tweed slacks are a wardrobe must-have for dress and professional wear.

Hats disappeared rapidly in the 1960s. Some blame the hatless style of President John F. Kennedy, who took office that year. The hatless man and the upside-down women in the montage are taken from a 1961 department store ad that shows the man holding his narrow brim hat. Clockwise from top right: man's 1906 C&K Knapp-Felt derby for $4 (1906); Stetson western-wear hats for $40+ (1981); women's straw boaters for $4-$5 (1899); 1920s-style fedora for $100 (2014); background images and sales pitches from C&K's 1914 "Hatman" brochure; "The Playboy" Stetson for $5 (1941); Stetsons $8.50-$12.50 (1948); woman wearing hat (1949); "Chic" New York-style hat for $1.98 (1928); Easter hat for $5 (1910); "Stetson Hats have character" (1912); "A Broad Showing of Modish Hats" (1909); and woman with hat (1899).

FASHION

MEN'S JEANS

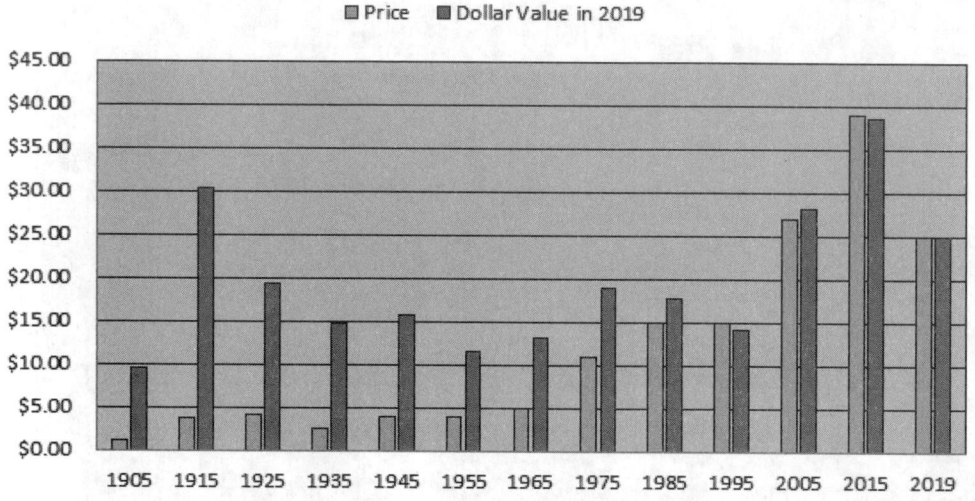

	1905	1915	1925	1935	1945	1955	1965
Price	$1.15	$3.75	$4.10	$2.45	$3.95	$3.98	$5.00
Dollar Value in 2019	$9.62	$30.24	$19.42	$14.68	$15.70	$11.56	$13.05

	1975	1985	1995	2005	2015	2019
Price	$10.99	$14.99	$14.88	$26.99	$39.00	$24.99
Dollar Value in 2019	$18.88	$17.78	$14.05	$28.13	$38.59	$24.99

FASHION

MEN'S SWEATER

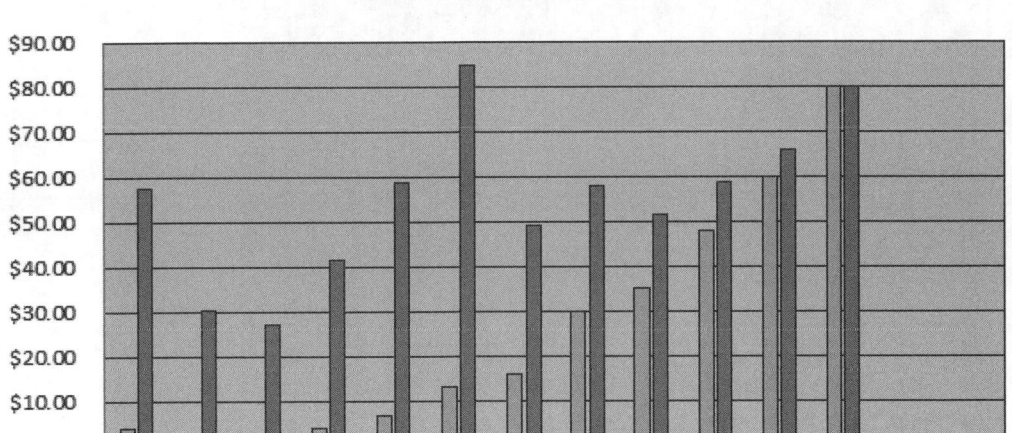

	1925	**1930**	**1940**	**1950**	**1960**	**1970**
Price	$3.98	$2.00	$1.49	$3.95	$6.86	$13.00
Dollar Value in 2019	$57.49	$30.27	$26.90	$41.43	$58.58	$84.69

	1980	**1990**	**2000**	**2007**	**2012**	**2019**
Price	$15.99	$29.99	$35.00	$48.00	$60.00	$79.97
Dollar Value in 2019	$49.05	$58.00	$51.38	$58.52	$66.06	$79.97

FASHION

MEN'S TWO-PIECE SUIT

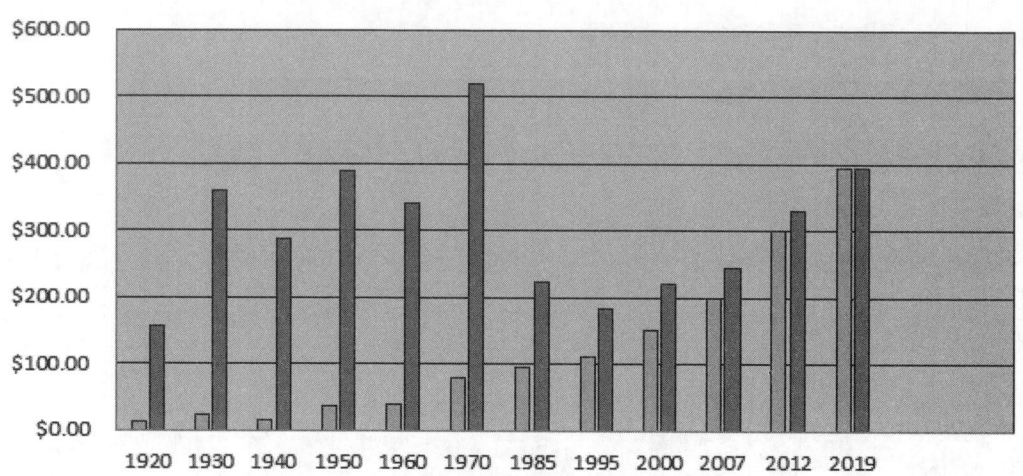

	1920	1930	1940	1950	1960	1970
Price	$12.45	$23.75	$15.95	$36.95	$39.90	$79.50
Dollar Value in 2019	$157.35	$359.49	$287.98	$387.55	$340.74	$517.93

	1985	1995	2000	2007	2012	2019
Price	$95.00	$110.00	$150.00	$200.00	$299.99	$395.00
Dollar Value in 2019	$223.18	$182.45	$220.19	$243.83	$330.28	$395.00

Excerpts from Ad Descriptions

1900: Men's Ready-Made Suits. A very handsome ready-made suit … dark background, covered with mixture of reddish brown and olive. Coat is satin piped throughout … pants made in first-class style.

1920: *Model S.* Gray striped worsted material, about 55 percent wool, 45 percent cotton. Well made in our popular waistline Model S. Well-fitted trousers have cuff bottoms.

1940: *2-Button Single Breasted Model.* Trim in every line. When you put it on you feel *progressive* … you *look* it … tyour boss and friends *believe* it.

1960: *A trend to quiet elegance.* A muted miniature check pattern in a year-around weight suit of 55% Dacron polyester fiber, 45% rich virgin wool worsted.

1985: *American Trend silk-blend.* Impeccably tailored … woven of a luxurious blend of polyester, silk and linen.

2012: *Lauren by Ralph Lauren.* Charcoal strip slim fit … gives your button-up look a modern appeal.

2019: *French Connection Slim Fit Black Suit.* A classic suit you can style your way.

FASHION

WOMEN'S BLACK PURSE

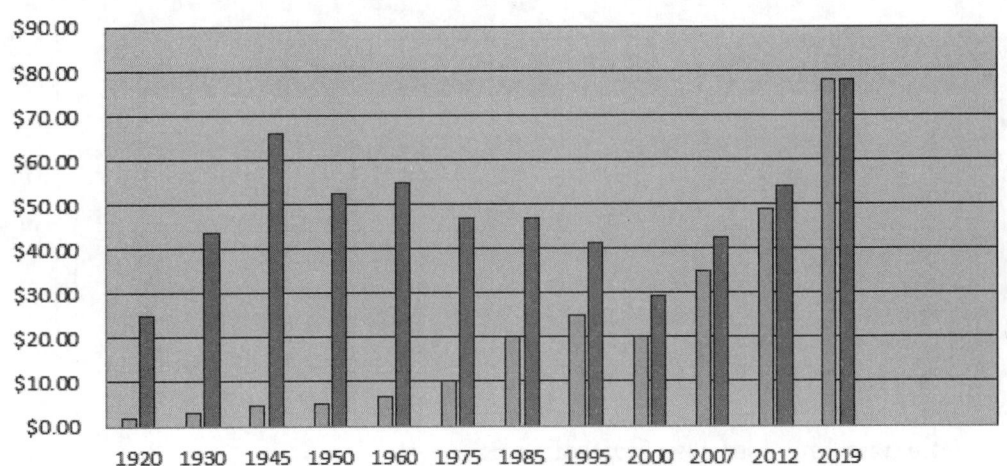

Price ☐ Dollar Value in 2019

	1920	**1930**	**1945**	**1950**	**1960**	**1975**
Price	$1.98	$2.89	$4.69	$5.00	$6.44	$10.00
Dollar Value in 2019	$25.02	$43.74	$65.86	$52.44	$55.00	$46.98

	1985	**1995**	**2000**	**2007**	**2012**	**2019**
Price	$20.00	$24.95	$19.99	$35.00	$49.00	$78.00
Dollar Value in 2019	$46.98	$41.38	$29.34	$42.67	$53.95	$78.00

Excerpts from Ad Descriptions

1920: *A beautifully embossed leather bag,* wide opening concealed frame and large inner pocket and coin purse to match bag.

1945: *Dressmaker-Detail Pouches,* Popular Capeskin in a tucked pouch with rayon Faille gussets, Lucite clasp. Has a strong metal frame. Rayon lined, coin case, mirror.

1960: *Kerrybooke Classics,* Roomy Swagger bag with 4-part frame has seven sections in all! Three are inside compartments with separate openings at top, two are outside swagger pockets.

1980: *The Handbag,* Polyester, rayon and flax bag. Beige plastic frame. Twist snap closure. Rope strap slips inside for use as a clutch.

2000: *Rosetti Bags,* Microfiber handbags.

2012: *Nine West Bag:* Croc print crossbody

2019: *Madewell Simple Crossbody Bag:* The kind of take-everywhere-stash-everything leather crossbody you'll want in every color (and, at this sweet price, why not?).

FASHION

WOMEN'S DRESS SUIT

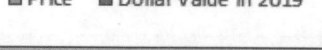

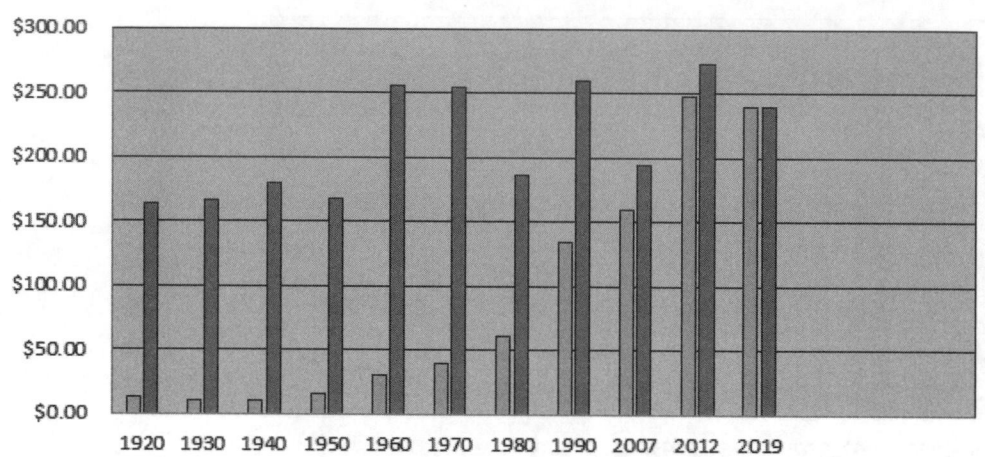

	1920	1930	1940	1950	1960	1970
Price	$12.95	$10.98	$9.98	$15.98	$29.90	$39.00
Dollar Value in 2019	$163.67	$166.20	$180.19	$167.61	$255.34	$254.08

	1980	1990	2007	2012	2019
Price	$60.54	$134.00	$159.00	$248.00	$240.00
Dollar Value in 2019	$185.72	$259.16	$193.84	$273.04	$240.00

Excerpts from Ad Descriptions

1920: *Smart Style with Youthful Lines.* … made of ALL WOOL DOUBLE TWISTED WARP SERGE, a material which is fashionable and wears well.

1940: *New Man-Tailored Suits.* Man-tailored suits and superb topcoats … like these have won Americans their name and their fame as the Best-dress Women and Girls in the world.

1960: *All Wool Worsted.* A fine lightweight fabric. Detailed with pretty acetate satin trim at lapels, hipline and sleeves; covered buttons to match. Jacket is rayon and acetate creped lined.

1980: *The Slender Suit.* Textured double-knit polyester … Jacket. Contrasting color piping edges shawl collar and front opening. Long sleeves; two slant pockets … Skirt. Zipper opening in back. A-line style.

2012: *Anne Klein Grey Suit.* Bolero Jacket with crisscross neckline mélange sheath dress

2019: *Le Suit Plus Size Open-Jacket Dress Suit*: A matching open-front jacket adds sophisticated coverage to this plus size suit with a sleeveless sheath dress

FASHION

WOMEN'S HIGH HEEL SHOES

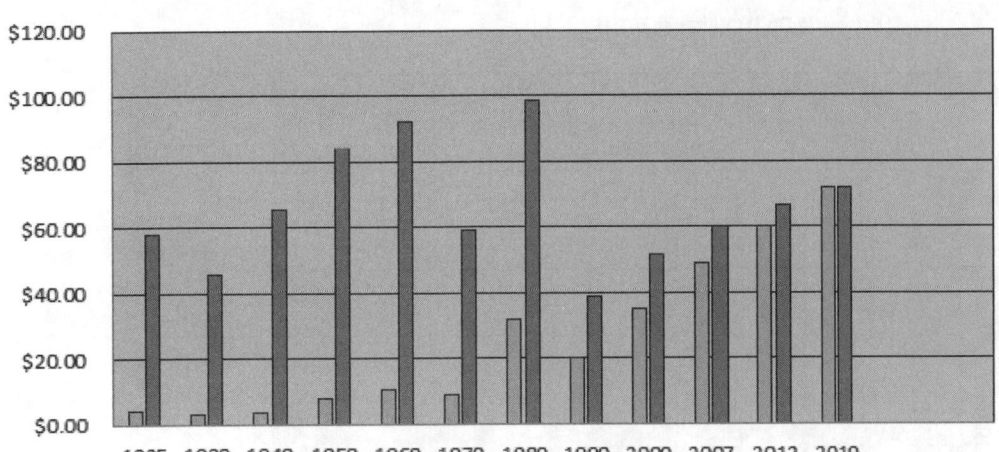

	1925	1930	1940	1950	1960	1970	1980	1990
Price	$3.98	$3.00	$3.59	$7.95	$10.70	$8.99	$31.99	$19.94
Dollar Value in 2019	$57.81	$45.67	$65.18	$83.86	$91.89	$58.90	$98.69	$38.78

	2000	2007	2012	2019
Price	$34.99	$49.00	$60.00	$72.00
Dollar Value in 2019	$51.65	$60.07	$66.43	$72.00

Excerpts from Ad Descriptions

1920: *The Pair.* Brown Kid Lace … French Hee l… Flexible Sewed Sole.

1940: *To Accent Foot Loveliness.* Elasticized gabardine step-in slips on so easily—then fairly molds itself to your foot as you walk. Softly pleated vamp. Leather sole, 2" Cuban heel.

1950: *Costume Drama.* High platforms, high heel … to star you as a leading lady … wherever you go. Superbly beautiful bracelet sandal for dining, dancing hours; soaring high on a 1/ 2" platform and slender 3" heels.

1960: *The classic Spectator.* Flexible Featherlite pointed toe pump of supple textured leather. Leather sole and 2 1/81" heel.

1970: *Step into the Classic Pump.* Neatly stitched topline and softly shaped toe … here's the perfect underscore for your dressy as well as tailored clothes. Choose uppers of smooth leather or gleaming patent vinyl.

1980: *The Spectator Pump.* A classic shoe to complement this year's suit styles.

2012: *Calvin Klein.* Pumps that offer incredible texture and style … with pretty peep toe.

2019: Go retro on your night out in America Rag's Reeta sandals featuring an ankle strap and sky-high platform block heel for amazing height.

FASHION

WOMEN'S ONE PIECE DRESS

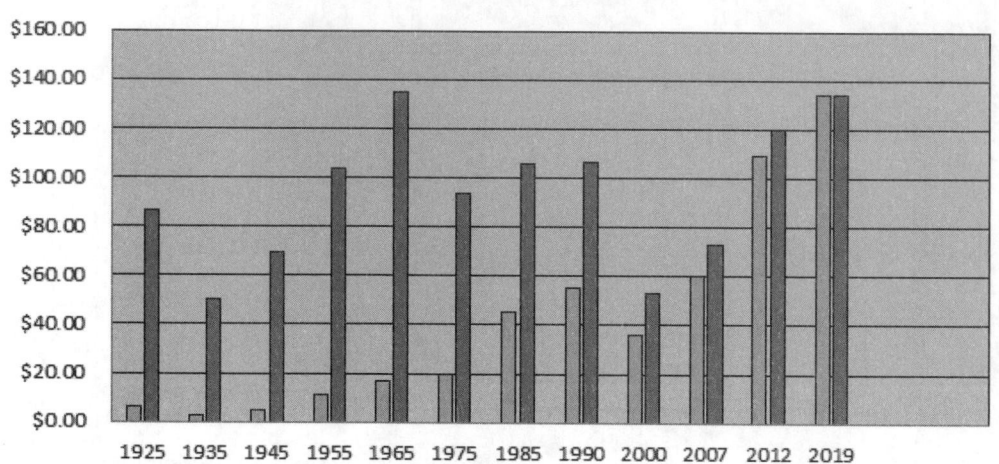

	1925	1935	1945	1955	1965	1975
Price	$5.98	$2.74	$4.95	$10.98	$16.81	$20.00
Dollar Value in 2019	$86.38	$50.56	$69.51	$103.56	$134.89	$93.97

	1985	1990	2000	2007	2012	2019
Price	$45.00	$55.00	$36.00	$60.00	$109.00	$134.00
Dollar Value in 2019	$105.71	$106.37	$52.85	$73.15	$120.01	$134.00

Excerpts from Ad Descriptions

1925: *Fine Quality Drawnwork Voile.* Just to see this dainty, demure summer wash frock of fine, sheet voile will convey to you its delicate loveliness.

1945: *The Peplum Dress.* ... Making fashion headlines everywhere with its jaunty newness. Gathered peplum covers skirt in front. Cinched in by set-in belt. Collar double looped. French-type rayon crepe.

1955: *This is the year for pleats ... and these wash!* 100% Nylon ... Crisp, sheer ribbon puckered nylon in a dress as cool as a tall lemonade. Printed roses float here and there ... pleated skirt whirls out to a full circle.

1975: *Softly Draped Dresses.* They are of Dacron polyester double-knit in a smooth interlock stitch ... Step-in style dress has a front zipper opening; elasticized waistband.

2012: *Black London Times.* Elevate your look to stunner status ... with graceful shutter pleats.

2019: Fit and Flare Dress with Pockets; The perfect retro treasure can be hard to come by— luckily, your style sense led you right to this grey fit and flare!

FASHION

WOMEN'S SKIRT

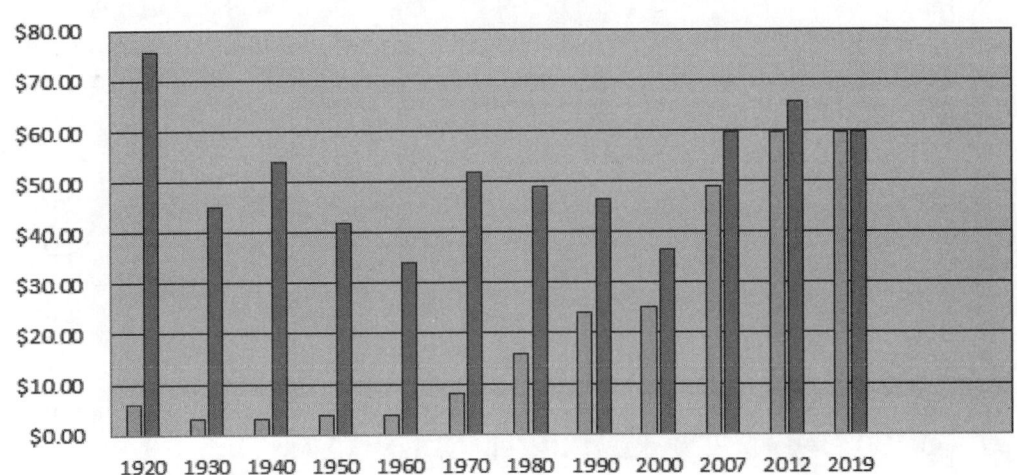

	1920	1930	1940	1950	1960	1970
Price	$5.98	$2.98	$2.98	$3.98	$3.97	$7.97
Dollar Value in 2019	$75.58	$45.11	$53.81	$41.74	$33.90	$51.92

	1980	1990	2000	2007	2012	2019
Price	$16.00	$24.00	$24.99	$49.00	$59.50	$59.50
Dollar Value in 2019	$49.08	$46.42	$36.68	$59.74	$65.51	$59.50

Excerpts from Ad Descriptions

1920: Typical of youth in every line, this fashionable skirt is all the miss wants for all around service.

1940: Fan Pleated; Handsomely tailored skirt in two fine fabrics that mate beautifully with blouses and jackets.

1960: Woven Plaid... Dan River wash-and-wear cotton. Simulated pockets; back zipper; kick pleats. Washable.

1980: The Slim Skirt; Ours is a lightweight gabardine that's classically styled with self-piped, button-down pockets in front and back.

2000: Apostrophe print ruffle skirt. A fun look.

2012: Maxi Skirt. A perfect complement to a colorful tank or chambray shirt.

2019: High Waisted Wrap Maxi Skirt; Flirty and flowy with a vibrant floral print, maxi length and wrap front; this skirt gives us major free-spirit vibes.

FASHION

WOMEN'S SWIMSUIT

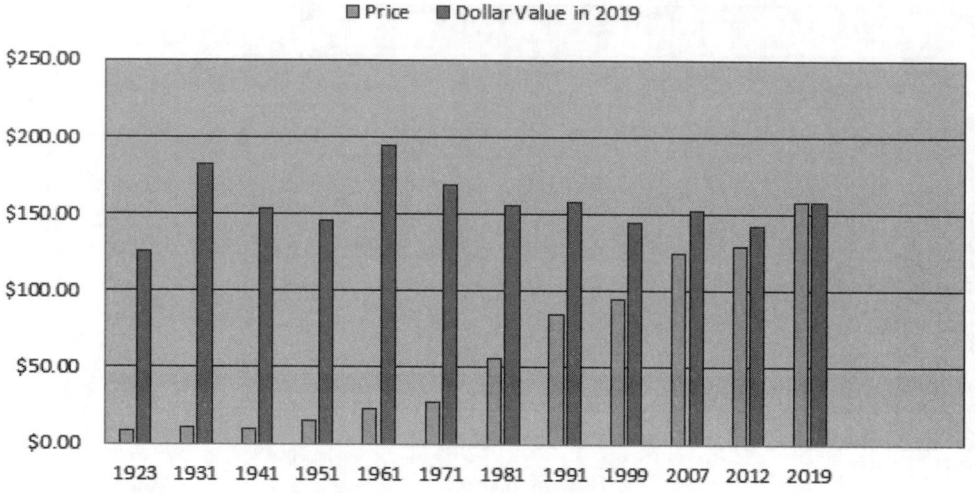

	1923	1931	1941	1951	1961	1971
Price	$8.50	$10.95	$8.95	$14.95	$22.95	$26.99
Dollar Value in 2019	$125.65	$182.10	$153.90	$145.35	$194.02	$168.45

	1981	1991	1999	2007	2012	2019
Price	$56.00	$85.00	$95.00	$125.00	$129.00	$158.00
Dollar Value in 2019	$155.73	$157.75	$144.14	$152.39	$142.03	$158.00

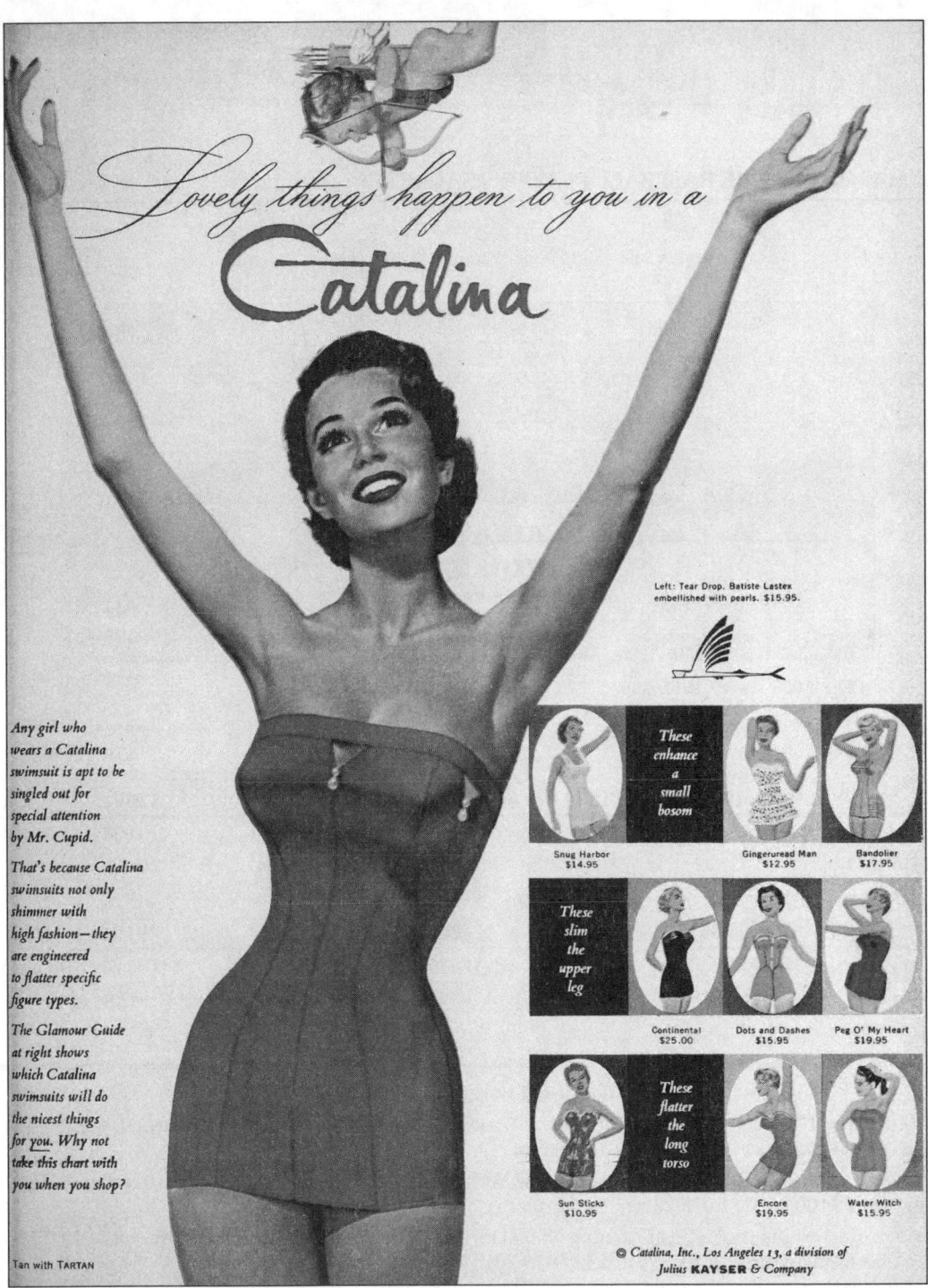

A 1955 advertisement for Catalina swimsuits. The text reads: Lovely things happen to you in a Catalina. Any girl who wears a Catalina swimsuit is apt to be singled out for special attention by Mr. Cupid. That's because Catalina swimsuits not only shimmer with high fashion—they are engineeres to flatter specific figure types. The Glamour Guide at right shows which Catalina swimsuits will do the nicest thing for you. Why not take this chart with you when you shop? (Via Wikimedia Commons)

HELP WANTED

AVERAGE MAJOR LEAGUE BASEBALL PLAYER'S SALARY

	1929	**1939**	**1946**	**1951**	**1967**	**1975**
Average Salary	$7,531	$7,306	$11,294	$13,300	$19,000	$44,676
Dollar Value in 2019	$37.92	$56.76	$90.28	$99.64	$98.21	$84.69

	1985	**1995**	**2007**	**2012**	**2019**
Average Salary	$371,157	$1,094,400	$1,176,928	$1,243,277	$4,095,686
Dollar Value in 2019	$95.10	$77.36	$72.66	$91.43	$101.29

Professional Baseball Salary Facts:

♦ Babe Ruth earned $10,000 in 1921 with the New York Yankees ($143,096 in 2019 dollars). By 1923, he earned a $52,000 salary ($778,914 in 2019 dollars).

♦ Joe DiMaggio earned $37,000 in 1941 on the New York Yankee payroll ($644,713 in 2019 dollars). In 1949, his salary was $100,000 ($1,076,231 in 2019 dollars).

♦ Willie Mays started his rookie year earning $5,000 in 1951 ($49,258 in 2019 dollars). He earned $170,000 near the end of his career in 1971 ($1,075,168 in 2019 dollars).

♦ In 2002, Alex Rodriquez earned $22 million ($31,323,768 in 2012 dollars) while playing for the Texas Rangers.

♦ Yoenis Céspedes of the New York Mets earned $29 million for the 2018 season.

HELP WANTED

AVERAGE US NATIONAL ANNUAL SALARY

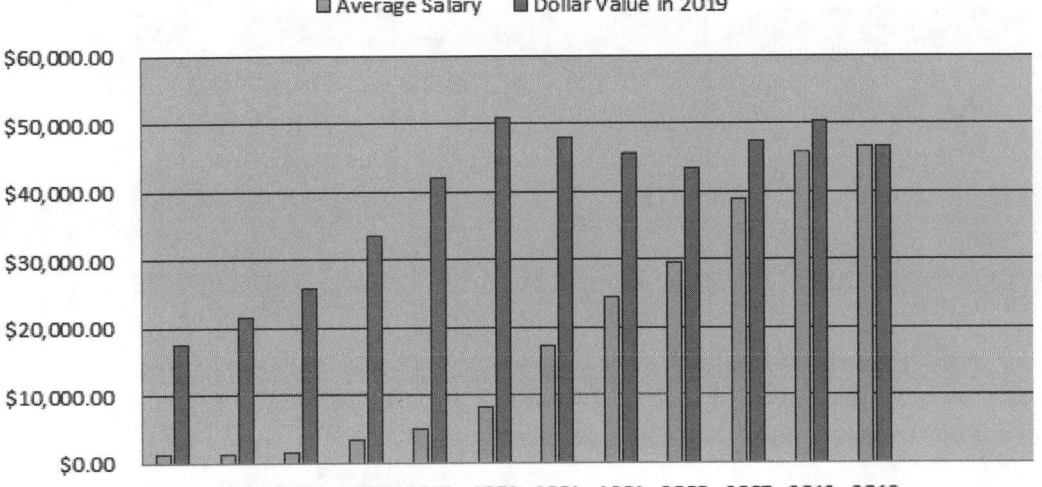

	1921	1931	1941	1951	1961	1971
Average Salary	$1,233	$1,289	$1,492	$3,452	$4,961	$8,144
Dollar Value in 2019	$17,412	$21,436	$25,656	$33,561	$41,941	$50,830

	1981	1991	2000	2007	2012	2019
Average Salary	$17,197	$24,578	$29,469	$38,760	$45,790	$46,644
Dollar Value in 2019	$47,822	$45,615	$43,258	$47,253	$50,413	$46,644

HELP WANTED

BOOKKEEPER ANNUAL SALARY

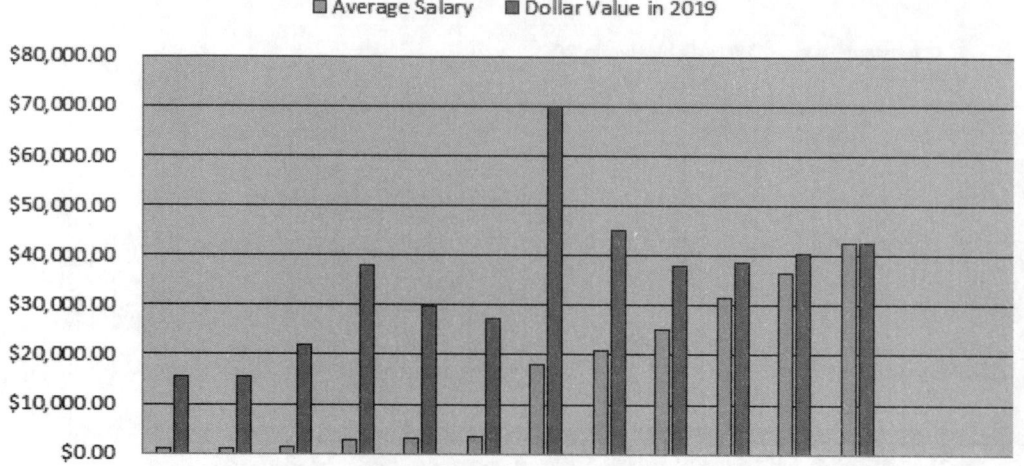

	1918	1929	1936	1943	1952	1964
Average Salary	$930	$1,040	$1,200	$2,600	$3,120	$3,360
Dollar Value in 2019	$15,568	$15,374	$21,822	$37,989	$29,761	$27,398

	1978	1988	1999	2007	2012	2019
Average Salary	$18,000	$21,000	$25,000	$31,560	$36,640	$42,454
Dollar Value in 2019	$69,785	$44,871	$37,932	$38,476	$40,340	$42,454

Year	Position Description Excerpts as Advertised
1918;	Assistant in office of large manufacturing concern
1929;	Manufacturing concern; experience a must, some typing involved
1936;	Complete charge of assistants
1943;	*No description in advertisement*
1952;	Accounts payable, dress manufacturing experience
1964;	Downtown company: good hours and benefits for keypunch experience
1978;	Full charge: CPA office
1988;	Manufacturer; supervise staff in all phases of computerized billing
2019;	Accurately record all day-to-day financial transactions of our company

HELP WANTED

COAL MINER ANNUAL SALARY*

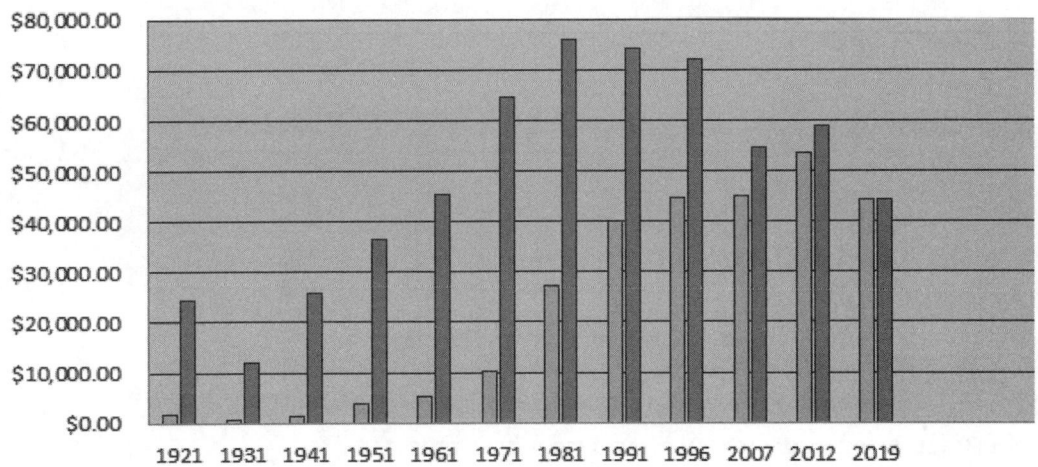

	1921	1931	1941	1951	1961	1971
Average Salary	$1,726	$723	$1,500	$3,762	$5,357	$10,331
Dollar Value in 2019	$23,374	$12,023	$25,973	$36,575	$45,288	$64,480

	1981	1991	1996	2007	2012	2019
Average Salary	$27,283	$39,988	$44,769	$44,930	$53,560	$44,304
Dollar Value in 2019	$75,869	$74,214	$72,126	$54,775	$58,968	$44,304

* Based on National Average

843

HELP WANTED

DOMESTIC WORKER ANNUAL SALARY*

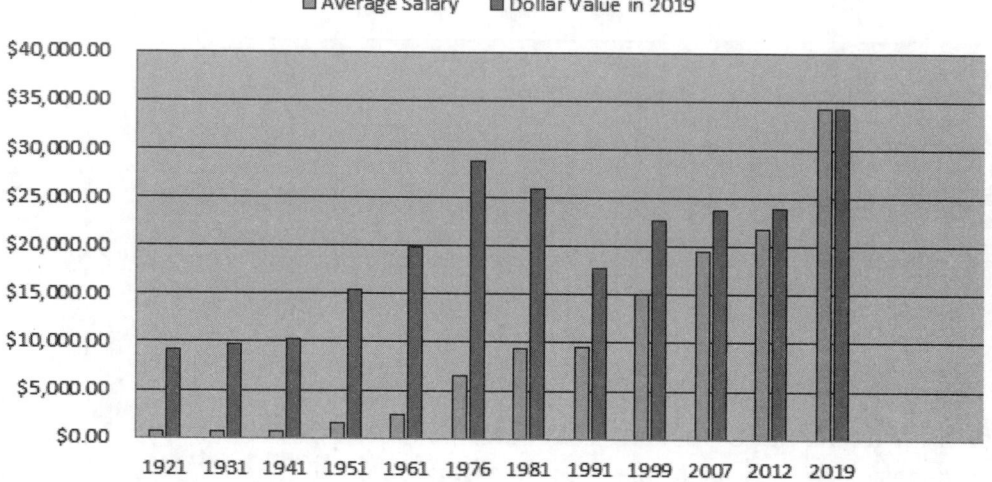

	1921	1931	1941	1951	1961	1976
Average Salary	$649	$584	$601	$1,588	$2,356	$6,479
Dollar Value in 2019	$9,165	$9,712	$10,335	$15,439	$19,918	$28,783

	1981	1991	1999	2007	2012	2019
Average Salary	$9,327	$9,527	$15,000	%19,550	$21,820	$34,244
Dollar Value in 2019	$25,937	$17,681	$22,759	$23,834	$24,023	$34,244

*Based on National Average

Clockwise from top left: RCA black-and-white television for $199.95+ (1950); Zenith color TV for $148.88+ (1963); "rabbit ears" TV antennae for 99 cents (1971); Portland TV with swivel cabinet for $599.95 (1979); cable-compatible TV for $369.99 (1985); TUSA cable connector (circa 1980); Proscan high-definition TV with LED screen for $129.99 (2013) headline about television exhibit (1928); and schematic drawing of television tube (1950).

HELP WANTED

DURABLE GOODS MANUFACTURER ANNUAL SALARY*

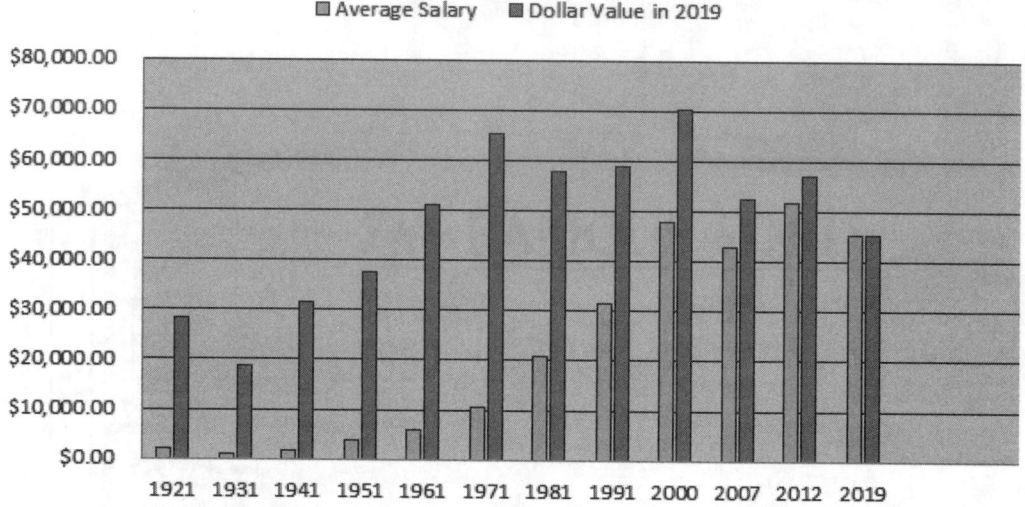

	1921	1931	1941	1951	1961	1971
Average Salary	$2,010	$1,127	$1,840	$3,862	$6,048	$10,473
Dollar Value in 2019	$28,384	$18,742	$31,640	$37,547	$51,130	$65,366

	1981	1991	2000	2007	2012	2019
Average Salary	$20,810	$31,658	$47,930	$42,993	$51,915	$45,531
Dollar Value in 2019	$57,869	$58,755	$70,357	$52,414	$57,157	$45,531

*Based on National Average

HELP WANTED

FEDERAL HOURLY MINIMUM WAGE

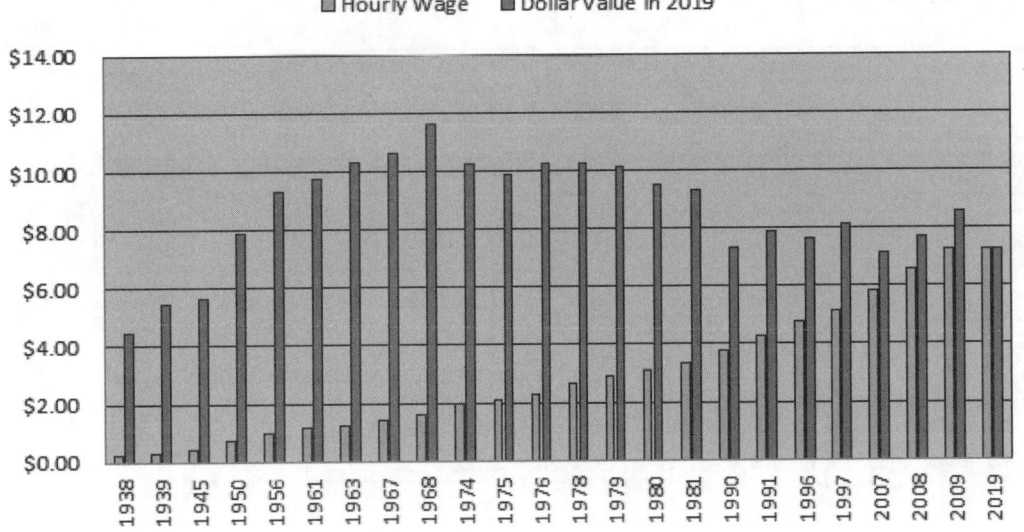

■ Hourly Wage   ■ Dollar Value in 2019

Year	Hourly Wage	Dollar Value in 2019	Year	Hourly Wage	Dollar Value in 2019
1938	$0.25	$4.48	1979	$2.90	$10.10
1939	$0.30	$5.46	1980	$3.10	$9.51
1945	$0.40	$5.62	1981	$3.35	$9.32
1950	$0.75	$7.87	1990	$3.80	$7.35
1956	$1.00	$9.29	1991	$4.25	$7.89
1961	$1.15	$9.72	1996	$4.75	$7.65
1963	$1.25	$10.33	1997	$5.15	$8.11
1967	$1.40	$10.60	2007	$5.85	$7.13
1968	$1.60	$11.62	2008	$6.55	$7.69
1974	$2.00	$10.25	2009	$7.25	$8.54
1975	$2.10	$9.87	2012	$7.25	$8.09
1976	$2.30	$10.22	2019	$7.25	$7.25
1978	$2.65	$10.27			

HELP WANTED

FOOTBALL CHAMPIONSHIP PRIZE MONEY: PLAYER'S SHARE*

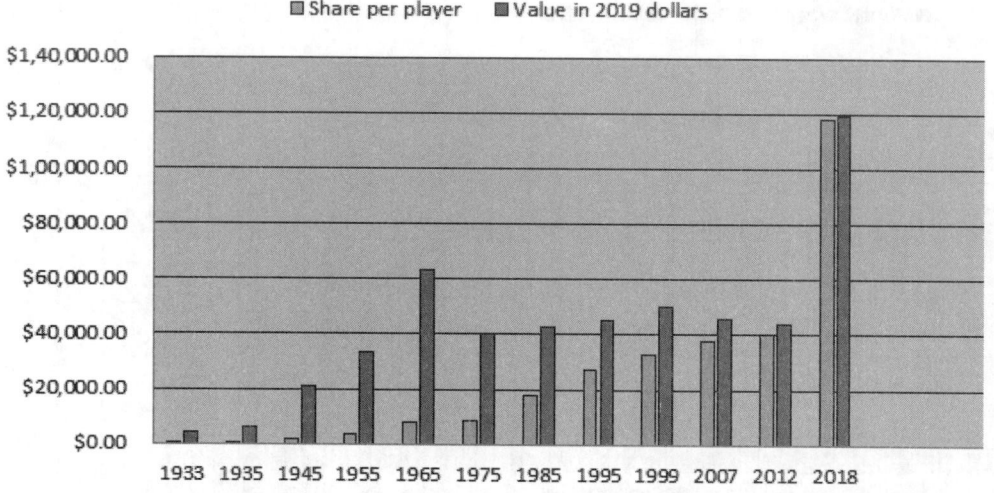

	1933	1935	1945	1955	1965	1975
Team	Chicago	Detroit	Cleveland	Cleveland	Green Bay	Dallas
Share per Player	$210	$313	$1,469	$3,508	$7,819	$8,500
Dollar Value in 2019	$4,106	$5,808	$20,746	$33,274	$63,099	$40,162

	1985	1995	1999	2007	2012	2018
Team	Chicago	Dallas	St. Louis	New York	New York	New England
Share per Player	$18,000	$27,000	$33,000	$37,500	$40,000	$118,000
Dollar Value in 2019	$42,525	$45,036	$50,352	$45,975	$44,287	$119,454

*The NFL Championship was not called the Superbowl until 1967

HELP WANTED

GAS & ELECTRIC WORKER ANNUAL SALARY*

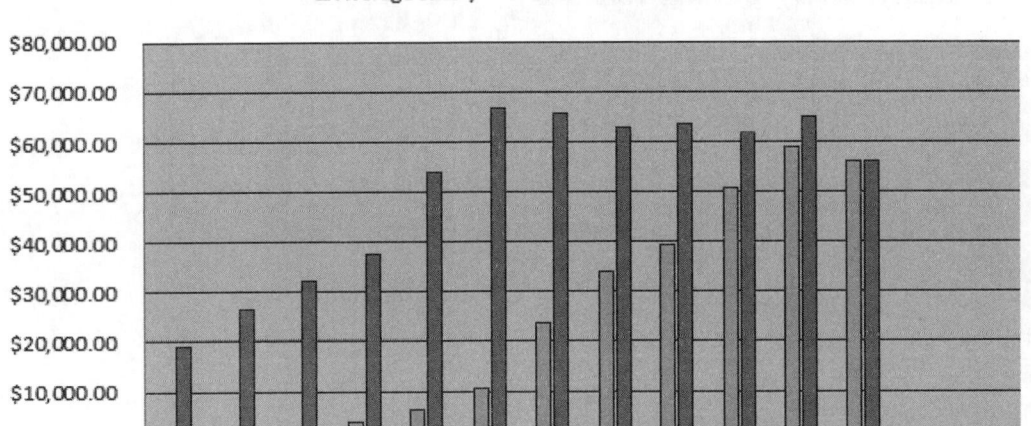

	1921	1931	1941	1951	1961	1971
Average Salary	$1,364	$1,600	$1,870	$3,851	$6,390	$10,696
Dollar Value in 2019	$19,262	$26,608	$32,156	$37,440	$54,021	$66,758

	1981	1991	1996	2007	2012	2019
Average Salary	$25,595	$33,940	$39,398	$50,772	$58,864	$56,000
Dollar Value in 2019	$65,613	$62,990	$63,473	$61,897	$64,807	$56,000

*Based on National Average

HELP WANTED

GOLF MASTER CHAMPIONS EARNINGS

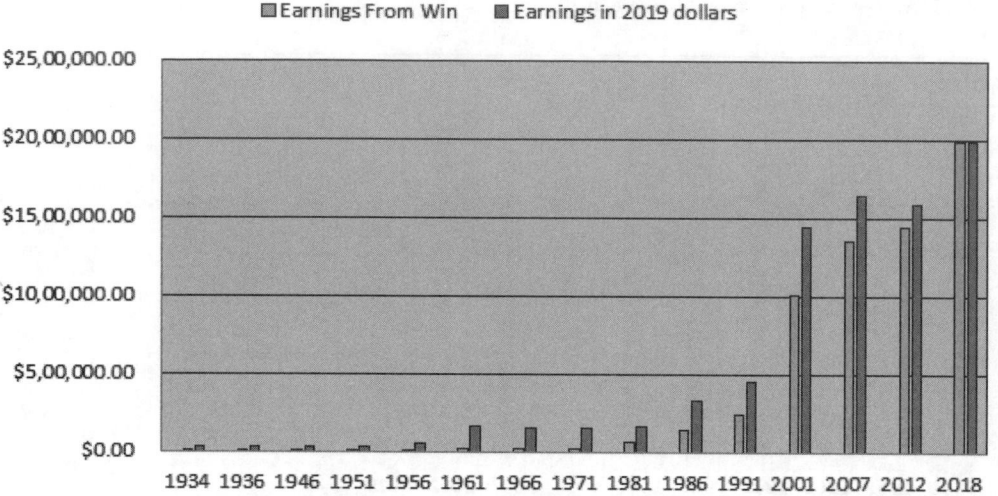

Year	Winning Player	Total Score	Earnings from Win	Earnings in 2019 Dollars
1934	Horton Smith	−4	$1,500	$28,295
1936	Henry Picard	−3	$1,500	$27,298
1946	Herman Keiser	−6	$2,500	$32,407
1951	Ben Hogan	−8	$3,000	$29,166
1956	Jack Burke, Jr.	1 over par	$6,000	$55,759
1961	Gary Player	−8	$20,000	$169,081
1966	Jack Nicklaus	Even	$20,000	$156,035
1971	Charles Coody	−9	$25,000	$156,035
1981	Tom Watson	−28	$60,000	$166,849
1986	Jack Nicklaus	−9	$144,000	$332,114
1991	Ian Woosnam	−11	$243,000	$450,988
2001	Tiger Woods	−16	$1,008,000	$1,439,538
2007	Trevor Immelman	−8	$1,350,000	$1,645,820
2012	Bubba Watson	−10	$1,440,000	$1,585,396
2019	Tiger woods	−13	$2,070,000	$2,070,000

HELP WANTED

MEDICAL/HEALTH SERVICE PROVIDER ANNUAL SALARY*

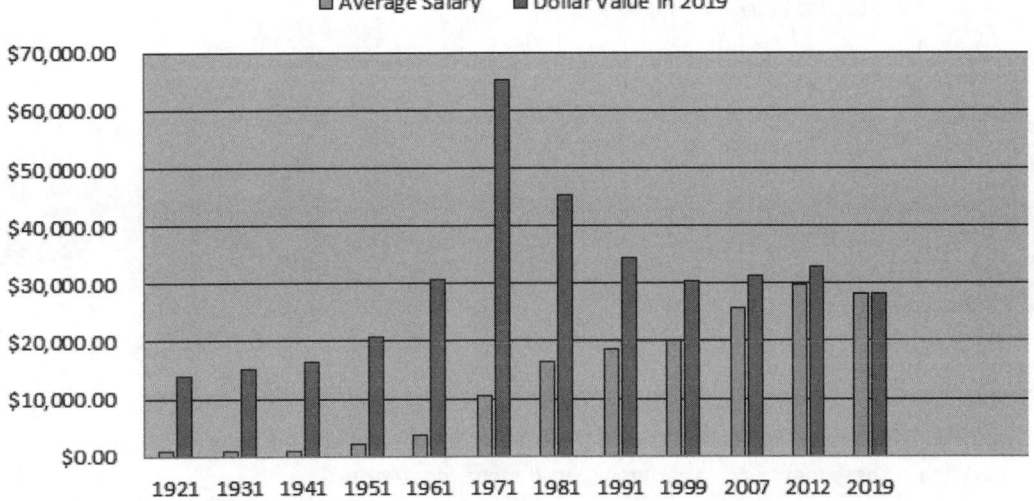

	1921	1931	1941	1951	1961	1971
Average Salary	$983	$919	$955	$2,143	$3,636	$10,465
Dollar Value in 2019	$13,882	$15,283	$16,422	$20,835	$30,739	$65,316

	1981	1991	1999	2007	2012	2019
Average Salary	$16,288	$18,522	$20,000	$25,600	$29,880	$28,331
Dollar Value in 2019	$45,294	$34,375	$30,345	$31,210	$32,897	$28,331

*Based on National Average

HELP WANTED

PRESIDENT OF THE UNITED STATES ANNUAL SALARY

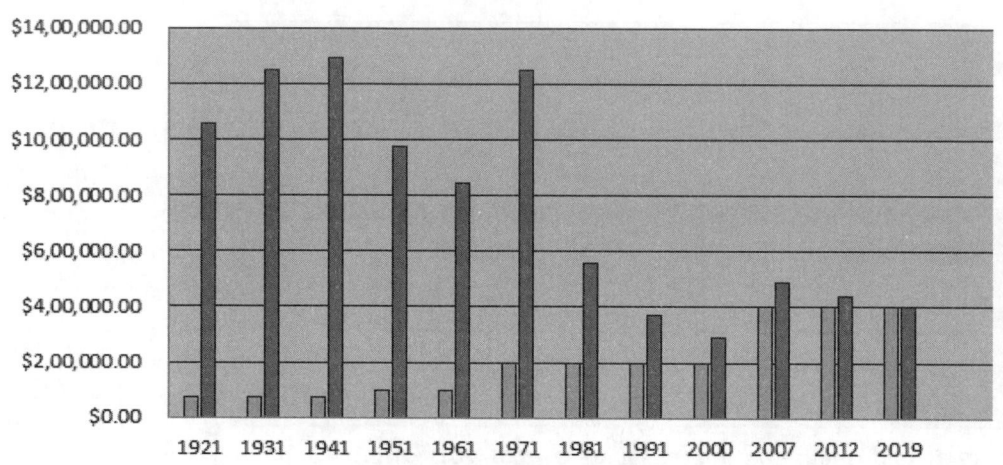

Year	President	Salary	Salary in 2019 Dollars
1921	Warren Harding	$75,000	$1,057,117
1931	Herbert Hoover	$75,000	$1,247,250
1941	Franklin D. Roosevelt	$75,000	$1,289,673
1951	Harry S. Truman	$100,000 + $50,000 expense account	$972,215
1961	John F. Kennedy	$100,000 + $50,000 expense account (refused by Kennedy)	$845,405
1971	Richard M. Nixon	$200,000 + $50,000 expense account	$1,248,277
1981	Ronald W. Reagan	$200,000 + $50,000 expense account	$556,163
1991	George H. W. Bush	$200,000 + $50,000 expense account	$371,184
2000	William J. Clinton	$200,000 + $50,000 expense account	$293,584
2007	George W. Bush	$400,000 + $50,000 expense account	$487,650
2012	Barack H. Obama	$400,000 + $50,000 expense account	$440,384
2019	Donald J. Trump	$400,000 + $50,000 expense account	$400,000

HELP WANTED

PUBLIC SCHOOL TEACHER ANNUAL SALARY*

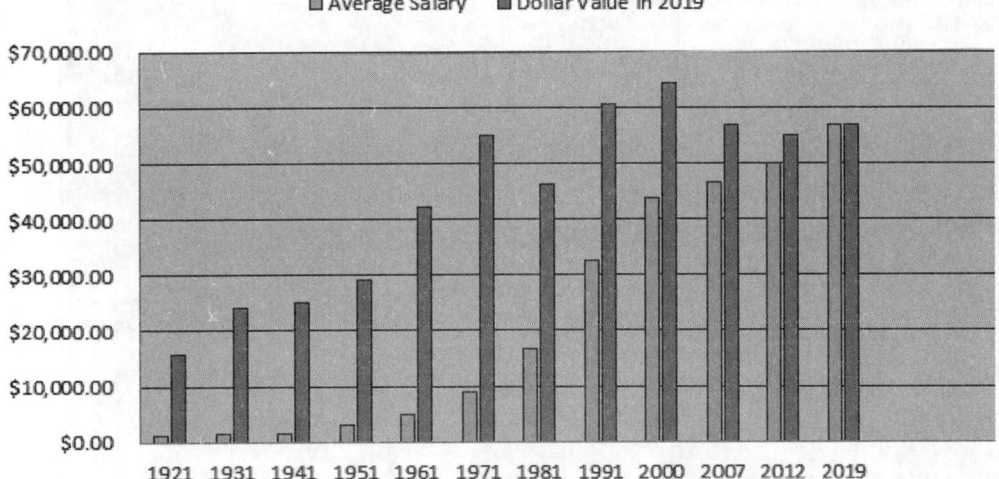

	1921	1931	1941	1951	1961	1971
Average Salary	$1,109	$1,463	$1,462	$2,998	$4,991	$8,813
Dollar Value in 2019	$15,661	$24,330	$25,140	$29,147	$42,194	$55.005

	1981	1991	2000	2007	2012	2019
Average Salary	$16,606	$32,638	$43,740	$46,610	$50,050	$56,753
Dollar Value in 2019	$46,178	$60,573	$64,207	$56,823	$55,104	$56,753

*Based on National Average

853

SAVE $10
$39^{99} sale

The horse, the automobile. The typewriter, the computer. The cassette tape, the Digital Recordable MiniDisc. Record music on your home deck and play it back anywhere. Just like tape. Digital sound and instant access to any song. Just like a CD. Record or mix up to 74 minutes from your CDs. All on one 2.5-inch MiniDisc. Then take it anywhere you go, and play it back on your car deck or portable player. Now that's progress.

O-OH — LET'S DANCE — I CAN'T RESIST THAT MUSIC!

HEADPHONES $25^{00}

A Victor

Don't let this Christmas go by without getting a Victor. It will bring more joy and entertainment than anything you can give.

Victor I, $25

OLYMPIA
There is no
"Just as Good"

$45

I LOVE YO

SONY

MDW-74

Clockwise from top right: "Wherever you may roam" ad for Ford automobile radios (1937); ad in Rolling Stone magazine for the Sony Digital Recordable MiniDisc (1997); Victrola's Automatic Electrola that "changes its own records" for $1,100 (1928); Pioneer headphones -- attached to one of the 1928 dancers -- for $25 (1979); The Olympia "with interchangeable tune-discs" for $45 (1899); "A Victor for Christmas" at $25 (1910); Stromberg-Carlson Labyrinth Radio from $190 to $1,050 (1937); and a Memorex CD and cassette player with AM/FM radio for $40 (2013).

HELP WANTED

PULITZER PRIZE AWARD AMOUNT

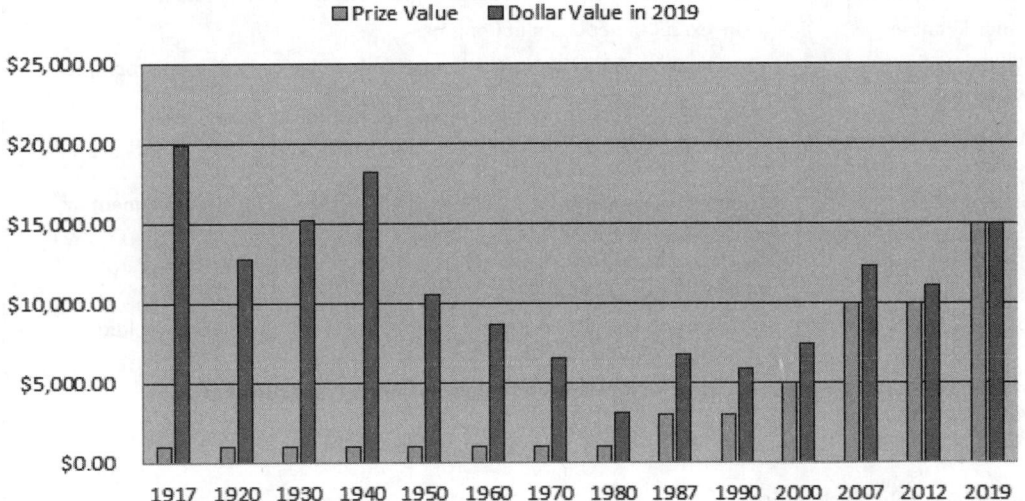

	1917	**1920**	**1930**	**1940**	**1950**	**1960**	**1970**
Prize Value	$1,000	$1,000	$1,000	$1,000	$1,000	$1,000	$1,000
Dollar Value in 2019	$19,860	$12,710	$15,222	$18,157	$10,548	$8,588	$6,552

	1980	**1987**	**1990**	**2000**	**2007**	**2012**	**2019**
Prize Value	$1,000	$3,000	$3,000	$5,000	$10,000	$10,000	$15,000
Dollar Value in 2019	$3,085	$6,713	$5,835	$7,381	$12,260	$11,072	$15,000

Awards in Journalism For National Reporting*

Year	Journalist(s)	Subject
1917	H.B. Swope	"Inside the German Empire"
1920	John J. Leary	National coal strike in the winter of 1919
1930	R.D. Owen	The Byrd Antarctic Expedition
1940	S. Burton Heath	The frauds perpetrated by Federal Judge Martin T. Manton
1950	Edwin O. Guthman	The clearing of Communist charges of Professor Melvin Rader
1960	Vance Trimble	The extent of nepotism in Congress
1970	William Eaton	Disclosures about the background of Judge Clement F. Haynesworth, Jr.
1980	Orsini & Stafford	Investigation of the Church of Scientology
1990	Anderson, Dietrich, Gwinn, & Nalder	The Exxon Valdez oil spill and its aftermath
2000	Staff of *Wall Street Journal*	Stories that question U.S. defense spending and military deployment in the post-Cold War era
2007	Charlie Savage	Revelations that President Bush often used "signing statements" to assert his controversial right to bypass provisions of new laws
2012	David Wood	Stories of physical and emotional challenges facing American soldiers severely wounded in Iraq and Afghanistan
2019	Staffs of *The New York Times* and *The Washington Post*	Coverage of Russian interference in the 2016 presidential

*Prior to 1948, the award was only for "Reporting."

HELP WANTED

RAILROAD WORKER ANNUAL SALARY*

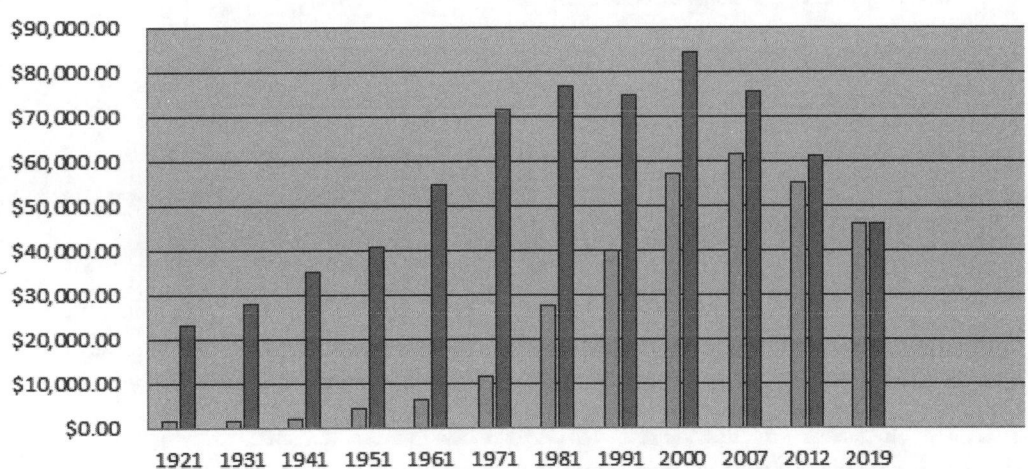

	1921	1931	1941	1951	1961	1971
Average Salary	$1,632	$1,661	$2,030	$4,163	$6,440	$11,360
Dollar Value in 2019	$23,176	$27,778	$35,104	$40,702	$54,751	$71,302

	1981	1991	2000	2007	2012	2019
Average Salary	$27,452	$39,987	$57,157	$61,480	$55,080	$45,846
Dollar Value in 2019	$76,770	$74,631	$84,375	$75,375	$60,984	$45,846

*Based on National Average

HELP WANTED

UNIVERSITY OF SOUTH CAROLINA YEARLY TUITION*

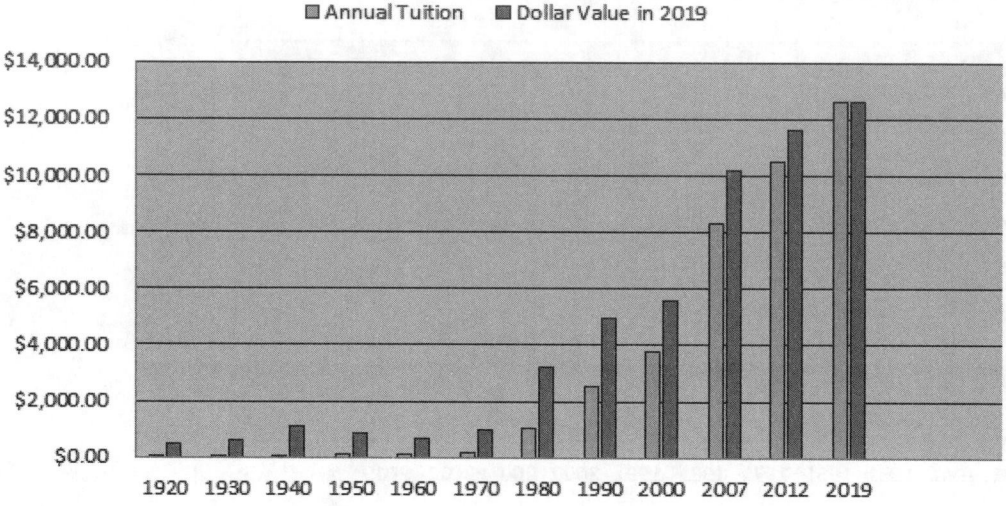

	1920	1930	1940	1950	1960	1970
Average Tuition	$40	$40	$60	$80	$80	$150
Dollar Value in 2019	$508	$609	$1,089	$844	$687	$983

	1980	1990	2000	2007	2012	2019
Average Tuition	$1,040	$2,560	$3,768	$8,307	$10,488	$12,618
Dollar Value in 2019	$3,208	$4,979	$5,562	$10,184	$11,612	$12,618

*Tuition does not include other university expenses.

HELP WANTED

UNITED STATES FEDERAL CIVILIAN ANNUAL SALARY*

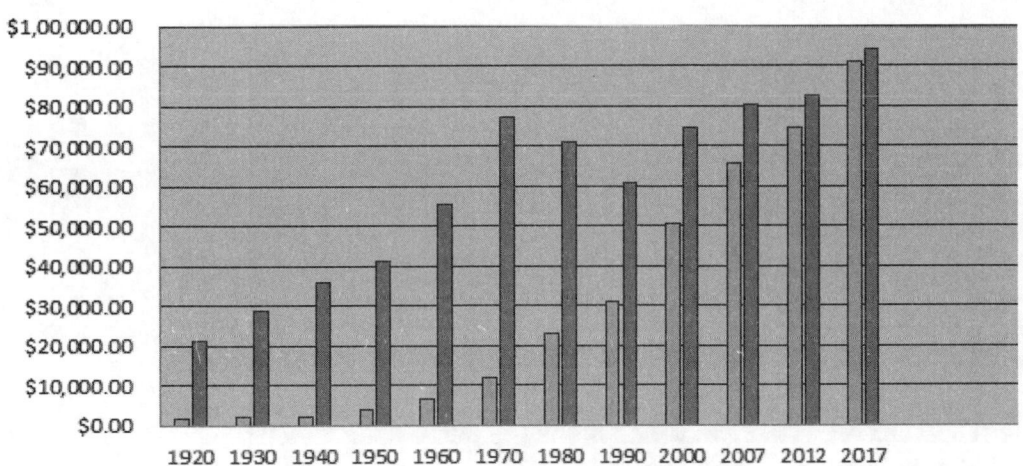

	1920	1930	1940	1950	1960	1970
Average Salary	$1,683	$1,895	$1,970	$3,924	$6,451	$11,767
Dollar Value in 2019	$21,391	$28,845	$35,770	$41,390	$55,401	$77,093

	1980	1990	2000	2007	2012	2017
Average Salary	$23,029	$31,174	$50,429	$65,473	$74,714	$90,794
Dollar Value in 2019	$71,044	$60,631	$74,443	$80,270	$82,722	$94,158

*Based on National Average

ITEMS IN THE REFRIGERATOR

BREAD (1 LOAF)

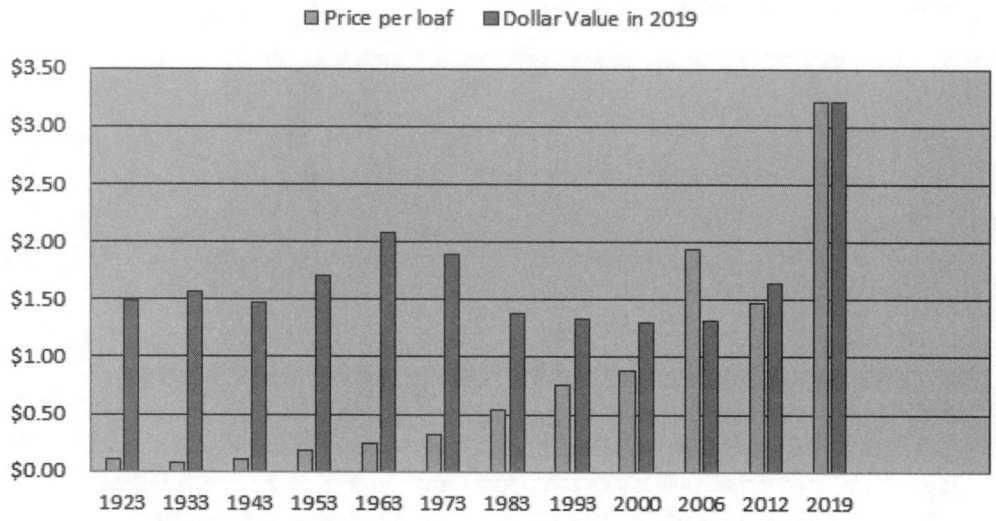

	1923	1933	1943	1953	1963	1973
Price per loaf	$0.10	$0.08	$0.10	$0.18	$0.25	$0.33
Dollar Value in 2019	$1.49	$1.56	$1.47	$1.71	$2.08	$1.89

	1983	1993	2000	2006	2012	2019
Price per loaf	$0.54	$0.76	$0.88	$1.94	$1.48	$3.22
Dollar Value in 2019	$1.38	$1.34	$1.30	$1.31	$1.64	$3.22

ITEMS IN THE REFRIGERATOR

BUTTER (1 POUND)

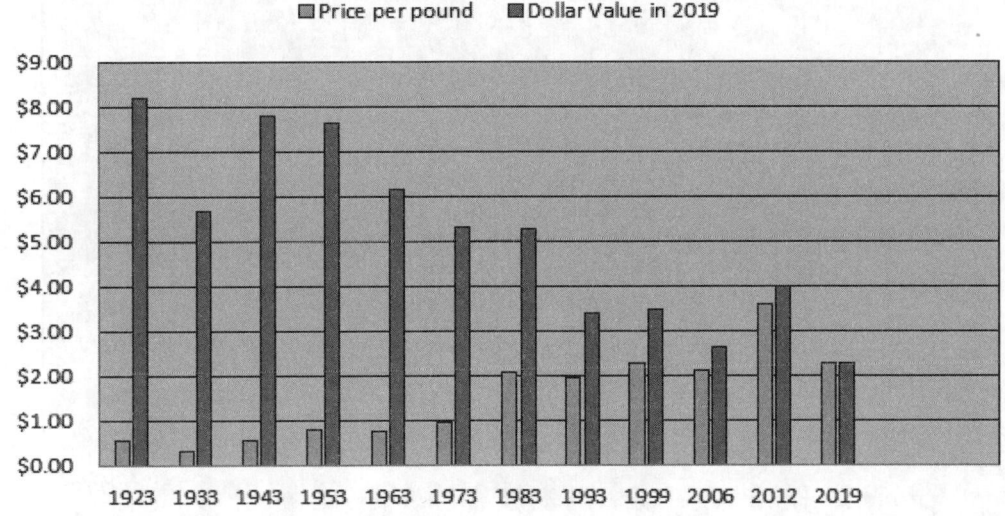

	1923	1933	1943	1953	1963	1973
Price per pound	$0.55	$0.29	$0.53	$0.80	$0.74	$0.93
Dollar Value in 2019	$8.18	$5.67	$7.79	$7.62	$6.15	$5.32

	1983	1993	1999	2006	2012	2019
Price per pound	$2.07	$1.93	$2.27	$2.09	$3.60	$2.27
Dollar Value in 2019	$5.28	$3.40	$3.46	$2.64	$3.99	$2.27

Clockwise from top: "Farmers Eat Quaker Oats," The Salt Lake Herald (1893); Quaker Oats priced at 9 cents per package, or 4.5 cents per pound, The Washington (D.C.) Times (1898); Quaker Oats, 42-ounce package, $3.49 (2013); Pillsbury's VITOS, Ladies Home Journal (1899); Honey Nut Cheerios, 17-ounce package, $3.79 (2013); "American Breakfast Cereals," The Wheeling Daily Intelligencer (1880); Rice Krispies, McCall's, (1933); "The Great Atlantic & Pacific Tea Company," Akron Daily Democrat (1899).

ITEMS IN THE REFRIGERATOR

CHICKEN (1 POUND)

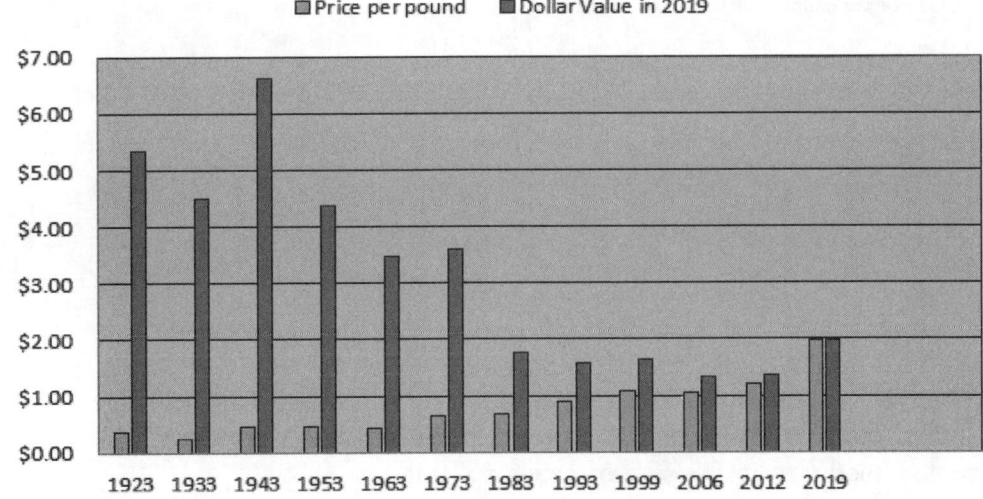

	1923	1933	1943	1953	1963	1973
Price per pound	$0.36	$0.23	$0.45	$0.46	$0.42	$0.63
Dollar Value in 2019	$5.35	$4.50	$6.61	$4.38	$3.49	$3.61

	1983	1993	1999	2006	2012	2019
Price per pound	$0.69	$0.90	$1.07	$1.06	$1.22	$1.99
Dollar Value in 2019	$1.76	$1.58	$1.63	$1.34	$1.35	$1.99

ITEMS IN THE REFRIGERATOR

COFFEE (1 POUND)

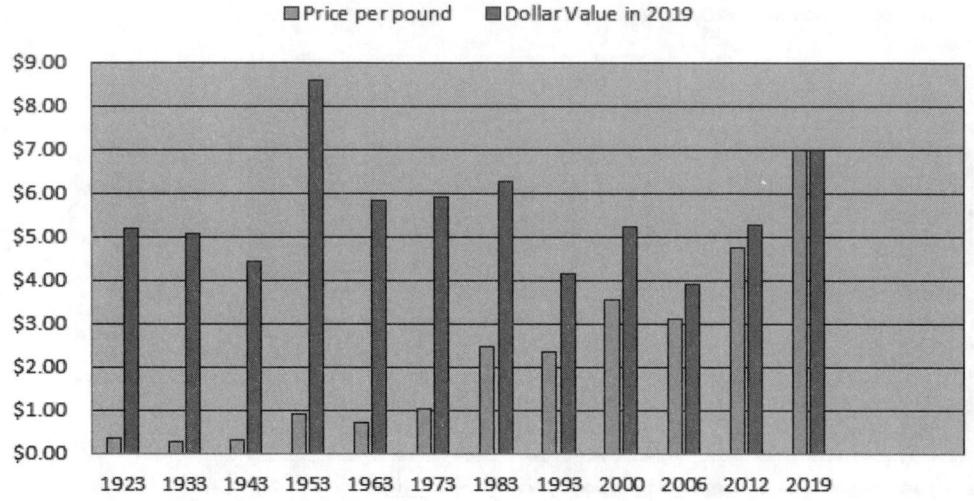

	1923	1933	1943	1953	1963	1973
Price per pound	$0.35	$0.26	$0.30	$0.90	$0.70	$1.03
Dollar Value in 2019	$5.20	$5.08	$4.41	$8.57	$5.82	$5.90

	1983	1993	2000	2006	2012	2019
Price per pound	$2.45	$2.35	$3.54	$3.11	$4.76	$6.99
Dollar Value in 2019	$6.25	$4.13	$5.23	$3.92	$5.27	$6.99

ITEMS IN THE REFRIGERATOR

DR. PEPPER (PER SERVING)

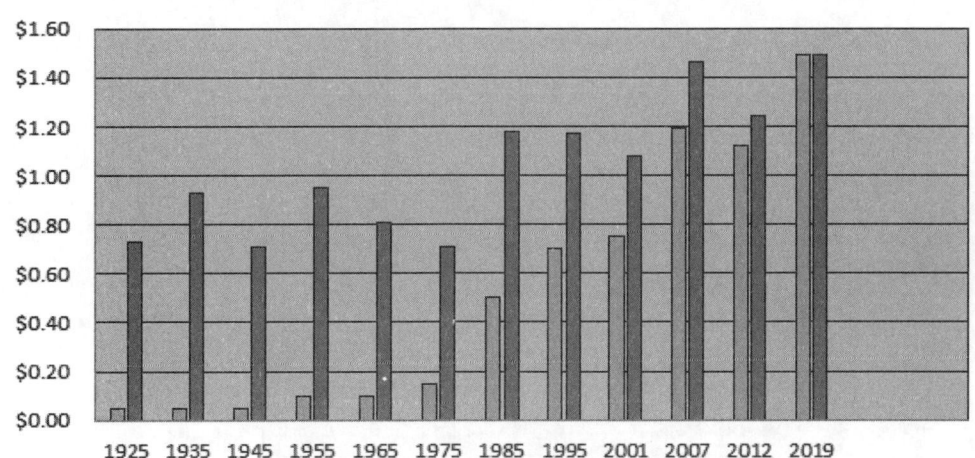

	1925	1935	1945	1955	1965	1975
Price per serving	$0.05	$0.05	$0.05	$0.10	$0.10	$0.15
Dollar Value in 2019	$0.73	$0.93	$0.71	$0.95	$0.81	$0.71

	1985	1995	2001	2007	2012	2019
Price per serving	$0.50	$0.70	$0.75	$1.19	$1.12	$1.49
Dollar Value in 2019	$1.18	$1.17	$1.08	$1.46	$1.24	$1.49

Excerpts from Ad Descriptions:

1909: Dr. Pepper contains no caffeine or any other heart-depressing drug. You contract no drug habit by drinking it.

1915: Dr. Pepper is liquid sunlight. As the sun rules and governs the day, so should you govern your appetite.

1927: For children from 3 to 90 years.

1936: Liquid snack puts Energy back.

1941: Swing your Energy UP.

1950: The Nicest Thing that Ever Happened to a Thirst.

1980: You'll love it HOT!

2011: Introducing: All 23 Flavors. Just 10 Manly Calories. It's Not for Women.

2019: Drink it Slow. Dr.'s Orders.

ITEMS IN THE REFRIGERATOR

EGGS (1 DOZEN)

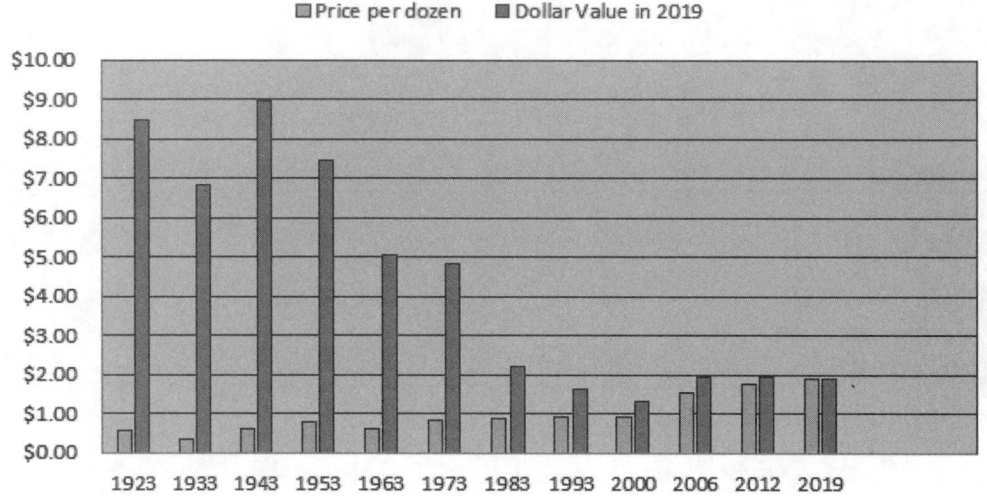

	1923	1933	1943	1953	1963	1973
Price per dozen	$0.57	$0.35	$0.61	$0.78	$0.61	$0.84
Dollar Value in 2019	$8.47	$6.84	$8.96	$7.43	$5.07	$4.81

	1983	1993	2000	2006	2012	2019
Price per dozen	$0.87	$0.92	$0.91	$1.54	$1.75	$1.89
Dollar Value in 2019	$2.22	$1.62	$1.34	$1.94	$1.94	$1.89

ITEMS IN THE REFRIGERATOR

HERSHEY'S MILK CHOCOLATE BAR

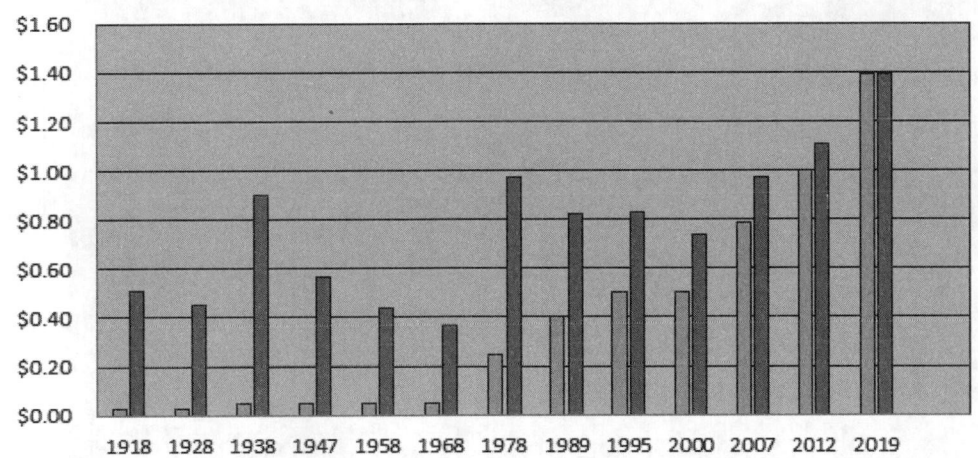

	1918	1928	1938	1947	1958	1968	1978
Price per bar	$0.03	$0.03	$0.05	$0.05	$0.05	$0.05	$0.25
Dollar Value in 2019	$0.51	$0.45	$0.90	$0.57	$0.44	$0.37	$0.97

	1989	1995	2000	2007	2012	2019
Price per bar	$0.40	$0.50	$0.50	$0.79	$1.00	$1.39
Dollar Value in 2019	$0.82	$0.83	$0.74	$0.97	$1.11	$1.39

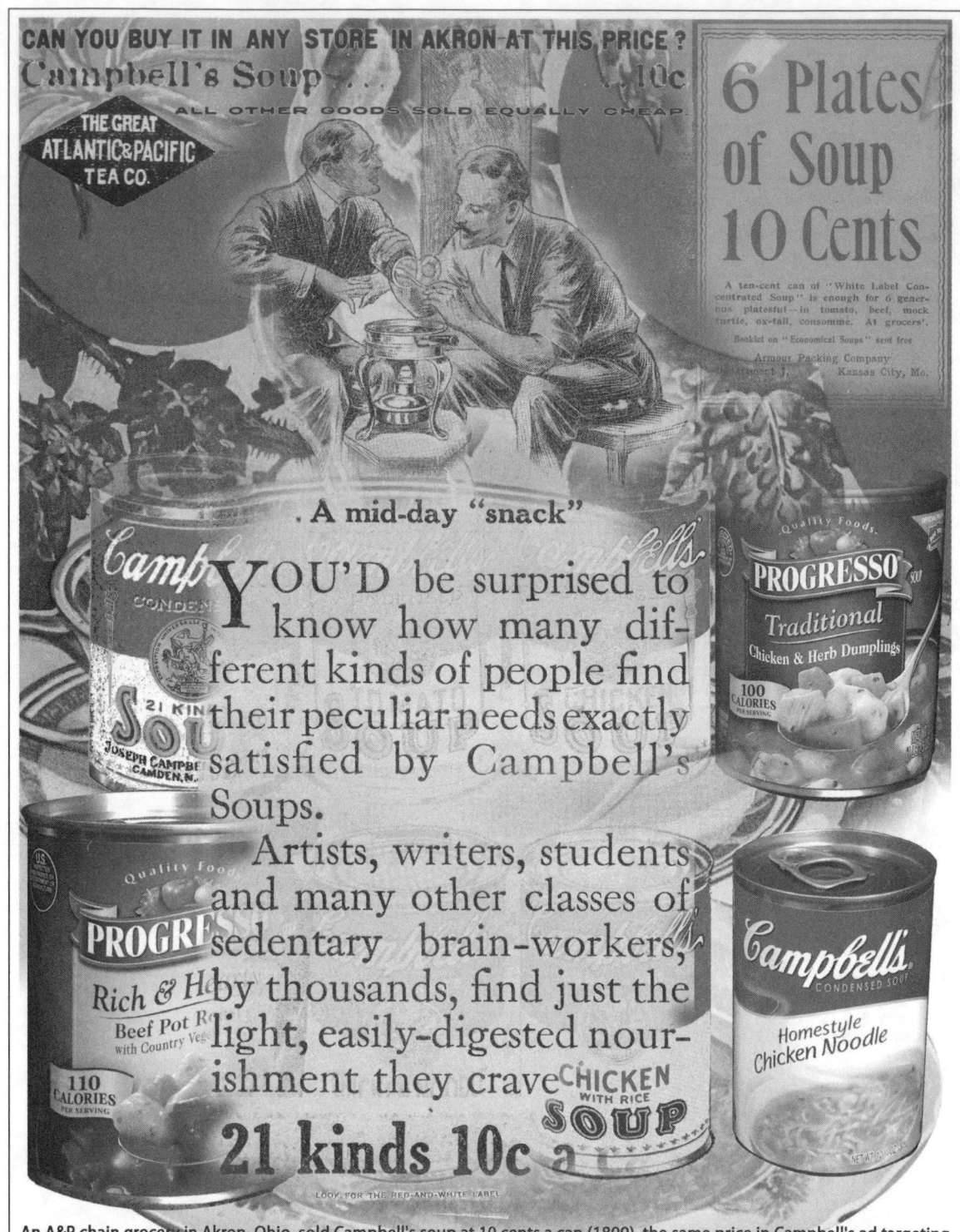

An A&P chain grocery in Akron, Ohio, sold Campbell's soup at 10 cents a can (1899), the same price in Campbell's ad targeting "brain-workers" (1910). Clockwise from top right: Armour soup for 10 cents a can (1899); three 19-ounce cans of Progresso soup for $5 (2014); and two 10.5-ounce cans of Campbell's soup for $1.50 (2014).

ITEMS IN THE REFRIGERATOR

MCDONALD'S HAMBURGER

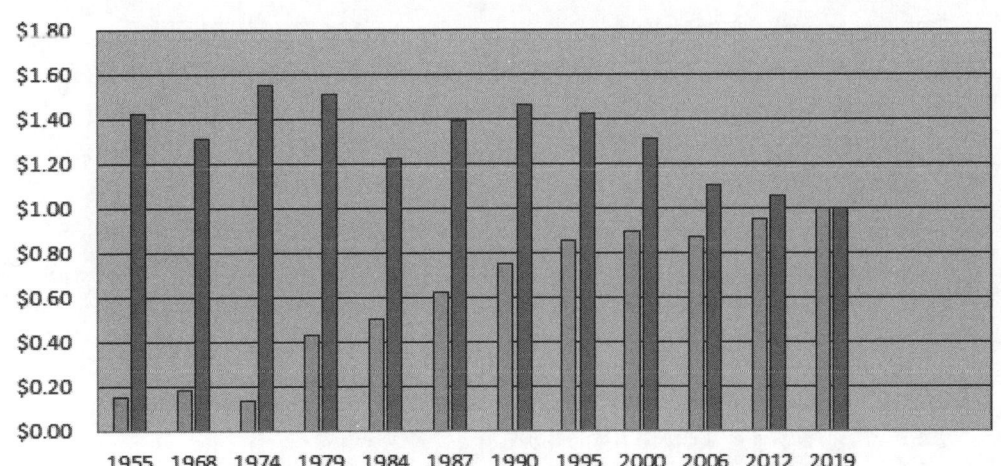

	1955	1968	1974	1979	1984	1987
Price	$0.15	$0.18	$0.13	$0.43	$0.50	$0.62
Dollar Value in 2019	$1.42	$1.31	$1.55	$1.51	$1.22	$1.39

	1990	1995	2000	2006	2012	2019
Price	$0.75	$0.85	$0.89	$0.87	$0.95	$1.00
Dollar Value in 2019	$1.46	$1.42	$1.31	$1.10	$1.05	$1.00

Excerpts from Ad Descriptions

1960: Look for the Golden Arches

1968: McDonald's introduces Big Mac. A meal disguised as a sandwich.

1970: You Deserve a Break Today

1975: When your job keeps you hoppin', you've got to eat when you can. So it's good to know McDonald's ® is always close by. The food is good and hot. The prices are low. And the service is right on time.

1980: McDonald's® invites you to break off a corner of our Filet-O-Fish™ and take a peek inside. See that sparkling white, flaky filet? That's North Atlantic Filet. Not a fishcake—but a real filet portion.

1990: We've Got your Size in Fries! Enjoy our World Famous Fries™ in Small, Medium and NEW LARGE size.

2003: I'm lovin' it.

2017: Mobile Ordering is here. Place your next order with the McDonald's app. Curbside Pick-Up, Inside the Restaurant or Drive Thru.

ITEMS IN THE REFRIGERATOR

MILK (1 QUART)

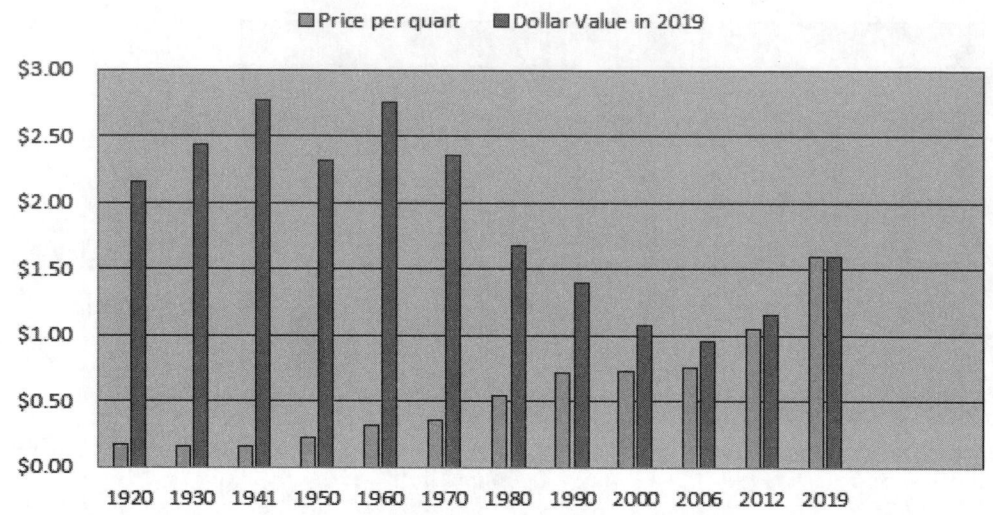

	1920	1930	1941	1950	1960	1970
Price per quart	$0.17	$0.16	$0.16	$0.22	$0.32	$0.36
Dollar Value in 2019	$2.16	$2.44	$2.77	$2.32	$2.75	$2.36

	1980	1990	2000	2006	2012	2019
Price per quart	$0.54	$0.72	$0.73	$0.75	$1.05	$1.59
Dollar Value in 2019	$1.67	$1.40	$1.08	$0.95	$1.16	$1.59

THE OUTDOORS

BICYCLE*

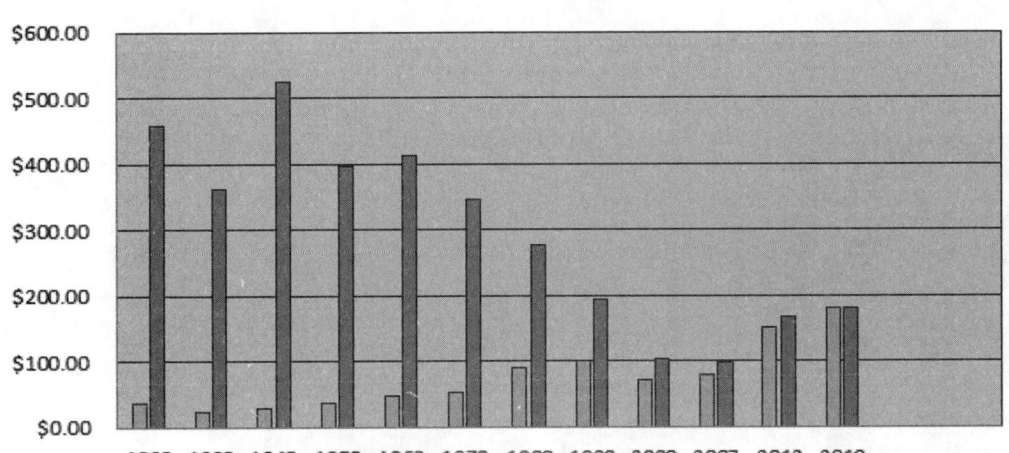

	1920	1930	1940	1950	1960	1970
Price	$35.95	$23.85	$28.95	$37.50	$47.95	$52.95
Dollar Value in 2019	$456.93	$363.04	$525.65	$395.54	$411.79	$346.91

	1980	1990	2000	2007	2012	2019
Price	$89.99	$99.99	$69.99	$79.64	$149.99	$179.99
Dollar Value in 2019	$277.62	$194.47	$103.32	$97.64	$166.07	$179.99

Excerpts from Ad Descriptions

1930: *The Elgin Redbird*-A sturdily built men's Elgin, single bar Motor Bike style. Red with white markings … Frame made of high carbon steel.

1940: *Sears 4-Star DeLuxe Twin Bar Elgin*—Like a greyhound straining at the lead, this champion Elgin fairly best to go places … and in a hurry!

1950: *J.C. Higgins Semi-Equipped Bicycle*—Keen-looking … smooth riding … a bike that will please the "extra-special" youngster.

1960: *Equipped Flightline r… Flo-bar frame.*-New for 1960. Regular coaster break for sure stops, effortless coasting. Boys' are metallic red; girls' are metallic blue.

2012: *Mantis Phoenix Men's Bike.* It is constructed around a steel frame, a material that absorbs the "buzz" of the road for extra comfort.

2019: *Men's L.L. Bean Acadia Cruiser Bike.* Inspired by the famous carriage paths at Acadia National Park, this cruiser bike is the perfect companion for pedaling unpaved roads without spending a fortune.

* Least Expensive Advertised

THE OUTDOORS

FISHING ROD

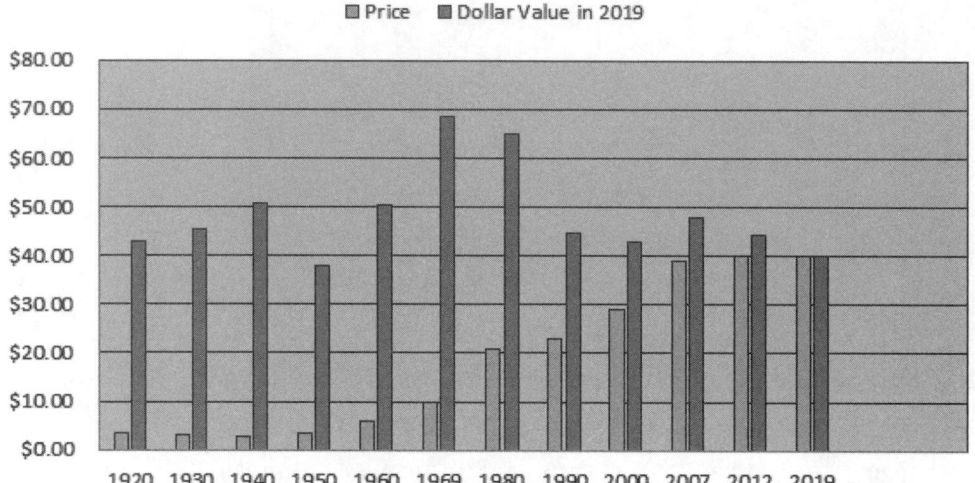

	1920	1930	1940	1950	1960	1969
Price	$3.38	$2.98	$2.79	$3.59	$5.87	$9.89
Dollar Value in 2019	$42.96	$45.36	$50.66	$37.87	$50.41	$68.50

	1980	1990	2000	2007	2012	2019
Price	$21.00	$22.99	$29.00	$39.00	$39.99	$39.98
Dollar Value in 2019	$64.78	$44.71	$42.81	$47.81	$44.28	$39.98

THE OUTDOORS

GARDEN HOSE

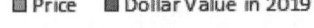

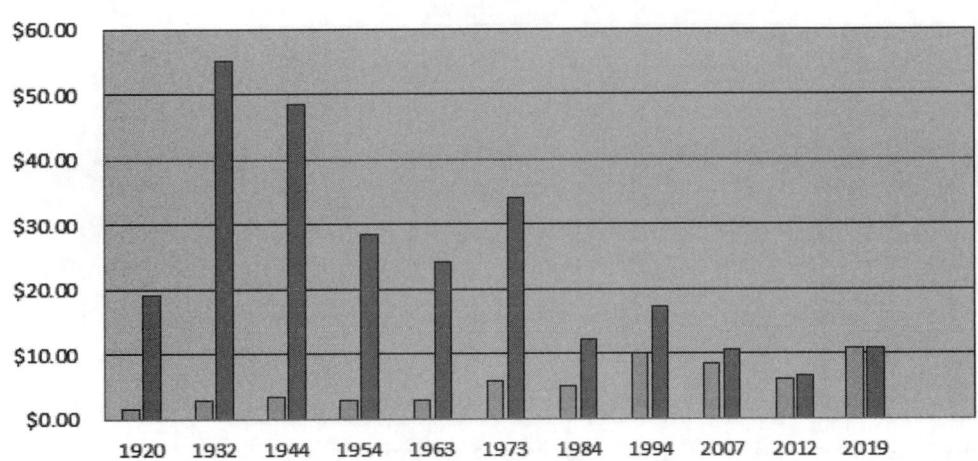

	1920	1932	1944	1954	1963	1973
Price	$1.50	$2.95	$3.33	$2.99	$2.88	$5.88
Dollar Value in 2019	$19.21	$55.15	$48.46	$28.47	$24.11	$33.92

	1984	1994	2007	2012	2019
Price	$4.99	$9.99	$8.49	$5.99	$10.92
Dollar Value in 2019	$12.30	$17.27	$10.49	$6.68	$10.92

THE OUTDOORS

GAS GRILL

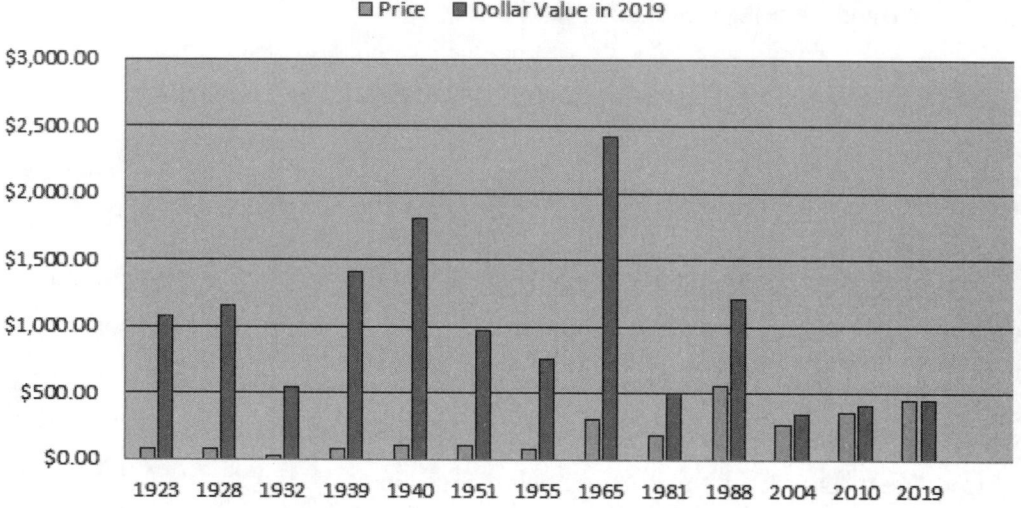

Price ▢ Dollar Value in 2019

	1923	1928	1932	1939	1940	1951	1955
Price	$72.75	$78	$28.95	$76.95	$100	$99	$79.95
Dollar Value in 2019	$1,074.04	$1,159.52	$537.35	$1,407	$1,815.73	$967.92	$758.34

	1965	1981	1988	2004	2010	2019
Price	$299.95	$179.99	$559.99	$259	$349.99	$449
Dollar Value in 2019	$2,420.57	$503.34	$1,203.30	$348.54	$408.01	$499

THE OUTDOORS

HAMMOCK

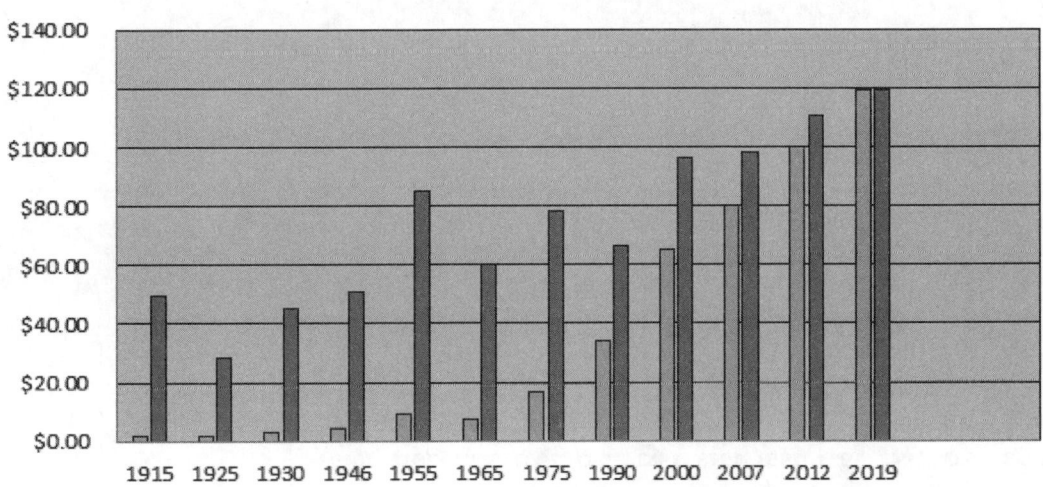

	1915	1925	1930	1946	1955	1965
Price	$1.98	$1.95	$2.98	$3.89	$8.95	$7.47
Dollar Value in 2019	$49.83	$28.33	$45.36	$50.71	$84.89	$60.28

	1975	1990	2000	2007	2012	2019
Price	$16.50	$34.00	$64.99	$80.00	$99.99	$119
Dollar Value in 2019	$77.96	$66.13	$95.94	$98.08	$110.71	$119

Excerpts from Ad Descriptions

1915: *Our Great Standard Leader*—A hammock of great strength and wearing qualities offered specially at a low price.

1925: *Fancy Weave Hammock*—Medium weight, fancy weave cotton hammock

1930: *For Summer Comfort*—A Jacquard weave hammock! Completely comfortable, thoroughly durable, made of strong tested warp yarn.

1955: *Heavy Jacquard Woven Cotton Hammock*—3-point suspension style. Colorful white diamond design on red background.

1965: *Sleeper Hammock won't rock or tilt*—Just swings gently to coax you to sleep. Green cotton plaid.

2008: *Byer of Maine Barados XL Hammock NEW 2007.* Perfect for one, cozy for two, the Barbados is the ideal hammock for sharing a relaxing afternoon, or dreaming of how nice sharing a hammock would be.

2019: *Coral Coast 13 ft. Unwind Quilted Double Hammock*—Enjoy spending time outdoors by yourself or snuggling with a loved one.

THE OUTDOORS

HARLEY-DAVIDSON MOTORCYCLE*

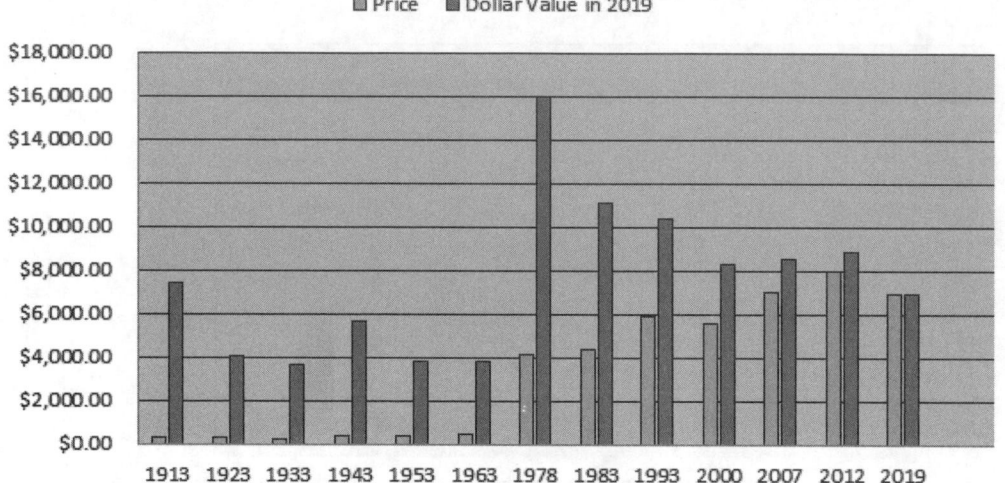

	1913	1923	1933	1943	1953	1963	1978
Price	$290	$275	$188	$385	$405	$460	$4,100
Dollar Value in 2019	$7,446	$4,088	$3,676	$5,657	$3,856	$3,821	$15,985

	1983	1993	2000	2007	2012	2019
Price	$4,345	$5,895	$5,595	$6,990	$7,999	$6,899
Dollar Value in 2019	$11,089	$10,370	$8,259	$8,570	$8,856	$6,899

Historical Information on Harley-Davidson

♦ In 1909, the company developed and introduced a new engine that permitted riders to travel at 60 miles per hour.

♦ By the end of World War I, twenty thousand Harley-Davidson motorcycles were utilized by the United States.

♦ During the 1930s, Harley-Davidson was one of only two motorcycle manufacturers to survive the Great Depression.

♦ During World War II, Harley-Davidson built over 90,000 motorcycles for the United States and its allies for military use.

♦ Black leather jackets developed as a "lifestyle" statement during the 1950s and 1960s.

♦ The company hired Elton John to headline their 100th anniversary event on September 1, 2003. Other performers included The Doobie Brothers, Kid Rock, and Tim McGraw.

*Prices listed are for least expensive Harley-Davidson motorcycles available during that year.

THE OUTDOORS

HIKING BOOTS

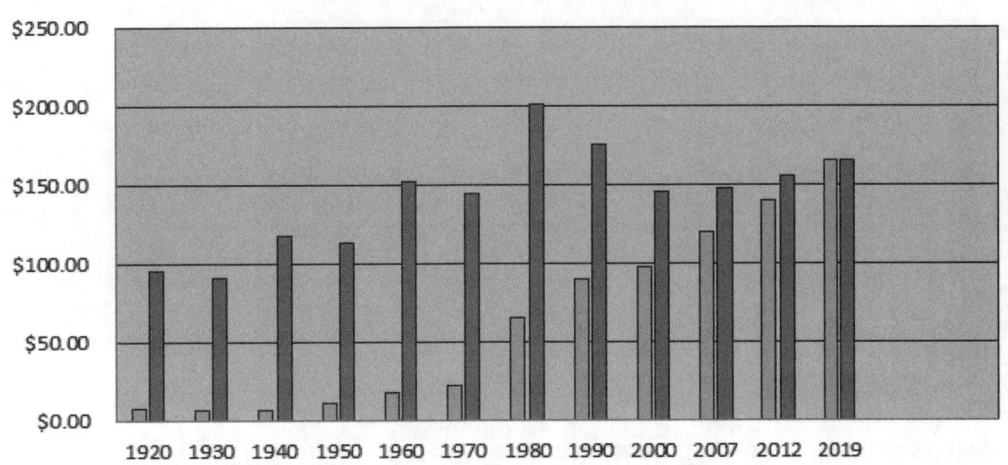

	1920	1930	1940	1950	1960	1970
Price	$7.50	$5.95	$6.45	$10.75	$17.70	$21.97
Dollar Value in 2019	$95.33	$90.57	$117.11	$113.39	$152.01	$143.94

	1980	1990	2000	2007	2012	2019
Price	$64.99	$89.97	$98	$120	$139.99	$165
Dollar Value in 2019	$200.49	$174.99	$144.67	$147.12	$154.99	$165

THE OUTDOORS

LAWN CHAIR

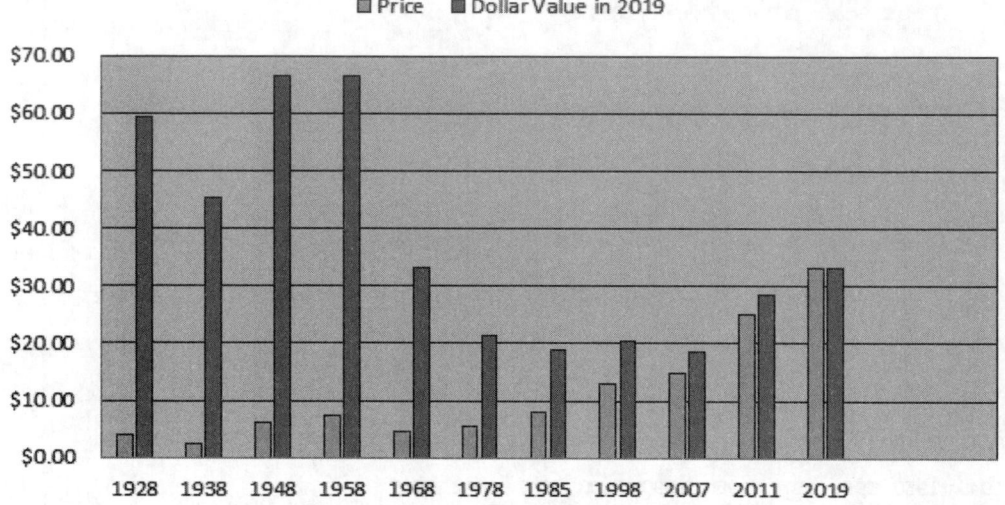

	1928	1938	1948	1958	1968	1978
Price	$3.95	$2.49	$6.25	$7.50	$4.49	$5.44
Dollar Value in 2019	$59.17	$45.23	$66.43	$66.47	$33.05	$21.37

	1985	1998	2007	2011	2019
Price	$7.99	$12.99	$15	$25	$33.19
Dollar Value in 2019	$19.02	$20.41	$18.53	$28.47	$33.19

THE OUTDOORS

LAWN MOWER*

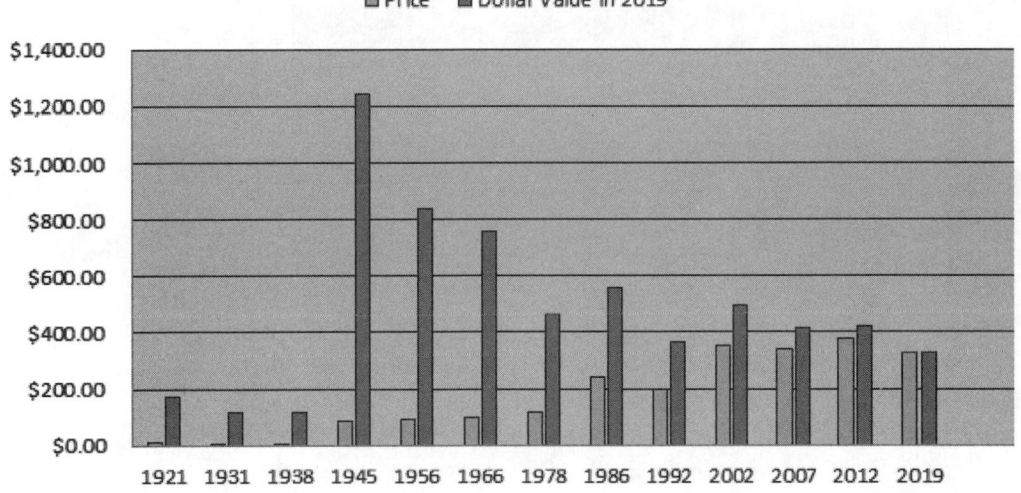

	1921	1931	1938	1945	1956	1966	1978
Price	$12	$6.85	$6.42	$87.95	$89.50	$96.50	$119
Dollar Value in 2019	$170.41	$114.56	$115.74	$1,242.06	$836.44	$757.11	$463.96

	1986	1992	2002	2007	2012	2019
Price	$239.99	$199.99	$350	$340	$379.99	$329.99
Dollar Value in 2019	$556.62	$362.35	$494.56	$416.84	$420.72	$329.99

*From 1920–1944 lawnmowers were push design. By 1945, power motors were available.

THE SPORTS PAGE

BASKETBALL

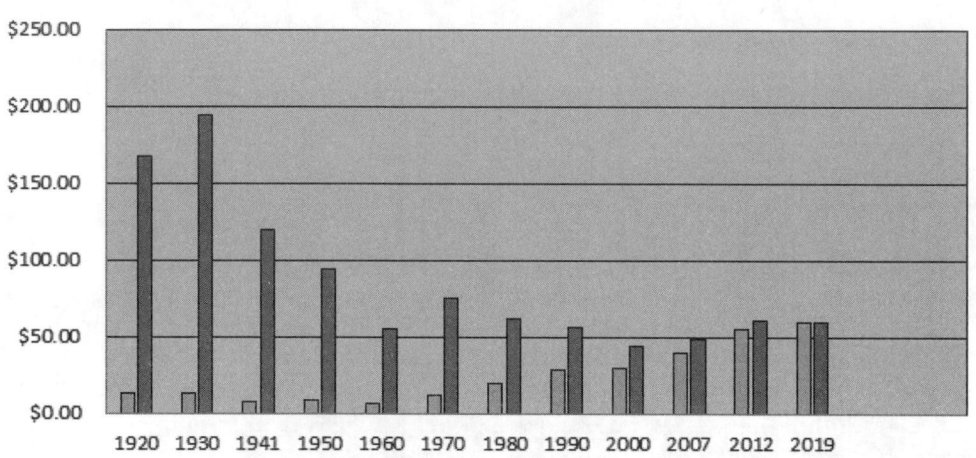

	1920	1930	1941	1950	1960	1970
Price	$13.20	$12.75	$6.95	$8.95	$6.47	$11.50
Dollar Value in 2019	$167.77	$194.08	$120.18	$94.40	$55.56	$75.34

	1980	1990	2000	2007	2012	2019
Price	$19.89	$28.88	$29.99	$39.99	$54.99	$59.95
Dollar Value in 2019	$61.36	$56.17	$44.27	$49.03	$60.88	$59.95

Excerpts from Ad Descriptions

1930: *"J.C. Higgins" Regulation Basketball* laced and ready to inflate. Sold to schools and colleges under Nationally Advertised Brand for $14.00. Save Money!

1950: *J.C. Higgins Official Laceless Basketball*-No laces. No dead spots. Official size, weight, handling ability. Select quality pebble-grained cowhide leather.

1960: *No Stronger Basketballs Made!* —Extra yards of nylon cord assure more wear, more games. Tan cover is heat and pressured cured.

1980: *5-Star Basketball with pebble-grained leather-look vinyl and nylon cover*-Ball is designed to minimize the effect temperature has on the bouncing ....

2012: *Wilson's Official Basketball.* Combines low-density rubber and ultra-durable butyl rubber producing ... exceptional feel and unmarked durability.

2019: *Spalding NBA Replica Official Basketball.* It's made for a consistent bounce and solid grip, so you can get your crossover just right.

THE SPORTS PAGE

GOLF BALL

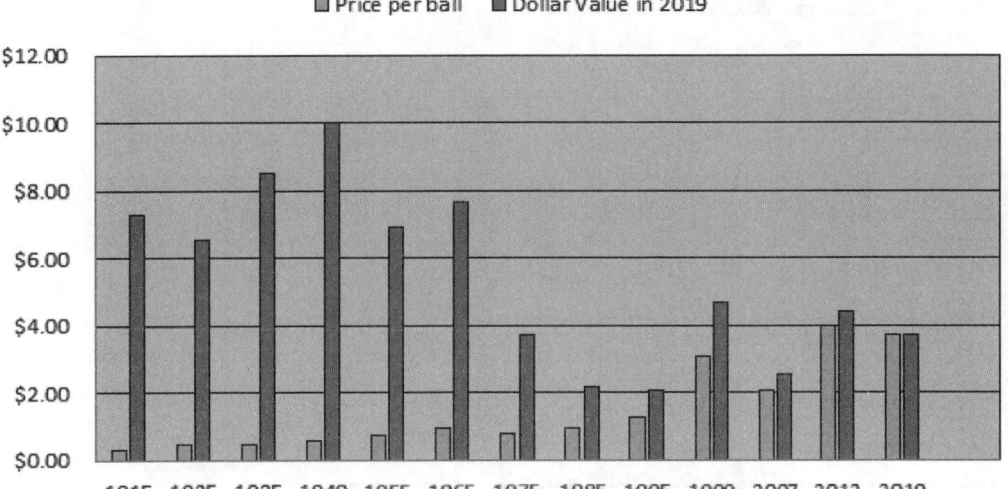

Year	Brand	Price/Ball	Price Dollars 2019
1915	Goodrich Stag	$0.29	$7.30
1925	Eclipse	$0.45	$6.54
1935	Aristo Cover Ball	$0.46	$8.54
1940	X-Pert High Grade	$0.55	$9.99
1955	Johnny Bulla Tournament	$0.73	$6.92
1965	Gene Sarazen	$0.95	$7.67
1975	Advisory Staff	$0.79	$3.73
1985	Power-Flite	$0.92	$2.17
1995	MacGregor	$1.25	$2.08
1999	Titleist DT Spin	$3.08	$4.70
2007	Callaway HX Hot	$2.08	$2.55
2012	Titleist Pro V1	$4.00	$4.43
2019	Bridgestone Tour B XS	$3.74	$3.74

THE SPORTS PAGE

KENTUCKY DERBY WINNERS

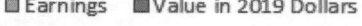

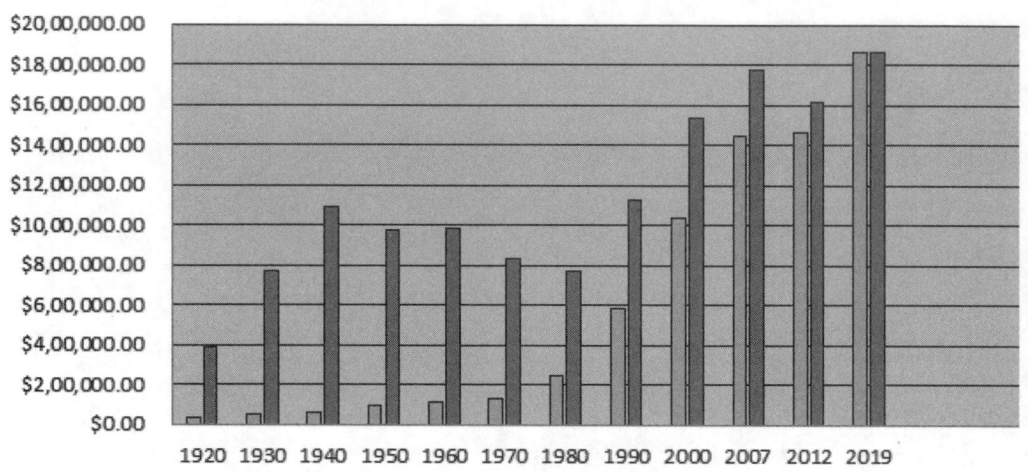

Year	Winning Horse	Earnings	Earnings value in 2012
1920	Paul Jones	$30,375	$386,069
1930	Gallant Fox	$50,725	$772,120
1940	Gallahadion	$60,150	$1,092,161
1950	Middleground	$92,650	$977,254
1960	Venetian Way	$114,850	$986,321
1970	Dust Commander	$127,800	$837,294
1980	Genuine Risk	$250,550	$772,941
1990	Unbridled	$581,000	$1,130,003
2000	Fusaichi Pegasus	$1,038,400	$1,532,888
2007	Street Sense	$1,450,000	$1,777,705
2012	I'll Have Another	$1,459,600	$1,616,041
2019	Country House*	$1,860,000	$1,860,000

*Country House won by default as the lead horse, Maximum Security, was disqualified for changing lanes without clearance.

THE SPORTS PAGE

NETWORK TV CONTRACTS WITH THE NBA (PER YEAR)

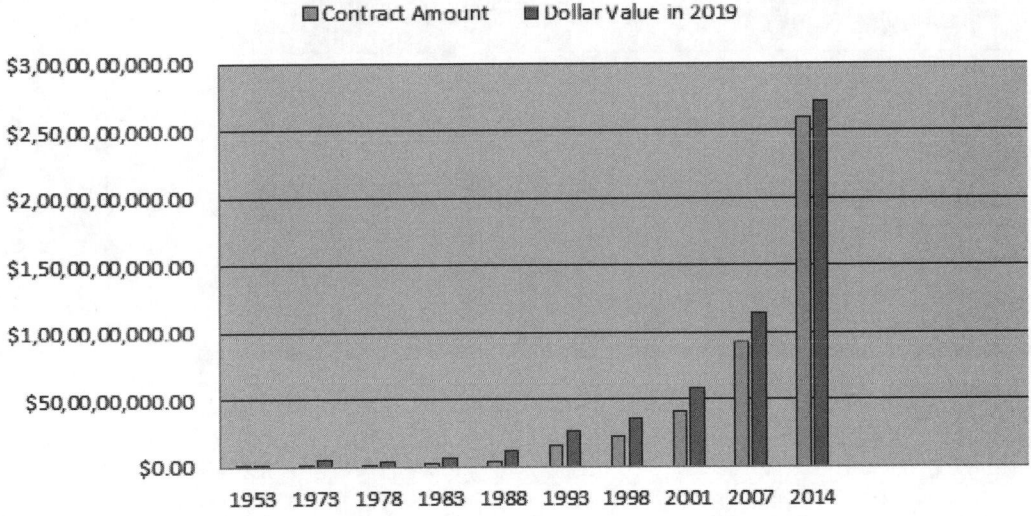

	1953	1973	1978	1983	1988
Network	DuMont	CBS	CBS	CBS	CBS
Contract Amount	$39,000	$9 million	$10.5 million	$22.9 million	$43.2 million
Dollar Value in 2019	$371,306	$51.5 million	$40.9 million	$58.6 million	$114 million

	1993	1998	2001	2007	2014
Network	NBC	NBC	NBC	ABC/ESPN	ABC/ESPN
Contract Amount	$150 million	$223 million	$404 million	$930 million	$2.6 billion
Dollar Value in 2019	$266 million	$350 million	$584 million	$1.1 billion	$2.6 billion

THE SPORTS PAGE

SUPER BOWL (FOOTBALL CHAMPIONSHIP) TICKET

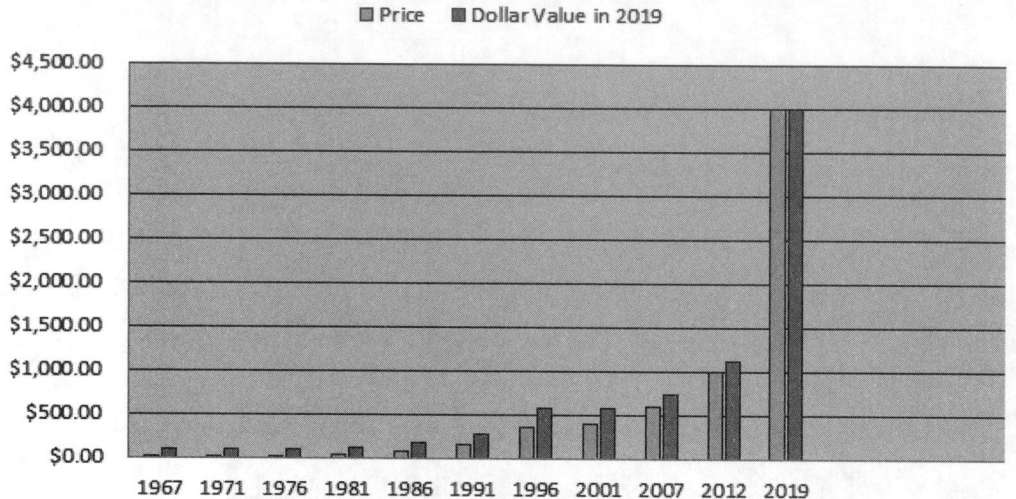

■ Price ■ Dollar Value in 2019

| | I | V | X | XV | XX | XXV |
	1967	1971	1976	1981	1986	1991
Avg. Ticket Price	$12	$15	$20	$40	$75	$150
Dollar Value in 2019	$91.33	$94.15	$89.35	$111.86	$173.95	$279.86

| | XXX | XXXV | XLI | XLV | LIII |
	1996	2001	2007	2012	2019
Avg. Ticket Price	$350	$400	$600	$1,000	$4,000
Dollar Value in 2019	$567.05	$574.47	$735.60	$1,107.18	$4,000

Super Bowl Facts:
- The Super Bowl was originally called the "AFC-NFC World Championship Game."
- The television audience for Super Bowl I was approximately 60,000 viewers.
- Super Bowl XIV had over 35 million television viewers, and Super Bowl XX was watched by over 127 million TV viewers.
- A one-minute television commercial sold for $75,000 to $85,000 during Super Bowl I (approximately $515,555 to $584,296 in 2012 dollars).
- Super Bowl V was the first played on artificial turf.

THE VALUE OF A DOLLAR 1860–2019

THE SPORTS PAGE

TENNIS RACQUET

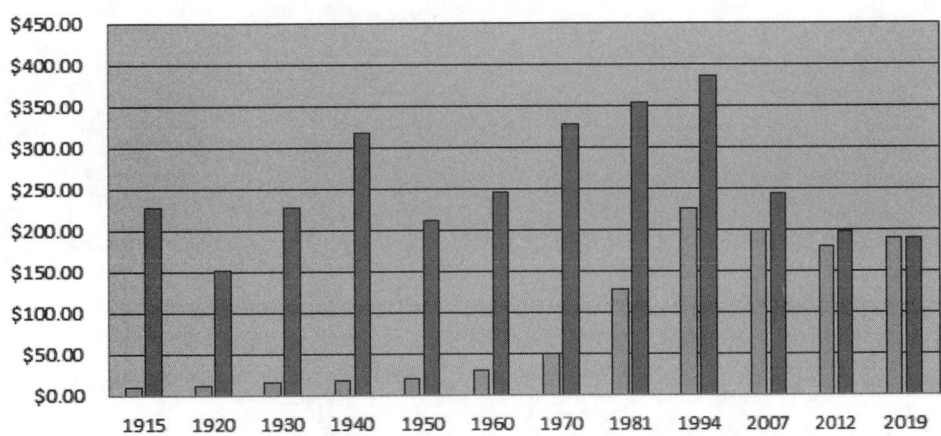

Year	Brand	Price	Dollar Value in 2019
1915	New Bancroft	$9.00	$226.52
1920	Invincible Driver	$12.00	$152.22
1930	Laminated AAA	$15.00	$228.33
1940	Squire	$17.50	$317.75
1950	Jack Kramer Autograph	$20.00	$210.96
1960	Kramer Autograph	$28.50	$244.76
1970	T-2000	$50.00	$327.58
1981	Bancroft Limited Edition	$126.50	$353.76
1994	Wilson Sledgehammer	$224.94	$385.83
2007	Dunlop Aerogel 220	$199.00	$243.97
2012	Dunlop Biomimetic	$179.00	$198.19
2019	Babolat Pure Aero	$189.00	$189.00

THE SPORTS PAGE

WORLD SERIES (BASEBALL CHAMPIONSHIP) TICKET (PER GAME)

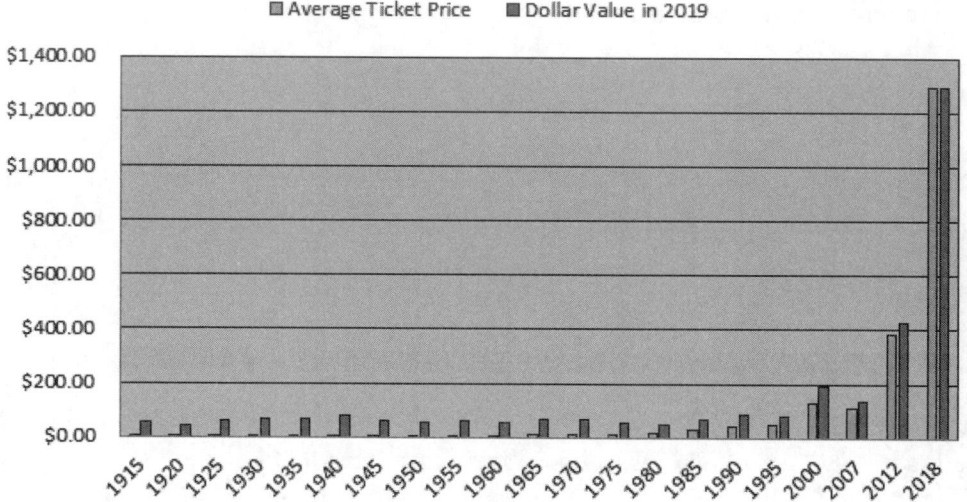

Year	# Games Played	Avg. Ticket Price	Dollar Value in 2019	Winning Team
1915	5	$2.23	$52.97	Boston Red Sox
1920	7	$3.16	$36.28	Cleveland Indians
1925	7	$4.18	$54.84	Pittsburgh Pirates
1930	6	$4.49	$61.73	Philadelphia Athletics
1935	6	$3.75	$62.85	Detroit Tigers
1940	7	$4.34	$71.17	Cincinnati Reds
1945	7	$4.48	$57.14	Detroit Tigers
1950	4	$4.87	$46.40	New York Yankees
1955	7	$6.45	$55.26	Brooklyn Dodgers
1960	7	$6.38	$49.49	Pittsburgh Pirates
1965	7	$8.17	$59.55	Los Angeles Dodgers
1970	5	$10.27	$60.77	Baltimore Orioles
1975	7	$10.97	$46.81	Cincinnati Reds
1980	6	$15.81	$44.05	Philadelphia Phillies
1985	7	$29.56	$63.07	Kansas City Royals
1990	4	$43.33	$76.12	Cincinnati Reds
1995	6	$46.31	$69.77	Atlanta Braves

Year	# Games Played	Avg. Ticket Price	Dollar Value in 2019	Winning Team
2000	5	$131.42	$175.22	New York Yankees
2007	4	$109.08	$120.81	Boston Red Sox
2012	4	$383.92	$383.92	San Francisco Giants
2018	5	$1,290	$1,290	Boston Red Sox

Clockwise from top right: billiard tables at $275+ (1877); Bicycle playing cards at 25 cents per pack (1910); Rook card game at 50 cents (1910); tabletop baseball at $3 (1910); Courtland billiard table at $299.99 (2013); "The Last of Us" computer game at $199.99 (2013); "Beyond" at $39.99 (2013); two packs of Bicycle cards for $6.79 (2014); and game controller at $44.99 (2013).

TRAVEL & ENTERTAINMENT

AIRLINE TICKET FROM NEW YORK CITY TO CHICAGO

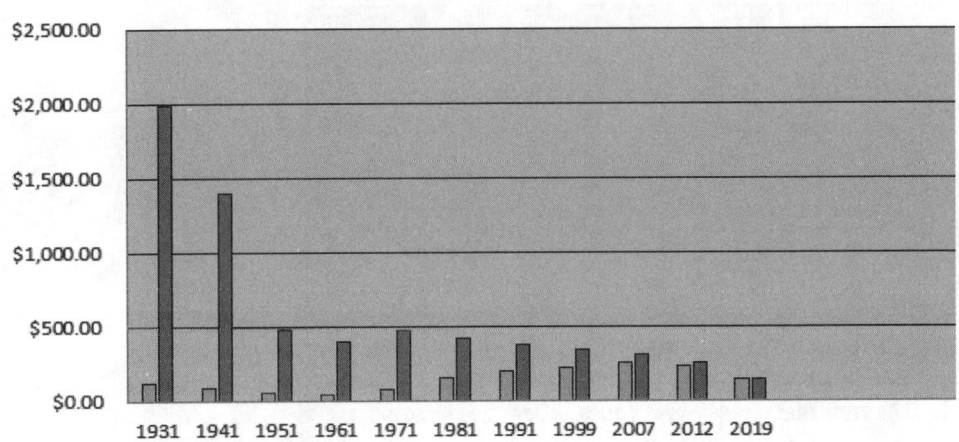

	1931	1941	1951	1961	1971	1981
Price	$119	$80.91	$48	$46.50	$75	$149
Dollar Value in 2019	$1,990.13	$1,399.15	$469.30	$395.53	$470.74	$416.68

	1991	1999	2007	2012	2019
Price	$198	$222	$249	$230	$147
Dollar Value in 2019	$369.54	$338.73	$305.27	$254.65	$147

Airline Ticket Facts:

♦ In 1931, Transcontinental & Western Air (TWA) advertised flights from New York City to Chicago.

♦ In 1941, TWA began flights from New York to Los Angeles for $149.94 one way ($2,612.66 in 2019 dollar value). The flights were "only 15 hours, 8 minutes" on "TWA's transcontinental Stratoliner."

♦ "Fast and luxurious" and "pressurized comfort" are examples of advertising phrases used from the 1930s through the 1960s.

♦ In 2007, JetBlue Airways Corporation began nonstop service to Chicago's O'Hare International Airport from New York's John F. Kennedy International Airport. It offered a special winter sale fare of $39 each way ($48.18 in 2019 dollar value) to promote the airline's new destination.

TRAVEL & ENTERTAINMENT

BOTTLE OF BEAULIEU VINEYARD WINE

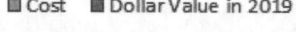

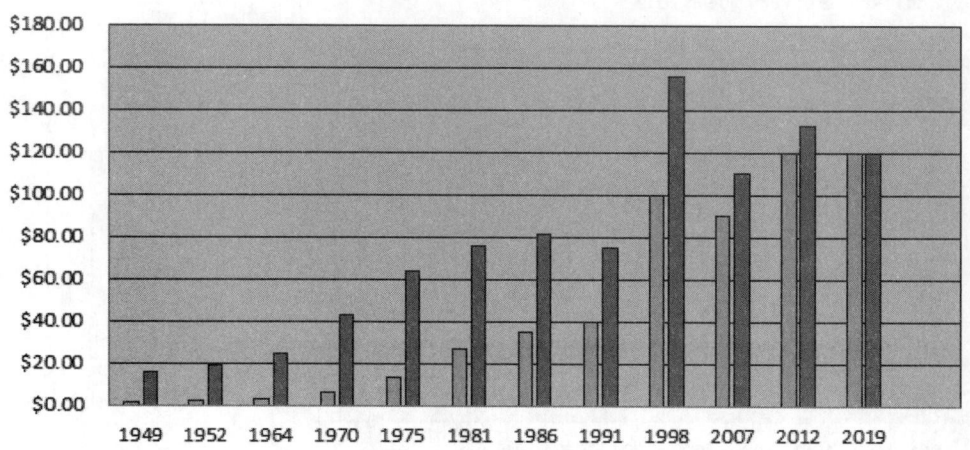

	1949	1952	1964	1970	1975	1981
Price	$1.50	$2.00	$3.00	$6.50	$13.50	$27
Dollar Value in 2019	$16.02	$19.19	$24.60	$42.59	$63.79	$75.51

	1986	1991	1998	2007	2012	2019
Price	$35	$40	$100	$90	$120	$119.94
Dollar Value in 2019	$81.18	$74.66	$155.95	$110.34	$132.86	$119.94

TRAVEL & ENTERTAINMENT

BROADWAY SHOW* TICKET

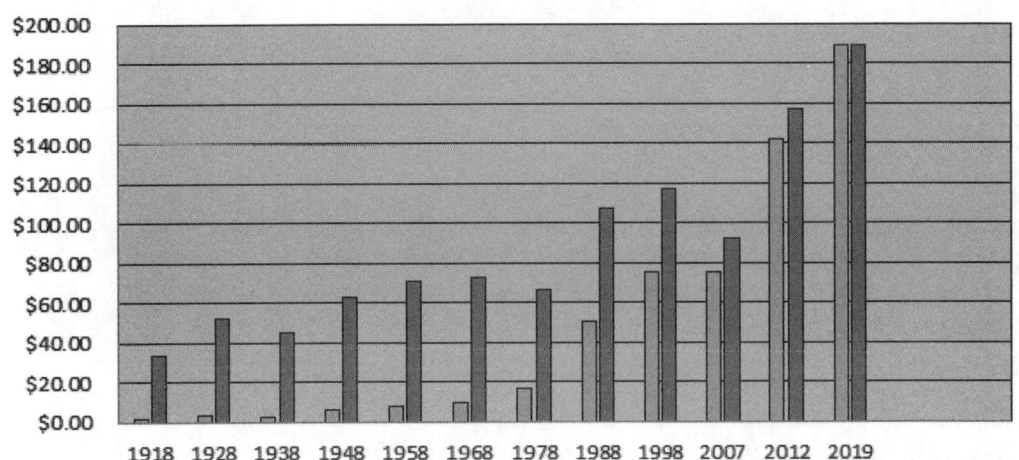

□ Price   ■ Dollar Value in 2019

	1918	1928	1938	1948	1958	1968
Price	$2.00	$3.50	$2.50	$6.00	$8.05	$9.90
Dollar Value in 2019	$33.67	$52.03	$45.07	$63.29	$70.81	$72.32

	1978	1988	1998	2007	2012	2019
Price	$17	$50	$75	$75	$142	$189
Dollar Value in 2019	$66.28	$107.40	$116.96	$91.95	$157.22	$189

Shows Performing on Broadway:	
1918: *Oh, Boy*	**1928:** The Five O'Clock Girl
1938: *Of Mice and Men*	**1948:** *Macbeth*
1958: *West Side Story*	**1968:** *Fiddler on the Roof*
1978: *A Chorus Line*	**1988:** *The Phantom of the Opera*
1998: *Chicago*	**2007:** *The Coast of Utopia*
2012: *Once*	**2019:** *Hadestown*

*Best seating

TRAVEL & ENTERTAINMENT

DISNEYLAND TICKET (ADULT)

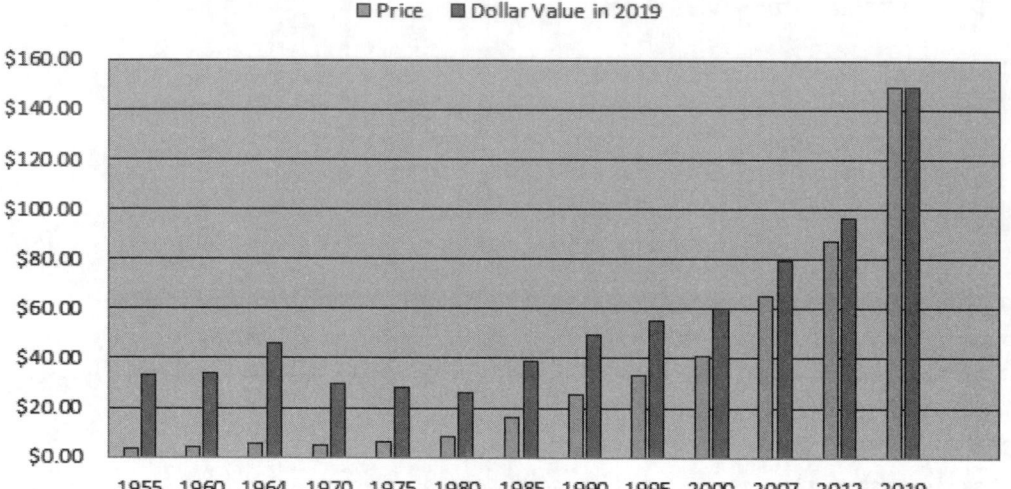

	1955	1960	1964	1970	1975	1980	1985
Price	$3.50	$3.95	$5.65	$4.50	$6.00	$8.50	$16.50
Dollar Value in 2019	$33.20	$33.92	$46.33	$29.48	$28.35	$26.22	$38.98

	1990	1995	2000	2007	2012	2019
Price	$35.50	$33	$41	$65	$87	$149
Dollar Value in 2019	$49.60	$55.04	$60.52	$79.69	$96.30	$149

Disneyland Ticket Facts:

♦ In **1955**, the general admission ticket was only $1, but that did not include any of the eight attractions at the park.

♦ When the park first opened, Disneyland sold books with coupons that permitted guests to ride select attractions. Each coupon permitted the guest to ride a select number of attractions, depending on the coupons' classification level.

♦ Many guests typically returned home with unused coupons, but could have used them in future visits.

♦ The park started phasing out the tickets in the late 1970s and early 1980s and instituted "unlimited passports." This occurred when other theme parks started selling all-inclusive tickets in the 1970s.

♦ Disneyland established the all-inclusive passport by June of 1982.

♦ In 2013, ticket prices were split with a higher cost for Magic Kingdom than the other parks

TRAVEL & ENTERTAINMENT

FORD AUTOMOBILE*

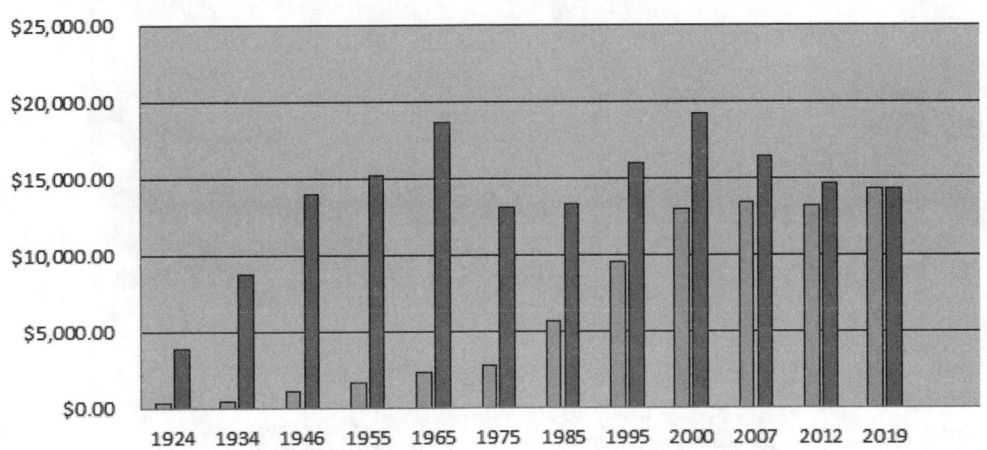

	1924	1934	1946	1955	1965	1975
Price	$260	$460	$1,074	$1,606	$2,313	$2,769
Dollar Value in 2019	$3,865	$8,726	$14,001	$15,223	$18,66	$13,083

	1985	1995	2000	2007	2012	2019
Price	$5,620	$9,560	$12,999	$13,425	$13,200	$14,260
Dollar Value in 2019	$13,277	$15,946	$19,189	$16,459	$14,615	$14,260

*Least expensive model

Clockwise from top right: Oldsmobile Six at $745+ (1936); Dodge Victory Six Coupe-Brougham at $1,095 (1928); Dodge Colt at $2,647 (1974); Triumph TR-4A about $2,500 (1965); interior of Olds Six; "The Famous Ford" Town Car at $950 (1910); Ford Escort ZX2 at $11,995 (1997); Mini Cooper at $16,975+ (2003); 2014 Fiat 500 at $12,990+.

TRAVEL & ENTERTAINMENT

HOTEL NIGHTLY RATE

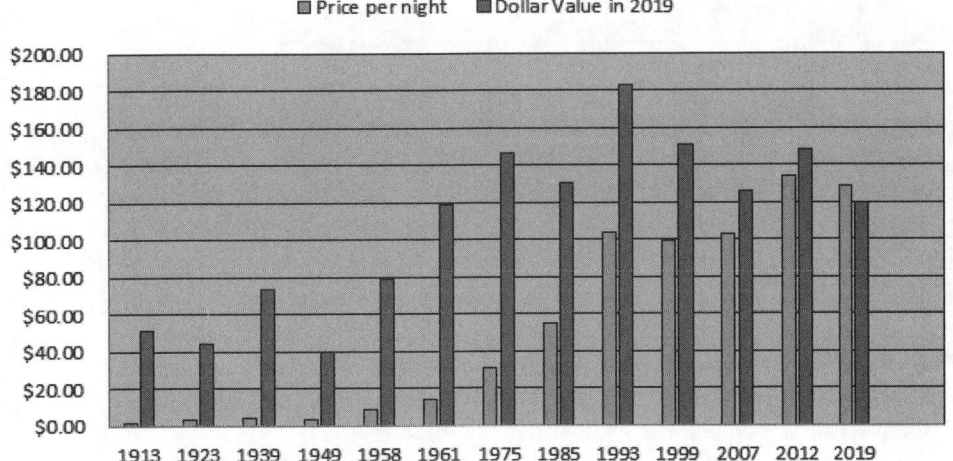

☐ Price per night   ■ Dollar Value in 2019

	1913	1923	1939	1949	1958	1961	1975
Price per night	$2.00	$3.00	$4.00	$3.75	$9.00	$14	$31
Dollar Value in 2019	$51.35	$44.60	$73.15	$40.05	$79.16	$119.02	$146.47

	1985	1993	1999	2007	2012	2019
Price per night	$55	$104	$99	$103	$134	$129
Dollar Value in 2019	$129.94	$182.96	$151.06	$126.28	$148.36	$119.94

TRAVEL & ENTERTAINMENT

MOVIE TICKET

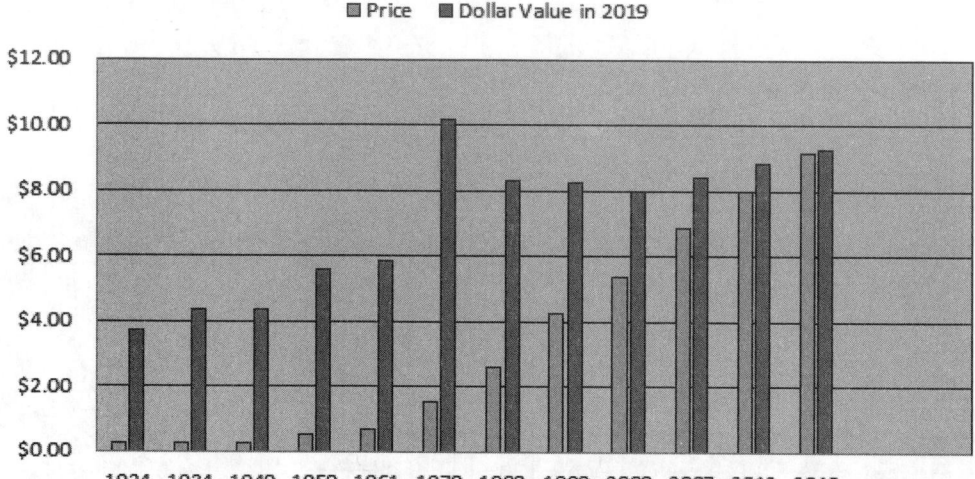

	1924	1934	1940	1950	1961	1970
Price	$0.25	$0.23	$0.24	$0.53	$0.69	$1.55
Dollar Value in 2019	$3.72	$4.36	$4.36	$5.59	$5.87	$10.15

	1980	1990	2000	2007	2012	2018
Price	$2.60	$4.23	$5.39	$6.88	$7.96	$9.16
Dollar Value in 2019	$8.30	$8.23	$7.96	$8.43	$8.81	$9.16

Top Grossing Movies by Year			
Year	Movie	Worldwide Gross	Dollar Value in 2019
1924	*The Sea Hawk*	$3.0 million	$44.9 million
1934	*The Merry Widow*	$2.6 million	$49.7 million
1940	*Pinocchio*	$87 million	$64 million
1950	*Cinderella*	$263 million	$2.8 billion
1961	*West Side Story*	$105 million	$899 million
1970	*Love Story*	$136 million	$897 million
1980	*The Empire Strikes Back*	$548 million	$1.7 billion
1990	*Ghost*	$505 million	$990 million
2000	*Mission: Impossible 2*	$546 million	$812 million
2007	*Pirates of the Caribbean: At World's End*	$963 million	$1.2 billion
2012	*The Avengers*	$1.5 billion	$1.7 billion
2018	*Avengers: Infinity War*	$2 billion	$2.1 billion

ON SALE TODAY at all Music and Department Stores, or at any Woolworth, Kresge or McCrory Store.

Other Popular "FEIST." Songs:

"You're A Dangerous Girl"   "My Old Rose"   "Don't Bite the Hand That's Feeding You"
"M-O-T-H-E-R"   "Moonshine Sally"   "Honolulu, America Loves You"
"Gila, Galah, Galoo"   "Honolulu Blues"   "'Way Out Yonder in the Golden West"
"I'm Saving up the Means to Get to New Orleans"   "Civilization" Peace song
"Some Girls Do and Some Girls Don't"   "Ireland Must Be Heaven, for my Mother Came from There"
"There's a Garden in Old Italy"   "The Sweetest Melody of All"
"Not so Very Far from Zanzibar"   "He May Be Old, but He's Got Young Ideas"
"Sweet Cider Time, When You Were Mine"   "It's Not Your Nationality, It's Simply You"

These songs are printed in the new "Feist" easy-to-read style. Complete song at a glance—no leaves to turn

SPECIAL NOTE: You should get all these songs from your dealer.   Please do so.   If you can't, send us eight 2c stamps for one, or a dollar bill for any seven pieces.   Orchestra or Band—25c each.   Male quartette—10c each.   These pieces may also be procured for your Talking Machine or your Player Piano from your dealer.   Be sure to get them.   Orchestra Leaders will gladly play them on request.

Top Songs

	Name	Album	Time	Price	
1	Royals	Pure Heroine	3:10	$1.29	View In iTunes ▸
2	Team	Pure Heroine	3:13	$1.29	View In iTunes ▸
3	Tennis Court	Pure Heroine	3:18	$1.29	View In iTunes ▸

THE DEAL
For $7.98 (or less, where possible) you get

TWO RECORDS AND A BOOK
Which is pretty cheap for a masterpiece

Clockwise from top: Feist songs sheet music ad (1916); songs by Lorde for sale online by iTunes for $1.29 each in 2013; Tommy Dorsey, "In a Sentimental Mood" (1952), album purchased for $2.98 from Miller & Rhoads department store, "Uncle Meat" double album by Frank Zappa advertised for $7.98 in the Chicago Seed alternative newspaper in May 1969 ; George Thorogood and the Destroyers, "Move It On Over " album (1979), sold for $4.99 at Wonderland record store in Newark, Del.

898

TRAVEL & ENTERTAINMENT

OCEAN CRUISE FROM NEW YORK CITY TO BERMUDA

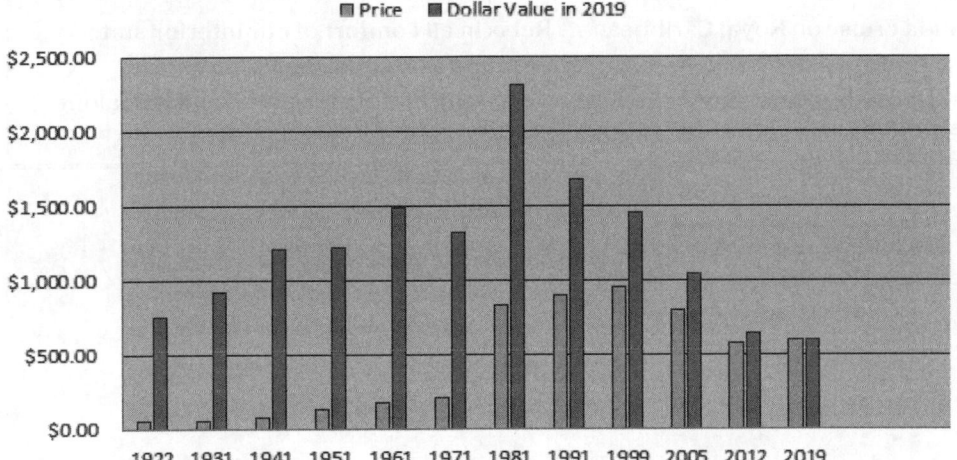

	1922	1931	1941	1951	1961	1971
Price	$50	$55	$70	$125	$175	$210
Dollar Value in 2019	$757	$920	$1,210	$1,222	$1,488	$1,318

	1981	1991	1999	2005	2012	2019
Price	$825	$895	$950	$799	$579	$599
Dollar Value in 2019	$2,307	$1,670	$1,450	$1,040	$641	$599

Excerpts from Cruise Descriptions:

1922: Go in May and June when Bermuda is ablaze with Flowers—perfect days for rest or play.

1941: Sail with Alcoa to Bermuda … a wonderful vacation combination! Expert Cruise Director, deck sports, movies, dancing to Al Donahue orchestra … round-the-clock enjoyment all the way.

1951: Sail into a world of Fun! Cruise on the "Queen of Bermuda" for the best vacation of your life! Take this gay cruise in one week or stay longer in Bermuda if you wish.

1971: This sparkling new ship will appeal to everyone … The Bermuda Government has selected SEA VENTURE as its official contract ship, a highly prized endorsement.

1991: Grand Resort to Bermuda. 7-night cruises from New York to Britain's beautiful crown jewel.

2012: Seven night Bermuda cruise on Royal Caribbean … Relax in all comfort of our interior staterooms.

2019: Sail on Carnival's Bermuda cruises and you'll experience this unique cultural cocktail, along with a serious helping of natural beauty.

TRAVEL & ENTERTAINMENT

PAPERBACK NOVEL

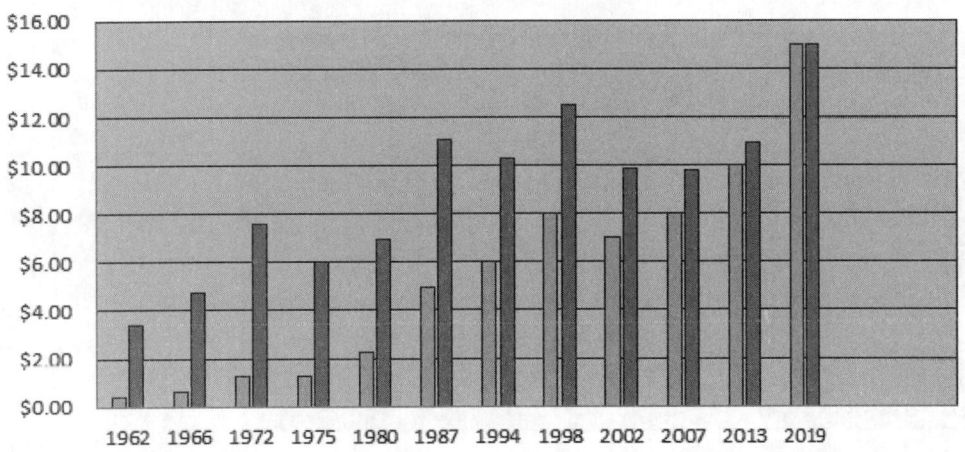

Year	Price	Dollar Value in 2019	Title	Author
1962	$0.40	$3.37	*The Lilies of the Field*	William Edmund Barrett
1966	$0.60	$4.71	*Flowers for Algernon*	Daniel Keyes
1972	$1.25	$7.60	*Death Wish*	Brian Garfield
1975	$1.25	$6.00	*Tuck Everlasting*	Natalie Babbitt
1980	$2.25	$6.94	*Firestarter*	Stephen King
1987	$4.95	$11.08	*Beloved*	Toni Morrison
1994	$5.99	$10.27	*Brother Cadfael's Penance*	Ellis Peters
1998	$7.99	$12.46	*The Magic Circle*	Katherine Neville
2002	$6.99	$9.88	*The Beach House*	Mary Alice Munro
2007	$7.99	$9.80	*Eclipse (Twilight Series)*	Stephenie Meyer
2013	$9.99	$11.00	*Choke Point*	Ridley Pearson
2019	$14.97	$14.97	*The Nickel Boys*	Colson Whitehead

TRAVEL & ENTERTAINMENT

RAIL FARE FROM NEW YORK CITY TO SAN FRANCISCO

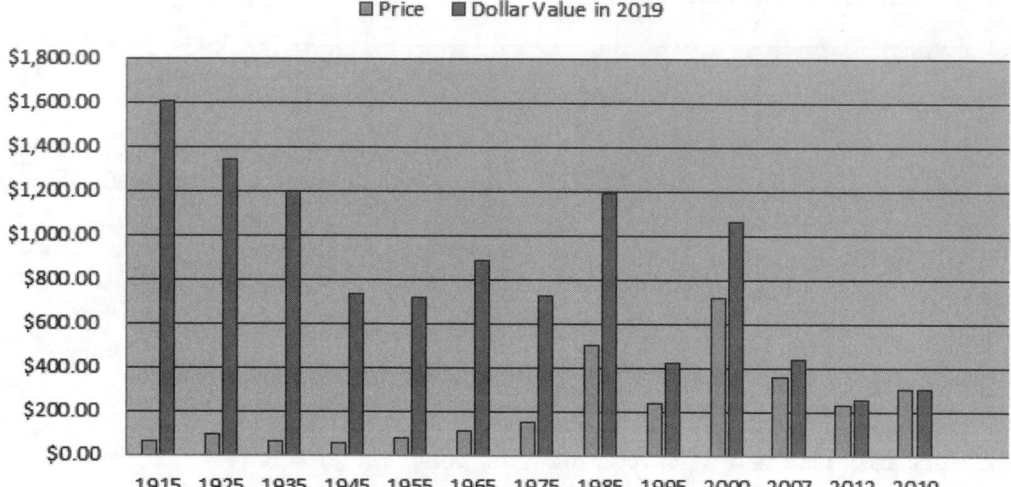

	1915	1925	1935	1945	1955	1965	1975
Price	$63.66	$92.55	$64.49	$51.77	$75.77	$109.55	$153.50
Dollar Value in 2019	$1,602.23	$1,344.37	$1,196.60	$731.11	$718.69	$884.06	$725.28

	1985	1995	2000	2007	2012	2019
Price	$504	$235	$720	$360	$230	$303
Dollar Value in 2019	$1,190.69	$422	$1,062.87	$441.36	$254.65	$303

TRAVEL & ENTERTAINMENT

ROLL OF FILM

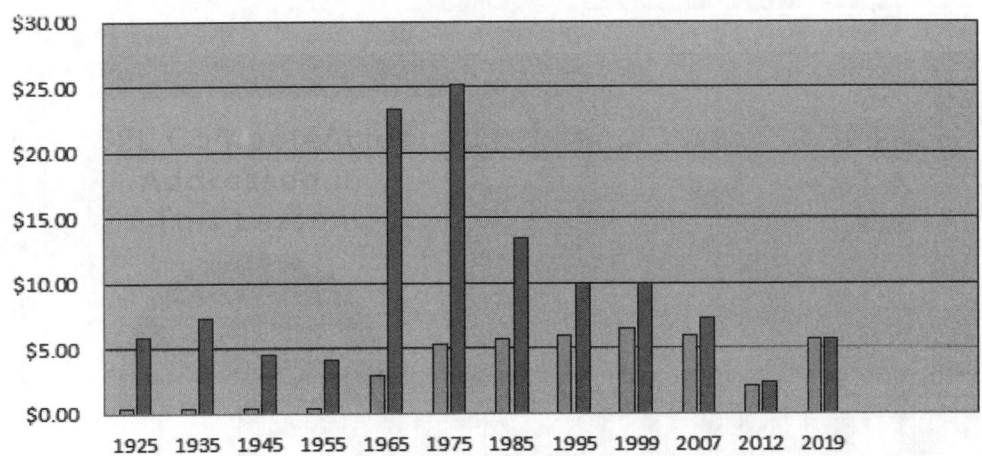

	1925	1935	1945	1955	1965	1975
Price	$0.40	$0.39	$0.32	$0.43	$2.89	$5.33
Dollar Value in 2019	$5.81	$7.24	$4.52	$4.08	$23.32	$25.18

	1985	1995	1999	2007	2012	2019
Price	$5.70	$6.00	$6.50	$5.99	$2.09	$5.75
Dollar Value in 2019	$13.47	$10.01	$9.92	$7.34	$2.31	$5.75

TRAVEL & ENTERTAINMENT

SUITCASE

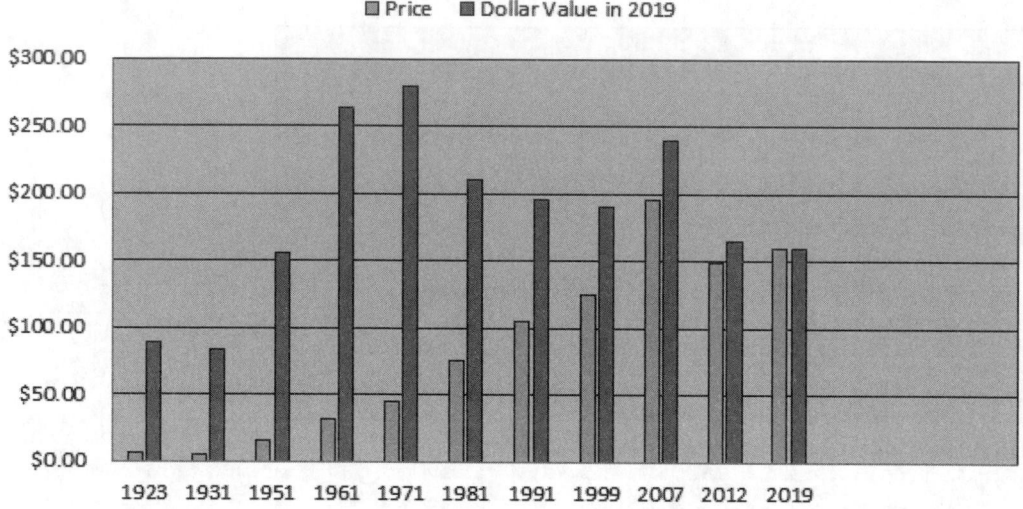

	1923	1931	1951	1961	1971	1981
Price	$6.00	$5.00	$15.95	$31	$44.50	$75
Dollar Value in 2019	$89.19	$83.62	$155.94	$263.55	$279.31	$209.74

	1991	1999	2007	2012	2019
Price	$105	$125	$195.40	$149	$159.99
Dollar Value in 2019	$195.97	$190.73	$239.56	$164.97	$159.99

GENERAL SOURCES

Backgrounds

Brinkley, Alan. *American History: A Survey*. 13th ed., McGraw-Hill Higher Education, 2009.

Freeman, Joshua B. *American Empire: The Rise of a Global Power, the Democratic Revolution at Home: 1945–2000*. Penguin Books, 2013.

Henry May, Neil R. McMillen, *A Synopsis of American History*. 8th ed., Dee, 1992.

Morris, Richard B., ed., *Encyclopedia of American History*. 7th ed., Harper & Row, 1996.

U.S. Bureau of the Census. *Historical Statistics of the United States, 1789–1945*, Washington, DC, 1949.

Tindall, George Brown., and David Emory. *America: A Narrative History*. 9th ed., W.W. Norton & Company, 2013.

Zinn, Howard. *A People's History of the United States*. Harper Perennial, 2015.

Publications:

Atlantic, The

Economist, The

Newsweek

New York Times, The

Time Magazine

Washington Post, The

Historical Snapshots

"America's Best History Timeline." *America's Best History*, americasbesthistory.com/abhtimeline.html.

Gordon, Lois and Alan Gordon. *Encyclopedia of American History; American Chronicle Year-by-Year Through the 20th Century*. Yale UP, 1999.

Greenspan, Karen. *The Timetables of Women's History*. Simon & Schuster, 1996.

Trager, James, ed. *The People's Chronology; A Year-by-Year Record of Human Events from Prehistory to the Present*. Holt, 1992.

"U.S. History Timeline." *Infoplease*, www.infoplease.com/history/us/us-history-timeline.

Consumer Expenditures

"Consumer Expenditure Surveys." *U.S. Bureau of Labor Statistics*, U.S. Department of Labor, www.bls.gov/cex/.

Department of Commerce, Bureau of Economic Analysis, *The National Income and Product Accounts, 1929–2018 Statistical Tables*. Government Printing Office, 2018.

Dewhurst, J. Frederick. *America's Needs and Resources: A New Survey*. Twentieth-Century Fund, 1955.

U.S. Bureau of the Census, *Current Population Reports*, series P–25, nos. 311, 1045, and 1069.

Investments

"Federal Reserve Bulletin." *Board of Governors of the Federal Reserve System*, www.federalreserve.gov/publications/bulletin.htm

"Survey of Current Business." *Bureau of Economic Analysis*, U.S. Department of Commerce, apps.bea.gov/scb/issues.htm.

U.S. Bureau of the Census. *Historical Statistics of the United States, Colonial Times to 1970*. Bicentennial ed., Government Printing Office, 1975.

Capital Changes Reports. Commerce Clearing House, 1993.

Yahoo! Finance. https://finance.yahoo.com/

Publications:

Wall Street Journal, The

Other factors affecting stock value, such as rights offered to debentures or other offerings, are omitted.

Selected Income

Sources are indicated in individual entries.

Standard Jobs

Douglas, Paul H. *Real Wages in the United States, 1890–1926*. Augustus Kelley, 1966.

Lebergott, Stanley. *Manpower in Economic Growth: The American Record Since 1800*. McGraw-Hill, 1964.

Department of Commerce, Bureau of Economic Analysis, *The National Income and Product Accounts, 1929–2018 Statistical Tables*. Government Printing Office, 2018.

"Quarterly Census of Employment and Wages." U.S. Bureau of Labor Statistics, U.S. Department of Labor, www.bls.gov/cew/home.htm.

Food Basket

"Average Retail Food and Energy Prices, U.S. City Average and West Region." *U.S. Bureau of Labor Statistics*, U.S. Department of Labor, www.bls.gov/regions/mid-atlantic/data/averageretail-foodandenergyprices_usandwest_table.htm.

"Consumer Expenditure Surveys." *U.S. Bureau of Labor Statistics*, U.S. Department of Labor, www.bls.gov/cex/.

Department of Commerce and Labor, *Bulletin of Bureau of Labor*. Government Printing Office, nos. 71 (1907), 105 (1912)

Department of Labor, Bureau of Labor Statistics, *Retail Prices*. Government Printing Office, nos. 140 (1914), 315 (1923), 366 (1925), 464 (1928), 495 (1929), 635 (1937), 707 (1942), 799 (1944), 899 (1947), 965 (1949), 1055 (1951), 1141 (1953), 1183 (1955), 1217 (1957), 1254 (1959), 1301 (1961), 1446 (1964), 1632 (1969)

Council for Community and Economic Research. *Cost of Living Index*.

Selected Prices

Sources are indicated in individual entries.

Miscellany

Sources are indicated in individual entries.

PRICING TRENDS SOURCES

Amtrak

Antiques Magazine

Apple, Inc.

Beaulieu Vineyard

Brooks Brothers

Cantigny First Division Foundation

Center of Disease Control

Chicago Historical Society

Chicago Tribune

Cleveland Public Library

CNN

Condé Nast

Consumer Digest

Delta Air Lines

Dublin Dr. Pepper Bottling Company Museum

Eureka

Ford Motor Company

Golf Digest

Hake's Auction, September

Harley Davidson Data Book

Harley Davidson Sales Company

Herman's

Hershey

Hilton Hotels

J.C. Penny

Kodak

Ladies Home Journal

Los Angeles Times

Major League Baseball

McDonald's

NASCAR Illustrated

National Association of Home Builders

National Association of Theatre Owners and Box Office Managers

National Basketball Association

National Football League

National Railroad Historical Society

Newsweek

New York Times

Playboy Magazine

Richland County Library

Sears Roebuck

Statistical Abstract of the United States

Sunbeam Corporation

Target Corporation

The Atlanta Constitution

The Atlantic Monthly Group

The Charlotte Observer

The Chicago Tribune

The Martinsville (Va.) Bulletin

The Sporting News Pro Football Guide

The Standard Catalog of Comic Books

The State

Time Warner

United States Census Bureau

United States Domestic Postage Rate: History

University of Oregon

University of South Carolina

US Treasury of the United States

USA Today

Yesterland Website

Zippo

FURTHER READING

Ahlstrom, Sydney E., and David D. Hall. *A Religious History of the American People*. 2nd ed., Yale UP, 2004.

Alter, Adam. *Irresistible: The Rise of Addictive Technology and the Business of Keeping Us Hooked*. Reprint ed., Penguin Books, 2018.

Bargeron, Eric. *American Decades 2000–2009*. vol. 11, Gale Research, 2011.

Batchelor, Bob. *American Pop: Popular Culture Decade by Decade*. Greenwood P, 2009.

Baughman, Judith. *American Decades: 1920–1929*. vol. 3, Gale Research, 1995.

Bondi, Victor. *American Decades: 1930–1939*. vol. 4, Gale Research, 1995.

Bondi, Victor. *American Decades: 1940–1949*. vol. 5, Gale Research, 1995.

Bondi, Victor. *American Decades: 1970–1979*. vol. 8, Gale Research, 1995.

Bondi, Victor. *American Decades: 1980–1989*. vol. 9, Gale Research, 1995.

Brands, H. W. *American Colossus: The Triumph of Capitalism, 1865–1900*. Reprint ed., Anchor Books, 2011.

Breslin, James E. B. *Mark Rothko—A Biography*. Reprint ed., U of Chicago P, 1998.

Brinkley, Douglas. *Wheels for the World: Henry Ford, His Company, and a Century of Progress, 1903–2003*. Penguin Books, 2004.

Bronski, Michael. *A Queer History of the United States*. Beacon P, 2012.

Brooks, John. *Telephone: The First Hundred Years*. Harper & Row, 1976.

Brown, Clair. *American Standards of Living: 1918–1988*. Wiley-Blackwell, 1995.

Bufwack, Mary A., and Robert K. Oermann. *Finding Her Voice: The Saga of Women in Country Music*. Crown Publishers, 1993.

Burch, Susan. *Encyclopedia of American Disability History*. Facts on File, 2009.

Burnham, John C. *Health Care in America: A History*. Johns Hopkins UP, 2015.

Cain, Louis P., et al., editors. *The Oxford Handbook of American Economic History*. Oxford UP, 2018.

Coombs, Danielle Sarver, and Bob Batchelor. *American History through American Sports: From Colonial Lacrosse to Extreme Sports*. Praeger, 2012.

Craven, Wayne. *American Art History and Culture*. McGraw-Hill, 2003.

Crawford, Richard. *America's Musical Life: A History*. W.W. Norton & Company, 2005.

Cullen, Jim. *Popular Culture in American History*. 2nd ed., Wiley-Blackwell, 2013.

Dalrymple, H., and C. Goodrum. *Advertising in America: The First 200 Years*. Harry N. Abrams, Inc, 1990.

Douglas, Susan J. *Inventing American Broadcasting: 1899–1922*. Johns Hopkins UP, 1989.

Eaklor, Vicki Lynn. *Queer America: A GLBT History of the 20th Century*. New P, 2011.

Egan, Timothy. *The Worst Hard Time: The Untold Story of Those Who Survived the Great American Dust Bowl*. Houghton Mifflin Co., 2013.

Epstein, Edward Jay. *The Hollywood Economist 2.0: The Hidden Financial Reality behind the Movies.* Melville House, 2012.

Evans, Sterling. *Farming across Borders: A Transnational History of the North American West.* Texas A&M UP, 2017.

Faderman, Lillian. *The Gay Revolution: The Story of the Struggle.* Simon & Schuster, 2016.

Fellow, Anthony R. *American Media History.* 3rd ed., Wadsworth, 2013.

Foner, Eric. *The Story of American Freedom.* W.W. Norton & Company, 1999.

Fox, Stephen R. *The Mirror Makers: A History of American Advertising & Its Creators.* University of Illinois P, 1997.

Foy, Jessica H., and Thomas J. Schlereth. *American Home Life, 1880–1930: A Social History of Spaces and Services.* U of Tennessee P, 1994.

Francisco, Frank. *Evolution of the Game: A Chronicle of American Football.* CreateSpace, 2016.

Friedman, Lawrence M. *A History of American Law.* 3rd ed., Simon & Schuster, 2005.

Gaustad, Edwin S., et al. *A Documentary History of Religion in America.* 4th ed., Eerdmans, 2018.

Geisst, Charles R. *Wall Street: A History.* Oxford UP, 2004.

Gertner, Jon. *The Idea Factory: Bell Labs and the Great Age of American Innovation.* Penguin Books, 2013.

Gray, Richard J. *A History of American Literature.* 2nd ed., Wiley-Blackwell, 2012.

Greenspan, Alan, and Adrian Wooldridge. *Capitalism in America: A History.* Penguin P, 2018.

Hazen, Don, et al. *The 99%: How the Occupy Wall Street Movement Is Changing America.* AlterNet Books, 2011.

Hechtlinger, Adelaide. *The Great Patent Medicine Era: or, Without Benefit of Doctor.* Galahad Books, 1974.

Hess, Stephen, and Sandy Northrop. *American Political Cartoons: From 1754–2010.* Transaction Publishers, 2010.

Hughes, Jonathan R. T., and Louis P. Cain. *American Economic History.* 8th ed., Pearson, 2011.

Hughes, Thomas P. *American Genesis: A Century of Invention and Technological Enthusiasm, 1870–1970.* 2nd ed., U of Chicago P, 2004.

Ikenson, Ben, and Jay Bennett. *Ingenious Patents: Bubble Wrap, Barbed Wire, Bionic Eyes, and Other Pioneering Inventions.* Black Dog & Leventhal Publishers, 2018.

Knowlton, Christopher. *Cattle Kingdom: The Hidden History of the Cowboy West.* Houghton Mifflin Harcourt, 2017.

Koplos, Janet, and Bruce Metcalf. *Makers: A History of American Studio Craft.* U of North Carolina P, 2010.

Kovel, Ralph M., and Terry H. Kovel. *Kovels' American Collectibles: 1900 to 2000.* Random House Reference, 2007.

Layman, Richard. *American Decades: 1950–1959.* vol. 6, Gale Research, 1995.

Layman, Richard. *American Decades: 1960–1969.* vol. 7, Gale Research, 1995.

Le Beau, Bryan. *A History of Religion in America.* Routledge, 2018.

Leuchtenburg, William Edward. *Franklin D. Roosevelt and the New Deal: 1932–1940.* Harper Perennial, 2009.

Longmore, Paul K., and Lauri Umansky, editors. *The New Disability History: American Perspectives*. New York UP, 2001.

McConnell, Tandy. *American Decades: 1990–1999*. vol. 10, Gale Research, 2000.

McElvaine, Robert S. *The Great Depression: America, 1929–1941*. Three Rivers P, 2009.

Monaco, Paul. *A History of American Movies: A Film-by-Film Look at the Art, Craft, and Business of Cinema*. Scarecrow P, 2010.

Morgan, Edmund S. *American Heroes: Profiles of Men and Women Who Shaped Early America*. W.W. Norton & Company, 2010.

Nyren, Chuck. *Advertising to Baby Boomers*. Paramount Market Pub., 2007.

Phillips, Kevin P. *Wealth and Democracy: A Political History of the American Rich*. Broadway Books, 2003.

Pohl, Frances K. *Framing America: A Social History of American Art*. 4th ed., Thames & Hudson, 2017.

Polchin, James. *Indecent Advances: The Hidden History of Murder and Masculinity before Stonewall*. Counterpoint, 2019.

Rothstein, Richard. *The Color of Law: A Forgotten History of How Our Government Segregated America*. Liveright, 2017.

Schwartz Cowan, Ruth. *A Social History of American Technology*. Oxford UP, 1997.

Smil, Vaclav. *Made in the USA: The Rise and Retreat of American Manufacturing*. MIT P, 2015.

Strasser, Susan. *Satisfaction Guaranteed: The Making of the American Mass Market*. Smithsonian Institution, 2004.

Taylor, Clarence. *Fight the Power: African Americans and the Long History of Police Brutality in New York City*. New York UP, 2018.

Thomson, David. *The Whole Equation: A History of Hollywood*. Vintage Books, 2006.

Tompkins, Vincent, editor. *American Decades: 1900–1909*. vol. 1, Gale Research, 1996.

Tompkins, Vincent. *American Decades: 1910–1919*. vol. 2, Gale Research, 1996.

Tungate, Mark. *Adland: A Global History of Advertising*. 2nd ed., Kogan Page, 2013.

Vecsey, George. *Baseball: A History of America's Favorite Game*. Modern Library, 2008.

Vries, Jan de. *The Industrious Revolution: Consumer Behavior and the Household Economy, 1650 to the Present*. Cambridge UP, 2009.

Wadman, Robert C., and William Thomas. Allison. *To Protect and to Serve: A History of Police in America*. Pearson, 2003.

Webber, Michael E. *Power Trip: The Story of Energy*. Basic Books, 2019.

Williams, Gregory Paul. *The Story of Hollywood: An Illustrated History*. BL P, 2011.

Wilson, Elizabeth. *Love Game: A History of Tennis, from Victorian Pastime to Global Phenomenon*. U of Chicago P, 2016.

Wolmar, Christian. *The Great Railroad Revolution: The History of Trains in America*. PublicAffairs, 2013.

INDEX